“In the chaotic aftermath of 9/11, Dr. Andrew Bostom embarked on an expedition through the institutional apologetics and semantic tiger traps constructed and set in order to further, through lies, the Islamic conquest of the West. His mission? To seek out the truth. The truth about Islam, the truth about Islamic conquest (jihad), the truth about the sharia (Islamic law), the truth about the dhimmi (Jews and Christians under sharia), the truth about Islam’s special hatred for Jews. A natural scholar trained in research medicine, Bostom has for a quarter century turned his skills to researching Islam — to revisiting, often unearthing, often translating into English for the first time, a vast literature of Islamic and Western sources from centuries unconstrained by the ideological straitjackets we know familiarly as ‘PC’ or ‘woke.’ What he has amassed, or, in many ways, restored, and brought forth in new works, is the essential record which eviscerates prevailing apologetics — valiant and valuable work, indeed. With *A Modern Qu’ranic Kampf Against the Jews*, Bostom, with translator Dr. Atef Ghobrial, now present a massive work from the center of Islamic learning to demonstrate that far from offering a practically liberal “alternative” to the harshest aspects of Islam — the apologist’s line -- it is a reiteration of them all, notably including the Qu’ranically correct hatred of Jews, currently poisoning world affairs.”

—Diana West, author of *American Betrayal*

“A must-read for those who want to comprehend the theological roots of the Islamic war against Israel and Jewish people introduced by one of the world’s most knowledgeable experts on jihadism and Islamic antisemitism. Understanding Islamic antisemitism is key to understanding all other aspects of jihad. Dr. Ghobrial's translation and Dr. Bostom's analysis are invaluable services to humanity.”

--Uzay Bulut, veteran Turkey-born journalist covering Islam worldwide

“This translation and Dr. Bostom’s analysis present an influential text by a significant Muslim scholar at Cairo’s Al-Azhar University, long the most important center of Sunni Islamic learning. Readers will find it unsettling, but undeniably relevant to the ongoing debate about Islam and antisemitism in the 21st century.”

—Clifford May, Founder and President of *The Foundation for the Defense of Democracies*

Translation Source, Acknowledgments, and Dedication

The original Arabic source for the translation can be found here: https://archive.org/details/tantawi-ph-d/mode/2up [Muḥammad Sayyed Ṭanṭāwī., Banū Isrā'īl fī al-Qur'ān wa-al-sunnah ("The Children of Israel in the Qur'an and the Traditions"), Print Book, Arabic, 1997, ©1968; 759 pp. Publisher: دار الشروق، al-Qāhirah, 1997, ©1968 / Dār al-Shurūq, al-Qāhirah, 1997, ©1968]

This book project would have been impossible to complete without the highly skilled, tireless efforts of my colleague, Dr. Atef Ghobrial. The Job-like patience and support of my beloved wife Leslie, and my dear friend Joyce, were also required, and deeply appreciated. Invaluable technical support was provided by Eddie Vincent, Jim Watson, Ned May, and the nonpareil artist and cover designer, Bosch Fawstin.

Any lingering, if unwitting errors are my responsibility.

As ***A Modern Qur'anic Kampf Against the Jews*** so starkly illustrates, wrenching reforms to the authoritative teaching of Islam's canonical, Jew-hating theology are required. The book is dedicated to those intrepid men and women of good faith who will demand Al-Azhar University, and its current Grand Imam, Ahmed al-Tayeb, specifically, initiate such a mea culpa-based reform process for institutional Islam.

Andrew G. Bostom, MD, MS

Table of Contents

Published by: www.andrewbostom.net

Date of publication: January, 2026

"As for those well-grounded in knowledge, they say, 'We believe in this Qur'an—it is all from our Lord.' But none will be mindful of this except people of reason."

—Qur'an 3:7

Introduction
Andrew G. Bostom, MD, MS

"The Koran of course, became a mine of anti-Jewish passages. The Hadith did not lag behind. Popular preachers used and embellished such material."
—Historian of Islam's Anti-Jewish polemic in the Middle Ages, Moshe Perlmann (d. 2001) [a.]

"[S]ome scholars argue that it is unfair to interpret the words of the Qur'an as the ulema (learned Muslim clerics) and (Muslim) mobs have done throughout history"...
—Holocaust and Middle East historian, Saul S. Friedman (d. 2013) [b.]

"The charge of antisemitism was invented by the Jews, as a means of pressuring the Arabs and Muslims and with the aim of implementing their conspiracies in the Arab and Muslim countries. It should be disregarded."
—Muhammad Sayyed Tantawi, as Al-Azhar Grand Imam, from an interview, November 20, 2002 [c.]

"Tolerance has its limits. Get it? Tolerance has its limits."
—Muhammad Sayyed Tantawi, as Al-Azhar Grand Imam, from an interview October 3, 2008 [d.]

"Love of the Prophet (Muhammad) requires hatred of the Jews"
—Al-Maghili, influential West African Muslim cleric, d. 1505 [e.]

"[T]he odium theologicum (theological hatred), in a sincere bigot, is one of the most unequivocal cases of moral feeling."
—John Stuart Mill, 1859 [f.]

Cairo's Al-Azhar University, and its mosque, founded in 972 C.E., have represented an authoritative sanctum of Sunni Islamic religious knowledge and education since the mid to late 13th century advent of Mamluk reign in Egypt.[1] At present, Al-Azhar maintains a Vatican-like status within Sunni Islam.[2] During a March, 2025 Ramadan event in front of Al-Azhar's mosque, celebrating its founding, Muslims were reminded of the words of the famous 16th century Egyptian Muslim scholar al-Haytami (d. 1567), *"There is no spot on the face of the earth that has gathered as many scholars and righteous people as Al-Azhar."* [3] Al-Azhar's contemporary Grand Imams, moreover, are generally recognized as the most authoritative Sunni Islamic religious leaders.[4] For example, when then Al-Azhar Grand Imam Abdel Halim Mahmoud visited North America in 1977, the Washington Post headline announced, "Leader of World Islam Begins Historic Tour of America," and the story opened with these lines: [4a]

> *"The man most widely recognized as the spiritual leader of Islam arrived in Washington (D.C.) last week, the first stop on a historic North American tour. 'It is for the first time that an incumbent of this high post visits the New World,'*

> *announced (Washington, D.C.) Islamic Center director Dr. Mohammad Rauf, as he presented His Eminence Dr. Abdel Halim Mahmoud, Sheikh Al-Azhar..."*

The late Al-Azhar University Grand Imam (appointed March 17, 1996),[5] and major contemporary Qur'anic exegete (commentator),[6] Muhammad Sayyed Tantawi (died March 10, 2010),[7] met with Israel's then Chief Rabbi, Israel Lau, in Cairo, December 15, 1997, within a year of becoming Grand Imam. Challenged during an interview shortly afterward by the Qatar-based, Muslim Brotherhood-affiliated Al-Jazeera media network [8] about the propriety of this meeting, Tantawi's acerbic retort alluded to his 1968 Ph.D. thesis—fully translated, and annotated, for the first time, herein—as follows: [9]

> *"The Prophet's [Muhammad's] stance, which is my own stance as well, was that anyone who avoids meeting with the enemies in order to counter their dubious claims and stick fingers into their eyes, is a coward. My stance stems from Allah's book [the Qur'an], more than one-third of which deals with the Jews.* ***You should know that you are interviewing a person who wrote a dissertation dealing with them [the Jews], all their false claims and their punishment by Allah. I still believe in everything written in that dissertation.*** (emphasis added)"

Rivka Yadlin characterized [10] "the major accusation hurled at Tantawi" after meeting with Rabbi Lau: their encounter constituted a violation of the broad consensus Egyptian societal position in 1997—still predominant today, some 30-years later [11]—against normalization of relations with Israel, *"and, as such, gave legitimacy to Jews and Judaism."* Tantawi summarily rejected all such interpretations of the meeting: [12]

> *"My son, normalization is an empty word. Whoever I meet with does not influence me; I influence him... I silenced his [Lau's] tongue."*

Elsewhere Tantawi elaborated on this view: [13]

> *"My animosity towards the normalization of relations [with Israel] is greater than that of others. I've been fighting normalization for over thirty years. This is proved by the dissertation that I wrote in 1966 [published 1968] entitled 'The Children of Israel in the Qur'an and Traditions'. In this dissertation I discussed their dark history, their ways of deceiving Islam and Muslims, their atrocities as depicted by the Qur'an, their false claims and the ways in which they were answered by the Qur'an, the punishments Allah imposed on them, and the stages of the Zionist invasion into Palestine. There is not a single Egyptian that maintains the normalization and whoever does so is a traitor to his religion and his nation."*

Some 7-months before his meeting with Rabbi Lau, Tantawi's own May 29, 1997 introduction to the 1997 re-publication of this Ph.D. thesis also confirmed his "updated" perspective was unchanged: [14]

"We Muslims have been harmed a great deal by the Jews... It was the Jews who fought the Islamic call with every possible weapon. They were the ones who usurped—with the help of the countries of the infidels- part of our holy land, Palestine—and established a country for them there in 1948...My main goal for choosing the topic of my dissertation 'The Children of Israel in the Qur'an and the Traditions' is to reveal—to Muslim youth in particular and to the rational, reasonable, and fair-minded people in general—the state of the Children of Israel [the Jews], their history, ethics, lies, depravity, and immorality, relying on what has been mentioned about them in the Holy Qur'an, the Sunna, and the correct and unequivocal historical facts."

Obituaries for Tantawi written by Western journalists uniformly stressed his "moderation," a sentiment reiterated and amplified by the U.S. and Western European leaders and diplomats quoted by the press.[15] An obvious, glaring omission in these encomiums (with one exception) [16] was any mention of Tantawi's Ph.D. thesis, and his strident re-affirmation of the views expressed in that thesis, for the remainder of his life. Muslim obituarists, in contrast, tended to condemn Tantawi's alleged "moderation," for example rejecting full face veils (niqabs) and female genital mutilation for Muslim women, while extolling the Qur'anic vitriol on Jews in his Ph.D. thesis, as "un-PC (politically correct) views of Jews." [17] Indeed, within three months of Tantawi's passing (June 10-13, 2010), *Al-Masry Al-Youm*, already by then Egypt's largest daily circulating newspaper,[18] published a series of articles lauding Tantawi's Ph.D. thesis, thusly: [19]

"Dr. Sayyed Tantawi, the late sheikh [Grand Imam] of Al-Azhar, debunked this illusion... that [Israel] is discriminated against and oppressed by its Arab neighbors...when he dedicated his 1969 [sic, 1968] doctoral dissertation to exposing what can be called the roots of violence in Jewish history, from [the Jews'] arrival in Egypt and their departure therefrom, to the establishment of the [Jewish] state, [attained] through the destruction of entire nations. Al-Masri Al-Youm rereads this important research in light of circumstances that demand an interpretation of and investigation into this culture of aggression throughout Jewish history... The sixth chapter of [Tantawi's] study deals with the Jews' abominations as they are described in the Qur'an. In this chapter, Tantawi explains that the sons of Israel are described in the Qur'an as people of various bad qualities, loathsome character, and contemptible behavior. The Qur'an describes them as infidels and liars, as ungrateful, selfish, arrogant and cowardly, as naggers and cheaters, rebels and lawbreakers, cruel and inherently inclined to deviate [from the straight and narrow]. [They are] quick to crime and aggression, and they steal people's money through lies and commit other such atrocities that are mentioned in the Qur'an and due to which [the Jews] deserve to be excluded from Allah's mercy and doomed to baseness and wretchedness. The abominations described in the Qur'an are demonstrated by [the Jews] throughout the ages and in different places. As time goes on, [these abominations] intensify and become more deeply entrenched among them."

Al-Masry Al-Youm rendered Tantawi's opening summation of chapter 6 from his Ph.D. thesis, "Banū Isrā'īl fī al-Qur'ān wa-al-sunnah" ("The Children of Israel in the Qur'an and the Traditions"), correctly. Here are Tantawi's observations, verbatim:[20]

> *"The reader of the Noble Qur'an will clearly see that it has depicted many of the inappropriate conducts, despicable manners and cunning and crooked behaviors that the Children of Israel indulged in. It has branded them with disbelief, ingratitude, egotism, cowardice, deceit, rebellion, transgression, cruelty, deviance, hastening to transgression and aggression, unjustly consuming people's wealth, and many more of the vices that are recorded in the Noble Qur'an. They therefore earned Allah's displeasure, were stripped of Allah's mercy and compassion, and they were stricken with disgrace and misery. These vices that the Noble Qur'an recorded can be clearly seen anywhere and throughout the ages. The passage of time has only made these vices more ingrained and rooted in them."*

Academic Tantawi apologist Jakob Skovgaard-Petersen alluded briefly and accurately in a 1997 book chapter to the contents of Tantawi's 1968 Ph.D. thesis as,[21]

> *"a vehement attack on everything Jewish. Demonstrating that the Prophet had a very bad relationship with the Jews of Medina, it interprets the many statements about the Jews in the Koran and Hadith to be valid as general rules also in the 20th century...The thesis then is a lengthy exposition of the Jews as they are described in the Koran and the Sunna, with occasional assurances that this picture is valid for our times. The conclusion is devoted to Zionism and Palestine and the faith that will secure the holy land for the Muslims again. It is indeed very difficult to imagine a peace with Israel if the Koran's warnings against the Jews are to be taken in their literal sense, and Sayyed Tantawi does not hesitate to denounce the idea of peace with Israel as haram (forbidden)...This is close to the outlook and discourse of the Muslim Brotherhood since the 1940s, and to Islamist groups of the 1970s and 1980s."*

Ignoring the thesis altogether in essays published in 2004,[22] and 2013,[23] Skovgaard-Petersen extolled Tantawi's alleged moderation, even ecumenism, but made no mention of the following: Tantawi's own validating introduction to the 1997 re-publication of his Ph.D. thesis, [24] Tantawi's hateful description of his 1997 meeting with Rabbi Lau, melded to his overt denunciation of Egyptian "normalization" of relations with Israel (and Jews), [25] Tantawi's repeated sanctioning of homicide bombing against Israeli Jews, including non-combatants, [26] or Tantawi's use of the canonical Qur'anic epithet (Q 5:60) "apes and pigs" when referring specifically to modern Jews. In 2004, Skovgaard-Petersen argued Tantawi's views, by default, including his bilious Jew-hatred, somehow presented, an "alternative" to, *"what...is seen as a rigid and conformist version of Islam. It is my impression that many non-Islamist Muslims are well aware that the State Mufti is under pressure from the state, and that they may disagree profoundly with the regime on many other issues. That they, in other words, sympathize with the Mufti, not for representing the State, but for the views he expresses."* [28] A decade later, 3-years after Tantawi's death,

Skovgaard-Petersen opined, *"Sayyed Tantawi (1996-2010) was much more maligned and attacked and often had to defend himself in the media. More politically involved than his predecessor, Tantawi actively sought a role in inter-religious dialogue accepting to meet with even Israeli rabbis..."* [29] Skovgaard-Petersen's narrowly resticted characterization, *"accepting to meet with even Israeli rabbis,"* negates Tantawi's own well-documented vitriolic assessment of the most publicized meeting. i.e., with Rabbi Lau. [30]

This pattern of Western, including Western academic apologetics, or frank denial, versus celebratory Muslim triumphalism regarding the unabashed Jew-hating rancor of Tantawi's thesis, persists with great ongoing relevance today. As I will demonstrate, the virulent Antisemitism permeating "Banū Isrā'īl fī al-Qur'ān wa-al-sunnah," has deep, mainstream Muslim historical and doctrinal roots, elucidated for the remainder of this introduction, prefaced by a related synopsis of Tantawi's biography.

A biographical sketch of Muhammad Sayyed Tantawi, 1928-2010, and an overview of Tantawi's public attitudes towards jihad, and Jews, in particular, with clarifying exegeses from his multi-volume Qur'anic commentary, *"The intermediate [balanced] interpretation of the Qur'an"*

The following biographical sketch of Tantawi draws, primarily, upon his official Al-Azhar University biography, [31] complemented by biographical materials included in two academic assessments of Tantawi's oeuvre, [32] and an interview by an academic, [33] with additional details from an obituarist. [34]

Muhammad Sayyed Tantawi, born on October 28, 1928 in Salim Sharqi, Sohaj Governorate, Upper Egypt, allegedly displayed "his brilliance when he was able to recite the whole Qur'an (i.e., he was a 'hafiz' [35]) while still in elementary school in his village." [36] Subsequently, Tantawi attended the Azhar Institute in Alexandria at the age of 16 in 1944. [37] According to obituarist Issandr El-Amrani, Tantawi, as a young man, at least fleetingly, joined the Muslim Brotherhood: [38]

> *"He came of age in the 1940s, and considered himself privileged to have been a young Muslim Brother and benefited from direct contact with the movement's founder, Hassan al-Banna (d. 1949). He shared with al-Banna and many other Brothers at the time a provincial origin, a fierce nationalism and disdain for the cosmopolitanism of Egypt's ruling elite under the monarchy."*

Charles Wendell, esteemed translator of al-Banna's most important treatises, summarized the quintessential Islamic ideology a youthful Tantawi, and countless Egyptian Muslims of his generation, imbibed from the Muslim Brotherhood's founder (emphases added). Wendell's observations remain critical to understanding the deep Islamic religious animus towards Israel—so much in evidence today—that Al-Banna and his movement both inspired and reflected. [39]

> *"Hasan al-Banna's fundamental conviction that Islam does not accept, or even tolerate, a separation of 'church' and state, or of either from society,* ***is as***

thoroughly Islamic as it can be. Any attempt to translate his movement into terms reducible to social, political, or religious factors exclusively simply misses the boat. The 'totality' created by the Prophet Muhammad in the Medinese state, the first Islamic state, was Hasan's unwavering ideal, ***and the ideal of all Muslim thinkers before him, including the idle dreamers in the mosque. His ideology then, before it was Egyptian or Arab or whatever, was Islamic to the core.*** *Since it embraced all aspects of human life and thought, it was at least as much religious as anything else. Practically all of his arguments are shored up by frequent quotations from the Qur'an and the Traditions, quite in the style of his medieval forbears.* ***If one considers the public to whom his writings were addressed, it becomes instantly apparent that such arguments must still be the most compelling for the vast bulk of the Muslim populations of today.*** *The nagging feeling that Islam must, and very quickly at that, catch up with the West, had even by his time filtered down from above to the masses after having been the watchword of the modernizing intellectual for almost a century. There was also the notion that all these Western sciences and techniques were originally adopted from Islamic culture, and were therefore merely 'coming home'—a piece of self-conscious back-patting that was already a cliché of most Muslim political writing...* ***To this [Islamic] revivalist mentality, nothing could be more hateful than further diminution of the lands traditionally dominated by Islam. I believe that much of the fury and unconcealed hatred of the Zionist state which is expressed by the majority of Arabs will become more comprehensible in light of what the Islamic domain as a concept really means to the Muslims, seen through the lens of Hasan's exposition.*** *Fascists were unable to endow their acts or beliefs with a religious dimension, except for the embarrassing juvenility of the Teutonic shrines reputedly raised in Germany. In the case of the Muslim Brotherhood, however, they had, on the basis of indisputable historical facts and clear religious traditions, a ready-made program for a world crusade that required only actors and a leader."*

Al-Banna himself is alleged to have declared about the Muslim Brotherhood's essential creed, [39a] "If (people) complain that you are vague, tell them ... 'O people! We are Islam'"

Tantawi graduated from The Faculty of Theology at Al-Azhar in 1958/59, receiving his Masters in Education. He was awarded an Al-Azhar Ph.D. in tafsir [40] (Qur'anic interpretation) and Hadith [41] (the traditions of Islam's prophet Muhammad, and his earliest votaries) in 1966, for the thesis, "Banū Isrā'īl fī al-Qur'ān wa-al-sunnah". [42] During the early 1960s, Tantawi was a preacher for the Egyptian Ministry of Waqf (Awqaf; Islamic charitable endowments), [43] and Laura Bariani claims he also studied in Iraq for several years. [44] Tantawi continued teaching at the Faculty of Theology through 1972, until his appointment as a lecturer at the University of Asiyut, becoming a Professor and Dean in 1976. [45] He was transferred, in 1978 to the Azhar Faculty of Islamic and Arabic Studies, albeit, as Skovgaard-Petersen observed, [46] "sometimes employed for short periods in Libya, Iraq, and Saudi Arabia, as were so many other Egyptian ulama (religious teachers) during this period." Tantawi was appointed Egypt's national Mufti (i.e., 10-years prior to becoming Grand Imam of Al-Azhar University) upon just having been elected Al-Azhar Dean of Faculty of Islamic and Arabic Studies, in late October, 1986. [47]

Tantawi's appointment as Mufti was unique given his complete absence of training or experience in Sharia (Islamic law) [48] jurisprudence, per se, "or even ordinary courts." [49] Skovgaard-Petersen emphasized [50] Tantawi's alternative rigorous academic religious background, "concentrated on the Koran, theology, and Islamic propagation." Before his designation as Mufti, Skovgaard-Petersen noted, [51]

> *"...apart from the thesis On the Children of Israel, from 1970 to 1986 he edited a 15-volume commentary to the Koran called at-Tafsir al-Wasit li'l-Qur'an al-Karim ("The intermediate [balanced] interpretation of the Qur'an"). According to Tantawi himself, this work aims at lay readers and is written in clear and simple language; for every verse it lists the context of its revelation (asbab an-nuzul), an explanation of every single term (tafsir al-alfaz), the meaning of the whole verse, and finally the rule and norms for behavior which may be deduced from it. Apart from these major works, he had published a book about prayer (du'a) in the Revelation, as well as minor treatises on the Prophet's (Muhammad's) life."*

Skovgaard-Petersen's academic portrayal of Tantawi, as discussed previously, was devoted to reinforcing the Egyptian cleric's putative moderation. [52] Accordingly, in describing Tantawi during his tenure as Egypt's Mufti (1986 to 1996), Skovgaard-Petersen added "a few personal details" to Tantawi's "portrait," writing, [53]

> *"Tantawi married in 1960 and has three children, a daughter who is a doctor of medicine and two sons who are working in a bank and with the police, respectively. It seems, then, that he does not oppose women working outside home, which he has also stated in several fatwas and interviews. His middle-class values are confirmed in an interview with the Leftist weekly al-Ahali, where he confesses that he listens to music (20th century classics) Umm Kulthum [54] and Muhammad abd al-Wahhab, [55] and although 'very ignorant' he likes and appreciates paintings and sculpture which he believes may refine the senses.* ***This is remarkable*** *(emphasis added); the status of music and, and especially sculpture are among the questions which have been directed to the Dar al-Ifta (body that issues fatwas or religious edicts) [56] all through the century, and not a few Muftis have regarded them as reprehensible. More than music, however, Sayyed Tantawi loves Arabic poetry, mentioning al-Mutannabi [57] and Ahmad Shawqi, [58] once again poets who encountered some opposition from the ulama of their day. He also watches TV (not only religious programs) but has no time to watch films. First and foremost, though, Tantawi is a hard-working man, as is amply shown by his output."*

After serving as Egypt's Mufti for a decade, Tantawi was appointed Grand Imam of Al Azhar University March 17, 1996, a position he held until his sudden cardiac death on March 10, 2010. [59]

The inaugural 2009 issue of *The 500 Most Influential Muslims in the World*, produced by the Amman, Jordan Royal Islamic Institute of Strategic Studies, created as an avatar of mainstream, moderate Islam, ranked Tantawi eighth in overall influence, and third among authoritative religious leaders (after The Islamic Republic of Iran's Ayatollah Khamenei, and Iraq's Ayatollah Sistani). [60] Tantawi's entry in *The 500* succinctly encapsulates his expertise, and the standard apologetic narrative of his tenure as both Egyptian Mufti, and Al-Azhar Grand Imam. Under a section labeled, "Key Commentator on the Qur'an," *The 500* states, [61]

> *"Tantawi's ability to talk about Islam and his scholarly influence are founded on the Islamic practice of tafsir, that is, commentary on the Qur'an. His current influence is seen in his close participation with the creation of the first online tafsir database (www.altafsir.com)."*

In its conclusion, *The 500* characterized Tantawi as a "bastion of moderation," and "most influential as the moderate voice of the Islamic establishment." [62] Perhaps the most salient issue cited in support of this claim was Tantawi's alleged stance on terrorism: [63]

> *"On the issue of terrorism, Tantawi was quick to brand the perptrators of terrorist acts as heretics, stating that it is not courageous 'to kill an innocent person, or to kill thousands of people, including men and women and children.'...*

Tantawi's long term record on "terrorism"—namely jihad terrorism, and the Islamic institution of jihad, [64] generally—does not comport with *The 500*'s laudatory characterization, [65] or the Western journalistic hagiography of James Reston Jr., written following an arranged "audience with the grand sheikh," in mid-March 2002. [66] The analysis of Reston Jr. merits elaboration because its errors and omissions are pathognomonic of standard journalistic and academic treatments of Tantawi's legacy as an influential, "hard working" lead Muslim cleric, and renowned Islamic religious scholar. [67]

Reston Jr. sought his "audience" with "the grand imam of Egypt's al-Azhar mosque, and the most widely respected and influential moral voice for Sunni Islam," so that Tantawi might "clarify for me [Reston Jr.] the Islamic concepts of jihad, paradise, and martyrdom." Against the then recent backdrop of "the attacks on the World Trade Center and Pentagon, the suicide bombings by Palestinians and the murder of journalist Daniel Pearl," Reston Jr. averred, Tantawi "was the right person from whom to seek guidance," given how "Sunni Muslims from Malaysia to the Middle East to Middle America, representing more than 80 percent of Islamic believers worldwide, look to al-Azhar and its Academy of Islamic Research (of which Tantawi is chairman) for learned interpretation and moral counsel." [68] Here is how Reston Jr. framed his main query to Tantawi: [69]

> *"Can it be, I wondered, that any Muslim, with a few followers, can walk into the street and proclaim a legitimate and authentic jihad against the West or Israel? Is it possible that any group of a few thousand fanatics can attack three huge American buildings, kill 3,000 unsuspecting innocents and validly say that the act is justified by the Koran?"*

Before summarizing Tantawi's responses, Reston Jr. described the setting in which he met the Grand Imam, and the Grand Imam's demeanor: [70]

> *"In his vast office, decorated with lovely wood paneling carved with geometric Arabic designs and appointed with huge photographs of Islam's three holiest mosques, at Mecca, Medina and Jerusalem, the 73-year-old Tantawi spoke forcefully about the misconceptions in the West and, equally forcefully, of the perversions of Islam in the East that have led to the violence. A small man, with puffy eyes, deliberate speech and a gentle demeanor, he sat on his couch amid advisers and lesser imams, dressed in a simple red and white cap and a brown, floor-length caftan."*

When Tantawi provided his response—a disingenuous Muslim apologetic on jihad and jihad terrorism that negated their open ended doctrinal and historical aggressiveness [71]—Reston Jr. saw fit to interject a quotation of Qur'an 2:190, along with a personal benign inference about the verse's meaning: [72]

> *"The concept of jihad, Tantawi affirmed through an interpreter, is purely defensive and cannot be aggressive. It can only legitimately be proclaimed by a head of state or leader of all Arab peoples when Arab lands are invaded and occupied (in the manner 12th-century Islamic leader Saladin employed against the Crusader force of Richard I of England), or when great numbers of Arab peoples are displaced and exiled, or when the tenets of Islam are directly attacked or abused. Tantawi's explanation fit with the words I had read in the Koran (Q 2:190) and quoted back to him: 'Fight in Allah's cause against those who wage war against you, but do not commit aggression, for verily Allah does not love aggressors.'"*

First, consistent with his own apologetic, that amplified Tantawi's, Reston Jr.'s parenthetical reference to Saladin's jihad against Richard I, and the Crusader Kingdom in the Levant, ignored the aggressive, sanguinary jihad campaigns which ravaged the indigenous Christian communities of the Middle East, North Africa, and Western Europe—punctuated by massacre, pillage, enslavement, and deportation—for more than 450 years before the First Crusade in 1099 C.E., beginning in 634 C.E., with the jihad invasion of Syro-Palestine. [73] More broadly and significantly, the manner in which Reston Jr. posed his essential question to Tantawi, described the Grand Imam's setting and "demeanor," and even interjected his own quotation (and inferred meaning) of Q

2:190, all facilitated Tantawi's bowdlerized responses, which went unchallenged by the journalist. [74]

An objective, informed interview would have, at minimum, referenced Tantawi's own prodigious 15-volume Qur'anic commentary, *at-Tafsir al-Wasit li'l-Qur'an al-Karim ("The intermediate [balanced] interpretation of the Qur'an")*, characterized, aptly, by the Grand Imam as targeting "lay readers," and "written in clear and simple language." [75] Tantawi's magnum opus was published in 1986, over 15-years before Reston Jr.'s face to face encounter with the Grand Imam. Juxtaposing Tantawi's responses to Reston Jr. with the glosses on relevant Qur'anic verses on jihad (as well as jihad terror, martyrdom, and paradise) from *The intermediate [balanced] interpretation of the Qur'an*—Tantawi vs. Tantawi—demolishes the dishonest apologetics Reston Jr. so willingly and uncritically accepted from the late Grand Imam. [76]

Contra Reston Jr.'s interpretation, Tantawi's gloss [77] on the relatively unaggressive sounding verse Qur'an 2:190, incorporates its 15th century classical interpretation in the most important single volume Qur'anic commentary Tafsir al-Jalalayn, [78] which argues 2:190 was abrogated, cancelled, by all of sura 9 (a series of aggressive war proclamations against non-Muslims [79]), and "Allah's words in the following ayat (verse, i.e., 2:191)." Verse 2: 191 reads: [80] "And kill them wherever you overtake them and expel them from wherever they have expelled you , and fitnah is worse than killing. And do not fight them at al-Masjid al-îram (Holy Mosque of Mecca) until they fight you there. But if they fight you then kill them. Such is the recompense of the disbelievers."

Regarding Q 2:190, Tantawi maintains, [81]

> *"What is meant by fighting in the way of Allah is jihad to make His word supreme so that the people of His true religion will be honored, not oppressed by His enemies, and free to call to Him and establish His just laws under the shadow of an awe-inspiring authority. That is, fight, O believers, to make the word of Allah supreme and His religion honorable, your enemies who have prepared themselves to fight you and confront you, and you have realized their bad intentions and corrupt nature. This noble verse encourages and entices the believers to fight their enemies without hesitation or fear, and guides them to make their jihad for the sake of supporting the truth [i.e., Islam]..."*

Referring to four canonical hadith collections (of Abu Dawud, al-Tirmidhi, al-Nasai, and Ibn Majah), Tantawi avers a Bedouin was told by Muhammad, [82] , "Whoever fights so that the word of Allah is supreme is fighting in the cause of Allah." Tantawi, underscoring the open-ended, aggressive nature of jihad, notes, [83] "There are many hadiths calling for jihad in the cause of Allah to make His word supreme." Such aggression extends even to non-combatants—the elderly, infirm, children, women, etc.—"who have evidence that they have had an impact, whether through their opinion or action, in the war, and who support the fighters to defeat the mujahideen (Muslim holy warriors)." [84] For Tantawi, "polytheism," or paganism is intrinsically "persecuting" toward Muslims, justifying the formulation of the esteemed 19th century Qur'anic commentator al-Alusi, [85] "the polytheists have no right except Islam or the sword." The notion of fighting polytheists/polytheism until submission is reinforced by Tantawi's citation of Muhammad's proclamation from the "two Sahihs," [86] the most authoritative "sound" (=sahih) hadith collections of Bukhari and Muslim: "I have been commanded to fight the people until they testify that there is no god but Allah and that Muhammad is the Messenger of Allah, establish prayer, and pay zakat. If they do that, then their blood and properties are safe from me, except for the right of Islam, and their reckoning is with Allah."

Tantawi's pellucid endorsement of classical Islam's support for offensive, expansionist jihad warfare against "polytheists" in his commentary on Q 2:190 (-195), is complemented by his gloss on Q 2:215-217 which reminds Muslims of their obligation to wage jihad against the polytheists (in particular), "despite the difficulties and hardships it entails." Aggressive jihad against the polytheists or "disbelievers/ hypocrites" is re-emphasized in Tantawi's commentaries on Q 9:5 and Q 9:73, and expanded to include open ended jihad to subjugate Jews and Christians, specifically, in Tantawi's gloss on Q 9:29. A review of Tantawi's commentaries on Q 9:111, Q 8:60, and Q 47:4, demonstrates, further, Tantawi also shared the classical Islamic viewpoint that glorifies aggressive, murderous jihad terror "martyrdom" attacks on non-Muslims for Muslims to achieve entry to paradise. Below, res ipsa loquitur extracts from Tantawi's glosses on all these verses, preceded by the verses themselves, are presented. [87]

Qur'an 2:215-2:217, and key extracts from Tantawi's related commentary, follow: [88]

> *(Q 2:215) They ask you, [O Muhammad], what they should spend. Say, "Whatever you spend of good is [to be] for parents and relatives and orphans and the needy and the traveler. And whatever you do of good - indeed, Allah is Knowing of it."*
> *(Q 2:216) Fighting has been enjoined upon you while it is hateful to you. But perhaps you hate a thing and it is good for you; and perhaps you love a thing and it is bad for you. And Allah Knows, while you know not.*
> *(Q 2:217) They ask you about the sacred month - about fighting therein. Say, "Fighting therein is great [sin], but averting [people] from the way of Allah and disbelief in Him and [preventing access to] al-Masjid al-haram and the expulsion of its people therefrom are greater [evil] in the sight of Allah. And fitnah is greater than killing." And they will continue to fight you until they turn you back from your religion if they are able. And whoever of you reverts from his religion [to disbelief] and dies while he is a disbeliever - for those, their deeds have become worthless in this world and the Hereafter, and those are the companions of the Fire, they will abide therein eternally.*
>
> *(Key extracts from Tantawi's commentary) "[T]he fact that fighting is disliked by people does not contradict faith, nor does it mean that Muslims disliked its obligation, because obeying the command may involve hardship, but if one knows the reward in facing the hardships, there is no doubt that fighting in the*

way of Allah - despite the difficulties and hardships it entails - will result in honor in this world and happiness in the hereafter... Allah - the Most High - prescribed for the Muslims to fight their enemies because He knew that it was in their interest, so the believers responded with sincerity and devotion to what their Lord had imposed upon them...The bottom line is that fighting in the way of Allah is a cause for achieving security from enemies in this world and a cause for the mujahid (holy warrior) to obtain a great reward in the hereafter... Al-Qurtubi [89] *said: The meaning is that perhaps you hate the hardship in jihad, while it is good for you, because you will be victorious, triumph, gain booty, and be rewarded, and whoever among you dies as a martyr. And perhaps you love ease and abandoning fighting, while it is bad for you, because you will be victorious and your matter will be lost. This is correct and there is no doubt about it, as happened in the land of Andalusia (Muslim Spain)* [90] *...feelings of sorrow and pain in the soul. Muslims only became humiliated and weak when they abandoned jihad in the way of Allah, and swarmed to the earth, and were content with worldly life and felt secure in it, and preferred the pleasures and desires of this world over the noble and honorable life... [I]t is proven in the Sahih:* [91] *'Whoever dies without having fought or having thought of fighting, dies a death of the ignorant.' And the Prophet (peace and blessings be upon him) said on the day of the conquest: 'There is no emigration after the conquest, but jihad and intention, and when you are called to arms, then mobilize.'...jihad in order to raise the word of truth... this noble verse has called upon the believers to sacrifice their wealth and their lives in the path of supporting the truth in the wisest manner, and cleared them of the doubts raised by the polytheists around them, and warned them against following their path, and gave them good tidings of a good outcome when they responded to the teachings of their religion and held fast to its rope."*

Qur'an 9:5, and key extracts from Tantawi's related commentary, follow: [92]

(Q 9:5) And when the sacred months have passed, then kill the polytheists wherever you find them and capture them and besiege them and sit in wait for them at every place of ambush. But if they should repent, establish prayer, and give zakah, let them [go] on their way. Indeed, Allah is Forgiving and Merciful.

(Key extracts from Tantawi's commentary) The one who contemplates this noble verse will see that these four methods - killing, capturing, besieging, and monitoring - are the means sufficient to eliminate the enemy, and no era is devoid of the use of some or all of them during an attack. Thus, we see the teachings of Islam urging Muslims to use all legitimate means to plot against their enemies and work to defeat them, as long as these enemies persist in their tyranny, aggression, and violation of the limits set by Allah Almighty. ***However, if they open their hearts to the truth and respond to it, then the noble verse lifts the sword from them and commands the believers to set them free****... That is, you - O believers - when the four months of security are over, you must kill the polytheists who broke their covenants wherever you find them, and capture*

them, imprison them, and monitor them on every road until their power is weakened and they submit to you. ***"But if they repent" from polytheism by entering Islam, then leave them alone, cease fighting them, and open the paths and roads to them****... Allah's statement, "Indeed, Allah is Forgiving and Merciful" is a conclusion intended to explain the obligation to set them free, i.e., if they do that, then set them free and do not deal with them based on their polytheism, for Islam wipes out what came before it, and Allah has forgiven them their past disbelief and treachery by His grace and mercy... It was reported in the two Sahihs* [93] *on the authority of Ibn Umar that the Messenger of Allah, may Allah bless him and grant him peace, said: "I have been commanded to fight the people until they testify that there is no god but Allah and that Muhammad is the Messenger of Allah, establish prayer, and pay zakat." Imam Ahmad* [94] *narrated that the Messenger of Allah, may Allah bless him and grant him peace, said: "I have been commanded to fight the people until they testify that there is no god but Allah and that Muhammad is the Messenger of Allah. When they testify, face our Qiblah, eat our slaughtered animals, and pray as we pray, then their bloods and properties are sacred to us except for a right reason. They have what the Muslims have and are subject to what the Muslims are subject to."...* ***Thus, you see that this verse has combined in its guidance both encouragement and intimidation. It has commanded the believers [Muslims] to use all legitimate means to terrorize their enemies. Then, at the same time, it has commanded them to release them if they repent, establish prayer, and pay zakat. After Allah the Exalted explained the ruling on those who persist in polytheism, which is to fight them and seize them, and the ruling on those who turn away from it, which is to release them. After that, Allah, the Exalted, explained the ruling on the polytheists who seek safety because of knowledge of the laws of Islam.***"

Qur'an 9:73, and key extracts from Tantawi's related commentary, follow: [94a]

(Q 9:73) "O Prophet, fight against the disbelievers and the hypocrites and be harsh upon them. And their refuge is Hell, and wretched is the destination."

(Key extracts from Tantawi's commentary) "[G]ood treatment of them (the disbelievers and hypocrites) ***only increased their filthiness. Therefore, this Sura - which is one of the last Suras to be revealed in the Qur'an - came to tell the Prophet*** *- may Allah bless him and grant him peace -* ***that the time has come to replace leniency and kindness with severity and firmness****, for severity has its places and leniency has its places. The meaning is that you - O noble Prophet -* ***must fight the disbelievers with the sword if nothing else will reform them, and that you must fight the hypocrites - who outwardly display Islam but conceal their disbelief - with whatever you see fit to repel, deter, and terrorize them, whether that is by hand, tongue, or otherwise, until you are safe from their evil****...* ***It was previously reported from the Commander of the Faithful, Ali ibn Abi Talib,*** [94b] ***that he said, The Messenger of Allah - may Allah bless him and grant him peace - was sent with four swords. A sword for***

> ***the polytheists 'So when the sacred months have passed, then kill the polytheists wherever you find them...' (Qur'an 9:5) And a sword for the infidels, the People of the Book 'Fight those who do not believe in Allah or in the Last Day and do not forbid what Allah and His Messenger have forbidden and do not adopt the religion of truth from among those who were given the Scripture...' (Qur'an 9:29) And a sword for the hypocrites 'Fight against the disbelievers And the hypocrites' (Qur'an 9:73) and a sword for the rebels 'Then fight against those who rebel until they return to the command of Allah' (Qur'an 49:9)*** *This requires that they fight with swords if they display hypocrisy...His (Allah's)statement, 'And be harsh upon them' refers to both groups, the disbelievers and the hypocrites.* ***That is, strive against them with all that you are able to strive against them with, as the situation requires, and be strict with them in this striving to the point that you do not leave any room for kindness and leniency with them, because they are not worthy of that, after they have become blind and deaf to sincere advice, and after they have persisted in their transgression.*** *His statement, 'And their refuge is Hell, and wretched is the destination' is a conclusion intended to* ***explain their bad fate in the Hereafter*** *after explaining what the believers must do towards them in this world."*

Qur'an 9:29, and key extracts from Tantawi's related commentary, follow: [95]

> *(Q 9:29) "Fight those who do not believe in Allah or in the Last Day and who do not consider unlawful what Allah and His Messenger have made unlawful and who do not adopt the religion of truth from those who were given the Scripture - [fight] until they give the jizya willingly while they are humbled."*

> *(Key extracts from Tantawi's commentary) "The intended meaning of His statement, "of those who were given the Scripture" is to distinguish them from the polytheists who worship idols in terms of ruling, because the ruling for the latter is to fight them until they submit to Islam, while the ruling for the People of the Scripture (primarily Jews and Christians) is fighting, or Islam, or the jizya. His statement, 'until they pay the jizya willingly while they are subdued,' is an end to fighting. That is, fight those of the People of the Book who have these characteristics until they pay the jizya willingly and obediently... What is meant by giving it in His statement, 'until they pay the jizya,' is the obligation to pay it, even if the specific time is not mentioned. The hand here may be a metaphor for surrender and submission. That is, until they pay the jizya in submission and obedience. It may also be a metaphor and "about" means paying in cash without delay. That is, until they give it in cash without procrastination or delay. It may also be its literal meaning, with "about" in the sense of the preposition "with," that is, until they give it with their own hand to the Muslims, not send it with the hand of someone other than them... And His statement, 'and they are humiliated,' is from 'saghir,' meaning humiliation and disgrace. It is said that someone became humiliated, humiliated, and submissive to someone else. The meaning is:* ***Fight those among the People of the Book***

who have these characteristics until they pay you the jizya willingly and submissively, and are submissive and subject to your authority over them. For those who do not believe in Allah or the Last Day, and do not forbid what Allah and His Messenger have forbidden...And they do not take the true religion as their religion. They deserve this humiliation in this world, but in the Hereafter, their punishment will be more severe and lasting. *This. Among the rulings that scholars have taken from this verse are the following: 1- This verse is the basis for the legitimacy of the jizya, and that it is only taken from the People of the Book according to many jurists - because the People of the Book are the ones who have the choice between Islam, fighting, or the jizya... Taking the jizya from them is only equivalent to what they receive, and our refraining from fighting them, and their contribution to raising the status of the Islamic state that has secured them...* ***What is correct regarding the verse is that the humiliation is their commitment to the implementation of Allah's rulings upon them, and paying the jizya, because that is humiliation... After He (Allah) - Glory be to Him - explained some of the vices of the People of the Book in general, He followed that with a detailed account of these vices, so He narrated their false statements, reprehensible actions, and bad intentions***..." [96]

Qur'an 9:111, and key extracts from Tantawi's related commentary, follow: [97]

(Q 9:111) *Indeed, Allah has purchased from the believers their lives and their properties [in exchange] for that they will have Paradise. They fight in the cause of Allah , so they kill and are killed. [It is] a true promise [binding] upon Him in the Torah and the Gospel and the Qur'an. And who is truer to his covenant than Allah ? So rejoice in your transaction which you have contracted. And it is that which is the great attainment.*

(Key extracts from Tantawi's commentary) " ***That is, they fight in the cause of Allah, some of them kill the enemies of Allah, and some of them are killed by these enemies, and the reward of both the killer and the killed is Paradise***...*[B]y placing the passive verb before the active verb...* ***indicates that the eagerness of these sincere believers to be martyred is greater than their eagerness to escape being killed, because this martyrdom leads them to a Paradise as wide as the heavens and the earth, and to the everlasting life.*** *And His statement, 'a true promise binding upon Him in the Torah, the Gospel, and the Qur'an,' confirms the reward that Allah has promised them.* **That is, this Paradise, which is the reward of the mujahideen (holy warriors), has been made by Allah, glory be to Him, as a favor and generosity from Him, a right upon them, and He has confirmed this for them in the heavenly books that He revealed to His messengers**... *And His statement, 'So rejoice in your transaction which you have contracted, and that is what is the great attainment,' is an incitement to fight, and informing them that they are winners in this deal. Rejoicing is the feeling of joy at good news. A feeling that makes the face smile. That is, if this is the case, then rejoice in your transaction that you have made with the utmost joy, and be satisfied with it with the utmost satisfaction, because*

that transaction is the great victory than which there is no victory greater. ***Some scholars said: You will not find a better or more eloquent encouragement for jihad than this verse, because He presented it in the form of a contract made by the Lord of Glory, and its price is money that no eye has seen, no ear has heard, and no human heart has conceived. He did not make the contract only for them to be killed, but rather also for them to be killers to raise His word, support His religion, and make it recorded in the heavenly books, and that is enough for you as a deed****... He depicted the jihad of the believers, and the sacrifice of their wealth and lives in it, and Allah's reward for that with Paradise, through buying and selling. He said, "they fight," clarifying the place of surrender, which is the battle, and to this is the allusion in His (Muhammad's) saying, peace and blessings be upon him,* ***"Paradise is under the shade of swords."*** [98] *Then He confirmed it by saying, "And that is the great attainment." It is narrated from Al-Hasan Al-Basri* [99] *that he read this verse and said, "Look at the generosity of Allah, the Most High. He is the Creator of Souls, and wealth He is the Provider of, then He rewards us for them with Paradise when we sacrifice them in His cause."*

Qur'an 8:60, and key extracts from Tantawi's related commentary, follow: [100]

(Q 8:60) And prepare against them whatever you are able of power and of steeds of war by which you may terrify the enemy of Allah and your enemy and others besides them whom you do not know [but] whom Allah knows. And whatever you spend in the cause of Allah will be fully repaid to you, and you will not be wronged.

*(Key extracts from Tantawi's commentary) "****That is, prepare whatever force you can, while you are terrifying with this preparation the enemy of Allah and your enemy, from every disbeliever, polytheist, and one who has deviated from the path of truth. At the head of all of these are the disbelievers of Mecca who expelled you from your homes unjustly, and the Jews of Medina who did everything they could to harm you****. His statement, {And others besides them whom you do not know, but Allah knows them} is connected to what preceded it.* ***That is, with this preparation you terrify enemies known to you - such as the polytheists of Mecca and the Jews of Medina, and you also terrify other enemies besides them whom you do not know because they hide their enmity towards you****. But Allah, from whom nothing is hidden, knows them and will nullify their deeds. The commentators differed as to who is meant by these enemies whom Allah referred to with His statement, 'You do not know them, but Allah knows them.'* ***Some of them said that what is meant by them is Banu Qurayza,*** [101] ***and some of them said that what is meant by them is the people of Persia and Rome... When the rulers acted in accordance with this verse during the days of Islamic civilization, Islam was honorable, great, refused injustice, was strong in its spear, had great prestige, and was abundant in its brilliance, as it spread the banner of its authority over the entire earth, and seized control of the regions and cities...Today, Muslims have abandoned this***

noble verse and have inclined towards luxury and comfort, neglecting a communal obligation. The entire Ummah has become sinful for neglecting this obligation, and thus today it is suffering from its anguish... Isn't it time for them to wake up from their negligence and prepare the equipment that Allah has commanded for their enemies, *and make up for what they have neglected before the enemy attacks what is left of it with his cavalry and infantry?* ***The strength that Allah has asked the believers to prepare to terrorize the enemy includes everything that makes the believers strong, such as preparing trained armies and various weapons that differ according to time and place. The narrated interpretation of strength - mentioned in the verse - as archery is only an example, because archery was the strongest means of strengthening one's strength at that time. Al-Fakhr al-Razi*** [102] ***said in his interpretation of the verse, 'What is meant by strength here is that which is a cause for obtaining strength.'*** *... the reason for fighting protecting the Islamic call..., establish freedom of belief, and purify the earth from injustice and tyranny. The obligation of spending in the cause of Allah. One of the most honorable forms of spending in the cause of Allah is for a Muslim to spend what he can in jihad, which is the pinnacle of Islam, and which no people abandon except that they are humiliated and throw themselves into destruction. The noble verse has given glad tidings to those who spend in the cause of Allah that He, the Almighty, will fully reward them for their spending, without any deficiency or injustice."*

Qur'an 47:4 and key extracts from Tantawi's related commentary, follow: [103]

(Q 47:4-47:6) So when you meet those who disbelieve [in battle], strike [their] necks until, when you have inflicted slaughter upon them, then secure their bonds, and either [confer] favor afterwards or ransom [them] until the war lays down its burdens. That [is the command]. And if Allah had willed, He could have taken vengeance upon them [Himself], but [He ordered armed struggle] to test some of you by means of others. And those who are killed in the cause of Allah - never will He waste their deeds. He will guide them and amend their condition. And admit them to Paradise, which He has made known to them.

(Key extracts from Tantawi's commentary) "'So when you meet' is to arrange what comes after it, which is guidance for the believers on what they must do when killing their enemies, based on what came before it, which is a description of the state of the disbelievers. What is meant by "meeting" here is fighting, not just meeting and seeing. What is meant by 'those who disbelieved' here are the polytheists and all those who are like them, with whom we have no treaty, but rather between us and them is war and fighting. And His statement, the Most High, 'So strike the necks' is a command to the believers regarding what they must do when they meet their enemies... if the state of those who disbelieved is as I have mentioned to you, with their deeds being rendered worthless due to their following falsehood and turning away from the truth, then when you meet them for battle, do not be moved by pity for them, but strike their necks with a

severe strike. The expression of killing with the phrase {so he struck off the necks} is to portray it in its most horrific form, to exaggerate the severity of the fighting, and to guide the believers to what they must do... this expression contains harshness and severity that is not found in the word killing, because it depicts killing in the most horrific form, which is slitting the neck and severing the limb that is the head of the body... [M]eet your enemies, then strike their necks, and when you have overcome them and subdued them, and inflicted wounds upon them that make them unable to resist you, then secure the shackles of those you have captured from them, so that they cannot escape or flee from you... 'And those who are killed in the cause of Allah,' meaning those who were martyred while fighting to raise the word of Allah. 'He will never let their deeds go to waste,' meaning He will not waste their deeds or invalidate them. Rather, 'He will guide them,' meaning He will lead them to the path of happiness and success. 'And amend their condition,' meaning He will amend their conditions, affairs, and hearts. 'And He will admit them to Paradise, which He has made known to them.' That is, after all of that, He will admit them to Paradise on the Day of Resurrection and guide them to their homes and dwellings therein, so that they will not miss them, as if they have been living there since they were created... [F]rom the rulings that the scholars took from these verses are the following: 1- The obligation to fight the disbelievers with all severity and strength, until their power is weakened, their state is established, and they submit to the rule of Islamic law over them. Many verses have been reported in this meaning, including the saying of Allah the Almighty: [Q 9:73] 'O Prophet, fight against the disbelievers and the hypocrites and be harsh upon them. And their refuge is Hell, and wretched is the destination'. 2- Some scholars took from the saying of Allah the Almighty: 'Then either by conferring favor afterward or by ransom until the war lays down its burdens,' that the situation of the enemy prisoner is between these two states: either we release him without compensation, or we release him in exchange for a specific ransom that we take from him, and this ransom may be money, work, or something else that benefits the Muslims. Some scholars believe that this verse was abrogated by the verse in which Allah the Almighty says: Q 9:5: 'So when the sacred months have passed, then kill the polytheists wherever you find them and capture them and besiege them and lie in wait for them at every place of ambush.' ***The scholars who investigated the verse, which is the verse in which Allah the Almighty says: 'Then either by way of favor afterwards or by ransom,' describe specific situations in which the issue of prisoners of war is a matter of favor or ransom, because both are in the interest of the Muslims. There are other situations in which it is more appropriate to kill the enemy or enslave them. The issue of enemy prisoners of war is decided based on what is in the best interest of the Muslims...This opinion was favored by many scholars, including Imam Ibn Jarir (i.e., al-Tabari),*** [104] ***who said, in summary - after citing a number of opinions - that the correct opinion in our view is that this verse is decisive and not abrogated, because it is not objectionable that the choice of favor, killing, or ransom was given to the Messenger (peace and blessings be upon him) and to those who came after him in charge of the***

> ***affairs of the ummah****. Even though killing is not mentioned in this verse, Allah - the Almighty - has permitted their killing in other verses, including 'So kill the polytheists wherever you find them.' [Q 9:5] The Messenger - may Allah's prayers and peace be upon him - did all of that with the prisoners...* ***Therefore, the public interest alone is decisive, and it is the plan that is followed in wars, especially since war is deceit and trickery****. As long as it is deceit or trickery, let the schemers devise plans of deceit and trickery and do not outline for them how to scheme, otherwise they would not be schemers. 3-* ***The martyrs are given good tidings of a great reward and immense recompense.*** *Sufficient for this is the statement of Allah the Almighty: 'And those who are killed in the cause of Allah - never will He let their deeds go to waste. He will guide them and amend their condition and admit them to Paradise, which* ***He has made known to them.' Imam Ibn Kathir*** [105] ***mentioned a number of hadiths in his interpretation of these verses, including what Imam Ahmad*** [106] ***...said: The Messenger of Allah (peace and blessings be upon him) said: "The martyr is given six things at the first drop of his blood: all his sins are expiated, he is shown his place in Paradise, he is married to the houris with wide-eyed eyes, he is protected from the greatest terror and the torment of the grave, and he is adorned with the garment of faith."*** [107]

Bassam Tibi's concise elucidation of Islam's innate rejection of the Western conception of "just war" appositely contextualizes Tantawi's modern Qur'anic commentaries sanctioning open-ended, aggressive jihad war. [108]

> *"The Western distinction between just and unjust wars linked to specific grounds for war is unknown in Islam. Any war against unbelievers, whatever its immediate ground, is morally justified. Only in this sense can one distinguish just and unjust wars in Islamic tradition.* ***When Muslims wage war for the dissemination of Islam, it is a just war (futuhat, literally 'opening,' in the sense of opening the world, through the use of force, to the call of Islam): when non-Muslims attack Muslims, it is an unjust war ('idwan)." [emphases added]***

Lastly, Reston Jr., 7-years after his 2002 interview of Tantawi, offered a revisionist assessment of their encounter, which still failed to address Tantawi's full-throated endorsement of aggressive jihad against non-believers, published in 1986, in *at-Tafsir al-Wasit li'l-Qur'an al-Karim*. Here is Reston Jr.'s retrospective claim from 2009: [109]

> *"Several years ago* ***I was able to coax out of Mohammed Sayed Tantawi [emphasis added],*** *the grand imam of the Al-Azhar mosque, a strong denunciation of bin Laden and his followers. 'They are not martyrs but aggressors,' he said. 'They will not achieve paradise, but receive severe punishment for their aggressions. Whoever shall kill a man or a believer without right, the punishment is hell forever.' But then a short time later, the grand imam refused to deliver a similar denunciation of suicide bombers."*

Reston Jr.'s honest observation that Tantawi failed to "denounce suicide bombers," is a fitting segue to the nexus between Tantawi's exegetic support for aggressive jihad, including jihad terror "martyrdom," and Tantawi's public pronouncements in support of homicide bombing, particularly against Israel's Jews. Indeed, shortly after becoming Grand Imam, March 17, 1996, Tantawi lauded homicide bombing "martyrdom" operations after a series of such attacks in Israel killing primarily civilian, but also military personnel, during February and March of 1996. [110]

As reported in the New York Times April 19, 1996, Tantawi, [111]

> *"The Sheikh of Al Azhar, the spiritual guide for hundreds of millions of Muslims, said in an interview today that he considered those who blow up Israeli troops in suicide operations to be martyrs."*

Tantawi was quoted directly as having declared, [112]

> *"Someone who blows himself up among the enemies of Allah who have occupied our land and have killed our children and kills dozens of them and protects his own honor and religion, there's no doubt he is a martyr."*

The brief New York Times article concluded by noting Tantawi, widely touted as a "liberal" Muslim religious leader, maintained "resistance to" i.e., waging violent jihad waged against, so-called "injustice," took on, "religious duty, even at the cost of one's life. Muslims should arm the victims of injustice, and volunteers who die fighting for the victims of injustice are martyrs he said." [113]

Six years later, notwithstanding the gruesome March 27, 2002 Netanya Passover homicide bombing of a Passover seder celebration that killed 30 Israeli civilians, and injured 140, 20 seriously, [114] just a week prior, on April 4, 2002, Tantawi advocated such deliberate civilian attacks, in comments posted at the Al-Azhar associated website. [115]

> *"Grand Imam Muhammad Sayyed Tantawi, Sheikh of Al-Azhar, called on the Palestinian people, with all their factions, to increase martyrdom operations against the Zionist enemy. He described martyrdom operations as the most noble operations of Islamic Jihad, as these young people have sold what is most precious to them for the sake of Allah Almighty. He stressed that any martyrdom operation against any Israeli, whether children, women or youth, is a legitimate act and an Islamic obligation until the people of Palestine reclaim their land and repel the brutal Israeli aggression."*

A complementary translation was provided by the Middle East Media Research Institute: [116]

> *"The great Imam of Al Azhar Sheikh Muhammad Sayyed Tantawi, demanded that the Palestinian people, of all factions, intensify the martyrdom operations*

[i.e. self-immolating homicidal attacks] against the Zionist enemy, and described the martyrdom operations as the highest form of Jihad operations. He says that the young people executing them have sold Allah the most precious thing of all. ***[Sheikh Tantawi] emphasized that every martyrdom operation against any Israeli, including children, women, and teenagers, is a legitimate act according to [Islamic] religious law, and an Islamic commandment,*** *until the people of Palestine regain their land and cause the cruel Israeli aggression to retreat..."*

This same April 7, 2002 report referenced an independent, concurring discussion of such martyrdom operations by then Egyptian Mufti, and later (in 2010) Tantawi's successor as Al-Azhar Grand Imam, Ahmed al-Tayeb: [117]

"Until now, in all of his interviews with the Egyptian press since becoming Mufti, Sheikh Al-Tayeb has avoided discussing suicide bombings. But since Sheikh Tantawi's call for suicide attacks, Sheikh Al-Tayeb has declared that 'the solution to the Israeli terror lies in a proliferation of Fidal [martyrdom] attacks that strike horror into the hearts of the enemies of Allah (see Qur'an 8:60). The Islamic countries, peoples and rulers alike, must support these martyrdom attacks.'"

Two years later, in 2004, Tantawi made a broader pronouncement, [118]

"Don't specify countries and names. I determined a general rule which is based on [Islamic] religious law and that applies to everybody. Anyone who blows himself up amongst enemies who want to destroy his home and attack his land, and so he blows himself up amongst them, is a Shahid, Shahid, Shahid [martyr, martyr, martyr]."

A year earlier, in the wake of the U.S. invasion of Iraq, "to satisfy the anti-American sentiment of the street," Shmuel Bar described how Tantawi "began to open his Friday sermons cursing the Americans and called for jihad against them, even before the curses against Israel and the Jews." [119] Bar further observed, "it is not surprising to hear Sheikh Tantawi himself issue contradicting statements, compatible with the audiences listening to him." [120]

Sanctioning homicide bombings against Israeli Jewish non-combatants was certainly the worst example of Tantawi's visceral, religiously inspired Islamic Jew-hatred during his tenure as Grand Imam, but there were other less directly lethal manifestations of his hateful incitement worth noting, as well. During a sermon in April, 2002, Tantawi referred to Jews as "the enemies of Allah, descendants of apes and pigs," [121] a direct reference to Qur'an 5:60, [122]

"Say, 'Shall I inform you of [what is] worse than that as penalty from Allah? [It is that of] those whom Allah has cursed and with whom He became angry and

made of them apes and pigs and slaves of Taghut. [123] *Those are worse in position and further astray from the sound way.'"*

This public declaration was entirely consistent with Tantawi's definitive interpretation of Q 5:60, in his commentary *at-Tafsir al-Wasit li'l-Qur'an al-Karim*, which elaborated his traditional, "sacralized" Jew-hatred, as follows: [124]

> *His (Allah's) saying: 'he whom Allah has cursed' is the predicate of an omitted subject, meaning he is the one whom Allah has cursed, and what is meant is the Jews because the attributes mentioned in the verse apply only to them.* ***The meaning is: Say, O Muhammad, to these Jews who criticized the believers for their belief in Allah and in the heavenly books He revealed, and who said to you: We do not know of people of a religion less fortunate in this world and the Hereafter than you, nor of a religion worse than your world. Say to them, by way of rebuke and warning of their misguidance: Has anyone from the people of that religion informed you of a punishment from Allah on the Day of Resurrection? He is the one whom Allah 'cursed' meaning He distanced him from His mercy 'and became angry with' by withholding His pleasure from him 'and made of them apes and pigs' by transforming some of them into monkeys and some of them into pigs and making some of them worship the Taghut (i.e., those who worship every false deity other than Allah, such as idols and statues and other false deities that they followed because of their tyranny and the corruption of their souls).***
>
> *If it is said that His statement –* ***'Say, 'Shall I inform you of something worse than that as a reward?' indicates that what the Jews criticized the believers for regarding their faith in Allah is evil. However, what the Jews are, is more evil, even though the faith of the believers has no evil at all, rather it is the very essence of goodness****. How is that? The answer is that* ***the speech is presented by way of resemblance and imitation of the corrupt thinking of the Jews and their false claim. It is as if He - Glory be to Him - is saying to His Prophet, may Allah bless him and grant him peace, that these Jews - O Muhammad - deny your belief in Allah and the heavenly books and consider it evil - although it is the very essence of goodness. Say to them by way of rebuke and obligating them with the argument: If you criticize our belief and consider it evil with no good in it - in your opinion - then what you are upon is worse in consequence and outcome than what you are upon of cursing and expulsion from the mercy of Allah, and what happened to your ancestors of some of them being transformed into apes and some into pigs****, and what is known about you of worshipping other than Allah... Similar to this verse in imitating the opponent in his claim is His - Glory be to Him - saying:* ***'And indeed, we or you are upon guidance or in manifest error' and His saying: 'Those are worse' 'in a place and more astray from the right path' is a statement of their evil end and ugly status****. That is, those who are described with the aforementioned immorality, cursing, and expulsion from Allah's mercy,* ***those who are described with that 'are worse in status' than others and more astray from the straight***

path than others. In this world, they associate partners with Allah and violate His prohibitions, and in the Hereafter, their abode is the Fire, and what an evil resting place it is... Thus, we see that these noble verses (i.e., Q 5:60-5:63) have rebuked the Jews for their envy of the believers for what Allah has given them of His bounty, and described them with a number of reprehensible characteristics so that the believers would beware of them and make their loyalty to Allah, His Messenger, and their brothers in faith and religion.

As reported January 22, 2008, Tantawi, through his Al-Azhar University spokesperson, Sheikh Abdel Fattah Allam, cancelled a planned visit by the (Al Azhar-appointed) imam of the Great Mosque of Rome, to Rome's Synagogue. [125] Tantawi's Al Azhar surrogate expressed the Grand Imam's opinions, rooted in a view of Israel and the Palestinian territories seen through the prism of traditional Islamic jurisprudence on jihad, [126] "Dialogue between Islam and Judaism is not contemplated until the rights of those who own them are restored." Expatriate Egyptian journalist Magdi Allam of *Corriere della Serra*, a widely read Italian newspaper, [127] observed, "I translate: only after the Palestinians have the entire geographical entity called Palestine, therefore only after the elimination of Israel, will it be possible to dialogue with the Jews in Italy." [128] Citing Tantawi's support of homicide bombing "martyrdom" operations against Israeli non-combatants, [129] Allam concluded, [130]

"The cancellation of today's visit by the imam of the Great Mosque of Rome to the Synagogue, due to a decision by the Islamic University of Al Azhar based in Cairo, a sort of 'Vatican of Sunni Islam,' confirms that even the so-called 'moderate' Muslims share the ideology of hatred, violence and death towards the Jewish state."

A synopsis of the contents of Tantawi's *Banū Isrā'īl fī al-Qur'ān wa-al-sunnah*

Just over 14-months after becoming Al Azhar Grand Imam, Tantawi, on May 29, 1997, briefly introduced the re-publication (translated herein) of his 1968 Ph.D. thesis. Tantawi opened that introduction with these words, reiterating the central purpose of the thesis: [131]

"My main goal for choosing the topic of my dissertation 'The Children of Israel in the Qur'an and the Sunna' is to reveal- to Muslim youth in particular and to the rational, reasonable and fair-minded people in general the state of the Children of Israel (i.e., Jews), their history, ethics, lies, depravity and immorality, relying on what has been mentioned about them in the Holy Qur'an, the Sunna and the correct and unequivocal historical facts."

Noting the dissertation "comprises eight chapters and a conclusion," Tantawi provided this succinct overview of the entire work: [132]

In Chapter One, I talked about the history of the Jews and their conditions ever since they immigrated to Egypt under the leadership of Jacob- peace be upon him- approximately in the 19th century BC until the second destruction of Jerusalem at the hands of the Romans in the year 70 AD. I concluded this chapter by talking about the history of the Jews of Arabia and their social, economic and religious conditions.

In Chapter Two, I talked about the method displayed in the Noble Qur'an to invite the People of the Scriptures to Islam. I have also shown its fair, tolerant and sympathetic approach to them.

In Chapter Three, I talked in detail about the ways the Jews used to conspire against Islam and Muslims to entrap them. I discussed 10 devious and cunning methods they employed to plot against Islam and Muslims. I concluded this chapter by showing the position of the Messenger (SAW) concerning them.

As for Chapter Four, I talked about the confrontations (meetings of the sword) between the Muslims and the Jews: The Battle of Banu Qaynuqa, the Battle of Banu Nadir, the Battle of Banu Qurayza, and the battle of Khaybar. I also talked about the murder of some of the Jewish leaders such as Kaa'b Bin El-Ashraf and others.

In Chapter Five, I detailed the blessings that Allah granted the Children of Israel and their position concerning these blessings. I showed how their ingratitude and ungratefulness would lead to bad and undesirable consequences in this world and in the next.

In Chapter Six, I talked at length about the vices of the Jews as depicted by the Noble Qur'an. I investigated in detail many of the issues on which interpreters have differed.

In Chapter Seven, I talked about their false and deceitful claims as demonstrated in the Noble Qur'an, and how the Qur'an responded to their false claims in a way that shuts their mouths, arrests their tongues and shows their lies and deception.

In Chapter Eight, I mentioned the numerous penalties with which Allah inflicted punishment on the Children of Israel for their injustices and immorality in accordance with what has been mentioned in the verses of the Noble Qur'an.

In the Conclusion, I talked about Palestine and the Zionist invasion of Palestine at its various stages. I finally showed the most important reasons that led to the catastrophe that has befallen Palestine as well as the most important strategies that if we- as Muslims- follow, will restore Palestine to us.

Tantawi, in addition, notes these five points of emphasis in the thesis to which he "paid special attention": [133]

1- Collect the verses that talk about the Children of Israel in the Noble Qur'an, put them in the most appropriate places, explain and interpret them in an accurate, scientific and verifiable way.

2- Referencing the Holy Sayings of the Prophet that are in the same vein as those verses.

3- Alluding to historical facts and current events when interpreting these noble verses as is clearly seen when I explicate the Almighty's: "And remember, O Prophet, when your Lord declared that He would send against them others who would make them suffer terribly until the Day of Judgment." [Qur'an 7:167] In fact, I have mentioned numerous methods for the punishments that had been inflicted on the Jews at various times and ages...I have then explained the reasons why these punishments had been inflicted upon them.

4- When I explained these verses, I investigated other exegetes and commentators and chose the most appropriate amongst them explaining the reasons for my choice. Consider, for example, our interpretation of the Almighty's: "And We warned the Children of Israel in the Scripture, 'You will certainly cause corruption in the land twice, and you will become extremely arrogant.'" [Qur'an 17:4]

5- We have paid a noticeable attention to Palestine from the historical and political perspectives as it is clearly shown in Chapter One and in the Conclusion... We have conscientiously and faithfully enumerated some methods that would safeguard restoring Palestine to us.

These emphases laid out by Tantawi provide a useful framework for the subsequent discussion, complemented by other antisemitic themes from Islam's canon explored in the thesis. A particular focus is how the canonical Islamic antisemitic motifs Tantawi elaborates at great length from the Qur'an, seminal Qur'anic commentators, and traditions of Muhammad and the nascent Muslim community, are very briefly interwoven with—indeed form the basis for an authoritative Islamic understanding of—modern, non-Islamic antisemitic sources, such as the Czarist Russian forgery, "The Protocols of the Elders of Zion," Benjamin Franklin's factitious "prophecy" about the alleged "danger" posed to the nascent United States by its infinitesimal Jewish minority, or the Jew-hating fulminations of Karl Marx, and Adolph Hitler. [134]

A Granular, Chapter by Chapter Analysis of the Key Contents of Tantawi's *Banū Isrā'īl fī al-Qur'ān wa-al-sunnah*

The following discussion of *Banū Isrā'īl fī al-Qur'ān wa-al-sunnah* demonstrates how the earliest chapters establish the main features of Tantawi's entire thesis: complete negation, or at best, trivialization of praiseworthy Jewish accomplishment, and the obsessive leveling of theological and historical calumnies against the Jews. Tantawi compiles an almost interminable (and not infrequently, bizarre) litany of alleged offenses the Jews committed—described or predicted by their indelible Qur'anic characterization—which "proves" their timeless "corruption and immorality," as agents, ultimately, of pure, inveterate evil.

Chapter 1, primarily a synopsis of the history of the Jews of ancient Israel, with both Biblical and non-religious historical sourcing, includes a gratuitously pejorative "analysis" of Exodus 11:1-2, 12:33-36, and 3:21-22 (with additional detail in Deuteronomy 15:12-15, and 23:7), when the expelled Jews of Egypt took silver and gold from the Egyptians as expressly commanded [135] by God:

> *"Whatever the situation was, the mere recording of this matter in such a style indicates what was and still reigns supreme in the hearts and minds of the Children of Israel: legitimizing and making "lawful" others' money and taking and usurping it by any means possible, even when wars or self-defense are not an issue. This has undoubtedly had a strong impact on entrenching and cementing this strange behavior in their offspring and those other races that enter their religion."* [136]

After expropriating Biblical David ("Dawud") and Solomon ("Sulaiman,"; "Soliman") as "Muslim prophets," Tantawi's negative reductio ad absurdum encapsulation of the history of Israel's Southern and Northern Kingdoms avers,

> *"[W]e can say that the eras of David and Solomon- peace be upon them- were considered the golden era for the Children of Israel who enjoyed affluence, stability and high status during this time. Aside from this era, however, their history was a chain of catastrophes and misfortunes that befell them from other nations due to their corruption and immorality. We consider David and Solomon- peace be upon them- too exalted and far above whatever injustice and unfairness the Books of the Torah or history books have attributed to them."* [137]

Auguring the remainder of his thesis (chapters 2-8, and the conclusion, en bloc), chapter one's introductory discussion of the 7th century Jews of Northern Arabia (from "Medina and its outskirts"), cites derogatory Qur'anic verses pertaining to the Jews:

> *"These noble verses (Qur'an 2:40-41; 4:160; 2:211)- and others- help us assert that those Jews who resided in Medina and its outskirts were from the Children of Israel, not from an Arabic origin. Addressing them in such a way indicates that they were the offspring of those forefathers who harmed Moses, Jesus and other prophets, peace be upon them."* [138]

The Torah and The Talmud are similarly derided, criticism of the latter citing debunked Jew-hating screeds written by notorious Antisemites such August Rohling. [139.]

> *[on The Torah] "Whoever looks at these books will find contradictions, defamation and slander, deviation from the truth and poor expression that would*

> *direct the reader to believe that these books are- in general- not the Torah that Allah revealed to Moses...There is no connection to a verifiable document. The Torah that is in existence currently lacks a certified verification that links to Moses, peace be upon him."*

> *[on The Talmud] "These are some excerpts about the falsehoods and slanders in which the Talmud abounds. Many researchers and scholars have gathered these passages and commented on them. Among the most prominent books written on this topic are "The Treasure Found in the Rules of the Talmud" by Dr. Rohling (who was a professor at Prague University), which was translated by Dr. Youssef Nasrallah, "The Talmud and the Law of Israel" which was written by another researcher, and "The Barbarism of Zionist Teachings" by Mr. Boulos Hanna Saad."*

In chapter 2, Tantawi discusses the Jews' Qur'anic "invitation" to Islam, and its alleged "fair, tolerant, and sympathetic approach to them." When this ostensible "invitation," in reality, submission to Islam, is rejected, Qur'anic invective is unleashed at the obstinate, ungrateful Jews, as Tantawi dutifully records: [140]

> *"The Jews should have rushed to believe in this unlettered prophet who brought irrefutable proofs of the truthfulness of what he had received from his Allah. Yet, most of them were blind and deaf to the truth. They rejected Muhammad and refused to believe in him, even though they knew him as they knew their own sons. Then Allah showed that the Jews did not reject Islam because of proofs that they possessed, but because of their obstinacy, immorality and envy." (Qur'an 3:19)*

The "Noble" Qur'anic narrative, Tantawi continues, [141]

> *"...did not only point that the difference between the Jews in religion was caused by immorality and mutual envy, and that they should have abandoned these vices to follow the truth with which Muhammad came, but the Qur'an also told them that it had clarified those things on which they differed, and that it was time they opened their hearts to him, not to stand in his way and refrain from pushing other people not to follow him."*

Had the stubborn Jews, the Qur'an further avers, [142]

> *"opened their hearts, feared their Lord, abstained from clinging to their illusions, they would have rushed to believe in the Prophet (Muhammad), and what he had brought, but their lust for the luxuries of this world, their selling and rejection of religion in return for the comforts of this life, the tribal solidarity and fanaticism to which they were so accustomed, and their envy of the Prophet for the favors that Allah had granted him- all of these pushed them to blindness and illusion rather than guidance and direction. They therefore brought down Allah's wrath,*

and they became worthy of shame and degradation in this world and severe punishment in the next."

The Jews, in addition, *"corrupted and distorted their texts by moving around the words and forgot a good portion of what they were reminded of."* Accordingly, *"their hearts hardened, and many of them became debauched fornicators."* [143]

After extolling the "*fairness of the Noble Qur'an in its rulings*," Tantawi demonstrates [144] that it

> *"described the Jews, in particular, with degenerate characteristics, i.e., killing the prophets of Allah, corrupting His words by putting them in the wrong places, unjustly devouring people's wealth, refusing to abandon evil deeds, and other dreadful and appalling characteristics caused by their deeply ingrained lasciviousness and immorality...everywhere and at all times."*

The small minority of Jews "*who were upright*," were those *"who submitted, accepted Islam and followed what Muhammad brought them."* [145]

Chapter 2 also includes [146] Tantawi's apologetic on Qur'an 9:29, and the related "jizya," or Qur'anic poll-tax, ostensibly exemplifying the Qur'an's (and Islam's) "fair, tolerant, and sympathetic" approach to the Jews. Tantawi's subsequent reference to the jizya in chapter 8, [147] and more importantly, his commentary on Q 9:29 in his full Qur'anic tafsir, *The intermediate [balanced] interpretation of the Qur'an*, contradict this claim. As a reminder that payment of the jizya is symbolic of the Jews' "humiliation in this world," because of their "vices," here are key extracts from Tantawi's gloss on Q 9:29 from *The intermediate [balanced] interpretation of the Qur'an*, presented more fully earlier: [148]

> *The meaning is: Fight those among the People of the Book who have these characteristics [i.e., they do not submit/convert to Islam] until they pay you the jizya willingly and submissively and are submissive and subject to your authority over them. For those who do not believe in Allah or the Last Day, and do not forbid what Allah and His Messenger have forbidden...And they do not take the true religion as their religion. They deserve this humiliation in this world, but in the Hereafter, their punishment will be more severe and lasting...What is correct regarding the verse is that the humiliation is their commitment to the implementation of Allah's rulings upon them, and paying the jizya, because that is humiliation... After He (Allah) - Glory be to Him - explained some of the vices of the People of the Book in general, He followed that with a detailed account of these vices, so He narrated their false statements, reprehensible actions, and bad intentions*

S.D. Goitein, recognized for his meticulous and measured scholarship on Muslim-Jewish relations, in a seminal 1963 essay (which was partly a mea culpa as well), examined the practical impact of the jizya. Goitein's objective scholarly analysis highlighted the limitation of studying the potential economic and other adverse social consequences of the jizya, some catastrophic, without reference to non-Muslim sources: [149]

> *"**There is no subject of Islamic social history on which the present writer had to modify his views so radically while passing from literary to documentary sources, i.e., from the study of Muslim books to that of the records of the Cairo Geniza as the jizya…or the poll tax to be paid by non-Muslims**. It was, of course, evident that the tax represented a discrimination and was intended, according to the Koran's own words, to emphasize the inferior status of the non-believers. It seemed, however, that from the economic point of view, it did not constitute and heavy imposition, since it was on a sliding scale approximately, one, two, and four dinars, and thus adjusted to the financial capacity of the taxpayer. **This impression proved to be entirely fallacious, for it did not take into consideration the immense extent of poverty and privation experienced by the masses, and in particular, their persistent lack of cash, which turned the 'season of the tax' into one of horror, dread, and misery. The provisions of ancient Islamic law which exempted the indigent, the invalids, and the old, were no longer observed in the Geniza period [primarily, ~ 950-1250 C.E]) and had been discarded by the Shafi'i School of Law, which prevailed in Egypt, also in theory**. It is precisely persons of such descriptions about whose plight we read so much in our records. The payment of the poll tax constituted item number one in the budget of families with modest income, such as teachers or laborers. For a man could clothe inexpensively, he could eat at starvation level, as perhaps a very large section of the population did. But he could not escape the tax gatherer—at least not for long. **If he was caught, he was beaten and suffered otherwise corporal punishment, 'nquba,' and was thrown into prison, where, because of starvation and maltreatment, he faced death…A very considerable section of the non-Muslim population must have been unable to pay it and often suffered humiliation and privation on its account**. While, in the higher circles, the prospects of appointment to leading government posts acted as an inducement for embracing Islam, the mass conversions in the lower classes might well have been caused in part by the intolerable burden of the poll tax."*

Near the beginning of chapter 3, Tantawi inserts an apologetic discussion of the so-called "Constitution of Medina," including the verbatim text of this putative document, as a cardinal example of Muhammad's "munificent treatment of the Jews." Tantawi claims, [150]

> *"In addition to his munificent treatment of the Jews, the Prophet wanted to enhance cooperation and mutual interests with them. He held a fair agreement with them. In this contract, he assured them their safety, the safety of their possessions and money, and their worship and creed. He guaranteed all that was fair and beneficial for them and for Muslims."*

Thorough, unapologetic analyses by modern non-Muslim scholars maintain that this "Constitution" is better understood as part of Muhammad's design to neutralize the Jews and establish a hegemonic Islamic order, which in fact occurred. What follows, chronologically, are the concurring assessments of Wellhausen (1889), Wensinck (1908), and Gil (1974).

Julius Wellhausen: [151]

> *"I doubt that there was indeed a written agreement of which both parties had a copy. The Jews never referred to their document. The Banu Qurayza claimed that there was no agreement between them and Muhammad. Their leader Ka'b ibn Asad, did not tear up a document, rather a shoelace, to demonstrate symbolically the breach with the Medinans. In any case, there cannot have been a general agreement with the Jews, but only special arrangements with individual clans, for the Jews were no political unit, rather each of their clans formed a confederation with the neighboring Arab clan. As far as I am concerned, Muhammad left the existing relations of individual Jewish clans with the families or clans of the ansar and incorporated them in the ummah. This was all he did. Muhammad had no direct relationship with the Jews but only by way of the Ansar ('helper' tribes). It was only they who had obligations towards the Jews, and had to honor them. Muhammad's obligations derived from this, and it was only because of consideration for the ansar that he did not declare them fair game...In spite of what has been said, I do not doubt the authenticity of the constitution as transmitted by Ibn Ishaq. But it did not represent an agreement with the Jews. [Islamic] Tradition has a simple explanation why Muhammad's relation with the Jews was so little affected by the agreement: Every hostile act of Muhammad was precipitated by the Jews and justified by planned or accomplished treachery, even though they had no intention openly to break the agreement. Muhammad himself supplies the interpretation in Koran 8:55–58: 'Lo! the worst of beasts in Allah's sight are the ungrateful who will not believe. [8:55]; Those of them with whom thou madest a treaty, and then at every opportunity they break their treaty, and they keep not duty (to Allah). [8:56]; If thou comest on them in the war, deal with them so as to strike fear in those who are behind them, that haply they may remember. [8:57]; And if thou fearest treachery from any folk, then throw back to them (their treaty) fairly. Lo! Allah loveth not the treacherous. [8:58].' We, however, will find that it was Muhammad who committed the perfidy. He gladly used every chance to punish the Jews, and contrived to create reasons if there were none."*

A.J. Wensinck: [152]

> *'The constitution was no treaty concluded between muhajirun (emigrants; early Muslim converts and companions of Muhammad) ,..., and the Jews. It was an edict defining the relation of the parties; above them was Allah, i.e., Muhammad. It was evidence of his great authority that, after a short stay in*

Medina, he, the stranger could lay down the law for all segments of the population. In religious matters the break with the Jews was irreconcilable. Muhammad did not express his annoyance over this. For the time being, he needed the Jews and included them in the ummah. His first plan failed; he had come to Medina hoping the town would soon be a religious unity as a theocratic monarchy under his leadership. If the Jews would have recognized him, this hope might have been realized...But the Jews showed no such inclination. What to do? They could not be attacked openly because Muhammad's position was still insufficiently established. All he could do was to use them in his plans, or in any case, neutralize them. When he realized that in the long run a common basis was impossible, he looked for an alternative which he found in the dogma of the religion of Abraham. The proclamation of this dogma coincided with the break with the Jews. Therefore, the constitution must have been written in the middle of the year 2 A.H. [year 2 after the hijra of 622; year 1 starts July 16, 622, and year 2 on July 5, 623] because the terminus ad quem [goal or finishing point] for dating the document is the battle of Badr in Ramadan 2 A.H. Quite clearly, it is unthinkable that after the battle of Badr Muhammad should have promised the Jews help against internal or external enemies, freedom of worship, or declared the territory of Yathrib [Medina] inviolable ground since he was on the point of attacking Banu Qaynuqa. The battle of Badr gave Muhammad the opportunity to repeal all concessions made to the Jews. This victory was a success which increased his authority among Banu Qaylah [i.e., the Aws and Khazraj] and allowed him to act with far greater confidence. From then on, he felt he could do without the Jews; consequently he did not wait long to express his exasperation."

Moshe Gil: [153]

"The document is better understood as an act of preparation for war, and not as its result. Through his alliance with the Arab tribes of Medina the Prophet gained enough strength to achieve a gradual anti-Jewish policy, despite the reluctance of his Medinese allies, who had formerly been those of the Jews...It is therefore an obvious alibi that Muslim sources have developed a tradition about a treaty between Muhammad and the Jews, be it this document or a lost one, as presumed by some modern scholars. Elsewhere, it is declared in complete sincerity that Muhammad, without invoking any treaty, simply asked the B. Qaynuqa, before taking action against them, to accept Islam. One of the 'ulafa' [allies, confederates] Ubada b. al-Samit of the clan B. Awf declares that he takes as walis [ruler] God and His Prophet, and renounces [oath, sworn alliance] with B. Qaynuqa. Ubada also says further to 'Abdallah b. Ubayy: ("The disposition of the hearts has changed and Islam has cancelled [any] treaties").Usayd b. Hudayr, when reminded by the B. Qurayza about the fact that they are [clients, feudal tenants] of his tribe, the Aws, answers: "There is no[contractual obligation] between us." The document therefore, was not a covenant with the Jews. On the contrary, it was a formal statement of intent to

disengage the Arab clans of Medina from the Jewish neighbors they had been allied with up to that time."

The remainder of chapter 3—as a rationale for subjugating and neutralizing the Jews—describes how the Qur'an reveals their "ungratefulness," "the deceitful and devious methods" they "employed to entrap Muslims, and undermine Islam," how they "traded their religion for transient worldly gains, " believed in "illusions and fantasies," were "completely consumed by stinginess," acted with "malice and resentment" in response to "the goodness Allah bestowed upon others, and preferred idol worshippers over those who worshiped the all-Merciful (Allah)." [154] In addition, the *"Noble Qur'an also detailed their ignominies and perversions, their transgressions against Allah, and other inequities and depravities they committed... They neither abandoned their wicked and meandering behavior, nor did they listen to the Prophet's kind and gracious advice. They did not even learn from the penalties that were imposed on people like them or the calamities that befell them. They persisted in their injustices and immorality, their attempts to undermine Islam and their pernicious efforts to eliminate it in every way possible."* [155] Accordingly, *"Allah prepared severe punishment for them. He caused them to be struck with moral humiliation and disgrace."* [156] Tantawi further insists the Qur'an has captured the permanent characteristics of the Jews which are most glaringly evident in the factitious "massacres" he claims they committed in contemporary "Palestine": [157]

> *"Time has proved the truth of what the Noble Qur'an said about them: After they entered—with the help of colonial powers—some Islamic cities in Palestine, they expelled their legitimate inhabitants and seized and usurped all their wealth. They did not even allow the people of these cities to take the least amount of food or clothing or what could have satisfied their most essential needs. An example of this could be seen when they occupied-by treachery and deceit- the village of Deir Yassin* [158] *... and other Palestinian cities. They slaughtered women, children and old men. Those whose lives were spared from slaughter and killing were deprived of all their possessions."*

Chapter 4 elaborates on Muhammad's and the nascent Muslim community's "righteous" subjugation of the Jewish tribes of Arabia. These proto-jihad campaigns, unbowdlerized, featured targeted assassinations of Jewish leaders, accompanied by mass killing, enslavement, rape, plunder, and deportation of ordinary Jews, as described by the exclusively Muslim sources, including those Tantawi cites. [159] Importantly, no independent historical validation exists regarding the pious Muslim narrative about these events in the Qur'an, hadith, or sira (earliest sacralized biographies of Muhammad). [160] Notwithstanding its complete absence of historical merit, Tantawi's thesis illustrates how all this literature plays a critical role in shaping the Shari'a—Islamic law and societal mores—and the Muslim *Weltanschauung*, past as prologue. [160]

In chronological order, Tantawi recounts how Muhammad and the Muslims subdued the Jews of Banu Qaynuqa, Banu Nadir, Banu Qurayza, and the Khaybar Jews, ultimately expelling the vanquished survivors of Khaybar, the last remnants of all these Jews, from the Arabian peninsula, under Caliph Umar ibn al-Khattab. [161] Tantawi's triumphal assessment of these victories highlights the following points: [162]

> *[Banu Qaynuqa] "As a consequence of expelling them, the voices of the hypocrites were silenced, terror entered the hearts of the rest of the Jews, and Muslims regained their authority and dignity. Banu Qaynuqa reaped the fruits of the evil that they planted."*
>
> *[Banu Nadir] "...with that victory (over Bani Nadir) that the Muslims achieved almost without any sacrifices worth mentioning, their authority in Medina was established and secured. Medina became safe and secure, and the emigrants benefited from the wealth that Allah granted from the wealth of the Jews."*
>
> *[Banu Qurayza] "...he (Muhammad) approached their fortresses and said: 'Brothers of apes and pigs! (see Q 5:60) Has Allah disgraced and brought down His damnation upon you?' They said: 'Abou Al-Qasim! You are not ignorant!' This is the status quo of the Jews everywhere and at all time; when they feel safe, they curse, offend and exceed conventional limits. When the opportunity offers itself, they murder, blow up and destroy. However, when they are cornered and feel threatened, they cry, plead and entreat. They adapt to suit the changing circumstances around them in a way that is convenient and beneficial for them. As for covenants or pledges, moral principles and values, and humane propensities and considerations, these are of no consequence... By eliminating Banu Qurayza, the influence of the Jews in Medina and its outskirts was completely eradicated... The Muslims were now able to safely go out of Medina to spread the 'light of Allah on earth.'"*
>
> *[Jews of Khaybar] "The Prophet hastened to invade the Jews of Khaybar immediately after the Hudaybiyyah [163] treaty so as not to give them the chance to seek the assistance of the other warring tribes...when the Muslims conquered and took over Khaybar's forts, Zeinab bint Al-Harith (wife of a Jewish tribal leader) wanted to hurt the Prophet. She sent a poisoned lamb to him as a present... There are reports that the Prophet ordered to kill her. Other reports suggest that he pardoned her. Researchers agree that he did not kill her right away."*
>
> *[Final expulsion] "...before his death, he [Muhammad] recommended that the Jews be expelled out of the Arabian Peninsula to prevent having two religions there. After the Prophet's death, Abu Bakr Al-Sidiiq (a companion of Muhammad and his immediate successor, the "First 'Rightly Guided Caliph') acknowledged the same treatment that the Prophet followed. However, the Jews were expelled during the era of Umar bin Khataab (also a companion of Muhammad, and successor of Abu Bakr, i.e., the 'Second Rightly Guided Caliph') in accordance with the recommendations of the Prophet."*

Two Qur'anic references are emphasized in Tantawi's chapter 4 account of Muhammad's submission of the Jews of Arabia, Q 3:12-13, and Q 59:14. Regarding Q 3:12-13, Tantawi asserts, [164] *"The meaning of the two noble verses is: Muhammad! Tell those who rejected this religion (Islam)- especially the Jews who were overconfident and conceited because of their might and money- that they would be defeated and humiliated in this world, and that they would be gathered and driven to hell, an awful place for a final abode. Tell them that Allah was truthful in His promise to kill Banu Nadir, conquer Khaybar, and Muslims levying the jizya on all their enemies. These are clear proofs that the Prophet was truthful in what he had said about his Lord."* Tantawi's tafsir *The intermediate [balanced] interpretation of the Qur'an*, offers a consistent gloss: [165]

> *"O Muhammad, to these Jews and their likes from the polytheists who show off with their strength and are deceived, with their money, children, and clannishness... Tell them you will be defeated and overcome in this world at the hands of the believers, and you will be gathered together on the Day of Resurrection, then you will be driven to the fire of Hell to meet your painful fate. 'And wretched is the resting place,' meaning wretched is the place they have prepared for themselves in the Hereafter because of their evil deeds... You will be overcome," is a statement about something that will happen in the future, and it happened as Allah the Almighty had foretold. The tables turned on the Jews of Banu Qaynuqa, Banu Nadir, Qurayza, and others, a few years after the Hijra, and Makkah was conquered in the eighth year after the Hijra. His statement, 'And evil is the resting place,' is either a continuation of what will be said to them, or a resumption of the horrific nature of Hell and the terrible state of its people. Then the Qur'an cited a visible example that indicates Allah's victory for His friends and His abandonment of His enemies."*

Citing Q 59:14, Tantawi insists this verse confirms what has *"proven true in ancient and in modern times."* He continues, [166]

> *The Almighty said: 'Even united, they would not dare fight against you except from within fortified strongholds or from behind walls. Their malice for each other is intense: you think they are united, yet their hearts are divided. That is because they are a people with no real understanding.' (Q 59:14) Meaning: Allah cast horror in the hearts of those Jews; they would not fight united in one place or another because they had utterly succumbed to fear and horror. Rather, they would fight from behind their fortified strongholds and their walls which they use to hide behind.* ***The war in Palestine between the true believers and the Jews confirmed this fact. The Jews do not fight except from behind their fortified encampments in the land of Palestine. Once they confront the Muslims face to face, they flee in panic and terror. It is as though this noble verse was initially revealed concerning them.*** *Blessed is the Omnipotent who is all-Knowledgeable and cognizant of the nature of humans."*

Again, Tantawi's tafsir on Q 59:14 in *The intermediate [balanced] interpretation of the Qur'an* provides a consistent gloss, but without any contemporary allusion to modern Israel: [167]

> *"...meaning that these Jews and their allies from the hypocrites will not fight you all together in any location except in villages fortified with trenches and the like, or they will fight you from behind the walls behind which they hide, because they are unable to duel you or confront you face to face, due to their extreme fear of you. Ibn Kathir said that it means that in their cowardice and panic, they are not able to confront the army of Islam, in a duel or fighting, but rather they are either in fortresses, or from behind walls under siege, so they fight you to defend themselves out of necessity... And the statement of the Most High: 'Their violence among themselves is severe' is a new sentence, as if someone said: 'Why do they only fight the believers in this way?' So the answer was: Their violence among themselves is severe. That is, their enmity amongst themselves is intense, to the point that they do not agree on an opinion, and they use their strength extensively amongst themselves, but when they meet you, this strength turns into cowardice and panic."*

Tantawi also attempts to frame the assassination of the Jew K'ab bin al-Ashraf—ordered by Muhammad—as a betrayal. But Tantawi conceded the real reason was K'ab's preference for "pre-Islamic ignorance" over the "religion of Islam," and his public expression of "animosity toward the Muslims" and insulting Islam's prophet. [168] In other words K'ab's crime was blasphemy, whose Sharia-based punishment [169] was death. Invoking both the towering Muslim jurist al-Shafi'i (d. 820), [170] founder of the Shafiite school of Islamic jurisprudence, and the influential theologian Ibn Taymiyya (d. 1328) [171], Tantawi acknowledges: [172]

> *"Al-Shafi'i brought as justification that whosoever offends the Prophet is to be killed without blame or guilt. That was the story of Ka'b bin al-Ashraf, the Jew. Al-Khatabi said that Al Shafi'i said that a dhimmi (those conquered non-Muslims possessed of Scriptures, and submitted to debasing Islamic law, in lieu of being slain)* [173] *is to be killed if he insulted the Prophet. Such a killing would be without any sense of guilt or blame...On Ibn Taymiyya's rationale: 'by offending and insulting the Messenger Ka'b breached this agreement.'"*

Tantawi further maintains K'ab's five Muslim assassins, [174]

> *"...killed him because he insulted the Messenger. A person killed in such a way has no protection under agreements or pledges. This is similar to those who are to be killed because of committing adultery, or for apostatizing and abandoning Islam, etc. It is not permissible to have a contract to protect such people as those as they have crossed specific boundaries. He brought damnation upon himself by insulting the Prophet and Muslims... His killing was a fair and just punishment for he... openly declared his animosity towards the Muslims and insulted the Prophet."*

A striking example from the Sunna (i.e., sira and hadith, specifically) about Muhammad's interactions with the Jews of Arabia which reflects quite poorly on the character of Islam's prophet, is omitted, unsurprisingly, from Tantawi's account: Muhammad personally beheading all (some 600-900) of the surrendered post-pubescent males of the Banu Qurayza. Ibn Ishaq's sira records the grisly execution: [175]

> *"When they [the men, including post-pubescent boys, of the Jewish tribe] surrendered, and the apostle [i.e., Muhammad] confined them in Medina in the quarter of d. al-Harith, a woman of B. Al-Najjar. Then the apostle went out to the market of Medina (which is still its market today) and dug trenches in it. Then he sent for them and struck off their heads in those trenches as they were brought out to him in batches. Among them was the enemy of Allah Huyayy b. Akhtab and Ka'b b. Asad their chief. There were 600 or 700 in all, though some put the figure as high as 800 or 900. As they were being taken out in batches to the apostle they asked Ka'b what he thought would be done with them. He replied, 'Will you never understand? Don't you see that the summoner never stops and those who are taken away do not return? By Allah it is death!' This went on until the apostle made an end of them."*

Tantawi's summary conclusions from chapter 4 are predictably redolent with hagiography of Islam and its prophet, and simultaneous condemnation of Jews, and Judaism. [176]

> *"...the Jews lived in the Arabian Peninsula for hundreds of years. They ate of its yield and goodness and roamed its lands. Had they been peaceful towards the Islamic call, no killings or expulsions would have ever occurred. They were obstinate in their denial and rejection of Prophet Muhammad whom they knew as they knew their own children. They were thus worthy of condemnation and curses in this world and severe punishment and torture in the afterlife. Islam spread on this land after generations in which the Jews lived there as they pleased...Had the Jews stayed in the Arabian Peninsula a thousand years more, they would have only enhanced its division and discord, and other nations would not have benefited from their being there. They may have been able to get more of the grains and fruits that they produce. Yet, with these, more corruption will ensue due to the usury, dissipation and intemperance that the Children of Israel are bound to export along their products. As for Islam, ever since the day it dawned in the Peninsula, it has been a message of faith and guidance; its truth and righteousness made it worthy of victory...Once again, the Jews reaped the fruits of their labor. They brought all of this to themselves. They were only expelled out of the Arabian Peninsula because of violating their covenants with the Muslims, fighting the Islamic call and rejecting the message of the Prophet. 'Allah did not wrong the evildoers, but they wronged themselves.'" (Qur'an 16:33)*

Serious non-Muslim scholars of the pious Muslim sources analyzed by Tantawi, whom Tantawi reflexively dismisses as "orientalists" (echoing the howlingly uninformed, pejorative "orientalist" caricature view of Edward Said [177]) proffer illuminating and decidedly different interpretations of these same materials, which merit consideration.

Hartwig Hirschfeld's comprehensive assessment of Muhammad's interactions with the Jews includes this opening summary of the "mutual disappointment" that characterized their relationship, and the understandably catastrophic results for the Jews: [178]

> *The Jews, for their part, were singularly disappointed in their expectations. The way in which Muhammad understood revelation, his ignorance and his clumsiness in religious questions in no way encouraged them to greet him as their Messiah. He tried at first to win them over to his teachings by sweetness and persuasion; they replied by posing once again the questions that they had already asked him; his answers, filled with gross errors, provoked their laughter and mockery. From this, of course, resulted a deep hostility between Muhammad and the Jews, whose only crime was to pass a severe judgment on the enterprise of this Arab who styled himself "God's prophet" and to find his conduct ridiculous, his knowledge false, and his regulations thoughtless. This judgment, which was well founded, was nevertheless politically incorrect [une faute politique], and the consequences thereof inevitably would prove to be disastrous for a minority that lacked direction or cohesion.*

W. H. T. Gairdner, also relying exclusively upon Muslim sources characterizing the slaughter of the Banu Qurayza, highlights the pivotal and less than salutary role that Muhammad himself played in orchestrating the overall events: [179]

> *The umpire who gave the fatal decision (Sa'ad) was extravagantly praised by Muhammad. Yet his action was wholly and admittedly due to his lust for personal vengeance on a tribe which had occasioned him a painful wound. In the agony of its treatment he cried out—'O God (Allah), let not my soul go forth ere thou has cooled my eye from the Bani Quraiza (Qurayza).'* ***This*** *was the arbiter to whose word the fate of that tribe was given over. His sentiments were well known to Muhammad, who appointed him. It is perfectly clear from that that their slaughter had been decreed. What makes it clearer still is the assertion of another biographer that Muhammad had refused to treat with the Bani Quraiza at all until they had 'come down to receive the judgment of the Apostle of God.' Accordingly 'they came down'; in other words put themselves in his power. And only then was the arbitration of Sa'ad proposed and accepted—but not accepted until it had been forced on him by Muhammad; for Sa'ad first declined and tried to make Muhammad take the responsibility, but was told 'qad amarak Allahu takhuma fihim,' 'Allah has commanded you to give sentence in their case.' From every point of view therefore the evidence is simply crushing that Muhammad was the ultimate author of this massacre.*

The political rationale for Muhammad's campaign against Khaybar has been discussed by Hirschfeld and D. S. Margoliouth. Hirschfeld, in his review of Leone Caetani's *Annali dell Islam*, agrees with the latter's assessment: [180]

"The author [Caetani] is undoubtedly right in saying that the reasons given by the Muslim traditionalists are worthless, as Muhammad's real motive was a purely political one, an additional motive being the opportunity which it gave of employing a number of followers unskilled in work but eager for spoil."

Hirschfeld then adds, based upon his own research of the documentary record: [181]

"The expedition against Khaybar was a distinct breach of faith, as two years previously Muhammad had given the Jews of Khaybar and Maqna a charter of liberty which has fortunately been preserved, and traces of which are also to be found in the works of al-Wakidi and al-Baladhuri."

Margoliouth expands upon these arguments, and concludes, [182]

[I]n plundering Meccans he [Muhammad] could plead that he had been driven from his home and possessions: and with the Jewish tribes of Medina he had in each case some outrage, real or pretended, to avenge. But the people of Khaybar, all that distance from Medina, had certainly done him and his followers no wrong: for their leaving unavenged the murder of one [183] of their number by his emissary was no act of aggression. Ali, when told to lead the forces against them, had to enquire for what he was fighting: and was told that he must compel them to adopt the formulae of Islam. Khaybar was attacked because there was booty to be acquired there, and the plea for attacking it was that its inhabitants were not Muslims.

Finally, Georges Vajda, in turn, reminds us of the theological animus that motivated Muhammad's political subjugation of the Jews, specifically, which became an indelible part of Muslim attitudes toward Jews across space and time: [184]

"The more Mohammed advanced his career in Medina, the more his resentment against Jews grew. This evolution was rather natural since the Jews, not content with disappointing his expectations of seeing them rally unreservedly to his cause, riddled him with sarcasm, cast doubt on the authenticity of his prophetic mission, and lastly had the fault of possessing vast resources in chattels and land, which the prophet could not do without in order to secure his domination in Medina and the execution of vast projects of religious and political conquest."

Chapter 5 describes what Tantawi characterizes as the Jews' "ingratitude" for the "blessings Allah granted" them, justifying their punishment in both the corporeal world, and the Hereafter. [185] Tantawi asserts, in summary, [186]

"It is as though the Almighty is portraying them as they go through three stages: favors and blessings, ungratefulness and unappreciativeness, and vengeance and penalty. In their story, there is a warning and a lesson to guide people to worship

> *their Creator in truth and righteousness and give thanks to Him to avoid those punishments that had befallen the Children of Israel due to their injustices, denial and their rushing to sins and vices."*

Tantawi seeks to establish the veracity of this assessment by invoking and providing his own glosses on Q 45:16-17, Q 26:63-67, Q 2:51-52, and Q 2:54, complemented by the glosses of the authoritative classical Qur'anic commentators al-Razi (on Q 2:41), al-Zamakshari (on Q 62:5), and Tabari ("Ibn Jarir," on Q 5:24). First Tantawi: [187]

> *[Q 45:16-17] "The lessons that we gather from these and similar verses is that the Almighty Allah favored the Children of Israel above other communities prior to the Muslim community. He granted them numerous favors, but they did not accept them with gratitude and thankfulness. Rather, they showed rebellion, malice and unappreciativeness. Therefore, Allah took away those favors. He described them in His Book with the most appalling characteristics and the worst features such as cruelty of heart, violation of covenants, covetousness and hunger for the lusts of the world, aggression against others, crookedness and deceitfulness to permit what Allah prohibited, hatred of the truth, following falsehoods, and many other characteristics that are mentioned in the Noble Qur'an."*

> *[Q 26:63-67] "Thus, the noble verses reminded the Children of Israel with one of Allah's most astounding and stunning signs/miracles: the parting of the sea, to thank their Creator and follow His Prophet. However, they did not fulfill their obligation to be thankful and show gratitude to their Creator. That was why they deserved to be cursed in this world and be afflicted with severe punishment in the hereafter for their ingratitude, injustices and denial. And Allah does not deal unjustly to His servants."*

> *[Q 2:51-52] "These two noble verses comprised what indicated the stupidity of the Children of Israel and their short sightedness since they took the calf as a god even though they had witnessed evidence and proofs of the truthfulness of their Prophet. The verses also included some element of amusement to the Messenger of Allah as he witnessed the stance of his contemporary Jews concerning the Islamic call. It was as though the Almighty was saying that the harm and malice that he had endured at the hands of those Jews was more or less similar to what their forefathers did with Moses, their Prophet: they had taken an idol of a calf that made a lowing sound as a god, when he was absent, not even realizing that he could not talk to them or lead them to the straightforward path. They were rebellious wrongdoers."*

> *[Q 2:54] "The verse (Q 2:54) also included reminding the Children of Israel who were contemporary with the Prophet of Allah's favors, for had it not been for Allah's favors, they would have ceased to be. There was also a reference to the leniency and benevolence of the Islamic Doctrine that Muhammad brought and an appealing invitation for the Jews to accept Islam, for if their forefathers'*

penitence was not accepted except by executing themselves, the Islamic doctrine stated that the Prophet who lifted the shackles off of your forefathers had come. Believe in him and follow him, and you will obtain mercy."

Then the classical commentators: [188]

> *[al-Razi, on Q 2:41] "Imam Al- Razi said: This sentence (from Q 2:41) was a message to the Children of Israel before anyone else. It was as though the Almighty was saying to them: Don't disbelieve Muhammad. There would be disbelievers after you, so do not be the first, for being the first to disbelieve increases the gravity of your transgression. That is because if you preceded others to disbelief, others will follow in your footsteps. In that case, your disbelief as well as the disbelief of others would be heaped upon you till Judgement Day. And if nobody followed in your footsteps, two things would be taken against you: being the first to disbelieve and being the only disbelievers. Both of these are grave transgressions that lead to severe punishment."*

> *[al-Zamakshari, on Q 62:5] "Al-Zamakshari (in his gloss on 62:5) said: "Allah regarded the Jews as people who carried the Torah, read it and even learned what is in it by heart. However, they did not follow its precepts and tenets, and they failed to benefit from its verses since it foretold the Messenger of Allah and described him, but they did not believe in him. Allah likened them to a donkey who carries voluminous books containing weighty knowledge but knows nothing about their contents. It only labors under the heavy weight of the books. That is the story of he who knows but fails to act according to that knowledge. How dreadful!"*

> *[al-Tabari (Ibn Jarir), on Q 5:24 (and 2:58)] "Furthermore, they were told: 'enter the gate with humility, saying, 'Absolve us.' We will forgive your sins and multiply the reward for the good-doers.' (Qur'an 2:58) However, they played on the words, changed them and showed disrespect. They committed many other evil deeds, too numerous to count, and tried to offend and harm their prophet. It was no wonder, then, that those people- like their forefathers- would not believe Muhammad. Rather, they would follow in their predecessors' footsteps in disbelieving in Muhammad, rejecting his message and rebelling against it. After all, they had abandoned their religion on numerous occasions, attacked their Prophet many times despite the many blessings and favors that Allah gave them."*

Tantawi concludes chapter 5 by presenting Zamakshari's consensus [189] classical commentary on Q 2:61, then re-affirming and updating this gloss with his own consistent observations: [190]

> *"Al-Zamakshari said: 'Disgrace had encircled them encompassing them all like being together under a pavilion, a sign that disgrace and misery have become glued and stuck to them. It is like someone forcibly hitting a wall with mud so*

hard that it sticks to the wall. The Jews are always in disgrace and fully humbled.'"

(Tantawi averred): "The Jews lived for centuries and generations enslaved to other nations. They became feeble-hearted and psychologically inept unable to differentiate between a disgraceful dishonorable life and an honorable dignified one. They would even prefer the former kind of life to the latter as long as they could secure the pleasures of life. No matter how affluent and prosperous they become, they will always suffer this psychological deficiency and incompetence. They will always appear miserable and humbled before people...Also, the Almighty said: 'unjustly' even though killing a prophet could never be a just cause. It was meant to indicate that killing the prophets was unjust and contrary to what their doctrine and law stipulated. It is forbidden by their law: 'whoever takes a life—unless as a punishment for murder or mischief in the land—it will be as if they killed all of humanity.' (Q 5:32) So, this restriction was meant to oppose their conduct in the light of their religion. It immortalized their transgression and disgraced and demeaned their wrongdoing since they had killed their prophets knowingly without any misunderstanding. Rather, they committed these atrocities knowing the ugliness and viciousness of their deeds, and they rejected Allah's law knowingly and deliberately...The noble Verse (Q 2:61) has thus described the Children of Israel as an ungrateful, inappropriate, illogical, insensible and arrogant people who disregarded the truth and executed injustices against themselves and others. What the verse mentions about them has been confirmed throughout the generations, at all times and everywhere."

Chapter 6 elaborates the Jews' Qur'anic "vices," a thorough, if seemingly redundant exercise by Tantawi given the collective contents of his chapters 1-5. Tantawi provides an opening summary litany of the Jews' putative vices "in general," (and, as will be explored, in perpetuity) before "interpreting" them "in detail," peppered with appropriate Qur'anic citations, throughout the remainder of the chapter: [191]

"First: Violating covenants and breaking promises...'the disobedience and indifference to covenants described has been a fixed and deeply entrenched characteristic.'
Second: Their inappropriateness to Allah, animosity to His angels and murdering His prophets.
Third: Rejecting the truth and hating good and beneficial things for others out of egotism and envy.
Fourth: Maneuvering to legitimize what Allah has prohibited.
Fifth: Rejecting Allah's Book, believing in magic and satanic illusions.
Sixth: Altering and changing texts and forgetting what they were reminded with.
Seventh; Clinging eagerly to life and their cowardice to fight for the sake of Allah.
Eighth: Demanding that Moses, their prophet, make them a god like other nations.
Nineth: Worshipping the calf.

Tenth: Lack of sensitivity for religion and engaging in semantic bickering and argumentation."

Prior to expanding upon Tantawi's litany of Jewish vices as depicted in the Qur'an, I will summarize two analogous, independent Qur'anic litanies produced by Al-Azhar University-affiliated scholars known for issuing authoritative fatwas (Islamic religious edicts), one from 1968, and another published in 2003. Sheikh Abdullah Al-Mashhad (d. 1990), during October 1968, gave a presentation at The Fourth Conference of The Academy of Islamic Research (founded by, and intimately connected to, Al-Azhar University) that included this litany of "vicious qualities…inherent in them (the Jews)," which the "Holy Qur'an" elucidated: [192]

> *"1. Telling Lies about God [Allah] (Q 3:74); 2. Their Fondness for Listening to Falsehood [Lies](Q 5:41-42); 3. Mutiny (Disobedience) against Allah (Q 5:13); 4. Mutiny [Disbelief] against His Messengers [Apostles] (Q 2:55, 5:24, 5:70); 5. Facility of Assassination (Q 2:61); 6. Confuting the Covenants [Breaking Promises] (Q 8:56); 7. Hardheartedness (Q 2:74); 8. Argumentativeness and double-facedness (Q 2:247, 2:70); 9. Suppression of the truth and misguidance (Q 2:42); 10. Hypocrisy (Q 2:44, 3:167); 11. Egoism (Q 2:87, 2:41); 12. Desire for corrupting people (Q 5:64); 13. Their lack of good conscience (Q 5:79); 14. Loving malignancy for others (Q 3:69, 4:44, 3:99, 7:86); 15. Their resentment for benefaction done for people (Q 3:120, 4:54, 2:105); 16. Hastening to commit sins and disobedience to Allah's injunctions (Q 5:62); 17. Self-conceit and haughtiness (Q 5:18, 3:75, 4:49); 18. Exploitation and opportunism (Q 4:161, 5:42); 19. Trickery for transgression (Q 2:65); 20. Cowardice (Q 5:24, 59:13-14, 2:249); 21. Indecency in talking (Q 2:93, 4:46); 22. Miserliness (Q 4:53, 9:76, 3:180, 9:34); 23. The most excessive selfishness (Q 3:119, 3:75); 24. Fear of death (Q 2:96); 25. Garbling of the Holy Books (Q 4:46, 2:79)."*

Thirty-six years later, in 2004 (March 22), during Tantawi's tenure as Al-Azhar Grand Imam, Sheikh Atiyyah Saqr, a former head of Al-Azhar' s Fatwa Committee, who two years earlier (April 15, 2002) issued a fatwa declaring Jews "apes and pigs" (per Q 5:60), was asked in an online chat room, "What, according to the Qur'an, are the Jews' main characteristics and qualities?" Describing the Qur'anic characterization of the Jews as "quite impartial," the good Sheikh could find only one positive trait of Jews (i.e., Q 45:16, more of a squandered endowment than a positive trait: "Indeed, We gave the Children of Israel the Scripture, wisdom, and prophethood; granted them good, lawful provisions; and favored them above the others."), whereas he identified twenty negative traits "due to their bad qualities and the heinous acts they used to commit." [193] He went on to enumerate them, with justifying Qur'anic citations:

> *"They used to fabricate things and falsely ascribe them to Allah. (Q 3:75, 5:64, 3:181); They love to listen to lies. (Q 5:41); Disobeying Almighty Allah and never observing His commands. (Q 5:13); Disputing and quarreling (Q 2:247); Hiding the truth and supporting deception. (Q 3:78); Rebelling against the*

> *Prophets and rejecting their guidance (Q 2:55); Hypocrisy (Q 2:14, 2:44); Giving preference to their own interests over the rulings of religion and the dictates of truth (Q 2:87); Wishing evil for people and trying to mislead them (Q 2:109); They feel pain to see others in happiness and are gleeful when others are afflicted with a calamity. (Q 3:120); They are known for their arrogance and haughtiness (Q 5:18); Utilitarianism and opportunism are among their innate traits (Q 4:161); Their rudeness and vulgarity is beyond description (Q 4:46); It is easy for them to slay people and kill innocents (Q 2:61); They are merciless and heartless (Q 2:74); They never keep their promises or fulfill their words (Q 2:100); They rush hurriedly to sin and compete in transgression (Q 5:79); Cowardice and love for this worldly life are undisputable traits [of the Jews]. (Q 59:13-14, 2:96); Miserliness runs deep in their hearts (Q 4:53); Distorting Divine Revelation and Allah's Sacred Books (Q 2:79)."* [194]

Tantawi's discussion of the Jews' alleged predilection to ignore covenants maintains "numerous" Qur'anic verses (as examples, Q 2:83-86, 5:12-13) "described the Jews as covenant breakers." [195] He adds, [196] "Those who follow their history- both ancient and modern- will see that this vice is almost second nature to them." Citing Q 5:13, "The Almighty said: 'You O Prophet will always find deceit on their part, except for a few'", Tantawi opines at length on the eternal implications of this inveterate negative Jewish trait, melding anti-Jewish truculence with Islamic apologetics: [197]

> *"This means:* ***You Prophet will always see in those contemporary Jews the same image of their predecessors when it comes to treachery, disloyalty and breaking covenants****. Those who exist now have inherited the disloyalty and treachery of their forefathers. They are just as cruel and misguided as their forefathers were. Even though time separates them, they have the same manners and dispositions with the exception of a few of them who accepted Islam, kept their promises and fulfilled their covenants. This honorable statement amply depicts the nature of the Jews at all times and places. Before Islam, they broke their covenants with Allah and harmed His messengers and prophets. When Allah sent His Prophet whom they knew as the knew their own children, they disbelieved and rejected him. They broke their promises with him every time, and they fought him using all possible means.* ***They have persisted on doing this from the start of the Islamic call until the present day****. Loyalty and faithfulness are not known to them. Their Modus operandi with Muslims is disloyalty, treachery and breaching covenants. If they are found deficient in inflicting harm openly, they would resort to hidden and covert methods and conspire with any of the enemies of the Islamic call. If the chance offers itself to them, they would viciously and brutally pounce on its followers...Those who follow the history of the Islamic State will realize that the Prophet dealt with kindness and consideration with the Jews who lived in Medina after his migration to it. He made an agreement with them, he was tolerant and lenient with them notwithstanding their desire to inflict harm, and he pardoned their offenses wishing that by doing so he might be able to lead them to the right path. However, when they breached their covenants and persisted in their injustices, he punished every sect with the appropriate punishment, one that was*

congruous with the offense. Therefore, he expelled Banu Qaynuqa and Banu Nadir, killed Banu Qurayza and reconciled with the people of Khaybar in return for a portion of their earthly yield of fruits and vegetables on the condition that he could expel them whenever he wanted to. Near the end of his life, he ordered the expulsion of the Jews from the Arab Peninsula to make sure that two religions would never exist there. ***It is incumbent upon Muslims to apply this principle in dealing with the Jews who exist right now****. Those Jews who attacked our homes should be fought against and expelled. Other peaceful Jews may be treated with kindness and leniency, unless they betray their evil intensions.* ***Very few of them will betray good intensions****."*

Among the "many vices and depravities of the Jews" recounted in the Qur'an, Tantawi places special emphasis on the Jews' "inappropriateness to the Creator," rejection of Islam's prophet Muhammad and "murdering honorable prophets that came to them with guidance and true faith," hatred of the angel Gabriel, and derision of the Qur'an's encouragement of charitable giving: [198]

"...two noble verses (Q 2:97-98) branded the Jews as disbelievers and ignorant for their animosity towards Gabriel, and their disbelief in Muhammad. They also revealed their disgrace and humiliation for this animosity was merely due to envy and malice, their resentment that Allah revealed His favors and grace to whomsoever He wants."

"And the Almighty stated that their killing of the prophets was 'unjust'—(Q 3:21, 3:181) even though this could never be just—to state the target of His condemnation and reproof, because the object of His disapproval was their transgression against the truth by killing the prophets. It was also meant to point out that due to their blindness and going too far in committing evil, they became enemies of the truth, unfamiliar and uncomfortable with it, and to record that their killing of the prophets was unwarranted in their own religion which prohibited it. ***It was a statement that expressed objection to them presenting what their law prevented them from doing to eternalize their denunciation everywhere and at all times****...Thus, the noble verses (Q 5:70-71; earlier 3:21, and 3:181))* ***revealed one of the guileful and inherent habits of the Jews in all places and at all times: receiving Allah's prophets and those who stood up for justice with arrogance and denial sometimes and killing and harming them at other times****. That deeply ingrained habit had led them to disgrace in this world and painful torment in the hereafter."*

"They ridiculed the teachings of Islam that urge and encourage people to be generous, charitable and giving. They allude to the Almighty things that are unbecoming, and they try all possible means to encourage the believers to be tightfisted and miserly in order to cast doubts in their faith and cause them to become unresponsive to Allah's Book and His Prophet (Q 3:181; 5:64)."

Regarding Q 2:109, and the Jews' willful, stubborn efforts to turn Muslims from Islam, Tantawi adds: [199]

> *"...the Qur'an was fair* ***to the few believers among them [the Jews]*** *who did not want the Muslims to turn back to disbelief after Allah had guided them to Islam...Their disbelief was not because of ignorance; rather, it was on account of their obstinacy, rebelliousness and a state of stagnation in embracing falsehoods. That was the condition of their rabbis and scholars who had knowledge of the Torah and it's heralding the arrival of the Prophet."*

Tantawi identified as a "most conspicuous" vice of the Jews "reiterated" by the Qur'an was their alleged, " 'corrupting' the texts (altering and changing the texts and using words for purposes other than what they were originally meant to convey)." [200] Invoking Q 2:7, 2:74, 2:75-79, and 4:46, Tantawi explains the origins and consequences of this particular vice: [201]

> *"That was because their hearts were hardened and cruel and their vision was dim and blurry, and they were more interested in seeking fleeting short-lived gains (Q 2:7, 2:74)...the majority of those Jews, essentially imitators and followers, received their religious tenets through corrupt and immoral leaders who disregarded the truth and all means leading to it. Therefore, such people who were brought up as blind followers could not be expected to detect the light of guidance and the beauty of righteousness. A nation whose scholars and distinguished ones- the best and brightest in it- had deteriorated to such a degree that they dared to distort the words of Allah, could not be expected to mount to any good; its subjects could not be any better in any way, shape or form...They had reached an abominable state that could not promise their coming to guidance; their scholars distorted and corrupted Allah's Book to suit their lusts and desires, and the common people only knew the lies and illusions that their rabbis and scholars made available to them.* ***A nation whose scholars and common people were like that could not be expected to accept the truth or follow the straight path****...shame, disgrace and perdition would be the lot of those Jewish scholars who distorted and deliberately misinterpreted the Books- instead of delivering the facts that were contained therein (as they were)- then falsely informed their illiterate imitators and followers that those were from Allah and from the Torah that Allah revealed to Moses in order to seek a little ephemeral gain. Their punishment would be severe for distorting the words of Allah, and they would be humiliated and disgraced for the gains they had unlawfully earned...they wrote the Book with their own hands and deceitfully and falsely attributed it to Allah in order to earn a meager worldly gain such as unlawful wealth, a pretense to erudition and knowledge, lust for authority and power, pleasing the public and common people- all that suited their desires and lusts (2:75-79)."*

Tantawi concludes, regarding Q 2:75-79, and 4:46: [202]

"Thus, we see that these noble verses (Q 2:75-79; Q 4:46) have recounted that the Jews have distorted the words of Allah and the words of those people who commanded them to be fair and just. They also recorded their inappropriate behavior towards the Messenger and all who had called them to guidance and the upright path. Allah described them as circuitous and devious people who uttered ambiguous and equivocal statement and behaved impudently and insolently. He also depicted them as people who disparaged and ridiculed the faith using phrases that would ostensibly be taken as respectful and differential while in reality they were demeaning, derisive and condescending. ***People with such characteristics are truly deserving of condemnation and severe torture.****"*

A universal, particularly "ugly characteristic" of Jews "at all times and in all places" featured in Tantawi's Qur'anic litany is their "intense and eager clinging to life (to live a long-drawn-out life), their extreme love for life in this world regardless of its quality even if it were blemished with humiliation and disgrace." [203] This "voracious love for life and the world," Tantawi avers, engendered in the Jews, [204]

"...indescribable shameful cowardice, withdrawal and retreat from noble and honorable situations, and finding all kinds of pretexts to avoid fighting even for the sake of the truth. The Noble Qur'an has depicted these inherent vices of the Jews with precision and truthfully." (see Q 2:96 and its classical gloss) [205] *...Like the Jews, all people cling to life; however, the Jews cling to it more eagerly than all other people. Because of this unrestricted clinging, they are ready to sacrifice their faith, their dignity and everything else...There is no doubt that such an intemperate clinging to life could lead to cowardice, timidity and submission in the face of grievance and injustice. A nation in which such a vice runs rampant would not be expected to distinguish between a respectful honorable life and a life of dishonor and humiliation."*

Given that the Jews, "had long been accustomed to humiliation and enslavement at the hands of Pharaoh and his people," [206] Tantawi also argues they allegedly, [207]

"...did not attach great value to freedom. They didn't appreciate it, their sense of pride waned and their inherent sense of human dignity ceased to exist. ***An easy comfortable life in humiliation, slavery and servitude was far better than dignity, self-esteem and pride in a life filled with fighting and jihad.****" (****Q 5:20-26****)...From this story, we also learn that rebelliousness against Allah and His messengers would only lead to loss in this world and in the Afterlife, for when the Children of Israel were fearful of entering the Holy Land and disobeyed the commandment of Moses, their prophet, Allah punished them by wandering aimlessly in the desert for forty years. Thus far, we have mentioned some of the noble verses that documented the Jews' voracious desire to cling to life, their cowardice to fight, their rejection of sound counsels, and their refusal to comply with their prophet's command. This led to undesirable consequences in this life and in the Hereafter."*

Moreover, Tantawi insists the Jews, because of their "nature," are trapped in a recurring downward spiral: [208]

> *"...as soon as they find the straight path (i.e., Islam; see Q 1:6-7), they depart from it and go astray; they soon decline, deteriorate and go speedily down the minute they ascend and rise; they may find the righteous path but they quickly relapse, regress and revert."*

The Biblical narrative of the golden calf (Exodus 32:1-9) is transmogrified in the Qur'an (especially Q 7:150-153 and 20:83-98), and excitedly conveyed by Tantawi as a pathognomonic composite of eternal Jewish vices, reflecting, [209]

> *"...the ignorance of the Children of Israel, their crooked and twisted nature, their corrupt unsound mentality, their lack of vision and discernment and their reluctance to mend their ways was taking the calf-instead of Allah- as a god to worship and becoming wholeheartedly devoted to worshipping it. The Noble Qur'an ridiculed the Children of Israel for this vice that their souls craved. It showed them its vanity and irrelevance in many of its verses...[which] labeled the Children of Israel with the vice of ignorance and narrow-mindedness. They have shown their inability to make sound judgements and their propensity to choose misguidance rather than guidance as they indulged in worshipping the calf, the epitome of stupidity and absurdity, and abandoned worshipping the One Who is Worthy of obedience, submission and worship, the One to Whom nothing on earth or in the heavens is concealed."*

For Tantawi, the golden calf episode is also evidence of the [210]

> *"...deeply ingrained harshness and cruelty of the Children of Israel, their arrogant and inappropriate attitude towards their prophets, their endless persistent and excessive inquiries, their unwillingness to submit and comply with what their prophets bring them, their procrastination and stalling when it was time to comply, and their deviation from the righteous path."*

Before his closing summary assessment of the lasting impact of Jewish vices as portrayed in the Qur'an, Tantawi acknowledges candidly the core Muslim belief that Islam was "the religion that Allah sent to Moses," [211] and he decries the Jews' alleged [212]

> *"...callousness and insensitivity to religion, their ungratefulness and belittling what Allah bestowed upon them, their non-compliance with the word of truth, their distrust of the truthfulness of their prophets and their semantic bickering either to get away with their non-compliance because of their lack of vision and perceptiveness to understand the law and its tenets."*

Tantawi ends chapter 6, thusly: [213]

"In concluding our long discussion of the vices of the Children of Israel as portrayed by the Noble Qur'an, ***we say that their vices that we mentioned in this chapter were only examples of their wickedness and corruption which the successors inherited from their predecessors****. The Noble Qur'an mentioned these vices to record their deviation from the truth, their preference of misguidance and blindness over light and the straight path and to caution the believers against their wickedness and corruptions."*

Chapter 7 details the Jews' "long and unparalleled history" of making "false claims, untruthful statements, and insincere and dishonest assertions." [214] Tantawi, representing any believing Muslim reader of the Qur'an "who is equipped with discernment and sound logical judgment," proceeds to demonstrate in this chapter how Islam's "Noble" book, [215]

"...exposed these false claims and declarations that the Jews came up with. It demolished their excuses and shut their mouths, revealing their lies and falsehoods and exposing their vices, depravities and failings."

Referencing Q 2:91-93, Tantawi demonstrates how the Jews denial of prophethood—which devolved into alleged "prophet-killing," including the attempted assassination, and later, lethal poisoning of Muhammad—was rooted in ignorance, lies, wrongful acts, and ultimately, evil: [216]

"...the Jews—who claimed to believe in what was sent down to them—were lying because they did not believe in Muhammad who was prophesied in their Torah which commanded them to believe in him and which the Noble Qur'an confirmed it in this regard...dreadful criminal acts happen again and again and the [Jews'] successors blindly and thoughtlessly follow in the footsteps of their predecessors. The Jews who were contemporaneous with the Prophet tried to kill him, but the Almighty protected and saved him from their deceit and cunningness...It (the Qur'an) showed their (the Jews) blatant lies, denial and rejection, and it demonstrated that the disease of denial in them was an old disease, which they had imbibed in their hearts for centuries, until it became a chronic disease, and that what they had done today concerning disbelief in what was revealed to Muhammad was nothing but a connected link in the chain of their disbelief in what was revealed to them. It presented the horrific and undeniable historical evidence demonstrating their ignorance of Allah, their violation of the sanctity of His prophets, and their rebellion against His commands: 'Then why did you kill the prophets of Allah before, if you were believers?' (Q 2:91)...Then, consider how the Noble Qur'an that has recorded the most despicable of vices against the Children of Israel—i.e., taking the calf, the epitome of stupidity, as a god to glorify, and described the cruelty of their hearts in disregarding Allah's commandments after prompting them to obey through magnificent and awesome signs—after all of this, it just describes them as acting 'wrongfully' (Q 2:92) and that what they did was 'evil (Q 2:93). Is that all that can be said regarding all of these atrocities? Yes, these are two words that qualify to describe the crime, if understood appropriately!"

But Allah thwarted the Jews, as Tantawi explains, invoking Q 2:137: [217]

> *"Allah fulfilled His promise; He helped His Prophet gain victory over his enemies, and He spared him their evil and malice. The Prophet was able to sow the seeds of dissention and animosity between them, he expelled those who were deserving of being driven out, and he killed those who were deserving of death because of their treachery and betrayal. The noble verse comprised a promise of victory to the believers and a warning to the Jews and their likes of humiliation, disgrace and defeat."*

Tantawi champions unmitigated Islamic supremacism: [218]

> *"In sum, Islam for man should not be solely because he was brought up in Muslim environment or born to a Muslim father and mother." ... as the Almighty said: Those 'will have their reward with their Lord. And there will be no fear for them, nor will they grieve (Q 2:62)'."*

He further argues, this "noble verse" (Q 2:62), [219]

"...confirmed what they [the Jews] denied: others [i.e., the Muslims] will enter Paradise."

Indeed, if only the Jews had accepted Islam and its Shari'a they would have been spared their calamitous fate. Qur'an 2:62, [220]

> *"...showed that they [the Jews] are not the people of Paradise unless they submit to Allah and do good deeds. This was to encourage them to embrace Islam and show them how different they were from those who will enter Paradise...[Q 2:62] was also meant to encourage them to abandon their wicked deeds and desert their crooked ways...[Q 2:62] provided a statement to indicate that for Allah an acceptable deed should comprise two things: First, it should be done exclusively for the sake of Allah.; Second, it should be in agreement with the doctrine that Allah accepts: the Islamic Shari'a."*

Tantawi next rivets on Allah's (and Muhammad's) refutation of the Jews' (and Christians') claim to be the "children of God," invoking and glossing Q 5:18: [221]

> *"Interpreters believe that the word 'children' in their claim "We are the children of Allah" refers to true 'biological' childhood. In fact, from their Book, the Jews refer to Allah's (God's) words to His servant Israel: 'Israel is the first of my sons.' (Exodus 4:22) So, they added extra shades of meaning and distorted what was said from its original sense.* ***One of their sensible scholars, who embraced Islam,*** *maintained that it was merely meant as a way to honor and dignify (Israel)...Then the Almighty impugned and refuted their claim in His response: 'Say, O Prophet, 'Why then does He punish you for your sins?. 'That is, tell those frauds and liars,*

Muhammad, that if you were truly Allah's children and His most beloved- as you claim- He wouldn't have punished you. A true lover would not torture his beloved. ***However, your situation is quite the opposite, for Allah has punished you for your sins by murdering, capturing and transforming you (into apes and pigs, i.e., Q 5:60).*** *In the Books that are between your hands, it is written that you will be punished in the Hereafter for your transgressions in this world. The Jews conceded that torture will befall them for only a few days, and the Noble Qur'an recounted that: 'Some of the Jews claim, 'The Fire will not touch us except for a number of days (Q 2:80).''"*

The following verse, Q 2:81, of course negates that "concession," declaring they (the Jews), "will be the residents of the Fire…forever." [222] Tantawi then invokes Q 9:31 and a canonical hadith of Muhammad (Jami at-Tirmidhi 2954, which clarifies Q 1:7), identifying the Jews' (and Christians') alleged disavowal of monotheism—at least from the perspective of Islam—engendering, for the Jews specifically, Allah's anger: [223]

"The Almighty then showed that they were only commanded to worship none but One Allah, without associating any partner or son with Him. He said: 'they were commanded to worship none but One Allah. There is no god worthy of worship except Him. Glorified is He above what they associate with Him!' (Q 9:31). That is, they were commanded in their Books and by Moses and Jesus-peace be upon them- to worship Allah Alone with faithfulness and loyalty… He (Muhammad) said: 'The Jews are those who earned Your anger, and the Christians are those who went astray' (also a reference to Q 1:7)."

Tantawi then reminds the reader of Islam's "supremacy," admitting the Jews' refusal to accept Islam's "true guidance" is their cardinal sin. [224]

*"The Almighty thwarted the attempts of those disbelievers and rendered them helpless and disappointed while promising the believers the good tidings of victory. He said: '****He is the One Who has sent His Messenger with true guidance and the religion of truth, making it prevail over all others****…(Q 9:33) That is, it was the Almighty who sent Muhammad, His Messenger, with the Qur'an that would guide people to what is good and beneficial to them.* ***It was Allah who sent Muhammad with the religion of truth, Islam, to prevail and have supremacy over all other religions****…"*

Prior to continuing his Qur'anic litany of the Jews' mendacious statements and behaviors, Tantawi provides an interim summary assessment from Tafsir al-Alusi: [225]

"…the Jews were chastised for consuming others' money, following their wishes and desires, claiming things that Allah never promised, lying and distorting Allah's judgements, indulged in unlawful gains, and saying untruths about Allah."

Returning to his chapter 7 litany, Tantawi demonstrates how the Qur'an accuses the Jews of not abiding covenants, most prominent among them, "worshipping Allah alone (monotheism)," believing in His messengers, especially Muhammad," and "living in piety and fear of Allah." [226] In essence, Tantawi continues, [227] man should shun what Allah has prohibited, and do only what Allah has made permissible." Unsurprisingly, Tantawi avers, the Qur'an declares the Jews' lacking in all these attributes: [228]

> *"They did not fulfill the covenant that Allah took from them to believe in Muhammad. Consequently, they made permissible what Allah has forbidden, and they did not fulfill their trusts and they denied others their rights. They untruthfully claimed, 'We are not accountable for exploiting the Gentiles' (Q 3:75)."*

For Tantawi, this Qur'anic narrative is reflected in the Jews' alleged belief, [229]

> *"They would not be censured or impugned if they trespassed against them for those Gentiles do not believe in their religion. The Jews claim that their Book permits them to kill and take the money away from those who oppose them, and by any possible means. Sanctity and honoring others' possessions are not to be extended to non- Jews.* ***This contemptible and detestable attitude is deeply ingrained in the Jews.****"*

The Qur'anic hub of Jew-hatred for Tantawi is Q 5:64, as can be gleaned from its prominent placement as the opening quotation of his work, and the elaboration of its myriad "validations" in chapter 7. [230] Just before Tantawi's discussion regarding Q 5:64 in this chapter, he provides a gloss on Q 4:155-160, accompanied by a revealing fulmination about (an unnamed) "German priest" who allegedly "offered a proposal to the (also unnamed) Ecumenical Council to exonerate the Jews from Christ's blood." [231] Tantawi's anger about this noble effort to reject the deicide allegation against the Jews intensifies because the (unnamed) "Archbishop of the Anglican Church" purportedly endorsed the campaign. [232] Beyond the moral turpitude of Tantawi's rage, what is equally striking is how Tantawi ignored the monumental Vatican II/Nostre Aetate process of the Catholic Church in the early to mid-1960s (completed in 1965), with its far reaching, unequivocal rejection of the deicide allegation. [233]

Tantawi's commentary on Q 4:155-160 highlights the following: [234]

> *"It is because of breaking their covenant, their rejection of Our signs, their killing of the prophets and attributing lies and falsehoods to Us that We did what We did to them: We condemned and transformed them (into apes and pigs; Q 5:60; but also in Baydawi's gloss* [234a] *on Q 4:157), in addition to the other punishments that we inflicted upon them...it is the Almighty Allah Who has sealed their hearts because of their disbelief and wicked deeds. The Almighty created the human heart and inherently equipped it with the ability to choose good and evil. However, those Jews departed from what is good and righteous and pursued what is evil and wicked...Among the reasons why Allah condemned*

the Jews and cast humiliation and disgrace upon them was their disbelief and rejection of Jesus (Isa is the Muslim Jesus in Islam), the messenger who was sent to guide them to the truth, to a straightforward path, and their outrageous accusations and lies about Mary, Jesus' Mother, and the terrible falsehoods they attributed to her, namely, begetting Jesus without a father. She was innocent of all of these charges and untruths."

The Qur'anic narrative which denies Isa's crucifixion and death, however, does not exculpate the Jews, Tantawi affirms: [235]

"'But they neither killed nor crucified him.' (Q 4:157) That does negate that they unjustly killed the prophets. Nor does this negate that they sought all possible criminal ways to kill and crucify Jesus. Had the Almighty not miraculously saved Him from their cunning connivance, they would have killed and crucified Him. They would not have proceeded to kill the one who was 'likened' to Jesus had they not been fully convinced that their target was Jesus Himself... Thus, the noble verses impugned the Jews for the outrageous lies that they attributed to the Immaculate Virgin Mary. They also censured them for claiming that they killed Jesus, Son of Mary and Allah's messenger. The verses chastised them for their false allegations, brought the truth to light and abolished their lies and falsehoods, even to the dismay of the wicked."

Tantawi adds, [236]

"As things stand, they were like a group of bandits that sought to kill a certain man. They prepared themselves for that deed and they took all the measures to pursue it. However, they were unable to achieve their goal because of factors beyond their control. It is therefore reasonable to suggest that they should be condemned- as bandits- by just doctrines and fair laws. And we would like to add here that what they wanted to kill was one of the most distinguished amongst the prophets, One Who was sent by Allah to guide them to the truth. Yet, they rejected Him, disbelieved in Him, conspired against Him and planned to kill Him. In fact, they did kill one whom they thought was the Christ. They have been boastful of their crime throughout the generations."

The Qur'anic narrative of Isa's "rescue" by Allah—despite the murderous machinations of the perfidious Jews—is melded by Tantawi to yet another conspiratorial diatribe against the Jews, whose efforts to exonerate themselves from the deicide allegation, abetted by venal Christians, helps fulfill their immoral designs on "Muslim Palestine": [237]

"Thus, through cunningness and craftiness, the Jews were able to clutch an admission from some Christians that exonerated them from the blood of Christ... *The first goal behind the Jews' plan is to form a Jewish-Christian block that would stand in the face of the Muslims, support them in in usurping Palestine, and alleviate the intensity of the religious animosity between the Christians and* *the Jews considering that the mortal wound afflicting the Christian body is that Christ was killed and crucified by the Jews... We can therefore perceive that absolving the Jews from Christ's blood is—under current circumstances—politically motivated, an action that some Christians undertook to curry favor with the Jews and benefit from their money and world. Even if what they call for is what actually happened, the real motive is unethical and immoral: benefitting financially and forming a vile block to conspire against Islam and Muslims and divert the attention of those who follow in their footsteps and cause them to turn a blind eye to thousands upon thousands of the displaced Muslim Palestinian refugees."*

Tantawi concludes his putative chapter 7 discussion of Jesus Christ—in reality, the Christianity-destroying Muslim simulacrum of the Jesus of the Gospels, Isa the Muslim Jesus of the Qur'an and hadith—with a frank depiction of Isa's role in Muslim eschatology, according to the canonical hadith. [238] This closing reference is very odd. The author undermines his rancorous contentions of Jewish deicide against Christ, and modern Christian absolution of the Jews for that crime, as part of a Judeo-Christian conspiracy to "usurp Palestine," and "turn a blind eye to the thousands upon thousand of displaced Palestinian Muslim refugees." [239] As Tantawi acknowledges, Isa will return some forty years before the end of times as a full-throated Muslim to destroy Christianity—"break the cross, kill the pig, and end the payment of the jizya (poll tax per Q 9:29 paid by vanquished Christians and Jews who refuse to convert to Islam, in lieu of being slain)"—meaning Christians (and Jews) who truly understand their faith will become Muslims, and Isa will slaughter those who stubbornly refuse to accept Islam. [240]

Regarding Q 4:155-160, and the relevant hadith, Tantawi declares: [241]

"...what was narrated by the Sheikhan (the two Sheikhs; i.e., the hadith collections of Bukhari and Muslim) on the authority of Abu Hurairah, who said: 'By Him in Whose Hand is my soul, the Son of Mary will soon descend among you as a just judge. He will break the cross, kill the pig, and abolish the jizya.'...Then Abu Hurairah said: 'Read if you wish: 'Every one of the People of the Book will definitely believe in him before his death. And on the Day of Judgment Jesus will be a witness against them'...The statement: 'And on the Day of Judgment Jesus will be a witness against them.' means that He will be a witness against the Jews that they denounced and rejected Him...Thus, the noble verses impugned the Jews for the outrageous lies that they attributed to the Immaculate Virgin Mary. They also censured them for claiming that they killed Jesus, Son of Mary and Allah's messenger. The verses chastised them for their false allegations, brought the truth to light and abolished their lies and falsehoods, even to the dismay of the wicked."

What Tantawi leaves vague is that Isa will be a "witness against" Christians who retain their traditional faith, as well as Jews. The seminal Qur'anic commentary Tafsir al-Baydawi elucidates these points in its gloss on Q 43:61 (The verse reads, "And his

[Isa's] second coming is truly a sign for the Hour. So have no doubt about it and follow me. This is the Straight Path [i.e., Islam]."): [242]

> *"In the hadith, Jesus (Isa), peace be upon him, will descend on a pass in the Holy Land called Afiq, holding a spear with which he will kill the Antichrist. He will come to Jerusalem while the people are praying the dawn prayer, but the imam will delay, so Jesus, peace be upon him, will put him forward and pray behind him according to the law of Muhammad (i.e., the Sharia), peace be upon him. Then he will kill the pigs, break the cross,* ***destroy the churches*** *and synagogues,* ***and kill the Christians except for those who believe in him****. It was said that the pronoun refers to the Qur'an, as it contains information about the Hour and evidence of it. 'So have no doubt about it,' Do not have any doubts about it. 'And follow me,' and follow my guidance, or my law, or my messenger. It was said that it is the statement of the Messenger, peace be upon him, that he was commanded to say. 'This,' is what I call you to. 'A straight path,' whose follower will not go astray."*

Pre-eminent American scholar of Islam Duncan B. MacDonald's (d. 1943) entry on "Isa" in the *First Encyclopaedia of Islam*, paraphrases and clarifies the key narrative elements of Baydawi's Q 43:61 gloss, [243]

> *"The later doctrine of his [Isa's] return is given soberly by al-Baydawi on Q 43:61: that he will descend in the Holy Land at a place called Afik with a spear in his hand; that he will kill with it al-Dadjdal [The Muslim Anti-Christ] and come to Jerusalem at the time of the salat (prayer) of the morning; that the imam will seek to yield place to him but he will refuse and worship behind him according to the shari'a of Muhammad [i.e., as a Muslim]; thereafter he will the swine and break the cross and lay ruins the synagogues and churches and kill all Christians who do not believe in him."*

Tantawi's focal analysis of Q 5:64 in chapter 7 argues that the verse has myriad timeless historical manifestations of powerful, ugly Jewish conspiracies, from the advent of Islam, till the present era. However, Tantawi avers, also consistent with Q 5:64, there are "silver linings": the Jews' propensity to generate self-destructive hate among themselves, and Allah's tendency to quash their conspiracies. [244]
Here is Q 5:64: *"Some among the Jews said, 'Allah is tight-fisted.' May their fists be tied and they be condemned for what they said. Rather, He is open-handed, giving freely as He pleases. That which has been revealed to you O Prophet from your Lord will only cause many of them to increase in wickedness and disbelief. We have stirred among them hostility and hatred until the Day of Judgment. Whenever they kindle the fire of war, Allah puts it out. And they strive to spread corruption in the land. And Allah does not like corruptors."* [244a] As a prelude to Tantawi's commentary on Q 5:64 in chapter 7, extracts from his mature gloss on this verse published some two decades later in his full Qur'anic commentary, *"The intermediate [balanced] interpretation of the Qur'an,"* clarify the verse's centrality to his—and Islam's—eternal theological animus towards

the Jews, "updated" with a re-assuring (i.e., to Muslims) allusion to the fate of the modern "state" of the Jews "in Palestine." [245]

> *"His statement (in Q 5:64), 'Their hands are chained, and they are cursed for what they said,' is a prayer against them with bitter greed and hideous stinginess, that Allah Almighty will create in them, Allah's creation, and He decreed that they be expelled from Allah's mercy, the Most High, because of their bad manners toward Him, the Most High, and their ingratitude for His blessings. This sentence is a teaching from Allah to us to invoke curses upon those whose hearts are corrupted, and who are ill-mannered towards their Creator and Provider, and who say about Him what He is far above... Allah, the Almighty, further consoled His Messenger by issuing His ruling concerning them regarding the perpetuation of enmity and hatred between their sects and groups, saying, 'And We cast among them enmity and hatred until the Day of Resurrection.' The pronoun in His statement, 'among them,' refers to the various Jewish sects, including the Pharisees, Sadducees, Karaites, Scribes, and other diverse sects... The meaning is: We cast permanent enmity and constant hatred between the various sects of the Jews. You see their words differing, their hearts divided, and each group of them attributes shortcomings to the other, and they will remain in this state until the Day of Resurrection...* ***The cooperation and support shown by the Jews in this era, which led them to establish a state for themselves in Palestine, is a temporary matter. This state will not last long but will return to its Muslim people when they are sincere in their jihad and follow the teachings of their religion****. Al-Fakhr Al-Razi (the great classical Islamic exegete; see note [102]) said: 'Know that the connection between this verse and the one before it (Q 5:63: 'Why do their rabbis and scholars not forbid them from saying what is sinful and consuming what is unlawful? Evil indeed is their inaction!') is that Allah, the Almighty, made it clear that these Jews only denied his prophethood, peace and blessings be upon him, after the evidence of its authenticity had become clear, out of envy and the love of fame and money. Then He, the Almighty, made it clear that since they preferred this world over the hereafter, there is no doubt that just as He, the Almighty, deprived them of the happiness of religion, He also deprived them of the happiness of this world, because each group of them remained steadfast in their doctrine and opinion. This became a cause for severe enmity between their sects and groups. The matter ended with some of them declaring others infidels and fighting each other.',,, And His saying, 'And they strive to spread corruption in the land. And Allah does not like corrupters.' This is a conclusion confirming the previous reprehensible characteristics with which Allah - the Most High - branded the Jews. That is, the state of these Jews is that they strive hard to plot against Islam and its people and that they strive diligently to spread corruption on earth by stirring up sedition and awakening hatred among people. Allah - the Most High - does not like corrupters, rather He hates and detests them, because they prefer misguidance over guidance and evil over good. Thus, we see that the noble verse has responded to the Jews in their attribution of stinginess to Allah - the Most High - and made clear that He - the Most Generous - is the One who is*

bountiful and generous in giving. It revealed aspects of their vices and stubbornness and made it clear that He - the Most High - hates them because they spread corruption on earth and do not reform."

Tantawi's prior statements on Q 5:64 in *Banū Isrā'īl fī al-Qur'ān wa-al-sunnah* were concordant but much more expansive including a series of putative historical examples of conspiratorial Jewish behavior validating the "Qur'anic insight" of this verse. These "historical examples," which devolve into malevolent, ahistorical lunacy, merit careful attention, and will be discussed at some length, subsequently.

Consistent with the gloss on Q 5:64 in *"The intermediate [balanced] interpretation of the Qur'an,"* Tantawi's Ph.D. thesis maintains: [246]

> *"The Jews are known for their attempts to corrupt the land and entrap Islam and the Muslims. They have tried to erase the description of the characteristics of the Messenger from their Books. They also tried to sow the seeds of suspicion in the hearts of the Muslims concerning their faith. They stirred up dissentions and discords among them...We have sowed perpetual animosity and everlasting hatred amongst the different Jewish sects. Their views were different and ununified and their attitudes and desires were at variance. Moreover, whenever they sought to wage a war on the Messenger and the believers, Allah frustrated their schemes, foiled their plots and cast terror in their hearts. What this noble verse mentioned concerning the eternal animosity and hatred among the sects of the Jews is undoubtedly factual and true. Different Jewish sectors are still at variance warring with each other; the members of each sector betray evil and display animosity to members of other sectors. The hatred and enmity that is concealed and hidden is far greater.* ***The cooperation and collaboration and the cunningness and deceit that the Jews employed at this generation to establish a state for them in Palestine is only temporary and transitory. Their presence in Palestine will not last long, regardless of the assistance and support they receive. Palestine will be restored once the Muslims truthfully fight them, follow the teachings of Islam and adequately prepare themselves to restore their usurped land****... History bears witness that the Muslims were exposed a great deal to the harm of the Jews and their aggression; however, the Almighty granted the believers victory over them because of their faithfulness and trust in Him as well as their adequate preparedness to confront their enemies."*

Tantawi's barrage of vicious, ahistorical twaddle—allegedly "proving" the validity of Q 5:64—opens with this calumny: [247]

> *"Those who look at history in its various stages will soon realize that killing and assassination is second nature in the Jews throughout the generations."*

Immediately, Tantawi segues to an especially vile classic Medieval Christian blood libel—accusing Jews of ritually murdering Christians as an integral part of their religion, blending Christian blood in the Passover unleavened bread, or "matzot," (and for other evil magical, or sacerdotal applications). Riveting on a factitious incident, the 1840 Damascus Affair, a mid-19th century modern version of this calumny, Tantawi asserts: [248]

> *"Among the most acknowledged Jewish rituals is the shedding of blood of non-Jews and mixing this blood with the dough that is used for the Passover bread. This topic has been investigated, and it was found that the Jews have actually performed this criminal practice throughout the ages...One of the most well-known crimes was the one that took place in 1840. It was confirmed that they killed Father Toma (sic Tommaso; Thomas) and his servant. In sum, one of the Jewish rabbis wanted to get non-Jewish human blood to use for the Passover bread. They lured Father Toma and his servant, slaughtered them and drained their blood for that purpose. The murderers were convicted and sentenced to death."*

Week upon week, Muhammed Ali, the Egyptian viceroy overseeing Syria/Damascus, delayed the execution of the "convicted" Jews—whose spurious "confessions" were extracted through torture. (Then Austrian consul-general Laurin in Alexandria wrote that every "confession" had been extracted by five thousand blows of the bastinado.) During this delay, Jewish leaders Sir Moses Montefiore, the president of the Board of Deputies of British Jews, and Adolphe Cremieux, vice president of the French Jewish Consistoire Central (governing body), and a renowned courtroom lawyer, traveled to Alexandria, Egypt, and met with Muhammed Ali numerous times. Notwithstanding these appeals, four of the thirteen Jews imprisoned for the 1840 Damascus blood libel died as result of their incarceration and torture. A month after the intercession of Montefiore and Cremieux, the nine surviving Jewish prisoners in Damascus were released unconditionally. One of these survivors, Moses Abulafia (Abu el-Afieh), in the interim, had become a Muslim, and he gave false testimony for the prosecution to escape his repeated torture. The gruesome details of el-Afieh's torture warrant attentive reading. [249]

Historical analyses of the 1840 Damascus blood libel by Tudor Parfitt and Jonathan Frankel emphasize these two key features which were independent of Christian anti-Jewish motifs, per se: the general support th at the persecution of the Jews was given by the Arab Muslim population at large, in reaction against the various reforms introduced (under Muhammad Ali, in Syria and Palestine) which sought to ameliorate some of the most oppressive aspects of the Shari'a for non-Muslims, specifically; the fact that this negative reaction by the Muslim masses to these reforms had serious repercussions for both Jews and Christians during pogroms against the Jews of Safed (in 1834 and 1838), and the extensive anti-Christian pogroms which marred Damascus in 1860. [250] Indeed as Frankel observes, despite their own bigoted anti-Jewish attitudes, it was the European consuls who drew the line in 1840, [251]

> *... when it came to the threat of wholesale massacre...advising that the Jewish communities receive military protection. Just how real that danger was would*

become apparent twenty years later, when the Christian population of Damascus was decimated in a Muslim, primarily Druse, slaughter

Regardless, Parfitt notes how blood libels occurred often "throughout the entire region after the Damascus Affair." [252] He enumerates this depressing proliferation: [253]

> *"In the vicinity of Damascus there were nine blood libels between 1840 and 1900. In Palestine there were blood libels in 1847, 1848, 1870 and 1871. In 1844 there were two cases of blood libels in Egypt: one in Cairo instigated by Muslims, and the other in Alexandria, instigated by the Greek Orthodox; in 1866, in Hamadan in western Iran, eighteen Jews were massacred following a ritual murder allegation—two more were burnt alive while the rest of the community only managed to escape the fury of the mob by converting en masse to Islam; there were further libels in Alexandria in 1870, in Smyrna in 1871, and Damanhur (Egypt) in 1871 and 1873, initiated by Muslims, and again in Smyrna in 1873. In 1875 there was a blood libel in Aleppo, as a result of which the Pasha of Aleppo had to send troops to guard the Jewish quarter. In 1876 there was another blood libel in Constantinople, while 1877 saw libels in Damanhur and Mansura (Mansoura, also Egypt), where local Muslims accused the Jews of kidnapping a Muslim child and killing it in order to use its blood for matzot."*

Tantawi's allegations of the Jews' predilection for "killing and assassination" include so-called "appalling crimes that cause one to cringe and squirm," directed at the Arabs of Palestine "ever since their (the Jews') feet have trodden upon Palestinian soil." [254] Once again demonstrating his crude historical negationism, Tantawi's timeline for this criminal Jewish behavior—alleged massacring of Arab Muslim Palestinians, ostensibly "ever since their (the Jews') feet have trodden upon Palestinian soil," only begins [255] in 1948, i.e., during the war that established Israel as an independent state. [256] Quite predictably, Tantawi invokes the mythical "Deir Yassin Massacre" as epitomizing this trend (although his comments about the event are deferred until chapter 8, quoting a "contemporary writer"): [257]

> *"The Deir Yassin Massacre was one of the most atrocious that the Jews had perpetrated. They killed two **hundred and fifty (250),** mutilated their bodies, slaughtered the children in the arms of their mothers..."*

Eliezer Tauber's meticulous analysis of both Arab and Jewish testimony from primary source documents chronicles the essence of what occurred at Deir Yassin: a fierce ten-hour battle for the village. [258] After adducing voluminous evidence, Tauber's concluding assessment that in the military struggle for Deir Yassin, "people in Deir Yassin were killed, not massacred," includes these summary factual observations: [259]

> *"Seventy percent of the about 1,000 inhabitants of Deir Yassin managed to escape the attack (because the attackers let them escape), twenty percent were taken prisoner and later released, and ten percent were killed. As was shown...,*

> ***the ratio between Arabs killed and injured (about 100 each) did not suggest a massacre****. Even more indicative is the fact that double the number of Arabs were taken prisoner as were killed. This is an even better metric, because the decision to take individuals prisoner was an intentional act on the part of the captor (unlike when injuring people). Finally,* ***the very fact that the overwhelming majority, ninety percent, survived the attack is the clearest refutation of the accusation of a massacre. Sixty-one people out of the 84, whose circumstances of death were ascertained, were killed in battle conditions even if they themselves were not all active combatants. 'I believe that most of those killed were among the fighters and the women and children who helped the fighters,' one of the [Arab Muslim] fighters stated****. Forty-two percent of the people killed were males of an age fit for fighting. Twenty-four of the people killed were combatants. Relatively, many heads of families remained alive, while their family were killed...It was precisely because they were armed combatants that they had the ability and skills to succeed in escaping...[T]he battle for Deir Yassin took place in the presence of a civilian population. Combatants and non-combatants were present in the same houses. In many instances, heads of families, with their sons or other relatives, would shoot at the attackers from within the houses with the rest of their families with them. The attackers responded with a three-phase method of using explosives, hand grenades and automatic fire, successively, when bursting into the houses, The occupants did not stand much of chance to survive it. Some adherents of the massacre narrative claim that the events took place in two stages, asserting that, after the battle had ended and the Palmach [an elite branch of the Haganah, a Zionist military organization] had left, Etzel and Lehi [Jewish underground military organizations] staged a full-scale massacre. The available evidence negates this allegation. Most of the people killed in the village were killed during the battle and under battle conditions and not in a subsequent deliberate massacre. Generally speaking, when the battle ended, the killing stopped. There were no incidents of families being lined against walls and shot in Deir Yassin."*

Moreover, Tauber also provides a very measured synopsis of two Arab Muslim responses to the battle of Deir Yassin—which Tauber is even reluctant to label "reprisals"—that could quite reasonably be considered true massacres [260] of primarily non-combatant, or surrendered Jews: [261]

> *"On 13 April (1948) ...The Arabs attacked a Jewish convoy on its way to Hadassah hospital, killing 78 people (20 of them women), most of them medical staff. Many, including senior British officials, the High Commissioner among them, interpreted the attacks as a reprisal for Deir Yassin. While some of the assailants did shout 'Remember Deir Yassin!' and 'Avenge Deir Yassin!' it appears the attack would have been carried out anyhow. The Arabs believed the Haganah combatants were exploiting the convoy to reach Mount Scopus and operate from the hospital and university against them. The same applied to the attack a month later on Kfar Etzion, bringing about the death of 127 Jews (21 of*

them women), after they had surrendered. Some of the Arab attackers shouted Deir Yassin, Deir Yassin,' but the attack would have taken place anyway because of the settlement's strategic location. It might be said that the Deir Yassin affair aggravated the outcomes of these attacks but it did not cause them."

Tantawi not only ignores the attacks on the Hadassah hospital convoy and Kfar Etzion during the 1948 war—each of which included strong evidence that real massacres of Jews occurred [262]—he of course makes no mention of the nearly 13 century plight of the Jews in historical Palestine under Muslim rule. That legacy was one of brutal jihad conquest—massacre, pillage enslavement, and deportation of the indigenous Jewish population—and the subjection of the vanquished survivors to humiliating and pauperizing Sharia-based governance, interspersed with paroxysms of violence, including mass anti-Jewish pogroms. [263] Even under the British Mandate following World War I, the ugly dynamics of jihad persisted as evidenced by another event Tantawi conveniently ignores: the 1929 Hebron jihadist pogrom which metastasized to Jerusalem, Safed, Jaffa, Haifa, Ramla, Beisan, Acre, and Nazareth. [264]

Late August, 1929, the U.S. *Beatrice Daily Sun* (Beatrice, Nebraska), proclaimed, "***MOSLEMS SATE BLOOD LUST. Even Little Children Die By Knife in Jehad.***" This brief report conveyed with grisly accuracy the Arab Muslim jihad [jehad] depredations against the Jews of Hebron which began with the insolated stabbings (one fatal) of two yeshiva students on Friday, August 23rd, followed by a raging massacre the next morning, during which 66 Jews were butchered within two-hours: [265]

In practically every instance death was caused by swords or knives. Even young children of two and three years, many of them girls, did not escape the savagery of the attack.

While the greatest carnage of Jews was in Hebron, the Arab Muslim jihad rampages, which continued through August 29th, extended to Jerusalem 31 killed, 119 wounded; Safed 20 killed, 39 wounded; Jaffa 8 killed, 33 wounded; Haifa 6 killed, 67 wounded; Ramla 1 killed, 1 wounded; Beisan 25 wounded; Acre 3 wounded; and Nazareth 1 wounded. [266] Even a strained "balanced" account of the 1929 Arab Muslim jihad concedes, regarding the total [267] of 133 Jews killed, and 241 injured: [268]

A large majority of the Jews slain were unarmed and were murdered in their homes by Arabs. Most of the Arab dead were killed as they attacked Jewish settlements or neighborhoods. Most of the Arabs were felled by bullets fired by the British armed forces...

Jerusalem historian and journalist Pinchas Grayevsky (d. 1941) [269] provided this graphic 1929 description of the brutal murder of Hebron pharmacist Ben-Zion Gershon: [270]

For forty years, this Jew dressed the wounds and treated the illnesses of the most wretched Arabs, generally without asking for any compensation, as he received a

> *salary from the community or from Hadassah. Over his lifetime, this man saved hundreds and thousands of Arabs from dying of diseases of all kinds, from going blind or becoming handicapped...On the day of the riots Arabs broke into the home of this poor Jew,* ***and instead of having mercy on him for being one-legged, they cut off both of his hands. The very same Arabs whose eyes had been cured by him of trachoma*** *[a potentially blinding infection if untreated, caused by C. trachomatis]* ***and blindness stood over him and gouged out his eyes. The same Arabs whose wives and daughters he had saved from miscarrying and from gynecological illnesses now seized his eldest daughter, raped her, and killed her. They also stabbed his wife four times with a knife and brought a nail-studded club down on her head.***

Historian Jerold Auerbach's somber 2009 analysis ***Hebron Jews: Memory and Conflict in the Land of Israel*** summarizes the Muslim atmospherics, and offers harrowing details—rape, torture, beheadings, throat slitting, and mutilation—from eyewitness reports of other merciless assaults on Hebron's Jews: [271]

> *"In August 1929, Palestinian Arabs were incited to impassioned fury by the harangues of* ***Haj Amin-al-Husseini, the mufti of Jerusalem****. His allegations that Jews intended to "usurp" the Western Wall and endanger Muslim holy sites on the Temple Mount aroused his followers throughout Palestine... [Saturday, Aug.24th] cars filled with Arabs from nearby villages, screaming Allah akbar ("Allah is greater") and Itbach al Yahud ("Kill the Jews"), sped through the streets of Hebron. Rabbi Bemzweig recounted, "Right after eight o'clock in the morning we heard screams. Arabs, armed [with iron bars, sledgehammers, knives, and axes], had begun breaking into Jewish home...[F]amily members and yeshiva students, had crowded into Eliezer Dan Slonim's spacious house, where they believed that his esteem in the Hebron community would protect them...Virtually the entire Slonim family, including his wife Hannah and their son, his father-in-law, the chief rabbi of Zichron Yaakov, and his wife, was slaughtered. The sole survivor, one-year-old Shlomo, was discovered, blood drenched and wounded, beneath the corpses of his relatives. His look of abject terror, captured in a photograph, reflected the horror he had witnessed but could not begin to describe. A visiting tourist, Y. L. Grodzinsky, heard "the shrieks of the women and the babies' wailing" reverberate through the Slonim house. When he emerged from hiding, he saw "a sea of blood" from victims with "knife and hatchet wounds in their heads... A few bodies had been slashed and their entrails had come out." Twenty-two Jews were murdered there...Elsewhere in Hebron, Rabbi Hanoch Hasson, along with his entire family, was murdered... Four-year-old Shalom Goldshmidt and his sister survived by hiding under a bed; their mother and another sister were killed, and their father was tortured to death by Arabs who held his head over a burning kerosene stove. Two-year-old Menachem Segal, one of three children under the age of five who was murdered, had his head torn off... In the main room of the Anglo-Palestine bank, where twenty-three corpses were discovered, blood covered the tile floor "like thick jelly." Arabs "knocked down thirteen-year-old girls, mothers, and grandmothers in the blood*

and raped them in unison." Six yeshiva students were successively seated on the lap of Mrs. Sokolov; then, "one by one, [Arabs] slit their throats." Among the murdered students were eight Americans, including two sixteen-year-olds. One of the survivors, a student from Chicago, recounted that he "had seen greater horrors than Dante in hell." The grisly toll mounted. The entire Lazarovsky family, except for one son, was slaughtered. Rabbis Meir Kastel and Tzvi Drabkin, with five of their students, were tortured, castrated, and murdered. Rabbi Yakov Orlanski HaCohen had his brain removed from his skull. Moshe Arbiter, a yeshiva student from the United States, had two fingers chopped off; Elchanan Zeligroch, another student, had one hand severed at the wrist; and Liba Segal lost four fingers. There were reports of amputated penises and breasts.

Artist Nachum Gutman's poignant 1929 black and white drawings (see two, below)—quickly banned by the British Mandatory authorities—captured the Muslim incitement, and barbarity. [272]

"For every Jew killed, ten cigarettes. Mabrouk"

Auerbach's study refers to Hajj Amin el-Husseini's indirect role as key instigator of the Arab Muslim "fury" unleashed on Hebron. [273] Lt. Col. F.H. Kisch, Chairman of the Palestine Zionist Executive from 1923 to 1931 assigned culpability to el-Husseini, directly, in his 1938 memoir, *Palestine Diary*: [274]

"I mentioned...in regard to those whose active campaign of provocation ample evidence was in the hands of authorities...[local Hebron] ***Sheikh Taleb Morke, against whom there was abundant evidence of his having called upon the inhabitants of Hebron to kill the Jews, saying that an order to this effect had come from Hajj Amin****."*

The 1929 jihad carnage in Hebron had two major historical antecedents: large anti-Jewish pogroms by Muslims in Hebron punctuated the Ottoman Muslim period of rule in historical Palestine, one early (in 1517), and one in the last century of Ottoman control (1834).

A letter signed Japheth Ben Manasseh describing the 1517 events, whose Hebrew text was printed in *Sefer Hevron*, records the following: [275]

In the seventh month, on the holiday of Succoth in 1517, the cruel tyrant; the wrath of the Holy One Be He, Murad Bey, deputy of the Sultan and ruler of Jerusalem, decided in his heart to take out his fury on the Jews in his city and those living in Hebron. And he said 'I will take booty from them and take the Jews in the two cities captive so long as they have the power to see me.' And he carried out his decree. On that day, his men came to Hebron and killed many of the Jews who fought for their lives and plundered all their belongings until not one refugee or survivor was left in the Land. And a small remainder of those not felled by the sword fled to the Land of Beirut. And prior to departing, they hurried to bring along their Torah scrolls, and requested to remove their holy books. And in our numerous sins, we did not find anything. It is written and signed here by Rabbi Korpo on the sixth day of Tevet, 1519 - Yafeth ben Menashe."

Egyptian Muslim soldiers of Ibrahim Pasha sent to quell an Arab revolt, joined by local Arab Muslims on June 15, 1834, participated in a pogrom that killed 12 Jews, including 5 young girls. Ancient synagogues were desecrated, Jewish homes ransacked, and Jewish assets stolen, leaving the community destitute, in what became known to the Jews as "the great destruction." [276]

Apart from these pogroms (four centuries, and one century, respectively, before the 1929 jihad carnage), two complementary late 19th century travelogue accounts (by Marion Harland, published in 1896, and John Kelman, published in 1902) capture the chronic state of persecution the Jews of Hebron experienced under Muslim rule, entirely consistent with the application of the Sharia: [277]

[Marion Harland] "'Father Abraham' occupies an exalted place among saints revered by the Moslems, ***and the jealous hatred of the Jews, never absent from the creed and feelings of the worshiper of Mohammed, <u>is at fever-heat in Hebron</u>. Nowhere else in the Holy Land, or out of it, are they regarded with such intolerant suspicion as in the ancient city in which David reigned over Judah seven years and six months****. Hence, the approach of an Israelite to the tomb of the patriarchs is even more abhorrent to 'believers' than that of the 'Christian dog.'"*

[John Kelman]***"In Hebron they (the Jews) are a persecuted minority****...today the lowest and most insulting term of abuse among the Fellahin (Arab Muslim peasants) is to call each other Jews."*

The "Jewish experience" under Muslim rule in Hebron mirrors wider, persistent currents evident throughout 13 centuries of their Islamic Shari'a governance in historical Palestine: violent, catastrophically destructive jihad conquest, followed by chronic, grinding persecution and impoverishment, interspersed with paroxysms of violence (including further internecine Muslim jihad violence, simultaneously directed at Jews and Christians, as well). Understandably, Tantawi ignores these historical realities, or bowdlerizes them as uniformly tolerant, beneficent Muslim conquest, and administration, under the Shari'a.

The 7th century jihad depredations which established Islam in Palestine through devastating, sanguinary conquest and colonization are described at length by Moshe Gil, in his monumental analysis *A History of Palestine, 634-1099.* Gil emphasizes the singular centrality that Palestine occupied in the mind of its pre-Islamic Jewish inhabitants, who referred to the land as '*al—Sham.*' Indeed, as Gil observes, the sizable Jewish population in Palestine (who formed a majority of its inhabitants, when grouped with the Samaritans) at the dawn of the Arab Muslim conquest were, "the direct descendants of the generations of Jews who had lived there since the days of Joshua bin Nun, in other words for some 2000 years." [278] Jews and Christians speaking Aramaic inhabited the cities and the cultivated inner regions, devoid of any unique ties to the Bedouin of the desert hinterlands, who were regarded as bellicose and threatening, in the writings of both the Church Fathers, and in Talmudic sources. [279]

What follows is a brief summary of the spoliation wrought by the Arab Muslim jihad conquest of Palestine during the fourth decade of the 7th century, directed by the first two Caliphs, Abu Bakr and Umar b. al-Khattab. The entire Gaza region up to Cesarea was sacked and devastated in the campaign of 634, which included the slaughter of four thousand Jewish, Christian, and Samaritan peasants. Villages in the Negev were also pillaged, and towns such as Jerusalem, Gaza, Jaffa, Cesarea, Nablus, and Beth Shean were isolated. In his sermon on the Day of the Epiphany 636, Sophronius, Patriarch of Jerusalem, bewailed the destruction of the churches and monasteries, the sacked towns and villages, and the fields laid waste by the invaders. Thousands of people perished in 639, victims of the famine and plague wrought by this wanton destruction. The Muslim historian Baladhuri (d. 892 C.E.), maintained that 30,000 Samaritans and 20,000 Jews lived in Caesarea alone just prior to the Arab Muslim conquest; afterward, all evidence of them disappears. Archaeological data confirms the lasting devastation wrought by these initial jihad conquests, particularly the widespread destruction of synagogues and churches from the Byzantine era, whose remnants are still being unearthed. The total number of towns was reduced from fifty—eight to seventeen in the red sand hills and swamps of the western coastal plain (i.e., the Sharon). Massive soil erosion from the Judaean mountains western slopes also occurred due to agricultural uprooting during this period. Finally, the papyri of Nessana were completely discontinued after the year 700, reflecting how the Negev also experienced the destruction of its agriculture, and the desertion of its villages. [280]

Bat Ye'or elucidated the fiscal oppression inherent in eighth century Palestine which devastated the dhimmi Jewish and Christian peasantry: [281] "Over-taxed and tortured by the tax collectors, the villagers fled into hiding or emigrated into towns." She quotes from a detailed chronicle of an eighth century monk, completed in 774 C.E.: [282] "The men scattered, they became wanderers everywhere; the fields were laid waste, the countryside pillaged; the people went from one land to another." Perhaps the clearest outward manifestations of the inferiority and humiliation of the dhimmis were the prohibitions regarding their dress codes, and the demands that distinguishing signs be placed on the entrances of dhimmi houses. During the Abbasid caliphates of Harun al-Rashid (786-809) and al-Mutawwakil (847-861), Jews and Christians were required to wear yellow (as patches attached to their garments, or hats). Later, to differentiate further between Christians and Jews, the Christians were required to wear blue. In 850, consistent with Qur'anic verses associating them with Satan and Hell, al-Mutawwakil decreed that Jews and Christians attach wooden images of devils to the doors of their homes to distinguish them from the homes of Muslims. [283]

Muslim and non-Muslims sources establish that during the early 11th century period of al-Hakim's reign, religious assaults and hostility intensified, for both Jews and Christians. The destruction of the churches at the Holy Sepulchre (1009 C.E.) was followed by a large scale campaign of Church destructions (including the Church of the Resurrection in Jerusalem, and additional churches throughout the Fatimid kingdom), and other brutal acts of oppression against the dhimmi populations, such as forcible conversion to Islam, or expulsion. The discriminatory edicts al-Hakim imposed upon the dhimmis beginning in August 1011 C.E., included orders to wear black turbans; a five pound, 18-inch cross (for Christians), or five pound block of wood (for Jews), around their necks; and distinguishing marks in the bathhouses. Ultimately al-Hakim decided that there were to be separate bathhouses for the dhimmis use. [284] During the early through the mid-11th century, the Jews, in particular, continued to suffer frequently from both economic and physical oppression, according to Gil. [285]

Muslim Turcoman rule of Palestine for the nearly three decades just prior to the Crusades (1071-1099 C.E.) was characterized by such unrelenting warfare and devastation, that an imminent "End of Days" atmosphere was engendered. [286] A contemporary poem by Solomon ha-Kohen b. Joseph, believed to be a descendant of the Geonim, an illustrious family of Palestinian Jews of priestly descent, speaks of destruction and ruin, the burning of harvests, the razing of plantations, the desecration of cemeteries, and acts of violence, slaughter, and plunder. [287]

The brutal nature of the Crusader's conquest of Palestine, particularly of the major cities, beginning in 1098/99 C.E., has been copiously documented. [288] However, the devastation wrought by both Crusader conquest and rule (through the last decades of the 13th century) cannot reasonably be claimed to have approached, let alone somehow "exceeded," what transpired during the first four and one-half centuries of Muslim jihad conquests, endless internecine struggles for Muslim dominance, and imposition of dhimmitude. We also cannot ignore the testimony of Isaac b. Samuel of Acre (1270-1350 C.E.), one of the most outstanding Kabbalists of his time. Conversant with Islamic theology and often using Arabic in his exegesis, Isaac nevertheless believed that it was preferable to live under the yoke of Christendom, rather than that of Islamdom. Acre was taken from the Crusaders by the Mamelukes in 1291 by a very brutal jihad conquest. Accordingly, despite the precept to dwell in the Holy Land, Isaac b. Samuel fled to Italy and thence to Christian Spain, where he wrote: [289]

> *"...they [the Muslims] strike upon the head the children of Israel who dwell in their lands and they thus extort money from them by force. For they say in their tongue, ... 'it is lawful to take money of the Jews.' For, in the eyes of the Muslims, the children of Israel are as open to abuse as an unprotected field. Even in their law and statutes they rule that the testimony of a Muslim is always to be*

believed against that of a Jew. For this reason our rabbis of blessed memory have said, 'Rather beneath the yoke of Edom [Christendom] than that of Ishmael. [Islam]'"

Although episodes of violent anarchy diminished during the period of Ottoman suzerainty (beginning in 1516-1517 C.E.), the degrading conditions of the indigenous Jews and Christians living under the Sharia's jurisdiction remained unchanged for centuries. For example, Samuel b. Ishaq Uceda, a major Kabbalist from Safed at the end of the 16th century, refers in his commentary on *The Lamentations of Jeremiah*, to the situation of the Jews in the Land of Israel (Palestine): [290]

"...there is no town in the [Ottoman] empire in which the Jews are subjected to such heavy taxes and dues as in the Land of Israel, and particularly in Jerusalem. Were it not for the funds sent by the communities in Exile, no Jew could survive here on account of the numerous taxes... The [Muslims] humiliate us to such an extent that we are not allowed to walk in the streets. The Jew is obliged to step aside in order to let the Gentile [Muslim] pass first. And if the Jew does not turn aside of his own will, he is forced to do so. This law is particularly enforced in Jerusalem, more so than in other localities."

A century later Canon Antoine Morison, from Bar-le-Duc in France, while traveling in the Levant in 1698, observed that the Jews in Jerusalem are "there in misery and under the most cruel and shameful slavery," and although a large community, they suffered from extortion. [291]

Similar contemporary observations regarding the plight of both Palestinian Jews and Christians—subjected to the *jizya* [infidel poll tax, per Q 9:29], and other attendant forms of social, economic, and religious .. discrimination, often brutally imposed, were made by the Polish Jew, Gedaliah of Siemiatyce (d. 1716), who, braving numerous perils, came to Jerusalem in 1700. These appalling conditions, recorded in his book, <u>Pray for the Peace of Jerusalem</u>, forced him to return to Europe in order to raise funds for the Jews of Jerusalem. [292]

"No Jew or Christian is allowed to ride a horse, but a donkey is permitted, for [in the eyes of Muslims] Christians and Jews are inferior beings... The Muslims do not allow any member of another faith—unless he converts to their religion—entry to the Temple [Mount] area, for they claim that no other religion is sufficiently pure to enter this holy spot. In the Land of Israel, no member of any other religion besides Islam may wear the color green, even if it is a thread [of cotton] like that with which we decorate our prayer shawls. If a Muslim perceives it, that could bring trouble. Moreover, the Muslim law requires that each religious denomination wear its specific garment so that each people may be distinguished from another. This distinction also applies to footwear. Indeed, the Jews wear shoes of a dark blue color, whereas Christians wear red shoes. No one can use green, for this color is worn solely by Muslims. The latter are very hostile toward Jews and inflict upon them vexations in the

streets of the city...the common folk persecute the Jews, for we are forbidden to defend ourselves against the Turks or the Arabs. If an Arab strikes a Jew, he [the Jew] must appease him but dare not rebuke him, for fear that he may be struck even harder, which they [the Arabs] do without the slightest scruple. This is the way the Oriental Jews react, for they are accustomed to this treatment, whereas the European Jews, who are not yet accustomed to suffer being assaulted by the Arabs, insult them in return. Even the Christians are subjected to these vexations. If a Jew offends a Muslim, the latter strikes him a brutal blow with his shoe in order to demean him, without anyone's being able to prevent him from doing it. The Christians fall victim to the same treatment and they suffer as much as the Jews, except that the former are very rich by reason of the subsidies that they receive from abroad, and they use this money to bribe the Arabs. As for the Jews, they do not possess much money with which to oil the palms of the Muslims, and consequently they are subject to much greater suffering."

These prevailing conditions for Jews did not improve in a consistent or substantive manner even after the mid-19th century treaties imposed by the European powers on the weakened Ottoman Empire included provisions for the Tanzimat reforms. First introduced in 1839, these reforms were designed to end the discriminatory laws of dhimmitude for both Jews and Christians, living under the Ottoman Shari'a. European consuls endeavored to maintain compliance with at least two cardinal principles central to any meaningful implementation of the reforms: respect for the life and property of non-Muslims; and the right for Christians and Jews to provide evidence in Islamic courts when a Muslim was a party. Unfortunately, such efforts to replace the concept of Muslim superiority over 'infidels', with the principle of equal rights, failed. [293]

Nearing two decades later, three eyewitness accounts from Palestine, particularly Jerusalem, one written by itinerant rabbi Rabbi Israel Joseph Benjamin (Binyamin) form his 1847 visit, another from the missionary Gregory Wortabet, (published in 1856), and the third by British Jerusalem Consul James Finn, (reported November 8-11, 1858) make clear that the deeply ingrained Islamic religious bigotry, discriminatory regulations, and treacherous conditions for non-Muslims in Palestine had not improved, even after a second iteration of Ottoman "reforms" in 1856.

Israel Joseph (I.J.) Benjamin (1818-1864), was a "maggid," an itinerant Jewish preacher, best known for his extensive first hand mid-19th century travelogue accounts of the Jewish communities of Africa and Asia ("***Eight years in Asia and Africa from 1846 to 1855***"). Here are his comments based on what he witnessed during a sojourn in Palestine in 1847: [294]

"Deep misery and continual oppression are the right words to describe the condition of the Children of Israel in the land of their fathers. —-I comprise a short and faithful picture of their actual state under the following heads.
1) They are entirely destitute of every legal protection and every means of safety. Instead of security afforded by law, which is unknown in these countries,

they are completely under the orders of the Scheiks and Pashas, men, whose character and feelings inspire but little confidence from the beginning. It is only the European Consuls who frequently take care of the oppressed, and afford them some protection...
2) With unheard of rapacity tax upon tax is levied on them, and with the exception of Jerusalem, the taxes demanded are arbitrary. Whole communities have been impoverished by the exorbitant claims of the Scheiks, who, under the most trifling pretenses and without being, subject to any control, oppress the 'Jews with fresh burthens.; It is impossible to enumerate all their oppressions.
3) In the strict sense of the word the Jews are not even to complain when they are robbed und plundered; for the vengeance of the Arabs would be sure to follow each com plaint. Alas, alas, that such in the nineteenth century should be the condition of some of our people.
4) Their lives are taken into as little consideration as their property; they are- exposed to the caprice of any one; ever. the smallest pretext, even a harmless discussion, a word dropped in conversation, is enough to cause bloody reprisals. Violence of every kind is of daily occurrence. When, for instance in the contests of Mahomet Ali with the Sublime Porte, the City of Hebron was besieged by Egyptian troops and taken by storm, the Jews were murdered and plundered, and the survivors scarcely even allowed to retain a few rags to cover themselves. No pen can describe the despair of these unfortunates. The women were treated with brutal cruelty; and even to this day, many are found, who since that time are miserable cripples. With truth can the Lamentations of Jeremiah be employed here. Since that great misfortune up to the present day, the Jews of Hebron languish in the deepest misery, and the present Scheik is unwearied in his endeavours, not to allow their condition to be ameliorated, but on the contrary, he makes it worse.
5) The chief evidence of their miserable condition is the universal poverty which we remarked in Palestine, and which is here truly astounding; for nowhere else in our long journeys, in Europe, Asia and Africa did we observe it among the Jews. It even causes leprosy among the Jews of Palestine, as in former times. Robbed of their means of subsistence from the cultivation of the soil and the pursuit of trade, they exist upon the charity of their brethren in the faith in foreign parts. — The Writer, who has seen all their misery with his own eyes, and with his own hands has touched the deep and ever open and bleeding wounds of his brethren, has often repeated in his heart the words of Jeremiah: 'If I go forth into the field, there I behold the slain with the sword, and when I enter into the city then I behold those who are sick with famine! —How is my heart oppressed with sadness! how loudly does it throb, I can nowhere find peace.' But altho' he has grieved over their inexpressible misery, he has also admired the resignation with which his brethren in the faith have borne their misfortunes for hundreds of years up to this time, and the confidence, with which they continue to be steadfast in hope. Like shadows they steal over the hand, which nourishes their cruel and imperious tyrants. The ignorant and barbarous Arab tramples this sacred soil beneath his feet, and considers the Jew a disinherited and accursed being, unworthy of dwelling there; and yet

these ruins, these desolate cities, these wide-spreading fields now uncultivated and desolate, are the inheritance of Israel; and still does this fruitful land up to the present day bring forth abundantly every kind of grain, fruits of all countries, and excellent wine; and its air is also of exquisite purity and indescribable freshness...In a word the state of the Jews in Palestine, physically and mentally, is an unbearable one. This we vouch for and our assertion is the more deserving of credence as we devoted all our time and energies to obtain correct information on this point, and yet there the land yields most abundantly. If the possession of it were not too completely in the hands of the Arabs, — if one could only secure for the Jews some little portion of it, and give them the means for its cultivation, sufficient sources of industry would be open to them, wherewith to obtain a subsistence. We are thoroughly convinced of the correctness of this from our own personal observations on the spot. We paid very particular attention to this subject, as it is one that has been much agitated in Europe of late. But what does it benefit them to cultivate the ground, if the Arabs rob them of the harvest?"

Wortabet's narrative depicts the common, prevailing attitudes of Muslim Jew hatred derived from a purely Islamic perspective. Indeed, Wortabet refers, quite plausibly to the hadith about Muhammad's poisoning by a Khaybar Jewess as a primary source of such animus. Finn's report highlights the legal discrimination and physical insecurity suffered by both Jews and Christians. [295]

> [*Wortabet*'s account] *"The Jew is still an object of scorn, and nowhere is the name of "Yahoodi (Jew)" more looked down upon than here in the city of his fathers. One day, as I was passing the Damascus gate, I saw an Arab hurrying on his donkey amid imprecations such as the following: 'Emshi ya Ibn-el-Yahoodi (Walk, thou son of a Jew)! Yulaan abuk ya Ibn—el—Yahoodi (Cursed be thy father, thou son of a Jew)!' I need not give any more illustrations of the manner in which the man went on. The reader will observe, that the man did not curse the donkey, but the Jew, the father of the donkey. Walking up to him, I said: — 'Why do you curse the Jew? What harm has he done you?' 'El Yahoodi khanzeer (the Jew is a hog)!' answered the man. 'How do you make that out?' I said. 'Is not the Jew as good as you or I?' 'Ogh!' ejaculated the man, his eyes twinkling with fierce rage, and his brow knitting.By this time he was getting out of my hearing. I was pursuing my walk, when he turned round, and said: —'El Yahoodi khanzeer! Khanzeer el Yahoodi! (The Jew is a hog! A hog is a Jew!)' Now I must tell the reader, that, in the Mahomedan vocabulary, there is no word lower than a hog, that animal being in their estimation the most defiled of animals; and good Mahomedans are prohibited by the Koran from eating it. The Jew, in their estimation, is the vilest of the human family, and is the object of their pious hatred, perhaps from* ***the recollection that a Jewess of Khaibar first undermined the health of the prophet by infusing poison into his food****. Hence a hog and a Jew are esteemed alike in the eye of a Moslem, both being the lowest of their kind; and now the reader will better understand the meaning of the man's words, 'El Yahoodi khanzeer!'"*

[Finn's account] *"...my Hebrew Dragoman, having a case for judgment in the Makhkameh (Shari'a court) before the new Kadi (judge)...was commanded to stand up humbly and take off his shoes...during the process, although the thief had previously confessed to the robbery in the presence of Jews, the Kadi would not proceed without the testimony of two Moslems — when the Jewish witnesses were offered, he refused to accept their testimony—and the offensive term adopted toward Jews...(more offensive than Giaour for Christians) was used by the Kadi's servants... In continuing to report concerning the apprehensions of Christians from revival of fanaticism on the part of the Mahometans, I have... to state that daily accounts are given to me of insults in the streets offered to Christians and Jews, accompanied by acts of violence... the sufferers are afraid."*

Tudor Parfitt's study concluded that these problems persisted through the close of the 19th century: [296]

"...the courts were biased against the Jews and even when a case was heard in a properly assembled court where dhimmi testimony was admissible the court would still almost invariably rule against the Jews. Inside the towns, Jews and other dhimmis were frequently attacked, wounded, and even killed by local Muslims and Turkish soldiers. Such attacks were frequently for trivial reasons."

Ultimately, enforced abrogation of the laws and social practices of dhimmitude required the dismantling of the Ottoman Empire, which only occurred during the European Mandate period following World War I. Remarkably soon afterwards, however (i.e., within two years of the abrogation of the Shari'a), by 1920, Musa Kazem el-Husseini, former governor of Jaffa during the final years of Ottoman rule, and president of the Arab (primarily Muslim) Palestinian Congress, demanded restoration of the Shari'a in a letter to then British High Commissioner, Herbert Samuels: [297]

[Ottoman] Turkey has drafted such laws as suit our customs. This was done relying upon the Shari'a (Religious Law), in force in Arabic territories, that is engraved in the very hearts of the Arabs and has been assimilated in their customs and that has been applied... in the modern [Arab] states.... We therefore ask the British government... that it should respect these laws [i.e., the Shari'a]... that were in force under the Turkish regime.

After more than thirteen centuries of almost uninterrupted jihad in historical Palestine, it is not surprising, as late Papal Nuncio Pietro Sambi warned in 2003, that the finalized constitution for the proposed Palestinian Arab state—per the Palestinian Authority, not Hamas—declared all aspects of Palestinian state law to be subservient to the Shari'a. [298] Contemporary Palestinian Authority religious intelligentsia also openly support the restoration of the oppressive system of dhimmitude within a Muslim-dominated Israel. On July 6, 2001, Palestinian Authority Sheikh Muhammad Ibrahim Al-Madhi, at the Sheik Ijlin Mosque in Gaza, intoned, [299]

"We welcome, as we did in the past, any Jew who wants to live in this land as a Dhimmi, just as the Jews have lived in our countries, as Dhimmis, and have earned appreciation, and some of them have even reached the positions of counselor or minister here and there. We welcome the Jews to live as Dhimmis, but the rule in this land and in all the Muslim countries must be the rule of Allah..."

Two years earlier, an appropriate assessment of such anachronistic, discriminatory views toward non-Muslim Jews or Christians, was provided by then Catholic Archbishop of the Galilee, Butrus Al-Mu'alem, who, in a June 1999 statement, dismissed the notion of modern dhimmis submitting to Muslims: [300]

"It is strange to me that there remains such backwardness in our society; while humans have already reached space, the stars, and the moon... there are still those who amuse themselves with fossilized notions."

Tantawi sees many other alleged historical validations of Q 5:64's timeless wisdom on the Jews, whom he accuses, "throughout the ages, and in all places," of "stirring up seditions, fanning the embers of war, and provoking revolutions against the status quo…with history as a witness for what we say." [301] These additional ahistorical calumnies drip with Jew-hatred, and a number are also frankly bizarre. Here are some more salient examples from Tantawi's litany: [302]

—The Jews, Tantawi asserts, fought Muhammad's "call" (to Islam, i.e., Muslim dawa, or proselytization) by "stirring up seditions and conflicts." [303]

—Invoking the character of Abdallah ibn Saba, a "famous Jew, who pretended to have entered Islam and caused discord and disagreement among the Muslims," Tantawi alleges his "conspiracies and intrigues…led to the murder of Uthman Ibn Affan, the third ("Rightly Guided") Caliph. [304]

—Declaring the Jews were progenitors of the Donmeh sect in Ottoman Turkey, which "hid behind Islam to entrap it in modern times." Tantawi insists the Donmeh were "Jews," who "to pretended embrace Islam until they were able to eradicate the Ottoman Empire…and abolish its Caliphate." [305]

—Tantawi claims, in addition, the Jews, "pushed William, the Conqueror to enter England so that they could follow in his footsteps. They were also responsible for inciting Alexander the Great to most of his conquests. They came with him to Egypt where they settled. They encouraged the Spanish King, Philip the Second, to annex Portugal to his kingdom to dwell in it under his banner. They also provoked the flames of the two World Wars in this century. They were the only ones who amassed great fortunes as a result of these wars" [306]

—Perseverating on his specious allegations about fantastic Jewish wealth, Tantawi maintains, "the Jews [wealth] in the United States in 1926 was estimated at 500 thousand million (500 billion) dollars. Of this, the Rothschild family alone had 300 thousand million (300 million) dollars. The other wealthy non-Jewish people who live in America possessed 25 million dollars." As a corollary, Tantawi claims, "with this enormous amount of money and influence, the Jews were capable of planting the seeds of discord, arousing wars and inciting revolutions to serve their self-interest." [307]

—Continuing with the theme of "stirring up revolutions," Tantawi insists, "The Communist movement itself was in general the work of the Jews. It was Karl Marx, a Jew, who was its leader and founder." [308]

—According to Tantawi, The Protocols of The Elders of Zion are quite real, and were issued "…to corrupt the world in order to subjugate the world and bring it under their sole control… Some writers translated them into Arabic…excerpts from the Protocols of the Elders of Zion. They betray the evils and malicious intent of the Jews for the world, their plans to destroy the world and subjugate its people, communities and nations. The extracts also reveal their wide knowledge of the methods through which they can exploit others' weaknesses to serve their goals and satisfy their greed and desires. They are seeking to topple governments in all countries and replace them with governments under Jewish control. They never desist from sowing the seeds of discord and dissention in all countries." [309]

—Tantawi also avers, Jews (apparently as a perverse global "monopoly"), "Jews own the brothels in the world. They spread debauchery, decadence and depravity everywhere." [310]

Tantawi concludes, [311]

> *"These are some of the examples for the Jews' corruption of the land. We mention them to demonstrate and explain the Almighty's: 'And they strive to spread corruption in the land. And Allah does not like corruptors.' (Q 5;64)"*

While each of these "examples" is a false, grotesque calumny, as already documented in their accompanying notes, three deserve elaboration: Tantawi's Jew-hating calumnies about Abdullah Ibn Saba, Karl Marx, and *The Protocols of the Elders of Zion.*

The saga of Abdullah Ibn Saba illustrates Q 5:64's unabashed Jew-hating conspiracism in association with "the birth pangs" of Islam. It also captures Islam's anti-black racism. As put forth in early Sunni Muslim historiography (for example, by Tabari), Abdullah Ibn Saba, was an alleged renegade Yemenite Jew, and founder of the heterodox Shiite sect. [313] Sean Anthony's extensive modern analysis of Abdullah Ibn Saba adds another pejorative characteristic conferred upon this ostensible Yemenite Jew in the Muslim literature: his mother was black. Anthony notes that a "favorite derisive handle for him," was "son of the Black woman." [314]

According to Sunni dogma, Abdullah Ibn Saba is held responsible — identified as a Jew (and black) — for promoting the Shiite heresy and fomenting the rebellion and internal strife associated with this primary breach in Islam's "political innocence," culminating in the assassination of the third Rightly Guided Caliph Uthman, and the bitter, lasting legacy of Sunni-Shiite sectarian strife. [315] Here are key extracts from Tabari's account: [316]

> *'Abd Allah b. Saba' was a Yemenite Jew. . . . He later converted to Islam in the time of [Caliph] Uthman. Then he traveled through the lands of the Muslims trying to lead them into error. . . . [For example] in Egypt he promulgated to the people the [heterodox] doctrine of the Return [of Muhammad as Messiah]. So the Egyptians discussed this idea. Then, after that, he said that there were one thousand prophets, each of whom had an agent; and that Ali was Muhammad's agent. Then he said, Muhammad was the Seal of the Prophets and Ali was the Seal of the Agents. Also, he asked: "Who is more evil than those who denied Muhammad's designation of Ali as his agent-successor, pounced upon this successor- designate of Ali's messenger and seized (illegitimately) the rulership of the Muslim community?" [In answer to this question as it were,] he told the Egyptians that Uthman had seized power illegitimately while Ali was, in fact, the agent-successor of Allah's messenger. "Rebel against this illegitimate rule, provoke it, and challenge your rulers . . ." [said 'Abd Allah b. Saba'].*

The Shiite position on Abdullah Ibn Saba does not concede the discussion to Sunni traditionalist scholars. Authoritative Shiite authors countered that he was guilty of perverting and warping the message of Caliph Ali's true (Shiite) followers. Mainstream Shiites thus designated Abdullah Ibn Saba an archetypal avatar of extreme, heretical beliefs, notably, the profession of Ali's divinity. [317] This profession was an egregious heresy for which Caliph Ali purportedly had Ibn Saba burned alive, as described in a Shiite hadith: [318]

> *Muhammad b. Qūlawayh al-Qummī—Sa'd b. 'Abd Allāh b. Abī Khalaf al-Qummī—Muhammad b. 'Uthmān al-'Abdī—Yūnus b. 'Abd al-Rahmān—'Abd Allāh b. Sinān—his father (Sinān b. Tarīf)—Abū Ja'far (Muhammad al-Bāqir) said: "'Abd Allāh b. Saba' made a claim to prophecy while asserting that the Commander of the Faithful ('Alī) is God. This reached the Commander of the Faithful, and he called for him and questioned him. (Ibn Saba') reaffirmed this and said, 'Yes, you are he! It was cast into my heart that you indeed are God, and I am a prophet.' The Commander of the Faithful said to him, 'Woe to you, for Satan mocks you! Turn away from this, lest your mother be bereaved of you, and repent!' (Ibn Saba') refused.* ***('Alī) imprisoned him and urged him to repent for three days, but he did not repent. Then 'Alī burned him alive with fire and said, 'Satan led him astray with false imaginings He would come to him and cast such things into his heart.'"***

Caliph Ali is also claimed to have denounced Ibn Saba's blackness, allegedly declaring, [319]

What do I have to do with the vile, black man?

Although of Jewish descent, Karl Marx's father converted to Lutheranism, and young Karl was baptized at age six (along with all his siblings), and ostensibly attended classes that led to confirmation into the Lutheran Church by age fifteen. [320] Marxism's founding Dr. Crankley, [321] Karl Marx, was an annihilationist Jew-hater. Marx wished to extinguish Judaism, and its Jewish adepts—mere embodiments of "usury and money"— actions which would achieve his dystopian vision of "the emancipation of society from Jewry": [322]

> *Money is the zealous one God of Israel, beside which no other God may stand...The God of the Jews has become secularized and is now a worldly God. The bill of exchange is the Jew's real God. His God is the illusory bill of exchange...What is the foundation of the Jew in our world? Practical necessity, private advantage...The chimerical nationality of the Jew is the true nationality of the merchant, of the man of money. The law of the Jew, lacking all solid foundation, is only a religious caricature of morality and of law in general...What is the object of the Jew's worship in this world? Usury. What is his worldly God? Money...Very well then: emancipation from usury and money, that is, from practical, real Judaism, would constitute the emancipation of our time...As soon as society can abolish the empirical nature of the Jew, that is, usury and its preconditions, being a Jew will become impossible...The social emancipation of Jewry is the emancipation of society from Jewry" (The Jewish Question,* Braunschweig, 1843)

Additional statements of Karl Marx's reflexive, day-to-day Jew-hatred, include the following: [323]

> *It is the circumvention of law that makes the religious Jew a religious Jew. (Die Deutsche Ideologie, MEGA V, 162); The Jews of Poland are the smeariest of all races. (Neue Rheinische Zeitung, April 29, 1849); He called Ferdinand Lassalle,* ***"Judel Itzig—Jewish Nigger."*** *(Der Judische Nigger, MEKOR III, 82, July 30, 1862); Ramsgate [British coastal resort] is full of Jews and fleas. (MEKOR IV, 490, August 25, 1879)*

Marx was also the original proponent of a "Red-Green Alliance", circa 1878 (in a February 4, 1878 letter), championing the (final gasps of) Ottoman jihad to *defeat* Czarist Russia, and foment "revolution" there, and throughout Europe: [324]

> *"...the defeat of the Russians would greatly accelerate the social upheaval in Russia—the elements for which are plentiful—and thereby the reversal in all of Europe."*

The jihad pogrom against the Jews of Hebron, and beyond, in 1929, illustrates the dynamics of the Red-Green alliance in Palestine. Less than a week after the 1929 Haj

Amin El-Husseini-fomented Jew-hating carnage ended on August 29th, [325] "Morning Freiheit", the New York City-based, official Communist party Yiddish language newspaper, published the first of two vicious Der Stürmer-like [326] cartoons (Sept. 4, 1929; the second appearing Sept. 19th) condemning the self-defensive actions of Mandatory Palestine's Jews. Rabbi Benjamin Schultz's July 13,1949 testimony before the House Un-American Activities Committee on Communist Antisemitism, highlighted the "object" of these grotesquely bigoted caricatures—*"discredit Jewish aspiration for a homeland in Palestine and justify Stalin's power bid to the Arabs against the British".* [327] Schultz also displayed the images and provided these apt descriptions of them: [328]

"One cartoon ['The Mask Behind Which He Shoots'] appeared Sept. 4, 1929, and shows the Zionist as a pudgy monstrosity with a hooked nose using an old bearded Jew as a shield. This bearded Jew has an even bigger hooked nose. **[Julius] Streicher, the Nazi, could do no better.**"

"The other cartoon ['The Zionist Charity Givers'] was published in the *Freiheit* of Sept 19, 1929, and is labeled "Zionist Charity Giver." He is a gruesome Jew again with a hooked nose, and a shield of David on his stomach with the dollar sign over it. The other cartoon has the shield of David, or six-pointed Jewish star, on a big money bag. This was the Communist line in 1929."

Ex-Communist apostate Whittaker Chambers, in his searing 1952 autobiography *Witness* commented acidly about the same perverse 1929 American Communist Party phenomenon having served then as a writer/editor for the English language Communist organ *Daily Worker*: [329]

> *"Arab outrages were occurring in Palestine.* ***The Communist International chose that moment to call for the formation of a 'Soviet Arabistan,' and to attack the Zionists****. Day after day bludgeoning stories and editorials along this mad line appeared in the Daily Worker.* ***Editing them seemed less like a peculiarly trying exercise in party discipline than horseplay in a mental home.****"*

Historian Walter Laqueur's 1956 study, "***Communism And Nationalism In The Middle East,***" chronicled the same reaction—orchestrated by the Soviet Comintern—within the Communist movement of Palestine itself: full-throated support for Arab violence—pogroms—to destroy Jewish settlements. [330]

*"**In a country like Palestine a revolutionary movement without pogroms is impossible.**" This, in a nutshell, was the new line. Could a real revolutionist argue that such a movement should be disapproved of and discouraged merely because there was a danger of pogroms? Of course not If the Arab proletariat had not been so weak, pogroms would not have occurred at all...**The Zionist ideology was the real culprit**, but the Arab revolt, the pogroms, and the national struggle in general had given Zionism a death blow from which, in all probability, it would never recover. The main assignment for the Communist Party was to encourage the Arab revolt, to broaden it, and to lead it.*

Lastly, both Winston Churchill, in 1920, and journalist Eugene Lyons, in 1947, exploded the pernicious myth of "Jewish Communism." As Churchill observed, [331] aptly, nearly all of the small minority of so-called "Jews" of Leon Trotsky's ilk, were atheistic, and anti-Zionist, and had *"forsaken the faith of their forefathers, and divorced from their minds all spiritual hopes of the next world...Nothing could be more significant than the fury with which Trotsky has attacked the Zionists generally, and Dr. (Chaim) Weissmann in particular."* Lyons argued that the "silly myth of 'Jewish Communism'," was "brought to full flower by Nazi propaganda, part of the evil heritage of Hitlerism." [332] He pointed out regarding the Jews' alleged outsized role in the 1917 Bolshevik Revolution, and Bolshevism, more broadly, [333]

> *"...anti-Jewish propaganda conveniently forgets that Jews were even more numerous and more prominent in the Menshevik and Social Revolutionary camps—in the groups, that is, **opposing Bolshevism. Within the Bolshevik high command, Jews were always a distinct minority. The founders of the party and its most active leaders from 1903 to 1908 were Lenin, Malinovsky, Skvortzev-Stepanov, Vorovsky, Professor Pokrovsky, Bonch-Bruchevich. Rumyantzev—not a Jew among them.** Only much later some Jews began to achieve posts of leadership. Of the 124,000 Communist members in the Russian ruling party in 1918, the first Soviet year, **only 3,200 or 2.6 percent were Jews.***

When it came to Communism in the United States, Lyons noted, [334]

> *"Though there are some 5,000,000 (5 million) Jews in the United States, there is only one Jewish Communist daily, the Freiheit, with a circulation of about 12,000; the Forward, by contrast, has 140,000. **The whole of the Jewish English-language press (American Hebrew, Jewish Frontier, Commentary, etc.) is vigorously anti-Communist**...[P]ractically all Jewish labor leaders, with David Dubinsky, head of the International Ladies Garment Workers Union, Julius Hochman, head of the dressmakers, and Max Zaritsky, head of the cap and millinery workers [were also anti-Communist]. **The United Hebrew Trades, representing the vast majority of organized Jewish workers, has been militantly anti-Communist at a time when the general American labor movement was crawling with Communist borers-from within.**"*

Sixty-five years before Tantawi's adamant endorsement of the veracity of *The Protocols of the Elders of Zion*, [335] serious investigative journalism by Philip Graves, a former military intelligence officer, who served in the Middle East, proved they were a rather crude forgery. [336] Graves published his findings in *The Times* of London on August 18, 1921, concluding: [337]

> *"1. The Protocols are largely a paraphrase of the book here provisionally called the Geneva Dialogues.*
> *2. They were designed to foster the belief among Russian conservatives, and especially in Court circles, that the prime cause of discontent among the politically minded elements of Russia was not the oppressive policy of the bureaucracy but a worldwide Jewish conspiracy. They thus served as a weapon against the Russian liberals, who urged the Tsar to make certain concessions to the intelligentsia.*
> *3. The Protocols were paraphrased very hastily and carelessly.*
> *4. Such portions of the Protocols as were not derived from the Geneva Dialogues were probably suppled by the Okhrana (Russian imperial secret police), which organization very possibly obtained them from Jews it employed to spy on their co-religionists.*
>
> *So much for the Protocols. They have done harm not so much, in the writer's opinion, by arousing anti-Jewish feeling, which is older than the Protocols and will persist in all counties where there is a Jewish problem until that problem is solved; rather, they have done harm by persuading all sorts of mostly well-to-do people that every recent manifestation of discontent on the part of the poor is an unnatural phenomenon, a fictitious agitation caused by a secret society of Jews.*

The Times, on August 18th, concurrent with Graves' article, published an editorial declaring, "The fact that the plagiarism has now been conclusively established, …the legend may be allowed to pass into oblivion." [338] Yet as Ben-Ito, noted ruefully—Tantawi being a prime example, [339]

> *"For an entire century this lie has been published and disseminated in almost every language known to men in civilized countries, and time and again, it has been challenged and exposed by honest journalists, by learned historians, by politicians and by diplomats, by religious leaders and former police agents, and most of all by courageous, responsible, and unimpeachable judges in democratic countries. It has also been disproved by the horrible history of the twentieth century. Yet the lie endures and is still spreading its poison."*

Indeed, when an Egyptian television series "dramatization" validating The *Protocols* [340] was broadcast during Ramadan, 2002, Tantawi gave it his tacit endorsement, commenting, [341]

> *"I assume that the series contains criticism of some of the Jews' traits, or that it presents these traits. But this is no reason to make such an artificial uproar. I*

have proven that we were Semites even before they were, and it is inconceivable for anyone to show hostility towards himself. I am a Semite—how, then, should I be hostile towards myself? The charge of antisemitism was invented by the Jews, as a means of pressuring the Arabs and Muslims and with the aim of implementing their conspiracies in the Arab and Muslim countries. It should be disregarded."

Tantawi's discussion in chapter 8 describes the "numerous penalties with which Allah inflicted punishment on the Children of Israel for their injustices and immorality in accordance with what has been mentioned in the Noble Qur'an." [342] He enumerates six categories of such penalties/punishments, as a prelude to their Qur'anic elaboration: [343]

"First: Dispersing and scattering them and sending them mighty ones who would make them suffer terribly until the Day of Judgement.
Second: Allah's warning and decree for corrupting the land twice.
Third: Forbidding them good things because of their aggression and violations.
Fourth: Allah's condemnation and punishment by reducing them to apes and pigs.
Fifth: They earned Allah's wrath and condemnation; He cursed them.
Sixth: They were stricken with disgrace and misery."

Tantawi emphasizes the following Qur'anic verses in illustrating these points: Q 7:167-168, 17:4-8, 5:60, and 3:110-112. Additional verses alluded to are, Q 3:75, 5:42, 2:90, 4:51, 4:46, and 5:13. Tantawi also makes important related excursuses in chapter 8 redolent with anti-Jewish calumny. These include: alleged "Jewish massacres" of Christians in Rome at the outset of the 3rd century C.E., and during the brief interval of Persian rule in early 7th century Palestine; the Jews' putative machinations (some murderous) in Western and Eastern Europe from the 17th through the 20th centuries, as well as the Deir Yassin "massacre" (discussed in chapter 7); and the Jews' "appropriate" condemnation by Adolph Hitler.

Tantawi cites these historical examples validating **Q 7:167-168** (*"Remember, Muhammad, when your Lord informed the Children of Israel with His decision concerning them that He will- until the Day of Judgement- send others against them who would cause them to suffer terribly. They would humiliate, debase and disgrace them because of altering and distorting Allah's words, killing His prophets and persevering in committing vices and violations."*), and **17:4-8** (*"persevering in transgressions and evil deeds, allowing what Allah had forbidden and all the other vices that permeated and prevailed among them throughout the ages and everywhere."*): [344] the hugely destructive and mass murderous Assyrian (721 and 677 B.C.E.) and Babylonian (606, 599, and 586 B.C.E.) invasions of Israel; the Jews' conquest and subjection by the *"Alexandrian Greeks and their successors the Ptolemaic and Seleucid Kingdoms and then the Romans before and after the latter adopted Christianity"*; and their subjection by Muhammad and the Muslims because of the Jews' treacherous return to wrongdoing (per Q 17:8, i.e., not believing in Muhammad, and even seeking to kill him), as instructed by Allah, *"to punish them because of their treachery and injustice...He [Muhammad] killed Banu Qurayza, drove Banu Qaynuqa and Banu Nadir out of Medina and levied the Jizya tax on the rest.*

They would pay the tax, willingly submitting, fully humbled (per Q 9:29)." Tantawi further avers, [345] *"Everywhere they [the Jews] settled they were exposed to the condemnation of the inhabitants of those lands because of their egotism, aloofness, prejudice, inciting discord and spreading vices."* Riveting on (and quoting from) Q 7:167-168, Tantawi insists, [346]

> *"The world's resentment and scorn for them will continue and its hatred and vengeance will go on until the Judgement Day. This is due to their selfishness and their corruption of the land. The Noble Qur'an stated this clearly: "And ˹remember, O Prophet,˺ when your Lord declared that He would send against them others who would make them suffer terribly until the Day of Judgment (Q 7:167)."*

Then Tantawi immediately reminds Muslims that, [347] *"The Jews at the present time are the same Jews throughout the ages: corrupt and corrupting, belligerent and aggressive, and tyrannical and oppressive. They flagrantly and brazenly attacked the Muslims of Palestine. Infidel countries provided them with various types of assistance."* Following that statement, he assures his co-religionists, [348] *"Our anticipated role, Allah willing, is to eliminate all manner of disagreements and discord amongst ourselves to enable the religion of Allah to be firm and steadfast in the land through unity, strength, hard work and true worship and conduct our business unwaveringly with legitimate means and with resoluteness and stanchness. Then the believers will be gladdened with Allah's victory."*

As in the preceding chapters, especially chapter 7, Tantawi finds historical "validation" of the Jews' Qur'anic perfidy by adducing more calumnies against them. He maintains, for example, in chapter 8 (related, tangentially, to Q 7:167-168, and 17:4-8), "the Jews killed a great number of the Christians who lived with them in Palestine after the victory of the Persians [over the ruling Byzantine Christians]," during the interlude of Persian conquest and rule from 614 to 628 C.E. [349] The actual historical context indicates brutal Byzantine persecution of Jews who then saw the invading Persians as potential "liberators." During the last 2-years of Byzantine Emperor Phocas' reign (602-610 AD), he initiated [350]

> *"a series of bloody persecutions against Monophysites and Hebrews in Syria, Palestine and Egypt. These oppressions turned out to be directly responsible for the collapse of the Byzantine rule under the attacks of the Persians in the eastern provinces of the Empire, determining Monophysites and Hebrews to become the main allies of the Sassanids."*

However, although some Christian sources claim up to 90,000 Christians were killed in this period by Persian suppression of their rebellion against Sassanid Persian rule, [351]

> *'...the [contemporary Christian chronicler] eyewitness Sebeos, never mentions Jews in the killings...He clearly points out that Christian dead were victims of Persian troops involved in suppressing the Christian counter-rebellion. Similarly, the noted 7th century Christian chronicle of the world, known as the Chronicon*

Paschale, does not accuse Jews of any massacre...Straegius, whose writings later sources seem to follow, put the blame on the Jews only in a single case, where he gives no numbers. Therefore, the claim that a large number of Christians was killed by the Jews appears to be fabricated, or greatly exaggerated, to play it into a blood libel... Yet these figures were used by Christian writers, and are being used till today, not just as facts, but as hate literature against Jews who, in the first place, were not involved."

Tantawi also insists that four centuries earlier in history, the Jews were somehow responsible for the mass murder of Christians during the reign of Roman Emperor Marcus Aurelius: [352]

"In Rome alone, they killed one hundred thousand Christians in 204 A.D. (C.E.) at the behest of Emperor Marcus Aurelius."

But Aurelius died in 180 C.E.. a quarter century before the date Tantawi provides for the alleged "Jewish massacres" of Christians during his reign, while mass Roman persecution of the Christians did not begin until the reign of Decius, 249 to 251 C.E., and the Jews were not "accomplices." [353] Tantawi then opines, [354] "And why should we go so far back to bring evidence for their brutality when we have the wars in Palestine vividly itched and alive in our memory?" He segues to the debunked Deir Yassin "massacre" as an alleged modern example of the Jews' propensity for mass murder. [355]

The Jews, in a related series of additional Tantawi calumnies, were responsible for revolution, economic exploitation, and killing across Europe: [356]

"Britain had no Jews for approximately three centuries. [357] *The Jews returned to Britain in 1656, during the despot Cromwell, who usurped the Kingdom from Charles the First because of the Jews who offered him great amounts of money to achieve his goals* [358]*...The Jews were the target of the condemnation and resentment of the French people during many different epochs. That was because the Jews ruined their national economy and smothered it with their usury and immoral practices and interactions...During their stay there, they employed all their cunning and crafty methods to destroy and devastate* [359]*...They opened bars, traded in liquor, lent money in return for extremely high interest, seized a lot of the country's wealth by illegal forbidden means, killed many of the Russian citizens, when possible, formed secret societies that aimed to eradicate the Russian Orthodox Rule and continued their activities until they succeeded through the Communist Revolution in 1917 C.E.* [360]*...They appallingly exploited the German people until they were almost able to seize its wealth through extremely dreadful usury and through the use of different methods to amass forbidden money. The Germans revolted against them at different times."* [361]

Citing the Jews' putative "boundless selfishness and greed," "arrogance and conceit" (per Q 3:75), and the "inextricable" Jewish Qur'anic traits of "isolation, tribal solidarity, and fanaticism," along their purported "betrayal of the countries they live in," Tantawi rationalizes Hitler's treatment of the Jews by repeating the Nazi dictator's conspiratorial claims in Mein Kampf. [362]

> *"Hitler enumerated the deceptions of the Jews to Germany. He mentioned forcibly taking the people's money by usury and extortion, corrupting education, controlling the banks and trade companies, dominating publishing presses, and meddling in the politics of the country for the benefit of other countries and against the wellbeing of Germany. At the top of their treacheries came their spying against Germany, something that many of them perfected. Hitler concludes his long speech about the Jews, saying: 'If it were destined for a Jew to overcome the countries of this world, his crown would be Humanity's Funeral. And when our planet continues its march in the universe as it has done for millions of years, there will be no humans left on its surface... That is why, I believe that I dealt with them as our Creator wished: by defending myself against the Jew, I strive to defend the work of the Creator.'"*

Returning to a broader overview of the Jews' Qur'anic depiction, Tantawi emphasizes a critical transition in the Qur'an highlighting its final—and abrogating—Medinan narrative (as described by Sheikh Abdul-Mu'iz Abdul Sattar): [363]

> *"We may have noticed that the Almighty does not mention the Children of Israel in Meccan Suras except to mention their stance towards Moses and his commandments and their stance with Pharaoh and his soldiers. However, in Medinan Suras, the Almighty mentions them a lot. He mentions many forms and types of corruption and corrupting; He [Sattar]mentions breaching their pledges, their disbelief in Allah's miracles and signs, their unjust killing of the prophets, their saying that their hearts are unresponsive, their injustices and wrongdoing, their hindering others from Allah's way, their acceptance of usury and extreme high interest and their unlawful exploitation of others' wealth. He [Sattar]also talks about their violation of the Sabbath, their fear of death and consuming lust for a long life, their choosing a fleeting gain over Allah's revelations, their killing each other and driving one another from their homes; their aggression and animosity and their claiming that they could not be held accountable for exploiting the Gentiles."*

Additional specific Qur'anic citations by Tantawi, and the "Jewish traits" they frame, in perpetuity, include:

> [Q 4:161 and 5:42] *"...wherever Jewish transactions are conducted, there abounds the unjust consumption of people's money; it is not a- give- and- take kind of transaction, no reciprocity or mutual interest. Rather, their transactions are based on monopoly, domination and bribery... whatever they called or however they are described. Dealings without honor, without integrity..."* [364]

> [Q 2:90, 4:51, 4:46, and 5:13] *"...there are numerous noble verses that state the condemnation of the Children of Israel and earning Allah's wrath because of their immoralities and decadences."* [365]

Near the conclusion of chapter 8, Tantawi provides long explications of Q 5:60 and 3:110 to 112, the latter with an emphasis on Q 3:112, [366] It is noteworthy that verses Q 3:110-112 are also the opening words of the Hamas Covenant, even placed before the document's Preamble. [367]

Regarding Q 5:60, Tantawi's overview gloss maintains: [368]

> *"Among the punishments that Allah Almighty has inflicted upon the Jews is transforming them into apes and pigs, cursing them and becoming wrathful with them on account of their transgression, disobeying His commandments, and being consumed by their greed and desires...* ***The meaning is: Muhammad, tell those Jews who have taken Islam lightly and begrudge you for believing in Allah and what has been revealed to you, and what has been revealed before- tell them shall I inform you of far worse for what you begrudge us as a punishment from Allah? Then Allah revealed: '[It is that of] those whom Allah has cursed and with whom He became angry and made of them apes and pigs and slaves of Taghut.' (Q 5:60) This means what is even far more evil than the religion that you begrudge us for is the religion of those whom Allah has cursed and who arose His anger and made of them apes, pigs and slaves of Taghut****... 'Taghut' is a name for anything that is worshipped, honored or glorified, other than Allah Almighty. It can be an idol, a man, a demon or any other false god."*

Tantawi continues, [369]

> *"Some commentators [Tantawi references Al-Razi) maintain that the Almighty links the people of the Sabbath to apes and those who disbelieved in Jesus' Table- (reference is to the Last Supper)- to pigs. Others say that the transformations occurred to the people of the Sabbath: their (the Jews') youth were reduced into apes, and their elders were reduced into pigs... Having mentioned these traits about them, He moves from condemning them for their hatred for Muslims for entering (accepting) Islam into mentioning what is even more despicable and censure provoking, i.e., the attitude of their fathers towards their Prophets and Allah's punishment for them for their immorality and rebellion: He incurred upon them a punishment that was worse that His punishment for the unjust profligates and debauched: He cursed them and became wrathful and made them apes and pigs and slaves of Taghut...[the] Jews and their likes were different, however. They were not moved or affected by what they heard from the Prophet and his companions. That was essentially because their bad intensions, cunning and denial of the truth prevented them from discernment, learning and understanding. Rather, their bad intensions drove them to treachery and deceitfulness. They did not have the mentality to perceive and discern nor the contrite heart to consider and submit."*

He concludes, referencing two additional verses (Q 2:65 and 7:166) which denote the Jews transformation into apes, exclusively, by stating: [370]

> *"...these noble verses (Q 2:65, **especially 5:60**, and 7:166) that we have examined mentioned some of the punishments that Allah inflicted upon the Jews: He cursed them, He was indignant and wrathful with them, and He reduced them to apes and pigs. All of this was because of going beyond their limits and encroaching against Him, rushing into violations and wrongdoing, the inactivity of their rabbis and scholars and their neglecting to warn them against their encroachments."*

Tantawi's exegesis on Q 5:60 from his subsequent full Qur'anic commentary *"The intermediate [balanced] interpretation of the Qur'an,"* is very consistent in its essence with his Ph.D. thesis gloss, as these extracts confirm: [370a]

> *His (Allah's) saying: 'he whom Allah has cursed' is the predicate of an omitted subject, meaning he is the one whom Allah has cursed, and what is meant is the Jews because the attributes mentioned in the verse apply only to them. The meaning is: Say, O Muhammad, to these Jews who criticized the believers for their belief in Allah and in the heavenly books He revealed, and who said to you: We do not know of people of a religion less fortunate in this world and the Hereafter than you, nor of a religion worse than your world. Say to them, by way of rebuke and warning of their misguidance: Has anyone from the people of that religion informed you of a punishment from Allah on the Day of Resurrection?* ***He is the one whom Allah 'cursed' meaning He distanced him from His mercy 'and became angry with' by withholding His pleasure from him 'and made of them apes and pigs' by transforming some of them into monkeys and some of them into pigs and making some of them worship the Taghut (i.e., those who worship every false deity other than Allah, such as idols and statues and other false deities that they followed because of their tyranny and the corruption of their souls)...*** *If it is said that His statement – 'Say, 'Shall I inform you of something worse than that as a reward?' indicates that what the Jews criticized the believers for regarding their faith in Allah is evil. However, what the Jews are, is more evil, even though the faith of the believers has no evil at all, rather it is the very essence of goodness. How is that? The answer is that the speech is presented by way of resemblance and imitation of the corrupt thinking of the Jews and their false claim. It is as if He - Glory be to Him - is saying to His Prophet, may Allah bless him and grant him peace, that these Jews - O Muhammad - deny your belief in Allah and the heavenly books and consider it evil - although it is the very essence of goodness. Say to them by way of rebuke and obligating them with the argument: If you criticize our belief and consider it evil with no good in it - in your opinion - then what you are upon is worse in consequence and outcome than what you are upon of cursing and expulsion from the mercy of Allah, and what happened to your ancestors of some of them being transformed into apes and some into pigs,*

and what is known about you of worshipping other than Allah... Similar to this verse in imitating the opponent in his claim is His - Glory be to Him - saying: 'And indeed, we or you are upon guidance or in manifest error' and His saying: 'Those are worse' 'in a place and more astray from the right path' is a statement of their evil end and ugly status. That is, those who are described with the aforementioned immorality, cursing, and expulsion from Allah's mercy, ***those who are described with that 'are worse in status' than others and more astray from the straight path than others. In this world, they associate partners with Allah and violate His prohibitions, and in the Hereafter, their abode is the Fire, and what an evil resting place it is... Thus, we see that these noble verses (i.e., Q 5:60-5:63) have rebuked the Jews for their envy of the believers for what Allah has given them of His bounty, and described them with a number of reprehensible characteristics so that the believers would beware of them and make their loyalty to Allah, His Messenger, and their brothers in faith and religion.***

Historically, invocations of the Qur'anic epithets "apes" (Q 2:65 and 7:166), or "apes and pigs" (Q 5:60) for Jews have been employed by Muslim religio-political leaders to both humiliate Jews, and incite violence against them, since the advent of Islam. The Muslim prophet Muhammad used the epithets "apes/monkeys" and/or "pigs" (again, per Koran 5:60) to characterize Jewish victims of his jihadist campaigns, notably the Qurayza tribe, whose males Islam's prophet himself subsequently beheaded. Just prior to orchestrating the en masse execution of the adult males from the besieged Medinan Jewish tribe the Banu Qurayza (and distributing their women, children, and possessions as slave "booty" for the Muslims), Muhammad, according to his earliest Muslim biographer, Ibn Ishaq, addressed these Jews with menacing, hateful derision: "You brothers of monkeys (apes), has Allah disgraced you and brought His vengeance upon you?" (Another early Muslim biographer of Muhammad, Ibn Saad, reports that Muhammad stated, "brothers of monkeys (apes) and pigs, fear me, fear me!"). [371]

A fatwa written by the ninth-century jurist from Kairouan, Ifiqiyya (modern Tunisia), Qadi [Shari'a judge] Ahmed b. Talib (d. 889), *"compelled the dhimmis to wear upon the shoulder a patch of white cloth (riqa') that bore the image of an ape (for Jews) . . . and to nail onto their doors a board bearing the sign of a monkey."* [372] He further ordered, *"A Jew who dresses like the Muslims and fails to wear the clothing that distinguishes him from them will be incarcerated, beaten, and paraded ignominiously through the places inhabited by the Jews and the Christians as an example."* [373]

Abu Ishaq Elbiri's verse of condemnation against the vizier Joseph b. Samuel Naghrela and the Granadan Jewish community, which helped incite the 1066 Granada pogrom, with its massacre of some three thousand to four thousand Jews, annihilating the entire community, contains the following line, [374] *"Many a pious Muslim is in awe of the vilest infidel ape."* [375] Moshe Perlmann, in his analysis of the Muslim anti-Jewish polemic of eleventh-century Granada, notes, *"[Abu Ishaq] Elbiri used the epithet "ape" (qird) profusely when referring to Jews. Such indeed was the parlance."* [376] Perlmann then cites the related Qur'anic passages (i.e., 2:65, 5:60, and 7:166) upon which such "nomenclature" was based. [377] Despite this unparallelled carnage, as Perlmann lamented in 1966, on its 900th anniversary, "the Granada debacle...the first major pogrom on European soil…past unnoticed." [378]

Anti-Jewish riots and massacres by Muslims accompanied the 1291 death of Jewish physician-vizier Sa'd ad-Daula in Baghdad, the plundering and killing of Jews extending throughout Iraq (and possibly into Persia/Iran). [379] These events, which marked the collapse of a transient Jewish ascendancy (afforded by the ruling Mongols' abrogation of the system of *dhimmitude*), [380] were celebrated in an ode by the Muslim preacher Zaynu'd-Din 'Ali b. Said. [381] His verse opens with a debasing reference to the Jews as apes:

> *His name we praise who rules the firmament. These apish Jews are done away and shent [ruined or destroyed].* [382]

The bitter anti-Jewish sentiments of the theologian Al- Mahgili (d. 1504/1505) were expressed in both his writing and his preaching. [383] Referring to the Jews as "brothers of apes"—consistent with both Zamakshari's classical Qur'anic commentary on verse 5:60, and Tantawi's modern exegesis, [384] who incessantly blasphemed the Prophet Muhammad and whose entire conduct demonstrated their hatred of Muslims, Al-Maghili posed the rhetorical question: What should be done about them? [385] He "answered" this question by fomenting a Muslim pogrom (in ~1490) against the Jews of Touat, which plundered and killed them en masse, and destroyed their synagogue in neighboring Tamantit. [386]

Tantawi's glosses on Q 3:110, 3:111, and 3:112 reinforce stark contrasts delineated in the original Qur'anic text. While in Q 3:110, Muslims are told, [387] "Allah extolled the Islamic nation as the best community that was ever raised for humanity. He attributed many honorable traits that made it worthy of such praise and high status. They are an upright community, one that enjoins what is good and virtuous and forbids what is bad and ungodly. They believe in Allah," they are reminded in Q 3:112, "He censured and condemned the Jews and ascribed the worst descriptions to them. He warned them of severe and terrible punishment. He struck them with disgrace and humiliation for disbelieving His signs, killing the prophets and trespassing beyond bounds." Continuing, Tantawi avers, [388] per Q 3:110, "Encouraging good and forbidding evil for these are the bulwarks, the fortifications of religion. No nation can be solidly established on virtue and righteousness except by embracing them," but, per Q 3:112, "The Children of Israel were deserving of condemnation because they abandoned them." The "noble verse," Q 3:110, awards [389] "justice to the few of the People of the Book who believed like Abdullah Ibn Salaam and others who entered into Islam and embraced it. It also censures the majority of the People of the Scripture who denounced the truth and deviated from the straight path (i.e., Islam)." Tantawi warns [390] Muslims, regarding Q 3:111, "if the Muslim community does not want to be afflicted by any harms from the Jews, it must faithfully and loyally worship its Lord, embrace the Sunna (teachings) of its Prophet, abide by the tenets of its Book, and be well prepared to fight Allah's enemy and their own. If the Muslim community does not do this, their enemy will inflict harm upon it, its very foundation would be shaken and its enemy would be become enabled to do what they please." Amplifying this latter point, vis-a-vis the contemporary "Palestine conflict," Tantawi poses—and answers—the question, "Has Allah forsaken His promise?" [391]

> *"If someone said: 'But what we witness now is that the Jews- whom no one suspects are cowards and eager for prolonged lives- have triumphed over the Muslims and established a state in one of the most precious of all the Islamic countries, Palestine. Has Allah forsaken His promise?' The answer is: Allah's promise has not- nor will it ever be- changed or forsaken. The Almighty fulfilled this promise for our righteous predecessors who truly and devotedly believed in Him, those who enjoined what is good and forbade what is evil. However,* ***it is the Muslims of this generation that have changed. They have neglected their religion, they do not establish prayers, they have indulged in lusts desires, they have followed Satan's footsteps, they have become divided to parties and sects, they have stopped encouraging what is righteous and good, they have abstained from forbidding what is bad and ungodly, they have not been harsh enough on the infidels nor merciful enough among each other (Q 48:29), they have not adequately prepared themselves to fight against Allah's enemy and their own as were their predecessors, and they have not adequately shouldered the responsibility as mandated by the teachings and instructions of Islam.****"*

Tantawi's complementary gloss on Q 3:112 emphasizes that the Jews are the antithesis of the "best community" of Q 3:110, i.e., the Muslims, and how the Jews as a collective merit permanent humiliating punishment and only survive when protected by other nations. [392]

> *"Then, the Almighty showed some of the punishments that He inflicted upon the Jews. He said: 'They will be stricken with disgrace wherever they go, unless they are protected by a covenant with Allah or a treaty with the people' (Q 3:112)...[D]isgrace, ignominy and humiliation. They [the Jews] are surrounded and utterly wrapped in it...Those Jews have been besieged by disgrace in all aspects and wherever they exist or go except when they are protected by a covenant with Allah or a treaty with the people... Interpreters explain that 'a covenant with Allah' is a reference to the Jizya...The overall meaning of the verse is: Allah has stricken the Jews with disgrace and misery everywhere they go, everywhere and at all times because of their disbelief and rebellion. Their ability to self-determination and governance have been stripped from them; they live all over the land in the protection of other nations and according to treaties that they have with these nations...In addition to being struck with disgrace wherever they went, they have also earned Allah's wrath and became deserving of His anger. They have also been stricken with misery which causes them to feel small and demoralized regardless of their physical strength and wealth...[T]heir continuous defeats, being struck with Allah's wrath and misery, becoming the object of His anger and denunciation- all these and other punishments are because of their rejection of Our revelations, killing Our prophets deliberately, insisting on their wrongdoing. They would not have had*

the audacity to perpetrate these violations had they not relished and enjoyed committing these transgressions and gotten used to aggression and wrongdoing. It is easy for those with such proclivities to commit all kinds of offenses and crimes and, consequently, become deserving of Allah's most severe punishments. This is what has become of the Children of Israel."

As flimsy theoretical opposition to this eternal Qur'anic depiction, Tantawi mentions Israel's establishment: [393]

"Someone may say: 'They now have status, prestige and authority after they have been able to acquire international recognition by establishing the State of Israel.'"

Tantawi's "rejoinder" follows immediately: [394]

"The response to this is: Even though this State has been established, they still live under the protection of the other infidel world powers."

Tantawi adds, [395]

"The Jews have no power or authority; neither do they have self-esteem. They are commanded and controlled, harnessed to live in that part of the land to be the center, or springboard for these nations—that provide them with protection—to attack and fight the Muslims if the chance offered itself to them."

He then charts a clear path to renewed Muslim triumph: [396]

"If the Muslims changed their own state of faith, held tight to their faith, united and with common goals, these countries and those that protect them [the Jews] would be in fear and terror of the Muslims. We have great hope in Allah that the Muslims would become vigilant and aware of the dangers that surround them and push them away. We have great hope that they will hold firmly together to the rope of Allah to regain their strength and prestige."

Tantawi's summary assessment of chapter 8 invokes a canonical hadith that prioritizes violent jihad "by the hand" (i.e., with force) over non-violent methods: [396]

"The history of the Children of Israel abounds with violations and disobedience in various shapes and forms. These violations and wrongdoings were not individual actions; rather, they characterized the whole society, and their occurrence have become common and familiar. No one can deny these violations, and no one tries to eradicate them. When a nation descends to such a low stage, when evil is perpetrated by the old and the young, and when no one tries to change this with his hand (by force),[397] *tongue (speech) or heart, such a nation is destined*

to collapse and become annihilated, one deserving of punishment in this world and in the Hereafter."

One again, these key extracts from Tantawi's formal complete exegesis of Q 3:112 in his full Qur'anic commentary *"The intermediate [balanced] interpretation of the Qur'an,"* demonstrate his overall interpretation and emphases remained remarkably consistent with the earlier gloss in *"Banū Isrā'īl fī al-Qur'ān wa-al-sunnah"*: [398]

> *"...**[I]f someone says but what we see now is that the Jews, whose cowardice and eagerness for life is unquestionable, have defeated the Muslims and established a state for themselves in one of the most cherished spots in the Islamic lands, which is Palestine. So, will Allah's promise be broken? The answer to that is that Allah's promise - the Most High - does not and will not be broken**. He - the Most High - fulfilled it for our righteous ancestors who truly believed in Him. But the Muslims of this era are the ones whose conditions have changed. They have neglected their religion, neglected prayer, followed their desires, divided into sects and parties, deviated from the straight path, and did not take the necessary steps to achieve victory that Allah - the Most High - has prescribed. They did not feel responsible. When they did that, their condition changed from good to evil, and from strength to weakness... And if the Muslims return to their religion and fully apply its commands and prohibitions to themselves, then Allah - the Most High - will restore their dignity, pride and strength... He [Allah] - Glory be to Him - mentioned some of the punishments with which He inflicted on the Jews because of their disbelief and injustice, saying: 'Humiliation has been imposed upon them wherever they are found, except by a rope from Allah and a rope from the people.' ...What is meant by it is smallness, disgrace and insignificance. So, **the imposition of humiliation upon them is a metaphor for its adherence to these Jews and its enveloping of them, just as a tent envelops those inside it. The author of Al-Kashaf [i.e., Zamakshari] said: Humiliation has surrounded and encompassed them, so they are like someone who is in a dome that has been placed over him, or has stuck to them like clay thrown on a wall that sticks to it. The Jews are humiliated and submissive, people of poverty and abject poverty**... A rope is what connects two things and is used for a covenant because people are bound by covenants just as physical connection occurs with ropes, and this use is what is meant here. Therefore, **Ibn Jarir [al-Tabari] said: As for the rope that Allah - the Most High - mentioned in this topic, it is the reason by which they feel safe from the believers and their money and children from a covenant and security that was made before they were found in the lands of Islam. The meaning is that these Jews were surrounded by humiliation in all their circumstances wherever they were and wherever they settled except in the case of their clinging to a covenant from Allah or a covenant from people.** Scholars have interpreted the covenant of Allah as the contract of jizya that connects them with Muslims. The contract of jizya was a covenant from Allah to them... **The overall meaning of the verse is that Allah Almighty has afflicted the Jews with humiliation and poverty in every time and place because of their disbelief***

> ***and tyranny, and has stripped them of their authority and kingdom. They live in all parts of the earth under the protection of other nations, according to covenants they make with them. These covenants may or may not be in accordance with Allah's law. If someone says that they are now people of influence and power, after they established their state in Palestine, the answer is that with the establishment of this state, they live under the protection of other major infidel states. It is these states that protect them and provide them with the means of life and strength.*** *Therefore, in this case, it also applies that they are under the protection of the people.* ***The Jews have no power, nor any pride in their souls, but they are commanded and enslaved to live in that spot of land to be a center for those nations who pledged to protect them, from which they can leap to fight the Muslims, if they are given the opportunity. If only the Muslims would change what is in themselves, adhere to their Sharia, unite their hearts, unify their goals, develop a sense of responsibility towards their religion, themselves and their homelands, and prepare whatever force they can to fight the enemies of Allah and their enemies***... *If they had done that, their state would not be as you see it now: weakness, cowardice and division.* ***There is great hope that the Muslims will become aware of the dangers surrounding them, work to repel them and hold fast to the rope of Allah so that their strength and prestige may be restored."***

Lastly, real world implications for Jews of the dictates of Q 3:112 were perhaps best illustrated in Yemen, where Jews were the lone non-Muslim minority, and experienced more than a millennial continuum of humiliating Sharia-based Islamic persecution, into the present era. [399]

Yemenite Jews had to remove human feces and other waste matter (urine that failed to evaporate, etc.) from Muslim areas, initially in Sanaa and later in other communities such as Shibam, Yarim, and Dhamar. [400] Decrees requiring this obligation were issued in the late eighteenth or early nineteenth century and reintroduced in 1913. [401] Yehuda Nini reproduces an 1874 letter written by a Yemenite Jew to the Alliance Israélite in Paris, lamenting the practice: [402]

> *"[I]t is 86 years since our forefathers suffered the cruel decree and great shame to the nation of Israel from the east to sundown . . . for in the days of our fathers, 86 years ago, there arose a judge known as Qadi, and said unto the king and his ministers who lived in that time that the Lord, Blessed be He, had only created the Jews out of love of the other nations,* ***to do their work and be enslaved by them at their will, and to do the most contemptible and lowly of tasks. And of them all . . . the greatest contamination of all, to clear their privies and streets and pathways of the filthy dung and the great filth in that place and to collect all that is left of the dung****, may your Honor pardon the expression."*

Nini adds these pertinent details: [402a]

"The Muslim authorities ignored the (specific) 'class' of dung-gatherers and considered the entire Jewish community to be responsible for clearing the dung...[T]he (dung-gathering) decree started in 1806. It was in force until the Jews of Yemen emigrated to Israel in 1949-50, causing them great suffering and humiliation...In 1949 during the 'On Eagle's Wings' immigration from the Yemen the Muslims of Sanaa bullied the dung-gatherers and prevented their immigration (to Israel), and permission was only obtained after lengthy negotiations."

Y. D. Sémach of the Alliance Israélite described what he termed the "behavioral distortions" of Yemenite Jews, resulting from their relentless oppression. His eyewitness account published in 1910 included these observations: [403]

"They lack confidence in themselves, and beneath the weight of Arab oppression they cower and crawl in the dust...The Jew is not allowed to wear white or colored garments outside his quarter...[H]e must wear a ridiculously short garment that does not cover his legs, and he must walk barefooted and wear on his head a little blackcap...The Jew cannot ride within the town on a donkey and morning and evening he must walk on foot the two miles that separate his quarter from the marketplace... Every day young Arabs found amusement in throwing stones at passing Jews while they, pretending not to notice, would hasten their stride. If one spits in their face, they turn their heads. A high-ranking [Turkish] officer described to me a scene that he had witnessed more than once: some youths had caught hold of an elderly Jew and amused themselves by pulling his side locks, while their victim grinned and simpered stupidly. Constantly obliged to bear these insults, the Jew has lost all sense of dignity and has come to accept his fate; instead of fighting back, he smiles. What else can he do? A revolt would bring even more trouble. Every day our coreligionists suffer all kinds of humiliations and violence. They do not even complain: for them there is no justice, there cannot be. The Yemenite courts are all religious courts and the testimony of Jews is not accepted. A Muslim can knock down a Jew in front of fifty witnesses, yet he need only deny it to be acquitted; no Muslim would want to lodge a complaint against a brother for the sake of an infidel."

Yemenite Jews paid the *jizya* until the liquidation of their community after Israel was established in 1948. Yemen's twentieth-century rulers (Imam Yahya and his son Ahmad) continued the deliberately threatening and humiliating atmospherics of *jizya* collection. Aviva Klein-Franke described the collection process: [404]

"The Imam [Yahya, and later his son Ahmad] would nominate a respectable Jew to collect the Poll Tax. ...He was ordered to prepare a list of all the Jewish males in his community who had reached the age of thirteen years for the purpose of collecting the jizya . . . [His assistants] also had to mention those Jews who had emigrated. As we have seen, the Imam confiscated the property of anyone who left the Yemen. Jews were not allowed to sell their property before

leaving the country—everything would be forfeited to the Imam by his [Imam Yahya's] decree of 1920. Before the [designated Jew] collected the money, a street crier went through the Jewish quarter, proclaiming that the Imam expected everyone to pay the jizya without delay. Failure to do so meant that a soldier, might be billeted on those in default until such time as they paid... Usually the Jews paid without any objection...they could send a written appeal to the Imam. If a Jew still refused to pay the jizya, the Imam would accept no further excuses and would send his soldiers to the recalcitrant Jew."

October 8, 1983, historian Bat Ye'or interviewed Yemenite Jews Hannah [Lolou] and Sa'adya b. Shelomo Akiva [Aqua], born respectively at Dhamar and Menakha (Yemen). They left Yemen in 1949, became citizens of Israel, and lived in Nes Ziyyona. Their recorded testimony affirms the additional chronic humiliations and oppressions experienced by Yemen's Jews, resulting from the application of the sharia, right up until the community was effectively liquidated after the creation of Israel. [405]

> ***"Until our departure from Yemen in 1949, it was forbidden for a Jew to write in Arabic, to possess arms, or to ride on a horse or camel. The Jews could only ride on donkeys, both legs on one side [sidesaddle] and were obliged to jump to the ground when passing a Muslim, and had to make detours. Pedestrians went on the left of Muslims.*** *It was forbidden for Jews to enter mosques...* ***The Arabs forbade us to wear shoes, so that we hid them when, as children, we went searching for wood for cooking. When we were far enough away, we put on our shoes; on returning, we took them off and hid them in the branches. The Arabs frequently searched us, and if they found them, they punished us and forbade us to collect wood. We had to lower our head, accepting insults and humiliations. The Arabs called us 'stinking dogs.' Jewish children who became orphans before they were fifteen were forcibly converted to Islam.*** *The families tried to save them by hiding them in bundles of hay. Afterward, the children were sent to other villages where they hid with another family and were given other names. Sometimes the children were put into coffins and the Arabs were told that they had died with their parents. Then they were helped to escape."*

Even the barely visible, minute vestigial remnant of Jews left behind in Yemen continued to suffer similarly within the past decade. An eponymous *New York Times* story from February 19, 2015, was entitled, "Persecution Defines Life for Yemen's Remaining Jews." [406] Taking great umbrage at the sight of a Yemenite Jew accompanying the New York Times reporter, a local Shiite Muslim referred to his fellow human being as somehow "not" human, and "damned" by Allah. The Times reporter added that the Jewish community—then **perhaps a mere 70 souls between Raida, Yemen, and Sanaa, the capital, "where a small number live under what amounts to house arrest by the Houthi leadership"** — indeed, [407]

> *"...have more to fear than bad words. The encounter [above] in the souk took place a short distance from where a Yemeni Air Force pilot in 2008*

*accosted Moshe Yaish Nahari, the brother of a prominent rabbi and the father of eight children, as he stepped out of his home. The assailant coldly said, "**Jew, here's a message from Islam," and then fatally shot Mr. Nahari, who was unarmed, five times with an assault rifle**, according to Yemeni news accounts. The pilot was convicted and sentenced to death for murder, **but Mr. Nahari's family, pressured into accepting blood money from the killer's tribe to spare his life,** left Yemen **as soon as possible. In the next few years, nearly all of Raida's Jews followed.**"*

Tantawi's opus consists of eight chapters of Jew-hating invective rooted, primarily, in traditional Qur'anic exegesis. [408] This narrative, in chapters 7 and 8, is complemented with brief, ahistorical examples—some frankly deranged—allegedly validating these Qur'anic motifs with non-Islamic antisemitic conspiracism. [409] Tantawi introduces his short "Conclusion" chapter with these statements, consistent with the ethos of the entire work: [410]

"Most of my investigation concerning the Children of Israel in the previous chapters focused on expounding the noble verses that mention them in the Qur'an and examining their actions during the Prophet's era in relation to their betrayals, conspiracies and violations that led each group of them to the punishments which they deserved... My goal is to help reveal the crooked methods and the various conspiracies that World Judaism has played throughout the ages until it was able to establish a state in Palestine, in the heart (center) of the Islamic World, in 1948, after killing thousands of its children and displacing hundreds of thousands of its Muslim inhabitants."

Tantawi's concise, risibly ahistorical hagiography of the 7th century Muslim conquest and rule of Byzantine Palestine, ignores the sanguinary and wantonly destructive nature of the initial jihad campaign, internecine Muslim conflicts, and the continuous imposition of the Sharia till the First Crusade
in 1099. [411] He manages, however, to insert this "pious" howler about conquering Muslim Caliph Umar bin al-Khattab: [412]

*"...**he (Umar) entered the mosque (allegedly already built on the Temple Mount) from the door through which the Messenger of Allah entered on the night of the Isra' (so-called Night Journey of Muhammad)**. He prayed the greeting of the mosque in the niche of David. He also prayed with the Muslims the morning prayer the next day. He first recited Sura Sad (sura 38) and prostrated and the Muslims also did so. (He recited) a second Sura (the Children of Israel/ Al-Isra'; sura 17), when he came to the Rock and asked Ka'b Al-Ahbar about its location. Then, he removed some dirt from the Rock using the edge of his cloak, and the Muslims also did like him."*

There was no pre-existing mosque on the Temple Mount. When Caliph Umar b. al-Khattab visited Palestine and Jerusalem, specifically, during 638, mainly to end some of the excess destruction wrought by rival elements of his jihadist forces, he immediately built an unostentatious mosque on the Temple Mount. Umar's treaty of submission for the Christians, included abiding their prohibition on Jewish settlement in Jerusalem. Three years later (641), Umar did allow very limited Jewish re-settlement of Jerusalem, but for politico-religious reasons, advantageous to the Muslim rulers: to spur economic activity and weaken exclusive Christian claims to the city. By the end of the 7th century, the triumphal Dome of the Rock was constructed on the Temple Mount under the Umayyad Caliph Abd al-Malik, and his sons, giving Jerusalem a Muslim "*aura of sanctity*, "transforming it, "*into a center of attraction to visitors from all over the Muslim world.*" [413]

Devoid of any unintentional humor, Tantawi also includes a vicious, delusive calumny about alleged "Jewish bankrolling" of the First Crusade, a Christian counter-jihad which in 1099, transiently reversed over 450 years of Muslim jihad conquest and rule of Palestine. [414] Tantawi's calumny of course fails to mention that the First Crusade was punctuated by massacres of Jews in both Western Europe, during the Crusader rampages in the Rhineland (in 1096), [415] and the Crusader conquest of the Holy Land itself. [416]

Tantawi segues to these additional lunatic antisemitic conspiracy theories in developing his overarching conspiracy theory about "Jewish usurpation of Palestine." This antisemitic litany is presented without refutation, because the individual claims are too unhinged to warrant any rebuttal: [416a]

—Following the 1789 French Revolution, "...the activities of the Jews demanding creating a homeland for them in Palestine increased **because they were behind the French Revolution, as they admitted in their *Protocols (of the Elders of Zion*)**."
—In 1797, an unidentified "Jewish rabbi" demanded French Jews "return to Palestine," demonstrating for Tantawi, "...**the dreams, imagination and ambitions of the Jews to annex Lower Egypt**."
—Ottoman Sultan Abdul Hamid (d. 1918; ruled from 1876-1909) was deposed in a Jewish conspiracy
—The United States entered World War I because of the Jews.
—All British High Commissioners to Palestine were "faithful servants and obedient soldiers" to the Jews.

The final section of Tantawi's "Conclusion," written in the aftermath of the "Arab and Islamic nations...unparalleled humiliation and disgrace due to the June 1967 war," poses two central questions, the author then addresses: [417]

> *"What are the principal reasons for the tragedy of Palestine? How can we restore it as an Islamic Arabic country once again?"*

Tantawi enumerates the following principal causes of the June 1967 Six Day War debacle for the Arab Muslim umma, dividing these between internal (i.e., Arab Muslim) reasons, and external reasons (i.e., machinations of Great Britain and the United States). [418] The internal reasons: [419]

— "The weakening and dwindling of religious motives in the hearts of Muslims."
— "Negligence in identifying the threat that surrounds the Islamic World due to the spread of World Zionism."
— "(T)he lack of unity amongst their [Arab Muslim] leaders."
— Religious zeal and fervor for Palestine did not fill the hearts of the [Arab Muslim] fighters."

The external reasons: [420]

— "Making the Jewish State a basis for it (colonialism), a poisonous dagger that can be brandished in the face of Arab countries whenever they sense mutiny or resistance."
— "Making the Jewish State a wedge that separates the Arab countries in Asia from the Arab countries in Africa to cut off land connection between the two continents.
— "Making the Jews an obstacle to hinder the Arab countries from forging ahead in their vast territories which are located in the most important geographic, commercial and military centers in the world and whose numbers are ever-increasing and which colonialism wants to control and exploit."

Addressing the question, "How can we restore Palestine as an Arab Islamic country once again?"—whose premise assumes the jihad destruction of the sovereign state of Israel—Tantawi first reminds Muslims of the eschatological "trees and stones" hadith, a tradition of Muhammad sanctioning mass murder of Jews, i.e., genocide, not merely the "policide" of Israel. [421] This eschatological jihad to redress the "tragedy of Palestine," is coupled to the "tragedy of al-Andalus," i.e., the Christian reconquest of the Iberian Peninsula, not merely a call for the global Muslim umma to wage a jihad to destroy Israel, and "return" its territory to Muslim suzerainty under the Sharia. [422]

Here is Tantawi's discussion of the Islamic eschatology germane to restoring Muslim sovereignty to all of historical Palestine, and liquidating modern Israel: [422a]

"We should be aware a decisive war will take place between the Muslims and the Jews in which the Muslims will be victorious as long as they cling steadfastly to their religion, obey the teachings of their Quran, and follow the ways of their Prophet. Al-Bukhari and Muslim relate on the authority of Abdullah bin Umar that the Messenger of Allah said: 'You will fight the Jews and they will hide behind the stone which will yell: Servant of Allah! There is a Jew behind me...Kill him.' In another Hadith by the two Sheikhs, Abu Hurayra related that the Messenger of God said: "The hour will not come until the Muslims fight the Jews, and the Muslims will kill them. The Jews will hide behind trees and stones, and the trees and stones will shout: 'O Muslim, servant of Allah! There is a Jew hiding behind me. Come and kill him. Except for the Gharqad since they are from the trees of the Jews.' These two authentic Hadiths inform the Muslims that a ferocious fight will take place between the Muslims

and the Jews before the Hour has come, and that the Muslims will be victorious when they follow Allah's commandments. Allah will honor them; He will inform the stones and trees behind which the Jews hide to tell the Muslims about their hiding places, and that they have to kill them."

Tantawi's primary invocation of an eschatological jihad against the Jews has deep-seated ancient and modern Islamic roots, with baleful implications. Georges Vajda's pioneering research on the Jew-hating motifs in the hadith demonstrates how Sunni Muslim eschatology emphasizes the Jews supreme hostility toward Islam. Jews are described as adherents of the Dajjal—the Muslim equivalent of the Antichrist— and, as per another tradition, the Dajjal is in fact Jewish. [423] Armand Abel, the renowned Belgian scholar of Islam, includes this summary characterization of the Dajjal (from his official entry, "al-Dajdjal," in the Encyclopedia of Islam): [424]

*A giant, false prophet, king of the Jews, representations of him vary according to the degree of literary information available or the predominating prejudices... Abd al-Kahir al-*Baghdadi [425] *regards him as the ultimate term of comparison to describe false doctrine and going astray...he [the Dajjal] would perish at the hands of Jesus [i.e., Isa, the Muslim Jesus* [426]*] who, in that way, would be converted to Islam after killing pigs, scattering wine and taking his place for prayer at the [Meccan] Kaba.*

The "Muslim Jesus" (or "Isa") hadith variant which takes place in Jerusalem, is described by James Robson. [427]

[M]ost of the Arabs will be in Jerusalem when Jesus will descend. The imam will give place to him, but Jesus will tell him to lead the prayers. Afterwards, Jesus will order the door to be opened, and the Dajjal will be seen there with 70,000 armed Jews. The Dajjal will begin to melt, but Jesus will pursue and catch him and kill him at the east gate of Ludd. God will rout the Jews who will find that even the places where they shelter will shout out where they are hiding.

At his appearance, other traditions state that the Dajjal will be accompanied by seventy thousand Jews from Isfahan wrapped in their robes and armed with polished sabers, their heads covered with a sort of veil. When the Dajjal is defeated, his Jewish companions will be slaughtered—everything will deliver them up except for the so-called gharqad tree. Thus, according to several canonical hadith if a Jew seeks refuge under a tree or a stone, these objects will be able to speak to tell a Muslim: "There is a Jew behind me; come and kill him!" [428] Here are examples of these hadith: [429]

Anas b. Malik reported that Allah's Messenger said: "The Dajjal would be followed by seventy thousand Jews of Isfahan wearing Persian shawls."

Narrated Abu Huraira: Allah's Apostle said, "The Hour will not be established until you fight with the Jews, and the stone behind which a Jew will be hiding will say. "O Muslim! There is a Jew hiding behind me, so kill him."

Abu Huraira reported Allah's Messenger (may peace be upon him) as saying: "The last hour would not come unless the Muslims will fight against the Jews and the Muslims would kill them until the Jews would hide themselves behind a stone or a tree and a stone or a tree would say: Muslim, or the servant of Allah, there is a Jew behind me; come and kill him; but the tree Gharqad would not say, for it is the tree of the Jews."

Apropos to their longstanding Islamic relevance, Ibn Kathir's 14th century commentary on Qur'an 4:159, which discusses Isa's (the Muslim Jesus') role in defeating the *Dajjal*, and his Jewish minions, invokes these same apocalyptic canonical hadith of Jew annihilation. [430]

"Then Jesus, son of Mary, will be in my nation a just judge and a fair leader. He will break the cross, slaughter the pig, abolish the jizya, and abandon the zakat... The Messenger of Allah, may Allah bless him and grant him peace, said: 'You will fight the Jews, and kill them, until even a stone will say: O Muslim, this is a Jew, so come and kill him.' And he has on the authority of Suhayl ibn Abi Salih on the authority of his father on the authority of Abu Hurrayra that the Messenger of Allah, may Allah bless him and grant him peace, said, The Hour will not come until the Muslims fight the Jews and kill them, until a Jew hides behind rocks and trees, and the rocks and trees say, 'O Muslim, O servant of Allah, there is a Jew behind me, come and kill him. Except for the gharqad tree, for it is one of the trees of the Jews.'...Allah sends the Messiah, son of Mary, peace be upon him, and he descends near the white minaret east of Damascus between two angels, placing his hands on the wings of two angels...I heard the Messenger of Allah, may Allah bless him and grant him peace, say: 'The son of Mary will kill the Antichrist at the gate of Ludd - or to the side of Ludd.' Ahmad also narrated it on the authority of Sufyan ibn Uyaynah from the hadith of al-Layth and al-Awza'i, all three of them on the authority of al-Zuhri, on the authority of Abdullah ibn Ubayd Allah ibn Tha'labah, on the authority of Abd al-Rahman ibn Yazid, on the authority of his uncle Majma' ibn Jariyah, on the authority of the Messenger of Allah, may Allah bless him and grant him peace, who said : 'The son of Mary will kill the Antichrist at the gate of Ludd.' Al-Tirmidhi narrated it likewise on the authority of Qutaybah on the authority of al-Layth, and he said: This is a sahih hadith."

Vajda also emphasizes how the notion of jihad "ransom" extends even into Islamic eschatology: [431]

Not only are the Jews vanquished in the eschatological war, but they will serve as ransom for the Muslims in the fires of hell. The sins of certain Muslims will weigh on them like mountains, but on the day of resurrection, these sins will be lifted and laid upon the Jews.

This Judeo-centric Sunni eschatology resonates broadly, with an authoritative imprimatur, across Islamdom, in the modern era, and even within the Muslim diaspora. [432] For example, Hajj Amin El-Husseini concluded his compendious 1937 discourse on Islam's canonical Jew-hatred by reproducing the hadith (*Sahih Bukhari, Volume 4, Book 52, Number 177*; *Sahih Muslim, Book 041, Number 6985*) [433] about how the destruction of the Jews is requisite for ushering in the messianic times. Fifty years later Article 7 of Hamas' foundational 1988 charter re-stated the same canonical, apocalyptic hadith of Jew annihilation, which closed Hajj Amin el-Husseini's 1937 declaration: [434]

> *...the Islamic Resistance Movement aspires to realize the promise of Allah, no matter how long it takes. The Prophet, Allah's prayer and peace be upon him, says: "The hour of judgment shall not come until the Muslims fight the Jews and kill them, so that the Jews hide behind trees and stones, and each tree and stone will say: 'Oh Muslim, oh servant of Allah, there is a Jew behind me, come and kill him,' except for the Gharqad tree, for it is the tree of the Jews." (Sahih Muslim, Book 41, Number 6985)*

Current Palestinian Authority Grand Mufti of Jerusalem, Muhammad Hussein repeated this canonical tradition during a January 9, 2012 sermon. [435] And during a May 10, 2013 sermon at Al-Azhar University's mosque, Muhammad Al-Mahdi, a senior scholar and head of the Sharia association at Al-Azhar also proclaimed the same end of times Jew-annihilating hadith (and Qur'an 5:82, as well). [436]

Salah Khalaf, nom de guerre "Abu Iyad," was the founder of Black September, and second in command to Yasir Arafat in Fatah, whom Iyad met in Cairo while Iyad was a student at Al-Azhar University. [437] His January 21, 1974 essay published in *Le Monde*, when pseudo-secular [438] "Arab nationalism" still had some currency, included this admission: [439] **"We intend to fight so that our Palestinian homeland does not become a new Andalusia."** Abu Iyad's statement was a frank acknowledgement that Israel had a pre-Islamic Jewish heritage, like Spain's pre-Islamic Christian heritage. Both were conquered by jihad, and ruled under the Sharia, for seven (Spain) to thirteen (Israel) centuries, but then liberated from the Sharia, and their pre-Islamic cultures restored [440]—a phenomenon equally anathema to Tantawi and Abu Iyad.

Tantawi's 1968 call for the global Muslim umma to wage a jihad policide against Israel is entirely, if depressingly consistent with Al-Azhar's over 75-year continuum of such declarations (to be elaborated later in this Introduction), dating back to the November 1947 United Nations Partition Plan, and forward to within two weeks of Hamas' brutal jihad carnage on October 7, 2023. [441] Two salient examples 12-years prior to the publication of Tantawi's thesis were the twin Grand Mufti of Egypt, and Al-Azhar declarations of jihad issued in January 1956 some nine months before the outbreak of the 1956 Sinai War. [442]

Here are Tantawi's 1968 statements rallying Muslims for a "decisive jihad...to purge the Holy Land from the Jews," from the Conclusion of *Banū Isrā'īl fī al-Qur'ān wa-al-sunnah*: [443]

"The Arab and the Islamic nations should strengthen and reinforce the Palestinian fighters from all aspects. These fighters should be chosen from among the loyal and faithful ones who are strong believers in Allah, their religion and their country. They should be equipped with all the facilities that they could use to violently shake the Zionists (through guerrilla wars) because these wars threaten the security, stability and economy of Israel and all its structures. ***This jihad will be the prelude to that decisive jihad that the Islamic nation should wage against Israel to purge the Holy Land from the Jews…We should wage our next Palestinian war on a religious struggle (jihad) basis, not on a patriotic one only. That is because Palestine is a holy Islamic country, as we mentioned before. It is the land of all Muslims, and it is the obligation and duty of each Muslim on the face of world to defend and protect it.****"*

The two complementary 1956 fatwas were written January 5, 1956, by then grand mufti of Egypt, Sheikh Hasan Mamoun, and January 9, 1956, signed by the leading members of the Fatwa Committee of Al Azhar University, and the major representatives of all four Sunni Islamic schools of jurisprudence. These rulings elaborated the following key initial point: that ***all of historical Palestine***—modern Jordan, Israel, and the disputed territories of Judea and Samaria, as well as Gaza—having been conquered by jihad, was a permanent possession of the global Muslim *umma* (community), —fay territory— booty or spoils— to be governed eternally by Islamic law. [444]

Muslims cannot conclude peace with those Jews who have usurped the territory of Palestine and attacked its people and their property in any manner which allows the Jews to continue as a state in that sacred Muslim territory. ***[As] Jews have taken a part of Palestine and there established their non-Islamic government and have also evacuated from that part most of its Muslim inhabitants. . . . Jihad . . . to restore the country to its people . . . is the duty of all Muslims,*** *not just those who can undertake it. And since all Islamic countries constitute the abode of every Muslim, the Jihad is imperative for both the Muslims inhabiting the territory attacked, and Muslims everywhere else because even though some sections have not been attacked directly, the attack nevertheless took place on a part of the Muslim territory which is a legitimate residence for any Muslim…* ***Everyone knows that from the early days of Islam to the present day the Jews have been plotting against Islam and Muslims and the Islamic homeland.*** *They do not propose to be content with the attack they made on Palestine and Al Aqsa Mosque, but they plan for the possession of all Islamic territories from the Nile to the Euphrates.*

These 1956 fatwas are concordant with Tantawi's own 1968 "jurisprudence" on jihad, and share his conspiratorial Islamic Jew-hatred.

The last statements in Tantawi's Conclusion which close *Banū Isrā'īl fī al-Qur'ān wa-al-sunnah* are lines from the fraudulent antisemitic screed attributed, falsely, to one America's founding fathers, Benjamin Franklin. In reality, Franklin was quite philosemitic. [445] Tantawi's attribution for the so-called "Franklin Prophesy," was "American President, Benjamin Franklin," "from a speech he gave in 1789 in celebration of the Feast of the Constitution," punctuating the author's final descent into his own morass of virulent, ahistorical, and deranged, yet authoritative Islamic Jew-hatred.

Academic Discussions of *Banū Isrā'īl fī al-Qur'ān wa-al-sunnah*, Direct Comparisons of Tantawi's Qur'anic Interpretations with Those of Major Classical and Modern Muslim Qur'anic Commentators, and Seminal Non-Muslim Scholarship on Islamic Jew-Hatred

Islamologist Maxime Rodinson, in 1974, discussed the origins of the academic deification of Islam by "the anti-colonialist ideology of the Left," and its living legacy: [446]

> *"...[t]o some of those who were most deeply committed in this direction, Islam appeared intrinsically to be a naturally 'progressive' factor. There were even conversions to Islam...the anti-colonialist left, often goes so far as to sanctify Islam and the contemporary ideologies of the Muslim world...Understanding has given way to apologetics pure and simple"*

Two contemporary academic summary appraisals of Tantawi's *Banū Isrā'īl fī al-Qur'ān wa-al-sunnah* illustrate this apologetic mindset. While both treatments acknowledge the antisemitic content of Tantawi's thesis, each, in turn, dismisses the monotonous Jew-hatred as aberrant, non-traditional interpretation. [447]

Skovgaard-Petersen, discussed earlier, pigeon-holed Tantawi's antisemitic outlook as consistent, exclusively, with the Weltanschauung of the Muslim Brotherhood, and other "Islamist groups." [448] Tantawi's vitriol was mere "professed intransigence toward Israel," while Skovgaard-Petersen highlighted "new (then) illegal printings of *Banū Isrā'īl*," by the Muslim Brotherhood. He also described as simply a politicized campaign to "embarrass" Tantawi, the favorable publication of a full page of quotes in the "Islamist" weekly an-*Nur*, headed, "A reading of the book [thesis] of the Mufti which has caused the wrath of Israel: the glorious Koran warned us against the Children of Israel and confirmed that they will never honor a pact or a treaty." [448] According to Skovgaard-Petersen, the Jew-hatred redolent in Tantawi's thesis was solely a byproduct of "mythologization of the conflict" between Egypt and Israel. [449] Skovgaard-Petersen ignored how "the conflict"—sans any "mythology"—was widely perceived across Islamdom, at all societal levels, as the global Muslim umma's obligatory jihad against Israel. [450] Also scrupulously avoided by Skovgaard-Petersen was any discussion of how Tantawi's interpretations of the Qur'anic references to Jews he cited comported with authoritative classical or modern exegeses. [451]

Like Skovgaard-Petersen, Suha Taji-Farouki provides an apt characterization of the structure and antisemitic bent of *Banu Isra'il*. [452] She acknowledges the academic heft of Tantawi's methodology, [453]

> *"In a weighty exposition of seven hundred pages, he lists Qur'anic verses and hadiths addressing various aspects of his subject. A detailed discussion of these verses and hadiths is offered, incorporating extracts from various commentaries which are cited to substantiate and confirm his understanding of them. While his preference is for the classical commentaries including, for example, those of al-Zamakshari, al-Tabari, al-Razi, al-Qurtubi, and Ibn Kathir, he occasionally refers to the modern commentary al-Manar by Rashid Rida. In places he lists the opinions of several commentators in turn, ending with his own conclusions."*

Taji-Farouki also recognizes that, "as might be expected in the case of a study carried out under the supervision of specialists in exegesis at al-Azhar," the "style and presentation (of) Tantawi's work **deviates little from traditional Islamic exegetical scholarship**." Offering no evidence, Taji-Farouki nevertheless avers, "in insisting only on the negative characteristics of the Jews, however, it deviates significantly from traditional exegesis." [454] Similar to the earlier analysis of how journalist Reston Jr. bowdlerized Tantawi's views on jihad, based upon actual examination of Tantawi's own exegeses [455] in his 15-volume Qur'anic commentary, *al-Tafsīr al-wasīṭ lil-Qur'ān al-karīm*, juxtaposition of Tantawi's interpretations in *Banu Isra'il*, with the exegeses of authoritative classical and modern Qur'anic commentators—the latter including Tantawi's own (from *al-Tafsīr al-wasīṭ lil-Qur'ān al-karīm*) —thoroughly debunks Taji-Farouki's glib assertion. [456]

Tantawi's "point 4" of his introductory statements about *Banū Isrā'īl fī al-Qur'ān wa-al-sunnah's* "5 points of emphasis" provides a testable challenge to al-Farouki's unsupported claim. As Tantawi states, using Q 17:4 as a specific example, [457]

> *"I investigated other exegetes and commentators and chose the most appropriate amongst them explaining the reasons for my choice. Consider, for example, our interpretation of the Almighty's: "And We warned the Children of Israel in the Scripture, 'You will certainly cause corruption in the land twice, and you will become extremely arrogant.'" [Qur'an 17:4]*

I have compared Tantawi's gloss on Q 17:4 (combining Q 17:4-8, especially 17:4 and 17:8, for added contextualization) with those of the classical Muslim exegetes Farouki acknowledges are featured in *Banū Isrā'īl fī al-Qur'ān wa-al-sunnah*—Zamakshari, Tabari, Razi, Qurtubi, and Ibn Kathir. In addition, I have juxtaposed Tantawi's interpretation of Q 17:4/8 in *Banū Isrā'īl fī al-Qur'ān wa-al-sunnah* to his own exegesis in *"The intermediate [balanced] interpretation of the Qur'an,"* and the glosses of two other seminal modern Qur'anic exegetes, one Sunni, and the other Shi'ite. What follows is a direct comparison of the main elements of those exegeses, broken down further by grouping the classical exegetes (i.e., Zamakshari, Tabari, Razi, Qurtubi, and Ibn Kathir), first, followed by the modern exegetes (i.e., Shafi, Tabatabai, and Tantawi), for the most relevant comparisons.

Key extracts from the commentaries on Q 17:4/8 of the five classical exegetes are presented below, in chronological order (i.e., by date of death of the exegete).

Tabari (d. 923): [457]

> *"Your Lord has finished with the Children of Israel in what He revealed of His Book to Moses, peace and blessings be upon him, by informing them and telling them, 'You will surely cause corruption on the earth twice.' He says: You will disobey Allah, O Children of Israel, and you will surely defy His command in His land twice. "And you will surely become arrogant with great arrogance." He says: You will surely become arrogant towards Allah by your extreme audacity towards Him. And the scholars of interpretation have said something similar to what we have said about this...the first instance of* ***the Children of Israel's corruption on Earth*** *was their killing of the Prophet Zechariah, in addition to their previous and subsequent transgressions, until Allah sent against them one through whom He inflicted His wrath upon them for their disobedience to Allah and their defiance of their Lord. However, according to the account of Ibn Ishaq, from whom we have narrated, their first instance of corruption was what was described regarding their killing of the Prophet Isaiah, son of Amaziah. Ibn Ishaq mentioned that some scholars informed him that Zechariah died a natural death and was not killed, and that it was Isaiah who was killed, and that Nebuchadnezzar was the one who was given power over the Children of Israel the first time after they killed Isaiah...As for their corruption on earth the second time, there is no disagreement among scholars that it was their killing of John the Baptist. They differed, however, regarding the one whom Allah empowered against them as retribution at that time, and I will mention their differing opinions on this, Allah willing. As for His saying, {And you will surely attain great arrogance}, we have already mentioned the interpretation of those who said it refers to their arrogance towards Allah through their defiance of Him and their disobedience to His commands...The first instance of corruption by the Children of Israel in the land was as follows: Allah had made a covenant with the Children of Israel in the Torah: 'You will surely cause corruption in the land twice.' The first of these two instances of corruption was the killing of Zechariah. So Allah sent against them the king of the Nabataeans, who was called Dhuhabin... 'And if you return, We will return.' ...The people returned with the worst of what was present for them, so Allah sent upon them whatever He willed of His wrath and punishment.* ***Then the conclusion of that was that Allah sent upon them this tribe of Arabs, and they are in torment from them until the Day of Resurrection****. Allah, the Exalted and Glorified, said in another verse : 'And when your Lord proclaimed that He would surely send against them until the Day of Resurrection,' ...****so Allah sent upon them this tribe of Arabs****... 'Perhaps your Lord will have mercy on you, but if you return [to sin], We will return [to punishment].'* ***So they [the Jews]***

returned [to sin], and Allah sent Muhammad, peace and blessings be upon him, against them. Now they pay the jizya willingly and are humbled*...[In the afterlife] Allah has made Hell a bed and a resting place for those [like the Jews] who disbelieve in Him, as He said:* ***'For them there will be a bed of Hell, and over them coverings of fire.'*** *(Quran 7:17)."*

Zamakshari (d. 1144): [458]

"'And We decreed to the Children of Israel' and We revealed to them a decreed revelation, that is, a definitive and conclusive revelation, that they would inevitably cause corruption in the land, and they would become arrogant, that is, they would become haughty and transgress. {in the Scripture} in the Torah, and 'you will surely cause corruption' is the answer to an implied oath...'And you will surely cause corruption' (with the letter 'ta' pronounced with a fatha, from the root 'fasada') 'twice.' The first time was the killing of Zechariah and the imprisonment of Jeremiah when he warned them of Allah's wrath. The second time was the killing of John the son of Zechariah and the attempt to kill (Isa) Jesus, son of Mary. "Our servants" (also read as "Our slaves"). It is more commonly said that the servants of Allah are the servants of Allah, while the slaves of people are those of Sennacherib and his army, or, according to another opinion, Nebuchadnezzar. According to Ibn Abbas, it was Goliath. They [the 3 aforementioned] killed their [the Jews] scholars, burned the Torah, destroyed the mosque [i.e., the Temple—there was no mosque], and took seventy thousand of them captive. If you ask how it was permissible for Allah to send the disbelievers to do that and give them power over them, I would say it means that We left them to their own devices and did not prevent them. However, Allah, Exalted is He, attributed the sending of the disbelievers against them to Himself. This is similar to His saying, 'And thus We make some of the wrongdoers allies of one another because of what they used to earn.' (Q 6:129)...'Perhaps your Lord will have mercy on you,' after the second time if you repent again and refrain from sins. 'But if you return' a third time, 'We will return' to punishing you. And they did return, so Allah returned His wrath upon them by empowering the Persian emperors and imposing tribute upon them. And according to al-Hasan, ***they returned, so Allah sent Muhammad, and they pay the jizya willingly while they are humbled****..then the last of that was that Allah sent this tribe of Arabs upon them, and they are in torment from them until the Day of Resurrection"*

Razi (d. 1209): [459]

"Know that when Allah Almighty mentioned His favor upon the Children of Israel by revealing the Torah to them, and that He made the Torah a guidance for them, He clarified that they were not guided by His guidance, but rather fell into corruption, saying: 'And We decreed to the Children of Israel in the Scripture, You will surely cause corruption on the earth twice.' ... It was said: The Children of Israel became arrogant and proud, and they permitted what

was forbidden, and they killed the prophets and shed blood. That was the first of the two corruptions, so Allah gave power over them to Nebuchadnezzar, who killed forty thousand of them who read the Torah, and he took the rest to his own land, and they remained there in humiliation until Allah appointed another king who conquered the people of Babylon, and it happened that he married a woman from the Children of Israel. That woman asked that king to return the Children of Israel to Jerusalem, so he did, and after a period the prophets arose among them and they returned to the best of what they were, and that is what He said: 'Then We gave you back the advantage over them.' The second interpretation is that the meaning of His saying, 'We sent against you servants of Ours,' is that Allah Almighty empowered Goliath against them until he destroyed and annihilated them. And His saying, 'Then We gave you back the advantage,' means that He strengthened Saul so that he fought Goliath and granted victory to David until he killed Goliath. That is the return of the advantage. The third interpretation is that His saying, 'We sent against you servants of Ours,' means that Allah Almighty instilled fear of the Children of Israel in the hearts of the Magians. When sins increased among them, He removed that fear from the hearts of the Magians, so they targeted them and went to great lengths to kill, annihilate, and destroy them. Know that there is little benefit in knowing the identities of those peoples; rather, the point is that when they increased their sins, He empowered peoples against them who killed and annihilated them...Our scholars used this verse (17:4) to support their position on the issue of predestination and divine decree in several ways. First, Allah Almighty said: 'And We decreed to the Children of Israel in the Scripture, You will surely cause corruption on the earth twice, and you will surely reach a great degree of arrogance.' This decree, at the very least, implies a definitive judgment and an irrefutable statement. Thus, it is established that Allah Almighty informed them that they would commit corruption and sins with a definitive statement that cannot be abrogated, because, as we have explained, a decree means a definitive judgment. Furthermore, Allah Almighty further emphasized this decree by saying: 'And it was a promise fulfilled.' If this is established, then we say: the absence of such corruption on their part would necessitate the transformation of Allah's truthful word into falsehood, His decisive judgment into invalidity, and His true knowledge into ignorance—all of which are impossible. Therefore, their refraining from such corruption was impossible, and their perpetration of it was an obligatory duty, not subject to abrogation or repeal, even though they were commanded to refrain from it and cursed for committing it. This supports our statement that Allah may command something and then forbid it, and may prohibit something and then decree its occurrence. This is one way of arguing based on this verse. The second way of arguing based on this verse is through Allah's statement: 'We sent against you servants of Ours, possessing great might.' This refers to those who oppressed the Children of Israel through killing, plundering, and captivity. Allah clarifies that He is the One who sent them against the Children of Israel. Undoubtedly, the killing of the Children of Israel, the plundering of their wealth, and the capture of their children involved immense injustice and grave sins. Then He, the Exalted, attributed all of that to Himself by saying, "Then We sent against you." This indicates that good and evil, obedience and disobedience, are from Allah, the Exalted... The commentators said that it [17:8] refers to the final promise, and this final promise is their perpetration of murder against Zechariah and John, peace be upon them. Al-Wahidi [459a] *said: So Allah Almighty sent against them Nebuchadnezzar the Babylonian Magian, the most hateful of His creation to Him, and he took the Children of Israel captive, killed them, and destroyed the Temple in Jerusalem. I say: The histories testify that Nebuchadnezzar was many years before the time of Jesus, peace be upon him, and John and Zechariah, peace be upon them. It is known that the king who took revenge on the Jews because of these people was a king from the Romans called Constantine the King - and Allah knows best about their circumstances - and the purpose of interpreting the Qur'an is not related to knowing the identities of these people... We interpreted this verse [17:8] as referring to worldly punishment because of what Allah Almighty said in Sura Al-A'raf (sura 7), informing us about the Children of Israel: 'And when your Lord proclaimed that He would surely send against them until the Day of Resurrection those who would afflict them with the worst punishment.' [7:167]. Then He said: 'And if you return, We will return' [17:8] meaning that they returned to doing what is not appropriate, which is denying Muhammad, may Allah bless him and grant him peace, and concealing what was mentioned in the Torah and the Gospel, so Allah returned to them with punishment at the hands of the Arabs...* ***So what befell the Banu Nadir, Banu Qurayza, Banu Qaynuqa, and the Jews of Khaybar was what befell them in terms of killing and expulsion. Then the rest of them were subjugated by paying the jizya (tribute), with no kingdom or authority****. Then Allah Almighty said: 'And We have made Hell a prison for the disbelievers.'...The meaning is that although the punishment in this world is severe and intense, some people may escape it. Those who fall into that punishment are saved from it, either by death or by some other means.* ***As for the punishment of the Hereafter, it will be all-encompassing and surrounding a person, with no hope of escape from it. So these people will have the punishment in this world that we have described, and after that, they will have the punishment of the Hereafter that will surround them from all sides, and they will never escape from it****."*

Qurtubi (d. 1273): [460]

"His saying [from 17:4], may He be exalted: 'And We decreed to the Children of Israel in the Scripture.'... The meaning of 'We decreed' is that We informed and notified... We judged, and the root of 'decree' is to finalize something and complete it. It was also said: We decreed or revealed, and that is why He said, 'to the Children of Israel.'...'You will surely corrupt'...meaning if they corrupt, they will be corrupted, and what is meant by corruption is violating the rulings of the Torah. 'In the land' meaning the land of Syria, Jerusalem, and its surrounding areas. 'Twice, and you will surely become [arrogant]...'Great arrogance' meaning pride, transgression, tyranny, oppression, domination, and

*aggression...His saying [from 17:8], may He be exalted: 'Perhaps your Lord will have mercy on you'—this is something they were informed of in their scripture. 'Perhaps' is a promise from Allah that He will relieve them. And 'perhaps' from Allah is a certainty. '[T]hat He will have mercy on you,' after His vengeance upon you, and so it was; He increased their numbers and made kings from among them. 'And if you return, We will return.'...**So they returned, and Allah sent Muhammad, peace and blessings be upon him, against them, and they pay the jizya in humiliation... Punishment befell the Children of Israel twice at the hands of the disbelievers, and once at the hands of the Muslims. This was when they returned, so Allah returned upon them...'And We have made Hell a prison for the disbelievers,' meaning a place of confinement and imprisonment**..."*

Ibn Kathir (d. 1373): [461]

Allah Almighty informs us that He decreed to the Children of Israel in the Book, that is, He informed them in the Book that He revealed to them that they would cause corruption on earth twice, and become very arrogant, that is, they would become tyrannical and oppressive, and they would transgress against the people,...They ravaged your lands, meaning they conquered your countries, and they traversed your homes, meaning they moved about among them and within them, going back and forth, fearing no one. And it was a promise fulfilled. The commentators, both early and later, differed regarding who these soldiers were who were unleashed upon them. Ibn Abbas and Qatadah said that it was Goliath of Persia and his army, who were initially given power over them, and then they were later defeated. David killed Goliath, and that is why He said, {Then We gave you back the advantage over them} (Quran 3:11). It is narrated from Sa'id ibn Jubayr that he was the king of Mosul, Sennacherib, and his army. It is also narrated from him and others that he was Nebuchadnezzar, the king of Babylon...Allah informed us that when they transgressed and rebelled, He empowered their enemy against them, who seized their territory, invaded their homes, and humiliated and subjugated them as a just recompense. Your Lord is not unjust to His servants, for they had rebelled and killed many prophets and scholars...Nebuchadnezzar appeared in Syria, destroyed the Temple in Jerusalem, and killed its inhabitants...[T]he second time, that is, if you corrupt the second time, and your enemies come 'to disgrace your faces' meaning to humiliate and subdue you, 'and to enter the mosque' meaning the Temple in Jerusalem 'as they entered it the first time' meaning the time when they ransacked the houses. And that they might utterly destroy and ruin whatever they have conquered. Perhaps your Lord will have mercy on you, and turn them away from you. But if you return, We will return. And if you return to corruption, We will return to dominating you in this world, in addition to the punishment and torment We have reserved for you in the Hereafter. This is why He said, "And We have made Hell a prison for the disbelievers," meaning a place of confinement and confinement, a prison from which there is no escape...The Children of Israel have returned, so Allah has given power over them to this tribe, Muhammad, may Allah bless him and grant him peace, and his companions, who take the jizya from them willingly while they are humiliated.

The exegeses on Q 17:4/8 by these five classical commentators are remarkably concordant in their key points of emphasis: [462]

—Despite repeated admonishments, the Jews returned to their acts of "corruption," especially "prophet killing" (although the litany of alleged murdered prophets may differ, slightly)
—The Jews were variously punished for these alleged offenses by Nebuchadnezzar [463] (in particular), through perhaps the Roman Emperors [464] including Constantine [465] (who converted the Roman Empire to Christianity)
—With the advent of Islam under Muhammad, the "corrupted" Jews continued their sacralized humiliation under Muslim suzerainty as evidenced by their conquest and payment of the jizya (per Qur'an 9:29), with its attendant humiliating atmospherics. [466]
—Far worse than these corporeal world historical punishments, Hellfire awaits the "corrupted" Jews in the Afterlife. [467]

Tantawi's glosses on Q 17:4/8 will be compared, initially, to two renowned modern Qur'anic exegetes, Maulana Mufti Muhammad Shafi (d. 1976) and Muhammad Husain Tabatabai (d. 1981)

Ma'ariful Qur'an, [468] a definitive modern Sunni Qur'anic commentary, was written by Shafi (1898-1976), [469] the former Grand Mufti of (pre-Partition) India, who wrote over a hundred works explaining the Qur'an and Islamic law.

Shafi's gloss on Q 17:4/8 opens by averring the Jews who were attuned "to sin and disobedience," initially "increased the tempo of their hostility" until Allah "set their enemies upon them," which "shook them up." [470] After briefly giving "the impression of having been corrected," the Jews' "lust for mischief and misdeeds overtook them," resulting in renewed punishment, sanctioned by Allah, "at the hands of their enemies." [471] Although Shafi claims the Qur'an only mentions two [punishment] events, while there are six alleged historical examples (enumerated and described, below) of such punishments, he adds the caveat, "it is difficult to determine which…are the events mentioned by the Holy Qur'an." [472] Shafi then draws the "obvious" conclusion that the Qur'an must describe only "the major and serious among these in which the Jews were far too wicked and more seriously punished too, should be taken as the likely ones." He settles upon the fourth and sixth examples as being of Qur'anic origin based on an alleged hadith attributed to Hudhayfah ibn al-Yaman. [473] Here are Shafi's six examples: [474]

"1. The first event came to pass some time after the demise of Sulayman [King Solomon], the founder of Al-Masjid al-Aqsa [sic, The Temple], when the ruler of Baytul-maqdis became irreligious and corrupt. The ruler of Egypt attacked him

and took away the gold and silver of Baytul-maqdis. But, he did not demolish the city and the Masjid.

2. The second event relates to the period nearly four hundred years after that. Some Jews settled in Baytul-maqdis started idol-worship while the rest began disputing among themselves. This ill omen prompted another ruler of Egypt to attack them which somewhat affected the city and the Masjid both. After that, their condition took a turn for the better.

3. The third event came to pass after some years when Nebuchadnezzar, the King of Babylon ransacked Baytul-maqdis. He conquered the city, looted property and took back a lot of people as prisoners of war. When he left, he had a member of the family of the former king appointed a ruler of the city as his deputy.

4. When this new king, who worshipped idols and was corrupt, rebelled against Nebuchadnezzar, he returned, killed people, destroyed property en masse and burned the city razing it to rubbles. This happened nearly four hundred and fifteen years after the construction of the Masjid. After that, the Jews went out as exiles to Babylon where they lived in disgrace for seventy years. After that, the King of Iran attacked the King of Babylon and conquered it. Then the King of Iran [Cyrus] showed mercy to the Jewish expatriates and ordered that they should be sent back to Syria along with things looted from them. Now the Jews had repented having forsaken their habitual sins and misdeeds. When they resettled there, they restored the original structure of Masjid al-Aqsa with the support of the King of Iran.

5. Then came the fifth event. When the Jews had peace and prosperity once again, the first thing they forgot was their past. They returned to the kind of evil deeds they were used to. Then, it so happened that, one hundred and seventy years before the birth of Isa [the Muslim Jesus] the king who had founded Antakiah (Antioch) attacked, killed forty thousand Jews and took with him another forty thousand as prisoners and slaves, even desecrated the Masjid though its structure remained safe. But, later, the successors of that king rendered the city and the Masjid totally denuded. Soon after this, Baytul-maqdis came under the authority of Roman kings. They put the Masjid back into shape and it was after eight years that Isa was born.

6. Forty years after the physical ascension of Isa, the Jews chose to rebel against their Roman rulers. The Romans destroyed the city and the Masjid once again relegating it to what it was. The king at that time was called Titus who was neither Jewish nor Christian because long after him Constantine I was a Christian. From that time to the time of Umar [ibn al-Khattab] this Masjid lay desolate until he had it reconstructed. [This latter assertion is untrue. See note [413]]"

In what he dubs as his own "Commentary" on these verses, Shafi describes the "outcome" of the six examples/events: [475]

> *"The outcome of the events mentioned above is that Allah had decreed that the Bani Isra'il will be successful, having the best of both worlds, the material and the spiritual, as long as they continue to obey Allah. But, whenever they deviate from the dictates of Faith, they shall be put to disgrace, and that they would be subjected to punishment at the hands of enemies and disbelievers. Then, not only that the enemies will run over them destroying their lives and properties, but it would also happen that their Qiblah [direction of prayer], their sacred Baytul-maqdis, will also not remain safe against the onslaught of that enemy. Their disbelieving enemies will barge into the Mosque of Baytul-maqdis and defile and damage it. This too will be a part of the punishment of Bani Isra'il themselves. The Holy Qur'an has told us about two events relating to them. The first one dates back to the time of Mosaic religious law while the second pertains to the Christian. During both these periods, the Bani Isra'il rebelled against the divine law of the time. In the first case, a disbelieving monarch was made to sit over them, and Baytul-maqdis, who brought great destruction upon them. In the second case, a Roman emperor was set against them who killed and pillaged and made Baytul-maqdis all demolished and rendered desolate."*

Shafi continues, regarding Q 17:8, specifically: [476]

> *"After having mentioned these two events, Allah declared His Law in such matters by saying: ('If you do this again, We shall do that again' [Q 17:8]. This law which means—'if you return to disobedience and contumacy, We shall, once again, make a similar penalty and punishment zoom back upon you'—has been declared as valid right through the last day of Qiyamah [day of Resurrection]. That its addressees were the people of Banu Isra'il who were present during the blessed time of the Holy Prophet serves as a reminder to them. It is being pointed out to them that they should not forget that they were seized by divine punishment twice when they had first opposed the code of Musa [Moses], and then the code of Isa [the Muslim Jesus]. Now this was the period of the Code of laws brought by the Holy Prophet [Muhammad] This was a period that will continue up to the Last Day."*

The Jews, Shafi adds, [477] also "became hostile to Islam and the religious code of laws brought by the Holy Prophet." Accordingly, [478]

> *"...they were expelled and disgraced at the hands of Muslims, and finally Baytul-maqdis, their Qiblah, too came under Muslim control. However, the only difference was that their past conquering kings had treated them disgracefully and had desecrated their Qiblah too. Now when Muslims took over Baytul-maqdis, they reconstructed the great Mosque of al-Quds ash-Sharif which was lying demolished and desolate for centuries and thereby reinstated the honor and reverence of the Qiblah of prophets."*

Shafi concludes his exegesis of Q 17:4/8 by reminding Muslims of the relevance of these verses to contemporary interactions vis-à-vis them, and the Jews "in our time…the most disgraced in this world," admonishing Muslims to wage a "purely Islamic Jihad" to restore "Palestine" to Sharia jurisdiction. [479]

> *The calamity of the Jewish usurpation of Baytul-maqdis in our time and the added sacrilege of setting fire to it (a false allegation* [480]*) has thrown the world of Islam into acute anxiety. In reality, it is confirming the Qur'an. Muslims forgot Allah and His Messenger, ignored the life waiting for them in the Hereafter and opted to scrounge for their share in the glamour and grandeur of the mortal world. When they became aliens to the dictates of the Qur'an, and Sunnah, the same divine law stood activated before them. A few hundred thousand Jews overcame them. They also inflicted the loss of life and property on them. Worse still is the fate of one of the three greatest mosques of the world according to the religious law of Islam, a mosque that has the distinction of being the Qiblah of all prophets. It was snatched from them and those who took it over had a track record of being the most disgraced people in this world, that is, the Jews. In addition to that, it is common observation that these people stand nowhere close to Muslims in terms of their numbers, nor do they have some significant superiority over the current collective Muslim holdings of war materials. This also tells us that this event does not really give Jews any niche of honor in the annals of world nations. However, it does provide punishment for Muslims in return for their disobedience. It clearly shows that everything that came to pass came as the punishment of our own misdeeds. And it also shows that there is no remedy for it except that we should feel ashamed of our misdeeds, make a genuine taubah (repentance), start obeying the commandments of Allah, become true Muslims and shun the great sins of imitating and trusting others. If we were to do just that, Insha'Allah, true to the Divine promise, Baytul-maqdis and Palestine shall return to us. But, it is regrettable that the present-day Arab rulers and common Muslims living in Arab lands have yet to be alerted to that reality. They are still relying on foreign assistance while making plans of taking Baytul-maqdis back, something that does not appear to be probable, at least outwardly. Where else shall we lodge our plaint but Allah! The only weapon system and military hardware with which Baytul-maqdis and Palestine can return to Muslim hands are still there waiting to be picked up--Return o Allah, genuinely and passionately. Have certitude of Akhirah [the Hereafter]. Obey the injunctions of the Sharia. Stay away from imitating and trusting others in our social and political goals. Finally, let us place our trust in Allah and wage a purely Islamic Jihad as enjoined by the Sharia. May Allah give our Arab rulers and other Muslims the ability to answer the challenge effectively.*

A brief biographical introduction to Muhammad Hussein Tabatabai (d. 1981) is in order to appreciate the significance of his doctrinal interpretations. Also known as "Allamah (an honorific title for a profound scholar, a polymath, a man of vast reading and erudition) Tabatabai," he was a prolific writer whose influential Koranic studies, and philosophical works, remain widely read. Tabatabai's monumental twenty volume *Al-Mizān fi Tafsir al-Qur'an* ("The measure of balance in the interpretation of the Quran"), is generally regarded as the most important 20th century Shiite Qur'anic commentary.[481] Jane Dammen McCauliffe, an internationally recognized scholar of Qur'anic exegesis, is editor of both the six-volume *Encyclopaedia of the Qur'an,* [482] and *The Cambridge Companion to the Qur'an.* [483] Noting Tabatabai's Koranic commentary, "*included with some frequency…excerpts from hadith collections and from previous commentaries, particularly those of al-Ayyashi (d. 932), al-Qummi (d. 939), and al-Tabarsi (d. 1153).*," McCauliffe concluded that the massive work, [484]

> "*… testifies to his [Tabatabai's] broad scholarly background and abiding interest in comparative religion and philosophy. In addition to etymological and grammatical discussions,* ***it combines his own thoughts and elucidations of the passage under consideration with discourses on its moral implications or mystical-philosophical ramifications.***"

Renowned Iranian Professor of Islamic Studies at Georgetown University and prominent contemporary Muslim philosopher, Seyyed Hossein Nasr, translated and wrote the preface to Tabatabai's treatise, *Shi'ite Islam.* [485] Professor Nasr referred to Tabatabai as, "*a man who has devoted his whole life to the study of religion, in whom humility and the power of intellectual analysis are combined,*" a "*celebrated Shi'ite authority,*" who produced the "*monumental Quranic commentary, al-Mizan.*" [486] And Nasr reverently summarized Tabatabai's purported unique combination of scholarship and spirituality, as follows: [487]

> "*Allamah Tabatabai represents that central and intellectually dominating class of Shi'ite ulama who have combined interest in jurisprudence and Quranic commentary with philosophy, theosophy, and Sufism and who represent a more universal interpretation of the Shi'ite point of view. Within the class of the traditional ulama, 'Allamah Tabatabai possesses the distinction of being a master of both the Shari'ite [Sharia] and esoteric sciences and at the same time he is an outstanding hakim or traditional Islamic philosopher (or more exactly, 'theosopher).*"

Pace the hagiographies of McCauliffe and Nasr, Professor W. Montgomery Watt, in a 1977 review of the Tabatabai-Nasr collaboration, *Shi'ite Islam*, offered this alternative assessment of both Tabatabai and the Islamic apologist, Nasr: [488]

> "*…there is no sign in the present work of any attempt to come to terms with occidental thought. The author [Tabatabai] still lives in the world of traditional Islamic theology, virtually untouched by any 'impact of the West.'…Seyyed Hossein Nasr, a Persian who studied science and philosophy at the Massachusetts Institute of Technology and Harvard, is the most effective apologist for Islam to the West at the present time, as may be seen from his Ideals and Realities of Islam and various other books and articles.*"

Allameh [Allamah] Tabatabai University, named in honor of this celebrated Shiite authority and "theosopher," is the largest specialized state social sciences university in Iran and the Middle East, with 17000 students and 500 full-time faculty members. [489] Affirming his continued lofty stature, and relevance, an Iranian national conference was held on May 3, 2012, in Qom, dedicated to "recognizing the interpretative methods and principles used by Allameh [Allamah] Tabatabaee [Tabatabai] in [his] *Al-Mizan* exegesis." [490]

Here are key extracts from Tabatabai's modern gloss on Q 17:4/8: [491]

> *The apparent meaning of the opening verses of the chapter is that they are intended to explain that Allah's established pattern with humankind is to guide them to the path of servitude and monotheism, enabling them to attain this through their own choice. He bestows upon them blessings in this world and the Hereafter, and provides them with the means to both obedience and disobedience. If they obey and do good, He rewards them with happiness in this world and the Hereafter. If they do evil and disobey, He punishes them with worldly retribution and the torment of the Hereafter. Thus, these verses serve as an example of* ***this general pattern that occurred with the Children of Israel. Allah revealed the Book to their prophet, making it a guide for them to follow. He decreed that they would become arrogant, transgress, and commit sins, so Allah would punish them by allowing their enemies to conquer them through humiliation, killing, and captivity. Then they would return to obedience, and Allah would return to His blessings and mercy. Then they would become arrogant and transgress again, so Allah would punish them a second time, more severely than the first. It is then hoped that their Lord will have mercy on them and that they will return to the right path. From this, it can be concluded that these verses serve as an introduction to what will follow regarding the application of this general principle to this nation…*** *We informed and notified the Children of Israel definitively in the Book, which is the Torah. I swear and this statement is true:* ***You, the people of Israel, will cause corruption in the land—that is, the land of Palestine and its surrounding areas—twice, time after time, and you will become greatly exalted and transgress with immense tyranny****... His statement, "We sent against you servants of Ours, possessing great might," means that We raised them up and sent them to you to humiliate you and take revenge on you. The proof that the sending was for revenge and humiliation is His statement, "possessing great might," etc. There is no harm in considering their coming to the Children of Israel, with all the widespread killing, captivity, enslavement, plunder, and destruction that it entailed, as a divine sending, because it was a recompense for their corruption on earth, their arrogance, and their transgression without right. So Allah did not wrong them by sending their enemies and supporting them against them, but rather they were the ones who wronged themselves. Thus, it becomes clear that there is no evidence in the text*

*to support the claim that the meaning of "We sent against you," etc., is that We commanded a group of believers to fight and wage jihad against you, based on the apparent meaning of "We sent" and "servants." This is because, as you know, there is no objection to considering this a divine mission, given that it was a form of retribution. Similarly, there is no objection to considering the disbelievers as servants of Allah, given what follows in the verse, "possessing great might." A similar argument is made by those who say that these sent ones could be believers whom Allah commanded to fight against these people, or that they could be disbelievers whom a prophet sought to win over to fight these people and empower them against other disbelievers and transgressors... T]hat the Children of Israel will regain dominion over their enemies after the initial promise, overcoming and subjugating them, and freeing themselves from their enslavement and subjugation. This dominion will gradually return to them over a considerable period of time, as is necessary given the provision of wealth and offspring, and the increase in their numbers. The statement in the following verse, "If you do good, you do good for yourselves; and if you do evil, it is against yourselves," indicates—indeed, it is a clear indication, aided by the context—that this event, the restoration of dominance to the Children of Israel over their enemies, was due to their return to good after they had tasted the consequences of their previous evil. Similarly, the fulfillment of the promise of the Hereafter was due to their relapse into evil after this initial return to good... Many important calamities befell the Children of Israel since they became independent in kingship and sovereignty, more than two - according to what their history records - and what these verses contain can apply to two of them, but what is like a given among them is that one of these two calamities to which the verses refer is what happened to them at the hands of Nebuchadnezzar, one of the kings of Babylon, about six centuries before Christ. He was a powerful and influential king, one of the giants of his time. He protected the Israelites, but they disobeyed and rebelled against him. So he marched against them with armies they could not withstand, besieged their land, and then conquered it by force. He devastated the land, demolished the Al-Aqsa Mosque, burned the Torah and the books of the prophets, and massacred the people, leaving only a small group of women, children, and weak men. He took them captive and sent them with him to Babylon, where they remained without protection or defense for the duration of Nebuchadnezzar's reign and for a long time afterward. Then Cyrus, one of the great kings of Persia, marched on Babylon and conquered it. He showed kindness to the Israelite captives and allowed them to return to the Holy Land. He helped them rebuild the Temple—**the Al-Aqsa Mosque**—and renovate its structures... This occurred around 450 BC. It appears from Jewish history that the first one sent to destroy the Temple was Nebuchadnezzar, and it remained in ruins for seventy years. The second one sent was the Roman Emperor Vespasian, who dispatched his minister to them [who] destroyed the house and humiliated the people approximately one century before Christ... When the second promise of destruction came to pass, We sent them to disgrace you by displaying grief and sorrow, and by showing humiliation and wretchedness, and to enter the Al-Aqsa Mosque as they did the first time, and to* *utterly destroy those they conquered and annihilate those they passed over. His saying, may He be exalted, 'Perhaps your Lord will have mercy on you. But if you return [to sin], We will return [to punishment]. And We have made Hell a prison for the disbelievers.' The word "prison" (hasir) comes from the root meaning "to confine" or "to restrict," as they have mentioned. He, may He be exalted, said* **, 'And confine them'** *(Q 9: 5), meaning restrict them. His saying, 'Perhaps your Lord will have mercy on you', means after the second resurrection, as the context indicates. This is an expression of hope for mercy, assuming they repent and return to obedience and good deeds, as evidenced by His saying, 'But if you return [to sin], We will return [to punishment].'* ***That is, if you return to corruption and arrogance after you have turned away from it and your Lord has shown you mercy, We will return to punishment and retribution. And We have made Hell a prison for the disbelievers, a place of confinement from which they cannot escape****...The point here is to indicate that the fundamental principle of Allah's Lordship is that He should have mercy on His servants if they follow the path dictated by their creation and guided by their innate nature, unless they deviate from the path of creation and stray from the way of nature."*

The following are key extracts from Tantawi's gloss on Q 17:4/8 in his thesis: [492]

"The Almighty's 'And We warned the Children of Israel in the Scripture, You will certainly cause corruption in the land twice, and you will become extremely arrogant.' (Q 17:4) This means that We have disclosed to the Children of Israel and informed them in their Book, the Torah, of a sure revelation. We made it known to them through Moses, their prophet, that they will cause corruption in the land of the Levantine twice as the Almighty said: 'You will certainly cause corruption in the land twice, and you will become extremely arrogant.' That is, you will disobey Allah, become arrogant and refuse to comply with His commandments twice. You will become extremely and undeservedly haughty, and that would lead you to loss and destruction. Among the signs of their corrupting the land was twisting and distorting the Torah, their non-compliance with its teachings, their killing of the prophets, their aggression towards those who seek fairness and justice among people, and indulging in immoralities and iniquities... among the benefits of declaring this in the Noble Qur'an is to alert those Jews who were contemporaneous with the Prophet- as well as other disbelievers and polytheists like them- to one of Allah's ways of dealing with His creation, i.e., corrupting the earth, disobeying His commandments, transgressing, and disobeying His prophets- all of these will lead to loss in this world and in the Hereafter. So, it is imperative for the Jews and other people to believe in Muhammad- whose prophethood has been verified and confirmed- to secure happiness in this world and in the Hereafter... Among the examples of them corrupting the land this second time are killing Zachariah and John, attempting to kill Jesus, persevering in transgressions and evil deeds, allowing what Allah had forbidden and all the other vices that permeated and prevailed among them

throughout the ages and everywhere. Most exegetes believe that this time it was Nebuchadnezzar, the Babylonian, who was sent against them the second time... the Almighty showed that the destruction that befell them for corrupting the land twice could be for their own good, a way to lead them to penitence and righteousness if they became responsive to the truth, learned from previous examples and past events and understood that Allah's way with His creation is fixed, constant and unchangeable: good deeds lead unto happiness and corruption leads unto perdition and annihilation. The Almighty said: 'Perhaps your Lord will have mercy on you if you repent, but if you return to sin, We will return to punishment. And We have made Hell a permanent confinement for the disbelievers.' (Q 17:8)...The meaning is: Perhaps Allah will pardon and have mercy on you after His vengeance against you, Children of Israel, if you act rightly, do good deeds, worship Him truthfully, and shun depravities and transgressions. You have learned that Allah does not allow calamities to befall unless there are inequities and transgressions, and He does not lift them without penitence. For this reason, He said: 'but if you return to sin, We will return ...' That is: If you return to disobeying Me, disregarding My commandments and violating My sanctities for a third time after you have been clothed with My compassion, We will return to murder and torture, humiliate and disgrace you, and send enemies against you who would severely punish you in this worldly life. In fact, they did return to wrongdoing, and Allah did return to punishing them. They did not believe in Muhammad, and they concealed what was reported concerning him in the Torah and the Bible. They sought to kill him. So, Allah instructed Muhammad to punish them because of their treachery and injustice. He killed Ban Qurayza, drove Banu Qaynuqa and Banu Nadir out of Medina and levied the jizya tax on the rest. They would pay the tax, willingly submitting, fully humbled... they returned to their corruption during the ages that followed the advent of Islam, and Allah sent others from His servants who humiliated and displaced them. The Jews are still the object of people's contempt, resentment and hatred because of their selfishness, racism, ill manners and corruption in the land. And Allah has truthfully said: "And remember, O Prophet, when your Lord declared that He would send against them others who would make them suffer terribly until the Day of Judgment." (Al-A'raf; Q 7:167) He also reveals their end: 'And We have made Hell a permanent confinement for the disbelievers.' (Q 17:8) That is, Hell will be their abode; it is there that We have prepared an eternal prison for them, one from which they cannot escape. So, in this worldly life, they have faced annihilation and destruction. In the Hereafter, they will suffer in the eternal fire that surrounds them from every side. That is because of their corruption and for corrupting the land...[T]hose whom Allah sent against the Children of Israel after their first corruption of the land were Goliath and his warriors. As for the servants that Allah sent against the Children of Israel after their second corruption of the land, interpreters tend to think that they were the Babylonians headed by Nebuchadnezzar. We have shown before that Nebuchadnezzar attacked the Children of Israel three times: the first was in 606 BCE, the second was in 599 BCE and the third was in 588 BCE. The third time, he killed thousands of them, demolished their Temple and took those who were alive captives to Babylon, as we detailed when we treated the first perspective. This view has been adopted by a large number of exegetes. It is not far-fetched since it describes the severe punishments that they were subjected to. However, we tend to believe that it was the Romans headed by Titus who were sent against them the second time they corrupted the land... [T]he adversities and hardships that Titus and other Romans inflicted upon the Jews were- in our opinion- harsher and crueler than those that Nebuchadnezzar caused them... The Jews at the present time are the same Jews throughout the ages: corrupt and corrupting, belligerent and aggressive, and tyrannical and oppressive. They flagrantly and brazenly attacked the Muslims of Palestine. Infidel countries provided them with various types of assistance. Our anticipated role, Allah willing, is to eliminate all manner of disagreements and discord amongst ourselves to enable the religion of Allah to be firm and steadfast in the land through unity, strength, hard work and true worship and conduct our business unwaveringly with legitimate means and with resoluteness and stanchness. Then the believers will be gladdened with Allah's victory."

Lastly, here are extracts from Tantawi's gloss on Q 17:4/8 in his full Qur'anic commentary, *The intermediate [balanced] interpretation of the Qur'an*: [493]

"And His saying (Q 17:4), may He be glorified, 'And We decreed to the Children of Israel in the Scripture, 'You will surely cause corruption on the earth twice...,' is a statement from Allah, may He be exalted, to them, concerning what would befall them, according to what occurred in His all-encompassing knowledge, which contains no compulsion or coercion, but rather is a revealing attribute, indicating their fate and circumstances...The meaning is: We informed the Children of Israel in their book, the Torah, with certainty, and We revealed to them through Our messengers, saying to them, 'You will surely cause corruption on the earth twice, and you will surely become arrogant towards people without right, with great arrogance, which will lead you to loss and destruction.' The fact that their corruption is described as a divine decree and mentioned in the Book indicates its certainty... [W]hile their actions are certain and exist, they are accompanied by tyranny, pride, transgression, and aggression. Among the manifestations of their corruption on Earth were their distortion of the Torah, their abandonment of its rulings, and their killing of prophets and reformers. Then, Allah—exalted is He—explained that after their initial corruption on Earth, He would send against them those who would subdue them, violate their sanctities, and utterly destroy them, saying (Q 17:5)—exalted is He— 'So when the first of the two promises came to pass, We sent against you servants of Ours, possessing great might, and they ravaged the land. And it was a promise fulfilled.'...The meaning is: When the time came for your punishment, O Children of Israel, for the first instance of your corruption, We sent against you and directed towards you 'servants of Ours, possessing great might,' meaning those with great power in wars and battles. They humiliated and subjugated you, searching for you among your dwellings and homes to kill those of you who remained alive. This was the aforementioned

mission and its consequences: your killing, the plundering of your wealth, the violation of your honor, and the destruction of your homes...There is disagreement regarding the identity of these servants—those whom Allah sent to punish the Children of Israel after their first transgression... [whether] Goliath and his army... Sennacherib, the king of Babylon, and his army... the Amalekites, and some said Nebuchadnezzar... If someone were to ask, what is the benefit of Allah—Exalted is He—informing the Children of Israel in the Torah that they would cause corruption in the land twice, and that He would punish them for their arrogance and tyranny by sending against them those who would humiliate, subdue, and destroy them? The answer is that informing them of this demonstrates that Allah—Exalted is He—does not wrong people in any way. Rather, He punishes them for their transgressions and forgives much, and that His mercy is open to sinners whenever they repent, turn back to Him, and mend their ways. Another benefit of this account is to warn the wise among all nations against committing sins that lead to destruction, and to caution their people against such sins, making them aware of the dire consequences of straying from the path of righteousness, lest they expose themselves to the punishment of Allah Almighty. Among the benefits of including this account in the Holy Quran is to alert the Jews contemporary with the Prophet (peace and blessings be upon him) and those among the polytheists who shared their wickedness and disobedience to one of Allah's established laws in His creation: that corruption ultimately leads to loss. Therefore, the Jews and all other people should follow the Messenger (peace and blessings be upon him), whose prophethood is beyond doubt, so that they may find happiness in this life and the Hereafter...Allah Almighty concluded the verses by stating that this destruction that befell the Children of Israel due to their two acts of corruption in the land could be a path to His mercy and a reason for their repentance and return to Him, if they opened their hearts to the truth, learned from past events, and understood Allah's unchanging law: that good deeds lead to success and victory, while corruption leads to loss and destruction. The Holy Quran expressed these meanings most eloquently and wisely. Allah Almighty said (Q 17:8): 'Perhaps your Lord will have mercy on you. But if you return [to sin], We will return [to punishment]. And We have made Hell a prison for the disbelievers.' Perhaps your Lord will have mercy on you and forgive you, O Children of Israel, when you sincerely worship and obey Him, and rectify your words and deeds. For you know that He—exalted is He—does not send down calamity except for sin, and He does not lift it except through repentance...It would have been obedient for them to follow Jesus and Muhammad—peace be upon them—but they did not. And His—exalted is He—saying, 'And if you return, We will return,' is a warning to them of inflicting punishments upon them if they return to their corruption and wrongdoing. That is, if you return to sins and disobeying My commands and violating My prohibitions, after My mercy has encompassed you, We will return upon you with killing, torture, and the destruction of your homes. They returned to disbelief, immorality, and disobedience, as they turned away from the call of truth that the Messenger, may Allah bless him and grant him peace, brought to them. They were not satisfied with this turning away, but rather they plotted to kill him, may Allah bless him and grant him peace, and they supported everyone who lay in wait for Islam and the Muslims. As a result of that, the Prophet, may Allah bless him and grant him peace, and his companions punished them as they deserved, by expulsion, displacement, and killing...Then He, the Exalted, explained their punishment in the Hereafter, saying, 'And We have made Hell a prison for the disbelievers.' Meaning, if you return to disobeying Us in this world, We will return to you with a deterrent punishment. As for the Hereafter, We have made Hell a prison for the disbelievers...Thus we see that the noble verses have told us Allah Almighty's judgment on the Children of Israel, and have presented to us, so that we may consider and learn from the various laws of Allah Almighty that do not fail, the most prominent of which is that faith and righteousness result in success, and that disbelief and corruption result in misery, and the punishment of the Hereafter is more severe and lasting... Allah sent Goliath against them in the first instance, and he ravaged their lands. So they asked Allah - the Exalted - to send them a king, and He sent them Saul. They fought Goliath and were victorious over him, and David killed Goliath, and their kingship was restored to the Children of Israel. When they persisted in their corruption, Allah sent Nebuchadnezzar against them a second time, and he destroyed their temples and utterly razed their structures. These are some of the pieces of evidence that lead us to believe that the servants whom Allah Almighty empowered over the Children of Israel after their first corruption in the land were Goliath and his army. As for the servants whom Allah empowered over them after their second corruption, many commentators believe they were Nebuchadnezzar and his army. This view is not far from the truth, given what we mentioned earlier about his persecution of them and their captivity in Babylon in 588 BC. However, we prefer this view to the view that those who subjugated them after their second corruption were the Romans, led by their leader Titus, in 70 CE... The Roman attacks themselves were more severe and harsher on the Israelites than Nebuchadnezzar's attacks on them. For example, the number of Jews killed by the Romans under Titus reached one million, and the number of captives reached about one hundred thousand. In contrast, the number of those killed and taken captive by Nebuchadnezzar was far less. Historians have described the catastrophe inflicted upon them by the Romans in terms far exceeding that inflicted by the Babylonians under Nebuchadnezzar... After Titus and his soldiers stormed the city [Jerusalem], he ordered them to burn, plunder, and kill, declaring that the Jews' possessions and honor were fair game. The Romans burned and destroyed the Jewish temple... The calamity inflicted upon them by the Romans—in terms of its consequences—was far more devastating than the one inflicted by Nebuchadnezzar. For after Nebuchadnezzar's brutal treatment and taking them captive to his lands, where they remained imprisoned for nearly fifty years, they returned to their homes once more with the help of Cyrus, the Persian king, who defeated Nebuchadnezzar around 538 BC, and their numbers began to increase again. After Titus's brutal treatment of them, they were utterly destroyed and scattered throughout the land, their lineage as a nation coming to an end... [W]hat Allah has related to us in His Book is sufficient for us from all the other books that came before it. Allah and His Messenger did not make us in need of them. Allah Almighty informed us that when they transgressed and rebelled, He gave power over them to their enemy, who violated their sanctity, entered their homes, humiliated them, and subjugated them, as a just recompense. And your Lord is not unjust to His servants, for they had rebelled and killed a number of prophets and scholars. Imam al-Razi said, 'Know that there is little real purpose in knowing the identities of those peoples. Rather, the point is that because they committed many sins, Allah empowered peoples over them who killed and annihilated them.'"

The exegeses on Q 17:4/8 by these three seminal modern Qur'anic commentators are very consistent with each other, as well as the five classical commentators excerpted and juxtaposed earlier. [494] Moreover, any objective assessment of all these glosses on Q 17:4/8—classical and modern—reveals they emphasize, uniformly, indelible pejorative characteristics of Jews who therefore deserve worldly devastating humiliation, and Hellfire in the Afterlife. This hard evidence debunks Taji-Farouki's glib, unsupported assertion [495] that Tantawi's exegeses somehow "deviate(d) significantly from traditional exegesis." Even Tantawi's truculent remarks in his thesis commentary on Q 17:4/8 regarding modern Jews and their conflict with "Muslims of Palestine" are mirrored by Shafi in his influential contemporary *Ma'ariful Qur'an*. [496] Indeed Shafi's gloss calls for a global Muslim "purely Islamic Jihad" to destroy Israel and reimpose Sharia governance on all of "Palestine." [497]

Tantawi and Al Azhar's Living Legacy of Anti-Israel Jihad and Jew-Hatred—Relevance to the Post October 7, 2023 Jihad Carnage in Southern Israel, and the Raging Pandemic of Muslim Antisemitism

An Overview of the October 7, 2023 Jihad Carnage in Southern Israel

The carnage of October 7, 2023 in southern Israel was wrought by an unprovoked attack of the jihad terror organization Hamas, in conjunction with local Gazan Muslims. [498] Launched during an ostensible "truce," the attack had apparently been planned since 2014 by Hamas leadership. [499] Some 1200 Israelis were murdered, the victims being disproportionately (i.e., > 70 percent) non-combatant children, women, men, and the elderly. [500] Hamas' jihad carnage on October 7, 2023 was the largest mass killing terror attack, per capita (per 10,000 population), in over 50-years, and was ~2.6-fold more deadly than the next most lethal attack. [501] Atrocities committed against these largely non-combatant Israelis included, mutilation, torture, beheadings, and mass rape, followed by burning, with documentation in the jihadists' own videos and oral testimony (of captured jihadists), surveillance camera videos, surviving eyewitness testimony of the victims, and forensic pathology evidence. [502]

Sobering analyses of the similarities between the catastrophic Israeli military intelligence failures during the 1973 Yom Kippur War, and the Hamas October 7, 2023 jihad terror attacks, were provided by Drs. Uri Bar-Joseph, and Itai Shapira on January 26, 2024. [503] [8] Both emphasized the shared and fixed belief in 1973, and again in 2023, that Egypt, and Hamas, respectively, were allegedly "deterred." Dr. Shapira focused upon these specific features: [504]

> *"(Israeli Military Intelligence) did not pressure strongly enough the fact that Hamas wants to destroy Israel, and it will never give up its policy & strategy to destroy Israel. It (Hamas) is based, all its existence is based on the destruction of Israel. And when you don't repeatedly say to the Prime Minister who wants to believe that Hamas doesn't want to destroy Israel, or you can tame Hamas by providing it with money from Qatar, then you provide the Prime Minister with an intel estimate that comes closer to his political needs, and at the same time you diminish the level of alertness that should be among intel analysts with regard to what Hamas intends to do."*

Dr. Bar-Joseph emphasized Hamas' ideological motivation—it's raw determination to destroy Israel—and the self-fulfilling willful blindness to this obsession by both intelligence analysts, and Israeli Prime Minister Netanyahu: [505]

> *"[L]ack of intel about enemy capabilities (i.e., underestimation) to understand adversary strategy...That was a failure in 1973, and it might also have been a failure now (10/7/2023)...From an intelligence policy perspective, if Israeli intelligence in 2023 would have said that Hamas is capable of conducting a surprise military attack against Israel, and is not only capable, but intends to do that, this means, or would have meant, that the Israeli Defense Forces operation in 2021, 'Guardian of the Walls,' was not effective. This would have meant that the Israeli policy (allowing) Qatar to bring money (to Hamas), and so forth is not effective. And giving such an intel assessment to military commanders and to politicians is problematic."*

Neither Dr. Shapira nor Dr. Bar Joseph, in the end, ever elucidated, even in summary, Hamas' (and the much broader Palestinian Muslim populace's) animating "sacralized" Islamic jihadism, and Jew-hatred, which clearly underpin these annihilationist obsessions. [506]

The remainder of this concluding section of the Introduction will elaborate on those themes by reviewing hard polling data, and authoritative contemporary Islamic pedagogy—emphasizing Al-Azhar University pedagogy—on the jihad against Israel, and the Jews. Independent assessments of Islam's theological Jew-hatred by non-Muslim scholars will also be examined. A brief overview of an existing paradigm for serious reform of Islam's theological Jew-hatred closes this section, and the Introduction.

"Antisemitism" is Jew-Hatred

The late Robert Wistrich [507] emphasized the problematic nature of the term "antisemitism," derived from a group of cognate "Semitic" (i.e., stemming from the biblical Shem, one of Noah's three sons) languages—Hebrew, Aramaic, Arabic, Babylonian, Assyrian, and Ethiopic—and applied, inappropriately, to a pseudo-scientific racial designation by the German journalist Wilhelm Marr in the 1870s. Regardless, for over a century, as Wistrich noted, [508]

> *the illogical term "antisemitism" . . . [w]hich never really meant hatred of "Semites" **(for example, Arabs)** at all, but rather hatred of Jews, has come to be accepted in general usage as denoting all forms of hostility towards Jews and Judaism throughout history.*

An expanded working definition of Jew-hatred/Antisemitism by the International Holocaust Remembrance Association from May 26, 2016, now includes denying the State of Israel's right to exist, *a priori* defining its existence as "racist," and insisting Israel, alone, conform to unique standards of behavior relative to other democratic nations. [509]

Contemporary Jew-Hatred by the Numbers

Perversely, during the two-months immediately after the October 7th massacres, and accompanying atrocities, the Anti-Defamation League (ADL) documented an "unprecedented" increase in Jew-hating incidents within the United States, marking the *"highest number of incidents during any two-month period since ADL began tracking in 1979."* ADL recorded a total of 2,031 antisemitic incidents between 10/7/23 and 12/7/23, *"up from 465 incidents during the same period in 2022, representing a 337% increase year-over-year."* These incidents included 40 involving physical assault, 337 of vandalism, 749 of verbal or written harassment and *"905 rallies including antisemitic rhetoric, expressions of support for terrorism against the state of Israel and/or anti-Zionism."* ADL noted that on average, *"over the 61 days from 10/7/23/ to 12/11/23, Jews in America experienced nearly 34 antisemitic incidents per day."* Approximately 250 antisemitic incidents *"specifically targeted Jewish institutions such as synagogues and campus Hillels."* ADL further recorded a total of 400 antisemitic incidents on college and university campuses, compared to only 33 incidents during the same period in 2022. Of the total incidents, *"at least"* 1,411 *"could be clearly linked to the Israel-Hamas war."* ADL added, *"data includes one fatality that occurred at an anti-Israel protest in Los Angeles, where a Jewish man was killed after being hit in the head by a pro-Palestinian protester."* [510] What ADL failed to note was that the "pro-Palestinian protester," arrested and charged with involuntary manslaughter, was a devout Muslim Computer Science lecturer at California State University-Northridge, whose social media profile expressed support for Hamas jihadists. [511]

The Anti-Defamatiuon League has developed and validated simple questionnaires to gauge Jew-hatred, broadly, in population-based samples. Two closely related examples, from 2004, and 2014 through 2022-23, are depicted below. ADL's 2004 questionnaire, administered during 2004 in the United Kingdom, France, Germany, Denmark, Belgium, the Netherlands, Austria, Italy, Spain, and Switzerland, was modified, slightly, and employed globally during surveys whose results were reported between 2014, to 2022-23 [512,513] Each iteration of the questionnaire was designed to capture the prevalence—

occurrence, as a percentage—of extreme Antisemitism, defined as agreement with at least six of the eleven of the Antisemitic stereotypes queried.

2004 version
[1.] Jews don't care what happens to anyone but their own kind.
[2.] Jews are more willing than others to use shady practices to get what they want.
[3.] Jews are more loyal to Israel than to this country.
[4.] Jews have too much power in the business world.
[5.] Jews have lots of irritating faults.
[6.] Jews stick together more than other citizens. (of respondent's country of residence)
[7.] Jews always like to be at the head of things.
[8.] Jews have too much power in international financial markets.
[9.] Jews have too much power in our country today.
[10.] Jewish business people are so shrewd that others do not have a fair chance to compete.
[11.] Jews are just as honest as other business people.* (*frequency of respondents that disagreed with this)

2014-2022/23/24 version
[1.] Jews are more loyal to Israel than to (this country/the countries they live in).
[2.] Jews have too much power in the business world.
[3.] Jews have too much power in international financial markets.
[4.] Jews don't care about what happens to anyone but their own kind.
[5.] Jews have too much control over global affairs.
[6.] People hate Jews because of the way Jews behave.
[7.] Jews think they are better than other people.
[8.] Jews have too much control over the United States government.
[9.] Jews have too much control over the global media.
[10.] Jews still talk too much about what happened to them in the Holocaust.
[11.] Jews are responsible for most of the world's wars.

Attempted removal of "confounding" factors (or "bias") from the 2004 Western European survey data —specifically, age, country of residence, religion, income, sex, contact with Jews, commonality with other races/religions, and attitudes toward immigrants—was accomplished with the use of statistical modeling of the unadjusted raw data by multivariable logistic regression. This analysis demonstrated that relative to Christianity, as the "referent" religion, Islam conferred a nearly 8-fold increased risk (quantified as an "odds ratio") for extreme Antisemitism! [514]

By 2014, ADL was applying its slightly modified survey instrument, globally. These baleful findings, vis-à-vis, Muslim attitudes towards Jews, were reflected in the raw, unadjusted data: [515]

—*The world's 16 most Antisemitic countries were all in the Muslim Middle East, where 74% to 93% of the overwhelmingly Muslim denizens of these nations exhibited extreme Antisemitism*—Judea-Samaria/Gaza 93%; Iraq 92%; Yemen 88%; Algeria 87%;

Libya 87%; Tunisia 86%; Kuwait 82%; Bahrain 81%; Jordan 81%; Morocco 80%; Qatar 80%; United Arab Emirates 80%; Lebanon 78%; Oman 76%; Egypt 75%; Saudi Arabia 74%.
—*There was a 2 to 3-fold excess occurrence of extreme Muslim Antisemitism, globally, by religious affiliation*—Muslim, 49%; Christian, 24%; No religion, 21%; Hindu, 19%; Buddhist, 17%.

A decade later, ADL's 2024 global survey again confirmed the unabated—indeed slight worsened—disproportionate pandemic of extreme Muslim Jew-hatred even in the aftermath of the October 7, 2023 atrocities. [516] The 19 most antisemitic countries in the world were all predominantly, if not almost exclusively Muslim countries, both Arab and non-Arab Muslim societies, where the prevalence of extreme antisemitism ranged from 64 to 97 percent: Kuwait and Gaza/Judea-Samaria (The West Bank) 97%; Indonesia 96%; Bahrain 95%; Oman 94%; Saudi Arabia 92%; Jordan 91%; United Arab Emirates 91%; Lebanon 86%; Egypt 84%; Tunisia 83%; Libya 82%; Algeria 81%; Turkey 79%; Iraq 77%; Malaysia 75%; Sudan 72%; Morocco 70%; Qatar 64%. For comparison, key Western European and North American countries exhibited a much lower prevalence of extreme antisemitism, ranging from 8 to 13 percent: France 13%; United Kingdom 12%; Germany 9%; United States 9%; Canada 8%.

ADL published Western European data in 2015 that included large Muslim population samples. The disproportionate occurrence of Muslim Jew-hatred was again apparent: [517]

—*There was 2* to 4.5-fold excess *prevalence of extreme Muslim Antisemitism in Western Europe*—Belgium, 68% of Muslims vs. 21% of non-Muslims; Spain, 62% of Muslims vs. 29% of non-Muslims; Germany, 56% of Muslims vs. 16% of non-Muslims; Italy, 56% of Muslims vs. 29% of non-Muslims; United Kingdom, 54% of Muslims vs. 12% of non-Muslims; France, 49% of Muslims vs. 17% of non-Muslims.

Dr. Gunther Jikeli described unique United States ADL data from 2017 comparing the prevalence Muslim and non-Muslim extreme antisemitism (which the ADL itself has never reported to the public). [518]

> *"Anzalone Liszt Grove conducted the survey in January and February of that year with a representative sample of the American general population of 3600 participants and a sample of American Muslims of 805 participants. The margin of error for the U.S. general population was 1.6%, and the margin of error for the U.S. Muslim population was 3%. A total of 6% of the U.S. general population and 38% of the Muslim population agreed with 6 or more of the 11 antisemitic statements."*

Thus U.S. Muslims were ~6.3-fold more likely to exhibit extreme antisemitism relative to U.S. non-Muslims.

ADL released its 2019 survey data characterizing the prevalence of *extreme* Antisemitism within 18 countries assessed between April 15 and June 3, 2019. Six of these countries—Belgium, The United Kingdom, Germany, Spain, France, and Italy—again included a Muslim over-sample, allowing for a direct comparison of Muslims vs. Christians, those professing no religion, and the general populations. These findings confirmed the ongoing, disproportionate roughly 3-fold excess occurrence of extreme Antisemitism among Western Europe's Muslims. [519] Curiously, ADL's 22pp. summary report of its most recent survey of 6 Western and 4 Eastern European countries (published May, 2023), makes no mention of extreme Muslim Antisemitism, whatsoever. [520] Elsewhere, ADL's own raw 2023 tabulations of extreme Antisemitism for the only two countries where Muslim data are provided, i.e., France and Belgium, reveal the same nearly 20-year, repeated phenomenon: 62% of French Muslims exhibited extreme Antisemitism, vs. 15% of French Christians; for Belgium those numbers were 52% Muslims, 21% Christians. [521]

Independent validation of these ADL surveys was provided by European pollsters who reported their findings between 2005 and 2013. Data collected during the **2008** "Six Countries Study" (i.e., **The Netherlands**, Germany, France, Belgium, Austria, and Sweden) from ~9000 participants (3373 native Christians; 3344 Turkish Muslim immigrants; 2204 Moroccan Muslim immigrants) revealed that **45% of the Muslim immigrants, vs. 9% of native Christians, believed "Jews cannot be trusted." While such hostility to Jews among "fundamentalist" Christians doubled to ~18%, over 70% of fundamentalist Muslims were hostile to Jews**. [522] [26] "Antisemitism in Brussels' Schools," a 426-pp. study, included data on the views within the young Belgian Muslim community, primarily, 12–18-year-olds, during **2011**. [523] A 354-pp. follow-up study of Antwerp-Ghent youth was published in 2013. Thirty-two Dutch-speaking Brussels high schools were surveyed, including 2,837 students. **Muslim respondents agreed with the following four statements—i.e., Antisemitic stereotypes—at disproportionate, 3.7-fold, to 7.0-fold, rates!:** [I] "Jews want to dominate everything" (Muslims, 56.8%; non-Muslims, 10.5%); [II] "Most Jews think they're better than others" (Muslims, 47.1%; non-Muslims, 12.9%); (III) "If you do business with Jews, you should be extra careful" (Muslims, 47.5%; non-Muslims, 12.9%); (IV) "Jews incite to war and blame others" (Muslims, 53.7%; non-Muslims, 7.7%). Antisemitic Muslim attitudes were unrelated to low educational level or social disadvantage. The 2013 study of 863 students from Ghent and Antwerp, including 346 Muslim students, confirmed these results. **45-50% of Muslim students evidenced Antisemitic attitudes, versus 10% of non-Muslims, consistent 4.5 to 5-fold excess rates**. [524] Gunther Jikeli's earlier **2005 to 2007** study yielded concordant results. [525] Jikeli, a Muslim convert, [526] conducted 117 interviews with Muslims from Berlin, Paris, and London, whose mean age was 19 years old. **Jikeli** affirmed **the centrality of Islam,** *"references to the Qur'an or the Hadith (traditions of Muhammad),"* **in shaping the Antisemitic views of young Muslim adults in Western Europe.** [527] Finally, a **lone study of its kind**, assessing non-lethal violence and violent threats targeting Jews, was conducted by FRA – European Union for Fundamental Rights, in 2012. **Uniquely, it queried Jewish victims about the identity of those who attacked them, or threatened them with violence**, asking them to recall their past 5-year experiences: *"Thinking about the incident where somebody attacked or threatened you in a way that frightened you because you are Jewish–who did this to you?"* There was a gross 2.2-fold excess occurrence of non-lethal violence, or violent threats against Western European Jews, by Muslims, relative to non-Muslims, collectively, who held designated, "right-wing", "left-wing", or "Christian" views. [528]

Polling data obtained from Palestinian Muslims shortly before, and since October 7, 2023, [529] a massive survey of Muslims in the Middle East and North Africa (MENA) conducted after October 7, 2023, [530] and a survey with an oversample of American Muslims following October 7, 2023, [531] have all addressed sympathy with Hamas' jihad carnage. The extensive MENA survey further gauged Muslim willingness to recognize Israel's right to exist as a sovereign state in the aftermath of October 7, 2023. [532]

Three months prior to October 7, 2023, Palestinian polling data obtained by the Palestinian Center for Policy and Survey Research, (PCPSR) Bir Zeit University, Research from face-to-face interviews of 1270 adults, June 7th to 11th, 2023, confirmed the public preference for Hamas over Fatah: Hamas polled 10% higher than Fatah on the question of "deserving to represent the people," while Hamas leader Ismail Haniyeh was preferred by 23% more Palestinians than Fatah leader Mahmoud Abbas, to be President. [533]

A poll released Nov. 14, 2023 by the Arab World for Research & Development, surveyed 668 Palestinians polled (391 West Bank; 277 Gaza, asking: "How much do support the military operation carried out by the Palestinian resistance led by Hamas?" Seventy-five percent were extremely or somewhat supportive, 59.3% extremely; 15.7% somewhat. The survey also reported Hamas' favorability at 76%, but Palestinian Authority favorability was only 10%. Highest overall favorability occurred among designated military/jihad terror organizations: Al Qassam Brigades 89%; Islamic Jihad 84%; Al Aqsa Brigades 80%. [534] A PCPSR poll released December 13, 2023, interviewed 1231 adults face to face, 750 in the West Bank, and 481 in the Gaza Strip. Seventy-two percent (82% in the West Bank/57% in Gaza) affirmed the October 7th jihadist attack was the "correct decision". Satisfaction with the role of Hamas was the highest—72% (85% West Bank/ 52% Gaza) followed by the role played by Hamas leader Yahya Sinwar 69% (81% West Bank/ 52% Gaza), vs. only 14% for the Palestinian Authority (10% West Bank/21% Gaza), and 11% for Palestinian Authority /Fatah leader Mahmoud Abbas (7% West Bank/ 17% Gaza). Fifty-four percent believed that Hamas was the most deserving of representing and leading the Palestinian people, while 13% believed that Fatah under the leadership of Abbas was more deserving. For the Arab regional actors, the highest level of satisfaction went to Houthi-dominated Yemen 80% (89% West Bank/ 68% Gaza), followed by Qatar, 56%. [535]

A population-based sample of 8000 MENA Muslims (from Mauritania, Morocco, Algeria, Tunisia, Libya, Egypt, Sudan, Yemen, Oman, Qatar, Kuwait, Saudi Arabia, Iraq, Jordan, Lebanon, and the West Bank, Palestine [including Jerusalem]) were polled by the Doha, Qatar-based Arab Center for Research and Policy, between December 12, 2023, through January 5, 2024. The communities surveyed represented 95% of the population of MENA Muslims, including its far-flung regions, with 500 men and women sampled in each community. Eighty-nine percent of the respondents felt the October 7, 2023 jihad carnage by Hamas was "a legitimate resistance operation," 67%, unequivocally, 19%, believing the attack was "somewhat flawed, but legitimate," while 3% claimed the attack was "a legitimate resistance operation that involved criminal acts." An equivalent 89% of the sample refused to recognize Israel's right to exist as a sovereign state. [536]

Lastly, 58% of a United States Muslim oversample (total sample, n=2020) polled October 16-18, 2023 agreed Hamas' jihad carnage "was justified." [537]

<u>*From Polling Data to Animating Islamic Religious Ideology*</u>
In July, 2011, American pollster Stanley Greenberg reported the results from what was described as an *"intensive, face-to-face survey in Arabic of 1,010 Palestinian adults in the West Bank and the Gaza Strip."* [538] There were two salient, pathognomonic findings from this unique survey which directly queried the respondents about themes quoted from the Hamas Covenant. [539] One was that **73%** of the Palestinian Muslims surveyed ***"agreed with a quote from the (*Hamas*) charter (Covenant), (article 7) and a hadith, or tradition ascribed to the prophet Muhammad, about the need to kill Jews hiding behind stones and trees,"*** [540] i.e., the dictates of Islam's prophet Muhammad's canonical hadith of Jew-annihilation. [541] Eighty percent further agreed with *"a quote from the Hamas Charter about the need for battalions from the Arab and Islamic world to defeat the Jews,"* i.e., article 15 of the Hamas charter calling for the jihad destruction of the State of Israel by the world's Muslims. Per the charter, this ***"jihad becomes a personal duty of every Muslim…*** *[I]t is necessary to raise the banner of jihad. This requires the propagation of Islamic consciousness among the masses, locally (in Palestine), in the Arab world and in the Islamic world"*, [542] the same public admonition then Malaysian Prime Minister Mahathir Mohamad gave to the heads of all the nation states of the global Muslim umma at the 2003 Organization of the Islamic Conference meeting in Putrajaya. [543]

From January 1989, till his death **in May, 2012, [544] historian David Littman's toiled ceaselessly to cajole the United Nations Human Rights Commission into condemning Hamas' "sacralized" Covenant of genocidal Islamic Jew-hatred. [545]**

January 31, 1989, addressing the United Nations Human Rights Commission, less than 6-months after the Hamas Covenant was made public, Littman plaintively warned that the document was, [546]

> *"a blatant blueprint for genocide, undoubtedly inspired by its spiritual leader, Sheikh Ahmed Yassin. I have with me a copy of the Arabic text and an English translation. Its aims are clearly defined in article 8, under the title, "Slogan": "Allah is its target, the Prophet is its model, the Koran its constitution;* ***Jihad is its path****, and death for the sake of Allah is the loftiest of wishes." Article 13 declares: "There is no solution for the Palestinian question except through jihad." And article 28 does not beat about the bush: "Israel, Judaism, and Jews challenge Islam and the Muslim people: 'May the cowards never sleep.'"*

Littman concluded, [547]

> *"These realities cannot be brushed aside simply because they are embarrassing, but should rather serve as a serious warning to the gullible for whom an appeasing, misguiding, 'peace in our time,' will-o'-the-wisp remains a constant obsession."*

Focus on Hamas' covenant as a binding documentary record of the organization's specific beliefs and goals is required because it expresses, unabashedly, as I will demonstrate, the same conjoined jihadism and Jew-hatred mainstream Islam inculcates. This indoctrination—sanctioned by Islam's leading religious teaching institutions, and clerics—in turn animates, and unifies the global Muslim umma's relentless efforts to destroy Israel as an autonomous state by jihad, and return Israel to Sharia jurisdiction. **Apropos to the analysis of *Banu Isra'il fi al-Qur'an wa al-Sunna* herein, when reading the following brief discussion of the central antisemitic motifs of the Hamas Covenant one cannot avoid noting its striking concordance with the identical thematic elements developed (albeit much more extensively) by Tantawi in his thesis. At the conclusion of this specific discussion, I will elucidate that concordance**.

The very first statement of Hamas' foundational Covenant, before the document's preamble, features Qur'an 3:112. Although discussed earlier, as a reminder, here is the Sahih International translation of 3:112: [548]

> *They have been put under humiliation [by Allah] wherever they are overtaken, except for a covenant from Allah and a rope from the Muslims. And they have drawn upon themselves anger from Allah and have been put under destitution. That is because they disbelieved in the verses of Allah and killed the prophets without right. That is because they disobeyed and [habitually] transgressed.*

In classical and modern Qur'anic exegeses by seminal, authoritative Islamic theologians this central motif (repeated at Qur'an 2:61) is coupled to Qur'anic verses 5:60, and 5:78, which describe the Jews transformation into apes and swine (5:60), or simply apes, (i.e. verses 2:65 and 7:166), having been "...cursed by the tongue of David, and Jesus, Mary's son" (5:78). [549] Muhammad himself repeats this Qur'anic curse in a canonical tradition or hadith, *"He (Muhammad) then recited the verse (5:78): '...curses were pronounced on those among the children of Israel who rejected Faith, by the tongue of David and of Jesus the son of Mary'"*. [550]

Salah al-Khalidi [551] made clear how these motifs of Qur'anic Jew-hatred **are interpreted by Hamas** in a manner that is entirely consistent with both classical, and modern authoritative exegeses. Extracts are provided below from Khalidi's major work *Haqa'iq Koraniyya al Qadiyya al-Filastinniya* ["Qur'anic Facts Regarding the Palestinian Issue"] **which was first published in 1991 by the Hamas Publishing House** *Manshūrāt Filastin al-Muslima*, and translated into Urdu, Hindi, Turkish, Russian, and English, due to its international popularity. [552]

*Humiliation is attached to the Jews for their entire lifetime: they were humiliated in Egypt, and when they arrived in [sic] Palestine, and when they were exiled from Palestine, and when they dispersed into the valleys of the earth. What concerns us here-in our discussion of the Jewish character-is to indicate that this humiliation is to be considered as an inveterate Jewish character trait, and a destructive Jewish perversion. Humiliation is one of their historical attributes, a fixed fact of their existence, and a basis of their life... (Qur'an 3:112) The Jews are humiliated because they disbelieved in Allah, killed His prophets, disobeyed His emissaries, transgressed His prohibitions-all of this is humiliation. They are humiliated-and this is why they search out lustful indulgences, and have become their slaves. All of this is humiliation...It is impossible that the Jews could not be cursed. How could they not be accursed when they are attributed with such degenerate inveterate character traits, twenty of which we have demonstrated above. (**Note**: Khalidi earlier states, 'We have extracted from the Qur'an twenty Jewish traits. The Jews are: liars, perverters (of the Text), envious, tricky, fickle, mercurial, sardonic, treacherous, in error, causing others to be in error, merchants, fools, humiliated, dastards, misers, avid for (this) life, disloyal to their firm contracts, rush into sinful aggression, concealers of true evidence, corrupters in the earth, and obstructors in Allah's path.'* ***For specific Qur'anic citations confirming his litany see*** *[553]). They are worthy of eternal curse because of the villainous traits they display and the corrupt evils they have perpetrated...The Jews are in a condition of mal`ana, i.e. everyone pours out curses on them; Allah has cursed them, the angels have cursed them, their prophets have cursed them, the good people among them have cursed them, and everyone has cursed them. They are deserving of this eternal and continual damnation until the day of resurrection when they will encounter Allah's wrath, fury, and punishment. They were accordingly exiled from Allah's mercy, and kept afar from His goodness... Many Koranic verses were revealed emphasizing...the judgment upon them of cursed damnation, and exile from His mercy, e.g. Qur'an 5:13: "For breaking their covenant, We curse them, and have made their hearts hard." And Qur'an 5:60...And Qur'an 5:64...And Qur'an 5:78..."*

As noted earlier, [554] annihilationist sentiments regarding Jews are also rooted in Islamic eschatology (end of times theology) and incorporated permanently into the foundational 1988 Hamas covenant. [555] Muslim eschatology highlights the Jews' supreme hostility to Islam. Jews are described as adherents of the Dajjâl—the Muslim equivalent of the Anti-Christ—or according to other traditions, the Dajjâl is himself Jewish. At his appearance, some traditions maintain that the Dajjâl will be accompanied by 70,000 Jews from Isfahan wrapped in their robes, and armed with polished sabers, their heads covered with a sort of veil. [556] When the Dajjâl is defeated, his Jewish companions will be slaughtered—everything will deliver them up except for the so-called gharqad tree as per the canonical hadith (Sahih Muslim, Book 41, Number 6985; [557]) included in the 1988 Hamas covenant (in article 7). This hadith is cited in the covenant as a sacralized, obligatory call for a Muslim jihad genocide of the Jews: [558]

> ***...the Islamic Resistance Movement aspires to realize the promise of Allah, no matter how long it takes.*** *The Prophet, Allah's prayer and peace be upon him, says: "The hour of judgment shall not come until the Muslims fight the Jews and kill them, so that the Jews hide behind trees and stones, and each tree and stone will say: 'Oh Muslim, oh servant of Allah, there is a Jew behind me, come and kill him,' except for the Gharqad tree, for it is the tree of the Jews."* (Sahih Muslim, Book 41, Number 6985)

Ibn Kathir's still widely used, authoritative 14th century Qur'anic commentary's gloss on verses 4:155 through 4:159–which discusses Isa's (the Muslim Jesus') role in defeating the Dajjal, and his Jewish minions—also invokes this same apocalyptic canonical hadith of Jew annihilation, indicative of the fact that its contemporary invocation is not a modern "*sui generis*" phenomenon. [559] Such Judeo-centric Sunni eschatology has resonated, broadly, with an authoritative imprimatur, across Islamdom, for over a thousand years into the modern era, and even within the Muslim diaspora, before and since October 7, 2023. Hajj Amin El-Husseini, jihadist "Godfather" of the modern Palestinian Muslim movement, concluded his compendious 1937 discourse on Islam's canonical Jew-hatred by reproducing Sahih Muslim, Book 41, Number 6985, and reiterating how the destruction of the Jews is requisite for ushering in the messianic times. [560] The current Palestinian Authority Grand Mufti of Jerusalem, Muhammad Hussein [561] repeated this canonical tradition in a January 9, 2012 sermon. [562] Subsequently, during a May 10, 2013 sermon at the mosque of Al-Azhar University, Muhammad Al-Mahdi, a senior scholar and head of the Sharia association at Al-Azhar also proclaimed the same end of times Jew-annihilating hadith. [563] Such ignoble Jew-hating eschatological incitement by contemporary Palestinian and American clerics continued even in the aftermath of October 7, 2023. Less than 2-weeks following the October 7th massacres, the Palestinian Authority Ministry of Religious Affairs posted guidelines for mosques Wednesday, October 18, 2023, at its Facebook page. Muslim preachers were instructed to include Sahih Muslim, Book 41, Number 6985 in their upcoming Friday sermons. [564] Lastly, Colorado U.S. imam Karim Abu Zaid, is described as a "prolific author," and "dynamic leader" within his suburban Denver community, with "a steadfast dedication to scholarly pursuits," who is currently seeking a Ph.D. at The Islamic University of Minnesota. [565] Imam Abu Zaid, in a November 10, 2023 *Friday sermon streamed live on the Facebook page of the Colorado Muslims Community Center, extolled murderous jihad martyrdom operations, and "modernized" the canonical hadith of Jew-annihilation, as follows:* [566]

> *"Remember, one day Allah will give Muslims drones too – rocks. A rock, one day, will call upon the Muslim: 'Come, behind me there is [a Jew].' A drone, that is a drone. The rock will call a Muslim: 'Come, he is behind me.'*

Returning to the Hamas covenant, Article 28, which is free of any eschatological references, clearly "widens the circle of hate" towards Jews, as David Littman observed, [567] targeting *all* contemporary Jews: *"Israel, Judaism and Jews challenge Islam and the Muslim people: 'May the cowards never sleep.'"* Articles 22 and 32 invoke modern conspiratorial themes reminiscent of European (secular) antisemitic motifs, especially the latter (article 32), which makes explicit mention of the Czarist Russian forgery, *The Protocols of the Elders of Zion.* [568] However, even these articles are peppered with Qur'anic citations, including references in both articles 22 and 32 to Qur'an 5:64, a sort of ancient antecedent of *The Protocols*. (Sahih International translation, Qur'an 5:64: "And the Jews say, 'The hand of Allah is chained.' Chained are their hands, and cursed are they for what they say. Rather, both His hands are extended; He spends however He wills. And that which has been revealed to you from your Lord will surely increase many of them in transgression and disbelief. And We have cast among them animosity and hatred until the Day of Resurrection. Every time they kindled the fire of war [against you], Allah extinguished it. And they strive throughout the land [causing] corruption, and Allah does not like corrupters.") [569]

Jihad [570] is the other pillar of Hamas' foundational Jew-annihilationist ideology featured in the 1988 covenant. Once again, this is already suggested in the opening statement before the preamble which includes the following quote attributed to Hasan al-Banna, founder of the Egyptian Muslim Brotherhood: "Israel will exist, and will continue to exist, until Islam abolishes it, as it abolished that which was before it." Hamas, it should be noted, claims to be a wing of the International Muslim Brotherhood. Article 2 of the Hamas covenant, for example, states: "The Islamic Resistance Movement is one of the wings of Muslim Brotherhood in Palestine. The Muslim Brotherhood Movement is a universal organization which constitutes the largest Islamic movement in modern times." [571]

The body of the Hamas Covenant includes unequivocal statements of Hamas' irredentist commitment to the annihilation of Israel via jihad. Jihad martyrdom is lauded in article 8 "the Hamas slogan," which states, "Allah is its target, the Prophet is its model, the Qur'an its Constitution; Jihad is its path, and death for the sake of Allah is the loftiest of its wishes." Article 13 makes plain that Hamas' jihadism is completely incompatible with any meaningful Middle East peace settlement: [572]

> *Initiatives, and so-called peaceful solutions and international conferences, are in contradiction to the principles of the Islamic Resistance Movement. Abusing any part of Palestine is abuse against part of religion. Nationalism of the Islamic Resistance Movement is part of its religion. Its members have been fed on that...There is no solution to the Palestinian question except by Jihad. All initiatives, proposals, and International Conferences are a waste of time and vain endeavors.*

Finally, article 15 (subtitled, "Jihad for the Liberation of Palestine is a Personal Duty") elucidates classical jihadist theory, including murder "martyrdom" operations , as well as their practical modern application to the destruction of Israel by jihad: [573]

> *The day the enemies conquer some part of the Muslim land, jihad becomes a personal duty of every Muslim. In the face of the Jewish occupation of Palestine, it is necessary to raise the banner of jihad. This requires the propagation of Islamic consciousness among the masses, locally [in Palestine], in the Arab world*

and in the Islamic world. It is necessary to instill the spirit of jihad in the nation, engage the enemies and join the ranks of the jihad fighters. The indoctrination campaign must involve ulama, educators, teachers and information and media experts, as well as all intellectuals, especially the young people and the sheikhs of Islamic movements...It is necessary to establish in the minds of all the Muslim generations that the Palestinian issue is a religious issue, and that it must be dealt with as such, for [Palestine] contains Islamic holy places, [namely] the Al-Aqsa mosque, which is inseparably connected, for as long as heaven and earth shall endure, to the holy mosque of Mecca through the Prophet's nocturnal journey [from the mosque of Mecca to the Al-Aqsa mosque] and through his ascension to heaven thence. "Being stationed on the frontier for the sake of Allah for one day is better than this [entire] world and everything in it; and the place taken up in paradise by the [horseman's] whip of any one of you [jihad fighters] is better than this [entire] world and everything in it. Every evening [operation] and morning [operation] performed by Muslims for the sake of Allah is better than this [entire] world and everything in it." (Recorded in the Hadith collections of Bukhari, Muslim, Tirmidhi and Ibn Maja). "By the name of Him who holds Muhammad's soul in His hand, I wish to launch an attack for the sake of Allah and be killed and attack again and be killed and attack again and be killed." (Recorded in the Hadith collections of Bukhari and Muslim)

The quintessential jihadism and theological (including eschatological) Islamic Jew-hatred espoused in Al Azhar-trained Tantawi's *Banū Isrā'īl fī al-Qur'ān wa-al-sunnah*—a Ph.D. thesis which launched a career culminating in his leadership of this pre-eminent Sunni Islamic religious education center as Grand Imam of Al Azhar—is simply a far lengthier and more erudite elaboration of the identical Islamic religious animus directed at Jews, compendiously, and 20-years later, in the Hamas Covenant.

Tantawi invokes the same two central Qur'anic motifs of Jew-hatred featured in the Hamas Covenant:
—Qur'an 3:112 which consigns the Jews as "prophet killers," and overall "transgressors against the will of Allah," to permanent subjugation and humiliation, especially under Muslim rule; [574]
—Qur'an 5:64, which demonstrates the eternal predilection of the Jews to sow corruption and discord, validating, for example, the fraudulent modern Protocols of the Elders of Zion, that both Tantawi and the Hamas Covenant connect, seamlessly, to this Qur'anic verse. [575]

Banū Isrā'īl fī al-Qur'ān wa-al-sunnah and article 7 of the Hamas Covenant similarly reference Muhammad's canonical hadith of Jew annihilation reminding Muslims that the jihad against Jewish Israel is a sacralized imperative of Islam's broader eschatological—and genocidal—war against the Jews. [576] Finally, Tantawi and the Hamas Covenant advocate, vociferously, a real world military jihad by the entire global Muslim umma to destroy the modern State of Israel—a policide. [577] In fact, Tantawi's zealous jihadism vis-à-vis Israel was indistinguishable from the position taken four decades earlier by Muslim Brotherhood founder and ideologue Hasan al-Banna who insisted pre-empting, or destroying the establishment of Israel, was only achievable by Muslims "prepared to bear the burdens of a long-term jihad." [578]

<u>*Islam's Jew-Hating Canon Per Authoritative Muslim and Non-Muslim Scholars*</u>
Although the Qur'an's basic organizing principle across 114 chapters (or "suras"), is simply longer duration chapters to shorter duration chapters, absent any chronological, orienting narrative, the terse fatiha, chapter 1, is a glaring exception to this order. [579] Pious Muslims repeat the fatiha a total of 17 times daily during their requisite five prayers sessions. [580]

Muslims are directed on their appropriate, righteous path as set forth in the fatiha's initial six verses, but they are cautioned, at concluding verse 7, to follow "the path of those upon whom You (Allah) have bestowed favor (Islam), not of those who have evoked (Your) anger or of those who are astray." Islam's prophet Muhammad, in a canonical tradition (or hadith), clarified that it is the Jews who evoked Allah's anger and the Christians who went astray. [581] This clarifying interpretation is reinforced, with rare exceptions, by over 13 centuries of authoritative classical and modern Quranic commentaries which have glossed verse 1:7. [582]

The Qur'an: An Encyclopedia is a modern compendium of analyses written by 43 Muslim and non-Muslim mainstream academic experts, edited by Oliver Leaman, and published by Routledge. These excerpts serve as a "summary verdict" on how Muslims and non-Muslims, both, are to understand the Fatiha's last verse: [583]

> *"The Prophet (Muhammad) interpreted those who incurred God's [Allah's] wrath as the Jews and the misguided as the Christians. The Jews, we are told killed many of their prophets and through their character and materialistic tendencies (usurious 2:275, 4:161; greedy/hedonistic 2:96; envious 2:109; hard-hearted 2:74; liars 2:78) have contributed much to moral corruption, social upheaval and sedition in the world (5:32–33; 5:64) ... [T]hey were readily misled and incurred both God's [Allah's] wrath and ignominy (2:61; 2:90; 3:112). As for the Christians ... over time they succumbed to the influence of those who had already deviated from the chosen path (5:77)"*

Tantawi's passing reference to Q 1:7 in *Banū Isrā'īl fī al-Qur'ān wa-al-sunnah* is consistent with the predominant interpretation that the Jews have incurred Allah's anger. [584] His formal gloss on Q 1:7 in *The intermediate [balanced] interpretation of the Qur'an* reiterates this interpretation: [585]

> *"Those who have incurred Allah's anger are the Jews…This interpretation comes from Muhammad, in a tradition narrated by Imam Ahmad (ibn Hanbal) in his Musnad and Ibn Habban (al-Busti) in his Sahih. Some exegetes say those who have incurred Allah's anger [the Jews] knew the truth, but departed from it out of stubbornness and denial."*

As alluded to by many of the most authoritative glosses on Quran 1:7, [586] the Quran's overall discussion of the Jews is marked by a litany of their sins and punishments, as if part of a divine indictment, conviction, and punishment process. [587] The Jews wronged themselves (16:118) by losing faith (7:168) and breaking their covenant (5:13). The Jews (echoing an ante-Nicaean, Marcionite polemic) are a nation that has passed away (2:134; repeated in 2:141). Twice Allah sent his instruments (the Assyrians/or Babylonians, and Romans) to punish this perverse people (17:4-5)—their dispersal over the earth is proof of Allah's rejection (7:168). The Jews are further warned about both their arrogant claim that they remain Allah's chosen people (62:6), and continued disobedience and "corruption" (5:32-33; 5:64) Other sins, some repeated, are enumerated: abuse, even killing of prophets (4:155; 2:91), including Isa (Jesus) (3:55; 4:157), is a consistent theme. The Jews ridiculed Muhammad as Ra'ina (the evil one, in 2:104; 4:46), and they are also accused of lack of faith, taking words out of context, disobedience, and distortion (4:46). Precious few of them are believers (also 4:46). These "perverse" creatures claim that Ezra is the messiah and they worship rabbis who defraud men of their possessions (9:30). Additional sins are described: the Jews are typified as an "envious" people (2:109), whose hearts are as hardened as rocks (2:74). They are further accused of confounding the truth (2:42), deliberately perverting scripture (2:75), and being liars (2:78). Ill-informed people of little faith (2:89), they pursue vague and wishful fancies (2:111). Other sins have contributed to their being stamped (see 2:61/ 3:112) with "wretchedness/abasement and humiliation," including usury (2:275), sorcery (2:102), hedonism (2:96), and idol worship (2:53). More (and repeat) sins, are described: the Jews' idol worship is again mentioned (4:51), then linked and followed by charges of other (often repeat) iniquities—the "tremendous calumny" against Mary (4:156), as well as usury and cheating (4:161). Most Jews are accused of being "evil-livers" / "transgressors" / "ungodly" (3:110), who, deceived by their own lies (3:24), try to turn Muslims from Islam (3:99). Jews are blind and deaf to the truth (5:71), and what they have not forgotten they have perverted. They mislead (3:69), confound the truth (3:71), twist tongues (3:79), and cheat Gentiles without remorse (3:75). Muslims are advised not to take the Jews as friends (5:51), and to beware of the inveterate hatred that Jews bear towards them (5:82). The Jews' ultimate sin and punishment are made clear: they are the devil's minions (4:60) cursed by Allah, their faces will be obliterated (4:47) if they do not accept the true faith of Islam. The Jews who understand their faith become Muslims (3:113). Otherwise, they will be made into apes (2:65/ 7:166), or apes and swine (5:60), and burn in the Hell fires (4:55, 5:29, 98:6, and
58:14-19). [588]

Already by the mid-9th century, the renowned Muslim polymath of the Abbasid (Baghdad) Caliphate, al-Jahiz (d. 869), observed that Qur'an 5:82 ("You will surely find the most intense of the people in animosity toward the believers [to be] the Jews...") was the "most potent" cause of Muslim animus toward Jews, which greatly exceeded their hatred of Christians. [589]

This verse continues to shape Muslim attitudes towards Jews. Consider the modern glosses on Qur'an 5:82 two of the most important Qur'anic commentators of our era,

Shiite exegete Muhammad Husayn Tabatabai characterized earlier, [590] and his Sunni counterpart, Tantawi the subject of this Introduction, whose translation of his 1968 thesis *Banū Isrā'īl fī al-Qur'ān wa-al-sunnah*, is presented herein.

Here is Tabatabai's gloss on Qur'an 5:82—the central Qur'anic verse defining Islam's eternal attitudes towards Jews and Judaism—from *al-Mizan*: [591]

> *"...the Jews, they had their own scholars, no doubt; but they behaved proudly, and their arrogance and stubbornness did not let them be prepared for accepting the truth...Jews, although they had the same alternatives as the Christians, and they could retain their religion with payment of the jizya [Qur'anic poll tax, per verse 9:29], yet they continued in their haughtiness, became harder in their bigotry, and turned to double dealing and deception. They broke their covenants, eagerly waited calamities to befall the Muslims and dealt to them the bitterest deal...[T]he enmity of the Jews...toward the divine religion [Islam] and their sustained arrogance and bigotry, have continued exactly in the same manner even after the Prophet... These unchanged characteristics...confirm what the Mighty Book [the Qur'an] had indicated."*

Tabatabai further provides this general description of the Qur'anic portrayal of the Jews, beginning at Qur'an 2:40 to 2:44, and continuing for over a hundred verses thereafter: [592]

> *"Now begins the rebuking of the Jews that continues for more than a hundred verses. Allah reminds them of the bounties bestowed, of the honors given; contrasting it with their ingratitude and disobedience; showing how at every juncture they paid the favors of Allah with disregard of their covenant, open rebellion against divine commands and even with polytheism. The series reminds them of twelve events of their history — ... all of which shows how they were chosen to receive the especial favors of Allah. But their ingratitude runs parallel to it. They repeatedly broke the covenants made with Allah, committed capital sins, heinous crimes, and shameful deeds; more despicable was their spiritual poverty and moral bankruptcy — in open defiance to their book and total disregard for reason. It was all because their hearts were hardened, their souls lost and their endeavors worthless."*

Tantawi gloss on Qur'an 5:82 from this authoritative full Qur'anic commentary *The intermediate [balanced] interpretation of the Qur'an*, comports with Tabatabai's: [593]

> *"The Almighty's (Allah's) words, 'You will surely find the most intense of the people in animosity toward the believers to be the Jews"...is a statement that serves, in continuation, to reinforce other verses that preceded it, verses that documented the many despicable characteristics, and crooked and cunning ways of the Jews. The Almighty asserted—through linguistic devices—the content of the message entailed in the statement, and the addressee is the Prophet (Muhammad), and it can also be anyone who is entitled to preach to warn that their (the Jews) condition is no secret to anyone. Their enmity is*

rooted in envy, spite, stubbornness, and pride. Once these vices overcome the soul, it will not be able to find the way to the righteous path and the true religion (Islam)...The first object to His (Allah's) saying 'You will surely find,' is 'the most intense of the people.' The second object is 'the Jews.' Al-Alusi [594] *said that it is apparently the Jews in general that are meant here. That is to say, those who were in the presence of the Apostle (Muhammad) from the Jews of Medina, and others. This view is supported by the Apostle who said, 'Whenever a Jew is alone with a Muslim, he (the Jew) will strive to kill him (the Muslim).'* [595] *...It was said that one of the doctrines of the Jews is to cause harm to those who disagree with them in matters of religion by any means possible. Mentioning Jews before those who associate others with Allah is a declaration that they are more intense and far surpass the other group in their animosity (toward Muslims)."*

Islam conjoins such theological Jew-hatred—as expressed by Qur'an 5:82, its authoritative gloss, and myriad other Qur'anic verses, and related hateful motifs in the traditions of Islam's prophet Muhammad, and their interpretations—with the animus of the perpetual jihad war against Jews (and Christians/"scriptuaries"), to be waged (and renewed) until their complete submission to an Islamic, Sharia-based order. [596] Qur'an 9:29 elucidates this eternal jihad mandate, succinctly: [597]

"Fight those who do not believe in Allah or in the Last Day and who do not consider unlawful
what Allah and His Messenger have made unlawful and who do not adopt the religion of truth
(Islam) from those who were given the Scripture (Jews/other 'scriptuaries') - [fight] until they give the jizya (Qur'anic poll-tax, in lieu of being slain) willingly while they are humbled (such as the humiliating jizya collection 'rituals', blows, mock beheadings, etc.)."

Again, we can turn to the pre-eminent modern Qur'anic exegetes, Tabatabai and Tantawi, for definitive instruction on how Muslims are to understand Qur'an 9:29, today. These glosses on Qur'an 9:29, extracted, below, reiterate an overarching principle, established across a millennium of uniform commentary on this verse: [598] Jews (and other "scriptuaries," or "People of the Book," including Christians, and perhaps Zoroastrians) must be fought, subdued, and humbled because they constitute a chronic danger to an Islamic, Sharia-based society, and its mores. Tabatabai emphasizes the Jews'/scriptuaries' corrupting "lunacies" in the corporeal world, while Tantawi's gloss adds a comment on their "excruciatingly painful" punishment in the hereafter: [599]

(Tabatabai) "Regarding their characteristics that necessitate fighting them, as mentioned in the beginning of the verse, followed by them giving the jizya to uphold their protection [i.e., from renewal of the jihad war against them!], it informs [us] that the purpose of humiliating them is their submission to an Islamic lifestyle and to a righteous religious government within an Islamic society. They shall not be equal to Muslims nor stand out against with them as

an independent identity, free to express anything their souls feel like, nor to publicize the doctrines and activities invented by their lunacies that corrupt human societies. This all relates to them handing over money from their hands out of a contemptible position. So the meaning of the verse (and Allah knows best) is: Fight the People of the Book who do not [truly] believe in Allah or in the Last Day, with a faith that is acceptable and uncorrupted from being proper, and who do not forbid what is forbidden in Islam namely those [crimes] that, when committed, corrupt human society, and who do not abide by a religion that conforms with the divine creation. Fight them and persist in fighting them until they are humbled among you and submit to your rule."

(Tantawi) "The reasons for the order to fight them are: they do not believe in Allah and the Last Day, they do not prohibit what Allah and His Messenger [Muhammad] have prohibited, and they do not adopt the religion of truth (Islam)...The meaning is fight those who have these attributes from among the People of the Scripture until they pay the jizya willingly and submissively (while) they are humbled, humiliated and subservient to your rule over them...Taking the jizya from them...is also a way of contributing to the advancement and prosperity of the Islamic state...It is an acknowledgement on their behalf to submit to the instructions of this state...Those who do not believe in Allah and the Last Day, those who do not prohibit what Allah and His Apostle [Muhammad] have prohibited, and who do not adopt the religion of truth (i.e., Islam) as their religion deserve this humiliation and ignominy in this world. As for the afterlife, their torture would be excruciatingly painful and everlasting."

Seminal analyses by non-Muslim scholars published in 1940, 1937, and the mid-1880s, anticipated the subsequent, independent conclusions of Muslim religious authorities Tabatabai and Tantawi. [600]

Professor Moshe Perlmann (1905-2001) was a meticulous scholar of Arabic and Islam, whose research focus was the Medieval religious polemic, especially Islam's anti-Jewish and anti-Christian tracts. [601] [105] Perlmann rejected the fatuous notion—still regnant today—that Arab Muslim Antisemitism was somehow a modern European export to the Islamic Middle East (and Islamdom, more broadly). Here is his rather understated debunking of that meme, written in 1955: [602]

..."neither the popular attitude nor the Arab literary heritage are exactly favorable to the Jew. **A goodly layer of derogatory notions, contempt and misgivings antedates the penetration of Western Jew-baiting**. *The sunnah foundations (i.e., traditions of Muhammad and the nascent Muslim community, which, along with the Koran, formed the basis for Islamic law) may have 'clearly defined' the infidel's position (i.e., as debased, and humiliated but at least 'protected' from a resumption of jihad war)...However, this definition never deterred the people and the legislators throughout the centuries from questioning again and again the rights of the infidel to buildings for worship,*

> *the holding of office, amenities of everyday life.* ***In agitated times sunnah could not prevent Jew-baiting riots; in normal or static periods to eliminate either its own outlook—social disqualification and humiliation for the infidel—or the masses' guarded, suspicious, and negative attitude.*** *"*

But it was Perlmann's compendious discussion of Islam's theological animus towards Jews which may be **his most remarkable contribution**. He wrote a chapter entitled, "The Jews in the Koran and the Traditions," within his 1940 PhD thesis, *"A Study of Muslim Polemics Directed Against Jews,"* which stands as a permanent testament to his informed intellectual honesty. Here are key extracts from that discussion: [603]

> *[Jews in the Koran]*
> *"Forgetting the Divine Dispensation, the Jews transgressed God's commandments and flouted the prophets, and even slew them (3:181). Therefore, many punishments fell upon them (2:61); e.g., some of them were turned into apes for desecrating the sabbath (2:65; 7:166). Muhammad came to confirm their scriptures (3:3; 4:51), but they did not accept him. They concealed the revelation (2:42; 3:71), or did not understand it (2:78); they tried to mislead people (3:69; 3:99), having no compunction about deceiving the pagan Arabs (3:69). Therefore, although they knew from their books all about Muhammad 'as they knew their own children,' (2:146), they made false statements about the scriptures (4:51; 5:49) distorting the texts. In contradiction to them, the Prophet declares that Ibrahim [Abraham] and Ismail [Ishmael] were Muslim prophets (2:124; 3:67; 3:68), who built the Meccan temple (2:125; 3:97) before the revelation of Musa [Moses], to which the Jews refer. Thus, Islam is the original revelation. This cuts the ground from under the feet of the unbelievers. They make blasphemous statements: That God's hand is chained up (5:64); that Uzair [Ezra] is the son of God (9:30). At the same time, they are stubborn in their opposition to the true prophet. They must be regarded as enemies (3:28; 5:51; 5:57). The believers will find that they are their fiercest enemies, the Christians being much more friendly (***5:82***). Therefore, after they had rejected many friendly overtures (2:59; 5:81), it was decided that they must be fought against, made tributaries, and compelled to pay poll-tax, as a mark of their humiliation (***9:29***)...In the Fatiha [i.e.,* **1:7***], the words* **al-maghdub alayhim ('those who earned Your (Allah's) anger')** *are supposed to refer to the Jews."*
>
> *[Jews in the Traditions]*
> *"Persisting in their obduracy, they did not shrink from plotting, practicing sorcery and poisoning, until they were finally crushed and driven out of Arabia. The Jews extended their hatred of the Prophet to all Muslims. They mispronounced the usual "Peace be unto you", so that it came to mean: "Poison be upon you"; for which reason it is wiser and safer to reply with a mere: "The same to you"...They always try to trick the unsuspecting Muslim. To imitate them is positively forbidden...* **They became, in a way, the incarnation of evil.** *No wonder that, when the world comes to an end, and when Dajjal [the Muslim Antichrist] threatens to destroy those of the true faith, the Jews will be betrayed*

*in their hiding-places even by the crying of the rock: 'Here is a Jew behind me. Kill him.' (*Sahih Muslim, Book 41, Number 6985)"

Georges Vajda (1908-1981) was considered the "dean of European scholars of Judaica," who dedicated a considerable part of his scholarly activities to the study of the relationships between Islam and Judaism. [604] Vajda's 70pp. 1937 essay "Juifs et Musulmans Selon Le Hadit" ("Jews and Muslims According to the Hadith"), was a singularly comprehensive, defining study of the subject. [605] Vajda demonstrated that stubborn malevolence is the Jews defining worldly characteristic in these traditions. Rejecting Muhammad and refusing to convert to Islam out of jealousy, envy, and even selfish personal interest, lead them to acts of treachery, in keeping with their inveterate nature: **"…sorcery, poisoning, assassination held no scruples for them."** These archetypes sanction Muslim hatred towards the Jews, and the admonition to at best, **"subject [the Jews] to Muslim domination"**—Jewish dhimmis, treated "with contempt," under certain "humiliating arrangements." [606] As alluded to earlier, [607] Vajda's research on the hadith described how Sunni Muslim eschatology highlighted Jewish hatred toward Islam. Jews are adherents of the Dajjâl—the Muslim equivalent of the Antichrist, and the Dajjâl, per other traditions, is identified as Jewish. When the Dajjâl is defeated, his Jewish companions will be slaughtered—everything will reveal them to the Muslims except for the so-called gharqad tree. Thus, according to several canonical hadith, Muhammad himself reportedly declared if a Jew seeks refuge under a tree or a stone, these objects will be able to speak to tell a Muslim: "There is a Jew behind me; come and kill him!" Vajda also emphasizes how the notion of jihad war "ransom" extends even into Islamic eschatology: [608]

> *"Not only are the Jews vanquished in the eschatological war, but they will serve as ransom for the Muslims in the fires of hell. The sins of certain Muslims will weigh on them like mountains, but on the day of resurrection, these sins will be lifted and laid upon the Jews."*

Hartwig Hirschfeld (1854-1934) was a renowned scholar of Semitic languages, the Qur'an, Hebrew-Arabic literature, and the relationship between Jewish and Arab culture. [609] [113] Hirschfeld's detailed analysis of Muhammad's interactions with the Jews, "Essai sur l'histoire des Juifs de Medine" ("Essay on the History of the Jews of Medina"), as noted earlier, reminded us of the "mutual disappointment" that characterized their encounters, and the predictably disastrous results for the Jews. [610] As also discussed previously, Georges Vajda, in turn, recounted the theological animus which motivated Muhammad's political subjugation of the Jews, specifically, and became an indelible part of Muslim attitudes toward Jews across space and time. [611]

Two Muslim canonical source examples from the earliest pious Muslim biographies of Muhammad, the sira of Ibn Ishaq (d. 761) and Ibn Saad (d. 845), [612] illustrate the dark themes summarized by Vajda and Hirschfeld.

According to these sira, Muhammad used the Qur'anic epithets "apes/monkeys," and/or "pigs" (per Qur'an 2:65, **7:166,** 5:60) to characterize the Qurayza tribe Jewish victims of his jihadist campaign (allegedly in 627), whose males Muhammad himself subsequently beheaded. Just prior to orchestrating the en masse execution of the adult males from the besieged Medinan Jewish tribe (and distributing their women, children, and possessions as slave "booty" for the Muslims), Muhammad, per his earliest Muslim biographer, Ibn Ishaq addressed these Jews with menacing, hateful derision: [613] *"You brothers of monkeys, has Allah disgraced you and brought His vengeance upon you?"* Ibn Sa'd [d. 845] **reported** that Muhammad stated, [614] *"brothers of monkeys and pigs, fear me, fear me!"* Here is Ibn Ishaq's description of Muhammad's mass beheading of the surrendered Banu Qurayza males: [615]

> *"When they (the men, including post-pubescent boys, of the Jewish tribe) surrendered,* ***and the apostle (Muhammad) confined them in Medina*** *in the quarter of d. al-Harith, a woman of B. Al-Najjar.* ***Then the apostle went out to the market of Medina (which is still its market today) and dug trenches in it.*** *Then* ***he sent for them and struck off their heads in those trenches as they were brought out to him in batches****. Among them was the enemy of Allah Huyayy b. Akhtab and Ka'b b. Asad their chief. There were 600 or 700 in all, though some put the figure as high as 800 or 900. As they were being taken out in batches to the apostle they asked Ka'b what he thought would be done with them. He replied, 'Will you never understand? Don't you see that the summoner never stops and those who are taken away do not return? By Allah it is death!'* ***This went on until the apostle made an end of them****."*

As recounted by the venerated early 20th century scholar of Islam's origins, David Margoliouth, within a year after the massacre of the Banu Qurayza, Muhammad waited for some act of aggression on the part of the Jews of Khaybar, whose fertile lands and villages he had destined for his followers, to furnish an excuse for an attack. But no such opportunity offering, he resolved in the autumn of that year (i.e., 628), on a sudden and unprovoked invasion of their territory. Ali (later, the fourth "Rightly Guided Caliph", and especially revered by Shiite Muslims) asked Muhammad why the Jews of Khaybar were being attacked, since they were peaceful farmers, tending their oasis, and was told by Muhammad he must compel them to submit to Islamic Law. Thus, Margoliouth, observed aptly, [616]

> *"Now the fact that a community was idolatrous, or Jewish, or anything but Mohammedan, warranted a murderous attack upon it."*

In the aftermath of Muhammad's murderous jihad conquest of Khaybar's Jews, Ibn Sa'd's sira recorded the ostensible "Jewish conspiracy"—orchestrated by the surviving prototype Jewish dhimmis—resulting in Muhammad's poisoning, protracted illness, and eventual death several years later. Per Ibn Sa'd's "approved version" of events: [617]

> *"When the Apostle of Allah, may Allah bless him, conquered Khaybar...Zaynab Bint al-Harith...inquired: Which part of the goat is liked by Muhammad? They said: The foreleg. Then she slaughtered one from her goats and roasted it (the meat). Then she wanted a poison which could not fail. The Jews discussed about*

poisons and became united on one poison. She poisoned the she-goat, putting more poison on the forelegs and shoulder. When the sun had set and the Apostle of Allah, may Allah bless him, returned after leading the people in Maghrib (sunset) prayers, she sat by his feet...She said, ... 'here is a present which I wish to for you...The Prophet ordered it to be taken. It was served to him and his Companions who were present...The Apostle of Allah took the foreleg, a piece of which he put into his mouth...Then the Apostle of Allah said: 'Hold back your hands!' 'Because this foreleg,' and according to another version, 'the shoulder of the goat has informed me that it was poisoned.'... The Apostle of Allah sent for Zaynab Bint al-Harith and said to her: 'What induced you to do what you have done?' She replied: 'What you have done to my people. You have killed my father, my uncle, and my husband, so I said to myself: If you are a prophet, the foreleg will inform you; and others have said: If you are a king we will get rid of you.'...He (Ibn Sa'd) said: 'The Apostle of Allah, may Allah bless him, handed her over to the heirs of Bishr ibn al-Barra (who was also poisoned, and died), who put her to death... The Apostle of Allah, lived three years after this, till as a consequence of his pain, he passed away. During his illness he used to say: I did not cease to find the effect of the (poisoned) morsel I took at Khaybar, and I suffered several times (from its effect)..."

<u>*Jihad and Jew-Hatred Sanctioned by Authoritative Islam After October 7, 2023*</u>

Beginning mere hours after the October 7, 2023 attacks, Al-Azhar University—its Grand Imam Ahmed al-Tayeb, leading ancillary clerics, and formal "Fatwa (religious edict) Committee"—sanctioned and celebrated Hamas' jihad carnage, on Al-Azhar's social media platforms. [618] During October 7th itself, ignoring Hamas' precipitating murderous atrocities, which were not mentioned at all, and well before the Israel Defense Forces' counter-offensive in Gaza, Al-Azhar, with al-Tayeb's imprimatur, declared officially: [619]

> *"Al-Azhar salutes with utmost pride the resistance efforts of the proud Palestinian people...Al-Azhar supports the hearts and hands of the proud Palestinian people who have imbued us with spirit and faith and restored us to life, after we thought that would never happen, and prays that Allah grant them steadfastness, peace of mind and strength."*

Muhammad Omar Al-Qady, dean of the Faculty for Islamic and Arabic Studies at Al-Azhar University, addressed Hamas' October 7th attacks in posts on his personal Facebook account October 17 and 18, 2023. He praised the Hamas attackers and longed for the liquidation of the Jews, whom he called "the descendants of apes and pigs (Qur'an 5:60)." Al-Qady's October 17, 2023 post intoned: [620]

> *"[When I say] resistance I mean the jihad fighters in Palestine, who defend their honor and land, those who fight against their enemy and ours, namely the Jews... I ask Allah to strengthen His soldiers and His camp and grant our brothers in Gaza, in Palestine and in the rest of the Muslim countries victory*

> *over their enemy and ours, the enemy of Allah and humanity, the cursed descendants of apes and pigs [i.e., the Jews]."*

Referencing additional Qur'anic condemnations of Jews, Al-Qady wrote on October 18, 2023: [621]

> *"Allah, bring perdition upon the cursed (Qur'an 5:78) and treacherous (Jews), the murderers of prophets (Qur'an 2:61, 3:112)..."*

Abbas Shuman, current inspector general of Al-Azhar's Fatwa committees, at his Facebook account, October 7, 2023, expressed support for Hamas' terror attack earlier that day, and on October 18, 2023 "rejoiced" over "the demise of the descendants of apes and pigs." [622]

October 18-19, 2023, Al-Azhar's "Global Center for Online Fatwas" issued a formal religious ruling declaring that all Israelis, including non-combatants, were legitimate targets of jihad terror. Specifically, it claimed, "the term 'civilians' does not apply to the Zionist settlers of the occupied land." [623] This sentiment is entirely consistent with the Islamic legal logic of Al Azhar fatwas, or the resolutions of Al-Azhar Conference Proceedings, issued since immediately after the 1947 United Nations Partition Plan, during Israel's 1948 War of Independence, prior to the 1956 Sinai War, before the 1967 Six-Day War, and at The Fourth Conference of the Academy of Islamic Research, September, 1968. [624]

That "Islamic legal logic" has always been rooted in jihad, and sacralized Islamic Jew-hatred. Reconsider, briefly, the complementary fatwas issued in January, 1956, discussed earlier by Egypt's then Grand Mufti, and the heads of Al-Azhar's four schools of Islamic jurisprudence, as well as the six key resolutions from Al-Azhar's 1968 Fourth Conference of the Academy of Islamic Research. The two 1956 fatwas were written January 5, 1956, by Egyptian Grand Mufti Sheikh Hasan Mamoun, and January 9, 1956, by the leading members of the Fatwa Committee of Al Azhar, representing all four Sunni Islamic schools of jurisprudence. These rulings elaborated the following key initial point: that **all of historical Palestine**—modern Jordan, Israel, and the disputed territories of Judea and Samaria, as well as Gaza—having been conquered by jihad, was a permanent possession of the global Muslim *umma* (community)—"fay territory," booty or spoils—to be governed eternally by Islamic law. This jihad ideology was conjoined to conspiratorial Muslim Jew-hatred. [625]

A year after Israel's decisive victory during the 1967 war, [626] Al-Azhar convened the 4th Conference of the Academy of Islamic Research in Cairo, which assembled prominent Muslim theologians not only from the Middle East, but Asia, Africa, and Europe. [627] This seminal Conference, marked the formal abandonment of pseudo-secular "Arab Nationalism" [628] as a guiding ideological rationale for the simmering conflict with Israel. Published in English as a 935pp. tome in 1970, the Conference Proceedings were the subject of historian David Littman's pioneering analysis, in 1971. Littman summarized the Conference's six key "recurring themes," as follows: [629]

1) "Jews are frequently denoted as the 'Enemies of Allah'"
2) "Jews manifest in themselves an historical continuity of evil qualities...as described in the Qur'an"
3) "The Jews do not constitute a true people or nation"
4) "The State of Israel is the culmination of the historical and cultural depravity of the Jews...It has to be destroyed by a Jihad"
5) "The superiority of Islam over all other religions is brandished as a guarantee that the Arabs will ultimately triumph"
6) "It is outrageous for the Jews, traditionally kept by Arab Islam in a humiliated, inferior status, and characterized as cowardly, to defeat the Arabs, have their own State, and cause the contraction of the 'abode of Islam'"

Littman concluded plaintively, over 50 years ago, Al Azhar was then promoting ideas which, [630]

> *"...lead to the urge to liquidate Israel, politicide, and the Jews, genocide. If the evil of the Jews is immutable and permanent, transcending time and circumstances, and impervious to all hopes of reform, there is only one way to cleanse the world of them—by their complete annihilation."*

Current Al-Azhar Grand Imam Ahmed al-Tayeb embodies that living legacy of annihilationist
Jew-hatred. [631]

Each year, The Royal Islamic Strategic Studies Center (RISSC)—a pre-eminent avatar of interfaith dialogue, and mainstream, "moderate Islam," issues its annual rankings of "The World's 500 Most Influential Muslims." Al-Tayeb, was the number 1 ranked Muslim figure for 2017 in "The Muslim 500". His "The Muslim 500" profile stated, [632]

> *"Influence: Highest scholarly authority for the majority of Sunni Muslims, runs the foremost and largest Sunni Islamic university. School of Thought: Traditional Sunni"*

Notwithstanding his 2017 lionization by the RISSC, as Egypt's Grand Mufti, and since 2010, till now, Al Azhar Grand Imam, Al-Tayeb has sanctioned homicide bombing murder of Israeli Jews, including non-combatants, [633] and twice publicly condemned Jews, eternally, while invoking Qur'an 5:82—a central Antisemitic verse—for causing *"Muslim distress...since the inception of Islam 1400 years ago."* [634] He has also accused "Global Zionism" (Jews) of midwifing ISIS, and related jihad terror groups, to *"destroy the Middle East,"* [635] and claimed the "Zionist entity," i.e., Israel, was plotting to *"march on the Kaaba (in Mecca) and on the Prophet's Mosque (in Medina). This is on their minds and in their hearts."* [636]

The RISSC's top ranking for 2024 was bestowed upon Yemeni theologian Habib Umar bin Hafiz, *"one of the foremost scholars, spiritual guides, and preachers within the*

Islamic tradition today," whose direct influence extends to *"hundreds of millions of Muslims around the globe."*[637]

October 10, 2023 23, ignoring the precipitating murderous brutality wrought by Hamas just 3-days earlier, and anticipating Israel's understandable defensive response, bin Hafiz launched into a diatribe against Jews employing standard Qur'anic motifs of sacralized Jew-hatred, "spreading corruption" (Q 5:33; 5:64), and "propagating falsehood" (Q 3:75; 5:41). He further invoked Qur'an 41:15 condemning Israel's/the Jews' "arrogance", "without right", and threatening Allah's retribution. Illustrating Islam's religious supersession and negation of Judaism (and Christianity), bin Hafiz intoned, *"They do not belong to our Master Moses, nor our master Jesus, nor our master Muhammad. They have falsely claimed a connection to Moses."* Habib Umar bin Hafiz concluded his diatribe with a genocidal declaration, repeating the canonical tradition of Jew-annihilation featured in Hamas' Covenant, article 7: *"When one of them seeks refuge under a tree and stone, the trees and the stones will cry out, 'Oh Muslim, Oh servant of Allah! Behind me is a Jew, come and kill him.' This was repeated by the most truthful of people. No doubt that day will surely come."* [638]

In follow-up pronouncements issued 10/21/23 and 11/1/23, bin Hafiz denied there was any evidence Palestinian Muslims killed Israeli children on October 7th (notwithstanding gruesome video and forensic findings, confirmed by captured Hamas jihadists), contended the Jews were *"even more debased than insects and animals* (Q 2:26; 98:6)," reiterated the Jews/*"Zionist oppressors"* sought only *"corruption on earth* (Q 5:33; 5:64)," and claimed those among them who died, like (the ancient Egyptian) Pharoah and his minions, are burning in Hell (Q 40:46). [639]

Finally, bin Hafiz's later, lengthier pronouncement (on 12/15/23) repeated the charge that Jews/Zionists fuel discord and corruption, and claimed they lie and deceive in a manner that *"is more disgusting and foul than people realize,"* before insisting all Muslims have always been the target of the Jews' conspiratorial treachery: [640]

> *"The war they wage is the same type of war from the very beginning [of Islam]. It is a war born of hatred (Q 5:82)...You are their target. Your religion [Islam] is their target. Their aim is to destroy the Islamic laws! Their aim is to claim the earth is theirs! It is hostility towards Muhammad...It is hatred toward his divine message and revelation...It is hatred towards companions, pure family, and his Ummah (entire Muslim community). It is hatred towards the laws of the religion [Islam]...[The Jews are] the leadership of disbelief on the earth! 'If they attack your faith, fight the leaders of disbelief. They never honor their oaths, so fight them (Q 9:12).'...They killed prophets (Q 2:61; 2:91: 3:112; 3:181). They have been doing this from the very beginning...So what do you expect from them? 'Hatred has become evident from their mouths (3:118)'...'If good befalls you it grieves them, and if harm afflicts you, they rejoice (Q 3:120).'"*

<u>*Jihad and Jew-Hatred Preached Openly in U.S Mosques After October 7, 2023*</u>

Mansour Al-Hadj is Director of the Middle East Research Institute Project for Reform in the Arab and Muslim World. Despite his own apologetic interpretation of canonical Islam, after studying "hundreds of Friday mosque sermons" across the U.S. since October 7, 2023 he acknowledged, [641]

> *"...almost all the sermons seemed to share similar themes in their framing of the attack, amplifying a single narrative which justifies Hamas's attack as a legitimate act that is based on the command of Allah and the teachings of the prophet Muhammad. Therefore, they did not condemn or hold Hamas responsible for killing and abducting civilians, including children and the elderly, and sexually assaulting several women. They did not condemn Hamas for starting a war, miscalculating Israel's response, using the Gazans as human shields, or causing the death of thousands of Palestinians and the destruction of large areas of Gaza. Instead, in their sermons, these preachers and imams focused on highlighting the similarities between Hamas' attack and the wars fought by the prophet and his companions, demonizing Israel, narrating historical antisemitic stories attributed to the prophet Muhammad, founder of Islam, such as the hadith about the stones and the Gharqad Tree, and citing verses from the Qur'an that characterized Jews as corrupt, treacherous, untrustworthy, and the killers of prophets."*

Three examples of this preaching are presented in summary, and chronological order.

Gambian born Imam Alhagie Jallow, completed his memorization of the Qur'an while studying in Senegal, and later studied at the Islamic University of Imam Muhammad bin Saud in Riyadh, Saudi Arabia. He became the Imam of the Masjid Us-Sunnah shortly after his visit to Madison, Wisconsin, in 2009. Less than a week after October 7th (on 10/13/23), he delivered this annihilationist diatribe during a sermon: [642]

> *"The only thing that can bring glory to this Islamic nation is the Jihad, which is mentioned in the Quran and the hadiths (traditions) of the Prophet Muhammad. The only thing that can bring honor and glory to this nation is Jihad... Oh Jews, you unjust, criminal, corrupt oppressors – stop! You will all most definitely be killed. The Jews, the aggressors, the evil... You describe them, what they do. By Allah, all of them [Jews] will be killed by Muslims. They all will be executed by Muslims. They will all be killed, this is a divine promise (likely referencing the hadith in the Hamas Covenant, article 7) that will inevitably be fulfilled. This is a promise from Allah and it is going to happen. They will all be killed. They will all be killed, and on that day, the believers will rejoice in Allah's victory."*

Imam Umar Mitchell of Masjid Umar Ibn Al-Khattab in Aurora, Colorado taught a Qur'anic lesson to primary school age children at the Colorado Muslims Community Center, October 22, 2023, outlining for his young audience central indelible, pejorative characteristics of the Jews as depicted in the Qur'an. He intoned that the Jews are inveterate liars (Qur'an 2:10; 3:75) who never abide their contracts and covenants (Q 2:61; 3:112; 4:155; 5:13), murdered their prophets (Q 2:61; 3:112; 3:181; 4:155), and even attempted to murder Jesus (actually "Isa," a decidedly non-Christian "Muslim Jesus," Q 4:157). Imam Mitchell also recounted the Qur'anic story of Jewish fishermen who were allegedly transformed by Allah into "literal physical monkeys" for fishing on Saturday (2;65; but elaborated in 7:163 , 7:164; 7:165, 7:166; again, verse 5:60 refers to the Jews as "apes and pigs"). The good imam concluded that not all Jews are as despicable as their portrayal in the Qur'an but consistent with Qur'an **3:113**, he asserted only *"a couple of them"* aren't. [643]

During a Friday sermon in suburban Dallas, Texas, on 12/29/23, Ghaith Arodaki, an entrepreneur and recent graduate of San Jose State University, serving as "guest imam," declared, [644]

> *"Every single day, we recite the Al-Fatiha (opening) chapter of the Qur'an five times a day, and at the end (Qur'an 1:7), we recite: 'Guide us along the Straight Path, the Path of those You have blessed—not those who have incurred Your wrath, or those who were misguided.' The interpreters explained this verse to mean three categories of people: 'Those who You have blessed,' and they said it means the Muslims.* **'Those who have incurred Your wrath.' 'Those that You have cursed,' they said it [is] meant to be the Jews.** *'Those who were misguided,' and it was said to be the Christians."*

As described earlier, Arodaki's interpretation of Qur'an 1:7 is in accord with the gloss of Islam's prophet Muhammad, from a canonical tradition *(at-Tirmidhi, Vol. 5, Book 44, Hadith 2954),* and the formal exegeses of 90% of classical and modern authoritative Qur'anic commentaries, Sunni and Shiite alike. [645]

Finally, an ominous threshold may have been crossed on Tuesday, February 18, 2025. On that evening, hordes of Muslims marched into the largest U.S. orthodox Jewish—not "Zionist" neighborhood—Boro Park Brooklyn, openly calling for Jew-annihilation targeting "Zionists," who in their parlance are interchangeable with Jews. In the middle of the street, a Muslim leader took to the microphone and bellowed: [646]

> *"Oh Allah, annihilate the plundering Zionists. Oh Allah, annihilate the criminal Zionists. Oh Allah, kill them one by one, count them one by one, and do not leave a single one of them."*

Can Islam Follow the Path of Those the Qur'an Claims (Q 1;7, 5:77) "Went Astray," i.e., Christians?: A Nostre Aetate/Vatican II Model For Islam

Ignoring his own public fulminations espousing blatant Jew-hatred, present Al Azhar Grand Imam Ahmed al-Tayyeb, in 2018, denied the very existence of antisemitism, *claiming, "the issue of antisemitism is a lie that continues to deceive nations to this day."* [647] *The context of this denial was even more bitterly ironic. Al-Tayyeb's comments were made in concert with his vehement rejection of an appeal from French public intellectuals, following two brutal murders of elderly French Jewish women by Jew-hating French Muslims, that* [648]

"Qur'anic verses calling to kill and punish Jews, Christians and non-believers be declared obsolete by the theological authorities – just as the inconsistencies of the Bible and Catholic antisemitism were abolished by the Second Vatican Council (in 1962-1965) – so that no believer can rely on a sacred text to commit a crime."

Over the long term, Islam must undergo Vatican II analogous reforms, and that process should begin immediately.

During 1947, in the aftermath of World War II and the Holocaust, the International Emergency Conference on Antisemitism took place in Seelisberg, Switzerland. Its aim was to combat the roots of the antisemitism still rampant in many countries despite the fall of National Socialist (Nazi) rule. Its objective, within this context, was also to address Christian anti-Judaism and help establish a new relationship between Christianity and Judaism. [649] At Seelisberg, the French Jewish historian and Holocaust survivor, Jules Isaac, admonished his contemporaries to confront Christianity's antisemitic New Testament theology—especially what the leading New Testament commentaries, and commentators glossed—circulating his book manuscript *Jésus et Israël* (*Jesus and Israel*), [650] Isaac argued that, [651]

"In the Christian's eyes, the Gospels are inspired texts. They are nonetheless texts set down by the hand of man, and for that reason necessarily subject to the laws of criticism, textual, literary, historical, which no exegesis, even the most orthodox, may evade."

The 21 propositions, around which Isaac had organized his book, directly inspired the Ten Points of Seelisberg. This statement adjured Christians to recall that Jesus and his first disciples were Jewish, and that Christ's directive to love one's neighbor applied to all peoples, including Jews. Christians must therefore refrain from speaking of Jews collectively as "enemies of Christ," killers of Christ, or accursed by God as punishment for deicide. Isaac, working with willing Christian colleagues (including direct appeals to Pope Pius XII and Pope John XXIII), thus helped catalyze a movement culminating in the Second Vatican Council, whose deliberations begot the declaration *Nostra Aetate* (1965), an unprecedented, mea culpa-based document text that would entirely alter Christian-Jewish relations. [652]

Vatican II/Nostre Aetate, as illustrated by a sentence from the pronouncement issued October 28, 1965, unambiguously condemned antisemitism, from The Church's perspective: [653]

"Moreover, mindful of her common patrimony with the Jews, and motivated by the gospel's spiritual love and by no political considerations, she deplores the hatred, persecution, and displays of antisemitism directed against the Jews at any time, and from any source."

Catholic Theologian John T. Pawlikowski, observed in 1996 (from the essay collection, appositely entitled, "Removing Anti-Judaism from the Pulpit"), that the noble ideals articulated in the October 28, 1965 pronouncement were only advanced when The Vatican Council, [654]

> *… "formally launched the process of uprooting the classic theology of Jewish displacement from the covenant in light of the Christ event and replaced it with a theological work based on the notion of the ongoing validity of the Jewish covenant to which Christians have been joined."*

The "Phase I cleansing" stage in this overall process, as Dr. Pawlikowski characterized it, involved, [655]

> *"… the removal from mainline Christian educational texts of the charge that Jews collectively were responsible for the death of Jesus, that the Pharisees were the arch enemies of Jesus and spiritually soulless, that Jews had been displaced by Christians in the covenantal relationship with God as a result of refusal to accept Jesus as the Messiah, that the Old Testament was totally inferior to the New and that Jewish faith was rooted in legalism while the Christian religion was based on grace."*

Indeed by 1995, current St. Joseph's University Professor Philip Cunningham's study "Education for Shalom: Religion Textbooks and the Enhancement of the Catholic-Jewish Relationship," noted that, [656]

> *"… the elements of the patristic anti-Judaic theological system had pretty much been eliminated from the textbooks."*

Judging from the angry rejection of the inchoate 2018 French appeal to authoritative Islam to eliminate Qur'anic Jew-, and other non-Muslim hatred, invoking Nostre Aetate/Vatican II, there is no cause, at present, for any optimism that Islam's major religious teaching centers will soon begin their own desperately needed process to remove canonical Islamic antisemitism from the minbar. [657] However, we must still hope that non-Muslim religious and civic leaders, notably Jews, will redouble their efforts, overcome their timorous, stifling cultural relativism, and demand such a momentous Islamic initiative as Jules Isaac did of the Catholic Church. Isaac, it must be remembered, refused to be dissuaded by the mealy-mouthed "nonconfrontational" arguments of his era: [658]

> *"I am told that I would do better to devote myself to some constructive task: rather than denounce the teaching of contempt, why not initiate the teaching of respect? But the two ends are inseparable. It is impossible to combat the teaching of contempt and its modern survivals, without thereby laying the foundations for the teaching of respect; and, conversely, it is impossible to*

establish the teaching of respect, without first destroying the remnants of contempt. Truth cannot be built upon error."

References

[a.] Moshe Perlmann. Proceedings of the American Academy for Jewish Research, 1964, Vol. 32, *Samau'al Al-Maghribī Ifḥām Al-Yahūd: Silencing the Jews* (1964), p. 19. Professor Moshe Perlmann (1905-2001) was a meticulous scholar of Arabic and Islam, with great fluency in not only Arabic and Hebrew, but also Russian (having been born in Odessa), and German, as well as further written proficiency in Persian, Syriac, French and Italian. The focus of Perlmann's work was the Medieval religious polemic, especially Islam's anti-Jewish and anti-Christian tracts. Unearthing and providing unique annotated translations of pathognomonic texts (catalogued here: Sabine Schmidtke. "Moshe Perlmann (1905-2001): a bibliography." *JERUSALEM STUDIES IN ARABIC AND ISLAM*, 2009, Vol. 36, pp. 33-61), with insightful commentary, Perlmann, as obituarist Herbert A. Dawson, observed, allowed the original writings, "to speak for themselves," leaving readers "to draw whatever moral they can." (Herbert A, Dawson. "Moshe Perlmann, Near Eastern Languages and Cultures: Los Angeles," in, *University of California: In Memoriam, 2001*, Micki Conklin, Editor, pp. 209-211.)

[b.] Saul S. Friedman. *Without future: the plight of Syrian Jewry*, Praeger, New York, 1989, p. 7.; "In Memoriam: Saul S. Friedman, 1937–2013." *Holocaust and Genocide Studies*, Volume 27, Number 2, Fall 2013, p. 384. https://doi.org/10.1093/hgs/dct034 Regarded as a "pillar of both the academic and Jewish communities," Professor Friedman (1937-2013) published broadly on the Middle East, antisemitism, Jewish oppression, and the Holocaust, in particular. Three of Friedman's books focused on the Middle East: *Land of Dust* (1982), *Without Future* (1989), and *A History of the Middle East* (2006).

[c.] *Akher Sa'a* (Egypt), November 20, 2002, translated and cited in, "Arab Press Debates Antisemitic Egyptian Series 'Knight Without a Horse'- Part III," *The Middle East Media Research Institute,* Egypt—Inquiry & Analysis Series No. 114, December 10, 2002 https://www.memri.org/reports/arab-press-debates-antisemitic-egyptian-series-knight-without-horse-part-iii#_edn4

[d.] "Sheik of Al-Azhar Muhammad Sayyed Tantawi Appalled after Newspaper Depicted Him in Christian Garb," *The Middle East Media Research Institute*, October 3, 2008, #1928 https://www.memri.org/tv/sheik-al-azhar-muhammad-sayyed-tantawi-appalled-after-newspaper-depicted-him-christian-garb

[e.] H. I. Gwarzo, "The Life and Teachings of al- Maghili with Particular Reference to the Saharan Jewish Community," (PhD diss., University of London, 1972), p. 134. Al-Maghili (1440–1503/1505). A theologian/jurist of Tlemcen, known for his persecution of the Jewish community of Tuwåt [Touat] in the Algerian Sahara and for the advice he gave to Sudanic rulers. He wrote a treatise which maintained that the Jews of Tuwåt had broken their pact with the Muslims, and thus forfeited their protection, by not paying *jizya* regularly in a state of "abasement and humiliation" and by "rebelling against Islamic laws" through too close an association with their Muslim overlords. He also claimed that the existence of the Tuwåt synagogue was contrary to Islamic law and demanded its destruction. Al-Maghili's writings were widely circulated in Morocco and continued to influence the treatment of Moroccan Jewry through the early twentieth century.

f. John Stuart Mill. *On Liberty*, Second Edition, London, John W. Parker and Son, 1859, p. 18.

1. "Azhar," in H.A.R. Gibb and J.H. Kramers, *Shorter Encyclopaedia of Islam*, Indian Edition, Pergamon Press, New Delhi, 2008, p.70.; "Al-Azhar University," Britannica Online, last updated April 4, 2025 by Adam Zeidan. https://www.britannica.com/topic/al-Azhar-University; Referring to Al-Azhar's importance, popular Sheik Muhammad Metwalli al-Sha'rawi (1911–1998), averred, "Islam was revealed in Mecca, but taught in Egypt." Quoted from Jacqueline Brinton. *Preaching Islamic Renewal: Religious authority and media in contemporary Egypt*. University of California Press, 2015. Brinton's quotation was cited in Ahmad Sobhy Mustafa. "Al-Azhar's Renewal of Religious Discourse and Power after the 2011 Egyptian Revolution," M.S. thesis, University of Kansas, May 13, 2021. p. 2. https://www.academia.edu/100313530/Al_Azhars_Renewal_of_Religious_Discourse_and_Power_after_the_2011_Egyptian_Revolution In the same thesis, Mustafa, a representative of Al-Azhar, declared (p.1), "The al-Azhar Mosque is one of the oldest Islamic institutions, madrasas, and degree granting universities in the Middle East. It is renowned as the most prestigious university in the Middle East for Sunni Islamic inquiry."

2. Malika Zeghal.
"Cairo as Capitol of Islamic Institutions," in, Diane Singerman, Editor, *Cairo Contested—Governance, Urban Space, and Global Modernity*, 2009, The American University in Cairo Press, pp. 65-66. Zeghal dubbed Al-Azhar "one of the most important centers of transmission of religious knowledge in the Sunni Muslim world." She further conceded that the prototypical Cairene Egyptian tourist guide who refers to Al-Azhar as "the Vatican of Islam," is "not totally wrong." Zeghal noted, "Despite the doctrinal absence of a clergy in Islam," for example under Egypt's modern authoritarian regimes, "Al-Azhar monopolized religious discourse."'; See too, Mary Fitzgerald, "For Sunnis, A First Among Equals," *The Irish Times*, June 30, 2006: "In a religion with no central authority and no clerical hierarchy, Al Azhar became the closest thing Sunni Islam had to a Vatican. Its ulama (scholars) were renowned, its edicts considered definitive, and millions of Muslims looked to it for guidance."

See also, Magdi Allam. "La fatwa dell'odio anti-Israeleche condiziona anche i 'moderati'," ["The fatwa of anti-Israel hatred that also affects the 'moderates'"] *Corriere della Sera*, January 22, 2008.
https://www.corriere.it/esteri/08_gennaio_22/fatwa_odio_antisraele_2e310ff0-c8b3-11dc-8074-0003ba99c667.shtml. Allam, an expatriate Egyptian journalist, described Al-Azhar as a "sort of "Vatican of Sunni Islam'," issuing fatwas, Islamic religious edicts, that dictated the behavior of Muslims in Rome, Italy.; Skovgaard-Petersen's entry on Al-Azhar in the 3rd edition of the *Encyclopedia of Islam* traces Al Azhar's modern prominence back to the post-World War I collapse of the Ottoman Caliphate: "A new era was ushered in for Egypt and al-Azhar in the 1920s. The 1924 abolition of the caliphate and the office of Shaykh al-Islam in Istanbul resulted in al-Azhar becoming the best-known Islamic institution internationally." Skovgaard-Petersen, J. (2008). al-Azhar:

modern period. In G. Krämer, D. Matringe, J. Nawas, & E. Rowson (Eds.), *Encyclopedia of Islam Three* (3. ed., Vol. 1). Brill.

3. Al-Azhar "X" account, May 7, 2025 https://x.com/AlAzhar/status/1898149370333163773 " 'There is no spot on the face of the earth that has gathered as many scholars and righteous people as Al-Azhar'" - Imam Ibn Hajar Al-Haytami. Al-Azhar celebrates the 1085th Hijri year since the first prayer held in Al-Azhar Mosque on the 7th of Ramadan in the year 361 AH, corresponding to June 21, 972 AD."; Al-Haytami was a famous scholar and prolific writer of the Shafiite school of Islamic jurisprudence who died in 1567. See: Arendonk, C. and Schacht, J. (2012). Ibn Ḥadjar al-Haytamī. In P. Bearman (ed.), *Encyclopaedia of Islam New Edition Online (EI-2 English).* Brill. https://doi.org/10.1163/1573-3912_islam_SIM_3179

4. For contemporary examples, see: "Grand Imam of Al-Azhar's historic visit to Iraq: Significance and implications," *The Atlantic Council*, https://www.atlanticcouncil.org/, Tuesday, November 16, 2021 https://www.atlanticcouncil.org/event/grand-imam-of-al-azhars-historic-visit-to-iraq-significance-and-implications/, "Considered to be the world's highest Sunni Islamic authority, the landmark tour will take Grand Imam Ahmed al-Tayeb and a senior delegation of Azhari scholars to stops that include Baghdad, Najaf, Erbil, and Mosul."; See also, Zayed Award For Human Fraternity given to current Al-Azhar Grand Imam, Ahmed al-Tayeb, 2019: "The most prominent Sunni Muslim religious authority in the world, the Grand Imam of Al-Azhar...etc.," https://www.zayedaward.org/en/recipient/ahmed-al-tayeb;
Earlier, see a brief entry on Muhammad Sayyed Tantawi, then Al-Azhar Grand Imam, and ranked eighth in the inaugural edition of "The 500 Most Influential Muslims in the World," Chief Editors John Esposito and Ibrahim Kalin, *The Royal Islamic Strategic Studies Center,* 2009, first edition, p. 36: "He is the leading authority for the vast majority of Sunni Muslims, and the head of the foremost Islamic educational institution."

4a. Constance D'au Vin. "Leader of World Islam Begins A Historic Tour of America," *The Washington Post*, November 25, 1977, p. 62.

5. " The Grand Imams of Al-Azhar, '*Shuyukhul Azhar*'" https://web.archive.org/web/20030105093431/https://sunnah.org/history/Scholars/mashaykh_azhar.htm#tantawi (accessed 4/9/2025)

6. Johanna Pink. "Tradition and Ideology in Contemporary Sunnite Qurʾānic Exegesis: Qurʾānic Commentaries from the Arab World, Turkey and Indonesia and their Interpretation of Q 5:51," *Die Welt des Islams*, New Series, Vol. 50, Issue 1 (2010), pp. 3-59 https://www.jstor.org/stable/20788347; Johanna Pink. "Tradition, Authority and Innovation in Contemporary Sunnī tafsīr: Towards a Typology of Qur'an Commentaries from the Arab World, Indonesia and Turkey," *Journal of Qur'anic Studies*, Vol. 12 (2010), pp. 56-82. https://www.jstor.org/stable/25831165;

7. Trevor Mostyn. "Sheikh Mohammed Tantawi obituary. Leading moderate Muslim cleric and an advocate of dialogue between civilisations," *The Guardian*, March 10, 2010. https://www.theguardian.com/world/2010/mar/10/sheikh-mohammed-tantawi-obituary; "Sheik Mohammed Tantawi, Egypt's Highest Cleric, Dies," *ABC News*, March 10, 2010

https://abcnews.go.com/International/sheik-mohammed-tantawi-egypt-highest-cleric-dies/story?id=10062072#:~:text=Tantawi%2C%20who%20was%2081%2C%20was%20the%20grand,plane%20and%20suffered%20a%20massive%20heart%20attack.

8. Suzan Quitaz. "Al Jazeera – Feeding the Muslim Brotherhood's Political Agenda to the Arab World", *Jerusalem Center for Security and Foreign Affairs*, Vol. 24, No. 12, June 18, 2024. https://jcpa.org/article/al-jazeera-feeding-the-muslim-brotherhoods-political-agenda-to-the-arab-world/

9. "The Meeting between the Sheik [Grand Imam] of Al-Azhar and the Chief Rabbi of Israel." *The Middle East Media Research Institute* (MEMRI), February 8, 1998 Special Reports No. 3. https://www.memri.org/reports/meeting-between-sheik-al-azhar-and-chief-rabbi-israel

10. Rivka Yadlin. "Inter-Faith Strife: The Al-Azhar Discourse on Israel," *Israel Affairs*, Vol.12, No.1, January 2006, pp.52–64, pp. 58-59.

11. "Arab Public Opinion about the Israeli war on Gaza," Arab Center for Research and Policy Studies, Doha, Qatar; Released January 10, 2024 https://arabindex.dohainstitute.org/EN/Pages/APOIsWarOnGaza.aspx; Full report here: https://www.dohainstitute.org/en/Lists/ACRPS-PDFDocumentLibrary/arab-opinion-war-on-gaza-full-report-en.pdf; See data from this population-based sample of 16 Middle East and North African countries (~500 per country) totaling 8,000 respondents, collected during the period between December 12, 2023, to January 5, 2024, in Mauritania, Morocco, Algeria, Tunisia, Libya, **Egypt**, Sudan, Yemen, Oman, Qatar, Kuwait, Saudi Arabia, Iraq, Jordan, Lebanon, and the West Bank in "Palestine." These countries represent more than 95 percent of the population across the Arab region. Eighty-nine percent of the Egyptians surveyed were in accord with the rest of the sample whose opinion was "almost unanimous in rejecting recognition of Israel."

12. Al-Jazeera interview, quoted in Rose al-Yousef, January 5, 1998, translated by MEMRI, Special Report No. 3, February 8, 1998.

13. Al-'Ahd Wal-Mithaq, December 12, 1998, translated by MEMRI, Special Report No. 3, February 8, 1998.

14. Andrew Bostom, Atef Ghobrial. *A Modern Qur'anic Kampf Against The Jews*, Published by www.andrewbostom.org, 2025, p. 1 of Tantawi's Introduction.

15. Michael Slackman. "Mohamed Tantawi, 81, Top Egyptian Cleric," *New York Times* March 11, 2010,
p. B19; "Sheikh Tantawi, Egypt's top cleric dies aged 81," *BBC News*, Wednesday, March 10, 2010.; Trevor Mostyn. "Sheikh Mohammed Tantawi obituary. Leading moderate Muslim cleric and an advocate of dialogue between civilisations," *The Guardian*, March 10, 2010. https://www.theguardian.com/world/2010/mar/10/sheikh-mohammed-tantawi-obituary; David A. Graham. "Tantawi May Have Been Moderate, But He Was Ignored," *Newsweek*, March 11, 2010 https://www.newsweek.com/tantawi-may-have-been-moderate-he-was-ignored-69235; Judith Miller. "A Courageous Voice Silenced In the Middle East," *Fox News Opinion*, March 11, 2020 https://www.foxnews.com/opinion/a-courageous-voice-silenced-in-the-middle-east; "Sheikh Mohammed Sayyed Tantawi," *The Telegraph*, March 11, 2010. https://www.telegraph.co.uk/news/obituaries/religion-obituaries/7423395/Sheikh-Mohammed-Sayyed-Tantawi.html; "Egypt's top Sunni Islam cleric was a moderate

Muslim voice," *The Washington Post*, March 13, 2010.
https://www.washingtonpost.com/archive/local/2010/03/13/egypts-top-sunni-islam-cleric-was-a-moderate-muslim-voice/8c5d4217-2e50-43a5-bbb4-58e7d73610bf/

[16.] Andrew Rosemarine. "Sheikh Mohamed Sayyed Tantawi: Controversial Imam who preached tolerance," *The Independent* (U.K.), Friday, March 19, 2010.
https://www.independent.co.uk/news/obituaries/sheikh-mohamed-Sayyed-tantawi-controversial-imam-who-preached-tolerance-1923670.html

[17.] Issandr El Amrani. "Sheikh Tantawi, 1928-2010," *The Arabist*, March 10, 2010,
https://www.arabist.net/blog/2010/3/10/sheikh-tantawi-1928-2010.html

[18.] Caryle Murphy. "The Future of Print. The digital revolution and the prospects for Arab newspapers," *The Majalla*, December 18, 2012
https://web.archive.org/web/20130723032742/http://www.majalla.com/eng/2012/12/article55236690

[19.] "Egyptian Daily Publishes Antisemitic Dissertation by the Late Al-Azhar Sheikh Tantawi; In It, He States 'The [Jews'] Abominations Described in the Koran Are Demonstrated Throughout the Ages'," *The Middle East Media Research Institute (MEMRI)*, July 20, 2010, Special Dispatch No. 3108.
https://www.memri.org/reports/egyptian-daily-publishes-antisemitic-dissertation-late-al-azhar-sheikh-tantawi-it-he-states

[20.] *A Modern Qur'anic Kampf Against The Jews*, p. 324.

[21.] Jakob Skovgaard-Petersen. "The Dar Al-Ifta Today\: Sayyed Tantawi," Chapter 9, in, *Defining Islam for the Egyptian state: muftis and fatwas of the Dār al*-Iftā, Leiden, the Netherlands, New York: Brill, 1997, pp. 253-54.

[22.] Jakob Skovgaard-Petersen. "A Typology of State Muftis," in Yvonne Haddad and Barbara Stowasser (eds): *Islamic Law and the Challenges of Modernity*. New York: Altamira Press, 2004, pp. 81-98.

[23.] Jakob Skovgaard-Petersen. "Egypt's Ulama In The State, In Politics And In The Islamist Vision," in Arjomand & Brown: *The Rule of Law, Islam and Constitutional Politics in Egypt and Iran*. State University of New York Press, 2013, pp. 279-302.

[24.] Reference 14

[25.] References 9, 10, 12, and 13

[26.] "The Deputy Permanent Representative of Israel requests that this note and its enclosure be circulated as an official document of the fifty-second session of the Commission on Human Rights under agenda item 4. MARCH 5, 1996,"
https://www.un.org/unispal/document/auto-insert-181410/; "Sheik Defines Path to Heaven," *New York Times*, April 20, 1996, p. 6.; www.lailatalqadr.com, archived here:
https://web.archive.org/web/20020611054245/http://www.lailatalqadr.com/stories/n040401.shtml; "Leading Egyptian Government Cleric Calls For: 'Martyrdom Attacks that Strike Horror into the Hearts of the Enemies of Allah," *The Middle East Media Research Institute*, Special Dispatch No. 363, April 7, 2002,
https://www.memri.org/reports/leading-egyptian-government-cleric-calls-martyrdom-attacks-strike-horror-hearts-enemies; "Sheik of Al-Azhar, Muhammad Sayyed Tantawi: Those Who Carry Out Suicide Operations Are Martyrs," *The Middle East Media Research Institute*, August 19, 2004, #209
https://www.memri.org/tv/sheik-al-azhar-muhammad-sayyed-tantawi-those-who-carry-out-suicide-operations-are-martyrs

[27.] Aluma Dankowitz. *The Middle East Media Research Institute*. "Based on Koranic Verses, Interpretations, and Traditions, Muslim Clerics State: The Jews Are the Descendants of Apes, Pigs, And Other Animals," October 31, 2002, Special Reports No. 11, https://www.memri.org/reports/based-koranic-verses-interpretations-and-traditions-muslim-clerics-state-jews-are#_edn56
[28.] Skovgaard-Petersen. "A Typology of State Muftis"
[29.] Skovgaard-Petersen. "Egypt's Ulama In The State, In Politics And In The Islamist Vision."
[30.] refs 9,10, 12, and 13, above.
[31.] **"Shaykh Muhammad Sayyed Tantawi (1928-2010)."** *The Grand Imams of Al-Azhar (Shuyukhul Azhar).*
https://web.archive.org/web/20030105093431/https://sunnah.org/history/Scholars/mashaykh_azhar.htm#tantawi
[32.] Skovgaard-Petersen, "The Dar Al-Ifta Today\: Sayyed Tantawi," pp. 251-55; Pink, "Tradition and Ideology in Contemporary Sunnite Qur'ānic Exegesis," p. 11.
[33.] Laura Bariani. "Intervista al Muftī d'Egitto, šayḫ Muḥammad Sayyed Ṭanṭāwī" ("Interview with the Muftī of Egypt, Muḥammad Sayyed Ṭanṭāwī"), *Oriente Moderno*, Nuova serie, Anno 11 (72), Nr. 1/6 (Gennaio-Giugno 1992), pp. 135-36.
[34.] Issandr El-Amrani. "Sheikh Tantawi, 1928-2010," *The Arabist*, March 10, 2010. https://www.arabist.net/blog/2010/3/10/sheikh-tantawi-1928-2010.html
[35.] *E.J. Brill's First Encyclopaedia of Islam*, 1913-1936, edited by M.Th. Houtsma, A.J. Wensinck, T. W. Arnold, W. Heffening, and E. Lévi-Provençal. Volume III, p. 210: "When used of men a hafiz is one who knows the Qur'an by heart, literally 'preserves it' (in the memory)."
[36.] **"Shaykh Muhammad Sayyed Tantawi (1928-2010)."** *The Grand Imams of Al-Azhar.*
[37.] Skovgaard-Petersen, "The Dar Al-Ifta Today\: Sayyed Tantawi," p. 251.
[38.] El-Amrani. "Sheikh Tantawi, 1928-2010"
[39.] Nancy E. Gallagher. "In Memoriam: Charles Wendell, 1919-1982," *International Journal of Middle East Studies*, Vol. 14, No. 4 (Nov., 1982), p. 559: "Charles Wendell held a joint appointment as associate professor in the departments of Religious Studies and Germanic and Slavic languages at the University of California-Santa Barbara, where he taught the history of Islam and Arabic. He was a learned figure in the classical sense of the term, an erudite scholar in Islamic culture and languages, and a man of depth and sensitivity... In 1960 he came to UCLA and completed his Ph.D. there in 1967. He joined the UCSB (Santa Barbara) faculty in 1967 as an assistant professor of Arabic. He spoke Arabic, Persian, French, and Spanish and did research in those languages as well as in German, Italian, Hebrew, Turkish, Latin, and Greek. His scholarly interests ranged from the culture and history of early Islam to intellectual developments in modern Egypt. His books include: *The Evolution of the Egyptian National Image: From its Origins to Ahmad Lutfi al-Sayyed*, and *Five Tracts of Hasan al-Banna*, both published by the University of California Press."; Quotes from, Charles Wendell. *Five tracts of Ḥasan Al-Bannā' (1906-1949): a selection from the Majmū'at rasā'il al-Imām al-shahīd Ḥasan al-Bannā*, University of California Press, Berkeley, CA, 1978, pp. 3-8.
[39a.] Hazem Kandil. *Inside The Brotherhood*, Polity, Malden, MA, 2015, p. 86.

[40.] *E.J. Brill's First Encyclopaedia of Islam*, Volume VII, p. 603: "In Islam the word 'tafsir' means particularly the commentaries on the Qur'an and the science of interpreting the sacred book."
[41.] *E.J. Brill's First Encyclopaedia of Islam*, Volume III, p. 189: "The word 'hadith' means primarily a communication or narrative in general whether religious or profane, then it has the particular meaning of a record of actions or sayings of the Prophet and his companions."; p.192: "Six of these works (collections of hadith) were in course of time generally recognized by the orthodox Muslim world as authoritative; they all arose in the third century A.H. (9th century C.E.); they are the collections by 1.) Al-Bukhari (died 870), 2.) Muslim (died 875), 3.) Abu Dawud (died 888), 4.) Al-Tirmidhi (died 892), 5.) Al-Nasa'i (died 915), and 6.) Ibn Madja (died 886). These works are usually called briefly the 'six books' or also 'the six Sahih's," i.e., the 'sound' (i.e., the correct, reliable collections)."
[42.] Skovgaard-Petersen, "The Dar Al-Ifta Today: Sayyed Tantawi," p. 251.
[43.] Ibid.
[44.] Bariani. "Intervista al Muftī d'Egitto, šayḫ Muḥammad Sayyed Ṭanṭāwī," p. 136.
[45.] Skovgaard-Petersen, "The Dar Al-Ifta Today: Sayyed Tantawi," p. 251.
[46.] Ibid.
[47.] Ibid.
[48.] Andrew Bostom. *Sharia Versus Freedom—The Legacy of Islamic Totalitarianism*, Prometheus Books, Amherst, New York, 2012, pp. 99-130.
[49.] Skovgaard-Petersen, "The Dar Al-Ifta Today\: Sayyed Tantawi," p. 251.
[50.] Ibid.
[51.] Skovgaard-Petersen, "The Dar Al-Ifta Today\: Sayyed Tantawi," p. 252.
[52.] See references 28 and 29.
[53.] Skovgaard-Petersen, "The Dar Al-Ifta Today: Sayyed Tantawi," p. 252.
[54.] Danielson V. Listening to Umm Kulthūm. *Middle East Studies Association Bulletin.* 1996;30(2):170-173.
[55.] Habeeb Salloum. "Mohammed Abdul Wahab: The Father of Modern Egyptian Song," *Al Jadid Magazine*, Vol. 1, No. 2, December 1995 https://aljadid.com/content/mohammad-abdul-wahab-father-modern-egyptian-song
[56.] See https://www.dar-alifta.org/en/about/history-of-dar-alifta: "Egypt's Dar Al-Ifta is one of the first pioneering foundations to issue fatwas (religious verdicts) throughout the Islamic world. It was founded and affiliated with the ministry of Justice in 1895 by the high command of Khedive Abbas Helmi. The organization began as one of the divisions of the Egyptian Ministry of Justice. Since its foundation, Egypt's Dar Al-Ifta has played a significant role in religious consultation, capital punishment sentences, and other legal chores referred to the institution seeking the Grand Mufti's judgment. Egypt's Dar al-Ifta's role does not stop at this point; it is not limited by domestic boundaries but extends beyond Egypt as an expertise house to issue guidance for Muslims worldwide. Since its establishment, Egypt's Dar Al-Ifta has been the primary institution representing Islam and the importance of Islamic legal research. The leadership role of the Dar is best shown by its records of fatwas since its establishment to the present day. Dar Al-Ifta plays a significant role in giving rulings (fatwas) to Muslims all over the world and consultation for the judiciary in Egypt. It serves a historic and civic purpose by keeping Muslims in touch with their Islamic ideals and principles in our modern society;

clarifying issues, removing doubts concerning religion and life, and revealing religious laws for new issues. Egypt's Dar al-Ifta is perceived as a scholarly reference for adopting a moderate methodology in understanding rulings derived from inherited jurisprudence, creating a consistency between Islamic law and the needs of society."

57. Reynold A. Nicholson. *A Literary History of the Arabs*, New York, Charles Scribner's Sons, 1907, p. 270: "Mutanabbi, in the opinion of his countrymen [was] the greatest of Moslem poets." He lived from 915 to 965 C.E. (see Nicholson, *A Literary History of the Arabs*, p. 304)

58. Arthur Goldschmidt Jr. and Robert Johnson. "Shawqi, Ahmad, (1868-1932)" *Historical Dictionary of Egypt*, Scarecrow Press, 2003, p. 363: "Distinguished Arabic poet and playwright, often called Amir al-shu'ara (Prince of Poets). He came from a wealthy family of mixed Turkish, Arab, Kurdish, and Greek origin that was closely connected to the khedivial family... His enemies called him the 'poet of Arab princes' because of his close ties with Abdin Palace, but his work remains a model for neoclassical Arabic poetry. He is still widely read and admired throughout the Arab world. His Giza mansion is now a museum."

59. See references 15 to 17, and 31, above.

60. "The 500 Most Influential Muslims in the World," Chief Editors John Esposito and Ibrahim Kalin, *The Royal Islamic Institute of Strategic Studies Centre*, Amman, Jordan, 2009, p. 36.; *Royal Islamic Institute of Strategic Studies Centre*: "The primary goal of The Royal Islamic Strategic Studies Centre ('the Centre') is to protect, preserve and propagate traditional, orthodox, 'moderate' Islam as defined by the international Islamic Consensus on the 'Three Points of the Amman Message' arrived at over the years 2005-2006." https://rissc.jo/about-us/

61. Ibid.

62. Ibid.

63. Ibid.

64. Andrew Bostom. *The Legacy of Jihad*, Prometheus Books, Amherst, New York, 2005, pp. 24-124.

65. "The 500 Most Influential Muslims in the World," p. 36.

66. James Reston, Jr. "Seeking Meaning From a Grand Imam," *The Washington Post*, March 31, 2002.
https://www.washingtonpost.com/archive/opinions/2002/03/31/seeking-meaning-from-a-grand-imam/378f8145-e525-4259-a2d7-4b0d6e7dc212/

67. Ibid.; See also this Ph.D. thesis which repeats the same counterfactual, disingenuous Tantawi apologetics, albeit within an "academic" milieu, absent any mention of Tantawi's own full-throated views clearly expressed in his *at-Tafsir al-Wasit li'l-Qur'an al-Karim*, Safaa M. Afifi El-Scheikh. "Die westlichen Kirchen im Bild der zeitgenössischen ägyptischen und arabischen Religionsgelehrten. Ein Beitrag zum Dialog im Offenen Brief an Papst Benedikt XVI," Dissertation zur Erlangung des akademischen Grades Doktorin der Philosophie (Dr. phil.) ["The Western churches as seen by contemporary Egyptian and Arab religious scholars.A contribution to the dialogue in the Open Letter to Pope Benedict XVI," Dissertation for the academic degree of Doctor of Philosophy (Dr. phil.)], Humboldt University of Berlin, Oral defense, July 24, 2012, pp. 47-48. https://edoc.hu-berlin.de/server/api/core/bitstreams/1d37ed25-47ae-43c1-8e93-b80fb06097dd/content

[68]. Ibid.
[69]. Ibid.
[70]. Ibid.
[71]. See Bostom, *The Legacy of Jihad*, especially, pp. 24-250; 368-517.
[72]. Reston, Jr. "Seeking Meaning From a Grand Imam"
[73]. See Bostom, *The Legacy of Jihad*, especially, pp. 39-59; 368-432.
[74]. Reston, Jr. "Seeking Meaning From a Grand Imam"
[75]. See reference 51.
[76]. I have used the Arabic version of *at-Tafsir al-Wasit li'l-Qur'an al-Karim ("The intermediate [balanced] interpretation of the Qur'an")* posted at the website Tantawi helped organize, (*www.altafsir.com*), here: https://www.altafsir.com/Tafasir.asp?tMadhNo=0&tTafsirNo=57&tSoraNo=1&tAyahNo=1&tDisplay=yes&UserProfile=0&LanguageId=1
[77]. Tantawi's gloss on 2:190 is a combined discussion of verses 2:190 through 2:195. https://www.altafsir.com/Tafasir.asp?tMadhNo=0&tTafsirNo=57&tSoraNo=2&tAyahNo=190&tDisplay=yes&UserProfile=0&LanguageId=1
[78]. Jalalu'd-din Al-Mahalli and Jalalu'd-din As-Suyuti. *Tafsir Al-Jalalayn*, Translated by Aisha Bewley, Dar Al Taqwa, London, 2007, p. 69. Tafsir al-Jalalayn — meaning "The Commentary of the Two Jalals," named after its two Egyptian authors: Al-Suyuti (1445-1505), a brilliant multidisciplinary scholar; and his mentor Jalalu'd-Din al-Mahalli (1389-1459). The late Dutch Islamologist Johannes J.G. Jansen noted in his treatise *The Interpretation of the Koran in Modern Egypt* (Brill, Leiden, 1974, pp. 16-17), Tafsir al-Jalalayn remains one of the most popular as well as the most authoritative Koranic commentaries in Egypt..; See also, Anwarul Haqq. *Abrogation in the Koran*, Methodist Publishing House, Lucknow, India, 1926, p. 15, which indicated that verse 2:190 was abrogated by verse 9:36, while verses 2:191 and 2:192 were abrogated by verse 9:5.
[79]. Bostom, *The Legacy of Jihad*, pp. 125, 127-135.
[80]. The Quranic Arabic Corpus, www.corpus.quran.com, Sahih International translation, https://corpus.quran.com/translation.jsp?chapter=2&verse=191
[81]. Tantawi's gloss on 2:190 to 2:195 https://bit.ly/3EUtIUN
[82]. Ibid; See also, Andrew Bostom, *The Legacy of Islamic Antisemitism*, www.andrewbostom.net, 2020, pp. 56-57, for an introduction to the hadith collections of Abu Dawud, al-Tirmidhi, al-Nasai, and ibn Majah
[83]. Tantawi's gloss on 2:190 to 2:195 https://bit.ly/3EUtIUN
[84]. Ibid.
[85]. Ibid; Al-Alusi wrote a monumental 19th century Qur'anic commentary, *Ruh al-Maani* ("The Spirit of Meaning[s]"). See: Basheer M. Nafi. "Abu al-Thana' al-Alusi: An Alim, Ottoman Mufti, and Exegete of the Qur'an." *International Journal of Middle East Studies*, 2002; Vol. 34; pp. 465-494 https://www.jstor.org/stable/3879672
[86]. Tantawi's gloss on 2:190 to 2:195 https://bit.ly/3EUtIUN; see also, Bostom, *The Legacy of Islamic Antisemitism*, pp. 56-57, for an introduction to the hadith collections of Bukhari and Muslim
[87]. See Quranic Arabic Corpus, www.corpus.quran.com, Sahih International translations, and reference 76 for *at-Tafsir al-Wasit li'l-Qur'an al-Karim*, respectively, for all the

quoted Qur'anic verses and commentaries to follow regarding Q 2:215-217, Q 9:5, Q 9:29, Q 9:11, Q 8:60, and Q 47:4, below.

[88.] Q 2:215 https://corpus.quran.com/translation.jsp?chapter=2&verse=215;
Q 2:216 https://corpus.quran.com/translation.jsp?chapter=2&verse=216;
Q 2: 217 https://corpus.quran.com/translation.jsp?chapter=2&verse=217
Tantawi's commentary extracts on Q2:215-217:
https://www.altafsir.com/Tafasir.asp?tMadhNo=0&tTafsirNo=57&tSoraNo=2&tAyahNo=216&tDisplay=yes&UserProfile=0&LanguageId=1

[89.] al-Qurtubi (d. 1272) was Muslim scholar of the Maliki school of Islamic law, who was "an expert on hadith and well known for his commentary on the Qur'an... The commentary of al-Qurtubi is principally distinguished by the recourse to a very great number of hadiths." He was "more interested in the content (of the hadith) than in the process of transmission. The hadiths are therefore assembled for the purpose of the reply that they offer to the question raised by the verse under discussion. Above all, the work consists of exegeses designed to clarify the meaning and implication of the (Islamic) Law." Arnaldez, R. (2012). al-Ḳurṭubī. In P. Bearman (ed.), *Encyclopaedia of Islam New Edition Online (EI-2 English)*. Brill. https://doi.org/10.1163/1573-3912_islam_SIM_4553

[90.] Andalusia, Muslim Spain, was the name given to the Iberian territories initially conquered in an aggressive jihad invasion during the early 8th century, which for 700 years afterward became a land of jihad par excellence, punctuated by massacre, pillage, enslavement, and the imposition of rigid Maliki jurisprudence with harsh discrimination against non-Muslims, per Qur'an 9:29. In 1066, Granada was the scene of the largest Western European pogrom of Jews up until that time—an entire community of 4000 exterminated, incited by the "profuse" usage of the Qur'anic epithet "apes" for Jews (Q 2:65; Q 5:60, and Q 7:166), along with the notion the Jews had breached the limits of their prescribed humiliated status, per Q 9:29. These events, obviously, are not what Tantawi refers to in his lament, but rather the Reconquista of Spain completed in the 15th century, which ended Muslim rule. See, Bostom, *The Legacy of Islamic Antisemitism*, pp. 97-105.; See also, this strikingly consistent warning/lament from then Yasir Arafat lieutenant, Abu Iyad (nom de guerre of Salah Khalaf, founder of Black September), published in Le Monde (RÉVOLUTION ET RÉALISME Par ABOU AYAD (*) Publié le 21 janvier 1974:
https://www.lemonde.fr/archives/article/1974/01/21/revolution-et-realisme_2520176_1819218.html), during 1974: "We intend to fight so that our Palestinian homeland does not become a new Andalusia." ("Nous entendons lutter pour que notre patrie palestinienne ne devienne poas unde nouvelle Andalousie.") His statement was an acknowledgement that Israel had a pre-Islamic Jewish heritage, like Spain's pre-Islamic Christian heritage. Both were conquered by jihad, and ruled under the Sharia, for 7 (Spain) to 13 (Israel) centuries but then liberated from the Sharia, and their pre-Islamic cultures restored—a phenomenon anathema to Tantawi and Abu Iyad!

[91.] See reference 86 for discussion of the "two Sahihs."

[92.] Q 9:5 https://corpus.quran.com/translation.jsp?chapter=9&verse=5; Tantawi's commentary
https://www.altafsir.com/Tafasir.asp?tMadhNo=0&tTafsirNo=57&tSoraNo=9&tAyahNo=5&tDisplay=yes&UserProfile=0&LanguageId=1

[93.] See reference 86 for discussion of the "two Sahihs."

[94.] Ahmed b. Hanbal (d. 855), known as Ibn Hanbal, "celebrated Islamic theologian," among whose works, "the great encyclopedia of traditions, *Musnad*, compiled by his son 'Abd Allah, from his lectures and amplified by supplements, containing 28,000 to 29,000 traditions, acquired great renown." From, Ignaz Goldziher, *First Encyclopaedia of Islam*, Vol. 1, p. 188.

[94a.] Q 9:73 https://corpus.quran.com/translation.jsp?chapter=9&verse=73; Tantawi's commentary https://www.altafsir.com/Tafasir.asp?tMadhNo=0&tTafsirNo=57&tSoraNo=9&tAyahNo=73&tDisplay=yes&UserProfile=0&LanguageId=1

[94b.] Ali ibn Abi Talib, "was a cousin and the son-in-law of the Prophet Muhammad and the fourth orthodox caliph…He was one of the ten to whom Paradise was expressly promised by the Prophet, and one of the six councilors on whom the Prophet on his death bed set his hopes…Ali accompanied Muhammad in the battles of Bedr (Badr), Ohod (Uhud), al-Khandak ('the ditch'), and in nearly all his expeditions…and on the day when (the Jewish oasis of) Khaibar was stormed he carried the (Muslim) banner…**Ali is said to have transmitted 586 hadith [emphasis added]**…By the Shiites…Ali is pre-eminently the saint of Islam, by which quality he is clearly distinguished from Muhammad, who is only the *nabi*, 'the prophet of Allah.' All Shi'ism, with its numberless sects, is based on this conception." Clement Huart, *First Encyclopaedia of Islam*, Volume 1, pp. 283-285.

[95.] Q 9:29 https://corpus.quran.com/translation.jsp?chapter=9&verse=29; Tantawi's commentary https://www.altafsir.com/Tafasir.asp?tMadhNo=0&tTafsirNo=57&tSoraNo=9&tAyahNo=29&tDisplay=yes&UserProfile=0&LanguageId=1

[96.] See Bostom, *The Legacy of Jihad*, pp. 29-53, for a brief introduction to the collection of the Qur'anic poll-tax, per Q 9:29, jizya, or the tax paid "as though it were compensation for not being slain," and other attendant restrictions and humiliations actually imposed; pp. 127-135 for classical and modern Qur'anic commentaries on Qur'an 9:29; see also p. 199 for the great Sufi al-Ghazali on jihad against the "People of the Book," and the imposition of the jizya and related restrictions and humiliations upon them, and pp. 383-404 for an overview of the early Muslim jihad conquests of the Christian Near East, i.e., the application of Q 9:29.

[97.] Q 9:111 https://corpus.quran.com/translation.jsp?chapter=9&verse=111; Tantawi's commentary https://www.altafsir.com/Tafasir.asp?tMadhNo=0&tTafsirNo=57&tSoraNo=9&tAyahNo=111&tDisplay=yes&UserProfile=0&LanguageId=1

[98.] al-Hasan al-Basri (d. 728), "He exercised a lasting influence on the development of Sufism, by his ascetic piety…Numerous sayings are placed on his lips and the Sufis see in him a predecessor, whom they quote as often as do orthodox Sunnis." *Shorter Encyclopaedia of Islam*, p. 195.

[99.] Full hadith: Sahih al-Bukhari 3024 https://sunnah.com/bukhari:3024 "(the freed slave of 'Umar bin 'Ubaidullah) I was Umar's clerk. Once Abdullah bin Abi Aufa wrote a letter to Umar when he proceeded to Al-Haruriya. I read in it that Allah's Messenger in one of his military expeditions against the enemy, waited till the sun declined and then he got up amongst the people saying, 'O people! Do not wish to meet the enemy, and ask Allah for safety, but **when you face the enemy, be patient, and remember that Paradise is under the shades of swords**.' Then he said, 'O Allah, the Revealer of the Holy Book, and the Mover of the clouds and the Defeater of the clans, defeat them, and grant us victory over them.'''

100. Q 8:60 https://corpus.quran.com/translation.jsp?chapter=8&verse=60; Tantawi's commentary https://www.altafsir.com/Tafasir.asp?tMadhNo=0&tTafsirNo=57&tSoraNo=8&tAyahNo=60&tDisplay=yes&UserProfile=0&LanguageId=1

101. For a discussion of the Medinan Jewish tribe Banu Qurayza (based on primary Muslim sources, i.e., Qur'an and Qur'anic commentary, hadith, and sira [earliest pious Muslim biographies of Muhammad especially Ibn Ishaq's]), and how and why Muhammad labeled them with the Qur'anic epithet (Q 5:60) "apes and pigs," besieged and subdued them, and orchestrated their "trial" and subsequent massacre—personally beheading up to an alleged 700 of their post-pubescent males, enslaved their wives and children, and seized their property and possessions as "booty" for the Muslims, see: Andrew Bostom, "Muhammad and the Banu Qurayza: The Bloody, Living Legacy of Islam's Willing Jew-Executioner, and Meshugga 'prophet'," November 23, 2019, https://andrewbostom.net/2019/11/muhammad-and-the-banu-qurayza-the-bloody-living-legacy-of-islams-willing-jew-executioner-and-meshugga-prophet/

102. Fakir al-Din al-Razi (d. 1209), famous philosopher of religion, and theologian, and author of the monumental Qur'anic commentary, al-*Tafsir al-Kabir*. "At the end of his life al-Razi excelled as a preacher…and he declared that he found his highest satisfaction and peace of mind in the reading of the Qur'an." *Shorter Encyclopaedia of Islam*, pp. 667-668.

103. Q 47:4-6 https://corpus.quran.com/translation.jsp?chapter=47&verse=4; https://corpus.quran.com/translation.jsp?chapter=47&verse=5; https://corpus.quran.com/translation.jsp?chapter=47&verse=6; Tantawi's commentary https://www.altafsir.com/Tafasir.asp?tMadhNo=0&tTafsirNo=57&tSoraNo=47&tAyahNo=4&tDisplay=yes&UserProfile=0&LanguageId=1

104. al-Tabari (d. 923) was a precocious, versatile, and prolific scholar. Alleged to have memorized the Qur'an by age 7, he would later compose renowned works on history, Islamic law, and Qur'anic exegesis, but also dedicated himself "to poetry, lexicography, grammar and ethics, and even mathematics and medicine." Tabari's great commentary on the Qur'an, *Djami al-bayan fi tafsir al-Quran*, "collected for the first time the ample material of traditional (Qur'anic) exegesis and thus created a standard work upon which later Qur'anic commentators drew; it is still a mine of information for historical and critical research by western scholars." *Shorter Encyclopaedia of Islam*, pp. 788-789.

105. Ibn Kathir (d. 1373), was "one of the best-known historians and traditionists of Syria under the Babri Mamluk dynasty." According to Laoust, "by far the most important of Ibn Kathir's works is his great history of Islam, *al-Biddya wa 'l-nihaya*," but he also contributed a "vast commentary on the Qur'an."
Henri Laoust, *Encyclopaedia of Islam*, 2nd edition, Vol. 3, H-Iram, pp. 817-818. https://archive.org/details/ei2-complete/Encyclopaedia_of_Islam_vol_3_H-Iram/page/818/mode/2up

106. "Imam Ahmad," Ahmed b. Hanbal, see reference 94.

[107]. From Ahmed b. Hanbal's *Musnad*, 17783: "Qais Al-Jadhami narrated that the Prophet said: 'The martyr is given six rewards as soon as the first drop of his blood falls: every sin of his is forgiven, he finds his abode in Paradise, he is married to the beautiful Hur-e-Ayn (houris; wide eyed virgins), he is protected from the greatest terror, he is protected from the torment of the grave, and he is clothed with the garment of faith'" https://al-hadees.com/musnad-ahmed/17783; From the hadith collection of Ibn Majah: "The martyr has six things (in store) with Allah: He is forgiven from the first drop of his blood that is shed; he is shown his place in Paradise; he is spared the torment of the grave; he is kept safe from the greatest terror; he is adorned with a garment of faith; he is married to (wives) from among the wide-eyed houris; and he is permitted to intercede for seventy of his relatives." https://sunnah.com/ibnmajah:2799 ; From the hadith collection of at-Tirmidhi: "There are six things with Allah for the martyr. He is forgiven with the first flow of blood (he suffers), he is shown his place in Paradise, he is protected from punishment in the grave, secured from the greatest terror, the crown of dignity is placed upon his head - and its gems are better than the world and what is in it - he is married to seventy two wives of Paradise, and he may intercede for seventy of his close relatives." https://sunnah.com/tirmidhi:1663;
Interestingly, the jihad terror organization, "ISIS-K" cited the same traditions in 2022 in one of their monthly publications. See: "Article In Issue 12 Of ISIS-K Magazine 'Voice Of Khurasan' Cites Hadith To Highlight Rewards Of Martyrdom: 'If You Carry Out Five Mine Planting Operations, You Will Be Rewarded With 300 Years Of Worship Of Another Non-Mujahid Muslim, By The Will Of Allah'," *Middle East Media Research Institute*, *Jihad and Terrorism Threat Monitor*, September 9, 2022 https://www.memri.org/jttm/article-issue-12-isis-k-magazine-voice-khurasan-cites-hadith-highlight-rewards-martyrdom-if-you

[108]. Bassam Tibi, "War and Peace in Islam," in *The Ethics of War and Peace: Religious and Secular Perspectives*, editor Terry Nardin, (Princeton University Press, 1996), pp. 128-45, essay reproduced in full, and specific extracts quoted from, Bostom, *The Legacy of Jihad*, p. 329.

[109]. James Reston, Jr. "Purification starts with the truth," *USA Today*, July 6, 2009 https://web.archive.org/web/20090707104610/http://blogs.usatoday.com/oped/2009/07/purification-starts-with-the-truth-.html

[110]. "The Deputy Permanent Representative of Israel requests that this note and its enclosure be circulated as an official document of the fifty-second session of the Commission on Human Rights under agenda item 4. MARCH 5, 1996," https://www.un.org/unispal/document/auto-insert-181410/

[111]. "Sheikh Defines Path to Heaven," *The New York Times*, April 20, 1996, p.6.

[112]. Ibid.

[113]. Ibid.

[114]. "Passover suicide bombing at Park Hotel in Netanya," https://www.gov.il/en/pages/passover-suicide-bombing-at-park-hotel-in-netanya

[115]. "The Grand Imam of Al-Azhar calls for an increase in martyrdom operations," lailatalqadr.com, April 4, 2002 (the website is directly "associated with Al-Azhar). Archived link:

https://web.archive.org/web/20020611054245/http://www.lailatalqadr.com:80/stories/n040401.shtml

116. "Leading Egyptian Government Cleric Calls For: 'Martyrdom Attacks that Strike Horror into the Hearts of the Enemies of Allah," *The Middle East Media Research Institute*, Special Dispatch No. 363, April 7, 2002, https://www.memri.org/reports/leading-egyptian-government-cleric-calls-martyrdom-attacks-strike-horror-hearts-enemies

117. Ibid.

118. "Sheik of Al-Azhar, Muhammad Sayyed Tantawi: Those Who Carry Out Suicide Operations Are Martyrs," August 19, 2004, #209 https://www.memri.org/tv/sheik-al-azhar-muhammad-sayyed-tantawi-those-who-carry-out-suicide-operations-are-martyrs

119. Shmuel Bar. "The Conflict between Radical Islam and the West—Origins, Prognosis, and Prescriptions," Hudson Institute and the Institute for Policy and Strategy at Herzliya, January 5, 2006, p. 69, note 6. https://www.esd.whs.mil/Portals/54/Documents/FOID/Reading%20Room/Other/15-F-0990_DOC_03_Radical_Islams_Confrontation_with_the_West_Final.pdf

120. Ibid, p. 95.

121. Dankowitz, "Based on Koranic Verses, Interpretations, and Traditions, Muslim Clerics State: The Jews Are the Descendants of Apes, Pigs, And Other Animals."

122. Q 5:60 https://corpus.quran.com/translation.jsp?chapter=5&verse=60;

123. Taghut is a reference to pre-Islamic pagan deities, later "applied to Satan, sorcerer, and rebel, and to any power opposed to that of Islam." F.H. Stewart, *Encyclopaedia of Islam New Edition Online (EI-2 English)* https://archive.org/details/ei2-complete/Encyclopaedia_of_Islam_vol_10_T-U/page/93/mode/2up

124. Tantawi's commentary on Q 5:60 groups it with the following verses, Q 5:61, Q 5:62, and Q 5:63
https://corpus.quran.com/translation.jsp?chapter=5&verse=61;
https://corpus.quran.com/translation.jsp?chapter=5&verse=62;
https://corpus.quran.com/translation.jsp?chapter=5&verse=63;
Commentary (Q5:60-63): https://corpus.quran.com/translation.jsp?chapter=5&verse=60;

125. Richard Owen. "Imam's historic visit to synagogue in Rome cancelled," *Times (London) Online*, January 22, 2008 https://web.archive.org/web/20080214155635/http:/www.timesonline.co.uk/tol/comment/faith/article3230397.ece; Also, Allam, "La fatwa dell'odio anti-Israeleche condiziona anche i 'moderati'," ["The fatwa of anti-Israel hatred that also affects the 'moderates'"]

126. On the relevant doctrinal aspects of jihad, see two complementary fatwas, one written January 5, 1956, by then grand mufti of Egypt, Sheikh Hasan Ma'moun, and another January 9, 1956, signed by the leading members of the Fatwa Committee of Al Azhar University—Sunni Islam's Vatican—and the major representatives of all four Sunni Islamic schools of jurisprudence. These rulings elaborated the following key initial point: that ***all of historical Palestine***—modern Jordan, Israel, and the disputed territories of Judea and Samaria, as well as Gaza—having been conquered by jihad, was a permanent possession of the global Muslim *umma* (community), —"fay territory"—booty or spoils—to be governed eternally by Islamic law. See, Document declassified and released under the Nazi War Crimes Disclosure Act, 2006, PL105-246 State

Department Telegram 1763/Embassy (Cairo) Telegram 1256 D441214. English translation (by the US embassy) of two fatwas written by the grand mufti of Egypt, Sheikh Hasan Ma'moun, January 5, 1956, and another dated January 9, 1956, signed by the leading members of the Fatwa Committee of Al Azhar, that is, its chairman and ex-mufti of Egypt, and major representatives of all four Islamic schools of jurisprudence, the ex-sheikh of the Shari'a College (Shafi'i sect), Mahmoud Shaltout (Hanafi sect), the director of Religious Guidance (Maliki Sect), and the director of the Azhar Inspectorate (Hanbali sect), and published the following days in the Egyptian newspaper, *Al Ahram*. The expression "fay" is found in Qur'an 59: 6-10, which describes Muhammad's attack upon the Jewish tribe Banu Nadir. In the traditional Muslim interpretation of these verses the theocratic conception of property rights is confirmed, as voiced by the Prophet—Allah returns to the Believers the possessions of His foes, what is properly His. See Leone Caetani, *Annali dell' Islam*, Milan: 1905–1926, vol. 5, p. 332.

Quote is from Allam, "The fatwa of anti-Israel hatred that also affects the 'moderates'"

127. Owen. "Imam's historic visit to synagogue in Rome cancelled."

128. Allam, "The fatwa of anti-Israel hatred that also affects the 'moderates'"

129. See references 115 and 116.

130. Allam, "The fatwa of anti-Israel hatred that also affects the 'moderates'"

131. *A Modern Qur'anic Kampf Against The Jews*, p. x

132. Ibid, pp.

133. Ibid, p.

134. Haddasa Ben-Ito. *The Lie that Wouldn't Die: The Protocols of the Elders of Zion*, 2005, Vallentine Mitchell, 390pp. https://archive.org/details/liethatwouldntdi0000beni; "Benjamin Franklin vindicated: an exposure of the Franklin 'prophecy." *International Benjamin Franklin Society*, 1939, Pamphlet, American Jewish Congress, New York. Cover title. "Most of this material is reprinted from the November 1938 issue of Contemporary Jewish record," p. 15. https://ia601202.us.archive.org/23/items/306346/306346.pdf; "Antisemitism in Europe: hearing before the Subcommittee on European Affairs of the Committee on Foreign Relations, United States Senate, One Hundred Eighth Congress, first session, October 22, 2003. https://www.govinfo.gov/content/pkg/CHRG-108shrg95528/html/CHRG-108shrg95528.htm:
"The Franklin 'Prophecy' is a classic antisemitic canard that falsely claims that American statesman Benjamin Franklin made anti-Jewish statements during the Constitutional Convention of 1787. It has found widening acceptance in Muslim and Arab media, where it has been used to criticize Israel and Jews."; Saul J. Singer. "Benjamin Franklin And The Jews," The Jewish Press, June 28, 2023 https://www.jewishpress.com/sections/features/features-on-jewish-world/benjamin-franklin-and-the-jews/2023/06/28/;
Karl Marx. *A World Without Jews*, translated by Dagobert David Runes, Philos, New York, 1959, 83pp.;
Adolf Hitler. *Mein Kampf ("My Struggle")*, (originally 1925-1926), Reissue edition (September 15, 1998), Publisher: Mariner Books, English, paperback, 720pp.

[135.] Rabbi Jonathan Sacks. *The Rabbi Sacks Legacy*. "Letting Go," January 15, 2005 https://rabbisacks.org/covenant-conversation/bo/letting-go/
[136.] *A Modern Qur'anic Kampf Against The Jews*, p. 13.
[137.] Ibid, p. 29.
[138.] Ibid, p. 45.
[139.] Ibid, pp. 50, 56; Isidore Singer, Gotthard Deutsch. "Rohling, August," *The Jewish Encyclopedia* https://www.jewishencyclopedia.com/articles/12807-rohling-august
[140.] *A Modern Qur'anic Kampf Against The Jews*, p. 89.
[141.] Ibid, p. 92.
[142.] Ibid, p. 95.
[143.] Ibid, p. 96.
[144.] Ibid, p. 97.
[145.] Ibid, p. 98.
[146.] Ibid, pp. 96, 102-104.
[147.] Ibid, p, 219, chapter 4 refers to jizya humiliation; chapter 8 reference is on p. 550.
[148.] See reference 96.
[149.] S.D. Goitein. "Evidence on the Muslim Poll Tax from Non-Muslim Sources," *Journal of Economic and Social History of the Orient*, 1963, Volume 6, pp. 278-95; extracts from reproduction of this entire essay in Bostom, *The Legacy of Islamic Antisemitism*, pp 481,486.; Shlomo Dov [S. D.] Goitein (1900–1985) was a historian of Muslim-Jewish relations and a Jewish ethnographer, renowned for his expositions of Jewish life in the High Middle Ages (c. 950–1250 CE), based on the careful analysis of thousands of Geniza documents, an accumulation of almost two hundred thousand Jewish manuscripts that were found in the "geniza," or storeroom depository of the Ben Ezra synagogue (built 882) of Fostat, Egypt (now Old Cairo), the Basatin cemetery east of Old Cairo, and a number of old documents that were brought to Cairo in the latter part of the nineteenth century. Goitein's seminal research findings were widely published, most notably in the monumental five-volume work *A Mediterranean Society: The Jewish Communities of the Arab World as Portrayed in the Documents of the Cairo Geniza (1967–1993)*.
[150.] *A Modern Qur'anic Kampf Against The Jews*, p. 111.
[151.] Julius Wellhausen. "Muhammad's Constitution of Medina" (first published as "Muhammads Gemeindeordnung von Medina," in *Skizzen und Vorarbeiten* [Berlin, 1889] vol. 4, pp. 67–83), published as an excursus in Arent Jan Wensinck, *Muhammad and the Jews of Medina*, trans. Wolfgang H. Behn (Berlin: 1982), pp. 137, 136.
[152.] Arent Jan Wensinck. (first published as *Mohammed en de Joden te Medina* [Leiden, 1908]), with an excursus [appendix] from Julius Wellhausen's "Muhammad's Constitution of Medina" (first published as "Muhammads Gemeindeordnung von Medina" from *Skizzen und Vorarbeiten* [Berlin, 1889], vol. 4, pp. 67–83). English translation by Wolfgang H. Behn (Berlin: 1982), pp. 70–71.
[153.] Moshe Gil. "The Constitution of Medina: A Reconsideration," *Israel Oriental Studies* 4 (1974): 64–65.
[154.] *A Modern Qur'anic Kampf Against The Jews*, p. 197.
[155.] Ibid, p. 211.
[156.] Ibid.
[157.] Ibid, p. 196.

[158] See Eliezer Tauber. *The Massacre That Never Was—The Myth of Deir Yassin and the Creation of the Palestinian Refugee Problem*, London, The Toby Press, 2021, 322 pp.
[159] See Bostom. *The Legacy of Islamic Antisemitism*, pp. xx, yy, etc.; Andrew Bostom. "Islam and the 'Sexual Ethics' of Jihad Slavery," Video and text of a speech delivered Friday, January 29, 2016, at The Education Policy Conference, St. Louis, MO, USA https://andrewbostom.net/2016/05/video-text-islam-and-the-sexual-ethics-of-jihad-slavery/; *A Modern Qur'anic Kampf Against The Jews*, reference section to Tantawi's chapter 4, pp. 270-273.
[160] Bostom, *The Legacy of Islamic Antisemitism*, pp. 56-57; Bostom, *Sharia Versus Freedom*, pp. 107-118.
[161] See note 159.
[162] *A Modern Qur'anic Kampf Against The Jews*, pp. 222, 239, 245, 256, and 269.
[163] *"...the treaty of Hudaybiyya(h), [was] negotiated by the Prophet with the (Meccan pagan tribe) Quraysh in a state of war: it was a limited truce. If the Muslims are powerful, they may not hold an armistice for more than one year; if they are militarily inferior, an armistice of ten years is allowed."* From Bassam Tibi. "War and Peace in Islam," cited in Bostom, *The Legacy of Jihad*, p. 334.
[164] *A Modern Qur'anic Kampf Against The Jews*, p. 219.
[165] Tantawi, *The intermediate [balanced] interpretation of the Qur'an*, https://www.altafsir.com/Tafasir.asp?tMadhNo=0&tTafsirNo=57&tSoraNo=3&tAyahNo=12&tDisplay=yes&UserProfile=0&LanguageId=1
[166] *A Modern Qur'anic Kampf Against The Jews*, p. 237.
[167] Tantawi, *The intermediate [balanced] interpretation of the Qur'an*, https://www.altafsir.com/Tafasir.asp?tMadhNo=0&tTafsirNo=57&tSoraNo=59&tAyahNo=14&tDisplay=yes&UserProfile=0&LanguageId=1
[168] *A Modern Qur'anic Kampf Against The Jews*, p. 220.
[169] Bostom, *Sharia***Error! Bookmark not defined.** *Versus Freedom*, pp. 131-139, 320-322.; See also, Andrew Bostom. "Ten Key Points on Islamic Blasphemy Law," *The American Thinker*, March 15, 2013 https://www.americanthinker.com/blog/2013/03/ten_key_points_on_islamic_blasphemy_law.html
[170] Al-Shafi'i (d. 820), a theologian and jurisconsult, was born in Gaza, and became a disciple of the Medinan jurist, Malik b. Anas (d. 795), founder of the Maliki school of Islamic jurisprudence. Shafi'i, after whom the Shafi'ite school of jurisprudence is named, is considered to have developed the "legal science" of *usul al fiqh*, i.e., understanding the sources of Islamic law and the scholarly pursuit dedicated to elucidating these sources, and their relationship to substantive Islamic legal rulings
[171] Ibn Taymiyya (d. 1328) was a Syrian theologian and jurisconsult of the Hanbali school of jurisprudence under the Mamluks, who was active in Damascus. He left a considerable corpus of jurisprudence, which later inspired the Wahhabi movement in 18th century Arabia.
[172] *A Modern Qur'anic Kampf Against The Jews*, p. 226.
[173] See Bostom, *The Legacy of Jihad*, pp. 29-37.
[174] *A Modern Qur'anic Kampf Against The Jews*, p. 226.

[175] *The Life of Muhammad—A Translation of Ishaq's Sirat Rasul Allah*, with an Introduction and Notes by A. Guillaume, Oxford, U.K. Oxford University Press, 1955, 1967, 2004 (Printed in Pakistan by Mas Printers), p. 464, section 690. https://ia801606.us.archive.org/13/items/IbnIshaqMuhammad/Ibn%20Ishaq%20-%20Muhammad.pdf

[176] *A Modern Qur'anic Kampf Against The Jews*, p. 269.

[177] See Ibn Warraq, *Defending the West—A Critique of Edward Said's Orientalism*, Prometheus Books, Amherst, N.Y., 2007, pp. 53-54. *"The most pernicious legacy of Said's Orientalism is its implicit support for religious fundamentalism, and its insistence that 'all the ills [of the Arab world] emanate from Orientalism and have nothing to do with the socio-economic, political, and ideological makeup of Arab lands or the cultural backwardness behind it.' Thus ironically, Said, a Christian agnostic, becomes a de facto apologist and protector of Islam, the least Christian religion and certainly the religion least given to self-doubt. Despite his claims that he does not know anything about Islam, and despite the fact that he has never written a single scholarly work devoted to Islam, Said has always assumed the role in the West of an Islamic expert and has never flinched from telling us in unscholarly journalistic articles what the real Islam is. One's reaction is 'stop telling us what Islam is, let us Muslims do that, stop talking for Muslims.' Said is a secularist defending Islam, so one wonders how he will be able to argue for a non-theocratic state once Palestine becomes a reality—in a theocratic Islamic Palestine, he would be put in his dhimmi place. If Islam is such a wonderful religion, why does he not convert to it, and why does he not accept it as the basis for any new constitution? At some stage, Said will have to do what he has always been avoiding all his adult life—criticize Islam, or at least indirectly the idea of a theocracy. Said has much to answer for. Orientalism, despite its systematic distortions and its limited value as intellectual history, has left Western scholars in fear of asking questions—in other words, it has inhibited their research. Said's work, with its strident anti-Westernism, has made the goal of modernization of Middle Eastern societies that much more difficult. His work, wherein all the ills of Middle Eastern societies are blamed on the wicked West, has rendered much needed self-criticism by Muslims, Arab and non-Arab alike, nearly impossible. His work has encouraged Islamic fundamentalists, whose impact on world affairs needs no underlining."*

[178] Hartwig Hirschfeld. "Essai Sur l'Histoire des Juifs de Medina," *Revue Des Etudes Juives*, 1885, vol. 10, p. 11. English translation in Bostom, *The Legacy of Islamic Antisemitism*, p. 67.; Hirschfeld (d. 1934) was born in Thorn, Germany (now Torun, in Poland), received his doctorate in Strasbourg, France (then in Germany), and moved to England in 1889. Hirschfeld taught initially at Montefiore College, Ramsgate, and in 1901 was appointed librarian and professor of Semitic languages at Jews' College, London. He also taught Hebrew, Semitic epigraphy, and Ethiopian at University College. His major work was on the interaction between Jewish and Arabic cultures as well as the Arabic literature of the Jews. Hirschfeld published Judah Halevi's Kuzari in its original Judeo-Arabic and in Hebrew, German, and English translations. Among his many other works is a series of essays on Arabic fragments.

[179] W. H. T. Gairdner, "Muhammad without Camouflage," *Moslem World* 1919, vol. 9, p. 36.; Gairdner (d. 1928) was an Anglican theologian who spent three decades in Cairo, Egypt, acquiring renown as a very accomplished Arabic linguist, and teacher. His

scholarship included the publication of a seminal translation of Al-Ghazali's "*Mishkat Al-Anwar*" ["*The Niche For Lights*"]. A dedicated student of Islam, while respectful of the creed, Gairdner paid considerable attention to its expansion, and wrote unapologetically about the challenges that it posed to Christianity.

180. Hartwig Hirschfeld, "The Annals of Islam," review of *Annali dell'Islam compilati de Leone Caetani, Principe de Teano*, vol. 2 (Milan: 1907), in *Jewish Quarterly Review* 1908; vol. 20, p. 876.

181. Ibid. Regarding the breached treaty, Hirschfeld refers to its existence in his own essay "The Arabic Portion of the Cairo Genizah at Cambridge," *Jewish Quarterly Review* 1905; vol. 15, 170–74.

182. D. S. Margoliouth , *Mohammed and the Rise of Islam*, London, 1905, reprint New Delhi, 1985, pp. 362–63. See these extracts from "David Samuel Margoliouth, 1858-1940," an obituary by the great Islamic scholar H. A. R. Gibb, published in the *Journal of the Royal Asiatic Society of Great Britain and Ireland*, No. 3 (July., 1940), pp. 392-394: *"It would be no exaggeration to say that for the last thirty five years Professor Margoliouth was, in the eyes of lay and learned alike, the leading Arabic scholar in England. By virtue of his publications, learning and personality, and the position which he held in this Society, he was regarded in the international circle of Orientalists as the chief representative of Oriental Studies in Great Britain, while his long tenure of the Laudian Professorship at Oxford had contributed to give him an almost legendary reputation amongst non-Orientalists and even in the Islamic countries of the East...With the appearance of Mohammed and the Rise of Islam in the "Heroes of the Nations" series in 1905, Margoliouth for the first time came before the wider public as an interpreter of Islam. This essay was followed by Mohammedanism in the Home University Library in 1911, and a more important series of Hibbert Lectures on the Early Development of Mohammedanism, published in 1914, as well as a number of articles contributed to various encyclopedias. All three books had a substantial success, and have stood for a generation as the standard English works on their subjects...The solid learning which had gone into the making of them was universally respected, and the last of the three especially threw new light on many disputed questions."*

183. Hirschfeld discusses two assassinations of Khaybar Jews, prior to the Muslims' assault on Khaybar (Hirschfeld, "Essai sur l'histoire des Juifs de Medine," pp. 27–28.; English translation in Bostom, *The Legacy of Islamic Antisemitism*, p.74.), which is confirmed by Ibn Ishaq (Guillaume, *The Life of Muhammad*, pp. 665–66, and 482–83).

184. Georges Vajda. "Juifs et musulmans selon le Hadit," *Journal Asiatique* 1937, vol. 229 (January–March, 57–127.; Extracts from p. 85. English translation in Bostom, *The Legacy of Islamic Antisemitism*, p. 76.; Vajda (d. 1981) was born in Budapest and educated in the local rabbinical seminary. He moved to Paris in 1928, where he resided until his death. Possessing a sound knowledge of classical languages and Arabic, Hebrew, Persian, and Turkish, from 1933 he was a member of the editorial committee of *Revue des Études Juives*, and professor of the Bible and of Jewish theology at the Séminaire Israélite de France, where, in 1931, Vajda began his teaching career as a lecturer. He gained a faculty appointment in 1937 at the École Pratique des Hautes Études, Paris. After escaping the German occupation by hiding in Haute-Loire, Vajda resumed his work with unparalleled vigor, rising to Directeur D'Etudes in 1954, and professor at the Sorbonne. He published his seminal analysis of the characterization of the Jews in the hadith ("Juifs et Musulmans

Selon le Hadit") in 1937. Vajda's other major studies among more than 1,600 articles and books, included *Introduction a la Pensee Juive du Moyen Age* (1947), *Repertoire de Catalogues et Inventaires de Manuscrits Arabes* (1949), and *Judische Philosophie* (1950).

185. *A Modern Qur'anic Kampf Against The Jews*, p. 2.

186. Ibid, p. 274

187. Ibid, pp. 285, 293, 295, and 299.

188. Ibid, pp. 277, 296, and 300.

189. The great Muslim historian and Qur'anic exegete Tabari (d. 923) interpreted the Qur'anic curse upon the Jews in Q 2:61 as follows: *"[A]basement and poverty were imposed and laid down upon them," as when someone says "the imam imposed the poll tax (jizya) on free non- Muslim subjects," or "The man imposed land tax on his slave," meaning thereby that he obliged him [to pay] it, or, "The commander imposed a sortie on his troops," meaning he made it their duty. Allah commanded His believing servants not to give them [i.e., the non-Muslim people of the scripture, including Jews]] security—as long as they continued to disbelieve in Him and His Messenger—unless they paid the poll tax to them; Allah said: 'Fight those who believe not in Allah and the Last Day and do not forbid what Allah and His Messenger have forbidden— such men as practice not the religion of truth [Islam], being of those who have been given the Book [Bible]—until they pay the poll tax, being humble.' (Qur'an 9:29) Ibn Zaid said about His words 'and abasement and poverty were imposed upon them,'... 'These are the Jews of the Children of Israel.' I said: 'Are they the Copts of Egypt?' He said:* ***'What have the Copts of Egypt to do with this? No, by Allah, they are not; but they are the Jews, the Children of Israel.*** *' By 'and slain the prophets unrightfully,' He means that they used to kill the Messengers of Allah without Allah's leave, denying their messages and rejecting their prophethood."* From Tabari, The Commentary on the Qur'an, with an introduction and notes by J. Cooper, ed. W. F. Medlung and A. Jones (Oxford: Oxford University Press, 1987), pp. 353–55.; Baydawi (d. 1316), in his important Qur'anic exegesis *Anwaar al-Tanziil wa-Asraar al-Ta'wiil*, provided this analysis of Qur'an 2:61: " *'[H]umiliation and wretchedness' covered them like a dome, or stuck to them like wet clay to a wall—a metaphor for their denial of the bounty.* ***The Jews are mostly humiliated and wretched either of their own accord, or out of coercion of the fear of having their jizya doubled.*** *. . . Either they became deserving of His wrath [or] . . . the affliction of "humiliation and wretchedness" and the deserving wrath which preceded this. "[B]ecause they disbelieved and killed the prophets unjustly" by reason of their disbelief in miracles, e.g. the splitting of the sea, the clouds giving shade, and the sending of the manna and quails, and splitting of the rock into twelve fountains or, disbelief in the revealed books, e.g. the Gospel, Qur'an, the verse of stoning, and the Torah verse in which Muhammad is depicted; and their killing of the prophets like Shay'aa [Isaiah], Zakariyyaa, Yahyaa, et al., all killed unjustly because they considered that of these prophets nothing was to be believed and thus they deserved to be killed. In addition [Allah] accuses them of following fantasy and love of this world, as he demonstrates in His saying 'this if for their transgression and sin,' i.e.* ***rebelliousness, contrariness, and hostility brought them into disbelief in the signs, and killing the prophets****. Venal sins lead to serious sins, just as small bits of obedience lead to larger ones...* ***[Allah] repeated this proof of what is inveterate [in the Jews], which is the reason for their unbelief and murder, and which is the cause of their***

committing sins and transgressing the bounds Allah set. *"* Baydawi, Commentaius in Coranum: Anwaar al- Tanziil Wa-Asraar al-Ta'wiil, ed. H. O. Fleischer (1846–48; reprint, Osnabrück: 1968), p. 63; English translation by Michael Schub, in Bostom, *The Legacy of Islamic Antisemitism*, p. 35.; Ibn Kathir (d. 1373), another prominent Qur'anic commentator, emphasized the Jews' eternal humiliation in accord with Qur'an 2:61: "This ayah indicates that the Children of Israel were plagued with humiliation, and this will continue, meaning it will never cease. They will continue to suffer humiliation at the hands of all who interact with them, along with the disgrace that they feel inwardly. Al-Hassan commented, 'Allah humiliated them under the feet of the Muslims, who appeared at a time when the Majus (Zoroastrians) were taking the jizya from the Jews. Also, Abu Al-'Aliyah, Ar-Rabi bin Anas and As-Suddi said that 'misery' used in that ayah means poverty. 'Atiyah Al-'Awfi said that 'misery' means, 'paying the tilth (tax).' In addition, Ad-Dahhak commented on Allah's statement, 'and they drew on themselves the wrath of Allah,' 'They deserved Allah's anger'. Also, Ibn Jarir (al-Tabari) said that, 'and they drew on themselves the wrath of Allah' means, 'They went back with the wrath.' Similarly, Allah said, 'Verily, I intend to let you draw my sin on yourself as well as yours' (Qur'an 5:29) meaning, 'You will end up carrying my and your mistakes instead of me. Thus the meaning of the ayah becomes, "They went back carrying Allah's anger: Allah's wrath descended upon them; they deserved Allah's anger.' Allah's statement, 'That was because they used to disbelieve in the Ayat (proofs, evidence, etc.) of Allah and killed the Prophets wrongfully,' means 'This is what We rewarded the Children of Israel with: humiliation and misery.' **Allah's anger that descended on the Children of Israel was a part of the humiliation they earned, because of their defiance of the truth, disbelief in Allah's Law, i.e., the Prophets and their following. The Children of Israel rejected the Messengers even killing them. Surely there is no form of disbelief worse than disbelieving in Allah's ayat and murdering the Prophets of Allah**."; English translation from: Ibn Kathir, Tafsir Ibn Kathir (Riyadh: 2000), vol. 1, pp. 245–46.

190. *A Modern Qur'anic Kampf Against The Jews*, p. 318

191. Ibid.

192. "D.F. Green" (compound pseudonym for David Littman and Yehoshafat Harkabi). *Arab Theologians on Jews and Israel—Extracts from the proceedings of the Fourth Conference of the Academy of Islamic Research*, 1971, 1976, Geneva, (Cairo, October 1968), pp. 29-32, from Sheikh Abd Allah Meshad (Mashhad)'s presentation, "*Jews' Attitude Towards Islam and Muslims in the First Islamic Era*"; "Sheikh Abdullah Al-Mashhad (Meshad) was born in Dayrut, a district of Mahmoudiya in the Beheira Governorate. He received a traditional religious education, beginning with a kuttab (a school where he memorized the Quran). He continued his education until he earned the ancient global certificate from Al-Azhar Al-Sharif. He rose through the ranks at Al-Azhar Al-Sharif, starting by teaching at the Alexandria Institute, then the Cairo Institute, and finally the Faculty of Sharia, where he excelled... He held several scholarly and advocacy positions, most notably, since the late 1950s, he was the Director of Preaching at Al-Azhar, a corps of scholars spread across various regions encompassing the entire country. Sheikh Abdullah Al-Mashhad was also chosen as Dean of Arabic and Islamic Studies in its new Higher Department in 1964. These studies began during the reign of Sheikh Al-Baqouri and were later transformed during the reign of Dr. Abdel Halim

Mahmoud into the college known by this name in 1976, which has become a prestigious college today. Sheikh Abdullah Al-Mashhad was chosen as a member of the Islamic Research Academy and Assistant Secretary-General of the Academy. He concluded his tenure by becoming Chairman of the Fatwa Committee at Al-Azhar. Toward the end of his life, Sheikh Al-Mashhad served as a religious advisor for Sharia supervision at several national banks." From, Dr. Mohammed al-Jawady. "Abdullah Al-Mashhad (Meshad), the jurist and mujtahid who issued a fatwa permitting the slaughter of sacrificial animals outside the Hijaz," *Al-Jazeera online*, 8/24/2020 https://rb.gy/dsue5y

193. "Former Al-Azhar Fatwa Committee Head Sets Out the Jews' 20 Bad Traits as Described in the Qur'an," April 6, 2004, *Middle East Media Research Institute*, February 27, 2004, Special Dispatch Series # 691.; Sheikh Atiyyah Saqr (d. 2006), "received his education at al-Azhar University, graduating with the al-Alamiyah degree in 1941. Alongside being a prolific writer, he was a consultant for the Egyptian Ministry of Awqaf, (the ministry of religious endowments). He sat in various religious councils, such as the Al-Azhar's Islamic Research Academy, Higher Council for Islamic Affairs and Al-Azhar's Fatwa Committee." October 13, 2022 https://www.islamopediaonline.org/atiyyah-saqr/

194. "Former Al-Azhar Fatwa Committee Head Sets Out the Jews' 20 Bad Traits as Described in the Qur'an,"

195. *A Modern Qur'anic Kampf Against The Jews*, p. 324.

196. Ibid.

197. Ibid, p. 336.

198. Ibid, pp. 349, 350, 353, and 343.

199. Ibid, pp. 368, and 369.

200. Ibid, p. 382.

201. Ibid, pp. 382, 384, 386, and 387.

202. Ibid, p. 392.

203. Ibid.

204. Ibid, pp. 392 and 393.

205. Tantawi, translation herein, p. xy; See *Tafsir Al-Jalalayn*, on Q 2:96 p. 34: *"In fact the Jews are even greedier for life than the idolators, because they know they will end up in the Fire…Allah will give them their just deserts."* Also see note 78.

206. *A Modern Qur'anic Kampf Against The Jews*, p. 403.

207. Ibid, pp. 403 and 405.

208. Ibid, p. 407.

209. Ibid, pp. 409 and 425.

210. Ibid, p. 436.

211. Ibid, p. 419.

212. Ibid, p. 425.

213. Ibid, p. 435.

214. Ibid, p. 244.

215. Ibid.

216. Ibid, pp. 452, 452, and 459.

217. Ibid, p. 465.

218. Ibid, pp. 473, and 474.

219. Ibid, p. 474.

220. Ibid.
221. Ibid, pp. 479 and 480.
222. Ibid, p. 447 (Qur'an 2:81)
223. Ibid pp. 483, and 484. (Jami at-Tirmidhi 2954 https://sunnah.com/urn/639380)
224. Ibid, p. 484.
225. Ibid, p. 487. (also see reference 85 on al-Alusi)
226. Ibid, p. 491.
227. Ibid.
228. Ibid.
229. Ibid, p. 489.
230. Ibid, pp. 503-524.
231. Ibid, p. 497.
232. Ibid.
233. "DECLARATION ON THE RELATION OF THE CHURCH TO NON-CHRISTIAN RELIGIONS, NOSTRA AETATE, PROCLAIMED BY HIS HOLINESS POPE PAUL VI, ON OCTOBER 28, 1965" https://bit.ly/2sKp5HI; Norman C. Tobias. *Jewish Conscience of The Church—Jules Isaac and the Second Vatican Council*, 2017, Palgrave MacMillan, Switzerland, 307pp.
234. *A Modern Qur'anic Kampf Against The Jews*, pp. 492 and 493.
234a. Tafsir al-Baydawi, from the gloss on Q 4:157 https://www.altafsir.com/Tafasir.asp?tMadhNo=0&tTafsirNo=6&tSoraNo=4&tAyahNo=157&tDisplay=yes&UserProfile=0&LanguageId=1 "It was narrated that a group of Jews insulted him [Isa] and his mother [Mary], so he prayed against them, and Allah transformed them into monkeys and pigs."
235. *A Modern Qur'anic Kampf Against The Jews*, pp. 498 and 503.
236. Ibid, p. 498.
237. Ibid, pp. 497 and 498.
238. Ibid, pp. 499-503, also, Tantawi, translation herein, p. xy; Sahih al-Bukhari 3448 https://sunnah.com/bukhari:3448; also from Sahih Muslim, see: Sahih Muslim Book 1, Hadith Number 289. https://hadithcollection.com/sahihmuslim/sahih-muslim-book-01-faith/sahih-muslim-book-001-hadith-number-0289, and Sahih Muslim Book 1, Hadith Number 293. https://hadithcollection.com/sahihmuslim/sahih-muslim-book-01-faith/sahih-muslim-book-001-hadith-number-0293; Mark Durie. "Isa, the Muslim Jesus" https://www.answering-islam.org/authors/durie/islamic_jesus.html; Duncan B. MacDonald, "Isa" *First Encyclopaedia of Islam*, Vol. III, pp. 524-526, especially p. 525.; and from *Tafsir al-Baydawi* (Baydawi's, *Anwar al-Tanzil wa Asrar al Ta'wil*), his glosses on Q 4:157 (see note 234a), and Q 43:61: https://www.altafsir.com/Tafasir.asp?tMadhNo=0&tTafsirNo=6&tSoraNo=43&tAyahNo=61&tDisplay=yes&Page=2&Size=1&LanguageId=1
239. See reference 237.
240. *A Modern Qur'anic Kampf Against The Jews*, p. 499.
241. Ibid, pp. 499, 500, and 503.
242. Tafsir al-Baydawi on Q 43:61 https://www.altafsir.com/Tafasir.asp?tMadhNo=0&tTafsirNo=6&tSoraNo=43&tAyahNo=61&tDisplay=yes&Page=2&Size=1&LanguageId=1; Baydawi [Baidawi], d. 1282, was a jurist and Qur'anic commentator. The *First Encyclopaedia of Islam*, Vol. II, pp.

590-591 entry on him notes, "His chief work *Anwar al-Tanzil wa Asrar al Ta'wil*, (was) a commentary on the Qur'an, based on the Kashshaf of Zamakshari, but considerably simplified from other sources. His commentary is regarded by the Sunnis as the best and almost a holy book. He is especially noted for the fact that his work contains much material in small compass…"

[243.] MacDonald, *First Encyclopaedia of Islam*, Vol. III, p. 525; Duncan B. MacDonald, 1863-1943, "For close on fifty years [he] was the foremost Islamic scholar and teacher on the American continent… The first of his published works, issued in 1903, on the *Development of Muslim Theology, Jurisprudence, and Constitutional Theory,* already showed his remarkable power to clothe the dry bones of his subject with living tissue. All his later work was instinct with the same vitality—the vitality of one who has thought and felt deeply and whose vision has penetrated through the outer husks to the essential core."

From his obituary by Sir Hamilton Gibb, Gibb HAR. "Duncan Black Macdonald 1863–1943". *Journal of the Royal Asiatic Society*. 1944;76(1-2):87-88; p. 87.

[244.] See reference 230.

[244a.] https://quran.com/5?startingVerse=64

[245.] Tantawi, *"The intermediate [balanced] interpretation of the Qur'an,"* gloss on Q 5:64
https://www.altafsir.com/Tafasir.asp?tMadhNo=0&tTafsirNo=57&tSoraNo=5&tAyahNo=64&tDisplay=yes&UserProfile=0&LanguageId=1

[246.] *A Modern Qur'anic Kampf Against The Jews*, pp. 507 and 506.

[247.] Ibid, p. 507.

[248.] Ibid, p. 508.

[249.] Jonathan Frankel. "'Ritual Murder' in the Modern Era: The Damascus Affair of 1840," *Jewish Social Studies*, Winter, 1997, New Series, Vol. 3, No. 2 (Winter, 1997), pp. 1-16; see especially p, 2; Also, Jonathan Frankel. *The Damascus Affair. "Ritual Murder," Politics and the Jews in 1840*, Cambridge University Press, 1997, especially pp. 79, 100-101, 136, 344-345, 437-438.; From pp. 46-47, here are some of the details Frankel provides of Moses Abu el-Afieh's (and his wife's) torture that extracted his false confession: *"Abu el-Afieh, about forty years old, was…a rabbi by training but a merchant by profession. He was one of the accused subjected to the greatest cruelties, being twice deprived of sleep for three days at a time, twice dragged around by the genitals, and twice flogged. (Many months later he was still lame from the beatings applied to the soles of his feet.) On March 1 [1840] he was taken to find the bottle of blood which, according to the confessions up to that moment, including his own, was hidden in his house. Among those accompanying him were Count de Ratti-Menton, the chief of police, and Francis Salina, who was one of the French consul's closest confidants. What followed was described in a written statement drawn up in June by Ora Abu el-Afieh, the prisoner's wife. She, of course, was astounded to hear her husband constantly asking her for the blood, until he managed to say to her he had lied in order to be brought home, 'so that I would be killed; so that they would take my blood; so that they could say, 'Here is Father Thomas's blood,'…I'd prefer death to these tortures.' [Ora Abu el-Afieh stated] 'The consul did not want to believe that my husband had lied and that there was no blood…[He; The consul] began hitting me, saying 'Tell me, where's blood?' Salina [confidant of the consul], on orders of the consul, hit me very hard on the head ad body. A cord was tied around my husband's neck; the consul and Saline dragged him across the courtyard...causing him terrible pain—his feet, torn to pieces by the blows [in prison]...showed only the bones...This scene went on for about three hours.' She was the taken off, carrying her small baby, to the palace, and the consul sent a request to the governor-general to 'have me beaten and tortured.' Only an appeal, it seems, by a high official persuaded Sherif Pasha not to comply with the request, but orders were given to have her husband flogged again 'and he was given another two hundred lashes in my presence.' His sufferings on that day were, in all probability, the straw that broke the camel's back. On 2 March he declared that he wished to become a Muslim and it was now that he changed his original story, saying that he had delivered the bottle of blood to the chief rabbi."*

250. Tudor Parfitt. " 'The Year of the Pride of Israel': Montefiore and the Blood Libel of 1840," in *The Century of Moses Montefiore*, Oxford University Press, London, 1985, pp. 135-148, see pp. 133-134.; On the Safed pogroms, see Bostom, *The Legacy of Islamic Antisemitism*, pp. 594-596.; On the Damascus pogroms, see Consul James Brant to Sir Henry Bulwer, Damascus, 25th July, 1860, Consul James Brant to Lord John Russell, Damascus, 28th July, 1860, Consul James Brant to Sir Henry Bulwer, Damascus, 9th August, 1860, and Consul James Brant to Sir Henry Bulwer, Damascus, 16th August, 1860, all in Bat Ye'or, *The Decline of Eastern Christianity Under Islam*, Farleigh Dickinson University Press, Teaneck, N.J., 1996, pp. 404-408.

251. Frankel. *The Damascus Affair. "Ritual Murder," Politics and the Jews in 1840*, pp. 437-438.

252. Parfitt, "'The Year of the Pride of Israel': Montefiore and the Blood Libel of 1840," p. 144.

253. Ibid, pp. 144-145.

254. *A Modern Qur'anic Kampf Against The Jews*, p. 508.

255. Ibid.

256. Efraim Karsh. *The Arab-Israeli Conflict: The Palestine War 1948*, Osprey Publishing, Oxford, 2002, 96 pp.; Efraim Karsh. "1948, Israel, and the Palestinians—The True Story," *Commentary*, May 2008. https://www.commentary.org/articles/efraim-karsh/1948-israel-and-the-palestinians-the-true-story/

257. *A Modern Qur'anic Kampf Against The Jews*, p. 542.

258. Eliezer Tauber. *The Massacre That Never Was—The Myth of Deir Yassin and the Creation of the Palestinian Refugee Problem,* ASMEA, The Toby Press, New Milford, CT, USA, 2021. Error! Bookmark not defined.

259. Ibid, pp. 206-207.

260. On the Hadassah attack, see Dov Joseph. *The faithful city: the siege of Jerusalem, 1948*, Simon and Schuster, New York, 1960, pp. 74-75: https://archive.org/details/thefaithfulcity0000unse/page/74/mode/2up; "*...in the Hadassah massacre...seventy-seven Jewish nurses or teachers were killed or burned alive on the road to Mount Scopus...* ***The attack had been commanded by an Iraqi officer, it was claimed by the Arab Higher Committee, which praised the massacre as an heroic exploit. It censured the British for their last minute intervention: "Had it not been for Army interference, not a single Jewish passenger would have remained alive.";*** On the Kfar Etzion attack, see Benny Morris. "Before the Kidnappings, There

Was a Massacre," *Tablet*, June 25, 2014 https://www.tabletmag.com/sections/israel-middle-east/articles/kfar-etzion: "…151 Jewish fighters—of whom 21 were women—[were] killed during the two-day battle; **127 of them died on the second day of the battle, May 13, 1948, the day before the State of Israel was established and proclaimed. Of these, most were murdered in the center of Kfar Etzion, the core settlement of the bloc, while surrendering or after they had surrendered**."

261. Tauber, *The Massacre That Never Was*, p. 170.

262. See reference 260 above.

263. Andrew G. Bostom. "Negating the Legacy of Jihad in Palestine", *Israel Affairs*, 2007, Vol. 13:4, pp. 819-836.; Also, Bostom, *The Legacy of Islamic Antisemitism*, pp. 78-91.

264. Hillel Cohen. *Year Zero of the Arab-Israeli Conflict 1929*, translated by Haim Watzman, Brandeis University Press, 2015, 312 pp.; Jerold S. Auerbach. *Hebron Jews: Memory and Conflict in the Land of Israel,* Roman and Littlefield, 2009, 240 pp. For a compelling post-October 7, 2023 re-analysis see, Yardena Schwartz. *Ghosts of a Holy War: The 1929 Massacre in Palestine That Ignited the Arab-Israeli Conflict,* Union Square & Company, New York, 2024, 432 pp.

265. "MOSLEMS SATE BLOOD LUST Even Little Children Die By Knife In Jehad," *Beatrice Daily Sun* (Nebraska), August 29, 1929, p. 8. https://www.newspapers.com/newspage/506702795/

266. Cohen, *Year Zero of the Arab-Israeli Conflict 1929*, p. xxi.

267. Ibid.

268. Ibid.

269. "Pinchas Tzvi Grayevsky and Family - Jerusalem - 1873-1941" https://jr.co.il/richman/pinchas-grayevsky.htm; Born in Jerusalem in 1873, "Grayevski was a well-known Jerusalem historian. Between 1896 and 1926 he wrote over 600 articles for newspapers in Israel and abroad under different pen names. He collected historical Jerusalem documents, biographical sketches, articles about institutions, events and life of the old Jewish yishuv in Jerusalem. His research was published in many Hebrew booklets and books. Titles include: 'B'not Tzion VeYerushalim', 'B'not Tzion HaMetzuyanot', 'Zichronot Kedumim', 'MiGinzei Yerushalaim', 'Zichron LaChovevim HaRishonim', 'Avnei Zikaron', 'K'neset Yerushalaim', 'Sefer HaZikaron' and more…"

270. Cohen, *Year Zero of the Arab-Israeli Conflict 1929*, p. 123.

271. Auerbach. *Hebron Jews: Memory and Conflict in the Land of Israel,* pp. 66-69ff.

272. Chen Malul. "Banned by the British: Caricatures of the 1929 Palestine Riots. Meet the artist who risked time in prison by drawing the massacre of the Jews in the Land of Israel in 1929." August 23, 2018 https://blog.nli.org.il/en/banned_drawings/

273. Auerbach. *Hebron Jews\: Memory and Conflict in the Land of Israel,* p. 66.

274. Frederick Hermann Kisch. *Palestine Diary*, AMS Press, 1974, p. 263.

275. "The 1517 Hebron Massacre" https://hebron.org.il/en/the-1517-hebron-massacre/ "The Hebrew text is printed in *Sefer Hevron* by Oded Avisar" See: https://hebron.org.il/en/out-of-print-sefer-hevron-now-available-online-in-full-text/

276. "The 1834 Hebron Massacre" https://hebron.org.il/en/the-1834-hebron-massacre/ ; Georges Bensoussan. "Pogroms in Palestine before the creation of the state of Israel (1830-1948)." https://www.fondapol.org/en/study/pogroms-in-palestine-before-the-creation-of-the-state-of-israel-1830-1948/

277. Marion Harland. *The Home of the Bible: What I Heard and Saw in Palestine*, 1896, The Christian Herald, pp. 328-29 https://archive.org/details/homeofbiblewhati00mari; John Kelman, *The Holy Land*, A. and C. Black, (London), 1902, pp. 97-98. https://archive.org/details/holyland00kelm_0

278. Moshe Gil. *A History of Palestine, 634-1099*, translated by Ethel Broido, Cambridge and New York, 1992, p. 2

279. Gil, *A History of Palestine*, 634-1099, pp. 15, 20; Demetrios Constantelos, "Greek Christian and Other Accounts of the Moslem Conquests of the Near East," in *Christian Hellenism: Essays and Studies in Continuity and Change*, New Rochelle, N.Y., A.D. Caratzas, 1998, pp. 126-130.

280. Bat Ye'or, *The Decline of Eastern Christianity Under Islam*, p. 44.; Bat Ye'or, "Islam and the Dhimmis," *The Jerusalem Quarterly*, 1987, Vol. 42, p. 85. Moshe Gil, *A History of Palestine, 634-1099*, pp. 61, 169-170; Naphtali Lewis, "New Light on the Negev in Ancient Times," *Palestine Exploration Quarterly*, 1948, vol. 80, pp. 116-117; Constantelos, "Greek Christian and Other Accounts of the Moslem Conquests of the Near East," pp. 127-128; *Al-Baladhuri The Origins of the Islamic State* (Kitah Futuh al-Buldan), translated by Philip K. Hitti, London, Longman, Greens, and Company, 1916, p. 217.

281. Bat Ye'or, *The Decline of Eastern Christianity Under Islam*, p. 74.

282. Chronique de Denys de Tell-Mahre, translated from the Syriac by Jean-Baptiste Chabot (Paris, 1895), part 4, p. 112. English translation in: Bat Ye'or, *The Decline of Eastern Christianity Under Islam*, p. 74.

283. Gil, *A History of Palestine, 634-1099*, p.159; Q 16:63: "By Allah! We have surely sent messengers to communities before you O Prophet, but Satan made their misdeeds appealing to them. So he is their patron today, and they will suffer a painful punishment."; Q 5:72 "Those who say, 'Allah is the Messiah, son of Mary,' have certainly fallen into disbelief. The Messiah himself said, 'O Children of Israel! Worship Allah—my Lord and your Lord.' Whoever associates others with Allah in worship will surely be forbidden Paradise by Allah. Their home will be the Fire. And the wrongdoers will have no helpers."

Q 58:19: "Satan has taken hold of them, causing them to forget the remembrance of Allah. They are the party of Satan. Surely Satan's party is bound to lose."; Bat Ye'or, *The Decline of Eastern Christianity Under Islam*, p. 84

284. Gil, *A History of Palestine*, 634-1099, pp. 371-379.

285. Moshe Gil. "Dhimmi Donations and Foundations for Jerusalem (638-1099)", *Journal of the Economic and Social History of the Orient*, Vol. 37, 1984, pp. 166—167.

286. Moshe Gil, *A History of Palestine*, 634-1099, pp. 412—416.

287. Julius Greenstone, in his essay, "The Turcoman Defeat at Cairo," The *American Journal of Semitic Languages and Literatures*, Vol. 22, 1906, pp. 144-175, provides a translation of this poem (excerpted, pp. 164-165]) by Solomon ha-Kohen b. Joseph (believed to be a descendant of the Geonim, an illustrious family of Palestinian Jews of priestly descent), which includes the poet's recollection of the previous Turcoman conquest of Jerusalem during the eighth decade of the 11th century. Greenstone comments (p. 152), "As appears from the poem, the conquest of Jerusalem by Atsiz was

very sorely felt by the Jews. The author dwell at great length on the cruelties perpetrated against the inhabitants of the city..."

288. For example, Steven Runciman, *A History of the Crusades— Vol. 1— The First Crusade and the Foundation of the Kingdom of Jerusalem*, Cambridge, 1951, Pp. 286-87; Gil, *A History of Palestine, 634-1099*, p. 827 notes, "The Christians violated their promise to the inhabitants that they would be left alive, and slaughtered some 20,000 to 30,000 people, a number which may be an exaggeration..."

289. Isaac b. Samuel of Acre. *Osar Hayyim* (Treasure Store of Life) (Hebrew). Ms. Gunzburg 775 fol. 27b. Lenin State Library, Moscow. (English translation in, Bat Ye'or, *The Dhimmi: Jews and Christians Under Islam*, pp. 352-54.)

290. Samuel b. Ishaq Uceda, *Lehem dim'ah (The Bread of Tears)* (Hebrew). Venice, 1606. [English translation in, Bat Ye'or, *The Dhimmi: Jews and Christians Under Islam*, pp. 354.

291. Bat Ye'or, *Islam and Dhimmitude— Where Civilizations Collide*. Cranbury, NJ.: Associated University Presses, 2001; p. 318.

292. Gedaliah of Siemiatyce, *Sha'alu Shelom Yerushalayim (Pray for the Peace of Jerusalem),* (Hebrew), Berlin, 1716. [English translation in, Bat Ye'or, *The Decline of Eastern Christianity Under Islam*, pp. 377-80.]

293. Edouard Engelhardt, *La Turquie et La Tanzimat, 2 Vols*., 1882, Paris, Vol. p.111, Vol. 2 p. 171; English translation in, Bat Ye'or. Islam *and Dhimmitude— Where Civilizations Collide*, Fairleigh Dickinson University Press, 2001, pp. 431-432; *Reports from Her Majesty's Consuls Relating to the Condition of the Christians in Turkey*, 1867 volume, pp. 5,29. See also related other reports by various consuls and vice—consuls, in the 1860 vol., p.58; the 1867 vol, pp. 4,5,6,14,15; and the 1867 vol., part 2, p.3 [All cited in, Vahakn Dadrian. Chapter 2, "The Clash Between Democratic Norms and Theocratic Dogmas", *Warrant for Genocide*, New Brunswick, New Jersey, Transaction Publishers, pp. 26-27, note 4]; See also, extensive excerpts from these reports in, Bat Ye'or, *The Decline of Eastern Christianity*, pp. 409-433; and Roderick Davison. "Turkish Attitudes Concerning Christian-Muslim Equality in the Nineteenth Century," *American Historical Review*, Vol. 59, pp. 848, 855, 859, 864.

294. Isidore Singer, E. Schwarzfeld. "BENJAMIN II., J. J. (real name, Joseph Israel)," *The Jewish Encyclopedia* https://www.jewishencyclopedia.com/articles/2948-benjamin-ii-j-j; J.J. Benjamin II. *Eight years in Asia and Africa from 1846 to 1855*, Hanover, 1863, published by the author, pp. 31-34.
https://archive.org/details/eightyearsinasi00benjgoog

295. Gregory Wortabet, *Syria and the Syrians. Vol. II*, London, 1856, pp. 263-264; Consul James Finn, published in, Albert M. Hyamson. The *British Consulate in Jerusalem (in relation to the Jews of Palestine)*, Edward Goldstein Ltd., London, 1939, p. 261.

296. Tudor Parfitt, *The Jews of Palestine, 1800-1882*, Suffolk, England, The Boydell Press, 1987, pp. 168, 172-173.

297. Musa Kazem el-Husseini (President Palestinian Arab Congress), to High Commissioner for Palestine, 10 December 1920 (translated 2 January 1921), *Israel State Archives*, R.G. 2, Box 10, File 244.

298. David Bedein. "Essential Questions not Being Asked of Nations that will Recognize a Planned Palestinian State," *The Times of Israel*, August 17, 2025.

https://blogs.timesofisrael.com/essential-questions-not-being-asked-of-nations-that-will-recognize-a-planned-palestinian-state/
299. "A Friday Sermon on PA TV:..We Must Educate our Children on the Love of Jihad," *Middle East Media Research Institute* (MEMRI), July 11, 2001, https://web.archive.org/web/20171002174807/https://www.memri.org/reports/palestinian-authority-sermons-2000-2003
300. "Muslim–Christian Tensions in the Israeli- Arab Community', *Middle East Media Research Institute* (MEMRI), August 2, 1999, https://web.archive.org/web/20170411153707/https://www.memri.org/reports/muslim-christian-tensions-israeli-arab-community
301. *A Modern Qur'anic Kampf Against The Jews*, p. 514.
302. Ibid, pp. 514-516.
303. Ibid, p. 514. (For analyses of the Muslim sources by respected Western scholars, see references 178-184.)
304. Ibid, p. 512. (On Abdullah Ibn Saba, see Bostom, *The Legacy of Islamic Antisemitism*, pp. 41,100, 319, 337, 389-390.; Sean W. Anthony, *The Caliphs and the Heretic: Ibn Saba, The Sabaiya and Early Shi'ism Between Myth and History*, Ph.D. Dissertation, University of Chicago, August, 2009 http://bit. ly/1ckyFfF; Sean W. Anthony, "The Legend of Abdallāh ibn Saba and the Date of Umm al- Kitāb," *Journal of the Royal Asiatic Society*, 2011, Vol. 21, pp. 1-30 http://bit.ly/1eG7rpy)
305. Ibid, p. 513. (Here are relevant citations with extracts on the Donmeh: Kaufmann Kohler, Richard Gottheil. "DÖNMEH," *The Jewish Encyclopedia*, https://www.jewishencyclopedia.com/articles/5278-donmeh "The community is outwardly Mohammedan; but in secret observes certain Jewish rites, **though in no way making common cause with the Jews, whom they call 'koferim' (infidels)**... The women wear the 'yashmak' (veil); the men have two sets of names: a religious one, which they keep secret, and a secular one for purposes of commercial intercourse. They are assiduous in visiting the mosque and in fasting during Ramadhan, and at intervals they even send one of their number on the 'ḥajj' (pilgrimage) to Mecca. But they do not intermarry with the Turks."; Marc David Baer. "An Enemy Old and New: The Dönme, Anti-Semitism, and Conspiracy Theories in the Ottoman Empire and Turkish Republic," *The Jewish Quarterly Review,* FALL 2013, Vol. 103, No. 4 (FALL 2013), pp. 523- 555. From pp. 528-529: "From 1908 to today, the Dönme character—a secret Jew hiding in the guise of the nation's leader who surreptitiously aims to destroy Turkish culture, nation, and people on behalf of world Jewry—has been the stock figure in antigovernment conspiracy theories promoted by Islamists dispossessed of their authority, extreme rightists, and most recently leftists and secularists divested of their power. Long indoctrinated by official historiography's belief that internal Christian enemies allied with foreign Christians always seek to destroy Turkey, the secularists were prepared to accept conspiracy theories about local minority puppets of world powers. The Islamists' rise to power and the decline of the secular elite's control of Turkey's wealth, power, and culture, triggered the secularists acceptance of the idea of a crypto-Jewish prime minister. **Antisemitic conspiracy theories gain traction among all elements of Turkish society based on the essentialist and racist assumption that only an ethnic Turkish Muslim can have Turkey's interests at heart, while a Jew—**

here the false convert, the secret Jew Dönme—can only serve foreign interests at odds with those of the Turks.")

306. Ibid, p. 515. (The following citations and extracts debunk Tantawi's assertions about William The Conqueror, Alexander The Great, King Philip II, and the Jews, and the alleged "Jewish accumulation of wealth" after World Wars I and II.

Mark Carlson. "Invasion 1066," *Naval History* (U.S. Naval Institute), October 2021 https://www.usni.org/magazines/naval-history-magazine/2021/october/invasion-1066#:~:text=Initially%2C%20this%20man%20who%20would,his%20wife%2C%20Matilda%20of%20Flanders

"Initially, this man who would be king was unsuccessful at raising the support of the Norman nobles for his invasion. Historian David Howarth claims in his book *1066: The Year of the Conquest* that William's "outraged pride gave them too much assurance and not enough persuasion." It was generally known that the English could mass a large fleet and at least 10,000 men at arms. But William declared, "Wars are not won by numbers but by courage." **He finally convinced Normandy's nobles that Harold indeed had sworn on holy relics to give William the crown. Then he used two very powerful incentives—greed and the church. An invasion of England would mean great riches for the barons who supported him. But his greatest coup was in convincing Pope Alexander II of the righteousness of his claim. Receiving a papal blessing for a now ostensibly holy crusade was his most potent weapon in the war to come. The Regent of France, Count Baldwin, provided French cavaliers and their horses, while William's representatives scoured Brittany, Flanders, Burgundy, Aquitaine, and Poitou for veteran foot and mounted men-at-arms**."

Steve Hurley. "Why the Pope Supported William's Invasion of England," *Regia Anglorum*, 1993

https://regia.org/research/history/papalpolitics.htm#:~:text=The%20Pope%20supported%20William%20of%20Normandy%20for,by:%20*%20**Prior%20Lanfranc**%20*%20**Archdeacon%20Hildebrand**

"Papal support in the form of the Papal Banner, a Relic and a Papal Blessing were issued. While copies of the Papal Blessing were made and sent from the Abbey of Bec to all those heads of state who may wish to join William in his crusade, clearly indicating the position of the Church."

How did William the Conqueror Fund? https://publish.obsidian.md/american-exodus/How+did+William+the+Conqueror+Fund%3F+Proprietary+Claims#:~:text=The%20root%20of%20William%20the,the%20world%20of%20feudal%20Europe

"The root of William the Conqueror's conquering of England was funded by a webbed network of informal promises to **financial elites around the world of feudal Europe**."

Isaac Broydé, Kaufmann Kohler, Israel Lévi. "ALEXANDER THE GREAT," *The Jewish Encyclopedia*,

https://www.jewishencyclopedia.com/articles/1120-alexander-the-great

"…**there are no personal details which connect him (Alexander) with Jewish history, save that after the siege of Tyre, 332 B.C., he marched through Palestine unopposed, except in the case of Gaza, which was razed to the ground**."

Jonathan Israel. "King Philip II of Spain as a symbol of 'Tyranny' in Spinoza's Political Writings," *Revista Co-herencia* Vol. 15, No 28 Enero - Junio de 2018, pp. 137-154. From p. 138 http://www.scielo.org.co/pdf/cohe/v15n28/1794-5887-cohe-15-28-00137.pdf
"After the battle for Lisbon, the historic liberties and privileges of Portugal, like those of Aragon subsequently, in 1591-1592, were ruthlessly suppressed by the Spanish monarch [i.e., King Phillip II]. **One ominous consequence of this 1580 'revolution' in Portugal for the 'New Christians', or *conversos* of Jewish descent, was that the powers of the Inquisition in Portugal, as might have been expected, were further extended. Faced by this crisis and disaster in Portugal, and marked intensification of persecution of all New Christians [i.e., Jews]…"**

Chase Peterson-Withorn. "From Rockefeller to Ford, See Forbes' 1918 Ranking Of The Richest People In America," *Forbes*, September 19, 2017. https://www.forbes.com/sites/chasewithorn/2017/09/19/the-first-forbes-list-see-who-the-richest-americans-were-in-1918/ No Jew was among the top 5 men with the greatest net worth in 1918 according to Forbes: John D. Rockefeller (\$1.2 billion); Henry Clay Frick (\$225 million); Andrew Carnegie (\$200 million); and George F. Baker and William Rockefeller were tied (\$150 million, each); After World War II, Henry Ford (1940s) and J. Paul Getty (1950s) had amassed the greatest wealth. Neither was a Jew. https://www.madisontrust.com/information-center/visualizations/a-timeline-of-the-richest-person-on-the-planet-since-1900/)
[307.] Ibid, pp. 516-518. (Also see note 306, above, and for realistic, scholarly assessment of Rothschild assets that debunk Tantawi's risible and undocumented claims, see Niall Ferguson. *The House of Rothschild THE WORLD'S BANKER, 1849-1998.* Penguin Books, New York, 2000. Appendix 2, Selected Financial Statistics, Table f: N. M. Rothschild & Sons: balance sheets, 1873-1918 (£, end of calendar year). 1918 (latest year) Total Assets=12,701,677 £ = **\$17,205,506** (U.S.) calculated per Lawrence H. Officer, "Dollar-Pound Exchange Rate From 1791," MeasuringWorth, 2025. URL: (1918= \$4.76 per £)]
http://www.measuringworth.com/exchangepound/; Regarding Tantawi's lunatic claim about "Jewish wealth in the United States" amounting to \$500 billion, that figure exceeds total U.S. assets by almost \$150 billion! See, "National Wealth and Income: A Report By the Federal Trade Commission in Final Response to Senate Resolution No. 451, Sixty-Seventh Congress, Fourth Session," Agreed to February 28, 1923 United States. Federal Trade Commission, May 25, 1926, p. 2: "The estimate of national wealth is shown in general for 1922, with comparisons for most items with 1912, on the basis of the census estimates, but with some modifications. **The total amount, as already noted, is about \$353,000,000,000 (\$352 billion) for 1922**…"; In addition, see this New York Times article from 1927: "AMERICAN WEALTH," *The New York Times*, Feb. 21, 1927, p. 16 https://www.nytimes.com/1927/02/21/archives/american-wealth.html
"America's prosperity is not mainly nor even largely the fruit of Continental misery. Our profits are not very largely war profits." This conclusion is clear from the tabulated income of the American people going back to the year 1909. Translating both 1909 dollars and 1926 dollars into 1913 dollars, we find that the increase has been from something over twenty-eight billions to nearly fifty-three billions. For the five-year

period 1909-13 the increase was something less than four billions, or an annual increase of 760 millions. For the nine-year period 1914-22, counting the four years after the armistice as 'war years,' the increase was nine billions, or a billion annually. For the four-year period 1923-26 the increase was twelve and a half billions, or more than three billions annually. In other words, in the four years since the beginning of European recovery the income of the American people increased one and a half times as much as during the nine preceding years of actual war and post-war prostration.")

308. Ibid. (See Karl Marx. *A world without Jews*, translated from the original German, with an introduction by Dagobert D. Runes, Philosophical Library, Inc. New York, 1959; Bill Potter. "The Baptism of Karl Marx, August 28, 1824," *Landmark Events*, August 24, 2020 https://landmarkevents.org/the-baptism-of-karl-marx-1824/ "when the Prussian government imposed the requirement of belonging to the state church in order to practice law, Heinrich (Marx, Karl's father) agreed to baptism for himself and his children…at the age of six, he (Karl) and six siblings were baptized into the Lutheran Church on August 28, 1824…When Karl reached the age of fifteen, he presumably went through the classes that led successfully to his confirmation in the Lutheran Church.")

309. Ibid, pp. 516-518 (Ben-Ito, *The Lie that Wouldn't Die: The Protocols of the Elders of Zion)*

310. Ibid, p. 523. (**The "world's largest brothel" is found in Muslim Bangladesh, and it is decidedly not "run by Jews."** See, Mohammed al-Amin. "'World's largest brothel' pushed into crisis by COVID-19 lockdowns, bounces back with vaccination," June 22, 2023 https://www.gavi.org/vaccineswork/worlds-largest-brothel-pushed-crisis-covid-19-lockdowns-bounces-back-vaccination; See also, Claudia Hammond, "I'm Just Here For Survival, " *The Guardian*, January 9, 2008 https://www.theguardian.com/world/2008/jan/09/gender.humantrafficking "Daulatdia, in Bangladesh, is one of the largest brothels in the world - a village of 1,600 women who sell sex to 3,000 men every day. As Claudia Hammond found, it is a punishing place that few will ever leave."; Moreover, see Nazra Amin. "Daulatdia: A Look Into One of the World's Largest Brothels," September 5, 2019, https://www.newsecuritybeat.org/2019/09/daulatdia-worlds-largest-brothels/: "An infamous example of sex trafficking in Asia can be found in Bangladesh, in the village of **Daulatdia, home to one of the world's largest brothels**. Nearly 2,000 women and girls work there as prostitutes—sometimes voluntarily, most of the time not. Located in the Rajbari District of central Bangladesh, Daulatdia is so large it is often referred to as a "brothel village." **Bangladesh is one of the few Muslim countries where both the purchase and sale of sex work is legal**… People become sex workers in Bangladesh through a legal process. **The (Muslim) government, police, and religious institutions oversee the process.**")

311. Ibid, p. 524.

313. See refence 304, "On Abdullah Ibn Saba."

314. Anthony, *The Caliphs and the Heretic: Ibn Saba, The Sabaiya and Early Shi'ism Between Myth and History*, p. 68.

315. See especially, Bostom, *The Legacy of Islamic Antisemitism*, pp. 41,100, 319, 337, 389-390.

316. Ibid., p. 319.

[317.] Anthony, *The Caliphs and the Heretic: Ibn Saba, The Sabaiya and Early Shi'ism Between Myth and History*, p. vii; Anthony, "The Legend of Abdallāh ibn Saba and the Date of Umm al-Kitāb," p. 2.
[318.] Anthony, *The Caliphs and the Heretic: Ibn Saba, The Sabaiya and Early Shi'ism Between Myth and History*, pp. 167-168.
[319.] Ibid., p. 75.
[320] Potter. "The Baptism of Karl Marx"
[321.] Bertrand Russell. Freedom and Organization, 1814-1914, Routledge Classics, London and New York, First Edition, 1934, p. 164, reproduces Marx's letter to his daughter, from 1865, signed "Dr. Crankley" https://shorturl.at/VQiaA; Whittaker Chambers wrote a biting critique of Marx, and Marxism-Socialism in 1948, on the 100th anniversary of publication of The Communist Manifesto, entitled, "Communists: Dr. Crankley's Children," Time Magazine, February 23, 1948 https://time.com/archive/6600575/communists-dr-crankleys-children/
[322.] Karl Marx. *A world without Jews*, Runes translation and introduction, pp. v, vi, 37, 45.
[323.] Ibid, p. vii
[324.] Karl Marx. Friedrich Engels. *WERKE-BAND 34*, Dietz Verlag, Berlin, 1966, p. 317, "Marx an Wilhelm Liebknecht in Leipzig," [London] 4. Februar 1878 https://marx-wirklich-studieren.net/wp-content/uploads/2012/11/mew_band34.pdf; See also, G.-H. Bousquet. "Marx et Engels se sont-ils intéressés aux questions islamiques?", *Studia Islamica*, 1969, No. 30, pp. 119-130. https://www.jstor.org/stable/1595201 On p. 128, Bousquet observes, "This Turkophilia is largely explained by the hope of seeing the revolution break out in Russia (January 11, 1878, to J. P. Becker). This is also Marx's idea (February 4, 1878, to Liebknecht): he hopes to see it spread to all of Europe."
[325.] See refences 264-274.
[326.] Der Stürmer. *"Die Juden sind unser Unglück!" [Slogan printed on the bottom of the anti-Semitic newspaper* Der Stürmer] http://www.holocaustresearchproject.org/holoprelude/dersturmer.html
[327.] Andrew Bostom. "The Leftist American Rabbinate's 70-Year War on Anti-Totalitarian Rabbis," *Pajamas Media*, November 14, 2017 https://web.archive.org/web/20190825072815/https:/pjmedia.com/homeland-security/leftist-american-rabbinates-70-year-war-anti-totalitarian-rabbis/; HEARINGS BEFORE THE COMMITTEE ON UN-AMERICAN ACTIVITIES, HOUSE OF REPRESENTATIVES, EIGHTY- FIRST CONGRESS, FIRST SESSION, JULY 13, 14, AND 18, 1949, pp. 433-445, "July 13, 1949, Testimony of Rabbi Benjamin Schultz." https://shorturl.at/RuDbk
[328.] "July 13, 1949, Testimony of Rabbi Benjamin Schultz," 94413 049 pt. 1 (Face p. 440)
[329.] Whittaker Chambers. *Witness*, 1952, 1969, 2014, Regnery History, Washington, DC, p. 212.
[330.] Walter Z. Laqueur. *Communism and Nationalism in the Middle East*, Frederick A. Praeger, New York, 1956, p. 84. https://dn720704.ca.archive.org/0/items/dli.ernet.151886/151886-Communism%20And%20Nationalism%20In%20The%20Middle%20East.pdf

[331.] Winston Churchill. "Zionism Versus Bolshevism—A Struggle for the Soul of the Jewish People," *Illustrated Sunday Herald* (London), February 8, 1920, p. 5. https://en.wikisource.org/wiki/Zionism_versus_Bolshevism Reproduced by WikiSource
[332.] Andrew Bostom. "Eugene Lyons–'The Myth of Jewish Communism,' April, 1947: Full Text and Brief Background," andrewbostom.org, https://andrewbostom.net/2018/11/eugene-lyons-the-myth-of-jewish-communism-april-1947-full-text-and-brief-background/
[333.] Ibid.
[334.] Ibid.
[335.] *A Modern Qur'anic Kampf Against The Jews*, p. 538.
[336.] Ben-Ito, *The Lie that Wouldn't Die: The Protocols of the Elders of Zion*, pp. 94-102.
[337.] From Our Constantinople Correspondent (i.e., Philip Graves), "The Protocol Forgery," *The Times* (London, England), Thursday, August 18, 1921, p. 9ff.
[338.] Ben-Ito, *The Lie that Wouldn't Die: The Protocols of the Elders of Zion*, p. 101.
[339.] Ibid, p. xv.
[340.] Sarah Gauch. "Egyptian TV 'Knight' crusades against US, Jews," *The Christian Science Monitor*, November 22, 2002, https://www.csmonitor.com/2002/1122/p07s02-wogi.html
"As the series begins, its main character - played by well-known Egyptian actor Mohamed Sobhi, who also co-wrote the script - discovers the *Protocols of the Elders of Zion*, a discredited 19th-century Russian tract that purportedly proves the existence of a Jewish plot for world domination. From its content, the hero learns that his true enemy is not the British, but the Zionists."
[341.] "Arab Press Debates Antisemitic Egyptian Series 'Knight Without a Horse'- Part III," *Middle East Media Research Institute*, Egypt, Inquiry & Analysis Series, No. 114, December 10, 2002 https://web.archive.org/web/20200519140726/https://www.memri.org/reports/arab-press-debates-antisemitic-egyptian-series-knight-without-horse-part-iii
[342.] *A Modern Qur'anic Kampf Against The Jews*, p. 2.
[343.] Ibid, p. 528.
[344.] Ibid, pp. 529 and 550.
[345.] Ibid, p. 532.
[346.] Ibid, p. 574.
[347.] Ibid, p. 575.
[348.] Ibid.
[349.] Ibid, p. 533.
[350.] Remus Mihai Feraru. "THE RELIGIOUS POLICY OF EMPEROR HERACLIUS (610-641) IN REGARDS TO HEBREWS: PREMISES, ACCEPTANCE AND CONSEQUENCES," *Theologica Orthodoxica*, 2018, Issue No. 1, pp. 27-40; pp. 27-28, quoted. https://www.academia.edu/47477963/The_Religious_Policy_of_Emperor_Heraclius_610_641_in_regards_to_Hebrews
[351.] Daniel Graupe. "JEWISH RULE OF JERUSALEM 614-617 C.E.—Jewish Revolt Against Byzant with Persian Support" July, 2020. Pp. 50-51. https://www.academia.edu/44363024/JEWISH_RULE_OF_JERUSALEM_614_617_C_E_Jewish_Revolt_Against_Byzant_with_Persian_Support

[352.] *A Modern Qur'anic Kampf Against The Jews*, p. 542.

[353.] There is no evidence Aurelius was engaged in active persecution of Christians, let alone that it was somehow meted out by Roman Jews. See H.D. Sedgwick. *Marcus Aurelius*, Yale University Press, 1921, https://dn790006.ca.archive.org/0/items/marcusaureliusbi00sedguoft/marcusaureliusbi00sedguoft.pdf, i.e., the Preface, and also pp. 241-242, where Sedgwick analyzes the lone hard allegation against Aurelius pertaining to the Christians of Lyon in Gaul (France), supposedly in 177 C.E. From Sedgwick's Preface: *"And in my defence to sundry criticisms made upon Marcus by ancient and modern writers, I give by far the most space to the gravest, that he persecuted the Christians, for I think no accusation would have surprised him more, or have seemed to him more unreasonable."*
See also Donald J. Roberston, "Did Marcus Aurelius Persecute the Christians?," January 13, 2017 https://donaldrobertson.name/2017/01/13/did-marcus-aurelius-persecute-the-christians/
Roberston points out (among eight points of rebuttal) the flimsiness of the lone specific allegations against Aurelius by Christian chronicler Eusebius in a letter written "well over a hundred years" after the event ostensibly occurred, and the fact that contrastingly, *"...we have the surviving text of an Imperial edict from Marcus that provides evidence he actually tried to* ***prevent*** *the persecution of Christians by provincial authorities."*; During the brief reign of Decius, widespread Christian persecution did occur (in 249-251 C.E.) following an imperial edict mandating pagan sacrifice for the Emperor. This edict was defied by "a number of Christians," who were then killed, "among them Pope Fabianus at Rome," accompanied by "anti-Christian feeling [which] led to pogroms at Carthage and Alexandria." See Chris Scarre. *Chronicle of the Roman Emperors*, Thames and Hudson, London, paperback edition, 2012, p. 170

[354.] *A Modern Qur'anic Kampf Against The Jews*, p. 542.

[355.] The Deir Yassin "massacre" calumny was discussed in the analysis of chapter 7. See references 259-261.

[356.] *A Modern Qur'anic Kampf Against The Jews*, pp. 536-538..

[357.] See, Jennifer Jahner & John Tolan (2025) Violence, Letters, and the Law: Jewish-Christian Interaction and Episcopal Sanction in Thirteenth-Century England, *Global Intellectual History*, 10:3, 236-253. From pp. 236-237: "On 18 July 1290, King Edward I of England issued letters directing his sheriffs to provide safe-conduct to all Jews in England as they 'pass[ed] out of the realm' at the king's command…A crucial moment in medieval Jewish European history, the edict of 1290 marks, too, a crucial moment in English legal history…[and] the largest expulsion of a Jewish population from a Christian territory to date…**over the course of the twelfth and thirteenth centuries, the English Crown tested its powers to generate and regulate finances through its control and exploitation of Jewish economic activity.** Such control typically came accompanied by legal 'protection', promising royal prosecution of anyone who committed a violent crime against Jewish persons, **even as royal lawmaking itself proved responsible for decades of punitive taxation and restriction. This dynamic characterizes even the letters of eviction themselves, extending the promise of safe-conduct to individuals forcibly migrating under royal command**."

[358]. Barbara Coulton. "Cromwell and the 'Readmission' of the Jews in England, 1656," *CROMWELLIANA*, 2001 edited by Peter Gaunt, pp. 21-38. https://www.olivercromwell.org/Cromwelliana_Archive/2001.pdf
Contra Tantawi's calumny, there is no historical record of "Jewish financing" of Cromwell's ascension to power. From Coulton, p. 23: "The return of the Jews to England was important to both sides: the new chosen people, protestant England, would convert them; their reaching England would help the progress of Jewish messianism... Another factor in the acceptance of the Jews was the interest of puritan divines in the Hebrew language and its religious literature."

[359]. An example from the actual historical record of Jewish scapegoating in France based on discriminatory socio-economic spoliation, rooted in religious prejudice, from: Stéphane Mechoulan, "The Expulsion of the Jews from France in 1306: a Modern Fiscal Analysis," Department of Economics, University of Toronto, June 2004 https://www.economics.utoronto.ca/public/workingPapers/tecipa-209-1.pdf
"...having been heavily taxed prior to being chased out, the **displaced and impoverished English Jews fled to the kingdom of France**. In 1291, Philippe the Fair ordered a stop to the influx of refugees, but then accepted them in return for a tax...Philippe 'did not use the Jews as an object to make a major statement of his authority' at the beginning of his reign. Instead, **he continued the more traditional royal attitude, developed during the half century prior to his reign: restrictions were imposed, both economic and social, to encourage conversion. In short, the Jews were merely tolerated but not accepted. The expulsion of the Jews in 1306 was a direct result of the early-fourteenth century French currency crisis**.... It certainly helped matters that the Jews were an obvious target because of their precarious social status... Other circumstantial motives played upon Philippe's decision. In 1306, the Parisian populace were enraged against the king. Not only was currency constantly being manipulated, but there had been a flood and a subsequent shortage of food. Currency reinforcement, affecting renters and debtors, could only worsen the plight of the city's poor: **a scapegoat was needed and the Jews were available**... Outside of purely economic grounds, **religious factors must also be considered in reviewing the expulsion... at the time, various religious-based stories circulated to justify the king's move. French monks, for example, viewed the expulsion as the consequence of a trial, fifteen years earlier, against a Jew for host desecration. Augustine's doctrine, moreover, was frequently cited: do not kill the Jews but chase them out and force them into exile**."

[360]. This group of vicious Tantawi calumnies about the Jews of Russia, notwithstanding, see previous discussion related to the "Jewish Bolshevism/Communism" calumny and references 331-334; See also, for example, Robert Weinberg. (1992). "The Pogrom Of 1905 In Odessa: A Case Study". *Pogroms: Anti-Jewish Violence in Modern Russian History*. Pp. 248-289., Quotes from pp. 248,250-51, and 277. https://works.swarthmore.edu/fac-history/326
"...the Jews of Odessa were no strangers to anti-Jewish animosity, which generally remained submerged but did assume ugly and violent form several times before 1905. Serious pogroms in which Jews were killed and wounded and Jewish houses and businesses suffered substantial damage had occurred in 1821, 1859, 1871, 1881, and 1900. Anti-Jewish sentiment was common among Odessa's Russian population ...

Every year at Eastertime rumors of an impending pogrom circulated through the city's Jewish community. Pogrom mongering intensified after the turn of the century as militantly patriotic and pro-tsarist organizations emerged and engaged in Jew-baiting and other antisemitic activities. These pogroms stemmed in part from deep-rooted anti-Jewish feelings and reflected a Judeophobia prevalent among many non-Jewish residents of the city… The heritage of antisemitism made Odessa particularly ripe for a pogrom: the legal disabilities and mistreatment endured by the Jews of Russia engendered an attitude that accepted antisemitism and tolerated anti-Jewish violence… Similarly, the depressed state of the Odessa economy also helped set the stage for the outbreak of the pogrom. The straitened economic circumstances of 1905 produced a situation especially ripe for anti-Jewish violence… In the port city of Odessa alone, the police reported that at least 400 Jews and 100 non-Jews were killed and approximately 300 people, mostly Jews, were injured, with slightly over 1,600 Jewish houses, apartments, and stores incurring damage. These official figures undoubtedly underestimate the true extent of the damage, as other informed sources indicate substantially higher numbers of persons killed and injured. For example, Dmitri Neidhardt, City Governor of Odessa during the pogrom and brother-in-law of the future Prime Minister Peter Stolypin, estimated the number of casualties at 2,500, and the Jewish newspaper *Voskhod* reported that over 800 were killed and another several thousand were wounded. Moreover, various hospitals and clinics reported treating at least 600 persons for injuries sustained during the pogrom. 3 Indeed, no other city in the Russian Empire in 1905 experienced a pogrom comparable in its destruction and violence to the one unleashed against the Jews of Odessa.";

And on the specific issue of alcohol sales by the Jews of Eastern Europe/Russia, see Rabbi Ken Spiro. "Jews and Booze: The Fascinating History of Jews and Alcohol" https://aish.com/jews-and-booze-the-fascinating-history-of-jews-and-alcohol/ "The distillation and sale of alcohol became **one of the biggest money-makers for the Polish nobility who earned the lion's share of the profit from its sale to the peasantry**. The nobility also believed that only Jews, unlike many eastern Europeans, could remain sober enough to profitably run an inn… **After the Polish-Lithuanian Commonwealth was partitioned between Russia, Prussia and Austria, antisemitic restrictions forbade Jewish involvement in innkeeping, alcohol and many other jobs, greatly increasing poverty within the Jewish communities of Eastern Europe**. Jews were often able to circumvent these discriminatory restrictions by using a non-Jews as the 'front man' in the local inn, but **ever-increasing restrictions and violent antisemitism drove Jews almost completely out of the alcohol business, and also drove millions of Jews physically out of Eastern Europe. Two and a half million Eastern European Jews immigrated to the United States between 1882 and 1920**."

361. Tantawi is merely regurgitating the odious theme of "Jewish Parasitism," exploited by the Nazis, in particular, as explained by Bein in 1965. See Alexander Bein. "'Der jüdische Parasit'.Bemerkungen zur Semantik der Judenfrage," *Vierteljahrshefte für Zeitgeschichte* , Apr., 1965, 13. Jahrg., 2. H. (Apr., 1965), pp. 121-149 https://www.jstor.org/stable/30195054, and stated plainly by Hitler in *Mein Kampf*: "[The Jew] is and remains the eternal parasite, a parasite that spreads more and more

like a harmful bacillus, as well as inviting only a favorable culture medium. The effect of its existence, however, is similar to that of parasites: where it occurs, the host people die after a shorter or longer time." (Hitler, Adolf (1942). *Mein Kampf*. München: Eher-Verlag. p. 334.)

362. *A Modern Qur'anic Kampf Against The Jews*, p. 541, is a paraphrase; (The original is in, Adolf Hitler, *Mein Kampf*, Houghton Mifflin, New York: Hutchinson Publ. Ltd., London, 1969, p. 60.: "The Jewish doctrine of Marxism rejects the aristocratic principle of Nature and replaces the eternal privilege of power and strength by the mass of numbers and their dead weight. Thus it denies the value of personality in man, contests the significance of nationality and race, and thereby withdraws from humanity the premise of its existence and its culture. As a foundation of the universe, this doctrine would bring about the end of any order intellectually conceivable to man. And as, in this greatest of all recognizable organisms, the result of an application of such a law could only be chaos, on earth it could only be destruction for the inhabitants of this planet. If, with the help of his Marxist creed, the Jew is victorious over the other peoples of the world, his crown will be the funeral wreath of humanity and this planet will, as it did thousands of years ago, move through the ether devoid of men. Eternal Nature inexorably avenges the infringement of her commands. **Hence today I believe that I am acting in accordance with the will of the Almighty Creator: *by defending myself against the Jew, I am fighting for the work of the Lord.*"**)

363. Ibid, pp. 561-562. (See also Anwarrul Haqq. *ABROGATION IN THE KORAN*, Lucknow, India, 1926 https://www.muhammadanism.org/Quran/abrogation_koran.pdf; and David Bukay, "Peace or Jihad," *The Middle East Quarterly*, Fall 2007, Volume 14, Number 4 https://www.meforum.org/middle-east-quarterly/peace-or-jihad-abrogation-in-islam

364. Ibid, p. 579.

365. Ibid, p. 588.

366. Ibid, pp. 581-595.

367. "The Covenant Of The Islamic Resistance Movement – Hamas," *Middle East Media Research Institute*, February 14, 2006, Special Dispatch No. 1092. a translation of the Hamas Covenant, originally published in Arabic, August 18, 1988. https://web.archive.org/web/20161218190022/https://www.memri.org/reports/covenant-islamic-resistance-movement-%E2%80%93-hamas

368. *A Modern Qur'anic Kampf Against The Jews*, pp. 580 and 581.

369. Ibid, pp. 581, 582, and 584.

370. Ibid, p. 585.

370a. Key extracts from Tantawi's gloss on Q 5:60 from *"The intermediate [balanced] interpretation of the Qur'an,"* https://www.altafsir.com/Tafasir.asp?tMadhNo=0&tTafsirNo=57&tSoraNo=5&tAyahNo=60&tDisplay=yes&UserProfile=0&LanguageId=1

371. See earlier reference 175.; and M. J. Kister, "The Massacre of the Banu Qurayza: A Re-Examination of a Tradition," *Jerusalem Studies in Arabic and Islam* 8 (1986): 61–96; W. H. T. Gairdner, "Muhammad without Camouflage," *Moslem World* 9 (1919): p. 36.; *The Life of Muhammad*, A Translation of Ibn Ishaq's *Sirat Rasul Allah*, trans. by A. Guillaume (Oxford: 2001), p. 461.; Ibn Sa'd, *Kitab Al-Tabaqat Al-Kabir*, trans. S. *A Survey of Its Theological-Juridical Origins and Historical Manifestations* 181

Moinul Haq and H. K. Ghazanfar (New Delhi: 1993), p. 95. (The translators wrote: "Brothren [*sic*] of monkeys and boars fear me, fear me!")

372. H. R. Idris, "Contributions a histoire de l'Ifriqiya" (*Riyad an Nufus d'Al-Maliki*), *Revue des Etudes Islamiques* (1935); English translation in Bat Ye'or, *The Dhimmi,* p. 186.

373. H. R. Idris, "Tributaries in the Medieval Muslim West, according to the *Mi'yar* of al-Wansharisi"; English translation by Michael J. Miller of "Les tributaries en Occident Musulman medieval d'apres 'miyar d'al Wansarisi,'" in *Melanges d'islamologie: Volume dediae a la memoire de Armand Abel par ses colleagues, ses aeleves, et ses amis* (1974), pp. 172–96, selected extracts.

374. Reinhard Dozy. *Spanish Islam: A History of the Muslims in Spain.* Trans. by Francis Griffin Stokes, London, 1915. Kessinger Reprint, p. 653; M. Perlmann, "Eleventh Century Andalusian Authors on the Jews of Granada," *Proceedings of the American Academy for Jewish Research*, 1948-1949, Vol. 18 (1948-1949), pp. 269-290.

375. Perlmann, "Eleventh Century Andalusian Authors on the Jews of Granada," p. 286.

376. Perlmann, "Eleventh Century Andalusian Authors on the Jews of Granada," pp. 287–88.

377. Ibid, p. 288 note 56a.

378. Moshe Perlmann. *Jewish Social Studies*, July, 1968, Vol. 30, No. 3 (July, 1968), pp. 177-179, p. 178, from his review of *A History of the Jews in Muslim Spain.* Vol. II by E. Ashtor.

379. Bar Hebraeus. *The Chronography of Bar Hebraeus*. Translated by E. A. W. Budge. London, 1932.p. 491; W. J. Fischel. *Jews in the Economic and Political Life of Medieval Islam*. London, 1937.pp. 116, 117 n. 5.

380. Bar Hebraeus, *The Chronography*, p. 490; Ghazi b. al-Wasiti, "An Answer to the Dhimmis." Treatise. English translation by Richard Gottheil. *Journal of the American Oriental Society (JAOS)* Vol. 41 (1921) p. 449; Fischel, *Jews in the Economic and Political Life of Medieval Islam*, p. 91.

381. E.G. Browne. *A Literary History of Persia*. 4 vols. Cambridge, 1902–1924.With a new introduction by J. T. P. de Bruijn, 4 vols., Bethesda, 1997. vol. 3, pp. 35–36.

382. Ibid., p. 35.

383. See Georges Vajda, *Études d'Orientalisme dédiées à la mémoire de Lévi-Provençal.* 2 vols. Paris, 1962. See essay, in vol. 2, p. 811, "Un Traite Maghrebin 'Adversos Judaeos: Ahkam Ahl Al-Dimma Du Sayh Muhammad B. 'Abd Al-Karim Al-Magili.'"; John O. Hunwick, "Al-Maghili and the Jews of Tuwat: the Demise of a Community." *Studia Islamica* volume 61 (1985), pp. 155–83.

384. See reference 370a for Tantawi's "mature" gloss on Q 5:60; Also, Zamakshari, *Al-Kashshaaf `an Haqaa'iq GhawaamiD al-Tanziil wa-`Uyuun al-Aqaawiil fii Wujuuh alTa'wiil*, ed. M. H. Ahmad (Cairo: 1365/1946), p. 684, referring to Qur'an 5:60/61:

"Some say that when this occurred, the Muslims taunted them, saying, 'O brothers of apes and pigs,' and the Jews would bow their heads. 'These' the cursed transformed ones 'are the lowest in stature' they were put in the evil place they deserved. The emphasis here is intended as 'lowest and most erring' for it became a by-name for them beyond mere metaphor. The reason for this revelation is that a group of Jews approached Muhammad with the worst intentions, being hypocritical in feigning belief,

and Allah revealed to Muhammad that they would leave in the same state in which they entered, and would heed nothing he would say in unbelief and pretending."
385. Vajda, "Un Traite Maghrebin 'Adversos Judaeos," p. 809.
386. See H.Z. Hirschberg. *A History of the Jews of North Africa.* Vol. 1. Leyden, 1974., p. 402; Jane Gerber. *Jewish Society in Fez 1450-1700: Studies in Communal and Economic Life.* Ann Arbor, 1975.
Leyden, 1980, p. 18; and Hunwick, "Al-Maghili and the Jews of Tuwat: the Demise of a Community."
387. *A Modern Qur'anic Kampf Against The Jews*, pp. 588 and 589.
388. Ibid, p. 590.
389. Ibid.
390. Ibid, p. 590.
391. Ibid, pp. 592-593.
392. Ibid, pp. 593, 594, and 595.
393. Ibid, p. 594.
394. Ibid.
395. Ibid.
396. Ibid.
397. Sahih Muslim Book 1, Hadith Number 79.
https://hadithcollection.com/sahihmuslim/sahih-muslim-book-01-faith/sahih-muslim-book-001-hadith-number-0079 ; This hadith is also discussed in John Ralph Willis, p. 399, "Jihad fi sabil Allah- Its doctrinal basis in Islam and some aspects of its evolution in 19th century West Africa," ***The Journal of African History***, 1967, Vol. 8 [No. 3], pp. 395-415. Willis explains this canonical hadith from Sahih Muslim **reverses the priority of jihad, i.e., jihad by force assuming *highest* priority, *not lowest*, as purportedly espoused by some Sufis on the "basis" of a disputed hadith, which even the Islamophilic scholar Reuven Firestone could not authenticate as being from any of the six canonical collections:** "*Its (i.e., the alleged Sufi tradition of the greater jihad being inner spiritual struggle; the lesser jihad being warfare, etc.) source is not usually given, and it is in fact nowhere to be found in the canonical collections* [of hadith]; Reuven Firestone. *Jihad-The Origin of Holy War in Islam*, Oxford University Press, 1999, pp. 139-140, note 19.)"
398. Tantawi, *"The [balanced] interpretation of the Qur'an,"* gloss on Q 3:112
https://www.altafsir.com/Tafasir.asp?tMadhNo=0&tTafsirNo=57&tSoraNo=3&tAyahNo=112&tDisplay=yes&UserProfile=0&LanguageId=1
399. Andrew Bostom. "The Houthi 'Motto,' and My Limited Sympathy for War-Torn Yemen," *Pajamas Media*, April 2, 2015 https://pjmedia.com/andrew-g-bostom-2/2015/04/02/the-houthi-motto-and-my-limited-sympathy-for-war-torn-yemen-n6458
400. Tudor Parfitt, *The Road to Redemption—The Jews of the Yemen 1900–1950*, Leiden: Brill, 1996, p. 187.
401. Ibid., p. 87; Yehuda Nini, *The Jews of the Yemen, 1800–1914*, translated by H. Galai, Harwood Academic Publishers, Chur, Switzerland, 1991, pp. 24–25.
402. Nini, *The Jews of the Yemen,* p. 24.
402a. Ibid, p. 25, and p. 25 note 17.
403. Y. D. Sémach, *Une Mission de l'Alliance au Yémen*, Paris, 1910, pp. 72–73; English translation reproduced from Bat Ye'or, *The Dhimmi*, pp. 341–43.

404. Aviva Klein-Franke, "Collecting the Djizya (Poll-Tax) in the Yemen," in *Israel and Ishmael: Studies in Muslim-Jewish Relations*, editor Tudor Parfitt, New York, 2000, pp. 182–83, 186.
405. Bat Ye'or's interview (October 8, 1983) with Hannah [Lolou] and Sa'adya b. Shelomo Akiva [Aqua], born respectively at Dhamar and Menakha (Yemen). Since 1949 they have been citizens of Israel and live in Nes Ziyyona. Reproduced from Bat Ye'or, *The Dhimmi*, pp. 380–82.
406. Rod Norland. "Persecution Defines Life For Yemen's Remaining Jews," *The New York Times*, February 19, 2015, p. A8.
407. Ibid.
408. *A Modern Qur'anic Kampf Against The Jews*, pp. 1-598.
409. Ibid, pp. 444-598.
410. Ibid, p. 599.
411. See references 278-289.
412. *A Modern Qur'anic Kampf Against The Jews*, p. 600.
413. Gil, *A History of Palestine, 634-1099*, pp. 50, 65, 73-74, and 101-102.
414. *A Modern Qur'anic Kampf Against The Jews*, p. 601; See also note 411
415. David Nirenberg. "The Rhineland Massacres of Jews in the First Crusade, Memories Medieval and Modern," in *Medieval Concepts of the Past: Ritual, Memory, Historiography*, Cambridge University Press, 2002, pp. 279–309.
416. See note 288.
416a. *A Modern Qur'anic Kampf Against The Jews*, pp. 605, 606, 611, 625, 513, 514, and 613.
417. Ibid, p. 617.
418. Ibid, pp. 617-620.
419. Ibid, pp. 617, 618, and 619.
420. Ibid, p. 619.
421. Ibid, pp. 620-621.
422. Ibid, pp. 621-622.
422a. Ibid, pp. 620-621.
423. Bostom, *The Legacy of Islamic Antisemitism*, p. 63.
424. Armand Abel, "al-Dadjdjal" *Encyclopedia of Islam*, Edited by B. Lewis, Ch. Pellat, and J. Schacht, 1991, Leiden, E.J. Brill, Vol. II C-G, pp. 77-78. For additional confirmation that the Muslim Antichrist "Dajjal" is accompanied by Jews, and may be identified as "Jewish," see Cook, "Dajjāl,"; Cook, *Studies in Muslim Apocalyptic* section, "The Jewish Dajjal," pp. 110ff., and pp. 341, 367; and Cook's 'Hadith,' Authority and the End of the World: Traditions in Modern Muslim Apocalyptic Literature," *Oriente Moderno,* Nuova serie, Anno 21 (82), Nr. 1, *Hadith in Modern Islam*, 2002, p. 36.
425. abu-Mansur abd-al-Kahir ibn Tahir al-Baghdadi (d. 1037) was a Muslim theologian, esteemed for his erudition in Islamic law and the hadith, as well as a noted mathematician; See the introduction *to Moslem Schisms and Sects* (*Al-Fark Bain Al-Firak*) *by abu-Mansur abd-al-Kahir ibn Tahir al-Baghdadi (d. 1037)*, translated by Kate Chambers Seelye, 1920, New York, Columbia University Press, pp. 7-8.
426. Mark Durie, "Isa, the Muslim Jesus," in *The Myth of Islamic Tolerance*, edited by Robert Spencer, 2005, Amherst, NY, pp. 541–55.

427. James Robson, "The material of Tradition II," *The Muslim World*, 1951, Vol. 41, pp. 257–270; p. 259 http://bit.ly/1lWt6xQ
428. Bostom, *The Legacy of Islamic Antisemitism*, p. 63.
429. *Sahih Muslim, Book 041, Number 7034* https://hadithcollection.com/sahihmuslim/sahih-muslim-book-41-turmoil-and-portents-of-the-last-hour/sahih-muslim-book-041-hadith-number-7034; *Sahih Bukhari, Volume 4, Book 52, Number 177* https://hadithcollection.com/sahihbukhari/sahih-bukhari-book-52-fighting-for-the-cause-of-allah-jihaad/sahih-bukhari-volume-004-book-052-hadith-number-177; *Sahih Muslim, Book 041, Number 6985.* https://hadithcollection.com/sahihmuslim/sahih-muslim-book-41-turmoil-and-portents-of-the-last-hour/sahih-muslim-book-041-hadith-number-6985
430. From Ibn Kathir's gloss on Q 4:159 https://www.altafsir.com/Tafasir.asp?tMadhNo=0&tTafsirNo=7&tSoraNo=4&tAyahNo=159&tDisplay=yes&Page=10&Size=1&LanguageId=1
431 Bostom, *The Legacy of Islamic Antisemitism*, p. 63.; Regarding the ransoming of prisoners of Muslim enemies vanquished by jihad (see Bostom, *The Legacy of Jihad*, p. 149), the great Maliki jurist and polymath Averroes (d. 1198), wrote: "Most scholars are agreed that, in his dealings with captives, various policies are open to the Imam [head of the Islamic state, caliph]. He may pardon them, kill them, or release them . . . on ransom"...
432. Andrew Bostom, "Islam's Jew-Hating Hadith In Context," *The Jewish Press*, April 17, 2013 https://jewishpress.com/indepth/analysis/islams-jew-hating-hadith-in-context/2013/04/17/0/
433. Andrew Bostom, The Mufti's Islamic Jew-Hatred—What The Nazis Learned From the Muslim Pope, 2013, Washington, D.C., Bravura Books, p. 31.
434."The Covenant of the Islamic Resistance Movement–Hamas", *Middle East Media Research Institute*, February 14, 2006, Special Dispatch No.1092 https://www.memri.org/reports/covenant-islamic-resistance-movement-%E2%80%93-hamas
435. Itamar Marcus, Nan Jacques Zilberdik, "Muslims' destiny is to kill Jews," *Palestinian Media Watch,* January 15, 2012, https://palwatch.org/page/3447
The following is an excerpt from the Fatah ceremony broadcast on PA TV: Moderator at Fatah ceremony: "Our war with the descendants of the apes and pigs (i.e., Jews) is a war of religion and faith. Long Live Fatah! [I invite you,] our honorable Sheikh." ***PA Mufti Muhammad Hussein*** *comes to the podium and says: "47 years ago the [Fatah] revolution started. Which revolution? The modern revolution of the Palestinian people's history. In fact, Palestine in its entirety is a revolution, since [Caliph] Umar came [to conquer Jerusalem, 637 CE], and continuing today, and until the End of Days. The reliable Hadith (tradition attributed to Muhammad), [found] in the two reliable collections,*
Bukhari and Muslim, says: "The Hour [of Resurrection] will not come until you fight the Jews. The Jew will hide behind stones or trees. Then the stones or trees will call: 'Oh Muslim, servant of Allah, there is a Jew behind me, come and kill him.' Except the Gharqad tree [which will keep silent]." Therefore it is no wonder that you see Gharqad

[trees] surrounding the [Israeli] settlements and colonies…[PA TV (Fatah), Jan. 9, 2012]

436. "Antisemitism in Al-Azhar University's Friday Sermon: The Jews Are The Muslims' Worst Enemies," *The Middle East Media Research Institute*, Clip No. 3871, May 10, 2013

Following are excerpts from a Friday sermon at Al-Azhar University in Cairo, delivered by Muhammad Al-Mukhtar Al-Mahdi, which aired on Channel 1, Egyptian TV, on May 10, 2013: Muhammad Al-Mukhtar

Al-Mahdi: "The Islamic nation, which is the guardian of Truth, must be aware of the conspiracies of Falsehood, and of the snares of those who lie in wait. ***Allah has taught [Muslims] that their worst enemies are those about whom He said: "You shall find the Jews and the polytheists to be the most hostile towards the believers" [Qur'an 5:82].*** *Thus, Allah made Jihad for His sake and endurance of pain and hardship effective means to fight the people of Falsehood. [...] The confrontation [with the Jews] is inevitable.* ***Our Prophet does not lie. He told us that there would be a confrontation between the Muslims and the Jews before the Day of Judgment, and that the Muslims would vanquish them to the point that the Jews would hide behind the stones and the trees, but the stones and the trees would say: 'Oh Muslim, oh servant of Allah, there is a Jew behind me, come and kill him.'*** *Prepare for that day, for it will surely arrive, because the divine revelation harbors no lies."*

437. "Salah Khalaf (Abu Iyad) (1933-1991)," *Yasser Arafat Foundation* https://yaf.ps/page-1115-en.html; Abu Iyad attending Al-Azhar University is noted in, Ghasan Charbel. "Farouk al-Qaddoumi: We Visited Assad and He Ordered Arafat's Release from Mezzeh Prison," *Asharq al-Awsat*, August 24, 2024 https://english.aawsat.com/features/5053690-farouk-al-qaddoumi-we-visited-assad-and-he-ordered-arafat%E2%80%99s-release-mezzeh-prison "I was in Cairo in 1954. Along with Arafat, Salah Khalaf (Abu Iyad), and I were members of the General Union of Palestine Students. Arafat was its president. I was a student at the American university, Arafat was a student at Cairo University **and Abu Iyad went to al-Azhar University**. I was a member of the Baath part, **Abu Iyad of the enlightened Muslim Brotherhood** and Arafat was religious but independent."

438. Sylvia Haim, a renowned expert on the Arab national movement, identified its Islamic jihad quintessence in a 1955 essay: **"***Another feature of the modern doctrine which fits in with the Muslim past is the emphasis which both of them lay on communal solidarity, discipline and cooperation.* ***The ummain Islam is a solidary entity, and its foremost duty is to answer the call of the jihad.*** *[emphasis added] This brings us to the third feature which both modern and ancient systems have in common, to wit the glorification of one's own group. The traditional attitude of the Muslims to the outside world is one of superiority, and the distinction between the Dar al-harb, Dar al-Islam, and Dar as-sulh, is an ever present one in the mind of the Muslim jurist.* ***It may therefore be said in conclusion of this modern doctrine of nationalism, that although it introduces into Islam features which may not accord with strict orthodoxy, it is the least incompatible perhaps of modern European doctrines with the political thought and political experience of Sunni Islam*** *[emphasis added]."* From: Sylvia Haim,

—Islam and the Theory of Arab Nationalism,‖ *Die Welt Des Islams* Vol. 4, Issue 2/3, 1955, pp. 124–49; quote from her p. 149 conclusion.

Subsequently, in her 1962 anthology on Arab nationalism, Haim quoted the non-Muslim (i.e., Christian) founder of the Arab nationalist Baath Party, Michel Aflaq's own confirmatory pronouncement: "*Muhammad was the epitome of all the Arabs, so let all the Arabs today be Muhammad. ... Islam was an Arab movement and its meaning was the renewal of Arabism and its maturity ... [even]Arab Christians will recognize that Islam constitutes for them a national culture in which they must immerse themselves so that they may understand and love it, and so that they may preserve Islam as they would preserve the most precious element in their Arabism.*" From: Sylvia Haim. *Arab Nationalism—An Anthology*, Berkeley and Los Angeles: University of California Press, 1962, pp. 63–64.

439. Abou Iyad. "Revolution et Realisme," *Le Monde*, January 21, 1974 https://www.lemonde.fr/archives/article/1974/01/21/revolution-et-realisme_2520176_1819218.html

440. Bostom, *The Legacy of Islamic Antisemitism*, Palestine, pp. 78-97; Spain, pp: 97-112.

441. Andrew Bostom. "Al-Azhar's Ongoing 75-Year Annihilationist Jihad Against the Jews of Israel," www.andrewbostom.net, November 9, 2023 https://andrewbostom.net/2023/11/al-azhars-ongoing-75-year-annihilationist-jihad-against-the-jews-of-israel/

442. Document declassified and released under the Nazi War Crimes Disclosure Act, 2006, PL105-246 State Department Telegram 1763/Embassy (Cairo) Telegram 1256 D441214. English translation (by the US embassy) of two fatwas written by the grand mufti of Egypt, Sheikh Hasan Ma'moun, January 5, 1956, and another dated January 9, 1956, signed by the leading members of the Fatwa Committee of Al Azhar, that is, its chairman and ex-mufti of Egypt, and major representatives of all four Islamic schools of jurisprudence, the ex-sheikh of the Shari'a College (Shafi'i sect), Mahmoud Shaltout (Hanafi sect), the director of Religious Guidance (Maliki Sect), and the director of the Azhar Inspectorate (Hanbali sect), and published the following days in the Egyptian newspaper, *Al Ahram.* The redundant extracts from each fatwa were pooled for simplicity.; On the start of the 1956 Sinai War, see Michael Oren. Origins of the Second Arab-Israel War—Egypt, Israel, and the Great Powers, 1952-1956, Routledge, London and New York, , 1992; Paperback 2016, 199 pp.; The outbreak of full-fledged hostilities occurred October 29-30, 1956, on p. 145.

443. *A Modern Qur'anic Kampf Against The Jews*, p. 622.

444. See note 442.; The expression "fay" is found in Qur'an 59: 6-10, which describes Muhammad's attack upon the Jewish tribe Banu Nadir. In the traditional Muslim interpretation of these verses the theocratic conception of property rights is confirmed, as voiced by the Prophet— Allah returns to the Believers the possessions of His foes, what is properly His. See Leone Caetani, *Annali dell'Islam*, Milan: 1905–1926, vol. 5, p. 332.

445. *A Modern Qur'anic Kampf Against The Jews*, p. 624.; See also Tantawi's "Conclusion," pp. 625-626, references 31, and 31a.

[446]. Maxime Rodinson. "The Western Image and Western Studies of Islam," in *The Legacy of Islam*, edited by Joseph Schacht and C.E. Bosworth, Oxford at The Clarendon Press, 1974, pp. 58-59 https://archive.org/details/legacyofislam0000jose/page/n11/mode/2up

[447]. Skovgaard-Petersen, *Defining Islam for the Egyptian State*; Suha Taji-Farouki. "A Contemporary Construction of Jews in the Qur'an: A Review of Muhammad Sayyid Tantawi's *Banu Isra'il fi al-Qur'an wa al-Sunna*, and 'Afif 'Abd al-Fattah Tabbara's *Al-yahud fi al-Qur'an*, in Ronald L. Nettler and Suha Taji-Farouki, editors, *Muslim-Jewish Encounters Intellectual Traditions and Modern Politics*, Routledge, 1998, pp. 15-37

[448]. See reference 21; also, Skovgaard-Petersen, *Defining Islam for the Egyptian State*, p. 254.

[449]. Ibid, p. 254, including note 10.

[450]. See reference 263.

[451]. Ibid, pp. 253-54.

[452]. Taji-Farouki, "A Contemporary Construction of Jews in the Qur'an"

[453]. Ibid, p. 16.

[454]. Ibid.

[455]. See earlier references 66-109, and related discussion.

[456]. Muhammad Sayyid (Sayyed) Tantawi. *al-Tafsīr al-wasīṭ lil-Qur'ān al-karīm* ("The intermediate [balanced] interpretation of the Qur'an"), al-Qāhirah, 1992-1993, Dār al-Ma'ārif, al-Qāhirah, 15-volumes https://search.worldcat.org/title/27272751; The full Arabic text is also available at altafsir.com: (https://www.altafsir.com/Tafasir.asp?tMadhNo=0&tTafsirNo=57&tSoraNo=1&tAyahNo=1&tDisplay=yes&UserProfile=0&LanguageId=1)

[457]. Tabari's glosses on Q 17:4/8 can be found here: https://www.altafsir.com/Tafasir.asp?tMadhNo=0&tTafsirNo=1&tSoraNo=17&tAyahNo=4&tDisplay=yes&UserProfile=0&LanguageId=1; https://www.altafsir.com/Tafasir.asp?tMadhNo=0&tTafsirNo=1&tSoraNo=17&tAyahNo=8&tDisplay=yes&UserProfile=0&LanguageId=1; See reference 104 for biographical background on Tabari.

[458]. Zamakshari's glosses on Q 17:4/8 can be found here: https://www.altafsir.com/Tafasir.asp?tMadhNo=0&tTafsirNo=2&tSoraNo=17&tAyahNo=4&tDisplay=yes&UserProfile=0&LanguageId=1; https://www.altafsir.com/Tafasir.asp?tMadhNo=0&tTafsirNo=2&tSoraNo=17&tAyahNo=8&tDisplay=yes&UserProfile=0&LanguageId=1; For historical background, see Andrew Lane. "You can't tell a book by its author: A study of Muʿtazilite theology in al-Zamakhsharī's (d. 538/1144) Kashshāf." *Bulletin of SOAS*, 75, 1 (2012), 47–86. From pp. 47 and 85: **Lane emphasizes Zamakshari's traditionalism in his major Qur'anic commentary**, noting he "was a Muʿtazilite (a non-traditionalist medieval school of Islamic thought) man of letters and grammarian from Khwārazm. The author of about fifty works, two-thirds of which have survived (many in print), his main fields of interest were adab (i.e., manners, ethics), grammar and lexicography, but he also composed works in theology and law, as well as works on the Quran and the Tradition. He is best known, however, for his Quran commentary, **al-Kashshāf** ʿan ḥaqā'iq ghawāmiḍ al-tanzīl wa-ʿuyūn al-aqāwīl fī wujūh al-ta'wīl (The Discoverer of the Truths of the Hidden Things of Revelation and the Choicest Statements concerning the Aspects

of Interpretation) **which he completed in Mecca** in 528/1134… **Al-Zamakhsharī's Kashshāf is a traditional Quran commentary** written by a member of the Muʿtazilite school of theology, **that sometimes incorporates Muʿtazilite comments into a traditional framework**."

459. Razi's glosses on Q 17:4/8 can be found here: https://www.altafsir.com/Tafasir.asp?tMadhNo=0&tTafsirNo=4&tSoraNo=17&tAyahNo=4&tDisplay=yes&UserProfile=0&LanguageId=1; https://www.altafsir.com/Tafasir.asp?tMadhNo=0&tTafsirNo=4&tSoraNo=17&tAyahNo=8&tDisplay=yes&UserProfile=0&LanguageId=1; See reference 102 for biographical background on Razi.

459a. Walid Saleh. "The Introduction to Wahidi's al-Basit: An Edition, Translation, and Commentary," in *Contexts of Qur'anic Exegesis (2nd/8th-9th/15th C.)*, edited by Karen Bauer, Oxford University Press, 2013, pp. 67-100. From p. 67, we learn that al-Wahidi (d. 1076) was "one of the leading exegetes and literary critics of the medieval Islamic world, wrote three Qur'an commentaries: al-Wajīz (The Short Commentary), al-Wasīt (The Middle Commentary) and al-Basīt (The Large Commentary). The popularity of each of these commentaries was such that they have all survived."

460. Qurtubi's glosses on Q 17:4/8 can be found here: https://www.altafsir.com/Tafasir.asp?tMadhNo=0&tTafsirNo=5&tSoraNo=17&tAyahNo=8&tDisplay=yes&UserProfile=0&LanguageId=1; https://www.altafsir.com/Tafasir.asp?tMadhNo=0&tTafsirNo=4&tSoraNo=17&tAyahNo=8&tDisplay=yes&UserProfile=0&LanguageId=1; See reference 89 for biographical background on Qurtubi

461. Ibn Kathir's glosses on Q 17:4/8 can be found here: https://www.altafsir.com/Tafasir.asp?tMadhNo=0&tTafsirNo=7&tSoraNo=17&tAyahNo=4&tDisplay=yes&UserProfile=0&LanguageId=1; https://www.altafsir.com/Tafasir.asp?tMadhNo=0&tTafsirNo=7&tSoraNo=17&tAyahNo=8&tDisplay=yes&Page=2&Size=1&LanguageId=1; See reference 105 for biographical background on Ibn Kathir.

462. See references 457, 458, 459, 460, and 461.

463. From, "Nebuchadnezzar II, king of Babylonia," Henry W.F. Saggs, Britannica Editors, Nov. 7, 2025
https://www.britannica.com/place/Hanging-Gardens-of-Babylon
Nebuchadnezzar II (d. 561 BCE) was the second and greatest king of the Chaldean dynasty of Babylonia (who ruled from 605 to 561 BCE), renowned for his military prowess, the magnificence of Babylon, his capital, and the prominent role he played in Jewish history. Some of his key "military activities are known not
from extant chronicles but from other sources, particularly the Bible, which records another attack on Jerusalem and a siege of Tyre (lasting 13 years, according to the Jewish historian Flavius Josephus) and hints at an invasion of Egypt. The siege of Jerusalem ended in its capture in 587/586 and in the deportation of prominent citizens, with a further deportation in 582."; See also references 457, 458, 459, 460, and 461.

464. Although none of the classical exegetes mention him, Tabatabai's modern gloss mentions Vespasian (d. 79 CE), the Roman governor of Judea who spearheaded the efforts to suppress a Jewish revolt in Judea before becoming Emperor in 69 CE. See, Scarre, *Chronicle of the Roman Emperors*, pp. 60-72.

[465]. For Constantine (d. 337 CE), see, Scarre, *Chronicle of the Roman Emperors*, pp. 213-221. Also from "Jews and the Later Roman Law 315-531 CE," *Fordham University*: "Constantine the Great (306-337)…was the first Roman emperor to issue laws which radically limited the rights of Jews as citizens of the Roman Empire…," https://sourcebooks.fordham.edu/jewish/jews-romanlaw.asp; See also references 457, 458, 459, 460, and 461.
[466]. See previous discussion of the jizya in references 96, 149, 189, and 404; See also references 457, 458, 459, 460, and 461.
[467]. On the Jews being consigned to Hellfire, see Bostom, *The Legacy of Islamic Antisemitism*, pp. 34, 41, 44, 54, 166, 292, 351, and 431.
[468]. Maulana Mufti Muhammad Shafi. *MA'ARIFUL QUR'AN*, Translated by Prof. Muhammad Hasan Askari, Prof. Muhammad Sbamim, and revised by Justice Mufti Muhammad Taqi Usmani, with a Foreword written by Usmani July 9, 1995, Darul-Uloom, Karachi. https://archive.org/details/MaarifulQuranEnglsih8Volumes/mode/2up
[469]. Asad Ullah. "Research Study of the Contribution of Mufti Muhammad Shafi' in Sīrah Studies," *Journal of Islamic and Religious Studies* 2018, 3 (1). Haripur, Pakistan: 95-105.
[470]. Shafi, *MA'ARIFUL QUR'AN*, volume 5, p. 463.
[471]. Ibid.
[472]. Ibid, p. 464.
[473]. Hasan ibn Muhammad Al Daylami. *The Narration (Hadeeth) of Hudhayfah Ibn Alyaman*, Translated by Jerrmein Abu Shahba, *Al-Islam.org* https://web.archive.org/web/20200511012231/https://www.al-islam.org/articles/narration-hadeeth-hudhayfah-ibn-alyaman-hasan-ibn-muhammad-al-daylami
[474]. Shafi, *MA'ARIFUL QUR'AN*, volume 5, pp. 463-464.
[475]. Ibid, pp. 466-467.
[476]. Ibid, p. 467.
[477]. Ibid.
[478]. Ibid.
[479]. Ibid, pp. 468-469.
[480]. The August 23, 1969 Al-Aqsa Mosque fire was set by a psychotic Australian Christian, acting out a sexual fantasy. See, Abraham Rabinovich, "How an Australian sheepshearer's al-Aqsa arson nearly torched Middle East peace—On August 23, 1969, kibbutz volunteer Denis Rohan listened to the voices in his head and started a fire on the Temple Mount, nearly igniting a regional war," *The Times of Israel*, August 23, 2019 https://www.timesofisrael.com/how-an-australian-sheepshearers-al-aqsa-arson-nearly-torched-middle-east-peace/ "His most revealing testimony came on the last day, when he related what the voice had said to him in his cell a few days before. 'Because you have done everything I have told you even to your own hurt,' he quoted, 'I shall exalt you above the whole earth and bring all the maidens of Israel to you to bear forth your offspring to my glory. You shall build the temple, and Zipporah will be your queen.' Zipporah was a young teacher of Hebrew to the volunteers at the kibbutz. She would testify that Rohan had one day chosen a seat next to her on the bus out of the kibbutz, but had been too shy to converse. Instead of his usual enthusiasm, Rohan bowed his head and had to force himself to share this most intimate of revelations. **Psychiatrists**

who testified were in agreement that the underlying cause for his act had been neither religious nor political, but sexual."

481. "Tabatabai, Muhammad Husayn," in *The Oxford Dictionary of Islam.*, edited by John L. Esposito. *Oxford Islamic Studies Online*, https://www.oxfordreference.com/display/10.1093/oi/authority.20110803101820826 (accessed December 12, 2013).; *Al-Mizan fi Tafsir-il-Qur'an* by Allamah as-Saiyed Mohammad Husain at- Tabataba'i, al-A'lami lil-Matbu'at, Beirut, Lebanon, 1972/1392 AH.

482. *Encyclopaedia of the Quran Online*, https://referenceworks.brill.com/display/db/eqo?language=en

483. *The Cambridge Companion to the Qur'an*, edited by Jane Dammen McCauliffe, Cambridge, U.K., Cambridge University Press, 2006.

484. Jane Dammen McCauliffe, "Christians in the Quran and Tafsir", in *Muslim Perceptions of Other Religions—A Historical Survey*, New York, 1999, edited by Jacques Waardenburg, pp. 107-108.; Elsewhere, in Jane Dammen McCauliffe, *Qur'anic Christians—An Analysis of Classical and Modern Exegetes*, 1991, Cambridge, U.K., p. 85, **after dubbing the Sunni Sheikh, Rashid Rida (d. 1935), one of the "preeminent exegetes of this [the 20th] century," McCauliffe maintains, "Rashid Rida's counterpart for 20th century Shi'i commentary is undoubtedly Muhammad Husayn Tabatabai."**

485. Allamah Sayyed Muhammad Husayn Tabatabai, *Shi'ite Islam*, translated and edited by Seyyed Hossein Nasr, SUNY Press, 1975.

486. Ibid., p. 20.

487. Ibid., p. 19.

488. W. Montgomery Watt, *Religious Studies*, 1977, Vol. 13, pp. 377-378, a review of *Shi'ite Islam* by Allāmah Ṭabāṭabā'ī; Seyyed Hossein Nasr, https://www.jstor.org/stable/20005436

489. "Introduction: Allameh Tabatabai University" http://web.archive.org/web/20110722013508/http:/atu.ac.ir/index_en.htm

490. "Allameh Tabataba(e)i's Interpretive Methods and Principles Nat'l Congress to be Held," *https://navideshahed.com/en*, May 1, 2012 https://navideshahed.com/en/news/346955/%E2%80%9Callameh-tabatabaei%E2%80%99s-interpretive-methods-and-principles%E2%80%9D-nat%E2%80%99l-congress-to-be-held

"Speaking in a news conference on April 29, executive secretary of the congress Hojat-ol-Islam Amir Reza Ashrafi said that the congress is aimed at recognizing the interpretative methods and principles used by Allameh Tabatabaee [Tabatabai] in *Al-Mizan* exegesis as well as different attitudes of Quran researchers toward the subject."

491. The extracts quoted from Tabatabai's gloss on Q 17:4/8 can be found here: https://www.altafsir.com/Tafasir.asp?tMadhNo=0&tTafsirNo=56&tSoraNo=17&tAyahNo=4&tDisplay=yes&UserProfile=0&LanguageId=1

492. *A Modern Qur'anic Kampf Against The Jews*, pp. 547, 548, 549, 550, 551, 555, 557, 558, and 575.

493. The extracts quoted from Tantawi's Qur'anic commentaries on Q 17:4/8 can be found here: https://www.altafsir.com/Tafasir.asp?tMadhNo=0&tTafsirNo=57&tSoraNo=17&tAyah

No=4&tDisplay=yes&UserProfile=0&LanguageId=1;
https://www.altafsir.com/Tafasir.asp?tMadhNo=0&tTafsirNo=57&tSoraNo=17&tAyahNo=8&tDisplay=yes&UserProfile=0&LanguageId=1

494. See reference 467.

495. See reference 454.

496. See references 479 and 492

497. See reference 479.

498. See "The Covenant of the Islamic Resistance Movement—Hamas," Special Dispatch, No. 1092, *The Middle East Media Research Institute* https://www.memri.org/reports/covenant-islamic-resistance-movement-%E2%80%93-hamas; The Covenant was translated from the Arabic original, found here: https://web.archive.org/web/20070325201016/http://www.islamonline.net/Arabic/doc/2004/03/article11.SHTML; For an overview of the attacks see: Morton Klein, "Palestinian Arabs Overwhelmingly Support Hamas And Its Genocidal Aspirations," *The Federalist*, October 25, 2023. https://thefederalist.com/2023/10/25/palestinian-arabs-overwhelmingly-support-hamas-and-their-genocidal-aspirations/

499. Ibid.; For apparent planning since 2014, see "'Al-Aqsa Flood': Initiated by 70 Elite Fighters, Crafted by 5 Hamas Leaders," *Asharq Al-Awsat*, January 10, 2024 (accessed 4/19/24) https://english.aawsat.com/arab-world/4780421-%E2%80%98al-aqsa-flood%E2%80%99-initiated-70-elite-fighters-crafted-5-hamas-leaders

500. Daniel Byman, Riley McCabe, Alexander Palmer, Catrina Doxsee, Mackenzie Holtz, and Delaney Duff. "Hamas' October 7th Attack: Visualizing the Data," The Center for Strategic and International Studies, December 19, 2023 https://www.csis.org/analysis/hamass-october-7-attack-visualizing-data#:~:text=Hamas%27s%20October%207%20terrorist%20attack,years%20of%20the%20Second%20Intifada

501. Ibid, See Figure 2.

502. "Israel Revises October 7 Death Toll After Agonizing Forensics," *Foundation for the Defense of Democracies*, November 12, 2023 https://www.fdd.org/analysis/2023/11/12/israel-revises-october-7-death-toll-after-agonizing-forensics/ (accessed 4/19/24); Natalya Vasilyeva. "Why the full extent of Hamas's sex crimes may never be known, " *The Telegraph* (London), December 30, 2023 https://www.telegraph.co.uk/world-news/2023/12/30/truth-about-hamas-sex-crimes-may-never-be-known/; "Israel Shares Raw Footage of the Oct. 7 Attacks," The New York Times, October 23, 2023 https://www.nytimes.com/2023/10/23/world/middleeast/israel-hamas-attack-video.html; Julia Frankel. "Israeli video compilation shows the savagery and ease of Hamas' attack," *The Associated Press*, October 17, 2023 https://apnews.com/article/israel-palestinians-hamas-attack-military-war-a8f63b07641212f0de61861844e5e71e

503. "Examination of Israel's Intelligence and Policy Failures in the Yom Kippur War and Hamas Attack." Streamed live on Jan 26, 2024 https://www.youtube.com/watch?v=D0sqTLemeqE

504. Ibid.

505. Ibid.

[506.] Ibid.; Also, "The Covenant of the Islamic Resistance Movement—Hamas,"; Andrew Bostom. "Hamas' Jihad And Jew-Hatred Are Islam's Jihad And Jew-Hatred," April 1, 2019, https://www.andrewbostom.org/2019/04/hamas-jihad-and-jew-hatred-are-islams-jihad-and-jew-hatred/; For much more extensive background see both Bostom, "Negating the Legacy of Jihad in Palestine," and Bostom, "The Legacy of Islamic Antisemitism"

[507.] "Obituary: In Memoriam: Robert S. Wistrich," *Holocaust and Genocide Studies*, vol. 29 no. 2, 2015, p. 351-351. *Project MUSE* muse.jhu.edu/article/589000.

[508.] Robert Wistrich, *Antisemitism—The Longest Hatred*, New York, 1991, p. xv.

[509.] "Working definition of antisemitism" https://holocaustremembrance.com/resources/working-definition-antisemitism; "Defining Antisemitism" https://www.state.gov/defining-antisemitism/

[510.] "ADL Reports Unprecedented Rise in Antisemitic Incidents Post-October 7." December 11, 2023. https://www.adl.org/resources/press-release/adl-reports-unprecedented-rise-antisemitic-incidents-post-oct-7

[511.] Hannah Nightingale. "California professor Loay Alnaji arrested, charged with involuntary manslaughter after death of Jewish man at anti-Israel protest." *The Post Millennial*, November 16, 2023 https://thepostmillennial.com/breaking-california-professor-loay-alnaji-arrested-charged-with-involuntary-manslaughter-after-death-of-jewish-man-at-anti-israel-protest#google_vignette

[512.] "Attitudes Toward Jews, Israel and the Palestinian-Israeli Conflict in Ten European Countries." April, 2004. 34pp. **https://www.adl.org/sites/default/files/documents/assets/pdf/israel-international/european_attitudes_april_2004.pdf**; Questions were 1 to 10 were created by asking whether the negative stereotypes are "probably true"; Respondents who said at least 6 out of 11 statements are "probably true" for statements 1 to 10, or probably false" for statement 11, are considered to harbor extreme antisemitic attitudes.

[513.] "ADL Global 100: A Survey of Attitudes Toward Jews in Over 100 Countries Around the World" (2014) https://web.archive.org/web/20190401023041/http:/global100.adl.org/public/ADL-Global-100-Executive-Summary.pdf; Methods: "The Anti-Defamation League commissioned First International Resources to research attitudes and opinions toward Jews in more than 100 countries around the world. Fieldwork and data collection for this global public opinion project were conducted and coordinated by Anzalone Liszt Grove Research. All interviews were conducted between July 2013 and February 2014. The data is a result of 53,100 total interviews among citizens aged 18 and over, across 101 countries and the Palestinian Territories in the West Bank & Gaza. Expected margin of sampling error for the weighted global average is +/- 0.97%, for the countries/territories surveyed with n=500 interviews it is +/- 4.4% and for countries sampled with n=1,000 interviews it is +/- 3.2%. The margin of error is higher for sub-groups within each geography. Interviews were conducted via landline telephones, mobile phones and face-to-face discussions in 96 languages (including many dialects and pidgin/creole versions). All respondents were selected at random. Telephone respondents were selected using random-digit dial sampling; face-to-face respondents were selected using geographically stratified, randomly selected sampling points in each country and at the household level, using a Kish grid."

Religion as a percentage of population source for this survey, from: "The World Fact Book," *Central Intelligence Agency*, 2013-2014 https://web.archive.org/web/20130116012027/https://www.cia.gov/library/publications/the-world-factbook/geos/xx.html

"New ADL Poll Finds Dramatic Decline in Anti-Semitic Attitudes in France; Significant Drops in Germany and Belgium" (2015) https://www.adl.org/news/press-releases/new-poll-anti-semitic-attitudes-19-countries#.Vn8RAMtOnqA; As I have noted, ADL has decided not to allow access to these data any longer. Unfortunately, data from the 6 Western European countries which included a Muslim oversample some time between 2015 to 2022/23, as described for each country, can no longer be found at the following hyperlink, https://global100.adl.org/map/weurope and related internal specific country hyperlinks: See the following discussions of this unfortunate phenomenon and the concealed data: Andrew Bostom. "ADL Western European Data From 2015 (full) & 2019 (press release) demonstrating 2- to 4-fold excess prevalence of Extreme Antisemitism among Muslims vs. Non-Muslims; Update: Images of 2023 data scrubbed," www.andrewbostom.net, April 5, 2025 https://andrewbostom.net/2025/04/adl-western-european-data-from-2015-full-2019-press-release-demonstrating-2-to-4-fold-excess-prevalence-of-extreme-antisemitism-among-muslims-vs-non-muslims/;
Andrew Bostom. "UPDATED with ADL email exchange: ADL 2023 & 2019 Western European Muslim Antisemitism Data Previously Available Now Scrubbed, Either Inadvertently or By Design," www.andrewbostom.net, April 7, 2025

Jikeli G. "How Do Muslims and Jews in Christian Countries See Each Other Today? A Survey Review," *Religions*. 2023; 14(3):412. https://doi.org/10.3390/rel14030412 See p. 32.

"ADL Global Survey of 18 Countries Finds Hardcore Anti-Semitic Attitudes Remain Pervasive," (2019) https://www.adl.org/resources/press-release/adl-global-survey-18-countries-finds-hardcore-anti-semitic-attitudes-remain;

"The ADL Global 100: An Index of Antisemitism," (2023) https://www.adl.org/sites/default/files/pdfs/2023-05/ADL-Global100-2023_1.pdf;
514. Edward H. Kaplan. Charles A. Small. "Anti-Israel Sentiment Predicts Anti-Semitism in Europe." *Journal of Conflict Resolution*, 2006; vol. 50, no, 4, pp, 548-561.
515. "ADL Global 100: A Survey of Attitudes Toward Jews in Over 100 Countries Around the World" (2014)
516. Andrew Bostom. "Just Released Global ADL Data Confirm Muslim Nations Exhibit Disproportionate Extreme Antisemitism, Including "Moderate and Tolerant" Indonesia, Where Its Prevalence is Now 96%!," www.andrewbostom.net, January 16, 2025 https://andrewbostom.net/2025/01/just-released-global-adl-data-confirm-muslim-nations-exhibit-disproportionate-extreme-antisemitism-including-moderate-and-tolerant-

indonesia-where-its-prevalence-is-now-96/; The original ADL data can be found here: https://www.adl.org/adl-global-100-index-antisemitism
517. "New ADL Poll Finds Dramatic Decline in Anti-Semitic Attitudes in France; Significant Drops in Germany and Belgium" (2015)
518. Jikeli, "How Do Muslims and Jews in Christian Countries See Each Other Today? A Survey Review"
519. "ADL Global Survey of 18 Countries Finds Hardcore Anti-Semitic Attitudes Remain Pervasive," (2019)
520. "The ADL Global 100: An Index of Antisemitism," (2023); See Bostom. "ADL Western European Data From 2015 (full) & 2019 (press release) demonstrating 2- to 4-fold excess prevalence of Extreme Antisemitism among Muslims vs. Non-Muslims; Update: Images of 2023 data scrubbed," www.andrewbostom.net, April 5, 2025
521. France: https://global100.adl.org/country/france/2023; Belgium: https://global100.adl.org/country/belgium/2023; See Bostom. "ADL Western European Data From 2015 (full) & 2019 (press release) demonstrating 2- to 4-fold excess prevalence of Extreme Antisemitism among Muslims vs. Non-Muslims; Update: Images of 2023 data scrubbed," www.andrewbostom.net, April 5, 2025
522. Evelyn Ersanilli, Ruud Koopmans. "The Six Country Immigrant Integration Comparative Survey (SCIICS)" – Technical report Discussion Paper SP VI 2013–102 July 2013. WZB Berlin Social Research Center Research Area Migration und Diversity Research Unit Migration, Integration, Trans nationalization. https://bibliothek.wzb.eu/pdf/2013/vi13-102.pdf
523. Jong in Brussel: bevindingen uit de JOP-monitor Brussel Broché – 30 septembre 2011 Édition en Néerlandais Nicole Vettenburg, Mark Elchardus, Johan Put. https://www.amazon.fr/Jong-Brussel-bevindingen-uit-JOP-monitor/dp/9033484145
524. Nicole Vettenburg, Mark Elchardus, Johan Put, Stefaan Pleysier. Jong in Antwerpen en Gent: bevindingen uit de JOP-monitor Antwerpen-Gent Paperback – 22 Jan. 2013 https://www.amazon.co.uk/Jong-Antwerpen-Gent-bevindingen-Antwerpen-Gent/dp/903349230X
525. Gunther Jikeli. "Interviews with Young Muslim Men in Europe," in "European Muslim Antisemitism," Indiana University Press, 2015. https://www.jstor.org/stable/j.ctt16gzdvm.7
526. Gunther Jikeli. "Antisemitism in youth language: the pejorative use for the terms for 'Jew' in German and French." Conflict and Communication Online. Vol. 9. No. 1. 2010. https://web.archive.org/web/20140617154317/https://www.cco.regener-online.de/2010_1/pdf/jikeli.pdf
527. Jikeli, "Interviews with Young Muslim Men in Europe"
528. Technical report: "FRA survey - Discrimination and hate crime against Jews in EU Member States: experiences and perceptions of antisemitism," November 6, 2013. https://fra.europa.eu/en/publication/2013/technical-report-fra-survey-discrimination-and-hate-crime-against-jews-eu-member
529. Public Opinion Poll No (88). **Palestinian Center for Policy and Survey Research (PSR), June 7-11, 2023.** https://pcpsr.org/en/node/944; Public Opinion Polls Gaza Survey 7th October. Arab World for Research and Development (AWRAD), November 14, 2023.

https://www.awrad.org/files/server/polls/polls2023/Public%20Opinion%20Poll%20-%20Gaza%20War%202023%20-%20Tables%20of%20Results.pdf;
Public Opinion Poll No (90). **Palestinian Center for Policy and Survey Research (PSR), November 22, 2023-December 2, 2023. Released December 13, 2023** https://pcpsr.org/en/node/961

530. "Arab Public Opinion about the Israeli War on Gaza," Arab Center for Research and Policy Studies, Doha, Qatar, January 10, 2024 https://www.dohainstitute.org/en/Lists/ACRPS-PDFDocumentLibrary/arab-opinion-war-on-gaza-press-release-en.pdf

531. Cygnal. "Survey of General Population Israel - Hamas Awareness and Attitudes," October 20, 2023. https://www.cygn.al/wp-content/uploads/2023/10/Cygnal-National-Israel-Deck.pdf

532. "Arab Public Opinion about the Israeli War on Gaza"

533. Public Opinion Poll No (88). **Palestinian Center for Policy and Survey Research (PSR), June 7-11, 2023.**

534. Public Opinion Polls Gaza Survey 7th October. Arab World for Research and Development (AWRAD), November 14, 2023.

535. Public Opinion Poll No (90). **Palestinian Center for Policy and Survey Research (PSR), November 22, 2023-December 2, 2023.**

536. "Arab Public Opinion about the Israeli War on Gaza," Arab Center for Research and Policy Studies, Doha, Qatar, January 10, 2024.

537. Cygnal. "Survey of General Population Israel - Hamas Awareness and Attitudes," October 20, 2023.

538. Gil Stern Hoffman. "6 in 10 Palestinians reject 2-state solution, survey finds," The Jerusalem Post, July 15, 2011 https://www.jpost.com/Diplomacy-and-Politics/6-in-10-Palestinians-reject-2-state-solution-survey-finds

539. "The Covenant of the Islamic Resistance Movement—Hamas"

540. "6 in 10 Palestinians reject 2-state solution, survey finds."

541. Sahih Muslim Book 041, Hadith Number 6985 https://hadithcollection.com/sahihmuslim/sahih-muslim-book-41-turmoil-and-portents-of-the-last-hour/sahih-muslim-book-041-hadith-number-6985

542. "The Covenant of the Islamic Resistance Movement—Hamas"

543. Mahathir's full speech October 22, 2003 — 10.00am. Dr Mahathir bin Mohamad at the opening of the tenth session of the Islamic Summit conference at Putrajaya Convention Centre. https://www.smh.com.au/world/mahathirs-full-speech-20031022-gdhmg3.html

544. Andrew Bostom. "David Littman, 1933-2012: He Showed Us The Mettle of His Pasture," May 21, 2012 https://www.andrewbostom.org/2012/05/david-littman-1933-2012-he-showed-us-the-mettle-of-his-pasture/

545. "Human rights and human wrongs," World Union for Progressive Judaism, 1986-1991, The Union, Genève (Geneva) https://search.worldcat.org/title/762567903; Littman made his first statements about the Hamas Covenant during the January 31, 1989 session as documented in "Human rights and human wrongs," No. 6, p.3.; See also: "The Charter of Hamas," – HRC first special session – NGO statement (World Union for Progressive Judaism, Association for World Education). Joint written statement submitted by the Association for World Education and the World Union for

Progressive Judaism (WUPJ), non-governmental organizations on the Roster. The Secretary-General received the following written statement which is circulated in accordance with Economic and Social Council resolution 1996/31.(July 4, 2006) https://www.un.org/unispal/document/auto-insert-182893/; "The 1988 Charter of Hamas and its evil legacy of 'jihadist-martyrdom' bombings," (E/CN.4/Sub.2/2003/NGO/41, of 21 July 2003). Written statement by the WUPJ, circulated officially as a document at the 55th session of the UN Sub-Commission on Human Rights (July 28-15 August 2003) https://web.archive.org/web/20110128180743/http://www.unhchr.ch/Huridocda/Huridoca.nsf/e06a5300f90fa0238025668700518ca4/99cdd287d4323f56c1256d780034ba6f/$FILE/G0315092.pdf

546. "Human rights and human wrongs," January 31, 1989, No. 6, p.3

547. Ibid.

548. Qur'an 3:112, https://corpus.quran.com/translation.jsp?chapter=3&verse=112; All Qur'anic translations are from the online "The Qur'anic Arabic Corpus" https://corpus.quran.com/ which provides seven pious Muslim and/or non-Muslim academic translations of each verse: Sahih International; Pickthall; Yusuf Ali; Shakir; Muhammad Sarwar; Mohsin Khan; Arberry. I have chosen to use the Sahih International translation for consistency.

549. "The Legacy of Islamic Antisemitism—From Sacred Texts to Solemn History," 2020, pp. 34-37, 164.
5:60 http://corpus.quran.com/translation.jsp?chapter=5&verse=60;
5:78 http://corpus.quran.com/translation.jsp?chapter=5&verse=78;
2:65 http://corpus.quran.com/translation.jsp?chapter=2&verse=65;
7:166 http://corpus.quran.com/translation.jsp?chapter=7&verse=166

550. Sunan Abu Dawud, Book 39, hadith 36 https://sunnah.com/abudawud/39/46

551. "Jordanian Professor Salah Al-Khalidi: The Palestinians Will Rid the World of the Jews," The Middle East Media Research Institute, December 28, 2015, #5260. https://www.memri.org/tv/jordanian-professor-salah-al-khalidi-palestinians-will-rid-world-jews

552. Bostom, *The Legacy of Islamic Antisemitism,* 2020, pp. 429-454; For similarities and differences between Sunni and Shiite apocalyptic literature, see Andrew Bostom, "Iran's Final Solution for Israel," Bravura, Washington, D.C., 2014, pp. 148-154; For Qur'anic citations, see reference 52, above, and:
5:13 https://corpus.quran.com/translation.jsp?chapter=5&verse=13;
5:65 http://corpus.quran.com/translation.jsp?chapter=5&verse=64

553. "Former Al-Azhar Fatwa Committee Head Sets Out the Jews' 20 Bad Traits As Described in the Qur'an," The Middle East Media Research Institute, April 6, 2004. https://www.memri.org/reports/former-al-azhar-fatwa-committee-head-sets-out-jews-20-bad-traits-described-quran; For an earlier, similar litany, which included 25 "personality traits," see: Sheikh Abd Allah Al Meshad, "Jews' Attitudes Toward Islam and Muslims in the First Islamic Era," presented at The Al-Azhar University sponsored Fourth Conference of the Academy of Islamic Research, Cairo, September,1968 (see: https://babel.hathitrust.org/cgi/pt?id=uc1.b3938025), and cited in Bostom, *The Legacy of Islamic Antisemitism,* pp. 384-386.

554. See references 422a to 436.

[555] "The Covenant of the Islamic Resistance Movement—Hamas"
[556] "The Legacy of Islamic Antisemitism—From Sacred Texts to Solemn History," 2020, p. 63.
[557] Sahih Muslim, Book 41, Number 6985 https://quranx.com/Hadith/Muslim/USC-MSA/Book-41/Hadith-6985
[558] "The Covenant of the Islamic Resistance Movement—Hamas"
[559] Tafseer (Tafsir) Ibn Kathir (English, 114 Sura's Complete); Sura 4, pp. 358-359 https://archive.org/details/TafseerIbnKathirenglish114SurahsComplete/004Nisa/mode/2up;
Born in Basrah in 1300, Ibn Kathir died in Damascus in 1373. He was one of the best-known historians and traditionalists of Syria during the reign of the Bahri Mamluks, compiling an important history of Islam, as well as a Qur'anic commentary that foreshadows in its style the commentary of Al-Suyuti.; For background on Ibn Kathir's Tafsir, see Younus Y. Mirza, "TAFSĪR IBN KATHĪR A Window Onto Medieval Islam and a Guide to the Development of Modern Islamic Orthodoxy," 2021, Routledge Companion to the Qur'an
https://www.academia.edu/61582430/TAFS%C4%AAR_IBN_KATH%C4%AAR_A_Window_Onto_Medieval_Islam_and_a_Guide_to_the_Development_of_Modern_Islamic_Orthodoxy?hb-sb-sw=2020221
4:155 https://corpus.quran.com/translation.jsp?chapter=4&verse=155
4:156 https://corpus.quran.com/translation.jsp?chapter=4&verse=156
4:157 https://corpus.quran.com/translation.jsp?chapter=4&verse=157
4:158 https://corpus.quran.com/translation.jsp?chapter=4&verse=158
4:159 https://corpus.quran.com/translation.jsp?chapter=4&verse=159
[560] Bostom, *The Mufti's Islamic Jew-Hatred*, p. 31.
[561] "Palestinian Muslims mark sad and tense 'holiest Ramadan night' in Jerusalem,' *Agence France-Presse*, April 5, 2024 https://www.france24.com/en/live-news/20240405-palestinian-muslims-mark-sad-and-tense-holiest-ramadan-night-in-jerusalem
[562] Itamar Marcus, Nan Jacques Zilberdik. "PA Mufti: Muslims' destiny is to kill Jews," *Palestinian Media Watch*, January 15, 2012. https://palwatch.org/page/3447
[563] "Antisemitism in Al-Azhar University's Friday Sermon: The Jews Are The Muslims' Worst Enemies," *The Middle East Media Research Institute*, May 10, 2013, Clip # 3871 (transcript)
https://web.archive.org/web/20140413130150/http://www.memritv.org/clip_transcript/en/3871.htm
[564] Itamar Marcus. "PA teaches about Muslim destiny to kill Jews just 2 weeks after Oct. 7 massacre of Jews," *Palestinian Media Watch*, October 22, 2023.
https://palwatch.org/page/34677
[565] About Karim Abu Zaid https://karimabuzaid.com/about/, at https://karimabuzaid.com/
[566] "Colorado Islamic Scholar Karim Abu Zaid: Muslims Should Not Shy Away From Talking About Martyrdom, There Is A Prize For Being Killed For The Sake Of Allah – It's Like The Airline Upgrading You From Economy To First Class," *The Middle East Media Research Institute*, November 10, 2023, #10643.

https://www.memri.org/tv/colorado-islamic-scholar-karim-abuzaid-muslims-not-shy-away-martyrdom-prize

567. David Littman. HUMAN RIGHTS COUNCIL Ninth special session A/HRC/S-9/NGO/3, January 8, 2009 https://digitallibrary.un.org/record/645886/files/A_HRC_S-9_NGO_3-EN.pdf

568. "The Covenant of the Islamic Resistance Movement—Hamas"; See for example, Hadassa Ben-Itto. "The lie that wouldn't die: The Protocols of the Elders of Zion, London," 2005. https://search.worldcat.org/title/57750903

569. "The Covenant of the Islamic Resistance Movement—Hamas"; 5:64 https://corpus.quran.com/translation.jsp?chapter=5&verse=64

570. See Bostom, *The Legacy of Jihad*, for a general juridical and historical analysis of jihad

571. "The Covenant of the Islamic Resistance Movement—Hamas"; The specific quote attributed to al-Banna in the Hamas covenant is not sourced. Regardless, see Abd Al Fattah El-Awaisi, *The Muslim Brothers and the Palestine Question*, London, 1998, p. 109 for a discussion of al-Banna's conviction during the World War II years that armed, violent jihad was the only way to "solve" the "Palestine problem." Al-Banna stated that preventing (or destroying the establishment of) a Zionist state, could only be achieved by those Muslims "prepared to bear the burdens of a long-term jihad."

572. "The Covenant of the Islamic Resistance Movement—Hamas"

573. Ibid; For jihad martyrdom, see Bostom, *The Legacy of Jihad*, pp. 136-139 (in the hadith); 249-50.

574. See for Tantawi references 387-396.; See for the Hamas Covenant references 548-552.

575. See for Tantawi references 198, 230, 244-248, 302, 309, 311, and 335; See for the Hamas Covenant references 568 and 569

576. See for Tantawi references 421-422a; See for the Hamas Covenant references 540 and 558.

577. See for Tantawi reference 443; See for the Hamas Covenant references 542, 546, and 570.

578. See reference 571. For al-Banna, see reference 39.

579. "This variation in length is noteworthy because the Qur'an uses length as an organizing principle. The canonical text is arranged by roughly descending order of sura length. In other words, the longer suras appear earlier in the text, the very shortest ones toward the end." Jane Dammen McAuliffe (Editor). *Encyclopaedia Of The Quran*, Vol 1, 2002, Preface, p i.
https://archive.org/details/EncyclopaediaOfTheQuranVol1/page/n5/mode/2up

580. Tafsir Ibn Kathir, Vol. 1, Darussalam, Riyadh, 2000, p. 49, "Reciting Al-Fatihah is required in Every Rak'ah (subdivision) of the Prayer (daily prayer sessions)"; See also: Muiz Bukhary." Why Do We Read Surat Al-Fatihah 17 Times a day?"
https://www.youtube.com/watch?v=OnQMrhAuNd0

581. 1:1 https://corpus.quran.com/translation.jsp?chapter=1&verse=1;
1:2 https://corpus.quran.com/translation.jsp?chapter=1&verse=2;
1:3 https://corpus.quran.com/translation.jsp?chapter=1&verse=3;
1:4 https://corpus.quran.com/translation.jsp?chapter=1&verse=4;
1:5 https://corpus.quran.com/translation.jsp?chapter=1&verse=5;
1:6 https://corpus.quran.com/translation.jsp?chapter=1&verse=6;

1:7 https://corpus.quran.com/translation.jsp?chapter=1&verse=7
Jami at-Tirmidhi, Vol. 5, Book 44, Hadith 2954 https://sunnah.com/urn/639380
582. Sami A. Aldeeb. "The Fatiha and the Culture of Hate—Interpretation of the 7th verse through the centuries," Centre of Arab and Islamic Law, 2015.
https://www.researchgate.net/publication/356598834_The_Fatiha_and_the_culture_of_hate_interpretation_of_the_7th_verse_through_the_centuries/link/61a40fee7323543e211175ef/download?_tp=eyJjb250ZXh0Ijp7ImZpcnN0UGFnZSI6InB1YmxpY2F0aW9uIiwicGFnZSI6InB1YmxpY2F0aW9uIn19;
See also: Andrew Bostom. "The Opening Salvo of 'Calming' Qur'anic Jew-Hatred," December 10, 2023, https://www.andrewbostom.org/2023/12/the-opening-salvo-of-calming-quranic-jew-hatred/
583. Oliver Leaman (Editor). "The Qur'an: an encyclopedia," Routledge, Abingdon, 2006, p. 614.
2:275 https://corpus.quran.com/translation.jsp?chapter=2&verse=275;
4:161 https://corpus.quran.com/translation.jsp?chapter=4&verse=161;
2:96 https://corpus.quran.com/translation.jsp?chapter=2&verse=96;
2:109 https://corpus.quran.com/translation.jsp?chapter=2&verse=109;
2:74 https://corpus.quran.com/translation.jsp?chapter=2&verse=74;
2:78 https://corpus.quran.com/translation.jsp?chapter=2&verse=78;
5:32 https://corpus.quran.com/translation.jsp?chapter=5&verse=32;
5:33 https://corpus.quran.com/translation.jsp?chapter=5&verse=33;
5:64 https://corpus.quran.com/translation.jsp?chapter=5&verse=64;
2:61 https://corpus.quran.com/translation.jsp?chapter=2&verse=61;
2:90 https://corpus.quran.com/translation.jsp?chapter=2&verse=90;
3:112 https://corpus.quran.com/translation.jsp?chapter=3&verse=112;
5:77 https://corpus.quran.com/translation.jsp?chapter=5&verse=77
584. See reference 223.
585. Tantawi's formal gloss on Q 1:7 is found here: https://www.altafsir.com/Tafasir.asp?tMadhNo=0&tTafsirNo=57&tSoraNo=1&tAyahNo=7&tDisplay=yes&Page=1&Size=1&LanguageId=1
586. al-Deeb, "The Fatiha and the Culture of Hate"; Bostom, "The Opening Salvo of 'Calming' Qur'anic Jew-Hatred".
587. Bostom, "The Legacy of Islamic Antisemitism," 2020, pp. 33-38;
See also within "The Legacy of Islamic Antisemitism," Haggai Ben-Shammai, "Jew-Hatred in the Islamic Tradition and the Koranic (Qur'anic) Exegesis," pp. 221-225.
588. Ibid; Note: Below will be the last series of full The Qur'anic Arabic Corpus links to individual verses
16:118 https://corpus.quran.com/translation.jsp?chapter=16&verse=118;
7:168 https://corpus.quran.com/translation.jsp?chapter=7&verse=168;
5:13 https://corpus.quran.com/translation.jsp?chapter=5&verse=13;
2:134 https://corpus.quran.com/translation.jsp?chapter=2&verse=134;
2:141 https://corpus.quran.com/translation.jsp?chapter=2&verse=141;
17:4 https://corpus.quran.com/translation.jsp?chapter=17&verse=4;
17:5 https://corpus.quran.com/translation.jsp?chapter=17&verse=5;
7:168 https://corpus.quran.com/translation.jsp?chapter=7&verse=168;
62:6 https://corpus.quran.com/translation.jsp?chapter=62&verse=6;

5:32 https://corpus.quran.com/translation.jsp?chapter=5&verse=32;
5:64 https://corpus.quran.com/translation.jsp?chapter=5&verse=64;
4:155 https://corpus.quran.com/translation.jsp?chapter=4&verse=155;
2:91 https://corpus.quran.com/translation.jsp?chapter=2&verse=91;
3:55 https://corpus.quran.com/translation.jsp?chapter=3&verse=55;
4:157 https://corpus.quran.com/translation.jsp?chapter=4&verse=157;
2:104 https://corpus.quran.com/translation.jsp?chapter=2&verse=104;
4:46 https://corpus.quran.com/translation.jsp?chapter=4&verse=46;
9:30 https://corpus.quran.com/translation.jsp?chapter=9&verse=30;
2:109 https://corpus.quran.com/translation.jsp?chapter=2&verse=109;
2:74 https://corpus.quran.com/translation.jsp?chapter=2&verse=74;
2:75 https://corpus.quran.com/translation.jsp?chapter=2&verse=75;
2:78 https://corpus.quran.com/translation.jsp?chapter=2&verse=78;
2:89 https://corpus.quran.com/translation.jsp?chapter=2&verse=89;
2:111 https://corpus.quran.com/translation.jsp?chapter=2&verse=111;
2:61 https://corpus.quran.com/translation.jsp?chapter=2&verse=61;
3:112 https://corpus.quran.com/translation.jsp?chapter=3&verse=112;
2:275 https://corpus.quran.com/translation.jsp?chapter=2&verse=275;
2:109 https://corpus.quran.com/translation.jsp?chapter=2&verse=109;
2:96 https://corpus.quran.com/translation.jsp?chapter=2&verse=96;
2:53 https://corpus.quran.com/translation.jsp?chapter=2&verse=53;
4:51 https://corpus.quran.com/translation.jsp?chapter=4&verse=51;
4:156 https://corpus.quran.com/translation.jsp?chapter=4&verse=156;
4:161 https://corpus.quran.com/translation.jsp?chapter=4&verse=161;
3:110 https://corpus.quran.com/translation.jsp?chapter=3&verse=110;
3:24 https://corpus.quran.com/translation.jsp?chapter=3&verse=24;
3:99 https://corpus.quran.com/translation.jsp?chapter=3&verse=99;
5:71 https://corpus.quran.com/translation.jsp?chapter=5&verse=71;
3:69 https://corpus.quran.com/translation.jsp?chapter=3&verse=69;
3:71 https://corpus.quran.com/translation.jsp?chapter=3&verse=71;
3:79 https://corpus.quran.com/translation.jsp?chapter=3&verse=79;
3:75 https://corpus.quran.com/translation.jsp?chapter=3&verse=75;
5:51 https://corpus.quran.com/translation.jsp?chapter=5&verse=51;
5:82 https://corpus.quran.com/translation.jsp?chapter=5&verse=82;
4:47 https://corpus.quran.com/translation.jsp?chapter=4&verse=47;
3:113 https://corpus.quran.com/translation.jsp?chapter=3&verse=113;
2:65 https://corpus.quran.com/translation.jsp?chapter=2&verse=65;
7:166 https://corpus.quran.com/translation.jsp?chapter=7&verse=166;
5:60 https://corpus.quran.com/translation.jsp?chapter=5&verse=60;
4:55 https://corpus.quran.com/translation.jsp?chapter=4&verse=55;
5:29 https://corpus.quran.com/translation.jsp?chapter=5&verse=29;
98:6 https://corpus.quran.com/translation.jsp?chapter=98&verse=6;
58:14 https://corpus.quran.com/translation.jsp?chapter=58&verse=14;
58:15 https://corpus.quran.com/translation.jsp?chapter=58&verse=15;
58:16 https://corpus.quran.com/translation.jsp?chapter=58&verse=16;
58:17 https://corpus.quran.com/translation.jsp?chapter=58&verse=17;

58:18 https://corpus.quran.com/translation.jsp?chapter=58&verse=18;
58:18 https://corpus.quran.com/translation.jsp?chapter=58&verse=19

589. "A Risala of Al-Jahiz," translated by Joshua Finkel. *Journal of the American Oriental Society* 1927; Vol. 47: 311–34, p.324; Sahih International translation of Qur'an 5:82, "You will surely find the most intense of the people in animosity toward the believers [to be] the Jews and those who associate others with Allah;..." https://corpus.quran.com/translation.jsp?chapter=5&verse=82
590. **See references 481-490.**
591. Tabatabai's original Arabic gloss on 5:82 from al-Mizan at Al-Tafsir.com: https://www.altafsir.com/Tafasir.asp?tMadhNo=0&tTafsirNo=56&tSoraNo=5&tAyahNo=82&tDisplay=yes&UserProfile=0&LanguageId=1; Extracts of Tabatabai's gloss on 5:82 in English translation, from: Sayyid Muhammad Husayn at-Tabataba'i, "Al-Mizan fe Tafsir al-Quran," translated by Sayyid Saeed Akhtar Rizvi, 1982, vol. 11, pp. 96-97, 99 https://wofis.com/pdfs/books/42/AL-MIZAN%20An%20Exegesis%20of%20the%20Qur%E2%80%99an%20Vol.%2011.pdf
592. *Al-Mizan*, (translated by Rizvi), 1983, Vol. 1, p. 256 https://www.wofis.com/pdfs/books/32/AL-MIZAN%20An%20Exegesis%20of%20the%20Qur%E2%80%99an%20Vol.%201.pdf
593. Tantawi's gloss on Qur'an 5:82 in al-Tafsīr al-wasīṭ lil-Qur'ān al-karīm, was translated by Dr. Atef Ghobrial from the original Arabic at Al-Tafsir.com, which can be found here https://www.altafsir.com/Tafasir.asp?tMadhNo=0&tTafsirNo=57&tSoraNo=5&tAyahNo=82&tDisplay=yes&UserProfile=0&LanguageId=1
594. Author of a monumental 19th century Qur'anic commentary, Ruh al-Maani ("The Spirit of Meaning[s]"). See: Basheer M. Nafi. "Abu al-Thana' al-Alusi: An Alim, Ottoman Mufti, and Exegete of the Qur'an." *International Journal of Middle East Studies*. 2002; Vol. 34; pp. 465-494 https://www.jstor.org/stable/3879672
595. See: Ghazi al-Wasiti, "Anti-Jewish Anecdotes from an Anti-Dhimmi Treatise," in Bostom, *The Legacy of Islamic Antisemitism*, p. 327
596. Bostom, *The Legacy of Jihad*, pp. 24-37; 125-250.
597. Qur'an 9:29, https://corpus.quran.com/translation.jsp?chapter=9&verse=29
598. "Classical and Modern Qur'anic Commentators on Qur'an 9:29," in Bostom, *The Legacy of Jihad*, pp. 127-135.
599. Tabatabai's gloss on Qur'an 9:29 from "Al-Mizan," at Al-Tafsir.com, https://www.altafsir.com/Tafasir.asp?tMadhNo=0&tTafsirNo=56&tSoraNo=9&tAyahNo=29&tDisplay=yes&UserProfile=0&LanguageId=1, translated by Prof. Sjimon den Hollander https://hunter-cuny.academia.edu/SjimonDenHollander/CurriculumVitae; Tantawi's gloss on Qur'an 9:29 from "al-Tafsīr al-wasīṭ lil-Qur'ān al-karīm," at Al-Tafsir.com, https://www.altafsir.com/Tafasir.asp?tMadhNo=0&tTafsirNo=57&tSoraNo=9&tAyahNo=29&tDisplay=yes&UserProfile=0&LanguageId=1, was translated by Dr. Atef Ghobrial.
600. Moshe Perlmann. "The Jews in the Koran and the Traditions," in "*A Study of Muslim Polemics Directed Against Jews,*" Thesis submitted to the University of London for the

degree of Ph.D. (Internal) in History, Faculty of Arts. September 1940 https://eprints.soas.ac.uk/29128/1/10731223.pdf.;
Georges Vajda. "Juifs et Musulmans Selon Le Hadit" ("Jews and Christians According to the Hadith"), *Journal Asiatique*, 1937, Vol. 229, pp. 57-127 https://gallica.bnf.fr/ark:/12148/bpt6k933293/f59.item. A first time English translation of this essay, in full, is provided in Bostom, "*The Legacy of Islamic Antisemitism*," pp. 235-260.;
Hartwig Hirschfeld, "Essai sur l'histoire des Juifs de Medine" ("Essay on the History of the Jews of Medina"), Revue Des Etude Juives 7 (1883): pp. 167–93 https://www.persee.fr/doc/rjuiv_0484-8616_1883_num_7_14_6499; 10 (1885): pp. 10–31 https://www.persee.fr/doc/rjuiv_0484-8616_1885_num_10_19_6532. A first time English translation of these essays, in full, is provided in Bostom, "*The Legacy of Islamic Antisemitism*," pp. 299-312.

601. "Moshe Perlmann, Near Eastern Languages and Cultures: Los Angeles" http://texts.cdlib.org/view?docId=hb987008v1&doc.view=frames&chunk.id=div00059&toc.depth=1&toc.id=; Moshe Perlmann. "'Abd al-Ḥaḳḳ al-Islāmī, a Jewish Convert," *The Jewish Quarterly Review*, Vol. 31, No. 2 (Oct., 1940), pp. 171-191 https://www.jstor.org/stable/1452603?origin=crossref;
Moshe Perlmann. "Samau'al al-Maghribī Ifḥām Al-Yahūd: Silencing the Jews," *Proceedings of the American Academy for Jewish Research*, Vol. 32, (1964), 234pp. https://www.jstor.org/stable/3622414?origin=crossref;
Moshe Perlmann. "Notes on Anti-Christian Propaganda in the Mamlūk Empire," Bulletin of the School of Oriental and African Studies, University of London, Vol. 10, No. 4 (1942), pp. 843-861 https://www.jstor.org/stable/609129;
Aḥmad ibn ʻAbd al-Munʻim Damanhūrī, Moshe Perlmann (Translator). "Shaykh Damanhūrī on the churches of Cairo (1739)," University of California Press, Berkeley, 1975, 87 pp. https://search.worldcat.org/title/1583677

602. Moshe Perlmann. "Arabic Antisemitic Literature: Comment on Sylvia G. Haim's Article," *Jewish Social Studies*, Vol. 17, No. 4 (Oct., 1955), pp. 313-314 https://www.jstor.org/stable/4465373

603. Perlmann, "The Jews in the Koran and the Traditions," pp. 5-7.

604. "Georges Vajda Dead at 73," The Jewish Telegraphic Agency, October 21, 1981. https://www.jta.org/archive/georges-vajda-dead-at-73; "Vajda, Georges, (Budapest, 1908—Paris, 1981," in Francois Pouillon (Editor). "Dictionnaire des Orientalistes de Langue Française, Paris, 2008, p. 947.

605. Vajda, "Jews and Christians According to the Hadith," in Bostom, "*The Legacy of Islamic Antisemitism*," pp. 235-260.

606. Ibid.

607. See references 423 and 431.

608. Vajda, "Jews and Christians According to the Hadith," in Bostom, "*The Legacy of Islamic Antisemitism*," pp. 235-260.

609. Hartwig Hirschfeld Obituary. *Journal of the Royal Asiatic Society*, Volume 67 , Issue 1 , January 1935 , pp. 229 – 230 https://www.cambridge.org/core/journals/journal-of-the-royal-asiatic-society/article/dr-hartwig-hirschfeld/DE2B4A21E51E091A5754A79B0D97AFE8; Rubinstein, William D.; Jolles,

Michael A.; Rubinstein, Hillary L., eds. (2011). "The Palgrave Dictionary of Anglo-Jewish History," London: Palgrave Macmillan. p. 429.

[610.] Hirschfeld, "Essay on the History of the Jews of Medina," in Bostom, *The Legacy of Islamic Antisemitism*, p. 299.

[611.] Vajda, "Jews and Christians According to the Hadith," in Bostom, *"The Legacy of Islamic Antisemitism,"* p. 240.

[612.] "The Life of Muhammad," a translation of Ishaq's "Sirat Rasul Allah" with an introduction and notes by Alfred Guillaume, The Oxford University Press, first published London 1955, Karachi 1967.
https://archive.org/details/GuillaumeATheLifeOfMuhammad/mode/2up;
Ibn Sa'd, "Kitab Al-Tabaqat Al-Kabir," vol. 2 (New Delhi: 1993), pp. 31–33, 35–39, 68–71, 91–96, 131–46, 244–52. English translation by S. Moinul Haq and H. K. Ghazanfar. Reproduced in Bostom, *The Legacy of Islamic Antisemitism*, pp. 283-295.

[613.] Ishaq, *The Life of Muhammad*, p. 461.

[614.] Ibn Sa'd, *Kitab Al-Tabaqat Al-Kabir*, in Bostom, *The Legacy of Islamic Antisemitism*, p. 287. The original translation used the word "boars" instead of "pigs".

[615.] Ishaq, *The Life of Muhammad*, p. 464.

[616.] D. S. Margoliouth. *Mohammed and the Rise of Islam*, London, 1905, (reprint New Delhi: 1985), pp. 362–63.; Obituary Prof. D. S. Margoliouth, F.B.A. *Nature* 1940, vol. **145**, p. 542 https://doi.org/10.1038/145542a0:
"Margoliouth's knowledge of the Arabic language and literature was universally recognized as unrivalled in either Europe or the East. His unremitting activity in this branch of Oriental studies was devoted to the editing and elucidation of the more difficult and obscure of classical Arabic texts... His profound knowledge of the early development of Islamic belief is to be observed in some degree in his Hibbert Lectures delivered in 1913 and in the two books which appeal to a wider audience, *Mohammed and the Rise of Islam*, and *Mohammedanism*..."; For background on Ali, see: Manouchehri, F. H., Melvin-Koushki, T. b. M., Bulookbashi, A. A., Negahban, T. b. F., Waley, T. b. M. I., Alizadeh, M., Gholami, Y., Shah-Kazemi, R., Bahramian, A., Pakatchi, A., Tareh, M., Brown, T. b. K., Reza Jozi, M., Sajjadi, S., & Gholami, T. b. R. (2015). "ʿAlī b. Abī Ṭālib," In W. Madelung and F. Daftary (eds.), "*Encyclopaedia Islamica Online*," Brill, https://doi.org/10.1163/1875-9831_isla_COM_0252

[617.] *Kitab Al-Tabaqat Al-Kabir*, in Bostom, The Legacy of Islamic Antisemitism, pp. 294, 295.; For Khaybar's Jews as the prototypical dhimmis, see Bostom, *The Legacy of Jihad*, pp. 73, 140.

[618.] "Egypt's Al-Azhar Salutes Hamas Terror Attack In Which Over 600 Israelis Were Killed, Over 100 Were Kidnapped, And Over 2,000 Were Wounded," The Middle East Media Research Institute, October 8, 2023, Special Dispatch No. 10834
https://www.memri.org/reports/egypts-al-azhar-salutes-hamas-terror-attack-which-over-600-israelis-were-killed-over-100;
Al-Azhar Fatwa Center: "The classification of "civilians" does not apply to Zionist settlers (i.e., all Israelis, since all are considered 'Zionist settlers')," October 19, 2023
https://www.youm7.com/6344848;
"Virulent Incitement By Al-Azhar: Praise For Palestinian Jihad Fighters; Israel Is Destined To Perish; U.S. Is The Greatest Satan; Jews Are Descendants Of Apes And Pigs," The Middle East Media Research Institute, November 10, 2023, Special Dispatch

No. 10952 https://www.memri.org/reports/virulent-incitement-al-azhar-praise-palestinian-jihad-fighters-israel-destined-perish-us;
"UN Secretary-General Antonio Guterres Praises Al-Azhar Sheikh Ahmad Al-Tayeb, Who Glorified Hamas' October 7 Massacre: 'His Permanent Engagement To Foster Peace And Solidarity Must Be An Example To All'," The Middle East Media Research Institute, April 11, 2024, Special Dispatch No. 11269
https://www.memri.org/reports/un-secretary-general-antonio-guterres-praises-al-azhar-sheikh-ahmad-al-Tayeb-who-glorified#_edn14

619. "Egypt's Al-Azhar Salutes Hamas Terror Attack"

620. "UN Secretary-General Antonio Guterres Praises Al-Azhar Sheikh Ahmad Al-Tayeb, Who Glorified Hamas' October 7 Massacre"

621. Ibid.

622. "Virulent Incitement By Al-Azhar; Jews Are Descendants Of Apes And Pigs"

623. Al-Azhar Fatwa Center: "The classification of "civilians" does not apply to Zionist settlers"; See also, "Virulent Incitement By Al-Azhar; Jews Are Descendants Of Apes And Pigs"

624. For an overview, see: Andrew Bostom. "Al-Azhar's Ongoing 75-Year Annihilationist Jihad Against the Jews of Israel, " www.andrewbostom.org, November 9, 2023. https://www.andrewbostom.org/2023/11/al-azhars-ongoing-75-year-annihilationist-jihad-against-the-jews-of-israel/;
Kermit Roosevelt. "Will the Arabs Fight?", The Saturday Evening Post, December 27, 1947, pp. 20, 21, 55, 56. https://ia902302.us.archive.org/1/items/sim_saturday-evening-post_1947-12-27_220_26/sim_saturday-evening-post_1947-12-27_220_26.pdf;
Roosevelt warned, *"The danger is a jihad, a holy war, preached from the mosques in every village. If a jihad is proclaimed, its scope and ending are unpredictable. The Arab governments might, in time, have to recognize it and join in."* His concerns were promptly realized. See, "Al-Azhar University calls for jihad against the Jews of nascent Israel in 1947 after the UN partition plan was announced, and after Israel's declaration of independence in 1948" https://www.andrewbostom.org/2023/11/al-azhar-university-calls-for-jihad-against-the-jews-of-nascent-israel-in-1947-after-the-un-partition-plan-was-announced-and-after-israels-declaration-of-independence-in-1948/;
See also, Benny Morris. "1948—A History of the First Arab Israeli-War," Yale University Press, New Haven, 2008, pp. 65, 232, 395.
https://dn790004.ca.archive.org/0/items/islamichistory_201406/1948.%20A%20History%20of%20the%20First%20Arab-Israeli%20War.pdf;
For the 1956 fatwas, see, "Document declassified and released under the Nazi War Crimes Disclosure Act, 2006, PL105-246 State Department Telegram 1763/Embassy (Cairo) Telegram 1256 D441214," English
translation (by the U.S. embassy) of two fatwas written by the Grand Mufti of Egypt, Sheikh Hasan Ma'moun, January 5, 1956, and another dated January 9, 1956, signed by the leading members of the Fatwa Committee of Al Azhar, that is, its chairman and ex-mufti of Egypt, and major representatives of all four Islamic schools of jurisprudence, the ex-sheikh of the Shari'a College (Shafi'i sect), Mahmoud Shaltout (Hanafi sect), the director of Religious Guidance (Maliki Sect), and the director of the Azhar Inspectorate (Hanbali sect), and published the following days in the Egyptian newspaper, Al Ahram. The redundant extracts from each fatwa were pooled for simplicity. The expression

"fay" is found in Koran 59: 6-10, which describes Muhammad's attack upon the Jewish tribe Banu Nadir. In the traditional Muslim interpretation of these verses the theocratic conception of property rights is confirmed, as voiced by the Prophet—"Allah returns to the Believers the possessions of His foes, what is properly His." See Leone Caetani, "Annali dell'Islam," Milan: 1905–1926, vol. 5, p. 332.; *The fourth conference of the Academy of Islamic Research, Rajab 1388, September 1968*, Cairo, 1970, 935pp. https://search.worldcat.org/title/680594625

625. 1956 fatwas, "State Department Telegram 1763/Embassy (Cairo) Telegram 1256 D44121"

626. Michael B. Oren. "Six Days of War—June 1967 and the Making of the Modern Middle East," Oxford University Press, 2002, 446pp. https://archive.org/details/sixdaysofwarjune0000oren

627. *The fourth conference of the Academy of Islamic Research*

628. Sylvia Haim. "Islam and the Theory of Arab Nationalism," *Die Welt Des Islams*, Vol. 4, Issue
2/3, 1955, pp. 124–49. Haim, a renowned expert on the Arab national movement, identified its Islamic jihad quintessence at the conclusion her 1955 essay, p. 149: "Another feature of the modern doctrine which fits in with the Muslim past is the emphasis which both of them lay on communal solidarity, discipline, and cooperation. **The umma in Islam is a solidary entity, and its foremost duty is to answer the call of the jihad**. [emphasis added] This brings us to the third feature which both modern and ancient systems have in common, to wit the glorification of one's own group. The traditional attitude of the Muslims to the outside world is one of superiority, and the distinction between the Dar al-harb, Dar al-Islam, and Dar as-sulh, is an ever present one in the mind of the Muslim jurist. It may therefore be said in conclusion of this modern doctrine of nationalism, that although it introduces into Islam features which may not accord with strict orthodoxy, **it is the least incompatible perhaps of modern European doctrines with the political thought and political experience of Sunni Islam** [emphasis added]."

629. David Littman, with Yehoshafat Harkabi ("D.F. Green"). *Arab Theologians on Jews and Israel—Extracts from the proceedings of The Fourth Conference of the Academy of Islamic Research*, 1971, 1976, 2011, pp. 8-9 https://www.centerforsecuritypolicy.org/wp-content/uploads/2011/08/Arab-Theologians-on-Jews-and-Israel-4th_Ed_082011.pdf

630. Ibid, p. 9

631. For an overview see, Andrew Bostom, "Ahmed al-Tayeb, Sunni Islam's Jew-Hating Papal Equivalent, In His Own Words," www.andrewbostom.org, April 19, 2019. https://www.andrewbostom.org/2019/04/ahmed-al-tayeb-sunni-islams-jew-hating-papal-equivalent-in-his-own-words/; "Ahmad Al-Tayyib (Tayeb), Al-Azhar University President and Former Mufti of Egypt, Justifies Palestinian Suicide Bombings," The Middle East Media Research Institute, October 10, 2007, #1622 https://www.memri.org/tv/ahmad-al-tayyib-al-azhar-university-president-and-former-mufti-egypt-justifies-palestinian; "Sheik of Al-Azhar Ahmad Al-Tayeb Justifies Antisemitism on the Basis of the Koran," The Middle East Media Research Institute, October 25, 2013, #4048 https://www.memri.org/tv/sheik-al-azhar-ahmad-al-tayeb-justifies-antisemitism-basis-koran; "Sheikh of Al-Azhar on Jewish-Muslim Animosity:

The Jews Started It," The Middle East Media Research Institute, May 4, 2017, #6019 https://www.memri.org/tv/sheikh-al-azhar-jewish-muslim-animosity-jews-started-it; "Sheik of Al-Azhar: Global Zionism Behind Islamist Terror Organizations," The Middle East Media Research Institute, September 8, 2014, #4488 https://www.memri.org/tv/sheik-al-azhar-global-zionism-behind-islamist-terror-organizations;
"Sheikh of Al-Azhar Ahmed Al-Tayeb: People Blame Us for Terrorism, But If Not for Israel, There Would Be No Problem, the Region Would Have Prospered," The Middle East Media Research Institute, January 26, 2018, #6438 https://www.memri.org/tv/sheikh-al-azhar-people-blame-us-for-terrorism-if-not-for-israel-there-would-be-no-problem

632. Mackenzie R. Poust. "'Made' in Jordan: Assessing the Legacy of the Amman Message," Berkley Forum, September 15, 2022 https://berkleycenter.georgetown.edu/posts/made-in-jordan-assessing-the-legacy-of-the-amman-message; See multiple examples of "The Muslim 500" here: https://themuslim500.com/download/
See "The Muslim 500" 2017, here: https://www.themuslim500.com/wp-content/uploads/2018/05/TheMuslim500-2017-low.pdf

633. "Ahmad Al-Tayyib (Tayeb), Al-Azhar University President and Former Mufti of Egypt, Justifies Palestinian Suicide Bombings"

634. "Sheik of Al-Azhar Ahmad Al-Tayeb Justifies Antisemitism on the Basis of the Koran"; "Sheikh of Al-Azhar on Jewish-Muslim Animosity: The Jews Started It"

635. "Sheik of Al-Azhar: Global Zionism Behind Islamist Terror Organizations"

636. "Sheikh of Al-Azhar Ahmed Al-Tayeb: People Blame Us for Terrorism, But If Not for Israel, There Would Be No Problem, the Region Would Have Prospered"

637. "The Muslim 500" 2024, https://themuslim500.com/wp-content/uploads/2023/10/The-Muslim-500-2024-Free.pdf

638. Habib Umar bin Hafiz. "Palestine Will Be Free!" (English subtitles), October 10, 2023 https://www.youtube.com/watch?v=ejHM0vHHXAM;
Qur'an 41:15 https://corpus.quran.com/translation.jsp?chapter=41&verse=15;
See, "The Covenant of the Islamic Resistance Movement—Hamas," article 7

639. Habib Umar bin Hafiz. "Palestinian Oppression!" (English subtitles), October 21, 2023 https://www.youtube.com/watch?v=2HaFQHUido8, and "The Oppressors of Gaza!" (English subtitles), November 1, 2023 https://www.youtube.com/watch?v=gND7EgcwvLA; Carrie Keller-Lynn. "IDF shows foreign press Hamas bodycam videos, photos of murder, torture, decapitation," The Times of Israel, October 23, 2023 https://www.timesofisrael.com/idf-shows-foreign-press-raw-hamas-bodycam-videos-of-murder-torture-decapitation/; Elana Kirsh. "Trained to analyze ancient carnage, archaeologists locate victims among kibbutz ashes," The Times of Israel, November 7, 2023 https://www.timesofisrael.com/trained-to-analyze-ancient-carnage-archaeologists-locate-victims-among-kibbutz-ashes/; "Kill, behead, rape: Interrogated Hamas members detail atrocities against civilians," The Times of Israel, October 24, 2023 https://www.timesofisrael.com/kill-behead-rape-interrogated-hamas-members-detail-atrocities-against-civilians/; Qur'an 2:26

https://corpus.quran.com/translation.jsp?chapter=2&verse=26; Qur'an 98:6 https://corpus.quran.com/translation.jsp?chapter=98&verse=6; Qur'an 40:46 https://corpus.quran.com/translation.jsp?chapter=40&verse=46

640. Habib Umar bin Hafiz. "The Zionist Goal!" (English subtitles), December 15, 2023 https://www.youtube.com/watch?v=TbkqnFSbfx8;
Qur'an 9:12 https://corpus.quran.com/translation.jsp?chapter=9&verse=12;
Qur'an 3:118 https://corpus.quran.com/translation.jsp?chapter=3&verse=118;
Qur'an 3:120 https://corpus.quran.com/translation.jsp?chapter=3&verse=120

641. Mansour Al-Hadj. "Challenging The Dominant Radical Narrative Preached In Mosques Across The U.S. Regarding The Israel-Hamas War," *The Middle East Media Research Institute*, April 3, 2024, MEMRI Daily Brief No. 589. https://www.memri.org/reports/challenging-dominant-radical-narrative-preached-mosques-across-us-regarding-israel-hamas-war

642. "About Imam Alhagie Jallow" https://madisonmuslims.org/imam-alhagie/; "Madison, Wisconsin Friday Sermon By Imam Alhajie Jallow Following October 7 Attack: Our Brothers In Gaza Are Heroes; Only Jihad Can Bring Glory And Victory To The Muslims; The Jews Will Be Killed, Executed By The Muslims," *The Middle East Media Research Institute*, October 13, 2023, #10799 https://www.memri.org/tv/madison-wisconsin-friday-sermon-imam-alhajie-jallow-october-7-brothers-gaza-heroes-jihad-jews-killed-executed

643. "Colorado Imam Teaches Children At Mosque: Jews Cannot Be Trusted; Allah Turned Jewish Fishermen Into Monkeys; The Jews Killed Their Prophets, Tried To Kill Jesus," *The Middle East Media Research Institute*, October 22, 2023, #10565 https://www.memri.org/tv/colorado-imam-children-jews-not-trusted-allah-fishermen-monkeys-killed-prophet-jesus; Qur'an 2:10 https://corpus.quran.com/translation.jsp?chapter=2&verse=10; Qur'an 4:155 https://corpus.quran.com/translation.jsp?chapter=4&verse=155; Qur'an 5:13 https://corpus.quran.com/translation.jsp?chapter=5&verse=13; Qur'an 3:181 https://corpus.quran.com/translation.jsp?chapter=3&verse=181; Dr Mark Durie. "'Isa, the Muslim Jesus," Answering Islam—A Christian Muslim Dialogue," https://www.answering-islam.org/authors/durie/islamic_jesus.html

644. "Friday Sermon At Islamic Center Of Frisco, Texas, By Ghaith Arodaki: This Did Not Start On October 7 — The Jews Are Cursed By Allah; They Control The Media, Financial, Political, Social Systems, Spread Corruption, Fornication, Murder," *The Middle East Media Research Institute*, December 29, 2023, #10776 https://www.memri.org/tv/friday-sermon-islamic-center-frisco-texas-october-seven-jews-cursed-control-media-finance-politics-spread-corruption

645. For exegeses of Qur'an 1:7, see canonical hadith of Muhammad https://sunnah.com/urn/639380, and previous references 223, and 581 to 585.

646. "Anti-Israel Protesters in Boro Park, Brooklyn Pray: 'Oh Allah, Annihilate the Criminal Zionists, Kill Them One by One, Do Not Leave a Single One of Them,'" *The Middle East Media Research Center,* February 18, 2025, #11837 https://web.archive.org/web/20250220115606/https://www.memri.org/tv/islamic-prayer-boro-park-ny-allah-annihilate-kill-zionists

647. Bostom, "Ahmed al-Tayeb, Sunni Islam's Jew-Hating Papal Equivalent, In His Own Words"

648. See Qur'an 9:29 and 9:5 at references 92, 95, 96, 148, 223, 292, 466, 591, 593, 597-599, 603, *and* Y. Graff. "French Manifesto Calling To 'Declare Obsolete' Violent Quranic Verses Sparks Fury From Islamic Religious Establishment, Writers In Arab Media," *The Middle East Media Research Institute*, August 20, 2018, Inquiry & Analysis Series, No. 1413 https://www.memri.org/reports/muslims-furious-over-french-

manifesto-on-quran#_edn3; "Manifeste 'contre le nouvel Antisémitisme'" ("Manifesto 'against the new Antisemitism'"), Le Parisien, May 2, 2018 https://www.leparisien.fr/societe/manifeste-contre-le-nouvel-antisemitisme-21-04-2018-7676787.php; Michel Gurfinkel. "Sarah Halimi: Beaten, tortured and killed — yet France turned a blind eye," The Jewish Chronicle, August 24, 2017 https://www.thejc.com/news/features/sarah-halimi-beaten-tortured-and-killed-yet-france-turned-a-blind-eye-o80r0ddx ; "Killer of French Holocaust survivor Mireille Knoll sentenced to life in prison," France 24, November 10, 2021 https://www.france24.com/en/europe/20211110-killer-of-french-holocaust-survivor-mireille-knoll-sentenced-to-life-in-prison

[649.] Christian Rutishauser. "The 1947 Seelisberg Conference: The Foundation of the Jewish-Christian Dialogue", *Studies in Christian-Jewish Relations*, 2007; vol. 2, pp. 34-53. https://www.prchiz.pl/storage/app/media/pliki/Seelisberg_70.pdf

[650.] Norman C. Tobias. *Jewish Conscience of The Church—Jules Isaac and the Second Vatican Council*, 2017, Palgrave MacMillan, Switzerland, 307pp.; p. xxi, of the book's Prologue includes Isaac's own January, 1960 mini-biography composed for Rev. James Parkes, to accompany the publication in English translation of a December 15, 1959 lecture Isaac had delivered at the Sorbonne: "Of a Jewish family and Alsacien-Lorrainer, through Rennes, Brittany (1877). Son and grandson of soldiers, Jules Isaac was a professor and historian, cut from a combative cloth. He never ceased to fight for truth, for liberty, and for peace. In his youth, during the Dreyfus Affair, he was the friend and companion-in-arms of the great writer (Charles) Péguy…In his adulthood, by his Cours d'Histoires ("Storytelling Course") (Hachette), he taught the majority of French youth, and he continues to do so. Combatant in the Great War (1914-18); wounded at Verdun, decorated with Croix de Guerre, he made efforts to prevent a new French-German conflict, proposing a Locarno Pact of a moral nature (1936), provoking first meetings between French and German historians, and publishing principally two books: 1914, Le problème des origins de la guerre ("The problem of the origins of the war") (Rieder, 1933), and Paradoxes sur la science homicide et autres hérésies ("Paradoxes about the science of homicide and other heresies") (Rieder, 1935). From 1934, he was an active member of the Comité de Vigilence des intellectuels antifascists ("Vigilance Committee of Antifascist Intellectuals"). After the disaster of 1940, Vichy legislation stripped him of his high office as Inspecteur Générale de l'Education Nationale. While a refugee in Aix, he wrote under the pseudonym of Junius, Les Oligarches, essai d'histoire partiale for les Éditions de Minuit. He then turned his attention to the fight against antisemitism, principally in the religious context, and began to write Jésus et Israël. It was during that time that drama took place, a Gestapo raid that he avoided by mere happenstance, the majority of his family arrested and deported. From that moment forward, that in which he was engaged took on the character of a sacred mission. Continued from safe house to safe house, Jésus et Israël was published in 1948. At the International Jewish-Christian Congress of Seelisberg (1947), Jules Isaac contributed to the adoption of a program of rectification of Christian teaching in ten points. In France, he was a founder and facilitator of the Amitié Judéo-Chrétienne, of which (in 1960) he is, together with Jacques Maritain, president d'honneur. He gave to Jésus et Israël an addendum: Genèse de l'antisemitisme (Calmann-Levy, 1956). His last effort (1960) was to obtain from the leader of the Catholic Church, Pope John XXIII, a position in favor of the rectification of Catholic teaching concerning the Jews. The [papal] reception gave him cause for hope. In France, both in Catholic and Protestant circles, a purifying tendency is making its way with ever more strength." See also, Edward H. Flannery. "Jesus, Israel, and Christian Renewal," Journal of Ecumenical Studies, 1972, vol. 9 (Winter), pp. 74-92, especially p. 80, and the discussion of Isaac's use of New Testament commentaries.

651. Jules Isaac, "Jésus et Israël," 1948, Paris, Albin Michel, p. 178. English translation in Tobias, "Jewish Conscience of The Church," p. 98.

652. Tobias, "Jewish Conscience of The Church," p. 100ff. and p. 104ff.

653. "DECLARATION ON THE RELATION OF THE CHURCH TO NON-CHRISTIAN RELIGIONS, NOSTRA AETATE, PROCLAIMED BY HIS HOLINESS POPE PAUL VI, ON OCTOBER 28, 1965" https://www.vatican.va/archive/hist_councils/ii_vatican_council/documents/vat-ii_decl_19651028_nostra-aetate_en.html

654. John T. Pawlikowski. "Accomplishments and Challenges in the Contemporary Jewish-Christian Encounter", in *Removing Anti-Judaism from the Pulpit*, edited by Howard Clark Kee and Irwin J. Borowsky, New York, Continuum Publishing, 1996, p. 29.

655. Ibid, pp. 29-30.

656. Philip A. Cunningham. *Education for Shalom—Religion Textbooks and the Enhancement of the Catholic and Jewish Relationship*, American Interfaith Institute, Philadelphia, 1995, p. 134.

657. See reference 648.

658. Jules Isaac. *The Teaching of Contempt: Christian Roots of Antisemitism*, Translated by Helen Weaver. Biographical Introduction by Claire Huchet Bishop. New York, 1964; Author's Foreword, p. 18. (Published in France under the title, "L'Enseignement du Mépris," 1962.)

The Honorable Grand Imam
Dr. Muhammad Sayyed Tantawi
Sheikh of Al-Azhar Mosque

The Children of Israel In The Quran And The Sunna

In the name of Allah, the Compassionate, the Merciful

Almighty Allah said:

“Whenever they kindle the fire of war, Allah puts it out. And they strive to spread corruption in the land. And Allah does not like corruptors.”

Sura Al-Ma’ida: 64 (Qur’an 5:64)

In the name of Allah, the Compassionate, the Merciful

Introduction

Thanks be to Allah, Lord of the Universe, and peace and prayers on our Master the Messenger of Allah:

The reader of the Noble Qur'an will find that the Qur'an has most talked about the Children of Israel in great detail. It describes their conditions, ethics and their position concerning the prophets, peace be upon them. It has done this in sumptuous detail.

In the Meccan verses (Meccan Suras), the Noble Qur'an mentions many stories about them: the pain and torture that Pharaoh inflicted upon them as well as their various conditions during the times that preceded the mission of the Prophet, Allah's peace and prayers be upon him (SAW).

As for the Medina verses (Medinan Suras), the Qur'an mentioned their stance and reaction concerning the Islamic call, the blessings that Allah had bestowed upon them, and the curses that had befallen them due to their rejection of Allah's call. It had also mentioned in great detail their morals, their vices, and their false claims and various methods to entrap Islam and Muslims.

In speaking about the Children of Israel, the Qur'an tightly connects the behaviors, ethics, and characteristics of those who were contemporaneous with the Prophet and their forefathers who lived during the times of Moses and Jesus and other prophets, thereby revealing that their depravity, disobedience, rejection, and hostility to the call to Islam were merely the natural heritage of bad behaviors that had passed on from the forefathers to their offspring.

And evidence to the truthfulness of the Noble Qur'an can be found in the characteristics that had been attributed to them and which we can always see applicable to them everywhere and throughout the generations. The passage of time has only made these attributes stick even more. For example, throughout the ages, we can see their consuming desire and obsession to live a long life.

We Muslims have been harmed a great deal by the Jews... It was the Jews who fought the Islamic call with every possible weapon. They were the ones who usurped- with the help of the countries of the infidels- part of our holy land- Palestine- and established a country for them there in 1948.

Against this historical background, writers have written hundreds of books and articles and did a lot of research on the Jews and Palestine. However, most of what has been written concentrates on political, historical, economic, and military aspects. Religious aspects and perspectives are still in dire need of sound scientific writings that base their delineation of the Jews on the Book of Almighty Allah (the Qur'an) and the Sunna (sayings) of His Messenger, (SAW)

My main goal for choosing the topic of my dissertation "The Children of Israel in the Qur'an and the Sunna" is to reveal- to Muslim youth in particular and to the rational, reasonable and fair-minded people in general- the state of the Children of Israel, their history, ethics, lies, depravity and immorality, relying on what has been mentioned about them in the Holy Qur'an, the Sunna and the correct and unequivocal historical facts.

This dissertation comprises eight chapters and a conclusion.

In Chapter One, I talked about the history of the Jews and their conditions ever since they immigrated to Egypt under the leadership of Jacob- peace be upon him- approximately in the 19th century BC until the second destruction of Jerusalem at the hands of the Romans in the year 70 AD. I concluded this chapter by talking about the history of the Jews of Arabia and their social, economic and religious conditions.

In Chapter Two, I talked about the method displayed in the Noble Qur'an to invite the People of the Scriptures to Islam. I have also shown its fair, tolerant and sympathetic approach to them.

In Chapter Three, I talked in detail about the ways the Jews used to conspire against Islam and Muslims to entrap them. I discussed 10 devious and cunning methods they employed to plot against Islam and Muslims. I concluded this chapter by showing the position of the Messenger (SAW) concerning them.

As for Chapter Four, I talked about the confrontations (meetings of the sword) between the Muslims and the Jews: The Battle of Banu Qaynuqa, the Battle of Banu Nadir, the Battle of Banu Qurayza, and the battle of Khaybar. I also talked about the murder of some of the Jewish leaders such as kaa'b Bin El-Ashraf and others.

In Chapter Five, I detailed the blessings that Allah granted the Children of Israel and their position concerning these blessings. I showed how their ingratitude and ungratefulness would lead to bad and undesirable consequences in this world and in the next.

In Chapter Six, I talked at length about the vices of the Jews as depicted by the Noble Qur'an. I investigated in detail many of the issues on which interpreters have differed.

In Chapter Seven, I talked about their false and deceitful claims as demonstrated in the Noble Qur'an, and how the Qur'an responded to their false claims in a way that shuts their mouths, arrests their tongues and shows their lies and deception.

In Chapter Eight, I mentioned the numerous penalties with which Allah inflicted punishment on the Children of Israel for their injustices and immorality in accordance with what has been mentioned in the verses of the Noble Qur'an.

In the Conclusion, I talked about Palestine and the Zionist invasion of Palestine at its various stages. I finally showed the most important reasons that led to the catastrophe that has befallen Palestine as well as the most important strategies that if we- as Muslims- follow, will restore Palestine to us.

These are the chapters of the dissertation. In writing it, I have paid special attention to:

1- Collect the verses that talk about the Children of Israel in the Noble Qur'an, put them in the most appropriate places, explain and interpret them in an accurate, scientific and verifiable way.
2- Referencing the Holy Sayings of the Prophet that are in the same vein as those verses.
3- Alluding to historical facts and current events when interpreting these noble verses as is clearly seen when I explicate the Almighty's: "And remember, O Prophet, when your Lord declared that He would send against them others who would make them suffer terribly until the Day of Judgment." (Qur'an 7:167) In fact, I have mentioned numerous methods for the punishments that had been inflicted on the Jews at various times and ages... I have then explained the reasons why these punishments had been inflicted upon them.
4- When I explained these verses, I investigated other exegetes and commentators and chose the most appropriate amongst them explaining the reasons for my choice. Consider, for example, our interpretation of the Almighty's: "And We warned the Children of Israel in the Scripture, "You will certainly cause corruption in the land twice, and you will become extremely arrogant." (Qur'an 17:4)
5- We have paid a noticeable attention to Palestine from the historical and political perspectives as it is clearly shown in Chapter One and in the Conclusion... We have conscientiously and faithfully enumerated some methods that would safeguard restoring Palestine to us.

We ask the Almighty Allah to accept this work for the benefit of His servants. Prayers and peace be upon our master Muhammad and his people and companions.

Sheikh of Al-Azhar
Dr. Muhammad Sayyed Tantawi

May 29, 1997

Chapter One

The History Of The Children of Israel And Their Conditions In Arabia

***

In this chapter, we will deal with the following topics:

First: Why were the Jews called the Hebrews, or Israelites or Jews?

Second: A general look at their history ever since they immigrated to Egypt under the leadership of Jacob—peace be upon him—in 1900 BC until the (second) destruction of Jerusalem at the hands of Titus, the Roman, in the year 70 AD.

Third: Their immigration to Arabia and a look at their religious, social and economic conditions there.

Topic # 1

Among the most famous names for the Children of Israel are the Hebrews, the Israelites, and the Jews. There are many different reasons why they were called "the Hebrews:"

1- It is said that they were called the Hebrews in relation to Abraham himself. In the Book of Genesis, he was named (Abraham the Hebrew/ the crosser) since he crossed the Euphrates River and many other rivers.
2- It is said that they were called the Hebrews in association with "Iber," the fifth grandfather of Abraham, peace be upon him.
3- Dr. Israel Wolfensohn differed with these two previous views and voiced a third opinion as to why they received this name. He said: "the word Hebrew goes back to the original place for the Children of Israel. Originally, they were Bedouins who did not settle in one place; rather, they would move from one place to another with their livestock in search for water and pasture. The word Hebrew is originally driven from the verb عَبَرَ(to cross), which means crossed or covered a certain distance, or crossed the valley or the river. All such meanings exist in Arabic or Hebrew. In general, the meaning indicates moving, which is a major characteristic of Bedouins and people who roam the deserts. Therefore, the word Hebrew is similar to the word Bedouin, i.e., an inhabitant of the desert. The Canaanites, the Egyptians and the Palestinians used to call the

Children of Israel "the Hebrews," because of their association with the desert and to distinguish them from urban people. When the Children of Israel resided in Canaan and came to know city life and stability, they started to deride and disparage the word Hebrew as it reminded them of their rough and rugged early life as Bedouins. They started to like being regarded only as the Children of Israel."[1]

From the words of Dr. Wolfensohn we can conclude that calling the Children of Israel "Hebrews" is not due to a specific incident or a specific person. Rather, it is due to their living lifestyle in the desert and their moving from one place to another in search of food and sustenance.

A magazine published research[2] written by Father Isaac Saka titled "The Meaning of the Names of the Three Major Semitic Peoples..." In this article he favored the first opinion. He said: "Most learned and scholarly scientists- amongst whom the Syriac scientists Ibn El-Saleebi (who died in 1171 AD) and Ibn El- Abri (who died in 1286 AD)- favor the first opinion which is the naming that is driven from the crossing of Abraham - peace be upon him- of the Euphrates River. Ibn El-Abri supported his opinion by using the Greek translation (Akobola) which translated (Hebrew) as (the crosser) or passing through. This opinion is also adopted by Dr. Levin who said: "It is taken from a verb which means crossing the river." This is a reference to Abraham's crossing the Euphrates River. In this case, the word can be translated into (an immigrant). This may show the way the Canaanites talked about Abraham). This opinion is also confirmed by what is mentioned in Joshua (24:2): "Thus saith the Lord God of Israel, Your fathers dwelt on the other side of the flood in old time, *even* Terah, the father of Abraham, and the father of Nachor: and they served other Gods. And I took your father Abraham from the other side of the flood, and led him throughout all the land of Canaan."

Father Saka continued his argument confirming that: "In addition to this, the term was not used until Abraham crossed the Euphrates River." Moreover, adopting this view is closer to the truth than the other two views. And why not? It is the view adopted by the most erudite and knowledgeable of scientists.

Adopting the second view is rather difficult. First: there are six consecutive generations between Abraham - to whom this name was first attributed- and Aber. If Abraham was to be associated with one of his forefathers, it would have made more sense to have him associated with Sam, one of his most well-known forefathers.

Second: If the association was made to Aber, why hasn't it occurred in the Scriptures for 600 years? And why wasn't Abraham named after it before crossing the Euphrates River while he was still in his land and among his people? And how does connecting him to Aber- and not others- make sense? And why didn't the writer of the Torah hint at that? All of these urge us to discard this view.

Third: Dr. Wolfensohn's view cannot be adopted for if this naming is the result of immigration and movement from one place to another, it would have been attributed to most Semitic nations. When speaking about the original cradle of the Semites and the movements of most Semitic peoples such as the Babylonians, the Armenians, the Israelites, and the Arabs, Dr. Wolfensohn himself says:

"It is noticeable that the most obvious characteristic of these nations is that they are almost desert-like. The passions, imagination and thoughts of these nations evoke the spirit of the desert." Therefore, if this naming is the consequence of moving around and leading a Bedouin-like lifestyle- as he claims- why wasn't the name attributed to all Semitic nations? And why has that name been particularly attributed to the Israelites who have shown aversion to it- as he himself claimed? And if Dr. Wolfensohn's claim that the Israelites didn't like that name and that after settling down and becoming civilized, they changed that name to Israelite, why didn't they also change the name of their language from Hebrew to Israelite? Therefore, his view is not well-grounded or convincing. For this reason, adopting the first view is the most reasonable, makes the best sense, and should be adopted."

These are some of the ideas and opinions for naming the Children of Israel as Hebrews. It seems to us that the most valid among these is the first view for- according to Fr. Isaac Saka- it is the opinion of the most learned, knowledgeable, and erudite of scientists.

We now move to the reason why they were called the Israelites or the Children of Israel:

They were named the Israelites or the Children of Israel after their father Israel who was Jacob, son of Isaac, son of Abraham- peace and prayers be upon them. Israel is a Hebrew word which is made up of "Isra," which means servant or chosen, and "eel," meaning Allah. Thus, the meaning of the word is the servant of Allah or the chosen by Allah.

Jacob begot 12 male children; with Leah he got six. These were Reuben, Simeon, Levi, Judah, Issachar and Zebulun. Rachel bore him two: Joseph and Benjamin. With Zilpah (Leah's handmaid) he had two: Gad and Asher. Bilhah (Rachel's handmaid) bore him two children: Dan and Naphtali.

The children of Jacob- peace be upon him- and their offspring formed the Children of Israel, and it was attributed to him.

Jacob- peace be upon him- is mentioned in many verses in the Noble Qur'an: "Or did you witness when death came to Jacob? He asked his children, "Who will you worship after my passing?" They replied, "We will ⌜continue to⌝ worship your Allah, the Allah of your forefathers—Abraham, Ishmael, and Isaac—the One Allah. And to Him we ⌜all⌝ submit."[3]

We now proceed to discuss why they were called Jews:

1- It was said that they were called Jews when they repented and abandoned worshipping the calf, saying: we repented and turned to you. The author of "Lisan al-Arab" says: (Alhud الهَوْد= righteousness) comes from the verb "يهود"which means "repent and return to righteousness." The Qur'an says: "Ordain for us what is good in this life and the next. Indeed, we have turned to You ⌜in repentance⌝هدنا إليك." In other words, we have repented and returned to you. This is supported by Mujahid and Sa'id Ibn Jubayr and Ibrahim. "Jew" is the name for the tribe. They added the definite article الـ to become اليهود=the Jew. The Qur'an's "For those who are Jewish, We forbade every animal with undivided hoofs," means those who entered into Judaism. The verb "هوَّدَHawada the man" means returned him to Judaism. Sibawayh says that in the Saying: "'Every newborn is born without a religion; the parents turn the infant either to Judaism or to Christianity,' means that they teach the infant Judaism or Christianity and make him adopt one or the other." [4]

2- It was said that they were called Jews because they يتهوَّدون, In other words, they move and gesticulate when they read the Torah.

3- It was also said that they were called يهود =Jews in connection to (يهوذاJudah) , the fourth son of Jacob, peace on him.

Some scientists exclusively favored this view. In support of this view, Al-Birouni says: "They were called Jews because of their link and relationship to Judah, one of the tribes. In his offspring, the kingdom was established, the sound "th"/ ذ was changed into the letter "d" /د . It was a practice of the Arabs to change some letters when they borrow foreign names."[5]

Judah was the ruler among his father's eleven children. He was appointed by his father. He remained the ruler until his death. After his death, his tribe was the most prominent amongst all the other tribes until his kingdom was divided into two parts after the death of Suliman, peace on him:

The Kingdom of Judah- founded in Jerusalem- which consisted of the Tribe of Judah and the Tribe of Benjamin, and the Kingdom of Israel- in Samaria- and which comprised all the other ten Tribes.

After the fall of the state of Israel at the hands of the Assyrians in 721 BC, all that remained pledged allegiance to the kings of Judah until the fall of the Kingdom of Judah at the hands of Nebuchadnezzar in 586 BC. He led those who were still alive to Babylon as captives where they were known as the Children of Judah. Each one was called a Jew, a name that became widely used to include all the Hebrews, the Children of Israel and all those other races that came to adopt Judaism.

Dr. Jawad Ali writes: "The term Jew (يهود) is more common than the term Hebrew or the Children of Israel. That is because the term Jew is used for Hebrews and others who adopt the religion of the Jews, even if not from among them. The Israelites and the people of Judah called themselves and all those who adopted their religion Jews (يهود) in order to distinguish themselves from others who were not followers of their religion- the foreigners."[6]

So far, we have shown why the Jews were called the Hebrews or the Children of Israel or Jews (يهود)

Topic # 2

An Overall Look into the History of the Children of Israel

This topic comprises a comprehensive outlook about the history of the Children of Israel and their conditions since they left to Egypt in 1900 BC under the leadership of Jacob- peace be upon him- until the second destruction of Jerusalem at the hands of the Roman Emperor, Titus, in 70 AD.

Our research- on the History of the Children of Israel and their conditions during this period that stretches for almost 20 centuries- will be as follows:

A- Their history since they went to Egypt until they left it during the thirteenth century BC.
B- Their history since they left Egypt until establishing their kingdom at the hands of Talut (Saul) in (1082-1010) BC approximately.
C- Their history ever since they established their kingdom until it split into two kingdoms- Judah and Israel- in 975 BC.
D- Their history from the time of the split into two kingdoms until the first destruction of Jerusalem at the hands of Nebuchadnezzar in 586 BC.
E- Their history from the first destruction of Jerusalem to its second destruction at the hands of the Roman Emperor, Titus, in the year 70 AD.

We now talk in detail about each of these 5 periods:

A- Some historians maintain that Jacob- peace be upon him- immigrated with his people from Palestine to Egypt approximately in the nineteenth century BC. [7] That was because of the famine that befell Palestine and drastically affected its pastures causing drought, scarcity, and barrenness. The children of Jacob- peace be upon him- went to Egypt frequently for trade and food. There, they recognized their brother Joseph who was treasurer collector (chief Steward) of the land of Egypt. He was hospitable and welcomed them all and asked them to bring everyone- including Jacob, their father- to the land of Egypt and immigrate from Palestine to live there (in Egypt). Jacob accepted Joseph's request, and they all came to dwell in Egypt. There were 66 of them other than his children's women.[8]

Joseph- peace be upon him- honored his father and brothers. He also asked pharaoh to be kind and compassionate to them. The Children of Israel asked the pharaoh of Egypt to allow them to live in Goshen.[9] Pharaoh granted them their request, and he said to Joseph: "Your father and your brothers have come to you, and the land of Egypt is before you;

settle your father and your brothers in the best part of the land. Let them live in Goshen... So, Joseph settled his father and his brothers in Egypt and gave them property in the best part of the land... Joseph also provided his father and his brothers and all his father's household with food, according to the number of their children."[10]

In the Yusuf Sura (Joseph), there is a magnificent portrayal of what took place between him and his brothers. There is also a reference to Jacob's immigration with his children to Egypt. In the first half, there is a description of what happened between Joseph and his brothers, their jealousy and resentment because of his special place in their father's heart, their throwing him in the well, and their returning to their father in the evening crying: "They cried, "Our father! We went racing and left Joseph with our belongings, and a wolf devoured him! But you will not believe us, no matter how truthful we are.... And they brought his shirt, stained with false blood.[1] He responded, "No! Your souls must have tempted you to do something ˹evil˺. So ˹I can only endure with˺ beautiful patience! It is Allah's help that I seek to bear your claims."[11]

Then the chapter (Sura) describes how merchant travelers saved Joseph and brought him out of the well. They sold him to the Chief Minister for a cheap price, just a few silver coins—only wanting to get rid of him. The chapter continues to depict what later happened to Joseph-peace be upon him- at the hands of the Chief Minister's wife who threatened to imprison him if he refused to succumb to her desires. About her, the Noble Qur'an says: "I did try to seduce him but he ˹firmly˺ refused." In other words, he did not do what she wanted him to do with her. "And if he does not do what I order him to, he will certainly be imprisoned and ˹fully˺ disgraced."[12] That is to say, if he refused to carry out her command in the future, he will be put in prison and become one of the most disgraced and humiliated of all.

Joseph resorted to Allah and asked for His help: "Joseph prayed, 'My Lord! I would rather be in jail than do what they invite me to" - this wickedness and immorality. "And if You do not turn their cunning away from me" by Your power, might and confirming me in your obedience, "I might yield to them and fall into ignorance." In other words, if I yielded and surrendered to their wicked desires, I will be like one of those foolish and ignorant people who are easily lured by their desires. There is no pain or gain except through Your power, might and help.

The Noble Qur'an then shows that Almighty Allah heeded his prayers and supplications: "So his Lord responded to him, turning their cunning away from him. Surely, He is the All-Hearing, All-Knowing."[13] This is an indication that Allah Almighty surrounded him with His care and protection in all his ways.

Then the Almighty says: "And so it occurred to those in charge, despite seeing all the proofs of his innocence, that he should be imprisoned for a while."

Imam Ibn Kathir says: "Almighty Allah says that it appeared convenient to them that they imprison him for a while even though they have become convinced of his innocence and there were many proofs to ascertain and verify his virtue, integrity and righteousness. It is as though- and only Allah knows- they decided to imprison him for the rumor, the tittle-tattle itself, falsely trying to convince themselves that he tried to seduce her. Thus, they imprisoned him. For this reason, when the great King asked to bring him out of the prison at the end of his jail period, he refused to leave the prison until his innocence was proven and the deception attributed to him cleared. When this was accomplished, he came out of the prison, his integrity intact. Peace be upon him." [14]

The Sura (Chapter) then mentions Joseph's going to prison, how Allah had given him the ability to interpret dreams, how he invited his fellow prisoners to monotheism, how he had rightly interpreted the King's dream and thus rescued Egypt from an all- consuming and devouring famine, and how the King summoned him and appointed him minister.

I concluded these events which those verses have portrayed by emphasizing one of Allah's eternal doctrines and everlasting principles: the Almighty Allah never wastes or ignores the rewards of the righteous and the benevolent. He provides for them on earth and grants them His blessings: "This is how We established Joseph in the land to settle wherever he pleased. We shower Our mercy on whoever We will, and We never discount the reward of the good-doers. And the reward of the Hereafter is far better for those who are faithful and are mindful ⌜of Allah⌝."[15]

This- in short- has been a quick overview of what is contained in Yusuf (Joseph): the events, instructions and recommendations in the first half, while the final half revolves around the arrival of his brothers, recognizing them, trying to elicit some information about his brother Benjamin who did not come with them, preventing Benjamin from leaving when they brought him under the pretext that he was a thief... then revealing his identity to them and inviting them all to come to Egypt with their families. On this the Almighty Allah says: "And Joseph's brothers came and entered his presence. He recognized them but they were unaware of who he really was. (Q 12:58) When he had provided them with their supplies, he demanded, "Bring me your brother on your father's side. Do you not see that I give full measure and I am the best of hosts? (Q 12:59) But if you do not bring him to me 'next time', I will have no grain for you, nor will you ever come close to me again. (Q 12:60) They promised, "We will try to convince his father to let him come. We will certainly do ⌜our best⌝. (Q 12:61) Joseph ordered his servants to put his brothers' money back into their saddlebags so that they would find it when they returned to their family and perhaps they would come back." (Q 12:62)

Imam Ibn Kathir said: "El-Sadi, Muhammad Ibn Ishaq and other interpreters mention the reason behind the coming of Joseph's brothers to the land of Egypt. Joseph- peace be upon him- became Chief Minister in charge of the store houses in the land of Egypt. The seven years of plenty and abundance were followed by seven years of barrenness and great hardships. Barrenness and infertility swept all the land of Egypt and reached Canaan, where Jacob and his children lived. Joseph adeptly and proficiently oversaw the storehouses, collected and saved enough grain for the people. People from various other provinces came to him to get food for themselves and their children. He would just provide them with what was enough to satisfy their needs, no more. He-peace be upon him- would even restrain himself from food... Joseph's brothers were among those who came to get food as instructed by their father who learned that the Chief minister of Egypt provided food to people at a low price. They took some money to purchase food, and they rode 10 donkeys to go. Jacob-peace be upon him- kept Benjamin, Joseph's brother, with him. He was his dearest son after Joseph. When Joseph's brothers came and entered his presence in all his majesty and grandeur, he recognized them. However, they were unaware of who he was since they departed when he was very young, and he was sold to the travelers and nobody knew where they took him. They never could have imagined that he would be what he had become. That is why, they were unaware of who he was while he recognized them. Al-Sadi and others mention that when Joseph started talking with them, he addressed them with "apparent" suspicion: "Why have you come to my land?" They responded: "O Chief Minister! We have come for food." He said: "Maybe you are spies?" They responded: "Allah forbids!" He asked: "Where are you from?" They said: "We are from the land of Canaan, and our father is Jacob, a prophet of Allah." He asked: "Does he have other children?" They said: "Yes. There were 12 of us. Our youngest perished in the wilderness. He was the most loved by our father. Our father kept his brother with him to keep him company." Joseph ordered his men to welcome and make the necessary accommodations for them.[16]

After I mentioned the verses that depict what had transpired between Joseph and his brothers and how he kept his brother Benjamin, I showed that Jacob- peace be upon him- ordered his children to go to the land of Egypt to gather information about Joseph and his brother Benjamin: "O my sons! Go and search ⌜diligently⌝ for Joseph and his brother. And do not lose hope in the mercy of Allah, for no one loses hope in Allah's mercy except those with no faith." (Qur'an 12:87) In other words, go to the land of Egypt and use your eyes and ears to gather information about Joseph and Benjamin to become aware of where you stand. Do not lose heart or become despondent for only the faithless who do not trust in Allah's might and mercy will do so.

The Noble Qur'an then describes what had occurred between Joseph and his brothers: "When they entered Joseph's presence, they pleaded, "O Chief Minister! We and our family have been touched with hardship." In other words, after complying with their father's directions when he asked them to go and search for Joseph and his brother, they went to Egypt. When they entered the presence of Joseph, they told him: O Chief Minister, we have become weak and frail because of the famine that has afflicted us.

"And we have brought only a few worthless coins;" meaning, we have only brought useless and valueless goods, "but please give us our supplies in full" as we have been accustomed because of your generosity, "and be charitable to us. Indeed, Allah rewards the charitable."[17]

Then the Noble Qur'an narrates Joseph's response: "Do you remember what you did to Joseph and his brother in your ignorance?"[18] which means your unawareness of the ugliness and viciousness of what you did.

Upon which they asked in amazement and shock: "Are you really Joseph?" He replied: "I am Joseph, and here is my brother Benjamin! Allah has truly been gracious to us." He brought us together again after being separated. "Surely whoever is mindful ˹of Allah˺ and patient, then certainly Allah never discounts the reward of the good-doers."[19]

They responded saying: "By Allah! Allah has truly preferred you over us" and He endowed you with knowledge, patience and blessings, "and we have surely been sinful "in the way we dealt with you.

Joseph- peace be upon him- responded: "There is no blame on you today. May Allah forgive you! He is the Most Merciful of the merciful! (Qur'an 12:92) Go with this shirt of mine and cast it over my father's face, and he will regain his sight. Then come back to me with your whole family." In other words, bring to me in Egypt all your people: the men, the women and the children… everyone.

The Noble Qur'an then recounts what had taken place between Joseph, his father and his brothers when they came to Egypt from Palestine: "When they entered Joseph's presence, he received his parents graciously." He hugged and embraced them and said, "Enter Egypt, Allah willing, in security. Then he raised his parents to the throne." (Qur'an 12:99-100) He had them sit on his own bed with him. "And they all fell down in prostration." His parents and his brothers knelt down as a sign of respect and honor NOT as a sign of worship. This kind of kneeling down was acceptable in their doctrine.

Imam Ibn Kathir maintains "This was acceptable and customary in their doctrine. When they greeted an elder, they would kneel down to him. This had been the case from Adam until Issa (Jesus)- peace be upon him. This has been forbidden in Islam; kneeling down is exclusively restricted to the Lord Allah Almighty."[20]

Joseph said, "O my dear father! This is the interpretation of my old dream. My Lord has made it come true." This means that this prostration from you and my 11 brothers is the consequence of my interpretation of the dreams I had before when I was young: Joseph said to his father, "O my dear father! Indeed, I dreamt of eleven stars, and the sun, and the moon—I saw them prostrating to me!... He (Allah) was truly kind to me when He freed me from prison, and brought you all from the desert after Satan had ignited rivalry between me and my siblings. Indeed my Lord is subtle in fulfilling what He wills. Surely, He alone is the All-Knowing, All-Wise." (Qur'an 12:4-6)

Al-Hassan said: Joseph was thrown into the well when he was seventeen. Eighty years passed before they were brought back together. He lived 23 more years and died at the age of 120. [21]

The Children of Israel lived in Egypt after that. What spurred and encouraged them to dwell there was the abundance and plenty as well as the peace and stability that they enjoyed after wandering and roaming from one place to another and after experiencing the famines that afflicted them.

But who was ruling Egypt when Jacob and his children arrived there?

Historians maintain that the Hyksos were ruling Egypt when Jacob and his offspring immigrated to it in the nineteenth century BC?

The Hyksos were groups of shepherds of Asian descent, and they came to Egypt as a result of the famines that afflicted their countries. They seized the chance of the disintegration of the Thirteenth Pharaonic Dynasty and the discord and conflict among the members of the nobility, and they usurped the authority and power in Egypt. They formed four of the ancient Dynasties that ruled Egypt. Their rule lasted from around 2098 to 1587 BC.

The children of Israel enjoyed a safe and abundant life during the rule of the Hyksos, who were foreigners in the land of Egypt.

When Ahmose conquered the Hyksos, drove them out of Egypt and founded the Eighteenth Dynasty in the sixteenth century BC, fears and worries started to haunt the Children of Israel who became concerned with the new regime. When the Nineteenth Dynasty (amongst whose kings was Ramses the Second) was founded, the Egyptians publicly displayed their animosity towards the Children of Israel. They imposed various forms of punishments and retributions because they had witnessed how arrogant, proud and distant they were. They saw how artfully and ingeniously they maneuvered and schemed to usurp their money. They also witnessed how they devised plots- with the Hyksos- against the original inhabitants of the land of Egypt, and how they tried to overthrow the existing ruling administration.

The writer of "The History of the Children of Israel from Their Travels" reports that: "It was clear that the state of the Children of Israel had changed after ending the rule of the Hyksos in the sixteenth century BC and establishing the Egyptian Empire. From the Papyrus, we have evidence that harnessing and enslaving them reached its peak during the reign of Ramses the Second, the greatest King of the Nineth Dynasty which ruled from 1350 to 1250 BC according to (James Henry) Breasted, the historian, or from 1462 to 1288 according to Sharobeem, another historian. There is evidence that indicates that the Children of Israel played a role in the religious upheaval that Akhenaten (one of the kings of the Eighteenth Dynasty from 1580-1350) caused. Akhenaten's goal behind this coup was Atenism, which is centered on worshipping the sun, and he called his Allah "Aten," which is believed to be taken from the Hebrew "Adon" or "Adonai," which the Hebrews used for Allah. [22] Dr. Ahmed Badawi describes the relationship of the Egyptians with the Children of Israel during that period. He says:

"It is evident from what was written in the heavenly books, on the one hand, and what the antiquities and ancient monuments display, on the other, that the Hebrews came to know Egypt at least during the Middle Kingdom. First, they came to it as refugees seeking their livelihood and searching for an easy and comfortable way of life among its noble and hospitable people. On other occasions, they came as captives following the victorious Pharaoh when he triumphantly came back from his wars in the eastern provinces. He would then send them to houses of worship to work in construction. They worshipped their Gods with freedom; nobody forced or coerced them to adopt a certain religion or doctrine. They enjoyed a lifestyle of ease and comfort in Egypt and their lives ran smoothly. When hardships befell the Egyptians and adversities afflicted them, the Children of Israel would then ignore and snub them and look the other way. They lurked in wait and tried to impoverish them. They weakened the morale among the different classes of the people in order to monopolize the means of living in the country to impose their own authority through economic pressure, at times, or through religion at other times."[23]

In many verses, the Noble Qur'an mentions various patterns of tortures and punishments with which Egypt's Pharaoh and his soldiers afflicted the Children of Israel. In the Sura of Ibrahim (Abraham), the Almighty says: "Consider˺ when Moses said to his people, "Remember Allah's favor upon you when He rescued you from the people of Pharaoh, who afflicted you with dreadful torment—slaughtering your sons and keeping your women. That was a severe test from your Lord." [24] And in Sura Al-Qasas (the Stories), the Almighty says: "Indeed, Pharaoh arrogantly elevated himself in the land and divided its people into ˹subservient˺ groups, one of which he persecuted, slaughtering their sons and keeping their women. He was truly one of the corruptors."[25] And in Sura Al-Baqarah (The Cow), we read: "Remember how We delivered you from the people of Pharaoh, who afflicted you with dreadful torment, slaughtering your sons and keeping your women. That was a severe test from your Lord."[26]

During these hardships and calamities that befell the Children of Israel at the hands of Pharaoh and his soldiers, Allah Almighty had compassion upon them and wanted to save them from the adversities they were experiencing. He sent His prophet Moses[27]- peace be upon him- to save and guide them.

The Noble Qur'an narrates in many verses that Moses- peace be upon him- asked Pharaoh to stop harming the Children of Israel, to abandon arrogance and disbelief, and to worship Allah alone with no partners. In Sura Al-A'raf (the Heights), He says: "And Moses said, "O Pharaoh! I am truly a messenger from the Lord of all worlds, obliged to say nothing about Allah except the truth. Indeed, I have come to you with clear proof from your Lord, so let the children of Israel go with me."[28] In other words, Moses debated with confidence and proof with pharaoh saying: I am a messenger from Allah, the Creator and owner of everything, and I can say nothing about Allah except the truthful saying with which He commanded me. I have to be heedful that I do not say anything about Allah except the truth, so let the children of Israel go with me. In other words, release them from captivity and oppression and leave them worship the Lord, their Allah. Let them go so they can return with me to the Levant.

The Noble Qur'an then recounts that the chiefs of Pharaoh's people asked him to add to the afflictions and sufferings of the Children of Israel and to coerce them to worship his gods. It says: "The chiefs of Pharaoh's people protested, "Are you going to leave Moses and his people free to spread corruption in the land and abandon you and your gods?" He responded, "We will kill their sons and keep their women. We will completely dominate them."[29] In other words, the chief of Pharaoh's people said to him: Are you going to leave Moses and his people free to corrupt your subjects and force them to worship the Allah of Moses? Are you going to let them forbid your people from worshipping your gods? Moses responded to them: We will kill their children and keep their women. We will dominate them thoroughly.

Interpreters maintain that the meaning of "abandon you and your gods" lies in the fact that Pharaoh had made small idols for his people and ordered them to worship them. He called himself "the most high," as he was described in the Qur'an: Then he summoned his people and called out, saying, "I am your lord, the most high!"[30]

Al-Hasan said that he worshipped the planets and believed that they are the gods of the underworld.

The Noble Qur'an then reveals Moses's advice to his people: "Moses reassured his people, "Seek Allah's help and be patient. Indeed, the earth belongs to Allah alone. He grants it to whoever He chooses of His servants. The ultimate outcome belongs ˹only˺ to the righteous."[31] In other words, Moses asked his people to trust in Allah to deliver them from this tyrant and oppressor. He advised them to have patience and endure his oppression for the land does not belong to Pharaoh, but it is Allah's land, and He will give it to whomsoever He pleases. He confirmed that good rewards from Allah await those who are righteous, fear Him, observe His statutes and stay away from what He had forbidden.

What was the effect of this advice on the Children of Israel? How did they respond to their prophet Moses- peace be upon him? They did not benefit from that precious advice. They responded with brusqueness and asperity and said: "We have always been oppressed before and after you came to us." They meant that they benefited nothing from his message or prophethood. They were oppressed at the hands of Pharaoh before Moses- peace be upon him- came with his message, and this oppression and humiliation continued after he came with his message. In both cases there was torture, oppression and anguish.

Upon hearing their response, Moses- peace on him- with words of hope and forewarning: "Perhaps your Lord will destroy your enemy and make you successors in the land to see what you will do."[32] Meaning: will you be thankful or will you be ungrateful? Will you destroy and corrupt the earth or fix and restore it?

Some historians believe that the Children of Israel departed from Egypt under the leadership of Moses- peace be upon him- (during the reign of Merneptah, son of Ramses II) around 1213 BC after Moses-peace be upon him- asked him more than once to send the Children of Israel with him to go to the Levant.

In Numbers Chapter 1, Moses counted the Children of Israel when they departed from Egypt. He found that those who were able to go forth to war, that is, those who were twenty years old and upward reached 603,500. This means their overall number exceeded 1 million.

One of the interpreters comments on the story of the Children of Israel's taking the jewelry of the Egyptians when they left Egypt. He says: "What attracts the attention- particularly from what was written in the Torah- is about the men and women of the Children of Israel who would take the golden and silver possessions of their neighbors under the pretext of borrowing them and attribute this act to Allah- the Almighty. Whatever the situation was, the mere recording of this matter in such a style indicates what was and still reign supreme in the hearts and minds of the Children of Israel: legitimizing and making "lawful" others' money and taking and usurping it by any means possible, even when wars or self-defense are not an issue. This has undoubtedly had a strong impact on entrenching and cementing this strange behavior in their offspring and those other races that enter their religion." [33]

The story of the departure of the Children of Israel from Egypt to the Levant is reported in many places in the Noble Qur'an. In Sura "Taha" the Almighty says:

"And We surely inspired Moses, saying, "Leave with My servants ˹at night˺ and strike a dry passage for them across the sea. Have no fear of being overtaken, nor be concerned of drowning". (Q 20:77) "Then Pharaoh pursued them with his soldiers—but how overwhelming were the waters that submerged them! And ˹so˺ Pharaoh led his people astray, and did not guide ˹them rightly˺. O Children of Israel! We saved you from your enemy, and made an appointment with you[1] on the right side of Mount Ṭûr, and sent down to you manna and quails, ˹saying, ˺ "Eat from the good things We have provided for you, but do not transgress in them, or My wrath will befall you. And whoever My wrath befalls is certainly doomed. But I am truly Most Forgiving to whoever repents, believes, and does good, then persists on ˹true˺ guidance." (Q 20:78-82)

And in Sura Ash-Sh'ara (The Poets): "And We inspired Moses, ˹saying, ˺ "Leave with My servants at night, for you will surely be pursued." (Q 26:52) Meaning, we inspired Moses to leave with My servants at night or at the beginning of night to leave Egypt and depart to the Levantine because Pharaoh and his soldiers will follow you to harm and inflict pain on you.

Imam Ibn Kathir said: As Moses-peace be upon him- stayed in Egypt for a long time and he presented Allah's proofs and testimonies to Pharaoh and his chiefs who persevered in their arrogance and denial, nothing remained for them except oppression and persecution. Therefore, Allah commanded Moses-peace be upon him- to leave Egypt with the Children of Israel at night and to lead them to where He would command him. Moses- peace be upon him- did what Allah ordered him to do. They left after borrowing from Pharaoh's people a lot of jewelry. According to all commentators except one, he left with them when the moon appeared in the sky. Mujahid mentioned that there was an eclipse of the moon that night. When morning came and Pharaoh's people discovered that they were gone, Pharaoh was furious and extremely angry with the Children of Israel, and he wanted to inflict pain and destruction on them. He sent messengers all over the land to gather soldiers to go after and destroy them.

This is revealed in His saying: "Then Pharaoh sent mobilizers to all cities." (Q 26:53) In other words, Pharaoh called upon his people seeking their help and sending them to various provinces to gather people and bring them around him to be at his command.

Then the Qur'an shows how Pharaoh describes Moses' people: "These outcasts are just a handful of people." (Q 26:54) Pharaoh said to his people that those (meaning Moses and his people) who left our country are just few people compared to our big army.

A handful of people "who have really enraged us." (Q 26:55) They manage to do things that enrage us on every occasion and fill our hearts with hatred towards them. "But we are all on the alert." (Q 26:56) In other words, we are always watchful, and we take precautions against their wickedness and malevolence. We are always ready to discipline them, bring them down and get rid of them.

Then Allah- the Almighty- displays the calamities that befell Pharaoh and his soldiers on account of their oppression and tyranny: "So We lured the tyrants out of ˹their˺ gardens, springs, treasures, and splendid residences. So it was. And We awarded it all to the Children of Israel." (Q 26:57-59) This means that We deprived Pharaoh and his soldiers of the abundance and lavishness in which they lived and brought pain and suffering on them because of their ingratitude and disbelief. We gave these riches and wealth to the Children of Israel.

Then Allah- the Almighty-shows what happened to Moses' people when Pharaoh and his soldiers caught up with them: "And so they pursued them at sunrise." (Q 26:60) This means that Pharaoh and his soldiers caught up with Moses and his people at sunrise. "When the two groups came face to face," (Q 26:61) that is, the two parties came too close to each other and were able to see each other, "the companions of Moses cried out, "We are overtaken for sure." (Q 26:62) Filled with fear and terror, Moses' people said that Pharaoh and his men were about to overtake them to inflict the severest pain and torture on them, as he was accustomed to doing. But Moses responded with confidence and poise: "Absolutely not! My Lord is certainly with me—He will guide me." (Q 26:62) Meaning: Moses will not overtake you, for Allah has promised you that he will protect you from him. So do not be afraid, for Allah is with me. He will support and help me, and he will guide me to what is good and beneficial.

Then Allah inspired Moses to: "Strike the sea with your staff." When Moses did, the sea was divided into two parts: "and the sea was split, each part was like a huge mountain." (Q 26:63)

Ibn Abbas said: the sea had formed 12 paths, one path for each one of the 12 tribes.

Then Allah showed what had befallen Pharaoh and his soldiers: "We drew the pursuers to that place." (Q 26:64) Meaning: We brought Pharaoh and his soldiers to the sea until they entered behind the Children of Israel between the two parts. The result was as Almighty Allah said: "and delivered Moses and those with him all together. Then We drowned the others" (Q 26:65-66) when we closed the sea on them after the Children of Israel crossed it.

Almighty Allah concluded this story by showing a lesson to those who will weigh and consider: "Surely in this is a sign. Yet most of them would not believe. And your Lord is certainly the Almighty, Most Merciful." (Q 26:67-68)

Thus, these honorable verses have vividly, thoroughly and exquisitely depicted the story of the exodus of the Children of Israel from Egypt, pharaoh's pursuing them, and his drowning in the end right in front of their eyes.

Now that we have recounted the state of the Children of Israel since their immigration to Egypt under the leadership of Jacob- peace be upon him- until their departure from it at the hands of Moses- peace be upon him-, we are going to recount another stage of their history, namely,

B- Their history from their exodus from Egypt until establishing their Kingdom around 1095 BC

The departure of the Children of Israel from Egypt took place around the thirteenth century BC. After witnessing the drowning of Pharoah with their own eyes, Moses- peace be upon him- led them to the land of Palestine in the Levant. He was hoping that they would become a strong nation through their faith and good deeds. A natural consequence of their departure from Egypt and witnessing the perdition of Pharaoh in front of their eyes was that they became free to manage and run their own affairs after the suffering and torture that they received at the hands of Pharaoh and his men.

The writer of the History of the Israelites narrates: "Their history until their departure from Egypt was the history of a small family that had grown and became bigger until it became a big tribe without a specific character or a government. There were no legislators or representatives that would look into various matters or help the weak against the powerful. They were scattered all over the land of Egypt, and they were exposed to slavery, harness, oppression and humiliation. However, after the exodus, they formed one people and one nation with a leader from among its sons, an army to protect it, and a ruler in charge of its various affairs. The characteristics of an independent nation started to take shape and crystalize. No sooner had they departed from Egypt than the legislator started to pass laws and issue regulations governing civil, social and religious matters... just as it is the case with every independent nation. Thus, the history of the Israelites started after their exodus from Egypt. This history covered many centuries during which they had been exposed to many ordinary events such as wars, progress and degeneration."[34]

However, the Children of Israel did not appreciate the value of freedom. They did not thank Allah for their deliverance from the hands of their enemy. And they did not obey their prophet Moses- peace be upon him- who came to guide, protect and mend their ways. In fact, they severely maltreated and harmed him. These are some of the vicious and vile things they did on their way to the land of the Levant.

1- After Moses- peace be upon him- led them for a period of time in Sinai in the direction of the land of Palestine in the Levant, they revolted against him and his brother Aaron. As mentioned in the Torah, they said: "Oh, that we had died by the hand of the Lord in the land of Egypt, when we sat by the pots of meat *and* when we ate bread to the full! For you have brought us out into this wilderness to kill this whole assembly with hunger." [35]

The Torah also recounts that Moses- peace be upon him- was incensed and greatly annoyed by their ignorance and evil deeds. He implored the Lord saying: "So Moses said to the Lord, "Why have You afflicted Your servant? And why have I not found favor in Your sight, that You have laid the [d]burden of all these people on me? [12] Did I conceive all these people? Did I beget them, that You should say to me, 'Carry them in your bosom, as a guardian carries a nursing child… I am not able to bear all these people alone, because the burden *is* too heavy for me. [15] If You treat me like this, please kill me here and now—if I have found favor in Your sight—and do not let me see my wretchedness!'"[36]

2- After the Children of Israel witnessed the drowning of Pharaoh with their own eyes, they marched with Moses- peace be upon him- to the Levant. They saw people[37] worshipping idols. As soon as they saw those pagans, the Children of Israel asked their prophet Moses- peace be upon him- to make idols for them to worship just as those people were worshipping their idols. The paganism that they witnessed in Egypt was still rooted in their weak spirits. The Noble Qur'an talks about this vice: "We brought the Children of Israel across the sea and they came upon a people devoted to idols. They demanded, "O Moses! Make for us a Allah like their Gods." He replied, "Indeed, you are a people acting ignorantly! What they follow is certainly doomed to destruction and their deeds are in vain. He added, "Shall I seek for you a Allah other than Allah, while He has honoured you above the others? And ⌜remember⌝ when We rescued you from the people of Pharaoh, who afflicted you with dreadful torment—killing your sons and keeping your women. That was a severe test from your Lord. [38]"

3- During Moses' march with his people through the Sinai desert heading towards the Levant, Almighty Allah promised to give Moses the Torah as a guide to the Children of Israel after he had fasted forty days. When the time came, Moses left the Children of Israel in the care of Aaron, his brother. He went to the mountain to receive the Torah. The Noble Qur'an recounts this: "We appointed for Moses thirty nights then added another

> ten—completing his Lord's term of forty nights. Moses commanded his brother Aaron, "Take my place among my people, do what is right, and do not follow the way of the corruptors."[39]

Imam Ibn Kathir said: "Almighty Allah- Benevolent and bountiful to the Children of Israel- by talking to Moses and giving him the Torah, which contains their statutes and the specifics of their doctrine- appointed Moses 30 nights. Exegetes report that Moses fasted this period, and when the time had come, Allah appointed 10 more days to complete 40 days. Interpreters differ in their interpretation of those ten days. Most agree that the thirty days are the (month of) Dhul-Qa'dah ذو القعدة and the ten days are Dhul-Hijjah ذو الحجة. Mujahid, Masruq and Ibn Jurayj maintain that the term was thus completed on the Day of Slaughtering (the tenth day of Dhul-Hijjah), in which Allah talked to Moses- peace be upon him. So, when the term was completed, Moses decided to go to the mountain, as mentioned in the Qur'an: "O Children of Israel! We saved you from your enemy, and made an appointment with you[1] on the right side of Mount Ṭûr, and sent down to you manna and quails." Moses left Aaron behind him with the Children of Israel and asked him to take his place, do the right thing and to stay away from corruption. It was an advice and a counsel, for Aaron-peace be upon him- is a noble prophet, and he has his distinction and nobility in Allah's eyes. [40]

But what did the Children of Israel do after Moses left them to receive the Torah?

They abused Aaron's lenience and malleability and started worshipping a calf that made a lowing sound molded by the Samaritan out of the jewelry they borrowed from the Copts of Egypt. Being led astray, Aaron tried to turn them away from the wrongdoing and waywardness in which they indulged, but they opposed him defiantly- as mentioned in the Noble Qur'an in Sura Taha: "We will not cease to worship it until Moses returns to us." When he intensely forbade them from worshipping the calf, they attacked and nearly killed him.

Almighty Allah informed Moses that his people were led astray by the Samaritan, and he returned to them furious and sorrowful. He harshly reproached and scolded them and warned of the wrath and dreadful torment that would befall them. They apologized and told him that the Samaritan had led them astray.

Moses- peace be upon him- thought that his brother Aaron did not do enough for them. He scolded and reprimanded him for that. But Aaron- peace be upon him- informed Moses that he did everything he could to provide them with good counsel and turn them away from worshipping anything except Allah alone. However, they opposed him, rebelled against him, overpowered him and were about to kill him.

Upon hearing this, Moses poured his anger on the Samaritan, the chief plotter responsible for this revolt and disturbance. After listening to his weak defense of himself, Moses said to him: "Go away then! And for the rest of your life you will surely be crying, 'Do not touch me!' Then you will certainly have a fate that you cannot escape. Now look at your god to which you have been devoted: we will burn it up, then scatter it in the sea completely (Qur'an 20:97)." Then Moses addressed his people: "Your only god is Allah, there is no god worthy of worship except Him. He encompasses everything in His knowledge (Qur'an 20:98)."

In the presence of the Children of Israel, Moses- peace be upon him- carried out his promise to the Samaritan: he burned the calf up and threw its dust in the sea thereby proving to all that only "Allah" is worthy of worship and that the calf that they worshipped- in their ignorance and folly- benefitted them nothing.

The Noble Qur'an recounts the story of the Children of Israel's worshipping the calf in many lengthy verses in Sura Al'Araf and Sura Taha. We have interpreted it in detail in another section.[41]

Then Almighty Allah revealed to Moses that the repentance of the calf worshippers will not be acceptable until they eliminated the worshippers. When they did what Allah asked them to do, they were forgiven, hoping that they would become thankful for Allah's blessings and forgiveness: "And remember when Moses said to his people, "O my people! Surely you have wronged yourselves by worshipping the calf, so turn in repentance to your Creator and execute ˹the calf-worshippers among˺ yourselves. That is best for you in the sight of your Creator." Then He accepted your repentance. Surely, He is the Accepter of Repentance, Most Merciful." (Qur'an 2:54)

In general, the meaning of the noble verse (Q 2:54) is: O Children of Israel, remember- to your advantage and benefit- what Moses said to his people who worshipped the calf when he was away talking to his Allah: You did yourselves great injustice when you worshipped something other than Allah. If you wanted to atone for your sins, repent to your Allah and Creator and offer a true and genuine penitence. Kill yourselves in atonement for your sins. Or else, those who did not worship the calf, let them kill the calf worshippers. Your humiliation, that is, killing yourselves or killing those who worshipped the calf, is best for you in the sight of your Creator. You did this, so Allah accepted your repentance: "He is the Accepter of Repentance, Most Merciful." [42]

4- After all these events and the offences that the Children of Israel made, Moses-peace be upon him- continued marching to the Levant. Before arriving with them to the Holy Land that was inhabited by the mighty Canaanites, he ordered them to get ready to enter the land, and to be prepared to fight for the sake of Allah. He chose 12 deputies to go before them to enter the Holy Land to gather information about it and about the conditions of its inhabitants. The deputies did what Moses- peace be upon him- instructed them to do. They came back after accomplishing their mission and becoming acquainted with the condition of the inhabitants; They said: the Holy Land overflows with milk and honey, but its inhabitants are mighty and strong. The deputies tried to dissuade their people from entering the land. Only two deputies commanded the Children of Israel to obey their Prophet Moses-peace be upon him. They insisted on entering the Holy Land that Allah destined for them. They anticipated victory if they trusted in Allah and were wholeheartedly committed to fight. However, the Children of Israel were opposed to the advice of the two men- as they disobeyed their prophet Moses before. The result was Allah's punishment to them to wander in the wilderness for 40 years.

The Noble Qur'an eloquently recounts this story in Sura Al-Ma'idah: "And remember when Moses said to his people, "O my people! Remember Allah's favors upon you when He raised prophets from among you, made you sovereign, and gave you what He had never given anyone in the world. O my people! Enter the Holy Land which Allah has destined for you to enter. And do not turn back or else you will become losers. They replied, "O Moses! There is an enormously powerful people there, so we will never ˹be able to˺ enter it until they leave. If they do, then we will enter! Two Allah-fearing men—who had been blessed by Allah—said, "Surprise them through the gate. If you do, you will certainly prevail. Put your trust in Allah if you are ˹truly˺ believers. Yet they said, "O Moses! ˹Still˺ we will never enter as long as they remain there. So go—both you and your Lord—and fight; we are staying right here!" Moses pleaded, "My Lord! I have no control over anyone except myself and my brother. So set us apart from the rebellious people." (Qur'an 5:20-5:25) [43]

After the death of Moses and Aaron- peace be upon them- Joshua, son of Nun, became in charge of the Children of Israel. That generation- that was brought up in servitude and humility and which once said to Moses: "Go—both you and your Lord—and fight; we are staying right here!"- had perished. Another generation- brought up during the time in the wilderness- learned austerity and rigor and Bedouin life. It was this generation that Joshua led to enter the Holy Land.

The Torah recounts that Joshua crossed the Jordan River with the Children of Israel to enter the Holy Land. The first city that Joshua and his men were able to enter was Jericho. Then they proceeded to "Ai" a city between Nablus and Jerusalem from the east. When the Children of Israel entered these two cities, they killed most of the inhabitants and crucified the king of the city "Ai" at the city gate. Then the Torah recounts Joshua's victory over the Canaanites, who inhabited Palestine at that time. It also recounts how the Children of Israel killed the men, women and children of the cities that fell to their hands at the Lord's command.

In Joshua Chapter 10, we read: "So Joshua conquered all the land: the mountain country and the South and the lowland and the wilderness slopes, and all their kings; he left none remaining, but utterly destroyed all that breathed, as the Lord God of Israel had commanded. And Joshua conquered them from Kadesh Barnea as far as Gaza.... because the Lord Allah of Israel fought for Israel." [44]

What we can glean form these passages is that after the Children of Israel conquered the Canaanites under the leadership of Joshua, they put them to the sword, burned their cities, and demolished their homes. Nobody was saved except those who fled.

The author of The Story of Civilization describes what the Children of Israel did to the Canaanites. He says: "The defeat of the Canaanites provides a clear example of a hungry group bouncing on a safe and secure group. The Hebrews killed whomsoever they were able to kill. They captured whoever remained of their women and made them captives. The blood of the slaughtered flowed like rivers. And that killing was- as indicated in the Holy Bible- instituted by the law with which the Lord commanded Moses. It was "زكاة" Alms" to the Lord. When they captured one of the cities, they killed 12 thousand of its inhabitants, burned it, and they crucified its ruler. We have never seen this kind of excess and profusion in killing and taking delight in it... Joshua had instituted his rule on the principle of a law of nature which says: "The killer of the most people is the one that remains alive." Thus, in this way that is devoid of feelings, the Jews took over and usurped the Promised Land."[45]

Joshua divided the land that he took from the Canaanites amongst the 12 tribes. Joshua Chapter 13 to 19 recounts the names of the cities and borders that were assigned to each of these tribes. These chapters also show that some provinces and cities remained in the possession of their original inhabitants. They were not taken by the Children of Israel until after Joshua's death. Still, some were never taken by the Children of Israel and were never part of their possession like the southern part of Palestine.

Joshua died when he was one hundred and ten years old as mentioned in Joshua Chapter 24. He was buried within the border of his inheritance in the mountains of Ephraim, near modern day Nablus.[46]

Dr. Ali Abd el-Wahed describes how the Children of Israel entered- and lived in- Palestine under the leadership of Joshua. He says: "Around the thirteenth century BC, the Children of Israel under the leadership of Joshua, who came after Moses- peace be upon him- invaded the land of Canaan/Palestine and its surroundings which is the Promised Land that Allah had destined for them. They occupied it and usurped all its riches and treasures after they had eradicated most of its inhabitants. They enslaved whoever they kept alive. That is how the roughness, coarseness and Bedouin-like style of moving from one place to the other came to an end. They started a new era of civilization and stability, and they resided in the cities, villages, houses and mansions that they inherited from the Canaanites. Their religious matters started to follow well informed and disciplined laws under the supervision of their rabbis, jurists, the learned ones and the leaders in their synagogues and altars. Most of those were from the offspring of Levi, one of Jacob's children, kindred of Moses and Aaron." [47]

The Noble Qur'an had referred to the story of the Children of Israel's entering the Promised Land under the leadership of Joshua in many verses. In Sural Al-Baqarah, we read: "And remember when We said, "Enter this city and eat freely from wherever you please; enter the gate with humility, saying, 'Absolve us.' We will forgive your sins and multiply the reward for the good-doers. But the wrongdoers changed the words they were commanded to say. So, We sent down a punishment from the heavens upon them for their rebelliousness." (Qur'an 2:58-59) [48]

Imam Ibn Kathir recounts that "That was after they came out of the wilderness with Joshua, son of Nun, after forty years. Allah enabled them to enter. He even stopped the sun for some time until they were able to enter it. And when they entered it, they were commanded to go in with humility as a sign of gratitude to Allah for His grace and assistance for them to become victorious and for His help in rescuing them from the wilderness."[49]

But they did not do that. Therefore, Allah sent His punishment upon them from the heavens for their depravity, wickedness and injustice. He followed the death Joshua, son of Nun, with an era known as the era of the Judges because the leaders that led the Children of Israel after Joshua were called Judges. Their rule continued until the establishment of the kingdom of the Children of Israel at the hands of "Taloot" known as "Saul" in the Torah. The number of Judges that ruled over the Children of Israel during this period was about 15 Judges. Among them were Othniel, Samuel, Ehud, Shamgar, Barak, Jephthah, Gideon and samson, etc.

The author of The History of the Israelites describes the era of the Judges: "The country during the era of the Judges was more like united kingdoms. In each kingdom there was a tribe from the twelve tribes, ruled by the elders therein. These tribes were all united with one bond... They took part in major religious ceremonies. Oftentimes, they would forsake Allah and resort to worshipping idols. In the Torah: 'that was a reason for being dominated by foreigners.' Among them, there were Judges that tried to bring them back together. None of those Judges had any royal privileges or enjoyed specific prestige. Some of those Judges' responsibilities were merely limited to repelling an invasion or pushing an enemy back. Some ruled all their lives because of their wisdom and expertise." [50]

The book of judges recounts their life story and their conditions, what calamities they had to face during their reign which is said to be four hundred years according to the Book of Judges itself. Some historians believe their reign lasted one hundred years only.

Professor Muhammad Izzat Darwaza maintains: "According to the Book of Judges, the period they ruled might be around 400 hundred years even though it might not exceed 100 years. We know that the official rule for the Children of Israel began in the middle of the 11th century BC (approximately in 1030 BC), and that the Children of Israel departed from Egypt at the end of the 13th century BC (approximately in 1210 BC), and that the leadership of Moses and Joshua after him lasted for almost eighty years. This number- the 400 years- is an exaggeration in the Book of Judges, just like the other books when numbers are concerned." [51]

He who reads the Book of Judges will conclude that: The era of the Judges was one of the worst eras in the history of the Children of Israel. During this time, many vices and depravities proliferated and became widespread; they worshipped idols, killed reformers and prophets, and adultery ran rampant. Consequently, they were exposed to raids and invasions, including the invasion of Sheanaim, king of the two rivers, and Heglon, king of the Moabites, and Jabin, king of the Canaanites and others...

Chapter Two of the Book of Judges offers an overall account of the life of the Children of Israel during the era of the Judges. It says: "Another generation arose after them, meaning, Joshua, son of Nun, and his followers. It was a different generation that did not know the Lord nor what He had done to Israel. The Children of Israel did evil in the sight of the Lord. They bowed down and worshipped Baal. They abandoned the God of their fathers who brought them out of the land of Egypt, and they followed other Gods from among the Gods of the other peoples around them. They bowed down and worshipped those Gods. Therefore, the Lord was wrathful and furious, and He pushed them to the hands of looters and plunderers who exploited and looted them. He sold them to their enemies around them, and they were unable to stand against their enemies anymore. Wherever they went, the hand of the Lord was upon them dealing harshly with them as He had said and sworn. They were exceedingly anguished and distressed."[52]

Samuel was the last Judge for the Children of Israel during this era. During his time, corruption and perversion ran rampant. When he became advanced in age, he authorized his children to manage the judicial affairs. Those children were corrupt; they took bribes and ruled unjustly. The Children of Israel revolted against him and his children. That brought the era of the Judges to an end. The era of the Kings followed. We now offer a brief account of the Kings' era.

C- The History of the Children of Israel Since Establishing Their Kingdom in 1095 BC Until its Division in 975 BC

The Kings during this era in the History of the Children of Israel are Talut (Saul), David, and Solomon, peace be upon them.

Their biographies are recorded in 1 Samuel from the Chapter 13 onwards, and in 2 Samuel. Then it is recorded in 1 Kings from Chapter 1 to Chapter 12, and in 1 Chronicles, and from Chapter One to Chapter Ten in 2 Chronicles.

The Jewish Kingdom was established approximately in 1095 BC. Their first King was Talut (Saul). This era which includes him, David and Solomon- peace be upon them- is called the era of the First Kings. It ended with the death of Solomon-peace be upon him- around 975 BC. The era that followed Solomon- peace be upon him- until the eradication of the Kingdom of the Children of Israel at the hands of Nebuchadnezzar 586 BC, is called the era of the Second Kings. During the reign of Talut (Saul), he courageously led the Children of Israel in many wars with other nations. For instance, he led them against the Ammonites who inhabited east of Jordan and vanquished them.

One of the most well-known battles is the one in which Saul led the Children of Israel against the Palestinians under the leadership of Goliath- "Galoot" as he is called in the Noble Qur'an. David- peace be upon him- took part in that battle, and he himself killed Goliath.

This is a synopsis of the battle as recounted in 1 Samuel, Chapter 17: "The Palestinians (Philistines) gathered to wreak vengeance against the Children of Israel. Saul and his soldiers encamped in preparation to confront them. Goliath emerged from among the Palestinians (Philistines) and challenged the Children of Israel: "Choose one from your men and let him come to me. If he is able to kill me, the Palestinians (Philistines) will become your servants. But if I prevail and kill him, you will become our servants." Saul and the Children of Israel were dismayed and greatly afraid... David emerged with his sling and staff... With a sling and a stone, he struck Goliath who fell to the ground on his face. David ran and stood over the Philistine, took his sword and drew it out of its sheath and killed him, and cut off his head with it... When the Palestinians witnessed the death of their mighty one, they fled. The Children of Israel chased and killed them and plundered their tents."[53]

There are also some noble verses in Sura "Al-Baqarah" that refer to choosing Talut (Saul) as King over the Children of Israel, and the battle that took place between them and Goliath: "Have you not seen those chiefs of the Children of Israel after Moses? They said to one of their prophets, "Appoint for us a king, ⌜and⌝ we will fight in the cause of Allah." He said, "Are you not going to cower if ordered to fight?" They replied, "How could we refuse to fight in the cause of Allah, while we were driven out of our homes and ⌜separated from⌝ our children?" But when they were ordered to fight, they fled, except for a few of them. And Allah has ⌜perfect⌝ knowledge of the wrongdoers (Qur'an 2:246)."

The meaning of this noble verse is: You were well informed, Mohammed, with what the chiefs among the Children of Israel- who came after Moses- peace be upon him- wanted. They got together after their unity was shattered and their opinions differed, and they asked their prophet to "Appoint for us a king, ⌜and⌝ we will fight in the cause of Allah" in order to restore our usurped pride and our occupied land. However, their prophet -who tried them before and was aware of their frailty and weaknesses- questioned their sincerity and earnestness of what they were saying and asked them- as recounted in the Noble Qur'an: "Are you not going to cower if ordered to fight?" The meaning of this is: Is that what I should expect from you, or will you cower and become afraid to fight? The interrogation herein was a confirmation of the fact that what was anticipated was the status quo.

Al-Zamakhshari, the author of Al-Kashaaf says: "The meaning: Is it going to be as I expect... that you are not going to fight. In other words, I expect that you will become cowards when called to fighting. He used the interrogative "Hal /هل" to inquire about what was most expected. The interrogation was meant to confirm that what was expected would be true, and that he was correct in his prediction." [54]

Then, the Noble Qur'an (Q 2:246) mentions their response to their prophet's question: "How could we refuse to fight in the cause of Allah, while we were driven out of our homes and ⌜separated from⌝ our children?"

In other words, the Children of Israel were opposed to what their prophet expected concerning their unwillingness to fight: "How can we not fight when we were driven out of our homes and were separated from our children?" Then the Noble Qur'an reports that their prophet was right concerning the weakness and cowardice that he had expected. What they said with their tongues was not really what was in their hearts, for when it was time for them to fight, they fled. Only few of them remained with their leader: "But when they were ordered to fight, they fled, except for a few of them. And Allah has ˹perfect˺ knowledge of the wrongdoers." (Q 2:246)

Then, the Noble Qur'an relates the story of choosing Talut (Saul) as king, and how they had objected to that choice: "Their prophet told them, "Allah has appointed Saul to be your king." Meaning: their prophet told them that the all-Knowledgeable and Omniscient- who knows their state perfectly- was the One who chose Saul to become their king. But what was their reaction? The Qur'an relates: "How can he be our king when some of us are more deserving of kingship than he, and he has not been blessed with vast riches?" (Qur'an 2:247)

In other words, the Children of Israel- rejecting the choice of Saul to be king over them- said: How could he be king when we are more worthy of kingship because we are far better and he is poor and we are richer than him? Their wrong understanding and misconceptions concerning the correct criteria and standards led them to believe that it was lineage and riches, rather than mental acuteness, adeptness and strong physique, that were required for kingship.

Imam Ibn Kathir said: "Saul was one of their soldiers, but he was not from the king's lineage, for the king was from the tribe of Judah. Saul was not from that tribe. That is why, they said: "How can he be our king?" [55]

As recounted in the Qur'an, their Prophet firmly and decisively responded to them, saying: "Allah has chosen him over you and blessed him with knowledge and stature. Allah grants kingship to whoever He wills. And Allah is All-Bountiful, All-Knowing." (Q 2:247)

That is, it was Allah who chose him for you, and it was not appropriate to oppose Allah's commandments. Moreover, Allah had granted Saul plenty of knowledge and good stature. He far exceeded you in both knowledge and physique. Those who are that well-endowed were most worthy of the highest of ranks. They were more deserving than those who have the money but lack knowledge and good stature.

The verse concludes stating that everything is in the hand of Allah, and that everything in the universe is under His dominion and power: "Allah grants kingship to whoever He wills. And Allah is All-Bountiful, All-Knowing." (Q 2:247)

The Noble Qur'an states that in order to reassure them and comfort their hearts, their prophet informed them that Saul will bring along a sign that shows his worthiness and competence to become their king: "Their prophet further told them, "The sign of Saul's kingship is that the Ark[56] will come to you—containing reasSurance from your Lord and relics of the family of Moses and the family of Aaron, which will be carried by the angels. Surely in this is a sign for you, if you truly believe." (Qur'an 2:248)

That is, their prophet- in order to convince them that Saul was worthy to be king over them- said that the sign of the blessings of Saul's kingship was that "the Ark will come to you." The Ark- the box of the Torah- that was taken from you "containing reasSurance from your Lord "will be returned. Its return means reasSurance, comfort and mercy to you from your Lord. Or, in the Ark itself you have what comforts and reassures you, i.e., the Torah.

"And relics of the family of Moses and the family of Aaron" means that he will bring to you some of the things that were left by Moses and Aaron.

The author of Al-Kashaaf maintains that "relics," "refers the tablets and Moses' staff and clothes and some of the Torah. Almighty Allah had lifted them after Moses- peace be upon him. Now the angels came down carrying them as they were looking. That was a sign from Allah to choose Saul. It was said that these were with Moses and the prophets of the Children of Israel after him. With its blessing, they were able to conquer their enemies. But when they went astray, the unbelievers vanquished them, and they ended in the land of Goliath. When Allah willed that Saul become king, He inflicted Goliath and his people with a scourge, and five cities were destroyed. They attributed this to the Ark behind them. They therefore put the Ark on two bulls, and the angels directed them to Saul. Now, if you ask who are "the family of Moses and the family of Aaron? "I will answer: the prophets from the children of Jacob because Amram- Moses' father- was the son of Kohath, son of Levi, son of Jacob.[57]

"Carried by the angels:" Ibn Jurayj said that Ibn Abbas said: "The angels came carrying the Ark between the heavens and the earth until they placed it between the hands of Saul as the people were looking."[58]

"Surely in this" meaning that which Saul brings to you was "a sign" to show and ascertain the truth of what you were told "if you 'truly' believe" in Allah and the Last Day.

The Noble Qur'an then reveals what transpired between Saul and his soldiers when he led them to fight: "When Saul marched forth with his army," and left the place in which he resided with the Children of Israel, he led them out of Jerusalem to fight Goliath and his army. "He cautioned: "Allah will test you with a river". Meaning: Allah will test you with a river on your way to fight your enemies. "So whoever drinks his fill," meaning: from the river, "is not with me." In other words, he who would drink from it would not be one of my soldiers. He would have to leave; he couldn't accompany me to this fight. "And whoever does not taste it" meaning: he who would not drink much but would be content with just "a sip from the hollow of his hands" would be among my soldiers and fight with me against Goliath and his soldiers. (Qur'an 2:249)

What was the position of the Children of Israel concerning this order from their leader? Many of them disobeyed the order of their leader and drank and filled their bellies heedless of his order: "They all drank 'their fill' except for a few!" Only "a few" did not drink and showed obedience to their leader.

Then Almighty Allah shows the panic and horror that came upon those who were with Saul when they saw Goliath and his men. He also reveals what the loyal soldiers said: "When he and the remaining faithful with him crossed the river, they said, "Now we are no match for Goliath and his warriors." But those believers who were certain they would meet Allah reasoned, "How many times has a small force vanquished a mighty army by the Will of Allah! And Allah is ⌜always⌝ with the steadfast." (Q 2:249)

That is, when Saul and his men crossed the river and saw the great multitudes of Goliath's army, they said to one another that they could not fight Goliath and his men that day. However, the faithful believers among them who were confident of meeting Allah and expected His reward, encouraged and reassured them, telling them that there was no reason for panic or fear for oftentimes small forces overwhelm and vanquish bigger and mightier armies by the will of Allah who always supports those who persevere and rewards them with victory despite the great number of their enemies.

Then Allah revealed what the faithful believers said when they faced their enemy. He said, "When they advanced to face Goliath and his warriors, they prayed, "Our Lord! Shower us with perseverance," that is to say, grant us patience and perseverance and "make our steps firm" when we meet our enemies and Yours; support us so that we do not escape or feel incompetent to face them, and give us victory over the unbelievers. (Qur'an 2:250)

What was the fruit of these faithful and sincere supplications? They resulted in Allah's rewarding the few faithful believers under the leadership of Saul victory over the great number of unbelievers under the leadership of Goliath. In this respect, the Almighty Allah says: "So they defeated them by Allah's Will", that is, they defeated and vanquished them because Allah granted them this victory, and "David killed Goliath. And Allah blessed David with kingship and wisdom and taught him what He willed." (Qur'an 2:251) In other words, Allah blessed David and made him King over the Children of Israel. He gave him wisdom, that is, prophecy. And He bestowed all kinds of knowledge upon him. The Almighty's "what He willed" points to the breadth and depth of the knowledge that Allah granted David-peace be upon him. It was vast, unbound and unlimited knowledge except by Allah's will.

Then the Almighty says: "Had Allah not repelled a group of people by the might of another, corruption would have dominated the earth." (Q 2:251) This means: if the Almighty Allah did not cause some people to go against others, the world would become corrupt and immoral, for if the evildoers are left uncurbed to do as they please, abomination, infamy and devastation would prevail. That is why, Allah did not leave them free to spread corruption and do as they please. He intervenes at a time of His choosing, for He is the Omnipotent and All Knowledgeable.

Then, the Almighty concludes these enlightening verses for those who are open to ponder conscientiously and consider diligently with a statement that this message is from Allah and that He, the Almighty, revealed it to Muhammed, His Messenger and Prophet, in complete truth. He said: "These are Allah's revelations which We recite to you O Prophet in truth." (Qur'an 2:252) Meaning: These, Muhammed, are the signs and revelations from Allah that We revealed to you concerning the Children of Israel. We recite them to you with pure and unadulterated truth that those who were led astray may come to their senses, walk in the right path, follow you and believe that you are truly one of the messengers that Allah sent to bring people out of the darkness and into the light.

This is the story of King Saul's ascension of the throne to become King over the Children of Israel, and their war against Goliath and his warriors- eloquently depicted in the Noble Qur'an and abounding in moral lessons and ethical messages: "Hardships soften the spirit and make it seek help and munificence of the Almighty; religion is the basis of honor and uprightness for those who are afflicted and distressed; no authority or dignity except through one clothed with righteousness and virtue to dispel and repel the decadent and corrupt; a prince should have the mental prowess and competence, the width and profundity of knowledge, and the expertise and capability to lead his people to what is beneficial and useful for them; the most important factor in victory is the control of the self for no one can control his enemy unless he controls himself first; no one can vanquish and suppress his foe unless he suppresses his desires first; and after you prepare yourself and get ready for the battle, you trust in Allah wholeheartedly and leave the rest to Him."[59]

We now continue to talk about what happened between Saul and David after that battle in which David killed Goliath: Some books in the Torah recount that after David- peace be upon him- killed Goliath, the people became enamored and captivated by him. He captured their minds and their hearts, and they started to draw near to him. Saul offered him his daughter, Michal, for a wife. He made him commander over his army. A strong friendship between Jonathan, Saul's son, and David- peace be upon him- also bonded the two. These verses then mention that some conflict between Saul and David took place. This conflict led to David's leaving Saul and departing to the land of the Palestinians. The verses also mention that the Palestinians seized the opportunity that David was not with Saul and started their raids on the Children of Israel. These raids culminated in the death of Saul and some of his children and a humiliating defeat for the Israelites. [60]
Saul remained King until his death. His rule lasted two years.[61]

After the death of Saul, David[62]- peace be upon him- became King over the Children of Israel. His reign lasted for forty years. Hebron[63] was the capital of his kingdom during the first seven years. As for the rest of his years as King, the capital was Jerusalem.[64]

During the reign of David- peace be upon him- many wars took place between the Children of Israel and other nations. Among the nations that they waged a war against was the Jebusites who inhabited the city of Jerusalem. David waged a war against them, drove them out, of there and made Jerusalem the capital of his kingdom. He was also able to gain control of the fortress of Zion, and he called it after his name, "the City of David." This stronghold was a castle that was built on high hills in the middle of Jerusalem.[65]

Prosperity and affluence spread throughout the land during the reign of David- peace be upon him. Commercial relations and transactions with other nations were widespread. His kingdom dominated other peoples and kingdoms in the east and west of Jordan.

Some exegetes recount that "The era of David- peace be upon him- witnessed a variety of conditions. At first, there was confusion and unrest. Then, David-peace be upon him- was able to overcome the other nations surrounding him. That was followed by a period of unrest that lasted until the end of his days. During these periods of unrest and turbulence, the Palestinians were able to break away from David's control. Fighting resumed between them and the Children of Israel, but there was no decisive conclusion."[66]

Solomon [67], David's son, became King after David. His rule lasted for approximately forty years. This period was characterized by stability and affluence.

Shaheen Makarios, the author of the History of the Israelites, describes the era of Solomon- peace be upon him. He says:

"During his era, the Israelites were greatly dignified and exalted. They were feared by neighboring nations. Solomon- peace be upon him-married Pharoah's daughter. He made a treaty with Hiram, King of Tyre. He built his famous Temple. He brought the most prominent builders, craftsmen and designers to build it, and he sent his ships all over the world, and they reached as far as southern Spain. His reputation spread all over the world and to all the kingdoms. The queen of Sheba came from Yemen and visited his court to test his wisdom by asking him to solve a number of riddles. She was stunned by his wisdom. His reign lasted for forty years during which the Israelites enjoyed prosperity and affluence. His era is regarded as the Golden Age of their nation. Industries made giant leaps and architecture well advanced due to the luxurious buildings and sumptuous constructions that Solomon planned to build: the Temple, the castle, many cities, strongholds and fortresses..."[68]

Yet, even though the author of the History of the Israelites describes Solomon's era in such a manner, we find that the Books of the Torah attribute many acts- that we deem he was far above them- abound. For instance, in 1 Kings Chapter Two, we read that Solomon started his reign by killing Adonijah when he requested to marry Abishag, the Shunammite, then he killed Joab, the commander of his father's army, and he removed Abiathar, the High Priest, from the priesthood of the Lord, for conspiring with Adonijah.[69]

Mr. Muhammad Izzat Darwaza states that "If we are to outline the era of Solomon- peace be upon him-, it would be fair to say that his authority did not go beyond the land of Canaan- west of Jordan, and his era was more stable and peaceful with less troubles and turbulences than his father's. However, it was not completely free from problems and internal and external disturbances. [70]

The author of Landmarks of Human History says: "The story of King Solomon and his wisdom as narrated in the Holy Bible was subject to verbiage, additions and verbosity on a large scale. 1 Kings excessively and profusely portrays the splendor and grandeur of Solomon but, in reality if Solomon's edifices are compared to those of Thutmose III, Ramses II or Nebuchadnezzar, they would pale in comparison and appear to be trivial and insignificant." [71]

Gustave Le Bon argues that "we should not talk about the architecture or photography of the Children of Israel, or their design and construction. Look at their famous Temple (Solomon's Temple) about which boring articles and research were published. We will find that it is a structure that was built on the Assyrian Egyptian style, by foreign builders, as the Torah indicates. And Solomon's mansions were nothing but a poor reflection of Egyptian or Assyrian mansions."[72]

With these passages having been narrated, we can say that the eras of David and Solomon- peace be upon them- were considered the golden era for the Children of Israel who enjoyed affluence, stability and high status during this time. Aside from this era, however, their history was a chain of catastrophes and misfortunes that befell them from other nations due to their corruption and immorality. We consider David and Solomon- peace be upon them- too exalted and far above whatever injustice and unfairness the Books of the Torah or history books have attributed to them.

They were two honorable and infallible Prophets, incapable of doing what Allah forbade.

The Noble Qur'an mentions David and Solomon- peace be upon them- in many verses. Most of these verses describe the multitude of blessings that Allah granted them. In Sura Al-Anbya, the Almighty says:

"And remember when David and Solomon passed judgment regarding the crops ruined at night by someone's sheep, and We were witness to their judgments. We guided young Solomon to a fairer settlement, and granted each of them wisdom and knowledge. We subjected the mountains as well as the birds to hymn Our praises along with David. It is We Who did it all. We taught him the art of making body armor to protect you in battle. Will you then be grateful? And to Solomon We subjected the raging winds, blowing by his command to the land We had showered with blessings. It is We Who know everything. And We subjected some jinn that dived for him, and performed other duties. It is We Who kept them in check." (Qur'an 21:78-82)

The meaning of these noble verses: Remember, Muhammed, the story of David and Solomon- peace be upon them- as they were passing "judgement regarding the crops". It was believed to be bunches of grapes. These crops were ruined at night by sheep that were without a shepherd. "We were witness to their judgments" and "We guided ⌜young⌝ Solomon." In other words, we showed Solomon how to judge.

Imam Ibn Kathir's interpretation of these verses can be summed up as follows:

"Some sheep spoilt the crops of other people. David- peace be upon him- said to them that he would bring the necks of the sheep to the owners of the crops. They left David and went to Solomon who asked how David would settle the situation. They told him his judgement. Solomon said that if he were to judge between them, he would judge differently: he would have been kinder to the two parties. When this came to David- peace be upon him- he called Solomon and asked how he would settle the issue. Solomon said that he would give the sheep to the owner of the crops to benefit from their young, milk and wool, and the owner of the sheep would plant for the owner of the crops the same way as he would plant for himself. When the crops become ripe and ready, he would give them to his friend and take his sheep back. David said: The judgement is as you decreed, and so it was."[73]

The listener may misunderstand His Almighty's "We were witness to their judgments" and think that David- peace be upon him- was not completely willing to judge after him. The saying is immediately followed by He "granted each of them wisdom and knowledge. "In other words, Almighty Allah granted both David and Solomon the ability to judge between people and the knowledge to direct them along the right path.

"We subjected the mountains as well as the birds to hymn ⌜Our praises⌝ along with David." The mountains and the birds sing Allah's praises with David. It could be the sound of real singing or Allah is endowing them with the capacity to sing in a way that only David could understand.

The honorable Sheikh Hasaneen Mahkloof said: it is one of the miracles just like the pebbles sang in the palm of the Messenger of Allah (SAW) and the people heard.

And His saying: "It is We Who did it all means that We did this subjecting of the mountains and the birds. Even though it might be strange to you, We did it.

Then the Almighty Allah revealed other blessings he bestowed upon David- peace be upon him. He said: "We taught him the art of making body armour" and He showed that the purpose for this teaching was "to protect you in battle" if they were to go to war. So, will you then be grateful for this blessing? The question here implies a command. In other words, you should thank Allah for these blessings. It is in the form of a question to urge them to be thankful and grateful.

Then Almighty Allah revealed some of His blessings He granted Solomon: And to Solomon We subjected the raging winds, blowing by his command, as he wished, to the land We had showered with blessings, which was the Levant.

It is We Who know everything. We run everything with sound counsel and good judgement according to Our wisdom and will.

And ⌜We subjected⌝ some jinn that dived for him. Some Jinn dive into the sea for Solomon to extract pearls and corals, and they performed other duties such as build castles and statues. It is We Who kept them in check," so they could not disobey him or fail to follow his commands.

These are some of verses that recount the blessings that Allah granted to David and Solomon- peace be upon them. We mention them because of our explanation concerning their time which was considered the Golden Age for the Children of Israel. There are many more verses in the Noble Qur'an that relate the blessings that Allah bestowed upon these two honorable prophets. We will postpone talking about them now to look at the conditions of the Children of Israel after that era.

D- Their history after the death of Solomon- peace be upon him- until the first destruction of Jerusalem in 586 BC:

Solomon- peace be upon him- died approximately in 975 BC.[74] After that the second era- for the kings who governed the Children of Israel- started. The first era for the kings of the Children of Israel started with Saul and ended with the death of Solomon- peace be upon him. After the death of Solomon, peace be upon him, his son Rehoboam declared himself king of the children of Israel, and the tribes of Judah and Benjamin, who were residing in the area of Jerusalem and its environs to southern Palestine, pledged allegiance to him. Rehoboam then headed towards Shechem[75] (also spelled Sichem) to get the allegiance of the other tribes, but they refused to pledge allegiance to him. Their elders assembled around him and asked him to give up his viciousness and cruelty, but he talked harshly and threatened them saying: "I will scourge you with scorpions."[76]

Thus, the Kingdom of the Children of Israel was divided into two kingdoms after the death of Solomon:

1- The Kingdom of Judah in the south and its capital was Jerusalem and its first king was Rehoboam. Twenty kings ruled after him. The kingdom lasted until 586 BC when it fell to Nebuchadnezzar, the Babylonian. So, this Kingdom lasted almost 4 centuries. The following is a list of its kings in the order they ruled, the period of time they ruled and the year they became kings.

King	Years of Reign	Ascension Year
1) Rehoboam, son of Solomon	17 years	975 BC
2) Abijam, son of Rehoboam	3 years	958 BC
3) Asa, son of Rehoboam	41 years	955 BC
4) Jehosaphat	35 years	914 BC
5) Jehoram, son of Jehosaphat	8 years	888 BC
6) Ahaziah, son of Jehoram	1 year	885 BC
7) Athaliah, son of Ahaziah	6 years	884 BC
8) Jehoash, son of Ahaziah	40 years	878 BC
9) Amaziah, son of Jehoash	39 years	847 BC
10) Uzziah, son of Amaziah	51 years	808 BC
11) Jotham, son Uzziah	16 years	757 BC
12) Ahaz, son of Manasseh	15 years	741 BC
13) Hezekiah, son of Ahaz	29 years	726 BC

14) Manasseh, son of Hezekiah	55 years	697 BC
15) Amon, son of Manasseh	2 years	642 BC
16) Josiah, son of Amon	31 years	640 BC
17) Jehoahaz, son of Josiah	3 months	609 BC
18) Jehoiakim, son of Josiah	11 years	609 BC
19) Jehoiachin, son of Jehoiakim	3 months	598 BC
20) Zedekiah, son of Jehoiakim	21 years	586 BC

Zedekiah was the last King in the Kingdom of Judah. It was during his reign that this kingdom came to an end at the hands of Nebuchadnezzar.

2- The Kingdom of Israel in the north and its capital most of its days was Shechem. The first king who ruled it was Jeroboam, and around 19 kings reigned it after him. It lasted approximately 250 years and was destroyed by Sargon II, the Assyrian King, in 721 BC.

King	Years of Reign	Ascension Year
1) Jeroboam, of Nevat	32 years	975 BC
2) Nadab, son of Jeroboam	2 years	953 BC
3) Baasha, son of Achiyah	22 years	952 BC
4) Elah, son of Bashaa	2 years	930 BC
5) Zimri	7 days	930 BC
6) Omri	7 years	929 BC
7) Ahab, son of Omri	24 years	922 BC
8) Ahaziah, son of Ahab	2 years	898 BC
9) Joram, son of Ahab	12 years	896 BC
10) Yeho, son of Yehoshafat	28 years	884 BC
11) Jehoahaz, son Jeho	17 years	856 BC
12) Jehoash, son of Jehoahaz	41 years	840 BC
13) Jeroboam II	31 years	800 BC
14) Zachariah, son of Jeroboam	6 months	770 BC
15) Shallum, son of Yavesh	1 month	770 BC
16) Menachem, son of Gadi	10 years	769 BC
17) Pekahiah, son of Menachem	2 years	760 BC
18) Pekah, son of Remalyahu	28 years	758 BC
19) Hoshea, son of Elah	8 years	729 BC

Hoshea son of Ela was the last of its kings for it came to an end during his reign at the hands of the Assyrian King Sargon II.

1 Kings, 2 Kings and 2 Chronicles record many of the events that took place in the Kingdoms of Judah and Israel. They relate their internal and external conditions, the discords, conflicts, civil wars and unrest they went through, the religious aberrations and

immoralities they experienced, and the external incursions and raids to which they were exposed.

We will now outline our account of these two kingdoms in two points:

First: We will give an account of the relationship between the two kingdoms and their internal affairs.

Second: We will give an account of their relations with neighboring countries.

First point:
Since their division, the relationship between the two kingdoms became worse. 1 Kings relates that the wars between Rehoboam and Jeroboam continued and that the discord between the two kingdoms reached a point in which Jeroboam, the King of the of Israel, molded two calves of gold and told his people: 'These are your Gods that brought you out of Egypt. Offer them your sacrifices and celebrate your feasts here, and do not go to Jerusalem.' The people did as he had asked them to do. He did this to avoid the consequences of his people going to Jerusalem and to avoid the impact that Rehoboam's propaganda might have on them." [77]

The wars and discords between the two kingdoms lasted most of the days of their existence. It reached a point in which each one of them would seek the help of another country or countries to destroy the other kingdom. Judah's King, Asa son of Rehoboam, sought the assistance of the King of Damascus to kill Baasha son of Achiyah, King of Israel. These same acts were also performed by other kings from the two kingdoms.

The author of the History of the Israelites describes the wars and conflicts between the two kingdoms: "Many wars and conflicts took place between the two kingdoms because of the rivalry and competition between their kings and the lack of a consistent policy of governance in each kingdom. Those kings would sometimes go hand in hand to fight together in solidarity. However, that spirit of competition would still be ingrained and divisive between them. That was because the kings of Israel feared that their subjects would abandon them and go to the kings of Judah to worship in the Temple of Jerusalem. Therefore, some of those kings took great measures to have their subjects abandon that habit by all means possible. They would sometimes mold idols for them to worship. At other times, they would forcefully forbid their subjects from observing the rituals of worshipping.

Thus, all aspects of unity and harmony disintegrated and crumbled. Discord and disagreement worsened. Consequently, the two kingdoms weakened. Enemies and invaders vanquished one kingdom after the other.[78]

Corruption ran rampant in the two kingdoms. Internal disturbances and turbulence became widespread during many of the eras of these kingdoms. However, the Kingdom of Judah- in general- was in a better shape than the Kingdom of Israel. In this respect, Mr. Muhammad Izzat Darwaza says:

“The state of Israel had the most tribes. It was more spacious than the state of Judah. However, its people, kings and subjects alike, diverted from the right path ever since the establishment of their state. They continued their perverseness and depravity until the end of the state. Many upheavals and coups took place in the state of Israel. That led to the shedding of blood and eliminating whole ruling families for the sake of grabbing power and authority. Even the capital changed many times because of these disturbances. “Shechem” (Nablus) was the capital at first. Then it was changed to “Tirza” then to “Shamer” which was close to Shechem and where a village named Sebastia exists in its place today. It was renovated during the Roman era. It was also named by the Romans. The state of Judah, on the other hand, was in a better shape- in general- than the state of Israel from the stability and righteousness perspectives. Some books in the Torah recount that its kings made considerable efforts in a variety of fields. These accounts also hint at the power, riches and glory that its kings enjoyed. Yet, they also reported the depravity and injustices that many of its kings committed. The periods of aberrations and deviations were longer than those of righteousness and uprightness. The chain of the kings of Judah continued in the offspring of Solomon- peace be upon him. As for the Kingdom of Israel, many kings from various tribes ruled it.” [79]

We now start discussing the second issue:

The relationship of the two Kingdoms with other countries was- in general- characterized by hostilities and wars.

1- During the era of Rehoboam and Jeroboam, Egypt’s Pharoah, Sheshonq, invaded Palestine (sic; Judah/Judea, and Israel). He marched towards Jerusalem and plundered it. He gained control over the Kingdom of Judah. After that he controlled the Kingdom of Israel and his dominion reached to Al-Galeel (Galilee). [80a]

2- In the year 740 BC, Tiglath-Pileser III, the Assyrian King, invaded the Kingdom of Israel. The King of the Kingdom of Israel, Menahem, son of Gadi, gave him one thousand loads of silver to leave him as king, and Tiglath-Pileser III accepted.

3- In 727 BC, Shalmaneser III ascended the Assyrian throne, and Israel revolted against him. He marched towards it, but Hoshea, son of Elah, the last king of Israel, presented many gifts to him. The Assyrian King accepted the presents, and marched back to his country. However, no sooner had he reached Nineveh than the Israelites resumed their disobedience and rebellion. He marched back to them and imposed a great siege around Samaria, their capital. He died before conquering it, though.

4- In 721 BC, his successor, Sargon II, invaded the Kingdom of Israel. He besieged and encircled the city from all sides. A battle ensued between them, and it ended in the complete demise of the Kingdom of Israel. Sargon took the tribes as captives and sent them away from their country to beyond the Euphrates. He appointed an Assyrian deputy.

Thus, the Kingdom of Israel was completely eradicated in 731 BC.

5- Sargon's son, Ashur-Akhi-Adan, was able to assert his control over the Levant- including the Kingdom of Judah- after his father. Judah was still within the boundaries of its borders after the elimination of the Kingdom of Israel, whose provinces were under the administration of the Assyrians. King of Judah, Manasseh, son of Hezekiah, offered gifts to please Ashur-Akhi-Adan. However, he later rebelled against the Assyrians. Ashur-Akhi-Adan attacked him and subjugated the Kingdom of Judah to Assyria. Manasseh was led as a captive in shackles to Babylon where he once again pledged allegiance and promised obedience. He was reinstated on his throne. That was in 677 BC.

6- In 610 BC, Egypt's Pharaoh, Necho, seized the chance of the disintegration of the Kingdom of Assyria. He gathered his army and marched to invade it. Josiah, son of Amon, King of Judah, intercepted him, but Josiah was defeated and killed. Necho continued his journey with his army towards the Levant. Many of its cities fell to his hands. He continued his march until he reached the Euphrates. When news that the Jews had once again rebelled and became resistant, he went back and disciplined them. He dethroned their King and appointed another one in his place.

7- It was at the hands of the Babylon Nebuchadnezzar that the Kingdom of Judah came to an end. Nebuchadnezzar, King of Babylon, invaded Jerusalem in 606 BC and plundered and ransacked it. He dislocated and drove many of its inhabitants. He captured Jehoiachin, son of Jehoiakim, its King at the time, and he banished him along with a large number of his women and family members. He appointed Zedekiah, son of Jehoiakim, in his place. Zedekiah, however, rebelled against him. Nebuchadnezzar invaded Jerusalem once again in 599 BC and, this time, he deported tens of thousands of their nobles and chiefs to Babylon. He also looted the treasures of the Temple and royal mansions. Once again, Zedekiah declared his rebellion for the second time in 593 BC. Nebuchadnezzar marched with his army to Jerusalem, for the third time, in 586 BC. This time, he brutally killed Zedekiah along with his children and other members of his family. He demolished the city of Jerusalem, its walls and its Temple. He set fire to the city, plundered its treasures and drove the people of Judah as captives to Babylon. They remained in captivity there for 50 years during which time Jerusalem remained in a state of destruction and desolation.

Thus, the Kingdom of Judah came to an end in 586 BC just as its sister, the Kingdom of Israel, came to an end in 721 BC.

Mr. Muhammad Izzat Darwaza describes the relationship of the two Kingdoms with other countries: "It seems that the relationship of the two Kingdoms with other states was characterized by hostility, animosity, uncertainty, disloyal and treacherous, or took the form of humility, subjugation and self-effacement. And it is also evident that the other states dealt with them in the same fashion. They dealt with them in the same way. Therefore, throughout their existence, these two Kingdome were constantly in a state of hostility and wars with other states. They were subject to invasions and raids and the consequent subjugation and suppression of other nations. All of this ended in the demolition and destruction of their kingdoms and their deportation and expulsion from their country because the Assyrians and the Chaldeans saw that that was the most decisive remedy because of the treachery, disloyalty, tricks and deceit they suffered because of them."[81]

A western writer describes the end of the two Kingdoms:
"The Hebrews did not enjoy a state of luxury except for a short time. Hiram died, and the assistance that was provided by Tyre- and that sustained and strengthened Jerusalem- came to an end. Egypt became strong once again. The history of the kings of Judah and Israel was nothing but a history of two small states in the middle of adversity, subsequently exposed to hostilities from Syria and Babylon from the north and Egypt from the south. It was a story of calamities and disasters, a story of freedoms and autonomies that only postpone the inevitable: the complete and final blow, the deadly demise. It was the story of barbarian kings ruling barbarian subjects until 721 BC when the Assyrians completely wiped out the Kingdom of Israel and its people from history. The Kingdom of Judah continued to struggle until the Babylonians ended it in 586 BC."[82]

Wells describes the condition of the two Kingdoms:
"The life of the Hebrews in Palestine was like a man insisting on residing in an overcrowded path. He was thus constantly run over by trucks and buses... From the very beginning and until the end, their Kingdoms were nothing but an incidental occurrence in the history of Egypt, Syria, Assyria and Phenicia, whose history was far greater and more splendid than theirs."[83]

Thus far, we have presented the condition of the two Kingdoms: Judah and Israel ever since their inception until their demise. Now let us look at what happened to the Children of Israel after that!

E- Their history from the first destruction of Jerusalem to its second destruction at the hands of the Roman Emperor, Titus. in the year 70 AD.

Many countries ruled over Palestine ever since its first destruction at the hands of Nebuchadnezzar to its second destruction at the hands of the Romans.

These countries ruled Palestine according to the following order:

1- The Babylonians from 586 to 538 BC
2- The Persians from 538 to 330 BC
3- The Greeks from 330 to 323 BC
4- The Ptolemies from 323 to 200 BC
5- The Seleucids from 200 to 167 BC
6- The Seleucids and the Maccabees from 167 to 63 BC
7- The Romans from 63 BC to 614 AD

The following is a short outline for each of these periods:

1- After the fall of Jerusalem at the hands of Nebuchadnezzar in 586 BC, there were virtually no Jews in Palestine. They lived for almost 50 years as captives in exile in Babylon. There, they adopted many of their doctrines and lifestyles. They had jobs and assumed responsibilities under the supervision of the Babylonians.

During this period- as indicated in some of the Books of the Torah- many prophets, preachers and ministers came to the Children of Israel. The Books of Jeremiah, Ezra, Nehemiah, Esther, Ezekiel and Daniel abound with preaching and forewarnings directed by these prophets to the Children of Israel during this period.

2- In 538 BC, the King of Persia, Cyrus the Great, overtook Babylon. He was kind to the Jews and treated them extremely well because he was brought up in the tender care of Esther who was a Jew. Cyrus issued a decree announcing that the Jews could go back to Jerusalem and rebuild their Temple. He helped by providing them with money and men.

However, most of the Jews had become accustomed to the luxurious lifestyle in Babylon. They enjoyed the easy living, affluence and the profitable commerce that life provided there. That is why they were reluctant to go back to Jerusalem and most of those who returned were from the tribe of Judah and Benjamin.

"The return of the Jews from exile was the return of the people, not the state. The Children of Israel returned, but their state did not. They had become subjects of the Persian rule and were governed by the Persians. Still, the skirmishes between them and their Persian rulers never ceased."[84]

During their dominion and control over Palestine, many Persian kings ruled. Among them were Cambises, Komata, Dariash I, Dariash II, and Dariash III. During their rule, the Persian kings would appoint deputies to govern Palestine. Oftentimes, the Persian king would appoint a Jew to govern under the supervision of the Persians. For example, the Persian King Loghiamanus appointed Ezra, a Jew, as a governor over Jerusalem in 445 BC.

3- In 330 BC, there was a war between Alexander the Macedonian and the Persians under the leadership of Darius III, their King. The war ended with the victory of Alexander and the defeat of the Persians and driving them away from the Levant. The Levant- including Palestine- became under the control of Alexander of Macedon.

Some books in the Torah and some history books relate that during his reign Alexander treated the Jews well and that he visited Jerusalem and the Temple.

4- After the death of Alexander in 323 BC, his great empire was divided amongst his chief commanders. Palestine fell to Ptolemy I, King of Egypt, and the Ptolemaic rule over Palestine lasted until 200 BC.

Ptolemy I, ruled from 323 to 285 BC. During this time, many wars and conflicts took place between him and neighboring countries. He was able to overcome all of his enemies. He was also able to gain power over Jerusalem after the Jews declared their rebellion against him. He led more than one hundred thousand of them as captives to Egypt.

Ptolemy II reigned after him from 285 to 247 BC. Palestine remained under his control. He treated the Jews fairly allowing 120 thousand who lived in Egypt to return to Judaism.

The author of the History of the Israelites says: "Ptolemy II was the founder of the famous library of Alexandria which historians claim that the Arabs burned after the conquest of Egypt."[85]

Mr. Muhammad Izzat Darwaza says: "Ptolemy II asked Eliezer, the High Priest, to send him seventy-two Jewish Sheikhs (elders)- six from each of the twelve tribes- to translate the five books of Moses into Greek. Eliezer was at the head of those elders. The mission was accomplished in seventy-two days. This is what is known as the Septuagint, the translation of the Hebrew Bible (five books) into Greek." [86]

Ptolemy III succeeded him. He ruled Egypt and Palestine from 247 to 222 BC. Bishop Debs mentions that "Adina, the High Priest of Jerusalem- failed to pay the Jizya for some years during the era of Ptolemy III. The Jizya was 20 loads annually. Ptolemy III sent someone to Jerusalem to force the Jews to pay the jizya. He threatened them with deportation if they did not pay. Concern and apprehension prevailed in Jerusalem. The

Jews sent an intelligent man to Ptolemy III, and he was able to convince him to exempt the Jews from most of the taxes that accrued." [87]

During the reign of Ptolemy IV which lasted almost from 222 to 202 BC, wars were waged between him and Antiochus III, the Seleucid King of Syria. Antiochus was victorious. He went to Jerusalem and humiliated the Jews. A little while later, Ptolemy IV was able to avenge himself against Antiochus. He drove him out of Palestine (Judea/Israel) and restored it to his rule. However, the Seleucids were able to take Palestine (Judea/Israel) back to their fold in 200 BC, and they gained victory over Ptolemy V.

5- From 200 to 167 BC, the Seleucids were able to keep Palestine (Judea/Israel) under their control. They treated the Jews harshly and brutally. They exerted great effort to convert the Jews away from their Jewish social and religious traditions to adopt and observe Greek traditions. The Seleucid Wali (governor) Athenaeus, built a Greek idol in the Temple of Jerusalem and offered sacrifices to it. He kept on inviting the Jews to participate in the Greek rituals, and he severely punished those who refused to respond to his instructions and teachings. Many Jews accepted his teachings and started abandoning their religion and traditions and observe Greek rituals and traditions.

In sum, during their reign, the Seleucids demeaned and humiliated the Jews and sought to seek vengeance against them in the most horrible ways possible.

6- This harsh and cruel treatment that the Jews received at the hands of the Seleucids led to a revolution from a group of Jewish priests known in history as the Maccabees.[88] Their revolution took place around 166 BC.

Mattathias, A Jewish priest, was in charge of this revolution along with his five children: John, Simon, Judah, Eleazar, and Jonathan.

The books of the Maccabees relate that Mattathias immigrated with his children to a city called Modeen.[89] He was extremely sorrowful and sad for what had befallen Jerusalem. When messengers from the Seleucid king later came to coerce the inhabitants to spurn and deride the laws of the Torah, Mattathias refused to obey. He then jumped and attacked one of the king's messengers and killed him. Then he went into the mountains and said: "Whoever loves and wants to preserve the Law, let him follow me." A great multitude followed him. That was a declaration of the revolution."[90]

After the death of Mattathias, his son Judah took charge of the rebels. He confronted Apollonius, the leader of the Seleucids, in a fierce battle which ended with the victory of Judah and his followers.

Many more battles between Judah and the Seleucids followed, and Judah was able to capture Jerusalem in 165 BC.

In 161 BC, the Seleucids were able to conquer and vanquish Judah and his followers. They restored Jerusalem to their control. However, the Maccabees continued their revolt against the Seleucids.

In 104 BC, the Maccabee leader Aristobulus was able to become king, but his rule did not last long. Confrontations between him and his brother, Antigonus, led to the demise of both. The Maccabees were able to control Jerusalem for a period of time. They were also able to enjoy some semblance of independence. Yet, their independence was mostly under the control of the Seleucids. It was also an independence that was subject to- and governed by- changing conditions.

What aided the Maccabees to succeed during some of these periods was the conflicts that arouse between the Seleucids and the Ptolemaists, on the one hand, and between the Seleucid leaders themselves, on the other.

The revolutions of the Maccabees revealed instances of bravery and courage. However, not all the Jews were committed to these revolutions. On many occasions and by all means possible, a lot of Jews conspired against these revolutions and the men participating in them. Also, in the Maccabee revolution itself, cooperation did not last long between the individuals participating in it. Oftentimes they would divide, turn and wage wars against each other.

In 63 BC, a conflict over the throne between Hyrcanus, the Maccabee, and his brother, Aristobulus, arouse. The Romans seized that chance and used it to spread their influence to Palestine (Judea/Israel). Pompey, the Roman leader, came for that reason. He came with his army to Damascus and waited there to observe how the situation between the two brothers would resolve. Aristobulus and Hyrcanus went to him and offered him precious gifts, each asking him to be appointed king. However, Pompey refused and ordered them both to submit to him. Aristobulus refused to follow Pompey's order and sought refuge in Jerusalem. Pompey besieged him until he forced him to submit and surrender.

The priests were determined to resist and fight Pompey. They sought shelter in the Temple. Pompey surrounded them for almost three months until they finally entered the Temple and mercilessly and heartlessly put the Jews to the sword.

Ever since, Palestine (Judea/Israel) became under the Roman rule which lasted until 614 AD.

The following is an account of the Jews and their history since the Romans gained control over Palestine until the second destruction of Jerusalem at the hands of Titus, the Roman, in 70 AD.

7- During the period extending from 63 BC to 70 AD in which the Romans ruled Palestine, they would sometimes appoint Jewish deputies who behaved in compliance with the expectations of the Roman Empire.

Oftentimes, however, the Jews would fail to obey the Romans who, in turn, would discipline and punish them with whatever measures they deemed appropriate.

A- In 57 BC, Alexander (son of Aristobulus, the Jew) revolted against the Romans. He made war against his uncle, Hyrcanus, who was appointed as a deputy by the Romans, and he defeated him and entered Jerusalem. Alexander's victory was short lived, for the Romans sent Gabinios, one of their leaders, to discipline him. Gabinios marched to Jerusalem and defeated Alexander. When Alexander realized that the only option for him was to surrender, he asked the Roman leader to spare his life, and he accepted. He restored Hyrcanus to govern in Jerusalem.
B- In the same year, Alexander's father, Aristobulus, was able to escape from Rome with one of his children. When he reached Jerusalem, a big number of Jews joined him, and declared war on the Romans. The Roman leader, Gabinios, crushed them, killed most of the Jews who joined Aristobulus, and captured him and sent him as captive to Rome for the second time.
C- In 49 BC, Alexander, son of Aristobulus, attempted once again to revolt against the Romans, but the Wali (governor) of Syria (who was appointed by the Romans) captured and killed him most viciously in Antioch.
D- In 37 BC, with the help of some of the rebels, Antigonus, son of Aristobulus, had been able to rule over Jerusalem. The Romans prepared an army to discipline him. They surrounded Jerusalem for six months. They stormed the city and after they entered it, they killed many of its inhabitants, plundered their possessions, captured Antigonus, led him as captive to the Roman Ceaser who killed him.

With Antigonus' death, the Maccabee state was completely eradicated. Antigonus was their last leader.

But, did the Jews stop their revolts and rebellions against the Romans?

The author of the History of the Israelites states: "The Jews were not content after they became governed by the Romans. It was hard for them to accept that the Romans occupied the capital of their kingdom and their holy Temple. Sometimes they would threaten the Walis (governors). At other times, they would kick the Roman soldiers out of Jerusalem. And at other times, they would show contentment and satisfaction with the rule of the Romans. Many Roman governors ruled over them. They brutally punished and harshly treated them, so they sent their grievances to Rome. When their pleas went unheeded, they feigned rebellion and caused excessive unrest and disturbance. Rome sent its experienced and skillful leader, Vespasianus, who besieged Jerusalem, fought the Jews, and continued to fight against them until the Romans elected him Emperor. Titus, his son, succeeded him in surrounding and killing the Jews. Titus was also a skillful, knowledgeable and proficient leader. He had also suffered a lot from the Jews. He persevered in the fight against them. He brought his best- and well-known soldiers. The Jews were divided amongst themselves; there were many disagreements and disputes between their leaders. They became weak and disintegrated. Titus attacked them forcibly and dispersed them. He marched on Jerusalem and completely destroyed and demolished it. Almost one million Jew died during that siege, and blood flew like rivers.

He continues to say: The history of the Israelites as a nation ends here. For after the second destruction of Jerusalem at the hands of Titus, the Jews were scattered all over, and their history during the ages is appended to the history of the kingdoms in which they inhabited. They suffered all kinds of torture and calamities during their sojourn. The Romans forbade them from entering Jerusalem."[91]

Josephus[92], a Jew who was also contemporaneous to these events, describes what befell Jerusalem at the hands of Titus, the Roman. The following is a brief statement of his description:

Titus' siege of Jerusalem lasted for a long time. All the food therein had been consumed. The inhabitants were forced to eat carcasses and organisms that creep on earth. Many people perished because of hunger. The living busied themselves with their own concerns and left the dead without burial. The houses and streets were filled with corpses and decomposed bodies... Thousands of people would go to the Romans without being prevented. They would swallow the gold and silver they had and later get it from their stool after they arrived at the Romans. When news reached the Romans, they would kill them to get the gold and silver they had in their bellies. Finally, the Romans were able to break through the walls of Jerusalem, and they entered the city, killed the Jews and destroyed whatever they found on their way. Thus was Jerusalem destroyed, and the Temple was demolished for the second time. The Jews perished in the city; they were either killed or died of hunger. Some of them killed each other, and some died at the hands of the Romans." [93]

Titus' destruction of Jerusalem took place in 70 AD. After that destruction, those Jews who remained alive fled to neighboring countries like Egypt, Cyprus, Libya and the Arabian Peninsula.

The following is a detailed account of those Jews who fled from the face of Titus and went to the Arab Peninsula.

Topic # 3

Third: The Jews of the Arabian Peninsula & Their Social and Religious Conditions

By "the Jews of the Arabian Peninsula" we mean those who inhabited the Medina and its outskirts like Banu Qaynuqa, Banu Nadir and Banu Qurayza. We also mean the Jews of Khaybar, Tamim and Wadi Al-Qura.

Our account of the Jews of the Arabian Peninsula will treat the following issues:

A- The opinions of historians concerning the time of their arrival to the Arabian Peninsula.
B- Their ethnic background, their dwellings and their economic and social conditions.
C- Their religious conditions and their holy books.
D- Their relationship with Banu Aws and the Khazraj

Concerning the first point we say:

A- There is a lot of disagreement amongst historians concerning the time in which the Jews immigrated to the Arabian Peninsula. Some believe that they immigrated to it during the era of David, peace be upon him. Others see that they went there during the time of King Ezekiel who ruled Judah from 717 to 690 BC.

These two opinions are not historically verifiable. For this reason, cautious and meticulous historians did not rely on these accounts.

What historians find acceptable is the view that the great immigration of the Jews to the Arabian Peninsula took place during the first century after the Romans maltreated and abused them in 70 AD.

That does not negate the fact that there were some Jews who lived in the Arabian Peninsula before that time.

Dr. Israel Wolfensohn says: "After the war between the Jews and the Romans in 70 AD which ended in the demolition of Palestine, the destruction of the Temple and the scattering of the Jews to different parts of the world, a great number of Jews went to Arab countries as mentioned by Josephus, the Jewish historian, who witnessed these wars and was a leader to some of the army units."

He continues: "Arabic sources confirm this. The author of Al-Aghani mentions that when the Romans appeared against the Children of Israel in the Levant, they killed them and raped their women. The tribes of Banu Nadir Banu Qurayza, and Banu Yahadal fled to the Hijaz. The Romans followed them, and they died of thirst and hunger in the gap between the Levant and the Hijaz, which was a desert land without food and water, a place that was called Thamad al-Rum. It is called that until today."[94]

Dr. Gawad Ali is also favors the view that the immigration of the Jews to the Arabian Peninsula took place after being invaded by the Romans:

"What has been mentioned- concerning the immigration of the Jews to Yathrib and the Hijaz following the appearance of the Romans in the Levant and the killings and massacres that forced them to flee to distant places away from the Romans-is confirmed by sound historical evidence. What we know is that the Roman conquest of Palestine led to the immigration of a large number of the Jews. Therefore, it is very plausible that the Jews of the Hijaz were the offspring of those immigrants. The tribes of Banu Qurayza, Banu Nadir and Banu Yahadal were among those immigrants. They marched to the south in the direction of Yathrib. When they reached the place of the forest, they found it detestable, and they hated to stay there. They sent a surveyor to explore and find a decent place and fertile land for them. When he reached (Al-Aliyya), which are Wadi Bathan and Wadi Mahzur, two valleys with clean water and springs, they decided to settle there. Banu Nadir and their companions settled in Bathan, and Banu Qurayza and Banu Yahadal settled in Mahzur."[95]

Thus, we believe that the view which is the closest to the truth is that the majority of the Jews of the Arabian Peninsula came to it in the first century, that is, after the second destruction of Jerusalem at the hands of Titus, the Roman. The most important reason for them to go there was to flee from the Romans and save themselves from their viciousness and brutality.

B- As regards the second point:

Some writers believe that the Jews of the Hijaz descend from Arab tribes that converted to Judaism and not from the Children of Israel. This can be corroborated by the fact that most of their names and the names of their tribes are Arabic names such as Rifa'a, Wahab, Ka'ab, Zaid, Abdallah... etc. and Banu Nadir, Banu Awf, Banu Tha'labah...etc.

We refute this view and say: The Noble Qur'an addressed the Jews in many verses as "O Children of Israel." In various places in the Qur'an, they are referred to with this phrase, or the Jews or those who turned to Judaism. In many of the verses, a connection was made between the moral standards of the Jews who were contemporary with the Prophet-(SAW)- and the standards of their forefathers who descended from Moses, Issa (Jesus) and other prophets, and their disbelief, aggression and hostility against the prophets who came to guide them to the righteous path. In Sura Al-Baqarah: "O children of Israel! Remember My favors upon you. Fulfil your covenant and I will fulfil Mine, and stand in awe of Me alone. Believe in My revelations which confirm your Scriptures. Do not be the first to deny them or trade them for a fleeting gain. And be mindful of Me." (Qur'an 2:40-41) And in Sura An-Nisa: "We forbade the Jews certain foods that had been lawful to them for their wrongdoing, and for hindering many from the Way of Allah." (Qur'an 4:160) And in Sura Al-Baqarah: "Ask the Children of Israel how many clear signs We have given them. And whoever trades Allah's favor—after receiving it—ʳfor disbeliefˀ should know that Allah is indeed severe in punishment." (Qur'an 2:211)

These noble verses- and others- help us assert that those Jews who resided in Medina and its outskirts were from the Children of Israel, not from an Arabic origin. Addressing them in such a way indicates that they were the offspring of those forefathers who harmed Moses, Jesus and other prophets, peace be upon them.

In addition, during the prophetic era, the Jews had their own neighborhoods and villages, Hebrew was the language of communication among them and they also had their own rituals, schools and synagogues that were particularly theirs, not to be shared with others. They even regarded Judaism, their religion, restricted to them alone.

Mr. Muhammad Izzat Darwaza provides a detailed account on this topic. We sum up what he says: In the Hijaz there were no Arab tribes that turned to Judaism. It is possible, however, that some Arab individuals might have turned to Judaism, even though there is no valid evidence to confirm this. And naming tribes as Banu Nadir, Banu Qurayza, or Banu Qaynuqa cannot be held as evidence. What this naming indicates is that the Israelites adopted names and phrases that were appropriate with the environment in which they stayed for lengthy periods of time. Moreover, these Arabic names with which some Jews were named are oftentimes followed by the Israeli names of the parents as in Abdallah ben Souriyya, Tha'labba ben She'ah, Rifa'a ben Yazid ben A-Taboot and No'maan ben Ad'a.

We can even go farther and say that in all of the Arabian Peninsula- especially in Yemen- there were no Arabic Jewish masses during the time of the Prophet, (SAW). The reports that state that some Jews in the Hijaz were able to spread Judaism in the Yemen during the Al-Tuba' era are without merit and lack solid evidence. Ancient books and chronicles never suggested that there were Jews in Yemen during the time of the Prophet, (SAW). Neither did they mention that Omar- may Allah be pleased with him- drove Jews out of Yemen when he drove Arab Christians out of Najran/Yemen to fulfill the Prophet's commandment that the Arabian Peninsula Should not have two religions. Abu Ubaida- may Allah be pleased with him- related that the last words the Prophet said were his directive to send the Jews of the Hijaz and the Christians of Najran of Yemen out of the Arabian Peninsula. This indicates that there were no Jews in Yemen during the time of the Prophet- (SAW)- but there were some remaining in the Hijaz.[96]

This shows us that the Jews of the Peninsula were from a Jewish origin. They were sporadic and random groups when they were driven out of Medina and its outskirts. They did not leave any original or impressive landmarks that the residents of these places can attest to or vouch for.

As for the dwelling places of the Jews: some were inside Medina, some were close to it, and some were far away from it.

Banu Qaynuqa lived inside Medina in a section that they considered theirs after their brothers Banu Nadir and Banu Qurayza drove them out of their dwellings that were outside Medina.

Banu al-Nadir's dwelling places were in Al-A'liyya in the valley of Bathan, two or three miles away from Medina, a place with plenty of palm trees and vegetations.

Banu Qurayza lived in the valley of Mahzur which is a few miles south of Medina.

There were many other small Jewish tribes that lived in Medina and its outskirts such as Banu Ikrimah, Banu Tha'labah, Banu Muhammar, Banu Za'ura, Banu Awf, Banu Hadal, Banu al-Qusis and others. These small tribes followed the policies of the bigger ones such as Banu Qaynuqa, Nanu al-Nadir and Banu Qurayza.

Dr. Jawad Ali states: "Banu Qurayza and Banu al-Nadir were known as the 'Two Priests.' They were thus called because of their lineage to their grandfather who was called 'the Priest.' He was son of Aaron, son of Amran, according to some chroniclers. Therefore, they were from a noble descent in which they took great pride and gave them the excuse to feel superior to others of the same religion."[97]

Banu Khaybar lived some distance away from Medina in the direction of the Levant. The Jews of Khaybar were known for their wealth and affluence because of the richness of their fertile soil and the great number of farms and orchards they had. They were also known for their enormous and gigantic fortresses and strongholds.

Close to them other Jewish tribes-such as Wadi al-Qura, Tamim and Fadak- lived. In general, the dwellings of the Jews were known for their isolation and sturdiness. They built them like that to give them the protection they needed at times of danger, and to use them as a shelter to defend themselves from behind them. The Noble Qur'an pointed to this in His saying: "They would not ⌜dare⌝ fight against you except ⌜from⌝ within fortified strongholds or from behind walls." (Qur'an 59:14) [98]

Among the strongest Jewish fortresses are the Forts of al-Nutah, Al-Saab bin Moaz, Na'am, Al-Zubayer, Al-Watih, Al-Qamous and Al-Salam. They all existed in Khaybar.

Most of those fortresses were also in areas that were fertile and bountiful and at the center of the commercial marine paths and land roads in the Arabian Peninsula.

The Jews worked mostly in trade. Some of them enjoyed great fame like Abi Raf' Salam son of Abi al-Haqeek who was called "the merchant of the people of the Hijaz." We can even say that the trade of dates, barley, wheat and wine was almost controlled by them in the north of the Hijaz. The Jews also worked in agriculture which was the main occupation for those who resided in the villages. They also raised cattle and chicken, and -in certain places such as Maqna- they worked in fishing, and their women worked in weaving fabrics. Among the industries that the Jews of the Arabian Peninsula performed was goldsmithing. Banu Qaynuqa were particularly known for this craft. In addition, they molded and shaped swords, breastplates and many other military tools.

Most of their interactions and dealings with others were based on gambling and usury. The nature of farming allowed them to do so since farmers would usually need to borrow money until harvest time.

The Noble Qur'an (Q 4:161) reprimanded them for their use of usury, a thing which Allah prohibited them from doing. The Almighty says: (We punished the Jews for) "taking interest despite its prohibition, and consuming people's wealth unjustly. We have prepared for the disbelievers among them a painful punishment." [99]

As a consequence of the monopoly of the Jews of the economic aspects in Medina and its outskirts, their financial influence and prestige grew and strengthened. They started to viciously control the markets and use them for their benefits and to serve their own interests. The majority of the people hated them because of their egotism, their inhumanity in taking high interest rates, and their achieving affluence and riches in cunning and crafty ways that an Arab would regard as despicable.

C- We now talk about their religious condition and their Holy Books.

The Jews who inhabited the Arabian Peninsula had schools in which they learned their doctrine, the Law, matters pertaining to their religion, their history, and other particular reports concerning their messengers and prophets. They also had especial places where they would practice and observe their rituals and other forms of worship.

These places were called "Madares" (schools), that is, the places in which the texts of the Torah and other issues pertaining to the Law were taught.

These "Madares" (schools) were not confined to worship, prayers and learning. Rather, they were places wherein the Jews gathered for counsel on various worldly, spiritual and religious matters. These were the places that were frequented by those who wanted to get the counsel of their rabbis and scholars on certain issues.

The Jews' rabbis, learned and all-knowledgeable ones were those who undertook the task of teaching the Jews matters about their religion. At the forefront of those learned ones was Abdallah bin Salam, may Allah be pleased with him- who announced his conversion to Islam after meeting the Messenger of Allah, (SAW). Also, and at the forefront, was Abdallah bin Soriyya al'Awar about whom it was said that no one in the Hijaz was more knowledgeable of the Torah at his time than him.

Verifiable accounts had been obtained that confirm this: After his migration to Medina- the Messenger, (SAW)- would go to the Jews in their madares (schools) to call them to Islam and warn them against disbelief and distrusting him. On the authority of Abu Hurairah, Al-Bukhari said, "While we were in the mosque, the Messenger of Allah would come and say: 'O Jews: come to Islam and you will be safe.' They said: 'You have informed us, Aba al-Kassem.' He said: that is what I want, and he said it again. They said:

You have informed us Aba al-Kassem. The third time, he would say: You should know that the world is Allah's and His messenger."[100]

Also, some of the Companions such as Abu Bakr Al-Siddiq- may Allah be pleased with him- would go to them in that place to command them to follow Mohammad whom they knew to be truthful about his messages about Allah just as they knew their own children.

The Noble Qur'an has recounted many of the religious arguments and obstinate and obdurate questions that the Jews asked the Prophet- (SAW)- for the purpose of embarrassing him and showing him incapable of responding to their questions and incompetent in debating with them. However, the Messenger (SAW) would respond to their question in a manner that would shake their reasoning and shut their mouths. [101]

The Jews also had their own doctrines and laws concerning offerings, punishments, inheritance, confession, purification, slavery, circumcision, marriage, women issues, and other matters. They took some of these regulations and rules from their books. Other rules and regulations were put forth by their rabbis and religious scholars.

An example of this is provided by a quote by Anas concerning what was mentioned in the Hadith: "When a woman menstruates, a Jew would not eat or have intercourse or stay in the same place with her." When the Companions asked the Prophet, Allah revealed (Qur'an 2:222) to him: "They ask you ʿO Prophetʾ about menstruation. Say, "Beware of its harm! So keep away, and do not have intercourse with your wives during their monthly cycles until they are purified.[1] When they purify themselves, then you may approach them in the manner specified by Allah. Surely Allah loves those who always turn to Him in repentance and those who purify themselves."[102] The Messenger of Allah said: "Do everything except intercourse. When the Jews heard of this, they said: that man does not want anything except contradict us on every issue. Aseed bin Hudeir and Abbad bin Basheer came to the Prophet and asked him: Oh, Messenger of Allah! The Jews say so and so. Aren't we supposed to have intercourse? The Prophet's face changed color, and they thought that he was angry with them. When they went out, the Messenger of Allah sent some milk after them to drink, and they knew he was not upset.[103]

They also had their special feasts. The most famous of these are the Harvest Feast, the Great Fast, the Passover which is called the feast of the unleavened Bread...[104] The Jews pay especial attention to this feast because it commemorates the day in which the Children of Israel got out of Egypt escaping from Pharoah and his injustice and cruelty.

The Jews also consider the sabbath as a feast, a day during which they are not supposed to work. Whoever fails to observe the sanctity of this day and defiles it by working has committed a great offense.

The Jews had especial days for fasting such as the Day of Ashura. Al-Bukhari and Muslim ibn Abbas- may Allah be pleased with them- said: "The Messenger of Allah went to Medina and saw the Jews fasting the Day of Ashura and asked what was that day that they were fasting. They said that that was a great day in which Allah saved Moses and his people and caused Pharoah and his men to drown. Moses fasted as an expression of gratitude and thankfulness. We also fast on that day. The Messenger of Allah said: "We are more worthy of Moses than you." He fasted and ordered his followers to fast during this day. He said to his companions: "You are more worthy of Moses than them, so fast on that day."

The Jews claim that the basis of their worship, law, conduct and interactions is what is mentioned in the Torah that the Almighty Allah revealed to Moses, peace be upon him.

Here, we would like to talk in more detail about the Torah, the Books therein, and the aberrations, alterations and changes that found their way to them.

The Torah: It is a Hebrew word which means the Law or religious instructions and directives.

The Jews attest to 39 Books to which they refer as the "Old Testament" to distinguish them from the other Books that Christians corroborate and regard as the "New Testament." It is traditionally the case that the name "Holy Bible" is used to refer to both the books of the Old Testament and those books in the New Testament.

The Jews consider the 39 Books as Holy Books, that is, divinely inspired. They call five of those Books the "Torah" or the Books of Moses because -according to them-Allah revealed them to Moses-peace be upon him- and Moses wrote them himself.

These 5 Books are, the Book of Genesis, the Book of Exodus, the Book of Deuteronomy, the Book of Leviticus, and the Book of Numbers.

1- The Book of Genesis or "the Creation" is thus called because it recounts the story of the creation of the heavens and the earth. It also narrates the story of the creation of Adam and his eating of the tree and subsequent descent to earth. It also gives an account of the story of Noah- peace be upon him- the Flood, and the story of Abraham- peace be upon him- and his children. The Book ends with the story of Joseph- peace be upon him- until his death.

2- The Book of Exodus is so called because it tells the history of the Children of Israel in Egypt, and how they departed from it. It also recounts how they lived after that, their story in the wilderness, and what happened between them and Moses.

3- The Book of Deuteronomy is thus called because it repeats and reiterates the instructions and commands that Allah revealed to Moses- peace be upon him. Most of it revolves around the political, economic and legislative issues pertaining to the Children of Israel.

4- The Book of Leviticus revolves around matters of worship, the instructions, the statutes, the rituals, the feasts and the vows. The Levites are the offspring of Levi, one of the sons of Jacob, peace be upon him. Moses and Aaron were among them. This Book was attributed to the Levites because they were the custodians of the Temple and protectors of the Law. Most of the Book revolves around matters of worship and interactions that they oversaw.

5- As for the book of Numbers, it mostly revolves around the division of the Children of Israel, listing the number of their tribes, their armies, their wealth and their males and females. In addition, it also contains some directives related to matters of worship and dealings with others.

The other 34 Books are attributed to individuals that wrote these books after Moses at various epochs. These are "Joshua, Judges, Ruth, 1 Samuel, 2 Samuel, 1 Kings, 2 Kings, 1 Chronicles, 2 Chronicles, Ezra, Nehemiah, Esther, Job. Psalm, Proverbs, Ecclesiastes, Song of Songs, Isaiah, Jeremiah, Ezekiel, Daniel, Hosea, Joel, Amos, Obadiah, Jonah, Micah, Nahum, Habakkuk, Zephaniah, Haggai, Zachariah and Malachi."[105]

These 34 Books are also considered holy to the Jews. Together with the other previously mentioned books, they are called the Torah.

In general, these books are religious in nature. Some, however, are more historical in nature such as Genesis, Exodus, Joshua, Judges, Chronicles, Ezra and Nehemiah. Some are more ethical and legislatively- oriented and provide directives and advice such as Leviticus, Psalms, Ecclesiastes, Isaiah and Jeremiah. Some are long like Genesis, Psalms, Isaiah and Jeremiah, and some are short like Obadiah, Haggai and Habakkuk.

After this brief definition of the Holy books of the Jews which they call the Torah, we ask if these holy books are the Torah that Allah revealed to Moses, peace be upon him!

To respond to this question, we say: Whoever looks at these books will find contradictions, defamation and slander, deviation from the truth and poor expression that would direct the reader to believe that these books are- in general- not the Torah that Allah revealed to Moses. The following are some proofs of this:

First: The Noble Qur'an acknowledged the Torah that the Almighty Allah revealed to Moses- peace be upon him. In many verses the Qur'an praises the Torah. In Sura Al-Imran (Qur'an 3:2-3), the Almighty says: "Allah! There is no God worthy of worship except Him—the Ever-Living, All-Sustaining. He has revealed to you O Prophet the Book in truth, confirming what came before it, as He revealed the Torah and the Gospel."

The Noble Qur'an informs us that the evil hands of the Jews have stretched to the Torah, and they changed and altered it, concealing those things that were not agreeable and pleasing to their inclinations and aspirations. In Sura Al-Baqarah, the Almighty says: "Do you believers still expect them to be true to you, though a group of them would hear the word of Allah then knowingly corrupt it after understanding it? (Qur'an 2:75) When they meet the believers they say, "We believe." But in private they say to each other, "Will you disclose to the believers the knowledge Allah has revealed to you,[1] so that they may use it against you before your Lord? Do you not understand? (Qur'an 2:76) Do they not know that Allah is aware of what they conceal and what they reveal? (Qur'an 2:77) And among them are the illiterate who know nothing about the Scripture except lies, and so they ˹wishfully˺ speculate. (Qur'an 2:78) So woe to those who distort the Scripture with their own hands then say, "This is from Allah"—seeking a fleeting gain! So, woe to them for what their hands have written, and woe to them for what they have earned" (Qur'an 2:79)

And in Sura Al-Ma'idah (Q 5:15), the Almighty says: "O People of the Book! Now Our Messenger has come to you, revealing much of what you have hidden of the Scriptures and disregarding much. There certainly has come to you from Allah a light and a clear Book."

Also, in Sura Al-Ma'idah (Q 5:13), the Almighty says: "But for breaking their covenant We condemned them and hardened their hearts. They distorted the words of the Scripture and neglected a portion of what they had been commanded to uphold."

Second: There is no connection to a verifiable document. The Torah that is in existence currently lacks a certified verification that links to Moses, peace be upon him. On the contrary, there is valid evidence (in it) that it was written a long time after him. In Deuteronomy, for example, we read the following text concerning the death of Moses, peace be upon him: "And Moses the servant of the Lord died there in Moab, as the Lord had said..., but to this day no one knows where his grave is." It is extremely unlikely that Moses wrote such a statement. We also read in the same chapter: "Since then, no prophet has risen in Israel like Moses."

It is evident that these statements were written after the death of Moses, peace be upon him. The late Sheikh Rahmatuallah al-Hindi mentions many proofs for the lack of a verifiable link. He says what can be summed up in the following:

"Know, may the Almighty Allah guide you- that in order to fully commit to a heavenly book, that it must be proven- with strong and valid evidence-that that book was written by a certain prophet, and that it then reached us by verifiable means without changes or alterations… There is no such proof or verification that this Torah that is attributed to Moses belongs to him. The link of this Torah was cut off before the era of Josiah, son of Amon,[106] and the copy that was found 18 years after he sat on the throne cannot be verified, or relied upon, with certainty. In addition to not being verifiable, it also disappeared and was lost, most probably before the events of Nebuchadnezzar, during whose incidents the Torah and most of the books of the Old Testament were utterly erased and destroyed. When Ezra wrote these books, as they claim, they were lost-along with most of what was documented- during the events of Antiochus."[107]

Dr. Ali Abd-el-Wahid Wafi discusses the times during which these books that are attributed to Moses-peace be upon him- were written:

"The most important books in the Old Testament are Genesis, Exodus, Deuteronomy, Leviticus and Numbers. The Jews attribute these books to Moses-peace be upon him- and believe that were divinely inspired by Allah, and that they comprise the Torah. However, by observing the languages and styles in which these books were written, by looking at the subjects, edicts, laws and the social and political environments reflected therein, modern scholars and researchers found out- from these observations- that they were written at times that were subsequent (and not by short intervals) to Moses. Moses lived probably during the 13th or 14th century BC. Most of the books of Genesis and Exodus were written around the 9th century BC. The book of Deuteronomy was written at the end of the 7th century BC. Numbers and Leviticus were written during the 5th and 4th centuries BC… All of these books were written by the Jews. These books include the various doctrines and statutes that represent and reflect the numerous ideas and systems that prevailed among them throughout their long history. …Therefore, they are vastly different from the Torah that the Qur'an mentions as the holy and divinely inspired book that the Almighty Allah revealed to Moses, peace be upon him."[108]

Thus, we can see that a verifiable connection to the Torah to Moses does not exist, and that it was written after Moses-peace be upon him- by many individuals and in different epochs.

Third: If we look at the current Torah from the content perspective, we will find it replete with stories, expressions and contradictions that truthful heavenly books will find unbecoming and not worth mentioning. Here are some examples:

A- The Book of Genesis states: "And on the seventh day Allah ended His work which He had done, and He rested on the seventh day from all His work which He had done. Then Allah blessed the seventh day and sanctified it, because in it He rested from all His work which Allah had created and made."[109]

The Almighty Allah- as well as any heavenly book- rise above such a description; they are far exalted and sublime for such a false and untrue statement.

The Noble Qur'an (Q 50:38) has shown that the Almighty Allah had created the heavens and the earth and what is contained betwixt them without getting tired or being touched with fatigue: "Indeed, We created the heavens and the earth and everything in between in six Days, and We were not even touched with fatigue."[110]

Also, there are some references in the books that indicate that the Children of Israel believed in many gods and that their Allah is different from the gods of human beings. "Some books contain many situations in which Allah resembles a human being in his weakness and might, his deviation and discretion, his ignorance and forbearance… as though Allah had taken residence in a tent with the Jews and dwelt among them.

Numerous examples are found that show this; it is unlikely to find one page in the Old Testament that does have an example of this." [111]

B- The current Torah connects some prophets- peace be upon them- to reprehensible and disgraceful deeds that are in direct opposition to the infallibility which the Almighty Allah had granted them. Such deeds can be expected from only the most despicable and contemptible of people. An example of this is what is mentioned in Genesis: (Lot-peace be upon him- and his two daughters: Lot and his two daughters were the only survivors after the destruction of his people. After that, all three dwelt in a cave. The firstborn said to the younger "Our father *is* old, and *there is* no man on the earth to come in to us as is the custom of all the earth. Come, let us make our father drink wine, and we will lie with him, that we may preserve the lineage of our father." (Genesis 19: 31-32) They carried out their plan, and the firstborn bore a son and called him Moab. The younger daughter also bore him a son and she called him Ammon. The Moabites and the people of Ammon were the descendants of these two children.[112]

In addition, there are passages in the current Torah that contain insolent and forward reference to some prophets [113]such as Adam, Noah, Abraham, Isaac, Jacob, Moses, Aaron, David and Solomon- peace be upon them all-. These passages contain impertinent and despicable acts unbecoming of, and in opposition with, the sublime conduct and exalted nature with which the Almighty Allah endowed them.

C- In the current Torah, there many signs of contradictions and conflicts in statutes.

For example, in Exodus and Deuteronomy, there are texts that show that if an Israelite decided to voluntarily sell himself to his brother in case he was in need of money, his enslavement would not last more than 6 years. However, in Leviticus, we read that the enslavement of a person would not end except with the advent of the Israeli Jubilee, (a feast that occurs once every 50 years) regardless of the period of time he had spent in enslavement before that. So, according to the book of Leviticus, it was possible that his enslavement may last one day or a few days short of fifty years if he were enslaved immediately after the feast.[114]

And there are numerous examples for the contradictions and inconsistencies in the statutes, the laws and the decrees in the current existing Torah.

Some of the Books contain graphic and vivid carnal courtship... lascivious and lewd expressions… and such things that would compel any rational human being to discard that these books are divinely inspired. The Book of Song of Songs, for example, abounds with such lascivious and lustful types of courtship: "All night long on my bed I looked for the one my heart loves; I looked for him but did not find him. I will get up now and go about the city, through its streets and squares; I will search for the one my heart loves. So I looked for him but did not find him. The watchmen found me as they made their rounds in the city. "Have you seen the one my heart loves?" Scarcely had I passed them when I found the one my heart loves. I held him and would not let him go till I had brought him to my mother's house, to the room of the one who conceived me."[115]

The author of "The Story of Civilization" talks about the abundance of expressions that provoke lustful inclinations and carnal desires in these books. He says: "These strange flirtatious and coquettish writings pave the way to a great deal of guesswork and speculation. They could have been a group of Babylon songs… They could have also been songs written by Hebrew courtship poets. No matter what their origins were, their very existence is enigmatic, a sheer mystery. We do not know how religious and holy men have failed to recognize and understand the lascivious and lewd nature of these songs and allowed them to find their way to the writings of Isiah and Jeremiah." [116]

To sum up, the current Torah- in general- was written after Moses- peace be upon him- during various epochs, and from various viewpoints and perspectives. The Jews wrote it to reflect their morals, their history, their aspirations and their sufferings. Their main objective behind this was to show that the Israelites were people closest to Almighty Allah, and that they were favored than other nations. Due to the many writers that contributed to the writing of the Torah, it abounds in in errors, exaggerations and contradictions.

May Allah rest the soul of Rahmutulahh Al-Hindi who investigated the books of the Old and new Testaments- that is, the Torah and the Bible- and quoted their historians and scientists to indicate the contradictions in their verses. He had shown, through valid and unquestionable evidence, that their scientists did not possess a verifiable document to either of the two testaments. He then investigated the contradictions and inconsistencies that the two testaments contain. He then allocated a specific chapter to prove the aberrations and deviations in the old and new testaments in collaboration with the Almighty's saying: "They distorted the words of the Scripture and neglected a portion of what they had been commanded to uphold." (Qur'an 5:13) And he proved that some of these deviations were deliberate. He also proved that some of these deviations were accomplished through addition, deletions or altering certain words. Concerning deviation through additions he provided 45 proofs. For altering certain words, he provided 35 examples. As for deletions, he provided 20 proofs. This proves a conscientious effort and meticulous approach in finding evidence against them from their books."[117]

These books- that we have mentioned- are not the only holy books for the Jews. They have another book that they consider of equal status as the Torah. This book is the Talmud.

Jewish scholars and intellectuals undertook the task of explaining and interpreting the Torah. These interpretations and elucidations deal with the doctrine, history and statutes of the Jews. They also gathered the oral anecdotes that Jewish scholars and intellectuals exchanged throughout the generations. Those scholars collected 63 books that were written during the first and second centuries BC. These were called the Mishnah; that is, the repeated doctrine or law, because the Mishnah is a repletion and explanation and a continuation of what is mentioned in the Torah.

Other assiduous Jewish scholars who resided in Palestine and Babel offered more explanations related to the Mishnah. These were called Gemara which is a discussion and commentary. These discussions and explanations took place over an extended period of time lasting from the second to the six century AD.

The Talmud is a combination of the Mishnah and Gemara. It contains the instructions and religious statutes and principles of the Jews. Thus, the Talmud consists of two parts:

The Mishnah, which is explanations and elucidations of the Torah.
The Gemara, which is interpretations and commentaries on the Mishnah.

The commentaries that the rabbis of Palestine (Judea/Israel) added to the Mishnah are called the Jerusalemite Talmud, and those interpretations that were added by the rabbis of Babel to the Mishnah are called the Babylonian Talmud. The Babylonian Talmud is more comprehensive, expansive and widely circulated than the Jerusalemite Talmud; if the Jews find something ambiguous or vague in the Jerusalemite Talmud, they turn to the Babylonian Talmud because they consider it to be their guide and the standard book among them.

Most Jews consider the Talmud a holy book, and place it in the same status as the Torah. They feel that the Almighty Allah gave Moses the Torah in writing on the Mount of Sinai, but He also sent down with him the Talmud orally (the Oral Torah). Some Jews even place the Talmud at a higher status than the Torah. Some had attributed to Isaiah the saying that "The Torah is like water, the Mishnah is like wine, and the Gemara is like distilled, aromatic wine. The world cannot live without water, wine and aromatic wine. A rich man would have all of these. That is why, the world cannot survive without the Torah, the Mishnah and the Gemara. The Torah is like salt, the Mishnah is like the spices, and the Gemara is like the flavor and relish. The work of those who study the Torah may be regarded as virtuous or not virtuous. Those who study the Mishnah practice virtue and will be rewarded for it. As for those who study the Gemara, they are granted the greatest and most sublime of virtues...He who disparages the words of the rabbis is deserving of death." [118]

The Talmud contains numerous falsehoods and slanders that are unacceptable. For example, it mentions that "The Almighty God has divided the day into 12 hours: in the first 3 hours, He teaches the Law of the Jews; in the second 3 hours, He condemns the world; in the following 3 hours, He feeds the world; in the last final 3 hours, He plays with the king of the fish..."[119]

It also mentions that "God regretted what He did to the Temple of the Jews, and He bemoaned saying, 'Woe to Me for allowing My house to be plundered and ransacked, My temple scorched and burned, and My children dispersed and scattered..."[120]

And about the Jews, it mentions that "The spirits of the Jews are distinguished from the spirits of other people in that they are part of the Almighty God just as a son is a part of his father. Therefore, every Jew should do his best to prevent other nations from dominating the world… Also, God considers a Jew at a higher status than the angels; a Jew is a part of God. Therefore, if a gentile hits a Jew, it is as though that gentile has struck the Divine Majesty. The difference between a human and an animal is the difference between a Jew and a non-Jew. It is permissible for a Jew to swindle and deceive a non-Jew and swear and assert falsehoods."[121]

These are some excerpts about the falsehoods and slanders in which the Talmud abounds. Many researchers and scholars have gathered these passages and commented on them. Among the most prominent books written on this topic are "The Treasure Found in the Rules of the Talmud" by Dr. Rohling (who was a professor at Prague University), and which was translated by Dr. Youssef Nasrallah, "The Talmud and the Law of Israel" which was written by another researcher, and "The Barbarism of Zionist Teachings" by Mr. Boulos Hanna Saad.

After this brief discussion of the Jews' Holy Books, we conclude our talk with a short word on their religious sects:

The Jews have many sects, and each one of them claims that it adheres most vehemently to the fundamentals of the Jewish religion. Among their most well-known sects are:

A- The Pharisees: Which means the isolated or detached from the rest of the people. This sect came into existence during the era of the Maccabees around the second century BC. Their goal was to preserve the Law and literally adhere to its instructions, without attempting to interpret or study it.

The Pharisees believe in resurrection, reckoning and rewards. Most of them do not marry, and they preserve their lineage through adoption.

"The Pharisees believe that the Torah is not the only holy book to rely on. Rather, in addition to it, there are spoken and oral narratives, and a number of interpretations and explanations which are considered the oral Torah, and which rabbis have passed over from one generation to the next. These oral stories and narratives were written in what is called the Talmud. And in order to ascertain and guarantee that the Jews sanctify the Talmud, the Pharisees announced that the rabbis have a higher authority, that they are infallible, that what they say proceeds from the Almighty Allah, and that fearing them is just like fearing Allah."[122]

As for the conduct of the Pharisees, the author of the History of the Israelites maintains that "It is evident from the Talmud that not all the Pharisees were appropriate. Many of them 'appeared' to be righteous on the surface but, inwardly, they disregarded the statutes and teachings of their sect. The Talmud had divided the Pharisees into seven sections and regarded six of them unworthy of consideration for violating and disregarding the intended goal. The members of the seventh section are the true Pharisees who work according to the will of Allah because they love Him."[123]

B- The Sadducees: They derive their name from their leader Zadok, the High Priest, who lived during the third century AD.

They do not acknowledge resurrection, reckoning, rewards, paradise or hell. They maintain that man gets his reward or punishment in the world.

They also deny the Talmud. They even think that the Torah does not have absolute and unconditional holiness; a man may interpret and introduce what he deems appropriate. Most of those who belong to this sect are amongst the richest and most affluent of the Jews. Some researchers believe that they are more of a political party than a religious sect.

C- The Karaites: At first, this sect comprised few Jews only. It became bigger and the number of its members grew after the conditions of the Pharisees deteriorated.

This group believe in the Torah only. They do not acknowledge the interpretations and teachings of the rabbis as absolute. Rather, they believe that these could likely be correct and truthful or erroneous and false. In their view, these interpretations are also prone to be added to or detracted from. This is in contrast with the Pharisees who regard the interpretations of the rabbis as holy as the words of the Torah.

This sect was founded in the second century BC under the leadership of David Bin Annan, a Jewish Rabbi in Baghdad.

D- The Scribes: The task of the members of this group is to write the Law to whoever asks for it. They are more like copiers. And because of doing this kind of work for a long time, a number of them came to be known as well-versed and knowledgeable of their Law. That is why, they took up teaching and preaching as a profession for them.

With the passage of time, they occupied important positions, helped rulers attain their goals, and they became the shepherds of schools and temples.

These are the most well-known Jewish religious groups. There are other groups that scholars in religious sects have mentioned, but there is no reason to mention them here. Thus, we have gathered some understanding concerning the religious conditions of the Jews.

We now move to the fourth point which is their relationship with the Aws and the Khazraj. We say:

Historians maintain that the origin of the Aws and Khazraj was the Al-Azd tribe in Yemen, and they came to Medina after the great flood of the Ma'rib Dam to look for a new place after their houses were destroyed by the flood. When they arrived, they were poor and helpless, so they accepted whatever was offered them: poor infertile land and insufficient and scarce livelihood. With the passage of time, the Aws and the Khazraj mixed with the Jews who were residing in Yathrib and who were rich, affluent and influential.

The Aws and the Khazraj remained weak until the appearance of their leader, Malik Bin Ajlan, among them. His shrewdness, discernment and bravery enabled him to destroy the Jews and make the members of his tribe more influential and have the final word.

Dr. Jawad Ali describes the weakness and humiliation that the Jews experienced. He says: "Even though the Jews lived clumped together and independently in fortresses and villages, they were unable to spread their influence and authority on the lands in which they built their settlements. Neither were they able to establish kingdoms or governments wherein they ruled. Rather, they were independently defending the chiefs and heads of tribes. They paid them taxes every year in return for their protection and defending them and preventing Arabs from attacking them. They often had to make treaties with them, so every Jewish chief had an Arab ally or one of the chiefs among Arab tribes."[124]

The Noble Qur'an pointed out that some Jews joined the Aws, while others sided with the Khazraj at fighting. In Sura Al-Baqarah (Q2:84-85) we read: "And remember when We took your covenant that you would neither shed each other's blood nor expel each other from their homes, you gave your pledge and bore witness. But here you are, killing each other and expelling some of your people from their homes, aiding one another in sin and aggression; and when those expelled come to you as captives, you still ransom them—though expelling them was unlawful for you. Do you believe in some of the Scripture and reject the rest? Is there any reward for those who do so among you other than disgrace in this worldly life and being subjected to the harshest punishment on the Day of Judgment? For Allah is never unaware of what you do."

Yet, even though the Jews did not have any noticeable political or military influence on Medina since the Aws and the Khazraj were influential in these respects, some verses in the Noble Qur'an state that from the religious perspective, the Jews described themselves as the people of knowledge and expertise in matters of religion and the Law. They claimed that they were the children of Allah and His beloved ones. They were also preaching the advent of a new prophet, and they told the Aws and the Khazraj that they would follow the new prophet and kill you like Aad and Iram."

The Noble Qur'an pointed to what they said: "Although they used to pray for victory by means of the Prophet over the polytheists, when there came to them a Book from Allah which they recognized, confirming the Scripture they had in their hands, they rejected it. So may Allah's condemnation be upon the disbelievers."[125]

To sum up, the relationship of the Jews with the Aws and Khazraj was governed by personal interest and financial gains. They would kindle the flames of war between the two parties whenever they see that it would promote their self-interest as had happened in the many wars that wore out both the Aws and the Khazraj. Their main objective was to gain financial control over Medina. Their talk about the promised coming prophet encouraged both the Aws and the Khazraj to enter into Islam.

The relationship between the Jews and the Aws and the Khazraj continued along that pattern until the Prophet- (SAW)- immigrated to Medina. They took part in receiving him. Then many things took place between them. We will talk about these issues in the following chapters.

Now, after talking about the history of the Jews and their conditions during various periods of time, we will now move to Chapter Two to discuss the methods of the Noble Qur'an in calling them to Islam.

---

[1] History of Semitic Languages P.77, Dr. Israel Wolfensohn. He was a Professor of Semitic Languages in Dar Al-Eloum College, then he immigrated to Palestine and died there before the State of Israel was established.
[2] The Kuwaiti Arabic Magazine: # 91/ June 1966 P. 151
[3] Al-Baqarah: verse 133
[4] Lisan al-Arab by Ibn Manzour Vol.15 P.439. Beirut
[5] History of Religions by Amin al-Khouli Vol. 2 P. 4
[6] The History of the Arabs Before Islam by Dr. Jawad Ali, Vol.6 P. 95. The Research Institute in Baghdad, Iraq.
[7] History of the Children of Israel from Their Travels by Muhammad Izzat Darwaza P. 40
[8] Genesis Chapter 46
[9] Gochen is now called Suft al-Henna in the Governate of el-Sharqiyya in Egypt
[10] Genesis Chapter 47
[11] Verses 17 & 18
[12] Verse 32
[13] Verse 34
[14] Ibn Kathir Interpretation Vol. 2 P. 477
[15] Verses 56 & 57
[16] Ibn Kathir Interpretation Vol.2 P. 438
[17] Verse 88
[18] Verse 89
[19] Verse 90
[20] Ibn Kathir Interpretation Vol.2 P. 491
[21] Ibn Kathir Interpretation Vol. 2 P. 493
[22] History of the Children of Israel from Their Travels by Muhammad Izzat Darwaza P. 41
[23] In the Procession of the Sun Vol. 2 P. 589 by Dr. Ahmed Badawi
[24] Verse 6
[25] Verse 4
[26] Verse 49

[27] Moses is son of Amran from the offspring of Levi son of Jacob- peace on him. Some historians maintain that he was born approximately during the thirteenth century BC and that his mission was during Merneptah, son of Ramses the Second.
[28] Verses 104 & 105
[29] Al-A'raf: Verse 127
[30] An-Nazi'at: Verses 23 & 24
[31] Al-A'raf: Verse 128
[32] Al-A'raf: Verse 129
[33] History of the Children of Israel from Their Travels by Muhammad Izzat Darwaza P. 43. We have also recounted the story of borrowing the jewelry of Egypt's women in the chapter title The Vices of the Jews under the topic of Worshipping the Calf.
[34] History of the Israelites by Shaheen Makarios P. 15 (Al-Muqtataf Edition 1904)
[35] Exodus Chapter 16
[36] Numbers Chapter 11
[37] It was said that they were Canaanites.
[38] Al-A'raf
[39] Al-A'raf Verse 142
[40] Ibn Kathir Interpretation Vol. 2 P. 243
[41] Review the Chapter "The Vices of the Children of Israel" under the topic "Continuing to Worship the Calf."
[42] We interpreted this verse in full in chapter "The Graces of Allah to the Children of Israel and Their Stance Concerning Them." Topic: (The Grace of Guiding Them to What They Can do to Rid Themselves of Their Sins."
[43] We explain these verses in the Chapter: "The Vices of the Jews" Topic: "Their Cowardice in Fighting."
[44] Joshua Chapters One, Seven, Eight & Ten
[45] The Story of Civilization Vol. 2 P. 326
[46] History of the Children of Israel from Their Travels P. 77
[47] The Holy Books in Pre-Islamic Religions by Dr Ali Abdel Wahed Wafi P. 8
[48] We interpreted these two verses in the chapter titled "Allah's Grace for the Children of Israel" under the Topic "Enabling them to Enter the Holy Land."
[49] Ibn Kathir's Interpretation Vol. 1 P. 98
[50] The History of the Israelites P. 19
[51] History of the Children of Israel from Their Travels P. 82
[52] Judges, Chapter Two
[53] 1 Samuel, Chapter 17
[54] Al-Kashaaf Interpretation Vol. 1 P. 392, Dar Al-Kitaab Al- Arabi, Bierut
[55] Ibn Kathir Interpretation Vol. 1 P. 301
[56] تابوت The ark, the Box of the Torah. From the Arabic word to repent, meaning to return (Tabout)
[57] Al-Kashaaf Interpretation Vol. 1 P. 293, Dar Al-Kitaab Al- Arabi, Bierut
[58] Ibn Kathir Interpretation Vol. 1 P. 301
[59] Quoted from Interpretation of the Noble Verses the honorable Sheikh Muhammad Abi-Zahra. Loua' al-Islaam # 2: Seventh Year.
[60] 1 Samuel from Chapter 18 to Chapter 26. These Chapters also narrate Saul's malice and hatred for David and his attempt to kill him on numerous occasions. We have decided not

to mention these verses because of our belief that they are not becoming to attribute to a man who was described by the Almighty Allah as chosen over the Children of Israel and was granted width and depth of knowledge and a strong physique and stature.

[61] The History of the Israelites by Shaheen Makarios P. 31, 1904

[62] Son of Jesse, born in Bethlehem approximately in 1085 BC and died in Jerusalem in 1015 BC.

[63] Hebron: al-Kahlil city now

[64] Jerusalem القدس(al-Quds) meaning the city of peace

[65] World Zionism and the Promised Land by Ali Imam Attiyya P. 64

[66] History of the Children of Israel from Their Travels by Muhammad Izzat Darwaza P. 112.

[67] Solomon was born in Jerusalem around 1043 BC and he died around 975 BC

[68] The History of the Israelites by Shaheen Makarious P.25

[69] 1 Kings/ Chapter 2

[70] History of the Children of Israel from Their Travels by Muhammad Izzat Darwaza P. 123.

[71] Landmarks of Human History by Wells. Quoted from Judaism by Dr. Ahmed Shalaby P. 59

[72] The Jews in Early Civilizations by Gustave Le Bon P. 45

[73] Ibn Kathir's Interpretation Vol. 3 P. 186

[74] It was also said: He died in 953 BC

[75] Shechem is Nablus now

[76] I Kings, Chapter 12

[77] 1 Kings, Chapter 13. (Quoted from the History of the Children of Israel from Their Travels P. 121)

[78] The History of the Israelites by Shaheen Makarious P.30

[79] History of the Children of Israel from Their Travels (with outlining and abbreviation) P. 128, 164 & 177

[80] Yigal Levin. "Did Pharaoh Sheshonq Attack Jerusalem?" *Biblical Archaeology Review* 38.4 (2012): 43–45, 48–52. https://library.biblicalarchaeology.org/article/did-pharaoh-sheshonq-attack-jerusalem/

[80a] The History of Egypt from the Earliest Tomes to the Persian Conquest by Breasted P. 357

[81] History of the Children of Israel from Their Travels P. 157

[82] Judaism by Dr Ahmed Shalaby P. 63

[83] H. G. Wells from Encyclopedia of Our Country, Palestine by Mustafa Murad Al-Dabbagh Vol. 1 P. 564, Dar El- Taleeha, Beirut.

[84] Judaism by Dr Ahmed Shalaby P. 66

[85] The History of the Israelites by Shaheen Makarious P. 36

[86] The History of the Children of Israel from Their Travels P. 236

[87] History of Syria by Bishop Debs Vol. 2 P. 123

[88] It is said that they were called Maccabees because the word Maccaba, in Hebrew, means a hiding place.

[89] Now, it is called Medea, a village in Lydda

[90] Maccabee Chapter 2

[91] The History of the Israelites by Shaheen Makarious P. 71 & 77, Al-Muqtataf Edition 1904

[92] Josephus, a Jewish Historian. He was born in 37 AD and died in 103 AD. He was contemporaneous with the destruction of Jerusalem, and he wrote a voluminous book on it.

[93] History of Josephus, quoted from The History of the Children of Israel from their Travels P. 351

[94] The History of the Jews in Arab Countries P. 9

[95] The History of the Arabs Before Islam by Dr. Gawad Ali Vol. 6 P.10

[96] History of the Arab Race Vol. 5 P. 148/ The Age of the Prophet and his Invronment Before His Mission P.105/ The Qur'an and the Jews P. 24 by Mr. Muhammad Izzat Darwaza

[97] The History of the Arabs Before Islam by Dr. Jawad Ali, Vol.6 P. 13

[98] Sura Al-Hashr. We have interpreted this verse in the Chapter "The punishment of the Jews."

[99] Sura An-Nisa Verse 161

[100] Sahih al-Bukhari, the Book of Coercion Vol.9, P. 46

[101] We have talked in detail concerning the heated debates that took place between the Messenger and the Jews in the chapter "The Methods that the Jews used to entrap Islam and Muslims" under the topic (Religious Debates).

[102] Sura Ai-Baqarah: Verse 222

[103] Muslim in the book of "Menstruation" Vol. 1 P. 246/ Abu Dawod in "Eating with a Menstruating Woman "Vol. 1 P. 59

[104] It is said that this feast is called the Feast of the Unleavened Bread because the Jews left Egypt quickly and did not have the time to prepare it as they usually did. Rather, they prepared the dough without yeast to make it rise. This is still the custom of the Jews during this feast which they celebrate for 7 days. They eat unleavened bread. These seven days start each year on the 14th of April and end on the 21st of the month.

[105] These are the 39 Books that the Protestant church certifies. The Catholic church adds 7 more. These are Tobit, Judith, Wisdom, Sirach, Baruch, 1 Maccabee and 2 Maccabee. As such, their Holy Books are 46.

There are also some Books that historians believe existed but they disappeared or were concealed and hidden. Sheikh Rahmat allah el-Hindi attested to this in his valuable book "Revealing the Truth."

[106] Josiah son of Amon was one of the kings of the Jews. He ruled over them from 640 to 609 BC, that is, almost 6 centuries after the death of Moses, peace be upon him.

[107] Antiochus who ruled over Syria from 174 164 BC. During his reign, he severely humiliated and mortified the Jews. Review "Revealing the Truth" by Sheikh Rahmat allah el-Hindi Vol. 1 P.56-58. Al-Wehda al_Maghribiyya, Morocco.

[108] The Holy Books in Religions Before Islam P. 16 (Nahdat Misr Library)

[109] Book of Genesis, Chapter Two

[110] Sura `Qaf

[111] Christ in the Qur'an by Mr. Abdul Karim Al-Khatib

[112] Genesis Chapter 19

[113] These passages are discussed in detail by the honorable Sheikh Abdu-Rahman A—Jizeeri in his book "Evidence of Proof in Responding to the Book the Scale of righteousness from Preachers," P. 431- 454

[114] The Holy Books by Dr. Ali Abdu Wahid Wafi P. 33

[115] Song of Songs, Quoted from Christ in the Qur'an by Dr. Abdul Karim Al-Khatib P. 52

[116] The Story of Civilization by Will Durant Vol. 3 P. 388

[117] The Introduction to "Revealing the Truth": by Omar El- DOsouki.

[118] The Barbarism of Zionist Teachings by Mr. Boulos Hanna Saad (Beirut Edition 16)

[119] Previous reference. P. 24

[120] Previous reference. P. 25

[121] The treasure Found in the Rules of the Talmud. Translated by Dr. Youssef Nasrallah from P. 48.

[122] Judaism by Dr Ahmed Shalaby P. 196.

[123] The History of the Israelites by Shaheen Macarious P. 119.

[124] The History of Arabs Before Islam Vol. 6 P. 23

[125] Sura Al-Baqarah: Verse 89

Chapter Two

The Methods that the Noble Qur'an Used to Call Jews To Accept Islam And Proofs Of Its Fairness Towards Them

In this chapter, we will essentially deal with two basic topics.

First: Present the most important methods that the Noble Qur'an used to invite the People of Scriptures to accept Islam and believe in the prophesy of Muhammad (SAW).

Second: Show the most important indications of fairness and leniency with which Islam treated the People of the Scriptures.

To speak about the first topic, we maintain that inviting people to Monotheism, utter loyalty in worshipping Allah Almighty, and submitting to His statutes and decrees, is the first reason for which Allah sent the prophets and messengers, and ordered them to guide people- everywhere and at all times- to them.

The Noble Qur'an recounts that every messenger that Allah Almighty sent was unstructured to order this people into Monotheism, belief in only one Allah: "We never sent a messenger before you O Prophet without revealing to him: "There is no God˹worthy of worship˺ except Me, so worship Me alone." (Qur'an 21:25)

The Noble Qur'an states that inviting/calling people to worship Allah alone was mentioned unanimously and in unity from various messengers offering advice to their people.

About Noah- peace be upon him- the Almighty said: "Indeed, We sent Noah to his people. He said, "O my people! Worship Allah—you have no other Allah except Him." (Q7:59) [1] And about Hud-peace be upon him- the Almighty said: "And to the people of 'Âd We sent their brother Hûd. He said, "O my people! Worship Allah—you have no other God except Him." (Q 7:65) [2] And concerning Salih, peace be upon him- the almighty said, "And to the people of Thamûd We sent their brother Ṣâliḥ. He said, "O my people! Worship Allah—you have no other Allah except Him." (Q 7:73) [3] And about Shu'aib- peace be upon him- the Almighty said: "And to the people of Midian We sent their brother Shu'aib. He said, "O my people! Worship Allah—you have no other Allah except Him." (Q7:85) [4]

There is no doubt that every prophet directed this statement to his people verbatim (as stated) or in a manner that captures its purport simply because, by following this directive- faithfully and wholeheartedly- their happiness and success exist.

It was Almighty Allah's wisdom to send Muhammad, His Messenger, as a seal to all other prophets and messengers, make his message a general message to all the people, his doctrine- the major miracle of all (i.e., the Noble Qur'an) confirm and validate previous divinely inspired books while having dominance over them, and his call, in spirit and essence, in agreement with the calls and messages of previous prophets. By virtue of these advantages that the Almighty Allah exclusively granted His Prophet (SAW), he-with unwavering faith, clear and undeniable evidence and steadfast patience- called all the people to Monotheism, presenting clear evidence and verifiable proofs that what he was telling them to -about His Allah- is true.

Among the people to whom the Messenger (SAW) directed his call to follow him and accept his message were the People of the Book, in general, and the Jews who were neighbors to the Arabs of the Peninsula, in particular.

In his attempt to call them to accept Islam, the Prophet (SAW) pursued all possible methods to convince and alert them to the truth of his message. He brought forth verses from the Noble Qur'an that would urge and incentivize them to accept Islam if they were among those who were willing to open their hearts and be receptive of the truth and if they truly fear Allah.

The following are some of the methods that the Noble Qur'an used to call on the Children of Israel to accept Islam and believe and follow Muhammad (SAW):

First: Presenting proofs to them that the Prophet is truthful through:

A- Alerting them that Muhammad (SAW) is the prophet who is mentioned in their Torah and Bible.

B- Alerting them that Muhammad (peace and prayers be upon him) is the prophet about whom Issa (Jesus)- peace on him- prophesied

C- Alerting them that this is Muhammad (SAW), and that they used to pray for victory 'by means of the Prophet' over the polytheists.

D- Turning their attention that the Noble Qur'an that was sent to Muhammad confirms previous Scriptures and divinely inspired books.

Second: Turning their attention to the fact that Muhammad's call is essentially and at its very core in agreement with what other prophets had called for.

Third: Enticing them- through wisdom and good counsel- to accept Muhammad's call.

Fourth: Warning them of punishment- in this world and the next- if they failed to accept the message of the Prophet, (SAW).

Fifth: Informing them that disputing religion was due to debauchery and wanton envy.

Sixth: Informing them that the Noble Qur'an tells them the truth about that with which they disagree.

Seventh: Providing proofs against them by quoting them to prove the truthfulness of the Prophet, (SAW).

These are some of the points that the Noble Qur'an presented as proofs of the truthfulness of Prophet Muhammad (SAW), and the call to the People of the Book to understand with loyalty and discernment in order to hasten into accepting Islam and Muhammad (SAW). Having mentioned these points in brief, we will now discuss each in detail:

First: Presenting proofs to them- and others- that the Prophet is truthful:

Among the methods that the Noble Qur'an used to call the Children of Israel to accept and believe in Muhammad was presenting proofs that what Muhammad was informing them about his Allah is truthful and correct. One of these proofs was alerting them that Muhammad (SAW) was the Prophet that was mentioned in their Torah and Bible. We find this forewarning in Sura Al-A'raf: "My mercy encompasses everything. I will ordain mercy for those who shun evil, pay alms-tax, and believe in Our revelations. They are˺ the ones who follow the Messenger, the unlettered Prophet, whose description they find in their Torah and the Gospel. He commands them to do good and forbids them from evil, permits for them what is lawful and forbids to them what is impure, and relieves them from their burdens and the shackles that bound them. Only those who believe in him, honor and support him, and follow the light sent down to him will be successful. Say, O Prophet, "O humanity! I am Allah's Messenger to you all. To Him alone belongs the kingdom of the heavens and the earth. There is no Allah ˹worthy of worship˺ except Him. He gives life and causes death." So believe in Allah and His Messenger, the unlettered Prophet, who believes in Allah and His revelations. And follow him, so you may be ˹rightly˺ guided." (Qur'an 7:156-58)

(The Interpretation of the noble Verses)

Allah Almighty described His mercy as all-encompassing; it "encompasses everything". In this world, it descends upon the believers and the disbelievers, the righteous and the unholy. As for the world to come, the Almighty Allah mentioned that it will be confined to those who have these three qualities: First: righteousness in their secret and public lives; Second: those who pay alms-tax generously to those deserving and worthy of alms; Third: those who believe in Allah's revelations with which He has inspired His prophets and messengers: "I will ordain mercy for those who shun evil, pay alms-tax, and believe in

Our revelations." To these qualities the Almighty added a statement clarifying that those are the ones who believe- in truth and faithfulness- in Muhammad, His Servant and Messenger, and in his revelation: "the ones who follow the Messenger, the unlettered Prophet."

The Almighty Allah had attributed honorable characteristics and qualities that would invite the just, reasonable and fair-minded to accept him, support him and venerate him.

The first characteristic: He is the Messenger of Allah to all the people.

The second characteristic: He is a prophet to whom Allah revealed guidelines, an eternal doctrine.

The third characteristic: He is unlettered. He did not read, he did not write, he did not sit with a teacher or receive his knowledge from anyone. It was Almighty Allah that revealed the Noble Qur'an to him through Gabriel- peace be upon him- and He lavishly bestowed upon him useful knowledge and principles that clarify what the Noble Qur'an had revealed to him. He therefore was ahead of philosophers, legislators, historians and scholars of physics and science. Being unlettered while having this knowledge concerning the world and the hereafter is the greatest evidence that what he says is divinely inspired:

The Almighty said: "And so We have sent to you 'O Prophet' a revelation by Our command. You did not know of 'this' Book and faith 'before'. But We have made it a light, by which We guide whoever We will of Our servants. And you are truly leading 'all' to the Straight Path." Q 42:52) [5] And: "You O Prophet could not read any writing even before this revelation, nor could you write at all. Otherwise, the people of falsehood would have been suspicious." (Q 29:48) [6]

The fourth characteristic: And this has been pointed out in His saying: "whose description they find in their Torah and the Gospel." In other words, the People of the book can find this unlettered Messenger in their Torah and Bible, and that his name and description in their books are the main causes to believe, accept and follow him. The Jews presaged the emissary of the Prophet (SAW) long before it came to pass, and they read in their books what ascertains that. when Allah sent His Messenger with the religion of truth and straight path, those who opened their hearts to the truth believed in him, feared their Lord and stayed away from immoral and evil. Yet the haughty and arrogant who envied Muhammad for what His Allah has favored him with started to delete, change or hide from the public what was mentioned in their books about the Prophet (SAW). Yet, despite their efforts and caution to delete, change or keep from the illiterate among them what was mentioned about the Messenger in their books, the Almighty Allah would not allow it. His message shone forth in the Torah and the Bible; the Prophet's (SAW) characteristics, qualities and his very name remained there, clearly.

Scholars have recounted the predictions of prophets about Muhammad (SAW). They gathered tens of passages that mentioned his qualities and characteristics. We will now recount just a few of these instances that scientists and scholars have recounted in this respect.

In his "Signs of Prophethood," Imam Al-Mawardi said: "There were many predictions that were heralded from prophets who preceded concerning the emissary of Muhammad (SAW). These were evidence to their people and a miracle indicating his truthfulness, to help the Prophet and urge others to accept him. Some of them were mentioned by name, some by a certain quality, some in relation to their people or country, some specifically by their deeds, and some were distinguished through fame and prominence. The Almighty Allah granted him all of these that he became a distinct certainty after looming as a possibility, and an undeniable fact after suspicion." [7]

In "The Wish of the Intelligent in the Stories of the Prophets," it is mentioned that "Previous prophets have anticipated Our Prophet (SAW). They testified that his prophecy was truthful, and described him in such a way that eradicated all manner of suspicion; they identified his name, country, gender, manners and qualities. Even though the People of the Book removed his name from their recent editions, they were not successful, for the characteristics- that historians from all races and religions agreed upon- remained. These were more indicative and revealing than the name itself. For two individuals may have the same name, but it is unlikely that two individuals will share all the qualities and characteristics. However, not too long ago, they started to distort some qualities so that they would not apply to the Prophet (SAW). Every later edition would therefore differ in certain places from previous ones. A discerning intelligent person would be able to detect such distortions and understand the reason behind them. They benefitted nothing from these distortions except that the suspicion against them became stronger due to the widespread use of printing and ease of juxtaposing editions against each other." [8]

The honorable Sheikh Rahmat Allah El-Hindi in his "Revealing the Truth" said: "The accounts that relate to Muhammad are numerous so far alongside the distortions in these books. He who knew the accounts concerning the earlier prophet then the later prophet and then looked fairly and without bias to the accounts that the Evangelists brought concerning Issa (Jesus)- peace on Him- would conclude with the utmost certainty that the Muhammadian accounts are extremely strong."[9]

The author of "Revealing the Truth" and other scientists and historians gathered many of the predictions (good tidings) that are mentioned in the Torah and the Bible concerning Muhammad (SAW) and which indicate his qualities and characteristics.

Concerning what was mentioned in the Torah about the Prophet (SAW), Al-Bukhari relates on the authority of Abdallah Ibn Amr Ibn Al-As- Allah be pleased with them. He said: (I read in the Torah the Traits of the Prophet (SAW) "Muhammad, the Messenger of Allah, My servant and My Messenger, the trusting, not coarse nor quarrelsome, nor will anyone hear his voice in the marketplace. He does nor repay evil with evil, but he will pardon and forgive. I will not take him until he had straightened out the crooked unbelievers and say 'There is no Gog but Allah.'"[10]

Also, what ascertains the existence of the quality of the Prophet (SAW) is what Imam Ahmad relates on the authority of Abi Sakher Al-a'qeeli. He said: "A Bedouin told me that he asked a milkwoman who came to Medina during the time of the Prophet (SAW) to meet that man to hear from him. Soon after, Abi Bakr and Omer were walking, so I followed them. They came to a Jew who was reading the Torah to console himself for the looming death of his son, one of the best looking and handsome amongst the youth. The Messenger of Allah (SAW) said to him: "Prithee, in the name of Him who revealed the Torah, do you find in your book something related to me and my characteristics?" The man shook his head indicating "No." His son: "Yes, by Him who revealed the Torah, we find you in our book, and I testify that there is no God but Allah and that you are the Messenger of Allah." The Messenger (SAW) then said that that Jew was a brother. He then undertook the business of enshrouding and praying upon him.[11]

Those who desire to get more information concerning this issue can review what scholars have written. [12]

Then the Almighty Allah attributed a fifth characteristic to His Messenger: "He commands them to do good and forbids them from evil." (Qur'an 7:157) This means that among the characteristics of this unlettered messenger- whom the People of the Book find in their Torah and Bible- is that he commands them to do good, i.e., believe in Allah, His angels, books, messengers, and Judgement Day. It is also a command to be moral and ethical and be clothed in righteousness and such virtues that are in the Hanafi doctrine and which reasonable people and pure hearts find comforting and reassuring. He also forbids them evil, i.e., disbelief, transgressions and immorality.

Then, the Almighty Allah attributed a sixth quality to Muhammad: He "permits for them what is lawful and forbids to them what is impure." (Q 7:157) This means he allowed what Allah had forbidden- such as (pork) grease- as a punishment for their injustice and cruelty. He also allowed those things that they had denied themselves without Allah's permission such as the meat of camels and their milk. He forbade them blood, dead meat, and pork (in foods), and he forbade them usuary and devouring peoples' money unjustly (in dealings). All of this was for their success, happiness and well-being.

Then, the Almighty Allah attributed a seventh quality to His Messenger (SAW): He "relieves them from their burdens and the shackles that bound them." الاصر is a "burden" in Arabic; it is that thing that prevents someone from moving freely because of its heaviness. It also means a covenant as in the Almighty's: "He added, "Do you affirm this covenant and accept this commitment?"

Al-Qurtubi said: "This verse comprises the two meanings, for the Children of Israel were under a covenant that they undertake heavy and difficult tasks. Muhammad (SAW) relieved them from that covenant and the burden of these tasks such as the washing of urine soiled garments, the legitimizing of spoils, and accompanying, eating and sleeping with a menstruating woman. Thus, if someone's garment is soiled, he would give it away. If they gathered spoils, these spoils would be devoured by fire from the heavens. If a woman was menstruating, they would not come close to her, etc. All of this had been verified in Al-Sahih and others."[13]

"Shackles" are the iron chains that are on the hand or the neck. The statement "relieving them from their burdens and the shackles that bound them" is a metaphor that refers to the difficult tasks and heavy burdens in their Law such as the stipulation to kill oneself to ascertain true repentance. The Almighty likened the burdens that the Children of Israel had to endure in worship and interactions and food to someone groaning under the yoke of a heavy burden that he is unable to carry. Moreover, he is chained with shackles on his neck, hands and feet. The meaning is that among the characteristics of this unlettered Messenger is that he came to them to lift up these burdens and relieve them from the shackles with which Allah had punished them for their injustices because the Messenger (SAW) came with good tidings and to alleviate burdens, he came to preach the wonderfully delightful Hanafi doctrine. Amongst his commandments "Preach and do not alienate and repel, make it lighter and easier not harder and cumbersome."

Imam Ibn Kathir said that the doctrines of the nations that preceded us were distressing for them. Allah lightened the burdens of this nation and made it easier for them. Therefore, the Prophet said: "The wrong, the oblivion and compulsion were lifted and removed." So, Allah guide this nation to say: "Our Lord! Do not place a burden on us like the one you placed on those before us. Our Lord! Do not burden us with what we cannot bear. Pardon us, forgive us, and have mercy on us. You are our only Guardian. So grant us victory over the disbelieving people." (Qur'an 2:286) It was proven in Sahih Muslim that after each of these questions, the Almighty said: "I did, I did."[14]

It is therefore the duty of all the Children of Israel to accept and follow Muhammad (SAW) whose description was revealed to them. Their happiness- in this world and the next- lie in accepting him. That is why, the Almighty concluded these noble verses with a statement showing the rewards of those who believe in His Messenger: "Only those who believe in him, honor and support him, and follow the light sent down to him will be successful." (Q 7:157) This means that those amongst the Children of Israel who believed, accepted and supported that unlettered Messenger, those who defended him against those who opposed him, those who revere, honor and sustain him by all means possible, those who follow the light sent down to him- the Qur'an and the revelation- that he invited people to accept and believe in- those are the successful ones, the ones who will be granted Allah's mercy and forgiveness and will find favor in Allah's eyes.

Thus, the noble verses described the Prophet (SAW) with the most brilliant qualities and the most exquisite characteristics. They presented evidence against the People of the Book that what he brought to them- by bringing to their attention that what they have in their books and what proceeded from the mouths of their prophets- was for their guidance and happiness and that if they believed and trusted him, they would be among "those who listen to what is said and follow the best of it. These are the ones rightly guided by Allah, and these are truly the people of reason." (Qur'an 39:18)

Then Allah commanded His Messenger to show all people that he was sent for everyone. The Almighty says: "Say, 'O Prophet, O humanity! I am Allah's Messenger to you all.'" (Qur'an 7:158) Meaning: Tell all the people, Muhammad, Arabs and Ajam (none Arabs) alike, that you are Allah's Messenger to all of them and that there is no difference between Christians and Jews. Tell them that your message is for all of them. The Noble Qur'an and the Sunna contain evidence that validates the general nature of his message.

In the Noble Qur'an, for example, the Almighty says: "We have sent you O Prophet only as a mercy for the whole world." (Q 21:107) And: "We have sent you O Prophet only as a deliverer of good news and a warner to all of humanity." (Q 34:28) And the Almighty's saying: "And this Quran has been revealed to me so that, with it, I may warn you and whoever it reaches." (Q 6:19) That is to say, those whom the Qur'an reached- all over the world- have been warned. This indicates that the message of the Prophet (SAW) was directed to all and that the statutes of the would apply to all in the Day of Judgement.

As for the Sunna, Al-Bukhari relates on the authority of Gaber Ibn Abdullah that the Messenger of Allah (SAW) said: " I was given five things that were not given to anyone before me: I made the earth a mosque and purification and when it is time for any man from my people to pray, let him pray; booty is permitted to me and it was not allowed before; I was awarded the blessing of intercession."[15] The Prophet would preach his people in particular and all the others in general.

And in Sahih Muslim, on the authority of Abi Mosa Al-A'shari- may Allah be pleased with- the Messenger of Allah said: "Those who hear from me from this nation, whether a Jew or a Christian, and do not believe me, will go to hell."[16]

Imam Ibn Kathir said: "The verses relating to this issue are numerous. Also, the sayings are innumerable and uncountable. It is known in religion of Islam that he is a messenger to all the people."

Then, Almighty Allah attributed to Himself those particular qualities- indicating ability and omniscience- that are exclusively His: "To Him alone belongs the kingdom of the heavens and the earth. There is no God worthy of worship except Him. He gives life and causes death." (Q 7:158) That is to say, O Muhammad, tell the people that you are a Messenger to you from Allah who is omniscient and omnipotent, who has authority over the heavens and the earth and who is the only one worthy of worship, and who can give life and cause death. He who possesses such a status is to be obeyed; what He had forbidden should be abandoned, and His Messenger should be accepted and trusted. Then, on the bases of these glorious traits that He attributed to Himself, the Almighty Allah built the call to the faith and said: "So believe in Allah and His Messenger, the unlettered Prophet, who believes in Allah and His revelations. And follow him, so you may be rightly guided." (Q 7:158) Meaning, believe, all of you people, in Allah, the One and the Only Allah, and also believe in His Messenger, Muhammad (SAW), the unlettered Prophet who believes in Allah and His revelation, those prophets who came before him. Follow him and walk in his footsteps; abide by everything he commands and shun everything he forbids that you may be guided to the straight and righteous path.

And in describing him once again as unlettered, there is a reference to the perfection of his knowledge, for though he was not familiar with books or instructors, Allah had opened for him the doors of knowledge and erudition, and He taught him what he did not know before concerning all the fields of knowledge that others learned and by which they excelled and became amongst the most prominent of scientists and the most distinguished leaders of thought. He thereby honored this illiteracy against which all the erudition and knowledge of scientists, anywhere and everywhere, waxed poor and insignificant.

Thus, the two noble verses had described the Messenger (SAW) with the most exquisite and dignified qualities. They presented the clearest and strongest evidence of his truthfulness concerning his message. They invited the Jews, indeed all the people, to believe and accept him, for the other previous heavenly and divinely inspired books foretold his coming. He (SAW) only came to preach what is good, asking them to stay away from evil deeds. And since his statutes are characterized with ease, felicity and good tidings, and his followers and supporters would be the successful ones, and his message is for all, it is worthy to follow, believe and obey him. Those who reject his call are the transgressors who prefer this present worldly life.

B- Alerting them that Muhammad (peace and prayers be upon him) is the prophet about whom Issa (Jesus)- peace on him- prophesied

Amongst the methods that the Noble Qur'an used in calling the Children of Israel to Islam was bringing to their attention that Muhammad (SAW) who called them to monotheism was the prophet that Issa (Jesus) -peace on Him- prophesied. This meaning is mentioned in Sura As-Saf: "And remember when Jesus, son of Mary, said, "O children of Israel! I am truly Allah's messenger to you, confirming the Torah which came before me, and giving good news of a messenger after me whose name will be Aḥmad." Yet when the Prophet came to them with clear proofs, they said, "This is pure magic." (Qur'an 61:6) [17]

The meaning of the noble verses: Mention, Muhammad, to those Jews what Jesus, son of Mary, said to them: 'O Children of Israel, I am a messenger from Allah to. I believe in the Torah of my brother Moses, peace be upon him. I also believe in Ahmad, the unlettered Arab Prophet, who will come after me. I foretell his coming, and I call upon you to believe him when he comes with guidance and the religion of truth.

Then the Noble Qur'an shows the position of the Children of Israel concerning the Messenger whom Jesus predicted: "When the Prophet came to them with clear proofs, they said, "This is pure magic." This means that when Ahmad- who was foretold before with clear proofs and astounding miracles- came, they met his invitation with obstinacy and ungratefulness, and they said to him: what you brought was nothing but clear pure magic and worthless nonsense.

The noble verse mentions that Jesus, son of Mary, peace be upon him, who was the seal of the prophets of the Children of Israel portended the Prophet (SAW), after whom there would be no other messages or prophesies. He mentioned him to them by name in order to believe and accept him when he arrived. Yet, when he arrived, they said, "This is pure magic." This constitutes proofs against them, a chastisement for their arrogance and ungratefulness.

There are numerous sayings in which the Prophet (SAW) stated that among his names is Ahmad, and that Jesus foretold his coming. Among these sayings was what was recounted by Al-Bukhari who relates on the authority of Gubayr Ibn Mut'im. He said that the Messenger of Allah (SAW) said: "I have names. I am Muhammad and I am Ahmad. I am the Eraser by whom Allah will erase disbelief." [18]

After mentioning a number of sayings concerning the names of the Prophet (SAW) and predictions concerning his coming, Imam Ibn Kathir said that the prophets- peace upon them- kept on describing and mentioning him in their books. They would talk about him to their people, and they would command them to follow, accept and support him. Among the well know anecdotes among the people of the earth what was recounted by the son of Mary and Abraham, the Father of the Prophets, when he interceded for the people of Mecca that Allah may send a messenger from among them. When they asked to tell them about himself, he said: "The intercession of my father, Abraham, and the prophesy of Jesus, son of Mary, and the vision that my mother saw."[19]

Thus, the noble verse called the Jews to believe in the Prophet (SAW) with clear and formidable evidence to his truthfulness for even Jesus, the last one of their prophets, foretold his coming and asked them to believe and follow him, but they closed their eyes and shut their ears so they could not see or hear the truth. They disbelieved these two honorable Prophets as they disbelieved others before.

E- Alerting them that that was Muhammad (SAW), and that they used to pray for victory 'by means of the Prophet' over the polytheists.

Also, among the proofs that the Noble Qur'an had against the Jews to urge them to acknowledge the truth of the Prophet (SAW) and to follow him were to inform them that that was the Messenger whom they used to invoke his name before his arrival to gain victory over the polytheists. The Noble Qur'an clarified this in a number of verses, as in: "Although they used to pray for victory by means of the Prophet over the polytheists, when there came to them a Book from Allah which they recognized, confirming the Scripture they had in their hands, they rejected it. So may Allah's condemnation be upon the disbelievers." (Qur'an 2:89) [20]

Meaning: A Book from Allah, which is the Noble Qur'an, came to the Jews, confirming the Scripture, i.e., in agreement with Torah which Allah revealed to them in order to guide them concerning the emissary of the Prophet (SAW). Although they used to pray for victory by means of the Prophet over the polytheists," meaning, the Jews used pray for victory against their enemies by invoking the name of Mohammad before his emissary.

They would say: Allah grant us victory through the name of Mohammad whom we find in the Torah.

The Noble Qur'an presents their stance concerning the Prophet (SAW) when he came: "when there came to them a Book from Allah which they recognized… they rejected it. So may Allah's condemnation be upon the disbelievers." Meaning: When there came to them what they knew was truthful, which is the message of the Prophet whose description they find in their book- applying to him alone- they distrusted him because he was not one of them. Therefore, Allah's condemnation will be upon them and those disbelievers- who knew the truth yet knowingly suppressed it- will be thrown away and denied Allah's mercy.

It is worth mentioning what lured the Aws and Khazraj to accept Islam was that they heard a lot from the Jews concerning the eminent emissary of the Prophet (SAW), and that they were waiting for this to believe in him and thereby attain a better status with him.

Scholars have mentioned many examples of this. [21]Asem Ibn Amer Ibn Qitada el-Ansari said: "What brought us to believe in Islam- alongside the mercy of Allah and His guidance- was that we often heard from the Jews. We were disbelievers then, and they were the People of the Book who had knowledge of things we didn't have knowledge of. There were still hostilities and enmities between us and them. Whenever we were able to gain something in spite of them, they would say: 'The time of a prophet to be sent was fast approaching; we will follow him and kill you like Aad and Iram. When Allah sent Muhammad (ASW) as a Messenger, we accepted him when he called us unto Allah. We knew what they were promising and forecasting, and we took the initiative and believed in him, and they did not. About them and us the Almighty says: "Although they used to pray for victory by means of the Prophet over the polytheists, when there came to them a Book from Allah which they recognized,[2] confirming the Scripture they had in their hands, they rejected it. So may Allah's condemnation be upon the disbelievers." (Q 2:89) [22]

This noble verse alerted the Jews to their misguidance, obstinacy and ungratefulness in order to abandon this attitude, come to their senses and accept the Prophet (SAW) who was spoken of in their books and whose name they used to invoke- before his emissary- to have victory over the infidels and polytheists.

F- Turning their attention that the Noble Qur'an that was sent to Muhammad confirms previous divinely inspired books and having supreme authority on them. predominates and surpasses them.

Among the methods that Islam used to call the People of the Book to pay allegiance and adhere to Islam and follow its Prophet was to alert them that the Noble Qur'an- Muhammad's (SAW) greatest miracle- corroborates and confirms previous Scriptures (divinely inspired books) and has supreme authority on them. The Noble Qur'an reiterates this in many of its verses. Among them: "We have revealed to you O Prophet this Book with the truth, as a confirmation of previous Scriptures and a supreme authority on them." (Qur'an 5:48) [23]

Meaning: Just as We revealed the Torah to Moses and the Bible to Jesus- peace be upon both of them-, We have revealed to you, Muhammad, the Book, that is, the Noble Qur'an with the truth, the unquestionable truth that it came from Allah, as a confirmation of previous Scriptures, that is, supporting and confirming the other divinely inspired books that had preceded it such as the Torah and the Bible.

And after the Almighty Allah described the Noble Qur'an as a confirmation of previous Scriptures, He added another trait and said: "a supreme authority on them."

Ibn Abbas said the words "supreme authority" refer to faithfulness and honesty. That is to say, the Qur'an is faithful to every book preceding it. Mujahid and Qatada said that the words "supreme authority" refer to the Qur'an witnessing for previously inspired books. Ibn Juryj said that the Qur'an is faithful and loyal to previous books and that what is in agreement with it is truthful and what is at variance with it is worthless and futile.

Imam Ibn Kathir said that all of these sayings are close in meaning and that the words "supreme authority" denote and reflect these meanings. It is a faithful and honest witness and judge of all the previous books. Allah made this magnificent book the last and concluding book, the most comprehensive, the greatest and the most thorough. In it, He gathered together all the splendid and exquisite things in the previous books while also adding magnificent and glorious things that were not in the previous books. For this reason, Allah made it a witness faithfully judging everything, and He kept it well-preserved. He said: "It is certainly We Who have revealed the Reminder, and it is certainly We Who will preserve it."

Our honorable Professor Dr. Muhammad Abdullah Draz said that the Noble Qur'an added another quality in addition to its being "a confirmation of previous Scriptures." It declared that it also came with a supreme authority over these books. In other words, it was a guardian and a keeper for them. And an honest protection of these books would not be limited to the guardian's support of what history had immortalized in these books of what is righteous and just. Rather, it should go beyond that to protect them from intruders and meddlers who may unlawfully and dishonestly add to them and to highlight- when necessary- the facts that might have been submerged and hidden.

Therefore, the Qur'an had to abolish additions and challenge those who claimed certain things existed in these books "Say, O Prophet, Bring the Torah and read it, if your claims are true." (Qur'an 3:93) It also had to reveal what was necessary to reveal of the things that they hid and concealed: "O People of the Book! Now Our Messenger has come to you, revealing much of what you have hidden." (Qur'an 5:15) [24]

One of the verses that show that the Noble Qur'an confirmed the previous Scriptures is His saying: "This is a blessed Book which We have revealed—confirming what came before it—so you may warn the Mother of Cities (Mecca) and everyone around it. Those who believe in the Hereafter ⌜truly⌝ believe in it and guard their prayers." (Qur'an 6:92) [25]

The Almighty also said: "In their stories there is truly a lesson for people of reason. This message cannot be a fabrication, rather it is a confirmation of previous revelation, a detailed explanation of all things, a guide, and a mercy for people of faith." (Qur'an 12:111) [26]

And His saying: "It is not possible for this Quran to have been produced by anyone other than Allah. In fact, it is a confirmation of what came before, and an explanation of the Scripture. It is, without a doubt, from the Lord of all worlds." (Qur'an 10:37) [27]

These noble verses indicate that the Noble Qur'an that descended upon Muhammad (SAW) confirmed the previous Scriptures that were revealed to prophets before him, and that it has supreme authority over them. Therefore, the People of the Book should believe in him because it brought them what confirms what is in their books of the correct statutes and the true and straight meanings. It had also eradicated the corruptions and alterations that found their way to these books while revealing what their rabbis and monks had unjustly concealed and hid. Moreover, it detailed accounts of the law: what is permissible and what is forbidden, what is good and what is evil.

A book such as this can only be Divinely inspired, revealed from Allah Almighty, and any reasonable person will only have to strongly and profoundly believe in- and most vehemently trust- whatever is contained therein.

Second: Turning their attention to the fact that Muhammad's call is essentially and at its very core in agreement with what other prophets had called for.

This was another method that the Noble Qur'an used to call the Jews to accept Islam and believe in Muhammad (SAW). This method can be summed up in: The Noble Qur'an mentioned to them that the religion of Islam- to which Muhammad (SAW) called them to accept- was in essence and at its very core in agreement and harmony with what most of the previous prophets called for. Many verses in the Noble Qur'an reflect this meaning. Among them is the Almighty's saying: "He has ordained for you believers the Way which He decreed for Noah, and what We have revealed to you O Prophet and what We decreed for Abraham, Moses, and Jesus, commanding: "Uphold the faith, and make no divisions in it." What you call the polytheists to is unbearable for them. Allah chooses for Himself whoever He wills, and guides to Himself whoever turns to Him." (Qur'an 42:13) [28]

This means that the Almighty Allah had ordained for you, O Muslims, the same things He had decreed to Noah and the other prophets who came after him until the arrival of Muhammad.

Noah, Abraham, Moses and Jesus are specifically mentioned for their higher status and prominence, for they are- along with the Prophet (SAW)- the most distinguished among all messengers. Also, all prophets who came with similar messages calling people to monotheism, belief in Allah, His Divine Books and the Day of Judgement. About them, the Almighty says: "We never sent a messenger before you O Prophet without revealing to him: "There is no God worthy of worship except Me, so worship Me alone." (Qur'an 21:25) [29]

Then the Almighty showed His commandment to all of them: "Uphold the faith, and make no divisions in it." (Qur'an 42:13) Meaning: keep this religion, i.e., the belief that there is only one Allah (Monotheism) forever, and faithfully and devotedly worship Allah. Keep the religion unadulterated, without changes or alterations, and make sure that nothing is added to it that Allah did not ordain or allow, and do not take some parts from it and leave other parts.

Commanding them not to be divided amongst themselves is part and parcel of the religion and its basic tenets and foundation. These include belief in Allah and His angels, his Books and Messengers, and the Day of judgement. However, some laws may differ from others in matters pertaining to the specifics and particular details, as Allah Almighty mentioned: "To each of you We have ordained a code of law and a way of life." (Qur'an 5:48) [30]

The Almighty then presented the position of the polytheists from the religion of monotheism. He said: "What you call the polytheists to is unbearable for them." (Qur'an 42:13) Meaning: it was difficult and beneath the polytheists to accept what you are calling them to- believing in one Allah and abandoning worshipping other Gods, because they had inherited this wanton wickedness and polytheism from their spoiled elite, their forefathers. When they were called to accept the religion of truth, they would say- as recounted by the Noble Qur'an: "We found our forefathers following a particular way, and we are walking in their footsteps." (Qur'an 43:23)

Then Almighty Allah indicated those who are worthy of His favor and guidance. He said: "Allah chooses for Himself whoever He wills, and guides to Himself whoever turns to Him." (Qur'an 42:13)

In other words, the Almighty chooses whomsoever He wants from amongst His servants, brings them closer to Him, facilitates the obedience of those who draw closer to Him, and those who show true and genuine penitence.

Thus, the honorable verse indicated that the messages of most of the prophets were basically the same in so far as their core, essence, spirit, and intentions were concerned.

The Noble Qur'an mentioned that Abraham and Jacob- whom the Jews claim to follow- had both urged and advised them to accept the religion of Islam. In Sura Al-Baqarah, the Almighty says: "And who would reject the faith of Abraham except a fool! We certainly chose him in this life, and in the Hereafter he will surely be among the righteous. (Qur'an 2:130) When his Lord ordered him, "Submit to My Will," he responded, "I submit to the Lord of all worlds." (Q 2:131) This was the advice of Abraham—as well as Jacob—to his children, saying, "Indeed, Allah has chosen for you this faith; so do not die except in a state of full submission. (Q 2:132) Or did you witness when death came to Jacob? He asked his children, "Who will you worship after my passing?" They replied, "We will continue to worship your God, the God of your forefathers—Abraham, Ishmael, and

Isaac—the One Allah. And to Him we all submit." (Q 2:133) "That was a community that had already gone before. For them is what they earned and for you is what you have earned. And you will not be accountable for what they have done." (Q 2:134)

In His saying, "And who would reject the faith of Abraham except a fool!" The meaning is: Nobody would reject the religion of Abraham, abandon it and follow many Gods except for the undignified fool, the heedless and misguided who is likely to do himself an injustice because of his erroneous judgement and lack of discernment and would thus abandon the religion of truth and go astray.

Then the Almighty Allah revealed the high status of His Prophet Abraham- peace on him- and the erroneous conduct of those who steer away from his sublime and lofty ways. He said: "We certainly chose him in this life, and in the Hereafter, he will surely be among the righteous." Meaning: We had chosen him as a messenger to guide people in this world. Also, in the next world, he is among the righteous ones who followed the straight path. Anyone who steers away from the path of someone of such a status and follows unrighteous and wicked ways will be found unparalleled in his folly, recklessness and misguidance.

Then the Almighty Allah showed Abraham's thorough perfection which lifted him to such a high status. He said: "When his Lord ordered him, "Submit ⸢to My Will⸣," he responded, "I submit to the Lord of all worlds." Meaning: The Almighty Allah chose Abraham because He commanded him to obey and submit to Him in every situation, and Abraham submitted utterly and obeyed wholeheartedly: "I submit to the Lord of all worlds," which is, I am completely devoted to Allah who created all the creation. The Noble Qur'an also recounts this about him: "I have turned my face towards the One Who has originated the heavens and the earth—being upright—and I am not one of the polytheists." (Al-An'am:79; Q 6:79)

After the Almighty Allah showed that Abraham- peace on him- was complete and thorough in perfection, He followed that with a statement that he was also working to perfect others and call them to monotheism. The Almighty said: "This was the advice of Abraham—as well as Jacob—to his children, ⸢saying⸣, "Indeed, Allah has chosen for you this faith; so do not die except in a state of full submission."

The demonstrative "this" refers to the religion (the way) that was previously mentioned in His saying: "who would reject the faith of Abraham." Abraham urged and pressed his children to follow in his footsteps. So did Jacob who also urged and advised his children to do the same. Both told their children: "do not die except in ⸢a state of full⸣ submission." Meaning: Be firm in your belief in Islam- the upright religion- and which is the only religion that Allah accepts, and adhere to it steadfastly until death.

The Noble Qur'an then denounced the calumny that the Jews levelled against Jacob claiming that he was a follower of Judaism which they followed abandoning the religion of Islam (i.e., Islam being the "true" Judaism). The Almighty said: "Or did you witness when death came to Jacob? He asked his children, "Who will you worship after my passing?" (Q 2:133)

It was said that the Jews asked the Prophet (SAW): "Don't you know that Jacob advised his children to follow Judaism. That is why this verse was revealed.[31]

The meaning: O Jews! You were present when Jacob was on his deathbed, and he said to his children: "Who will you worship after my passing?" How can you claim that he followed Judaism- that you are following- and that he pressed his children to adopt? The meaning of Jacob's question was to have them pledge to steadfastly follow the doctrine of their father Abraham after his passing in order for them to live happily in this world and in the hereafter. Their answer to him showed their resolve and steadfast and unwavering faith. They replied, "We will ˹continue to˺ worship your God, the God of your forefathers—Abraham, Ishmael, and Isaac—the One Allah. And to Him we ˹all˺ submit." (Q 2:133)

This response indicated that they adhered to the doctrine of Abraham- peace be upon him. It is a doctrine where there is no Trinity and no likening (Allah) to other creatures. It is worshipping One Allah only, in complete submission and utter obedience.

Then the Almighty Allah warned the People of the Book against relinquishing His obedience relying on their lineage to their forefathers who were righteous prophets. He said: "That was a community that had already gone before. For them is what they earned and for you is what you have earned. And you will not be accountable for what they have done." (Q 2:134)

The word "that" refers to Abraham and his children. In other words, it refers to Abraham and his offspring. It was a community that had disappeared; it was gone. They will have their recompense for their good or evil deeds. On the Day of Judgement, you will not be asked about their deeds while they were alive; you will not be accountable or responsible, and you will not be asked why did they do this and that. You will only be accountable for your own deeds, so mend them and do the best you can, and believe in Muhammad (SAW) and his religion, for he is what Abraham had called upon you to accept.

This noble verse is mentioned to emphasize one of Allah's general and basic decrees: that everyone is solely responsible for their deeds, i.e., everyone will be rewarded for their good deeds, and they will be punished for their evil ones. Thus, the noble verses clearly showed the Children of Israel- and others- that the religion of Abraham was Islam, and that he and Jacob- peace be upon them- had advised and encouraged their children to staunchly hold unto this religion until death. The children of Jacob promised their father that they unwaveringly stick to his religion- and Abraham's- peace be upon them.

Those things that the noble verses have demonstrated- believing in the Almighty Allah- accepting His Messenger and following the decrees and teachings of Islam- are in agreement with Muhammad's (SAW) call and his message to them.

Also, there are other verses in the Noble Qur'an that explicitly stated that Islam is the name of the religion that all prophets called for and which their followers adopted. Noah said to his people: "And if you turn away, remember I have never demanded a reward from you ˹for delivering the message˺. My reward is only from Allah. And I have been commanded to be one of those who submit to Allah." (Qur'an 10:72) [32]

And Moses said to his people: "O my people! If you do believe in Allah and submit to His Will, then put your trust in Him. "[33]

And the disciples of Jesus told Him: "We will stand up for Allah. We believe in Allah, so bear witness that we have submitted." (Q 10:84) [34]

Moreover, upon hearing the Qur'an recited to them, the hearts of a group of the People of the Scriptures were filled with light and joy, and they were fascinated by its call and they said, "We believe in it. This is definitely the truth from our Lord. We had already submitted even before this." (Qur'an 28:53) [35]

So far, we have mentioned some of the noble verses that show that what Muhammad (SAW) brought them was in agreement with what previous prophets called for. Therefore, they had to believe and trust in him, for disbelieving him meant a suspicion and distrust of all the previous prophets.

Before concluding this topic, we would like to alert you to an important issue. As we mentioned before, what the Prophet (SAW) brought was in agreement with what other prophets before him called for concerning such issues as the basic tenets of religion, i.e., believing in One God only, worshipping Him and no other, believing in what the previous prophets called for about Allah Almighty, believing in the Resurrection and the afterlife and the rewards and punishments entailed therein, encouraging rectitude and righteousness, etc. As for issues related to the specifics concerning certain ways of worship and manners of interactions, codes of law generally differ as to what is fitting and suitable to the community to which Allah sent a messenger: "To each of you We have ordained a code of law and a way of life." (Q 5:48)

From this concept the Islamic Law came with something that was not in existence in previous laws and doctrines. The Noble Qur'an declared to people that Muhammad's doctrine had its advantages as it made it permissible to people to partake of all that was good and prohibited all that was evil. It also relieved them from their burdens and rid them of the shackles that tie them, as it endorsed ways pertaining to manners of worship and interactions characterized by ease and felicity.

I would like to seize this chance and commend what our late Professor Sheikh Muhammad Abdullah Draz said in this respect: "It must be understood that amending an earlier code of law by a later one is not considered rescinding or repealing it. Rather, it is to have it cater for the needs of the moment."

Here is an example for this. Three physicians: the first one came to see a child at an early stage in his life and restricted his diet to milk. At a later stage in the child's life, the second physician allowed the child milk and some food containing some carbohydrates. At yet a later stage in the child's life, the third physician recommended the child to take a complete well-balanced diet.

There is no doubt here that each one of these physicians implicitly agreed that the other physicians were thoroughly successful in dealing with the child's condition as it manifested itself at a specific time. Indeed, there are general health rules concerning sanitation, ventilation, heating and the like. These do not change, and they are not subject to alteration or modifications. On such issues Pediatrics and Geriatrics do not differ.

So is the case with the Heavenly Laws. They are all truthful and just whether as a whole or in their details and specifics. They all validate each other from A to Z. This endorsement takes two forms:

Endorsing the old and allowing it to stay and continue while keeping it within the boundaries if its past circumstances. That is because the Heavenly Doctrines contain two kinds of decrees:

Eternal decrees: These do not change and can not be amended when there are changes in circumstances (such as the Nine Commandments and the like).

Temporary decrees: These could last for either a long or a short time. They end when they are no longer needed. Other decrees- that are better equipped to handle sudden rising situations- are instituted.

The decrees of the Torah, for example, were concerned with instituting the basic fundamental laws of conduct: "Do not kill… Do not steal." The most prominent feature of these laws was to specify rights and seek justice and equality.

The decrees of the Bible came after the decrees of the Torah and validated what was contained therein. It then went a step farther and added things that are more sublime: "Do good unto those who do you harm."

And finally, the decrees of the Qur'an that combine both precepts in one verse: "Allah commands justice and benevolence." (Qur'an 16:90)

Thus, the heavenly decrees ascending steps in building higher codes of conduct and morality to maintain the structure and policies of the community. The last step had completed this structure and filled in whatever was, lacking, deficient and unfulfilled. At the same time, it was like the cornerstone that held together all the parts of the structure.

Truthful was the Messenger of Allah when he aptly and most fittingly depicted the heavenly decrees in their totality, saying: "Me and those prophets before me are like a man who built a house, beautified and perfected it except for a brick. He made the people go around the house to look at and admire. They said: 'What about that brick?' I am the brick and I am the seal of the prophets." [36]

Thus, it is evident that the harmony and agreement of the Islamic decrees with the other preceding decrees is in the basics and generalities, not the specifics and particulars.

Third: Enticing them- through wisdom and good counsel- to accept Muhammad's call.

The Noble Qur'an used many different types of incentives and attractions to entice the People of the Book to accept Islam. The Qur'an showed them that in accepting the Prophet (SAW) lie their happiness and well-being, the protection of their money and their blood in this world, their success and affluence, and finding favor in the sight of Allah in the afterlife. It had also demonstrated that what Muhammad (SAW) was calling them to follow should be accepted by all those reasonable and sound-minded. It was something that would please the righteous hearts, and instill peace and comfort in their souls. Reasonable people would never disagree that it was righteousness and mercy.

Among the verses which reveal how the Noble Qur'an persuaded the People of the Book to enter into Islam is the Almighty's saying: Say, "O Prophet, "O People of the Book! Let us come to common terms: that we will worship none but Allah, associate none with Him, nor take one another as lords instead of Allah." But if they turn away, then say, "Bear witness that we have submitted to Allah alone." (Qur'an 3:64) [37]

Meaning: Tell Muhammad the People of the Book "Let us come to common terms" and draw near to a just and impartial word between you and us, a word that the Qur'an, the Torah and the Bible agree upon. This word is "we will worship none but Allah, associate none with Him," none of His creatures. We will not "take one another as lords instead of Allah." That is to say, we will not follow or obey one another when it comes to wrongdoing. Rather, we obey to shun and veer away from the things that Allah had prohibited and vilified. We will all pay homage to Allah's decrees and ordinances: what He had commanded us to do and what He had prohibited us from doing, what He made "Halal" permissible and what He assigned as "Haram" or unallowable.

Then the Almighty Allah showed the believers what they should say to the People of the Book if they failed to listen and obey this word of truth. He said: "If they turn away, then say, 'Bear witness that we have submitted to Allah alone'". This means: If those whom you call to Allah's unicity turn away and disregard your call, then you believers should tell them 'Bear witness, O you People of the Book- that we are submitting to Allah alone, devoutly following the word of truth. We were fair to you; we invited but you did not accept it. We have our religion, and you have yours. Allah will judge us and He is the best of Judges."

This Noble verse manifests the most prudent and discreet method in this righteous call. It invited the People of the Book to Monotheism, to associate none with Allah. This was a message that was revealed in all the heavenly revelations. It contained what convinces the reasonable and judicious and what instills peace and comfort in one's heart in the best and most pleasant of styles and with eloquence and persuasiveness. For this reason, the Prophet (SAW) used it in calling others to Allah. He would mention it in his messages to kings and princes- when he invited them to Islam- as he did in his message to Hercules, the Roman King.

Also, among the verses in the Noble Qur'an that judiciously and serenely invited the People of the Book to accept Islam was: "O People of the Book! Now Our Messenger has come to you, revealing much of what you have hidden of the Scriptures and disregarding much. There certainly has come to you from Allah a light and a clear Book, through which Allah guides those who seek His pleasure to the ways of peace, brings them out of darkness and into light by His Will, and guides them to the Straight Path." (Qur'an 5:15-16) [38]

The meaning of these two verses is: "O People of the Book! Now Our Messenger has come to you," i.e., Muhammad (SAW), "revealing much of what you have hidden of the Scriptures." That is to say, he will show you, O Jews, many of the decrees and laws that your books had mentioned, but you hid and concealed from your people, i.e., concealing the trait of the Prophet (SAW) that was mentioned in your books as well as concealing the good tidings about his coming, and others. These are some of the issues that you concealed from your people, but the Prophet (SAW) made sure to reveal them, bring the truth to light and set matters straight.

Then, the Noble Qur'an revealed that the Messenger (SAW) did not reveal other things that they concealed. The Almighty said: "disregarding much." In other words, he did not reveal what you had concealed. Rather, he opted to disregard it as there was no necessity to reveal it, and it would avail people nothing if it were to be disclosed. Not revealing it was a sign of compassion and mercy unto people, a way of avoiding reproach, criticism and admonition.

It is noteworthy that revealing much of what they had concealed, and pardoning much of what they had hidden entailed a miracle and a great feat. Since he did not read a book or sat in the presence of an instructor, being informed about the secrets of what is contained in their books was to be considered a miraculous awareness of what was hidden, what was not manifest or apparent. In a sense, it was a miracle that should have pressed them to believe and accept his call and become loyal to him.

Then, the Almighty praised the goodness and guidance that His Messenger had brought: "There certainly has come to you from Allah a light and a clear Book." You, People of the Book, a light and a clear Book, i.e., the Noble Qur'an- which will dissolve the darkness of disbelief and guide people to what was good and beneficial for them in this world and in the hereafter- had come to them.

The Almighty revealed to the People of the Book the advantages of this light that came from Allah and the benefits that they would enjoy when they follow this light: "through which Allah guides those who seek His pleasure to the ways of peace, brings them out of darkness and into light by His Will, and guides them to the Straight Path." In other words, Allah will guide those who walk in this light to peace and safety from all misery and misfortune.

And His saying He will "bring them out of darkness and into light by His Will" means that He will bring them from disbelief and associating others with Allah to the light and brigtness of Islam, by His will.

And His He "guides them to the Straight Path" means that He will guide and lead them to the right and upright religion, the straight path that is devoid of aberrations and deviations.

Thus, the two verses had invited the Jews to follow Muhammad (SAW) in the most decent of ways, eloquently, and with astounding clarity. They showed them such great benefits and wonderful privileges that should have pushed them to hasten to believe and accept him, that is, if they were among those who would follow good counsel.

And among the noble verses that invited the People of the Book to believe Muhammad (SAW) and erased any excuse for them: "O People of the Book! Our Messenger has indeed come to you, making things clear to you after an interval [39] between the messengers so you do not say, 'There has never come to us a deliverer of good news or a warner.' Now there has come to you a deliverer of good news and a warner. And Allah is Most Capable of everything." (Qur'an 5:19) [40]

In this verse, the Almighty shows the value of the Mohammaden (Islamic) message. It came when the world was in a dire need for such a message. Speaking to the People of the Book, the Almighty said: "O People of the Book! Our Messenger has indeed come to you, making things clear to you after an interval between the messengers." Meaning: O you People of the Book- whose awareness and knowledge of the Book should have directed you to obey. Our Messenger Mohammad had come to you to show you what you had been commanded to do and what you had been instructed to abandon when there was an interval in which no messengers were sent and a time wherein there were no guidance or instructions. There was no messengers or prophets between him and Jesus as mentioned in the honorable saying: I am the closest of people to Jesus, son of Mary.... there is not a prophet among us." [41]

For Allah sent Muhammad (SAW) at a time of blurry and indistinct doctrines, distorted and corrupt religions and growing idol worshipping. His coming was the perfection of all blessings.

Then the Noble Qur'an mentioned what deprived them of any excuses: "so you do not say, 'There has never come to us a deliverer of good news or a warner.'" Meaning: O, People of the Book, Our Messenger, Mohammad, had come to you after an interval between the messengers. He had come to show you the correct and straight path. You have no excuse now and, in the Day of Judgement- you will not be able to say we did not have a deliverer of good news who promised goodness for our obedience. You will not be able to claim that you did not have a warner who warned you of punishment for your disobedience. In short, this statement denied them any excuse and deprived them of any justification and pretexts if they were to feign ignorance and claim- in the Day of Judgement- that no messenger came to guide them to what is good and forbid them from what is evil. Therefore, the Almighty said: "Now there has come to you a deliverer of good news and a warner."

That is, We sent him to you and you had no excuse. You cannot say that no deliverer of good news and a warner had come to us. Muhammad (SAW) came to you as a deliverer of good news and a warner. He promised good tidings if you believed and did good deeds. He forewarned you with severe punishment if you continued your disbelief and obstinacy and defiance of the truth. You should accept and believe him because he guides you to the truth and the straight path.

Allah Almighty concluded this honorable verse by showing His power and authority. He said: "Allah is Most Capable of everything." Thus, the noble verse showed the nobility of the Muhammadian message and its magnanimity. It came when people were in dire need for it. The Jews should have believed this unlettered Prophet, a deliverer of good tidings and a warner, who removed the pretext of ignorance from them in order to obtain the favor of the Almighty.

Fourth: Warning them of severe punishment if they did not accept Muhammad (SAW)

As the Noble Qur'an used many methods to attract and encourage the Jews in calling them to Islam, as we demonstrated earlier, it also warned them to shun disbelief, immorality and disobedience and to press them to do good deeds, believe and submit.

Among the verses that marks that warning of punishment to the People of the Book if they failed to accept the truth is His saying: "O you who were given the Book! Believe in what We have revealed—confirming your own Scriptures—before We wipe out your faces, turning them backwards, or We condemn the defiant as We did to the Sabbath-breakers. And Allah's command is always executed! Indeed, Allah does not forgive associating others with Him in worship, but forgives anything else of whoever He wills. And whoever associates others with Allah has indeed committed a grave sin." (Qur'an 4:47-48) [42]

Ibn Jarir relates on the authority of Ibn 'Abbas- may Giod be pleased with them- that the Messenger of Allah (SAW) talked with Jewish scholars and rabbis like Abdullah bin Soriya and K'ab bin Asad. He told them: "O, Jews, fear Allah and submit. By Allah, you know that what I am calling you to accept is the truth." They responded saying: "We do not know that Muhammad." They rejected what they knew and insisted on their disbelief. In reference to them, Allah revealed: "O you who were given the Book! Believe in what We have revealed—confirming your own Scriptures—before We wipe out ˹your˺ faces, turning them backwards, or We condemn the defiant as We did to the Sabbath-breakers.[1] And Allah's command is always executed!" [43]

The Almighty Allah started the first verse by calling the People of the Book commanding them to believe Muhammad: "O you who were given the Book! Believe in what We have revealed—confirming your own Scriptures."

This honorable statement contains two incentives for them to believe:
First: They were given the Book and knowledge of what is therein, and because of this knowledge they should have rushed to believe in the Prophet's call. They should have refrained from their religious fanaticism and prejudice just as the people of Mecca were consumed by their tribal and pre-Islamic strife and fanaticism.

Second: That faith to which they were called to accept was believing in what Allah' revelation to Muhammad (SAW)- the Qur'an- because it was essentially and fundamentally in agreement with what He had revealed to other previous prophets in whom the People of the Book claim they believe. Since the Revealer was ONE, this should have necessitated that they believe in all that the Almighty Allah had revealed to all His messengers. Otherwise, they would be regarded as a people that make a distinction between Allah and His messengers, by saying: "We believe in some and disbelieve in others," desiring to forge a compromise." From Qur'an 4:150)

Then, the Almighty Allah warned them of severe punishment in this world and in the next if they did not accept Muhammad. He said: "before We wipe out your faces, turning them backwards, or And Allah's command is always executed."

This means: You people who were given the Divine Book- the Torah-, you ought to believe in the Qur'an which We revealed to you and which confirms the basic tenets and pillars of your religion before We afflict you with one of these two penalties:

The First: The Noble Qur'an pointed at this punishment by saying "before We wipe out [44]'your' faces, turning them backwards."

Mujaahid said it means "we turned their faces away from the True Path, and so we will turn them unto their backs for their error.

Al-Suddi said that it means that we will blind them to the truth and turn them back to their former state of disbelief.

Al-DaHaak said that it means that we will turn them away from clear guidance and vision, for he had already turned them over on their backs, so they disbelieved in Muhammad (SAW) and the messages he brought.

What is obvious from these interpretations is that they refer to moral humiliation and annihilation.

And the meaning is: Believe before your hearts harden and eradicate them because of your hearts' persistence in clinging to disbelief and their abominable obstinacy. It is similar to the Almighty's: "O believers! Respond to Allah and His Messenger when he calls you to that which gives you life. And know that Allah stands between a person and their heart, and that to Him you will all be gathered." (Qur'an 8:24) [45]

The heart is the mind. Standing between a person and his heart means to deprive him from sound judgement and clear sightedness. This is similar to the Almighty's "and have placed a barrier before them and a barrier behind them and covered them all up, so they fail to see the truth. It is the same whether you warn them or not—they will never believe." (Qur'an 36:9-10) [46]

It is obvious that the word "barrier" here refers to an intangible moral hindrance which will lead to their inability to behold guidance and perceive and reach the truth.

As for the second punishment, it was mentioned in His: "Or We condemn the defiant as We did to the Sabbath-breakers." (Q 4:47)The meaning of "condemn" here is exile and moral humiliation.

In sum, the verse is an invitation to the Jews before the Almighty Allah deprives them of their ability to discern and takes away their capacity to judge rightly, and they will thus be unable to march in the ways of truth nor will they be able to feel inclined to it. It is an invitation to them before He condemns them and exiles them from His mercy and compassion, an invitation before He proclaims exile and moral humiliation and inflicts severe punishment.

The word "or" in this verse indicates that the Almighty may punish a group of them with one of these two punishments and the other group with another punishment if they were to continue in their disbelief and ungratefulness.

Yet, some scholars offered other interpretations:

The Almighty's: "before We wipe out your faces, turning them backwards" may have meant to indicates a tangible and concrete punishment. That would mean wiping out the features of the face, the nose, the eyes and the mouth- and changing it to be utterly indistinguishable. And His saying: "Or We condemn the defiant as We did to the Sabbath-breakers" means that we would change them into disdained apes as We did to those who did not preserve the Sabbath. This interpretation is taken from Ibn Abbas- Allah be pleased with him- and it was adopted by a number of interpreters. Then, they differed amongst themselves as to when that was likely to pass. Some said that it would be at the end of time, others said that it would be in the afterlife.

In short, what the verse means is: Believe in the Qur'an before one of these two forms of punishment come upon you:

The first: Allah will instruct the believers to fight you, and you will retreat in defeat, and only the back of your heads will be apparent.

The second: We will condemn you as We condemned the men of the Sabbath, and you would be exiled from Our mercy. We will stamp your hearts and minds, and you will be left without discernment and understanding. You will be left on earth scattered and in miserable wretchedness.

It was said that “wiping out” could mean utter change. Also, “faces” is a reference to chiefs and heads (superiors).

The meaning is: Believe in the Qur’an before We change the conditions of your chiefs and superiors, deprive their faces of their good looks, cover them with humiliation and disgrace, or condemn them as We condemned the men of the Sabbath.

It is also possible that the meaning of “wipe out your faces” as mentioned, i.e., Believe before we send you nobles and chiefs to Adhra’at (in the Levant) in miserable shame and sycophantic servility, or before We condemn them as We condemned the men of the Sabbath.

So, Allah had caused humiliation and shame to be the lot of the chiefs and heads, a punishment for their disbelief for they were the most distinguished and prominent in the nation, a symbol thereof. If they were to be humiliated and shamed, the whole nation is humiliated and shamed.

Concerning this interpretation, Abdul Rahman Ibn Zeid said that that warning did in fact come true to the Jews. Banu Qaynuqa and Banu Nadir were forced to leave the Levant. They were thus forced to flee to Adhra’at and Jerico, just as they came from there.

We believe that the first interpretation which we advanced in interpreting these verses as the most viable since it agrees the most with the meaning of the verse. It is also devoid of contradictions and incongruities, as it is the most widely adopted interpretation by the greatest number of exegeses. Other interpretations suffer incongruities, and we thought it would make the best sense not to deal with them here. Some interpreters such Al-Razi and Al-Alusi dealt with this in detail.

The Almighty’s “And Allah’s command is always executed” (Q 4:47) means that all the things that Allah had ordained were undoubtedly bound to pass for nothing- on earth or in heaven- would stand in Allah’s way.

The pronoun in “We will curse them” (Q 4:47) refers to the owners of the faces, or, by way of object switching, it refers to those who were given the Book.

Then the Almighty reiterated that He would not forgive anyone who ascribes partners with Him. Except for this sin, He may forgive whomever He wills: “Allah does not forgive associating others with Him in worship, but forgives anything else of whoever He wills. And whoever associates others with Allah has indeed committed a grave sin.” (Qur’an 4:48, and 4:116)

Meaning: Allah would not forgive the Jews who did not believe in Muhammad (SAW) their grievous sins and dreadful transgressions. Associating others with Him ⌜in worship, and ascribing partners to Allah is "a grave sin."

Thus, the two noble verses (Q 4:47-48) had specifically asked the Jews to believe in Muhammad (SAW). They showed that their disbelief would lead humiliation and shame in this world and severe punishment and torture in the next. The Almighty would not forgive those who ascribe partners with Him. Other than that, He may forgive whomever He wills.

Fifth: Informing them that disputing religion was due to debauchery and wanton envy.

In essence, the heavenly laws are the same. They are all revealed by Allah to guide mankind to what is good and beneficial for them in this world and the next. They differ only in the details, not the essentials, in minute aspects, not the basics. This difference in the details and minute aspects between laws is a sign of Allah's mercy for His people, for He instituted for each community that which is appropriate for them in accordance with their particular needs and circumstances.

Muhammad (SAW) brought the final revelation, the seal of all religious laws, having superiority and dominance over them and confirming their basic and fundamental tenets, i.e., worshipping One God (i.e., Allah) only (Monotheism), belief in Allah's messengers, possessing moral integrity and demonstrating noble qualities and behaviors.

The Jews should have rushed to believe in this unlettered prophet who brought irrefutable proofs of the truthfulness of what he had received from his Allah. Yet, most of them were blind and deaf to the truth. They rejected Muhammad and refused to believe in him, even though they knew him as they knew their own sons. Then, they fiercely and feverishly differed among themselves.

The Noble Qur'an stated in many verses that the refusal of the People of the Book to enter Islam and follow Muhammad was due to their stubbornness, immorality and wanton envy, not logical evidence and indisputable proofs. One of the verses that clearly stated that is in Sura Al Imran (Qur'an 3:19-20): "Certainly, Allah's only Way is Islam. Those who were given the Scripture did not dispute ⌜among themselves⌝ out of mutual envy until knowledge came to them. Whoever denies Allah's signs, then surely Allah is swift in reckoning. So if they argue with you O Prophet, say, "I have submitted myself to Allah, and so have my followers." And ask those who were given the Scripture and the illiterate ⌜people, "Have you submitted yourselves to Allah?" If they submit, they will be rightly guided. But if they turn away, then your duty is only to deliver the message. And Allah is All-Seeing of His servants."

Allah said: "Allah's only Way is Islam."

Qataada said that Islam means the Shahaada that "There is no Allah but Allah," and acknowledging what was revealed by Allah, i.e., the religion that He had legislated for Himself and with which He sent His messengers and asked His awliyaa (friends) to proclaim. He only accepts these, and the reward comes from Him alone. [47]

Then Allah showed that the Jews did not reject Islam because of proofs that they possessed, but because of their obstinacy, immorality and envy: "Those who were given the Scripture did not dispute among themselves out of mutual envy until knowledge came to them." (Q 3:19) That is to say, those who were given the book did not disagree among themselves concerning Islam, and refused to accept it until knowledge came to them or, in other words, when they had learned that it was the undeniable and undisputable truth. Their disputing/rejection was not due to ignorance, doubt or lack of clarity. Rather, it was out of mutual envy. This means that their dispute and repudiation of the truth was caused by their wantonness and envious attitude to Muhammad whom Allah had favored and granted esteem and nobility. It was also because of their lust for power and perpetual pursuit of the pleasures and luxuries of this life. It was because of their degenerate wantonness, envy and their love for this world which, once it had penetrated one's heart, it removes the light of knowledge from it, makes it deny and denounce the truth and veer away from the path of belief and sink and wallow in disbelief, disobedience and debauchery.

Then the Almighty concluded the noble verse with a strong threat to anyone who would disbelieve in His verses: "Whoever denies Allah's signs, then surely Allah is swift in reckoning." (from Q 3:19) Meaning: whoever repudiates or denies Allah's signs which He had manifested as proofs for the sensible and judicious, and evidence for those who will weigh and consider, Allah will inflict a severe punishment upon him, for Allah is quick to judge and bring to account.

Then Allah guided His Messenger as to how to respond to them if they argued with him: "So if they argue with you O Prophet, say, 'I have submitted myself to Allah, and so have my followers.'" (Qur'an 3:20)

Meaning: If the People of the Book argued with you- Muhammad- concerning the religion of Islam (after it had been proven that it is the truthful religion), do not be concerned about arguing with them. Just tell them: "I have submitted myself to Allah." That is, I worship Allah Alone, with my tongue, with all my heart, and with all my being. I submit to Him alone, and I associate none of His creatures as a partner with Him. Also, those who follow me- "And so have my followers-" submit to Him.

The writer of Al-Kashaaf said: The Almighty's saying "if they argue with you" in matters related to the religion, say that you had submitted to Allah Alone and had not ascribed partners with Him. You only serve and worship Him Alone. In other words, the religion of Monotheism is the straight and right religion. And this was the religion that that was confirmed by your books, as I had been informed. I did not bring anything novel or new to argue with me about. This was also confirmed by the Almighty's: "O People of the Book! Let us come to common terms: that we will worship none but Allah, associate none with Him." In other words, Muhammad, and other believers with him, are on the right and straight path, one that is undoubtedly clear and flawless, so there was no need for controversy or arguments.[48]

Then the Almighty commanded His Messenger (SAW) to ask the People of the Book to follow his example and worship Allah with complete and utter loyalty and submit to Him thoroughly. He said: "And ask those who were given the Scripture and the illiterate people, 'Have you submitted yourselves to Allah?" This means: Muhammad, tell those who were given the Scriptures, especially the Jews- but also the gentiles who were not with a book- tell them all that If I had submitted to Allah along with those who followed and accepted my message, are you going to follow suit and do what I- and my followers- did now that you had learned the truth of what I had informed you about my Allah? The interrogation in the noble verse was meant to press and urge them to submit to Allah and to faithfully and devotedly worship Him just as the Prophet (SAW) and his companions did, and to abandon these false and pointless arguments since they would not to anything profitable. In seeking the truth, the important thing is to pursue it with pure hearts and faultless and impeccable intensions. Pointless and meaningless arguments avail nothing.

The author of Al-Kashaaf- may Allah rest his soul- had been poignant and effective in explaining this meaning. He said: "And ask those who were given the Scripture and the illiterate people, 'Have you submitted yourselves to Allah?'" (Q 3:20) In other words, you had been given enough proofs and evidence that necessitated your submission to Islam. Did you submit or are you still in this state of disbelief? You had made it very clear; you made everything clear and saved no effort to explain everything! So, did you understand? The questioning here indicates their stubbornness and unfairness. If they were fair and just, they would have succumbed to the truth. However, for the willful and stubborn, submission is not an option. In His "did you understand?'" was a reproach for idleness and slothfulness. In His "Will you not then abstain?" was a reproach for their apathy and their doing what they were forbidden (note: the latter possibly a reference to Qur'an 5:91) to do.

Then the Almighty showed their reward if they submitted to Him and their fate if they turned away. He said: "If they submit, they will be rightly guided. But if they turn away, then your duty is only to deliver the message. And Allah is All-Seeing of His servants." (Q 3:20) Meaning: If they submitted to Allah and worshipped Him faithfully, they would have been on the right path, rightly guided, and thus departed from disbelief and misguidance to uprightness and the correct direction. But if they turn away, refrain from stop calling them to the right path, for you only had to deliver 'the message'. You only inform them what We had commanded you to tell them, and it is up to Us to hold them accountable and "Allah is All-Seeing of His servants." That is to say, He is knowledgeable and cognizant of those who deserve guidance and those who deserve misguidance, for He is the One who "cannot be questioned about what He does, but they will all be questioned." (Qur'an 21:23)

The appendix to this noble verse is a consolation to the Prophet (SAW) for their disbelief, a reference to their state, and a warning to them of a grievous fate if they persevered in their stubbornness and disbelief.

Among the verses that clearly stated the reason for the difference of the People of the Book and their deviation from the truth and uprightness was dissipation and wanton envy. In Sura Al-Jathiyah, the Almighty says: "Indeed, We gave the Children of Israel the Scripture, wisdom, and prophethood; granted them good, lawful provisions; and favored them above the others. We also gave them clear commandments regarding their faith. But it was not until knowledge came to them that they differed out of mutual envy. Surely your Lord will judge between them on the Day of Judgment regarding their differences." (Qur'an 45:16-17)

Also, in Sura Ash-Shuraa: "They did not split into sects out of mutual envy until knowledge came to them. Had it not been for a prior decree from your Lord for an appointed term, the matter would have certainly been settled between them at once. And surely those who were made to inherit the Scripture after them are truly in alarming doubt about this Quran." (Qur'an 42:14)

These noble verses indicate that the reason for their difference and split concerning the upright religion- when knowledge came to them and they were certain that it came from Allah- was their mutual envy and degradation and their substituting the mean and lowly for the good and sublime. The Noble Qur'an mentioned that to them to become alert and go back to their senses, abandon their tribal solidarity and fanaticism, walk in the right path, and rush into believing in Muhammad whose truthfulness had been proven without a doubt and with clear proofs and undeniable evidence. They unquestionably knew all of that. In addition, the Qur'an also mentioned that accepting Islam meant their guidance and happiness and their rejection meant wretchedness and misery.

Sixth: Informing them that the Noble Qur'an tells them the truth about that with which they disagree.

The Noble Qur'an did not only point that the difference between the Jews in religion was caused by immorality and mutual envy, and that they should have abandoned these vices to follow the truth with which Muhammad came, but the Qur'an also told them that it had clarified those things on which they differed, and that it was time they opened their hearts to him, not to stand in his way and refrain from pushing other people not to follow him.

Among the verses that demonstrated to the People of the Book that the Noble Qur'an guides to what was truthful concerning the things with which they disagree is what Allah said in Sura An-Naml: "Indeed, this Quran clarifies for the Children of Israel most of what they differ over. And it is truly a guide and mercy for the believers. Your Lord will certainly judge between them by His justice, for He is the Almighty, All-Knowing. So put your trust in Allah, for you are surely upon the Path of clear truth." (Qur'an 27: 76-79)

Meaning: This Noble Qur'an that Allah revealed to His Messenger, Muhammad, informs the Children of Israel the truth of most of that about which they differed. It is the Book that confirms the other books and it has superiority over them. Where the books agree would be right and truthful, and where they do not agree is false and untrue.

The Children of Israel differed on many issues: they differed on the topic of abrogation. Some said that it was impossible logically and inapplicable legally. Others maintained that it was logically possible, but forbidden legally. They differed concerning Jesus- peace on Him- and related his lineage to Joseph, the carpenter. They attributed to His mother that of which she was innocent and without blemish. They differed concerning Abraham- peace on him- and said that he was a Jew. They also differed with the Prophet (SAW) on many issues that we mentioned in detail in another place.[49]

The Noble Qur'an narrated most of these differences and presented the truthful and righteous decisions and sayings. It called the Children of Israel to obey Allah and His Messenger and to follow what the Noble Qur'an called them to follow if they were among the rational and sensible who can heed an advice, follow the truth and pursue what is right and just.

Allah described the Noble Qur'an as "truly a guide and mercy for the believers." (Q 27:77) In other words, in addition to narrating to the Children of Israel most of the issues on which they differed while providing the word of truth on these issues, this Noble Qur'an was also a guide and mercy to the hearts of the believers who adopted its teachings, followed its upright ways which provided profitable advice and good counsel that would make them happy in this world and the next.

Then Allah showed that it was Him alone who judge among the Children of Israel concerning the things on which they differed: "Your Lord will certainly judge between them by His justice, for He is the Almighty, All-Knowing." (Q 27:78) Meaning: It is your Allah, Muhammad, who will judge between those who differed among the Children of Israel by passing His Judgement and justice on them on Judgement Day. He will reward those who had done good deeds, and He will punish those who had done evil deeds. He is the "Almighty" in His vengeance, and no one would be able to escape His judgement. He is the "All-Knowing" concerning all that they differed on, whom He will judge for and reward and whom He will judge against and punish.

Then Allah commanded His Prophet (SAW) to trust in Him, to continue and persevere in spreading the religion, to uplift His word, to take no heed of the enemies of the religion that stand in the way of the righteous path: "So put your trust in Allah, for you are surely upon the Path of clear truth." (Q 27:79) Whosoever follows Him will not be disappointed. Only the blind who can noy see the truth will abandon Him to be led astray.

Thus, these noble verses showed the Children of Israel that the Noble Qur'an contained and dealt with most of the issues on which they differed, and it treated these issues in accordance with what is right and just. They therefore had to come back to their senses, think rationally and soundly, abandon obstinacy and envy, and follow what Muhammad

(SAW) brought them to enjoy happiness in this world and Allah's pleasure and favor in the next.

Seventh: Providing proofs against them- by quoting them- to prove the truthfulness of the Prophet, (SAW).

Among the methods that the Noble Qur'an used in calling the People of the Book to enter Islam was quoting their books to prove the truthfulness of the Prophet (SAW) and ascertain that the Noble Qur'an was the revelation of the Omnipotent.

The Noble Qur'an had reiterated its push for them to follow the path of truth and uprightness through checking their own books and what their own prophets had brought them. The Qur'an did this in many of its verses that they might return to their senses and accept what they were called to.

Among the verses that point in this direction and reflect this meaning is Allah's saying: If you ˹O Prophet˺ are in doubt about ˹these stories˺ that We have revealed to you, then ask those who read the Scripture before you. The truth has certainly come to you from your Lord, so do not be one of those who doubt." (Qur'an 10:94) [50]

Which means: If you, O Messenger, had any doubts concerning any of the accounts, teachings or decrees that We had revealed to you in this Qur'an, you could ask the People of the Book who read the Torah and the Injil (Gospel). They know without the shadow of a doubt that you are right, and they know with certainty that the Qur'an that you brought them came from Allah, because their knowledge of these books provided them with this knowledge and asSurance. This noble verse does not mean that the Messenger (SAW) doubted what Allah revealed to him or that he should have asked the People of the Book for clarification or validity of truth. Rather, it was a mere hypothetical rhetorical device.

The author of Al-Kashaaf did a wonderful job in explaining this verse. He said: If you say how could the Almighty say to His Messenger (SAW) "If you O Prophet are in doubt about these stories that We have revealed to you" and His saying about the infidels that they were "truly in alarming doubt about this ˹Quran˺," I would say that the difference is great. That is to say, in saying they were "truly in alarming doubt about this Quran," there is a confirmation of the suspicion and doubt they felt experienced. On the other hand, in saying "If you … are in doubt" is merely a proposition, a suggestion. This means if you are in doubt and Satan tried to play a trick on you, then ask those who read the Scripture before you." The meaning is: Allah mentioned the Children of Israel as readers of the Books, that knowledge came to them, that the Messenger of Allah was revealed to them in the Torah and the Bible, and that they know him as they know their own sons. Allah was confirming their knowledge of the truth of the Qur'an, and the truthfulness of Muhammad's message. He went further and said: if -for any reason-you had any doubts, you could ask the learned ones among the People of the Book. They are well aware of the truth of what we revealed to you. The purpose behind this was confirming the knowledge that those scholars and rabbis had concerning the truth that was revealed to the Messenger of Allah, not attributing doubt to the Messenger of Allah concerning what was revealed. [51]

This eloquent Qur'anic expression had brought numerous and unquestionable evidence to strengthen one's belief and conviction, and establish undefeatable evidence to prove what should be proven or negate what ought to be discarded. The verse had proven that the People of the Book know- from their books- the undeniable truth of the Prophet (SAW).

Allah then commanded His Messenger to persevere in his call: "The truth has certainly come to you from your Lord, so do not be one of those who doubt." (Q 10:94) Meaning: It had become undoubtedly clear to you, O Muhammad, that what you had received from your Lord is the truth, the undeniable truth that is supported by overwhelming and striking evidence, so do not be one of those who doubt.

Thus, this noble verse presented an argument against the Children of Israel that they most certainly know the truth of the Prophet (SAW) through their divinely revealed books. It was therefore appropriate and becoming for them to accept, follow and believe in him. Otherwise, they would be perceived as among those who knowingly conceal the truth.

We have now concluded mentioning the most important methods that the Noble Qur'an had used to call the People of the Book in general, and the Jews, in particular, to enter and accept Islam.

Had they opened their hearts, feared their Lord, abstained from clinging to their illusions, they would have rushed to believe in the Prophet (SAW), and what he had brought, but their lust for the luxuries of this world, their selling and rejection of religion in return for the comforts of this life, the tribal solidarity and fanaticism to which they were so accustomed, and their envy of the Prophet for the favors that Allah had granted him- all of these pushed them to blindness and illusion rather than guidance and direction. They therefore brought down Allah's wrath, and they became worthy of shame and degradation in this world and severe punishment in the next.

We now proceed to discuss the second topic:

Showing the most important indications of fairness and tolerance with which Islam treated the People of the Scriptures.

We maintain that Allah Almighty sent His Messenger, Muhammad (SAW), with guidance and the true upright religion. At that time, the world was beaming with waves of false beliefs, corrupt fables, despicable moral behaviors and loathsome habits and practices. Muhammad called two types of people to Islam:

First: The polytheists, the idol worshippers, who believed that Allah had other partners they must worship in humility and submission.

Second: The People of the Book who corrupted and distorted their texts by moving around the words and forgot a good portion of what they were reminded of. With the passage of time, their hearts hardened, and many of them became debauched fornicators. Those who carefully follow the Islamic call will find that the position of Islam concerning idolatry was one of utter opposition and complete antagonism. Islam would eradicate their beliefs and destroy their illusions. It was, therefore, bound to save no effort to eliminate these idols from existence by any means possible as this was in direct opposition with Monotheism, worshipping One Allah Only.

Islam openly and clearly declared war against idolatry. It publicly announced its disgust and aversion of the idol worshippers. It forbade their sacrifices, prevented marriages with them, and they were prohibited from holding their pagan rituals in or around the Kaaba. Islam also forbade them from building mosques, and they were informed that Allah had mothing to with them during the greatest Day of Hajj, and they were given a period of time to reconsider and manage their affairs. If they failed to come to the Islamic fold, they would be killed, taken as slaves, and closely monitored wherever they were found. The Jizya (tax on dhimmis)- which would have been used to protect and allow them and to observe their pagan rituals- was not levied on them. The only choice was the sword or Islam.

Thus, idolatry was not tolerated by Islam which waged a war against it until Islam completely destroyed and purged the earth of it. On the day of the conquest of Mecca, the Prophet (SAW) would stab the idols saying: "And declare, "The truth has come and falsehood has vanished. Indeed, falsehood is bound to vanish." (Qur'an 17:81) [52]

This, in short, was the position of Islam concerning idolatry and its followers. As for its position concerning the People of the book, it was characterized by striking tolerance, unreserved fairness, thoughtful and benevolent treatment, and calling them to the truth through presenting clear proofs and overwhelming evidence for the truthfulness of the Prophet (SAW). He even hated doing things following the practices of the polytheists, while he embraced the practices of the People of the Book if he was not ordered otherwise. Al-Bukhari relates on the authority of Ibn Abbas that "the Prophet would let his hair down following the practice of the Jews. He would not part his hair as the idolaters were used to doing. That was a sign of his solidarity with the People of the Book. He later began to part his hair." [53]

Here are some of the features that indicate the tolerance of Islam towards the People of the Book and its fairness to them.

First: The Noble Qur'an described them in many of its verses as the People of the Book:

The "Book" is the Torah which Allah revealed to Moses, peace on him, to guide the Children of Israel. It is also the Injil (the Gospel) that Allah revealed to Jesus, peace on Him, as a shining path for His followers. This description, in itself, is a recognition of them, their past and their present. It is a praise and a commendation that distinguish them from others who did not inherit the divine revelations that they inherited. The Noble

Qur'an used this description to praise and commend those among them who were worthy of praise. At other times, it was used to chide and reproach them for their low morals and evil deeds.

In the first case, its praise for them was meant to incentivize them to accept the truth, to remind them that they were a group of people who received a divine revelation. Thus, it would have been becoming to rush to believe in Muhammad, and accept what he brought because he was the Messenger whom they find mentioned in their Torah and Bible. In Sura Al-Qasas, we encounter one of the praises of the Qur'an: "As for those faithful to whom We had given the Scripture before this Qur'an, they do believe in it. When it is recited to them, they declare, 'We believe in it.' This is definitely the truth from our Lord. We had already submitted even before this. These believers will be given a double reward for their perseverance, responding to evil with good, and for donating from what We have provided for them." (Qur'an 28:52-54)

In the second case, it chastised them for knowingly concealing the truth and for not believing Muhammad whose truth they knew just as they knew their own sons. It was a reprimand for their obstinacy, ungratefulness and the contradictions they fell into since describing them in such a way meant that they did not abide by the decrees of their own books that commanded them to follow Muhammad.

In Sura Al Imran, we encounter an example of this censure even though they were given the Book, "Say, O Prophet, O People of the Book! Why do you deny the revelations of Allah, when Allah is a Witness to what you do? Say, O People of the Book! Why do you turn the believers away from the Way of Allah—striving to make it appear crooked, while you are witnesses to its truth? And Allah is never unaware of what you do." (Qur'an 3:98-99)

Therefore, we see that describing the Jews as the People of the Book acknowledged the guidance they inherited, and set them apart from idolaters. If the Noble Qur'an used the description to chastise and admonish them, it was because they did not abide by what their Book commanded them and failed to follow the truth that they indubitably and unquestionably knew.

Second: The fairness of the Noble Qur'an in its rulings

In general, the Qur'an described the People of the Book with negative attributes like their fanaticism in religion and following a false path. It described the Jews, in particular, with degenerate characteristics, i.e., killing the prophets of Allah, corrupting His words by putting them in the wrong places, unjustly devouring people's wealth, refusing to abandon evil deeds, and other dreadful and appalling characteristics caused by their deeply ingrained lasciviousness and immorality. Yet, those who look studiously and thoughtfully at the verses of the Noble Qur'an would conclude that it makes a distinction between their righteous and virtuous ones and the unrighteous and unholy ones. It punishes and rewards them according to what each deserves. Its system of rewards and punishments is based on fairness and justice. The following are some of the verses that show the exemption of some of them from these vices. They hint at their appropriate and moderate positions and point at their faith, loyalty and their positive response to the truth.

In Sura Al-Baqarah: "And remember˺ when We took a covenant from the children of Israel stating, 'Worship none but Allah; be kind to parents, relatives, orphans and the needy; speak kindly to people; establish prayer; and pay alms-tax.' But you Israelites turned away—except for a few of you—and were indifferent." (Qur'an 2:83)

Allah's "But you Israelites turned away—except for a few of you" is an indication of the fairness for the few among the Children of Israel who did not break their promise with Allah. It was a testimony for those few who did not deviate from the truth nor succumb to illusion and misguidance.

In Al-Imran, Allah said, "Yet they are not all alike: there are some among the People of the Book who are upright, who recite Allah's revelations throughout the night, prostrating in prayer. They believe in Allah and the Last Day, encourage good and forbid evil, and race with one another in doing good. They are truly among the righteous. They will never be denied the reward for any good they have done. And Allah has ˹perfect˺ knowledge of those mindful of Him." (Qur'an 3:113-114)

These noble verses mean that the Children of Israel are not all the same when it comes to evildoing and misdemeanor. There are some among the People of the Book who are upright. In other words, there were some who were upright and followed Allah's decrees. Those were the ones who submitted, accepted Islam and followed what Muhammad (SAW) brought them.

Then Allah attributed wonderful traits to them. He said, they "recite Allah's revelations throughout the night, prostrating in prayer. They believe in Allah and the Last Day, encourage good and forbid evil, and race with one another in doing good. They are ˹truly˺ among the righteous." (Q 3:113)

These good qualities are restricted to only the believers among the Children of Israel; the infidels among them are far removed from these qualities, because they deviated from the truth, and they do not believe in Allah and the Last Day.

Then Allah said, "They will never be denied the reward for any good they have done. And Allah has perfect knowledge of those mindful of Him." (Qur'an 3:115)

Meaning: The righteous ones will be rewarded for the good that they do, for Allah will never neglect to reward good deeds, and He is most knowledgeable of those who are righteous. On those He bestows what is pleasing and profitable on them.

These noble verses have depicted splendid and magnificent qualities for the believers among the People of the Book. They have brought good tidings of complete and perfect rewards to them who have such qualities.

This is also reiterated in Sura Al Imran. Allah said, "Indeed, there are some among the People of the Book who truly believe in Allah and what has been revealed to you believers and what was revealed to them. They humble themselves before Allah—never trading Allah's revelations for a fleeting gain. Their reward is with their Lord. Surely Allah is swift in reckoning." (Qur'an 3:199)

The verse reflects many of the praises and commendations for the believers among the People of the Book.

Sura Al-Ma'idah provides many verses that attribute the most despicable and abhorrent qualities to the Children of Israel. However, a few of them were fairly and justly spared these contemptable qualities. Among these verses are:

A- Allah said, "Say, O Prophet, "O People of the Book! Do you resent us only because we believe in Allah and what has been revealed to us and what was revealed before—while most of you are rebellious (Q 5:59)?"

B- And He also said, "You see many of them racing towards sin, transgression, and consumption of forbidden gain. Evil indeed are their actions! (Q 5:62)"

C- And, "And had they observed the Torah, the Gospel, and what has been revealed to them from their Lord, they would have been overwhelmed with provisions from above and below. Some among them are upright, yet many do nothing but evil (Q 5:66)."

D- Allah also said, "You see many of them taking the disbelievers as allies. Truly wicked are their misdeeds, which have earned them Allah's wrath. And they will be in everlasting torment (Q 5:80)."

These noble verses described a lot of Jews, or many of them, with immorality, transgression, racing towards sin and wrongdoing and consuming forbidden gain. These qualities were not applied to all of them, though. This precaution reflects the fairness and justice with which the few who believed were regarded. They were spared the abhorrent qualities with which the Noble Qur'an had described the greatest majority of the Children of Israel.

In Sura An-Nisa, Allah said, "But those with solid knowledge among them and those with true faith believe in what has been revealed to you O Prophet and what was revealed before you—especially those who establish prayer—and those who pay alms-tax and believe in Allah and the Last Day, to these people We will grant a great reward." (Qur'an 4:162)

This noble verse was revealed following a strong campaign waged against the Children of Israel to whom the Qur'an attributed breaking promises, disbelief in Allah's verses, the killing of prophets and expressing false rumors about Mary. It was because of their injustices that Allah forbade them from eating what was made permissible, and He prepared severe punishment to those disbelievers. Then, this verse was revealed to exclude those with solid knowledge, and those who believed in Allah and His messengers. It praised those who established prayer, paid alms tax and believe in the day of Reckoning (the Last Day). The verse promised them that Allah will reward them bountifully because they followed His commandments and did not commit- unlike many of the Jews everywhere and at all times- what He had forbidden them from doing.

The words "those" refers back to the Children of Israel who were mentioned before.

These are some of the noble verses that commented on the few righteous believers among the Children of Israel, and excluded them from the censure and reproach that was levelled at the majority of the Jewish disbelievers. This was to make a distinction between the honorable and righteous and the despicable and wrongdoer. The good will be rewarded, and the evildoer will be punished. Each one will receive according to their deeds, i.e., praise or censure, fairly and justly.

Third: Argue gracefully with them:

The Noble Qur'an directed Muslims to the best methods of arguing with the People of the Book in both style and topic. As far as style was concerned, the Qur'an suggested that arguments should be conducted with them with grace and poise as long as they were not hostile obstinate deniers.

In so far as the topic was concerned, the Qur'an recommended that arguments should be based on persuading them that Allah's religion is one, that our Allah and theirs is one, and that we want nothing except that they follow the truth we followed and to abandon their obstinacy and ungratefulness.

In this respect, Allah said in Sura Al-'Ankabut: "Do not argue with the People of the Book unless gracefully, except with those of them who act wrongfully. And say, 'We believe in what has been revealed to us and what was revealed to you. Our Allah and your Allah is only One. And to Him we fully submit.'" (Qur'an 29:46)

The meaning of the noble verse is: You, Muslims, should not argue with the People of the Book except in a graceful and poised manner. Your argument should be lenient and tolerant, not rough and harsh since this would only lead to stubbornness and obstructing others from the path to Allah. On the other hand, gentleness and tolerance help bring about peace, understanding and reconciliation.

Then the Noble Qur'an excluded those who had done evil and injustices from this favorable and graceful treatment. Allah said, "except with those of them who act wrongfully." (Q 29:46) In other words, argue with all the People of the Book in the best possible manner except those who those who went overboard in their hostility and denial. Since gentle persuasion can do no good with them, use force with them, and treat them the way you deem suitable to turn them away from evildoing while protecting yourselves, the sanctity of your religion, your possessions and your country.

The Qur'an gave an example of elegant and graceful argument "And say, "We believe in what has been revealed to us and what was revealed to you. Our Allah and your Allah is only One. And to Him we fully submit." That is, you can argue gracefully with them except for the unjust wrongdoers. Be harsh with them. And if they argue with you in matters related to your religion, tell them: We believed in what was revealed to us, i.e., the Noble Qur'an, and we also believed in what was revealed to you, i.e., the Torah and the Bible, and we believe that your Allah and our Allah is only One. He is the Lord of the Worlds. To Him we submit as Muslims.

Imam Ibn Kathir said: "The almighty's And say, 'We believe in what has been revealed to us and what was revealed to you,' means if they told something that we do not know whether it is true or false, we cannot claim that it is false right away because it may be true, and we cannot accept it right away because it can be untrue. Our belief in what they said is dependent on one condition: it should be something that was revealed not altered or interpreted. Al-Bukhari narrates on the authority of Abu Hurayra that the People of the Book used to read the Torah in Hebrew and explain it in Arabic to Muslims. The Messenger of Allah (SAW) told them to neither believe nor disbelieve the People of the Book: 'And say, "We believe in what has been revealed to us and what was revealed to you'."

So, the noble verse guided the believers to argue with grace with the People of the Book, and to deal harshly with those obstinate wrongdoers and denials. This reflects tolerance, compassion and empathy.

Other verses reflect the same meaning. In Sura An-Nahl, Allah said, "Invite all to the Way of your Lord with wisdom and kind advice, and only debate with them in the best manner. Surely your Lord ⸢alone⸣ knows best who has strayed from His Way and who is rightly guided." (Qur'an 16:125)

Fourth: Making their food lawful and allowing interactions with- and marrying- them:

Islam's tolerance with the People of the Book can also be seen in the following examples: making their food lawful, allowing interactions such as selling and buying, and other dealings.

Aisha- Allah be pleased with her- said, "Muhamad (SAW) bought food from a Jew, and he pawned an armor made of iron to him." [54]

She also said, "The Messenger of Allah died and his shield was pawned with a Jew." [55]

Also, Islamic Law made it lawful for Muslim men to marry their women, not the women of the disbelieving idol-worshippers. In Sura Al-Ma'ida, Allah said, "Today all good, pure foods have been made lawful for you. Similarly, the food of the People of the Book is permissible for you and yours is permissible for them. And permissible for you in marriage are chaste believing women as well as chaste women of those given the Scripture before you—as long as you pay them their dowries in wedlock, neither fornicating nor taking them as mistresses." (Qur'an 5:5)

The meaning of "chaste" is virtuous, and His saying "the food of the People of the Book is permissible for you and yours is permissible for them" is a straightforward permission to allow Muslims to eat their food, and His saying "permissible for you in marriage are chaste believing women as well as chaste women of those given the Scripture before you" is a clear permission to marry their women.

Uthman Ibn Affan married Na'ila bint al-Furafisa, a Christian woman; Hudhayfah married a Jewish woman, and Talha marries a Jew from the people of the Levant.

Ibn Qudamah said: There is no disagreement among scholars that marrying the virtuous among the People of the Book was permissible. Among those who were mentioned in this respect were Omar, Uthman, Talha, Hudhayfah ibn al-Yaman, Salman and Gaber and others from among the Companions. Then, Qudamah quoted Ibn al-Munzir as saying: "none of the early Companions had ever forbidden this."[56]

Islamic Law (Shari'a) has given wives from the People of the Book all the legal rights that other Muslim wives enjoy. She has equal shares with a Muslim wife; she has the right to live under the protection of her Muslim husband who fulfills her financial needs. Also, she can enjoy the same decent and graceful physical intimacy like her Muslim counterpart. And she cannot be coerced into abandoning her religion.

These are all proofs of Islam's tolerance towards the People of the Book provided that they do no harm to the Islamic community and as long as they do not abuse this tolerance in inflicting harm on Muslims.

Fifth: Receiving the Jizya from the Jews, not from the polytheists:
Islam did not accept the Jizya from the polytheists, the idol-worshippers. It gave them one of these two options: fighting or accepting Islam. However, Islam accepted the Jizya from the People of the Book who were permitted to live under the protection, maintain and keep their beliefs and not be forced or coerced into entering into Islam. In return, they should enable the Islamic nation to carry out its responsibilities through paying the Jizya in return for their protection and caring for them.

The Jizya in Islam is rightful and legal: the Muslim ruler receives it from the People of the Book in return for a certain duty he has towards them, i.e., making sure that their possessions, their souls, and their women are not harmed in any way.

Some people misunderstood Allah's saying, "until they pay the tax, willingly submitting, fully humbled." (Qur'an 9:29)They took these words to mean cruelty, humiliation and degradation. This is a wrong understanding. What the noble verse means is that the People of the Book would pay a certain amount of their money in order to be participants in building the Islamic state which is attentive and mindful of their needs. They should be obedient and submissive to this nation, unable to revolt against it, cause any harm to it, or disturb or threaten its peace and security.

This complete and utter submission to the rules of the Islamic state under which they enjoy protection is something that every state demands from its subjects and citizens who are under its care and protection. Thus, these states can carry out their obligations and responsibilities in peace and security. They will not be exposed to disturbances and disruptions, their power and authority will not be weakened, their dignity and respect will not be diminished, and their stability and strength will not be shaken or threatened.

Also, among the proofs of Islam's tolerance towards the People of the Book was that the jizya was only levied on their men, not their women or children. It was also levied on those who were able to pay it; the unable was exempted from paying the jizya.

In the Book of Absence by Abu Yusuf said that Omar- Allah be pleased with him- passed by a group of people who were sitting exposed to the sun some where in the Levant. So, he asked what was the matter with these people. He was told that they were unable to pay the Jizya. He hated that, and he asked what they had to say for an excuse. They said that they were unable to pay. So, he told his men to let them go and not to burden them with anything they could not do. They were let go.[57]

Abu Yusuf- may Allah have mercy upon his soul- also advised the Muslim Caliph of his time, say: "And you, Commander of the Believers- may Allah support you- should deal compassionately with the people of Dhimma, the people of your Prophet and cousin, Muhammad, and make sure that they are not harmed or burdened beyond their means, and that their property is not unjustly taken. He said that the Messenger of Allah said, "Anyone who unjustly treats or forces a Dhimmi beyond his capacity, has me as an opponent." At his death, Omer Ibn Al-Khataab also advised his follower, saying, "I advise the Caliph who comes after me- in the name of the Messenger of Allah- to honor their agreements and their pledges, to fight beside them, and not to burden them beyond their abilities."[58]

Sixth: Treating them according to the principle of "they have the same rights that we have, and they owe the same responsibilities:"

When the People of the Book were committed to living in peace under the protection of the Islamic, refraining from siding with others who fight against it, and not displaying anything that would harm it, then Islam orders its followers to treat them according this merciful rule: "they have the same rights that we have, and they owe the same responsibilities:"

Here are some of these rights that the People of the Book enjoyed because of this golden rule:

A- Protecting their lives, possessions and women (honor) from attacks, and giving them the same rights as Muslims in jobs and employment as long as they were loyal to the state's wellbeing and interests and as long as they were committed to assuming their responsibilities diligently and if these jobs would not be adversely impacted by non-Muslims. Islamic history throughout the ages had preserved the names of a great number of the People of the Book who occupied important positions in the Islamic state. However, some Muslim rulers removed some of the People of the Book from their positions because they abused the positions with which they were entrusted and took advantage of them to harm the Islamic state.

B- Showing compassion and mercy when they were incapable:

Imam Abu Yusuf said: Omar once passed by a gate where there was a group of people. One of them was a beggar. He was a blind old man. Omar asked him to which group of the People of the Book he belonged. The old man replied that he was a Jew. Omar asked, "What brought you to this condition?" The old man said, "I blame the jizya, poverty, and old age." Omar led him by the hand, brought him to his house, and gave him whatever he found. Then, he sent him to the treasury, and said to him, "Look at all this wealth from taxes. By Allah, we did not do him justice; we consumed his youth, and we forsook him at his old age. 'Alms giving is for the poor and the needy.' The poor are the poor among the Muslims. This man is one of the wretched People of the Book." Then, he relieved him of the jizya and other taxes. Abu Bakr said, "I witnessed this of Omar, and I saw that old man."[59]

In sum, this is Islam's fair and just position towards the People of the Book. It was its clear and upright method in calling them to accept Islam. They are only some of the proofs of its tolerance, fairness, and compassion towards them. The Children of Israel- as People of the Book- should have met kindness with kindness. They should have followed the Prophet (SAW) and accepted what they were called to. However, the Jews were not worthy. They stood defiantly against the Islamic call trying hard to make it dubious and suspicious. They were hostile to its Messenger, and they spread riots and revolutions among its followers sparing no means to eliminate and eradicate it.

In the following chapter, we will talk- Allah willing- about their evil ways to entrap Islam and Muslims.

---

[1] Sura Al-A'raf: Verse 59
[2] Sura Al-A'raf: Verse 65
[3] Sura Al-A'raf: Verse 73
[4] Sura Al-A'raf: Verse 85

[5] Sura Ash-Shuraa: Verse 52
[6] Sura Al-Ankabut: Verse 48
[7] Chapter 15 (The predictions of Prophets Muhammad SAW)
[8] Tafsir Al-Qasimi (The Merits of Interpretation) Vol:7 P. 2874
[9] "Revealing the Truth" by Rahmat Allah El-Hindi
[10] Sahih Al-Bukhari, Chapter "Hatred of Shouting in the Marketplace." From the book "Al-biyou' البيوع Vol: 3 P. 83
[11] Ibn Kathir Interpretation Vol:2 P. 251
[12] Review, for example, "Interpretation of Al-Manar" Vol:9 P. 291. Also "Revealing the Truth" by Rahmatullah Al-Hindi. Also "Evidence of Certainty in Responding to the Missionaries' Attacks" by Sheikh Abul Rahman Al-Jizeri.
[13] Interpretation of Al-Qurtubi Vol: 7 P. 300
[14] Ibn Kathir Interpretation Vol:2 P. 254
[15] Sahih Al-Bukhari Vol: 1 P. 87
[16] Sahih Muslim (The Book of Mosques and Places of Prayer)
[17] Sura Al-Saf Verse: 6
[18] The Crown of all Origins in the Sayings of the Prophet Vol: 1P. 232
[19] Ibn Kathir's Interpretation Vol: 4 P. 360
[20] Sura Al-Baqarah Verse:89
[21] Imam Ibn Tamyiyyah mentioned more than ten examples concerning this when he talked about this noble verse in his book "The Correct Answer to Whoever Changed the Religion of Christ." Vol: 3 P. 282 and after.
[22] "The Correct Answer to Whoever Changed the Religion of Christ." Vol: 3 P. 284 by Imam Ibn Tamyiyyah.
[23] Ibn Kathir's Interpretation Vol:1 P.65.
[24] Liwaa Al-Islam Magazine, Year 11 P.68
[25] Sura Al-An'am: Verse 92
[26] Sura Yusuf: Verse 111
[27] Sura Yunus: Verse 37
[28] Sura Ash-Shuraa: Verse 13
[29] Sura Al-Anbya: Verse 25
[30] Sura Al-Ma'idah: Verse 48
[31] The Reasons for the Revelation P. 22 By Al-Naysaburi (Mustafa Halabi Edition)
[32] Sura Yunus: Verse 72
[33] Sura Yunus: Verse 84
[34] Sura Ali'Imran: Verse 52
[35] Sura Al-Qasas: Verse 53
[36] From valuable research by the late Sheikh Muhammad Abdullah Draz. The topic is "The Position of Islam Concerning Other Religions and Its Relationship to Them." Published in Lewaa' Al-Islam Magazine # 11 Year 11 P. 681. The honorable Sheikh prepared this research to present it in the Islamists World Symposium which was held in Lahore in the late 1957. However, he died before the end of the Symposium. May Allah have mercy upon his soul.
[37] Sura Ali'Imran: Verse 64
[38] Sura Al-Ma'idah: Verse 15 & 16

[39] Al-Raghib said the word فتر from الفتور means silence or quietness after commotion and fury, leniency after harshness, and weakness after strength. The Almighty said: "O People of the Book! Our Messenger has indeed come to you, making things clear to you after an interval[39] between the messengers," meaning silence. P. 371 Al-Halabi Edition
[40] Sura Al-Ma'ida: Verse 19
[41] Al-Bukhari in "The Beginning of Creation" Vol 4, P. 203 (Sabeeh Edition)
[42] Sura An-Nisa: Verse 47& 48
[43] Ibn Garir's Interpretation Vol. 5 P. 124 (Mustafa Al-Halabi's Edition)
[44] Al-Raghib said: "wiping out" means removing traces by eradicating them. The Almighty said: So when the stars are put out" ... and "Our Lord, destroy their riches and harden their hearts" which means wipe them out. He also said: Had We willed, We could have easily blinded their eyes. "This means, We could have taken away their ability to see, wipe it out and make it disappear without a trace. Ibn Garir said: the word refers to levelling things and from this, we say that the traces (landmarks) of the road have been erased and completely gone. Now, they are levelled with the earth. Vol. 5 P. 123
[45] Sura Al-Anfal: Verse 24
[46] Sura Ya-Sin: Verses 9 & 10
[47] Ibn Garir's Interpretation Vol. 2 P.312.
[48] Al-Kashaaf's Interpretation Vol. 1 P. 298

[49] Look at the Chapter: "The Methods that the Jews Used to Entrap Islam and Muslims" Under (Their Religious Argumentations)
[50] Sura Yunus: Verse 94
[51] Al-Kashaaf, Vol. 2 P.70. (Al-Zamakhshari)
[52] Sura Al-Isra: Verse 81
[53] Sahih Al-Bukhari, Chapter "When the Jews Came to the Prophet when he came to Medina" Vol. 5 P. 90.
[54] Sahih Al-Bukhari (Chapter on Pawning) Vol. 2 P. 176
[55] Sahih Al-Bukhari: What was said about the armor of the Prophet, Vol. 4 P. 44.
[56] The Singer by Ibn Qudamah Vol. 7 P.50
[57] The Book of Absence by Abu Yusuf P. 125
[58] The Book of Absence by Abu Yusuf P. 134
[59] The Book of Absence by Abu Yusuf P. 126

Chapter Three

The Methods That The Jews Used To Entrap Islam And Muslims

In the previous chapter, we revealed some of the methods that the Noble Qur'an used to call the Children of Israel to accept Islam. We also provided some examples that reflect Islam's tolerance, lenience and kindness towards them.

We have also noted that the Jews did not receive this kindness with kindness and appreciation. Rather, they sought all means possible to destroy and nip the Islamic call in the bud.

In this chapter, we will discuss some of the evil methods that the Jews used to entrap Islam and Muslims after the emigration of the Messenger (SAW) to Medina.

Before we talk about these evil methods, we will discuss the following questions:

First: Were the Jews in Medina aware of the appearance of the Prophet (SAW) before he emigrated to it?

Second: How did the Jews receive the Prophet (SAW) when he arrived in Medina as an emigrant?

Third: Why were the Jews- in general- peaceful and serene towards the Islamic call at first and then opposed and showed hostility and animosity later?

In response to the first question:

The Jews in Medina were not unaware of the appearance of Muhammad (SAW) in Mecca. Here are some reasons:

First: Some Jews were used to visiting Mecca to conduct business and other activities. The Meccans themselves used to frequent Khaybar to buy the jewelry and ornaments of Abu al-Huqayq clan, with which their women and girls used to adorn themselves for their weddings. Even the Aws and Khazraj inhabitants of Medina used to go to Mecca for commercial reasons, to circumambulate Al- Kaaba and for various other business purposes.

There can be no doubt that some talk- concerning the new religion that Muhammad Ibn Abdullah (SAW) brought- must have taken place during these various interactions and business dealings among the various parties.

Second: While the Messenger was still living with Quraysh, some members of the tribe sent Nadir bin Harith and Uqba bin Abi Muait to Jewish rabbis and scholars in Medina. They asked them to inquire about Muhammad, give them his description, and to tell them about his message since they were the People of the first Book, and they had knowledge about the prophets that was not available to them. The two men went to Medina, and they asked the rabbis about the Messenger of Allah (SAW) after describing him and informing them with some of what he said. They inquired, "You are the People of the Torah, and we came to you to inform us about this man (our friend)."

The Jewish scholars said: "Ask him three questions that we will command you to do. If he told you about them, then he is a sent prophet. If he failed to inform you, then he is an imposter."

Ask him about three young men who perished a long time ago. What happened to them? What was their wonderous story.

Ask him about a man who travelled around the world and reached the east and west of the earth. What was his prophesy?

Ask him about the spirit. What is it?

If he told you, then follow him, for he is a prophet; if he did not, then he is an imposter and deal with him in whatever manner you deem fit.

So, Nadir bin Harith and Uqba bin Abi Muait returned to Mecca and told Quraysh what the Jewish scholars told them. Then, they went to the Messenger of Allah (SAW) and said, "Muhammad tell us about three young men who perished a long time ago. They had an amazing story. And tell us about a man who travelled around the world and reached the east and west of the earth. And tell us about the spirit. What is it?

Then the Messenger of Allah told them, "I will inform you of what you asked tomorrow." He did not say "in sha'a Allah" (Allah willing). They departed from Muhammad. The Messenger spent 15 nights during which Allah brought him no revelation, and Gabriel-peace on him- did not appear to him either. The Meccans were agitated and perplexed. They said, "Muhammad promised to tell us the following day. Now 15 days had passed. He never informed us about the things which we asked." The Messenger was saddened because no revelation had come to him. However, what he should be telling the people of Mecca was finally revealed to him. Allah sent Gabriel with Sura Al-Kahf * (*actually in Sura al-Isra, sura 17; see note 1) in which He blamed him for feeling sorry for the Meccans. It also contained the response to their inquiry concerning the young men and the wanderer who traveled around the world: "They ask you O Prophet about the spirit. Say, 'Its nature is known only to my Lord, and you O humanity have been given but little knowledge.'" (Qur'an 17:85) [1]

Third: When tensions and conflicts arose between the Jews and the Aws and Khazraj, they would threaten them saying: A prophet has been sent. Now, his time has passed. We will follow him and kill you with him like the killing of Ad and Iram.

The Noble Qur'an pointed to this: "Although they used to pray for victory ʿby means of the Prophetʾ over the polytheists, when there came to them a Book from Allah which they recognized, confirming the Scripture they had in their hands, they rejected it. So may Allah's condemnation be upon the disbelievers." (Qur'an 2:89) [2]

The verse indicates that they used to invoke the name of the sent prophet and ask Allah for victory over the polytheists "by means of the prophet" whose description and attributes were mentioned in the Torah. Yet, when that prophet- whose name they invoked to help them in their wars- came, they rejected him; they did not follow him. Allah's curse be upon the disbelievers.

Fourth: When presenting his call to the tribes during the Hajj season in the few years preceding the migration, the Prophet (SAW) used to meet members of the Aws and the Khazraj. Whenever he invited them to Islam, they would look at each other and say, "By Allah, he is truly the prophet that the Jews told you about his coming. Be the first to follow him."

After the First Pledge (of allegiance) of Aqaba, the Prophet (SAW) sent Musab bin Umair to the people of Medina to read the Qur'an to them and to teach them Islam and boost their understanding of religion. Islam spread in many houses in Medina.

Then came the Great Pledge of Aqaba in which twelve deputies from among the Aws and the Khazraj participated. One of the Khazraj leaders, Abu Al-Haytham bin Al-Tayhan, said to the Messenger of Allah, "O Messenger of Allah! There are ties between us and the men (the Jews), and we will break them. Would it be possible that if we did that and Allah made you victorious that you would return to your people and leave us?"

The Messenger smiled and said, "Blood for blood…and You are with me and I am with you. I wage wars against those you wage wars against, and I make peace with الهدم هدم [3] those with whom you make peace."

What is important and needs to be emphasized here is that the Jews were not unaware of the pledges that took place between the Messenger of Allah and the people of Medina before his migration. They were knowledgeable of the course and direction of the Islamic call as it extended to Yathrib and spread among its people.

And how could they not be aware when Islam did not surreptitiously spread in Medina? Musab bin Umair went among the people in public calling them to Allah and His Messenger. He moved- his heart overflowing with joy and ecstasy- from one neighborhood to the other, one clan to the other, spreading the word and witnessing a fertile soil for the Islamic call among the people of Medina whose followers were increasing in numbers and authority and power.

But what are the most important reasons that made the Aws and the Khazraj joyfully and wholeheartedly accept the Islamic call?

The Aws and Khazraj were mixed and mingled with the Jews of Yathrib. That had a profound spiritual impact on them. The Jews- being monotheists and People of the Book- used to reproach and censure them for worshipping idols. They forewarned them about the appearance of a new prophet who would end idol worshipping and eradicate it. These religious disputes- in addition to the rebellions and wars that decimated the Aws and the Khazraj by the Jews' insidious and devious attempts to sow the seeds of discord between them- made the inhabitants of Yathrib readily and cheerfully accept the call to Islam, and see its caller, Muhammad, as their savior from all their trials and tribulations.

Thus, we may conclude our answer to the first question by saying that the Jews were not only cognizant of the appearance of the Prophet and his message; rather, their very presence in Medina and its environs was in itself one of the main reasons for the spread of Islam there, if only indirectly and inadvertently, as Dr. Israel Wolfensohn maintains.

Now, we will answer the second question, that is, how did the Jews receive the Prophet when he emigrated to Medina?

On a certain day in recorded history, while the Muslims in Medina were waiting- in anticipation as usual- for the arrival of the Prophet after the news of his migration had reached them, a Jew shouted out to them that the Prophet's entourage had come into view. He exclaimed, "Sons of Qayla, your grandfather has arrived."[4]

Al-Bukhari notes a hadith in his section on Hegira (Hijra; migration to Medina)):" When the Muslims of Medina heard of the emissary of Allah's exit from Mecca, they would go out every morning to Al-Hurra to see him before they were forced to go back because of the noon heat. One day, when they had gone home after waiting for him for a long time, a Jew who was watching his arrival saw the Prophet and his Companions appear- and disappear- in a desert mirage. The Jew could not restrain himself from calling out loudly, saying, "You Arabs! Here comes your grandfather for whom you have been waiting."[5] Thereupon, the Muslims reached for their weapons, and they met the Emissary of Allah on the plain of Al-Hurra.

The Jews- in general- participated with the Muhajereen (Emigrants) and the AnSaar (supporters) in welcoming the Bringer of Allah's call. The reason we say "in general" is that some of the genuine hadiths (sayings) that have come down to us tell us that some Jews rejected the Islamic call and demonstrated premonitions concerning the messenger from the first day of the emigration.

On the authority of Safya bint Hayy ibn Akhtab, may Allah be pleased with her, "When the Prophet (SAW) came to stay with Banu Amr bin Awf, my father and uncle, Abu Yasser Akhtab, came to visit him… They did not return until the sun had set… Then they came, two lazy and fallen people, walking slowly... So, I ran towards them as I used to do, and by Allah, not one of them turned to me, despite the grief they were in… I heard my uncle Abu Yasser saying to Abu Huyay bin Akhtab: Is it him? He said: Yes, by Allah. He said: Do you know him and confirm him? He said: Yes, he said: What is in your mind about it? He said: His enmity, by Allah, as long as I live."[6]

And on the authority of Al-Zahri, Mousa Ibn Aqba mentioned that when the Prophet arrived at Medina, Aba Yasser Ibn Ahtab went to see him and talk to him. Then, he went back to his people and said to them: "Obey me people! Allah has brought to you him whom you have been waiting for. Follow and do not oppose him. His brother, Huyayy ibn Akhtab, one of the chiefs among the Jews of Banu Nadir, rushed to sit and talk with the Prophet. He then returned to his people among whom he was highly respected and obeyed. He told them that he had come after meeting a man that would be his enemy forever. His brother, Abu Yasser, son of my mother, just obey me on this one thing, and do not listen to me on everything else. But Huyayy swore by Allah that he would never obey him on this matter. Satan had completely possessed and had control over him. His people also followed him. Abu Yasser's fate was not known. As for Huyayy, he was filled with hatred and animosity towards the Prophet and never changed course until his perdition. [7]

These two excerpts show us that the Jews were dead set on opposing the Islamic call ever since the Messenger's arrival in Medina. However, the Prophet (SAW) knowingly and intentionally disregarded the animosity of those opposers, and he worked to spread the spirit of cooperation and tolerance with the Jews. He talked to their chiefs and they talked with him. He tried to get closer to them, and he encouraged them to draw nearer to him as well. He allowed Muslims to eat with them and marry their women. The Jews were exceedingly glad to that the Prophet and Muslims face Jerusalem when praying since it was also the Qiblah for the Children of Israel when praying.

In addition to his munificent treatment of the Jews, the Prophet wanted to enhance cooperation and mutual interests with them. He held a fair agreement with them. In this contract, he assured them their safety, the safety of their possessions and money, and their worship and creed. He guaranteed all that was fair and beneficial for them and for Muslims. Imam Ibn Kathir said that Muhammad Ibn Ishaq said that the Messenger of Allah (SAW) wrote a contract involving the Muhajereen (Emigrants), the AnSaar (Supporters) and to which he invited the Jews and made a covenant with them and pledged to safeguard their religion and their wealth. The contract reflected their rights and stipulated their responsibilities:[8]

In the name of Allah, the Most Gracious, the Most Merciful

1- This is a letter (Al-Madina Newspaper) from Muhammad the Prophet (Messenger of Allah) (between the believers and Muslims from Quraysh and (the people of) Yathrib and whoever follows them and joins them and strives with them.
2- They are one nation.

3- The Emigrants of the Quraysh, they deal with each other, and they ransom their captives with kindness and fairness as known to the believers.

4- And the Banu Awf, deal with their former strongholds, and each sect ransoms its captives with kindness and fairness among the believers.

5- And the Banu al-Harith (Ibn al-Khazraj) deal with each other in their first strongholds, and each sect ransoms its captives with kindness and justice among the believers.

6- And the Banu Sa'idah, treat their first strongholds, and each sect of them ransoms its captives with kindness and justice among the believers.

7- And the Banu Jashm on their quarters deal with their first strongholds, and every sect ransoms its captives with kindness and justice among the believers.

8- And the Banu al-Najjar, on their quarters, deal with their first strongholds, and each sect ransoms its captives with kindness and justice among the believers.

9- And the Banu Amr bin Awf, on their quarters, deal with their first strongholds, and each sect ransoms its captives with kindness and justice among the believers.

10-And the Banu al-Nabit, on their quarters, treat their first strongholds. And every sect ransoms its captives with kindness and justice among the believers.

11-The Banu Aws, on their quarters, deal with each other in their former strongholds, and each group ransoms its captives with kindness and justice among the believers.

12- And the believers do not leave any burdened [9] among them but deal with him with kindness in the form of redemption or compensation.

13- And that the pious believers have put their hands together against whoever among them transgresses, or seeks a [10] دسيعة profit through injustice, sin, hostility or corruption among the believers, and that their hands are against him, all of them, even if it is the child of one of them.

14- A believer does not kill a believer for the sake of an infidel, nor will he support an infidel against a believer.

15- The protection of Allah is one, the lowest of them are subject to protection, and that the believers are allies of one another, to the exclusion of other people.

16- And whoever of the Jews follows us will have victory and success, they will neither be oppressed nor taken advantage of.

17- And the peace of the believers is one. No believer will be at peace with another believer in a fight for the sake of Allah, except on the basis of equality and justice between them.

18- And every invader that invaded with us followed [11] one another.

19- And the believers protect each other on behalf of each other, they shed their blood for the sake of Allah.

20- And the pious believers follow the best and most correct guidance. And that no polytheist will lend money or lives to the Quraysh, nor will he deny it to a believer.

21- And whoever commits the killing of a believer without clear evidence [12], he will be charged with it, unless the guardian of the murdered person is satisfied (with reason), and that the believers are all responsible for it, and it is not permissible for

them to do so except to stand up for him.
22- It is not permissible for a believer who acknowledges what is in this document, and believes in Allah and the Last Day, to support or shelter an infidel, and whoever supports him or shelters him will be subject to the curse of Allah and His wrath on the Day of Resurrection, and no compensation or justice will be taken from him.
23- And no matter how much you disagree about it, it is due back to Allah Almighty and to Muhammad, (SAW).
24- And the Jews spend with the believers as long as they are warriors.
25- And that the Jews of Bani Awf are a nation with the believers. The Jews have their religion and the Muslims have their religion, their friends and themselves, except for those who are unjust and sinful, for he does not commit sin [13] except against himself and his family.
26- And the Jews of Banu Al-Najjar have the same as the Jews of Banu Awf.
27- And the Jews of Banu al-Harith have the same as the Jews of Banu Awf.
28- And the Jews of Banu Sa'idah have the same rights as the Jews of Banu Awf.
29- And the Jews of Banu Jashm have the same as the Jews of Banu Awf.
30- And the Jews of Banu Aws have the same as the Jews of Banu Awf.
31- And the Jews of Banu Tha'labah are like the Jews of Banu Awf, except those who do injustice and sin, for he does not harm anyone but himself and his family.
32- And the belly of Thalabah is like their own selves.
33- And that the Banu Shatiba have the same status as the Jews of Banu Awf, and that righteousness is less than sin.
34- And the loyalists of Tha'labah are like themselves.
35- And the inner circle of the Jews is like themselves.
36- And that none of them will leave except with the permission of Muhammad, (SAW). And that no one is to avenge an injury, and that whoever kills himself and his family, it is only one who is unjust, and Allah is most righteous.
37- And that the Jews are responsible for their maintenance, and that the Muslims are responsible for their maintenance, and that victory is among them over those who fought the people of this document, and that among them is advice, council, and righteousness without sin. And that no one commits a sin by having an ally, and that victory belongs to the oppressed.
38- And the Jews spend with the believers as long as they are warriors.
39- And that Yathrib and what is haram is forbidden for the people of this paper.
40- The neighbor is like the self, not to be harmed nor sinful.
41- And there are no merchants in the sanctuary except with the permission of its people.
42- And whatever incident or quarrel occurs between the people of this document should be referred back to Allah Almighty and to Muhammad, the Messenger of Allah, (SAW), and that Allah is the most pious and knowledgeable of what is in this document.
43- And that neither the Quraysh merchants nor those who helped them.
44- And that among them there was victory over those who attacked Yathrib.
45- And that if they call for reconciliation, they will reconcile it and adhere to it, and that when they call for the like of that, they have authority over the believers, except for those who wage war over religion. Every person must have their share from the

side before them.
46- And that the Jews of Aws, their masters and themselves, are in the same position as the people of this document, with the pure righteousness of the people of this document, and that righteousness is beneficial to those who are dressed in righteousness, and that Allah is the most truthful and righteous of what is in this document.
47- And that this book favors no oppressor or sinner, and that whoever leaves is safe, and whoever stays in Medina is safe, except for those who are unjust and sinful, and that Allah is close to those who are righteous and pious, and Muhammad is the Messenger of Allah, (SAW).[14]

This was the agreement that the Prophet (SAW) held with the various sects of the Jews. It contained many of the sublime principles and basic precepts that govern relations among nations. The following are some of these principles that we can take away from the agreement:

First: The agreement guaranteed freedom of religion to the Jews, and it allowed them to observe their religious doctrines and practices. A proof for this is the statement (the Jews have their religion and the Muslims have their religion).

Second: The agreement reflected high sense of community and societal solidarity. It declared that whoever decides not to abide by one of the items included therein, and attacked one of the parties that were promised peace and security, the people of this agreement would declare war against the aggressor. This was a clear indication of the communal identity, the community's common interests, the rights that the individuals enjoy, the responsibilities they have towards the community, and that the safety of Medina was the responsibility of every one of its inhabitants.

Third: The agreement clearly affirmed the authentic desire of the Muslims to cooperate with the Jews in order to establish peace and security in Medina, fight the aggressors and conspirators who sow the seeds of sectarian strife, regardless of their religion or race, and without any discrimination or favoritism. If a foreign aggression on Medina was to take place, Muslims and Jews would unite and take part in defending it.

Fourth: The agreement included many sublime human principles: helping the oppressed, protecting the neighbors, safeguarding private and public rights, paying ransoms and saving captives, helping those in debt, and many other exalted principles that make the residents of one nation feel as though they are one family.

Fifth: The agreement stated the animosity that existed between the Muslims and Quraysh, and it forbade all Muslims and Jews from siding or assisting Quraysh or giving refuge to anyone of them. Those who would do such a thing were deserving of the curse of Allah, His condemnation and His wrath in the Last Day.

Sixth: The Agreement stipulated that the Jews should contribute and pay along with the Muslims the expenses that were incurred because of wars. It had also stipulated the necessity of supporting and assisting Muslims with all possible means. In the document, we read: "And the Jews spend with the believers as long as they are warriors... and that victory is among them over those who fought the people of this document, and that among them is advice, council, and righteousness without sin. And that no one commits a sin by having an ally, and that victory belongs to the oppressed... And that among them there was victory over those who attacked Yathrib."

Seventh: The agreement stated that if there was any disagreement between the people of the document, the final arbitrator was the Prophet (SAW) since he was the highest authority in Medina.

Eighth: The agreement stipulated that whoever committed a sin should be subject to punishment, and that being a member of this agreement should not exclude him from due punishment, and that "this book favors no oppressor or sinner."

Ninth: One of the gains that Muslims achieved by virtue of this agreement was that they were to confront only one enemy, namely, Quraysh. The agreement shielded them against the Jews if they were to abide by the principles contained therein and would not violate them after a short while.

Tenth: Among the gains that the Jews secured by virtue of this agreement was that they secured the protection of the Muslims against any aggression against them: "And whoever of the Jews follows us will have victory and success, they will neither be oppressed nor taken advantage of." However, the Jews did not enjoy these gains since they failed to abide by- and adhere to- their pledges.

Mr. Abdul Rahman Azzam commented on this document saying:

"This treaty is one of the most precious and exquisite international contracts. It is worthy of the consideration and appreciation of all people. It is considered a shinning beacon between Muslims' international relations and their opposers from other religions. In addition, this treaty heralded the beginning of the Islamic state; others started acknowledging Muslims as a state.

With this treaty, Muslims made a contract with others who adopt other religions. There ensued the first Charter for the "League of Nations," one founded on assisting the oppressed, good council, righteousness and opposing sin, the sanctity of neighboring countries, and the inviolability of those who enter into this charter, all within the framework of acknowledging and protecting the doctrines, beliefs and freedoms of the participants in this contract.Thus, with this treaty Islam anteceded the current League of Nations by more than thirteen centuries. The Messenger of Allah (SAW) laid a solid foundation for the global state and international interactions in this charter on the basis of the freedom and independence of the participants." [15]

From all that has been mentioned so far, we can conclude that the Jews were well aware of the Islamic call in Mecca especially in the few years that preceded the Hegira (emigration). In general, they received the Prophet well upon his arrival in Medina. A period of peaceful relations- not for long, though- prevailed between the Jews and the Muslims after the emigration.

We will now answer the third question, that is, why did the Jews make peace with the Messenger (SAW) in the months following the Hegira (Emigration), and why did they turn against him and became hostile and antagonistic in various shapes and forms?

To answer the first part of this question, we say:

First: The Jews did not take part in welcoming the Messenger upon his arrival in Medina out of love. Rather, they were hoping to draw him to their side and to have him as an ally, so he and his Muslim followers could help them form a united front in the Arabian Peninsula to resist the Christians who drove them out of Palestine, dispersed and soundly defeated them. They thought that the Islam that Muhammad (SAW) brought would never accept the tritheism of the Christians. Thus, it was crucial for them to get the help they needed from the Muslims to eradicate Christianity that expelled them from the Promised Land.

Second: The Jews made peace with Muhammad on his arrival in Medina in the few months after the Hegira only because they believed that he would leave them out of the scope of his call, considering themselves better guided and, thus, above being called to accept his message or be included under his stewardship. They also believed that he would not bring new teachings that would oppose those of the Torah, nor would he point accusingly to any corruptions, changes or alterations in it. Perhaps, they might have even expected him to join them, especially after they witnessed him face their Qibla, and fast on the day of "Ashura" (day of commemoration in Islam) with them. He would also say: "We are more deserving of Moses than them." He would announce his belief in Allah, His angels, His emissaries, and the Last Day.

Third: When the Messenger of Allah emigrated to Medina, the Jews were in in a state of disarray. They were divided and differed among themselves. That dire condition they found themselves in made them incapable of showing open hostility to the Messenger (SAW). They thought it would be more advantageous for them to delay publicly displaying their animosity to the Islamic call until a more propitious time.

The Noble Qur'an pointed to the dissentions and animosities that existed among the various sects of the Jews. In Sura Al-Baqarah, we read: "And remember when We took your covenant that you would neither shed each other's blood nor expel each other from their homes, you gave your pledge and bore witness. But here you are, killing each other and expelling some of your people from their homes, aiding one another in sin and aggression; and when those expelled come to you as captives, you still ransom them—though expelling them was unlawful for you. Do you believe in some of the Scripture and reject the rest? Is there any reward for those who do so among you other than disgrace in this worldly life and being subjected to the harshest punishment on the Day of Judgment? For Allah is never unaware of what you do." (Qur'an 2:84-85)

The meaning of these two honorable verses:

The Almighty Allah made a covenant with the Children of Israel that they would not kill each other or expel each other from their homes. They pledged to abide by that covenant. However, they killed each other and expelled each other from their homes. For example, when hostilities arose between the Aws and the Khazraj, Banu Qaynuqa and Banu Nadir would join the Khazraj and fight alongside with them while Banu Qurayza would join the Aws and fight along with them. As a result of this, Jews were fighting against each other. When the wars were finished, all the Jews would use their money to ransom their captives that had fallen into the hands of the Aws and the Khazraj. The Arabs used to mock and reprimand them saying:

"How come you fight them then and ransom them with your money?" The Jews would respond, saying that Allah prohibited us from fighting them, but we would loathe to disappoint our allies, and that Allah had commanded them to rescue our captives. For this, Allah reproached them, saying: "Do you believe in some of the Scripture and reject the rest? Is there any reward for those who do so among you other than disgrace in this worldly life and being subjected to the harshest punishment on the Day of Judgment? For Allah is never unaware of what you do." (Q 2:84)

Fourth: After the emigration of the Messenger (SAW) to Medina, the Aws and the Khazraj were allied together and brought to a state brotherhood under the flag of the Islamic state after they had differed with one another. They now held the real power in Medina, and they renewed their pledges with the Prophet (SAW) to defend him with their wealth and lives. This position of utter power that the Aws and the Khazraj enjoyed after their entrance into Islam prevented the Jews from opposing the Prophet with open hostility at the time of his emigration. So, they preferred to wage war against him using devious and deceitful ways, the most important of which was using tricky theological questions, stirring up religious dissentions, and evoking arguments and disputes. We will show this shortly.

These are the most important reasons that made the Jews adopt a peaceable attitude towards the Islamic call in the first months after the Hegira. They adopted a wait-and-see attitude, vigilantly waiting to see what will become of it. But will they continue in this condition and leave the Islamic call to spread, flourish and gain power, content with the security they enjoyed under its umbrella and the peace that helped their commerce prosper and their wealth increase? NO! they did not continue this peaceful attitude for long; neither did they leave the Islamic call take its natural course under the sun. Fears began to haunt them, and anxiety disturbed their sleep, and worries gnawed at them. They began thinking deeply about entrapping Islam and Muslims.

Their conniving and calculations consumed their minds and emotions. That was because they foresaw that the course of events was going in the opposite direction of their vain hopes and aspirations. Here are the reasons:

1- They were disheartened that the Islamic teachings were becoming widely accepted by many, and the number of Muslims were increasing, not decreasing. With each passing day, Muslims grew in power, and they gained more independence in their thinking and in their actions.
2- They were extremely dispirited and alarmed when they felt that their political and economic power- which is essentially based on dissention and lack of unity among the Arabs- were dwindling and disappearing. The Aws and Khazraj entered into Islam and became united in brotherhood by the Grace of Allah. They became loving and cooperated with each other after being sworn enemies in the past.

3- The Jews realized that their desire to have the Muslims join them to gain more power and become more formidable in their war against the Christians in the Arabian Peninsula was nothing but a delusion and a mere fantasy because the teachings of Islam do not deny the laws of Moses, peace be on him. Indeed, the teachings of Islam confirm what is truthful in the laws of Moses. However, Islam was now taking on the appearance of renewal and independence. After the Hegira, Muslims in Medina were starting to become an independent state with an independent moral personality. In their wars and in their peace and in all their other affairs, the Muslims followed the religious mandates of their Prophet; they were not ready to follow the leadership of the Jews or anyone else.

4- The Jews are intrinsically the most eager to live a long life and they are the greediest amongst all people in accumulating wealth. They felt that the commercial transactions that they had monopolized in Medina for hundreds of years, and which they had exploited to acquire and gain things forbidden, began to slip through their fingers to the Muslim Muhaajereen who were just as knowledgeable and had similar expertise in financial and economic matters and were thus able to compete with them. This competition encouraged the Muslims to save no effort to attend to their own benefit and free themselves from having to borrow from the Jews.

5- The Jews were terrified when they saw that the Prophet did not exclude them from his call to Islam. He called them to enter Islam just as he called all others since his is universal directed to all mankind. The reason behind their fright for being called to Islam was their vainglorious belief that the Israelite people was above all other peoples, and that it was Allah's chosen people preferred over all other nations. It would thus be impossible that Allah would send a messenger from these nations and inspire him with a new law, whose teachings would go beyond those of the Torah.

6- The Jews were angered because they saw the Prophet as a dangerous competitor who would vitiate their religious superiority, undermine their special status and threaten their cultural dominance. People had already started to desert them and regard the Prophet as their primary authority and most trusted guide. They looked at him as the leader that should be obeyed as he was a messenger from Allah, of true Arab blood, and he brought with him religious and secular happiness.

7- The Jews were depressed to witness the teachings of Islam call for the revival of the spirit of brotherhood and equality among all mankind, so that an Arab would have no advantage over the non-Arab, nor the Israelite over the non-Israelite except in respect to piety. The teachings of Islam had also drawn some of the most prominent scholars among the Jews. For example, their rabbi Abdallah ibn Salaam became a Muslim shortly after meeting with the Prophet, and he ordered all the members of his household to become Muslims as well. Not only did he announce his acceptance of Islam, but he also went on to describe the Jews as mendacious people and warned the Prophet of their cunningness and conniving nature. Al-Bukhari reported on the authority of Anas ibn Maalik, who said: "Abdallah ibn Salaam heard about the arrival of the Messenger of Allah while he was reaping fruits in a verdant meadow, and he asked him three questions which could be answered only by a prophet: I- What are the first signs of the end of the world? II- what was the first food for the people in the Garden of Eden? III- Whom would a child resemble, the father or the mother? The Prophet said that Gabriel had given him the answers already. Abdallah ibn Salaam retorted, "Gabriel?" The Prophet responded in the affirmative. Then Abdallah ibn Salaam said, "But he is the enemy of the Jews." Then the Prophet recited this verse: "Whoever is an enemy to Gabriel"….. (Qur'an 2:97) Then, the Prophet answered: I- The first sign of the Hour is the fire which will gather all the people of the east and the west. II- The first food that the people of the Garden of Eden ate was whale liver, and III- If the father's liquid squirts out before the mother's liquid is released, the child will resemble his father, and vice versa. Abdallah ibn Salaam exclaimed that there is no God but Allah, and that you Mohammad is His Prophet. He also said that the Jews are a mendacious people and that when they find out that I became a Muslim, they will reject me. Then the Jews came to the Messenger of Allah. He asked them, "Which of you is Abdallah ibn Salaam?" They said, "The best of us, and the son of the best of us, our leader and the son of our leader." So, he asked them, "Do you know whether he accepted Islam or not?" They answered, "Allah forbid!" Then, Abdallah ibn Salaam came out and said: "I testify that there is no Allah but Allah and that Muhammad is the Messenger of Allah." So, the Jews said, "He is the worst of us, and the son of the worst of us." They ridiculed him. Abdallah ibn Salaam told Muhammad, "That was exactly what I feared." [16]

These were the most important reasons that made the Jews fight the Islamic call in Medina. They took every measure they could to extinguish its fire, stifle its authority and vitiate its power. They loathed the fact that this al-Hanif (monotheistic) religion was taking root and gaining support. It exceedingly troubled them that they would have to live in its shadow and under its authority. Had they accepted the safety and security that it provided, they would have lived prosperously in that environment. However, they opted to unite to entrap the Prophet of Allah and the believers. They decided to reject the Islamic call, and they preferred to obstruct and distort it. They dedicated all their resources, their power and their wealth to kill it in the cradle. In their quest to achieve their ends, they saved no effort. And what wouldn't they do to do so?

To answer this question, it is no exaggeration to say that the Jews left no stone unturned in the attempt to snuff out the Islamic call. No means were considered out of bounds in their attempt to denigrate Islam and its Prophet. They exploited all the methods that were available to carry out their goals.

The following are some of the ways they used to undermine Islam and entrap the Muslims. They are briefly mentioned here before we explore them in detail below:

A- Religious argumentation and semantic bickering.
B- Use of conniving and devious questions to discredit and embarrass the Prophet.
C- Attempting to eradicate trust between the Muslims.
D- Attempting to make Muslims abandon their faith/ religion.
E- Finagling with Allah's laws and attempting to arouse rebellion against the Prophet.
F- Allying themselves with the hypocrites against the Muslims.
G- Allying themselves with the polytheists against the Muslims.
H- Slandering the Prophet.
I- Mocking the religion and its tenets
J- Attempting to assassinate the Prophet.

First: <u>Religious argumentation and semantic bickering</u>:

It appears to us that the first method that the Jews used to harm the Prophet was by inciting rebellion among the various groups of Muslims. They did this through increasing religious contentions and semantic argumentations and nit-picking. It is in the very nature of the Israelites (Jews) to be contentious and rebellious in the face of the truth. The story of their sacrificing the cow (2:67-71) and the story of the chiefs of the Children of Israel who asked one of their prophets to "appoint a king for them to fight in the cause of Allah," (2:246) and other stories in the Qur'an that reflect their stubbornness- provide evidence and proof of what we say. We are not interested in analyzing their psychology; we are merely providing some instances and examples of their disputations and squabbling to demonstrate that evil intentions were the source of their resistance of the truth. They were not seeking the truth; rather, they were attempting to depict the Prophet as incapable of disproving their arguments or confronting their religious evidence. By so doing, they were hoping that the Muslims would begin to doubt the truth of their Prophet and convert out of the religion of Islam to which Allah had guided them.

However, the Jews failed in using this method just as they failed in other methods they adopted. Allah instructed His Prophet and gave him the responses with which to silence them and debunk their arguments: "Allah's word stands, even if they disapprove." (Qur'an 9:32)

The following are some of the ways which the Jews used to make their case against the Prophet. They are briefly mentioned here before we explore them in detail below:

I- They argued against the prophethood of the Prophet to undermine it.
II- They argued about Abraham and his مِلَّة religion.
III-They argued about the prophecy of Jesus.
IV-They disputed the issue of the *naskh* النسخ abrogation (in tafsir, or Qur'anic interpretation).
V-They disputed the matter concerning the change of the direction of the qibla.
VI-They disputed the foods that Allah allowed and prohibited.

We will now discuss these issues in detail.

A- They argued against the prophethood of the Prophet to undermine it.

The Jews tried to undermine the legitimacy of the Prophet's prophethood. They tried to cast doubts concerning his truthfulness so that people would abandon his call. They adopted many ways to do so. Amongst the most important were:

First: They claimed that Muhammad was not the prophet they had been expecting, the one who had been heralded in the heavenly books, even after they knew his truth as well as they knew their own sons. The Noble Qur'an mentioned this, "Although they used to pray for victory by means of the Prophet over the polytheists, when there came to them a Book from Allah which they recognized,[2] confirming the Scripture they had in their hands, they rejected it. So may Allah's condemnation be upon the disbelievers." (Qur'an 2:89) [17]

On the authority of Ibn Abbaas: "The Jews tried to dominate the Aws and the Khazraj before the Prophet's mission. When Allah sent him from among the Arabs, the Jews rejected him and denied what they had been saying about him. So, Mu'aadh ibn Jabal and Bishr ibn Al-Barraa' said to them, 'O you Jews! Obey Allah and become Muslims! You used to dominate us before Muhammad when we were a polytheistic people. You would announce his coming, and you would provide us with his description'. Then Salaam ibn Muskham, a member of Banu Nadir, said to them, 'No one we recognize has come to us; Muhammad is not the prophet we described.' That is when Allah revealed this Noble verse." [18]

The meaning of the noble verse is that even though the Jews tried to dominate their enemies and told them that a prophet will come with whom we will kill you like Ad and Erm, when a book, i.e., the Noble Qur'an, came to them, confirming the Torah that they had in their hands, with the same description and qualities they had in the Scriptures, they rejected and disbelieved him because he came from an Arab origin, not from among the Jews. So, Allah's condemnation be upon the disbelievers who rejected the truth that had been revealed and stubbornly and willfully hid it.

Thus, the verse censures them for their lies and dishonesty and their attempt to cast doubt on the truthfulness of the Prophet.

Second: They appeared as though they were the guardians of Allah's covenants and statutes, and that they did not disbelieve in Muhammad out of envy. Rather, they did not believe in him because he did not perform any miracles as previous prophets had done. So, they were not to blame for not believing in him because, in their view, he was not a truthful prophet.

The Noble Qur'an mentions their claim and effectively counters that claim. In Sura Al 'Imran: "Those are the same people who say, "Allah has commanded us not to believe in any messenger unless he brings us an offering to be consumed by fire from the sky." Say, O Prophet, "Other prophets did in fact come to you before me with clear proofs and even what you demanded—why then did you kill them, if what you say is true?"" (Qur'an 3:183)

In sum, they claimed that Allah told them in their books not to believe a messenger unless a fire comes from the heavens to consume an accepted offering that had been offered by one of his people.

Allah had commanded His Prophet to respond to them in a way that would silence them by reminding them of their evil history: "Say to them, O Muhammad, prophets before me came with proofs," with evidence and testimonies, and with "that which you demanded," meaning, a fire that would consume accepted offerings. So, why did you kill them if you were truthful in claiming that you follow the truth and are led by genuine emissaries?" (Q 3:183)

In interpreting this noble verse, Imam Al-Razi said: "Through these signs, Allah had shown that they were demanding such a miracle not by way of honest inquiry, but rather by way of deception and obstinacy. Their forefathers had demanded miracles from previous prophets like Zechariah, John the Baptist and Jesus. However, even after they made miracles, the Jews hastened to kill them accusing them of deceit, dissension and obstinacy. Their demands for miracles were merely out of trickery and deception. Otherwise, they would not have sought to kill them. Contemporary Jews are also content with the deeds of their predecessors, which indicates that they, too, are obstinate in their demands. That is why, Allah does not answer them." [19]

Thus, the noble verse nullifies the Jews' demands, demonstrates their lies, and supports the Prophet's truthfulness concerning what his Lord had informed him.

Third: The Jews made deceitful and unrealistic demands of Muhammad in order to challenge him and make him appear incompetent and unable to respond to their demands and fulfill them. They were hoping that by doing so they would make people abandon Muhammad and believe that he was not truthful.

Al-Tabari and Ibn Haatim, on the authority of 'Ikrama, on the authority of Ibn Abaas, said: "Raafi ibn Huraymala, a Jew, said to Muhammad, 'Muhammad! If you were truly a messenger from Allah as you say, tell Allah to speak to us so that we may hear Him.' To this Allah responds in Qur'an 2:118, "Those who have no knowledge say, "If only Allah would speak to us or a sign would come to us!" The same was said by those who came before. Their hearts are all alike. Indeed, We have made the signs clear for people of sure faith." [20]

The meaning of this noble verse is that there were "Those who did not know" any useful knowledge like those Jews who made deceitful demands of Muhammad, asking him, "if only Allah would speak to us," not you, either directly, or through a revelation, or show us proof to establish the truth of your prophethood. They would say this in stubborn denial that the signs that Allah established to prove the truth of his prophethood would be true indeed.

Allah replied to them saying, "The same was said by those who came before." (Q 2:118) In other words, their deceitful words were like the deceitful speeches of their forefathers to whom Allah sent messengers to bring them out of the darkness into the light.

"Their hearts are all alike," (Q 2:118) that is, the minds of the forefathers and their successors are alike in their erroneous and willful stubbornness.

"We have made the signs clear for people of sure faith." (Q 2:118) That is, we made these signs clear and transparent for those who seek the truth-wherever it may be found-sincerely. In such a case, they would search for the truth diligently, examine genuine evidence with hearts devoid of prejudicial illusions, adhere and follow the grandeur of the truth.

To ascertain the likeness of the forefathers to their successors, Imam al-Razi said that if a wise man wanted to get something, he would choose the closest way to get to it. So, the Jews requested that since Allah had spoken to Moses and to you, O Muhammad, why wouldn't he speak to us directly, or assign a miracle specifically to you that might reveal the truthfulness of your prophethood? This was meant as nullifying that the Qur'an is a miracle, because had they acknowledged that, it would have been impossible to say what they said.

Allah responded saying, "The same was said by those who came before." This means that: We have supported Muhammad through signs, and We revealed his truthfulness through the Qur'an and various evidences. Your asking for more and more is by way of stubbornness and obstinacy. Your requests, therefore, will not be granted. Here are some reasons:

1- If they were to believe if Allah gave them signs, He would have given them. Yet Allah knows that if He gave them what they demanded, they would have only multiplied their demands and asked more obstinately for more.
2- If one evidence would be sufficient, yet one would regard it is inadequate and insufficient, then continuing to demand reveals a stubborn and opposing attitude.
3- Having many signs subsequently would calumniate the marvelous nature of these signs. Miracles and signs lose their significance when they occur repeatedly and in sequence. Therefore, not responding to them by giving them signs did not vitiate the prophecy. [21]

Some interpreters see that "those who have no knowledge" was a reference to the Jews. Others believe that it was a reference to the polytheists from among the Arabs. While others suppose that it was the Christians that the phrase referred to. We suppose that the it could refer to all of these groups; however, we are more prone to believe that it was the Jews who were targeted by the verse for the following reasons:

1- The verse comes within a long chain of previous and succeeding verses that all refer to the conditions and morals of the Children of Israel.
2- The sentence "The same was said by those who came before" presupposes that the Jews who were contemporaneous with the Prophets era were the ones who had no knowledge. That is because, their forefathers used to make similar demands of Moses. They said to Moses, "O Moses! We will never believe you until we see Allah with our own eyes." They also demanded, "Make Allah visible to us!" They made many such devious and deceitful demands of him.
3- This verse is in Sura Al-Baqarah. It was among the very first verses revealed to Muhammad in Medina. It is well known that the people of the Scriptures, in general, and the Jews, in particular, were mentioned more that the polytheists among the Arabs. That is because the people of the Scriptures were more attached and closely linked to the environment of Medina.
4- The reason for revealing the verse that we mentioned supports that it was the Jews who were meant and referred to in this verse.

5- Those who suggest that it was the polytheists from among the Arabs that were meant by "those who have no knowledge" supported their claim by recounting that the Qur'anic verses that recite such claims about them are numerous, as though such demands and requests were unlikely to proceed from the Jews.

We respond by saying that the Noble Qur'an recounted similar requests and questions made by the Jews. In Sura Al-Nisa: "The People of the Book demand that you O Prophet bring down for them a revelation in writing from heaven. They demanded what is even greater than this from Moses, saying, "Make Allah visible to us!" So a thunderbolt struck them for their wrongdoing. Then they took the calf for worship after receiving clear signs. Still, We forgave them for that ⌜after their repentance⌝ and gave Moses compelling proof." (Qur'an 4:153)

6- Iman Ibn Jarir was more inclined to believe that "those who have no knowledge" is a reference to the Christians. He based his conclusion on the context of Allah's account of Christians, as the previous verse says, "They say, "Allah has offspring." Glory be to Him! In fact, to Him belongs whatever is in the heavens and the earth—all are subject to His Will." (Qur'an 2:116) And it was the Christians who said that.

However, we disagree on his conclusion for the following reasons:

A- The verse is not in the context of Allah's report about the Christians, but it was within the context of Allah's account of the Jews. Sura Al-Baqarah abounds with verses that recount the position of the Jews, their reasonings and their morals. There are more than 100 verses that come before and after this verse.

B- It was not only the Christians who said "Allah has offspring." The Jews also said the same thing: "The Jews say, "Ezra is the son of Allah," while the Christians say, "The Messiah is the son of Allah." (Qur'an 9:30) [22]

C- Imam Ibn Jarir did not come up with one single evidence to oppose those who suggested that "those who have no knowledge" was a reference to the Jews. He did not consider the excerpt of Ibn Abbas or looked at it to support or reject it. However, he criticized those who believed that the reference was to the polytheists from among the Arabs.

Yet, despite the abundant evidence, we once again do not mind accepting that the statement "those who have no knowledge" could be applied to all the disbelievers, even though we feel more inclined that it was the Jews who were primarily meant by the verse, and that it was revealed in response to their crooked demands, unprofitable suggestions and their attempts to vitiate the prophethood of Muhammad.

Fourth: One of the methods the Jews used to undermine Muhammad was to dispute his prophethood, trying to negate the fact that the Qur'an was brought down from Allah's presence to Muhammad.

Ibn Abbas related that Ibn Surayyyaa al-Fityuuni [23] said to the Messenger of Allah, "O Muhammad! You have not brought anything we recognize. Allah has not revealed to you any clear sign for which we should follow you." The reason for such a declaration was to reject that the Qur'an was Allah's miracle to the Prophet. Thereupon Allah revealed Qur'an 2:99: "Indeed, We have sent down to you O Prophet clear revelations. But none will deny them except the rebellious." [24]

The word "faasik/فاسق," meaning "rebellious" is a reference to those who leave one thing and go to another thing. It is often used in association with disbelief and disobedience. This is especially the case as it refers to abandoning Allah's "fitra/فطرة" which goodness, righteousness and truth and heading towards wantonness and corruption.

The meaning of this noble verse is "We have revealed to you, O Muhammad, clear signs. Their inimitability and exclusivity for mankind is unquestionable. No one needs further evidence of their genuine proofs of theological matters or their veracity. They are self-evident and transparent in their brilliance and clarity. Whosoever denies their validity and truthfulness as clear revelations is nothing but a rebellious disbeliever with a corrupt and devious nature, rejecting what is good, rational and legitimate. Any one in his right mind who would consider these revelations, O Muhammad, would certainly be led to the right faith and straight path. There is no doubt about that.

Thus, the noble verse responds to the Jews who tried to undermine the truth of the prophethood of Muhammad by denying that the Qur'an is a miracle.

Fifth: Among the devious and cunning ways that the Jews adopted to undermine and invalidate the prophethood of Muhammad was refuting that these revelations came to him from heaven. By this they meant to accuse the Prophet that what he was saying was from him, not what he received from Allah.

Ibn Abi Hatim related on the authority of Sa'id ibn Jubayr, he said: A Jewish man called Malik bin Al-Sayf came and quarreled with the Prophet. Then the Prophet said: I adjure you by the One who sent down the Torah to Moses. Do you find in the Torah that Allah hates a fat priest? He was a fat man, so he became angry and said: Allah has not sent down anything to a human being. So, his companions who were with him said to him: Woe! Nor to Moses. Then Allah Almighty revealed:"And they did not estimate Allah according to His value." (Qur'an 39:67) [25]

Al-Nisabawi said that Muhammad bin Kaab al-Qurazi said that Allah ordered Muhammad (SAW) to ask the People of the Scriptures regarding how they find him in their books. Their malicious envy of Muhammad prompted them to disbelieve Allah's Book and His Apostle and they said that: Allah has not sent down anything to a human being. So, Allah revealed this verse. [26]

The meaning of the noble verse is: Be aware, Muhammad, and let your people know that, by rebuffing these heavenly revelations, those Jews- who rejected the revelation and refused to believe that Allah sent you these revelations- did not estimate Allah according to His worth nor even knew Him the right way. It was Allah's mercy not to leave people without guidance, or allow evil and corruption to spread on earth without someone to stand against it. Giving Allah His true esteem necessitates faith that Allah will certainly send the people someone who will lead them out of the darkness and into the light, the belief that He will send His messengers revelations to instruct them of His commandments, what to do and what is forbidden. Ask them, Muhammad. Seek evidence from what they already know. Reproach them for their ignorance and reprimand them for their crookedness. Despite their general obstinate rejection, ask them a specific question: "Who sent the Book that Moses brought? Who sent the Torah as a guiding light in the midst of the darkness?" But you, O Jews, had shredded it to scraps of scattered pages, revealed some of its texts to the people and hid most out of fear for your authority and affluence and concealed those texts that show evidence concerning Muhammad. In response to this question, tell them, O Muhammad, that it is Allah- whom they deny that He sent down anything to any human being- who sent down the Torah to Moses, and it is He who taught you and your forefathers what you did not know. Yet, even after the evidence was made clear, they persevered in their obstinate blindness and continued their dishonesty and deceitfulness. That obstinate denial is futile and frivolous, and it is not even worth paying attention to.

Thus, the noble verse addressed the Jews' attempt to deny Allah's sending down the revelation to Muhammad.

These are some of arguments that the Jews used to undermine the prophethood of Muhammad. They all ended in failure because the Noble Qur'an was keen on examining these contentious arguments which can described as "cold wars" at the present time. The Qur'an pursued the various claims of the Jews, analyzed them, responded in a way that would render them ineffective and futile, and proved the truthfulness of the Prophet "that those who were to perish and those who were to survive might do so after the truth had been made clear to both. Surely Allah is All-Hearing, All-Knowing" (Qur'an 8:42)

B- They argued with the Prophet about Abraham and his مِلَّة religion.

Abraham's religion and the Prophet's following and calling others to follow it were the topic of numerous verses during the Meccan era. These verses recognized that Abraham, peace be upon him, was a monotheist, not a polytheist. In Sura An-Nahl (A Meccan Sura; the 16th) Allah says: "Indeed, Abraham was a model of excellence: devoted to Allah, perfectly upright—not a polytheist." (Qur'an 16:120) [27] After that, Allah says in the same Sura: "Then We revealed to you O Prophet, saying: 'Follow the faith of Abraham, the upright, who was not one of the polytheists.'" (Qur'an 16:123) [28]

When the Prophet immigrated to Medina, numerous Medina verses- that also ascertain that Abraham was devoted to Allah, upright and not a polytheist- were revealed. These verses show that the claims of the People of the Book that Abraham was a Jew or a Christian were false and dishonest.

Here, we will interpret only four verses from the Medina Sura, Al-Imran, where there was a debate between the Prophet and the People of the Book concerning Abraham and his religion. The Almighty said: "O People of the Book! Why do you argue about Abraham, while the Torah and the Gospel were not revealed until long after him? Do you not understand? Here you are! You disputed about what you have little knowledge of, but why do you now argue about what you have no knowledge of?[2] Allah knows and you do not know. Abraham was neither a Jew nor a Christian; he submitted in all uprightness and was not a polytheist. Indeed, those who have the best claim to Abraham are his followers, this Prophet. and the believers. And Allah is the Guardian of those who believe. Some of the People of the Book wish to mislead you believers. They mislead none but themselves, yet they fail to perceive it." (Qur'an 3:65-69)

Ibn Abbas said: Christians of Najran and Jews met at the Prophet and argued. The rabbis said that Abraham was a Jew, and the Christians maintained that Abraham was a Christian, so Allah revealed "Why do you argue about Abraham." (Q 3:65) [29]

The meaning of the verse is that it is not appropriate for you, Jews and Christians, to argue about Abraham concerning whether he was a Jew or a Christian, whether you followed him closely or shunned him entirely, or the true worth of his message. The Torah and the Injil (Gospel) revealed after him, so how could he be a Jew or a Christian? How could he have believed in either before they were revealed? This argument is remarkably fraudulent clearly dishonest. Do you not understand? Don't you understand the logic that if something happened before something else, it cannot follow something that happened later.

Then the second verse (Q 3:66) exposed another aspect of their defiance of lucid and logical conclusions, i.e., their argument concerning something about which they had no knowledge. It said: "Here you are! You disputed about what you have little knowledge of, but why do you now argue about what you have no knowledge of? Allah knows and you do not know." This means that you People of the Book argued about issues you had some knowledge of such as what you found in your books concerning your religion, your claim that the doctrines in the Torah and the Bible contradict the law of the Qur'an, and the reports about the Prophet whose description you found in your Books. But why do you argue about issues you have no knowledge of, i.e., that Abraham was a Jew or a Christian? There is no mention of the religion of Abraham in either Book!

You should have followed what Allah had revealed to His Messenger, Muhammad, concerning Abraham, because it is the Almighty who is knowledgeable of Abraham's situation, his state and his religion. You don't. The wise and prudent would steer away from arguments on issues about which they have no knowledge.

The third verse (Q 3:67)- "Abraham was neither a Jew nor a Christian; he submitted in all uprightness[1] and was not a polytheist-" had clearly declared Abraham's innocence of any religion that conflicts with monotheism. It also negates his connection to Judaism and Christianity. This negation also exposes the deceit and dishonesty inherent in attributing things unbecoming to Abraham, the Friend of Allah. It also conveys certain aspects concerning Abraham and sets him far above any of the attributes of those corrupt others.

The noble verse points to his true attributes. It uses three adjectives to describe him. All of these attributes are in direct opposition to the topsy-turvy and chaotic aberrations and deviations with which the People of the Book came.

First, it described him saying "he submitted in all uprightness." That is to say, he steered away from any false religion and followed the true religion, which is Islam.

Second, it described him as "not a polytheist." That means he would not associate other Gods with Allah in any way, shape or form. This description exposes their disbelief in the One true God and their polytheism. How, then, could they claim that they were followers of the religion of Abraham and that he was following their religion?

Then the fourth verse decisively settles the dispute and clearly and candidly announces those people who have the best claim to Abraham (Q 3:68): "Indeed, those who have the best claim to Abraham are his followers, this Prophet, and the believers. And Allah is the Guardian of those who believe."

The meaning is: There are three categories for those who followed Abraham:

First: "his followers," that is to say, those who answered his call during his life and followed his teachings after his death. Had those Jews avoided associating partners with Allah, they would have been able to become his followers. But they preferred blindness to true guidance and traded belief for disbelief. Thus, they were not Abraham's followers.

Second: "this Prophet," that is, Muhammad, who came from his offspring and called others to worshipping Allah alone (monotheism), like Abraham. The verse did not mention him among the others who followed Abraham, but it mentioned explicitly, as one who received guidance from heaven, like Abraham, and as the seal of the prophets and messengers.

Third, and the believers, that is, those who believed in Muhammad and followed him. Thus, the verse admits that this group of people-not the Jews- had the best claim to Abraham, because they sought after the truth and worshipped Allah with dedication and honesty.

The Almighty's "And Allah is the Guardian of those who believe" heralds Allah's support, assistance and guardianship in all matters pertaining to their lives.

In interpreting this verse, Imam Ibn Kathir said, "The Almighty says that those who are most worthy of Abraham (The Friend of Allah) are those who followed his religion, and the Prophet, i.e., Muhammad, those who believed from the Immigrants, Supporters and

Companions, and those who came after them. On the authority of Ibn Mas'ud, the Messenger of Allah said, "Every Prophet had a Wali (best friend) from among the Prophets. My Wali among them is my father Abraham, the Khalil (intimate friend) of my Lord, the Exalted and Most Honored. Then he read that verse: "Indeed, those who have the best claim to Abraham are his followers." [30]

This is the position of the Noble Qur'an concerning the Jews' arguments about Abraham and his religion. It chastised and censured them for arguing about Abraham even though the Torah and the Injil came after him. It rebuked them for arguing about an issue they had no knowledge of, and vehemently rebuffed and negated that Abraham was one of them. It proclaimed that those who had the best claim of Abraham were those monotheists headed by Muhammad and the believers who followed him.

Thus, the Noble Qur'an refuted the untrue and dishonest claims of the People of the Book concerning Abraham presenting clear evidence, undisputed proofs and unquestionable testimonies "to firmly establish the truth and wipe out falsehood—even to the dismay of the wicked." (Qur'an 8:8)

C- They argued about the prophecy of Jesus.

Among the issues that were the subject of heated debates between the Prophet and the Jews was the prophecy of Isa (Jesus) because Islam acknowledges the prophecy of Jesus and that Jesus is one of the messengers: "Indeed, the example of Jesus in the sight of Allah is like that of Adam. He created him from dust, then said to him, "Be!" And he was!" (Al Imran:59; Q 3:59). Islam also acknowledges that His mother is virtuous, righteous and immaculate, innocent of anything that tarnishes honor and integrity.

However, the Jews do not admit that. They do not concede His prophecy; rather, they believe that he was disgracefully conceived, and they believe that His mother was a harlot.

Ibn Jarir relates on the authority of Ibn 'Abbas, he said: "A group of Jews- (Abu Yasser bin Akhtab, Rafi 'ibn Abi Rafi and Azaar 'ibn Abi Azaar)- came to the Prophet asked him about who among the prophets did he believe. He said: 'I believe in Allah and what was revealed to us, what was revealed to Abraham, Ismail, Isaac, Jacob and the tribes, and what was revealed to Moses and Jesus. We do not differentiate between them, and we submit to them.' When he mentioned the name of Jesus, they repudiated His prophecy and said: 'We do not believe in what he believed in, and we do not know of any people who are less fortunate in this life or in eternity than you. No religion is more wicked and evil than yours.' So, Allah revealed this verse: "Say, O Prophet, 'O People of the Book! Do you resent us only because we believe in Allah and what has been revealed to us and what was revealed before—while most of you are rebellious?'" (Qur'an 5:59) [31]

The meaning of this honorable verse is: Muhammad, tell those Jews- by way of censure, condemnation and reproach for rejecting the prophecy of Jesus- that you resent us because we believe in Allah and associate no partners with Him, we believe in what Allah had revealed to us, and we believe in the prophets who had preceded us- and in Jesus as one of them- and in what was revealed to them. You only resent us because of your debauchery and rebelliousness, as people outside the circle of faith. The very thing that you hate and dislike us for is the essence of what is right and true; it is the very core of what is virtuous, noble and upright; it is the principal of happiness in this world and the hereafter.

The noble verse disclosed the worst kind of rebelliousness and ingratitude on the part of the Jews who made belief in the Messengers of Allah a reason for resentment and antipathy, even though it should have been looked at as something worthy of the Almighty's approval, pleasure and compassion.

The eloquence of the Noble Qur'an and its fairness in its judgement of the People of the Book are manifested abstaining from generalization It did not condemn all of them for their immorality and licentiousness. Rather, it merely condemned most of them to exclude the few among the People of the Book who believed and followed the straight and righteous way.

Al-Zamakhshari (in Al-Kashshaaf) said: Why do we have the conjunction (و/WAW= and) in the Arabic version of "(and) while most of you are rebellious?" I would say that there are a number of possibilities. It can be a connection relating it back to only because we believe in Allah. That is, you resent the fact that there is a linkage between our faith and your rebelliousness and disbelief. In other words, you resent us because we are in disagreement since we entered the faith while you rejected it. It is also possible that the "WAW" has the meaning of "مع/Ma'a=with." In this case, the meaning would be that you resent us for our faith "مع أنّ/even though" most of you are immoral and rebellious. It could also be an explanation linking a justification to another omitted justification as if the verse says: You resent us for nothing but "the faith due to your lack thereof, your immorality and following your carnal desires and lusts." It is because of your immorality that you resent us. [32]

Thus, the verse had chastised the Jews for their hatred of the believers for their belief in Allah and His books and their unbiased belief in His Messengers. It would have been more appropriate and becoming for those Jews to follow what the believers believed in, acknowledge the prophecy of Jesus as the Prophet and his true and genuine followers did. But the Jews are a people who are unable to comprehend.

D- They disputed the issue of the *naskh* النسخabrogation.

Also, among the issues that provoked heated debates between Muhammad and the Jews was the issue of abrogation. Their intention was to incite contention and dispute and to undermine the Islamic Law (Shari'a شريعة).

The Jews denounced that Allah would substitute a verse or a ruling for another verse or ruling. They would say: Do you not see how Muhammad commands his followers to do something then asks them not to do it and comes up with a different command? Do you not see how he says something today only to retract it the following day? This is not prophet-like! This Qur'an is but a fabrication of Muhammad's creation; it abounds with contradictions and incongruities.

However, the Noble Qur'an did not allow these allegations concerning the validity of the Islamic Law to go unanswered. Allah revealed Noble verses to eradicate them and remove them from the hearts and minds of people, and to enhance and strengthen the faith of the believers: In Sura Al-Baqarah (Qur'an 2:106-108), we read: "If We ever abrogate a verse or cause it to be forgotten, We replace it with a better or similar one. Do you not know that Allah is Most Capable of everything? Do you not know that the kingdom of the heavens and the earth belongs ⌜only⌝ to Allah, and you have no guardian or helper besides Allah? Or do you ⌜believers⌝ intend to ask of your Messenger as Moses was asked before? But whoever trades belief for disbelief has truly strayed from the Right Way."

Since this Abrogation issue- which the Jews used as a pretext to assault the Islamic Law- has been one of the most important issues that has continued to provoke debate in the past and at present, we found it imperative to discuss it in more detail to elucidate and clarify the facts and put things in the right perspective "that those who were to perish and those who were to survive might do so after the truth had been made clear to both."

We will discuss the following topics:

First: Interpreting the Noble Verses.
Second: The importance of abrogation and the wisdom behind its legitimacy.
Third: Testimonies for its existence theoretically and legally/practically.
Fourth: Suspicions that were raised around it and responding to them.
Fifth: Scientists' attitudes to Abrogation.

The Almighty said: "If We ever abrogate a verse or cause it to be forgotten, We replace it with a better or similar one." (Q 2:106)

First: Interpreting the Noble Verses.

The afore-mentioned verse was preceded by His Almighty's: "The disbelievers from the People of the Book and the polytheists would not want you to receive any blessing from your Lord, but Allah selects whoever He wills for His mercy. And Allah is the Lord of infinite bounty." (Qur'an 2:105)

This verse openly admits that the polytheists, in general, and the Jews, in particular, did not want the prophecy to come to Muhammad, who came from an Arab descent. That was why they denounced his message, invalidated his call and cast doubts and allegations around it. Therefore, Allah's clear and outright response was: Allah selects whoever He wills for His mercy. Then, He responded to the most important allegation that they raised, i.e., abrogation, to attack the Islamic Law and cast doubt on it. He said, "If We ever abrogate a verse or cause it to be forgotten, We replace it with a better or similar one." (Q 2:106)

Linguistically, abrogation means annulment, repealing or revocation. Legally, it is a declaration to announce the end of a ruling through a written letter without which the ruling would remain valid and legal, in accordance with the original written text.

The abrogation of a verse in the Almighty's "If We ever abrogate a verse" means lifting the ruling while remaining in the Qur'an.

The meaning of making it forgotten in the Almighty's "cause it to be forgotten" is removing it completely from the Qur'an. Completely removing a verse from the Qur'an was called causing that verse to be forgotten because once something was not there, recited, used by people or quoted as evidence, it was bound to be forgotten. It was possible to cause something to be forgotten by eradicating it thoroughly from the hearts and the minds, only if it were Allah's will to abrogate/ repeal it. And the reason we say only if it were Allah's will to abrogate a verse, because causing people to forget a verse that had not been abrogated would be equal to losing something from the Qur'an. And Allah has said, "It is certainly We Who have revealed the Reminder, and it is certainly We Who will preserve it" (Qur'an 15:9) [33]

Abrogating a forgotten verse, that is, ending the validity of its ruling, is indicated in the Almighty's: "We replace it with a better or similar one."This means that a better or similar verse would replace the forgotten abrogated one. That is why, His saying "cause it to be forgotten" expresses what would happen after some verses were to be abrogated: people will forget them because they would not remain in their hearts. That was only possible when Allah allowed abrogation to take place, as we mentioned.

Ibn Kathir and Abou 'Amro read it " ننسأها/ to be forgotten" with a Hamza/ أ from the word "النسئ" which is delaying. Accordingly, it could be abrogating the verse as a ruling only, or the expurgation of both the verses and their rulings.

The meaning of ننسأها is not to reveal it until another time. In its place, we reveal some other verse that would carry out the benefits it was revealed to achieve.

As for revealing something "better or similar" in His saying "We replace it with a better or similar on" refers to the appropriateness and privilege obtained by using the abrogated verse, for it could be more beneficial to apply the abrogated verse than the one it replaced. It could also be similar.

After the Almighty established that abrogation is possible by saying "If We ever abrogate a verse or cause it to be forgotten, We replace it with a better or similar one," He- in an eloquent statement- used the interrogative form (not to ask a question, but to confirm a point) to address the Islamic nation in the person of its Prophet to confirm this: "Do you not know that Allah is Most Capable of everything?" (also Q: 2:106) This means that the Almighty is capable of doing whatever He wants to do according to His wisdom and His will. Therefore, He is capable of making commands, replacing and changing them at any time, according to conditions and the necessities and demands of the time.

Then the Almighty established evidence for His authority and power: "Do you not know that the kingdom of the heavens and the earth belongs only to Allah, and you have no guardian or helper besides Allah?" (Qur'an 2:107)

In other words, the Almighty is the All-Powerful, the Owner of all creatures in heaven and on earth. He is the One who manages everything concerning them. He conducts their lives as He deems proper and beneficial to them. He is the All-Knowing, and He knows best what verses (abrogated or not) would best suit them. He is the only One who provides for them and supports them against their enemies. He who has Allah as a guardian undoubtedly knows that Allah will only provide what is good, beneficial and profitable for him in this world and in the afterlife.

Therefore, you Jews did not esteem Allah appropriately by claiming that abrogation is impossible for Him, because as the Owner of everything, He has the right to remove or establish whatever He wants according to His will and wisdom.

Thus, the honorable verse confirms what is stated in the previous one concerning Allah's Omnipotence and authority over everything.

Then the Noble Qur'an warns the believers against heeding the delusions of the Jews in order to fortify their hearts and confirm them in their faith. He said: "Or do you believers intend to ask of your Messenger as Moses was asked before? But whoever trades belief for disbelief has truly strayed from the Right Way." (Qur'an 2:108)

This means that it is inappropriate, O believers, to make suggestions to your Prophet that are in opposition with the true faith. It is unfitting to ask unwarranted and unprofitable questions, because if you did this, you would have become like the Children of Israel who asked their Prophet, Moses- who brought them clear evidence- for signs that only betrayed their ignorance and stubbornness. They demanded: "Make Allah visible to us!" (Qur'an 4:153) [34] and: "O Moses! Make for us a god." (Qur'an 7:138) [35] Had you behaved like them, you would have been like those who trade disbelief for belief, and you would have gone astray from the right path to which your Prophet had called you.

The question in the honorable verse is a sarcastic denunciation put in an eloquent style to emphatically warn the believers from being stubborn with their Prophet like the Jews before them. It made their intention to question the Prophet the target of derisive sarcasm. Forbidding someone from wanting something is forbidding him from doing it, in an eloquent style.

In Sura An-Nahl, there are two verses that confirm abrogation: "When We replace a verse with another—and Allah knows best what He reveals—they say, 'You Muḥammad' are just a fabricator.' In fact, most of them do not know." (Qur'an 16:101) Say, "The holy spirit has brought it down from your Lord with the truth to reassure the believers, and as a guide and good news for those who submit to Allah." (Qur'an 16:102)

The meaning of the two noble verses (i.e., Q 2:106, and 16:101): "When We replace a verse with another" through abrogation, with the new verse taking the place of the abrogated verse both verbally and statutory, "Allah knows best what He reveals," for what could have been beneficial and profitable at one time could be unprofitable at another time, and what could have been unprofitable then could be profitable now. That is, He would, therefore, confirm it. "They say-" that is, the disbelievers, on account of their ignorance- to the Prophet, "You Muḥammad are just a fabricator "who would command something and retract it. It was not as they claimed, but the fact was that most of them did not know the wisdom behind these statutes/rulings and they were incapable of distinguishing between right and wrong.

Then the Almighty asked His Messenger to respond to them, "Say, "The holy spirit has brought it down from your Lord." (Q 16:102) That is, tell them, Muhammad, that the Noble Qur'an was revealed gradually from your Lord, through Gabriel, according to events and what was best for the people, as a revelation clothed in truth and wisdom, so Allah would reassure and confirm the believers in the faith, "and as a guide and good news for those who submit to Allah," those who were led by His statutes and commands, who when they hear the verses that had been replaced, and understand and fathom the benefits and wisdom entailed therein, become more assured, more firm in their beliefs, with hearts content and fortified, knowing that the Almighty is All wise, incapable of doing anything except what is wise and right.

From these two noble verses, abrogation means replacing or removing something and replacing it with something. Accordingly, replacing a verse means removing it and placing another verse in its place. This is the very essence and meaning of abrogation.

Al-Zamakhshari (in Al-Kashshaaf) said: Replacing a verse with another verse is abrogation. The Almighty Allah replaces statutes with other statutes according to what is good and profitable. What was good and profitable yesterday could be harmful and corrupt today, and vice versa. The Almighty knows what is good and what is bad. He confirms what He wants according to His will and wisdom.[36]

The significance of the *آية verse- here- as a Qur'anic verse*آية : (Not a miracle)

First: Their claim, as recounted in the Qur'an, that "You, Muhammad, are just a fabricator," is most unlikely to be used in a cosmic sign (miracle=آية) *, because of the use of the word "fabrication." The style of the Qur'an confirms that in many places: "Who then does more wrong than those who fabricate lies against Allah?" [37] Also, in Sura An-Nahl, we read, "No one fabricates lies except those who disbelieve in Allah's revelations, and it is they who are the ˹true˺ liars." [38]

Al-Zamakhshari (in Al-Kashshaaf) said what can be summed up as follows: "They used to say, 'You, Muhammad, are just a fabricator,' claiming that Muhammad was mocking his followers by commanding them to do something today then forbidding them from doing it the next day, and ask them to do something easier. They were reprehensibly disreputable and scandalous, for he would merely replace what was difficult with something easier, what was easy with something difficult, what was easy with something easy, and what was difficult with something more difficult. The sole purpose behind that was to provide what was good and beneficial; it was not a matter of ease and difficulty. [39]

Second: The Almighty's saying: "Say, "The holy spirit has brought it down from your Lord." (Q 16:102) The holy spirit is Gabriel, and "holy" indicates sanctification and purification. It is a well- known fact that Gabriel would reveal Qur'anic verses, not cosmic signs (miracles).

Third: The Almighty's saying in the following verse "And We surely know that they say, "No one is teaching him except a human" (Qur'an 16:103) indicates that the polytheists' strikes were directed against the Noble Qur'an, its source and its intentions, and that it was a human being who was teaching him (the Prophet). This supports the notion that what was meant by the verse "When We replace a verse (آية) with another," the reference was to a Qur'anic verse آية, not a cosmic sign آية (miracle).

Fourth: The Polytheists had previously asked the Messenger for cosmic miracles/ signs (آيات) such as blowing up the earth or ascending to the heavens, among other signs. Their demands were not fulfilled because they were arbitrary and unreasonable. The Noble Qur'an refuted that and firmly shut the door in their faces. From this style of reasoning, we can infer that replacing verses (آيات), meaning miracles, with other miracles was uncommon with his people during the time of the Prophet. What was common- and was often attacked and denounced by the Jews and the Polytheists- was replacing the ruling purpose of the verses in accordance with what was good and profitable.

From this brief exposition of some of the noble verses that confirm abrogation, we can see that they had shushed the Jews and others regarding this issue as they brought ample proofs and clear evidence to the believers that reveal and prove that abrogation was not impossible for the Almighty Allah and that whatever He decreed was for their best interest.

Second: The importance of abrogation and the wisdom behind it:

Abrogation was an issue that the companions and followers of the Prophet had acknowledged from the very beginning of the Islamic Law (Shari'a شريعة). Their abundant talk about it- despite the differences therein- had been enough proof for its existence in the Islamic Law. The sayings of the companions and followers first, and the interpreters and exegetes later, would convince us that abrogation was one of the issues that were a fait accompli, a fixed reality, in the minds of the Muslim scientists.

Scientists were keen on investigating abrogation from all facets, and they appropriated rules and guidelines that would thoroughly and accurately distinguish it from other issues. That was because the knowledge of abrogation (what replaced what) would lead to a proper understanding of statutes and rulings, eliminate contradictions, and eradicate confusions and mix-ups that might ensue once a distinction had been made between what was right and what was not, and what came early and what came later. Lack of awareness and knowledge of what replaced what would oftentimes lead to misguidance and misleading. Also, awareness of abrogation (what replaced what) uncovers the veil and reveals the Islamic statutory proceedings and makes Muslims cognizant of the Almighty's wisdom in His management of people and His policies towards mankind. It will also enable Muslims to defend their religion against those who attack it.

It was Allah's will that abrogation be a genuine reality in the Islamic doctrine for noble practices and dignified and sublime intensions. The most important among these are:

A- Attending to the people's well-being and guiding them during their different stages with appropriate religious interventions. It is noteworthy that- at its inception- the Islamic nation was going through a hard stage of transition as it was uprooted from its customs and traditions. Had it been suddenly entrusted with all the commandments of this religion- i.e., what people were permitted to do, and what they were prohibited from- it would have been a very difficult task. It might have even pushed people to loathe and shun it. Therefore, the Islamic doctrine gradually introduced these commandments and prohibitions to the followers of the religion. It progressively led them on the way of climbing the ladder of uprightness and integrity. It proceeded from the easiest to the easier, from the easier to the difficult and, sometimes, from the difficult to the most difficult. Thus, they were successful and fruitful, because their immortal doctrine - (which led them slowly)- provided the best rules and guidance for every condition, and it clothed them in the best suitable and most appropriate attire for every stage. That reflects the splendor, grandeur and perfection of the Islamic doctrine.

B- Reminding the believers of Allah's graces and blessings and His mercy and compassion for lifting the difficulties in many of the abrogated verses, and replacing them with easier verses. This was reason enough to entice them to be indebted and grateful and obey His commandments and prohibitions.

C- Trial and testing: A true believer would receive Allah's statutes, commandments and prohibitions with compliance, obedience and submission. The wavering and indecisive one would receive them with suspicion, doubt and disbelief. This distinguished the good believer from the bad one, the resolute and firm from the irresolute and fickle.

D- A confirmation that the Islamic doctrine is the most perfect and flawless Shari'a (doctrine/law) as it fulfills the needs of humanity at the various stages reached. By abrogating other preceding doctrines, it had become worthy of being described as the perfect and complete doctrine for all times and places.

Third: Evidence and proofs for abrogation:

Legislators agreed that abrogation was theoretically and logically possible and legally and legislatively viable. No Muslim had objected to the occurrence of abrogation except for Abu Muslim [40] who admitted its logical possibility but denied its legal viability. Before we respond to the allegations of the Jews and Abu Muslim, we would first like to prove the existence of abrogation. We say:

A- Abrogation is logically not impossible. As evidence for this, we maintain that it is a legislative act of the All-knowledgeable Almighty who has the authority to command His subjects to do what He wills, and prohibit them from what He does not want them to do. He has the authority to keep whatever statutes He wants to preserve. No one can contest His judgement or dispute His or second guess His rules.
Numerous verses in the Qur'an indicate that the Creator had instituted what is good and beneficial to help His servants conduct their lives uprightly. He demanded only what is bearable and tolerable. The Almighty said: "And it is Allah's Will to lighten your burdens, for humankind was created weak" and "He ʳWhoˀ has chosen you, and laid upon you no hardship in the religion," and "Allah intends ease for you, not hardship." There are many more verses that revolve around the same meaning.

B- The existence of abrogation and its occurrence confirms the prophecy of Muhammad because had it not occurred, the previous doctrines would have remained valid and in effect, thereby nullifying the prophecy of Muhammad. However, since indisputable evidence exist concerning the validity of the prophecy of Muhammad, this means that preceding doctrines had been abrogated by Muhammad's doctrine. This confirms that abrogation is valid and did take place.

C-Among the evidence that confirms abrogation are the noble verses that we had previously interpreted: "If We ever abrogate a verse or cause it to be forgotten, We replace it with a better or similar one. Do you not know that Allah is Most Capable of everything?" And His: "When We replace a verse with another—and Allah knows best what He reveals—they say, "You Muḥammad are just a fabricator." In fact, most of them do not know. Say, "The holy spirit has brought it down from your Lord with the truth to reassure the believers, and as a guide and good news for those who submit to Allah."

D-Previous revealed (heavenly) books have confirmed that abrogation took place in the Torah, we read: "The Almighty said to Noah when he came out of the ship: 'I have made every animal food for you and your offspring as well as all the vegetation in the land, except for blood which you are not to eat.'" Later, Allah prohibited the Children of Israel from eating many animals. This is a proof that abrogation took place within the Law of Moses. Another example is: "God ordered the Children of Israel to kill those who worshipped the calf." (Exodus 32:27) Then He asked them to stop putting them to the sword.
These are proofs that abrogation is an actuality that had taken place.

Fourth: Charges that were raised around it and responding to them.

Scientists have taken great interest in responding to those who have denied abrogation, and those who have knowledge of Tafsir (interpretation) books and el-usul (roots) of laws, will notice a great interest in this issue. Abu Muslim's stance was not the reason behind this great interest; rather, it was the Jews - who expressed opposition to abrogation before Abu Muslim- who instigated this great interest.
It was the Jews who tried to undermine the Islamic Law and the prophecy of the Prophet on account of abrogation. They regarded abrogation as evidence that the Qur'an was not revealed by the Almighty Allah. Therefore, we regard the Jews as evidently at the top of those who denounced abrogation.

We now recount the contentions/charges that the Jews raised to denounce abrogation, and we will bring evidence to invalidate them. We say:

A- The Jews said: We forbid abrogation because it necessitated al-bada' البداء which is "appearance after being hidden," and this was impossible to Allah. As evidence for this is that when Allah commands us to do something, that thing must be good and beneficial. If He then rescinds it and forbids us from doing it, then that previous command is not good or beneficial, but rather unpleasant and ugly. That ugliness and unpleasantness which are hidden (not known) to Allah at first when He orders us to do it are now made manifest and clear, so the Almighty forbids us from doing it.

حاشاAllah forbid! The Almighty Allah is far above what they say!

This was the charge/pretext to which they clung to denounce abrogation. The answer is clear and simple: the wisdom behind abrogation was known to the Almighty. It is not new knowledge that the Almighty came to acquire. It was not something that was unknown to Him before; it was wisdom that took place in a new form. This did not mean ignorance or lack of knowledge; nor did it mean something that was hidden or unknown that was now made manifest. It was simply a way of leading people from one ruling to another, with a view to what was profitable and beneficial.

Abrogation is a change of what is to come to pass NOT what is known; it is a revelation of Allah's all-encompassing knowledge. No one in his right mind would ever doubt that different times and conditions have their effect on what is good and beneficial or harmful and damaging to people. A thing could be beneficial and useful at a certain time and harmful and injurious at another. People's daily activities and the way they conduct their lives can furnish evidence for this:

Practicing some sport activities like wrestling and lift-weighting, for example, can be useful and beneficial to man in his youth and are therefore recommended and required; however, they can be harmful and injurious at an advanced age and are therefore prohibited and shunned. The decision to command or prohibit in this case has nothing to do with the soundness of vision. How much more appropriate would it be if it proceeds from the Almighty all-knowing? Therefore, if Allah commanded his people to do something at a certain time and forbad them from doing it at another time, this does not mean ignorance or lack of knowledge on His part.

B- They said: We reject abrogation because it is absurd and futile. This is because an abrogated ruling that has been passed for prudent purposes would be absurd when abrogated. And absurdity is impossible for Allah.

Our response to this is that both the original and abrogated rulings are made possible by Allah for prudent reasons, and that both were appropriate to people at the time when they were legislated. It could well be the case that proceeding according to the abrogated ruling would be more beneficial than following the original ruling, or it could be similar. The point is that both rulings are better and more useful to people at the time when they were appointed. This proves that there is no absurdity or futility in abrogating a ruling for all Allah's decrees manifest wisdom and prudence and the benefits that people would experience as a result.

C- They said: We prohibit abrogation because it necessitates the existence of two opposing entities at the same time, and that is impossible, because a commandment to do something entails that this thing is good, and prohibiting to do it entails that it is bad. Therefore, if a commandment was given to do something, then it was prohibited, or vice versa, these opposing and contradictory attributes would simultaneously exist within the same action associated with the commandment and the prohibition.

This charge is contingent on the fact that both the commandment and the prohibition occur at the same time. Abrogation is different, though. One of its basic conditions is that the abrogated ruling comes after the original one. Now, since different times have been proven, the contention concerning the simultaneous existence of opposing contradictory attributes does not hold.

D- They said: We oppose abrogation because it was possible to abrogate a ruling, that would be either with Allah's knowledge that it would last forever, or His knowledge that it is temporary. Both are vain, for the first entails that His knowledge has turned into ignorance, and the second entails ending the ruling at the appointed specified time.

Our response to this charge is that the Almighty knows the termination of a ruling at a certain time. He also knows that He will abrogate it at that specific time. He knows the ending of a ruling because it has been abrogated, and He knows the reasons- and why they have come to pass- beforehand.

E- They said: The Torah that Allah revealed to Moses relates that this doctrine is as eternal as the heavens and the earth. In it there is also "Observe the Sabbath always." This proves that abrogation is not possible, because abrogating a ruling in the Torah is invalidating it, and this is not possible.

Our response to this is that the true Torah no longer exists. As evidence of this is the existence of different versions among the different sects of the Jews. The chain of transmissionالتواتر (through recounting from one person to another) that they claimed concerning it is not valid. Otherwise, they could have used it to argue against the Prophet. This was not the case. What happened was that some of their scholars- like Abdullah Ibn Salaam- entered Islam after becoming aware of the truthfulness of the Prophet. Thus, we see that the texts that they attributed to the Torah could not be taken as valid for argumentation and debate, and their charges and claims are baseless and untrue.

Now, we would like to briefly consider the position of Abu Muslim who objected to the possibility of abrogation in Islamic Law by reference to His Almighty's: "It cannot be proven false from any angle. It is a revelation from the One Who is All-Wise, Praiseworthy." His position is that the rulings of the Qur'an can never be annulled or abrogated, because abrogation entails voiding previous rulings.

Scholars countered by saying that the word "false" in the verse means what is contrary to what is right, and that abrogation is right.

The meaning of the noble verse is that nothing came before or after the Noble Qur'an that would invalidate or void it. Rather, all the rulings and statutes that it brought are in agreement with other revealed books and are supported by rational and sensible minds.

Also, abrogation was not voiding a ruling, but it was a new statement, that was not known before, for the benefit and best interest of the people.

It is noteworthy to mention that many scholars have denounced Abu Muslim's position concerning abrogation and waged harsh campaigns against him. However, many scholars have looked deeply- and understood- Abu Muslim's position concerning abrogation and found that it does indeed agree with what Muslim scholars believe. They said "the meaning of Abu Muslim's denunciation of abrogation is that the rulings that were abrogated were constricted to the appearance of other rulings that contradict our doctrines. Therefore, abrogation- to him- is constricted to the time it took place. Therefore, his difference with others is merely attributed to lexicon and terminology." [41]

Fifth: Scholars' position concerning abrogation:

There are three categories:

A- The exaggerators who had tried to deny abrogation altogether- following Abu Muslim's position. Those were mistaken and adopted crooked ways in interpretation through specification - (attributing certain characteristics to one entity to the exclusion of others)- and attached irrelevant meanings to the verses. No matter how much we notice the number of quotations regarding abrogation according to them, and which are not in agreement with the scholars of usul-al-fiqh (roots of law), the sayings of the companions and followers are enough to ascertain abrogation and its validity in the Islamic law.

B- The extravagates: Those have added to abrogation what should not belong because of mixing between abrogation and specification, and because of their erroneous thinking that there is an apparent conflict between the verses, even though there is, in fact, no contradiction. They were unable to see that abrogation is the ultimate understanding of the verses of the Noble Qur'an by the agreement of scholars. They were also blind to the fact that the predecessors did not regard abrogation in the limited meaning of the term, but rather more general and encompassing including the use of المجمل (having many possible meanings) and limiting المطلق(meanings that are not restricted), etc. Among the advocates of this position are Abou Gafar En-Nahas in his book "En-Nasihk u we-l-Mansuhk," and Heba Ibn Salaama.

C- The moderates: Those who confirm abrogation within reason, for they have not negated it altogether, nor have they added to it unnecessarily or without limitations. They admit it within the boundaries of necessity which are warranted when there is an actual conflict between evidence, to know what preceded and what followed and ensure truthful transmissions to verify their conclusions with clarity.

Scholars have gone to great lengths to prove abrogation (An-Naskh), its importance and the wisdom behind its legitimacy. They defined it in such a way that would prevent any manner of ambiguity. They showed ways to understand and discern its existence, and they explained the issues in which it is not appropriate to count on using it. They categorized it and instituted conditions for it. They detailed their explanations of the differences that exist between it and other rulings. They countered the charges and allegations that were raised concerning it. It is clear, therefore, that these charges that the Jews raised to undermine the Muslim's faith in their religion were annulled and voided by the Noble Qur'an, and Muslim scholars responded in detail to these charges and terminated them.[42] Allah knows

V-They disputed the change of the direction of the Qibla from Jerusalem to Al- Kaaba (Masjid al-Haram).

Among the issues in which debate between the Prophet and the Jews raged was changing the Qibla direction from Jerusalem to the Kaaba (Ka'bah). We will discuss the following topics:

First: How did the Muslims pray before changing the direction of the Qibla to Masjid Al-Haram (the Sacred Mosque)?
Second: What charges were raised by the Jews after changing the Qibla to Masjid Al-Haram?
Third: How did the Noble Qur'an pave the way for this change?

Fourth: Interpretation of the honorable verses that were revealed concerning the Qibla.
Fifth: Why did the Noble Qur'an discuss detailed discussing the change of the Qibla issue even though it is a subsidiary issue?

Now, we will answer each one of these questions.

First: Prayers were instituted and demanded of the Prophet in Mecca during the Night Journey and Mi'raj ليلة الاسراء والمعراج. Scholars believe that the Prophet would face Jerusalem while praying in Mecca. However, he would not avert Al- Kaaba, but he would have it between him and Jerusalem by standing between the Yamani and Black corners.

Some scholars believe that the Prophet would face the Sacred Mosque (Al-Masjid al-Haram) during prayer in Mecca. This view is the most likely in our opinion, because Masjid al- Haram is his father Abraham's Qibla, and because the Prophet is an Arab and came from an Arab descent. There is no doubt that Muslims take more pride in Masjid al-Haram than any other mosque. Therefore, it is both natural and logical that when Muslims prayed in Mecca, they would face the Holy Kaaba.

Regardless of the differences or disagreements that might exist between scholars concerning the Prophet's direction (Qibla) during prayer in Mecca, there is no disagreement that after the immigration to Medina, the Prophet would face Jerusalem only as was commanded by the Almighty. Numerous sayings (Hadith) are available to prove this. Al-Bukhari narrates on the authority of Al-Baraa bin Azib that the Prophet prayed sixteen or seventeen months facing Jerusalem, but he liked his Qibla to be the Sacred House, and he performed the first prayer that he prayed facing the Kaaba. It was the afternoon prayer, and a group of people prayed with him. A man who had prayed with him came out and passed by the people while they were kneeling, and he said: I bear witness to Allah, I prayed with the Messenger of Allah before Mecca, so they turned as they were before the House. The Jews liked that he would face Jerusalem, but when he turned in the direction of the House, they became indignant and resentful. [43]

Ibn Omar also narrated that while people were at the morning prayer, a man came to them and said, "Allah sent down a Qur'an to the Prophet that he should face the Kaaba", so they did. Their faces were directed towards the Levantine, but they turned and faced the Kaaba. [44]

Thus, we see that the Prophet used to face Jerusalem while praying in Medina before Allah commanded him to turn and face the Sacred Mosque (Al- Masjid al-Haram)

Second: The charges that were raised by the Jews after changing the Qibla to Al- Masjid Al-Haram:

We mentioned that after the immigration (hegira/hijra) to Medina, the Messenger of Allah faced Jerusalem during his prayers as a commandment from Allah to comfort the Jews since Jerusalem was their Qibla and a symbol of their unity.

The Jews were pleased that the Messenger and Muslims faced Jerusalem. It was the Prophet's hope that they would accept his call and hasten to enter Islam. However, they became deaf and blind. They started to spread rumors among the people that the Prophet faced their Qibla and would soon follow their doctrine and beliefs. They regarded the Muslim's facing Jerusalem (their Qibla) as a kind of being guided by them. The Messenger was disturbed by their ungrateful stance. An intense yearning and an overwhelming desire burst in his heart to change the direction of prayer towards Al-Kaaba. He prayed and supplicated to Allah that He might direct him to the Qibla of his father Abraham.

Allah heard His Prophet's prayers and supplications and granted him the Qibla that he desired. The Muslims were exceedingly glad to be directed to the Sacred Mosque. It was a symbol of their unity, the center of their aspirations, and the desire of their hearts. They received this this change with compliance and obedience to Allah and His Messenger.

However, the Jews and their likes- whose hearts are filled with malice and evil- received this scornfully and derisively. They were in ungrateful denial, and they raised doubts and tried to cast suspicions in the hearts of Muslims to undermine their faith.

This is some of what the polytheists said: Muhammad is uncertain about his religion, and he is about to come back to our religion just as he turned to our Qibla.

And the hypocrites said: Look at those Muslims! They had a Qibla then they abandoned it.

The Jews- who took upon themselves the responsibility of casting the greatest suspicions concerning the changing the direction towards the Sacred Mosque- said: "The first Qibla, i.e., Jerusalem, had it been the true and correct one, you righteous Muslims should not have abandoned it. Had it been false and incorrect, then your previous worship was false and invalid. And had Muhammad been a true prophet, he would not have abandoned the Qibla of the prophets who came before him and changed direction to another, nor would he have done something today only to abandon and forsake it the following day."

Their first goal behind these spiteful and vicious claims was to undermine Islam and weaken and damage the Prophet and his message.

Third: But the Noble Qur'an thwarted their plans and prevented and foiled their cunningness. The Almighty Allah told His Prophet that those fools would say even before they uttered anything. He paved the way for changing the Qibla by heartening and reassuring the spirits, asserting the faith in the hearts, and preparing them to accept that very significant and consequential matter. For this reason, in the verses coming before that change, Allah mentioned (Q 2:106) that if "If We ever abrogate a verse ... We replace it with a better or similar one," because the Omnipotent, the Owner of the heavens and the earth is most capable of everything, and He knows what is best for His people in matters of life and worship.

Then the Almighty mentioned that He is the All-Encompassing "To Allah belong the east and the west, so wherever you turn you are facing towards Allah" (Al-Baqarah: 115; Qur'an 2:115). He also warned His Messenger that he would not find favor in the eyes of the Jews and the Christians until he had followed their doctrine, an indication that the benefits of facing Jerusalem had come to an end and that they would continue in their obstinate denial and rejection as long as they had rejected Allah's guidance.

Then the Noble Qur'an talked in detail about the dignity and grandeur of the Sacred Mosque as a site for pilgrims who frequent it throughout the years from all nations and corners of the world.

Finally, Allah appointed two honorable prophets -Abraham and his son, Ishmael, - to build it, and He commanded them to purge it from all filth and purify it from all uncleanliness.

The verses that talked about the Sacred Mosque (Al-Masjid Al- Haram) before revealing the commandment to change the direction of the Qibla should have been sufficient to any rational human being: a house with this nobility and holiness was worthy to be the Qibla to people in their prayers. However, the Jews- and those who sick in their hearts- refused to accept the truth. It was not because they were in doubt or that they lacked sufficient evidence; rather, their rejection was due to obstinate wantonness and arrogance. These were enough to make them blind and deaf. It was no wonder then that when they spoke, they uttered blasphemies and their tongues produced nothing but evil and wicked foolishness.

Yet, the charges and allegations that were raised against changing the direction of the Qibla fell on deaf ears. The believers were aware of the true nature of these charges because the Almighty- as we mentioned before- paved the way for this change. He filled their hearts with assurance and confidence and taught His Prophet how to respond to them even before they were uttered. Thus, his responses were more forceful and vigorous in vanquishing their various claims and silencing their tongues.

Fourth: Interpretation of the honorable verses that were revealed concerning the changing the Qibla to the Sacred Mosque.

1- The Almighty revealed honorable verses in Sura Al-Baqarah (Qur'an 2:142-150) [45] concerning changing the Qibla to the Sacred Mosque. In these verses, He taught the believers how to respond to the oppositions of the Jews and others. He uplifted the Islamic nation and heralded the good tidings by responding favorably to the supplications of its Prophet and granting him the Qibla that he had desired. He also relieved him from his aspiration and concern that the Jews- and other ungrateful ones- be guided to the right path. That was because their objections and denial did not stem from suspicions that could be eliminated through valid and clear evidence. Rather, it was out of malice and ungrateful stubborn wantonness. Proof and evidence can scarcely help the malicious and spiteful.

The Noble Qur'an repeated the commandment to face the Kaaba three times in three verses. With each commandment, the Qur'an mentioned a new benefit, because the significance of that even required repetition to plant and confirm it in the hearts and firmly settle in the minds.

After this short introduction of the intensions included in the verses concerning changing the Qibla, we will now consider them in detail. We say: "The foolish among the people will ask, "Why did they turn away from the direction of prayer they used to face?" Say, O Prophet, "The east and west belong only to Allah. He guides whoever He wills to the Straight Path." (Qur'an 2:142ff. [46]) This verse informed the Prophet and the believers that a group of foolish and stupid people who preferred harm to benefit will object to changing the direction of the Qibla to the Sacred Mosque and say: what had had caused the believers to abandon their Qibla, i.e., Jerusalem.

Al-Zakhmshari said "If you said what benefit is there in informing them of something before it happens? I would say that facing something loathsome suddenly would more forcible. Knowing it beforehand would lessen confusion when it happens as it prepares people to adjust to what is coming." [47]

The "foolish" is a reference to the Jews who resented changing the direction of the Qibla. It is also a reference to those who adopted their stance and the polytheists from among the Arabs. Allah referred to them as fools because they spurned the truth, they were obstinately ungrateful, and they rejected the message of the Prophet even though they knew he was truthful.

Al-Bukhari- may Allah rest his soul- states that the "foolish" are the Jews. He narrates on the authority of Al-Baraa bin Azib: "The Messenger of Allah liked to turn his face towards the Kaaba, so Allah revealed 'We see the turning of thy face for guidance to the heavens,' and he turned to the Kaaba. And the foolish among the people- that is, the Jews- said: 'Why did they turn away from the direction their Qibla that they used to face before?'" [48]

Then the Almighty instructed His Prophet with what would silence the tongues of the Jews and other polytheists: "The east and west belong only to Allah. He guides whoever He wills to the Straight Path." (Q 2:142)

That is, tell them, Muhammad, if they showed opposition to changing the direction of the Qibla, that all places belong to Allah, and that they are all equal to Him. He has the authority to assign whatever rulings to certain places, and not others. If He commanded us to face a certain direction at prayers, it is for a good and wise reason. People should only obey and comply. The believers took the Kaaba as a Qibla to abide by Allah's commandment, not out of a whimsical preference to certain places, for it is Allah who guides whoever He wills to a straight path. He directed people to face Jerusalem for a certain period of time according to His wisdom. Then He directed them to face the Kaaba because in His prudence and wisdom He gives commands for the best interest of His people.

2- Then the Almighty described the Islamic community as just, upright, rich in knowledge and obdurate in perseverance: “And so We have made you believers an upright community so that you may be witnesses over humanity and that the Messenger may be a witness over you.” (Qur’an 2:143)

This means that just as we made your Qibla, O Muslims, the Sacred Mosque, in the middle as a safe and guiding light to people, We have also made you a moderate and “upright community,” that is, just and fair among the nations, to have balance between you and the Qibla that you face in your prayers. Thus, you may be witnesses over preceding nations that their prophets had delivered their messages and advised them of what was good and beneficial to them. Also, the Messenger will be a witness over you that you have believed him and entered the faith.

Al- Bukhari reported on the authority of Abu Saeed Al-Khadri, he said: “The Messenger of Allah said: “Noah will be called on the Day of Resurrection, and it will be said to him: Did you convey the message? He will say: Yes. Then, his people will be called, and it will be said to them: Did he convey the message to you? They will say: No warner/ harbinger came to us. Then it will be said to Noah: Who will bear witness for you? And he will say: Muhammad and his nation. And they will witness that he conveyed the message. That is His saying in (Q 2:143): “And so We have made you believers an upright community so that you may be witnesses over humanity and that the Messenger may be a witness over you.”[49]

Then Allah showed the wisdom behind changing the Qibla in the direction of Al- Kaaba. He said: “We assigned your former direction of prayer only to distinguish those who would remain faithful to the Messenger from those who would lose faith.” (Q 2:143)

Meaning: We had only assigned the Qibla that you faced before, that is, Jerusalem, to test people and know who would follow the Messenger and always comply with his commandments from those who were not true believers and were likely to waver and fluctuate and leave the faith upon encountering the least opacity or hurdle. This had taken place from the feeble hearted and shaky faith when the direction of the Qibla changed to the Kaaba. The All-Knowledgeable willed that the unseen (which is known to Him) be witnessed publicly. This is evidence and proof upon which rewards and punishment are based.

For this reason, Al-Zakhmshari said: If you said: How did He say “to distinguish,” and He is the All-Knowing? I would say to teach him something upon which reward and punishment depend, for it is not related to what he knows in the unseen, but rather it relates to what exists. Similarly, the Almighty’s saying: “Do you think you will enter Paradise without Allah proving which of you ⌜truly⌝ struggled ⌜for His cause⌝ and patiently endured?” (Al-Imran:142; Qur’an 3:142). And it was said: so that the Messenger and the believers may know, but he attributed their knowledge to Himself, the Most High, because they are His elite and the people of Zulfi with him. It was said: its meaning is to distinguish the follower from the renegade, as Allah Almighty said: "So that Allah may distinguish the bad from the good" (Al-Anfal: 37; Qur'an 8:37)), so knowledge was placed in the place of the follower's distinction, because with knowledge discrimination occurs. [50]

Then Allah almighty showed the result of changing the direction of the Qibla in the hearts of the believers and others. He said: "It was certainly a difficult test except for those rightly guided by Allah." (Q 2:143)

Meaning: We gave you permission, O Muhammad, to face Jerusalem at first. Then, We asked you to change the direction from there to Al-Kaaba to show who follows you and obeys your every condition from those who do not. Even though this action- changing the direction from Jerusalem to Al-Kaaba- must have been a difficult test, it was not for those in whom Allah instilled confidence and guidance in their hearts. Those received the commandments with submission and complete compliance. They said: We heard and obeyed all that was from our Lord.

And His saying: "And Allah would never discount your previous acts of faith. Surely Allah is Ever Gracious and Most Merciful to humanity" (Q 2:143)was a wonderful and reassuring message to the believers, a fulfillment of their hearts' desires, and a denunciation and denial of the Jews' claims that the believers' worship during the period that preceded changing the direction of the Qibla was useless.

Al-Bukhari narrates on the authority of Al-Baraa bin Azib. He said: Men died and were killed before changing the direction of the Qibla took place, and we did not know what to say concerning them. So, Allah revealed (Q 2:143): "And Allah would never discount your ⌜previous acts of⌝ faith." [51]

And Ibn Abas said: People from among the companions of the Messenger died at the time when they were facing the first Qibla. Among them were As'ad ibn Zarara and Abu Amama, and others. Their folks came to the Prophet and said: O messenger of Allah, our brethren died while they were still praying in the direction of the first Qibla. Now, Allah has directed you to Abraham's Qibla. So, what about our brethren? So, Allah Almighty revealed: "And Allah would never discount your previous acts of faith." [52]

It was also reported that Hui ibn Akhtab and a group of Jews said to the Muslims: Tell us about your prayers facing Jerusalem. It they were appropriate and correct (righteous), you have turned away from it. It they were misguided and unacceptable, you have done it for a long time, and those who died like that must have misguided and lost. The Muslims retorted: True guidance is following Allah's commandments, and misguidance is doing what He prohibited. The Jews said: what do think of those who died while facing our Qibla? - A group of Muslims had died before changing the direction of the Qibla, and their folks went to the Prophet and asked him about the fate of their brethren who died while facing Jerusalem in their prayers. Allah Almighty revealed: "And Allah would never discount your ⌜previous acts of⌝ faith. Surely Allah is Ever Gracious and Most Merciful to humanity."

The meaning is that Allah will never disregard the prayers and good deeds that you performed when you faced Jerusalem because He is gracious and merciful to His people, and He will never discount good and benevolent deeds.

3- Then Allah Almighty addressed His Prophet and promised him that the Qibla that He will order him to face is the one that he wishes for. The Almighty said: "Indeed, We see you ˹O Prophet˺ turning your face towards heaven. Now We will make you turn towards a direction ˹of prayer˺ that will please you. So, turn your face towards the Sacred Mosque ˹in Mecca˺—wherever you are, turn your faces towards it. Those who were given the Scripture certainly know this to be the truth from their Lord. And Allah is never unaware of what they do." (Qur'an 2:144)

Imam Ibn Kathir said: Ali Ibn Abi Talha said: Ibn Abas said: The Qibla was the first thing that was abrogated in the Qur'an. When the Messenger of Allah migrated to Medina that was mostly populated by Jews, Allah commanded him to face Jerusalem. The Jews were happy. The Messenger faced Jerusalem for a number of months. However, he liked the Qibla of his father Abraham. He would often look at the heavens and entreat his Allah, so Allah revealed this: "Indeed, We see you ˹O Prophet˺ turning your face towards heaven. Now We will make you turn towards a direction ˹of prayer˺ that will please you. So turn your face towards the Sacred Mosque in Mecca—wherever you are, turn your faces towards it." [53]

This means: We have seen and learned, O Muhammad, how you turn your face and gaze towards the heavens seeking a revelation. In anticipation to what you have been going through concerning changing the Qibla towards Al-Kaaba to encourage the Arabs to enter into Islam, and the opposition of the Jews who kept on saying: He opposes our religion, yet he faces our Qibla, We answered your prayers, gave you what you desired, directed you to the Qibla that you love and prefer. So, "turn your face towards the Sacred Mosque in Mecca."

That is, turn your face towards the Sacred Mosque (Al-Masjid Al-Haram).

Then the Noble Qur'an generalized this ruling to include the entire Muslim community. The Almighty said: "wherever you are, turn your faces towards it." (Q 2:144)

This means: Wherever you are- on land or at sea- turn your faces towards the Sacred Mosque. This statement was directed to the whole community to alleviate any suspicions that the message was just directed to the Prophet. Since changing the direction of the Qibla was a consequential matter, the Almighty directed a message specifically to them for assurance and emphasis.

So, the noble verse entails a commandment to every Muslim to take Al-Kaaba as their Qibla and face it whenever praying whether they are in Medina or Mecca or any other place.

We mentioned at the beginning of our discussion of this issue some sayings (Hadith) that indicated that when the Companions learned that the Prophet was ordered to turn and face Al-Kaaba, they all turned while praying, and they took it for their Qibla. As a testimony to their unwavering faith and earnest compliance to Allah's rulings, we mention what Nuwailah bint Aslam said: "We prayed the noon or afternoon prayers in the Banu Haritha Mosque, then we faced the Iliya (Elijah) Mosque, and we prayed two rak'ahs (prostrations), then someone came to tell us that the Messenger of Allah had faced the Sacred Mosque, so the women took the place of the men, and the men took the place of the women, so we prayed the remaining two prostrations while facing the Sacred Mosque. A man from Banu Haritha told me that the Prophet said when he heard that: "These are people who believe in the unseen." [54]

The honorable verse demonstrates that the People of the Book knew that changing the direction of the qibla to Al-Kaaba was the untainted and irrefutable truth. The Almighty said: "Those who were given the Scripture certainly know this to be the truth from their Lord. And Allah is never unaware of what they do." (Q 2:144)

This means: The Jews- who renounced your turning away from Jerusalem to face al-Kaaba- know that facing Al-Kaaba was the valid and correct. Clear and indisputable verses in their books show that he who was informed of this change of direction was a Messenger from Allah. He prayed the two Qiblas. Their position concerning changing the direction of the Qibla was merely out of stubbornness. Allah is thoroughly aware of your deeds, and He will punish you most severely on the Day of Resurrection.

4- Then, the Almighty mentions the Jews' disbelief and stubbornness and that they would not follow the truth even if the Messenger brings them all kinds of proof: "Even if you were to bring every proof to the People of the Book, they would not accept your direction of prayer, nor would you accept theirs; nor would any of them accept the direction of prayer of another. And if you were to follow their desires after all the knowledge that has come to you, then you would certainly be one of the wrongdoers." (Qur'an 2:145)

The meaning is: Even if you, Muhammad, brought the Jews and other disbelievers like them all kinds of evidence and proof that the truth- (the commandment to change the direction of the Qibla during prayer from Jerusalem to the Sacred Mosque)- was what you brought them, they would not have believed it. Their opposition to follow you was not because of suspicions that could be removed by presenting proof. Rather, it was due to their obstinacy and arrogance, even though they knew from their books that you were clearly truthful.

And you, Muhammed, would not accept their Qibla because you were rightly guided while they were misguided. The noble verse clinched their greed and determined the legitimacy of changing the Qibla in the direction of Al-Kaaba, after they spread rumors that if the Prophet continued to follow their Qibla, they would have believed that he was the awaited (expected) prophet. Thus, the Noble Qur'an decisively eradicated their hopes that the Prophet might turn and face their Qibla. It stated that the Prophet was not accepting it anymore.

The Noble Qur'an mentioned the differences between the People of the Book concerning the Qibla. It explained that each sect did not follow the Qibla of the other sects: "nor would any of them accept the direction of prayer of another." (Q 2:145) In other words, the Jews do not accept the Christians' Qibla, and the Christians would not follow the Jews' Qibla. So, even though they agreed with each other in opposing you, they are both misguided for the Jews face Jerusalem, and the Christians face sunrise.

Then the Noble Qur'an directed a warning to the whole community against following the People of the Book. That warning was directed to the person of the Prophet: "And if you were to follow their desires after all the knowledge that has come to you, then you would certainly be one of the wrongdoers." (Q 2:145)

Which means that if you, Muhammad, were to -(hypothetically)- accept their Qibla after the clear evidence and My informing you of their misguidance- then you would be one of the wrongdoers who oppose My commandments.

In sum, the noble verse was a warning to the Islamic community not to follow the opinions of the Jews that were rooted in wicked desires and cravings. It was also a warning in the form of a message to the Prophet concerning the wicked desires of the People of the Book, whom he was not expected to follow. It was as if the verse was saying: If the most favored in My creation, the most highly ranked one, would follow their evil desires, I would have punished him as a wrongdoer. Thus, those who are far beneath him in position and status, mainly the Jews and other polytheists, would be more deserving My severe punishment if they were to follow their wicked desires.

Al-Zakhmshari said: If you said: How could He say "nor would you accept theirs," and there are two Qiblas: one for the Jews and another for the Christians?

I would respond by saying that both Qiblas useless; they are null and void as they are at variance with the Qibla of the truth and righteousness. Accordingly, since they are both united in terms of their invalidity and uselessness, they are referred to as one Qibla.[55]

5- Then the Noble Qur'an showed that the People of the Book indisputably know the truthfulness of the Prophet. There was no room for any doubts on this: "Those We have given the Scripture recognize this Prophet as they recognize their own children." (Qur'an 2:146)

That is the Jewish scholars and Christian scientists knew that the Prophet was truthful, and they knew that turning in the direction of the Sacred Mosque was the right thing to do. They knew this just as they knew their own children. It was likening the rational knowledge acquired through reading the heavenly books to tangible knowledge; both reflect indubitable and irrefutable certainty.

Ibn Kathir said: "The Almighty indicates that the scholars among the People of the Book knew the truth of what the Messenger brought just as they knew their children. The Arabs oftentimes used such likening to prove the validity of certain things as was narrated in the Hadith: The Prophet said to a man who was walking with a young boy 'Is this your son?' He said: Yes, O Messenger of Allah. He said: Really? He said: I bear witness to it. Then he said: As for him, he will not commit injustice against you, and you should not commit injustice against him.' It was also narrated that Omar said to Abdullah bin Salam: 'Do you know Muhammad as you know your son? He said: Yes, and more. Allah sent His trustworthy person in heaven to His trustworthy person on earth with his name'... Omar kissed his head." [56]

Then, the Almighty said: "Yet a group of them hides the truth knowingly." (Q 2:146) This means that despite the clear evidence and certain and assured knowledge that you were truthful in every single thing, a group of the People of the Book would painstakingly continue in their malicious attempt to conceal the truth, even though they knew the severe punishment that awaits them in this life and the next.

6- Then, the Almighty assured His Prophet and the believers. He confirmed that what the Prophet brought was the indisputable and unquestionable truth: "This is the truth from your Lord, so do not ever be one of those who doubt." (Qur'an 2:147)

That is, know, O Muhammad, that what was revealed to you- concerning turning the Qibla in the direction of the Sacred Mosque- was the truth that came to you from your Lord. What the Jews and other polytheists claim was untruthful and void. So, do not doubt that they are concealing the truth despite their knowledge, and do not doubt the truth that came to you from your Lord or all the other issues concerning you like changing the direction towards the Sacred Mosque.

Suspicion is not expected from the Prophet. Therefore, interpreters expounded that prohibition (in the verse) was directed to the whole community through the person of its Prophet. New converts to Islam- and those in whose hearts the faith had not taken root- could have been particularly susceptible to be fooled or mislead by the ornate stylistic devices of the People of the Book.

Ibn Jarir clarified that meaning. He said: If someone said: "Was the Prophet doubtful that the truth came from His Lord, or that the Qibla to which Allah directed him was the truth from Allah, that he was prohibited from doubting through His saying: 'Do not ever be one of those who doubt.' (Qur'an 2:147; also 10:94)." I would respond by saying that that was often what Arabs would do; they use the form of prohibition or negative command to address someone even though the targeted audience was someone else, as in His saying: "O Prophet, fear Allah and do not obey the disbelievers and the hypocrites," (Qur'an 33:1) and "And follow what is revealed to you; Allah is the All Knowing of all that you do."

(Qur'an 10:109) So even though the commandment and prohibition seemed to be directed to the Prophet, it was his companions, the believers, who were targeted by this prohibition.

7- Then, the Almighty said: "Everyone turns to their own direction of prayer. So, compete with one another in doing good." (Qur'an 2:148)

That is, every religious community has their Qibla which they face when they worship, so hasten to obey the works that Allah had decreed for you that you may attain happiness in this world and the life to come. Among these works that Allah assigned was facing the Sacred Mosque.

Then the Almighty gave a promise and a warning: a promise to those who obey and a warning to those who forsake the truth. He said: "Wherever you are, Allah will bring you all together for judgment. Surely Allah is Most Capable of everything." (Qur'an 2:148)

That is to say, wherever you die, Allah will bring you together on the Day of Judgement, to stand before Him and give your accounts. The Almighty is All-Powerful and will gather you from your graves, no matter where you are. Therefore, hasten to do good and righteous deeds to show thankfulness to your Allah, preserve the Qibla, and do not go astray or be misguided as the Jews and those who are like them in their obstinacy and disbelief.

8- Then the Almighty confirmed the change of the direction of the Qibla. He also revealed that there was no difference when facing the Sacred Mosque in the event of travelling or when in its proximity: "Wherever you are O Prophet, turn your face towards the Sacred Mosque. This is certainly the truth from your Lord. And Allah is never unaware of what you all do." (Qur'an 2:149)

This means: wherever you went, O Muhammad, always turn your face towards the Sacred Mosque when you pray. Turning towards it is the irrefutable truth from your Allah. Therefore, keep it always, o believers. Obey Allah Almighty in everything He orders you to do or prohibits you from doing. He is not unaware of your deeds; He knows them well, and He will recompense you according to your deeds in the Day of Resurrection.

9- Then, the Almighty repeated His commandment to the believers to turn in the direction of the Sacred Mosque: "Wherever you are O Prophet, turn your face towards the Sacred Mosque. And wherever you believers are, face towards it, so that people will have no argument against you, except the wrongdoers among them. Do not fear them; fear Me, so that I may continue to perfect My favor upon you and so you may be rightly guided." (Qur'an 2:150)

Meaning: Wherever you are, Muhammad, turn your face towards the Sacred Mosque. And you, believers, wherever you are on Allah's earth, turn your faces towards it.

This is the third time in which the commandment to the believers- to turn their heads towards the Sacred Mosque- was made. This repletion was to emphasize the order concerning the Qibla. Changing the Qibla was the first abrogation in Islam- as mentioned by many scholars. It was therefore necessary to emphasize it so that it would be confirmed and planted in the hearts and minds of the believers, and to disperse the suspicions around this change and eradicate it them altogether. Allah assigned a reason that was different and specific for each one of the three orders as though He was saying to His Prophet and the believers:

*Stick to this Qibla since it is the one that you desired and had always wished for.
*Stick to it because it is the Qibla that will not change (be abrogated).
*Stick to it because this would eradicate the arguments of the ungrateful Jews and all other obstinate losers.

The third commandment (in this noble verse) to turn towards the Sacred Mosque was associated with three judicious reasons:

First: His saying: "so that people will have no argument against you, except the wrongdoers among them. Do not fear them; fear Me." The word people refers to the Jews and those who acted like them and opposed the Islamic call.

The meaning is: You, O Prophet, and the believers, should turn towards the Holy Kaaba when you pray to eliminate and abolish the arguments of the Jews. In addition to many other fraudulent and pathetic accusations, they told you when you were facing Jerusalem: If you Muslims have a religion that is different from ours, why then do you face our Qibla? Therefore, turning towards the Sacred Mosque would eradicate these arguments which might still be acceptable to the feeble-hearted.

And His saying: "except the wrongdoers among them" (Q 2:150) is excluding some of the people. The meaning is:

Lest any of the Jews should have an argument against you, except for those obstinate ones who say that he abandoned our Qibla for his love for the religion of his community and because of his longing to Mecca. Do not fear their assaults. Fear Me only. Do not even think twice about those who argue concerning the Qibla and other related matters. I am capable of rebuff their cunningness and thwart their evil intentions. You, believers, faced Jerusalem at first and then turned to the Sacred Mosque only to follow your Lord's commandments and obey Him. In both cases you manifested compliance and obedience to your Creator, the Almighty.

In interpreting the honorable verse, Al-Zakhmshari said that "except the wrongdoers among them" could also be a reference to the Arab polytheists. He said:

"Except the wrongdoers among them" is an exclusion of some people. It means: so that people will have no argument against you except for the antagonistic recalcitrant Jews who say: He left our Qibla and turned towards Al-Kaaba because of his strong proclivities

and leanings to the religion of his community and his love for his homeland. Had he been truthful and on the right path, he would have adhered to the Qibla of the prophets who preceded him. If you said: What argument could the fair-minded have raised had he not turned to avoid this argument and did not heed the argument of the disobedient and rebellious?
I would say: They used to say why didn't he turn to the Qibla of his father Abraham as is described in the Torah. If you then asked: How was the name "argument" used for the claims of the disobedient? I would say they drove him through arguments. The meaning can also be: Lest the Arabs could have an argument against you, an objection for not turning to Al-Kaaba which was the Qibla of Abraham and Ishmael- the father of the Arabs- except the wrongdoers among them, namely, the people of Mecca who would say: he returned to the Qibla of his fathers, and he is about to return to their religion.[57]

Second: His saying: "so that I may ⌜continue to⌝ perfect My favor upon you" (Q 2:150) means turn your faces towards the Sacred Mosque "so that people will have no argument against you," and to have a separate Qibla from the Jews and others.

Third: His saying: "and so you may be rightly guided" (Q 2:150) means that you will be guided to the right path in everything. Where other nations have gone astray and been misguided, We will guide you to the truth and make it specifically yours. It was for this reason that your community was the best nation that has ever come to be.

Thus, the noble verses that were revealed concerning changing the direction of the Qibla towards the Sacred Mosque confirmed the believers in their faith, made them steadfast and unfaltering, and eliminated all arguments brought forth by the Jews and others in this regard.

<u>Fifth</u>: In conclusion of this research, we would like to answer the fifth question, which is:

Why did the Noble Qur'an talk about changing the direction of the Qibla in detail?

Allah decreed that Muslims turn towards Al-Kaaba after they had faced Jerusalem for some time. He reiterated His commandment to face the Sacred Mosque during prayers. He provided clear and irrefutable evidence that that change was the truth, and He brought forth many warnings to those who would disobey His orders. In addition, He mentioned many proofs that indicated a great interest in this matter.

This great interest and detail given to this change of direction- even though it is only one aspect of the many aspects of religion- was because the change of direction from Jerusalem to the Sacred Mosque was the first abrogation in Islam, as many scholars maintain. And abrogation is one of the topics that was open to arguments, discussions and the deceit of Satan. It was therefore necessary to talk about the Qibla in detail so that Muslims would remain steadfast and unfaltering in their faith.

Also, this change came contrary to the desires of the Jews. They vehemently wanted the Muslims to continue to face Jerusalem since it was their Qibla. Therefore, when Muslims changed their Qibla to the Sacred Mosque, the Jews utilized this to undermine the prophecy to weaken and shake the faith of the less resolute and devoted. They saved no effort to shake the faith and beliefs of the Muslims.

They claimed that abrogating a ruling is contrary to judiciousness and diverges from reason and logic, and it should therefore not be considered among the heavenly doctrines. They came up with various charges and fabrications as we have explained when we interpreted some of the noble verses.

These contentions and arguments seemed to have had some impact on those whose faith was feeble and shaky. For this reason, this topic- unlike other secondary topics- occupied a certain importance and had to be explained in detail and be supported with ample clear irrefutable evidence. The Noble Qur'an did exactly this while dealing with the topic of the Qibla. It repeated and reiterated its position and confirmed its stances and position. It gave promises and issued warnings. It explained things with clarity to drive away all charges, encounter all arguments and augment the faith of the believers and confirm it. It strengthened the feeble and shaky to make them firm, resolute and devoted. It confronted the Jews and those who followed in their footsteps and dealt fatal blows to them. Allah is All-Powerful, but most people do not know.

E- Their contentions/charges concerning the foods that were prohibited, and the preference of the Sacred Mosque:

Two of the issues in which the Jews argued with the Prophet were:

Concerning the first issue/charge:
When the following verse in Sura Al-An'am was revealed: "For those who are Jewish, We forbade every animal with undivided hoofs and the fat of oxen and sheep except what is joined to their backs or intestines or mixed with bone. In this way We rewarded them for their violations. And We are certainly truthful," (Qur'an 6:146) the Jews said: We were not the first to be forbidden from eating these foods, and they were not prohibited as a way of punishment or because we were unfair. Abraham and the prophets before and after him were also prohibited from these foods.

Concerning the second issue/charge:
When the Qibla was changed from Jerusalem (Al-Aqsa Mosque) to the Sacred Mosque, they said: Muhammad! Jerusalem is better and more worthy than Al-Kaaba; it is the land of gathering and the land of Resurrection. All the prophets who descended from Isaac paid homage and faced its direction while praying. The Almighty Allah promised Abraham to bless his offspring through Isaac, his son. Therefore, if you were like them, you should have also exalted Jerusalem and kept on facing its direction while praying and never changed the direction to the Sacred Mosque. By changing the direction of the Qibla to the Sacred Mosque you had disagreed with the prophets who preceded you and rejected their Qibla.

These were two charges that the Jews raised to undermine the prophecy of the Prophet. The Noble Qur'an countered these charges decisively and clarified the lies and falsehoods they entailed. In response to the first claim, the Almighty said: "All food was lawful for the children of Israel, except what Israel made unlawful for himself before the Torah was revealed. Say, O Prophet, 'Bring the Torah and read it, if your claims are true. Then whoever still fabricates lies about Allah, they will be the true wrongdoers. Say, 'O Prophet,' "Allah has declared the truth. So follow the Way of Abraham, the upright—who was not a polytheist." (Qur'an 3:93-95) [58]

And in dispelling the second charge, the Almighty said: "Surely the first House of worship established for humanity is the one at Makkah (Mecca)—a blessed sanctuary and a guide for all people. In it are clear signs and the standing-place of Abraham. Whoever enters it should be safe. Pilgrimage to this House is an obligation by Allah upon whoever is able among the people. And whoever disbelieves, then surely Allah is not in need of any of His creation" (Qur'an 3:96-97) [59]

Let us now start interpreting these honorable verses.

His saying: "All food was lawful for the children of Israel, etc.," (Q 3:93) is a refutation of the Jews' claim that the foods that they were prohibited from eating were also forbidden for others before revealing the Torah, and a renunciation of their claim that Allah did not forbid them from these foods due to their violations and injustices- as we will explain shortly.

The meaning is: All food were permissible and lawful (Halal) for the Children of Israel except what was forbidden even before the Torah was revealed, which was what Israel made unlawful for himself. When Allah revealed the Torah, He forbade them from some food on account of their violations and injustices. So, tell them, Muhammad- if they argued with you concerning what We told you- tell them to bring the Torah and read it if they were truthful about their claims that what Allah forbade them was also forbidden for Noah, Abraham, Isaac and Jacob, peace be upon them.

So, the noble verse states a number of issues. The most important are:

<u>First</u>: annulling their argument concerning abrogation since they claimed that abrogation was impossible. They used the legitimacy of abrogation in Islam as a pretext to undermine the prophecy of Muhammad. So, the Noble Qur'an rescinded their claim and annulled it. It countered their argument through their Book. It mentioned that all food were lawful prior to the revelation of the Torah except for what Israel made unlawful for himself. That situation continued until the Torah was revealed, and Allah forbade them other foods because of their injustices and violations. In fact, forbidding certain foods that were lawful to them before revealing the Torah is abrogation itself. Imam Ibn Kathir said: The verse is a response to the Jews; it is a statement that the abrogation that they denied its possibility and legality had taken place. Allah Almighty had stated in their Book, the Torah, that when Noah came out of the ark, Allah permitted him to eat from all the animals on the earth. After that, Israel made unlawful certain food like camels and their milk. His children

also followed him and made unlawful the same things he made unlawful. The torah then came making these foods- in addition to other things - unlawful. This is abrogation itself. [60]

Ibn Kathir as well as other exegetes stated that Israel had made unlawful the meat of camels and their milk. Similar accounts were told of the Prophet. His shunning them was by way of exercising asceticism, austerity and self-control to obtain Allah's pleasure and favor. It was said that he abstained from veins. That was recounted on the authority of Ibn Abas, Al-Zahhak, Al-Suddi and others. They said that he was often attacked and tormented by sciatica at night, so he pledged that if he were to be cured of these onslaughts, he would abandon eating them. When Allah healed him, he abandoned eating veins as he promised.

Second: The verse repudiates their claim that what was forbidden them was not because of their injustices and wrongdoing, and it also renounces that it was also forbidden to other nations before them. Al-Zakhmshari illustrated this point. He said that "the verse renounces the Jews' claims and untruths; they wanted to exonerate themselves of what was attributed to them in His saying: "We forbade the Jews certain foods that had been lawful to them for their wrongdoing, and for hindering many from the Way of Allah, taking interest despite its prohibition, and consuming people's wealth unjustly. We have prepared for the disbelievers among them a painful punishment." (Qur'an 4:160-161) [61] Also, His saying: "For those who are Jewish, We forbade every animal with undivided hoofs and the fat of oxen and sheep except what is joined to their backs or intestines or mixed with bone. In this way We rewarded them for their violations. And We are certainly truthful." (Qur'an 6:146) [62] Since they (the Jews) wanted to confront and repudiate what made them wrathful, and because they were extremely displeased and disgusted with what the Qur'an said- concerning their being forbidden from certain foods because of their wrongdoing and injustices- they said that they were not the first to be forbidden from certain things, and that others were forbidden as well; it (forbidding things) was an old practice. These things were forbidden to Noah and Abraham and the Children of Israel after him, etc. until it reached us. We were thus forbidden just as others before us were forbidden. Their main purpose was to denounce Allah's testimony that they were unjust, wrong, a hindrance to others from Allah's path, taking interest which was prohibited and consuming people's wealth unjustly. Allah would continue to prohibit certain things as they continued to commit evil deeds." [63]

Third: The verse also comprises a command from the Almighty to His Prophet to challenge them through the Torah and rebuke them using what the Torah itself mentioned. The Almighty said: "Bring the Torah and read it, if your claims are true." (Qur'an 3:93) It is as if Allah is telling them: Well! Since you Jews claim that what you were forbidden is not unique (a new thing), and that it occurred in the past for other nations before you, then bring your Torah (since it is current), read it carefully and diligently to see if your claims are true.

The use of "if" in the verse points to their untruthfulness; it indicates suspicion in the condition sentence. In other words, they are not truthful concerning what they claimed.

Therefore, they neither recited the Torah nor read it. And if they were to bring it, it would have confirmed what the Noble Qur'an has mentioned. For this reason, they did not dare to bring the Torah, were silenced and became slavish. This was clear evidence for the truthfulness of the Prophet.

Imam Ibn Jarir said: His saying "Say, Bring the Torah and read it, if your claims are true," means if you were truthful in claiming that Allah prohibited camel meat and their milk in the Torah, then show this and recite this prohibition to us from it. But that was a declaration from Allah concerning their untruthful fabrications, because they could not produce such evidence. So, Allah revealed their lies to His Prophet. He made the Prophet's awareness and knowledge of their lies an argument against them, because if others from their religion were in the dark concerning this, Muhammad, who was illiterate and not from their religion, was informed. Allah revealed that to him. This was, therefore, one of the greatest pieces of evidence that he was the prophet sent to them by Allah. This was information that their forerunners had and which they concealed, and only the very elite among them knew."

Then Allah warned them for their lies and rejection of the truth: "Then whoever still fabricates lies about Allah, they will be the true wrongdoers." (Qur'an 3:94) Which means whoever deliberately lies and continues to claim that what the Children of Israel were forbidden in the Torah because of their wrongdoing and violations was also forbidden to others before revealing the Torah "will be the true wrongdoers." In other words, those were the liars who overstepped the legitimate boundaries, fabricated untruths about Allah after learning what was right.

Then Allah ordered His prophet to invite them to follow Abraham. He said: "Say, O Prophet, Allah has declared the truth So follow the Way of Abraham, the upright—who was not a polytheist." (Qur'an 3:95) Meaning: Muhammad, tell those Jews who deceitfully and untruthfully argued with you that "Allah has declared the truth" in His "All food was lawful for the children of Israel, except what Israel made unlawful for himself before the Torah was revealed." (Qur'an 3:93) Tell them that they were lying when they claimed that what they were forbidden in the Torah because of your injustices was also forbidden to other nations before them. The statement exposes their lies and fabrications.

Then, the Almighty said: "follow the Way of Abraham, the upright." (Q 3:95) This means: follow Islam, the religion of Muhammad and his followers for they are the true followers of Abraham, peace be upon him. Abraham was neither a Jew nor a Christian; he was an upright Muslim. That is, he was honorable and upright submitting to- and facing- Allah alone. Then the Almighty negated any likelihood of him (Abraham) worshipping more than one Allah in the most eloquent of statements: "who was not a polytheist." (Q 3:95) In other words, in all his ways, Abraham was never one of those who would have partners with Allah. He worshipped Allah alone. Allah had commanded His Prophet Muhammad to follow the faith of his father Abraham. In Sura An-Nahl, the Almighty said: "Then We revealed to you O Prophet, saying: "Follow the faith of Abraham, the upright, who was not one of the polytheists." (Q 3:95)

This exposes the polytheism of the Jews and other people who are in misguidance and disbelief.

Now that the Noble Qur'an had annulled their first charge and provided them with guidance (if they were among those who seek it), it embarked on responding to the second charge, namely, their claim that Jerusalem (Al-Aqsa Mosque) is better than Al-Kaaba. The Almighty said: "Surely the first House of worship established for humanity is the one at Makkah (Mecca)—a blessed sanctuary and a guide for all people." (Qur'an 3:96)

The word "house" refers to the Sacred Mosque in Mecca. The meaning of "the first house" is that it was the first house of prayer that Allah had established for people to worship in.

The meaning is: The first house that Allah had established for people to worship in was the Sacred Mosque which is in Mecca where people gather in great multitudes to circumambulate around it. On the authority of Abu Dharr, he said: "O Messenger of Allah, which mosque was first established on earth?" He said: "The Sacred Mosque." I said: "Then, which one?" He said: "The Al-Aqsa Mosque." I said: "How many years between them?" He said: "Forty years." Then he said: "When it is time to pray, pray. The ground is the mosque to you." [64]

Then, the Sacred Mosque is older than Al-Aqsa Mosque (i.e., bizarre reference to the Temple Mount!; see below for validation). It is the first house which Almighty Allah made for people to visit as pilgrims and circumambulate around it as a form of worshipping. There is no other house (mosque) to which pilgrimage is assigned as one of the pillars of Islam.

Thus, the Jews' claims- that the Al-Aqsa Mosque (Temple Mount) was better than the Sacred Mosque and that the Prophet's facing Al-Kaaba during his prayers was in opposition to the prophets before him- were confirmed as lies and untrue.

Then the Almighty described His Sacred Mosque as a blessed sanctuary. That is to say, it is most bountiful and munificent because of the good things that befall those who visit it, meditate in it, and circumambulate around it. For them, many good things and great rewards will come to pass. They will be doubly rewarded; their supplications will be answered and their sins will be forgiven. It is replete with physical/material as well as spiritual blessings.

As for the material/physical blessings: These are brought along with the people who come from all corners of the world with goods and much of the material comforts with which they are blessed. They offer these as alms to those people who live around the Sacred Mosque as a way of fulfilling the call of Abraham: "Our Lord! I have settled some of my offspring in a barren valley, near Your Sacred House, our Lord, so that they may establish prayer. So make the hearts of believing people incline towards them and provide them with fruits, so perhaps they will be thankful." (Qur'an 14:37) [65]

As for its spiritual blessings: It is the place for the gathering of the greatest multitudes of Muslims, i.e., the pilgrimage (Hajj), one of the pillars in Islam. Muslims face it during their prayers regardless of their nationalities, color or their places.

The Almighty described it as "a guide for all people." (Qur'an 3:96) It is their Qibla, the place they turn to when they worship and pray. In facing it, the hearts and minds are directed to the Almighty.

He also describes it as a place that has "clear signs," signs that point to its prominent place and lofty status. Then the Almighty shows these signs by referring to it as "the standing-place of Abraham." (Qur'an 3:96)

Jabir Ibn Abdullah said: The Messenger of Allah went to the standing-place of Abraham and read "You may take the standing-place of Abraham as a site of prayer." (Q 3:96) So, he appointed the standing-place between him and the Sacred Mosque, and he performed two prostrations (Rakaat).[66]

Abraham's standing-place is the place where he stood to face al-Kaaba when he prayed to Allah. There is no doubt that preserving this commandment to "take the standing-place of Abraham" as a place to pray and supplicate is a sign that Muhammad and his followers follow the faith of Abraham and that Islam is the religion of Abraham, peace be upon him.

Then the Almighty mentioned another verse that indicates the dignity and exalted status of the Sacred Mosque: "Whoever enters it should be safe." This means that whoever resorts to it would be safe from hurt or murder: "Have they not seen how We have made Mecca a safe haven, whereas people all around them are snatched away?" (Qur'an 29:67) [67] This was an answer to Abraham's prayer: "Remember' when Abraham prayed, "My Lord! Make this city of Mecca secure, and keep me and my children away from the worship of idols." (Qur'an 16:35) [68] The security and safety that the Sacred Mosque provides is undoubtedly the greatest sign for the grandeur and highly exalted status for Allah. It is a place of security for people in a hostile environment as it is void of vegetation and plants.

Then Allah showed the necessity of performing pilgrimage for those who are able to do so. He said: "Pilgrimage to this House is an obligation by Allah upon whoever is able among the people. And whoever disbelieves, then surely Allah is not in need of any of His creation." (Qur'an 3:97) That is, Allah imposed pilgrimage on people at certain times and in a certain manner whenever they are able to carry out this obligation. And whoever disbelieves, that is, whoever denies this obligation- if he is able- then Allah does not need him, his pilgrimage or anyone else.

Al-Zakhmshari said: These words indicate emphasis. The Almighty's words "Pilgrimage to this House is an obligation by Allah" show the duty and obligation of people to Allah. It is a binding pledge that should be performed. First, He mentioned people. Then He referred to those who are able. He clarifies and specifies. When He said whoever disbelieves, referring to those who perform this obligation, He mentioned that He has no need of him, to show disapproval and displeasure. His reference to creation, as opposed to referring to him (who doesn't do the pilgrimage), provides proof for not needing him, for if He is not in need of any of His creation, this would certainly include him (who doesn't do the pilgrimage). This complete disavowal of all is a strong indication of the Allah's disapproval and displeasure. [69]

Thus, the noble verses responded to the claims of the Jews that what Allah prohibited them from eating was not because of punishing them for their injustices and violations. They also responded to their untruthful claim that the Aqsa Mosque was better than the Sacred Mosque.

This response includes evidence taken from history to show their untruthfulness and fabrications. For example, Allah commanded the Prophet to ask them to bring their Torah if their claims were valid and truthful, but they became submissive and slavish. The Noble Qur'an also proved that the Sacred Mosque was the first house established on earth for people to pray in. It comes before the Aqsa Mosque, both in time and status. Therefore, the Jews arguments with the Prophet concerning these issues were rooted in stubbornness and rejection of the truth. Neither proofs nor evidence would avail when one is dealing with stubborn and ungrateful people. Allah's words are truthful when He said: "Indeed, a group of them conceal the truth while they know it." (Qur'an 2:147)

Second: <u>Use of conniving and devious questions to discredit and embarrass the Prophet.</u>

In the previous section which we discussed in detail, the Jews used religious argumentation and semantic bickering in order to shake the faith in the hearts of the followers of the Islamic call. They were disappointed and frustrated when these religious argumentations failed as the Noble Qur'an instructed the Messenger of Allah of what to say to silence them, renounce their claims and repudiate their accusations. Therefore, they resorted to other methods to shake the faith of the believers, namely, asking the Prophet conniving and devious questions to embarrass him and show him as incompetent and unable to respond to their requests.

The Noble Qur'an recounted this devious method that the Jews adopted, and it rebuked them for that. In Sura An-Nisa, the Almighty said: "The People of the Book demand that you O Prophet bring down for them a revelation in writing from heaven. They demanded what is even greater than this from Moses, saying, 'Make Allah visible to us!' So, a thunderbolt struck them for their wrongdoing. Then they took the calf for worship after receiving clear signs. Still, We forgave them for that after their repentance and gave Moses compelling proof. We raised the Mount over them as a warning for breaking their covenant and said, 'Enter the gate (of Jerusalem?) with humility.' We also warned them, 'Do not break the Sabbath,' and took from them a firm covenant." (Qur'an 4:153-154)

Ibn Jarir narrates on the authority of Muhammad bin Kaab Al-Qarzi, he said: A group of Jews came to the Messenger of Allah and said: 'Muhammad! Moses came with tablets from Allah, so bring us tablets from Allah so that we can believe you.' Allah revealed:

"The People of the Book demand that you O Prophet bring down for them a revelation in writing from heaven...." (Q 4:153)

"The people of the Book" here is a specific reference to the Jews since the noble verses depicts specific things that can only be attributed to them.

The Almighty's: "The People of the Book demand that you 'O Prophet' bring down for them a revelation in writing from heaven..." means that the Jews- out of obstinacy and stubbornness-asked you, Muhammad, to bring down from heaven a revelation in writing, just as Moses brought down the Torah to their forefathers written on tablets. They asked you to bring to them books from heaven that command them to believe you. But know, Muhammad, even if they were given what they requested, they would not have believed in you. Their requests were out of malice and spite, and malicious and spiteful people would not be persuaded even if they were presented with clear proofs and undoubtful evidence. Had they really been after the truth, they would not have asked you, for clear and flawless evidence had proven your truthfulness.

Then Allah rebuked them- and regaled His Prophet- for demanding such a thing. He said: "They demanded what is even greater than this from Moses." (Qur'an 4:153) Which means, do not be upset, Muhammad, on account of their requests. Neither be disheartened because of their stubbornness. Their forefathers had asked Moses, their Prophet, greater things than what they asked you. They also asked him to bring down a book from heaven. Now their descendants follow in their footsteps in their stubbornness and arrogance. So, the present time for those Jews is just like past time of their forerunners; they do not care about convincing and reliable evidence. All they want is to showing stubbornness and hostility towards the messengers, peace be on them.

Al-Zakhmshari said: "'They demanded what is even greater than this from Moses' is a response statement to the preceding conditional statement. That is, if you thought that what they asked you was great, they had demanded greater things from Moses. Their forefathers did this and the current Jews follow suit; they are happy to make such demands and they are far more stubborn than their forefathers." [70]

The Almighty then showed what the Children of Israel demanded from Moses and what befell them because of their stubbornness and intransigence. The Almighty said: "Make Allah visible to us!" (Q 4:153) That is, the forefathers of the Children of Israel asked their Prophet, Moses- peace be upon him- for greater things than what the contemporary Jews had asked you. Despite clear proofs and undeniable evidence that proved his truthfulness, they asked Moses to "Make Allah visible to us!" They wanted to see Allah with their own eyes. Because of their audacity and arrogance towards Allah "a thunderbolt struck them for their wrongdoing." (Q 4:153) That is to say, fire came thundering down from the heavens to strike them on account of their wrong doing and evil deeds.

Then the Almighty mentioned another vice, one of their many great vices: "Then they took the calf for worship after receiving clear signs. Still, We forgave them for that after their repentance and gave Moses compelling proof." (Q 4:153) This means: Those who asked Moses- peace be upon him- to make Allah visible to them, to see Him with their eyes, - after Allah saved them from the thunderbolt that struck them, after He saved them from the Pharaoh and his injustices and cruelty, and after they witnessed signs and miracles that undeniably proved the truthfulness of their prophet Moses- after all of these proofs, they took the calf for worship. Yet, "Still We forgave them" because they repented to Allah and killed themselves. And We "gave Moses compelling proof." That is. We gave Moses clear evidence, astounding miracles, might and strength to vanquish whoever stood against him.

The Almighty then revealed another kind of their stubbornness and intransigence. "He said: 'We raised the Mount over them as a warning for breaking their covenant and said, 'Enter the gate of Jerusalem with humility.' We also warned them, 'Do not break the Sabbath,' and took from them a firm covenant." (Q 4:154)

Imam Ibn Kathir said: "We raised the Mount over them as a warning for breaking their covenant" means that when they did not comply with the instructions of the Torah, and they rejected what Moses- peace be upon him- brought them, Allah raised a mountain over their heads. They were instructed to comply, and they did fell on their knees and worshipped looking at the mountain, fearing it might fall and engulf them, as the Almighty said: "And when We raised the mountain above them as if it were a canopy and they thought that it was falling upon them: 'Take what We have given you with strength and remember what is in it that you may become righteous'." (Al-Araf:171; Q 7:171) [71]

Then, the Almighty said: And We "said, "Enter the gate of Jerusalem with humility." We also warned them, "Do not break the Sabbath," and took from them a firm covenant." (Q 4:154) That is, We told them when we commanded them to enter the gates of Jerusalem to enter with modesty and meekness, obeying their Lord's commandments, and in submission and gratitude. However, they did not comply, neither in words, nor in deed.

We also asked them "not break the Sabbath," (Qur'an 4:154) that is, not to trespass or violate the boundaries concerning the Sabbath, namely, whale (great or big fish)-hunting. They broke the commandment, adopted wayward and conniving methods and did what Allah prohibited them from doing, so Allah transformed them to disgraced apes. (Qur'an 7:166)

And We "took from them a firm covenant," (Q 4:154) a pledge to commit to what Allah commanded and abandon what He prohibited. Yet, they broke their promises heedless of Allah's signs, killed His prophets unjustly, and indulged in immoralities and wrongdoing. So, the Almighty punished them most severely.

Thus, the two noble verses revealed how inclined the Jews were to embarrass the Messenger through conniving and devious questions. They admonished the Jews and revealed their vices and wickedness so that the believers would be able to know them for who they were to avoid and stay away from them. The Jews' crookedness and deviousness availed them nothing.

Among the devious and scheming questions that the Jews directed to the Prophet were questions about the spirit, the food of the people in paradise, funerals, monotheism, the Two-Horned One and the Almighty Allah Himself. All these questions- and more- were meant to attack, embarrass and offend the Prophet. They were not asked to seek knowledge or to reach the truth.

1- Abdullah bin Masoud narrated: "While I was walking with the Prophet, in a field, and he was leaning on a stick, a group of Jews passed by. They said to one another: 'ask him about the spirit.' He asked 'What's wrong?' Meaning 'Why do you ask a question you may dislike its answer? 'Some said: 'He will not respond with anything you dislike.' So, they asked him about the spirit. The Prophet remained silent and did not respond to the question. So, I knew it was being revealed to him, and I stood in my place. When the revelation came down, he said: 'And they ask you about the spirit, say the spirit is from the command of my Lord, and you have not been given of knowledge except a little.'" [72]

2- In Sahih Muslim, Thawban said: "I was standing with the Messenger of Allah when a Jewish rabbi came and said: 'Peace be upon you, Muhammad!' So, I pushed him, and he almost collapsed, and he said: 'Why did you push me?' So I said:' Didn't you say: O Messenger of Allah?' And the Jew said: 'We call him by his name, the one his family called him.' Then the Messenger of Allah said: 'My name is Muhammad, which my family called me.' Then the Jew said: 'I came to ask you where will the people be when the earth and the heavens will be changed?' So, the Messenger of Allah said: 'They will be in darkness Without the bridge.' The Jew said: 'Who are the first people to be permitted?' He said: 'The poor immigrants.' The Jew said: 'What is their reward when they enter Paradise?' The Prophet said: 'an abundance of cod liver oil.' The Jew said: "What is their food after that?" "The bull of Paradise, which used to eat from its edges.' He said: What do they drink on it? He said: "Whoever springs from it, it is called: Salsabila." He said: You are right.

He said: 'I came to ask you about something that no one on earth knows, except a prophet, or a man, or two men.' He said: 'It will benefit you if I tell you?' He said: 'I hear with my ears'. He said: 'I came to ask you about the gender of the fetus.' The Prophet said: 'The man's water is white. A woman's water is yellow. If they come together, the man's semen is more than the woman's semen, it would be male, Allah willing. If the woman's semen is higher than the man's semen, it would be a female, Allah willing.' The Jew said: 'You are right. And you are a prophet.' Then he left and left." [73]

3- Abou Dawud narrated on the authority of Abi Namlah al-Ansari, he said: While I was sitting with the Messenger of Allah in the company of a Jew, a funeral passed by. The Jew asked: ‘Is it permissible to speak during a funeral?’ The Prophet said: ‘I do not know.’ The Jew said: “It is possible.’ The Prophet said: ‘Do not believe the people of the Book and do not disbelieve in them. Say ‘We believe in Allah and His prophets revealed to us; if untrue, you did not believe it; if true, you did not disbelieve in it.” [74]

4- Ibn Ishaq said: “An-Nahaam bin Zeid, Qurdom bin Kaab, and Bahri bin Omer came to the Messenger of Allah. They said: ‘Muhammad! Don’t you know that there is another God beside Allah?’ the Messenger of Allah said: ‘Ask them, O Prophet, “Who is the best witness?” Say, “Allah is! He is a Witness between me and you. And this Quran has been revealed to me so that, with it, I may warn you and whoever it reaches. Do you ⌜pagans⌝ testify that there are other Gods besides Allah?” ⌜Then⌝ say, “I will never testify ⌜to this⌝!” And say, “There is only One Allah. And I totally reject whatever idols you associate with Him. Those to whom We gave the Scripture recognize him to be a true prophet as they recognize their own children. Those who have ruined themselves will never believe.” [75]

5- He also said: “Jabal bin Abi Qusher and Shamuel bin Zeid came to the Messenger of Allah and said: ‘Muhammad! If you were a prophet as you say, tell us when is the hour?’ Then Allah revealed: ‘They ask you O Prophet regarding the Hour, “When will it be?” Say, “That knowledge is only with my Lord. He alone will reveal it when the time comes. It is too tremendous for the heavens and the earth and will only take you by surprise.” They ask you as if you had full knowledge of it. Say, “That knowledge is only with Allah, but most people do not know.’” [76]

6- He also said: “Huyayy ibn Akhtab, Ka’ab ibn Asad, Abou Rafi’, Ashei’, and Shamuel bin Zeid said to Abdullah bin Salaam when he converted to Islam, ‘What is the prophecy for Arabs?’ They then went to the Messenger of Allah and asked him about the Two-Horned One. The Prophet told them what Allah had made known to him, of which Quraysh was knowledgeable. It was them who ordered Quraysh to ask the Messenger about him when they sent Al-Nadr bin Harith and Aqaba bin Abi Mi’et.” [77]

7- He also said that Said bin Jubir said: "A group of Jews came to Muhammad and asked him: 'Muhammad! Allah created this creation. Who created Allah?"

He said that the Messenger of Allah was extremely angry and his face changed color. He attacked them because of his jealousy for Allah. Gabriel- peace be upon him- came and calmed him down and brought from Allah the response to their question: 'Say: He is Allah, the One! (1) Allah, the eternally Besought of all! (2) He begets not, nor was begotten. (3) And there is none comparable unto Him. (4)' When he recited the verse, they said: 'Describe Him for us, Muhammad. How does He look. How is His arm? His upper arm?' Muhammad was now more furious than before, but Gabriel came once again with a response from Allah: 'They have not shown Allah His proper reverence—when on the Day of Judgment the ⸢whole⸣ earth will be in His Grip, and the heavens will be rolled up in His Right Hand. Glorified and Exalted is He above what they associate ⸢with Him⸣!' [78]

These are some examples for the devious and conniving questions that the Jews asked the Prophet. They were questions that were meant bother and annoy him. They wanted to depict him as incompetent and unable to address and respond to their questions. However, they failed. The Prophet was able to silence them and turn them away thwarted and in defeat. "Allah refuses except that His light be made perfect even if the disbelievers hate it."

A-Third: <u>Attempting to eradicate trust between the Muslims.</u>

One of the crooked and cunning ways that the Jews employed to enmesh Muslims and diminish and weaken Islam was sowing the seeds of contention and dissention between Muslims. The Noble Qur'an reported this method and vehemently rebuked the Jews for behaving in that fashion. It also guided them to the best way that would lead them to the straight path. In Al-'Imran, the Almighty said: "Say, O Prophet, 'O People of the Book! Why do you deny the revelations of Allah, when Allah is a Witness to what you do?'" "Say, 'O People of the Book! Why do you turn the believers away from the Way of Allah—striving to make it appear crooked, while you are witnesses to its truth? And Allah is never unaware of what you do.'" "O believers! If you were to yield to a group of those who were given the Scripture, they would turn you back from belief to disbelief." "How can you disbelieve when Allah's revelations are recited to you and His Messenger is in your midst? Whoever holds firmly to Allah is surely guided to the Straight Path." "O believers! Be mindful of Allah in the way He deserves. and do not die except in ⸢a state of full⸣ submission to Him." "And hold firmly together to the rope of Allah and do not be divided. Remember Allah's favor upon you when you were enemies, then He united your hearts, so you—by His grace—became brothers. And you were at the brink of a fiery pit and He saved you from it. This is how Allah makes His revelations clear to you, so that you may be rightly guided." (Qur'an 3:98-103)

The reason for revealing these verses: Al-Tabari narrated on the authority of Zayd bin Aslam, who said: "Shas bin Qays - who was an old man in pre-Islamic times, a great disbeliever, very envious of Muslims, and very malicious to them - passed by a group of the companions of the Messenger of Allah from the Aws and Khazraj. They were in a gathering that gathered them together to talk. He was angered when he saw their unity, brotherhood, and the reconciliation that took place between them because of Islam after the enmity that had existed between them in pre-Islamic times. He said: 'The people of Banu Qayla (meaning the Ansar of Aws and Khazraj) have gathered in this country. No, by Allah, we will have no stability with them if their people gather there.' So, he ordered a young boy from among the Jews who was with him and said to him: 'Go to them and sit with them.' He reminded them of the day of Baath and what had happened before it, and recited to them some of the poetry they had been discussing. So, he did, and the people spoke at that time, and they quarreled and bragged until two men from the groups (Aws bin Qayzi from the Aws tribe and Jabaar bin Saqer from the Khazraj) jumped on their knees and argued, and said to each other: 'If you wish, we will return to war now in a violent manner,' and the two groups became angry and said: 'We have taken the weapon and the weapon is your date.' This reached the Messenger of Allah, and he went out to them with his companions until he came to them and said: 'O community of Muslims, Allah bless you. Allah! Are we back to the pre-Islamic era while I am among you, after Allah has guided you to Islam and honored you with it, cut off from you the affairs of pre-Islamic times, saved you from disbelief, and united your hearts? Will you now return to the times of disbelief?' So, the people knew that it was a temptation of Satan and a plot of their enemy, so they laid down their weapons and cried. The men of the Aws and the men of the Khazraj hugged each other, then they departed with the Messenger of Allah, listening and obedient. Allah had extinguished from them the plot of Allah's enemy, Shas bin Qais, and what he did. So, Allah Almighty revealed: Say, 'O People of the Book, why do you disbelieve in the verses of Allah, when Allah is a witness of what you do?' (Qur'an 3:98)

And it was revealed about Al-Aws and Al-Khazraj: 'O you who have believed, if you obey a party of those who were given the Scripture, they will turn you back into disbelief after you have believed... It is they who will suffer a tremendous punishment." [79]

The Almighty's "O People of the Book, why do you disbelieve in the verses of Allah, when Allah is a witness of what you do?' (Q 3:98) means: Muhammad, tell those Jews who rejected the truth after they were presented with clear and unfailing evidence, why they resist the truth and oppose it? Why do they dispute the logical and rational verses that confirm the truth of what I say about my Lord? Indeed, Allah is All-Seeing and He knows your hidden and manifest deeds, and He will reward you accordingly.

The honorable verse comprises rebuking them for their disbelief, warning them with severe punishment if they continue with their evil deeds. And in order to make this admonition more poignant and painful, the Almighty commanded His Prophet to call them "O People of the Book," since their knowledge of the Scriptures necessitated accepting the faith and the truth. However, they used this knowledge to spread evil and misguidance. Their method betrayed their intrinsic and natural corruption, evil and abominable intentions and detestable and obnoxious behavior.

After the Noble Qur'an informed them with their disbelief and misguidance, it revealed another verse to chastise them for trying to mislead and misguide others: "O People of the Book! Why do you turn the believers away from the Way of Allah—striving to make it appear crooked, while you are witnesses to its truth? And Allah is never unaware of what you do." (Qur'an 3:99)

The meaning is: Ask those Jews-, Muhammad, - once more, to emphasize chastising and rebuking them and to eliminate any pretexts or excuses they might have- ask them why they have been trying to turn the believers away from the true faith? Why they have been trying to prevent those who believe in you from continuing to follow you? Why they have been trying to sow the seeds of contention and strife among the Muslims' ranks?

Then, the Noble Qur'an disclosed their intentions concerning turning people away from the path of Allah. He said striving to make it appear crooked, which means that you want the clear and straight paths of Allah to look crooked and deviate from the noble and righteous ways, in the eyes of the guided ones, just as your spirits have become deviant and crooked and your minds corrupted and degraded.

Al-Zakhmshari said: If you said: "How did He say striving to make it appear crooked" when this is impossible?"

I would respond by saying that there are two meanings: The first one is that you deliberately misguide people make them believe that it is "crooked" by saying that the Laws of Moses cannot be abrogated, and by changing the description of the Messenger of Allah from the true one. The second one is that you laboriously tire yourselves trying to conceal the truth and striving to incur what you do not have: finding crookedness in something that most straight and noble. [80]

His "while you are witnesses" means that you are aware that Islam is the right path and the true religion. You know this just as anyone who sees and witnesses the truth visibly. So, your rejection of the truth is done knowingly, and your disbelief is not due to ignorance or lack of knowledge.

His "Allah is never unaware of what you do" is a warning and an admonition for their misguidance and their attempt to mislead others. The Almighty is the All-Knowledgeable; He is aware of their deeds, and He will severely punish them for their devious and evil deeds: failure and humiliation in this life and torture and suffering in the next.

Imam Ibn Kathir said: "This is a severe admonition from the Almighty Allah to the infidels (disbelievers) from among the People of the Book for their intransigence and resistance to the truth, their disbelief in the verses of Allah, and for trying to turn away from the path of Allah those believers who vehemently and painstakingly try to follow this path. They did all of this even though they knew that what the Messenger brough was the truth from Allah. They also had knowledge about the former messengers and prophets, peace be upon them all. They learned about- and were foretold of- the illiterate, Hashemite, Arab,

Meccan prophet, the seal of the prophets, and the Messenger of the Lord of the heavens and the earth. Allah warned them. He told them that He witnessed their deeds: their deliberate rejection of the prophets, the way they dealt with the foretold Messenger, and how they rejected him and how they received him with ungratefulness and intransigence. The Almighty told them that He is not unaware of what they did. He will reward them on that Day 'when neither wealth nor children will be of any benefit.'" [81]

After the Noble Qur'an demonstrated that the Jews had the two vices: being misguided as well as trying to misguide others, it temporarily left them in their blindness and misguidance, and it called upon the believers to be wary of their plots and schemes, and cautioned them against paying attention to their conspiracies or heeding their collusions. It said: "O believers! If you were to yield to a group of those who were given the Scripture, they would turn you back from belief to disbelief." (Q 3:100)

Which means: If you believers listened to the Jews and heeded their schemes, they would not only cause enmity between you- as it was the case in pre-Islamic times-, but they would also go beyond that and attempt to turn you back to idol-worshipping and disbelief. Allah Himself addressed the believers in this verse after He commanded His Messenger to address the People of the Scripture in the previous two verses. This shows that Allah holds the believers in high esteem; they are made aware that they are worthy of being addressed by the Almighty Allah Himself.

And He called them using the word "believers" to kindle the fire of belief in their hearts and ignite their faith. He was also calling them to be watchful and vigilant, just as a believer should be.

The use of "If" indicated that yielding to the Jews was not expected; their faith would fortify them against this. The Almighty described those who tried to sow the seeds of discord between the believers as "a group of those who were given the Scripture" to fairly exclude those who did not do that. He also described them as a group who were "given the Scripture" to indicate that their attempt to mislead others was intentional and their plotting to harm the believers deliberate. After all, they were people of the Scripture and of knowledge. However, they used their knowledge to commit evil and malicious deeds.

Then the Noble Qur'an showed that it was unbecoming for the believers to yield to this group who were given the Scripture, turn to disbelief after believing, or become divided after they were united. The Almighty said: "How can you disbelieve when Allah's revelations are recited to you and His Messenger is in your midst? Whoever holds firmly to Allah is surely guided to the Straight Path." (Qur'an 3:101)

The question was to show the unlikely scenario of their turning back to disbelief when they had been equipped with all the reasons to remain firm and steadfast in the faith.

And the meaning is: How could you turn back (to disbelief)? How could it ever occur to you that you might do that when Allah's verses are recited day and night and when the Messenger of Allah is in your midst bringing you back to the correct path if you erred, and eradicating any ambiguities or suspicions. This was bound to cast despair in the hearts of the Jews as they would not be able to realize their goals (plots) with the believers as the Prophet repeatedly reminded the believers with what was profitable and beneficial to them and warned and cautioned them against what was injurious and harmful.

Then Allah directed His servants (the believers) to the path that would protect them from the conniving and cunning Jews. He said: "Whoever holds firmly to Allah is surely guided to the Straight Path."

Meaning: Whoever resorts to Allah in all conditions, trusts and relies on Him thoroughly, holds firmly to his faith, will be surely guided to the Straight Path, one without deviation or crookedness.

Then He ordered them to be obedient and deferential: "O believers! Be mindful of Allah in the way He deserves, and do not die except in a state of full submission to Him." (Qur'an 3:102)

In other words, be extremely pious and virtuous and make sure that you are Muslims when you die. So, continue holding firmly to your correct religion until death overtakes you.

His "And hold firmly together to the rope of Allah and do not be divided" (Qur'an 3:103) means that you should all hold firmly to the Book of Allah, which the strong rope of Allah and His shinning light. Rely on Him and trust in Him. Do not be divided as you were during pre-Islamic times when you were sworn enemies killing one another. Do not differ among yourselves in matters related to your religion and believe in some verses and disbelieve in others for that would lead you away from the straight path.

"Remember Allah's favour upon you when you were enemies, then He united your hearts, so you—by His grace—became brothers." (Q 3:103) Meaning: Remember Allah's favor when He united your hearts and eradicated the enmity between you in pre-Islamic times. By His grace you were united in a relationship of Islamic brotherhood. You became brothers, united and in harmony.

Then, the Almighty reiterated His warning concerning the consequences of disagreements and division and the evils that might ensue because of them after he had pointed out the blessings of living in harmony. He said: "And you were at the brink of a fiery pit and He saved you from it." (Q 3:103) That is to say, because of your disagreements and misguidance, you were about to fall in a fiery pit, but I saved you from it by guiding you to Islam.

Their differences and disagreements, their idol-worshipping, and their immorality and misguidance before Islam were likened to a person at the very brink of a fiery pit into which he was about to fall.
And Gog's guidance was depicted as a person pushing another person away from the fiery pit to save him.

Then Allah shoed that He makes His revelations (verses) clear in every situation: "This is how Allah makes His revelations clear to you, so that you may be rightly guided." (Q 3:103)

Meaning: Like this clear statement that you heard in these noble verses, Allah shows to you what will bring joy and happiness to you in this life and the next, and what will lead you by the hand to all means of guidance, hoping that you will be among those who found favor with Allah and in whom He is pleased.

Thus, the noble verses demonstrated another deceitful and devious method that the Jews employed to entrap Muslims and undermine Islam. The verses strongly rebuked them and exposed their slanders and calumnies throughout the ages and generations. They also cautioned the believers against their crooked and evil deeds, guided them to what might shield and protect them from their cunning, and reminded them with Allah's bounty and favor upon them in order to return to the straight path.

Fourth: <u>Attempting to make Muslims abandon their faith by means of duplicity and trickery:</u>

Among the methods that the Jews used to entrap Muslims and undermine Islam was pretending to be believers for a period of time then returning to disbelief. The Noble Qur'an recounted this deceitful and cunning method of trickery in many of its verses. In Al-Imran: "A group among the People of the Book said to one another, "Believe in what has been revealed to the believers in the morning and reject it in the evening, so they may abandon their faith. And only believe those who follow your religion." Say, O Prophet, "Surely, the only true guidance is Allah's guidance." They also said, "Do not believe that someone will receive ˹revealed˺ knowledge similar to yours or argue against you before your Lord. Say, O Prophet, "Indeed, all bounty is in the Hands of Allah—He grants it to whoever He wills. And Allah is All-Bountiful, All-Knowing. He chooses whoever He wills to receive His mercy. And Allah is the Lord of infinite bounty." (Qur'an 3:72-73)

These noble verses related a cunning and sneaky method that the Jews used: pretending to accept Islam so that the naïve and trusting- (those who did not have experience with their methods of trickery and deception)- would be inclined to think highly of them. Once people started feeling comfortable around them, they would openly declare their disbelief, and go back to their religion (Judaism) to give new believers and those who were shaky in their faith the impression that they were looking for the truth, and they had no feelings of animosity towards the Prophet, and that what truly happened was that after entering Islam and following Muhammad, they found that the religion is false and dishonest and that Muhammad was not the anticipated Prophet. They returned to Judaism after diligently examining and thoroughly inspecting the religion of Islam and closely looking at it.

There was no doubt that this method which they used to turn Muslims away from their religion was one of the most powerful methods that their evil minds satanic plans could come up with. Announcing disbelief in Islam after pretending to believe in it would instill uncertainty and suspicion in the hearts and cause perplexity and confusion for those whose faith was still feeble and faint, especially that the Arabs were an illiterate people, and some among them thought that the Jews were more knowledgeable in matters of religion and creed, and that they must had abandoned Islam after becoming aware of deficiencies in its teachings.

Anyone who follows the stages of history, ancient and modern, know that those are savvy, witty and astute in politics and wars adopt this trick to cause confusion and spread disturbances amongst groups and nations.

The late Sheikh Muhammad Abdu said: "This type of people that the verses talk about who abandon Islam (after "apparently" entering it is based on a natural rule in humans, which is that one of the signs for the truth of anything is that those who know it do not turn away from it. Hercules (Heraclitus), the king of the Romans, understood this, and one of the matters he asked Abu Sufyan about regarding the affairs of the Prophet, was that he said to him: 'Does any of Muhammad's followers apostatize out of dissatisfaction with his religion after he enters it?' Abu Sufyan said: 'No, this sect wanted to deceive people in this regard: it is as if they are saying: Had it not been apparent to them that Islam is incorrect and invalid, they would not have renounced it after they had entered into it and learned of its interior and hidden secrets, since it is inconceivable for a person to abandon the truth after knowing it, and turn away from it- for no reason- after wanting it." [82]

Moreover, the commentators have narrated multiple stories concerning the reason for revealing these verses and which revolve around the meaning that we have decided. Among these narrations is what Ibn Jarir narrated on the authority of Qatada. He said: 'Some of the People of the Book said to each other: 'Give them contentment with their religion at the beginning of the day, and disbelieve it at the end of the day, for it is more likely that they will believe you and know that you have seen what you hate in their religion, and in this case, it is more likely that they will turn away from their religion. [83]

Ibn Jarir narrated on the authority of Al-Sada concerning the Almighty's saying: "A group among the People of the Book said to one another, "Believe in what has been revealed to the believers in the morning and reject it in the evening, so they may abandon their faith." (Q 3:72) He said: 'There were the rabbis of Arab villages, twelve rabbis, and they said to each other: 'Enter the religion of Muhammad at the beginning of the day, and say: We bear witness that Muhammad is true and truthful. At the end of the day, disbelieve and say: 'We returned to our scholars and rabbis and asked them, and they told us that Muhammad is a liar, and that your beliefs are groundless and baseless, and we have returned to our religion, for it is more preferable to us than your religion.' Perhaps they will be thankful and say: 'These were with us at the beginning of the day, so what is the matter with them?' So, Allah Almighty informed His Messenger about that." [83]

After this introduction, we now return to interpreting His saying: "A group among the People of the Book said to one another, "Believe in what has been revealed to the believers in the morning and reject it in the evening, so they may abandon their faith." (Q 3:72) This means:

A group of Jews said: "Believe in what has been revealed to the believers in the morning and reject it in the evening, so they may abandon their faith." That is: be hypocrites and pretend that you believe in Islam and its prophet and what was revealed to him in the morning, then go back to your religion/Judaism at the end of the day so that the believers may hopefully be deceived by your trick and start having doubts about their religion and turn to disbelief after belief.

And His saying: "so they may abandon their faith" revealed their wicked and cunning intentions, namely, that the faithful believers would abandon their true religion.

Imam Al-Razi said: "The Almighty's revealing their collaboration in this plot entails a foretelling of what they had connived to do, frustrating and thwarting their plans to ascertain that nothing similar might come to pass for He had divulged their secret conspiracy, frustrated their intentions and vanquished and eradicated their goals." [84]

The Noble Qur'an then proceeds to reveal their racism and fanaticism, strong adherence to what is false and untrue and their teaming together to make certain that they only believe those who their religion. The Almighty said: "And only believe those who follow your religion." That is, do not submit or reveal your secrets that point to the truthfulness of this prophet except to those who follow Judaism like you. They knew that the Prophet was truthful, but they refused to acknowledge this to others.

And, here, the Noble Qur'an commands the Prophet- in a parenthetical expression - to hasten to bring them to the truth to which they had been blinded "Do not believe that someone will receive revealed knowledge similar to yours or argue against you before your Lord." (Q 3:73) Meaning: Hide your belief and do not disclose it except to those who follow your religion lest the Muslims believe that they- like you- have similar revealed books and become even more fervent and devout in their faith. Do not reveal this except to the children of your faith lest the Muslims argue against you because of your belief.

And, for the second time, the Almighty Allah commanded His Prophet to chastise them for their egotism, and to explain that guidance is a favor that the Almighty grants to whoever He wills: "Say, ʻO Prophet, ʼ "Indeed, all bounty is in the Hands of Allah—He grants it to whoever He wills. And Allah is All-Bountiful, All-Knowing." (Q 3:73)

Meaning: Muhammad, tell those Jews- who refused to acknowledge the truth of your message because of their envy and fear that another one would have what they had- tell them that prophecy, success and guidance unto the faith of Islam is a favor that the Almighty grants to His servants. The munificent bountiful is under no obligation to grant a specific kind of people. If prophecy had come to the Children of Israel for a period of time, this was because of Allah's favor, mercy and bounty. He was under no obligation to do this. And it was inappropriate that they tried to prevent and deny it from other Arabs. They had to yield and submit to the truth whether it came from an Arab or a Jew. Only Allah is All-Knowing; only He knows to whom His revelations would come down.

"And Allah is All-Bountiful, All-Knowing." This means that Allah is gracious and benevolent to whomsoever He wants to bestow His favors upon. He is also All-Knowing of who is worthy of His favors and blessings. Then He said: "He chooses whoever He wills to receive His mercy. And Allah is the Lord of infinite bounty." (Q 3:73) This means that Allah chooses whoever He wants to receive His prophecy and guidance. It is His great favor and mercy and infinite bounty and mercy. Those Jews who wanted prophecy to be confined to them were only limiting, indeed restricting, what Allah had made available. They envied the Prophet for the favors that Allah had granted him. They ignored that great and conspicuous reality that all was in the hands of Allah and that He alone chooses whoever He wills to receive His mercy. His decision is irrevocable and His judgement is finite.

Thus, the noble verses disclosed one of the cunning and crooked methods that the Jews used to entrap Muslims and undermine Islam so that Muslims would become watchful and guard themselves against these crooked methods and become wary and respond to them using the appropriate tools and weapons.

Fifth: <u>Finagling with Allah's laws and attempting to arouse rebellion against the Prophet</u>.

This was one of the new cunning and duplicitous methods that the Jews used to undermine and demoralize Islam. They used their intrinsic crafty and sneaky natural instincts as they sought to seek the counsel of the Messenger in some of their legal matters, hoping that he would come with a ruling at variance with what Allah had revealed. They would then openly announce that among the people, proclaim his untruthfulness in his prophecy, because had he been truthful, his judgement would have corresponded with Allah's revelations.

However, the Prophet judgements were in agreement with what Allah revealed. Thus, he thwarted their plots and frustrated their attempts. Here are some noble verses from Sura Al-Ma'idah (Qur'an 5:41-50) "O Messenger! Do not grieve for those who race to disbelieve—those who say, "We believe" with their tongues, but their hearts are in disbelief. Nor those among the Jews who eagerly listen to lies, attentive to those who are too arrogant to come to you. They distort the Scripture, taking rulings out of context, then say, "If this is the ruling you get from Muḥammad, accept it. If not, beware!" Whoever Allah allows to be deluded, you can never be of any help to them against Allah. It is not Allah's Will to purify their hearts. For them is disgrace in this world, and they will suffer a tremendous punishment in the Hereafter. They eagerly listen to falsehood and consume forbidden gain. So if they come to you O Prophet, either judge between them or turn away from them. If you turn away from them, they cannot harm you whatsoever. But if you judge between them, then do so with justice. Surely Allah loves those who are just. But why do they come to you for judgment when they already have the Torah containing Allah's judgment, then they turn away after all? They are not true believers. Indeed, We revealed the Torah, containing guidance and light, by which the prophets, who submitted themselves to Allah, made judgments for Jews. So too did the rabbis and scholars judge according to Allah's Book, with which they were entrusted and of which they were made keepers. So do not fear the people; fear Me! Nor trade my revelations for a fleeting gain. And those who do not judge by what Allah has revealed are ˹truly˺ the disbelievers. We ordained for them in the Torah, "A life for a life, an eye for an eye, a nose for a nose, an ear for an ear, a tooth for a tooth—and for wounds equal retaliation." But whoever waives it charitably, it will be atonement for them. And those who do not judge by what Allah has revealed are truly the wrongdoers. Then in the footsteps of the prophets, We sent Jesus, son of Mary, confirming the Torah revealed before him. And We gave him the Gospel containing guidance and light and confirming what was revealed in the Torah—a guide and a lesson to the Allah-fearing. So let the people of the Gospel judge by what Allah has revealed in it. And those who do not judge by what Allah has revealed are truly the rebellious. We have revealed to you O Prophet this Book with the truth, as a confirmation of previous Scriptures and a supreme authority on them. So, judge between them by what Allah has revealed, and do not follow their desires over the truth that has come to you. To each of you We have ordained a code of law and a way of life. If Allah had willed, He would have made you one community, but His Will is to test you with what He has given ˹each of˺ you. So, compete with one another in doing good. To Allah you will all return, then He will inform you of the truth regarding your differences. And judge between them ˹O Prophet˺ by what Allah has revealed, and do not follow their desires. And beware, so they do not lure you away from some of what Allah has revealed to you. If they turn away ˹from Allah's judgment˺, then know that it is Allah's Will to repay them for some of their sins, and that many people are indeed rebellious. Is it the judgment of ˹pre-Islamic˺ ignorance they seek? Who could be a better judge than Allah for people of sure faith?"

Many reasons had been recounted concerning revealing these noble verses. Among them:

1-Al-Bukhari narrated on the authority of Abi Omar that "a group of Jews came to Muhammad and told him that a man and a woman committed adultery, so the Messenger of Allah told them: "What do you find in the Torah concerning stoning?' They said: 'Exposing what they whipping.' Abdulla bin Salam said: 'You lied. The Torah includes stoning. Bring the Torah and look at it.' So, one pointed to the verse concerning stoning. They said: "Muhammad is truthful. There is stoning in the Torah." So, the Messenger ordered stoning, and they were. Abdullah bin Omar said: I saw the man bending over the woman to protect her from the stones." [85]

2- Muslim narrated on the authority of Al-Baraa' bin Azib, he said: "The Prophet passed by a flogged, bathed Jew. He called them and said: 'Is this how you find the punishment for an adulterer in your book?' They said: 'Yes.' So, he called one of their scholars and said: 'I adjure you by Allah who sent down the Torah to Moses. Is this how you find the punishment for the adulterer in your book?' He said: 'No, and had you not adjured me by Allah, I would not have told you about this, but it is stoning. It has become so widespread among our nobles, so that if we caught the honorable, we would leave him. And when we take the weak person, we impose punishment on him. So, we decided on something that we will impose on the honorable and the lowly, so we made it bathing and flogging at the place of stoning.' The Messenger of Allah said: 'Oh Allah, I am the first to revive your command if they killed him.' So, he ordered that he be stoned, so Allah Almighty sent down: 'O Messenger, let not those who hasten into disbelief grieve you' to His saying 'If you are given this, take it.' That is, they say: 'Go to Muhammad and if he commands that should be bathed and flogged, then take it, and if he gives you a fatwa of stoning, beware." [86]

4- Al-Zuhari narrated on the authority of Abu Hurairah:

A Jewish man and a woman committed adultery, and some Jews said to each other, 'Let us go to this prophet, for he is a prophet sent with relief/ mitigating punishment. If he gives us a fatwa short of stoning, we will accept it and use it as evidence before Allah. We will say, this is a fatwa to a prophet from among your prophets.' So, they came to the Prophet while he was sitting in the mosque with his companions, and they said, 'O Abu Al-Qasim, what do you say concerning a man and a woman who committed adultery?' He did not speak a word to them until he came to their school house and stood at the door and said, 'I adjure you by Allah who sent down the Torah to Moses. What do you find in the Torah regarding one who commits adultery when he is married?' They said, 'He should be bathed and must be beaten and whipped. Also, they would be seated on a donkey back-to-back and go down the streets in public (tajbiyya).' A young man among them remained silent, and when the Messenger of Allah saw him silent, he insisted that he talk He said, 'O Allah, since you had adjured us, we find stoning in the Torah.' Then the Prophet said, 'Why you made concessions to the command of Allah?' He young man said, 'A relative of one of our kings committed adultery, so he postponed stoning for him. Then a man in a family of ours committed adultery, and he wanted to stone him, but his people prevented him and said, 'Our man shall not be stoned until you bring your relative and stone him.' So, they agreed on this punishment among themselves, so the Prophet said, 'I judge according to what is in the Torah.' So, he ordered them to be stoned, and they were. Al-Zuhri said, 'We have been informed that this verse was revealed about them: 'Indeed, We revealed the Torah, containing guidance and light, by which the prophets, who submitted themselves to Allah, made judgments for Jews.'" (Qur'an 5:44) The Prophet was among them. [87]

5- Imam Ahmad narrated on the authority of Ibn Abas, he said: Allah revealed: 'And whoever does not judge by what Allah has revealed, those are the disbelievers' (Q 5:47) and 'those are the wrongdoers' and 'those are the transgressors.' He said: Ibn Abbas said: Allah sent the verses down concerning the two groups of Jews, one of them had subjugated the other in pre-Islamic times. They then reconciled and agreed that for every dead person killed by the triumphant tribe, the ransom was fifty wasqs, and for every dead person killed by the vanquished tribe, the ransom was one hundred wasqs. They remained like that until the Prophet came to Medina. The submissive tribe killed one of the other triumphant tribe. The triumphant tribe sent to the ask for a hundred wasqs. The submissive tribe said: could there be such unfairness between two neighborhoods whose religion was the same, whose lineage was the same, and whose country was the same? We only accepted out of fear. Now that Muhammad came, we will not give you that. So, war almost broke out between them, and they agreed to make the Messenger of Allah a judge between them. Then the triumphant tribe said: By Allah, Muhammad would not give you twice as much, and they were truthful. They did not give us this except out of grievance and subjugation. So, they sent to Muhammad someone who would tell you his opinion. If he gave you what you wanted, you would judge him, and if he did not give you, you would beware, and you would not take his opinion. So, they sent to the Messenger of Allah some hypocrites to inform them of the opinion of the Messenger of Allah. When they came to the Messenger of Allah, Allah informed His Messenger about their entire plot, and what they wanted. Then Allah Almighty revealed: O Messenger, let not those who hasten into disbelief grieve you (Q 5:41) to His words, "The transgressors," (Q 5:47) for it is about them, by Allah, that it was revealed, and to them Allah has narrated it. [88]

After narrating some of the Hadiths that related, Imam Ibn Kathir said that these sayings indicate that the Messenger of Allah did judge in accordance with the rulings of the Torah. That was not meant to dignify or acknowledge what they believed to be correct and sound. Undoubtedly, they are commanded to follow the Muhammad's doctrine. That was merely the result of a Divine revelation to Muhammad. He was asking them to reveal what they had conspired to conceal and deny, what they had refused to follow for long generations. When they acknowledged it- despite doing what was at variance and contrary- their falseness, stubbornness and denunciation of what they knew as true in their Book - (which is in their hands)- were made manifest and apparent. Resorting to seek the ruling/decision of the Messenger of Allah was merely a whim and a fancy, a desire that he would agree with their opinions, not out of belief in the truthfulness or validity of his judgement. That is why they said: "If this is the ruling you get from Muḥammad, accept it-" meaning accept bathing and flogging- and "If not, beware!"- do not accept or follow. [89]

When we look at these sayings that have been mentioned concerning the reason for revealing these verses, we will find that all of them have been accompanied with reliable and undoubtful evidence in the verifiable documented Sunna books. The first three indicate that the noble verses were revealed in relation to a case of adultery in which the Jews sought the counsel of the Prophet. The fourth Hadith indicated that the reason for the verses was a matter of animosity and blood-shedding. There are no contradictions between these sayings: the two reasons could have occurred at the same time or close to each other, and the verses were revealed to address both of them together. Scholars maintain that there is no problem having many reasons for revealing one verse or a number of verses.

Interpretation of the noble verses

The Almighty's saying: "O Messenger! Do not grieve for those who race to disbelieve." (Q 5:41)

The verses open with Allah's call to His Prophet to honor and dignify and announce what should not be a cause for grievance. This is because he is a messenger whose duty is to inform. Since he had informed others with the message and performed his duty, what he should have been concerned about was how some people would hasten disbelief.

Prohibiting grief is a natural matter that man has no say in. It was meant to prohibit other things that were associated with it such as renewing calamities and magnifying them, for this would renew pain and suffering and decrease comfort and solace.

The meaning is: O Messenger, do not heed those hypocrites who rush willingly into disbelief and demonstrate it whenever the chance allows them for I will give you victory over them, and I will protect you from their wickedness.

Then, the noble verse reveals their reality. The Almighty said: "—those who say, "We believe" with their tongues, but their hearts are in disbelief." (Q 5:41) This means do not be concerned about those who race to disbelief, those who believe with their tongue and not their hearts. Their hearts are devoid of faith, and those are the hypocrites.

Then the Noble Qur'an chastised those Jews who lied and manipulated the rulings of their religion. The almighty said: "Nor those among the Jews who eagerly listen to lies, attentive to those who are too arrogant to come to you." (Q 5:41) In other words, there were those Jews, Muhammad, who eagerly and willingly listened to the lies from their rabbis and scholars who falsified and distorted the truth about you. They listened attentively to others who did not "to come to you." That is, they did not seek your company or sat at your assembly. Rather, they shunned you because of their exceeding hatred and animosity towards you. The verse was thus meant to lend support and strengthen the Prophet.

The "to" in "listen to lies" سَمَّٰعُونَ لِلْكَذِبِ could be meant to indicate reason. In this case, the meaning would be: there were Jews, Muhammad, who listened to your words, not to benefit from them, but in order to lie to you through distorting what they heard. They also listened to what you said to transmit it to other people among them who did not attend your assemblies. They acted as spies in your assemblies to inform their nobles what they heard after distorting it.

The author of Al-Manar: "they told their nobles and the other enemies of Islam everything they were able to gather and make what they had distorted acceptable, as it was based on actual occurrences that they added to, subtracted from, and distorted and misrepresented what they wanted. Those who lie to you when they do not know you well, will not be able to make their lies acceptable as easy as those who know you. Their lies could be easily detected. For this reason, those who fabricated falsehoods about Islam at that time used to read some of the books of the Muslims to clothe their lies in known issues. They distorted the Scriptures, taking rulings out of their context. For example, the lies they fabricated concerning Zeinab bint Jahsh, Zeid bin Hartha, and others."

Then, the Noble Qur'an cited another despicable attribute/vice, and it related the evil that they conspired to perpetrate. It said: "They distort the Scripture, taking rulings out of context, then say, "If this is the ruling you get from Muḥammad, accept it. If not, beware!" (Q 5:41)

Meaning: In addition to their listening to lies (or listening in order to lie), those Jews also distorted the Scripture, taking rulings out of context." That is, they removed certain things in their Book to interpret them differently from what Allah intended. They added things and subtracted others just as we have seen in the story of the two Jews who committed adultery. The Jews abandoned and discarded stoning, which is the ruling of the Torah- which they could find written therein and which they were commanded to enact- and changed that ruling- on their own- with another ruling, namely, bathing and flogging. This act was a vivid proof of their decadence, deceit and arrogance towards Allah.

"(They) say, "If this is the ruling you get from Muḥammad, accept it. If not, beware!" (Q 5:41) This means that those Jews- who distorted the Scripture and took rulings out of context- said to those whom they sent to Muhammad to seek his judgement- that if Muhammad came with a Fatwa indicating bathing and flogging, accept his ruling and follow his counsel for it was the truth. If not, then beware, and do not accept his ruling, for it was incorrect.

After the Noble Qur'an disclosed one aspect of their vices and slanders, it informed the Prophet: "Whoever Allah allows to be deluded, you can never be of any help to them against Allah. It is not Allah's Will to purify their hearts. For them is disgrace in this world, and they will suffer a tremendous punishment in the Hereafter." (Q 5:41)

Which means: If Allah allowed someone to be deluded, that is, tested in his faith, and he is shown as misguided and in disbelief, you will not be able to help guide or counsel him. So do not be concerned about them rushing to disbelief, neither do heed their being restored to the path of guidance, for you will avail them nothing. You only have to inform and deliver the message, and We will reward and punish.

The Noble Qur'an then announced its fair verdict on those Jews who took their faith frivolously and lightly. It said: "It is not Allah's Will to purify their hearts." (Q 5:41) That is, those Jews and the other hypocrites like them who persevered in their misguidance and deviation from the truth did not find favor in Allah's eyes, and it was not His will to purify their hearts. "For them is disgrace in this world" by revealing their secrets, disclosing their lies and humiliating them. "And they will suffer a tremendous punishment in the Hereafter," (Q 5:41) which is eternal hellfire because of their refusal of-and aberration from- the straight path.

Then the Almighty revealed that in addition to eagerly listening to lies and fabrications, those Jews consume forbidden gain: "They eagerly listen to falsehood and consume forbidden gain." (Qur'an 5:42)

Al-suht السُّحت is a reference to anything that is acquired in a sneaky or cunning way, like using usury or accepting bribes (ill-gotten gain). It is well known that the Jews are the most eager among people in amassing forbidden and unlawful (haram) money.

Some scholars explained Al-suht السُّحت here as bribery in ruling. Ibn Omar said: "The messenger of Allah said: 'Everybody that grows from unlawful things, hell is more deserving of it.' So, the asked the Messenger: 'What is Al-suht?' He said: 'Bribery in ruling.'" [90]

The meaning is: In addition to their lies, which is the worst among all vices, those Jews consume unlawful and ill-gotten gains through various methods. Accordingly, their religious as well as worldly affairs became unethical, immoral and corrupt.

Then, the Almighty addressed His Messenger saying: "So if they come to you O Prophet either judge between them or turn away from them." (Qur'an 5:42) That is if those Jews came to ask you for a decision on one of their affairs, you have a choice: you may judge between them since they sought you as a judge, even though they did not believe in you, or you may ignore and disregard their request, since they came to you seeking a decision not for the sake of reaching the truth but to give a ruling according to their wishes and desires.

Then the almighty said: "If you turn away from them, they cannot harm you whatsoever." (Q 5:42) Meaning: If you decided not to judge between them and disregarded their request and they became hostile and antagonistic towards you, they would not be able to cause you any harm because Allah is with you. He will preserve you and grant you victory over them.

Then the Almighty said: "But if you judge between them, then do so with justice." (Q 5:42)

If you, Muhammad, decided to judge between them, then do so with the justice that you have been commanded to administer. Do not succumb to their wishes or surrender to their needs. Allah likes those who judge equitably and fairly between people, those who judge in accordance with Allah's commandments and the rulings of Islam.

Abdullah bin Omar bin 'Aas said that the Messenger of Allah said: "The just and the fair are -to Allah- placed on a pedestal of light, at the right hand of Allah." [91]

It is noteworthy mentioning that scholars have expounded their opinions in Fiqh الفقه books. They debated whether the Imam had a choice in judging between the Dhimmi people if they sought his counsel, or if that choice had been abrogated, and it had become imperative that he judges between them.

In response to this question, Sheikh Al-Qasmi said: "The Imam has a choice in judging between the Dhimmi people; he may accept or reject doing it. The choice mentioned had been abrogated in the Almighty's saying: 'And judge between them according to what Allah has revealed.'" (Qur'an 5:47)

It is like a law court. The choice is there. It had been corroborated by Al-Hassan, Al-Sho'abi, Al-Nakh'I and Al-Zuhari. There is no contradiction between the two verses: His saying 'judge between them according to what Allah has revealed' (Q 5:42) entails choice, and His saying 'and I judge between them according to what Allah has revealed' entails how to judge if he were to judge between them." [92]

The honorable Sheikh Hassanin Makhloof said that the Almighty's saying "So if they come to you O Prophet, either judge between them or turn away from them," indicates that the Messenger of Allah had the choice to either judge between the People of the Book or refrain from doing so. Then that choice had been abrogated by the Almighty's: 'and I judge between them according to what Allah has revealed.' It was said that choice had been confirmed by that verse, and His 'and I judge between them according to what Allah has revealed' was a statement to how to judge if he opted to judge, and that the rulings should be according to Islamic rulings. However, if a Muslim and a Dhimmi were to be judged, the rulings should be in accordance to Islamic rulings as previously agreed upon. [93]

The Noble Qur'an then denounced their cunning wayward methods, and decried their willingness to have someone- whom they did not believe in- judge between them, even though rulings were specified in the Torah between their hands. It said: "But why do they come to you for judgment when they already have the Torah containing Allah's judgment, then they turn away after all? They are not true believers." (Qur'an 5:43) In other words, it was really flabbergasting, Muhammad, that those Jews sought your ruling in their affairs even though they did not follow your faith and their Torah indicated Allah's clear judgement in those matters in which they sought your opinion and ruling. In fact, their conduct was a clear indication that they did not believe in their book the way they should have believed in it, since if they truly did, they would not have resorted to other sources. Also, they did not believe in your rulings which corresponded to those in the Torah because they rejected them since they did not agree with their desires and wishes. Indeed, His words "They are not true believers" are true. This means that those Jews were neither believers in their Book since they did not accept what rulings it entailed, nor did they believe in you, Muhammad, because ruling was in correspondence with the truth, not their wishes.

Imam Al-Razi said that the honorable verse revealed their vices and wickedness to warn others that they were not truly People of the Book or that they kept and followed Allah's commandments. This could be seen in:

One: Refusing the ruling of their Book. Second: Seeking the ruling of someone whom they thought to be false and untruthful. Third: Not accept his ruling after they had appointed him as a judge between them. Thus, their ignorance and stubbornness were made manifest. [94]

After the Almighty recounted the astonishing attitude of the Jews for knowingly forfeiting Allah's ruling, He exalted the Torah that he had revealed to Moses, peace be upon him. He said: "We revealed the Torah, containing guidance and light, by which the prophets, who submitted themselves to Allah, made judgments for Jews. So too did the rabbis and scholars judge according to Allah's Book, with which they were entrusted and of which they were made keepers." (Qur'an 5:44)

The meaning is: We had revealed the Torah as guidance to lead people to the truth and the straight path, and as a light to help them when there is ambiguity or opacity. Jewish prophets, who had submitted to Allah and were loyal and faithful worshippers from the time of Moses to the time of Isa (Jesus), would make judgements for the Jews. Also, the rabbis and scholars among the Jews, those who followed the path of their prophets, judge according to the Allah's Book, "with which they were entrusted and of which they were made keepers." That is to say, the rabbis and scholars judged according to Allah's Book, for Allah entrusted them with it and made them its keeper so that no changes or alterations would find their way to it. They were all witnesses that the Book was truthful and correct, and that it came from the Almighty Allah.

It might be plausible that the pronoun in with which they were entrusted was a reference to the rabbis and scholars, and that they were entrusted by the prophets. In this case, the meaning would be: Also, the rabbis and scholars judged between the Jews according to the Torah because their prophets entrusted, indeed ordered, them to keep Allah's Book impervious to changes and alterations, and because they were made keepers of the Book.

Regardless of the two meanings, the noble verse indicates that the prophets of the Children of Israel and their loyal, faithful and true worshippers and scholars judged with fairness in accordance with the truth that Allah revealed in His Book. However, those Jews- who abandoned the rulings of the Torah and came to ask the Messenger of Allah to judge between them in a way that is at variance with Allah's rulings- were not on the right path. They did not follow the prophets, rabbis or scholars that they should have followed. It was therefore fitting to say "It is not Allah's Will to purify their hearts. For them is disgrace in this world, and they will suffer a tremendous punishment in the Hereafter." (Q 5:41)

Then the Almighty Allah commanded them to fear Him alone and not to trade their faith for passing transient material gains: "So do not fear the people; fear Me! Nor trade my revelations for a fleeting gain." (Qur'an 5:44)

The meaning is: you Jews, who were contemporaneous with the Prophet, ought to have followed your prophets, rabbis and scholars. You should have followed the rulings of the Almighty Allah that were revealed in Hos Book. Beware of distorting or altering My rulings out of fear of the people. Fear Me alone, for I alone have the authority to benefit or harm you. Do not forfeit My revelations or trade them for transient, short-lived or worldly gains such as bribery, social status or satisfying peoples' wishes. These things, no matter how great they might appear, are loathsome trifles and of little importance compared to the bountiful and magnanimous blessings what Allah has prepared for those who fear Him and abstain from succumbing to their own wanton wishes and desires.

The Almighty then revealed the status of those who did what the Jews had done and judge differently from what Allah had decreed: "And those who do not judge by what Allah has revealed are truly the disbelievers." (Qur'an 5:44)

Which means that those who diverged from judging according to what Allah had revealed and followed other ways to judge were the disbelievers for they had concealed the truth which they were supposed to disclose, revealed other rulings and used them to judge.

According to scholars who investigated that issue, this description as "disbelievers" can be attributed to the Jews- and others- in general who stubbornly, persistently and ungratefully veer away from what Allah has revealed and judge differently.

Sheikh Al-Qasimi said in his interpretation: Muslim narrated on the authority of Al-Bara' that the almighty's saying "And those who do not judge by what Allah has revealed" targeted all disbelievers. Likewise, Abou Dawud narrated on the authority of Ibn Abas, he said that the description targeted the Jews particularly Qurayza and Nadir, but that did not exclude others since the words "those who" were meant to generalize.

Al-Hakim and Ibn Abi Hatim narrated on the authority of Abul Raziq and Ibn Abbas, they said: Those who do not judge according to what Allah has revealed are disbelievers. Their disbelief is not attributable to specific religion, as is the case for those who do not believe in Allah, His angels, Books, Messengers, Judgement Day, and the like. He said: "It is disbelief that greater than disbelief, injustice that is greater than injustice and immorality that is greater than immorality."

In Al-Lubab fi Ulum al-Kitab, it was said on the authority of Ibn Masoud, Al-Hasan and Al-Nakh'i that "these verses generally describe the Jews, those who received bribery, altered rulings and judged differently from Allah's rulings and were thus described as disbelievers, unjust and immoral... This pertained to those who deliberately and knowingly rejected Allah's rulings and judged differently after becoming aware of Allah's rulings. As for those who were not knowledgeable or wrongly misinterpreted something, those were not targeted by this warning."

In Ahkam al-Qur'an Provisions of the Qur'an, Ismail Al-Jahdhami said that the verses indicated that whosoever did like what the Jews did- fabricating a ruling at variance with Allah's rulings- was targeted by the chastisement stated in the verses, whether a ruler or nor." [95]

And Sheikh Hassanein Makhlouf said that commentators differed concerning the target of the verse "and those who do not judge by what Allah has revealed" (Qur'an 5:44) and the two verses that came after it. It was said, the first two targeted the Jews, and the third targeted the Christians. If disbelief is attributed to a believer, he would be severely and intensely admonished and chastised, not because of the disbelief itself which is an expression of a specific religion. If the disbeliever is described as immoral and unjust, it is the intensity of the disbelief and the rebellious attitude that are stressed. Ibn Abbas said:

whosoever did not rule with what was revealed by Allah showing stubbornness and ingratitude is a disbeliever, and whosoever acknowledged rulings other than Allah's is immoral, iniquitous and dissolute. [96]

The Noble Qur'an reiterated admonishing the Jews and chastising them for abandoning the rulings that were revealed in their Books. It said: "We ordained for them in the Torah." That is, We imposed on the Jews in the Torah, which Allah revealed to Moses, "A life for a life..., an ear for an ear, a tooth for a tooth—and for wounds equal retaliation" (Qur'an 5:45) which means, retribution is permissible as in the arm or the leg. There are things that are not permissible such as bone breaking.

"But whoever waives it charitably, it will be atonement for them." (Q 5:45) This means that whosoever had the right and forgave the wrongdoer, it will be considered atonement for them. The pronoun "them" refers to the charitable.

"And those who do not judge by what Allah has revealed are truly the wrongdoers." (Q 5:45) This means that those who forfeit Allah's rulings which is rooted in justice and equity, and opted to rule differently are considered wrongdoers since they have not followed the principles of justice and fairness.

After indicating that the Torah and the Injil (the Gospel) contained guidance and light, the Almighty proceeded to mention the Noble Qur'an. He said: "We have revealed to you O Prophet this Book with the truth, as a confirmation of previous Scriptures and a supreme authority on them." (Qur'an 5:48) That is, just as We revealed the Torah to Moses and the Gospel to Jesus- peace be upon them- We revealed the Book, i.e., the Noble Qur'an, to you, Muhammad, with the truth, that is, with unquestionable certainty that it came from the Almighty Allah, and that that Qur'an that was revealed to you, Muhammad, confirmed previous Scriptures in matters related to the faith and the essence and principles of the law.

Having "supreme authority on them" means that the Qur'an confirmed previously revealed Books that were preserved without alterations. It shielded and protected them, was a witness to their truth and an authority in deciding the principles of jurisprudence. Ibn Jurayj said: "The Qur'an was just and loyal to the Scriptures that preceded it; whatever agreed with it was authentic and true, and whatever was at variance with it was false and untrue."

Ibn Jarir (al-Tabari) said: "The origin of authority comes from the words preserve and watch. It is said that if a man watches and preserves something then he has complete authority over it." [97]

Ibn Kathir said: "The almighty made this great Book which He revealed the last and seal for all the others; it is the most comprehensive, the greatest, the most inclusive and all-encompassing, because the Almighty presented the greatest things in all the previously revealed Books, and He added extras that the others Books lacked. Therefore, He made this Qur'an a true preserver with supreme authority on the others. The Almighty Himself preserved the Qur'an: "Indeed, it is We who have sent down the Remembrance, and indeed, We will preserve it." (Qur'an 15:9) [98]

Then, the Almighty commanded his Prophet to judge between the Jews according to what He had revealed and not to follow their desires. He said: "So, judge between them by what Allah has revealed, and do not follow their desires over the truth that has come to you." (Qur'an 5:48) This means, if those meandering Jews asked you to judge between them, Muhammad, judge according to the truth that Allah had revealed to you, and do not deviate from the truth to follow their desires.

The Almighty said: "To each of you We have ordained a code of law and a way of life." (Q 5:48)

"A code of law is the clear path that leads to springs of water. This is a reference الشرعة to religion which is called Shari'a likening it to paths leading to water because both are المنهاجindispensable to life.
"[A] way of life" is the clear way in religion

The meaning is: We had ordained a particular and specific clear path and a well-defined way to all communities and nations. The nation that existed from the time of Moses to the time of Jesus- peace be upon them- had the Torah as a doctrine and a path. The nation that existed from the time of Jesus to the time of Muhammad, peace be upon them- had the Gospel as its law and doctrine. As for this Islamic nation, the Qur'an is its law and doctrine. It contains all the basic principles and tenets of religion that were brought in previously revealed Books and which do not differ regardless of the times. In addition, it contains additional tenets and creeds that are appropriate and fit the time in which it was revealed and the ages that follow until the Day of Resurrection.

The people of the Book were commanded to follow the rulings and tenets of their books before they were abrogated by the Noble Qur'an. After the revelation of the Qur'an and the advent of the Prophet as a seal to all the heavenly revelations, it is becoming imperative that they enter into Islam and follow its tenets and doctrines that had abrogated previous ones. They should also believe the Messenger of Allah and all that he had brought from his Allah. No faith is acceptable except through accepting him, believing in him and following him in all his sayings and deeds.

Abu Al- Sa'ud said: the Almighty's statement: "To each of you We have ordained a code of law and a way of life" (Q 5:48) is meant to incline the People of the two Books to follow his rulings that were revealed in the Noble Qur'an, and to indicate that it is the Book that they were now supposed to follow, not the other two Books, that they followed previously before they were abrogated. [99]

Imam Ibn Kathir said: "This announcement concerning nations with different religions and Allah's sending His honorable messengers with diverse codes of law that still agree on monotheism just as confirmed in Sahih Al-Bukhari who narrated on the authority of Abu Hurairah, he said: The Messenger of Allah said "We prophets are brothers for reasons. Our mothers are different, but our religion is one, that is, the message of monotheism with which Allah sent everyone of His messengers and which He manifested in every book He revealed. As the Almighty said: "And We did not send before you any messenger except that We revealed to him that there is no Allah but Me, so worship Me." (Qur'an 21:25) Codes of law are different when it comes to what is permissible and lawful and what is prohibited and forbidden. Something could be prohibited in a certain doctrine but lawful in another. As the Almighty said concerning Jesus: "and legalize some of what had been forbidden to you." (Qur'an 3:50) Conversely, something could be legal and permissible in a certain doctrine but is forbidden in another doctrine. It is Allah's infinite wisdom and immeasurable prudence. [100]

Then the Almighty said: "If Allah had willed, He would have made you one community, but His Will is to test you with what He has given each of you." (Qur'an 5:48) This means that if Allah had willed to make one community out of all the nations, one that would follow one code of law throughout the ages, He would have done so because He is the all-Powerful Omnipotent. But the Almighty is all-Knowledgeable; He knows exactly the rulings and doctrines that are suitable for all nations and all times. He knows what is best and beneficial for them, and what fits their nature and characteristics. Therefore, He revealed various codes of law which all agree in essence and basic tenets but differ in minor and subsidiary applications depending on the time and the makeup of the community. It was natural that certain rulings would be abrogated. In His infinite wisdom, He willed that all of these codes of law would be finalized and consolidated by one comprehensive, complete and perfect doctrine that would ensure the wellbeing of people in all ages and in all places. This doctrine was the doctrine if Islam which Muhammad brought.

Then the Almighty reiterated His commandment to Muhammad to judge between them according to what He had revealed. He cautioned him against their cunningness and craftiness: "And judge between them O Prophet by what Allah has revealed, and do not follow their desires. And beware, so they do not lure you away from some of what Allah has revealed to you. If they turn away from Allah's judgment, then know that it is Allah's Will to repay them for some of their sins, and that many people are indeed rebellious." (Qur'an 5:49)

Ibn Abbas said: "Ka'b ibn Assad, Ibn Sloba, Abdullah bin Soriyya, Shas bin Qeis said to each other: Let us go to Muhammad and try to lure him away from his faith. When they came to him, they said: 'Muhammad! You know that we are Jewish scholars, the chiefs among the Jews. If we followed you, other Jews will follow us. We have some disagreements with some of our people. We want you to judge between us and to take our side, and we will believe in you.' The Messenger of Allah rejected their request, and Allah revealed that verse (Q 5:49) about them: "And judge between them O Prophet by what Allah has revealed, and do not follow their desires. And beware, so they do not lure you away ...." [101]

And the Almighty's saying "And judge between them O Prophet by what Allah has revealed" is a reference to "Book," a continuation of the verse that was previously mentioned "We have revealed to you O Prophet this Book with the truth." (Q 5:48)

This means: We have revealed the Book to you, Muhammad, and We have revealed how to judge, so judge between them according to what Allah has revealed, and do not follow the desires of those Jews who have taken their religion lightly and frivolously. “And beware, so they do not lure you away from some of what Allah has revealed to you.” (Q 5:49) Meaning: Be careful not to be enticed or tempted to depart from what we have revealed to you, even slightly or minimally, through their presenting untruths as true, through lying and denying the rulings of the Torah, and through luring you to judge according to their desires. “If they turn away from Allah’s judgment, then know that it is Allah’s Will to repay them for some of their sins.” (Q 5:49) That is, if those Jews do not accept your judgement, Muhammad, and refuse to comply with it because it does not agree with their desires, then know that that is because of Allah’s prudence and wisdom. He wants to hasten His punishment of them in this world because of the sins they have committed in their lives. Allah did in fact execute His punishment of the Jews: Some were expelled from Medina while others were killed on account of their debauchery, immorality, trickery and wickedness.

Al-Zakhmshari said: “If they turn away” from Allah’s judgement and sought a different judgement, then “then know that it is Allah’s Will to repay them for some of their sins.” That is, the wrongdoers who rejected Allah’s judgement and sought a different one had been considered as culprits and responsible for many grievous sins. [102]

Then the Almighty said: “many people are indeed rebellious.” (Q 5:49) That is, many had persisted in their disbelief and opted to depart from the straight path that Allah had prepared for His servants. By ending the verse with this statement, Allah had shown His Messenger how they persevere in rejecting the truth.

The Almighty Allah then rebuked them for rejecting the truth and embracing falsehoods and untruths. He said: “Is it the judgment of pre-Islamic ignorance they seek?” (Qur’an 5:50) This means: Do they want to shun your ruling that is in accordance with what Allah has revealed and seek the times of pre-Islamic ignorance, even though they have Allah’s Book which contains the truth concerning the judgement you have decreed? “Ignorance” could be either a reference to pre-Islamic religions that were rooted in following desires, whims and favoritism. In this case, it was meant as an expression to rebuke the Jews for seeking pre-Islamic codes of law despite the fact that they were People of the Book and learning.

Or, it could be a reference to the people of pre-Islamic times and their rulings that were based on nepotism and inequality among people. In this case, it was meant as a chastisement to the Jews for following the people of the times of ignorance.

Then Allah denounced the notion that there could be a better judgement than His, or even one that could be equal to His judgement: “Who could be a better judge than Allah for people of sure faith?” (Q 5:50) This means that no one could render a better judgement than Allah’s judgements to His people, those who have faith, abide by His rulings, acknowledge His Lordship, and follow His prophets and messengers.

Imam Ibn Kathir vehemently denounced those who depart from Allah's judgement and seek the judgement of people/humans. He described those as infidels and made a Fatwa (a decision) calling for the necessity of fighting those until they return the judgement of Allah and His Messenger. He said: "In this verse, Allah denounces those who depart from His perfect and sound judgements that comprise everything that is profitable and beneficial and prohibit all evil, and seek other judgements based on opinions, desires and other notions that people come up with without verification from Allah's doctrine and law. This is just similar to the people in pre-Islamic ignorance who used to resort to delusions and ill-conceived opinions and crooked desires to judge their affairs. It is also similar to the royal policies in the Al-Yasaq law that was drawn by Genghis Khan to govern the Mongol Empire. It was a book composed of a group of rulings that he adopted from different doctrines such as Judaism, Christianity and Islam. There were also many rulings that he adopted merely out of personal opinion and desires. These became laws that his offspring followed over and above the rulings that were based on Allah's Book and the Sunna of His Messenger. Those who do this are infidels and should be resisted and fought till they return to the rulings of Allah and His Messenger. The Almighty said: 'Is it the judgment of ⌜pre-Islamic⌝ ignorance they seek?" (Q 5:50) Which means: they veer away from Allah's ruling. "Who could be a better judge than Allah for people of sure faith?" (Q 5:50) Which means: who is fairer than Allah in judgement? To the rational and sensible, to him who believes in- and acknowledges- Him, is not Allah the wisest of judges? Isn't He more merciful and compassionate than a mother to her son? Isn't He the All-Knowledgeable, the All-Powerful and the most just in everything?

Al-Tabarani narrated on the authority of Ibn Abbas, he said: "The most despicable in Allah's sight is the one who relinquishes Islam for the law of pre-Islamic ignorance and the one who unjustly seeks to shed the blood of an innocent man." [103]

Thus far, these noble verses have revealed in detail one of the most calculating and crafty methods that the Jews used to entrap Muslims and undermine Islam. They tried to lure the Messenger of Allah away from his faith and join their fold by asking him to rule between them in a way that was incongruent with what Allah has revealed, and to agree with them in their desires and wishes. The noble verses reiterated chastising and rebuking them, and denounced the way they manipulated their religion, deviated from the path of truth, succumbed to their greed and vices, and refused to judge in accordance with what Allah has revealed. The noble verses also repeated cautioning the Prophet and Muslims from their trickery, cunning, and evil and directed them to what is good and profitable and what would make them happy in their faith and this world.

Six: <u>Allying themselves with the hypocrites against the Muslims</u>:

Among the methods that the Jews used in fighting the Islamic call was siding with those who demonstrated hostility towards it in general and allying themselves with the hypocrites to eliminate that call in particular.

In Al-Ma'ida, the Almighty says: "O believers! Take neither Jews nor Christians as guardians—they are guardians of each other. Whoever does so will be counted as one of them. Surely Allah does not guide the wrongdoing people." (Qur'an 5:51) "You see those with sickness in their hearts racing for their guardianship, saying in justification, 'We fear a turn of fortune will strike us.' But perhaps Allah will bring about your victory or another favor by His command, and they will regret what they have hidden in their hearts." Qur'an 5:52)

Ibn Jarir narrated on the authority of Attiah Ibn Saad, he said: Ubadah bin Al-Samit went to the Messenger of Allah - and he was one of the Banu Al-Harith bin Al-Khazraj - and he had an alliance with them similar to the one they had with Abdullah bin Ubay. So, he renounced them to the Messenger of Allah and said: 'I swear by Allah and His Messenger that I disavow the alliance of the Jews, and seek alliance with Allah and His Messenger.' In him and in Abdullah bin Abi the verses were revealed: "O believers! Take neither Jews nor Christians as guardians—" up to His saying "they will regret what they have hidden in their hearts." (Q 5:52) [104]

Interpreting the Two Noble Verses

"O believers! Take neither Jews nor Christians as guardians..." (Q 5:51) The two verses began with a general call to the believers in which the Almighty forbade them from taking the People of the Book as guardians, trusting them and allying themselves with them after revealing that their mouths utter nothing but what was hateful and vile, and their hearts concealed even more animosity and acrimony. This prohibition from forming alliances with the Jews and the Christians was due to their strong aversion and antipathy towards Islam, and their open, flagrant as well as hidden and concealed hostility towards the Muslims. Had there been no reason, the prohibition would have been nonexistent, since the Noble Qur'an commands its followers to do good to the people of the Book if they do not seek to harm Muslims.

In Sura Al-Mumtahanah (sura 60), the Almighty said: "Allah does not forbid you from dealing kindly and fairly with those who have neither fought nor driven you out of your homes. Surely Allah loves those who are fair. Allah only forbids you from befriending those who have fought you for your faith, driven you out of your homes, or supported others in doing so. And whoever takes them as friends, then it is they who are the true wrongdoers." (Sura 60:8-9)

The two verses clearly indicate that this prohibition was due to enmity and waging a war against Muslims, not because of difference in religion.

Then the Almighty pointed out the reason for prohibiting that alliance to emphasize avoiding what was forbidden: "they are guardians of each other." (Q 5:51) In other words, they allied themselves with each other because of their unanimity in religion and their mutual animosity towards the Muslims. They might have differed with each other, but their mutual desire to undermine the Islamic call brought them together.

Then the Noble Qur'an issued its verdict concerning those who failed to abide by that prohibition and befriended them: "Whoever does so will be counted as one of them." (Q 5:51) Meaning: Whoever befriended or sided with them- notwithstanding their hostility towards the believers- would be considered as one of them, with views and beliefs similar to theirs, even if he claimed that he differed with them in faith and religion.

Ibn Jarir said: "Whoever took them as guardians and assisted them against the believers, would be one of their people having their religion, for no one would take a guardian unless he be content with their religion, and if he was content with his religion, then he would oppose those who differ and fight them." [105]

Al-Zakhmshari said: "This was a strong admonition from Allah to emphasize the necessity of dismissing those who differ in religion and excluding them." [106]

"Surely Allah does not guide the wrongdoing people." (Q 5:51) Allah does guide those who help and ally themselves with Allah's enemies because they have become unjust and wrong in allotting trust where it should not be placed. Such people are far removed from guidance and the right direction.

After presenting this strong prohibition from allying themselves with the Allah's enemies, the Noble Qur'an depicted one of the conditions of the hypocrites showing how they seek the guardianship of Allah's enemies and what happens to them. The Almighty said: "You see those with sickness in their hearts racing for their guardianship." (Qur'an 5:52) This means: You see, Muhammad, those hypocrites- whose faith was shaky and wobbly and did not manifest true belief and assurance in their faith- hasten to support and ally themselves with the Jews as if they were confident and sure of what they were doing, thoroughly heedless of the teachings of Islam while pretending to embrace them.

The Almighty's expression "in their hearts" is an exquisitely powerful and fitting expression with which the Jews were often described in the Noble Qur'an. The strength of the heart is often given as an example for steadfastness, firmness, assurance and psychological soundness and might. Conversely, the weakness of the heart which is portrayed here as "sickness" is likewise given as an example for feebleness, fickleness, lack of certainty, wobbliness and psychological ruin and collapse. This is the nature of a hypocrite at all times and in all places. It is impossible for a hypocrite to be clear, straightforward, showing an inclination or propensity towards a specific direction. He is always vacillating and oscillating, hesitating between two directions, seeking favors from both. His main objective is to feel safe, and secure his day and his tomorrow (the present and the future).

Then the Noble Qur'an disclosed the excuse that the hypocrites used as a pretext to take the Jews as guardians. The Almighty said: "saying in justification, 'We fear a turn of fortune will strike us.'" (Q 5:52) This means that they apologized for throwing themselves in the arms of the Jews because they were afraid that some calumny- a crisis, a hardship or distress- might befall them. Also, they claimed they were fearful lest victory would finally be theirs (the Jews); that was why, we ally with them to guard ourselves against their evil and wickedness and to secure their support when difficulties and hardships arose.

The Almighty responded to the ineffectual and futile justifications of the hypocrites and heralded the believers with victory and achieving what they hoped for: "But perhaps Allah will bring about your victory or another favor by His command, and they will regret what they have hidden in their hearts." (Q 5:52) This means that the Almighty Allah- by virtue of His grace and the truthfulness of His ever-faithful promises- would bring about a decisive judgement and conclusion, namely, victory for the believers over their enemies. Or, He would bring the Jews' attempts to no avail, and the hypocrites would feel remorseful for their hatred of the believers, support for the Jews, and their suspicion that victory would be the lot of the faithful followers of the Prophet. Allah was truthful and His promises came true; He humiliated the Jews, and gave their land, homes, and wealth to the believers. He also exposed and shamed the hypocrites: "Allah will certainly help those who stand up for Him. Allah is truly All-Powerful, Almighty." (Qur'an 22:40)

The two verses (Q 5:51-52) contain many examples for emphasizing prohibiting taking the enemies of Allah as allies or guardians. There is a straightforward and clear prohibition in the Almighty's saying: "O believers! Take neither Jews nor Christians as guardians..." Also stated is the reason for this prohibition as mentioned in the Almighty's "they are guardians of each other." Likewise, there is a clear declaration that whoever took them as guardians had become one of them as shown in the Almighty's: "Whoever does so will be counted as one of them." Also, there is this description of wrongdoing concerning those who ally themselves with the Jews: "Surely Allah does not guide the wrongdoing people" and informing them that siding with the Jews was the nature of those "with sickness in their hearts" for fear of difficulties and hardships ahead. Finally, among the clear examples of prohibiting this alliance with the Jews was thwarting the greed and blocking the desire of the hypocrites for victory and assuring the believers that victory would be theirs: "perhaps Allah will bring about your victory or another favor by His command." This wish- indicated by – was bound to materialize; it was issued by the Almighty and All-Powerful whose promises are forever faithful and true.

Thus, we see that these two noble verses have clearly demonstrated that the Jews and the hypocrites formed a united front to fight against the Islamic call.

In Sura Al-Hashr (Sura 59), the almighty said: "Have you O Prophet not seen the hypocrites who say to their fellow disbelievers from the People of the Book, "If you are expelled, we will certainly leave with you, and We will never obey anyone against you. And if you are fought against, we will surely help you."? But Allah bears witness that they are truly liars. Indeed, if they are expelled, the hypocrites will never leave with them. And if they are fought against, the hypocrites will never help them. And even if the hypocrites did so, they would certainly flee, then the disbelievers would be left with no help." (Qur'an 59: 11-12)

Exegetes agree that sural Al-Hashr was revealed concerning Banu Nadir. It recounts their defeat at the hands of the Muslims because of their wickedness. These two verses depict an aspect of the collaboration between the Jews and the hypocrites even though that partnership did not virtually take place.

Ibn Jarir and ibn Ishaq recounted that when the Muslims surrounded Banu Nadir, Abdullah bin Abi and other hypocrites with him sent to the Jews saying: 'fight and be firm, we will not abandon you. If you are fought against, we will fight with you, and if you are expelled, we will leave with you.' The Jews expected their support, but the hypocrites did not fulfill their promises. For this, Allah revealed these two verses. [107] The almighty's: "Have you 'O Prophet' not seen the hypocrites ...." means that you have become fully aware of the ways of these hypocrites- who told the Jews, their associates in infidelity and disbelief, when they were besieged by the Muslims-: "'If you are expelled, we will certainly leave with you, and We will never obey anyone against you. And if you are fought against, we will surely help you.'" That is, if you are driven out of your homes, we will come with you, and we will not obey anyone asking us stop helping you. If the Muslims fight against you, we are with you to support and help you against them, so do not be concerned; just fight them fiercely and do not worry about your homes and money.

But the Almighty, All-knowledgeable Allah responded to their claim, saying: "But Allah bears witness that they are truly liars." That is, Allah knows that they are liars concerning their promised to the Jews, for when the Muslims besieged Banu Nadir who expected help from the hypocrites according to their promises, they (the Jews) received no help and realized that their promises were false and unreliable.

After the Qur'an briefly exposed their lies, it detailed its delineation of their lies to emphasize their false position and to expose the extent of their cowardice "Indeed, if they are expelled, the hypocrites will never leave with them." Which means that if the Muslims expelled Banu Nadir from their homes, the hypocrites would not leave with them as they had promised, and if the Muslims fought against them, they would not support them, and if, the hypocrites hypothetically helped them, they would run away in humiliation. Thus, victory would be for the Muslims only.

Having investigated some of the verses that prove the alliance of the Jews with the hypocrites to entrap Muslims, we can now say that it was the Jews who helped create and strengthen a group of hypocrites in Medina through instilling doubts and suspicions in their hearts and through the lies, charges and allegations they spread concerning Islam. The hypocrites became strong only because of the help of the Jews. As evidence for this is that as soon as the Jews became weak after the Muslims dealt fatal blows them, we saw that the hypocrites weakened and power waned as described in the noble verse: "If only they could find a refuge, or a cave, or any hiding-place, they would rush headlong towards it." (Qur'an 9:57)

Affection and affability between the Jews and the hypocrites in Medina were extensive and far-reaching. As evidence for this, here is an example. When Abdullah bin Abi, the topmost hypocrite, was dying, the Jews surrounded his deathbed crying and weeping. One of Abdullah bin Abi's sones became angry and wanted to drive them out of the house. His father prevented him from doing this and said: 'Their nearness heals my heart.' The Jews said to him: 'Abdullah, we would willingly save you with our blood and money.' When he died, they wanted to bury him, but they were forbidden. After he was buried, the Jews hurled dust on their heads because of their grief and pain over the death of Abdullah ibn Abi, the chief among the hypocrites.

At the end of this brief exposition, we can also say that the existence of the Jews in Medina was one of the strongest reasons for teaching hypocrisy to some of the Arabs there. An Arab is frank and straightforward by nature. Hypocrisy did not manifest itself during the Meccan era because the people of Quraysh were open and straightforward in their hostility and wars against Islam and Muslims.

When the Hijra (Immigration) was completed and the Muslims were victorious in the battle of Badr, some Jews- followed by some Arabs- pretended to accept Islam. Ibn Hisham mentioned the names of a great number of the names of Jews who pretended to have accepted Islam. Among these were Zaid bin Al-Lasit, Sa'd bin Hanif, Rafi bin Huraymila and others. [108]

Thus, we see that the Jews were behind the hypocrites, encouraging them, providing them with money and instilling wicked ideas in their heads to fight the Muslims. With the waning strength of the Jews, the hypocrites power also declined and diminished.

Seven: <u>Allying Themselves with the Polytheists, and Proclaiming that They are Better Guided than the Believers</u>:

Some noble verses in Sura An-Nisa recount the Jews' shameful position. Despite the fact that they were People of the Scripture, their envy and malice incited and goaded them to embrace the idol-worshippers rather than the believers: "Have you O Prophet not seen those who were given a portion of the Scriptures yet believe in idols and false Gods and reassure the disbelievers[1] that they are better guided than the believers? It is they who have been condemned by Allah. And whoever is condemned by Allah will have no helper. Do they have control over shares of the kingdom? If so, they would not have given anyone so much as the speck on a date stone. Or do they envy the people for Allah's bounties? Indeed, We have given the descendants of Abraham the Book and wisdom, along with great authority. Yet some believed in him while others turned away from him. Hell is sufficient as a torment!" (Qur'an 4:51-55)

Ibn Jarir narrated on the authority of Ikrimah, he said: Ka'ab bin Al-Ashraf went to the polytheists among the people of Quraysh and incited them against the Prophet and ordered them to fight him. He said: 'We are with you, and we will fight him.' They said: 'You are people of the Scripture, and he is a man with a Book. If you really want us to go and fight against him, you have to kneel down, prostrate to these two idols and you have to worship and believe in them.' He did as he was told. Then they said to him: 'Who is better guided, us or Muhammad?' He said: 'Tell me about your religion.' Abou Sefian said: we are people who slaughter the kuma'a, and pour the milk over the water, and connect the relatives, and welcome the guest, and circumambulate this house, and Muhammad cut off his ties of kinship and left his country! He said: You are better guided! So, this verse was revealed: "Have you O Prophet not seen those who were given a portion of the Scriptures yet believe in idols and false Gods and reassure the disbelievers that they are better guided than the believers?" (Q 4:51) [109]

Ibn Ishaq narrated on the authority of ibn Abbas, he said: Among the people who formed alliances with Quraysh, Ghatafan and Banu Qurayza were Hayy bin Abi Al-Haqiq and Abou Rafi. Most of them were from Banu Nadir. When they came to Quraysh, they said: Those are Jews scholars and men of learning, and they are knowledgeable of the first Book. So, ask them if their religion is better than Muhammad's! They asked them, and they responded that their religion is better than Muhammad's and that they were better guided than Muhammad and his followers. Therefore, Allah revealed this verse: "Have you O Prophet not seen those who were given a portion of the Scriptures yet believe in idols and false Gods ..." up to "along with great authority." [110]

And the Almighty's saying: "Have you O Prophet not seen those who were given a portion of the Scriptures yet believe in idols and false Gods ...," (Q 4:51) [111] which means: Have you seen and ascertained, O honorable Messenger, the status of those Jews, who were given a portion of the Scripture and yet believe in unethical notions, false Gods and idol-worshippers?

Imam Ibn Jarir said that "the interpretation of "believe in idols and false Gods" is that they believe in two idols, not in Allah, and they regard them as two Gods. The words "gopt/الجبت" and "al-tagout/الطاغوت" are names for those who worship other than Allah, whether the worshiped is stone/statue, a human or Satan." [112]

Then the Almighty revealed their lies and the falsehoods they said to the polytheists. The Almighty said that (the Jews): "reassure the disbelievers that they are better guided than the believers?" (Qur'an 4:51)

In other words, to satisfy the polytheists, those Jews said that notwithstanding their idol-worshipping, they were better guided than the believers who had followed Muhammad.

Describing them as people who were "given a portion of the Scriptures," (Q 4:51) is a statement that explained their true status, for even though they were given a portion of the Scripture, they failed to act in accordance with what they received, for had they acted according to what they received, they would not have favored worshipping idols over worshipping the Al-Merciful, Compassionate Allah.

Then the Almighty revealed their awful fate because of their aberration from the truth. He said: "It is they who have been condemned by Allah. And whoever is condemned by Allah will have no helper." (Qur'an 4:52) This means that those who were overtaken and possessed by Satan, those who supported the polytheists by words or action, and those who prostrated and worshipped their idols, would be humiliated, disgraced and removed from Allah's mercies because of their lies, malice and their succumbing to their caprices and desires. Those whom Allah condemns will have no supporters or an intercessor to intercede on their behalf.

However, if the Jews went to the people of Mecca to seek their support against the Muslims, they would not get the help they sought. Even if they did, their support would not last for humiliation and disgrace would be for those who fought the truth.

The Noble Qur'an then went on from admonishing them for helping the polytheists and believing in idols and false Gods to rebuking them for their stinginess and parsimoniousness. The Almighty said: "Do they have control over shares of the kingdom? If so, they would not have given anyone so much as the speck on a date stone." (Qur'an 4:49) [113] This means that even if they were given authority and control, was it proven that they would demonstrate justice and fairness? No, that was not proven, for they capricious and whimsical, and such people who are overcome by their whims and fantasies are far from being fair and just.

The meaning is: Those Jews would not enjoy a fair share of rule or stability because of their tyranny and injustice and their obnoxious tribal solidarity. Even if they were to be given a share of that, they would not give others- whom they owe- even the minutest portion. This is because the Jews are only concerned about their own personal interest. They believe that they are the best of Allah's creation, and that they are Allah's children and His chosen people. Moreover, because of their egotism and tight fistedness, it is disconcerting for them to see other people, who do not belong to their religion, get any blessings or forge ahead in life. Time has proved the truth of what the Noble Qur'an said about them: After they entered- with the help of colonial powers- some Islamic cities in Palestine, they expelled their legitimate inhabitants and seized and usurped all their wealth. They did not even allow the people of these cities to take the least amount of food or clothing or what could have satisfied their most essential needs. An example of this could be seen when they occupied-by treachery and deceit- the villages of Deir Yassin, Qubiyya, Kafr Qasim, El-lad, El-Ramlla and other Palestinian cities. They slaughtered women, children and old men. Those whose lives were spared from slaughter and killing were deprived of all their possessions.

Then, the Noble Qur'an moved on from chastising them for their stinginess and tight fistedness to rebuking them for the vice of envy and malice which engulfed and consumed them, causing them to suffer on seeing other people enjoy any blessings, and even wishing for the eradication of such blessings from them and working to abolish and eliminate them. The Almighty said: "Or do they envy the people for Allah's bounties?" (Qur'an 4:54)

Which means: Those Jews were not only stingy and tightfisted, but they were also guilty of the vice of envy and spite. They begrudged the Arabs and resented them because the Prophet came from an Arab descent. They were jealous of the Prophet because Allah granted him the prophecy, and they were resentful of the believers because they were increasing, not decreasing, in numbers.

Some claim the word people referred to the Arabs, while others believe it referred to the Prophet. This meant that the Jews were jealous of the Prophet and the believers for the revelation and prophecy that Allah- out of His infinite bounty- bestowed upon them. The Jews were, thus, envious of those to whom Allah was benevolent and bountiful. In other words, they were stubborn and rebellious against the Creator who is Al-Knowledgeable with whom He should entrust His message and prophecy. The reason for this resentment and jealousy was their belief -out of conceit and vain sense of superiority- that they, not other people, were more worthy of the prophecy.

The Noble Qur'an then presented them some evidence by referring to what they knew concerning the Book and wisdom He gave the descendants of Abraham. The Almighty said: "Indeed, We have given the descendants of Abraham the Book and wisdom, along with great authority." (Q 4:54) In other words, if you begrudged the prophecy that Allah gave to the Prophet because you thought it should have been confined to you, Allah had shown you as liars and transgressors; the Almighty gave the descendants of Abraham- Ishmael (the grandfather of the Arabs), Isaac, Jacob and others- the Book without any discrimination between them. He also gave them wisdom and profitable knowledge. Moreover, He gave them great authority. Therefore, you Jews were not more worthy of the prophecy, neither were you more worthy of Abraham since the relationship between the Arabs and Abraham was like your relationship with him. If you are the descendants of Isaac, son of Abraham, the Arabs- and Muhammad among them- are the descendants of Ishmael, son of Abraham.

Then the Noble Qur'an showed the rewards for the good person and the punishment of the evil-doer: "Yet some believed in him while others turned away from him. Hell is sufficient as a torment!" (Qur'an 4:55) Meaning: Some of the Jews who were given the Book believed in and abided by the guidance that prophets had brought them. Others had rejected guidance and veered away from it. Severe punishment awaits them; hellfire is their lot. That also helped the Messenger persevere and become more patient and endure the rejection, ungratefulness and harm they manifested towards him.

Thus, we see that these noble verses recounted how the Jews traded their religion for transient worldly gains, their belief in illusions and fantasies, their being completely consumed by stinginess, their malice and resentment for the goodness and blessings that Allah bestowed upon others, and their preference for idol worshippers over those who worshipped the all-Merciful.

Dr. Israel Wolfensohn, a Jew, recounts what he regarded as a despicable alliance with the polytheists- that the noble verses related concerning the Jews- in his book "The History of the Jews in the Arabian Peninsula." He commented on this story saying: "It was imperative for those Jews not to be entangled in such a grave mistake; they should not have declared to the chiefs of Quraysh that idol-worshipping was better than the monotheism that Islam brought, even if they did not get what they wanted. That is because, the Children of Israel were for many centuries- and in the name of their forefathers- the carriers of the baton of monotheism among pagan nations in the world. For many centuries throughout history, they faced innumerable hardships and were plighted with many calumnies such as killing and persecution because of their belief in One Allah. It was their duty to sacrifice their lives and everything that they held dear and precious to them in order to defeat and humiliate the polytheists. In addition, in resorting to idol-worshippers, they were as though they were fighting themselves, contradicting the teachings of the Torah which instructed them to loathe the owners of idols and adopt a hostile attitude against them." [114]

There are two Noble verses in Sura Al-Ma'idah that clearly state that a lot of Jews allied with polytheists on account of their extreme aversion of Islam. These are: "You see many of them taking the disbelievers as allies. Truly wicked are their misdeeds, which have earned them Allah's wrath. And they will be in everlasting torment. Had they believed in Allah, the Prophet, and what has been revealed to him, they would have never taken those pagans as allies. But most of them are rebellious." (Qur'an 5:80-81)

The meaning is: You see, O honorable Messenger, a lot of the Jews ally themselves with the polytheists and support them against you, even though you believe in Allah, His angels, His Books and messengers without discrimination. Those polytheists with whom the Jews allied themselves do not believe in anything of the kind. "Truly wicked are their misdeeds, which have earned them Allah's wrath. And they will be in everlasting torment." (Q 5:80) Meaning: Their evil deeds earned them Allah's resentment, displeasure and wrath, and they will be suffering eternally.

The Almighty showed that the Jews' taking the disbelievers as allies as evidence for their inherent corruption and their going astray from the true faith. The Almighty said: "Had they believed in Allah, the Prophet, and what has been revealed to him, they would have never taken those pagans as allies." (Q 5:81) That is to say, if those Jews who took the disbelievers as allies were true believers in Moses and the guidance and revelations that were revealed to him as they claimed, they would have not taken them as allies or befriended them. Prohibiting alliances with the polytheists is confirmed in the Torah and in the Law of Moses. Therefore, that strong alliance between the Jews and the polytheists had no purpose other than holding an agreement between two parties to fight and undermine Islam and show hostility towards its followers.

Then the Noble Qur'an revealed the reasons that inclined the Jews to form an alliance with the polytheists. The Almighty said: "But most of them are rebellious." (Q 5:81) Which is to say, many of the Jews had deviated from the straightforward path of the law, that path which guides the heart and the mind and incline them to the true and straightforward path. However, many of them had veered away from true faith and had therefore chosen the infidels-not the believers- as allies.

Thus far, these noble verses have revealed the alliance that the Jews formed with the disbelievers to fight the Muslims. This revelation is a warning to the Muslims to be wary of their wickedness and to be careful not to fall victims to their tricks.

Eight: Slandering the Prophet.

By nature, the Jews are deceitful and fraudulent. They used their trickery and deceit as weapons to offend and harm the Prophet. They would often wiggle their tongues and resort to puns to get to the despicable purpose that they were after, namely, offending the Prophet, ridiculing him, belittling him, and using various methods to show him as incapable and incompetent in the company of his companions.

The Companions- my Allah be pleased with them- would utter words that had a clear and straight meaning to honor the dignify the Prophet. However, the Jews would pick these words and twist their tongues to make these words carry an ugly meaning when they produced them. The Noble Qur'an recounted that about them. It forbad Muslims from addressing the Messenger using certain words so that the Jews would not seize the chance, play on these words and offend the Prophet. An example for this is in Sura Al-Baqarah (sura 2): "O believers! Do not say, "Râ'ina." [Herd us!] But say, "Unẓurna," [Tend to us!] and listen attentively. And the disbelievers will suffer a painful punishment. The disbelievers from the People of the Book and the polytheists would not want you to receive any blessing from your Lord, but Allah selects whoever He wills for His mercy. And Allah is the Lord of infinite bounty." (Qur'an 2:104-105)

The word راعنا/ "Râ'ina" comes from a word that means excessive caring and looking what is in the best interest of others, guarding them and being patient with them. When the Messenger of Allah narrated a Hadith to the believers, they would often say to him: "Râ'ina" O Messenger of Allah, which meant watch over us and wait and be patient with us until we had understood and memorized your words. The Jews picked this word since it corresponds to a bad word they had and they would twist their tongues and "Râ'ina, Abou Al-Qasim." They thereby pretended to be asking him to be guarded and waited for while in fact the way they pronounced it meant frivolity and foolishness. So, Allah forbade the Muslims from using this word so that the Jews would use it as a way to offend the Prophet or diminish his status.

Qataada said: "The Jews said to the Prophet Râ'ina your hearing, mockingly. This word was a bad word in Judaism."

And Imam Ibn Kathir said: "The Almighty forbad the believers from associating themselves with the infidels in their words and their deeds. The Jews would use puns and play with words to diminish the status of the prophet. If they wanted to say "listen to us," they would say Râ'ina, to mean foolishness and frivolity. As the Almighty said: 'Some Jews take words out of context and say, "We listen and we disobey," "Hear! May you never hear," and "Râ'ina!" [Herd us!]—playing with words and discrediting the faith. Had they said ⌜courteously⌝, "We hear and obey," "Listen to us," and "Unẓurna," [Tend to us!] it would have been better for them and more proper. Allah has condemned them for their disbelief, so they do not believe except for a few." There are also some Hadiths that indicate that when they greeted others, they would say: "السام عليكم" (Saam be on you). "Saam" is death. Therefore, we were commanded to respond saying "and on you as well," hoping that our wishes- not theirs- be heard. Allah forbade the believers from doing what the infidels did both in words and in deeds [115].

Imam Ibn Taymiyya said: "The Muslims used to say 'Râ'ina, O Messenger of Allah, and listen attentively. The word 'Râ'ina' comes from shepherding and attending with care. However, it was a dirty word in Hebrew. When the Jews heard the Muslims use that word, they seized the chance. They said to one another: 'We used to curse Muhammad secretively. Now we can do it openly.' So, they would come to him and say 'Râ'ina, Muhammad' and laugh among themselves. Saa'd bin Ma'az heard them and understood since he knew their language. He said to the Jews: 'Allah's damnation descend upon you. I swear by my life if I ever heard one of you say it to the Messenger of Allah, O Jews, I would strike his neck.' They said: 'Don't you say it yourselves?' So, Allah revealed this verse: 'O believers! Do not say, "Râ'ina,' so that the Jews would not seize that chance to offend the Messenger." [116]

Then the Almighty guided the believers to what they should say instead: "But say, "Unẓurna." Meaning: Do not say Râ'ina, so that the Jews do not use it as a pretext to offend your Prophet. Instead, say "Unẓurna" which means wait for us and be patient with us so that we can understand what you say. It comes from a word that means "to wait for." This is the same meaning in the verse: "Wait for us that we may draw from your light."

The noble verse cautions and guides us to appropriate behaviors; when speaking to others, a man should avoid using words that may belittle the status of others especially when affection and honor are expected to surface.

Then the Almighty revealed the painful fate of the Jews due to their transgression: "And the disbelievers will suffer a painful punishment." (Q 5:80) This means that those Jews who used the word Râ'ina to offend and belittle the Prophet will suffer a painful punishment because they went overboard in their foolishness, arrogance and impudence with the Prophet.

Then the Almighty disclosed to the believers the resentment and envy that those Jews had: "And the disbelievers will suffer a painful punishment. The disbelievers from the People of the Book and the polytheists would not want you to receive any blessing from your Lord, but Allah selects whoever He wills for His mercy. And Allah is the Lord of infinite bounty." (Q 5:81)

Many authentic Hadiths recounted that the Jews used to greet the Messenger of Allah using distorted twisted words unrecognizable to many, meaning to wish him harm and death, but the Messenger would respond to them in a way that would silence them, thwart their attempts and sham them. Among these hadiths is what Al-Bukhari narrated on the authority of Ins ibn Malik, he said:

A Jew passed by the Messenger of Allah and said: 'السام عليك (Saam be on you).' The Messenger said: 'And on you, too.' And then he said to his companions: 'Do you know what he said?' They said: 'No.' the Messenger said: 'السام عليك (Saam be on you).' They said to the Messenger: 'Shouldn't we kill him?' He said: 'No. If the People of the Scripture greeted you, say and on you, too.'" [117]

Al Shaykhan (the two Sheikhs: Al-Bukhari and Muslim) narrated on the authority of A'isha, may Allah be pleased with her. She said:

A group of Jews came to the Messenger of Allah and said: 'السام عليك (Saam be on you).' She understood them and said: 'Saam and damnation be on you too.' The Messenger of Allah said; 'Take it easy A'isha. Allah likes us to be gentle.' A'isha said: 'Didn't you hear what they said?' He said: 'I said on you, too.'" [118]

Muslim narrated on the authority of Jaber ibn Abdullah, he said: "A group of Jews greeted the Messenger of Allah saying 'السام عليك (Saam be on you), Abou El- Qasim.' He said: 'On you, too.' A'isha was angry and said: 'Didn't you hear what they said?' He said, 'Yes, I did. And I responded. Our wishes, not theirs, are answered.'" [119]

Thus, this noble verse "O believers! Do not say, "Râ'ina" (Qur'an 2:104) along with the forementioned hadiths prove that the Jews used dreadful, obnoxious and crooked words and distorted speech as one of their crafty methods to undermine the Islamic call. However, the Almighty Allah thwarted their plans and frustrated their schemes and forbad the believers from using the words that the Jews used as a means to reach their goal. The Messenger also responded to them in a way that would shame and disgrace them. Thus, their attempts and schemes were to no avail, and the Almighty sustained and supported the Messenger and the believers.

Nine: Mocking the religion and its tenets:

Also, among the methods that the Jews used to undermine the Islamic call was taking Islam lightly and mocking its tenets. The Noble Qur'an exposed their conduct and prohibited the Muslims from taking them as guardians or allies. In Sura Al-Ma'idah (sura 5), the Almighty said: "O believers! Do not seek the guardianship of those given the Scripture before you and the disbelievers who have made your faith a mockery and amusement. And be mindful of Allah if you are truly believers. When you call to prayer, they mock it in amusement. This is because they are a people without understanding." (Qur'an 5:57-58)

The meaning is: O you- who have soundly believed in Allah, acknowledged His Books, Messengers and the Last Day- should not take as guardians those who had taken your faith- your source of happiness- frivolously, lightly, playfully and jokingly. That is, they made it an object of mockery and ridicule. As a sign for their conduct, they pretended to show that they were believers in Islam when around you. Once they were alone with their demons, they displayed all kinds of playfulness and mockery.

Calling the believers “O believers” was bound to evoke enthusiasm and zeal in their hearts for persuasion and faith that their enemies targeted as an object for their mockery and ridicule, for it was not becoming for a believer to befriend those that toyed with their faith.

The Noble Qur’an then displayed those who mock religion ant toy with its tenets. The almighty said: “those given the Scripture before you and the disbelievers.” In other words, do not take the Jews, the Christians or the disbelievers as guardian or allies, for they all united to fight you and mock your religion.

Describing them as “those given the Scripture” is a statement that showed how horrible they were and the extent of their misguidance, for had they truly been believers of their Book, they would not have mocked or ridiculed Allah’s religion or taken it lightly and playfully. Then, the Almighty commanded the believers to continue to obey Him and comply with his commandments. He said: “And be mindful of Allah if you are truly believers.” Indeed, faith requires earnest observance of Allah’s law and commandments. There is no other way.

Then the Almighty disclosed how the Jews- and others like them- mocked a certain and specific aspect of religion after He had stated in the first verse their sardonic and scornful attitude to religion in general. He said: “When you call to prayer, they mock it in amusement. This is because they are a people without understanding.” (Q 5:58)

The meaning is: When you called each other to prayer and when the Imam announced that the time for prayer had come, those Jews and others -whom you had been prohibited from taking as guardians-mock and laugh among themselves because they were people who were ignorant of the true nature of faith and they did not esteem Allah appropriately, nor did they know Him truly.

Imam Al-Qurtubi said: “When the Imam called Muslims for prayer, the Jews would laugh among themselves when the Muslims prostrated and worshipped. About the call to prayer, they said: ‘Muhammad! You came up with something novel that we never heard about in previous generations! The call to prayer is like the sound of the camels in a caravan. How despicable and abhorrent it is! And it was said that when the Imam called people to prayer, they laughed among themselves and winked to each other to show how lightly and frivolously they looked at it, to marginalize the believers and make people uncomfortable with the prayers and the caller.” [120]

The Almighty deprived them of the faculty of reasoning, because they didn’t use reason to benefit from it and they looked at Allah’s religion in a frivolous and thoughtless way. These were the deeds of those deprived of the faculty of reasoning.

Ten: Attempting to assassinate the Prophet.

It was not sufficient for the Jews to fight the Prophet using religious argumentation and semantic bickering, attempting to arouse dissention and stir discord among his companions, pretending to accept Islam at dawn and returning to disbelief at the end of the day, allying themselves with those who loathed Islam and hated Muslims, or mocking the religion and its tenets. The Jews were not content with all of these methods to eliminate and eradicate the Islamic call. They resorted to yet another method which their evil nature and wicked and malicious minds made possible.

The Noble Qur'an reminded the believers with Allah's blessings on them and how He protected their Prophet from the cunningness of the Jews and their attempts to harm the Prophet. In Sura Al-Ma'idah, the Almighty said: "O believers! Remember Allah's favor upon you: when a people sought to harm you, but He held their hands back from you. Be mindful of Allah. And in Allah let the believers put their trust." (Qur'an 5:11)

Ibn Jarir narrated the reason for revealing this verse on the authority of Ibn Abi Zeiyad, he said: "The Messenger of Allah came to Banu al-Nadir seeking their help in a matter that he had suffered. Abu Bakr, Omar, and Ali were with him. He said: Help me settle this blood money. They said: 'Yes, Abu Al-Qasim, it is time for you to come to us and ask us something! Sit down until we feed you and give you what you ask of us!' So, the Messenger of Allah sat and his companions were waiting for him. Huyay bin Akhtab, the chief among the people, came, and he said to his companions: 'You will not see him any closer than now. Throw stones at him and kill him. And never see evil again!' So, they came to a large millstone that they wanted to cast on him, but Allah withheld their hands from it, until Gabriel, may Allah bless him and grant him peace, came to him and raised him up. Then Allah Almighty revealed: "O you who have believed, remember the favor of Allah upon you, when they intended to extend their hands to you, so He withheld their hands from you, and fear Allah. And in Allah let the believers put their trust." (Q 5:11) So, Allah Almighty told His Prophet what they wanted to do to him. [121]

Imam ibn Kathir said: Muhammad ibn Ishaq ibn Yassar, Mujahid and Ikrimah mentioned that this verse was revealed concerning Banu al-Nadir when they wanted to throw a millstone on Muhammad's head when he went to them seeking their help in a blood money issue. Banu al-Nadir assigned Amro bin Jahash to do the job and ordered him to throw the millstone once the Prophet sat under the wall where they would gather to throw it from the top of the wall. Allah revealed their conspiracy to the Prophet, and he returned to Medina followed by his companions. Allah revealed that verse. [122]

There are other stories related to the reason for revealing this verse. One of these stories recounts that the verse was revealed when an Arab wanted to kill the Prophet, but Allah protected him. Another story mentions that it was revealed when Allah protected His Prophet from Banu Tha'labah and Banu Muharib when they plotted to kill him while he was praying with his companions.

It our conviction that it is likely that the verse could have been revealed after all these incidents took place. The events could be numerous, but the Revealer is one, as scholars believe.

However, we are more inclined to Ibn Jarir's interpretation that what the Qur'an recounts concerning the Jews and their breaching and violation of their pledges are strong evidence that the verse is a reminder to the believers of Allah's blessing in protecting His Prophet from the Jews' cunning conspiracies and malicious intent.

Imam Ibn Jarir said: Allah reminded the believers of the blessing of protecting their Prophet to thank Him for it. This is the most plausible scenario for that blessing with which Allah reminded the believers to be thankful for protecting their Prophet from what the Jews of Banu al-Nadir intended when he and his companions went to Banu al-Nadir to demand blood money from the two Amiris who were killed by Amr ibn Umayyah. We say it is the most plausible because Allah concluded that episode with the wicked and despicable deeds of the Jews and their betrayal their Allah and their prophets. Then He commanded His Prophet forgive and pardon them after saying "they intended to extend their hands to you." (Q 5:11) Who else extended their hands to them? If it were others who intended to extend their hands to them, it would have been imperative that the command to forgive be directed to them, not to others who were not mentioned, and attributing treachery in describing them in this place, not describing others who betrayal was not mentioned. For this reason, we believe that this is the most likely interpretation."[123]

The noble verse began with a command to the believers to remember Allah's favor to them: "they intended to extend their hands to you." Meaning: O you who believed in Allah and His Messenger, remember Allah's favor and thank Him for it and He will lavishly bestow more blessings and protect you from all evil.

Then the Almighty recounted the favor for which He ordered them to be thankful, along with other blessings. He said: "they intended to extend their hands to you, so He withheld their hands from you." That is: Remember Allah's favors when He protected you from the hands of the Jews who wanted to harm your Prophet and were about to successfully execute their cunning plot, but Allah thwarted it and saved your Prophet from their evil.

Then the Almighty commanded them to fear, obey and trust Him: "and fear Allah. And in Allah let the believers put their trust." (Q 5:11) In other words: Fear Allah, O believers, and always consider His grace and favors, and never stop thanking Him for them. He had shown you His Might and how He guarded and protected you, so trust Him alone. In Allah Only should the believers trust, those who acknowledge His monotheism, follow His Messenger, and comply with His commandments and prohibitions. This is part of your religion and the perfection of your faith. Whenever you abide by this, He will keep them safe and preserve them from anyone who wants to harm them: "And whoever puts their trust in Allah, then He alone is sufficient for them. Certainly, Allah achieves His Will. Allah has already set a destiny for everything." (Qur'an 65:3)

Thus, the noble verse reminded the believers of Allah's favor to increase their thanks and feelings of gratitude to Him. It also pointed out the harm that the Jews wanted to inflict upon the Messenger of Allah and How Allah frustrated their plans and defeated their purpose.

This is not the only incident that shows how the Jews attempted to kill the Prophet. There are others:

Al-Bukhari relates on the authority of Abu Hurairah: "When Khaybar was opened (Vanquished by Muslims), and the Prophet was content that it was under Muslim control, a poisoned lamb was sent to him as a present. After the Prophet took a bite, he spit it out and said: "Bring me all the Jews who were here." They did. Thereupon the Prophet said: "I will ask you a question. Are you going to be truthful in your response?" The Jews said: "Yes, father of Al-Qasim (Abou Qasim)." The Prophet asked: "Who is your father?" They responded and told him who their father was. The Prophet said, "You are lying because your father is not whom you said he is." Al-Hafez son of Hagar said: "It is Israel, Jacob, son of Isaac, son of Ibrahim (Peace be upon him)." They said to the Prophet, "You have rightly said the truth." The Prophet asked again: "Will you be truthful in your response if I asked you another question?" They responded: "Yes, Abou Al-Qasim. Well! If we lied, you will know that we have lied to you just as you knew who our father was!" The Prophet asked: "Who are the people of Hell?" They responded saying: "We will be there for just a short while, but then you will follow us there to stay." The Prophet said to them: "We will never be there, but you will stay there in wretchedness and humiliation." He then asked them: "Will you be truthful if I asked you another question?" They responded in the affirmative. He asked: "Did you poison this lamb?" He was referring to the lamb that was brought to him, and they did not deny it. Again, they responded in the affirmative. So, he asked them: "What made you do such a thing?" They said: "We wanted to get rid of you if you were lying, but if you were truly a prophet it would not hurt you." [123a]

Thus, we see that the Jews tried to kill the Prophet more than once, but Allah protected him from their cunning and artful schemes and saved him from their evil: "They want to extinguish the light of Allah with their mouths, but Allah refuses except to perfect His light, although the disbelievers dislike it." (Qur'an 9:32)

Now that we have reported various methods that the Jews employed to undermine the Islamic call, we want to ask this question: What was the Prophet's position concerning all of those evil deeds on the part of the Jews?

To answer this question, we say that the position of the Prophet comprised the following:

<u>First: Continuing to Call Them to Accept Islam:</u>

Despite the fact that the Jews left no method untried to diminish and eliminate Islam, the Prophet continued inviting them to enter into Islam. He brought them proofs and reliable evidence to his truthfulness so as to leave them no excuse and to show their injustice and aberrations from Allah's commands.

Among the verses that commanded the Jews to abandon their stubbornness, come back to their senses and follow what Muhammad brought is His saying in Sura Al-Baqarah: "Say, ⌜O believers, ⌝ "We believe in Allah and what has been revealed to us; and what was revealed to Abraham, Ishmael, Isaac, Jacob, and his descendants; and what was given to Moses, Jesus, and other prophets from their Lord. We make no distinction between any of them. And to Allah we all submit." (Qur'an 2:136)

Also, in Sura Al- 'Imran, the Almighty says: "Say, O Prophet, "O People of the Book! Let us come to common terms: that we will worship none but Allah, associate none with Him, nor take one another as lords instead of Allah." But if they turn away, then say, "Bear witness that we have submitted to Allah alone." (3:64)

<u>Second: Bringing Them back to the Right Path when They Argued or Asked Questions:</u>

At the beginning of this chapter, we mentioned many examples of the issues about which the Jews argued with the Prophet and the conniving and devious questions they asked him. Some of these arguments were related to his prophecy, the prophecy of Abraham and Jesus, the topic of abrogation, changing the direction of the Qiblah, and their demands to him to bring them a book from heaven, and many more arguments. The Prophet's position concerning these issues was to redirect them to the right path and respond to their questions and arguments by presenting indubitable evidence that disclosed their falsehoods and eliminated their allegations and charges, unveiled their lies, mocked their logic and rationale, challenged them to come and recite their Torah had they been truthful or to present just one solid and undeniable evidence to vouchsafe the truth of what they claimed. They were unable to do so, and they were unable to defend those questions and arguments that they raised, as we demonstrated before.

<u>Third: Prohibiting the Believers from Taking Them as Guardians and Associating with Them Closely</u>:

The Almighty prohibited the believers from taking the Jews and other infidels and hypocrites as guardians, warned not to trust them or listen to their charges or heed their allegations. This warning is recorded in numerous verses. Among these verses, we find in Sura Al-'Imran: "O believers! Do not associate closely with others who would not miss a chance to harm you. Their only desire is to see you suffer. Their prejudice has become evident from what they say—and what their hearts hide is far worse. We have made Our revelations clear to you, if only you understood. Here you are! You love them but they do not love you, and you believe in all Scriptures. When they meet you, they say, "We believe." But when alone, they bite their fingertips in rage. Say, O Prophet, "May you die of your rage!" Surely Allah knows best what is hidden in the heart. When you believers are touched with good, they grieve; but when you are afflicted with evil, they rejoice. Yet, if you are patient and mindful of Allah, their schemes will not harm you in the least. Surely Allah is fully aware of what they do." (Qur'an 3:118-120) [124]

Ibn Jarir narrated on the authority of Ibn Abbas, he said: "Muslim men were in close association with some jews because of their acquaintance, relationship and closeness in residence during pre-Islamic ignorance. The Almighty forbad them from associating with them or trusting them to protect them from their treason and duplicity. He revealed: "O believers! Do not associate closely with others who would not miss a chance to harm you." (Q 3:118) [125]

In these noble verses, Allah forbad the believers from associating closely, befriending or taking their enemies as guardians. Then He revealed the wisdom behind not associating themselves with them, namely, the treachery and betrayal that the Jews- and others like them- were capable of. He said: they (the Jews) "would not miss a chance to harm you. Their only desire is to see you suffer. Their prejudice has become evident from what they say—and what their hearts hide is far worse. We have made Our revelations clear to you, if only you understood." (Q 3:118)

The meaning is that those Jews and other hypocrites like them saved no effort to harm you. They wanted to harm you both in your faith and your lives. You had seen their enmity clear and manifest in what they said, for even though they tried to restrain themselves so as not to betray their hatred for you, they were incapable of controlling their tongues and did say what made you know of their animosity. Yet, the hatred that those Jews his and concealed in their hearts was far greater than what was displayed by their tongues. We had made things clear to you, O believers, through examples and evidence if you understood Allah's directives and commandments.

Then the Almighty revealed the big difference between the kind and pure hearts of the believers and those of the hostile antagonistic Jews. He said: "Here you are! You love them but they do not love you." (Qur'an 3:119) Meaning: You believers loved those Jews and those hypocrites who were like them. Because of this love for them, you invited them to Islam to enjoy happiness in this world and the next. However, they did not love you. Rather, they hated and loathed you. Also, "and you believe in all Scriptures." (Q 3:119) That is, you believe in all the heavenly books that were revealed to the messengers of Allah. They do not believe in the Qur'an, and they believe in some parts of the Torah and do not believe in other parts because of their malice and envy for your Prophet. And when those Jews and their likes "meet you, they say, 'We believe'" because they are deceitful and hypocrites, "But when alone, they bite their fingertips in rage." (Q 3:119) This means that when they depart after seeing how unified you are, they bite their fingertips because of their resentment for you for what you have of brotherhood, affection and guidance.

Then the Almighty commanded His Prophet to tell the Jews what would make them even more gloomy, despondent and melancholy. The almighty said: "Say, O Prophet, "⌜May you⌝ die of your rage!" Surely Allah knows best what is hidden in the heart." (Q 3:119)

Then the Noble Qur'an exposed them further and cautioned the believers against their evil to guard themselves against it. The Almighty said: "When you believers are touched with good, they grieve; but when you are afflicted with evil, they rejoice." (Qur'an 3:120)

In other words, if you believers are blessed with something good in your faith or in you daily lives, the Jews would become resentful and angry, but if some evil befalls you, they rejoice and become happy. That is because, they only wish you the worst. However, "if you are patient" despite their evil deeds "and mindful of Allah," comply with what you were commanded to do, and shun what you were prohibited from doing, no evil or harm would touch you, because the Almighty Allah would preserve you from their schemes, and deception, and He will grant you victory over them for "Surely Allah is Fully Aware of what they do," and He will punish them according to their deeds. (Q 3:120)

Thus, these noble verses forbad the Muslims associating closely with the Jews- and those like them- or having them as guardians. They warned the Muslims against their schemes and tricks and showed them various methods for their deceit, perfidy and treachery. They also encouraged the Muslims to adhere to piety to fear Allah and cling patience to guard themselves from their schemes and become deserving of Allah's favor and pleasure.

Fourth: Forbidding the Muslims from asking Them Religious Questions:

The Prophet prohibited the Muslims from asking the Jews questions that revolved around religion, and he ordered them to refer to their Qur'an or his Sunna. Ibn Abbas said: "O community of Muslims! How can you ask the People of the Book about something when your Book, which Allah sent down to your Prophet, may Allah bless him and grant him peace, is the clearest and newest news of Allah, and not distorted? Allah has told you that the People of the Book have altered some of the Books of Allah and changed them with their own hands. They traded it for a fleeting gain. Or doesn't the knowledge that has come to you forbid you from asking them? For, by Allah, we have never seen a man among them ask you about what was revealed to you!" [126]

Among the reasons why the Prophet prohibited his followers from asking the People of the Book was that whenever the believers asked the Jews questions, they would either conceal their knowledge from them or give them an untruthful and incorrect answer.

Al Shaykhan (the two Sheikhs: Al-Bukhari and Muslim) narrated that Marwan said to Rafi" "Go to Ibn Abbas and tell him that those who rejoice in their misdeeds that they had done and seek praise for what they had not done would be tormented."

Ibn abbas said that the Prophet invited some Jews and asked them a question. They concealed the true answer and gave him another response. They left having told him that they had provided him with the answer. They rejoiced for hiding the true answer to his question from him. Ibn Abbas then read: "Remember, O Prophet, ' when Allah took the covenant of those who were given the Scripture to make it known to people and not hide it, yet they cast it behind their backs and traded it for a fleeting gain. What a miserable profit! Do not let those who rejoice in their misdeeds and love to take credit for what they have not done think they will escape torment. They will suffer a painful punishment." [127]

Thus, we see that the teachings of Islam have forbidden the Muslims from asking the Jews concerning religious matters because they (the Jews) had distorted their books and were not honest concerning the knowledge Allah commanded them pass on.

Fifth: Cautioning the Believers from Following in Their Footsteps:

Many verses in the Noble Qur'an recount the various harms that the Children of Israel inflicted on their prophets, especially Moses, peace be upon him. The Qur'an narrates that they rebelled against him, refused to obey his command, and said to him: "So go, you and your Lord, and fight. Indeed, here we will sit," (Qur'an 5:24) and "We will not believe in you until we see Allah." (Qur'an 2:55) They also said: "We will never be patient with one kind of food." (Qur'an 2:61) In addition, they claimed that he had a physical deformity that was not fitting for his status as a prophet and messenger. However, Allah cleared him from these allegations. As a consequence to harming and slandering him and other prophets, Allah was displeased and angry with them, and they would suffer severe and eternal punishment.

The Noble Qur'an mentioned this so that the believers would weigh, consider and stay away from those Jews who slandered and harmed the messengers of Allah. Allah wanted them not to follow in their footsteps to avert the afflictions with which the Jews were plighted.

Among the verses that cautioned the believers against following in the footsteps of the Children of Israel who harmed the Messengers of Allah is what we read in Sura Al-Ahzab (sura 33): "O believers! Do not be like those who slandered Moses, but Allah cleared him of what they said. And he was honorable in the sight of Allah." (Qur'an 33:69)

Imam Al-Bukhari narrated on the authority of Abu Hurairah, he said: "The Messenger of Allah said: 'Moses, peace be upon him, was a man of great modesty. He loved to cover up and protect himself. He did not let anyone see any part of his skin, so the children of Israel offended him and said: 'He does not cover himself with this covering, except for a blemish on his skin: either leprosy, or أدرة [128] another defect, or illness. Allah wanted to clear him up and protect him from what they said about him. So, Moses went alone one day and placed his clothes on a stone, then washed himself. When he finished washing, he went to his clothes to take them, and he found that the stone had disappeared. So, Moses took his staff and ran naked behind the stone to get his clothes, and he said: 'Give me back my garment, O stone.' Until he passed by a group of the children of Israel, and they saw him naked, the best of what Allah created, and they knew that he had no sickness or blemish. Allah cleared him from what they said. Moses reached the stone, and he took his garment and put it on, and began hitting the stone with his stick, until the stone had traces remaining from Moses hitting it, either three traces, or four, or five. About which the Almighty's saying was revealed: "Oh you who have believed, do not be like those who harmed Moses, so Allah cleared him of what they said, and he was of honor in the sight of Allah." (Q 33:69) That is, you believers, be careful not to harm the Prophet like the Jews who slandered, and disobeyed and attributed to him things that were inappropriate to him as a prophet. Allah cleared him of the lies and foul things that they attributed to him, and He exalted him to a high status and prestige because of his straightforwardness, piety and fear of the Almighty. [128a]

We also read a verse that is close in meaning in Sura As-Saf (sura 61). The Almighty said: "Remember, O Prophet, when Moses said to his people, "O my people! Why do you hurt me when you already know I am Allah's messenger to you?" So, when they persistently deviated, Allah caused their hearts to deviate. For Allah does not guide the rebellious people." (Qur'an 61:5)

Which means: Remember, Muhammad, when Moses asked his people why they tried to hurt him with various kinds of mischief even though they knew perfectly well that he was truthful!

Al-Zakhmshari said: "They hurt him in many different ways: they claimed he had a deformity and not fit for the prophecy, they did not acknowledge his miracles and signs, they disobeyed him when they did not get what they wanted, they worshipped the calf, and they asked to see Allah visibly." [129]

And Imam ibn Kathir said: "This is regaling the Messenger of Allah for the harm he was exposed to from them. It is also a commandment for him to be patient. For this, he used to say: 'Allah rest Moses' soul; he was hurt even more, and he was patient.' There was also a prohibition to remind the Muslims not to extend any harm to the Prophet." [130]

Then, the almighty showed the fate of those Jews. He said: "So, when they persistently deviated, Allah caused their hearts to deviate." (Q 61:5) In other words, when the Jews knowingly deviated from- and rejected- the truth, Allah caused their hearts to digress from guidance, instilled doubts, confusion and humiliation in their hearts, for Allah does not guide hose who willingly and knowingly depart from his commandments, reject His signs, and prefer blindness and misguidance to guidance and the right path.

Thus, we see that the two noble verses sullied the Children of Israel for hurting their Prophet - peace be upon him. They therefore earned Allah's wrath and displeasure. The verses also cautioned the believers against following in their footsteps because this will only cause them misery and unhappiness in this world and the hereafter.

Seventh: reminding Them of Allah's Favors and His Punishment:

Also, the Prophet's position concerning those Jews who left no stone unturned in their attempt to fight the Islamic call comprised reminding them of Allah's favors, because that was bound to urge them to be grateful and comply with His commandments, if they were to listen and comprehend. The Noble Qur'an detailed the favors that Allah so lavishly bestowed upon the Children of Israel that they may be thankful, fulfill their pledges and believe in His messengers. However, in addition to describing these favors in detail, the Noble Qur'an also detailed their ungrateful attitudes concerning these favors and their trading fleeting transient pleasures and trifles with everlasting happiness. The Noble Qur'an also detailed their ignominies and perversions, their transgressions against Allah, and other inequities and depravities they committed. Because of this, Allah prepared severe punishment for them. He caused them to be struck with moral humiliation and disgrace.

Mentioning Allah's favors for the Children of Israel and their ungrateful churlish stance towards them is a reminder to the believers, a wake-up call to the slothful and unwatchful, to be watchful and careful not to follow in their footsteps and be subjected to the penalties and curses that they suffered. Allah's way does not change.

Seventh: Warning them of a Terrible Fate if They Persisted in Their Injustices:

The Prophet's position also included cautioning and alerting them to the severe punishment that awaited them if they did not change course and responded and reciprocated to the gentle call. He threatened to expel them from Medina if they continued to stir turbulence and unrest and sow the seeds of discord and dissention. This firm position was the final warning to them in order to come to their senses, abandon their stubbornness and misguidance, stop diverting people away from Allah's straight path and harming and slandering the Prophet and the Muslims.

Sura Al-Ahzab (sura 33) contains noble verses that warn them and others against continuing to hurt others and offend the Muslims. The Almighty said: "If the hypocrites, and those with sickness in their hearts, and rumor-mongers in Medina do not desist, We will certainly incite you O Prophet against them, and then they will not be your neighbors there any longer. They deserve to be condemned. If they were to persist, they would get themselves seized and killed relentlessly wherever they are found! That was Allah's way with those ⌜hypocrites⌝ who have gone before. And you will find no change in Allah's way." (Qur'an 33:60-62)

The meaning of these noble verses: "If the hypocrites... do not desist" from their schemes and deceit, "and those with sickness in their hearts" abandon their debauchery and immoralities, and those rumor mongers abstain from spreading evil and untruthful news, "We will certainly incite you ... against them" to shower them with penalties to coerce them to abandon their evil deeds and injustices. They would be your neighbors in Medina for a short while and, hopefully, they would get ready and depart from it forever. "⌜They deserve to be⌝ condemned. If they were to persist, they would get themselves seized and killed relentlessly." They would be undeserving of Allah's mercy. Wherever they are found, they would be seized and killed because of their cowardice. This is Allah's ruling concerning them because of their disbelief and their resistance to Allah and His Messenger.

Then, the Almighty revealed His way which never changes, namely, granting victory to the believers and humiliating the immoral and corrupt. The Almighty said: "That was

Allah's way with those hypocrites who have gone before. And you will find no change in Allah's way." That is, this is Allah's way with the hypocrites and the corrupt if they persisted in their hypocrisy and immorality; He sends the believers to vanquish, humiliate and inflict severe punishment on them. Allah's way does not change or alter.

Thus far, we have recounted some of the ways the Jews used to eliminate the Islamic call. We also mentioned some examples of the Prophet's position concerning them.

But, did the Jews abandon these cunning and devious methods that we mentioned before, like casting doubt concerning the truth of Muhammad's prophecy, attempting to stir disturbance and discord among Muslims, taking Allah's rulings playfully and regarding religion and its tenets lightly? Did they listen to the Prophet's advice to them? Did they heed his warning to them about the consequences of their evil and devious conduct?

No, they did not. They neither abandoned their wicked and meandering behavior, nor did they listen to the Prophet's kind and gracious advice. They did not even learn from the penalties that were imposed on people like them or the calamities that befell them. They persisted in their injustices and immorality, their attempts to undermine Islam and their pernicious efforts to eliminate it in every way possible.

It was therefore imperative to take a firmer stance concerning all these evil deeds that they committed, one that would punish and discipline them and stop their wickedness and evil. This is what we will investigate in the following chapter, Allah willing.

References

---

[1] Ibn Kathir's Interpretation (Tafsir) Vol.3 P. 71 Al-Halab Edition.
*(This verse is in Sura Al-Isra Verse 84, NOT in Sura Al-Kahf as mentioned in the original document)
[2] Sura Al-Baqarah Verse 89
[3]The shedding of blood: If anyone sheds your blood, they are shedding mine. This is an indication of the strong ties between them.
[4] Matriarch of Aws and Khazraj. The Aws and Khazraj were related through one father to their mother Qayla daughter of Kahel bin Azra. That is why, they were called sons of qayla.
[5] Sahih Al-Bhkhari "The Prophet's migration to Medina" Vol.5, P. 77 Sahih Edition.
[6] Siira (Life Story) by Ibn Hisham, Vol. 2, P.140
[7] The Beginning and the End by Ibn Kathir, Vol. 3, P.242
[8] The Beginning and the End by Ibn Kathir, Vol. 3, P. 224
[9] The reference is to a person whose burden weighs upon him and dissipates his joy.
[10] He who seeks money or profit through unjust and unfair ways.

[11] Invasions in turn one following the other.
[12] Kills him without committing a crime that warrants his killing
[13] He only destroys and corrupts
[14] The Siira (Life story) of the Prophet (SAW) by Ibn Hishaam, Vol. 2, P. 119
[15] The Eternal Message of Muhammad by Mr. Abdul Rahman Azzam P. 65
[16] Sahih Al-Bukhari, from the book of Interpretation, Vol. 6, P. 23
[17] Sura Al-Baqarah: Verse: 89
[18] Ibn Kathir Interpretation, Vol. 1, P. 124.
[19] Interpretation of Al-Razi, Vol. 9, P.122. Abdul-Rahman Muhammad Edition 1938.
[20] Al-Tabari's Interpretation, Vol. 1, P. 512. Al-Halabi edition.
[21] Al-Razi's Interpretation, Vol. 1, P. 461
[22] Sura AT-Tawbah: Verse 30.
[23] Al-Suhayli said: Al-Fityuun is a Hebrew word that is used for all those who are charged of the affairs of the Jews
[24] Al-Nishapuri, Reasons for the Descent, P. 17.
[25] Lubab al-Niqul fi Asbaab al-Nizul (The Core of the Discussion Regarding the Reasons for the Revelation) by Jalal al-Din al-Suyuti, P. 232
[26] Al-Nishapuri, Asbaab al-Nizul (Reasons for the Descent), P. 25
[27] Verse: 120.
[28] Verse: 123.
[29] Ibn Kathiir's Interpretation, Vol. 1, P. 372.
[30] Ibn Kathir Interpretation, Vol. 1, P. 372.
[31] Ibn Jarir's Interpretation, Vol. 6, P. 292. Sura Al-Ma'idah: Verse 59. The Arabic word تنقمونmeans to resent and deny because the word denotes rejection either verbally or through inflicting some sort of punishment.
[32] Al-Kashshaaf Interpretation, Vol. 1, P. 423
[33] Sura Al-Hijr: Verse 9.
[34] Sura An-Nisa: Verse 153.
[35] Sura Al-A'raf: Verse 138.
[36] Al-Kashshaaf Interpretation, Vol. 2, P. 634.
[37] Sura Al-Kahf: Verse 15.
*The word (آية) in Arabic could be a reference to either a miracle or a Qur'anic verse.
[38] Sura An-Nahl: Verse 105.
[39] Al-Kashshaaf Interpretation, Vol. 2, P. 634.
[40] Abu Muslim: Muhammasd ibn Bahr Al-Isfahani. He died in 322 Hegira.
[41] The Sciences of the Qur'an by the Honorable Sheikh Abu Salaama.
[42] To know what was written (from all various aspects) concerning abrogation, you may review "An-Naskh in the Islamic Doctrine" by Dr. Mustafa Zeid and "Sources of Gratitude in the Sciences of the Qur'an" by Sheikh Muhammad Abdul Azim Al-Zarqani and a lecture by the honorable Dr. Muhammad Sauad Galal.
[43] Al-Bukhari "Prayer and Faith," From the book "Faith," Vol. 1. P. 17.
[44] Al-Bukhari "What Occurred Concerning the Qibla," from the book "Prayer," Vol. 1. P. 106.
[45] Verses from 142-150
[46] Sura Al-Baqarah: Verses 142-150
[47] Al-Kashshaaf Interpretation, Vol. 1, P. 237.

[48] Sahih Al-Bukhari, Chapter "Facing the Qibla," Vol. 4, P. 104, from The Book of Prayer.
[49] Sahih Al-Bukhari, Chapter "We Have Made You an Upright Community," from the Interpretations, Vol. 6. P. 26
[50] Al-Kashshaaf Interpretation, Vol. 1, P. 238.
[51] Sahih Al-Bukhari, Chapter "Prayer and Faith," from The Book of Faith, Vol. 1, P. 18.
[52] Al-Nishapuri, Reasons for the Descent, P. 23.
[53] Ibn Kathir Interpretation, Vol. 1, P. 192.
[54] Ibn Kathir Interpretation, Vol.1, P. 193
[55] Al-Kashshaaf Interpretation, Vol. 1, P. 339.
[56] Ibn Kathir Interpretation, Vol. 1, P.194.
[57] Al-Kashshaaf Interpretation, Vol. 1, P. 240.
[58] Sura Al-Imran.
[59] Sura Al-Imran.
[60] Ibn Kathir's Interpretation, Vol. 1, P. 282
[61] Sura An-Nisa: Verses 160-161.
[62] Sura Al-An'am: Verse 146
[63] Al-Kashshaaf Interpretation, Vol. 1, P. 314.
[64] Sahih Al-Bukhari: Chapter "We granted David to Soliman, the best servant" from the book "The Beginning of Creation," Vol. 4, P. 197
[65] Sura Ibrahim
[66] Ibn Kathir Interpretation, Vol. 1, P. 170.
[67] Sura Al- 'Ankabut: Verse 67.
[68] Sura Ibrahim: Verse 35.
[69] Al-Kashshaaf Interpretation, Vol. 1, P. 316.
[70] Al-Kashshaaf Interpretation, Vol. 1, P. 394.
[71] Ibn Kathir Interpretation, Vol.1, P. 573
[72] Al-Bukhari, Chapter They Ask You about the Spirit from the book of Interpretation, Vol. 8, P. 109. It is also narrated by Muslim in Chapter "the Question of the Jews" in the book "Characteristics of the Hypocrites," Vol. 4. P. 2152, discussed by Muhammad Fouad Abdul Baqi.
[73] Sahih Muslim, the Book of Menstruation, Vol. 1, P. 252.
[74] Sunan Abi Dawud/Book of Knowledge, Vol. 2, P. 285.
[75] Sira Ibn Hashim, Vol. 2, P. 217. (Suah Al-'Anam)
[76] The previous source, P. 218. (Sura Al-'Araf
[77] The previous Source, P. 220.
[78] The previous Source, P. 220. (Sura Az-Zumar)
[79] Ibn Jarir Interpretation, Vol. 4, P. 23-24, Al-Halabi Edition.
[80] Al-Kashshaaf Interpretation, Vol. 1, P. 317.
[81] Ibn Kathir Interpretation, Vol. 1, P. 387
[82] Al-Manar Interpretation, Vol. 3. P. 333
[83] Ibn Jarir Interpretation, Vol. 3, P. 311.
[84] Al-Razi Interpretation, Vol., P. 101 / Abdul Rahman Muhammad Edition.
[85] Sahih Al-Bukhari: Chapter: "Say: Bring the Torah," from the book of Interpretation, Vol. 6, P. 46
[86] Sahih Muslim, Book of Borders, Vol. 3, P. 1227, Chapter "Stoning the Jews and Ahl al-Dhimmah for Adultery."

[87] Sunan Abi Dawud/Book of Borders, Vol. 2, P. 465 Al- Halabi Edition.
[88] Ibn Kathir Interpretation, Vol. 2, P. 60.
[89] Ibn Kathir Interpretation, Vol. 2, P. 59.
[90] Al-Alusi Interpretation, Vol. 6, P. 125.
[91] Sahih Muslim in "Emirate Book," Vol. 3, P. 1458, Al-Halabi Edition. Analysis by Fouad Abdul-Baqi.
[92] Al-Qasimi Interpretation, Vol. 5, P. 1992,
[93] Safwat al-Bayan by Hassanein Makhlouf, P. 193
[94] Al- Razi Interpretation, Vol. 10, P. 236, Abdul Rahman Muhammad Edition.
[95] Al-Qasimi Interpretation, Vol. 5, P. 1999.
[96] Safwat al-Bayan by Hassanein Makhlouf, P. 195.
[97] Ibn Jarir, Vol. 6, P. 266.
[98] Ibn Kathir Interpretation, Vol. 2, P. 65.
[99] Abu Al Saud Interpretation, Vol. 2, P. 34.
[100] Ibn Kathir Interpretation, Vol. 2, P. 66.
[101] Reasons for Descent (Asbab Al-Nuzul) by Naysaburi, P. 113.
[102] Al-Kashaf Interpretation, Vol. 1, P. 419.
[103] Ibn Kathir Interpretation, Vol. 2, P. 67.
[104] Ibn Jarir Al-Tabari Interpretation, Vol. 6, P. 275. We found that this story was sufficient to explain the reason for revealing the verse. There are other stories concerning the reason for the revelation and all of them revolve around one meaning, namely, prohibiting the alliance with the enemies of Allah and revealing the alliance of the two fronts, i.e., the Jews and the hypocrites against the Muslims.
[105] Ibn Jarir Interpretation, Vol. 6, P. 277.
[106] Al-Kashaf Interpretation, Vol. 1, P. 419.
[107] Sirah (Biography) of Ibn Hisham, Vol. 3, P. 321
[108] Sirah (Biography) of Ibn Hisham, Vol. 2, P. 174.
[109] Ibn Jarir Interpretation, Vol. 5, P.134.
[110] Ibn Jarir Interpretation, Vol. 5, P.135.
[111] gopt/ الجبت is originally الجبس/ al-gobs, but the س was changed to a ت. It means things that are evil and not profitable. It is a term that is used to refer to magic and idols. Al-tagout/الطاغوت is a word that refers to tyranny and its source, and it refers to going overboard in anything.
[112] Ibn Jarir Interpretation, Vol. 5, P. 135.
[113] The word أم/or here is used as an interrogative. It is used to move from rebuking them for believing in idols and false Gods to admonishing them for being miserly and stingy. النقير/speck is meant to indicate something that is extremely small (it is the little small hole out of which a palm tree sprouts).
[114] The History of the Jews in the Arabian Peninsula, P. 173.
[115] Ibn Kathir Interpretation, Vol. 1, P. 148.
[116] Al-Sarim Al-Maslul alaa Shatin Al-rasoul (the Unsheathed Sword) by Ibn Taymiyyah, P. 241.
[117] Sahih Al-Bukhari, Repentance of Apostates and Stubborn Ones, Vol. 9. P. 20.
[118] Narrated by Al-Bukhari, Chapter "How to Greet the Dhimmi People," Vol. 8, P. 70. Narrated by Muslim in (Asslaam/ السلام), Vol. 4, P. 1706. Muhammad Fou'ad Abdul Baqi.

[119] Sahih Muslim in Chapter How to Respond to the People of the Book. (Asslaam/السلام), Vol. 4, P. 1707.

[120] Al-Qurtubi's Interpretation, Vol. 6, P. 224, Dar Al-Kutub Edition.

[121] Ibn Jarir Interpretation, Vol. 6. P. 146.

[122] Ibn Kathir Interpretation, Vol. 2. P. 31.

[123] Ibn Jarir Interpretation, Vol. 1. P. 146.

[123a] Sahih al-Bukhari 3169; online here: https://sunnah.com/bukhari:3169

[124] Al-Zakhmshari said that the word بطانة (the inner underlay of a dress) is meant to indicate a very close friend in whom one trusts and confides. The meaning here is not to get into a close association the Jews.

[125] Ibn Jarir Interpretation, Vol. 4, P. 61.

[126] Sahih Al-Bukhari, the Book of Testimonies, Chapter "Polytheists are not Asked about polytheism," Vol. 3, P. 224.

[127] Sahih Al-Bukhari, the Book of Interpretation, Chapter, "Do not Think of Those Who rejoice in what They have." Vol. 6, P. 51. Also, in Sahih Muslim's Book "Characteristics and Rulings of the Hypocrites." Vol. 4, P. 2143.

[128] أدرة is a huge swelling in the testicles.

[128a] Sahih al-Bukhari 3404; hyperlink: https://sunnah.com/bukhari:3404

[129] Al-Kashaf Interpretation, Vol. 3, P. 183.

[130] Ibn Kathir Interpretation, Vol. 4, P. 359.

Chapter Four

Punishing of the Jews

1- A summary of what we related in the previous chapter.
2- The Jews' position after the Muslims' victory at the Battle of Badr.
3- Banu Qaynuqa's infringement and violation against the Muslims', and their non-compliance with the Prophet's advice.
4- The incidents of the Battle of Banu Qaynuqa.
5- The judicious plan that the Messenger executed in fighting them.
6- The consequences of expelling them.

1- In the previous chapter, we demonstrated how the Jews tried every method possible to eliminate the Islamic call, and we showed how they left no stone unturned to reach their goal to do so. Among these were: slandering the prophethood of the Prophet and mocking Islam and insulting its tenets, provoking suspicion and doubts to shake the Muslims' faith in their religion, trying to arouse discord and dissention between Muslims to break their unity, and the many other methods that we detailed in the previous chapter. We have also recounted that the Prophet endured their folly and dealt patiently with their cunningness and jealous animosity. He argued with them patiently despite their violations and infringements and lack of propriety hoping that they might find their way to guidance and the truth that they knew just as they knew their own children.

However, the Jews did not respond auspiciously to the Prophet's benevolent and thoughtful attitude. They met the Prophet's patience with more, treachery, deceit and animosity. In fact, they moved from rejecting the call and casting doubts among Muslims concerning their religion to downright open treason; i.e., violating pledges, openly announcing their hatred to the Muslims and resenting them for anything good they got.

2- When the Muslims came out victorious in the Battle of Badr, they thought that the Jews would welcome their victory with joy and contentment because they were the People of the Book, their neighbors and their allies according to a treaty that stipulated that they stood by the Muslims in defending Medina.

But the Jews were greatly dismayed because of the Muslims' victory, and they casted doubts about it. After ending the Battle of Badr and before going back with his army to Medina, the Messenger sent Zeid ibn Hartha and Abdullah ibn Rowaha to announce the victory of the Muslims to the people in Medina. When they arrived there, Abdullah ibn Rowaha started spreading the news of the victory to the people and recounting the names the polytheists who were killed. Zeid ibn Hartha was riding the Messenger's camel, (Al-Qaswa'). The people of Medina received these good tidings with joy shouting "Allah is great." However, this good news alarmed the Jews and greatly distressed them. Some of them shouted saying:

"Muhammad is killed and his companions are defeated. This is his camel that we all know. Had he been victorious, his camel would have been with him. These people are just saying that because they are extremely distraught and terrified..." Some Jews even went to Mecca to recite poetry for the dead among the polytheists and to incite Quraysh to avenge themselves against the Muslims.

Thus, the Jews betrayed their deeply-rooted feelings of malice and their open and downright hostility towards the Muslims after gaining victory in the Battle of Badr. Allah's will was revealed despite their hatred.

3- The Jews of Banu Qaynuqa[1] who lived in Medina in houses adjacent to the houses of the Muslims- were the first to betray these malicious and spiteful intentions and mock Islam and Muslims. They were not content to conspire and devise schemes against Islam and its followers. They overstepped their boundaries and violated the honor of a Muslim woman who came to their market with things to sell بِجَلَب [2]. She sat with a jeweler. Some Jews wanted her to show her face, but she refused. So, the jeweler came behind her and tied the hem of her dress to her back. When she rose, she unknowingly revealed her body. The Jews started laughing, and she cried and shouted for help. A Muslim man attacked the jeweler, who was a Jew, and killed him. The Jews gathered around the Muslim man and killed him. The family members of the Muslim man called other Muslims for help. They were furious, and fighting ensued between them and Banu Qaynuqa.[3]

The Messenger realized that by doing what they did, the Jews were not merely eager to cause dissention; rather, they wanted to challenge his authority, defy and weaken his word, dismantle his community, and show him and other Muslims around him as incompetent and unable to respond to others' acts of aggression or violations against their honor and dignity. Had the Jews succeeded in achieving what they were hoping for, the Muslim community would have suffered terrible humiliation. They would have been targeted at will by their enemy. Nothing is more detestable to Muslims than this; they are vehemently opposed to this and would save no effort to confront it.

In his Explanation of Talents, Al- Zarqani said: "Ibn Sa'ad mentioned that after the Battle of Badr, Banu Qaynuqa showed malice and Jealous animosity. They breached their pledges. Allah revealed: "And if you O Prophet see signs of betrayal by a people, respond by openly terminating your treaty with them. Surely Allah does not like those who betray." (Qur'an 8:58) The Prophet said: "I fear Banu Qaynuqa." [4]

The Prophet went to them and gathered them in their marketplace. He said to them: "Beware, you Jews, and fear Allah so that curses do not befall you as it happened with Quraysh. Embrace Islam for you know that I am a Messenger sent by Allah for you find this in your books and in Allah's covenant with you." However, counting on their strength, they said to Muhammad: "Muhammad! You think that we are like your people. Do not be fooled that you met with people inexperienced at battle. That is why you defeated them but, by Allah, if you were to fight against us, you will come to realize that we are (the formidable) people. That is why Allah revealed: "O Prophet! Tell the disbelievers, "Soon you will be overpowered and driven to Hell—what an evil place to rest! Indeed, there was a sign for you in the two armies that met in battle—one fighting for the cause of Allah and the other in denial. The believers saw their enemy twice their number. But Allah supports with His victory whoever He wills. Surely in this is a lesson for people of insight." (Qur' an 3:12-13) [5]

We thus see that the Jews of Banu Qaynuqa had persisted on being defiant, resistant and hostile. They met the Prophet's advice and warning with sarcasm and derision.

The meaning of the two noble verses is: Muhammad! Tell those who rejected this religion- especially the Jews who were overconfident and conceited because of their might and money- that they would be defeated and humiliated in this world, and that they would be gathered and driven to hell, an awful place for a final abode. Tell them that Allah was truthful in His promise to kill Banu Nadir, conquer Khaybar, and Muslims levying the jizya on all their enemies. These are clear proofs that the Prophet was truthful in what he had said about his Lord.

The Noble Qur'an did not address the Jews directly here. It commanded the Messenger to confront them: "'O Prophet! Tell the disbelievers." (Q 3:12) This was because they were arrogant and conceited because of their strength, overconfident because of the great number of their fighters and the amount of their weapons. It was thus more judicious to have the Prophet respond to them to make his threat and admonition more poignant.

After threatening them that they would be overpowered, the Noble Qur'an mentioned an actual event that testified to the truth of the Prophet, namely, the two armies that met in the Battle of Badr and in which the believers, a minority, vanquished the disbelievers, who far exceeded them in numbers and weapons. The Almighty said: "Indeed, there was a sign for you in the two armies that met in battle—one fighting for the cause of Allah and the other in denial. The believers saw their enemy twice their number." (Q 3:13) This means: You Jews had a sign and an indication that they would be overpowered and defeated, that Allah would uphold His religion and support His Messenger when the two armies met in the Battle of Badr. There was a small group of the believers, the Prophet and his companions who were fighting in the name of Allah, and there was a large group of denials and disbelievers, Mecca's polytheists. You had witnessed with your own eyes what you should have taken as a lesson: the Almighty Allah granted victory to the small group of believers over the large group of disbelievers.

Al-Zamakhshari (in Al-Kashshaaf) said: "The believers saw their enemy twice their number." The disbelievers saw the Muslims as though they were equal to them in numbers. That is, Allah made the disbelievers see the believers- who were smaller in numbers- as double, in order to instill fear in their hearts. That was Allah's plan for the believers. He also reinforced them with angels. Thus, the polytheists from Quraysh saw the believers' numbers a lot more that what they really were. If you said that this is in opposition to what the Almighty said in Sura Al-Anfal (sura 8): "made you appear as few in theirs (their eyes)," (Qur'an 8:44) I would contend that He made the believers few at first until the enemy was emboldened. When the disbelievers started fighting, they saw them at greater numbers. Thus, making them few or great in numbers was for different states to satisfy different conditions.: "So if there are a hundred steadfast among you, they will overcome two hundred. And if there be one thousand, they will overcome two thousand, by Allah's Will. And Allah is with the steadfast." (Qur'an 8:66) [6]

Then the Almighty reveals that victory and defeat are in His hand alone: "But Allah supports with His victory whoever He wills. Surely in this is a lesson for people of insight." (Q 3:13) This means that Allah supports those who trust in Him and give them insight. The victory of the few that do not have adequate weapons over the numerous who are well equipped is a lesson and an example for those who are prudent and insightful, those who are able to comprehend and discern matters in the right way, and as matters should be understood and discerned.

The two noble verses comprise good tidings for the believers and a threat to the infidels, mainly the Jews. There is also an invitation to ruminate and meditate on the tangible and palpable issues that occur in the universe, a call to guide and advise people that counting on one's strength only without consideration of the intangible and impalpable could lead to failure and disgrace and encounter unexpected and startling defeat. The Battle of Badr was provided a perfect example. The Jews heard and witnessed the events of that battle. Despite their fewer numbers, the Muslims overpowered the polytheists who outnumbered them. It was a perfect lesson to the level-headed and discerning.

4- We will now talk about the Battle of Banu Qaynuqa:

After that flagrant blatant defiance that the Jews of Banu Qaynuqa demonstrated, the Prophet was left with no other choice except to fight them because had the Muslims left them do as they pleased, i.e., breach their treaties and commit injustices and immoralities, their power and authority in Medina would have been gravely challenged, they would have been targeted by their enemies, and Medina would have become a den for conspiracies and seditions.

That was why the Prophet marched to fight Banu Qaynuqa in the month of Shwal in the second year after the immigration. The Muslims besieged their quarters for fifteen consecutive days. No one was allowed to exit, and no one was allowed to enter with food and sustenance. They were thus forced to surrender, and they accepted whatever the Messenger wanted to do with them, their lives their women, their offspring and their wealth. When Allah had enabled the Muslims to strike their necks, Abdullah ibn Abi Siluul came and said: "Muhammad, do good to my allies." Muhammad was patient with him. Again, he said: "Muhammad, do good to my allies. Muhammad continued to be patient. He then put his hand in the pocket of the Prophet, and Muhammad became angry to the extent that the color of his face changed.[7] The Prophet said: "Shame on you. Let go of me." Ibn Abi said: "I swear I will not until you do good to my allies. There are 400 حاسر [8] unarmored men and 300 armored ones… I do not like it when things turn around." The Prophet said: "They are yours on the condition that they leave Medina and do not become our neighbors anymore." [9]

Ibn Abi tried once again to have them stay in Medina, but the Prophet refused. Some Muslims fought with Ibn Abi until he became fearful. The Jews of Banu Qaynuqa saw that and were afraid. They said: "By Allah, we will not reside in a city in which you do not feel safe or where we can not defend you, Ibn Abi." [10]

Ubadah ibn al-Samit was among the Muslims who disagreed with Ibn Abi for defending the Jews of Banu Qaynuqa. He came to the Prophet and said: "I disavow the oaths of the Jews of Banu Qaynuqa, and I pledge allegiance to Allah, His Messenger and the believers. I have nothing to do with the oaths of the infidels or their allies. So, Allah revealed this verse concerning Ubadah and Ibn Abi: "O believers! Take neither Jews nor Christians as guardians—they are guardians of each other" (Qur'an 5:51) up to "it is certainly Allah's party that will prevail." (Qur'an 5:56) [11]

The Prophet then commanded that they be expelled. So, they left Medina leaving behind their weapons, and the instruments that they used to coin and shape gold. Ubadah bin al-Samit was in charge of getting them out of Medina. He accompanied them until they reached Zobab [12] As they were marching, he would say: "الشرف الأقصى الابعد فالابعد" which is as far away as possible to the north of the Levant. [13] They marched until they reached the valley of Qura and there they stayed for a while. Then they moved in the direction of the Levant until they reached Azra'aat [14] on the borders of the Levant. They resided there, but they did not stay there for long for most had perished.

Their exit lasted for three days, and their numbers reached 700 hundred. The Messenger delegated Abalbaba Al-Ansari as a Wali (governor) when he invaded them. Hamza ibn Abd-el Mutilib was assigned as head of the army. The Muslims took a lot of their weapons and instruments. Muhammad ibn Muslimah was entrusted with collecting their money. The prophet took one fifth and gave 4/5 to his companions. Their money was the first-after Badr- to be divided as such.

5- In concluding our talk about the Battle of Banu Qaynuqa, it is important to mention the judicious plan that the Messenger of Allah used in his fight against them, mainly, blockading them. This sagacious plan was the most successful one to get rid of them for two reasons:

First: Lack of self-sufficiency: Banu Qaynuqa had no palm trees or vegetation to use for food. They were jewelers who made their living by the jewelry they made and sold. They were thus dependent on others for sustenance. Therefore, being surrounded and cut off from others was the most successful method to overpower them. For how could they have survived when the most essential necessities of life were denied them?

Second: Weakness of their morale: This was due to their isolation from their kinsmen, residing by themselves in Medina, their being cut off from others outside Medina, and the depletion of their money (with which they were most concerned). All of these factors weakened their morale and pushed them to surrender faster. [15]

As a consequence of expelling them, the voices of the hypocrites were silenced, terror entered the hearts of the rest of the Jews, and Muslims regained their authority and dignity. Banu Qaynuqa reaped the fruits of the evil that they planted. It would have been better for them to keep their promises and comply with the agreements they made if they were sensible and could understand.

The Killing of Ka'b [16] (ibn al-Ashraf)

1- Ka'b ibn al-Ashraf stance when the Messenger of Allah arrived to Medina.
2- His stance concerning the Muslims' victory in the Battle of Badr.
3- The story of Ka'b bin al-Ashraf's murder as narrated by Al-Bukhari.
4- Responding to those who claimed that the killing of Ka'b bin al-Ashraf's murder was deceitful and mendacious.

1- Ka'b bin al-Ashraf was a Jew who declared his hatred and animosity towards the Prophet ever since he arrived in Medina as an immigrant. This is evidenced in "Explanation of Talents:" "Ibn Al-Ashraf was a tall, well-built man, a poet and an orator. He influenced the Jews of al-Hejaz because of his affluence and wealth. He had a strong sway over them, and he used to provide Jewish scholars with money. When the Prophet arrived in Medina, Jewish scholars from Banu Qaynuqa and Banu Qurayza tried to get money from him as they were accustomed to do. He asked them: "what kind of man he was?" They said: "It was him whom they were expecting." So, he said: "You have been denied a lot of favors. Go back to your folks empty handed!" They returned in disappointment. Then, they went back to him and said: "We had been hasty in our report about him. Now that we had investigated him thoroughly, we realized that we were mistaken, and he is not the expected prophet." Ka'b was pleased, and he gave them money. He also allocated a sum of money to all those scholars who followed them. [17]

2- When the Muslims gained victory over Quraysh in the Battle of Badr, the Jews were greatly alarmed and disappointed as they were hoping that things would turn against the Muslims at that battle. They were hoping to see the Muslims eliminated to gain back their religious leadership and prestige and their economic influence and commercial authority. Ka'b bin al-Ashraf was at the head of those Jews who were displeased, saddened and alarmed by the victory that the Muslims achieved.

Sheikh Al-Zarqani said: "Ka'b bin al-Ashraf had pledged not to incite anyone against the Prophet. He breached his agreement and cursed the Prophet and his companions. His enmity was so fierce that when Zeid bin Hartha and Abdullah bin Rwaha brought news about killing and capturing people from Quraysh, Ka'b said: "Is that true? Do you really think that Muhammad killed those people whom these two proclaimed he did? These are the noblest among the Arabs and the masters of the people. However, when he saw the captives led in disgrace and ignominy, he went to Quraysh to lament the dead and incite and inflame them against the Prophet... Then, he returned to Medina and started offending and hurting Muslim women there..." [18]

Counselors advised Ka'b bin al-Ashraf to stop hurting the Muslims. However, he persisted in his cruelty and betrayal, and he did not desist from his disloyalty, wickedness and iniquity. The Prophet shed his blood. Imam Al-Bukhari narrated the story of the murder of Ka'b bin al-Ashraf. He said "The Messenger of Allah said: 'What about Ka'b bin Al-Ashraf, because he has harmed Allah and His Messenger?' Then Muhammad bin Masalmeh got up and said: 'O Messenger of Allah, would you like me to kill him?' Muhammad said: 'Yes.' He said: 'So give me permission to say something.' He said: 'Say it.' So, Muhammad bin Masalmeh came to him and said: 'This man has asked us for charity, and he has been stubborn with us...We have followed him. We hate to leave him until we see what happens to him, and we wanted you to give us one or two wasqs in advance.' Ka'b said: 'What do you mortgage me?' They said: 'What do you want?' Ka'b said: 'Mortgage your wives to me.' They said: 'How can we mortgage our wives to you when you are the most beautiful of the Arabs?' He said: 'So give me a mortgage with your sons.' They said: 'How can we mortgage our sons with you? Then one of them curses, and it is said: 'He mortgaged one or two wasqs? This is a disgrace to us, but we will mortgage the lamah (meaning the weapon) to you.' So, he promised to come to him, so he came to him at night with Abu Na'ila, who was Ka'b's foster brother, and he invited them to the castle. His wife said to him: 'Where are you going out at this hour?' He said: It is Muhammad bin Masalmeh, and my brother, Abu Na'ila. She said: 'I hear a voice as if blood was dripping from it.' He said: 'It is my brother Muhammad bin Masalmeh, and my step brother, Abu Na'ila. If a noble man is called to a stabbing attack at night, he would accept.' A few conspired to kill the enemy of Allah: Muhammad bin Masalmeh, Salkan bin Salameh (Abu Na'ila, Ka'b's step brother), Abu Abbas bin Jabr, Al-Harith bin Aws, and Abbad bin Bishr. Muhammad bin Masalmeh said to them: 'When he comes, I will pick his hair and smell it, and when you see me seize his head, come and strike him.' He came down to them, clothed, exuding the fragrance of perfume, and said: I have never seen a more beautiful day.' Someone other than Amr said: He said: 'I have the most fragrant Arab women and the most perfect of Arabs.' Muhammad bin Masalmeh said: 'Do you permit me to smell your head?' He said: 'Yes.' So, he smelled it, then he smelled his companions. Then he said: 'May I have permission?' He said: 'Yes.' And when he gained control of him, he said: 'kill him.' So, they killed him. Then they came to the Prophet, may Allah bless him and grant him peace, and informed him.[19]

Ibn Ishaq and Ibn Kathir detailed the account of the murder of Ka'b bin al-Ashraf. They reported what could be summed up as follows: "When news of the defeat of the polytheists in the Battle of Badr reached Ka'b bin al-ashraf, he went to Mecca to Al-Muttalib bin Abi-Wadda' Al-sahmy and Atika daughter of Abi Al- 'aeis who warmly welcomed him. He incited people against the Messenger of Allah, he recited poetry and he lamented the people of Al-Qulaib from Quraysh who were harmed in the Battle of Badr (24 people thrown into the pit). He recited poetry lamenting their death:

The millstone of Badr that has its people crushed
Make the hearts bleed and tears flow
The best of folks are gone and have perished
Would even kings and nobles so lightly go?

Then, Ka'b bin al-Ashraf returned to Medina and started harming Muslim women. The Messenger said: 'Who is Ka'b bin al-Ashraf?' Muhammad bin Masalmeh said: 'He is the brother of Abd-el Ashhel. I can kill him Messenger of Allah.' The Messenger said: 'Do it if you are able to.' Muhammad bin Masalmeh returned and he spent three days without food or drink, only consuming the least that would sustain him. He mentioned that to the Prophet who asked him why he had abstained from eating and drinking. Muhammad bin Masalmeh said; 'Oh Messenger of Allah! Should I tell you or not?' The Messenger said: 'Say it. You are free to say whatever you want.' Thus, a few conspired to kill the enemy of Allah: Muhammad bin Masalmeh, Salkan bin Salameh (Abu Na'ila, Ka'b's step brother), Abu Abbas bin Jabr, Al-Harith bin Aws, and Abbad bin Bishr. They all came to the enemy of Allah, Ka'b. Salkan bin Salameh came to him first. They talked for an hour and exchanged poetry recitation. Abu Na'ila said to Ka'b: 'Shame Bin al-Ashraf! I came to tell you something.' Ka'b said: 'Go ahead.' Abu Na'ila said: 'The arrival of this man was a disaster that has plighted the Arabs.' Ka'b bin al-Ashraf said: 'Haven't I told you son of Salameh that things will turn out as I mentioned to you before?' So Salkan said to him: 'I wanted you to sell us food and mortgage you something.' Ka'b said; 'Will you mortgage me your children?' Salkan said: 'Do you intend to dishonor us? I have some friends who share my opinion, and you can trust them. We will mortgage you the weapons.' Ka'b accepted. Salkan went back to his companions and told them what transpired. He ordered them to take the weapons and go and get together at the Messenger's.

Ibn Ishaq said that the Messenger of Allah walked with them to a place called Buqe' al-Gharqad, and directed them saying: 'Go ahead in the name of Allah. Help them Allah.' Then, he returned home.

They came to Ka'b's castle and Abu Na'ila called him. Ka'b jumped in bed. His wife told him: You are a warrior and you know that warriors do not call at this time.' Ka'b told her: 'If a noble man is called to a stabbing attack, he would accept.' After walking together for an hour, Abu Na'ila picked his hair and said 'I have never seen a more beautiful night.' When he had control over him, he said: 'Strike the enemy of Allah.' And they did.

Muhammad bin Masalmeh said: 'I stabbed him in the chest with my knife, and kept pushing it until the enemy of Allah fell and gave out a howling shriek. Then we told the Messenger of Allah that we killed him. The Jews were frightened and terrified because of what we did. Every Jew panicked and became terrified.'[20]

This is the story of the murder of Ka'b bin al-Ashraf as recounted in Sahih Al-Bukhari and in verified and well-established biographies. Some orientalists and others who have "sickness in their hearts" that the killing of Ka'b bin al-Ashraf was out of betrayal and treachery. However, we rebuff this allegation:

First: Ka'b bin al-Ashraf had made an agreement with the Prophet that he would not support others against him. He broke his promise and breached that agreement. He went to Quraysh after they were defeated in the battle of Badr, lamented their dead and incited and provoked Quraysh to fight the Prophet. He preferred pre-Islamic ignorance to the religion of Islam and openly and publicly demonstrated his animosity towards the Muslims.

Numerous Hadiths (sayings) indicate that the Messenger of Allah did not give the permission to murder Ka'b bin al-Ashraf except after he preached his pledge and persisted in harming the Muslims. Among these Hadiths is what was narrated by ibn Abi Oeis, Ibrahim ibn Jafar ibn Muhammad bin Masalmeh, and Jaber bin Abdullah who said that Ka'b bin al-Ashraf promised the prophet not to assist anyone in fighting against him, but he broke his promise, went to Mecca and then headed to Medina declaring his animosity towards the Prophet. He began satirizing and mocking the Prophet, so the Prophet delegated some men to kill him. [21]

After the killing of Ka'b bin al-Ashraf, some Jews came to the Messenger of Allah. They said: 'Muhammad! Tonight, our friend was murdered. He was one of our masters. He was killed without a cause or a reason known to us.' The Messenger said: 'He would not have been murdered had he kept his promises, but he had harmed us, ridiculed and satirized us with his poetry. Anyone amongst you who would do such things would be targeted by the sword.' [22]

Second: By harming the Prophet and ridiculing and satirizing him, the shedding of Ka'b bin al-Ashraf's blood became legitimate. No prior contracts or agreements would have availed him.

Imam Ibn Taymiyya had reserved a whole chapter to investigate this matter. He said:

The third reason[23] is what Al-Safi'i brought as justification that whosoever offends the Prophet is to be killed without blame or guilt. That was the story of Ka'b bin al-Ashraf, the Jew.

Al-Khatabi said that Al Shafi'i said that a Dhimmi is to be killed if he insulted the Prophet. Such a killing would be without any sense of guilt or blame. He brought the incidence of bin al-Ashraf. Al Shafi'i said that no polytheists from amongst the People of the Scriptures were in close proximity to the Prophet except the Jews of Medina. These were allies to the Al-Ansar (Aws and Khazraj Supporters). After the battle of Badr, some Jews revealed their hostility towards the Prophet and they incited and provoked others to fight against him. The Messenger killed those who did so.

Ibn Taymiyya said that it was well known that Ka'b bin al-Ashraf was meant by this and that his story is well documented, detailed and well known.

Then he said that the evidence for murdering Ka'b bin al-Ashraf for insulting and cursing the Messenger is clear from two perspectives:

First: He had a truce and pledged to reconcile. There was no doubt about that, no difference whatsoever amongst scholars and biographers. This is common knowledge. However, by offending and insulting the Messenger Ka'b breached this agreement. As evidence for his breaching of that pledge is what was recounted in the Hadith: "What about Ka'b bin Al-Ashraf, because he has harmed Allah and His Messenger?" This saying indicates that he had offended Allah and his Messenger, a justification to delegate Muslims to kill those who do such things.

Second: The five Muslims who killed him- Muhammad bin Masalmeh, Salkan bin Salameh (Abu Na'ila), Al-Harith bin Aws, Abbad bin Bishr, and Abu Abbas bin Jabr- were given permission by the Prophet to trick him and pretend that they agreed and trusted him, then kill him. They killed him because he insulted the Messenger. A person killed in such a way has no protection under agreements or pledges. This is similar to those who are to be killed because of committing adultery, or for apostatizing and abandoning Islam, etc. It is not permissible to have a contract to protect such people as those as they have crossed specific boundaries.

Then, Ibn Taymiyya said that he had provided evidence to those fools who believe that the shedding of blood of such people as Ka'b bin al-Ashraf should not be allowed.

Al-Waqidi said that Ibrahim bin Jafar narrated that his father said that Marwan bin El-Hakam said while he had ibn Yamin al-Nidari in Medina, concerning the death of Ka'b bin al-Ashraf: Ibn Yamin said: 'It was treachery.' Sheikh Muhammad bin Masalmeh said: 'Marwan! Would the Messenger resort to trick? By Allah! We did not kill him without the orders of thew Prophet.'[24]

Third: By persisting in his inequities, harming the Muslims and provoking their enemies from Quraysh to fight them after their defeat in Badr, Ka'b became an enemy to the

Muslims, a threat to Medina's peace and security. It became incumbent upon the Muslims to defend themselves, initiate attacks and inflict punishment and exact retribution now that he had breached his promises, his evil had become conspicuously boundless and he rejected advice and counsel. Had the Muslims left him to do as he pleased, he would have gone overboard and corrupted the land, their authority would have been squandered and lost, their religion mocked and ridiculed, their community rendered to a state of chaos and turmoil, and they would have been targeted of loiters and exploiters.

For these reasons we can see that Ka'b bin al-Ashraf reaped what he sowed. He brought damnation upon himself by insulting the Prophet and Muslims. Had he kept his promise- as others did- he would not have been subjected to that fate that befell him. His killing was a fair and just punishment for what he did as he breached his promises, rejected counsel, openly declared his animosity towards the Muslims and insulted the Prophet.

The murder of Ka'b bin al-Ashraf took place in the month of Ramadan in the third year of migration.

The Prophet had also shed the blood of all those who followed Ka'b's footsteps and showed animosity towards the Muslims. Among those were Abu Afak, the Jew, because he wrote poetry ridiculing and insulting the Prophet and Muslims. He also incited people to wage war against Islam and its followers. Salem bin Umair al-A'meri was in charge of his killing.

Muhaisa bin Masoud also attacked a Jewish merchant called Ibn Sunaina, who used to harm Muslims, and he killed him. Huwayysa bin Masoud- who had not accepted Islam at that time- said to his brother, Muhaisa- who had embraced Islam if he would kill the enemy of Allah. Muhaisa said: 'By Allah, he has ordered me to kill him. If he had ordered me to kill you, I would have beheaded you.' Huwaisa said: 'By Allah, if Muhammad had ordered you to kill me, would you have killed me?' Muhaisa said: 'Yes, by Allah, if he had ordered me to behead you, I would have done so.' Huwaisa said: 'By Allah, this is a strange thing that has reached your religion,' and Huwaisa embraced Islam. [25]

Thus, after the Battle of Badr, Muslims killed and terrorized those who betrayed their allegiance, declared hostility towards Allah and His Messenger, supported Quraysh, its religion and way of life or showed sympathy for what had befallen them. They had to do so to be vigil and cautious, to prepare themselves to confront their enemies, and to purge Medina from a "Fifth Column" (spies) who knew their strengths and weaknesses and reported them to their enemies. Had they not done this, those instigators and offenders in Medina would have been able to cause confusion, strife and discord in battle and during peaceful times. However, by eliminating them, the Muslims restored their prestige and authority and secured their safety and wellbeing. They thus had the final say in their city.

The Battle of Bani Nadir [26]

1- The judicious policy that the Prophet used after the Battle of Badr.

2- Reasons for the Battle of al-Nadir.
3- Warning to expel them and their acceptance of the Prophet's rulings at the end.
4- Interpreting the noble verses that were revealed concerning them.
5- Consequences of expelling Bani Nadir

1- <u>The judicious policy that the Prophet used after the Battle of Badr.</u>

The Battle of Bani Nadir took place in the fourth year after migration, that is, approximately five months after the Battle of Uhud. As a consequence to the crushing defeat of the Muslims in the Battle of Uhud, many hypocrites and those who had pledged allegiance to support Muslims broke their promises. Some Arabians prepared themselves to raid Medina, eliminate the Muslims there and seize its wealth and riches. The Jews openly mocked and ridiculed Islam and Muslims and they made no secret of their joy for the victory that the polytheists were able to achieve.

The Prophet was well aware of the sensitivity of the situation. He knew that leading a nation after a crushing defeat and overwhelming circumstances would be much more difficult, arduous and demanding.

Under these difficult and sensitive circumstances, the Prophet adopted two judicious methods that enabled him to restore the Muslims' position, their authority and prestige, and their awe-inspiring stance:

First: He appointed some of the companions to roam the Peninsula to eliminate the rumors that were being spread against them and to gather news concerning the maneuvers and moves that hostile tribes were preparing to carry out their attacks. This method was exceedingly successful, and the Muslims became aware of their enemies' plots before they were taken by surprise.

Second: The Prophet adopted the policy of "attack is the best defense-" as war experts would have it. In other words, he would attack his enemies in their quarters before they had the chance to attack him.

At the heels of the Battle of Uhud, the Messenger sent his army to eliminate Bani Assad and Hudayl because they attempted to invade Medina. Theses forces succeeded in their mission and were able to counter the raids of the enemy while still at the preparation stage. The Prophet himself would lead his men to fight the traitors in their quarters as happened in the Battle of Dhat Al-Riqa.

So, the Prophet applied the "Principle of Protection" [27] in the best way imaginable. He had set the basis and principles that paved the way for the Muslims' victory, and restored their status and prestige after their defeat at the Battle of Uhud.

2- <u>Reasons for the Battle of al-Nadir</u>:

Among the reasons that drove the Prophet to engage in the Battle of Bani Al-Nadir and expel them were:

First: Banu Al-Nadir broke their promises which stipulated that they should not support or provide shelter for the enemies of the Muslims. However, not only did they do that, but they also informed their enemies of the weak points they had in Medina. This took place in the Invasion of Sawiq which can be summed up as follows: Two months after his defeat in the Battle Badr, Abu Sufyan ibn Harb sought to avenge himself against the Muslims. He marched with two hundred men to Medina until he reached Bani Al-Nadir quarters under the blanket of the night. He knocked at the door of Sallam ibn Mishkam who warmly received him, offered him wine to drink, and informed him of the Muslims' news and conditions. Together, they investigated the best ways to cause them harm and avoid retribution. Sallam and his men attacked a place called Al-'ureid, burned down two houses and palm trees and killed one of the supporters of the Prophet and an ally. Then they fled to Mecca. When the Muslims learned what happened they went after them. Abu Sufyan and his people fled swiftly and threw away whatever provisions they had (mostly from Sawiq) so as not to be encumbered by it. The Muslims returned to Medina after Abu Sufyan and his men succeeded in fleeing.

Second: The Jews of Bani Al-Nadir refused to provide the Muslims with weapons or money in the Battle of Uhud. Before the battle, they tried to dissuade the people from going out.

Third: The Prophet saw that the "Principle of Protection" which was a judicious choice he used against the treacherous tribes after the Battle of Uhud should also be used against Bani Al-Nadir after they tried to harm the Muslims with their words and deeds. Otherwise, Medina would have been exposed to internal strife and discord and the Muslims' authority would have waned and disintegrated.

Fourth: The Prophet felt that Banu Al-Nadir were lurking and waiting for a chance after the tragedy of Raji' and Bir Ma'una. [28] This tragedy reminded them of the Quraysh's victory at the Battle of Uhud. It also blurred their remembrance of the victories they achieved in Badr and other battles. The Prophet wanted to fathom their intentions. He went to them with some of the Companions to ask for their help in paying the compensation for the two men that Amr bin Umayyah mistakenly killed. The two men killed were from Bani Amer who were allies to the Bani Al-Nadir. The Jews pretended to accept the request of the Prophet. He sat next to the wall of one of their houses waiting for them to fulfill their promise. The Jews whispered among themselves and conspired against the Prophet betraying their treacherous and perfidious nature. They said to each other: "You will never find a better chance: Muhammad is by himself with only ten members of his Companions. Who would go to the house top and throw a rock on him to kill and relieve us of him?" Amro bin Jihash volunteered to carry out this mission. However, when the Jews were about to carry out their plot, Almighty Allah inspired His

Messenger who rose and pretended that he had to do something. He returned quickly to Medina.

When the Companions became aware that the Messenger of Allah left, they left after him. They met a man coming from Medina and asked him about the Prophet. He told them that he saw the Prophet enter Medina and walk in the direction of the mosque. When they caught up with him, they said: "You arose and left and we did not feel it." He told them about the Jews' treacherous intention and their attempt to kill him.

The Noble Qur'an revealed this verse in which it reminds the believers of Allah's favor for them as He saved their Prophet from the wicked and treacherous devices of the Jews of Bani al-Nadir: "O believers! Remember Allah's favor upon you: when a people sought to harm you, but He held their hands back from you. Be mindful of Allah. And in Allah let the believers put their trust." (Qur'an 5:11) [29]

Thus, the treacherous and deceitful nature of the Jews of Bani Al-Nadir became apparent, and their attempts to cause harm were numerous. It was therefore difficult and inconceivable to keep Medina as a safe haven to the Islamic call with the Jews residing next to it. The Prophet saw it fit to apply the "Principle/Law of Protection" which he applied and used with others after the Battle of Uhud, before their wickedness and evil became uncontrollable. So, what did he do to them?

3- <u>Warning to expel them and their acceptance of the Prophet's rulings at the end.</u>

The Prophet sent Muhammad bin Masalmeh to them. He said to him: "Go to Bani Al-Nadir and say: 'The Messenger of Allah sent me to you to tell you to leave my country and never to reside here again because of your deceitfulness and treachery. You have ten days to get ready to leave. Those who will not leave will have their necks struck.'"

So, he went to Bani Al-Nadir, and they could not find a response except that they said to Muhammad bin Masalmeh: "Oh Muhammad! We never expected to receive such news from a man like you." He said: "Hearts have changed." They said: "We will endure." They remained a few days there getting ready for departure.

During this period, Abdullah bin Abi Ibn Saluul sent a messenger to them saying: "Be steadfast and firm; we will not abandon you. If you are fought against, we will fight with you. If you are forced to leave, we will leave with you. Do not leave your homes and wealth. Remain in your strongholds, for I have two thousands of my men and others from the Arabs who will enter your barricades and fight until the last man has died." The Jews started to regain some of their confidence, and Huyay ibn Akhtab, one of their prominent masters, sent a messenger to the Prophet saying: "We will not depart from our homes. Do whatever you please!" The Prophet and the Muslims said: "Allahu Akbar/ Allah is Great." The ten days elapsed.

The Prophet and the Muslims got ready to fight them. He challenged any other Jewish tribes that might want to join them. He encircled them for twenty nights. The Prophet aimed a decisively devastating blow to the Jews: he burned their palm trees. This way he eliminated their very reasons to cling to their money or vegetations to strip them of their zeal to fight. The Jews were shocked and appalled. They shouted: "Muhammad! You had always decried corruption and railed against those who ruin things. So, what about burning these palm trees?"

Banu Al-Nadir realized that their departure was the only choice left, especially after Bin Abi Ibn Saluul breached his promise to support them and other tribes failed to defend them. They sent to the Prophet pleading him to protect and grant them time to leave their homes. He said to them: "Depart and you will save your lives and whatever the camels can carry except for the weapons." They accepted this, and they started to gather whatever food or money they could. They also demolished their homes so that the Muslims did not benefit from them when they were gone. They carried their possessions on six hundred camels. They left with music playing behind them so that the Muslims would not gloat and revel over their situation. Some went to Khaybar while others headed towards Daraa in the Levant. The hypocrites were exceedingly sorrowful and saddened for their departure, and they recited poetry to praise them.

The Prophet divided the money that Banu Al-Nadir left amongst the immigrants, and he allocated part of it for weapons. Thus, those Muslims who migrated to Medina did not have to rely on the help of the Al- Ansar (the Supporters of the Prophet), and they had money like them. The only Supporters who got part of that money were Abi Dijana and Sahil ibn Haneef who mentioned their poverty, so the Prophet gave them as he did to the immigrants.

Al-Baladhuri said: "The Muslims did not get the wealth of Bani-Al-Nadir through fighting by horsemen or footmen". The Messenger said: "Your brethren the emigrants do not have money, so if it pleases you, I can divide this money and yours between all of you. If you want to keep your money, I can divide this money between them." They said: "No, divide this money amongst them and give them whatever they need from our money as well." That is why this verse was revealed: "They give the emigrants preference over themselves even though they may be in need." (Qur'an 59:8) Abu Bakr said: "May Allah bless and be bountiful unto you, O Ansar (Supporters)" [30]

Most of the verses of Sura Al-Hashr (sura 59) were revealed concerning Bani Al-Nadir. Ibn Abas called Sura Al-Hashr as Sura Bani Al-Nadir. Al-Bukhari narrates on the authority of Ibn Jabir, he said: "I said to Ibn Abas Sura Al-Hashr. He said Sura Bani Al-Nadir."[31]

4- Interpreting the noble verses that were revealed concerning Bani Al-Nadir in Sura Al-Hashr:

The verses that relate to Bani Al-Nadir in Sura Al-Hashr relate three main themes:

First: Recounting what befell Bani Al-Nadir and their expulsion because of defying Allah and His Messenger.

Second: An account of the gains that Allah granted His Messenger as a result of this battle.

Third: An account of the hypocrites' alliance with the Jews and how they forsook and disappointed them when the flames of war raged. Revealing their cowardice and disagreements despite pretending to be united and in conformity.

The First Topic is revealed in these verses: "He is the One Who expelled the disbelievers of the People of the Book from their homes for their first banishment ever. You never thought they would go. And they thought their strongholds would put them out of Allah's reach. But the decree of Allah came upon them from where they never expected. And He cast horror into their hearts so they destroyed their houses with their own hands and the hands of the believers. So take a lesson from this, O people of insight! Had Allah not decreed exile for them, He would have certainly punished them in this world. And in the Hereafter they will suffer the punishment of the Fire. This is because they defied Allah and His Messenger. And whoever defies Allah, then Allah is truly severe in punishment. Whatever palm trees you believers cut down or left standing intact, it was ⸢all⸣ by Allah's Will, so that He might disgrace the rebellious." (Qur'an 59:2-5)

Concerning the Almighty's saying "first banishment," Al-Baidawi said that the word "hashr/banishment" means expelling a multitude of people and sending them to a different place. And the word "first" is a description of the first time they were driven out of the Arabian Peninsula, since no such humiliation had happened to them before. The last banishment took place at the hands of Umar who expelled them from Khaybar to the Levant. [32]

Then Allah showed how merciful and benevolent He was towards the believers as He facilitated their expulsion in a way that was not expected. He said: "You never thought they would go. And they thought their strongholds would put them out of Allah's reach." (Qur'an 59:2) That is, you believers never expected them to leave that easily because of their strength, their robust strongholds and their great numbers. They themselves never expected to leave their homes as they were proud of their fortifications and might. They were conceited and oblivious of Allah's unconquerable power, and they thought that the Muslims would never be able harm them because of their strong fortifications. However, they were terribly disappointed and utterly disillusioned.

"The decree of⸢ Allah came upon them from where they never expected." (Q 59:2) Allah's inevitable and unavoidable decree came upon them. It was a decree that could not be opposed or countered, and they never thought it could happen to them for after feeling confident in their power and strength, they felt horrified as the Muslims marched towards them.

“And He cast horror into their hearts.” (Q 59:2) They became frightened and their hearts were filled with horror especially after the murder of Ka’b bin al-Ashraf, their chief, and the hypocrites- who had promised to help them- abandoned and disappointed them.

Then the Noble Qur’an depicted their confusion and bewilderment when they failed to defend themselves. The almighty said: “They destroyed their houses with their own hands and the hands of the believers.” (Q 59:2) This means that they destroyed their houses with their own hands (from within) to use the lumbar and stones of the rubble and debris to block Muslims from entering to them and to make these homes useless after their departure. They also tried to get what wood and the doors they wanted. Also, the believers destroyed these homes (from the outside) to be able to get to them and remove their fortifications to fight them.

“So take a lesson from this, O people of insight!” (Q 59:2) Meaning: Take heed, be discerning and consider the great mishaps that befell these people. They never foresaw or expected that these calamities would ever befall them. Had they kept their promises, this well-deserved punishment that afflicted them would have never been. But they were blinded and deafened. They started a fire for which flames they became its wood. It fed on- and consumed- them.

Then the Noble Qur’an revealed that there was another kind of punishment that would have afflicted them in this world if they did not depart from their homes: “Had Allah not decreed exile for them, He would have certainly punished them in this world.” (Q 59:3) This means that had Allah not allowed them to depart from Medina and leave it because of their immorality and defiance, there would have been other kinds of torture for them i.e., murder and captivity. Allah had decreed that He would punish and torture them in this world.

His saying: “And in the Hereafter they will suffer the punishment of the Fire” (Qur’an 59:3) is a continuation of the punishment that they would experience in this world. In addition to it, they would also suffer hellfire in the hereafter. That would be even worse that their punishment in this world.

Then Allah displayed the reason for which they suffered this painful punishment: “This is because they defied Allah and His Messenger. And whoever defies Allah, then Allah is truly severe in punishment.” (Qur’an 59:4) That is, what they suffered and what they will still suffer was because they defied Allah and His Messenger. Whosoever does such a thing would suffer humiliation and disgrace in this world and a severe and everlasting punishment in the hereafter.

Then the Noble Qur’an comforted the believers and assured them that harming those who defied Allah and His Messenger by cutting down their palm trees was the best course of action: “Whatever palm trees you believers cut down or left standing intact, it was all by Allah’s Will, so that He might disgrace the rebellious.” (Qur’an 59:5) This means that whether you cut down the good palm trees that the Jews owned or left them intact, it was by Allah's will to put those Jews- who rejected Allah's orders- to shame and to rid the country of their evil and wickedness.

Al-Sheikan (the two Sheiks) narrated on the authority of Ibn Umar, they said: "The Messenger of Allah burned down the palm trees of Bani Al-Nadir – and cut down some of them- in Bouira, the place of their palm trees. The verse was revealed: 'Whatever palm trees you ⌜believers⌝ cut down or left standing intact, it was all by Allah's Will." [33]

Ibn Abas said: "When the Messenger of Allah ordered to cut down and burn the palm trees of Bani Al-Nadir, they said to him: 'Muhammad! You always stood against corrupting and ruining the land! What about cutting down and burning the palm trees?' That had an impact on the hearts of the believers, so they asked the Prophet: 'Do we earn wages for those trees we cut down? And for those that we left intact, would that be a sin for us?' So, Allah revealed the verse: "Whatever palm trees … rebellious." [34]

In other words, you had cut down palm trees following Allah's will. You also left some according to Allah's pleasure. That was not for ruining or damaging. It was done to strengthen the believers and terrorize the evildoers and rebellious. For cutting down their palm trees would fill their hearts with remorse, and it would fortify the hearts of the believers for what they did was in accordance with Allah's will.

<u>The Second Topic</u> which these verses reveal was an account of the gains that Allah granted: "As for gains [35] granted by Allah to His Messenger from the people of other lands, they are for Allah and the Messenger, his close relatives, orphans, the poor, and needy travelers so that wealth may not merely circulate among your rich. Whatever the Messenger gives you, take it. And whatever he forbids you from, leave it. And fear Allah. Surely Allah is severe in punishment. Some of the gains will be for poor emigrants who were driven out of their homes and wealth, seeking Allah's bounty and pleasure, and standing up for Allah and His Messenger. They are the ones true in faith." (Qur'an 59:7-8)

This means: The Messenger did not use the money of Bani Al-Nadir that Allah granted him after their departure as spoils. That is, he did not give the warriors 4/5 and kept 1/5 to himself, close relatives, the orphans, the poor and the travelers as he did with the spoils they seized at the Battle of Badr. Rather, Allah allowed the Messenger to allocate the money of Bani Al-Nadir as he liked because the Muslims did not acquire this money through fighting or through spurring on horsebacks or camels. For Allah had cast horror into the hearts of Bani Al-Nadir, and they submissively accepted the Messenger's rulings without any fighting worth mentioning. In fact, the Muslims headed on foot towards them since their houses were merely two miles away from Medina.

Al-Sheikan (the two Sheiks) narrated on the authority of Umar bin Khattab, they said: "Allah granted the wealth of Bani Al-Nadir to the Messenger. The Muslims did not spur into it by riding horses or camels. So, it was up to the Prophet to use it as he wished. He therefore gave money to his people, and he kept the rest to use for weapons and prepare for fighting for the sake of Allah." [36]

Then the Almighty Allah related the real reason for the Muslims' victory: "But Allah gives authority to His messengers over whoever He wills. For Allah is most capable of everything." (Qur'an 59:6) It is Allah's way that He sends messengers to His enemies, and they finally succumb and surrender. Messengers go to war or make peace only to uphold the Allah's word. Allah is capable of everything, and He will see to it that His messengers are crowned with victory over their enemies.

Now, after the Almighty showed what He had granted His Messenger from the money of Bani Al-Nadir, He showed what He had granted in general from the villages of other polytheists: "As for gains granted by Allah to His Messenger from the people of other lands, they are for Allah and the Messenger, his close relatives, orphans, the poor, and needy travelers." (Q 59:6)

This verse seems to answer a question that could have arisen in the light of what occurred previously. The question is: Well! Now that we know the rulings concerning what Allah granted His messenger from the wealth of Bani Al-Nadir, so what about the wealth that Allah granted from others?

So, this verse provides the answer and explains the previous verse.

The meaning is: What Allah made available to His messenger from the wealth of polytheists from other lands without war and fighting should be allocated to acts of goodness and righteousness. It should not be divided as spoils, but should be given to the Messenger, his close relatives from the believers of Bani Hashim and Bani Al-Mutilib, to the orphans who lost their supporters and breadwinners, to the poor and needy, and to the travelers who can no longer have access to their money.

The Noble Qur'an then reveals the reason for this Divine division of wealth: "so that wealth may not merely circulate among your rich." (Qur'an 59:7) In other words, this magnificent division of wealth was meant to make sure that would not be available merely to the rich and wealthy, but would also be available to the poor. That was the case in pre-Islamic times: the chief of the army would take ¼ of the spoils that they acquired from their enemies.

This noble verse "wealth may not merely circulate among your rich" is considered a basic rule among the rules of Islam. Every economic system that is not based on this rule is doomed to failure.

In fact, Islam built its system on this principle. It imposed Zakat (almsgiving), and it passed laws that aim at providing for the poor. It prohibited monopoly and usury. These are amongst the most important ways to circulate wealth between the rich and the poor. Thus, Islam established a unique economic and well-balanced system, with rights and responsibilities, to ensure happiness and prosperity to those who follow that system.

Then Allah commanded the followers of the Prophet at all times and places to obey his orders concerning what he allowed and what he prohibited: "Whatever the Messenger gives you, take it. And whatever he forbids you from, leave it. And fear Allah. Surely Allah is severe in punishment." (Q 59:7) This means: Do whatever the Messenger commands you to do and do not do what he had prohibited you from doing. And fear Allah, because His punishment is severe for those who oppose and fail to follow His commandments.

The Almighty commended the emigrants who left their homes and wealth seeking uphold and support Allah's religion and seek His pleasure. He also praised the Ansar who loved their emigrant brethren, opened their hearts to them, and even gave them (the emigrants) preference over themselves. He promised His followers with abundant favors and pledged to bestow His compassion and mercy on them.

After depicting this luminous picture of the emigrants and the Ansar and other followers bathing in Allah's mercies and favors until Judgement Day, the Noble Qur'an mentioned the Third Topic: The promise of the hypocrites to Bani Al-Nadir to stand beside them in thick and thin and how they abandoned and disappointed them in times of hardships and difficulties: "Have you O Prophet not seen the hypocrites who say to their fellow disbelievers from the People of the Book, "If you are expelled, we will certainly leave with you, and We will never obey anyone against you. And if you are fought against, we will surely help you."? But Allah bears witness that they are truly liars. Indeed, if they are expelled, the hypocrites will never leave with them. And if they are fought against, the hypocrites will never help them. And even if the hypocrites did so, they would certainly flee, then the disbelievers would be left with no help." (Qur'an 59:11-12)

The meaning is: "Muhammad! You had undoubtedly known those hypocrites who incited the Jews to fight against you. They said to them: 'We are coming with men and horses to help you. If you are expelled, we will leave with you. We will never deliver you to the Muslims. And if you are fought against, we will fight and support you.'" However, the Almighty Allah who knows them perfectly well knows that they are liars: If Bani Al-Nadir are expelled from their homes, the hypocrites will not leave with them. If the Muslims fight against them, the hypocrites will not support them. And if they hypothetically support them, they would run away and flee. Banu Al- Nadir would be left without help or support.

The Almighty was truthful in what He said and sworn would happen. The hypocrites were liars. They lied to their brothers and left them with no help.

Then the Noble Qur'an bore witness to a reality that exists in the hearts and souls of the Jews and hypocrites which rendered then as cowards who would be terrified at the prospect of confronting the believers: "Indeed, there is more fear in their hearts for you believers than for Allah. That is because they are a people who do not comprehend." (Qur'an 59:13)

This means that those Jews and those who defend them fear you more than they fear Allah. That is because they are a people who do not understand Allah's greatness and might. People such as these fear other people more than they fear Almighty Allah.

The Noble Qur'an confirmed this fact by citing other facts that were proven true in ancient and in modern times. The Almighty said: "Even united, they would not dare fight against you except from within fortified strongholds or from behind walls. Their malice for each other is intense: you think they are united, yet their hearts are divided. That is because they are a people with no real understanding." (Qur'an 59:14)

Meaning: Allah cast horror in the hearts of those Jews; they would not fight united in one place or another because they had utterly succumbed to fear and horror. Rather, they would fight from behind their fortified strongholds and their walls which they use to hide behind.

The war in Palestine between the true believers and the Jews confirmed this fact. The Jews do not fight except from behind their fortified encampments in the land of Palestine. Once they confront the Muslims face to face, they flee in panic and terror. It is as though this noble verse was initially revealed concerning them. Blessed is the Omnipotent who is all-Knowledgeable and cognizant of the nature of humans.

The Noble Qur'an then mentioned two reasons for their weakness and frailty: "Their malice for each other is intense: you think they are united, yet their hearts are divided." (Q 59:14)

That is, the animosity that these people have for each other is deeply ingrained. They are in such weakness, dissipation and degradation with which victory would be inconceivable. At first, some people may think that they are united and in agreement. The fact of the matter is that they are divided and in at variance because of their opposing interests and conflicting desires. They are a people who cannot comprehend or follow the truth. They follow falsehoods and pursue vanities.

Time has confirmed what the Noble Qur'an said concerning the Jews: "You think they are united, yet their hearts are divided." (Q 59:14)

Alfred Lilienthal said: "Those coward Jews who live in Zion, London, and America are the Zionist Jews who abandoned 6 million of their people to be burned, strangled and hanged without caring or offering any protection." He went on to say: "They knew ahead of time the time, the method and the place where these genocides were to take place, but they refused to even warn the victims." [37]

These noble verses encouraged the believers to fight them. They also lessened whatever might the enemy might have had because once a warrior becomes aware of the weaknesses of his enemy, he would no longer be intimidated. That helped warriors to gain victory over their enemies.

The Noble Qur'an then indicated that similar mishaps to those that plighted Bani Al-Nadir because of their deceitfulness and treachery had also happened to their brothers, namely, Banu Qaynuqa, as a result of their treachery and arrogance and conceit. The Almighty said: "They are both just like those who recently went down before them: they tasted the evil consequences of their doings. And they will suffer a painful punishment." (Qur'an 59:15)

That is to say, the punishments that the Jews of Banu Al-Nadir suffered were like those that their brothers from Banu Qaynuqa were also exposed to. The Muslims invaded Banu Qaynuqa because of their wrong doings and purged Medina from them. Their lot in the hereafter would also be severe punishment, one that is only known to Him Alone who knows the unknown.

Had Banu Al-Nadir been able to comprehend, they would have considered what happened to others before them and learned from it. However, they are a people who do not comprehend.

Then the Noble Qur'an gave another example for the hypocrites lured Banu Al-Nadir and encouraged them to resist only to forsake and disappoint them when hardships arose: "They are both just like those who recently went down before them: they tasted the evil consequences of their doings. And they will suffer a painful punishment. They are like Satan when he lures someone to disbelieve. Then after they have done so, he will say on Judgment Day, "I have absolutely nothing to do with you. I truly fear Allah—the Lord of all worlds." So they will both end up in the Fire, staying there forever. That is the reward of the wrongdoers." (Qur'an 59:15-17)

The meaning is: Those hypocrites promised victory to their brothers from Banu Al-Nadir then abandoned them to have such a miserable end. Banu Al-Nadir were tricked by their promises. These two groups are like Satan when he tricks a man and lures him to disbelieve promising him success and victory if he obeys him. When the man who surrenders to this temptation asks Satan to fulfill his promise, Satan abandons him and says: 'I fear Allah, the Lord of all worlds. If I support you, He will torture me with you.' However, this abandonment will not avail Satan just as the man who is promised will not get what he wants. Thus, the end of Satan who asks lures the man to disbelieve and the man who is asked- and does respond- to the request to disbelieve would be eternal hellfire.

This is the penalty for those who do not do justice to themselves and fail to follow their Lord.

With this moving example that touches the heart and the soul, the story of Banu Al-Nadir comes to an end. The story comprises abundant facts and directives. The noble verses show what they deserved by way of punishment for their wicked deeds and wrongdoing. They also show that the believers were granted much of their wealth without even fighting or riding on horsebacks. In addition, they show the end of those who rely on the created, not the Creator, for help.

The Noble Quran portrayed this story in a way that differs from how it is depicted in the books of humans with all the expectations for the innumerable and unparalleled differences between Allah's and man's work.

5- Consequences of expelling Banu Al-Nadir:

The expulsion of Banu Al-Nadir was a brilliant and perfect application of the "Principle of Protection" which the Prophet used especially after the Battle of Uhud because being adjacent to Medina- after their deceitfulness became apparent- was bound to create internal discord and dissention. That would have it impossible to become a safe haven for the Islamic call. In addition, being next to Medina meant another enemy other than Quraysh, and that would have compelled the Muslims to fight against two enemies instead of one. It was therefore imperative to expel them so that the Muslims would focus on one enemy, i.e., Quraysh.

Also, the expulsion of Banu Al-Nadir was a judicious plan and a decisive blow that targeted the Jews and the hypocrites at one and the same time. Together, they formed a united front against the Muslims; however, when this united front disintegrated and crumbled, the voices of the hypocrites were softened and their resolve and determination waned.

In addition, with that victory that the Muslims achieved almost without any sacrifices worth mentioning, their authority in Medina was established and secured. Medina became safe and secure, and the emigrants benefited from the wealth that Allah granted from the wealth of the Jews. The Muslims were also able to direct their attempts to suppress the Arabs that harmed the Muslims after the Battle of Uhud. They killed tens of them in Rujee', Beir Ma'ouna. That would have much more difficult had the Jews of Banu Al-Nadir remained a thorn in the side of Medina.

The Battle of Banu Qurayza

1- A brief exposition about the Battle of the Trench (Al-Ahzab/Allies) and the effect of the Jews in this battle.
2- Banu Qurayza's breach of their pledges and the impact of this in uplifting Al-Ahzab's morale.
3- Banu Qurayza persist in breaching their pledges and insult the Prophet.
4- Ka'b bib Assad suggestions to the Jews.
5- Delegating Sa'd bin Assad to rule among them and the Prophet's satisfaction with his rulings.

6- Executing the rulings of Sa'd. Any injustices in these rulings?
7- The verses that were revealed concerning the Battle of the Trench (Al-Ahzab)
8- The consequences of the Battle against Banu Qurayza.

1- We previously mentioned that after the expulsion of Banu Al-Nadir, the Muslims' prestige and authority in Medina (their base) were established and the Muslims felt safe and secure. At the same time, however, they were cautious and diligent and kept their ears and eyes open as to what was going on in the peninsula to avoid any sudden or unexpected attacks from others especially because their enemies were increasing: Quraysh was hostile and antagonistic and Arab tribes were out looking for a chance to attack. All the parties of the enemy realized that they were incapable of gaining victory over the Muslims if they fought separately against them because the Muslims- in just a few years- had become a formidable force that was capable of instilling fear and terror in the strongest and fiercest of Arab tribes.

The Jews were painfully aware of that fact. They thought of a method to eliminate Islam and Muslims. They finally concluded that the best way to reach their goal was to integrate all the enemies of Islam in one united army and confront the Muslims in a decisive battle to rid themselves of Islam and its followers.

To carry out that wicked and crafty plan that filled the heads of the chiefs amongst the Jews, Huyay bin Akhtab Al-Nadhari rushed accompanied by a group of Jews to the people of Mecca to incite and urge them to fight the Muslims. They told them that they would join them to fight Muhammad and his followers until they had completely annihilated them. They forgot that they were a People of the Scriptures and bowed down and worshipped the idols of the polytheists. The proclaimed a "Fatwa" (a statement) indicating that fighting against Muhammad was a right and his elimination a duty because "your religion is better than his and your traditions are better than his teachings."

In Sura An-Nisa (sura 4), this verse was revealed: "Have you O Prophet not seen those who were given a portion of the Scriptures yet believe in idols and false gods and reassure the disbelievers that they are better guided than the believers? It is they who have been condemned by Allah. And whoever is condemned by Allah will have no helper." (Qur'an 4:51-52)

The people of Mecca who were pleased to hear what the Jews told them, rushed to help them fight the Muslims and pledged to join them as they march towards Medina. Hayy bin Akhtab and other Jews were not satisfied with what they told Quraysh; they even went to the nomadic Arabs of Ghatafan and made a similar alliance with them as they did with Quraysh. They promised to provide them with a whole year worth of the fruits of Khaybar's farms if they were victorious. Then they left them and went to the tribes of Banu Murrah, Fazaza, Ashga', Salim and Assad and all those tribes that were affected by the Muslims. They commended their idol-worshipping and urged them to fight the

Muslims. They reminded them of Quraysh's stance against the Prophet, and they gave them tidings of certain victory over the Muslims. All these tribes agreed, and they proceeded to eliminate Islam and its followers.

Thus, the Jews, whom the Muslims were content to merely expel from Medina, were successful in provoking the disbelieving Ahzab (parties) to fight Islam. They thought that the end of Islam was only a few days away.

2- When the Prophet learned about the malicious plan of the Ahzab, he consulted his companions as to how to confront these thousands of men with all their horses, camels and weapons. Suleiman Al-Farisi suggested digging a trench along the northern border of Medina since it was the only side that was open and would therefore be easy for the enemy to penetrate through. The other borders were covered with thick orchards and other natural barriers. The Prophet and the Muslims liked the idea and they executed it in a few days. Then, they sturdily fortified Medina in a way that made it for the enemy to reach.

The Ahzab forces reached the outskirts of Medina. They were furious when they saw how fortified it was. They were exceedingly disappointed when they saw the trench as a barrier preventing them from breaking into Medina. Many days passed during which Muslims exchanged arrows (or spears) with their enemies. Disappointment crept into the hearts of the leaders of Ahzab because Medina was strongly and judiciously fortified, the trench was a major hindrance, the believers were determined to defend themselves, the weather was extremely cold and tempestuous, their tents were not adequate enough to protect them from the elements, a huge number of the Ahzab army were nomadic Arabs who were not used to stay in one place for an extended period of time, and Banu Qurayza were still complying with their pledge with the Prophet.

For all of these reasons, it was possible for the Muslims to resist for many months. It was also better for the Ahzab armies to withdraw, go back to where they came from, and come at a more appropriate time to resume fighting against the Muslims.

3- Huyay bin Akhtab and his men perceived the intention of the Ahzab to return back to their homes. They became frantic and extremely stressed since the withdrawal of the Ahzab armies meant that the Muslims would be able to strike the necks of the Jews. So, Huyay bin Akhtab and his followers tried their best to lure them to stay. He promised to facilitate matters for them. He even promised that he would convince Banu Qurayza to breach their agreement with the Muslims in order to cut off supplies from them, surround them from all sides, and find a way for the Ahzab armies to enter Medina from the southern border which Banu Qurayza inhabited. The Ahzab armies received Huyay's suggestions cheerfully, and their morale were uplifted. Huyay bin Akhtab hurried to

Ka'b bin Sa'd to lure him to renounce his agreement with the Muslims. When Ka'b heard what Huyay wanted, he closed the gates of his fortress. Huyay said to him: "Woe to you, O Ka'b!" Ka'b said: "Woe to you, O Huyay! You are an ill-fated man. I made an agreement with Muhammad, and I am not breaching it. I have seen nothing but loyalty and honesty from him."

However, Huyay kept waiting at his gate. He said to him: "By Allah! You closed your gates only because you are afraid I might take your food جشيشة [38]. Ka'b was angry, and he opened the gate. Huyay said: "Ka'b! I came to you with many of the best men بحر طام [39]. I came with the greatest among Quraysh and the chiefs and masters of Ghatfan. They have all pledged not to leave until we had eradicated Muhammad and his followers." Ka'b said: "You came to me with جهام [40]. It thunders, but there is no water in it. Woe to you Huyay! Leave me alone. I have seen nothing except truthfulness and loyalty from Muhammad." Huyay kept on الذروة [41] cajoling and flattering him until Ka'b bin Assad broke his promise with the Prophet and tore apart the contract that he had with the Muslims.[42] Hayy bin Akhtab was thus able to convince most of the Jews with his viewpoint. He was able to adorn treachery and embellish deceitfulness at the most critical of moments. He succeeded in bringing them to join the ranks of Ahzab that made the eradication of Islam and Muslims their goal.

Rumors spread among the Muslims that Banu Qurayza breached their agreement with them. The Prophet wanted to verify the truth of these rumors. He called Sa'd bin Ma'az, Sa'd bin Ebada, Abdullah bin Rowaha, and Khwat bin Jabeir and said: "Go and verify the truth of what we have been told about these people. See whether it is true or not. If true sing me a melody I know[43]. If they are still loyal and abiding by our agreement with them, announce this openly." When those messengers/companions reached Banu Qurayza, they found that they broke their promise and were indeed disloyal as they heard.

Sa'd bin Ma'az tried to remind them with their pledges with the Prophet. He also cautioned them of terrible the consequence of continuing to breach their pledge. They mocked him, and, Ka'b bin Assad, their eldest, said: "Who is the Messenger of Allah? We have no agreements or contracts with him." Sa'd bin Ma'az became extremely angry and he cursed them. They also cursed him. Sa'd bin Ebada said to him: "That is enough. No more cursing." The four companions returned to the Messenger, greeted him and said: "Adal w Alqara" which meant Banu Qurayza have become as treacherous to the Muslims just as "Adal w Alqara" have done to Khabeeb and his friends. Al-Ahzab were joyful because of the treachery of Banu Qurayza, and their morale was elevated. They prepared their forces to invade Medina from all sides. The Muslims were petrified and greatly shaken as their enemies were besieging them from every corner. One of the hypocrites said: "Muhammad's magic has appeared; he promised that we would seize Caesar's treasures, but now no one can even go alone safely."

The Muslims hearts were filled with anger and rage towards Banu Qurayza for deliberately breaking their covenant at a critical moment and siding with the Ahzab who had joined forces to eradicate Islam and its people, ransack and pillage Medina, kill its men, sell its women for slavery and sell their offspring in the markets.

However, the Messenger received the deception and treachery of Banu Qurayza with firmness and resolve. He employed all means possible to strengthen and elevate the morale of the believers and unsettle and disrupt the enemies' fronts. He shouted to his followers saying: "Allahu Akbar! I bring you promises of Allah's support and victory."

At the same time, he sent Salama bin Aslam with 200 men and Zeid bin Hartha with 300 men to guard Medina and to loudly say "Allahu Akbar" to frighten Banu Qurayza, and to protect women and children from their treachery. The Messenger also thought of breaking the unity of Al-Ahzab causing disagreements between them. He secretively negotiated with the leaders of Ghatfan. He promised to give them 1/3 of the fruits of Medina provided that they return back to their homes with their men.

He also used another weapon, namely casting doubts and using propaganda to break the unity and shake the trust between Al-Ahzab. It happened that during these critical hours, Nuaym ibn Masud Al-Ghatfani converted to Islam. He came to the Prophet to declare his conversion. He said: "Messenger of Allah! My people do not know of my conversion to Islam. Command me to do whatever you want." The messenger said: "You are only one man, so abandon us as much as you can, for war is a deception." That is, go into the people and see that they disagree with each other so that they cannot stand against us and continue their war.

Nuaym ibn Masud went to Banu Qurayza and said to them: "O Banu Qurayza! You have known my affection for you and the strong ties that bind us together." They said: "Certainly, we do." He said: "Quraysh and Ghatafan are not like you. This is your lands where you have your wealth, your women and your children. You cannot leave it and go to another land. Quraysh and Ghatafan came here to fight Muhammad and his followers and you have pledged your support to them. Their country and wealth are in other lands, not like yours. If they have (نهزة)[44] chance, they will seize it; otherwise, they would leave and go back to their lands and abandon you to that man. You will not have a chance if this is to happen. So, do not fight with them until you have secured a mortgage from among their nobles, to have them under your hands to ascertain that they will fight with you against Muhammad until you have eradicated him." They said: "You have fairly counselled us."

Then, he went to Quraysh and said: "You have known my affection for you, but I have been informed of something that I thought I should bring to your attention. It is an advice, so do not keep it between us." They said: "We will do." He said: "Some Jews have regretted what they have done with Muhammad, and they sent to him saying that they have been sorry. Would you be pleased if we take some men from Quraysh and Ghatafan to strike their necks and then we join you to eradicate the rest of them? They accepted. Therefore, if the Jews sent to you asking for men as mortgage, do not give them one single man."

Then he went to Ghatafan and told them what he had told Quraysh and cautioned them just like he cautioned Quraysh.

On a Saturday night in the month of Shawwal of the fifth year of Hijra, Abu Sufyan sent a messenger to Banu Qurayza who said: "We are not in our place of residence and the الخف و الحافر [45] have perished. Let us fight Muhammad until we have eradicated him." They sent a messenger who said: "It is Saturday (the Sabbath), a day in which we do not work... However, we will not fight with you until you give us a mortgage from your men, under our hands, until we eradicate Muhammad." When Quraysh and Ghatafan learned of what Qurayza said, they confirmed that what Nuaym ibn Masud told them was truthful. They therefore refused to give them any mortgage from their men. Consequently, Qurayza also thought that what Nuaym ibn Masud said was the truth. Allah had willed a state of discord and disagreement between the Ahzab.[46]

Thus, the crafty plan that Nuaym ibn Masud employe succeeded completely in sowing the seeds of doubt and discord amongst the leaders of Al-Ahzab. It was used in the most appropriate way possible and at the most propitious time.

Finally, after the fighting that had raged between the Muslims and Al-Ahzab, Allah's victory was manifested. He sent His soldiers and raging storms to afflict the infidels. Their fronts were in disarray and confusion, their tents crumbled and collapsed, and terror filled their hearts. They thought that the Muslims were surrounding them from all sides to annihilate and eradicate them. Tolayha ibn Khuwaylid shouted saying that Muhammad had intended evil to them and they had to seek refuge and safety.

Abu Sufyan said: "Oh People of Quraysh. You are not in your place of residence; the camels and horses have perished. Banu Qurayza had abandoned us, and we from them we received what we loathe. We have witnessed the raging storms, so depart for I am leaving." So, the people tried to gather whatever of their possessions they could gather, and they hurried to leave and the storms were still raging and getting the best of them. They fled: "And Allah drove back the disbelievers in their rage, totally empty-handed. And Allah spared the believers from fighting. For Allah is All-Powerful, Almighty." (Qur'an 33:25)

It was now time to punish Banu Qurayza:

4- The armies of Al-Ahzab returned home in humiliation, failure and disappointment. The Muslims sighed in relief and the were grateful for Allah Almighty for protecting them from their enemies.

As for Banu Qurayza, they remained alone in their fortresses aware of their appalling and despicable treason. Condemning solid evidences pointed to their duplicity and betrayal, and they waited in trepidation and terror their punishment and the execution of justice.

And as Allah willed, retribution was quick and decisive.

Al-Sheikan (the two Sheiks) narrated on the authority of Aiysha, they said: "When the Prophet returned from the trench, put down his weapon and washed, Gabriel came to him and said: 'You put down the weapon. We have not. Go out to them." The Prophet said: "where to?" Gabriel said: "Over there," as he pointed out in the direction of Banu Qurayza. The Prophet went to them." [47]

The Prophet ordered the Muslims to rush into fighting Banu Qurayza and not to be distracted from this mission by any other matters. On the authority of Ibn Umar, he said: "On the day of Al-Ahzab, the Prophet said: 'No one will pray the evening prayers except in Banu Qurayza's quarters.' The time for the evening prayer came while some were still marching towards Banu Qurayza. So, some said: 'We will not pray until we get there.' Others said: 'No! We pray, even though we are not supposed to.' The Prophet was not coarse with anyone when this was mentioned to him." [48]

5- The Prophet was careful to make sure that the Muslims rush speedily to Banu Qurayza to surprise them before they had enough time to prepare themselves, fortify their strongholds and recalculate and reconsider their plans. That is why, the Muslims rushed to them under the leadership of Ali bin Abi Talib who, upon reaching their homes, found them persevering in their deception and conceit and arrogance. They looked at the Muslims in a malicious and envious way, and they used the most despicable and appalling language to curse and offend the Prophet and his women. In order to divert the attention of the Prophet, Imam Ali asked Abi Quttada Al-Ansari to lead the men, and he headed to meet the Messenger a little distance away from the homes of these foolish loathsome people so that he would not hear their curses and foul language. He intercepted the Prophet as he was heading in their direction and said: "Messenger of Allah! Do not come close to those malicious people." The Prophet said: "Why? Have you heard foul language from them?" He said: "Yes, Messenger of Allah." The Prophet said: "If they saw me, they will not utter these obscenities." Then, he approached their fortresses and said: "Brothers of apes and pigs! Has Allah disgraced and brought down His damnation upon you?" They said: "Abou Al-Qasim! You are not ignorant!" [49]

This is the status quo of the Jews everywhere and at all time; when they feel safe, they curse, offend and exceed conventional limits. When the opportunity offers itself, they murder, blow up and destroy. However, when they are cornered and feel threatened, they cry, plead and entreat. They adapt to suit the changing circumstances around them in a way that is convenient and beneficial for them. As for covenants or pledges, moral principles and values, and humane propensities and considerations, these are of no consequence.

However, the offences and attempts of Banu Qurayza proved useless. The Muslims tightly besieged them for twenty-five nights during which they were unable to get out of their fortresses.

They realized that their fortresses would not save them from perdition if that besiege continues. In the midst of their despair, Ka'b bin Assad, their chief, said to them:

"As you see, things have come to that. I have three suggestions and it is up to you to choose one of them." They asked: "What are they?"

He said: "We follow this man and believe in him, for by Allah, it has been evident that he is a sent messenger, and that he is the one that you find mentioned in your Book. This way you can your lives, and wealth, and your children will be safe." They said: "We will never depart from the rulings of the Torah, nor will we replace them with anything else."

He said: "If you are averse to this, then let us kill our sons and women, then go out to Muhammad and his companions, men with drawn swords, leaving no burden behind us until Allah decides between us and Muhammad. If we perish, we will perish, and we have left behind us no offspring for whom we fear. If we vanquish them, we will find women and children." They said: "We kill these poor people, so what good is life after them?

He said: "If you refuse this, then tonight is the eve of the Sabbath, and it may be that Muhammad and his companions expect no attacks from us, so perhaps we can catch Muhammad and his companions by surprise." They said: "We will thus ruin our Sabbath by doing what no one of our predecessors had done except those whom you know, and whose plighted was transformation (physical transformation into apes and pigs).

Ka'b said: "Not a single man among you has spent one single night since his mother gave birth to him as firm and resolute."

Banu Qurayza then attempted to execute a reconciliation that would secure their lives. They sent Shas bin Qais to propose to the Prophet that they wanted to accept the terms that were offered Banu Al-Nadir, namely, they could take whatever their camels can carry except for weapons. The Prophet rejected their proposal. So, again they sent to indicate their willingness to give up their wealth provided that their lives, their women and their offspring be safe. Again, they were disappointed since the Prophet rejected this proposal and insisted that they accept his ruling without any conditions or stipulations.

Yet, the Jews of Banu Qurayza did not lose heart and they sent to the Prophet asking him to send Abu Lubaba to consult him concerning their situation. Abu Lubaba was one of the Aws, their allies. The Prophet sent him to them. When they saw him, the men went to meet him and the women and the children started crying. He felt sympathy for them. Ka'b bin Assad said to Abu Lubaba: "You have known what had taken place between us. We are being surrounded, and we are perishing. Muhammad won't leave our fortresses until we accept his terms. What do you think? Should we accept his conditions?" Abu Lubaba said: "Yes" as he pointed to his throat, as though he was cautioning them that it would be slaughter.[50] As soon as he said that, he realized that he was disloyal to the Prophet because what he told them implied causing them not to abide by the ruling of the Prophet. He roamed aimlessly feeling guilty and was unable to face the Prophet. He went inside the mosque and tied himself to one of the poles and pledged not to untie himself until Allah has forgiven him. He made a pledge with Allah never to tread on the lands of Banu Qurayza and never to be seen again in a land in which he was disloyal to Allah and His Messenger.

When the Prophet learned his story, he said: "Had he come to me I would have forgiven him, but since he did what he did, I will not untie him until Allah has forgiven him. [51] Allah accepted his repentance and revealed this verse: "Some others have confessed their wrongdoing: they have mixed goodness with evil. It is right to hope that Allah will turn to them in mercy. Surely Allah is All-Forgiving, Most Merciful." (Qur'an 9:102) [52]

People came to him to bring him the good tidings that his repentance had been accepted after he spent six nights never loosened except to pray, but he refused to allow anyone except the Prophet to loosen him. The Prophet untied him when he was going out for the morning prayer.

Finally, they resorted to a method to secure the sympathy of the Aws, their allies. They sent them messengers saying: "Don't you want to get for your brothers what the Khazraj got for theirs?" That was because Abdullah bin Abi Sulul who was one of Banu Khazraj stood by his allies from Banu Qaynuqa until their lives were spared, and the Prophet was content with merely expelling them from Medina. So, the Aws should do to Banu Qurayza, their allies, what one of the Khazraj did with Banu Qaynuqa, their allies.

6- Some men from the Aws went to the Prophet and said: "Messenger of Allah! Won't you accept from our allies what you have accepted from the Khazraj allies?" The Prophet said: "Community of the Aws! Don't you want to delegate a man between me and your allies?" They said: "Yes." He said: "Then, tell them to choose whomsoever they want." Banu Qurayza chose Sa'd ibn Mu'adh to decide concerning them as they thought that they would benefit from the bond they had with him during pre-Islamic times, and thus they would be able to get his sympathy and attenuate and often his ruling. They forgot (or appeared to have forgotten) that he himself came to them and advised them to remain loyal and cautioned them against the consequences of treachery. They offended both him and the Prophet.

That man whom the Jews chose to judge and issue rulings was the same man who was mortally wounded while fighting against Al-Ahzab. He pleaded with Allah and said: "Allah! If there is anything left in the Quraysh war, then keep me to fight against them, for there is people I would like to fight against than those who have harmed Your Messenger, looked at him as a liar and tried to drive him away. If there is a war between us and them, do not let me die until I am pleased with what befalls Banu Qurayza."

When Sa'd ibn Mu'adh was injured in the Battle of Al-Ahzab, the Prophet ordered that he be taken to the tent of Rafida [53] to be cared for. When the Prophet asked him to pronounce his judgement concerning Banu Qurayza, his people surrounded him and asked to be compassionate in his judgement. They told him that the Messenger delegated him to be lenient towards them.

However, regardless of all the pleas and supplications surrounding him, he never forgot that Banu Qurayza broke their covenant at a very critical time. He remembered how they had cursed the Messenger in the most despicable way possible, how the Muslims were besieged and surrounded from east and west and their eyes grew wild in horror, and how Medina, its fruits, its offspring and its women were saved- albeit miraculously- from the assault and cruelty of the armies of Al-Ahzab. He could not forget that Banu Qurayza turned around with their weapons to deliberately join the armies of the infidels and participate in killing the Muslims and taking them as captives.

Sa'd ibn Mu'adh never forgot any of those things that Banu Qurayza did despite all the pleas and entreaties around him. The Prophet said to him: "What is your judgement, Sa'd?" He said: "Allah and His Messenger are more worthy to decide their fate." The Messenger said: "Allah had commanded that you make a judgement."

Sa'd looked at the direction of Banu Qurayza and said: "Would you accept my judgement?" They said: "Yes." So, he said that the Prophet (without even looking at the Prophet out of respect and reverence) wants… The Prophet interjected: "Yes, Sa'd?" Then Sa'd said: "I rule that the men be killed, the money to be divided, and the women and offspring be enslaved." Thereupon, the Prophet said to Sa'd: "You have ruled in accordance with the judgement of Allah from the seventh heaven." [54]

Concerning the injuries that Sa'd ibn Mu'adh sustained during the Battle of the Trench and his judgement on Banu Qurayza, the two Sheikhs narrated a lengthy account that we think would be appropriate to mention here.

On the authority of Aiysha- may Allah be pleased with her- she said: "Sa'd ibn Mu'adh was injured on the day of the Battle of the Trench. A man from Quraysh struck him with an arrow in his arm where he could bleed to death. The Prophet installed a tent in the mosque to bring him there. When the Prophet returned from the trench, he put down his weapon and washed. Gabriel came to him and asked him to go out. The Prophet asked him: "Where?" He pointed to Banu Qurayza. The Prophet went to them and they succumbed to his ruling. He asked Sa'd to rule. Sa'd ruled that all warriors be killed, the women and offspring be enslaved, and the money divided.

Hisham said that his father said that Aiysha said that Sa'd said that Allah knows that nothing is more important to him than to fight those who did not believe His Messenger. He knew that Allah appointed this war between them and the infidels, so if there is anything left in the Quraysh war, he might survive to fight against them for Allah's name. If the war is ended, may Allah make him bleed to death and die. His wound started bleeding heavily, and he died. May Allah be pleased with him.[55]

Trenches were dug in the city market to execute Sa'd's ruling. Banu Qurayza's men were led there to pay the price of their treachery. There were between six and seven hundred men. In panic and terror, some of them asked Sa'd bin Assad, their chief, about what he was going to do to them. He said admonishing them: "In every situation, you people do not comprehend? The caller does not stop [56], and whoever among you is called, will not return back! By Allah, it is murder."

Yes, it is murder, the punishment of the deceitful traitors who stabbed the Muslims from behind at the most critical moment and most difficult time.

Finally, Hayy bin Akhtab, the chief corruptor and orchestrator of the dissention was brought to receive his just punishment. He was wearing a loose robe which he had split on each side. When he came close to the Messenger of Allah, he said: "By Allah, I did not blame my self in your enmity, but whoever fails Allah will be disappointed." Then he turned to the people and said: O people, there is nothing wrong with Allah's command: a book, a destiny, and an epic that Allah wrote for the children of Israel. Then he sat down and his neck was struck. About him the poet wrote:

By Allah, Bin Akhtab blamed not himself
But whoever abandons Allah will be forsaken;
He strives until the soul reached its full potential,
and was restless, seeking glory, as restless ones do.

Only one woman from Banu Qurayza was killed because she threw a rock on one of the Muslims and was killed. Those who were killed among their males were adults only.

The Prophet divided the wealth, women and children of Banu Qurayza among the Muslims.

7- Concerning the Battle of the Trench, nineteen verses were revealed in Sura Al-Ahzab (sura 33). [57] They were introduced by reminding the believers of Allah's favor upon them when He rescued them from their enemies at a time when their hearts jumped into their throats: He said: "O believers! Remember Allah's favor upon you when enemy forces came to besiege you in Medina, so We sent against them a bitter wind and forces you could not see. And Allah is All-Seeing of what you do. Remember when they came at you from east and west, when your eyes grew wild in horror and your hearts jumped

> into your throats, and you entertained conflicting thoughts about Allah. Then and there the believers were put to the test and were violently shaken." (Qur'an 33:9-11)

Then, the noble verses talked about the hypocrites and those who with sickness in their hearts. They described them as cowardly and fainthearted people with razor-sharp tongues, and they revealed their cunning and crafty intentions and groundless excuses as a group of them asked the Prophet's permission to leave, saying, "Our homes are vulnerable," while in fact they were not vulnerable. They only wished to flee, turn their back in retreat and abandon the fighting even though this would hardly save them from death, for no one could hope to be saved except by Allah's protection and grace.

The noble verses then directed the believers to follow the excellent example of the Prophet in his words and deeds. They praised the believers because they had proven true to what they pledged to Allah. Again, the verses reminded them at the end-as they did in the beginning- of Allah's favor upon them as He protected and saved them from the infidels who returned to their homes empty-handed, in defeat and humiliation: "And Allah spared the believers from fighting. For Allah is All-Powerful, Almighty." (Qur'an 33:25)

The noble verses concluded with an account of what had befallen Banu Qurayza as a result of their deceit and treachery: "And He brought down those from the People of the Book who supported the enemy alliance from their own strongholds and cast horror into their hearts. You believers killed some and took others captive. He has also caused you to take over their lands, homes, and wealth, as well as lands you have not yet set foot on. And Allah is Most Capable of everything." (Qur'an 33:26)

That is to say, remember Allah's favor upon you, O believers. He repelled the infidels and caused great harm to Banu Qurayza who helped them from their stronghold and fortresses. He cast horror into their hearts, and they thus submissively succumbed to your ruling: you killed their men and took their women and children captive. Allah gave you their land, fortresses, livestock and all their possessions and wealth. He even gave you lands you have not set foot on before, like Khaybar and others, for He is the Almighty and Capable Allah who supports whomsoever He wills and annihilates those who oppose and fight Him.

Now! Were the Muslims unfair towards the Jews by executing that ruling?

In order to respond to this question, we say: NO. The Muslims were not unfair. It was Banu Qurayza who brought that to themselves. They sought their own destruction because of their treachery. They were the ones who broke their covenant with the Muslims at a critical moment. All laws and regulations dictate that whoever breaks an agreement at such times should be stripped of life.

And what the Muslims did to them was out of self-preservation. Banu Qurayza kept their covenant with the Muslims before the Battle of the Trench only out of fear. However, when they found that the Muslims were besieged from all sides, they revealed their true nature, broke their promised and joined the belligerent polytheists.

8- The consequences of the Battle against Banu Qurayza.
By eliminating Banu Qurayza, the influence of the Jews in Medina and its outskirts was completely eradicated. Medina became a safe haven to the Muslims. All threats that could otherwise disturb its peace and security were eliminated. The status and prestige of the Muslims were reinforced in the hearts of their enemies, and those who previously regarded them lightly would, now, only talk about their strength and might. The Muslims were now able to safely go out of Medina to spread the "light of Allah on earth." Quraysh and its allies became aware that the Islamic call had assumed dominance and power that would transcend borders and overcome barriers. The Prophet gave his followers the good tidings that Quraysh would no longer be able to invade Medina after what happened in the Battle of the Trench.

Al-Bukhari narrated on the authority of Sulieman bin Sard, he said: "When the Prophet expelled the Ahzab out of Medina, I heard him say: 'Now, we can invade them, but they cannot invade us: We march to them.'"[58]

Later events had proven the truth of what the Prophet said.

The Killing of Abu Rafi Salam bin Abi Al-Haqiq

After eliminating Banu Qurayza because of their treachery, the Muslims pursued all those who were known for their animosity towards Islam. At the head of those Jews who harmed the Muslims was Abu Rafi Salam bin Abi Al-Haqiq who supported Ghatafan and other polytheists from among the Arabs by providing them with a lot of money to fight the Prophet. He was among the most prominent among the Jews who worked to join various parties (Ahzab) together to eradicate the Islamic call and its followers.
The competition to do what was good reached its peak between two tribes: the Aws and the Khazraj. Whenever one of those tribes did something pleasing to the Prophet, the other tribe would hasten to do something similar.

Ibn Ishaq said: "Muhammad bin Shihab said on the authority of Abdullah bin Ka'b bin Maalik, he said: "Allah had caused the two tribes: the Aws and the Khazraj compete like bulls [59] to please the Prophet. Whenever the Aws did something profitable to the Prophet or protected him from harm, the Khazraj would not become satisfied or content until they had done something similar. The Aws would say the same thing if the Khazraj did something beneficial or profitable to the Prophet. So, when the Aws helped in getting rid of Ka'b bin Al-Ashraf, the Khazraj insisted that they would have to do something similar. When they began thinking of a ferocious enemy to the Prophet like Ibn al-Ashraf, they determined that Salam bin Abi Al-Haqiq from Khaybar was such a man. They asked the Prophet's permission to kill him, and he granted them that permission. The Khazraj went out to him. There were five men in charge: Abdullah bin Atik, their chief, Masoud bin Sanan, Abdullah bin Anis, Abu Quttada Al-Harith bin Rub'i and Khuza'i bin Al-Aswad."[60]

Their mission to kill Abi Rafi was in the month of Ramadan in the sixth year of Hijra.

The story of his murder was reported in the authentic Sunna and in biographies. This is the story as recounted by Imam Bukhari. He said on the authority of Al-Bara' Ibn Azib:

"The Messenger of Allah sent some men from Al-Ansar to Abu Rafi, the Jew. He appointed Abdullah Ibn Atik as their chief. Abu Rafi used to plot against the Messenger of Allah to harm him. He was in a fortress in the land of Hijaz. They set out to him and approached his fortress at sun set when people were taking their cattle back to their sheds. Abdullah said to his companions: 'Sit here, and I will go to the gatekeeper and talk with him. Perhaps I can go inside.' When he came near the door, he pretended to be doing something so that he would not be identified as people were going in. When the porter saw him, he said: 'Abdullah! [61] If you want to go inside, you can go for I want to close the door.' When Abdullah and other people entered, he closed the door and hung the keys on a wedge. Ibn Atik said: 'There were people keeping his company at night to discuss different issues as he was the chief among the people of Khaybar. When these people were gone, I went upstairs to him. Every door I opened I would lock from the inside. I said to myself that even if people felt my presence, they would not get to me until I have killed him. I got to him while he was in a dimly lit place, and I was not able to know for sure where he was. I said: "Abu Rafi" to determine where he was. He said: 'Who is this?' I came close to his voice and hit him with the sword, perplexed. Abu Rafi yelled, so I stepped out of the house, but I didn't go far. I reentered as if I was trying to help, and I changed my voice. I said: 'what is that voice Abu Rafi?' He said: 'There is a man in the house who struck me with a sword.' Then Abdullah said: 'I hit him and severely injured him, but I didn't kill him.' Then, he said: 'I drove the pointed end of the sword in his stomach and it pierced all the way to his back. I knew that I killed him. I started opening the doors one by one. As I descended the stairs thinking that I reached the last step (since he had poor eye sight, according to some accounts), I fell and broke my leg, so I wrapped it in a band, and sat at the door. I said to myself that I would not leave until I knew whether I killed him or not. When the rooster crowed, a mourner said: 'I mourn the death of Abu Rafi, the merchant of the people of Hijaz.' I rushed hurriedly to my companions and said: 'Hurry! Allah has killed Abu Rafi.' Then, I went to the Prophet and told him what happened. He said to me: 'Stretch your leg.' I did. He wiped my leg, and it was as though I never injured it. According to another story about Abu Atik: 'We came to the Messenger of Allah as he was at the top of a pulpit, and he said: 'You have been successful.' " [62]

There many other accounts that report the murder of Abu Rafi. Some claim that Abdullah ibn Anis or all five companions took part in the assassination plot. However, we prefer the account narrated by Al-Bukhari which states thar Abdullah Ibn Atik was the person who killed him since it is more verifiable than others. For this reason, the author of Explanation of the Worldly Talents said: "What is right was that it was Abdullah Ibn Atik who went into his house and killed him, as reported by Al-Bukhari."[63]

Al-Hafiz Ibn Hajar said: "This Hadith reveals many benefits: the permissibility of assassinating the polytheist who has been informed of the call yet perseveres in his disbelief, the acceptability of killing those who assist or help others against the Messenger of Allah through providing money or through offending or insulting, the acceptability of spying on opposing aggressive parties and using force and severity in fighting polytheists; the acceptability of being elusive and tenuous for the common good..."[64]

With the death of Abu Rafi, terror crept into the hearts of the Jews of Khaybar, and a big obstacle that had long irked the Muslims was removed. His death was a prelude to the conquest of Khaybar.

The Killing of Asir bin Razam

Asir bin Razam took over leading the Jews of Khaybar after the death of Abu Rafi bin Abi Al-Haqiq. Asir used to meet with Banu Ghatafan to make agreements and deals to secure their assistance when he went to war against the Muslims. He encouraged the Jews to fight, saying: "By God! Every time Muhammad marched towards the Jews, or sent some of his companions, he had caused harm to those he wanted to harm, but I will do to him what nobody else ever did." They asked: "What do you intend to do?" He said: "I will gather Ghatafan and other tribes and go to his own home. Nobody was ever attacked in his own home unless he lost something to his enemy." They said: "Great idea!" [65]

The threats of Asir bin Razam reached the Muslims. The Prophet sent Abdullah bin Rawahah with three other Muslims to get more news about Asir bin Razam.

It was during Ramadan when they marched towards him. When Abdullah bin Rawahah arrived to Khaybar, he went inside its walls without anybody noticing. He sent his comrades in different directions towards the fortresses to gather information concerning Asir bin Razam. They learned about his evil intentions towards the Muslims and that he was preparing to attack them.

They returned to the Prophet and informed him with what they saw and heard and said: "We left Asir bin Razam preparing his battalions to invade us." The Prophet judiciously decided to send Asir bin Razam a delegate to invite him to come to Medina to negotiate what he wanted with him. He sent three men headed by Abdullah bin Rawahah. They arrived at Khaybar in the month of Shawwal in the six year of Hijra.

When they came to Asir bin Razam, they said: 'Are we safe to tell you what we have come to say?' He said: 'Yes, and am I also safe?'

They said: 'Yes.' Then, they said: 'The Messenger of Allah sent us to appoint you as head of Khaybar and do good to you.' He welcomed that suggestion and consulted some Jews, but they opposed him. However, he went with thirty Jews along with the Muslims. When they had reached "Alqarqara,"[66] Asir regretted that he was going in the direction of Medina. He unsheathed his sword intending to deceive and harm the Muslims. When Abdullah bin Aneis realized that he was reaching for his sword, he said: "Traitor! Oh, enemy of Allah!" He hit him with his sword and cut off his leg. Then Asir hit Abdullah bin Aneis. All Muslims hit the Jews who were with them and killed them all except for one Jew who fled. None of the Muslims was injured. They returned to the Prophet and told him what happened with Asir and his men. The Prophet said: "Allah had saved you from the wrongdoing people."

With the death of Asir bin Razam, the Muslims eliminated a Jewish tyrant who demonstrated treachery and betrayal and wanted to invade them in their very fortresses. He had thus reaped the fruit of his own perfidious and deceitful labor.

The Battle of Khaybar

1- What the Muslims accomplished by eliminating Banu Qurayza.
2- The good tidings of the Noble Qur'an concerning the conquest of Khaybar.
3- The reasons that caused the Muslims to invade Khaybar.
4- The Prophet leads the Muslims to invade Khaybar.
5- The Muslims' arrival to Khaybar, their battles and their conquest.
6- How the Prophet dealt with the people of Khaybar: dividing their wealth.
7- The conquest of Khaybar was by force; it was not a reconciliation.
8- The Prophet's marriage with Safia bint Huyay bin Akhtab.
9- The story of the poisoned lamb that was presented to the Prophet in Khaybar.
10- After the Battle of Khaybar.
11- Expelling the Jews out of the Arabian Peninsula.

1- After eradicating Banu Qurayza because of their treachery, the Muslims felt safe and secure. They started going out of Medina to safely spread

Islam among the tribes. However, there were two malicious and bitter enemies remaining: the people of Mecca and the Jews of Khaybar.

As for the people of Mecca, the Prophet was able- thanks to his judicious and wise policies, his far-sighted vision, and calculating and shrewd mentality- to hold Peace of Hudaybiyyah with them. About the Hudaybiyyah treaty, Al-Auhari said: "No other conquest in Islam was better than this." According to this peace treaty, people became comfortable and trusted each other. Accordingly, the Muslims activities became widespread in every aspect, and they spread their religion in all parts of the Arab Peninsula, and a great number of the polytheists accepted and entered Islam.

As for the Jews of Khaybar, the Prophet got ready to fight them in the month of Mahram in the seventh year of Hijra approximately 20 days after his return from Hudaybiyyah.

The Prophet hastened to invade the Jews of Khaybar immediately after the Hudaybiyyah treaty so as not to give them the chance to seek the assistance of the other warring tribes. The element of surprise that the Prophet adopted in this invasion is considered one of the most important military strategies that modern warriors rely on at the present time.

2- In Sura Al Fath (sura 48) which was revealed after the Hudaybiyyah treaty, there are numerous promises to those who attended the Hudaybiyyah treaty and the spoils they would receive for their loyalty to their religion: "Those who stayed behind will say, when you believers set out to take the spoils of war, "Let us accompany you." They wish to change Allah's promise. Say, O Prophet, "You will not accompany us. This is what Allah has said before." They will then say, "In fact, you are driven by jealousy against us!" (Qur'an 48:15) The truth is: they can hardly comprehend." It was the spoils of Khaybar that were referenced here.

The meaning of the noble verse is: Those who stayed behind and did not attend the Hudaybiyyah treaty because of their shaky and tenuous faith and their preoccupation with family and business matters will say: 'Fellow Muslims, let us follow you to the conquest of Khaybar.' By saying this, they want to change Allah's promise because the Almighty promised bestow the spoils of Khaybar solely on the people of Hudaybiyyah; none of those who failed to be present would have a share in them. Then the Almighty commanded His Messenger to reject their request to go out with him. He said: "You will not accompany us. This is what Allah has said before." (Q 48:15) Which means, do not allow them to go out with you to Khaybar since they did not go to Hudaybiyyah, for Allah had told you before returning from Hudaybiyyah to Medina that Khaybar's spoils were for those who were present and witnessed Hudaybiyyah, not for those who not there.

Then, the Almighty recounted that they would respond saying; "They will then say, "In fact, you are driven by jealousy against us!" (Q 48:15) This means that those who did not attend would say that Allah did not command us not to go out, but you wanted to keep

Khaybar's spoils all to yourselves. Therefore, you prevented us from going out with you. Allah therefore responded to them, saying: "they can hardly comprehend." (Q 48:15) Which means: It is not as these people claimed, for they did not attend Hudaybiyyah because of their ignorance about many of the issues pertaining to religion, for if they really comprehended, they wouldn't have been absent and would have joined the Messenger of Allah.

There are other verses in which the Almighty promised those believers who pledged to die at the Hudaybiyyah treaty to reward them with a victory at hand, and bestow upon them many favors and blessings. The almighty said: "Indeed, Allah was pleased with the believers when they pledged allegiance to you O Prophet under the tree. He knew what was in their hearts, so He sent down serenity upon them and rewarded them with a victory at hand, and many spoils of war they will gain. For Allah is Almighty, All-Wise. Allah has promised you believers abundant spoils, which you will gain, so He hastened this truce for you. And He has held people's hands back from harming you, so it may be a sign for the believers, and so He may guide you along the Straight Path." (Qur'an 48:18-20)

It is the conquest of Khaybar after leaving Hudaybiyyah that was meant by "a victory at hand." And "many spoils" was a reference to the spoils of Khaybar, and His words "hastened this" was a reference to the fact that Allah granted Khaybar's spoils a short time after the peace agreement at Hudaybiyyah.

The meaning of these noble verses is: Allah was pleased with the people of Hudaybiyyah who pledged allegiance to the Prophet. He knew the sincerity of their hearts and granted them peace and serenity. He richly rewarded them for their loyalty and obedience by conquering Khaybar after concluding Hudaybiyyah. In place of the spoils of Mecca, He abundantly compensated them by granting them the rich and precious spoils of Khaybar. Indeed, Allah's vengeance is magnificent and mighty, and His prudence in managing His creation is profound and unfathomable.

Then, Allah promised them with many spoils that they will get in the near future: "Allah has promised you believers abundant spoils, which you will gain, so He hastened this truce for you. And He has held people's hands back from harming you, so it may be a sign for the believers, and so He may guide you along the Straight Path." (Qur'an 48:20)

And in another verse in Sura Al-Fath, there is another promise that they would be victorious at Khaybar: "Indeed, Allah will fulfil His Messenger's vision in all truth: Allah willing, you will surely enter the Sacred Mosque, in security—some with heads shaved and others with hair shortened—without fear. He knew what you did not know, so He first granted you the triumph at hand." (Qur'an 48:27)

That is, Allah had promised you abundant spoils that you will be able to get from the polytheists at specific times. However, he had hastened the spoils of Khaybar, and prevented the Jews and other enemies from invading the city after leaving to Hudaybiyyah to thank Him and to understand that all of these blessings were evidence, a sign, of His protection and to guide you along the straight path.

“A victory at hand” is the conquest of Khaybar, as interpreters have suggested. And the meaning is:
The Almighty fulfilled the vision of His Messenger, i.e., safely entering the Sacred Mosque with his companions, unafraid of the polytheists, some with heads shaved and others with their hair shortened. “He knew what you did not know.” (Q 48:27) That is, the Almighty knew what was best for you. That is why, He did not allow you to go to Mecca that year because He did not want to see you sorrowful or in disgrace. Therefore, He allowed another conquest, i.e., that of Khaybar and the Hudaybiyyah Treaty before entering the Sacred Mosque which He promised in their Prophet’s vision.

These noble verses entailed promises to the believers that the conquest of Khaybar was bound to take place at their hands and they would benefit many blessings and abundant riches from it. They optimistically and confidently marched to it with their Prophet with hearts filled with faith that victory was theirs as Allah-whose promises are always truthful-had pledged.

3- The reasons that caused the Muslims to invade Khaybar:

A- From Khaybar came the Jewish delegate that went out to form parties to fight the Muslims in the Battle of the Trench. Had the Muslims not punished the Jews of Khaybar after the failure of Al-Ahzab, they would have probably tried some other time in the future. It was the judicious and wise policy for the Muslims to humiliate and break them once and for all.

B- After the defeat of Al-Ahzab, the Jews of Khaybar did not try to change their conduct and adjust their policies with the Muslims. On the contrary, they started making alliances with Ghatafan and Arab nomads to form a new front to fight the Muslims another time.

C- After eradicating Banu Qurayza, the Jews of Khaybar were angry. They sent delegates with money to Medina to pay ransoms for the women and children of Banu Qurayza. Then, they gathered together and decided to form an army made up of their own people along with the Jews of Wadi al-Qura وادي القرى and Wadi Taima تيماء to march to Medina while it was empty of its people because of the Hudaybiyyah Treaty to avenge Banu Qurayza. Asir bin Razam (whose death story was mentioned before) volunteered to lead this army.

D- After the Hudaybiyyah Peace Treaty, the Muslims became trusting of the people of Mecca and the southern parts of the Arabian Peninsula. However, the existence of the Jews of Khaybar in the northern part of Medina meant that the security of Medina was tenuous, for Hercules (Heraclius) could seek their assistance to fight the Muslims. It was certain that they would accept his request to avenge themselves against the Muslims whenever the opportunity presented itself.

These were the most important reasons that prompted the Prophet to wage war against the Jews of Khaybar to eradicate them and make sure they had no power left in them in the Arabian Peninsula. This way the Islamic call would enjoy peace, security and stability.

There are numerous Hadiths in the authentic Sunna concerning the Battle of Khaybar. Imam Bukhari narrated thirty Hadith related to this battle, as Ibn Hajar had mentioned. These Hadiths revolved around the events, incidents and the various other matters that had taken place in that battle. We will mention anything that is related to our present research in the appropriate place, Allah willing.

4- The Prophet leads the Muslims to invade Khaybar:

The Prophet left Numaila bin Abdullah Al-Laithi in charge in Medina. He went out with sixteen hundred of his companions: two hundred horsemen and the rest were footmen or riding camels. Those who did not attend the Hudaybiyyah Treaty came and proposed to march with him to Khaybar to share in the spoils, but he rejected that and told them they can come as volunteers, but they would not take any of the spoils.

Thanks to the Prophet's judicious policy, he deliberately made sure that Ghatafan was unable to provide assistance to the Jews, so went with his army to a valley called "Al-Raja'" lies between Ghatafan and Khaybar. The tribe of Ghatafan thought that the Muslim army was about to surround them, so they stayed indoors and did not dare assist the Jews of Khaybar. The Prophet's plan to isolate the Jews of Khaybar from their polytheist's allies proved successful.

Ibn Ishaq said: "When the Messenger of Allah left Medina on the way to Khaybar, he passed by "A'ser," [67] He built a mosque on the road to Khaybar there. Then, he came with his army to a valley called "Al-Raja'." He settled there between Khaybar and Ghatafan to prevent them from providing Khaybar with provisions. I was informed that when Ghatafan heard that the Prophet was heading to Khaybar, they went out to incite the Jews against him. When they had marched for a while, they heard sounds behind them and thought that the Muslims were pursuing them. They turned on their heels and remained indoors and left matters alone between the Messenger and Khaybar." [68]

In order to make their journey to Khaybar less arduous, the Prophet allowed Amer ibn Al-Akwa' to recite poetry to make the caravan march quickly and enthusiastically.

Imam al-Bukhari narrated on the authority of Salama bin Al-Akwa', he said: "We marched with the Prophet to Khaybar at night. One of the men said to Amer bin Al-Akwa'; 'Let us hear some of your "trifles." [69] Amer was a poet, and so he recited some poetry:

Oh Allah! Had it not been for you,
We would not have been guided, given charity or prayed,
Forgive us our errors and wrong doings

And make our feet firm when we meet the enemy,
Bestow tranquility upon us and give us peace,
They have attacked and wronged us.
And they wish to tempt us away from our faith
But help us remain firm and steadfast.

Amer was killed on the day of Khaybar.[70]

5- The Muslims' arrival to Khaybar, their battles and their conquest.

The Jews had fortified their lands and divided them to three areas, each consisting of a number of fortresses. These areas were Natat, Al-Shaq, and Al-Kateeba. Among the fortresses of Al-Natat were Ibn Muadh fortress, Na'em Fortress (soft port) and Al-Zubeir castle. Among the Al-Shaq fortresses were the fortress of Abi and Al-Nizar fortress. Among the fortresses of Al-Kateeba were Al-Qumus fortress, Al-Wateeh fortress and Al-Salalem fortress (which was the fortress of bin Abi al-Haqiq).[71]

The Jews had built these fortified strongholds on elevated areas to be safe from the raids of Arab nomads and to have the ability to defend themselves from the inside by shooting arrows and darts (and other projectiles). They also used them to store their grains, their money and everything that was valuable to them. During times of danger and uncertainty, they used to live on the provisions they stored in their fortresses. They strengthened their fortresses and made them sturdier after their brothers- Banu Qaynuqa, Banu Al-Nadir and Banu Qurayza who used to live in Medina and its outskirts- were disgracefully conquered and defeated.

However, these strong fortresses were of no use. When the Prophet approached these fortresses and the Muslims saw them with their eyes, the Prophet asked his companions to stand still, and they entreated the Almighty, saying: "O Allah, Lord of the heavens and what they overshadow, Lord of the earth and what they lower, Lord of the devils and what they lead astray, and Lord of the winds and what they produce. We ask You for the good of this village and the good of what is in its people and the good of what is in it; and we seek refuge in You from its evil and the evil of its people and the evil of what is in it. Let us proceed in the name of Allah." [71a]

In the early morning, the prophet and his companions progressed towards the fortresses of Khaybar at the time when its Jews were leaving their homes with their sweepers [72] and sacks to their fields. Surprised to see the Muslims heading towards them, they turned on their heels and headed in panic to their fortresses, shouting in horror and alarm: Muhammad and Al-Khamis.[73]

Muhammad exploited that horror that overtook the Jews to animate and embolden his comrades to fight and to mitigate and lessen the strength of the Jews of Khaybar. He said: "Allahu Akbar! Khaybar has been destroyed. When we camp at the courts of people, the morning of those who have been warned will be bad." The two Sheikhs narrated on the authority of Anis that the Messenger of Allah came to Khaybar at night. Whenever he came to people at night, he would not attack them until morning. When morning came, the Jews went out with their sacks and other instruments. When they saw him, they shouted, saying: 'Muhammad and Al-Khamis (the army).' Muhammad said: "When we camp at the courts of people, the morning of those who have been warned will be bad." [74]

The Muslims stood in front of the fortresses of Khaybar with hearts filled with Allah's assurance of victory. They were standing close to Al-Natat fortress. Al-Habab bin Al-Munther said: "Messenger of Allah! I have knowledge of the people of Al-Natat: no people can shoot far targets and more accurately better than them. They are on high hills, and that would help them shoot better at us. I think it would be better to move to another location." The Prophet moved to another location between the people of Khaybar and Ghatafan and which, at the same time- faces the fortresses of Al-Natat.

The Prophet built a mosque in that place where he prayed throughout his stay at Khaybar. Then he ordered his men to cut down the palm trees of the Jews of the Al-Natat fortress to force them to come out to fight. The Muslims cut down a number of those trees, and they stopped when he told them to.

As for the Jews, when they saw that the Muslims surrounded them and cut down their trees in front of their eyes, they consulted Salam Ibn Mushkim, their chief. He asked them to place their money and children in the Al-Wateeh and Al-Salalem fortresses and to put their ammunition in the Na'em Fortress. He also suggested that the warriors and fighters enter the Al-Natat fortress. They followed his suggestions, and he entered with them urging them to fight to the very end to defend themselves and protect their money.

After the Muslims strict and tight siege of the Al-Natat Fortress, the Jews came out without going too far away from it since, due to their craving for life, they hate fighting in open fields. As described by the Almighty: "they would not dare fight against you except from within fortified strongholds or from behind walls." (Q 59:14) The Muslims seized the chance of their being away from their strongholds and attacked them. The two parties fought a deadly fight near Al-Natat fortress. The Prophet fought ferociously riding on a horse called "Al-Zareb," wearing armor.

The Muslims fought the people of Al-Natat for seven consecutive days during which the Jews were fighting close to their fortress, not venturing away from it. When vanquished, they would return to their fortress and lock their gates. During the Muslims' besiege of the Al-Natat fortress, Salam Ibn Mushkim, the chief of the Jews of Khaybar, died. Al-Harith Ibn Abi Zeinab became their leader. He stepped out of the Na'em Fortress (one of the strongholds in the area of Al-Natat), and he wanted a duel against the Muslims. Banu Khazraj dissuaded him from this idea, and then forced him flee. The Muslims continued their tight siege of the Na'em fortress, while the Jews zealously defended themselves aware that their defeat in this battle meant the eradication of their existence in the Arabian Peninsula.

After ferocious battles between the Muslims and the Jews around the Na'em fortress, the Prophet brought his comrades the good tidings that the conquest would soon be near at the hands of a man who was loved by Allah and His Messenger.

Al-Bukhari narrated on the authority of Sahl Ibn Saad, he said: "On the Day of Khaybar, The Messenger of Allah said: 'Tomorrow I will give the banner to a man who loves Allah and His Messenger, and whom Allah and His Messenger love. Allah will grant victory at his hands.' So, the people spent the night wondering [75] which of them would have it. When the morning came, they went to the Messenger of Allah. Each one was hoping that he would be the one to get it. The Prophet said: 'Where is Ali bin Abi Talib?' They said: 'He complains about his eyes.' So, the Prophet asked them to send for him. So, they sent for him, and he was brought. The Prophet spat in his eyes. He prayed for him and he was healed, as if he had no ailment. Thereupon, the Prophet gave him the banner and said: 'When you go to their quarters, invite them to Islam, and inform them of what they are obligated to do regarding the Almighty. By Allah, if Allah would but guide one man through you is better for you than red camels.'" [76]

This sagacious and prudent advice that the Prophet gave to Imam Ali shows that the Prophet did not fight the people of Khaybar to acquire their wealth and money; rather, he fought them for challenging Allah and His Messenger. Had they accepted the truth and abandoned their animosity towards Islam and the Muslims, they would have lived in peace and serenity. However, they were blinded and deafened to the truth, and Allah had therefore deprived them of His favors and denied them His blessings.

Ali bin Abi Talib invited them to Islam, but they rejected the invitation. The Jew Marhab came out of their fortresses wearing armor and brandishing two swords trying to make a show of his might and saying:

Khaybar knows that I am Marhab
Wielding weapons, a proven hero,
I stab sometimes and strike at others,
Even when mighty forces draw near,
No one can outweigh what I do,
Those who know stay away.

So, Ali bin Abi Talib went to meet him. A fierce fight ensued between the two. It ended with Marhab's perdition. It was said that Muhammad ibn Maslama was the one who killed him to avenge himself on the death of his brother Mahmoud who was killed as a result of throwing a rock on him during the siege of the fortress. However, most biographies state that it was Ali bin Abi Talib who killed him.

Marhab's brother, Yassir, emerged, and Al-Zubeir Ibn Al-A'waam went out to confront him. Safiyya, mother of Al-Zubeir, had joined the army to help. She was worried about her son, but the Prophet assured her that her son would kill Yassir: "Your son will kill him, Allah willing." Indeed, Al-Zubeir killed Yassir, the Jew.

Fierce fights between the Muslims and the Jews resumed. The culminated in the conquest of the Na'em fortress (one of the areas of Al-Natat) at the hand Imam Ali after killing Al-Harith Ibn Ani Zeinab, the leader.

After the fall of the Na'em fortress, the Muslims headed towards Al-Sa'b Ibn Muadah. Ferocious fighting ensued around the fortress. Some of the Muslims were extremely worn out after their provisions were depleted. Some of them went to Muhammad and said: "We are exhausted, and we have nothing more to offer." Muhammad raised his hands towards the heavens and said: "Allah! You know their condition. They are weary, and I have nothing to offer them. Open unto them the richest fortress that has abundant food and sustenance." [77]

Allah gave the Muslims the fortress of Al-Sa'b Ibn Muadah. No other fortress had as much food and provisions as that fortress.

After that, the Muslims surrounded Al-Zubeir fortress. It was such a formidable fortress to the extent that the Muslims were unable to conquer it despite the strenuous efforts they made until they cut off the water from it. The Jews were thus forced to go out to fight, but they were incapable of withstanding the might of the Muslims. They fled to the Al-Shaq region. Thus, the Muslims were able to conquer the Natat area which comprised the Na'em, Al-Sa'ab and Al-Zubeir fortresses, which were among Khaybar's strongest and richest fortresses.

Then, the Muslims headed towards the Al-Shaq area and surrounded it. This area included the fortresses of Abi and Al-Nizar. The Jews forcefully defended them, but they eventually fell to the hands of the Muslims.

The Prophet ordered his companions to march to the Al-Kateeba area which contained Al-Qamous, Al-Wateeh and Al-Salalem fortresses. The Muslims started by surrounding Al-Qamous fortress which was one of Khaybar's most important fortresses. The Abi Al-Haqiq clan, the richest and most prominent leaders of the Jews, lived there. The Muslims tightly besieged that fortress until the Jews were forced run away and seek refuge in the Al-Wateeh and Al-Salalem fortresses. However, despair found its way to their hearts when the Muslims surrounded them there. They realized that there was no way out except through submitting. They proposed reconciliation, and the Prophet accepted. He stipulated that they should not conceal any of their wealth and possessions; otherwise, agreements will be null and void.

Thus, Khaybar's fortresses fell into the hands of the Muslims. Their people submitted to the conditions and rulings of the Prophet.

6- How the Prophet dealt with the people of Khaybar: dividing their wealth.

The lands of Khaybar were extensive and widespread. They abounded in gardens, orchards and farm lands that had required many laborers to farm and work in them for a long time. Its people were the most experienced in benefiting from these lands and using them to their advantage. As for the people of Medina, who were also essentially farmers, the Muslim army needed them to uphold Allah's word. Moreover, their own lands also needed their attention and efforts to till, farm and use them. Therefore, the Prophet accepted the reconciliation with the people of Khaybar, and he allowed them to stay in their lands provided that they gave half of their product to the Muslims.

Biographies and Sunna books related the way that the Prophet treated the Jews of Khaybar. Among these reports was what was narrated by Nafi' on the authority of Ibn Umar. He said: "The Messenger of Allah fought the people of Khaybar until he forced them to take refuge in their palaces. He had control of their crops, their land, and their palm trees. They agreed with him to evacuate their land and they would only have what their camels could carry. and the Messenger of Allah told them not to leave. However, they should report all they had and hide or conceal nothing. If they did, they had no obligation to bind them and no covenant to comply with. However, they concealed a sack containing money and jewelry for Huyay ibn Akhtab, which he had carried with him to Khaybar when Banu Al-Nadir was expelled. The Messenger of Allah said to Kinanah ibn Al-Rabi', husband of Safiyya daughter of Huyay ibn Akhtab, who had the treasure of Banu Al-Nadir: "What did Huyay do with the money he brought with him from al-Nadir?" He said, "It was spent on the wars." He said the time was close and the money was more than that." A Jew came to the Messenger of Allah and said, "I saw Kinanah going to this slum every morning." The Messenger said to Kinanah: "If we found this money hidden by you, you will be killed." The Messenger of Allah ordered to dig, and some of the treasure was concealed there. The Messenger ordered to kill him and take the women of Abi Al-Haqqiq and their children captives."

The Prophet wanted to expel them from Khaybar. They asked him to stay to till and improve the land. Since the Prophet did not have those who could attend to the land, he gave them Khaybar in return for a portion of all its fruits and produce. He said to them: "We will let you stay with our conditions."

Abdullah ibn Rawaha used to go to them every year and evaluate[78] the price of the products and to guarantee them half. They complained to the Messenger of Allah, about the severity of his pricing, and they wanted to bribe him. He said: "O enemies of Allah, do you want to feed me illicit things? By Allah, I have come to you from the people I love the most, and you are the most hateful and despicable people to me. My hatred for you and my love for him would not make me unfair to you.' They said: 'By this the heavens and the earth were established.' [79]

Imam Ibn Al-Qayyim said: "The Prophet divided the spoils of Khaybar into thirty-six shares, adding up to one hundred shares for each share , so it was three thousand and six hundred shares. Muhammad and the Muslims had half of that, which was one thousand and eight hundred shares, and he allocated the other half for unexpected calamities and the unforeseen affairs that could come upon Muslims. It was divided into one thousand and eight hundred shares because it was a gift from Allah to the people of Al-Hudaybiyyah, those who witnessed it and those who were absent, and they were one thousand four hundred, and they had with them two hundred horses , each horse having two shares, so it was divided into one thousand eight hundred shares. The only one who was absent from Khaybar from the people of Hudaybiyyah was Jafar ibn Abdullah, and the Prophet gave him the same shares that he gave to those who attended it.[80]

7- The conquest of Khaybar was by force; it was not a reconciliation.

Some researchers believe that Khaybar was taken partly by force and partly peacefully because in the Al-Wateeh and Al-Salalem fortresses in the Al-Kateeba region agreements were made. The Prophet divided the spoils that were acquired by force between the army and the spoilers, while he allocated what they acquired through agreements to unexpected events and what he might need to run the Muslims' affairs.

What seems to be true and most scientists agree on was that all the lands of Khaybar were conquered and taken by force. Anis ibn Malik said: "The Messenger of Allah invaded Khaybar and acquired it by force, and he took its people captive." [81]

Ibn Ishaq said: "I asked Ibn Shihaab Al-Zuhari, and he told me that the Messenger of Allah took over Khaybar by force after a fight."

And Ibn Abdu al- Bar said that the truth about the land of Khaybar was that it was all taken by force, and that the Messenger of Allah divided all of its lands between the spoilers: horsemen and footmen who were the people of Al-Hudaybiyyah.

Imam Ibn Al-Qayyim said: "When we looked deeply into biographies and invasions, we found that Khaybar was conquered and was taken by force, for if it was taken through reconciliation, why would the Messenger want to expel them. When he decided to expel them, they told him that they were more knowledgeable and experienced to take care of it. They asked to stay to take care of the land, till and improve it in return for a portion of its produce. This is clear evidence that it was taken by force." Then he said: "A lot of fighting took place, as it is known. If there was reconciliation, the lands and the wealth would have remained in the possession of the owners since this is the case with reconciliations. The unquestionable truth then is that it was taken by force. The imam has the choice to divide or not divide it, or divide part of it and not the other part." [82]

8- The Prophet's marriage with Safia bint Huyay bin Akhtab.

Numerous reports were recounted concerning the Prophet's marriage with Safia bint Huyay bin Akhtab. They mostly report that after the Muslims had conquered the Al-Qamous fortress, Bilal-may Allah be pleased with him- came to the Prophet with two women: Safia and her cousin. Safia was recently married to Kinanah ibn Al-Rabi' ibn Abi Al-Haqiq. The Prophet asked Bilal to accompany them to a certain place. While in his company, Bilal passed by the Jews who were killed. Safia's cousin cried bitterly and hurled dust over her head. When the Prophet learned about this, he was angry with Bilal.

He said: "Do you have no compassion, Bilal, that you pass by the women's killed husbands?" The Prophet invited Safia to Islam, and she converted. He freed her and married her, and made her emancipation his dowry. They consummated their marriage on his way to Medina from Khaybar. He saw her face glowing and asked about it. She said: "Messenger of Allah, I saw before you came to us as if the moon had moved from its place and fell into my lap, and by Allah I do not remember anything about you, so I related that to my husband, and he slapped me on the face. He said: "This is because you desire this king of Hijaz, Muhammad."

On the night when the Prophet was with Safia, Abou Ayyoub Khalid ibn Zeid spent the night going around the Prophet's place with his drawn sword to protect the him. When Abou Ayyoub saw the Prophet in the morning, he said: "Allahu Akbar." The Prophet asked: "What is the matter, Ayyoub?" He said that he was worried about him on account of the woman whose father, husband and people were killed and who was a disbeliever only a short time ago. The Prophet laughed and said: "May Allah protect Abou Ayyoub as spent the night protecting me."

Imam Al-Bukhari narrated on the authority of Ins ibn Malik who said: "The prophet stayed for three nights between Khaybar and Medina. He was with Safia, and he invited the Muslims to a banquet to celebrate. There was no bread or meat, only dates. The Muslims said: "One of the mothers of the Believers, or what his right hand possessed (a slave)?" They said: "If he extended the Hijab over her face, then she is one of the mothers of the believers. If not, then she is one of slaves. When he departed, he stepped behind her and extended the veil over her, so they were certain that she was one of the Mothers of the believers." [83]

9- The story of the poisoned lamb that was presented to the Prophet in Khaybar.

Malice and envy of the Prophet and the Muslims had completely consumed the Jews of Khaybar. Never did they expect that one day the Muslims will conquer and take their land and that they would submit and succumb to their conditions and rulings. Their fortresses were formidable and strong, their men were powerful, affluent and influential. Therefore, when the Muslims conquered and took over Khaybar's forts, Zeinab bint Al-Harith, Salam Mishkim's wife, wanted to hurt the Prophet. She sent a poisoned lamb to him as a present. When he ate from it, he felt the poison, and he spit it out. Bixr ibn al-Bara' ate from it, and he died a short time afterwards. The Prophet asked to bring the woman who placed the poison and asked her: "Why did you do that?" She said: "I have heard from my people what you all but know. That is why I did what I did. I said: 'If you were a king, we would be relieved. But if you were a prophet, then you would know.' The Prophet said: 'Allah would not set you against me.'"

There are reports that the Prophet ordered to kill her. Other reports suggest that he pardoned her. Researchers agree that he did not kill her right away. When Bixr ibn Al-

Bara' died, he killed her as a punishment for what she did. The Prophet then isolated himself to recover from the effect of the poison.

Al-Bukhari relates on the authority of Abu Hurayra: "When Khaybar was opened (Vanquished by Muslims), and the Prophet was content that it was under Muslim control, a poisoned lamb was sent to him as a present. After the Prophet took a bite, he spit it out and said: "Bring me all the Jews who were here." They did. Thereupon the Prophet said: "I will ask you a question. Are you going to be truthful in your response?" The Jews said: "Yes, father of Al-Qasim (Abou Qasim)." The Prophet asked: "Who is your father?" They responded and told him who their father was. The Prophet said, "You are lying because your father is not whom you said he is." Al-Hafez son of Hagar said: "It is Israel, Jacob, son of Isaac, son of Ibrahim (Peace be upon him)." They said to the Prophet, "You have rightly said the truth." The Prophet asked again: "Will you be truthful in your response if I asked you another question?" They responded: "Yes, Abou Al-Qasim. Well! If we lied, you will know that we have lied to you just as you knew who our father was!" The Prophet asked: "Who are the people of Hell?" They responded saying: "We will be there for just a short while, but then you will follow us there to stay." The Prophet said to them: "We will never be there, but you will stay there in wretchedness and humiliation." He then asked them: "Will you be truthful if I asked you another question?" They responded in the affirmative. He asked: "Did you poison this lamb?" He was referring to the lamb that was brought to him, and they did not deny it. Again, they responded in the affirmative. So, he asked them: "What made you do such a thing?" They said: "We wanted to get rid of you if you were lying, but if you were truly a prophet it would not hurt you." [84]

With the conquest of Khaybar, the Muslims gained many spoils. Abdullah ibn Umar said: "We never had enough until we conquered Khaybar."[85] Aisha said: "At the conquest of Khaybar we said that now we will be satisfied with plenty of dates."[86]

10- After the Battle of Khaybar.

During the Muslims' besiege of the Al-Wateeh and Al-Salalem fortresses in Khaybar, the Prophet sent Maheesa ibn Maso'd to the Jews of Fidik to call them to Islam. Yousha' bin Younan was their leader. When they learned that the two fortresses had fallen in the hands of the Muslims, they sent to the Prophet to ask for reconciliation, a settlement according to which they would offer the Muslims half of their wealth. The Prophet accepted their proposal and he used the wealth of Fidik to spend on what he saw as appropriate and fitting as that money was not acquired by horsemen or footmen.

When the Prophet was through with Khaybar, he made preparations to go to Medina through Wadi al-Qura, which was a place close to Medina, inhabited by some Jews. When they heard that the Muslims were approaching, they got ready to fight. The Prophet invited them to accept Islam, but they rejected his invitation. The Muslims surrounded them for four days, but when they insisted on rejecting the call to Islam, the Prophet got his men ready for fighting. He gave the banner to Sa'd ibn Abada. One of the Jews from Wadi al-Qura came out to fight, but Al-Zubayr bin Al-Awwam killed him. Another Jew came out, but he was also killed. Then a third who was also killed. Then a group of Jews came out to fight, but Abou Dajana killed them consecutively. Eleven Jews from Wadi al-Qura were killed. Every time a Jew was killed, the Prophet would reiterate his call to accept Islam. He told them that they would be able save themselves and keep their money and fortresses. When the Jews of Wadi al-Qura realized that they were incapable of standing against the might of the Muslims, they surrendered at sunrise the following day. The Prophet took it by fighting force. The Muslims acquired a lot of their wealth and possessions. The Prophet divided the spoils among his comrades, and he left the land and palm trees to the Jews who would share some of the products with them. He left Amer ibn Sa'eed ibn al-As behind him in Wadi al-Qura. [87]

When the Jews of Taima[88] learned about the defeat of the Jews of Wadi al-Qura, they reconciled with the Prophet and accepted to pay the jizya. They stayed in their land, and the Prophet appointed Yazid ibn Abi Sefein- who converted to Islam on the day of its conquest- as a Wali to govern its affairs. After that, the Muslims returned to Medina. Fifteen Muslims fell as martyrs during these battles. Approximately one hundred Jews were killed. These battles lasted around two months in which the Muslims were outside Medina to defend and uphold the word of Allah.

11- The consequences of the conquest of Khaybar and other Jewish villages:

The battle of Khaybar completely eliminated the power of the Jews in the lands of Hijaz. All their influence and prestige and prestige in the Arabian Peninsula was eradicated. The Muslims became confident that their city became safe and secure on the northern border after the conquest of Khaybar. They also felt that the southern border of their city was safe after the Al-Hudaybiyyah Treaty. The dissentions and discords- that the Jews used to stir in various parts of the Arabian Peninsula to trap the Muslims- ceased. Islam kept on spreading in that land which the Jews inhabited for some time and consumed and took advantage of its wealth without even thanking Allah for His favors. The enemies of the Islamic call came to the realization that Islam had taken their place under the sun and its light would be spreading to illuminate the horizon. The Prophet showed tolerance to those Jews who did not openly display animosity and belligerence. He only demanded the Jews of Bahrein to pay the jizya. He also agreed that the Jews of Banu Gadiyya and Banu Oreid to pay the jizya. He asked Mu'ad ibn Jabal not to lure the Jews of Yemen away from their Judaism. He reconciled with the Jews of Muqtana and Banu Huneina in return for one fourth of the yield of their land, and he wrote an agreement with them. And when the Jews of Khaybar asked the Messenger for their Torah scrolls- that fell to the hands of the Muslims after the conquest of Khaybar- he accepted and gave them back. In this respect, Dr. Israel Wolfensohn says:

"The Jews appreciated what the Prophet did as he did not do any harm to their holy writings. He did not do what the Romans did when they conquered Jerusalem in 70 A.D., when they burned the Holy Books and trampled them under their feet. He did not do what the Christians did when they persecuted the Jews in Al-Andalus where they burned Torah scrolls. This was a huge difference between the conquerors that we mentioned and the Messenger of Islam." [89]

12- Expelling the Jews out of the Arabian Peninsula:

The Prophet continued his fair treatment to the Jews who did not try to harm Islam and the Muslims. However, before his death, he recommended that the Jews be expelled out of the Arabian Peninsula to prevent having two religions there. After the Prophet's death, Abou Bakr Al-Sidiiq acknowledged the same treatment that the Prophet followed. However, the Jews were expelled during the era of Umar bin Khataab in accordance with the recommendations of the Prophet and also because they committed some crimes against the Muslims. For instance, they assassinated one of the Ansar and threw his body in a well. They also attacked Abdullah bin Umar while he was asleep. Nafi' narrated on the authority of Ibn Umar, he said: "Al-Zubeir, Miqdad ibn Umar and I went to Khaybar to get our share of wealth. Someone attacked me while I was sleeping in my bed, and my hand was broken. In the morning, my companions asked who did that to me. I said I didn't know. They treated my hand, and they took me to Umar who said: 'People! That was the deed of the Jews.' Umar stood among the believers and said: 'The Messenger had instructed us to expel the Jews if we wanted to. They attacked Abdullah bin Umar and broke his hand as you know. Before that, they attached one of the Ansar. We have no doubt that they are our foes. So, if you have money in Khaybar, join me. I will expel them.' ...And he did.

When Umar expelled the Jews out of Khaybar, he rode along with the Muhajereen and Ansar. Jabaar ibn Sakher went out with him. He was the evaluator of the prices of the products in Medina. He made the necessary financial interactions, and Umar expelled them to the Levant.

Al-Bukhari talked in detail about Umar's expulsion of the Jews of Khaybar. He said that Abou Ahmad narrated on the authority of Muhammad ibn Yehia on the authority of ibn Umar, who said: "When the people of Khaybar broke the hand of Abdullah bin Umar, Umar said: 'The Messenger of Allah had an agreement with the Jews of Khaybar concerning the division of wealth.' He added: 'We acknowledge what Allah acknowledged you. When Abdullah bin Umar went to get his share, he was attacked and his arms and legs were broken. We have no enemies there except for them. They are our foes, and I see that we expel them.' When Umar had decided to do this, one of the children of Banu Al-Haqqiq came to him and said: 'Commander of the faithful! Would you expel us when Muhammad made an agreement with us concerning the division of wealth as a condition?' Umar said: 'Do you think that I forgot that the Messenger of Allah said that after your expulsion out of Khaybar, your conquests will be repeated night after night?' He said: 'This was a poor harvest from Abu al-Qasim.' Umar said: You lied, O enemy of Allah.' So, Umar evacuated them and gave them the value of the fruits they had: money, camels, and provisions such as saddlebags, ropes, and other things." [90]

In conclusion, the Jews lived in the Arabian Peninsula for hundreds of years. They ate of its yield and goodness and roamed its lands. Had they been peaceful towards the Islamic call, no killings or expulsions would have ever occurred. They were obstinate in their denial and rejection of Prophet Muhammad whom they knew as they knew their own children. They were thus worthy of condemnation and curses in this world and severe punishment and torture in the afterlife. Islam spread on this land after generations in which the Jews lived there as they pleased.

The lesson that we learn from these battles and the evacuations that followed is that the land is the Lord's and He gives it to whomsoever He wills. He does not take the land away from one group of people and give it to another randomly; rather, the community that shows ingratitude and ungratefulness would be denied these favors and blessings which will, in turn, be granted to those who are grateful and thankful.

This principle was applied fiercely on the Children of Israel when they disregarded the precepts and rulings of the Torah and followed their own whims and caprices. Life is an ebb and flow. A quick look at the history of mankind reveals that a nation may become prominent and dominant for a while. However, it is just like the waves of the sea that rise and then fall and gradually disappear and break along the shore. It might rise up and become dominant once again only to weaken, falter and fall a new.

The Children of Israel ruled and were prosperous for some time. Then, their power and authority were taken away from them. The young Islamic nation inherited this power and authority, a change for the good of humanity at large.

Had the Jews stayed in the Arabian Peninsula a thousand years more, they would have only enhanced its division and discord, and other nations would not have benefited from their being there. They may have been able to get more of the grains and fruits that they produce. Yet, with these, more corruption will ensue due to the usury, dissipation and intemperance that the Children of Israel are bound to export along their products. As for Islam, ever since the day it dawned in the Peninsula, it has been a message of faith and guidance; its truth and righteousness made it worthy of victory. [91]

Once again, the Jews reaped the fruits of their labor. They brought all of this to themselves. They were only expelled out of the Arabian Peninsula because of violating their covenants with the Muslims, fighting the Islamic call and rejecting the message of the Prophet. "Allah did not wrong the evildoers, but they wronged themselves." (Qur'an 11:101)

---

[1] Al-Zarqani said in his "Explanation of Talents..." that Banu Qaynuqa were a sect of Jews in Medina. Their houses were close to Bathan. They were the bravest among the Jews, the richest and the most intense in their jealous animosity. The Battle of Banu Qaynuqa was on a Saturday in the middle of the month of Shawwal. Vol., P. 45

[2] جلب is everything that is brought to the market to be sold.

[3] Ibn Hisham Sira (Biography), Vol. 2, P. 427.

[4] Explanation of Talents, Vol. 1, P. 456.

[5] Sura Al 'Imran: verses 12 & 13.

[6] Al-Kashshaaf Interpretation, Vol. 1, P. 296.

[7] الظل، originally, the word means a cloud. It is used here to refer to how the face of the Prophet changed color because of anger.

[8] الحاسر a reference to an unarmored man.
[9] History of al-Tabari, Vol. 2, P. 480.
[10] The Life of Muhammad by Muhammad Hassanein Haikal, P. 247.
[11] Explanation of Talents. We previously explained these verses in Chapter "The Methods that the Jews Used..." Vol. 1, P. 457.
[12] ذباب (Zobab) is a mountain close to Medina.
[13] History of al-Tabari, Vol. 2, P. 481.
[14] A county in the Levant
[15] From an article titled:" The Art of Besieging in the Battle of Banu Qaynuqa," Al-Azhar Magazine, Vol. 25, P. 563, By Mr. Muhammad Jamal el-Din Mahfouz.
[16] Ka'b bin al-Ashraf, a poet and orator. It was said that his father was from Banu Nadir, a sect of Banu Nibhan from Tay. His mother was a Jew, according to all researchers. From her he took his Judaism and fanaticism. He was one of the fiercest opponents to the Prophet and Muslims.
[17] Explanation of Talents by Al-Zarqani, Vol. 2, P. 8.
[18] Explanation of Talents by Al-Zarqani, Vol. 2, P. 8.
[19] Sahih Al-Bukhari, Chapter "The Murder of Ka'b bin al-Ashraf," Vol. 7, P. 131 (Munir al-Dimishqi Edition). Also, Sahih Muslim in the Book of Jihad and Expedition in chapter on "The murder of Ka'b bin al-Ashraf,' Vol. 3, P. 1452. Report by Muhammad Fouad Abdul Baqi.
[20] The Beginning and the End by Ibn Kathir, Vol. 4, P. 6 And Ibn Hisham Biography, Vol. 2, P. 131.
[21] Al-Sarim Al-Maslul alaa Shatim Al-Rasoul (the Unsheathed Sword) by Ibn Taymiyya, P. 71.
[22] Al-Sarim Al-Maslul alaa Shatin Al-Rasoul (the Unsheathed Sword) by Ibn Taymiyya, P. 71.
[23] Imam Ibn Taymiyya mentioned two reasons prior to this reason as justifications for killing those who ridicule or offend the Prophet. This is the third reason.
[24] Al-Sarim Al-Maslul alaa Shatim Al-Rasoul (the Unsheathed Sword) by Ibn Taymiyya, P. 90.
[25] Ibn Kathir (al-Sira Al-Nabawiyya/ The Biography of the Prophet), Vol. 3, P. 16, reported by Mustapha abdul Wahid/ Al-Halaby edition.
[26] Al-Nadir is the name of one of the Jewish tribes that inhabited Bathan Valley, two or three miles away from Medina. They had palm trees next to their residence.
[27] مبدأ الوقاية is one of the principles or laws of war. Military laws define it as the devices that a leader employs to ascertain the safety of his forces from the element of surprise and to hide the position of his forces from enemy sight.
[28] The tragedy of Raji' and Bir Ma'una took place after the Battle of Uhud. More than fifty of the Companions were tricked and killed while they were on their way to teach traitors Islamic laws and rituals.
[29] We had previously interpreted this verse in the chapter titled "The Methods that the Jews Used to Entrap Islam and Muslims" under "Their Attempt to Assassinate the Prophet."
[30] Futuh Al-Buldan by Al-Baladhuri: research by Dr. Salah Al-Majid, Vol. 1, P. 21, Maktabat Al-NahDa edition.
[31] Sahih Al-Bukhari, Chapter on Hadith Bani Al-Nadir, Vol. 5, P. 113.

[32] Al-Baidawi's Interpretation, P.560.
[33] Al-Bukhari in chapter "Hadith Bani Al-Nadir," Vol. 5, P. 112. Also, in Muslim in "Jihad and Expeditions," Vol. 3, P. 1367, Al-Halabi Edition.
[34] Ibn Kathir Interpretation, Vol. 4, P. 333.
[35] أفاء to return/ What Allah returns to somebody. Legally, this is a reference to what the Muslims took from the polytheists without fighting as happened in the case of Bani Al-Nadir.The word الغنيمة /Spoils, on the other hand, is a reference to what the Muslims take through fighting.
[36] Al-Bukhari in chapter "Jihad and Expeditions," Vol. 4, P. 46. Also, in Sahih Muslim's in chapter "The rulings of Alfii'," Vol. 2, P.1376.
[37] From "the Price of Israel," P. 35, by the Jewish writer Alfred Lilienthal, Dar Al-Ilm for Millions, Beirut.

[38] الجشيشة Kind of food (flour that is thickly ground)
[39] A sea filled with water. He likens the great number of men to a seaبحر طام
[40]Thin clouds that have no precipitation; void of water.
[41] الذروة والغاربis a reference to the back of a camel. When camels are upset and unfriendly, the owners would pat their tops until they calm down and become friendly again. It means he kept tricking (and cajoling) him until he succeeded.
[42] Ibn Hisham Biography, Vol. 3, P.235.
[43] Meaning: Speak to me in a way in which words cover the real meaning and nobody would understand except me.
[44] النهزة Seizing a chance.
[45] الخف والحافر is a reference to camels and horses
[46] Ibn Hisham Biography, Vol. 2, P. 241 (a summary).
[47] Al-Bukhari in chapter "The Prophet's Position Concerning Al-Ahzab," Vol. 5, P. 142. Also, in Muslim in the Book of "Jihad and Expeditions," Vol. 3, P. 1389.
[48] Al-Bukhari in chapter "The Prophet's Position Concerning Al-Ahzab," Vol. 5, P. 143. Also, in Muslim in the Book of "Jihad and Expeditions," Vol. 2, P. 1391.
[49] Ibn Hisham Biography, Vol. 2, P. 245.
[50] The writer of "Talents" said: It was as though Abu Lubaba had understood this from the Prophet's unresponsiveness concerning their proposal not to shed their blood. He knew that he would slaughter them when they accepted his ruling.
[51] History of Al-Tabari, Vol. 2. P. 585.
[52] Sura At-Tawbah
[53] A woman from Al-Ansar who was in charge of the injured in battle.

[54] Ibn Hisham Biography, Vol. 3, P. 250.
[55] Al-Bukhari in the Book of Jihad, in chapter "The Prophet's Position Concerning Al-Ahzab," Vol. 5, P. 143. Also, in Muslim in the Book of "Jihad and Expeditions, "in chapter "The Killing of Those Who Break their Covenant," Vol. 3, P. 1389. Study by Muhammad Fou'd Abdul Baqi.
[56] Meaning: He who is calling them to be slaughtered does not stop, but keeps on calling.
[57] Verses 9-27.
[58] Sahih Al-Bukhari: chapter "The Battle of the Trench," Vol. 5, P. 141.
[59] Both of them did their best to defend Islam.
[60] Ibn Hisham Biography, Vol. 3, P. 43. Al- Halabi edition.
[61] It was meant to call a person "Oh, you servant of Allah," not a call using his actual name.
[62] Sahih Al-Bukhari, Chapter "The Murder of Abu Rafi," Vol. 5, P. 117.
[63] Al-Zarqani's Explanation of the Worldly Talents, Vol. 2, P. 170.
[64] Al-Maghazi or (The Conquests of the Messenger), Vol. 7, P.242.
[65] Al-Zarqani's Explanation of the Worldly Talents, Vol. 2, P. 170.
[66] القرقرةis a place about six miles away from Khaybar.
[67] عصر A'ser: This is a mountain between Medina and Khaybar.
[68] Ibn Hisham Biography, Vol. 3, P. 344.
[69] الهناة A reference to something trivial or worthless, as though poetry was something not highly regarded because of the lies it may contain. However, some poetry is highly judicious and sublime.
[70]Fath al-Bari, Book by Ibn Hajar Al-Asqalani, Vol. 7, P. 326.
[71] History of the Arabs before Islam by Gawad Ali, Vol. 6. P. 155.
[71a] "Fortress of the Muslim (Hisn al-Muslim)," (97) Chapter: "Upon entering a town or village."
https://sunnah.com/hisn:208
[72] مساحة A sweeper made of iron.
[73] الخميس the army.
[74]Sahih Al-Bukhari in chapter "The Conquest of Khaybar," Vol. 5, P. 167. Also, in Muslim in the Book of "Jihad and Expeditions," Chapter "The Conquest of Khaybar," Vol, 3, P. 1426.
[75] يدوكون wandering who would be receiving the banner.
[76] Sahih Al-Bukhari, Chapter "The Battle of Khaybar." Vol. 5, P. 171.
[77] Ibn Hisham Biography, Vol. 3, P. 383.
[78] The person who evaluates the price of productsالخارص
[79] The Beginning and the End" by Ibn Kathir, Vol. 4, P. 199.
[80] Zad al-Ma'ad fi Huda Khair al-Ibad: by Ibn Qayyim, Vol. 2, P.136.
[81] Sahih Muslim, "The Book of Jihad," chapter "The Battle of Khaybar," Vol. 3, P. 1426.
[82] Zad al-Ma'ad fi Huda Khair al-Ibad: by Ibn Qayyim, Vol. 2, P.137.
[83] Sahih Al-Bukhari, chapter "The Battle of Khaybar," Vol. 5, P. 172.
[84] Sahih Al-Bukhari, chapter "If the Polytheists deceived the Muslims," Vol. 4, P. 121.
[85] Sahih Al-Bukhari, chapter "The Battle of Khaybar," Vol. 5, P. 178.
[86] Sahih Al-Bukhari, chapter "The Battle of Khaybar," Vol. 5, P. 178.
[87] Al-Zarqani's Explanation of the Worldly Talents, Vol. 2, P. 248.
[88] Taima is a town between Medina and the Levant.

[89] The History of the Jews in the Arabian Peninsula, P. 170.
[90] Sahih Al-Bukhari, chapter on "Conditions," Vol. 3, P. 238.
[91] jurisprudence of biography, Fiqh of Biography, by Muhammad Al-Ghazali, P. 265.

Chapter Five

Allah's Favors To The Children of Israel And Their Attitude Concerning Them

The reader of Allah's Book will clearly see numerous verses in many of its Suras (chapters) that recount in great detail the various favors that the Almighty Allah had bestowed on the Children of Israel. They mention how Allah favored them over other nations, rescued them from their enemies, sent them many prophets, and many more favors and blessings. Allah's favors should have prompted them to offer thanksgiving to their Creator who had granted them such exclusive favors and they should have cautioned them from wrongdoing and transgression since falling in sins while privileged with abundant favors would lead to severe punishment in this world and the hereafter. His favors should have also implanted in them morality, goodness and integrity to shun wrongdoing, for enjoying Allah's favors often leads a reasonable sensible man to march in a righteous and straightforward path to acquire even more favors: "And remember when your Lord proclaimed, 'If you are grateful, I will certainly give you more. But if you are ungrateful, surely My punishment is severe.'" (Qur'an 14:7) [1]

It is also noticeable that after the Almighty mentioned the favors He granted the Children of Israel, He followed that with their ungrateful thankless stance concerning those favors and the just punishment they received as a consequence for their wrongdoing and transgressions. It is as though the Almighty is portraying them as they go through three stages: favors and blessings, ungratefulness and unappreciativeness, and vengeance and penalty. In their story, there is a warning and a lesson to guide people to worship their Creator in truth and righteousness and give thanks to Him to avoid those punishments that had befallen the Children of Israel due to their injustices, denial and their rushing to sins and vices.

In this chapter, we will examine these noble verses that revolve around this topic. We will interpret them and show their exalted wisdom, their rigorous directives and what they reveal about the mannerisms of the Children of Israel.

We will begin with some verses from Sura Al-Baqarah which detailed a number of the favors that Allah lavishly bestowed on the Children of Israel and which also comprised some of the penalties that befell them on account of their obstinate rejection and disbelief. Among these verses are: "O children of Israel! Remember My favors upon you. Fulfil your covenant and I will fulfil Mine, and stand in awe of Me alone. Believe in My revelations which confirm your Scriptures. Do not be the first to deny them or trade them for a fleeting gain. And be mindful of Me. Do not mix truth with falsehood or hide the truth knowingly. Establish prayer, pay alms-tax, and bow down with those who bow down." (Qur'an 2:40-43)

These verses relate to others that preceded them: the Noble Qur'an reminded all the people with Allah's favors to incite them to worship Him in truth and believe what His Messenger brought. Among these favors were the creation of Adam and His munificence towards the angels. Then the noble verses reminded a group of disbelievers who were contemporary to the Prophet, i.e., the Children of Israel, to lure their hearts to faith and believe in Him and His Prophet and abandon their stubborn denial and rejection. He said: "O children of Israel! Remember My favors upon you." (Q 2:40)

Israel was Jacob ibn Isaac ibn Ibrahim- peace be upon them. Adding them to their father, Israel, was an honor to urge them to comply with Allah's commands and prohibitions. It was as if it was said: children of My good and faithful servant and honorable prophet, follow in the footsteps of your father in being true worshippers and obedient.

Such an expression is used to encourage as well as to intimidate. The call "O children of Israel!" was the perfect way to call those with sound judgement and discernment to acknowledge the favor with which they were reminded and use these favors the right was they were supposed to be used.

The Almighty's "Remember My favors upon you" was a call to them to be aware- with their hearts and minds- of those favors that you received because of My grace and benevolence. Keep reminding yourselves with these favors, for talking about Allah's favors would prompt you to be thankful and grateful.

The word النعمة in the verse is singular. It occurred in the Noble Qur'an in the plural sense as in His saying: "If you tried to count Allah's blessings (نعمة), you would never be able to number them." (Qur'an 16:18) So, what is meant by the word نعمةis many blessings. There was no reference to a certain or particular blessing نعمة. Linguists regard the use of the singular to indicate the plural- relying on the principle of presumption- as one of the most effective stylistic devices.

The Almighty commanded them to fulfill their covenant: "Fulfill your covenant and I will fulfill Mine, and stand in awe of Me alone." (Q 2:40) A covenant- like a promise or a pledge- should be kept and fulfilled- by the party that promises to the party that is promised. We often hear: I have fulfilled my promise/pledge, which means I did what I promised I would do. Allah's covenant here refers to His commandments and prohibitions. To fulfill His covenant is to follow His commandments and avoid what He has prohibited. This included all that the Children of Israel received in the Torah concerning following Muhammad when he was sent, believing what he brought from Allah, and believing what he said about his Allah.

The meaning is: Abide by your promise to obey and believe in Me and My messengers, and I will fulfill My promise to you to inherit the land in this world and eternal happiness in the afterlife.

Then, the Almighty commanded them to fear Him alone: "and stand in awe of Me alone." That is, fear Me only, and let your hearts be filled with fear, for this would help you obey Me and turn you away from disobedience and noncompliance.

He commanded them saying: stand in awe of Me in everything you do so as not to afflict you with the punishments and curses that I had visited on those before you whom I had transformed (into apes and pigs; Qur'an 5:60)). The noble verses comprise both promises and cautions, encouragement and intimidation.

After the Almighty commanded the Children of Israel to fulfill their covenant to Him in general, He commanded them to fulfill a particular covenant, one that was concerned with the Noble Qur'an. Expressing it in this manner was an exaltation and a veneration. Allah specifically commanded them to believe in it within the same line in which He said "Believe in My revelations which confirm your Scriptures" (Q 2:41) to indicate that fulfilling their covenant could only be achieved only if they believed in it.

The meaning of لما معكم(what you have) is the Torah. The meaning is: Believe, Children of Israel, in the Book that was revealed to Muhammad, the Noble Qur'an, that confirmed your Torah. Among the signs that it confirmed your book was that it advanced the message of the Torah: it called people to monotheism, to cling to what is virtuous and righteous and to avoid vices and immoralities. It had also informed the Prophet of what it contained concerning his emissary and the perfect correspondence between him and his characteristics as revealed in the Torah. And it had indicated that it would have dominance (supreme authority) over it. That is why, the Messenger said: "If Moses were alive, he would have certainly followed me." [2]

Informing the Children of Israel that the Noble Qur'an confirmed what they had (the Torah) was bound to motivate them- if they were people who comprehended- to consider it and ruminate over its verses and realize that it was a call to truth and guidance that would lead them to joy and happiness in this life and the hereafter. That would have comforted their hearts and assured them that believing in it (the Qur'an) meant believing in what they had (the Torah), and that disbelieving in it meant disbelieving in what they had (the Torah) since it (the Torah) prophesied the emissary of Muhammad to whom the Noble Qur'an was revealed.

Imam Al-Razi said that that noble verse indicated the truthfulness of the Prophet from two perspectives:

First: Previous Books predicted and foretold the Prophet and their predictions could not be but truthful.

Second: The Prophet informed them of what they had in their books without prior knowledge. That can only be possible through Divine revelation.[3]

Then, after the Almighty directed them to straightforward unadulterated faith, He exposed them for their prurient and disbelieving disobedience. He said: "Do not be the first to deny them." (Q 2:41) That is, do not be the first among the people of the Scriptures to disbelieve and deny the Noble Qur'an and set an example for others to follow and thereby become the leaders of disbelievers. In fact, it was your duty to be the first to hasten to believe in him because you were aware that he was sent by Allah, and you knew that he was the

Messenger to whom this Qur'an was revealed and that he was truthful about what he said about his Lord.

The noble verse was an admonition; it was meant to rebuke them for their disbelief, ungrateful denial and their malicious intentions towards him.

Imam Al- Razi said: This sentence was a message to the Children of Israel before anyone else. It was as though the Almighty was saying to them: Don't disbelieve Muhammad. There would be disbelievers after you, so do not be the first, for being the first to disbelieve increases the gravity of your transgression. That is because if you preceded others to disbelief, others will follow in your footsteps. In that case, your disbelief as well as the disbelief of others would be heaped upon you till Judgement Day. And if nobody followed in your footsteps, two things would be taken against you: being the first to disbelieve and being the only disbelievers. Both of these are grave transgressions that lead to severe punishment. [4]

Then, the Almighty cautioned them against abandoning faith for worldly gain: "Do not be the first to deny them or trade them for a fleeting gain." Trading here is a metaphor for exchanging. In other words, what was exchanged here was a trifle in place of belief in the verses, i.e., evidence and proofs that confirm the truthfulness of the Prophet, mainly, the Noble Qur'an and the Torah.

The meaning of fleeting gain is worldly desires and lusts: the lust for money, power, prestige, authority and all such things that they feared would lose if they were to follow Muhammad.

The meaning is: do not exchange faith in what I revealed and which confirmed what you have for transitory worldly gains. Do not go after money in place of Allah's pleasure for no matter how much you get, these are ephemeral and short-lived. They pale in comparison to the abundant care and benevolence that the faithful believers receive in this world and the grace and blessings in the hereafter.

Describing gain as fleeting is convenient to the depiction of the of price of the verses, for it would be trivial and worthless; no matter how abundant the worldly gains were, they would be worthless and insignificant compared to Allah's pleasure.

The Almighty also made clear that the belief in these verses was in their hands, but they abandoned it and displayed aversion towards it. They traded a trifle for something grand and sublime. They had thus earned Allah's wrath for they rejected the Noble Qur'an and their Torah that foretold the Messenger of Allah.
Then, the Almighty warned them against persisting in disbelieving in what He had revealed confirming what they had: "And be mindful of Me." (Q 2:41) Being mindful means being careful. When we say "be mindful of Allah," we are saying be careful not to incur Allah's wrath and punishment. To avoid incurring Allah's wrath requires complying with His commandments and avoiding His prohibitions. In sum, "be mindful of Me" means believe in Me, follow righteousness and avoid wrongdoing.

After the Noble Qur'an had prohibited the Children of Israel from disbelief and misguidance, it proceeded to prohibit them from misleading others: "Do not mix truth with falsehood or hide the truth knowingly." (Q 2:42)

Misleaders use two ways to lure people away from guidance and truth:
The first one is mixing truths with falsehoods to make the lines between them blurry and indistinct. That is what is meant by "Do not mix truth with falsehood." The other way is hiding or concealing the truth to make it nonexistent. That is what is meant by "hide the truth."

The children of Israel used both ways to lure people away from Islam. Some of them would deliberately misinterpret the texts of their books that pointed to the truthfulness of the Prophet. They would mix truths with falsehoods to make people think that he was not the foretold anticipated prophet. Some would cast doubts around truths to perplex and confuse those whose faith was shaky or wobbly. Others would conceal or omit the texts that confirmed the truthfulness of the Prophet or those texts that did not suit their desires or aspirations. Allah warned them against these cunning and malicious deeds.

The meaning is: Do not mix the evident and conspicuous truth- that the heavenly Books revealed and that sound minds acknowledged- with the falsehoods that you fabricate to satisfy your whims and fulfill your desires. Do not conceal the truth that you knew as well as you knew your own children. The first prohibition was concerned with altering and mixing, while the second was concerned with hiding and concealing.

His saying: "knowingly" refers to people who were well informed and knowledgeable. It is not appropriate for this kind of people to conceal the truth or mix it with falsehoods. If this kind of deed- mixing truths with falsehoods, or concealing the truth and revealing untruths- is considered a grave and serious wrongdoing, it is even more despicable, more cancerous and more ominous in its effect when it ensues from a knowledgeable learned erudite who can distinguish between truths and falsehoods.

So, this statement disclosed the condition of the Children of Israel who were addressed with such a prohibition and rebuked because they did not do what they did out of ignorance or lack of knowledge. Rather, they did it knowingly, and they persisted in pursuing that crooked path.

In Tafsir al-Bahr al-Muhit, Abu Hayyan said: "A person who is ignorant concerning the condition of something does not know whether it is true or false. However, performing ugly deeds with the knowledge that they are ugly is a lot worse that doing them in ignorance." [5]

After the Almighty commanded them to be mindful of the most important tenets of religion which is believing in Him and in His Messenger, He directed their attention to two of its most practical pillars that would soften their hearts to the truth and instill in them fear of Allah Alone, if they were to observe them. He said: "Establish prayer, pay alms-tax, and bow down with those who bow down." (Q 2:43)

The meaning is: You Jews should establish prayer, which is the greatest form of physical worship, and pay alms tax, which is the greatest form of financial worship. You should be in complete submission to Allah's religion because by observing these forms of worship, you will cleanse your hearts, uplift your spirits, and sustain and enrich your feelings. If you don't observe these forms of worship- as Allah had commanded- you will suffer moral humiliation in this world and severe torment in the hereafter.

It is appropriate to conclude the interpretation of these noble verses and what they contained of sound advice and direction as well as solid rhetorical construction by citing what Abu Hayyan said in his Tafsir (Interpretation). He said:

"These sentences reflect an amazing chronological order from a rhetorical perspective and the way the sentences flowed one after the other: The almighty first ordered them to remember the favors He had granted them. This serves as an invitation to love the bestower of favors and the obligation and duty to obey Him. Then, He commanded them to fulfill their covenant and commitment to Him. He encouraged them by reminding them of His desire to fulfill His covenant to them. Then, He cautioned them to fear His wrath if they failed to fulfill their covenant. The command to fulfill their covenant was enfolded in His reminding them of His favors. He cautioned them against disobedience. Then, He followed that with the specific command to believe in what was revealed of the Qur'an, and He encouraged them to do so by indicating that confirmed what they had; it was not different from what they had. Moving in the direction of what is congruent and compatible is easier than moving in the direction of something incongruent and incompatible. Then, He cautioned them against trading what was precious and valuable for what is worthless and trivial. He followed that with a command to fear Him, and He prohibited them from mixing truths with falsehoods and from concealing the truth. Thus, the command to believe was clothed in a command to abandon disbelief and misguidance. And the prohibition not to confuse truths with falsehoods and not to hide the truth were calls to abandon misguidance. And since misguidance can be the result of either mixing the truth with falsehoods if evidence had already reached the follower of truth, or it can result due to concealing the evidence in case it is still unavailable, He referred to these two issues by "do not mix... or conceal." He emphasized that these two dreadful issues were all the more appalling if perpetrated with knowledge. Then He commanded them to faith and truth through establishing prayer and paying alms tax because praying is physically arduous and paying alms tax is financially demanding. He then concluded that commandment by the command to submit to Him with all the other worshippers "who bow down" in obedience and submission. Thus, introducing these verses by reminding them with His favors and concluding them with a call to submit to the Benefactor- in addition to all that was mentioned in between concerning matters related to creed, physical and financial actions, introductions, detailed explanations and a conclusion- all of these reveal Allah's favors. Yet, while these commandments and prohibitions were directed to the Children of Israel in particular, they are general precepts and guidelines that are applicable to all times and all places." [6]

Having issued all these commandments and prohibitions, the almighty rebuked them for doing things that were unbecoming to sensible, logical and understanding people: they asked people to do righteous and good deeds while they themselves did not do what they asked others to do: “Do you preach righteousness and fail to practice it yourselves, although you read the Scripture? Do you not understand?” (Qur’an 2:44)

That is, how could you Jews expect other people to practice righteous and virtuous deeds while you fail to practice them yourselves? How could you preach what you do not practice? Don’t you follow the commandments that you order others to follow while you read your Torah and know the severe punishment that befalls those who command others to do good deeds and fail to do them themselves? Don’t you have the reason and understanding to avert this travesty in which you have wallowed and know its undesirable and disagreeable consequence?

Ibn Abbas said: the Jews of Medina would often say to those Muslims that they had some relations with: stand firm and cling to what you have and what this man (meaning Muhammad) commanded you to do, for his commandments are right and true. They would command people to do that even though they didn’t do it themselves. [7]

The interrogation “Do you?” is meant to rebuke and admonish them and express astonishment at their strange demeanor.

And fail to practice which is تنسون in Arabic (literally, forget in the noble verse) means abandoning doing what they asked others to do. A person who actually forgot something could not be held accountable for what he had forgotten. He would not be liable for that severe admonition that occurred in the noble verse. In addition, the admonition here was not directed to them because they requested that others do good and righteous deeds, for such deeds are wholesome, welcome and desirable. Rather, the admonition was directed to them because they themselves knowingly abandoned doing the good deeds that they asked others to do. They seemed to be trying to cure others when their own hearts were filled with sicknesses and diseases.

And His “although you read the Scripture” (Q 2:44) made the admonition all the more poignant because their reading of their Books had abolished any excuse of ignorance or lack of knowledge to which disobedient degenerates cling when confronted.

And in His “Do you not understand?” (Q 2:44) we find the most appropriate kind of guidance and good counsel. Among the most pleasant methods in advising is that the person receiving the advice has a certain characteristic that could lead to righteousness. Yet, he is lured to some kind of evil which causes other people to marvel and wonder. The advisor would then mention this characteristic as a reminder that the conduct that the advisee displayed is at odds with what is known about him.

As an application of this principle, we say that those who were addressed “Do you not understand?” were people who had the ability to understand, comprehend and rationalize.

It was therefore because of these abilities to be cognizant and understanding that certain laws, tenets and principles were directed to- and expected from- them. However, they did not follow what their minds and understanding dictated. They ordered others to do righteous deeds, but they themselves neglected to do them. It was as though the Almighty was saying: "The unacceptable evil deeds that you had perpetrated make those who look at you think without hesitation that you have no reason and no virtue in you." This method combines the encouragement to do good with the intimidation- simultaneously- to stay away from evil.

And since the tasks that Allah had asked them to perform were rather difficult and not easily doable by everyone, He directed them to the methods that would strengthen their wills, purge their hearts and cure the sicknesses of their souls. He said: "And seek help through patience and prayer. Indeed, it is a burden except for the humble—those who are certain that they will meet their Lord and to Him they will return." (Qur'an 2:45)

His saying "And seek help through patience and prayer" was a call to them to abandon their love of the lusts of the world and to accept Islam and abide by its tenets and principles (even though you could not bring yourselves to do so) through patience which would help you accept what might seem unacceptable and through prayer which would help you avoid immoralities and wrongdoing.

Then He said: "Indeed, it is a burden except for the humble." (Q 2:45) The word كبيرة means difficult and cumbersome, a "burden" as it is in the verse. In Arabic, also refers to things that big and heavy. This meaning is evident in His: "What you call the polytheists to is unbearable for them." (Qur'an 42:13) "The humble" means flexibility and ease. إنها (it) is a reference to prayer. Thus, the verse means prayer has a great and wide-ranging effect. إلا (except) is to indicate exception. In sum, this is difficult for all people except for the humble and obedient.

The meaning is: prayer is difficult except for the submissive and humble whose hearts and feelings are given to Allah as they are confident that it is one of the most important ways to succeed in this world and attain happiness in the hereafter. They also experience joy and happiness when they pray and rush joyfully, faithfully and passionately to it when it is time to pray.

Imam Al-Razi said: "If it is said that since it is a 'burden' for those and easy for the submissive, the reward for those who find it burdensome should be greater, and the humble lesser. I would say that this is not acceptable because we are not saying that they toil and tire more than the humble. How could that be when the heart, feelings and emotions of the humble are inflamed during prayer? If that is so, then the burden on the humble because of his passionate prayers is greater. "It is a burden" is meant to refer to those who are not humble because they do not believe that there is neither reward in performing it nor a punishment in not performing it. It is thus burdensome for them to do. The polytheist does not believe there is a benefit behind doing it. It thus become difficult since doing something to no advantage or benefit

would be tedious and cumbersome. As for the monotheist- who believes that there are great benefits in praying and great harms in abandoning it- it is neither difficult or burdensome. He prays willingly and with joy and happiness. Consider the Prophet's saying: 'Prayer was made the apple of my eye.' He thus described it because it was not a 'burden' to him." [8]

Then the Almighty described the humble: "those who are certain that they will meet their Lord and to Him they will return." (Qur'an 2:46)

Those who are certain in the Arabic verse is الذين يظنون. The word الظن (suspicion/thinking) is used in most contexts to show and indicate certainty. It is certainty that transcends doubt and reaches unquestionable conviction. This is what is meant here. And it is similar to "Do not these people think يظنون that they will be resurrected for a great day?" (Qur'an 83:4) Meaning: don't these people know that they will be resurrected for a great day? And in His saying: "I thought I would meet His account." (Qur'an 2:249; 69:20) Meaning: I knew I would meet His account.

The humble who are certain to meet their Lord are those who will be going to meet Allah after death to be rewarded according to their deeds.

The meaning is: prayer could be a burden except for those who are humble who are certain to meet Allah on Judgement Day. They will return to Him to be rewarded according to their deeds.

Ibn Jarir said that the word (thinking/believing)الظن is most likely used in the sense of certainty. He said: "How could those who are humble and obedient 'think' (used here to indicate doubt) that they might meet Allah? Isn't he who doubts meeting Allah a disbeliever? But it is said that Arabs name certainty as doubt and doubt as certainty. This is similar to naming a helper as 'yeller' and the person screaming for help as 'yeller' as well. It is not uncommon to use a name and its opposite to refer to the same thing. As evidence of this is what Duraid bin Al-Sammah said: "So I told them, 'They thought يظنون there were two thousand Mudjaj.' By that he meant: be certain that there were two thousand Mudjaj. Then, he said that there is innumerable evidence that الظن (thinking/suspicion) is used to mean certainty. Among them is His saying: "The wicked will see the Fire and realize فظنوا that they are bound to fall into it." (Qur'an 18:53) Mujahid also said: "Every suspicion in the Qur'an is certainty." [9]

Those who said that الظن (thinking/suspicion) as used here in its true sense as a firm conviction or belief interpreted "the humble—those who are certain that they will meet their Lord" to mean their attaining His pleasure on Judgment Day. They also interpreted "and to Him they will return." to mean their closeness to His glorious and exquisite presence and dwelling in His Paradise. To sum up, prayer is a burden except to those who expect being close to Allah and dwelling in His Paradise when they return to Him.

This same interpretation was adopted by Al-Zamakhshari (in Al-Kashshaaf). He said: "If you asked: 'Why isn't it a burden to the humble even though humbleness in itself can be a burden?' I would say: 'Because they expect what has been preserved for the humble because of their toil and thus their toil would be worthwhile. Consider His saying: 'the humble—those who are certain that they will meet their Lord.' In other words, they expect His rewards; they expect to what He preserved for them.'" [10]

However, the humble person's feelings are only tentative and speculative, not a certainty. The end of life is unknown except to the All-knowledgeable Omnipotent. describing them using such words as "believe/think/suspect," highlights their fear and uncertainty of what Allah might bring them. That is why, the believer is always oscillating between fear and hope.

By explaining the meaning of this noble verse, we can see that those who interpreted الظن (thinking/suspicion) as certain and definite regard the meeting of the humble with their Lord as الحشر (al-Hashr), the gathering of people after their death to judge and reward them according to their deeds. The humble are firmly convinced of الحشر (al-Hashr) and the recompense.

Those who interpreted الظن (thinking/suspicion) as the most likely scenario see that the meeting of the humble with Allah means their expectation of His rewards. They see "returning" to Him as their gaining His Paradise. The humble see that it is "most likely" that they will get His rewards and Paradise, as these are contingent on Allah's grace and favor alone.

We believe that the first viewpoint is more suitable for the meaning of the noble verse. It is the viewpoint which interpreters such as Mujahid, Abu al-Aliyya and others expressed.

This noble verse admonished the scholars of the Jews for advising others while failing to practice what they preached. The verse also pointed out to the remedy, i.e., patience and continuous prayer, that could have cured them from this and other contemptible and despicable behavior if they truly and faithfully adopted it.

We will now talk about Allah's favors to the Children of Israel as mentioned in the Noble Qur'an.

First: Favoring them over the world:

"O Children of Israel! Remember all the favors I granted you and how I honored you above the others." (Q 2:40)

The Noble Qur'an reiterated its call to them to emphasize their duty to give thanks, draw their attention to the content of the message and the commandments and prohibitions entailed therein, and to enumerate the favors that Allah had bestowed upon them.

The Noble Qur'an typically uses this method of reiterating the sentences that comprise issues requiring more attention- as it is the case in mentioning the favors of Allah- since repeating them would lure the honorable and righteous to obey the provider of these favors and encourage them to walk in the straightforward path.

His saying "how I honored you above the others" follows "all the favors I granted you." This means, remember that I favored you above all the world. This was a special favor, favoring a specific group over a general group to indicate a special attention. It was meant to incite appreciation and prompt them to attempt to be worthy of such a favor.

The Almighty reminded the Children of Israel who were contemporary to the Prophet with these favors even though they were granted to their forefathers, as the following verses will show. The favors that were granted to the predecessors were also favors to the successors; after all, they are their lineage. That is why, reminding them with these favors was an honor that would clothe them, make them decent and reputable and lure them to faith and compliance, if they could comprehend.

Among the signs of Allah's favoring the Children of Israel over other people at that time were the many blessings that He bestowed upon them before the emissary of Muhammad. He granted them many favors, He sent many prophets to them, He saved them from their enemies, He did not punish them despite their defiance, aggression and committing many injustices and wrongdoings deliberately and insistently, and He did not eradicate them because of their transgressions as He did to others like the people of Aad and Thamud.

However, the Children of Israel did not show gratitude and appreciation for Allah's favors. Rather, they showed ungratefulness and inconsideration. So, Allah took these favors away from them and gave them to others who did not behave like them.

The Noble Qur'an recounted many of the favors that Allah granted to the Children of Israel. However, they received them with ingratitude and unappreciativeness, so Allah took them away from them: "Ask the Children of Israel how many clear signs We have given them. And whoever trades Allah's favor—after receiving it—'for disbelief' should know that Allah is indeed severe in punishment." (Qur'an 2:211) [11]

This means: Muhammad! Ask the Jews who are contemporary to you a question of admonition and rebuke: How many magnificent favors and wonderful miracles did Allah show them at the hands of their prophets, yet they received them scornfully and derisively showing no gratitude? These were meant to give them happiness and to guide them! For this, Allah humiliated and chastened them in this world and promised severe punishment in the hereafter.

Among the verses that stated that the Almighty granted the Children of Israel many favors and blessings for which they did not thank Him is His saying: "And We certainly delivered the Children of Israel from the humiliating torment of Pharaoh. He was truly a tyrant, a transgressor. And indeed, We chose the Israelites knowingly above the others. And We showed them signs in which there was a clear test." (Qur'an 44:30-33) [12]

Meaning: We saved the Children of Israel from the humiliating torture Pharaoh and his men were planning for them as We caused them to drown in front of their eyes because he was a tyrant. In addition, We favored the Children of Israel above all others- knowing what they would be doing- and We granted them favors and showed them signs to test their hearts and souls. They failed the test, showed no gratitude for Allah's favors, and disbelieved His messengers and killed them. Allah therefore warned to torment them with severe punishment in this world until Judgement Day, and with an evil place to rest, namely, hellfire, in the hereafter.

Also, among the verses that mentioned Allah's favors to the Children of Israel for which they did not thank Him is: "Indeed, We gave the Children of Israel the Scripture, wisdom, and prophethood; granted them good, lawful provisions; and favored them above the others. We also gave them clear commandments regarding ˹their˺ faith. But it was not until knowledge came to them that they differed out of mutual envy. Surely your Lord will judge between them on the Day of Judgment regarding their differences." (45:16-17) [13]

The meaning is: We brought the Torah to the Children of Israel to lead and guide them. We gave them wisdom and jurisprudence and granted prophethood to many of them. We provided them with the best foods and drinks, and we favored them above all others who were contemporary with them before the emissary of the Prophet. Moreover, their prophets performed many miracles and signs as proofs to strengthen their faith and guide them to the straight path. However, they did not benefit from all of those favors. Rather, they made their knowledge of the true religion a reason for dissention and discord, and they persisted in going astray on the path of misguidance. Allah will punish them for their ungratefulness and obstinate rejection.

The lessons that we gather from these and similar verses is that the Almighty Allah favored the Children of Israel above other communities prior to the Muslim community. He granted them numerous favors, but they did not accept them with gratitude and thankfulness. Rather, they showed rebellion, malice and unappreciativeness. Therefore, Allah took away those favors. He described them in His Book with the most appalling characteristics and the worst features such as cruelty of heart, violation of covenants, covetousness and hunger for the lusts of the world, aggression against others, crookedness and deceitfulness to permit what Allah prohibited, hatred of the truth, following falsehoods, and many other characteristics that are mentioned in the Noble Qur'an.

And this is the fate of any nation that exchange Allah's favors for wanton disbelief. Allah's scale is righteousness and good deeds, not race, color or connections.

Imam Al-Razi said what can be summed up as: "What is said concerning favoring them above the worlds would mean favoring them above the nation of Muhammad, but is incorrect. What is the response, then? We say that the most appropriate and correct response is that 'I favored you above other contemporary nations that co-existed during that time, because somebody would be there who was not there now and was not counted among 'the worlds.' The nation of Muhammad was not in existence at that time. The Children of Israel being favored above the worlds at that time did not mean that they were better than the Muhammadan nation. This is also the response to His saying: "Remember Allah's favors upon you when He raised prophets from among you, made you sovereign, and gave you what He had never given anyone in the world." (Qur'an 5:20) Also, His saying: "We have chosen them with knowledge over the world." (Qur'an 44:32) [14]

Thus, the Jews' claim that they are Allah's chosen people is incorrect according to this and similar noble verses. It is a claim that texts do not support and sensible people refute.

Then, the Almighty said: "Guard yourselves against the Day on which no soul will be of help to another. No intercession will be accepted, no ransom taken, and no help will be given." (Qur'an 2:48) After the Almighty reminded them in the previous verse with one of His great favors, He cautioned them in this one against not presenting good deeds because favoring them above all the others in their time could entice them to become conceited and cause them to imagine that they would be forgiven if they transgressed. This noble verse uproots any such illusions in a terse and succinct phrase.

"The Day" is a reference to Judgement Day. So, be careful of the torment and horror that happen on that Day. To "guard" oneself is to abide by Allah's commandment and not to violate or infringe upon them. The word "soul," which is mentioned twice in the verse, is used (in the plural sense) as a reference to all the souls: no soul will be able to help another soul.

And using the "Day" and not referring to it as Judgement Day is to convey that that Day is to Allah alone; there will be none of what people in this world got accustomed to, namely, defending each other.

The meaning is: Be careful, O Children of Israel, of that Day ahead in which you will present your account for nothing can save you then except righteousness and piety and being faithful and loyal to Allah in all conditions and in all your deeds. On that day, no soul (no matter how great) would be of help to another (no matter how small the offense was).

Then, the Noble Qur'an described that Day in a different befitting way. The Almighty said: "No intercession will be accepted." (Q 2:48) Intercession means joining another to fend for him. This means: no intercessor would be able to enumerate the things that could be beneficial or drive any harms away.

The noble verse definitively rejected accepting intercession. However, there are other noble verses that negate accepting intercession except by Allah's will. He said: "Who could possibly intercede with Him without His permission?" (Qur'an 2:255) [15] And in His: "On that Day no intercession will be of any benefit, except by those granted permission by the Most Compassionate and whose words are agreeable to Him." (Qur'an 20:109) [16]

It is noteworthy to mention that the verses that utterly reject intercessions are mentioned concerning the disbelieving infidels. Those verses that allow intercession are mentioned concerning the believers if Allah wills. Many authentic chains of transmission/Hadiths report that the Prophet will intercede and save believers from torment and reduce and attenuate the punishment of for major sins. Al-Bukhari narrated on the authority of Jaber bin Abdullah; he said: "The Messenger of Allah said: 'I was given five things that no one had been given before me: I was supported through terror for a month's journey, and the earth was made for me a place of mosque (prayer) and purification. My people were regarded as the best of nations, and I was given intercession.'" [17]

Imam Ibn Jarir said reciting this verse may give a general meaning, but its interpretation is specific because of what was said about what the Messenger of Allah said: "My intercession is for the people of my nation who commit major sins. Every prophet is given a supplication, and I have hidden my supplication as an intercession for my nation. It will come to whomsoever of my nation dies not associating any partners with Allah." Thus, the Almighty may forgive His servants, the believers, and refrain from punishing them, through the intercession of our Prophet Muhammad. His saying "No intercession will be accepted" is meant to those who die as unrepenting disbelievers."[18]

He then described that Day a third time as "the Day on which …no ransom (is) taken." (Qur'an 57:15)

Then He described that Day for the fourth time saying "and no help will be given." (Qur'an 2:48; 2:123)

All of these descriptions are meant to indicate that on that Day they will find nobody to help them and prevent Allah's punishment and torture on the Day of resurrection.

And since the Jews thought of themselves as a special chosen people and believed that their connection to the prophets will make them immune against punishment despite their prurient disobedience and depravity and that their forefathers will intercede for them, this noble verse was revealed to void and annul their illusion and eradicate all possibilities and avenues for salvation on Judgement Day except through faith and good and virtuous deeds.

The noble verse (Q 2:48) negated the existence of someone who would intercede on their behalf: "on which no soul will be of help to another." It also negated the possibility of benefiting from the intercession of intercessors on Judgement Day: "No intercession will be accepted." Also, it negated accepting a ransom for the sins they committed: "no ransom taken." Finally, it negated the possibility of finding someone who would support, help or defend them: "no help will be given."

Thus, the noble verse blocked all the ways they could imagine would help them avoid Allah's punishment and wrath as long as they persist on their prurient and disbelieving disobedience and ungratefulness.

These two verses (Qur'an 2:48, and probably, 20:109) employ a discreet wise way in counselling and guidance. It combines encouragement and intimidation. The first verse began by calling them using the name of their father, Israel, their pride, to instill the feelings of honor and dignity in their hearts and minds and to lure them away from all trifles and demeaning and undignified issues for he who feels that he comes from a noble origin would loathe to bother with trifles, lies and malicious matters. Then in the second verse, He guides them to righteousness which would lead to peace and success and cautioned them against the horrors of the Day of Judgement. The verse also made clear that their lineage and connection to their forefathers would avail them nothing on Judgement Day and that what would truly benefit them is accepting and following the teachings of Islam which the Prophet brought. That would curtail their conceit and eradicate their illusions.

Second: The favor of delivering them from their enemies:

The Almighty reminded them with a second great favor: the favor of delivering them from their enemies. The Almighty said: "Remember how We delivered you from the people of Pharaoh, who afflicted you with dreadful torment, slaughtering your sons and keeping your women. That was a severe test from your Lord." (Qur'an 2:49)

This verse comes after His saying "Remember My favors upon you" in the previous verse, thereby more detailed information is mentioned after the general concept: "Remember My favors upon you and Remember how We delivered you from the people of Pharaoh." The meaning is: remember the time when We delivered you. The use of "when" is meant to remind of the events that took place. The use of "test" is applicable to both good and evil as in "And We test you O humanity with good and evil as a trial." (Qur'an 21:35) [19]

The meaning is: Remember, Children of Israel, the time when We delivered you from the people of Pharaoh who afflicted you with outrageous and appalling torment. They wished nothing more than your degradation and humiliation, seeking to eradicate your offspring, debase you, and violate your dignity when they killed your children and took your women. It was dreadful torment humiliating and debasing you. Delivering you was a test to become thankful and grateful and abandon the wrongdoing and immoralities that would lead to your disgrace and humiliation in this world and punishment and torment in the hereafter.

Imam Al-Razi said what can be summed up as follows: "Know that the benefits of mentioning this favor, namely, delivering them from their enemies- are due to many facets. The most important of these are:

1- Since these things that Allah had mentioned constituted the greatest trials that people could experience from kings and the forces of darkness, Allah's deliverance had to be considered one of the greatest favors because they witnessed the destruction of those who wished them harm, and they saw the disgrace and humiliation of those who wanted to shame and humiliate them. It was undoubtedly one of the greatest favors ever, one that necessitated their utter and undivided submission and obedience and abandoning all wickedness and inequity. Allah mentioned that great favor to leave them without any excuses to follow Him.
2- They knew that they were in the final stages of humiliation and that their enemy was in their final stages of affluence and power. They were right and their adversary was wrong. Neither the disgrace of those who were right nor the strength of the wrongdoers were eradicated because of this knowledge. It was as though the Almighty was telling them not to count too much on their wealth or strength, and not to take the Muslims lightly because of their small numbers, since they were right and righteous, and those who were righteous would surely be rewarded with victory." [20]

The Jews who were contemporary with the Prophet were the ones who were reminded of this favor, even though it was their forefathers who were delivered from pharaoh. However, by delivering their forefathers, they themselves were essentially saved, for had Pharaoh continued to torment them, they would have been annihilated, and there would have been no trace of them (the successors). Thus, that deliverance was in fact twofold: the favor of delivering the forefathers from the torture with which they were afflicted, and second favor was for the successors whose very lives were simply the result of the first favor. It was the appropriate thing for all to show appreciation and gratitude and faithfully worship their Creator who delivered them from their enemies. Doing a favor to a nation is an act that is comprehensive and far-reaching, whether or not the people of this nation are directly impacted by it and also because the effects are often visited on the offspring. In other words, the offspring inherit the consequences of these favors from their predecessors. In addition, informing them would induce them to believe that what the Prophet was saying about his Lord was truthful for he informed them of the history of their predecessors truthfully and honestly. That was proof of the truthfulness of his message.

It is noteworthy that deliverance was from the people of Pharaoh, not Pharaoh himself, even though he was the one who gave the order to torture the Children of Israel. The Pharaoh's entourage and cortege (retinue) played a role in inflicting pain, torture, humiliation and suffering.

And the noble verse indicated that keeping their women was a punishment to the Jews. On the surface, that looked benevolent. However, they were kept to be dishonored and violated, to use them for menial work, and to enslave them. Thus, keeping the women as such was a form of degradation and humiliation, a painful torture that noble minds and compassionate and munificent natures reject and abhor.

Imam Al-Razi said: "Slaughtering the males, not the females, was injurious and detrimental for many reasons:

First: Slaughtering the sons would eradicate the males which, in turn, would cut off reproduction. Women would be unable to reproduce by themselves. This would ultimately lead to the annihilation of both men and women.

Second: The extinction of the men would result in the inability of the women to lead a decent respectful life. Women prefer death rather than being alone without the support of their male counterparts. Such a scheme was pernicious and delivering them from it was enormous.

Third: Killing an unborn after a long pregnancy- with all that those pregnancies entailed of hardships and difficulties as well as expectations of a useful and good help after delivery- was one of the most vicious forms of torture. Allah's favor in delivering them from this ordeal was astounding.

Fourth: Keeping the women without their male counterparts would make them sex objects for their enemy, and this was the ultimate form of degradation and disgrace." [21]

Many interpreters see that "slaughtering your sons" (Q 2:49) most likely meant the children, not the adults, because of the very meaning of the term "son." Also, the killing of the men would not benefit them much since they used them to perform difficult and menial work. Also, if "adult men" were the intended target of slaughtering, Moses's mother would not have thrown him in the river when he was a little child to rescue him from slaughtering.

Other interpreters believe that the term "son" referred to men, not children because the term "son" was juxtaposed against the term "women."

We are prone to believe that the first interpretation is the most likely since it highlights the favor of deliverance: the people of Pharaoh killed the young to get rid of the offspring; they kept the women to enslave them, and they preserved the lives of the adult men to serve until they start decreasing and become extinct which was even harsher for them than death itself.

The statement "slaughtering your sons" in this noble verse does not have the conjunction "and/ و." However, in Sura Ibrahim (sura 14) there is the conjunction "and/ و" [22] because here it is a statement and it explains "afflicted you with dreadful torment." In this case, "slaughtering your sons and keeping your women" is what was meant by (those who afflicted you with) "dreadful torment." (Qur'an 14:6)

In Sura Ibrahim, however, the verses enumerate the hardships that afflicted the Children of Israel. Therefore, being afflicted with "dreadful torment" was one of these hardships. "Slaughtering your sons" was another type of torment. That is why the conjunction is used because the second sentence does not explain the first one. Rather, it represents another type of the torments that afflicted them.

Delivering the Children of Israel from their enemies was repeated in many places in the Noble Qur'an because of its important significance and to encourage them to obey and thank the Almighty:

1- In sura Al-A'raf: "And remember when We rescued you from the people of Pharaoh, who afflicted you with dreadful torment—killing your sons and keeping your women. That was a severe test from your Lord." (Qur'an 7:141) [23]
2- In Sura Taha: "O Children of Israel! We saved you from your enemy, and made an appointment with you[1] on the right side of Mount Ṭûr, and sent down to you manna and quails, saying, "Eat from the good things We have provided for you, but do not transgress in them, or My wrath will befall you. And whoever My wrath befalls is certainly doomed. But I am truly Most Forgiving to whoever repents, believes, and does good, then persists on true guidance." ⌜Allah asked, ⌝ "Why have you come with such haste ahead of your people, O Moses?" (Qur'an 20:80-83) [24]

These noble verses and others that have similar purport and meaning were meant to remind the Children of Israel of Allah's favors as He delivered them from those who wished them harm and attempted to kill and exterminate them. That should have prompted and incited them to diligently thank Allah, if they were among those who could show appreciation and thankfulness when due.

Third: The favor of parting the sea:

The Almighty reminded them of a third magnificent favor that thoroughly saved them and reflected Allah's grace and munificence: parting the sea with them: "And remember when We parted the sea, rescued you, and drowned Pharaoh's people before your very eyes." (Qur'an 2:50)

The meaning is: Remember Children of Israel one of the many favors that We did for you: the favor of parting the sea when Moses struck the it with his staff, and it was split, with many dry paths that you walked through to flee from Pharaoh and his men. Thus, you were saved and your enemies drowned when they tried to follow you. You witnessed that with your own eyes, and you saw them overwhelmed by the waves of the sea. You saw all of this with clarity and without any confusion or ambiguity. That should have incited you to learn from these lessons; it should have prompted you become indebted and grateful to the Almighty.

The noble verse recounts the story of the deliverance of the children of Israel and the drowning of Pharaoh and his people. Here is the summary:

The almighty inspired Moses to depart at night with the Children of Israel from the land of Egypt where they had for long been tortured and to head to the land of Palestine. Moses obeyed Allah's command. Pharaoh was informed that Moses and his people were heading towards the Levant. He followed them with a big army. He caught up with them at sunrise near the coast of the Red Sea. When the Children of Israel saw him, they were convinced of their certain impending destruction. They turned to Moses in fear and horror, but he reassured them saying: "Absolutely not! My Lord is certainly with me—He will guide me." (Qur'an 26:62) Allah inspired him: "Strike the sea with your staff," "and the sea was split, each part was like a huge mountain." (Qur'an 26:63) Then Moses commanded his people to go safely between the two sides. They did, and no harm touched them. Pharaoh and his men pursued them thinking that they would be able to catch and overpower them. Once all of the Children of Israel crossed to the other side, the sea closed (as it was before) over pharaoh and his men who were still in the middle. They all drowned as the Children of Israel were looking in amazement, relief and happiness.

The Almighty made clear that the parting of the sea was His doing to ascertain that He was there with the people to take care of them as they crossed. He said: "We parted the sea, rescued you, and drowned Pharaoh's people." (Qur'an 2:50) It is a statement of Allah's great favor that he did for them and which resulted in the parting of the sea which had two outcomes. First, they were saved, and, Second, their enemy was destroyed. Both of these are magnificent favors.

True faith dictates that the parting of the Red Sea for Moses and his men be understood as a cosmic miracle. Some claimed that it was merely a natural phenomenon due to ebb and flow. Nothing supports this claim; there is no evidence for it.

And the verse here merely mentions the drowning of the people of Pharaoh, that is, his soldiers and supporters. This is reflected in His saying: "We drowned him and all of those with him." (Qur'an 17:103) [25] This is also apparent in His saying: "So We seized him and his soldiers, casting them into the sea while he was blameworthy." (Qur'an 51:40) [26] Such was Allah's great and all-encompassing favor: He caused the perdition of all those who were with Pharaoh along with Pharaoh himself.

His saying: "before your very eyes" (Q 2:50) means that We drowned the people of Pharaoh in your presence before your eyes to make you certain that your enemy was destroyed, to delight and gloat over their loss and to thank Allah for His favor. Those to whom that favor was done would undoubtedly rejoice with delight to witness such a favor. There was also a great lesson to learn from seeing the enemy perish. And witnessing the parting of the sea was bound to confirm and strengthen their faith, if they were like those who could benefit and learn from what they see and witness.

Imam Al-Razi said: "Know that this event- meaning the event of parting the sea, comprised many favors that benefited the Children of Israel in the world as well as in their religion and faith. Among the blessings in this world are:

First: When they approached the sea, they confronted a very critical moment: Pharaoh and his soldiers were behind them, and the sea was in front. If they stopped advancing, their enemy would have caught up and destroyed them. If they advanced, they would have drowned. Fear and horror overtook them. Deliverance came to them through the parting of the sea and the destruction of their enemy.

Second: The Almighty Allah did this great favor and astounding miracle to honor them and show His protection and care.

Third: By drowning Pharaoh and his people, they got rid of the torture and suffering they received at their hands. They finally felt safe and secure. That was a great favor, for if they were merely rescued without the destruction of Pharaoh, they would have lived in fear that he might resume his torture of them in the future. Drowning Pharaoh and his men meant safety and security to the Children of Israel.

Among the blessings for their faith and religion:

First: when Moses' people witnessed this dumbfounding and stunning miracle, suspicions, doubts and delusions were removed from their hearts because such an astounding feat proved the existence of the all-powerful all-Wise Allah and established the truthfulness of Moses as a fait accompli.

Second: Witnessing that miracle prompted them to become steadfast and resolute in faith and comply with the commands of their prophet.

Third: They realized that matters are in the hand of Allah. Nobody was as powerful and influential as Pharaoh, and no disgrace and degradation were as demeaning as what the Children of Israel suffered. Within the blink of an eye, all things reversed and changed course: the noble became disgraced and the disgraced noble, and the powerful became weak and the weak powerful. That should prompt one to dissociate oneself from the desires and lusts of the world and thoroughly commit to obey the Creator." [27]

The parting of the sea and the deliverance of the Children of Israel from their enemies occurred numerous times in the Noble Qur'an. In Sura Ash-Shu'ara (sura 26), the Almighty said: "So We inspired Moses: "Strike the sea with your staff," and the sea was split, each part was like a huge mountain. We drew the pursuers to that place, and delivered Moses and those with him all together. Then We drowned the others. Surely in this is a sign. Yet most of them would not believe." (Qur'an 26:63-67)

Thus, the noble verses reminded the Children of Israel with one of Allah's most astounding and stunning signs/miracles: the parting of the sea, to thank their Creator and follow His Prophet. However, they did not fulfill their obligation to be thankful and show gratitude to their Creator. That was why they deserved to be cursed in this world and be afflicted with severe punishment in the hereafter for their ingratitude, injustices and denial. And Allah does not deal unjustly to His servants.

Fourth: Allah's forgiveness after they worshipped the calf:

The almighty then reminded them of a fourth favor that He did for them: Forgiving them despite their ingratitude, disbelief and worshipping other than Him: "And remember when We appointed forty nights for Moses, then you worshipped the calf in his absence, acting wrongfully. Even then We still forgave you so perhaps you would be grateful." (Qur'an 2:51-52)

The "appointment" here is an action that involves two parties, and this not what is meant here. What is meant was Allah's command to Moses to dedicate forty nights to solely meditate and worship Him as a prelude to giving him the Torah. This meaning was supported by Abu Umara nd Abu Jafar. But it was also said that the "appointment" referred to the two parties involved: Allah promised Moses, His Prophet, that He would give him the Torah, and He commanded him to dedicate such a period of time to worship Him. Moses, on the other hand, promised his Allah to obey and comply with His order. Thus, the appointment did involve two parties.

The story can be summed up as follows: After Allah delivered Moses' people and drowned their enemy before their eyes, they asked Moses, their Prophet, to bring them a Book from Allah to follow its teachings and instructions. The Almighty promised Moses the Torah after forty nights during which Moses will wholeheartedly devote himself to worship Allah. By the time Moses received the Torah from his Allah after this period elapsed, the Children of Israel had taken an idol of a calf that made a lowing sound (deep, long sound of a cow) as a god which they worshipped. Allah informed Moses of what his people did after he left them, and Moses went back to them, saddened and furious. He informed his people that their repentance would not be acceptable unless they execute the calf- worshippers among themselves. When they did, Allah forgave them to give them the chance to thank Him and walk in the right straightforward path.

The meaning of the two noble verses is: remember Children of Israel when We made a covenant with Moses to give him the Torah after forty nights. When it was time and Moses came to Us, you worshipped the calf during his absence. Indeed, you have done yourselves a grave injustice by worshipping other than Allah. However, We did not rush to your punishment; We accepted your repentance and forgave you to be among the thankful.

Reminding them of these carries within its folds amazement and incredulity because they met Allah's favors by displaying the most abhorrent and repugnant forms of disbelief and ignorance as they fell for the calf, the epitome of foolishness and stupidity, during the absence of their Prophet.

Using the conjunction (ثم / then) in the statement "then you worshipped the calf in his absence" (Q 2:51) indicates their deterioration to the lowest and most despicable degrees of ingratitude and ignorance, and that what they perpetrated was most detestable, hateful and objectionable.

And His saying: "in his absence," which means after leaving to the mountain to meet his Allah, intensifies the degree of admonition and censure directed to them, since it tarnished their reputation, accusing them of disloyalty and betrayal. It was incumbent upon them to continue worshipping the One Allah during the absence of their Prophet, if they were people who could comprehend, especially after witnessing signs and miracles that should have strengthened their faith, assured their souls and ingrained obedience and compliance in their hearts.

And the sentence "acting wrongfully" (Q 2:51) indicated their condition, their state, making their taking the bull as a god part and parcel of their transgression and offensive conduct from start to finish, and leaving them without any possible excuse for what they did.

His saying: "Even then We still forgave you so perhaps you would be grateful" (Q 2:52) indicates that Allah did not rush to punish them. Rather, He forgave them after they repented for taking the calf as Allah, hoping that they would thank their Creator for pardoning them, appreciate His many favors and believe in His Messenger.

These two noble verses (Qur'an 2:51-52) comprised what indicated the stupidity of the Children of Israel and their short sightedness since they took the calf as a god even though they had witnessed evidence and proofs of the truthfulness of their Prophet. The verses also included some element of amusement to the Messenger of Allah as he witnessed the stance of his contemporary Jews concerning the Islamic call. It was as though the Almighty was saying that the harm and malice that he had endured at the hands of those Jews was more or less similar to what their forefathers did with Moses, their Prophet: they had taken an idol of a calf that made a lowing sound as a god, when he was absent, not even realizing that he could not talk to them or lead them to the straightforward path. They were rebellious wrongdoers.

Fifth: The favor of giving Moses the Torah to guide them:

The Almighty reminded them with a fifth favor that meant to guide and regulate their lives and various affairs, namely, giving the Torah to Moses, their Prophet: "And remember when We gave Moses the Scripture—the decisive authority—that perhaps you would be rightly guided." (Qur'an 2:53)

Meaning: Remember Children of Israel the blessing of giving your Prophet, Moses- peace be upon him- the Torah, which included the principles, tenets and rulings to guide you to success in this world and happiness in the hereafter.

The "Scripture" is the Torah which was given to Moses. The "Furqan/ الفرقان" is taken from a word that means divide (truths from falsehoods). The term "Furqan/ الفرقان" could be used to refer to a revealed book as in "Blessed is the One Who sent down the Decisive Authority to His servant." (Qur'an 25:1) [28] "It could also be used to refer to a sign/miracle as in: "Indeed, We granted Moses and Aaron the decisive authority," (Qur'an 21:48) [29] which means signs since Aaron was not given a revelation.

The word "Furqan/ الفرقان" here is a reference to the Torah.

Ibn Jarir said: "The most likely interpretation of the verse is what was recounted by Ibn Abbas, Abi Al-A'liyya and Mujaahid that the Furqan that Allah brought to Moses was the Book (the Scripture) that differentiated between truths and falsehoods. It is a description of the Torah. Thus, the meaning of the verse is: We brought Moses the Torah which We wrote on tablets and in which we differentiated between truths and falsehoods. Thus, the Scripture is a description of the Torah, taking its place and then referring to it as Al-Furqan (the decisive authority).[30]

His "perhaps you would be rightly guided" (Q 2:53) is a statement that reveals the result, the fruit of bringing the Torah since the goal of bringing the Torah to Moses was to guide them and bring them out of the darkness and into the light.

But what was the position of the Children of Israel regarding the Torah that Allah revealed for their guidance and happiness? As usual, they were ungrateful for Allah's favors. Their sinful evil hands altered and changed it according to their desires and wishes. The Noble Qur'an chastised them for this and likened them to donkeys that carry books filled with knowledge but they do not know what is in them. In Sura Al-Jumu'ah (sura 62), the Almighty said: "The example of those who were entrusted with observing the Torah but failed to do so, is that of a donkey carrying books. How evil is the example of those who reject Allah's signs! For Allah does not guide the wrongdoing people." (Qur'an 62:5)

This means that those Jews were expected to abide by the rulings of the Torah, but they did not do that. They were like a donkey who carries books but does not know what's in them. Nothing comes out of carrying them except toil and hardship, but there is no benefit. Woe to those Jews who did not believe Allah's verses that testified to the truthfulness of the Prophet and described his characteristics that were applicable to him alone. It has been Allah's way not to guide the likes of those errant and sinful people to the right path since they preferred blindness to light and traded their faith for the trifles and lusts of life.

Al-Zamakhshari said: "Allah regarded the Jews as people who carried the Torah, read it and even learned what is in it by heart. However, they did not follow its precepts and tenets, and they failed to benefit from its verses since it foretold the Messenger of Allah and described him, but they did not believe in him. Allah likened them to a donkey who carries voluminous books containing weighty knowledge but knows nothing about their contents. It only labors under the heavy weight of the books. That is the story of he who knows but fails to act according to that knowledge. How dreadful!" [31]

Imam Ibn Al-Qayyim said: "Allah likened those who carry His Book to diligently and attentively read it, apply its information and spread it to others and then fails to do so and reads recklessly without understanding or consideration to a donkey that carries a heavy weight of books but does not know their content. Such people get nothing from Allah's book just as the donkey that carries books on its back. This example, though directed to the Jews, is applicable to anyone who knows about the Qur'an but fails to apply its tenets and does not abide by its precepts." [32]

In sum, we see that Allah gave the Jews the Torah as a light and guidance, but they abandoned it and did not apply its principles and tenets. They liked blindness to guidance and light. Thus, "they have earned wrath upon wrath. And such disbelievers will suffer a humiliating punishment." (Qur'an 2:90)

Sixth: The favor of guiding them to what could absolve them of their sins:

The Almighty reminded them of a noble favor, namely, how they could rid themselves of their sins and telling them that their repentance was accepted. He said: "And remember when Moses said to his people, "O my people! Surely you have wronged yourselves by worshipping the calf, so turn in repentance to your Creator and execute the calf-worshippers among yourselves. That is best for you in the sight of your Creator." Then He accepted your repentance. Surely He is the Accepter of Repentance, Most Merciful." (Qur'an 2:54)

The meaning is: Remember, Children of Israel, for your own sake and benefit, the time when Moses told his people- who worshipped the calf when he was away alone worshipping his God- that they had wronged and degraded themselves by worshipping other than God and that if they wanted to absolve themselves of their transgressions, they should turn to their God (whom Tantawi believes is "Allah") in true and faithful penitence, execute the calf worshippers to receive Allah's forgiveness for that was better in the sight of Allah than their disobedience and transgression. Allah forgave and accepted your repentance when you did, for He is the One who accepts the penitence of His servants no matter how much they have sinned. He is the All-Merciful to those who come to Him and walk in His straightforward path.

Moses' call to his people "O my people!" was a gentle way of addressing them to entice them to listen, to encourage them to receive his commands obediently, and to make them feel that they were his folks: they all belong together. As such, he was undoubtedly seen as one who was not lying or trying to deceive them; rather, he was seen as someone seeking what was right and profitable to them.

The word البارى means the Creator of all creatures who created without any imperfections and without any confusion. It is therefore more specific than the meaning of creator. The Almighty said: "He is Allah: The Creator, the Inventor البارى, the Shaper." (Qur'an 59:24)

Therefore, using such a prudent sensible expression was a judicious way to induce them to repent and obey the Creator البارى, Who perfected everything He had created. It also implied an admonition for their foolishness when they abandoned worshipping the magnificent Inventor of the heavens and the earth and fell for worshipping the calf that was the epitome of stupidity and idiocy. It was referred to as "more stupid than a bull." It was as though the Almighty was telling them that they took that calf as a god because they resembled it in their ignorance, stupidity and folly.

Al-Zamakhshari said: "The البارى is He who created all creation without any discrepancies or imperfections: "You will never see any imperfection in the creation of the Most Compassionate." Everything is distinct from each other through different shapes and forms. It is as though there was an admonition for abandoning the worship of the All-Wise and All-Knowledgeable who had created them- according to His wisdom- in varied and distinct shapes and without any imperfections to worshipping the calf that was the epitome of stupidity and folly. They therefore incurred Allah's wrath when they did not thank Him for His favors and blessings which they ignored and submerged by worshipping something that could do nothing of the amazing things He did." [33]

His "execute ... yourselves" (Q 2:54) was a command by Moses to them so that Allah might accept their repentance; it was a command that Moses received from his God, since such a command would only be issues through a revelation.

The meaning of "execute ...yourselves" was to have those who did not worship the calf kill those who did. So, the meaning is, you should kill each other, as the Almighty said: "However, when you enter houses, greet one another with a greeting ⌜of peace⌝ from Allah, blessed and good." (Qur'an 24:61) That is, greet one another.

It was said that what was intended was that everyone who worshipped the calf should actually kill himself to atone for the sin of worshipping other than Allah. There were reports that they actually did that, but Allah lifted that punishment and forgave those who remained alive out of His Grace and kindness. That was the meaning of repentance in His: "Then He accepted your repentance." And that was the meaning of forgiveness in the previous verse: "Even then We ⌜still⌝ forgave you so perhaps you would be grateful." (Q 2:52)

Ibn Kathir and many other interpreters had reported on the manner of these killings. Among those views was what Sa'id ibn Jabir reported on the authority of ibn Abbas, who said: 'Almighty Allah told Moses that the repentance of calf worshippers was through killing them all; a father could kill his son with the sword, without blinking. Some of them repented, and Allah forgave them the sins they confessed. They did what they were ordered to do, and He forgave both the killer and the killed." [34]

Ibn Jarir reported on the authority of ibn Shihab al-Zuhari, who said: "When the Children of Israel were ordered to execute themselves, they came out with Moses and started to stick each other with their swords and daggers as Moses was raising his hands. When the killing had abated, some came to him and said: 'Entreat your God for our sake.' When God accepted their repentance, they threw the weapons away, and Moses and the Children of Israel were sorrowful for the dead among them. God instructed Moses not to grieve and told him that those who were killed were alive and well with Him, and those remaining had been forgiven. Moses and the Children of Israel were pleased." [35]

The statement “that is best for you in the sight of your Creator”(Q 2:54) is an explanatory sentence; it illustrates what is mentioned before. It was to encourage and incite them to comply with Moses’ commands. The demonstrative that refers to the repentance and executions that were mentioned before.

And His saying “in the sight of your Creator” rather “in His sight” is a repetition (of the word ‘Creator’) that was meant to provoke and push them to think, remember and obey. It was a way of pointing out that worshipping their Creator who had made them with perfection is better for them in this world and in the hereafter.

And the statement “Then He accepted your repentance” (Q 2:54) is a response to a conditional sentence that is omitted for brevity and pithiness. It means” you had complied, so the Creator accepted your repentance. Allah was addressing the Children of Israel through Moses to remind them of His favor and to guide them to the specific favor He granted them, namely, His acceptance of their repentance.

The coordinate conjunction “so/ then=فـ” in the sentence فتاب عليكم (Then He accepted your repentance) was to instill in them the feeling that He did not forsake them to execute themselves, but He overshadowed them with His mercy and compassion by accepting their repentance and lifting the penalty of execution from those remaining alive.

And His “Surely He is the Accepter of Repentance, Most Merciful” (Q 2:54) was a declaration of His forgiveness and mercy. The Almighty was confirming this to comfort and assure those who had extensively erred, transgressed and followed the devil’s path. Even those should not doubt Allah’s mercy and readiness to accept their repentance.

This noble verse recounted a great favor that the Almighty gave to the Children of Israel. He was compassionate and merciful. He accepted their repentance and pardoned them after exhibiting their truthfulness and earnestness in their repentance. The verse also included reminding the Children of Israel who were contemporary with the Prophet of Allah’s favors, for had it not been for Allah’s favors, they would have ceased to be. There was also a reference to the leniency and benevolence of the Islamic Doctrine that Muhammad brought and an appealing invitation for the Jews to accept Islam, for if their forefathers’ penitence was not accepted except by executing themselves, the Islamic doctrine stated that the Prophet who lifted the shackles off of your forefathers had come. Believe in him and follow him, and you will obtain mercy.

Seventh: The favor of bringing them back to life after their death:

The Almighty also reminded them with one of His wonderful favors despite their obstinate and unreasonable demands: bringing them back to life after their death. The Almighty said: “And remember when you said, “O Moses! We will never believe you until we see Allah with our own eyes,” so a thunderbolt struck you while you were looking on. Then We brought you back to life after your death, so that perhaps you would be grateful.” (Qur’an 2:55-56)

The word "جهرة" which here means "With our own eyes/ جهرة" is usually a reference to something that is read aloud, but it is borrowed here because of the clarity it indicates, since it can refer to things audible or visible.

The word "الصاعقة =thunderbolt-" as mentioned by Ibn Jarir- is "every amazing, astounding or mind-blowing issue- such as a great explosion, a fire, an earthquake or a tremor- that one may witness and which would cause destruction, perdition or some horrific consequence. Such "الصاعقة/thunderbolt" would cause amazement, shock and unconsciousness, but NOT death as in His saying "and Moses collapsed unconscious." Moses was not dead because of the shock; he was merely unconscious for Allah said that when he regained consciousness, he said: "Glory be to You! I turn to You in repentance." (Qur'an 7:143) [36]

The word("البعث "= resurrect or bring back) originally means to provoke something to make it move after a period of immobility or stillness as in he caused بعث the camel to move. It is also used in the sense of waking someone up as in the story of the cave people: "So We caused them to fall into a dead sleep in the cave for many years, then We raised them..." (Qur'an 18:11)

It can also be used to mean to raise up from the dead. And that is what is meant in our current verse as can be seen from "after your death." (Q 2:56)

The meaning of the two noble verses (Q 2:55-56): Remember, Children of Israel, when you went overboard and arrogantly made insensible and unreasonable demands of your Prophet, Moses, saying that you would not believe in him or acknowledge what he brought until you can see Allah with your own eyes. Because of your ignorance and wrongdoing, you were struck by a thunderbolt as you were watching. Yet, We kindly covered you with Our mercy and compassion and brought you back to life after you were struck by the thunderbolt, to thank Allah for His mercies and favor for bringing you back to life after your death.

Imam Ibn Jarir said: "Allah reminded them of the arrogance of their forefathers with their prophets despite witnessing many signs and wonderful miracles that should have confirmed their faith and comforted their hearts. Yet, despite the many proofs they had, and notwithstanding the numerous favors that Allah lavishly bestowed upon them, they would at one time ask their prophet to make them another Allah other than the Almighty and, at another time, they would worship the calf. On a third occasion, they would say that they would not believe in him until they see Allah with their own eyes. And at another time, when they were asked to fight, they said: "So go—both you and your Lord—and fight; we are staying right here!" (Qur'an 5:24) Furthermore, they were told: "enter the gate with humility, saying, 'Absolve us.' We will forgive your sins and multiply the reward for the good-doers." (Qur'an 2:58) However, they played on the words, changed them and showed disrespect. They committed many other evil deeds, too numerous to count, and tried to offend and harm their prophet. It was no wonder, then, that those people- like their forefathers- would not believe Muhammad. Rather, they would follow in their predecessors' footsteps in disbelieving in Muhammad, rejecting his message and rebelling against it. After all, they had abandoned their religion on numerous occasions, attacked their Prophet many times despite the many blessings and favors that Allah gave them." [37]

Exegetes believe that those who said to Moses: "O Moses! We will never believe you until we see Allah with our own eyes" (Q 2:55) were the seventy that Moses chose to accompany him when he went to meet his Lord on the mountain. There are reports that support this view.

Among those reports are what Ibn Jarir reported on the authority of Al-Rabi' ibn Anis concerning "so a thunderbolt struck you." He said 'Those were the seventy that Moses chose, and they marched with him. They asked him: 'Show us your Allah to believe you… We will never believe you until we see Allah with our own eyes.' They heard a sound, and they were stunned. They died. "Then We brought you back to life after your death." They were brought back to life because their death was merely a punishment. They remained alive for the rest of their appointed time." [38]

Ibn Kathir said: "Those who said to Moses: 'We want to see Allah with our own eyes' were the chosen seventy. Interpreters agreed on this view." [39]

It was reported that those who demanded to see Allah with their own eyes were the Children of Israel in general, without reference to the chosen seventy. Concerning the interpretation of this verse, Abdul Rahman ibn Zeid ibn Aslam was reported to have said: "When Moses returned with the tablets on which the Torah was written after his appointment with Allah, he found them worshipping the calf and commanded them to execute the calf worshippers. They did, and Allah forgave them. Moses said to them: 'These tablets are Allah's (God's) Book that contains what He commands you to do as well as what He prohibits you from doing.' They said to him: 'Why should we take your word for this? No, until we see Allah with our own eyes. Not until He appears to us and says 'This is My Book, so take it.' Why doesn't He talk to us like He talks to you. When they declared that they wanted to see Allah with their own eyes, a thunderbolt struck them after their repentance. They were stunned and, they died. Then Allah brought them back to life. "Then We brought you back to life after your death, so that perhaps you would be grateful." (Q 2:56)

Then Moses said: "Take Allah's Book." They refused. So, he asked: "What has gotten unto you?" They said: "We were struck dead, and we were brought back to life." He said: "take Allah's Book." Again, they refused, and Allah sent His angels that raised the mountain over them." [40]

It was not appropriate to call their Prophet by name "O Moses!". It was more becoming to address him as "Messenger of Allah" or "Prophet" to reverence and deference. They called him using his name like that on numerous occasions.

It is noteworthy that the Companions of the Messenger of Allah would address Muhammad saying "Messenger of Allah" in compliance with Allah's command: "Do not treat the Messenger's summons to you as lightly as your summons to one another." (Qur'an 24:63)

Their saying: "O Moses! We will never believe you until we see Allah with our own eyes" (Q 2:55) was an indication of their mutiny, rebellion and their indifference of the Allah's blessings and favors and the signs and miracles that they witnessed. They demanded that they see Allah with their own eyes; otherwise, they would doubt the truth of their Prophet.

The Noble Qur'an stated that they wanted to see Allah visibly with their eyes to discard any likelihood that they would be satisfied with seeing Him in a vision or a dream or through a rational mental conviction. Because of the cruelty of their hearts and their mean and vicious manners, they only believe in things that are concrete and tangible.

The Almighty's "so a thunderbolt struck you" (Q 2:55) indicates that the punishment took them by surprise after a very short time of their insensible and illogical demands since the "ف" (so) stresses the immediate consequences.

The statement "while you were looking on" (Q 2:55) indicates that the punishment befell them as they were watching it. In watching an approaching punishment, their hearts must have been filled with awe and terror, even before they felt the physical effect of the punishment that was incurred because of their wrongdoing, mutiny and voracity to get what they had no right to.

The noble verse indicates that the Children of Israel demanded from their Prophet that they see Allah with their eyes. Their faith was completely dependent on that. They did not heed the signs and miracles that attested to the truthfulness of Moses. In essence, they were essentially stubborn and defiant and they were, therefore, struck by a thunderbolt as punishment for this, not for merely asking to see Allah. Thus, the verse shows 'seeing" is not an impossibility as maintained by the Mu'tazilites.

"Then We brought you back to life after your death" (Q 2:56) is a statement that describes the blessing, the favor. It follows right after "so a thunderbolt struck you" using the conjunctionثم/ Then" indicating that between the thunderbolt and bringing them back to life a period of time had elapsed.

Bringing them back to life was a miracle in response to Moses' supplication on their behalf.

The two noble verses (Q 2:55-56) deliver a warning to those Jews who were contemporaneous with the Prophet against fighting the Islamic call to avoid being plighted with calamities- such as thunderbolts and others- that had befallen their ancestors. They also comfort the Prophet by indicating that whatever he experienced from the Jews was similar to what their forefathers had done to their own prophets. In addition, they report a new kind of favor that Allah bestowed upon them and for which they should have been grateful, if they were people who comprehended.

Eighth: The favor of shading them with clouds and sending down manna and quail:

After mentioning the favor of bringing them back to life after their death, the Almighty immediately followed it with another favor. In fact, He mentioned TWO favors: He shaded them with clouds, and He provided them with manna and quail. The Almighty said: "And remember when We shaded you with clouds and sent down to you manna and quails, saying, "Eat from the good things We have provided for you." The evildoers certainly did not wrong Us, but wronged themselves." (Qur'an 2:57)

Clouds الغمام are a visible mass of miniature liquid droplets. Some linguists refer to it as white clouds.

Manna المن is like a glue, rubbery substance that falls on trees. It resembles honey in its sweetness.

Quail السلوىis a wild bird that has delicious meat and is easy to catch. Winds blowing from the south would bring these birds to them every evening, and they could catch them with ease and felicity, without toil.

Shading them with clouds and bringing down manna and quail took place during the Israelites time wandering in the wilderness between Egypt and Levant. This is referenced in His saying: "Allah replied, "Then this land is forbidden to them for forty years, during which they will wander through the land. So do not grieve for the rebellious people." (Qur'an 5:26)

Al-Suddi said: When the Children of Israel went into the wilderness, they asked Moses- peace be upon him- where they could get food to eat! The Almighty brought down manna, which came down on ginger trees. He also brought them quails. If it were fleshy, they would slaughter it. Otherwise, they would let it go until it fattens. So, they said: Well! This is food. What about the drink? So, Allah ordered Moses to strike a solid rock with his staff. When Moses did that, twelve springs of running water burst from that stone to quench the thirst of the twelve tribes. Now that they drank, they asked Moses for a shade. Allah shaded them with clouds. Then they asked about the dress! Their clothes kept on covering them; they would expand to accommodate their needs, and none of their clothes were torn. That is seen in: "And … We shaded you with clouds and sent down to you manna and quails…." (Q 2:57) [41]

The noble verse means: Remember Children of Israel that among My favors for you was the favor of shading you with clouds while you were wandering in the wilderness to protect you from the sun and the heat. I also provided you with delicious food without having to work hard to get it. We told you to eat of that good food that we had provided and thank your Lord who gave you all those favors. However, you only wronged yourselves for your ungratefulness; it was not Me you wronged.

The noble verse points out their ungrateful stance towards Allah's favor: "The evildoers 'certainly' did not wrong Us, but wronged themselves." Describing their wrongdoing using (كانوا + the present tense يظلمون= they used to…) indicates that wronging themselves was a repeated occurrence, something that took place again and again.

Interpreting the Almighty's "The evildoers certainly did not wrong Us, but wronged themselves," (Q 2:57) Imam Ibn Jarir said: "They diverged from Our commandment, disobeyed their Allah and then opposed Our Messenger to them. 'They didn't wrong Us' by what they did means that their disobedience and wrongdoing did not affect Us; it did not harm in the least; rather, it harmed them. The Almighty would not suffer because of the transgression of an evildoer, nor would His treasures become less because of the injustices of the unjust. The disobedient would become regretful and the obedient would thrive and prosper" [42]

The favor of shading the Children of Israel with clouds is also mentioned elsewhere in the Noble Qur'an. In Sura Al-A'raf, the Almighty said: "And remember when it was said to them, "Enter this city [of Jerusalem] and eat from wherever you please. Say, 'Absolve us,' and enter the gate with humility. We will forgive your sins, and We will multiply the reward for the good-doers." But the wrongdoers among them changed the words they were commanded to say. So, We sent down a punishment from the heavens upon them for their wrongdoing." (7:161-162) [43]

Thus, these noble verses reminded the Children of Israel with one of the magnanimous favors that Allah granted them: shading them with clouds and sending down manna and quail. However, the Children of Israel did not show appreciation and gratitude to Allah. That was why, He sent down a severe punishment from the heavens upon them for their wrongdoing, rebelliousness and immorality.

Ninth: The favor of enabling them to enter Jerusalem and their desisting from doing that:

The Almighty then reminded them of a great favor that they did not receive well nor gave it its due weight and value: ending their laborious wandering in the wilderness and giving them permission to enter a town where they would find comfort and happiness. He also directed them to say what would save them from the punishments that they deserved, but they opposed Him. The Almighty said: "And remember when We said, "Enter this city القرية and eat freelyرغدا from wherever you please; enter the gate with humility, saying, 'Absolve us حطة.' We will forgive your sins and multiply the reward for the good-doers." (Q 7:161) But the wrongdoers changed the words they were commanded to say. So, We sent down a punishment from the heavens upon them for their rebelliousness."

Cityالقرية : A town that has houses. A reference to Jerusalem, most likely.

Freely رغدا : comfortable living

Absolve حطة: Asking for the forgiveness of sins.

Al-Zamakhshari said that the word حطة means to absolve of sin. [44]

The meaning: Remember Children of Israel- as an example and a lesson to learn from- that We commanded your predecessors to enter Jerusalem after ending their wandering in the wilderness and giving them permission to eat from the good food that We provided. We told them to enter through the gates in humility as a sign of gratitude and thankfulness to Allah for the blessing of opening the Holy Land for them. We asked them to implore the Almighty to forgive their sins. If they had just done this simple thing and said those few words, We would have forgiven their sins and multiplied the rewards of the good doers. However, they were ungrateful and disobeyed Allah's commandments. They changed the words that Allah commanded them to say and used other words that they came up with showing stubbornness and a mocking frivolous demeanor. So, we sent down a punishment from the heavens because of their rebelliousness.

Imam Ibn Kathir said: "They came out of the wilderness with Joshua bin Nun after forty years. They came to Jerusalem and besieged it. It was a Friday evening and the sun began to set. Allah withheld the sun on that day until they were able to enter the city. When it was opened for them, they were commanded to enter the gate with humility. That is, they should show gratitude and thank Allah for giving them the ability and the favor to enter the city victoriously and for saving them from wandering and drifting erratically in the wilderness." [45]

The Almighty's: "and eat freely from wherever you please" (Q 7:161) reflects the favor that was abundantly given to them. Allah gave them the permission to enjoy the fruits of the city and all its food anywhere they wanted.

And His: "enter the gate with humility, saying, 'Absolve us'" (Q 7:161) was a directive as to what they should do regarding their Creator: being thankful and humble. It was also an instruction to help them attain their goals in the simplest and easiest way possible. All they were commanded to do was to enter the gate of the city which Allah opened for them with thanksgiving and humility and to entreat Him to forgive their sins and wipe out their transgressions.

His saying: "We will forgive your sins" (Q 7:161) shows the consequence of their obedience and submission to their Creator. It should have encouraged them to comply with Allah's commandments and thank Him, if they were people who comprehended. After all, the ultimate goal of sensible and discerning people is the forgiveness of sins.

Imam Ibn Jarir said: "The meaning of the Almighty's 'We will forgive your sins' was that We would wipe out your sins because of My compassion, I will not bring My punishment down on you." [46]

The Almighty's "and multiply the reward for the good-doers" was a promise to increase- here in this world and in the hereafter- the blessings and rewards of the righteous who submitted to Allah and performed good deeds. In other words, those good doers would have their rewards multiply and increase, and those transgressors would have their sins covered and forgiven.

The Almighty commanded them to enter the gate of the city they opened with humility and to seek His forgiveness because vanquishing their enemies and entering the Holy Land that Allah assigned for them were great and magnanimous favors. It was their obligation and duty Allah for these favors both in words and in deeds so that He would increase His favors and multiply them. The good and righteous receive Allah's favors with thanksgiving.

That was why when the Prophet would overcome his enemies and attain his goals, he would show complete and thorough humility and submission to the Almighty. When he opened Mecca through the upper corner in complete humility to the extent that his honorable head almost touched his camel's neck, thanking Allah for the favor of conquest. After entering Mecca, he washed (performed ablution) and prayed eight Rak'ahs which some jurisprudents call "the prayer of conquest."

From the aforementioned example, jurisprudents encourage Muslims to perform eight Rak'ahs when they conquer/open a city in thankfulness and gratitude to Allah. Sa'd ibn Abi Waqaas when he opened Taq Kisra (Also known as the Arch of Ctesiphon). It was confirmed that he performed eight Rak'ahs inside it.

But, what did the Children of Israel do when Allah blessed them with the favor of opening (Jerusalem)?

They did not do what they were commanded to do, nor did they say what they were asked to say. They did not comply with what they were commanded to do either in words or in deeds. That was why, the Almighty said: "But the wrongdoers changed the words they were commanded to say." (Qur'an 2:59) Al-Bukhari related on the authority of Abi Hurayra, who said: "It was said to the Children of Israel; 'enter the gate with humility, saying, 'Absolve us حطة ' (Q 2:58), but they did not and they entered crawling on their steps, and they changed the words and said: 'a grain in a barley.'" [47]

Imam Kathir said: "According to what the interpreters mentioned and what the context implies, they altered the commandment of Allah to show humility in both words and deeds. They were commanded to enter the gate with humility; however, they entered arrogantly with their heads up high. They were commanded to say 'absolve us.' In other words, forgive us our sins and transgressions. However, they mocked the commandment and said 'grain in a barley,' playing on the words. That was the utmost act of defiance, obstinacy and opposition. That was why, Allah brought down His punishment and wrath. It was because of their immorality and obstinate opposition to obey Him." [48]

The Almighty's saying: "But the wrongdoers changed the words they were commanded to say" (Q 2:59) is a statement that relates the reason for sending down a punishment upon them and rebuking them for opposing Allah's commandments. "Changing" something means altering or removing it from its former form or purport and giving or adding a different meaning or form that is at variance with the original.

The verb changed requires two things: what it was changed into and what it was changed from. For the sake of brevity and terseness in the verse, only what it was changed into is mentioned, i.e., the saying that was not said to them. There is no mention of what it was changed from, i.e., what they were commanded to say. So, the wrongdoers chose other words other than what Allah commanded them to say. It was something that they came up with on their own by way of opposition and rebelliousness.

Al-Zamakhshari said: "But the wrongdoers changed the words they were commanded to say" means that instead of 'Absolve us حطة , they said something else. That is, they were commanded to say something that meant asking for forgiveness, but they opposed it and said something that did not mean what they were commanded to say. They did not comply with Allah's commandments. It was not that they were commanded to say the specific term Absolve usحطة , and they just used another term. For had they come up with another term that still had a similar meaning and fulfilled what they were commanded to say, they would blameless and irreproachable. Had they said 'we ask for Your forgiveness' or anything with a similar meaning instead of حطة, they would have been guiltless" [49]

The lesson we learn from this noble verse (Q 2:59) is that whosoever receives a commandment by the Almighty, rejects it and comes up with something other than what Allah has commanded would be considered one of the wrongdoers destined to punishment and an "evil destination."

The Almighty's saying: "So, We sent down a punishment from the heavens upon them for their rebelliousness" is a declaration that the torture that befell them was the result of their disobedience, rebellion and ungratefulness. The word "الرجز," in Arabic, means torture by different ways whether various diseases or other forms of torture and punishment.

Saying that this الرجز (torture) was sent down from heaven indicates that it was some punishment that could not be avoided or shunned. There was no earthly reason- such as contagiousness or the like- for it. Rather, it was the angels from heaven who sent it down and afflicted the wrongdoers only. It is worth mentioning that the Qur'an did not say "We sent down on them" in general. It said "We sent down on the wrongdoers," specifically mentioning a certain group, to emphasize the ugliest aspects of their qualities, i.e., wrongdoing, and to indicate that what befell them was the result of their injustices and jealous animosity.

The two noble verses Q 2:58-59) reveal that the Children of Israel were granted a favor, yet they rejected it; the doors of goodness and prosperity were opened to them, yet they refused to enter; they were directed to saying what would absolve them from their transgressions, yet they flagrantly and overtly opposed it. As a consequence of their ungratefulness and opposition of Allah's commandments, that favor was denied them for a while, and they were afflicted with a severe punishment. Rejecting a favor did not prevent it from it being a favor, and it must have provoked sorrow and regret in the hearts of those Jews who were contemporary with the Prophet for what their ancestors had wasted on account of their rebelliousness and opposition. There was also a warning to them not to follow in the footstep of their forefathers to avert the severe punishment that afflicted them.

Tenth: The favor of Quenching their thirst:

The Almighty also reminded them with one of His most marvelous favors, i.e., providing them with water to quench their thirst while wandering in the wilderness. The Almighty said: "And remember when Moses prayed for water for his people, We said, "Strike the rock with your staff." Then twelve springs gushed out, and each tribe knew its drinking place. We then said, "Eat and drink of Allah's provisions, and do not go about spreading corruption in the land." (Qur'an 2:60)

Moses asked Allah in submission and humility since there was no water or rain. He entreated Allah for water "الاستسقاء" so that the Children of Israel would quench their thirst while they were wandering in the wilderness. [50]Ibn Abbas said: "It was while they were wandering that Moses struck the stone with his staff and twelve springs of running water gushed out, one for each tribe." [51]

This favor was of significant importance to them in this life. It satisfied their overwhelming need to drink and quench their thirst. But for this great favor, they would have perished. It was also of great significance to their faith as it was one of the clearest proofs of the existence of Allah, His might and His knowledge. It was also one of the greatest proofs for the truthfulness of Moses' message.

The meaning of the noble verse: Remember Children of Israel when your forefathers were extremely thirsty in that barren desert and Moses, their Prophet, entreated that I provide them with water to quench their thirst and I inspired him to strike the rock with his staff. He did and twelve springs of water- the number of the tribes- gushed out. Each tribe knew its drinking place. And We said enjoy the delicious foods and drinks that Allah had provided you without toil and hard work. Just "do not go about spreading corruption in the land;" otherwise, these favors and blessing would be taken away from you, and you would regret what you had done.

The almighty's "when Moses prayed for water for his people "indicates that it was Moses-alone-who entreated his Lord for water so that Moses's high honor and status in the Lord's sight would be revealed to his people and in order for them to witness with their own eyes how Allah would honor him by granting him his request and causing water to gush out of the rock because of his prayers.

The "ال"in the word "الحجر"(the rock) was meant to indicate any rock at all, without a particular reference to a specific rock which, in that case, might be taken as a specific rock that Allah had revealed to Moses. Exegetes have researched that point and reached conclusions that investigators believe to be unfounded. That is why, we have decided not to consider them.

What we believe to be most likely is that the gushing of the water from any rock proved the truthfulness of Moses, and prompted the Children of Israel to believe him and follow the truth after it was made clear and transparent. Furthermore, it removed any doubts concerning Allah's honoring Moses, His Prophet, for had the gushing of the water come from a specific rock, they might have concluded the gushing of water had something to do with a particular rock, not because of Moses' status in the sight of his Lord.

There were twelve springs of water because there were twelve tribes for the Children of Israel. The tribes of the Children of Israel were the descendants of the children of Jacob. The gushing of the water from twelve springs was a completion of the favor that Allah bestowed upon them; each tribe had a spring to drink from; there were no altercations, clashes or disputes amongst them.

The Almighty said: فَٱنفَجَرَتْ "gushed out" (coming out with force) and in Sura Al-A'raf (Qur'an 7:160), He said: فَٱنۢبَجَسَتْ (coming out slowly). There is no contradiction between the two because the water flows slowly at first and then it gushes out with more force.

And His saying: "each tribe knew its drinking place" (Q 2:60) indicates the wisdom of having twelve different springs. Each tribe knew its drinking place, so there was no confusion or altercations between them. That must have comforted them and gave them feel secure and stable. There were no hostilities or acts of aggression between them.

And His saying: "Eat and drink of Allah's provisions" (Q 2:60) indicates that it was We (Allah) who told them to eat and drink.

The Almighty combined food and drink in this verse even though the focus was on drinking. That is because food was mentioned earlier when Allah provided them with manna and quail where the Almighty said: "Eat from the good things We have provided for you." (Q 2:60) Now that the water had gushed out of the springs, they had the two favors combined.

The Almighty's saying: "do not go about spreading corruption in the land" was to caution them against ungratefulness and conceit. He was warning them not to abuse the blessings and favors they were granted after He had given them the permission to enjoy the good things He offered them. Sometimes a person might forget his obligations and duty to his Creator and forsake Allah's law and corrupt the land when blessings abound. The Almighty said: "Most certainly, one exceeds all bounds once they think they are self-sufficient." (Qur'an 96:6-7)

The meaning is: Do not spread corruption in the land and receive favors and blessings with ungratefulness and thanklessness. Otherwise, they will be taken away from you.

Ibn Jarir said: "the origin of the word العثا (Corruption) indicates an excessive degree of corrupting something." [52]

Thus, the noble verse reminded the Children of Israel with another great favor, encouraged them to be thankful for it and cautioned them against spreading corruption in the land.

Eleventh: The favor of encompassing them with His favor and mercies despite violating their covenants:

The Almighty reminded them of the favor of encompassing them with His grace and mercy despite turning away and disobeying Him and violating their covenant. The Almighty said: "And remember when We took a covenant from you and raised the mountain above you saying, "Hold firmly to that Scripture which We have given you and observe its teachings so perhaps you will become mindful of Allah. Yet you turned away afterwards. Had it not been for Allah's grace and mercy upon you, you would have certainly been of the losers." (Qur'an 2:63-64)

Ibn Jarir said: "The reason for taking a covenant from them as mentioned by ibn Zeid, who said: 'When Moses returned with the tablets, he told his people, the Children of Israel, that those were the tablets with Allah's commandments and prohibitions, what He has permitted and what He had forbidden. They said to him: Why should we believe you? No, not until we see Allah with our eyes! Not until Allah appears and says: 'This is My Book, so take it. Why doesn't He speak to us like He speaks to you, Moses? Why doesn't he say to us: 'This is My Book. Take it.' Allah was wrathful and a thunderbolt struck them, and they all died. Then Allah brought them back to life. Moses said to them: 'Take Allah's Book.' They said: 'No.' He said: 'What has come over you?' They said: We all died and then we were brought back to life.' He said: 'Take Allah's Book.' They said: 'No.' Allah sent angels that raised the mountain over them. It was said to them: 'Do you know that?' They said: 'Yes. This is the mountain.' He said: 'Take the Book or We will cause to fall on you.' He said; 'they took it by a covenant.' He said: 'Had they taken it the first time, they would have taken it without a covenant.'" [53]

The meaning of the two noble verses (Q 2:63-64): Remember, Children of Israel, as a lesson for your benefit, the time when We made a covenant with you to worship Allah alone, follow the teachings of His messengers and comply with the Torah. Also, remember when We raised the mountain over your forefathers threatening them with severe punishment if they did not obey Allah's commandments, and when We told you to hold firmly to that Scripture which We had given you and to observe its teachings vigilantly, and follow its instructions and directives attentively to avoid perdition in this world and severe torment in the hereafter. However, you all failed to comply with what you had been instructed: you abandoned the teachings of your Scriptures, and you offended and harmed your prophets. Had not the Almighty had compassion upon you, guided you to repentance and forgiven your sins, you would have perished in this world and in the hereafter.

And the Almighty's saying: "and raised the mountain above you" means We raised it above your heads as a cloud.

الطُّورَis the name of the mountain on which Moses talked to his Lord. The Children of Israel were below it, so it was raised above their heads. They were reminded of this in many verses as in Sura Al-A'raf: "And remember when We raised the mountain over them as if it were a cloud and they thought it would fall on them. We said, "Hold firmly to that Scripture which We have given you and observe its teachings so perhaps you will become mindful of Allah. " (Qur'an 7:171) [54]

Imam Al-Qurtubi said: "نَتَقْنَا (raised) means shook and moved it from its place. A reference to anything that you pluck and throw. It was also said that نَتَقْنَا means we lifted it. Ibn Al-A'rabi said الناتق is a lifter." [55]

Interpreting the noble verse, the honorable Sheikh Muhammad Al-Khader Hussein said: "Taking a covenant from them took place before raising the mountain above them. It was to show them one of Allah's signs to strengthen their faith that the Torah was revealed by Allah because a strong faith encourages and stimulates to observe and hold firmly to what's in the revealed Scripture." [56]

His saying: "Hold firmly to that Scripture which We have given you" (Q 7:171) means We instructed you to adhere firmly to what you have in the Scripture, follow it attentively and observe it diligently accepting it wholeheartedly and without any hesitation and without wavering and faltering.

The statement "We have given you" refers to the Torah that Allah revealed to Moses as a guide and light to them. And His "observe its teachings" is a directive for them to memorize it, study it, follow it, avoid whatever it prohibits, and observe all that it had brought with diligence. (Q 7:171)

Imam Al-Qurtubi said that that was what is meant by Scriptures; they should be followed and observed assiduously and thoughtfully, not merely recited orally. Al-Nisa'i narrated on the authority of Abi Sa'id Al-Khadari that the Messenger of Allah said: 'The evilest person is immoral and corrupt who recites the Qur'an without understanding or following its tenets." [57]

The Almighty's "perhaps you لَعَلَّكُمْ will become mindful of Allah" (Q 7:171) is used either for "reasoning," in which case the meaning would be: Take the Scriptures seriously and earnestly and observe what's contained therein honestly and obediently in order to avert punishment in this world and in the hereafter. Or, it could be meant to indicate "pleading," in which case, it is directed to the addressees and it means: Take what We had given you firmly, hold firmly unto it, observe it and do not forget it if you wanted to be amongst the righteous.

And His: "Yet you turned away afterwards" (Q 2:64) is a statement of their failure and unwillingness to keep their covenant and throwing it behind their backs.

The Almighty's saying "مِنۢ بَعۡدِ ذَٰلِكَ afterwards" is a reference to the covenant taken from them and their acceptance of the Scriptures. The meaning: You turned away and disobeyed Me after taking the covenant from you and witnessing signs that should have assured and comforted your hearts because your hearts are like stones or even harder.

The Almighty's: "Had it not been for Allah's grace and mercy upon you, you would have certainly been of the losers" (Q 2:64) indicated Allah's mercy, His acceptance of their repentance and His forgiveness of their transgressions. It was as though the Almighty was saying: You had earned My wrath and punishment for your disobedience, violating My covenant, and neglecting to observe My Scriptures. However, I encompassed you with My grace, mercy and compassion. I had been lenient, tolerant and patient with you. Otherwise, you would have been losers in this world and in the hereafter because of violating your covenant.

Thus, the two noble verses (Q 2:63-64) reminded the Jews who were contemporary with the Prophet how ungrateful their ancestors were for the favor they received and how the violated their covenant. Through reminding them, they also cautioned them not to follow their ways, and they invited them to accept Islam and follow Muhammad.

They were ungrateful for the favor and they exchanged what was good and valuable for what was bad and worthless, what was better for what was worth.

The Almighty then reminded them of their ungratefulness and their taking Allah's favor lightly and exchanging- on account of their unsound and flawed decision- what was good and profitable for what was bad and worthless. The Almighty said: "And remember when you said, "O Moses! We cannot endure لَن نَّصۡبِرَ the same mealطَعَامٖ وَٰحِدٖ every day. So just call upon your Lord on our behalf, He will bring forth for us some of what the earth produces of herbs بَقۡلِهَا, cucumbers, garlicالفوم , lentils, and onions." Moses scolded them "Do you exchange what is better for what is worse? 'You can go down to any village and you will find what you have asked for." They were stricken with disgrace and misery, and they invited the displeasure of Allah for rejecting Allah's signs and unjustly killing the prophets. This is a fair reward for their disobedience and violations." (Qur'an 2:61)

(لَن نَّصۡبِرَ / We will not be patient). Patience is some kind of self-restraint or keeping oneself from something as in, for example, restraining oneself from transgressions and inequities. The "food" referred to here was what was provided for them in the wilderness: manna and quail. (herbs/ بَقۡلِهَا) is what the earth produces that people eat such as الفومgarlic (which was said to mean wheat) and وَقِثَّآئِ which was a kind of food bigger than cucumber in size.

Ibn Jarir said: "The reason for asking this of Moses as narrated by Ibn Quttada, who said: 'The people in the wilderness were protected from the sun by the clouds. They were also provided with manna and quail. They became bored, and they remembered their life in Egypt. They asked Moses, and the Almighty Allah said: ''You can go down to any village and you will find what you have asked for.'" (Qur'an 2:61) [58]

Then Ibn Jarir narrated a story in which he confirmed that their question to Moses was not in the wilderness but it was while they were wandering. He said: Younis ibn Abdul A'la said that ibn Wahab said that ibn Zeid said:

The food of the Children of Israel was the same, and their drink was also the same. They drank honey that came down to them from the heavens. It was called manna. They ate some kind of bird called quail. So, they ate quails and drank manna. They did not know bread or other foods. They said to Moses: 'We will not be patient with the same meal, so ask your Lord to bring forth the herbs that the land produces.' He read until he reached the Almighty's '⌜You can⌝ go down to any village and you will find what you have asked for.'" [59]

Abou Hayyan and Al-Zamakhshari also believe that the request was made during their wandering.

Interpreting the Almighty's "And ⌜remember⌝ when you said, "O Moses! We cannot endure the same meal every day," Abou Hayyan said: 'When they became bored of wandering and eating the same meal being away from the land in which they were accustomed to dwell and the things they were accustomed to get, they related their inability to endure and be patient, and they expressed their longing to what they were accustomed to, so they asked Moses to entreat Allah for them.' (Q 2:61) [60]

Al-Zamakhshari said: "They were farmers, and they felt that longing for their origin and habits.[61] They got bored and hated the blessing and favor they had, and they sought their own misery. They (did not!) want the manna and quail they had while wandering." [62]

In brief, the meaning of the noble verse is: Remember, Children of Israel, now that we had bestowed Our favors upon you how unsound and flawed your ancestors' decisions and how unbecoming and inappropriate their perceptions were. They maliciously rebelled against Moses, their Prophet, and arrogantly and inappropriately said to him: 'We will not endure the meal of manna and quail all the time. Ask your Allah to provide us with what the earth produces of its fruits, vegetables, herbs, lentils and onion. We have become sick and tired of Manna and quail.' Moses scolded them saying: 'Do you exchange what is less delicious and useful for manna and quail, which are more delicious and useful? Go down to any of the villages and you will find the herbs and these things that you are asking for.'

Disgrace, misery and Allah's wrath descended upon them.

Then, the Almighty showed the reason for their ungratefulness and that they were stricken with disgrace and misery and that they were deserving of His anger "for rejecting Allah's signs and unjustly killing the prophets." (Q 2:61) Rejecting Allah's signs had become deeply- rooted in them, and unjustly killing Allah's prophets was repeated again and again until it became like second nature to them. It was therefore not unexpected for such people as those to say 'we will not endure the favor of manna and quail.' And it was not unexpected that that would invite Allah's displeasure for all the injustices and ungratefulness they had shown.

The Almighty's saying: "O Moses! We cannot endure the same meal every day" reminded them with one of their desires that had its roots in their unwholesome and morbid inclinations and their inability to give favors their due value. The verse also revealed their propensities to follow their desires, lusts and folly as well as their inappropriate, impolite and arrogant behavior with Moses, their prophet. They expressed their rejection of manna and quail by using /لَنْ' (=will not) in لَن نَّصْبِرَ / (=will nit endure...). It was as though they were threatening him in order to push him to call upon his Lord speedily. In essence, they were saying: From this moment until we die, we will not endure the same meal everyday because we have become bored and sick of it, and we will not go back to it. Using /لَنْ' (=will not) betrayed their overwhelming and consuming anger and hatred for that food.

Al-Hasan al-Basri said: "They were ungrateful and hated the taste of the manna and quail and were unable to take it anymore. They remembered the life they had before. And they were people who lived on lentils, onions, herba and garlic." [63]

And they described the food they were getting as "طَعَامٍ وَاحِدٍ = same meal/one kind," even though manna and quail are two different things. They wanted to emphasize that it was one kind that was repeated every day. The Arabs usually refer to those who offer MANY kinds of food that do not change on their table as one kind.

They asked Moses, peace be upon him, to entreat Allah on their behalf, because it is more likely that Allah would answer the prayers and supplications of the prophets and the righteous because their supplications proceed from hearts that abound with piety and reverence to the Almighty. Accordingly, their prayers and supplications would be answered more likely than those who are consumed by their desires and overtaken by their evil deeds.

They said to Moses: "just call upon YOUR Lord on our behalf." (Q 2:61) They did not say "our" Lord. That was because their faith was shaky and wabbly; they did not have strong faith in their hearts. Also, Allah had given Moses a special status that He did not confer on them; He gave Moses the torah and the ability to talk to Him.

Their: "He will bring forth for us some of what the earth produces of herbs, cucumbers, garlic, lentils, and onions" (Q 2:61) showed the things they wanted from Moses. It implied "Tell your Lord to bring..."

The verb يُخْرِجْ = produce (used in the genitive) seemed to insinuate their certainty that if Moses called upon his Lord, He would answer his prayers. It was as if the yield of the earth was dependent on Moses' entreaties merely and that if he did not entreat his Lord, He would have been miserly in what would have been beneficial and useful to them. [64]

The noble statement: "Do you exchange what is better for what is worse?" (Q 2:61) was a strong admonition for their bad choice and feeble minds since they showed preference to something less, i.e., herbs and other similar choices, to what was better, i.e., manna and quail.

Interpreting this noble verse, Ibn Jarir said: "So, Moses asked them: 'would you choose what is less and worse in value over is better and more valuable?' That was the exchange that they wanted. "Exchanging" means leaving something and choosing another in its place. The meaning of ادنى is = less/worse/inferior/mean. For example, when we say; 'This is a mean man,' we mean to say that he is nasty, despicable and revolting. Then, he said: 'There is no doubt that he who exchanges manna and quail for herbs, lentils, onions and garlic has exchanged a sublime way of living for a despicable, shameful and mean one." [65]

Moses then added another admonition to the one previously mentioned concerning their ungratefulness and churlishness. He said: "You can go down to any village and you will find what you have asked for." (Q 2:61) In other words, if that is what you want, you can leave this place and go to one of the villages to get what whatever you want of herbs, garlic and the like because you will find what you seek in villages, not in this place where you are now.

Regarding His saying: " مِصْرًا" (village) Ibn Kathir said: "This is how it is written Qur'an of the Imam (alsi, the Qur'an of Othman) with the ا (Alif) and nunation." [66]

Ibn Jarir said: "The reading is with the ا (Alif) and nunation: آهْبِطُوا مِصْرًا (go down to any village). This is the only possible reading for me since all versions of the Qur'an as well as the reading of the public agree on this." [67]

In Al-Bahr Al-Muhit, Abou Hayyan said: "Al-Hasan, Talha, Al-A'mash and aban bin Taghlub read مِصْر without nunation which also occurred in the Abi ibn Ka'ab and Abdulah ibn Masoud and some of Othman's Qur'ans." [68]

According to the first reading, the meaning would be: Go down to one of the villages/ مِصْرًا because what you are seeking cannot be found here in this Bedouin land, but you can find it in villages and hamlets.

According to the second reading, the meaning is: Leave this place where you are now and go back to مِصْر /Egypt where you experienced all kinds of torture. There you will find what you want because you are a people who do not appreciate freedom or value psychological comfort. You would rather exchange what is better for what is worse.

Those who believe that by مِصْر - in that noble verse- Allah meant Egypt (Pharaoh's Egypt) cite the Almighty's saying in Sura Ash-Shu'ara (Qur'an 26:57-59): "So We lured the tyrants out of their gardens, springs, treasures, and splendid residences. So, it was. And We awarded it ˹all˺ to the Children of Israel."

In Sura Ad-Dukhan, the Almighty also said: "And leave the sea parted, for they are certainly an army bound to drown. Imagine how many gardens and springs the tyrants left behind, as well as various crops and splendid residences, and luxuries which they fully enjoyed. So, it was. And We awarded it all to another people." (Qur'an 44:24-28)

Ibn Jarir said: "Those who say that what Allah meant by آهْبِطُوا مِصْرًا was to go to any of the villages, not to Pharaoh's Egypt in particular, claim that the Almighty destined the land of the Levant for the Children of Israel to dwell in after bringing them out of Egypt. However, He plighted them with wandering when they refused Moses' command to fight against Amalek, an enormously powerful people there. He said: "O my people! Enter the Holy Land which Allah has destined for you to enter. And do not turn back or else you will become losers" (Qur'an 5:21) up to "O Moses! Still we will never enter as long as they remain there. So go—both you and your Lord—and fight; we are staying right here!" (Qur'an 5:24) For this reason, Allah prevented them from entering the Holy Land. They perished in the wilderness and Allah plighted them with wandering in the land for forty years. Then, He permitted their offspring to go to the Levant and made them dwell in the Holy Land, caused Amalek to perish at the hands of Joshua son of Nun after the death of Moses son of Amran. So, we see that the almighty had mentioned that He allotted the Holy Land to them, but He did not mention that He brought them back to Egypt after He brought them out of it. Therefore, it is likely that we read آهْبِطُوا مِصْرًا (go back to مِصْر /Egypt) and think that He caused them to come back to it. If someone is opposed to this and cites the Almighty's: "So We lured the tyrants out of their gardens, springs, treasures, and splendid residences. So, it was. And We awarded it all to the Children of Israel," (Qur'an 26:57-59) the response would be that Allah made them inherit the land, but He did not bring them back, and He made the Levant their dwelling place." [69]

In Al-Bahr Al-Muhit, Abou Hayyan said: "No historian or interpreter mentioned that they returned to Egypt after their wandering in the land." [70]

Although Ibn Jarir responded to those who claimed that what was meant by مِصْر /Egypt was Pharaoh's Egypt, he did not favor one view over the other. He said: "What we can say is that there is no evidence in Allah's Book concerning the validity of either interpretation. Interpreters also differ on this matter. It is most likely, however, to suggest that Moses asked his Lord to provide his people with what the earth produces while they were wandering in the land. Allah answered Moses' pleas and asked Moses and his people to go to a land that produces what they desired since what they wanted could only be found in villages and hamlets. He would provide them if they headed there. That could be Egypt, and it could also be the Levant." [71]

The aforementioned text from Ibn Jarir does not indicate decisively the place to which the Children of Israel were ordered to go. He does, however, believe that the Almighty did answer Moses' entreaties, and that Moses and his people did, in fact, go to a certain land that produced herbs and the like.

In his interpretation, Imam Ibn Kathir opposed Ibn Jarir's view. He said:

"What was meant by مِصْر was one of the villages or hamlets, as narrated by Ibn Abbas and others. It was as though Moses was telling them that what they were seeking was not of great value and would be available in great quantities in any village or town they enter. So, because what they were asking for was cheap and available, it was not becoming for

Moses to ask Allah for it. That was why he said: "Do you exchange what is better for what is worse? You can go down to any village and you will find what you have asked for." (Q 2:61) And since what they sought was out of ungratefulness and unappreciativeness, even unnecessary, they were not given what they wanted. Allah knows!" [72]

Thus, it seems evident that Ibn Kathir believed that what was meant by مِصْر was an unidentified place, and that Moses did not ask his Lord to answer their request because of their arrogant ungratefulness. Allah hates the arrogant and the ungrateful. And Moses' "You can go down to any village and you will find what you have asked for" (Q 2:61) was meant as an admonition and a rebuke, pointing, as it did, to their ignorance and witlessness since there was no close village or town nearby then.

On this issue, however, we favor Imam Ibn Kathir's views for the following reasons:

First: Reading with nunation [72a] was in accordance with the Chain of Interpretation. Ibn Jarir himself would only admit that it was the only way possible. Accordingly, the meaning of was any country- not Pharaoh's Egypt. It could not have been Pharaoh's Egypt because the villages that would have produced the herbs and vegetables that they desired were closer to them than Egypt. It would have been illogical and inconceivable to be ordered to go Pharaoh's Egypt which was very far away from them while they had villages that were closer and produced the same things they wanted.

Second: As mentioned by Abou Hayyan and others, no historian ever mentioned that they returned to Egypt after exiting it. It is well-known, however, that the Children of Israel departed from Egypt, and they were commanded to enter the Holy Land and fight Amalek (an enormously strong and powerful people). However, they disobeyed their prophet and were, therefore, tortured by wandering in the land for forty years for refusing to fight Amalek and for disobeying their prophet. They all died while wandering; only their children remained. They obeyed Allah's commandments and went to the Levant, fought Amalek and entered the Holy land under the leadership of Joshua son of Nun.

Third: There is nothing in the verse that gives the impression that Moses entreated his Lord to provide them with what they desired, so how could we claim something that was not supported by the Noble Qur'an?

Fourth: Their wandering in the land was their punishment for rejecting to fight Amalek to enter the Holy Land that Allah destined for them. Wandering and their pitiable state at the time was like a prison for them as a punishment, as can be gleaned from the Almighty's: "Then this land is forbidden to them for forty years, during which they will wander through the land." (Qur'an 5:26) So, how could the imprisoned get out of their prison as a response to satisfying their unbecoming and inappropriate desires? That is why, Moses 'saying: "'You can go down to any village and you will find what you have asked for" (Q 2:61) was essentially a threat, an admonition and a reference to their ignorance.

Then the Almighty showed the punishment that befell them because of their wrongdoing, rebellion and immorality. The Almighty said: "They will be stricken with disgrace الذلة

...They have invited the displeasure of Allah and have been branded with misery المسكنة ..." (Q 2:61)

To be stricken with disgrace and misery means to be constantly tarnished by them; they will always be plighted and surrounded by them just like a canopy that surrounds those inside it.

Al-Zamakshari said: "Disgrace had encircled them encompassing them all like being together under a pavilion, a sign that disgrace and misery have become glued and stuck to them. It is like someone forcibly hitting a wall with mud so hard that it sticks to the wall. The Jews are always in disgrace and fully humbled." [73]

The origin of the word "hit" in Arabic comes from: one object/body forcibly hitting another that they become stuck together. Various meanings sprang from this meaning that figuratively refer to the intensity of sticking.

Disgrace الذلةmeans humiliating, belittling or demeaning someone.

Misery المسكنة comes from "silence" because burden and oppression can make someone inactive and motionless (silent). In the verse, it means psychological weakness and ineptness that may engulf someone and make him feel worn out despite his physical strength.

The difference between the Disgrace الذلة and Misery المسكنة is:

Disgrace الذلة is caused by outside factors as when someone is vanquished by his enemy and becomes humbled and humiliated by that enemy.

As for Misery المسكنة, it is the outcome of internal factors such deviation from the truth, being consumed by greed and desires and being disgraced and humiliated for centuries. These factors cause a person to inherit this miserable المسكنة state to the extent that it might become like second nature to him. The Jews lived for centuries and generations enslaved to other nations. They became feeble-hearted and psychologically inept unable to differentiate between a disgraceful dishonorable life and an honorable dignified one. They would even prefer the former kind of life to the latter as long as they could secure the pleasures of life. No matter how affluent and prosperous they become, they will always suffer this psychological deficiency and incompetence. They will always appear miserable and humbled before people.

The almighty's "They have invited the displeasure of Allah" (Q 2:61) is a statement that indicates their horrid destiny in the hereafter. It also implies an exaggeration meant to humiliate and demean them for they are disgraced and dishonored in this world, and they will be fairly rewarded with Allah's wrath and displeasure in the hereafter because of their evil deeds and wickedness.

Ibn Jarir said: "The meaning of 'They have invited وَبَآءُو the displeasure of Allah' is to return or leave with either something good or bad as in His saying: 'I want to let you bear your sin against me along with your other sins.' (Qur'an 5:29) In other words, they returned bearing Allah's wrath as they became deserving of His displeasure." [74]

Al-Zamakhshari said: "'They have invited وَبَآءُو the displeasure of Allah' means it was a fair reward for them to receive His punishment." [75]

Then the Almighty recounted the reason for their being engulfed with disgrace and misery and why they richly deserved Allah's wrath and displeasure. He said: "They have invited the displeasure of Allah and have been branded with misery for rejecting يكفرون Allah's revelations and murdering ⌜His⌝ prophets unjustly. This is ⌜a fair reward⌝ for their disobedience and violations." (Qur'an 2:61) This verse answers the question: Why did He do all of this to them? And the response is: We did this because they rejected Allah's 'signs,' killed His prophets unjustly, disobeyed Him, transgressed and did evil deeds. The "signs" mentioned were clear evidence for monotheism, the belief that there is only One Allah, and they refer to the texts that the Scriptures contain and attest to the truthfulness of the prophets and what they say about the Almighty Allah. The Jews rejected all kinds of revelations and signs. They have been accustomed, even trained, to do so as indicated by the use of the present form of the verb يكفرون (reject).

The Almighty's saying: "murdering His prophets unjustly" means that they kill the messengers whom Allah sends as deliverers of good tidings or to warn them against wrongdoing. Among the prophets that the Jews murdered were Zechariah and John who refused to follow whims and desires.

Also, the Almighty said: "unjustly" even though killing a prophet could never be a just cause. It was meant to indicate that killing the prophets was unjust and contrary to what their doctrine and law stipulated. It is forbidden by their law: "whoever takes a life—unless as a punishment for murder or mischief in the land—it will be as if they killed all of humanity." (Qur'an 5:32) So, this restriction was meant to oppose their conduct in the light of their religion. It immortalized their transgression and disgraced and demeaned their wrongdoing since they had killed their prophets knowingly without any misunderstanding. Rather, they committed these atrocities knowing the ugliness and viciousness of their deeds, and they rejected Allah's law knowingly and deliberately.

Al-Zamakhshari said: "If you said that murdering the prophets cannot take place except unjustly, so what is the use of mentioning it? I would say that they killed them unjustly according to them, because they neither killed nor corrupted the land and thereby were not deserving of being killed. They instructed and advised them to what could be useful and beneficial to them. Yet they were killed. If they (the Jews) were asked and they were fair, they would find no reason for murdering them." [76]

Imam Al-Razi said: "Someone might say that the verse here reads 'وَيَقْتُلُونَ ٱلنَّبِيِّـۧنَ بِغَيْرِ ٱلْحَقِّ'(1) (= unjustly killing the prophets) while in Sura Al-Imran it is: 'وَيَقْتُلُونَ ٱلْأَنۢبِيَآءَ بِغَيْرِ حَقٍّ'(2) - What is the difference? I say that the "justice" that is known to Muslims which necessitates killing is recounted in one of the Hadiths: It is not permissible to shed the blood of a Muslim person except under one of these three conditions: Disbelief after faith, adultery after chastity and killing someone without a just cause. The justice mentioned here with the definite article أل (1) is a reference to these conditions. As for the justice that that mentioned without the definite article (2) emphasizes generalities. In other words, they had no reason and no right whatsoever to do what they did." [77]

Then, the Almighty said: "This is a fair reward for their disobedience and violations." (2:61)

"Disobedience" is noncompliance and rebellion against Allah. "Violation" is encroaching and going beyond specified limits. "This" refers to their disbelief in Allah's signs and revelations and their killing of the prophets. In this case, the meaning is: Those Jews have become accustomed to disobeying their Creator and recklessly and impudently trespass and go beyond their boundaries. Because of their rebelliousness and transgressions, they disbelieved the Allah's revelations and signs and their wicked blood-stained hands found their way to the prophets and killed them with hearts made of stone or even harder than stone.

The verse indicates that committing these transgressions repeatedly, doing what they were prohibited from doing and overstepping legal and permissible boundaries- all these led them from small errors and blunders into committing grave and serious sins and transgressions. When those Jews continued indulging themselves in committing these sins and persisted on disregarding boundaries, virtues shrank and diminished, and all sublime and high moral values dwindled and became insignificant in their eyes. Thus, they disbelieved Allah's signs and killed those who came with guidance and true faith.

The meaning is: Those Jews were stricken with disgrace and misery and earned Allah's displeasure because of disbelieving in Our signs, killing Our prophets, disobeying Our orders and overstepping Our boundaries.

Thus, the reasons for the punishments that descended on them were ordered in an excellent way. The Almighty began by mentioning the wrongdoing that was directed to Him, i.e., disbelieving in His signs and revelations. Then, the second most important reason: murdering His prophets. Then, He branded them with disobedience and noncompliance with His commandments. He concluded the reason for these punishments by denouncing them for overstepping boundaries and disregarding and floundering covenants. Such an order is one of the most striking styles of the Noble Qur'an in the realm of rulings and decrees, presented with solid justifications and reasons.

The noble Verse has thus described the Children of Israel as an ungrateful, inappropriate, illogical, insensible and arrogant people who disregarded the truth and executed injustices against themselves and others. What the verse mentions about them has been confirmed throughout the generations at all times and everywhere.

In conclusion, we have recounted some of the magnificent favors that Allah bestowed upon the Children of Israel. It was incumbent upon them to show appreciation and gratitude, but they didn't. Rather, they received these favors with ungratefulness, thanklessness and churlishness. As a result, Allah took them away from them, and He punished them for their ingratitude in accordance with their violations. We will detail Allah's punishments for their injustices and immorality after we discuss their vices and falsehoods- as mentioned in the Noble Qur'an- in the following two chapters.

References[78]

---

[1] Sura Ibrahim: verse 7.
[2] Interpretation (Tafsir) by Fakhr Al-Din Al-Razi, Vol. 1, P. 430.
[3] Interpretation by Fakhr Al-Din Al-Razi, Vol. 1, P. 342.
[4] Interpretation by Fakhr Al-Din Al-Razi, Vol. 1, P. 342.
[5] Tafsir al-Bahr al-Muhit, by Abu Hayyan al-Gharnati, Vol. 1, P. 180. Al-Sa'ada Printing Press, 1328 H.
[6] Tafsir al-Bahr al-Muhit, by Abu Hayyan al-Gharnati, Vol. 1, P. 181. Al-Sa'ada Printing Press: 1st Edition, 1328 H.
[7] Tafsir Al-Qurtubi, Vol. 1, P. 365, Dar al-Kutub Edition, 1345 H, 1935 M.
[8] Interpretation by Fakhr Al-Din Al-Razi, Vol. 1, P. 349.
[9] Tafsir Ibn Jarir, Vol. 1, P. 262.
[10] Tafsir Al-Kashshaaf, Al-Zamakhshari, Vol.1, P. 123.
[11] Sura Al-Baqarah, Verse 211.
[12] Sura Ad-Dukhan, verses: 30-33.
[13] Sura Al-Jathiyah, Verse: 16-17.
[14] Interpretation by Fakhr Al-Din Al-Razi, Vol. 1, P. 355.
[15] Sura Al-Baqarah: Verse 255.
[16] Sura Taha: Verse 109.
[17] Sahih Al-Bukhari, Vol. 1, P. 87.
[18] Tafsir Ibn Jarir, Vol. 1, P. 268.
[19] Sura Al-Anbya: Verse 35.
[20] Interpretation (Tafsir) by Fakhr Al-Din Al-Razi, Vol. 1, P. 360.
[21] Interpretation (Tafsir) by Fakhr Al-Din Al-Razi, Vol. 1, P. 358.
[22] Sura Ibrahim: Consider' when Moses said to his people, "Remember Allah's favor upon you when He rescued you from the people of Pharaoh, who afflicted you with dreadful torment (and/ (و) slaughtering your sons and keeping your women. That was a severe test from your Lord. Verse: 6.
[23] Sura Al-A'raf: Verse 141.
[24] Sura Taha: verses 80-83.
[25] Sura Al-Isra: Verse 103.
[26] Sura Adh-Dhariyat: Verse 40.
[27] Interpretation (Tafsir) by Fakhr Al-Din Al-Razi, Vol. 1, P. 360.
[28] Sura Al-Furqan: Verse 1.
[29] Sura Al-Anbya: Verse 48.
[30] Interpretation (Tafsir) by Fakhr Al-Din Al-Razi, Vol. 1, P. 285.

[31] Tafsir Al-Kashshaaf, Al-Zamakhshari, Vol.3, P. 175.
[32] Informing the Signatories about the Lord of the Worlds by Ibn Al-Qayyim, Vol. 16, P. 5800.
[33] Tafsir Al-Kashshaaf, Al-Zamakhshari, Vol.1, P. 215.
[34] Tafsir Ibn Kathir, Vol. 1, P. 92.
[35] Tafsir Ibn Jarir, Vol. 1, P. 287. Al-Halabi Edition.
[36] Tafsir Ibn Jarir, Vol. 1, P. 290. Al-Halabi Edition.
[37] Tafsir Ibn Jarir, Vol. 1, P. 282. Al-Halabi Edition.
[38] Tafsir Ibn Jarir, Vol. 1, P. 292.
[39] Tafsir Ibn Kathir, Vol. 1, P. 94.
[40] Ibn Kathir Interpretation, P.94.
[41] Ibn Kathir Interpretation, P.97.
[42] Tafsir Ibn Jarir, Vol. 1, P. 398. Al-Halabi Edition.
[43] Verse 161, 162.
[44] Tafsir Al-Kashshaaf, Al-Zamakhshari, Vol.1, P. 216.
[45] Tafsir Al-Kashshaaf, Vol.1, P. 216.
[46] Tafsir Ibn Jarir, Vol. 1, P. 302.
[47] Sahih Al-Bukhari, Chapter "We said: enter this city," Vol. 6, P. 22,
[48] Ibn Kathir Interpretation, Vol. 1, P.99.
[49] Tafsir Al-Kashshaaf, Al-Zamakhshari, Vol.1, P. 218.
[50] It was said that entreating for water took place in the wilderness, but there is evidence that indicate that it took place while wandering יציאת מצרים، Yeẓi'at Miẓrayim
[51] Ibn Kathir Interpretation, Vol. 1, P.100.
[52] Tafsir Ibn Jarir, Vol. 1, P. 308. Al-Halabi Edition.
[53] Tafsir Ibn Jarir, Vol. 1, P. 324.
[54] Sura Al-A'raf: Verse 171.
[55] Tafsir Al-Qurtubi, Vol. 1, P. 436.
[56] Liwaa Al-Islam Magazine, Second Year # 7, P. 4.
[57] Tafsir Al-Qurtubi, Vol. 1, P. 437.
[58] Tafsir Ibn Jarir, Vol. 1, P. 309.
[59] Tafsir Ibn Jarir, Vol. 1, P. 309.
[60] Tafsir Ibn Hayyan, Vol. 1, P. 231.
[61] فنزعوا الى عكرهم means they longed to their origin and customs.
[62] Tafsir Al-Kashshaaf, Vol.1, P. 217.
[63] Ibn Kathir Interpretation, Vol. 1, P.101.
[64] Tafsir Muhamad al-Taher ibn Ashur Al-tahreer w al-Tanweer (Liberating and enlightening), Vol. 1, P. 500, Esa Al-Halabi Edition, 1964.
[65] Tafsir Ibn Jarir, Vol. 1, P. 312.
[66] Ibn Kathir Interpretation, Vol. 1, P.101.
[67] Tafsir Ibn Jarir, Vol. 1, P. 315.
[68] Tafsir al-Bahr al-Muhit, by Abu Hayyan al-Gharnati, Vol. 1, P. 233.
[69] Tafsir Ibn Jarir, Vol. 1, P. 214.
[70] Tafsir al-Bahr al-Muhit, by Abu Hayyan al-Gharnati, Vol. 1, P. 234.
[71] Tafsir Ibn Jarir, Vol. 1, P. 314.
[72] See: Tafsir Ibn Kathir, (English translation, abridged), Darussalam, Riyadh, 2000, Vol. 1, P. 244.

[72a] Nunation or Tanwīn (تَنْوِين) stands for an extra نْ at the end of a noun (إِسْمٌ), which you pronounce (لَفْظًا) but do not write (لا خَطًّا). It practically means that you add a pronounced *"n"*-ending to an indefinite noun if you mark it with case endings.
[73] Tafsir Al-Kashshaaf, Vol.1, P. 217.
[74] Tafsir Ibn Jarir, Vol. 1, P. 215.
[75] Tafsir Al-Kashshaaf, Vol.1, P. 217.
[76] Tafsir Al-Kashshaaf, Vol.1, P. 217.
[77] Interpretation by Fakhr Al-Din Al-Razi, Vol. 1, P. 390.
[78]

Chapter Six

The Vices Of The Jews As Portrayed By The Noble Qur'an

The reader of the Noble Qur'an will clearly see that it has depicted many of the inappropriate conducts, despicable manners and cunning and crooked behaviors that the Children of Israel indulged in. It has branded them with disbelief, ingratitude, egotism, cowardice, deceit, rebellion, transgression, cruelty, deviance, hastening to transgression and aggression, unjustly consuming people's wealth, and many more of the vices that are recorded in the Noble Qur'an. They therefore earned Allah's displeasure, were stripped of Allah's mercy and compassion, and they were stricken with disgrace and misery.

These vices that the Noble Qur'an recorded can be clearly seen anywhere and throughout the ages. The passage of time has only made these vices more ingrained and rooted in them.

The following are some of their vices. We will mention them in general and then we will interpret the verses that talked about these vices in detail.

First: Violating covenants and breaking promises.
Second: Their inappropriateness to Allah, animosity to His angels and murdering His prophets.
Third: Rejecting the truth and hating good and beneficial things for others out of egotism and envy.
Fourth: Maneuvering to legitimize what Allah has prohibited.
Fifth: Rejecting Allah's Book, believing in magic and satanic illusions.
Sixth: Altering and changing texts and forgetting what they were reminded with.
Seventh; Clinging eagerly to life and their cowardice to fight for the sake of Allah.
Eighth: Demanding that Moses, their prophet, make them a god like other nations.
Nineth: Worshipping the calf.
Tenth: Lack of sensitivity for religion and engaging in semantic bickering and argumentation.

Now, we will talk in detail about each one of these vices which the Noble Qur'an ascribed to them.

<u>First: Violating Covenants and Promises</u>:

In numerous verses, the Noble Qur'an has described the Jews as covenant breakers. Those who follow their history- both ancient and modern- will see that this vice is almost second nature to them. Allah made many covenants with them through His prophets and messengers, but they violated them. The Prophet made many covenants with them, but they broke their covenants with him one time after the other.

There are noble verses in Sura Al-Baqara that report that- with the exception of a few of them- the Jews broke their covenant to worship Allah alone and do righteous and virtuous deeds. Among these verses are:

First: "And remember when We took a covenant from the children of Israel stating, "Worship none but Allah; be kind to parents, relatives, orphans and the needy; speak kindly to people; establish prayer; and pay alms-tax." But you Israelites turned away—except for a few of you—and were indifferent." (Qur'an 2:83)

The meaning of the verse is: Remember Children of Israel- to your benefit and to the benefit of others who may learn from this- when We took a covenant from you, commanded you to follow Our messengers and worship Allah alone. According to that covenant, We also asked you to be kind to your parents and fulfill all those duties that Allah instructed you to perform for them, to be kind to your relatives and those who lost their parents and the needy who do not have enough to sustain themselves with. We also commanded you to speak kindly to people and to guide and lead them to what is good and beneficial for them. We likewise commanded you to pray and pay alms-tax with honesty. However, you and your ancestors violated the covenant and did not comply with those commandments, except for a few of you who kept and followed it.

"The Children of Israel" in this noble verse refers to the predecessors and the successors because the commandments and prohibitions contained in the verses- and which comprise the essence of the covenant taken from them- were addressed to all of them through their prophets and messengers.

There is evidence that the successors who were contemporary with the Prophet were meant by "the Children of Israel." His saying "But you Israelites turned away—except for a few of you—and were indifferent-" at the end of the verse- indicates that He had pointed to their turning away from the covenant. Turning away from something indicates that they had received it first and then turned away, as we will discuss later.

And His saying: "'Worship none but Allah; be kind to parents…" up to "But you Israelites turned away—except for a few of you—and were indifferent" is a statement of the covenant and its details. The expression "'Worship none but Allah; be kind to parents…" is in the negative form in Arabic لَا تَعْبُدُونَ to emphasize and ascertain a prohibition to worship none but Allah. The combination of the command and the prohibition reflect their importance and the inevitability that they would be well received and obeyed: what should be done was established as a command; those commanded would follow what they were commanded to do and immediately shun what was prohibited. The style is emphatic and necessitated compliance with the command and shunning the prohibition.

The noble Verse (Q 2:83) comprised a unique and tightly-controlled style in directing this guidance- loaded command. Had they followed it, their relationship with both the Creator as well as the created would have improved and become better. The counsel starts with mentioning the highest and greatest obligation, i.e., their duty towards Allah. They were directed to worship Him alone adding no partners to Him. Then, it mentions their responsibilities towards people starting with the parents, those who are most worthy of their kindness for what they have done: birth, bringing them up and surrounding them with their compassion. Then, the verse mentions the relatives, those who are related to the father or the mother. They were asked to offer them whatever help they could offer them. Then the verse mentions the orphans since they need help having lost the kindness, help and compassion of their father. The verse then called them to be kind to all people by speaking kindly to them and treating them with benevolence and munificence because if people are not in need of money, they are at least in need of a kind and compassionate word. After mentioning this, the verse directs them to appropriate forms of worship that would cement their relationship with the Creator and His servants. It commanded them to establish prayer in humility and loyalty, to pay alms-tax with honesty, generosity and willingness. These two forms of worship, the physical and the financial, were especially mentioned after the commandment to worship Allah because of the importance of their specific- and to emphasize their- importance. The Children of Israel should have taken these judicious and wise commandments into consideration. Yet, they were blinded and the became deaf and could not heed or listen. The Noble Qur'an ridiculed them: "But you Israelites turned away—except for a few of you—and were indifferent."

In other words, you Jews had turned away and did not comply with the covenants taken from you. You assigned partners to Allah; you did not show kindness to your parents; you were inconsiderate of the relatives, the orphans and the needy; you had been insensitive to the people; you neglected prayers; you were not honest in alms-giving and you abandoned Allah's commandments.

His saying: "except for a few of you" shows fairness to those Jews who kept their covenant. There are in every nation those loyal who keep their pledges, pursue the truth and guide others. However, the presence of a few of those loyal ones in a nation would not prevent punishment to befall that nation on account of the misguidance and immorality of the majority.

His saying: "But you ...and were indifferent/وَأَنتُم مُّعْرِضُونَ" is an adverb meant to state their state or condition. It shows that the disobedience and indifference to covenants described has been a fixed and deeply entrenched characteristic.

In Tafsir Al-Manar, the author said: "A man may turn away from something with the intention of coming back to it to do what should have been done. Not everyone who turns away from something would continue to ignore it and show indifference forever. Therefore, the constraint "But you ...and were indifferent/وَأَنتُم مُّعْرِضُونَ" was out of necessity not repetition as might be construed... Then, he said their "turning away" coupled with their "indifference" was due to the fact that Allah commanded them to follow the principles and tenets of religion only from His Book. Yet, they took their rabbis and scholars as their gods; they permitted and prohibited things, allowed and prevented, and added rulings and doctrines following the resolutions and verdicts of their learned ones. That was how they made partners with Allah, those who allowed and permitted things that were neither allowed nor permitted by Allah. Allah is the sole arbitrator of religion; scholars are mere counselors to help understand His Scriptures and what His messengers bring." [1]

The difference between our interpretation and that of Al-Manar for His saying "But you ...and were indifferent/وَأَنتُم مُّعْرِضُونَ" is that this statement reveals a deeply ingrained habit in people, one that has become like second nature to them. Then, His "But you Israelites turned away" indicates that turning away is one of their established habits. In Al-Manar's interpretation, on the other hand, the statement reflects the kind of turning away. The first interpretation which we support stresses the element of admonition and rebuke and better describes the state of the Jews.

Second: The Almighty said: "And remember when We took your covenant that you would neither shed each other's blood nor expel each other from their homes, you gave your pledge and bore witness. But here you are, killing each other and expelling some of your people from their homes, aiding one another in sin and aggression; and when those expelled come to you as captives, you still ransom them—though expelling them was unlawful for you. Do you believe in some of the Scripture and reject the rest? Is there any reward for those who do so among you other than disgrace in this worldly life and being subjected to the harshest punishment on the Day of Judgment? For Allah is never unaware of what you do. These are the ones who trade the Hereafter for the life of this world. So, their punishment will not be reduced, nor will they be helped." (Qur'an 2:84-86) [2]

After the Almighty showed in the previous verse that He took a covenant from the Children of Israel to worship Him and establish prayer and then they did not comply with their covenant and turned away from it except for a few of them, He shows in these noble verses that He took another covenant from them. However, they broke that pledge as well as was customary with them.

This is a summary of that pledge that is mentioned in these noble verses: The Almighty took a covenant from them not to kill each other, not to expel each other from their homes, and to do their best to ransom those who become captives and deliver them from their enemies. However, when war broke out between the Aws and the Khazraj, Banu Qurayza joined the Aws while Banu Qaynuqa and Banu Nadir joined the Khazraj. Every sect from the Jews was fighting alongside its allies against the other sects. When the war had ended, all the Jews paid ransoms to free their captives from the hands of their enemies, as Allah had commanded them to do. Thus, they obeyed some of the scriptures, i.e., rescuing their captives, but they disobeyed other parts of the Scriptures, i.e., forbidding the shedding of each other's blood and expelling each other from their homes. History recounts that the Arabs ridiculed them by saying: How could you fight them and then pay ransom to rescue them? The Jews would respond to this saying: We were forbidden from fighting them, we could not fail our allies and we were commanded to rescue our captives.

The Almighty cautioned and threatened them with disgrace in this world and in the hereafter for breaking their covenant and choosing some of His commandments while neglecting others.

The overall meaning of these noble verses is: Also remember, Children of Israel, when We took a covenant from you and advised you not to kill or expel each other, and you accepted to comply with this pledge and commit to what was therein. Yet, after promising to abide by that pledge and after testifying that you accepted it, you turned away from the teachings of the Torah and you broke your promises: you shed each other's blood, and you aggressively and unjustly expelled your brothers- in blood and faith- from their homes. You also sided with others who were not related to you and who had different faith to kill and expel them. Yet, when your brethren with whom you fought and whom you expelled from their homes were taken captives, you paid their ransom to rescue them. So, why didn't you obey the Torah's commandment that prohibited fighting and expelling them just like you obeyed its commandment to rescue the captives? How could killing and expelling others from their homes be agreeable to you while you find leaving the captives in their enemies' hand objectionable? Disgrace in this world and severe punishment in the hereafter would be the lot of he who differentiated between Allah's rulings, accepting and obeying some and rejecting and disregarding others. Allah is knowledgeable and aware of what you do. And there is no doubt that those Jews who broke their covenants and disobeyed what they were commanded to do had traded life everlasting for the life of this world. Their torture would be severe and they would be without help or support.

The Almighty's saying: "And remember when We took your covenant that you would neither shed each other's blood nor expel each other from their homes" (Q 2:84) means remember, Children of Israel, the time when We took your covenant that you would not shed each other's blood nor expel each other from your homes. This is reminiscent of the Almighty's: "when you enter houses, greet one another with a greeting of peace from Allah, blessed and good." (Qur'an 24:61) [3]

The significance of this expression lies in the fact that a nation that is connected through religion and faith would enjoy a strong and profound feeling of unity and harmony. As such, a man's murder of another man is considered killing oneself, and a man expelling another is as like doing that to himself.

In Tafsir Al-Manar, the author said: "The Almighty expressed His prohibition against the shedding the blood and expelling each other from their homes and countries in a statement that solidified the unity of the nation and instill a noble and magnanimous feeling in the heart, one that would move and impel one to comply, if they had the sensitivity and feelings to be moved. The Almighty said (Q 2:84): "Neither shed each other's (YOUR) blood دماءكم ," thereby rendering the blood of each one in the nation as though it were one's own blood which, if shed, it would be as if he killed himself and committed suicide. He also said: "nor expel each other from their (YOUR) homes دِيَٰرِكُم" following the same style. This exquisite style is typical of the Noble Qur'an. [4]

And the Almighty's saying (Q 2:84): "you gave your pledge and bore witness" recorded their acceptance to comply with the covenant and follow its tenets. This means:

You Jews did not reject the covenant; you accepted it. It was therefore incumbent upon you follow its principles and rulings. But what was their position after giving their pledge and bearing witness?

The Noble Qur'an shows that they broke their promises and did what they were prohibited from doing. The almighty said (Q 2:85): "But here you are, killing each other and expelling some of your people from their homes." Which means: You broke your after accepting the covenant and you did to your brothers what you were prohibited from doing: you killed and expelled them. You perpetrated what levelheaded and sensible people- who should commit to their covenants and pledges- should have refrained from doing.

And since killing and expelling each other from their homes required strength and support, the Almighty showed that they committed these evils through overstepping their boundaries and seeking help and assistance from others. The Almighty said (Q 2:85): "aiding one another in sin and aggression." That is, you cooperated with those who were neither relatives nor held the same faith to kill your brothers and expel them from their homes. Thus, you had sinned and acted with aggression.

The Almighty's saying (Q 2:85): "and when those expelled come to you as captives, you still ransom them—though expelling them was unlawful for you" is a statement that depicts their inconsistencies and differentiations and discrepancies concerning Allah's rulings.

It means: When, you Jews, found those with whom you fought and expelled from their homes captives, you sought to ransom them and set them free. Killing and expelling them was unlawful to you just as leaving them captives in the hands of your enemies. So, why didn't you follow the Torah's decree that prohibited killing and expelling them just as you followed the decree of ransoming them?

And the noble statement "though expelling them was unlawful for you" explicitly indicates that that prohibition was a well-known and widely acknowledged one; it was not unknown to them.

And His saying (Q 2:85): "Do you believe in some of the Scripture and reject the rest?" is meant to censure and rebuke them for following some of Allah's rulings and rejecting others.

The meaning is: How could you comply with your Scriptures' rulings to rescue and ransom your captives and fail to follow the prohibition to not fight your brothers and expel them from their homes? The interrogation is meant to rebuke and admonish them for differentiating between Allah's rulings: believing some and disbelieving others.

Some of the Scriptures in which they believed was the prohibition to abandon their captives and leaving them in the hands of their enemies. The other part in which they disbelieved was the prohibition to kill and dispel each other from their homes. The admonition was directed to their combining disbelief and rejection with faith and belief.

The late Sheikh Muhammad Al-Khader Hussein said: "The Almighty called their noncompliance, i.e., killing and expelling from homes, disbelief. That is because those who rebel against Allah's commandments and do actual deeds thinking that their actions are wise and right, feeling no qualms or unease, no regrets or sorrow, for what they have done, are not to be considered as among the righteous believers. There is clear evidence in the honorable verse that those who believe in some of what was clearly stated in the faith and disbelieve in others would be considered among the disbelievers because faith cannot be cherry-picked; it is not a pick and choose matter." [5]

Then the Almighty revealed the punishment that awaits those who differentiate between Allah's decrees and rulings in this world and in the hereafter. He said (Q 2:85):. "Is there any reward for those who do so ذَٰلِكَ among you other than disgrace in this worldly life and being subjected to the harshest punishment on the Day of Judgment? For Allah is never unaware of what you do"

The demonstrative ذَٰلِكَ in the verse refers to killing and expelling from homes that they did violating their pledge to Allah out of rebellion and disbelief. Disgrace خِزْيٌ is the shame, ignominy and punishment that would come upon them. Among the signs of this disgrace was the humiliation and degradation that they suffered after these wars: Banu Qaynuqa and Banu Nadir were expelled from their homes, Banu Qurayza were murdered, and Khaybar was opened, and all the other forms of humiliation that had befallen them. This is Allah's way with every nation that does not hold fast to its faith and fail to comply with the tenets of its religion and its principles.

Some might think that the disgrace they will face in this worldly life may attenuate their punishment in the hereafter. The Almighty negated that illusion and revealed that they would be subjected to the "harshest punishment in the Day of Judgement." (Q 2:85) The Almighty is never unaware of their deeds to leave them unpunished.

What is meant by negating "unawareness" in "for Allah is never unaware of what you do" (Q 2:85) is to negate what could be caused as a result of leaving them without proper punishment for their evil deeds.

This is evidence that Allah punishes those who diverge from His straight path; there will be penalties in this world and in the hereafter for their transgressions and persistence in pursuing evil.

The Almighty then emphasized this serious threat and expounded its reasons. He said: "These are the ones who trade the Hereafter for the life of this world. So, their punishment will not be reduced, nor will they be helped." (Q 2:86)

The meaning is: Those Jews who differentiated between Allah's rulings and traded their faith for the pleasures and comforts of this world will be severely tortured, their punishment will not be reduced, and they will not help or support.

Thus, these noble verses stigmatized the Jews for breaking their vows and believing in some of the Scriptures and disbelieving in others. They therefore became deserving of Allah's wrath and displeasure. The infidels will surely have a humiliating punishment.

Third: In sura Al-Ma'idah (sura 5), there are two verses that clearly show that the Almighty took a covenant from the Children of Israel to follow and comply with what He had commanded them to do. However, they broke their promises and violated their covenant. These verses are: "Allah made a covenant with the Children of Israel and appointed twelve leaders from among them and then said, "I am truly with you. If you establish prayer, pay alms-tax, believe in My messengers, support them, and lend to Allah a good loan, I will certainly forgive your sins and admit you into Gardens under which rivers flow. And whoever among you disbelieves afterwards has truly strayed from the Right Way. But for breaking their covenant We condemned them and hardened their hearts. They distorted the words of the Scripture and neglected a portion of what they had been commanded to uphold. You O Prophet will always find deceit on their part, except for a few. But pardon them and bear with them. Indeed, Allah loves the good-doers." (Qur'an 5:12-13)

The covenant is the pledge that the Children of Israel made promising to follow Allah's commandments and follow the directives of the Torah that Allah revealed to Moses, their prophet.

The نَقِيبً [6] is the elder of the tribe who was well aware of their state and needs. He would always look for whatever his people needed.

The meaning is: Allah made a covenant with the Children of Israel to comply with the teachings of the Torah and preserve what they were commanded to observe concerning establishing prayer, paying alms-tax and obeying His messengers' instructions concerning what was permitted and what should be avoided. He appointed twelve leaders from among them to administer their religious matters and explore the conditions of those enormously strong men, Amalek, who inhabited the Holy Land that Allah had destined for them and commanded them to enter.

And here is the story: After the Almighty drowned Pharaoh and his men in the presence of the Children of Israel who witnessed that with their own eyes, He commanded Moses to march with them to the Holy land[7] in which the mighty Canaanites dwelt. Allah said to them: "I assigned it as a homeland to you. Go to it and fight those who live there, and I will grant you victory over them." Allah also commanded Moses to choose twelve leaders from among their twelve tribes to lead their tribes and carry out the commandments of Moses, their prophet. Moses did what Allah commanded him to do.

Before Moses reached the Holy Land, he sent these twelve leaders to investigate and gather information concerning those enormously powerful people who lived on that land to know how powerful and strong they were. He commanded them to inform him when they returned. He also commanded them not to inform his people about the strength or conditions of those powerful people so that his people would not lose heart and or the will to fight them.

When the leaders investigated the conditions of the Canaanites, they found out that they were an extremely powerful people. That made them fearful and unwilling to fight them. Ten of them also informed the Children of Israel what they had witnessed, which caused them to panic, and they refused to obey their prophet's command to fight them. They told him: "O Moses! There is an enormously powerful people there, so we will never be able to enter it until they leave. If they do, then we will enter!" (Qur'an 5:22)

So, we can see that the leaders of the Children of Israel were the first to violate their covenant. Only two of them complied with their pledge: Joshua son of Nun and Caleb son of Jephunneh.

We previously discussed this story in detail when we interpreted the noble verses that reported the story.[8]

Moses had appointed twelve leaders- representing the twelve tribes- from among the Children of Israel to manage and oversee their people because they had for long centuries been subjected to Pharaoh's cruelty and injustice. Consequently, they were stripped of their will, their confidence in themselves was shaken, and their values and ethics were depleted. A constant reminder was needed to be amongst them to control their voracity and greed when they wanted more and to uplift their morale when they were squeamish and terrified to instill strong will and courage in them.

His saying: "I am truly with you" (Q 5:12) means that the Almighty would assist you and grant you victory if you complied with My covenant, obeyed My messengers and followed the straightforward path that I had chartered for you.

Thus, the noble statement contained cautioning them against disobedience because the Almighty is always aware of everything. It also contained a promise to grant them victory if they obeyed Him, for if Allah is with you, nobody could defeat you. No matter how mighty the opponent might be, it would be nothing compared to Allah's invincible and indomitable might.

The Almighty then revealed the covenant He made with them. He did this in a conditional statement that comprised five issues. He said: "If you establish prayer, pay alms-tax, believe in My messengers, support them, and lend to Allah a good loan, I will certainly forgive your sins and admit you into Gardens under which rivers flow." (Q 5:12)

The first one of these issues that the covenant comprised was "establish(ing) prayer." (Q 5:12) That meant praying ceaselessly and performing it in the best possible way and with the utmost modesty and humility.

The second issue was "pay(ing) alms-tax" (Q 5:12) to those who were worthy of it because this was sure path to social justice and would generate cooperation and love between the rich and the poor.

The third issue- "believe(ing) in My messengers-" (Q 5:12) meant accepting the revelations they brought and complying with their messages without discrepancy or discrimination because Allah's message is one and His messengers all brought essentially the same message. At their core, there were no differences between these messages; the only difference was in some of the side issues.

The Almighty added His honorable messengers to dignify and exalt their messages and confirm them and to point out that believing in all of them was an obligation; those who obey them obey Allah, and those who disobey them disobey Allah.

Allah showed the fourth issue by saying: "support them." Al-Raghib said: "Supporting means backing and assisting in addition to dignifying." Thus, the meaning of the honorable verse is to empower, dignify and shield them from all harms.

The fifth issue was "lend to Allah a good loan" (Q 5:12) meant spend your money to support and back the truth that those messengers brought to you. You should support them with your money and your lives.

These were the five issues that were included in the covenant that Allah made with the Children of Israel. These were delivered in a conditional sentence to confirm the covenant. Allah revealed the response to the conditional sentence in His: "I will certainly forgive your sins and admit you into Gardens under which rivers flow." (Q 5:12) This response comprised two magnificent promises if they complied with their covenant: forgiving their sins in this world and obtaining His pleasure and dwelling in His gardens in the hereafter.

Then, after Allah had promised them this kindness and magnanimity if they were to keep their covenant, He cautioned them against violating His covenant and showing ingratitude towards His favors: "And whoever among you disbelieves afterwards has truly strayed from the Right Way." (Q 5:12) This means that those rejected and abandoned anything I commanded, or did something that I prohibited and their covenant with Me- after this condition confirming great promises- had erred and strayed from the right path and marched in a web of misguidance in which nothing avails them.

Al-Zamakhshari said: "If you said 'He who disbelieved before had also gone astray and departed from the right path.' When He said: 'How about those who disbelieve AFTER that? I would say: 'Yes, he who disbelieved before that had also gone astray, but misguidance and disbelief would be much worse after grace was made manifest and abundant. When grace increases and is abundant, disbelief is even more despicable; it has reached its worst stages.'" [9]

So far, the noble verse had shown that Allah made a covenant with the Children of Israel to carry out the commandments that He had asked them to fulfil. He encouraged them to comply with His demands and obey His requests, and He cautioned them against disloyalty and violating the covenant. So, what was their position concerning the covenant?

They violated the covenant and did not carry out the duties that Allah entrusted them with. They terribly offended the messengers of Allah; they killed some of them, and they disbelieved others. They were disloyal to the Prophet even though their scriptures commanded them to support, and they tried to kill him. Even their leaders acted just as the rest of them in breaching their covenant with Allah. Therefore, all of them were stripped of Allah's mercy and compassion. Their hearts became cruel and hardened incapable of doing good and righteous deeds. Allah showed this in His: "But for breaking their covenant We condemned them and hardened their hearts." (Qur'an 5:13)

The meaning is: Because of breaching the covenant that We made with them, We denied them Our mercy, and they became deserving of Our wrath and displeasure. We hardened their hearts and made them cruel and unyielding, void of compassion and mercy, unable to accept the truth. As they became accustomed to breaching covenants and became used to disobedience and opposition, their hearts hardened and they became cruel, cynical, unfeeling, and unable to be receptive to signs or responsive to miracles.

Describing them in such terms must have regaled the Prophet and comforted him for the treachery, harm and violations he had witnessed at the hands of those Jews who were contemporaneous with him.

For this reason, in his interpretation of this noble verse, Ibn Jarir said: "The Almighty says to His Prophet Muhammad: 'Muhammad! Do not wonder at those Jews who wanted to harm you and your companions and broke the promise they made with you out of treachery and disloyalty to you and your companions. These are their customs and the ways of their predecessors as well. I made a covenant with them during the time of Moses and I sent twelve leaders chosen from among their best to gather information about Amalek promising to grant them victory over them and to give them their land, their houses and their wealth after I showed them numerous signs and miracles. Yet, they breached the covenant and broke their promise with Me. I condemned them for doing what they did. If the best among them would do such a thing, do not be surprised what the worst ones would be capable of doing!" [10]

The most popular reading of "We ... hardened قاسيةtheir hearts" points to cruelty and viciousness.

However, Hamza and Al-Kisa'i's reading of "We … hardened قَاسِيَةً their hearts" can have two meanings: one that also refers to cruelty and viciousness and another meaning which means bad, impure or corrupt.

Accordingly, the meaning would be: "We made the faith in their hearts impure and contaminated. It was mixed with hypocrisy and disbelief just like the coins قَاسِيَةً where its silver is mixed with copper, lead and the like. It was adulterated impure silver.

Ibn Jarir said: "Of these two meanings, I am inclined to favor the one that refers to cruelty, simply because the Almighty described them as people who disbelieved and breached their covenant. He did not even remotely mention anything related to faith associated with them. Their hearts were not described as hearts that had faith mixed with disbelief like those silver coins that are mixed with other cheaper metals. Hardly!" [11]

However, Al-Zamakhshari combined the two meanings, that of impure and adulterated and cruel and vicious: " قَاسِيَةً which means impure as understood from a "قَاسِيَةً coin" which also refers to cruelty since pure unadulterated gold and silver are malleable and flexible whereas the impure and adulterated are hard and inflexible." [12]

Then the Almighty showed some of the consequences of their hardened hearts and condemning them for breaching their covenants. He said: "They distorted the words of the Scripture." (Q 5:13) This means they changed the place in which- and for which- certain words were mentioned. The did this through false and corrupt interpretations and by changing the vocabulary through adding or deleting.

The Jews did all of this in the Torah. Here is evidence for their doing so. The Torah forbade them from charging interest on loans: "Do not charge interest on your brother." What was meant by "brother" here was "brother in humanity," for the transactions that were prohibited with an Israelite were also forbidden for others. However, the Jews distorted this phrase and interpreted it in a narrow and unpleasant way, one that was in agreement with their greed, desires and lusts. They added the word "Israelite": "You may charge a foreigner interest, but not a fellow Israelite." (Deuteronomy, 20:23) Thus, the meaning changed significantly.

That distortion- for which they earned Allah's condemnation- took place after the time of Moses and it lasted until the time of our Prophet. Allah condemned the Children of Israel who were contemporary with the Prophet because they were their offspring, and they followed their forefathers' footsteps in their deception, lies and violation of the covenants in the Torah.

The Almighty then recounted that in addition "distorting the words in the Scriptures," they had neglected a great portion of what they were commanded to uphold. The Almighty said: "and neglected وَنَسُوا a portion of what they had been commanded to uphold." (Q 5:13) In other words, they abandoned a lot of what they were commanded to follow and comply with.

Al-Raghib said: "Neglecting النسيان is abandoning what man had acquired due to lack of a strong will/heart, out of oblivion, or on purpose so that it would no longer be present in the heart/mind." [13]

The three kinds that Al-Raghib mentioned as reasons for Neglecting النسيان were manifested in the actions of the Jews. They were too overtaken with neglect to attend to their scripture and comply with its principles and tents because of the frailty of their hearts and because they were consumed with their greed and lusts. They also neglected their faith and doctrine and did not follow their teachings and instructions in their lives and communities on purpose because being guided and constrained by these teachings would only impel them to walk on the straight path, something they were not inclined to do because of their untamed lusts and wild desires.

The admonition inherent in "neglected وَنَسُوا a portion ..."is meant to emphasize because a portion/ حظاً is indicative of something big, and those who get it are considered lucky. This indicates that the portion that those Jews ignored and neglected was the core of the scripture, its very essence. And this is the truth since the reader of the currently available Torah would not find in it any mention of the Final Day and the rewards and punishments it entails.

And this noble statement as well as others of similar purport in the Noble Qur'an are considered among the greatest miracles in the Noble Qur'an. Before the honorable prophetic emissary, people did were not aware that the Jews neglected a big portion of what they were commanded to uphold in their Torah. When the Noble Qur'an revealed that, they began to know what they did not know before.

And since the predecessors pass their moral values and ethics over to their successors which also take root and become deeply ingrained in them, Allah cautioned His Prophet against those Jews who were contemporary with him since they must have inherited the vices of their predecessors and their proclivity and proneness to breach their covenants. The Almighty said: "You O Prophet will always find deceit [14] on their part, except for a few." (Q 5:13)

This means: You Prophet will always see in those contemporary Jews the same image of their predecessors when it comes to treachery, disloyalty and breaking covenants. Those who exist now have inherited the disloyalty and treachery of their forefathers. They are just as cruel and misguided as their forefathers were. Even though time separates them, they have the same manners and dispositions with the exception of a few of them who accepted Islam, kept their promises and fulfilled their covenants.

This honorable statement amply depicts the nature of the Jews at all times and places. Before Islam, they broke their covenants with Allah and harmed His messengers and prophets. When Allah sent His Prophet whom they knew as the knew their own children, they disbelieved and rejected him. They broke their promises with him every time, and they fought him using all possible means. They have persisted on doing this from the start of the Islamic call until the present day. Loyalty and faithfulness are not known to them.

Their Modus operandi with Muslims is disloyalty, treachery and breaching covenants. If they are found deficient in inflicting harm openly, they would resort to hidden and covert methods and conspire with any of the enemies of the Islamic call. If the chance offers itself to them, they would viciously and brutally pounce on its followers.

The Almighty concluded the noble verse with His: "But pardon them and bear with them. Indeed, Allah loves the good-doers." (Q 5:13) To "pardon/ اعف" is to not respond to an offense with a similar offense. To "bear with them/اصفح" is to forgive and disregard blaming and upbraiding. They therefore claim that "bear with them/اصفح" is at a more sublime rank compared to "pardon/ اعف." That is because the former indicates abandoning the apparent conspicuous act of responding to an offense. The latter, however, comprises all of this in addition to a thorough clear conscience as thought the offense never happened in the first place.

The word الاحسان from which "good-doers ٱلْمُحْسِنِينَ" is derived refers to pardoning the offender and bearing with him.

Scientists have some opinions concerning those whom the prophet ordered to be pardoned:

1- Some believe that that was a reference to the few among the Jews who believed. Allah made an exception concerning them by saying "except for a few." Those were assured of safety; their wealth and their blood were protected. Thus, there was no need to pardon them.

2- Some believe that those whom the Prophet ordered to be pardoned were the majority of the Jews. However, they believe that the verse was abrogated by another one in Sura At-Tawbah : "Fight those who do not believe in Allah and the Last Day, nor comply with what Allah and His Messenger have forbidden, nor embrace the religion of truth from among those who were given the Scripture, until they pay the tax, willingly submitting, fully humbled. " (Qur'an 9:29) This view is not well grounded because abrogation does not take place unless combining the two verses is not feasible, and that was not the case as we will explain later.

3- Abou Muslim believes that it refers to the Jews who persisted on their disbelief but did not breach their covenants. He also sees that those were the intended people in His saying: "except for a few." [15]

4- What we are more inclined to believe is that pardoning and forgiveness were directed to all the Jews. As evidence for this was dwelling with them in peace and accepting the jizya (tax levied on dhimmis), debating with them in the best way possible, dealing with them according to the principle "They have the same (rights) that we have, and they have the same (obligations/duties) that we have," and pardoning and forgiving their blunders that did not impact the safety and integrity of the Islamic call. However, if they breached their covenants, proved disloyal and unfaithful to Allah, the Prophet and the believers, and forgiving them would adversely impact the Muslims, then they should be dealt with in a way that would safeguard the Muslims and protect them from their evil. This is because pardoning them when it is imperative to fight to protect their faith and lives is simply suicide, an act of self-annihilation. This view is very similar to Abou Muslim's view; it might even be considered an explanation of it.

Those who follow the history of the Islamic State will realize that the Prophet dealt with kindness and consideration with the Jews who lived in Medina after his migration to it. He made an agreement with them, he was tolerant and lenient with them notwithstanding their desire to inflict harm, and he pardoned their offenses wishing that by doing so he might be able to lead them to the right path. However, when they breached their covenants and persisted in their injustices, he punished every sect with the appropriate punishment, one that was congruous with the offense. Therefore, he expelled Banu Qaynuqa and Banu Nadir, killed Banu Qurayza and reconciled with the people of Khaybar in return for a portion of their earthly yield of fruits and vegetables on the condition that he could expel them whenever he wanted to. Near the end of his life, he ordered the expulsion of the Jews from the Arab Peninsula to make sure that two religions would never exist there.

It is incumbent upon Muslims to apply this principle in dealing with the Jews who exist right now. Those Jews who attacked our homes should be fought against and expelled. Other peaceful Jews may be treated with kindness and leniency, unless they betray their evil intensions. Very few of them will betray good intensions.

Fourth: There are numerous verses in the Noble Qur'an that state that Allah made a covenant with the Jews to believe in the Prophet whom they find in their Torah and Enjil (Injil; the Gospels), and to comply with whatever was revealed to him, i.e., the Noble Qur'an. However, when the Prophet came, they renounced and rejected his prophecy, abandoned what their scriptures commanded them to believe, breached the covenants that commanded them to believe in him, and disbelieved in the Noble Qur'an. They said: "Allah has revealed nothing to any human being." Among these verses are what the Almighty said in Sura Al-'Imran:

1- "Remember, O Prophet, when Allah took the covenant of those who were given the Scripture to make it known to people and not hide it, yet they cast it behind their backs and traded it for a fleeting gain. What a miserable profit!" (Qur'an 3:187)

Imam Ibn Kathir said: "This is an admonition from Allah, a rebuke and a threat to the People of the Book with whom Allah made a covenant through prophets to believe in Muhammad and proclaim him to other people to be receptive to him when he was sent. However, they concealed the truth and- instead of the good things they were promised in this worldly life and the happiness in the hereafter, they became deserving of nothing." [16]

Imam Ibn Jarir narrated on the authority of Ibn Abbas, who said: "This verse was revealed concerning Fanhas and Ashiya, two Jewish scholars, who concealed the characteristics written in their Torah concerning the Prophet even though Allah commanded them to reveal them." [17]

2- Also, among these verses are what we read in Sura Al-Baqara: "Now, when a messenger from Allah has come to them—confirming their own Scriptures—some of the People of the Book cast the Book of Allah behind their backs as if they did not know." (Qur'an 2:101)

The meaning of the verse: When Muhammad, a Messenger from Allah, was sent confirming what the Torah said about him as the expected prophet, a great number of the Jews cast the teachings of their Book behind their backs and thoroughly rejected this portion concerning that prediction about the prophet as if they knew nothing about it.

1- Imam Ibn Jarir said: "The meaning of the Almighty's 'as if they did not know' (Q 2:101) is that: It was as though those who hated Allah's Book from among the Jewish scholars and breached Allah's covenant by not complying with what was in it- did not know the Torah's command to follow Muhammad and believe in him. This was a assertion from Allah that they knowingly rejected the truth and opposed Allah's command even though they knew that it was incumbent upon them to follow those teachings." [18]

So, the noble verse provides a clear statement that the Jews breached the covenants that were in their Scripture that they should believe in Muhammad when he arrived and trust what he said about Allah.

These are three verses (Qur'an 5:13, 3:187, 2:101) that we referred to as evidence of the Jews breaching the covenants that Allah made with them in their Torah and not obeying their own prophets to believe in Muhammad. They took these covenants, but they breached and opposed them.

Fifth: We will now move to another kind of their breaching their covenants:

After The Prophet migrated to Medina, he entered into a treaty with the Jews who dwelt there. In that treaty he guaranteed them their freedom and stability. Among the most important articles in that treaty was: "In case of any act of aggression on Medina, the Jews should stand side by side with the Muslims to defend it, and the Jews should always agree with the Muslims as long as they were warriors."

Suffice it to say that all the different sects of Jews broke the pledge entailed in that text that called for helping the Muslims to defend Medina.

A- Banu Qaynuqa who lived inside Medina in houses that were adjacent to those of the Muslims not only refrained from helping them in the Battle of Badr, but they resented their victory over Quraysh, made no secret of their unhappiness for the defeat of the Meccans, and they began to provoke and harass the Muslims.

During that time, Gabriel came to the Prophet with this revelation: "And if you O Prophet see signs of betrayal by a people, respond by openly terminating your treaty with them. Surely Allah does not like those who betray." (Qur'an 8:58) [19] When Gabriel finished reading the verse, the Prophet said: "I fear Banu Qaynuqa." Then, he marched and went to them in their market place and said to them: "Take heed and beware, you Jews, lest a calamity such as the one that befell Quraysh befalls you. Submit for you have realized that I am a sent prophet, and you can find that in your Scripture and in Allah's covenant with you." They responded brandishing their might: "Muhammad! You think we are like your people. Do not be fooled by your victory over people who had no knowledge of fighting. If you fought against us, you will realize that we are people..."

When the Prophet realized that they were determined to persist in violating their covenants, fight the Islamic call and assist all those who opposed it, he expelled them from Medina and sent them to Daraa because of their betrayal and treachery. [20]

B- Banu Nadir were even worse than their predecessors in breaching their covenants with the Muslims. They were not content to merely desist from providing the Muslims with aid in the Battle of Badr but, rather, they helped the enemies that came to spread corruption in Medina after that. Here is what they did in the Battle of Suwaiq: Abu Sufyan bin Harb tried to avenge himself on the Muslims after his defeat at the Battle of Badr. So, he set out with his men to Medina and they arrived there at night. He knocked at the door of Salam bin Mishkam- brother of Banu Al-Nadir- who received him well. He told him the news of his people. Abu Sufyan then left and he and his men attacked a place called "al-'ureid." When the Muslims learned of this, they followed Abu Sufyan and his men. They escaped safely after throwing a lot of their provisions and what they got from Suwaiq.

Banu Nadir were also responsible for the attempt to assassinate the Messenger when he went to their homes to ask for their assistance to pay the compensation for a man who was wrongfully killed. [21]

Because of their treachery and breaching their covenants, the Muslims expelled them out of Medina like the others.

As for Banu Qurayza they were the worst of all. They surpassed all the other Jewish sects in breaching their covenants with the Muslims. They breached their covenants NOT at times of peace but at times of war, during difficulties and hardships, just as al-Ahzaab (the parties) of disbelief surrounded Medina (during the Battle of the Trench/ or the Battle of the Parties).

After the polytheists gathered their men at the Battle of Al-Ahzaab under the leadership of Abu Suyan and at the incitement and provocation of Huyayy bin Akhtab, the Jew, the Muslims learned that the Jews of Banu Qurayza had breached their covenant with them and joined the armies of the polytheists. The Messenger sent to them to caution and warn them of the consequences of their betrayal. They insisted on their path, and they used filthy and offensive language against the Prophet.

When Allah pushed those polytheists back away from Medina, the Messenger and the Muslims focused their attention on punishing the Jews of Banu Qurayza who breached their covenant at a difficult time. It was Allah's decree to murder them for their betrayal and treason. [22]

Thus, in concluding this section we can say that the verses that described the Jews as people who breach covenants are plenty. They are also confirmed by their actual history. Some of these verses declare that this vice appeared to be second nature to them, one of their very basic characteristics. The Almighty said: "Why is it that every time they make a covenant, a group of them casts it aside? In fact, most of them do not believe." (Qur'an 2:100) [23]

Interpreting this noble verse, Al-Zamakhshari said: "The Jews are stamped with treachery and breaching covenants. Allah made covenants with them and their predecessors many times, and they always breached them. They never fulfilled their promises: "namely those with whom you O Prophet have entered into treaties, but they violate them every time, not fearing the consequences." [24]

Ibn Jarir said: "Hardly had they made a covenant that they did not violate. They entered into treaties today only to be breached tomorrow." [25]

The use of "every time" (Q 2:100) indicates that these breaches and violations were recurrent and frequent. They took place all the time and everywhere, one after the other. That is why, Fakhr Al-Razi said:

"The interrogation emphasizes renouncing what they did and accentuating its gravity. That was a very effective and rhetorical way to admonish and reprove. Saying "that every time they make a covenant, a group of them casts it aside" is indicative of something "habitual." It was as though the Almighty is comforting the Messenger for their disbelief in the revelations that he brought. What they did was not unique or exceptional; it was their habit, something they were used to doing. It was the way their predecessors behaved as shown in previous verses; they breached their covenants again and again to the extent that it was not difficult to continue doing this, contrary to those who are not used to doing this.

Thus, these noble verses that we considered in this section described the Jews as people who breached the covenants that Allah took with them to worship Him, not to associate others with Him, and do good and righteous deeds. They breached the covenants that their Scripture commanded them to adhere to: They shed each other's blood, broke their pledges with their prophets, harmed them and rebelled against them. They also breached their covenants that called them to believe in Muhammad when he was sent. They broke their promises in every respect as long as that would agree with their whims and desires. For this, Allah condemned them and blinded their hearts: "In fact, most of them do not believe." [25a]

Second: Their inappropriateness to Allah, animosity to His angels and murdering His prophets.

The Noble Qur'an recounted many of the vices and depravities of the Jews. Among these vices and failings are their inappropriateness to the Creator and describing Him with things unfitting and are far beneath Him. Also, among the transgressions that the Qur'an recounted are their open animosity to Gabriel and murdering the honorable prophets that came to them with guidance and true faith as well as overstepping their boundaries with those people who stand up for justice.

Here are some of the verses that documented their vices, vices that would only be generated by those whom "Satan has taken hold of them, causing them to forget the remembrance of Allah. They are the party of Satan. Surely Satan's party is bound to lose." (Qur'an 58:19)

First: In Sura Al-'Imran the Almighty said: "Indeed, Allah has heard those among the Jews who said, "Allah is poor; we are rich!" We have certainly recorded their slurs and their killing of prophets unjustly. Then We will say, "Taste the torment of burning!" This is the reward for what your hands have done. And Allah is never unjust to His creation." (Qur'an 3:181)

Ibn Mardavieh and Ibn Abi Hatim narrated on the authority of Sa'id ibn Jubayr and Ibn Abbas, they said concerning the Almighty's: "Who is it that will lend to Allah a good loan which Allah will multiply many times over for them, and they will have an honorable reward?" The Jews said: O Muhammad! Allah has become impoverished and now He is asking His servants for a donation. Allah then revealed that verse. [26]

And Ibn Ishaq, Ibn Jarir, and Ibn Abi Hatim narrated on the authority of Ibn Abbas, who said: "Abu Bakr Siddiq went to a school where many Jews were gathered and were in the company of a man called Fanhas. Abu Bakr said to Fanhas: 'Woe to you, Fanhas! Fear

Allah and submit. By Allah, you know that Muhammad is the Messenger of Allah and that he came to you with the truth from Him. You will find that written in your Torah and Injil.' Fanhas said: 'Abu Bakr! What need do we have for Allah. He is poor. We do not supplicate to Him as He supplicates to us. We are rich without Him. If He were rich, He wouldn't have borrowed money from us, as your friend claims: He would forbid you from usury and give to us. And if He were rich, He wouldn't give us usury.' Abu Bakr became enraged, and he forcefully hit Fanhas in the face and said: "By the One in whose hand is my soul, had it not been for the covenant between us and you, I would have struck your neck, enemy of Allah.' Fanhas went to the Prophet and said: "Muhammad! Look what your friend did to me!" The Prophet said to Abu Bakr: "Why did you do that, Abu Bakr?" Abu Bakr said: "O Messenger of Allah, the enemy of Allah said something terrible. He claimed that Allah is poor and they have no need of Him. When he said that, I became angry, and I struck his face." Fanhas denied that and said: "I did not say that." Allah revealed this verse concerning what Fanhas said: "Indeed, Allah has heard those ʿamong the Jewsʾ who said, 'Allah is poor; we are rich!'" [27]

Ibn Al-Munzir narrated on the authority of Qataada who said: "It was said that this verse "Indeed, Allah has heard those ʿamong the Jewsʾ who said, 'Allah is poor'" was revealed of Huyayy ibn Akhtab When Allah revealed "Who is it that will lend to Allah a good loan ..." Huyayy said: "Allah borrows from us just as the poor borrows from the rich." [28]

These verses indicate that the Jews mocked and derided the Noble Qur'an when it calls people to donate and contribute. They ridiculed the teachings of Islam that urge and encourage people to be generous, charitable and giving. They allude to the Almighty things that are unbecoming, and they try all possible means to encourage the believers to be tightfisted and miserly in order to cast doubts in their faith and cause them to become unresponsive to Allah's Book and His Prophet. That despicable saying was not uncommon for the Jews; the Noble Qur'an reports in yet another verse that they said: "Allah is tight-fisted," (Qur'an 5:64) that is, He is stingy and doesn't give generously. In many other places the Noble Qur'an has also recounted how ignorant and arrogant they were in attributing to Allah things that are unsuitable and inappropriate and far below Him.

Allah showed that He is well aware of all that they say and do; He is the All-Knowledgeable: "Indeed, Allah has heard those among the Jews who said, Allah is poor; we are rich!" (Q 3:181) In other words, Allah heard what those Jews- who were uttering nothing but falsehoods and obscenities- were saying claiming that He is poor and they are rich.

Knowledge and awareness of these grave things they were claiming is what is meant by hearing. Afterwards comes presenting their accounts on that great day when people stand before their creator.

The noble statement therefore means that Allah is watching and listening to them fully aware of all that they say and do, and He will punish them for their inappropriateness and obscenities. The Almighty who owns the universe and all that is therein is aware of everything, nothing is hidden from Him, and He is able to punish those who do not give Him His true worth. That is why He said: "We have certainly recorded their slurs and their killing of prophets unjustly." (Q 3:181) Everything they said is recorded.

This poignant expression comprises a grave threat to them for the transgressions the perpetrated because what is really meant by "recording" is the consequences, the severe punishment and humiliating torture.

The Almighty also combined their despicable sayings with an appalling deed committed by their predecessors, i.e., unjustly killing the prophets. Thus, He pinpoints their inherent propensity for evil, their taking religious rights frivolously, and to indicate that their foul sayings and pernicious slurs were not their first offense or transgression. Their predecessors unjustly killed the prophets before. He is also showing that these two crimes were of the same kind, i.e., overstepping their boundaries with Allah since killing the prophets is a daring and audacious deed against Allah who had assigned these prophets to deliver His message, and their saying "'Allah is poor; we are rich!'" (Q 3:181) is trespassing against Allah Himself and attributing unbecoming characteristics to Him. Thus, they have gravely sinned, went astray and done dreadful deeds.

Adding the crime of murder to those who existed during the Prophetic era - despite the fact that it was committed by their predecessors- was right since they accepted and did not condemn it, even though they didn't do it that themselves. Those who accept crimes committed by others are just as guilty, as if they themselves commit them. In the Hadith: "If sin is committed on earth, he who witnesses it and does not acknowledge it as such is like one who is absent from it, and he who is absent and accepts it is like one who witnesses it."

The Almighty described killing the prophets as "unjust" (Q 3:181) even though it could never be just or justified. That emphasized the maliciousness of their deeds and their malevolence and viciousness, and their being heedless concerning the appropriateness (or lack thereof) of certain actions.

Then, He stated the punishment: "We will say, "Taste the torment of burning!"." That is, We will punish them for what they said and did, and we will cast them in Hellfire saying, "'Taste the torment of burning!'."

"Tasting" usually refers to something desired and requested. Using it here denotes sarcasm and mockery as in His saying: "So give them good news of a painful punishment." (Qur'an 84:24)

The Almighty then stated that they were responsible for bringing this punishment upon themselves: "This is the reward for what your hands have done. And Allah is never unjust to His creation." (Qur'an 8:51) That is, the severe punishment that befell you, O Jews, was the result of the evil that your hands have done and the slurs that your mouths have uttered. It is Allah's wisdom to punish only those who are deserving of punishment; He is never unjust.

Thus, these two noble verses ridiculed the Jews for their ignorance and unawareness. They also chastised them for their impoliteness and inappropriateness and threatened humiliating torture on account of their boldness and audacity towards their Creator.

Second: In Sura Al-Baqara the Almighty said: "Say, O Prophet, "Whoever is an enemy of Gabriel should know that he revealed this Quran to your heart by Allah's Will, confirming what came before it—a guide and good news for the believers." Whoever is an enemy of Allah, His angels, His messengers, Gabriel, and Michael, then let them know that Allah is certainly the enemy of the disbelievers." (Qur'an 2:97-98)

These two verses disclose one strange vice for the Jews, i.e., their animosity to one of Allah's angels, one who does not eat what they eat nor drink what hey drink, an angel who is so close to Allah, who always obeys what Allah commands him to do. Thus, this enmity towards him is not warranted or justified. So, why this open announcement of animosity and hatred?

They heard that Gabriel comes to Muhammad with revelations from Allah. Since they envied Muhammad for his prophecy, they also declared their animosity to Gabriel out of envy, malice and resentment. They were stupid and uninformed because Gabriel also came to them with good tidings for their lives and their faith. However, once is overpowered and consumed by envy and malice, they can no longer differentiate between good and evil.

The meaning of the two noble verses is: Muhammad, tell those Jews who declared their hatred to Gabriel that their animosity was unwarranted and unnecessary because he revealed the Qur'an to your heart in compliance with Allah's command to confirm the Scriptures that came before it, to guide people to the paths of happiness, and as good tidings to the believers. Also, tell them that whoever is an enemy of Allah or one of His angels or messengers is a disbeliever who earns Allah's displeasure and wrath who would be deserving disgrace and painful punishment.

Imam Ibn Jarir said; "Scholars agreed that this verse was revealed as a response to the Jews of the Children of Israel when they claimed that Gabriel was their enemy and Michael was their ally." [29]

Al-Bukhari narrated on the authority of Anas ibn Malik, who said that Abdullah bin Salam heard that the Prophet was coming to Medina while he was working in the fields. He said: 'I will ask you about three things that no one knows except a prophet. What are the first signs? What time? What is the first food that the people of paradise will eat? Why does a child turn towards his father or his mother?' He said: 'Gabriel told me about it earlier.' Ibn Salam said: 'That is the enemy of the Jews among the angels.' Then, the Prophet read this verse: 'Whoever is an enemy of Gabriel should know that he revealed this ⌜Quran⌝ to your heart by Allah's Will.' He said: 'As for the first signs of the Hour, a fire will gather them from the east to the west, and... What is the first food that the people of Paradise will eat? It is the liver of a whale. As for the child, if the man's fluid preceded the woman's fluid, the child will be a male. And if the woman's fluid preceded the man's, the child would be a female.' He said: 'I bear witness that there is no Allah but Allah, and that you are the Messenger of Allah.' He said, 'O Messenger of Allah: The Jews are a confused people, and if they know of my conversion to Islam, they would resent it.' The Prophet, said: 'Who is Abdullah? Which one of you?' They said: 'The best of us and the son of the best of us, our master and the son of our master.' Then the Prophet said: 'Do you know that Abdullah bin Salam converted to Islam?' They said: 'May Allah protect him from that.' So Abdullah went to them and said: 'I bear witness that there is no Allah but Allah, and that Muhammad is the Messenger of Allah.' They said: 'You are evil and the son of evil,' and they criticized him. He said: 'This is what I feared, O Messenger of Allah.' [30]

Imam Ahmad narrated on the authority of Ibn Abbas that after the Jews asked the Prophet questions that he answered, they asked him about his ally from amongst the angels so that they could determine whether to follow him or not. He said: "Amy ally is Gabriel. Allah has not sent a prophet without appointing Gabriel as an ally." They said: "Then, we will not follow you. Had you other angels as allies, we would have followed and believed in you." "What stops you from following him?" They said: "He is our enemy." Then, Allah revealed: "Say, ˹O Prophet, ˺ "Whoever is an enemy of Gabriel should know that he revealed this ˹Quran˺ to your heart by Allah's Will, confirming what came before it...." [31]

In a Hadith by Imam Ahmad, Al-Tirmidhi and An-Nisaa'i, the Jews said to Muhammad after they asked him some questions which he answered: "There is only one thing that you need to tell us in order to follow you: 'Every prophet has an angel that brings him tidings, so who is your angel?'" He said: "Gabriel." They said: "This Gabriel is our enemy, the one who brings tidings of war, fighting and death. Had you said that it is Michael, who brings us mercy, compassion, food, etc. we would have followed you." Allah therefore revealed the verse: "Say, O Prophet, "Whoever is an enemy of Gabriel should know that ...."

So, these Hadiths indicate that the Jews openly declared their enmity towards Gabriel- peace be upon him- and that their open assertions of animosity were repeated on various occasions between them and the Prophet. The reason for this was their envy and their resentment that it was Gabriel who brought Allah's revelations to Muhammad.

Sheikh Muhammad At-Taher bin A'shur said: "it is strange that their beliefs are that irrational and unreasonable since they believe that Gabriel is an angel of Allah yet they hate him. This is the lowest level of mental and religious degradation, for there is no doubt that religious misperception and confusion is one of the greatest indications for the degradation and dilapidation of a nation as it precludes their collective stance and shared belief in illusion and deception." [32]

Commanding the Prophet using "Say" to address the Jews was meant to comfort him and confirm the admonition for their animosity to Gabriel, the loyal protector of the revelation.

And His saying: “Say, O Prophet, “Whoever is an enemy of Gabriel” was a general call to indicate that Allah would not be mindful of them or others who would show animosity to Gabriel, if there were others who had a similar attitude towards him.

And “to your heart” (Q 2:97) was to further assert the revelation and to indicate that the reason he was able to recite the Noble Qur’an and inform the people was that it took root and was established in his heart.

Allah’s saying (Q 2:97): “... that he revealed this Quran to your heart by Allah’s Will” meant that the enmity they manifested was unwarranted because he revealed the Qur’an to your heart, Muhammad, by Allah’s will. Thus, any enmity towards him was, in fact, an enmity towards Allah Himself. It was the response, a reason, that is, to the condition statement implied in “Whoever.”

Al-Zamakhshari said: “If you say how could ‘...he revealed this ⌜Quran⌝ to your heart by Allah’s Will’ be the response statement for the conditional sentence? I would respond by saying that there are two sides to this. First: If one of the People of the Book showed animosity to Gabriel, this would be needless and unwarranted since a Book- one that confirmed the Books they had in their hands- had been revealed. If they were fair and just, they would have loved and become grateful to him for revealing what was good and beneficial to them and for correcting what they already had. Second: If someone became an enemy to him, the reason was that he revealed the Qur’an confirmed their Scriptures and agreed with what was contained therein. However, they hated the Qur’an and its agreement with their Scriptures. That was why they distorted their Scriptures and denounced its correspondence with the Qur’an.” [33]

The Almighty’s: by Allah’s Will” meant that the revelation was possible because it was Allah’s command. It was therefore a chastisement for their animosity to Gabriel who brought down the Qur’an following Allah’s command, not his own will. That was a first argument against their position.

And the Almighty’s saying: “confirming ...,” an adverb referring to “Quran” in describing the manner of the verb “revealed.” That is, He revealed the Qur’an as a Book that is in agreement with the Scriptures that were revealed before it including the Torah. And that was a second argument against their position.

He supported these arguments with a third and a fourth arguments. He said: “a guide and good news for the believers.” This means that the Qur’an that was revealed and which confirmed your Scriptures is a guide to success and good news. Sensible people would not reject the guidance that would save them from delusions and deceptions even if brought by an enemy. This Qur’an also brings the believers good tidings of Allah’s pleasure in this worldly life and in the hereafter. As for those who went astray, they were forewarned with undesirable and dreadful consequences. Therefore, follow the straightforward path of faith to be counted among the righteous. Thus, the Noble Qur’an had stated a number of arguments depicting their folly, obstinacy and rejection of the truth after it became clear to them. The noble verse also reflected five magnificent attributes in the Qur'an:

First: It came down from Allah and was revealed by His will. Second: It was revealed to the Prophet's heart. Third: It confirmed the Scriptures that came before it. Fourth: It firmly provided the best guidance and direction. Fifth: It brought good news for the believers.

Then, the Almighty revealed the truth concerning those enemies of Gabriel; they were enemies of Allah Himself because Gabriel was entrusted with bringing His revelations to His messengers, to inform them with what he was commanded to deliver. The almighty said; "Whoever is an enemy of Allah, His angels, His messengers, Gabriel, and Michael, then ˹let them know that˺ Allah is certainly the enemy of the disbelievers." This means: Being an enemy of Gabriel is like being an enemy of Allah. Also, being an enemy of Muhammad is like being an enemy of Allah. This is because belief in Allah, His angels and His messengers are indivisible and whoever disbelieves in one would become a disbeliever in all. When man becomes an enemy of Allah, this means that man disbelieves and opposes Allah's commandments and prohibitions. When man becomes an enemy of Allah's angels, this means that man denies and rejects their graces and favors and attributes aspects that run against their infallibility and flawlessness. And when man is an enemy of Allah's messengers, this means that man does not believe them and would deliberately try to harm and offend them. Allah's enmity to man, on the other hand, means Allah's pouring His wrath and displeasure on man and punishing him for his immorality and disbelief.

The Almighty mentioned Gabriel and Michael by name even though they under the group that combines all the angels because the Jews openly declared their animosity to Gabriel and their alliance with Michael. The Almighty specifically mentioned them to caution that if man is an enemy of one, he becomes an enemy of all, and if he disbelieves in one, he has shown disbelief in all.

Ibn Jarir said: "If someone said: 'Aren't Gabriel and Michael amongst the angels?' The response would be: 'Yes.' 'Then, what is the meaning of mentioning their names in the verse that refers to angels in general? 'The response would be: 'The meaning of specifically mentioning their names is: when the Jews said that Gabriel was their enemy and Michael was their guardian, and they claimed that they disbelieved in Muhammad because Gabriel was his friend, Allah informed them that whoever was an enemy to Gabriel, Allah would be his enemy and he would be among the infidels. That is why, He mentioned him and Michael by name so that no one would be able to say that Allah said whoever was an enemy to Allah, His angels and messengers- and we were not enemies to Allah, His angels and messengers- because "angels" is an inclusive name, so is the word "messengers." That was why Allah specifically mentioned the names of those who claimed to be his enemies in order to alleviate the confusion of those whose faith was shaky and wobbly." [34]

At the end of this noble verse, the Almighty said: "Allah is certainly the enemy of the disbelievers." (Q 2:98) The Almighty did not say that Allah was an enemy of "him" or “them” to indicate that the enmity of those who were mentioned in the noble verse was an act of disbelief and ingratitude, and to show that they were being placed under this inclusive ruling was a proof coupled with evidence, and to inform them that Allah’s enmity to them was due to their disbelief, for Allah does not show hostility to people because of who they are or to whom they are related. Allah only hates disbelief, and He punishes for infidelity.

In Tafsir Al-Manar, the author said: “This noble verse was cautioning them to the implausibility of the excuse with which they came up: they did not oppose all of the angels. So, the Almighty wanted to reveal what was actually happening: that they were enemies of the truth and anyone that represented the truth or called for it. An open declaration of enmity towards Gabriel was similar to an open announcement of enmity towards Michael whom they claimed to be their guardian that they loved, and that they would have believed in the Prophet had Michael been the one who came down with the revelations. Their animosity towards the Noble Qur’an was an enmity towards all the revealed Books, since they all point to the same goal and direction. Their animosity towards Muhammad was an animosity towards all the messengers of Allah since they all had the same vision, goal and responsibility. Therefore, their position indicated their animosity to all those who were mentioned. That was one of the Noble Qur’an’s terse and succinct eloquent styles that uniquely characterize the Noble Qur’an.” [35]

Thus, the two noble verses (Q 2:97-98) branded the Jews as disbelievers and ignorant for their animosity towards Gabriel, and their disbelief in Muhammad. They also revealed their disgrace and humiliation for this animosity was merely due to envy and malice, their resentment that Allah revealed His favors and grace to whomsoever He wants.

<u>Third</u>:

A. In Sura Al-‘Imran, the Almighty said: “Indeed, those who deny Allah’s signs, kill the prophets unjustly, and kill people who stand up for justice—give them good news of a painful punishment. They are the ones whose deeds are wasted in this world and the Hereafter. And they will have no helpers.” (Qur’an 3:21-22)

These two noble verses comprise a number of the vices that characterized the Children of Israel throughout the stages of their history.

The first vice was their disbelief in Allah’s signs, the revealed as well as the cosmic ones. In other words, they denied the clear signs that point to monotheism, the belief in one Allah, and they rejected the evident proofs of the truthfulness of His messengers, and avoided following the truth that they knew as they knew their own children.

The second vice was that they “kill the prophets unjustly.” They had committed that deed repeatedly throughout the generations.

The Jews killed Isaiah son of Amoz who lived in the middle of the eighth century BC. King Menesa ordered his men to kill him by tying him to a tree trunk and sawing his body in the year 700 BC because he advised him to abandon his evil deeds. They also killed Prophet Jeremiah by stoning him because he chastised them repeatedly for their immoralities and evil deeds. That was in the middle of the seventh century BC. Likewise, they killed Zechariah because he tried to defend his son, John. He was killed by Herod, king of the Jews appointed by the Romans. He also killed John, son of Zechariah, because his niece was enraged that John did not issue the Fatwa (the decree) that suited her whim, i.e., marrying Herod. One of the Jews, a judge, also killed Ezekiel, because he forbade him from certain transgressions. The Jews also claimed that they killed Jesus, and they were proud to have done it, but the Noble Qur'an reprimanded them: "But they neither killed nor crucified him—it was only made to appear so." (Qur'an 4:157)

They also tried to kill the Prophet many times; however, the Almighty foiled their attempts and protected him from their evil.

These confirmed historical facts show that killing the prophets at the hands of the Jews was something that was committed repeatedly at different times and throughout subsequent generations.

It might be argued that since the Jews did not kill all the prophets, why did the Noble Qur'an say that they "kill(ed) the prophets ...," not SOME prophets.

The answer to this question is: They disparaged the dignity of the prophecy and derided the call to the truth and, therefore, made these dreadfully outrageous onslaughts on some of the prophets. Those who did such things with a few had transgressed against the prophecy itself and would be considered transgressors and guilty of killing most of the prophets. In this respect, the Almighty said: "That is why We ordained for the Children of Israel that whoever takes a life—unless as a punishment for murder or mischief in the land—it will be as if they killed all of humanity." (Qur'an 5:32)

And the Almighty stated that their killing of the prophets was "unjust-" even though this could never be just- to state the target of His condemnation and reproof, because the object of His disapproval was their transgression against the truth by killing the prophets. It was also meant to point out that due to their blindness and going too far in committing evil, they became enemies of the truth, unfamiliar and uncomfortable with it, and to record that their killing of the prophets was unwarranted in their own religion which prohibited it. It was a statement that expressed objection to them presenting what their law prevented them from doing to eternalize their denunciation everywhere and at all times.

The honorable Sheikh Muhammad Abu Zahra said: "The Almighty mentioned the word "just" in the negative form of "unjustly" to indicate all kinds of justice or truth: fixed justice, alleged Justice, and delusional Justice. That is, they had no excuse whatsoever for this aggressive act: they did not believe it was the truth, they did not allege that it was the truth, and they were not delusional about it being the truth. They did what they did knowing that they were wrong, and their deed was therefore hideously criminal to the core and most despicable because of its intended target." [36]

Now that the Almighty stamped them with the crime of killing the prophets, which is the worst crime in this world, He followed it with their third crime, i.e., "kill(ing) people who stand up for justice." (Q 3:21) That is to say, they killed those who called for justice, and they were belligerent to those who were advocates for fairness and justice. They harmed those counsellors who wanted to instill virtues among people.

Their behavior was the direct consequence of their deafness to guidance, their rejection of good counsel, and their unresponsiveness to the word of truth. They were the kind of people who were adequately described in the Hadith: "Miserable are those people who kill those who stand up for justice. Miserable are those people who do not enjoin what is right and forbid what is wrong. Miserable are those people amongst whom the believer walks in piety." And in another Hadith, Abu Ubaidah Amer bin Al-Jarrah said that he asked the Prophet: "Messenger of Allah, who would receive the worst torture on the Day of Judgement? A man who kills a prophet? Or one who does not enjoin what is right and forbid what is wrong?" The Messenger of Allah said: "Indeed, those who deny Allah's signs, kill the prophets unjustly, and kill people who stand up for justice—give them good news of a painful punishment." (Q 3:21) Then he said: "Abu Ubaidah! The Children of Israel killed forty-three prophets at the beginning of the day. Then one hundred and seventy among them enjoined them to do what was good and forbid what was wrong, and they killed them all at the end of the day." [37]

The Almighty described those who stand up for justice as regular people, not prophets and not sent, but by likening them to prophets, the Almighty elevates their status and their righteous fight and faithful and worthwhile struggle. In His saying: "give them good news of a painful punishment," (Q 3:21) the Almighty was ridiculing and mocking the Children of Israel for they claimed that they were Allah's children and His chosen favorite people, and they were worthy of the prophecy because of lineage- not their deeds. Allah responded to their claim by telling them that the news that they should be expecting because of this alleged belief was a painful punishment, not an eternal bliss or grace.

The Almighty then showed that if a good deed was to come out of those people, it would avail them nothing because of the evil deeds in which they indulged. He said: "They are the ones whose deeds are wasted in this world and the Hereafter. And they will have no helpers." (Q 3:22) In other words, those who denied Allah's signs and killed His prophets and those who stood up for justice among people, would benefit nothing from their good deeds because of their disbelief and their unsound and corrupt thoughts. Their good deeds would even avail them nothing in the hereafter because good and virtuous deeds should be coupled with faith and belief. However, these people had persevered in their disbelief and were consumed by corruption. They therefore lacked the readiness to be recipients of what was good and righteous. Denying the truth, punishing those who were truthful, and killing those who stood up for the truth hardened their hearts and them like stones or even harder than stones.

The Almighty's: "And they will have no helpers" indicates that Allah's punishment was certain and inevitable and no one would be able to fend them against it, which also indicated that their deeds were wasted.

B. In Sura Al- Ma'idah, there are two verses that state that the Children of Israel would either reject and disbelieve or kill and attack any messenger who came to them with guidance that they found undesirable or incongruent with their whims. The Almighty said: "Indeed, We took a covenant from the Children of Israel and sent them messengers. Whenever a messenger came to them with what they did not desire, they denied some and killed others. They thought there would be no consequences, so they turned a blind eye and a deaf ear. Yet Allah turned to them in forgiveness after their repentance, but again many became blind and deaf. And Allah is All-Seeing of what they do." (Qur'an 5:70-71)

The meaning of the two noble verses (Q 5:70-71 is: We took a covenant with the Children of Israel to worship Allah only and do as We had commanded them to do and forsake what We had prohibited them from doing. We sent messengers to guide and caution them. However, every time a messenger was sent to them with what they did not desire, they either rebelled and denied him or killed or showed animosity towards him. Those transgressors from among the Children of Israel thought that they would not be punished for killing the prophets or denying them. They became blind to the truth and they thought that they would not be touched by Allah's wrath. They persisted in their denial, in turning a deaf ear to messages of guidance and turning a blind eye to the truth. Then they repented and Allah forgave them. However, most turned back to their blindness and deafness, and they rejected the truth and refused to do what their messengers commanded them to do. And "Allah is All-Seeing of what they do." (Q 5:71) He is All-Knowledgeable and well aware of all their deeds, and He will reward them accordingly on the Day of Resurrection. He will give them the appropriate punishment for their disbelief in His messengers and their acts of aggression towards them.

His saying: "Indeed, We took a covenant from the Children of Israel and sent them messengers..." was a statement for one of the many crimes they perpetrated, i.e., their transgression against the messengers of Allah- those who were sent to guide them- by disbelieving in them sometimes and killing them at other times.

What was meant by the "covenant" that was taken from them was the commandments that they received from their messengers to worship and obey Allah only, comply with His messengers and believe in Muhammad whose description they find in their Scriptures.

His saying: "We ... sent them messengers..." is a statement indicating the many important messengers that were sent to guide them to the straight path. But what was their position concerning those chosen messengers?

Their position was: "Whenever a messenger came to them with what they did not desire, they denied some and killed others."

In this noble statement, the Almighty illustrated one of the habits of the Children of Israel, an inherent one that could always be witnessed, i.e., every time a messenger was sent to them with something they didn't desire, they would receive him in one of these two ways: denial and rebellion or killing and shedding their blood.

Thus, the noble verse indicated that those Jews had reached the worst stages of corruption. Their hearts had hardened to such an extent that the good counsel of the messengers had no effect on them. On the contrary, the attempt to guide them only increased their denial and their acts of violence and aggression towards those messengers.

The Almighty then showed that they thought that they were not going to be touched by Allah's punishment despite their transgression and aggression. The Almighty said: "They thought there would be no consequences, so they turned a blind eye and a deaf ear." (Q 5:71) That is, those Jews who denied some messengers and killed others were under were almost certain that they would not be punished for denying and killing the messengers. They were therefore tempted to turn a blind eye to the path of truth and a deaf ear to the teachings and instructions that could have benefited them.

And that is the condition of nations when moral values deteriorate and decline. They are likely to trespass and commit immoralities and persist in depravities and decadences thinking that Allah will not punish them for their injustices, dissipation and corruption.

The Almighty then showed that He accepted their repentance, but they turned back to their debaucheries. He said: "Yet Allah turned to them in forgiveness after their repentance, but again many became blind and deaf. And Allah is All-Seeing of what they do." (Q 5:71) That is, Allah forgave them when they repented and returned to the truth and gave up their degeneracy and disobedience. However, that did not last since they turned back to their injustices and corruptions for they were people who were accustomed to breaching covenants. They preferred to march in the paths of unrighteousness and misguidance.

His saying: "but again MANY became blind and deaf" (Q 5:71) indicated that the greatest number among them were blind and deaf, NOT all of them. There were exceptions. This reflects the fairness of the Noble Qur'an to those pious and righteous people, even if only a few.

"And Allah is All-Seeing of what they do" was a warning to them for their wicked deeds. The Almighty was cautioning them because their despicable actions are well known and well documented to the Almighty. On the Day of Resurrection, He will say: "Taste the torment of burning! This is the reward for what your hands have done. And Allah is never unjust to His creation."

Thus, the noble verses revealed one of the guileful and inherent habits of the Jews in all places and at all times: receiving Allah's prophets and those who stood up for justice with arrogance and denial sometimes and killing and harming them at other times. That deeply ingrained habit had led them to disgrace in this world and painful torment in the hereafter.

Third: <u>Maneuvering to legitimize what Allah has prohibited.</u>

One of the vices that the Children of Israel committed as a result of their ignorance, decadence, greed, and lack of self-control was their maneuvering to breach pledges to attain their goals and satisfy their desires thinking- on account of their ignorance and unawareness- that by adopting manipulative strategies they would escape punishment.

Here is the story: The Almighty made a covenant with the Children of Israel to dedicate the Sabbath solely to His worship. He prohibited them from catching fish on that day, not the other days. He wanted to test their readiness to comply with their pledges. So, He tested them with plenty of whales/large fish coming to the shore on the Sabbath, not on the other days of the week. Abundant fish would come to the coast clearly visible to them and easy to catch. They said: 'If we dug ponds next to sea when fish becomes abundant on Saturday and cause the water to flow to them on that day, then we can catch the fish from these ponds on Sunday and the following days. This way we comply with our pledge for the Sabbath on the one hand and we secure the whales that we desire, on the other.' Some of the righteous ones advised them that it would be just an "apparent" compliance with Allah's commandments but, in reality, it was rebellion and noncompliance. The Sabbath breakers did not heed that advice and carried out their trick. Allah was wrathful, and He transformed them to humiliated apes making them an example to those who lived at the same time, those who came after them, and a lesson to the righteous.

The story of the Sabbath breakers was mentioned in detail in Sura Al-A'raf (sura 7): "Ask them O Prophet about '\the people of the town which was by the sea, who broke the Sabbath. During the Sabbath, abundant fish would come to them clearly visible, but on other days the fish were never seen. In this way We tested them for their rebelliousness. When some of the righteous among them questioned their fellow Sabbath-keepers, "Why do you bother to warn those Sabbath-breakers who will either be destroyed or severely punished by Allah?" They replied, "Just to be free from your Lord's blame, and so perhaps they may abstain." When they ignored the warning they were given, We rescued those who used to warn against evil and overtook the wrongdoers with a dreadful punishment for their rebelliousness. But when they stubbornly persisted in violation, We said to them, 'Be disgraced apes!'" (Qur'an 7:163-166)

The meaning of these noble verses: Muhammad, ask a question that is meant to rebuke and censure. Ask about the people who lived in the town that was close to the sea. They had broken the Sabbath that they were supposed to exalt, and they transgressed against Allah. On that day, abundant fish would come visibly on the surface of the water. On the other days of they week, they would not be seen in these great amounts as Allah was testing their will power and self-restraint.

That act of noncompliance on their part was that they dug ponds right next to the sea where fish was seen abundantly on the Sabbath. The water would flow into these ponds carrying plenty of fish with it on Saturday. When the fish wanted to return to the sea, they couldn't because of the shallowness of the water in the ponds. So, the fish would remain in the ponds until they got them after Saturday. Apparently, it seemed as though they were complying with Allah's command since they did not catch fish on Saturday. However, in reality, they were trespassing and far from complying with what Allah had prohibited; trapping the fish in the ponds was fishing, in essence.

A group of them advised (the Sabbath breakers) against doing that to avoid Allah's punishment from descending upon them, but they did not heed their advice and disobeyed their order. Still, they continued to advise, remind and counsel them.

Another group of people criticized those advisors for persisting on advising them since they did not listen to their advice. They asked: "Why do you keep warning and advising people whom Allah will either destroy or severely punish?" The advisors replied saying: "To avoid Allah's blame, we enjoin what is good and forbid what is wrong, and we hope that they repent, abstain from what they are doing and save themselves from perdition." When the Sabbath breakers ignored the advice, We saved the advisors and inflicted severe punishment on the violators because of their disobedience and rebellion. That severe punishment was that We transformed them into disgraced apes.

Questioning them was meant as a reproof for their noncompliance perhaps they would repent and return to the right path and avoid exposing themselves to penalties that their predecessors suffered. It was also meant to indicate to inform them that that story was a well-known story to them, one that they could not deny and could only be known either through a book or a revelation. Therefore, when the illiterate Prophet who did not read their Book told them about it, it was a miracle to him, one sure evidence that he was a truthful Prophet to whom that story was revealed.

Interpreting this noble verse, Imam Ibn Kathir said: "It means: ask Muhammad those Jews about the story of their friends who disobeyed Allah and were surprised by His wrath for what they did, their noncompliance and resorting to trickery and warn them from concealing your description that they have in their Scripture so that they might be able to avert the dire consequences that brothers and predecessors suffered. This town is Aila and it is located on the cost of the Red Sea." [38]

Imam Al-Qurtubi said: "This question was one of reproof and admonition. It was a sign for the truthfulness of the illiterate Prophet, who could not read, and whom Allah informed with these matters. They said: 'We are the children of Allah and His chosen ones: We are the descendants of the tribe of Israel, descendants of the tribe of Moses who spoke with Allah directly, and descendants of Aziz, Moses's son. We are their offspring.' So, Allah said to His Prophet: 'Ask them, Muhammad, about that town. Didn't they suffer there because of their transgressions when they wanted to change Allah's commands and make what He has forbidden permissible?'" [39]

Most researchers believe that it was Aila town that was referred to in the verse. It is located between Median and At-Tur. It was also said that it was Tiberias.

The meaning implied in is that it is close and directly overlooks its beaches. And the Almighty's saying: "During the Sabbath, abundant fish would come to them clearly visible, but on other days the fish were never seen" (Q 7:163)was a statement of the test, the challenge they were to face. The verse means: Abundant whales came to them on Saturday, the day they were supposed to exalt and dedicate to worshipping Allah. They appeared clearly and visibly, right on the surface of the water, close to their town, and easily catchable. When Saturday was over, these whales/large fish no longer come to them. It was a test from their Allah.

Ibn Abbas said: "The Jews were commanded to consecrate the same day that you were commanded dedicate to Allah. That day was Friday. Yet, they abandoned that day and chose Saturday instead. So, Allah tested them and prohibited fishing on that day. He commanded them to dedicate it to Him. On Saturdays, however, abundant whales were seen clearly in the sea. When Saturday was over, they disappear only to reappear the following Saturday. That was a test that Allah prepared for them. And that was the meaning of "but on other days the fish were never seen." [40]

Imam Al-Qurtubi said: "It was said that this story took place during the time of David when Iblis told them: 'Since you were forbidden from fishing on Saturday, why don't you dig ponds to entrap them there?" So, they lured the whales to those ponds on Saturday where they remained since they were unable to leave those ponds because of the shallow water. Then they would take them on Sunday." [41]

The Almighty's "In this way We tested them for their rebelliousness" meant that this testing-, i.e., the abundant fish visibly appearing to them on Saturday and not seen on the other days of the week- was meant challenge them, and test their will-power, to receive the appropriate punishment for their rebelliousness and transgression against Allah, and their resorting to trickery to make what Allah had forbidden permissible. This is Allah's way: Whoever obeys Him, He will facilitate their lives and lavishly reward them with what is good and beneficial. However, whoever disobeys Him, He will deal with them as an All-Powerful, Almighty, capable Allah.

The Almighty then described the position of all the different groups of people in that town. He said: "When some of the righteous among them questioned their fellow Sabbath-keepers, 'Why do you bother to warn those Sabbath-breakers who will either be destroyed or severely punished by Allah?' They replied, 'Just to be free from your Lord's blame, and so perhaps they may abstain.'" (Q 7:164)

It is therefore conceivable to garner from this verse that the town people were divided into three groups:

1- The Sabbath- breakers who deliberately and persistently trespassed and transgressed against Allah.
2- The counselors who advised the Sabbath breakers to abstain from their rebellion and transgression.
3- The blamers of the counselors for their failure to bring the Sabbath breakers to comply with the command concerning the Sabbath.

It was this third group about which the Noble Qur'an said: "'Why do you ˹bother to˺ warn those Sabbath-breakers who will either be destroyed or severely punished by Allah?'" In other words, a group of the people in the town asked their brethren- who saved no effort in advising the Sabbath breakers- why they kept on counselling those people who benefited nothing from their advice and availed nothing from being cautioned, since Allah had decreed to purge the earth from their wickedness and inflict severe punishment on them for their persistence in their wickedness and their deafness to instruction and counselling. The counsellors responding by saying: "'Just to be free from your Lord's blame, and so perhaps they may abstain.'" (Q 7:164)

That is, they gave two reasons for their continuing to advise the Sabbath breakers:

First: To apologize to Allah lest they would be found lacking in enjoining what was good and forbidding what was wrong.

Second: They were hoping that the Sabbath breakers might benefit from these advice and warnings and abstain and mend their ways.

It was said that the people of that town were divided into two groups: A group that transgressed and violated the Sabbath and another group that refrained from doing so and advised the sabbath breakers not to overstep their boundaries with Allah. When the second group (the advisors/counsellors) continued persisted on advising the transgressors (the Sabbath breakers) to refrain from their violations, the Sabbath breakers told the advisors- mockingly and disdainfully: "'Why do you bother to warn those Sabbath-breakers who will either be destroyed or severely punished by Allah?'" The advisors then responded, saying: "Just to be free from your Lord's blame, and so perhaps they may abstain."

We are inclined to believe- as most interpreters do- that the people of the town were divided into three groups. That can apparently be understood from the use of the pronouns in the Noble verse. Had there been two groups only, the advisors would have said وَلَعَلَّكُمْ تَتَّقُونَ using the (ك) instead of وَلَعَلَّهُمْ يَتَّقُونَ which indicates that the discussion took place between the blamers and the advisors.

Interpreting this noble verse, Imam Al-Qurtubi said: "The Children of Israel were divided into three groups: one that transgressed and rebelled which was composed of approximately 70 thousand, a second group that forbad and did not get involved any further which was about 12 thousand, and a third group that stayed away and did neither forbid nor transgress and that was the group that- most probably- told the advisors "'Why do you ˹bother to˺ warn those ˹Sabbath-breakers˺ who will either be destroyed or severely punished by Allah? And what would Allah do to disobedient nations?" [42]

The Almighty then showed the consequences to the advisors and the transgressors: "When they ignored the warning they were given, We rescued those who used to warn against evil and overtook the wrongdoers with a dreadful punishment for their rebelliousness." (Q 7:165) That is, when the transgressors persisted in their rebelliousness and turned a blind eye to advice and instruction, We rescued the advisors who warned against violations, and We plighted the wrongdoers with severe and ruthless punishment because of their violations of Allah's commands.

The noble verse clearly provides a statement that those who were severely punished where the unjust rebellious aggressors and that those who were rescued were the advisors against violations. As for the third group that blamed the advisors for advising the aggressors, it did not mention anything.

Many interpreters believe that that group was rescued because it hated what the Sabbath-breakers did on that Sabbath, and they did not commit any of their wrongdoings. They believe that they refrained from providing advice because they thought the transgressors would never abstain and mend their ways, and that they had definitely become the target of Allah's wrath and torture. Therefore, they thought it was useless to advise them. That was Al-Zamakhshari's and other interpreters' opinions.

Al-Zamakshari said: "If you said: 'That group of people (the blamers)- who asked why did you bother advising people who would be destroyed or severely punished- to which group they belonged? Were they the group that was rescued or were they the group that was tortured?' I would say: 'They were among the rescued because whatever they said was merely questioning the justification, or reason, for advising: They found no good reason to do so since they knew the nature of the aggressors and, accordingly, they that advising would avail them nothing and that it would absurd to advise them with this knowledge about them. The other group (the advisors), however, still had some hope; they were not as despondent as the blamers were. Or, maybe they were particularly the only ones concerned about their safety, as the Almighty described His Prophet: "Now, perhaps you O Prophet will grieve yourself to death over their denial, if they continue to disbelieve in this message." (Qur'an 18:6) [43]

Imam Ibn Kathir said: "When asked about the fate of the blamers, Ibn Abbas said: 'I do not know what happened to them.' Then, he conceded that they were saved on account of what Akramah, his son, said: 'Don't you see that they hated their stance and opposed them and spoke: 'Why do you bother to warn those Sabbath-breakers who will either be destroyed or severely punished by Allah?'(Q 7:165) Akramah said: 'I persisted on talking to him until I made him realize that they were saved.'" [44]

We are inclined to believe that the fate of that group of people was left undetermined since there was no clear reference to it. The noble verse clearly stated the consequences for both of the other two groups, the advisors and the transgressors, but it did not mention anything concerning the destiny of the group that blamed the advisors for persisting on advising the transgressors. That could have been because that took a negative stance regarding the Sabbath- breakers and was therefore worthy of being ignored, if not held accountable.

Then, the Almighty indicated the severe punishment that the violators received. He said, "But when they stubbornly persisted in violation, We said to them, 'Be disgraced apes!'" (Q 7:166) That is, when they arrogantly refused to abandon what the advisors asked them to do, We said "be disgraced apes," and they were so.

Al-Alusi said: "The command in the Almighty's "We said" (Q 7:166) is a formative, not an obligatory, command. انماIt was not a command they could accept or reject; it was a decree by Allah in front of which they were helpless. This is similar to His saying: 'If We ever will something to exist, all We say is: "Be!" And it is!' (Qur'an 16:40) It wasn't that there was a possibility that it might have been a mere saying or meant as an example." [45]

Concerning the interpretation of the verse, it was also said that the Almighty at first chastised the aggressors with such severe punishments like making them miserable, desolate and poverty-stricken. However, when they did not change course and failed to come to their senses, He physically transformed them into real apes. This is what we can clearly glean from the verse, and it is also supported by most.

It was also said that the Almighty deformed them morally and psychologically, so they became like apes in the evil and corruption that they caused to anything their hands reached. This view was supported by Mujahid.

That punishment was the result of their persistence in their violations, their rejection of advice, their lack of will-power, their succumbing to their greed and lusts and their relapsing to the world of animals being deficient in human characteristics. Thus, they became lowly, disgraced and submissive, and that was what they wanted.

There are two noble verses in Sura Al-Baqara that briefly mention the story of the Sabbath- breakers: "You are already aware of those of you who broke the Sabbath. We said to them, "Be disgraced apes!" So We made their fate an example to present and future generations, and a lesson to the Allah-fearing." (Qur'an 2:65-66) [46]

The meaning is: You know, Children of Israel, the fate of those who trespassed against Our law and commandment and violated the Sabbath, the day in which they were commanded to dedicate to worship and pray. As a result of this, We transformed them into disgraced apes. It was in Our wisdom that this penalty, i.e., becoming apes, would be an example to those who were present as well as those future generations who did not witness it. We also made it a lesson to those Allah-fearing, the pious people among them, who advised the transgressors and prohibited them from these violations. It was a lesson to those who could comprehend and benefit from these lessons.

The Noble Qur'an conveyed this story by His saying "وَلَقَدْ عَلِمْتُمُ/You are already aware" (Q 2:65) even though the previous verses related to the Children of Israel were mostly prefaced by "إِذْ /when" indicating the time of the story. That was because the story of the Sabbath- breakers was known to Jewish scholars and learned ones who wanted to conceal it from the general public. So, Allah revealed it to His Messenger- as a miracle- since he was able to inform them- through revelation- with what they were doing and what they were trying to hide and conceal. The expression "وَلَقَدْ عَلِمْتُمُ/You are already aware" indicates their confirmed awareness of a fact they would not be able to conceal or ignore.

The meaning of breaking the Sabbath: It was trapping the whales/big fish on that day because of the ponds they dug close to the sea. When the whales entered these ponds, they couldn't get out of them because the water in the ponds was shallow. They would then easily capture them after Saturday. It was also said that they set nets in the sea on Friday. These were filled by whales/big fish on Saturday, and they could not leave. They would take them after Saturday.

Ibn Jarir said: "The root of Saturday السبت signifies calmness and serenity. A person who is sleeping is said to be مسبوت because his body is quiet and resting. As the Almighty said: "and made your sleep for rest." (Qur'an 78:9) In other words, it is rest for your bodies." [47]

And Al-Zamakhshari said: Saturday السبت is a gerund (the source) indicating the Jews observing Saturday if they were to elevate and exalt Saturday. [48]

The Almighty's saying: "Be disgraced apes!'" (Q 2:65; Q 7:166) means be just like that. A "disgraced" is an isolated outcast. The statement means: Be like apes removed from what is good, in disgrace.

The Almighty's: فَجَعَلْنَاهَا / So We made" the punishment of transforming them into disgraced apes نَكَالًا / an example that others would learn from and desist doing what those transgressors did.

"To present and future generations" (Q 2:66) Means: those who existed before that punishment and lived to witness it, and also those who came after it and learned for certain that such a punishment took place. In short, that punishment was a lesson to those who came before it and lived until they witnessed it and also those who came after it and knew with certainty what happened to the sabbath- breakers who were transformed into apes because of their rebelliousness. It was a lesson to caution others against doing what they did and become deserving of such a punishment.

"And a lesson to the Allah-fearing" (Q 2:66) which the Almighty directs to the pious and righteous who are the ones who would benefit from such a lesson and reap its fruits.

In Sura An-Nahl, there is a reference to the punishment that afflicted the Jews because of breaking the Sabbath. The Almighty said: "Honoring the Sabbath was ordained only for those who disputed about Abraham. And surely your Lord will judge between them on the Day of Judgment regarding their disputes." (Qur'an 16:124)

And Sura An-Nisa states the curse that fell upon the Children of Israel because they resorted to trickery to make what Allah has forbidden permissible. The Almighty said: "O you who were given the Scripture, believe in what We have sent down [to Muhammad], confirming that which is with you, before We obliterate faces and turn them toward their backs or curse them as We cursed the sabbath-breakers. And ever is the decree of Allah accomplished." (Qur'an 4:47)

Researchers and scientists quote these noble verses to warn against and prohibit the despicable tricks that some might resort to as a pretext to attain their evil desires and unwholesome aspirations.

In his "Relief to the Anxious from the Traps of Satan," Imam Ibn Al-Qayyim detailed the many examples that support this prohibition. He said: Among the tricks that Satan used to trap Muslims and Islam were cunningness, deception and deceit to make permissible that which Allah has prohibited, to renounce what Allah has imposed, to reject His commandments and prohibitions. So, there are two opinions: one which corresponds with the texts and which should be upheld and viewed as right and sound and that was the one that the predecessors followed, and the other one contradicts the texts and should shunned, and that was what they censured and avoided. There are also two kinds of tricks: one that helps in doing what Allah has commanded and abandon what He has prohibited and avoid what has been forbidden, rescuing the oppressed from the cruel oppressor and saving the just from the unjust one. This is praiseworthy and those who do that are richly rewarded. The other kind of trick is the one that prompts abandoning responsibilities and duties, legitimizing what has been forbidden, changing the oppressed to an oppressor, the just unjust, the truth a falsehood and a falsehood a truth. That was what the predecessors censured and denounced. Then, he said: The Almighty Allah transformed the Sabbath-breakers into apes when they used tricks to legitimize what He had forbidden: They set the nets on Friday to take the trapped whales on Sunday. Some jurisprudents suggested that those who play tricks to get away with manipulating prohibitions would be deserving great reproof and admonition. Those are the kind who ostensibly appear to be a jurist while, in reality, he is not. A real jurist is one who fears Allah and complies with His commandments and respects and avoids His prohibitions. It is not the one who manipulates and makes permissible what He has prohibited. It is known that they did not do this for disbelieving in Moses and the Torah; it was merely to manipulate and operate within a religious context. It was a fraud and a cheat. On the surface, it appeared as though they were complying but, in actuality, it was a violation and aggression. They were therefore transformed into apes. So, those who transgressed against Allah and only observed what "appeared" to be superficially religious, the Almighty transformed them into apes, and they resembled the apes in their appearance. In the Hadith we read: "Do not commit what the Jews did and make lawful what Allah has forbidden by the slightest tricks." [49]

The two (sahihs) narrated on the authority of Abu Huriyyrah that the Messenger of Allah said: "Allah prohibited grease for the Jews, so they sold it and used the money to get food." [50] And Ibn Abbas said: "Omar learned that Samra sold liquor, so he said Woe to Samra! Didn't he know that the Messenger of Allah said: 'Allah prohibited Grease, so they melted and sold it?'" [51]

Thus, these noble verses have stamped the Sabbath-breakers as ignorant people who lacked restraint and self-control and who wickedly connived to make lawful what Allah has forbidden. That made them deserving of severe punishment and distortion. They persisted in their rebellion, and they were heedless of counsel and advice. Allah is never unjust to His servants.

Fourth: <u>Rejecting the truth and hating good and beneficial things for others out of egotism and envy</u>.

Among the vices that that was repeatedly used to describe the Jews in the Noble Qur'an is rejecting the truth deliberately and knowingly and their excessive selfishness which is engendered by their reprehensible fanaticism and abhorrent racism. This makes them intent on keeping good things to themselves and preventing it from other people. It also drives them to feel that any good thing that comes to others is a good thing that has been denied them. Thus, they become enraged when they witness any grace granted to other people who have a different faith.

First: the Noble Qur'an recounted these vices in numerous verses. The Almighty said: "Although they used to pray for victory by means of the Prophet over the polytheists, when there came to them a Book from Allah which they recognized, confirming the Scripture they had in their hands, they rejected it. So may Allah's condemnation be upon the disbelievers. Miserable is the price they have sold their souls for—denying Allah's revelation and resenting Allah for granting His grace to whoever He wills of His servants! They have earned wrath upon wrath. And such disbelievers will suffer a humiliating punishment." (Qur'an 2:89-90)

Abu 'Al-Aliya said: "The Jews used to pray for victory over the Arab polytheists by means of Muhammad. They used to say: 'Allah, send us this prophet who is mentioned in our Book to torment the polytheists and kill them.' When the Almighty sent Muhammad who was not from among them, they rejected and disbelieved in him out of envy and jealousy knowing that he is the Messenger of Allah. The Almighty said: 'when there came to them a Book from Allah which they recognized..., they rejected it. So may Allah's condemnation be upon the disbelievers.'" (Q 2:89)

The meaning of the two verses is: Even though the Jews used to pray for victory over their enemies by means Muhammad, when the anticipated Prophet and the Noble Qur'an- that Allah revealed to him and which confirmed what they know in their Scriptures concerning his emissary and his description -when he came to the Jews, they rejected his prophecy and his Book: "So may Allah's condemnation be upon the disbelievers." Woe to them for rejecting what Allah has revealed to His Prophet Muhammad. And that rejection and disbelief was out of the intense jealousy that overpowered and utterly consumed them for seeing the revelation coming to Muhammad, an Arab. Because of their disgraceful behavior and loathsome attitude, they earned Allah's multiplied wrath and condemnation. "And such disbelievers will suffer a humiliating punishment" (Q 2:90) on account of their disbelief and envy.

The two noble verses truthfully depict the Jews' innate propensity to reject the truth after it was revealed and their deeply ingrained jealousy that caused them to loathe what was good and beneficial for others.

It is the Noble Qur'an which is meant by "when there came to them a Book from Allah which they recognized, confirming the Scripture they had in their hands." (Q 2:89) There is more honor and glorification in rejecting it and in informing that it came from Allah, an indication that whatever is revealed by Allah should be affably accepted with obedience and compliance since it came from the All-Wise and All-Knowledgeable. What the Jews had was the Torah and the idea that the Qur'an confirmed what they had means that it supported the basics and principles of their religion and what it specifically recounted concerning the emissary of the Prophet and his description.

And the Qur'an's confirmation of what they had was a further admonition and censure for they essentially disbelieved in a Book that confirmed what they had in their hands; it was not something that was at variance with their basic tenets and principles.

The Almighty's saying: "Although they used to pray for victory by means of the Prophet over the polytheists" (Q 2:89) was a statement of their state before the Muhammadan emissary. It was well known that when there was strife between the Jews and others, they would pray for victory by means of the Prophet before he was sent. They would say: "Grant us victory by means of the prophet whose description we find in the Torah."

"الاستفتاح/ pray for victory" means asking for a final decision or judgement in a certain matter as it is conveyed in the Almighty's: "Our Lord! Judge between us and our people with truth." The word is also used to indicate victory as it is a decisive point between people. It is indicated in the Almighty's: "If you ⌜Meccans⌝ sought judgment, now it has come to you." In short, what is meant by the word "الاستفتاح/ pray for victory" in the verse was seeking victory.

Then, the Almighty revealed their true position after the Book and the Prophet came to them. He said: "when there came to them a Book from Allah which they recognized, confirming the Scripture they had ⌜in their hands⌝, they rejected it." (Q 2:89) That is, when the Prophet- whom they were waiting for and whose name they evoked to pray for victory over their enemies – came, they rejected him.

It is noteworthy that the Almighty said: "when there came to them a Book from Allah which they recognized, confirming the Scripture they had in their hands, they rejected it." (Q 2:89) He didn't say when the Book OR the Prophet came to them. It is more comprehensive to include both the Book and the Prophet who came with the Book, because the Book came only through the Prophet.

Their knowledge of the truthfulness of the Prophet and what was revealed to him was acquired through the correspondence of the Prophet's qualities and characteristics that were mentioned in the Torah. It was incumbent upon them to couple this knowledge with belief in him. However, the fear of losing their prestige and authority, coupled with the fact that the sent prophet was not from among them but from among the Arabs, filled their hearts with envy and malice until they were completely overpowered by them.

Consequently, that knowledge became useless as it was divorced from acceptance and belief.

Abdullah bin Salam, their leader, tried to caution them against their obstinate rebelliousness. He tried to persuade them that the Prophet brought was the truth that confirmed what they had and they had to follow him, but they turned a blind eye and a deaf ear and derided his position. Therefore, Allah condemned them and cast them out of His mercies: "So may Allah's condemnation be upon the disbelievers." (Q 2:89)

Also, the Almighty said "may Allah's condemnation be upon the disbelievers." He didn't say upon "them." That was to confirm that their condemnation was due to their "disbelief."

Then, the Almighty mentioned that they had sold their souls for a cheap price. He said: "Miserable is the price they have sold their souls for—denying Allah's revelation ..." (Q 2:90) That is to say, the Jews sold themselves by rejecting what Allah had revealed out of envy, but Allah grants His grace to whomever He wills of His servants.

Exegetes agree that the word آشْتَرَوْاْ (which literally means buy) means "sold" in this context. For those Jews who were capable of expressing faith that would have led them to eternal happiness deserted and rejected the truth when it came to them. They persisted in their disbelief out of envy and malice and because of their fascination with authority and beguilement with their race. Their choice of disbelief over belief was essentially eradicating themselves when they could have benefited through a true expression of belief. They sold what was good and profitable for something that was not worthwhile. Miserable is that price they have sold their souls for; it only confirmed their abominable and severe punishment.

The Almighty expressed their disbelief in the present tense (أَن يَكْفُرُوا/ denying Allah's revelation,) while He expressed their selling themselves in the past tense (آشْتَرَوْاْ/ they have sold) to indicate that they had declared their disbelief in the Noble Qur'an even before revealing the verse, and that their selling themselves and succumbing to disbelief was second nature to them, a deeply ingrained attribute, and that they still followed this deviant and aberrant nature.

The Almighty's "resenting Allah for granting His grace to whoever He wills of His servants!" (Q 2:90) explains their disbelief and states what prompted it: They rejected what Allah revealed to Muhammad, His servant and Messenger, out of envy, malice and resentment. They resented that Allah brought this revelation and granted His grace to whoever He wills of His servants. Resentment بَغْيًا in the context of the verse means being unjust, and envy is equated with injustice since injustice reflects interactions that are removed from the truth and avert it. Envy, on the other hand, means wishing something good and profitable to be taken away from others. Both the unjust and the envious have departed from the truth, and what is right; the envious would not benefit if grace disappeared and vanished from the envied, neither will he be harmed if it remained. Thus, the envious is being unjust towards the envied when he wishes grace and good things to disappear and vanish from others. How truthful were the poet's words:

"The worst of Allah's creation is the envious one
Who envies those who with affluence are inebriated."

The Jews rejected what Allah has revealed because they were envious of the Prophet- an Arab not one of them, for being granted the prophethood. They resented that Allah granted the revelation to whomsoever He chose. Their disbelief in what they had known and expected was the outcome of their vicious egotism and despicable favoritism which provoked them to envy other people for whatever graces Allah granted them and made them think that prophethood was confined to them. They were under the assumption that it was unlikely that Almighty Allah would take prophethood away from Isaac's offspring and grant it to Ishmael's descendants.

The Noble Qur'an did not state that the envied one was Muhammad since that was easily understood from the context of the noble verses. It was also with a view to drive home the fact that it was envy itself that was being denounced and decried, no matter what or who the envied one was.

The Almighty then depicted the clear loss they had to endure. He said: "They have earned wrath upon wrath. And such disbelievers will suffer a humiliating punishment." (Q 2:90) That is, because of their disbelief and envy towards the Prophet, they had coupled Allah's wrath to another wrath, one they had acquired on account of their disbelief in Jesus, distorting words from their proper meaning and context, and disregarding the rulings of the Torah. It was because of their continued disbelief and rebellion that they earned consecutive punishments from Allah.

It could also be feasible to suggest that the meaning of "They have earned wrath upon wrath" was that they were pushed back with severe punishment since it was a punishment that came from Allah.

The word "disbelievers" refers to the Jews about whom the Noble Qur'an talked previously. They were the ones who knew the truthfulness of the prophecy of Muhammad according to what the Torah has mentioned about him. Nonetheless, they rejected and disbelieved in him, preferring blindness and misguidance to discernment and guidance.

They were so described as to point out that the humiliating punishment that they suffered was because of their disbelief, and it was fitting to be so punished, for since their disbelief was due to their envy, malice, haughtiness, arrogance and selfishness, they were belittled and treated with humiliation and disgrace.

Thus, the two noble verses (Q 2:89-90) revealed one of the Jews' despicable attributes: rejecting Muhammad whose name they evoked- even before he was sent- to help them gain victory over their enemies. They also revealed their relinquished faith in an upright religion and a Noble Book to satisfy the jealousy that had consumed them utterly and their fanaticism that drove them to loath and reject a prophet who was not from the offspring of Children of Israel even though he brought them clear signs and unquestionable truths. The Almighty rightly described them saying: "We certainly know that what they say grieves you O Prophet It is not your honesty they question—it is Allah's signs that the wrongdoers deny." (Al-An'am 33; Q 6:33)

Second: There are two other verses in Sura Al-Baqara that cautioned the believers against the wickedness and evil that the polytheists and the People of the Book, especially the Jews, concealed in their hearts and their hatred for any blessings that Allah may grant them.

In the first Sura, the Almighty said: "The disbelievers from the People of the Book and the polytheists would not want you to receive any blessing from your Lord, but Allah selects whoever He wills for His mercy. And Allah is the Lord of infinite bounty." (Q 2:105) [52]

The words " مَا يَوَدّ /want or wish" indicate likening and wishing something to happen or not to happen.

Al-Zamakshari said: "The first noticeable thing in the verse is stating that the disbelievers are divided into two kinds: the People of the Book and the polytheists as the Almighty said (Q 2:105): "Those who disbelieved from among the People of the Book and the polytheists…" [53]

The meaning of the noble verse is: The disbelievers from among the People of the Book- both Jews and Christians- and the polytheists- the idol worshippers- do not want you believers to receive Allah's blessings and good and beneficial things because they envy and hate you. This is a kind of folly and ignorance because it is the Almighty Alone who has the absolute power to grant His blessings to whomsoever He chooses from among His servants, and He will not be harmed by the jealousy of the envious nor the malice of the malicious. He is the Bestower of good things upon His creatures.

The Almighty's: "The disbelievers from the People of the Book and the polytheists would not want you to receive any blessing from your Lord" (Q 2:105) recounted the hatred and malice that the disbelievers, especially the Jews, had for the Muslims and cautioned them against trusting them.

And His "The disbelievers from the People of the Book… would not want you -" NOT "the People of the Book-" is meant to draw attention to the fact that they disbelieved in their Books because had they believed in them, they would have believed in Muhammad because their Books commanded them to believe and follow him.

Then He followed "the People of the Book with "the polytheists" to show that the idol worshippers even surpassed the disbelievers from the People of the Book in their hatred for any blessings coming to the believers. All envied the believers for the graces and blessings that He bestowed upon them through His Prophet: an upright religion, a Noble

Qur'an, amazing guidance, inclusive brotherhood, peace and security after fear and trepidation and power and authority after weakness and insignificance.

The word خَيْرٍ referring to grace and blessings (in this verse) is a reference to prophecy and the truthful revelations that followed, the Noble Qur'an that includes wonderful wisdom, convincing arguments, brilliant eloquence and useful guidance.

The People of the Book hated the believers for being the recipients of these blessings because of their stubbornness and malice which caused them to resent seeing prophethood coming to an Arab, not one of them.

And the polytheists also hated that because the spread of the Islamic call and the revelations that descended on the Prophet meant losing hope in eradicating the Islamic call, weakening its authority and defeating its proponents.

The Almighty's saying (Q 2:105) "but Allah selects whoever He wills for His mercy. And Allah is the Lord of infinite bounty" was a response that revealed the ignorance and the witlessness of all the envious; it is out of stupidity and foolishness that the envious begrudges Allah's abilities and objects to His granting the envied and begrudged His blessings. It is Allah Almighty Who is the Lord of "infinite bounty" and has the absolute sovereignty to grant or deny His blessings. It was therefore more becoming for those who didn't want the believers to receive any blessings to save themselves the burden of these feelings of resentment and abandon their stupidity and foolishness because it is Allah alone Who grants His blessings to whomsoever He chooses.

And the word يَخْتَصُّ (select) is used to signal a particularly exclusive and specific person as a recipient of something specific. That something becomes exclusively his. It is in this sense that the word يَخْتَصُّ (select) is used in the noble verse.

The Almighty Allah had specifically restricted His mercy to whomsoever He يَخْتَصُّ (selects) so that all people would know that signaling certain individuals to receive His mercies is in accordance with His will alone. No one else has a say in such matters.

The "object" of His selection is omitted, but readily understood. It means He selects whoever He wills for His mercy, that is, prophethood, the Qur'an and victory. The disbelievers did not want the believers to receive any of these.

The Almighty's: "Allah is the Lord of infinite bounty" (Q 2:105) is a conclusion to what has preceded. It emphasizes that all the blessings that Allah's servants receive in their faith and in this world come from Allah alone. He is the One who grants the blessings. That was an invitation to the envious disbelievers to abandon their jealousy and envy. It was also a censure directed at the Jews who resented the prophethood that Allah granted Muhammad. It was as if the Almighty was telling them: "I assign for prophethood whoever I choose from My servants. It is not something that could be attained by wishful thinking. Rather, I grant it to those who are worthy of it."

Thus, the noble verse had warned the believers against the inherent hatred, envy and resentment of the disbelievers. It also brought them the good tidings that they will not be harmed by any of this as long as the abide by Allah's Book and follow their Prophet.

The second verse is: "Many among the People of the Book wish they could turn you believers back to disbelief because of their envy, after the truth has been made clear to them. Pardon and bear with them until Allah delivers His decision. Surely Allah is Most Capable of everything." (Q 2:109)

The verse means that a great number of the Jews- the People of the Book- wanted to turn you back from belief to disbelief because they envied you and hated your faith even after it was made clear to them that you were right in following Muhammad. Do not heed them; rather, stay away from their wickedness and malice, and bear with them until Allah gives you the permission to deal with them in a way that would ensure your safety and victory. The Almighty is Most Capable of everything.

The Almighty's "Many among the People of the Book wish they could turn you believers back to disbelief" (Q 2:109) is a statement that indicated one aspect of the wickedness and evil that the People of the Book, especially the Jews, concealed in their heart towards the believers, i.e., their desire to turn the Muslims from their upright religion into the disbelief from which Allah had saved them.

The desire of the disbelievers to do so was demonstrated by a great number of them. However, the Qur'an was fair to the few believers among them who did not want the Muslims to turn back to disbelief after Allah had guided them to Islam.
The Almighty's "بَعْدِ إِيمَـٰنِكُمْ /turn you believers back to disbelief" was meant to vehemently reprove and repudiate them for what they wanted: as People of the Book, they wanted disbelief in place of belief! It also indicated that that was not likely to happen because once belief takes hold and the hearts become content with this belief, it would be unlikely that the believers would turn back into disbelief.

Then the Almighty showed that the despicable wishes of disbelievers that the believers turn back to disbelief were prompted by their envy and malice. He said: "... because of their envy, after the truth has been made clear to them," to indicate that that wish was engendered by nothing but the envy and jealousy that consumed and overpowered them and made them envy the believers for the blessing of faith, hoping that they would go back to disbelief. The statement shows the reason for what the previous verse mentioned concerning their wish that the believers would go back to disbelief.

The late Sheikh Muhammad Al-Khadr Hussein said: "Envy- which is a feeling of uneasiness and discomfort that afflicts a person when he sees another person receiving a blessing and wishes that such a blessing be wiped out from that person- is reprehensible, unless it is a blessing that a licentious or unjust person has attained and which he will use to further increase evil, wickedness and corruption. In such a case, wishing that such a blessing be wiped out- because of hatred for evil and corruption- would not be considered reprehensible jealousy. If you do not wish another person to lose a blessing but desire to acquire to yourself something similar, this is a blissful and desirable competition. It is desirable, for it may well lead that person to acquire appropriate and desirable qualities he would not have been able to attain without this honorable competition. It is competition that has caused this person to become more aware (of the existence of these sought-after blessings). However, a person may completely succumb to jealousy and find himself unable to stop it because of the hatred he has for subject of his envy. Man is held accountable when he surrenders to it, becomes happy with these feeling of jealousy, continues to demonstrate hatred and jealousy hoping that blessings be wiped out from the other." [54]

The Almighty's "مِّنْ عِندِ أَنفُسِهِم/ their envy" (literally "of their own") demonstrated to the believers that those Jews were not commanded in their Book to behave in that way. On the contrary, their Book forbad them from that despicable and reprehensible conduct. However, because of their cunningness and unwholesome manners, envy became deeply ingrained in their hearts, and it became difficult to detach it from them or detach them from it.

And the noble statement "… because of their envy" indicates that those Jews believed in the truthfulness and uprightness of the religion of Islam because a man would not envy another man over religion unless he knows- deep down in his heart- that that religion is the upright and correct one and it is the way to success and happiness.

Then the Almighty said: "after the truth has been made clear to them." This statement shows that the desire of the Jews to turn the believers back into disbelief took place AFTER the truthfulness of the Prophet became evident and clear to them, and after the qualities that were written in the Torah about the promised Prophet became evident that they were only applicable to him. Their disbelief was not because of ignorance; rather, it was on account of their obstinacy, rebelliousness and a state of stagnation in embracing falsehoods. That was the condition of their rabbis and scholars who had knowledge of the Torah and its heralding the arrival of the Prophet.

Then, the Almighty Allah commanded the believers at the end of the verse to receive the wickedness of the Jews with pardon and forgiveness: "Pardon and bear with them until Allah delivers His decision. Surely Allah is Most Capable of everything." (Q 2:109)

To "pardon" means not to punish for some offense, and to "bear with" means to forgive. Therefore, "forgiving" indicates "pardoning," not vice versa.

And the meaning is: You believers should not punish those envious Jews, and you should abandon brandishing your swords in their faces until Allah grants you the permission to avenge yourselves and fight them and achieve victory over them. Allah is Most capable of everything.

The meaning of " يَأْتِيَ ٱللَّهُ بِأَمْرِهِۦٓ /until Allah delivers His decision" (Q 2:109) is until that time which Allah chose, the time in which they had the power to stand against their enemies.

In Tafsir Al-Manar, the author said: "In Allah's command to the believers to pardon and bear with the disbelievers, there is an indication that despite the fact that their numbers were fewer, they had the power and authority. It was as if Allah was saying 'Do not heed by the great numbers of the People of the Book for even though you are less in number, you are stronger because you are the righteous ones. So, deal with them as strong and just people deal with strong and foolish ones.' Depicting the believers as the mighty ones despite their smaller numbers, and the People of the Book as weak despite their great numbers was an indication that the righteous ones were the people who were supported by the Divine Providence, and that victory would be theirs as long as they remained steadfast in their faith, and whenever there was a conflict between right and wrong, right will always vanquish wrong and truth will always overpower falsehoods. Falsehoods exist only when truth is dormant and inactive." [55]

Allah confirmed His promise by saying (Q 2:109): "Surely Allah is Most Capable of everything." In other words, everything is under His Most Powerful and never-to-be-obstructed will.

And Allah did fulfil His promise to the believers; at the right time, He gave them permission to fight the Jews and discipline them. That ended in the victory of the believers and the dispelling and killing of the spiteful envious Jews.

Thus, the verses that we recounted in this section have stamped the Jews with the vice of rejecting the truth, hating to see others receive blessings, and their deep-rooted envy that had filled their hearts. These vices brought them misery and disgrace in this world and in the Hereafter. "And Allah is never unaware of what they do." (Q 2:144)

Fifth: <u>Rejecting Allah's Book, believing in magic and satanic illusions</u>.

Those who have sickness in their hearts, cunning intentions and feeble and frail minds are prone to exchange what is good and of a higher quality for what is unprofitable and of low value. The Children of Israel had their fair share of this, and their history throughout the generations reveals that the majority of them preferred blindness to guidance and exchanged good and valuable thing for bad and invaluable ones.

Among the vices with which the Qur'anic verses labelled them was their rejection of Allah's Book and following falsehoods and myths. In this respect, the Almighty said: "Now, when a messenger from Allah has come to them—confirming their own Scriptures—some of the People of the Book cast the Book of Allah behind their backs as if they did not know. They instead followed the magic promoted by the devils during the reign of Solomon. Never did Solomon disbelieve, rather the devils disbelieved. They taught magic to the people, along with what had been revealed to the two angels, Hârût and Mârût, in Babylon. The two angels never taught anyone without saying, "We are only a test for you, so do not abandon your faith." Yet people learned magic that caused a rift even between husband and wife; although their magic could not harm anyone except by

Allah's Will. They learned what harmed them and did not benefit them—although they already knew that whoever buys into magic would have no share in the Hereafter. Miserable indeed was the price for which they sold their souls, if only they knew!" (Q 2:101-102) [56]

The meaning is: When there came to the Jews and their scholars a Messenger from Allah, Muhammad, who is mentioned in their Torah, many people among them discarded the teachings of the Torah that attested to his truthfulness and they casted the Book behind their backs as if they were unaware that it was from Allah. They instead followed the magic, witchcraft, fantasies and slanders that the devils promoted during the reign of Solomon. Among these lies and slanders was their claim that Solomon was a magician and that his enormous kingdom and fabulous miracles in harnessing jinn and wind were only possible because of his witchcraft.

Yet Allah showed that that claim was false: "Never did Solomon disbelieve." That is, Solomon never learned witchcraft or dealt with it, as they claimed. "Rather the devils" were the ones who "disbelieved" by learning magic and teaching it to the people along with teaching them a different kind of magic: "what had been revealed to the two angels, Hârût and Mârût, in Babylon:" describing magic and how to use to swindle embezzle others. The two angels did not teach other people about magic unless they advise them, saying: 'This magic that we teach you is meant to guide you to distinguish between the obedient and the rebellious, magic and miracle. Beware of using it to do something that is prohibited or you will be considered one of the disbelievers.' The devils, on the other hand, learned magic and taught it to others to use it in mischievous and evil deeds, to cause a rift between a man and his wife. This magic in which the devils and their followers perform would not harm anyone by itself. This can only happen if Allah willed it to happen. Those who rejected Allah's Book and preferred magic learned that those who exchange Allah's Book for magic would not have an inheritance, share, in the Hereafter: "Miserable indeed was the price for which they sold their souls, if only they knew!" "If only they were faithful and mindful" of Allah and His Prophet Muhammad, as their Torah instructed them, had they avoided transgressions and rejected sins, they would have received a better reward from Allah. It was much better for them than what they chose for themselves and preferred over Allah's Book, if only they knew!"

The Almighty's (Q 2:101) "Now, when a messenger from Allah has come to them—confirming their own Scriptures—some of the People of the Book cast the Book of Allah behind their backs as if they did not know…" is a statement testifying the Jews' disbelief in the Prophet and their discarding the teachings of their Book which commanded them to follow him.

In Jarir narrated on the author of Al-Sudi who said concerning "Now, when a messenger from Allah has come to them—confirming their own Scriptures—some of the People of the Book cast the Book of Allah behind their backs as if they did not know. They ⌜instead⌝ followed the magic promoted by the devils during the reign of Solomon. Never did Solomon disbelieve." That is, when Muhammad came, they objected to him using the Torah. Yet, the Torah and the Qur'an agreed, and they rejected both of them and adopted the magic of Harut. That was Allah's saying: "as if they did not know." That is, as if those who rejected Allah's Book from among the Jewish scholars who breached their pledge with Allah did not know what was in the Torah concerning the commandment to follow Muhammad and believe in him. [57]

Describing the Prophet as coming from Allah was both a great honor to him as well as a strong condemnation of their rejection and disbelieving in him. It was also an alluring invitation to all people to accept his call since he was not coming on his own but was rather sent as a Messenger from Allah.

The statement "confirming their own Scriptures" is a reference to the Torah and "confirming their own Scriptures" (Q 2:101) means that the teachings that the Prophet brought were in agreement with the basic fundamentals of the Torah which described the characteristics of the anticipated Prophet- after Jesus- in a way that could only be applicable to him.

And the Almighty described their refusal to comply with the teachings of the Book that was revealed to them for their guidance by using the expression "threw away." This expression emphasizes their rejection and dismissal of the Book. The expression indicates throwing something away as invaluable or worthless.

And attributing the act of throwing away the Book to some of the People of the Book is meant to ridicule, disparage and belittle them because it was those who got the Book who threw it away and cast it behind their backs. Had it been the polytheists who threw the Book away, they might have been excused for their ignorance and unawareness. But those who abandoned the light were those who received the light and were honored with it. That is clear misguidance, a glaringly flagrant transgression.

And "Allah's Book-" which they cast behind their back when the Messenger came to them- is a reference to the Torah. Had they truly believed in the Torah, they would have followed the Messenger whose description was mentioned therein. By virtue of their Book, the Torah, it was incumbent upon them to believe in him. By rejecting his prophethood, they had rejected their own Torah that testified to his truthfulness.

It was also said that "Allah's Book" is a reference to the Qur'an because they did not believe in it; in fact, they forsook it after listening to it, and they forgot the guidance and direction it contained even though it was their duty to receive it willingly.

We are more inclined to adopt the first view since "throwing away" indicates that something was first acquired. This is true as far as the Torah is concerned, whereas in the case of the Noble Qur'an, they never accepted it before in order to throw it away later. Also, their censure was most vehemently pronounced and their rejection was all the more emphasized since the Book that was referred to as being thrown away was the same Book that was revealed to them to guide them and in which they believed: the Torah.

The Almighty's: "behind their backs" (Q 2:101) is a euphemism, a metaphor, to suggest their strong objection and refusal to abide by the teachings and instructions of the Torah.

When the Arabs say 'he threw this thing behind his back,' it means that he will no longer consider it since what is thrown behind one's back is not something that will be looked at again. So, this noble statement truthfully likens their abandoning Allah's Book to casting something behind one's back to indicate its triviality and insignificance.

Tafsir al-Manar said: "Throwing the Book behind their back does not mean they cast it all of it and abandoned believing in it altogether. Rather, what is meant is that they cast part of it, mainly, that part that foretells the coming of the Prophet, describes his attributes and commanded them to believe in, and follow, him. It likens abandoning and rejecting it to someone throwing something behind his back so as not to see-and remember- it. And abandoning part of it is like abandoning all of it because by abandon just a part, the sanctity of the revelation wanes and one is emboldened to abandon the whole..." [58]

The Almighty's "as if they did not know" (Q 2:101) is an adverbial statement that describes them as people who cast the Book behind their back as though they were unaware of anything it contained and as people who did not know that it was Allah's Book.

He described them as people who didn't know even though, in reality, they knew very well that it was from Allah. They cast it out of obstinacy and stubbornness. They did not instruct others in accordance with their knowledge and what they had learned. Those are therefore just like the ignorant and uninformed in their rejection of the truth and indulgence in inequities.

The Almighty's negation of the adverb in "as if they did not know" also suggests that it is not likely that these people will ever repent and change course. The days pass, and they hear sermons again and again, yet they do not repent or go back to the truth. They continue throwing away Allah's Book with obstinate persistence.

After chastising them for casting the Book of Allah behind their backs, the Almighty recounted another kind of their going astray and following falsehoods. He said: "They instead followed the magic promoted by the devils during the reign of Solomon." (Q 2:102)

"They followed" which means they followed in the footsteps. The pronoun "they" refers to the Jews who were living during the time of Prophet Muhammad.

"Promoted/ تتلو = recite" which means following someone's reading aloud. Al-Raghib said: he recited to someone means he lied to him.

The word "الشياطين/devils" is the plural of devil and it refers to a living being made of fire. It is also used to refer to human beings who are filled with evil.

The meaning is: Those Jews cast Allah's Book and followed the lies and falsehoods that the devils used to recite and promote during the reign of Solomon. Among these lies were their claim that Solomon's kingdom was founded on magic and that he became an atheist and worshipped idols at the end of his days to please his pagan women. They tried to attribute many other lies to him.

Al-Zamakhshari said: "The Almighty's 'during the reign of Solomon' means that during the time of Solomon's reign, the devils would listen attentively then add lies and falsehoods and pass them to priests who would then record them in books for people to read and learn from. That was rampant during the time of Solomon. They even claimed that the Jinn knew the unseen, and they said that all of Solomon's kingdoms were but founded on the knowledge of witchcraft which he used to harness man, the jinn and the wind according to his will." [59]

The Almighty's saying: "Never did Solomon disbelieve, rather the devils disbelieved" (Q 2:102) meant that the devils were the ones who disbelieved for they learned magic and taught it to others in order to mislead them and lead them away from worshipping Allah to the worship of other creatures.

The noble verse purges Solomon from disbelief and witchcraft. Those were the works of the devils who falsely and deceptively attributed these to him. The verse also indicates that that magic that the devils performed and misleadingly attributed to Solomon was a kind of disbelief.

The Jews believed that Solomon became a disbeliever and a renegade at the end of his days. They believed he worshipped idols and erected temples for them. When the Prophet mentioned Solomon among other prophets, they used to say: "Look how Muhammad mixes truths with falsehoods; he mentions Solomon- a magician who would ride the wind- with the other prophets!"

If someone asked: What is the wisdom behind negating the disbelief of Solomon?

The answer would be: Those Jews who discarded Allah's Book and followed the magic that they promoted claimed that Solomon used magic. They said: "He used magic to harness and control humans, the jinn and the wind." Allah showed them as liars by saying: "Never did Solomon disbelieve, rather the devils disbelieved," as we have shown before.

The pronoun in "They taught magic to the people" (Q 2:102) refers to the devils who fabricated lies about Solomon.

It could also refer to the Jews who threw away Allah's Book and followed what the devils promoted and attributed to Solomon.

Tafsir al-Manar said: "The Almighty's 'They taught magic to the people' points at two directions:

First: It could be related to "rather the devils disbelieved." In this case, it was the devils who taught magic to the people. Second, which is more apparent, it is related to the Jews. The talk about the devils has ended with the Almighty's "disbelieved." Taking up the teaching of magic was a well-known practice for the Jews then, and they still do it at the present time. In other words, a group of Jews cast Allah's Book behind and followed what the devils promoted during the reign of Solomon. Then, when someone asks: These devils who lied to Solomon and attributed disbelief to him, and claimed that magic was in his books under his throne- what did they follow? Through a rhetorical device called the eloquence of resumption: 'They taught magic to the people.' Solomon's disbelief was negated and attributed to the deceitful devils. The Jews followed the devils in performing witchcraft which was one of the vices they were known to have practiced to deceive, mislead and double-cross people." [60]

However, the Almighty added to the Jews that they followed what the devils promoted during the reign of Solomon in particular even though it was known before Solomon as mentioned in the Qur'an about Pharoah's magicians. He added that to them because it was a fact that was known and because the magic of these devils during the reign of Solomon was written in Jewish documents from ancient times and was passed over from the predecessors to the successors until it reached those who lived during the time of the Prophet. Allah also granted Solomon an enormous kingdom and gave him the ability to control humans, the jinn and the wind which the devils attributed to his knowledge of magic.

And وما (along) in His "along with what had been revealed to the two angels, Hârût and Mârût, in Babylon" (Q 2:102) is connected to magic in His saying "They taught magic to the people" by means of a conjunction (A conjunction is a dependent clause that is mediated between it and its antecedent by a conjunction letter). The meaning is: They taught magic to the people and they also taught what was revealed to the two angels.

And what was revealed to them was knowledge of what magic was and how to use it to mislead and deceive so that people might become cognizant and knowledgeable and shun it. As the poet said:

> "I knew evil not for its sake but only so that evil I may shun,
> He who does not know evil will someday to it will succumb."

The devils knew and promoted magic, and they taught it to people to use for evil and sinful deeds while the believers knew it and benefited from learning about it and shunned it. [61]

Babylon [62] was especially known for the widespread practice of witchcraft. Its magicians exploited magic to subjugate and control peoples' bodies, minds and wealth. They led them to worship idols and the planets. Corruption spread and falsehoods ran rampant. So, Allah inspired Harut and Marut to reveal the truth about magic and its intricacies to the people to realize that the magicians that turned them from worshiping Allah to worshipping the planets had mislead and deceived them. That way they could return to the right path.

Some exegetes reported that the two angels were two righteous men who became familiar with the secrets of magic that magicians used. They taught these secrets to the people to caution them against succumbing to the devils' traps. They were called angels even though they were human because of their righteousness and piety.

However, most interpreters believe that they were true angels sent by the Almighty to teach people magic in order to expose the claims of the magicians who falsely declared prophethood, controlled and subjugated the people and drove them away from worshipping Allah. Harut and Marut were the names of the two angels to whom magic was revealed.

The Almighty's: "The two angels never taught anyone without saying, 'We are only a test for you, so do not abandon your faith'" (Q 2:102) is a statement that reveals the advice of the angels to those who wanted to learn about magic from them.

The word فِتْنَةٌ means test as in 'Gold is tested in fire' to determine its true value and how good or bad it is.

The meaning is: The two angels did not teach anyone about magic unless they cautioned that the magic they were teaching was only meant as a test to distinguish between the obedient and the disobedient. Whoever uses it is deceived and misguided, and those who abandon it are guided by the light of Allah and know the difference between magic and miracle. So, be mindful not to use what you learned to do what you are prohibited from doing. Otherwise, you will be one of the disbelievers just like the magician who have disbelieved.

So, what was meant by teaching the people magic by the two angels was exposing the magicians and shaming them. The numbers of those magicians had increased at that time, and they claimed what Allah had not permitted. It was important to reveal the difference between magic and miracle so that people would be able to discern that those magicians that might claim that they were prophets are nothing but deceivers and liars. The magicians were only a test; they would not benefit or harm anyone. It was a test from Allah to discern the obedient from the rebellious.

Then, the Almighty revealed a kind of loathsome magic that those magicians used to harm people. He said: "Yet people learned magic that caused a rift even between husband and wife." (Q 2:102)

The statement is a branch of what has preceded in the Almighty's "The two angels never taught anyone without saying, 'We are only a test for you." It assumes that teaching was a fait accompli and that those taught have used it to cause a rift between a husband and his wife. The Almighty specifically mentioned this kind of magic to indicate its severe corruption and the gravity of the guilt of those who practice it since it has caused the separation of married people who were brought together by love and compassion.

Then the Almighty negated that magic would be the sole factor in causing any outcome: "although their magic could not harm anyone except by Allah's Will." (Q 2:102) This means that those magicians would not benefit or harm anyone with their magic except by Allah's will, for magic is a normal reason for causing harms, but it would not do so unless Allah allowed that. The sentence is a parenthetical statement to caution against the belief that magic could be harmful by itself.

The expression "by Allah's Will" shows Allah's separation between the charmed and the harms of magic. In other words, harm could occur if Allah allowed, but if He did not allow it, the enchanted would not be harmed or affected.

The Almighty emphasized the lack the effect of magic on its own, and He inspired people to not believe the magicians' claim that they have unseen powers. He also prompted them to use sound judgement and to be sensible and discerning.

The Almighty then showed that those who learned magic to harm others and cause a rift between lovers learned what could only harm them. He said: "They learned what harmed them and did not benefit them." (Q 2:102) That is, those who learned magic to harm others, not to distinguish between good and evil or push evil away from them, have chartered a path that would lead to their harm. They had thus become disobedient and failed to follow what the two angels had taught concerning magic.

The noble statement diligently alerts us to the feeble-mindedness, triviality and insignificance of those who perform magic to harm others. It likewise exaggerates the ignorance and unawareness of those who believe magicians for regardless of the skillfulness of a magician, he will undoubtedly fail to prevent anything that Allah wills, or bring about and cause something that Allah has prevented and will not allow. Accordingly, both the magician as well as those who believe in magic are in ill-advised and conspicuously misguided.

The noble statement combined a proof for the harm and a negation of the benefit to be gleaned from such practice. It was as if the Almighty was saying: "They had only learned what would only bring pure harm."

Then, the Almighty revealed what would happen to those Jews who abandoned the truth and followed falsehoods. He said: "they already knew that whoever buys into magic would have no share in the Hereafter." (Q 2:102) That is, those Jews- who abandoned the teachings of their Book and followed magic- knew that whoever replaces magic for Allah's Book will have no share in the Hereafter, for he has chosen misguidance and forfeited the light of discernment. Their knowledge of this is rooted in the fact that the Torah has prohibited learning and teaching magic to inflict harm. It has intensified the punishment on those who promote magic and those who follow the jinn, the devils and the soothsayers.

The pronoun "they" in "they already knew" refers to those Jews who abandoned Allah's Book and replaced it with magic.

And "buying" is getting something in return for something else. What the statement means is that they bought the magic that was promoted by the devils in return for their faith and share in paradise. Thus, they were deprived of their share in the Hereafter because of their deceitfulness and lies and because they exchanged what was good and valuable for what was bad and useless.

The Almighty confirmed that they were aware of the harms of magic. He said: "they already knew" to point out that their choice to use magic was not done in ignorance of its harms; rather, they deliberately and knowingly chose it fully aware of its undesirable and detrimental consequences.

Then the Almighty said: "Miserable indeed was the price for which they sold their souls, if only they knew!" (Q 2:102)

The word شَرَوْا here means "sold." And selling their souls means selling their share of paradise and its bliss.

The meaning is: Had they been people with true knowledge, understanding and discernment, they would not have performed magic.

The Almighty confirmed their knowledge: "they already knew that whoever buys into magic." Then, He immediately negated that knowledge, a rhetorical device to eloquently convey that if a person has acquired knowledge and then fails to use it properly, he is considered ignorant and ill-informed. In such a case, knowledge and discernment could not be attributed to him just as they could not be attributed to the ignorant and ill-informed.

Al-Zamakhshari pointed out to that same meaning that we have mentioned. He said:

"If you said, how did he confirm their knowledge at first by saying: "they already knew that whoever buys into magic" by using emphasis and confirmation then negating it by saying: "if only they knew?" I would respond by saying that the meaning is if they used their knowledge to do things. However, by not using their knowledge, they were made to appear stripped of knowledge altogether." [63]

Then the Almighty demonstrated the benefits they would have been able to enjoy had they pursued the truth after revealing the harms that occurred due to following falsehoods. He said: "If only they were faithful and mindful of Allah, there would have been a better reward [64] from Allah, if only they knew!" (Q 2:103) That is: Had those Jews- who threw away Allah's Book and followed delusions and misbeliefs- truly believed in Muhammad or the Torah and feared Allah, and avoided falsehoods and magic and all that caused them to transgress, they would have received a better reward from Allah. If they were truly people of knowledge and discernment, they would have understood that replaced magic with faith and piety. However, they were unable to comprehend.

His saying "there would have been a better reward from Allah" is the response to the conditional وَلَوْ / If. They would have been rewarded with something that was much better the evil they brought upon themselves. That meaning was pointed out by Al-Zamakhshari. [65]

Imam Al-Alusi said: "The Almighty did not say 'Allah's reward.' He said 'a reward from Allah' to indicate that a small reward from Allah (in Allah's eternal and everlasting Kingdom) was far better that many of the pleasures of this transient ephemeral life." [66]

And His saying: "if only they knew!" is another conditional statement where the response is omitted. It means if they knew Allah's reward, they would not have exchanged their faith and bought magic instead.

Thus, these noble verses (Q 2:102-1023) that we discussed in this section labelled the Children of Israel as people who rejected the truth, discarded the teachings of their Book, preferred to pursue lies and falsehoods, deliberately persisting in their evil ways, and not using their knowledge. That was due to the deviation of their nature, their foolish reasoning, their bad management and being utterly possessed by Satan. Thus, they earned wrath over wrath. The disbelievers will have severe punishment.

Before we conclude this section, we should briefly talk about magic:

Magic is a word that is literally driven from الصرف which means "diversion. "As in His saying: ""How are you then so deluded?" (Q 23:89) In other words, how would you be diverted from the truth to untruths and falsehoods?

Magic was mentioned in the Qur'an and the Sunna. Researchers agreed that magic does exist. However, they differed among themselves in describing and portraying it.

Sunni people entertained the idea that magic has real effects and that a magician can perform unnatural things. However, they maintained that the Almighty is the true actor in all things. They cite some evidence:

First: The Almighty commanded His Prophet to seek His refuge: "from the evil of those witches casting spells by blowing onto knots." (Q 113:4) Most likely, the reference here is made to magicians.

Imam Ibn Kathir said: "The Almighty's 'from the evil of those ⌜witches casting spells by⌝ blowing onto knots-' as pointed out by Mujahid, Akramah, Al-Hassan, Qatada and Al-Dahaak- is a reference to the magicians. [67]

The honorable verse indicates that magic has real effect; otherwise, Allah would not have ordered His Prophet to seek refuge from the evil of the magicians.

Second: In a Chapter on magic, Imam Al-Bukhari reported on the authority of Sufyan, on the authority of Hisham, on the authority of his father, on the authority of Aisha said: "The Messenger of Allah was bewitched to the extent that he began to imagine that he had done something- (i.e., sleeping with women)- when he did not. Sufyan said that that was the worst form of sorcery. So, he said: 'O Aisha, do you know that Allah has given me a fatwa regarding what I asked Him about? Two men came to me, one of them sat at my head and the other at my feet. The one at my head said to the other: 'What is the matter with the man?' He said: 'He has been bewitched.' The other said: 'Who bewitched him?' He said: 'Labid bin A'sam - a man from Banu Zurayq, an ally of the Jews and a hypocrite.' He said: 'And for what?' He said: 'For a comb and tongs.' He said: 'And where?' He said: 'In the trunk of a date palm, under a hump in the well of Dharwan.' She said: 'So the Prophet came to the well until he pulled it out, and he said: 'This is the well that I was shown, and its palm trees were as if they were the heads of devils.' He said: So, it (the spell) was pulled out. She said: 'have you been healed?' So, he said: "Allah has healed me, and I hate to stir up evil against anyone among the people." [68]

This authentic Hadith shows that magic had affected the physical condition of the Messenger of Allah. It caused him some kind of physical disease or heaviness, but it had no effect on his mind.

Imam Ibn Al-Qayyim said: "That was the Hadith that was narrated by Al-Bukhari. Researchers do not disagree concerning its validity. The authors of the two Sahihs agreed to modify and correct it. Exegetes, historians and jurisprudents are well aware of this story; they were the ones who were most knowledgeable of the Messengers life and state." [69]

Imam Al-Qurtubi said: "Plenty of evidence indicate that magic is real. The Almighty undoubtedly informed His messenger about its existence and reality. Scholars have agreed that it exists. They do not agree with the worthless Al-Mu'tazila and their stance against the people of the truth. Magic prevailed in olden times, and people often talked about it; the companions and the followers never denied it." [70]

Mr. Muhammad Fou'ad Abdul-Baqi said: "Al-Mazri said, 'Sunni people and the majority of the nation's scholars maintain that magic is just as real as other fixed truths. This is contrary to those who deny its existence and negate its presence and regard it as mere delusions and falsehoods that have no truth to them. The Almighty mentioned it in His Book, that it was something that could be learned and that it could cause a rift between a man and his wife. All of this is not possible if magic was not a reality. The previous Hadith confirms that magic is a reality; there are things (used in magic) that were buried and extracted. All of this annuls what they claimed concerning not being a reality. Some innovators rejected that Hadith claiming that vitiates the high status of prophethood and casts doubts around it. However, what those innovators have claimed is not true since there is reliable evidence that prove that the Hadith was true and correct. There were reports that showed that magic merely affected his physique, not his mind or beliefs. Accordingly, the meaning of the Hadith would be: "He would feel strong and energetic enough to make his advances. However, when he approached them (the women), he would become unable and behave as a bewitched person." [71]

The Mu'tazila maintained that magic does not exist; it is only a delusion and a figment of the imagination. As the Almighty said concerning the Pharaoh's magicians: "Moses responded, "No, you go first." And suddenly their ropes and staffs appeared to him—by their magic—to be slithering." (Q 20:66) The Almighty mentioned that what they thought was "slithering" was merely the work of the imagination. The Almighty also mentioned this concerning the Pharaoh's magicians: "Moses said, "You first." So, when they did, they deceived the eyes of the people, stunned them, and made a great display of magic." That is, when they threw their ropes and staffs, they deceived the people and made them think that they were slithering and instilled fear in their hearts with their great display of magic.

In our view, magic can be of many kinds:

First: A kind that could result in reversing facts such as transforming a human to an animal and vice versa. The Mu'tazila rejected that kind of magic believing that if a magician was able to do that, it would be confused with the miracles of the prophets. Sunni people believe that this kind of magic is possible even though it did not take place. They differentiate between this kind of magic and a miracle. To them, a miracle is something that supernatural that could be performed by a prophet to display rejection of something or challenging something. Magic, on the other hand, acknowledges no rejection or prophethood.

In addition, we have to notice that magic can be taught and learned. And contrary to a miracle, it can only be performed by the wicked.

The late honorable Sheikh Muhammad Al-Khder Hussein said: "There is no evidence that this kind of magic was performed. The need to distinguish between magic and miracle is important and should be made clear. A magician would not be able to transform a staff into a serpent, nor will he be able to part the sea to allow an army to pass through the sides, nor will he be able to cause water to spring out of rocks for people to drink. What I mean to say is that miracles could not be performed at the hands of a magician. Prophets, on the other hand, perform amazing and miraculous feats." [72]

Second: Some meandering and cunning people may perform certain acts that could harm others. Sunni people accept this kind of magic, but the Mu'tazila reject it. An example for this is what the magicians may do to cause a rift between a husband and his wife. The Noble Qur'an did mention that magicians learn how to use their magic to cause this rift in a relationship. In the Hadith, it was mentioned that Labid bin A'sam, a Jew, cast a spell on the Prophet.

Third: Performing acts that result in "apparent," not "real" effects. Both the Mu'tazila and the Sunni people agree on this. The Noble Qur'an mentioned this concerning the Pharaoh's magicians: "So, when they did, they deceived the eyes of the people, stunned them, and made a great display of magic." (Q 7:116) Also in His saying: "And suddenly their ropes and staffs appeared to him—by their magic—to be slithering." (Q 20:66)

The Noble Qur'an warned against using magic to cause harm. Its teachings censure and prohibit it. It threatens those who perform it with severe punishment. In the Hadith: "The punishment for a sorcerer is to strike him with a sword." [73]

Some Jurisprudents issued a Fatwa (decision) to kill the magician because he is a heretic. Some said that if the magician is a man, he should be killed (unless he repents); if the magician is a woman, she should be imprisoned until she abandons it. Some say that if the magician perpetrated a felony that necessities severe punishment, he should be killed. Otherwise, he should be fined in accordance with his mischievous act.

This is a brief review of magic. We did not want to embark on a lengthy investigation of its intricate details. We merely wanted to provide the reader with a brief idea since we are talking about the vices of the Jews: rejecting Allah's Book and following delusions and falsehoods.

Sixth: <u>Altering and changing texts seeking a fleeting gain</u>.

A- In Sura Al-Baqara the Almighty said: "Do you believers still expect them to be true to you, though a group of them would hear the word of Allah then knowingly corrupt it after understanding it? When they meet the believers they say, "We believe." But in private they say to each other, "Will you disclose to the believers the knowledge Allah has revealed to you, so that they may use it against you before your Lord? Do you not understand?" Do they not know that Allah is aware of what they conceal and what they reveal? And among them are the illiterate who know nothing about the Scripture except lies, and so they wishfully speculate. So woe to those who distort the Scripture with their own hands then say, "This is from Allah"—seeking a fleeting gain! So, woe to them for what their hands have written, and woe to them for what they have earned." (Q 2:75-79)

One of the most conspicuous vices of the Children of Israel that the Noble Qur'an reiterated was "corrupting" the texts (altering and changing the texts and using words for purposes other than what they were originally meant to convey). That was because their hearts were hardened and cruel and their vision was dim and blurry, and they were more interested in seeking fleeting short-lived gains.

The noble verses above open with denying the believers any hope of the Jews' ever accepting or entering into Islam. This was preceded with what supported and reinforced this negative outlook. The previous verses have portrayed the malicious and ungrateful attitude of the Jews towards Allah's blessings and favors. They also demonstrated how the Jews had knowingly snubbed and disregarded the tenets of their religion, their misconceptions of the instructions of their law, and their cruel hearts even after witnessing clear and undeniable miracles. Having thus delivered this negative picture indicating the improbability of responding to the truth, the Almighty addressed the believers, saying: "Do you ⸢believers still⸣ expect [74] them to be true to you, though a group of them would hear the word of Allah then knowingly corrupt [75] it after understanding it?"

The meaning of the verse is: You believers! Do you really expect those Jews to accept Islam after all that I had recounted to you concerning their stubbornness and ungratefulness? A group of their scholars and religious leaders would listen to Allah's words then distort and change them from their intended meaning after comprehending Allah's message. They knew that they were liars by changing Allah's words, and they were fully aware of the severe and painful punishment and humiliating disgrace that befall those who distort Allah's words.

It was the believers that were addressed in this honorable verse. The use of the interrogative here is meant to deny the believers' expectation of the Jews' positive response to the call of truth after learning about their deviation and corruption. However, prohibiting them from expecting that they would become believers did not mean NOT to invite them to the faith. The believers are expected to invite others to the faith so that they might use it against them in this world when they are judged as disbelievers, and to deny them any pretexts or excuses in the hereafter. Also, the Islamic call could find its way to the hearts of fair and just people who would embrace the call to the truth and find guidance to the straight path. That was what the Messenger did, and that was what his companions did after him. However, the Jews turned a deaf ear to the truth after they knew it and calling them to accept Islam became fruitless and unproductive. That is why there is this prohibition that was directed to the believers not to expect them to embrace the faith.

The Statement "a group of them would hear the word of Allah" is a circumstantial adverb that describes one of the reasons why believers should not expect that the Jews would ever believe. Thus, two reasons were mentioned regarding giving up hope that they would embrace the faith:

The first: Depicting their state prior to this verse.
The second: What this verse contains concerning knowingly and deliberately distorting the word of Allah.

The word group in His saying "a group of them" (Q 2:75) is a reference to their scholars and rabbis who lived during the honorable messengers and heard from them. It could also refer to those who came after them.

"Corrupt" (Q 2:75) refers to something that is deviant or going in the wrong direction. In this verse, it refers to distorting the revelation and the law and changing and altering the words by intentionally misinterpreting them.

His saying "then knowingly corrupt it after understanding it" (Q 2:75) rebukes them further since it indicates that they deliberately and knowingly distorted the words of Allah after comprehending them. It shows their bad intention, and it also reveals that they committed this abhorrent deed despite their knowledge of the punishment that the culprit would receive in this world and in the Hereafter. Thus, they had no excuse; they could attribute what they did to neither ignorance nor forgetfulness. What they did was recorded as deliberate disobedience.

The distortion and corruption of the Book at the hands of Jewish scholars and rabbis was a reason for the despair that crept into the hearts of the believers and caused them to lose heart in seeing most of those Jews embrace the faith. That was because the majority of those Jews, essentially imitators and followers, received their religious tenets through corrupt and immoral leaders who disregarded the truth and all means leading to it. Therefore, such people who were brought up as blind followers could not be expected to detect the light of guidance and the beauty of righteousness. A nation whose scholars and distinguished ones- the best and brightest in it- had deteriorated to such a degree that they dared to distort the words of Allah, could not be expected to mount to any good; its subjects could not be any better in any way, shape or form.

Then, the noble Qur'an recounted that in addition to the vice of distorting and corrupting Allah's words some of them also had another vice, mainly, hypocrisy and pretense. The Almighty said: "When they meet the believers they say, "We believe." But in private they say to each other, "Will you disclose to the believers the knowledge Allah has revealed to you, so that they may use it against you before your Lord? Do you not understand?" Do they not know that Allah is aware of what they conceal and what they reveal?" (Q 2:76)

The meaning is: If those hypocrites from among the Jews met the believers, they behaved with cunning and duplicity to deceive them. They would tell them: "We believe that that you are truthful and that Muhammad is a messenger from Allah." Yet, when the Jews were alone with one other, those who were not hypocrites or deceitful would reprimand their brethren who were, saying: "Do you inform the believers what Allah has revealed to you in your Book concerning their truth and upright faith so that they may use it against you in Judgement Day? Don't you understand that that would enable them to use this against you?" Thus, the noble verse (Q 2:76) states another kind of the vices and disgraceful attributes of the Jews, one that would lead to despair of their ever embracing the faith. In addition, the verse reveals their inherent deceitfulness and duplicity.[76]

Imam Al-Razi said: "They admonished them for doing that because if a Jew acknowledged that the Torah was correct and testified that it confirmed the Prophet's truthfulness, that would be powerful evidence against him. That was why some of them would prevent others from acknowledging this in the presence of the believers." [77]

And the use of the interrogative style in "Will you disclose to the believers the knowledge Allah has revealed to you?" (Q 2:76) was meant to severely censure and rebuke them. And the word فَتَحَ is used to refer to judgement as in the Almighty's: "Our Lord! Judge between us and our people with truth. You are the best of those who judge." (Q 7:89)

Ibn Jarir said: "The origin of the word الفتح in Arabic refers to ruling and judgement. The meaning is: 'Do you talk to them concerning Allah's judgement and decree concerning you? In His wisdom and Judicious judgement, He took a covenant with them to believe in Muhammad for the Torah has anticipated his coming." [78]

The Almighty's saying: "so that they may use it against you before your Lord" (Q 2:76) relates to talking about what Allah has revealed to them in the Torah. It was meant to intensify their admonition of their brethren who ostensibly displayed their faith out of hypocrisy. It was as though they were saying: "Are you really sharing with the believers what could be taken against you on Judgement Day in the presence of the Almighty Creator? They will tell you 'Haven't you discussed with us what your Book says concerning our religion and the truthfulness of our Prophet? That will further expose and dishonor you above all others on that majestic and fearful day. For those who confess the truth then conceal and hide it are in a worse position than those who deny it from the start.'"

The question: "Do you not understand?" (Q 2:76) continues their admonition of the hypocrites. It further chastised them so that they would not go back and speak with the believers.

The meaning is: Do you not have the mental ability and the acumen that would prevent you from talking to the believers and sharing with them what they could use against you on Judgement Day?

The Almighty then censured them for their unawareness of His knowledge. He said: "Do they not know that Allah is aware of what they conceal and what they reveal?" (Q 2:77) In other words, Did those- who had not behaved like their other hypocrite brethren say what they said, conceal what they had concealed of the Prophet's characteristics, and distort what they had distorted of Allah's Book- did they not know that Allah was Knowledgeable of all their malice and disbelief and all that that they had concealed as well as the faith and compassion that they had revealed?

The noble verse censured those Jews- who admonished the hypocrites for talking with the believers about the Torah's confirmation of the truthfulness of the Prophet- for their ignorance and unawareness. Had they been true and faithful believers, they would not have prohibited their brethren from talking with the believers about what the Torah has mentioned as it contains facts and characteristics about the Prophet that Allah commanded them to reveal and forbad them from concealing.

The Noble Qur'an continued to reveal the state of the common people after disclosing the condition and state of their scholars and hypocrites. The Almighty said: "And among them are the illiterate [79] who know nothing about the Scripture except lies, and so they wishfully speculate." (Q 2:78) That is to say: among the Jews were illiterate people who did not know how to write. They only knew the lies that their scholars had fabricated concerning the Torah. They had grasped these lies without understanding and discernment. They merely believed in lies and held them without irrefutable evidence or indisputable proof.

Thus, the honorable verse further reinforces the believers' despair and hopelessness of the Jews' embracing the faith. They had reached an abominable state that could not promise their coming to guidance; their scholars distorted and corrupted Allah's Book to suit their lusts and desires, and the common people only knew the lies and illusions that their rabbis and scholars made available to them. A nation whose scholars and common people were like that could not be expected to accept the truth or follow the straight path.

In Arabic, the word أَمَانِيَّ /⌜wishfully⌝ is derived from the desire to get something. It could also mean "to lie." Also, it could mean "to read a book."

If we look at أَمَانِيَّ according to the first interpretation, then إِلَّا أَمَانِيَّ would mean: They knew nothing except for their wishes that Allah would not chastise them for their sins and wrongdoing, that their fathers, the prophets, would intercede on their behalf, and that the fire would not touch them except for a number of days.

If we look at it according to the second meaning (lies), then إِلَّا أَمَانِيَّ would mean: They knew nothing except for the different lies that they heard from their scholars and which they accepted as followers and imitators.

If we look at أَمَانِيَّ according to the third meaning (reading), then His saying إِلَّا أَمَانِيَّ would mean: They knew nothing but what they read without discernment or understanding.

Ibn Jarir was more inclined to interpret أَمَانِيَّ as "lies." He said: "Those illiterates do not understand anything in that Book that Allah revealed to Moses. They lie and utter delusions and falsehoods. "أَمَانِيَّ /wishfully" in this context means lies and fabrications. As evidence for this is the Almighty's 'and so they wishfully speculate,' meaning that they desired lies because of their delusions, not certainty." [80]

However, we believe that all three meanings are applicable to the Jews; they were true and were manifested by the Jews. Since the term is applicable to all three meanings, then they are all valid, and there is no sense in becoming preoccupied with giving one sense more weight as Ibn Jarir and others did. Moreover, no matter what the interpretation of "أَمَانِيَّ /⌜wishfully⌝" is, there was no room for exceptions since all the meanings indicate that none knew the real meaning of the Book well.

His "and so they wishfully speculate" (Q 2:78) highlights and emphasizes their ignorance because their wishes were due to delusions that had no evidence and suspicions that were based on accepting one view out of two without compelling evidence or proof. This kind of knowledge could hardly be sufficient in grasping the tenets of religion on which deep and unshakeable faith is founded. They were uncertain of the tenets of their religion; they merely "felt" that they could be either this or that, and they didn't firmly-and with certainty- believed in those tenets.

After that, the Noble Qur'an warned those who distort the word of Allah. The Almighty said: "So woe [81] to those who distort the Scripture with their own hands then say, "This is from Allah"—seeking a fleeting gain! So, woe to them for what their hands have written, and woe to them for what they have earned." (Q 2:79)

In other words, shame, disgrace and perdition would be the lot of those Jewish scholars who distorted and deliberately misinterpreted the Books- instead of delivering the facts that were contained therein (as they were)- then falsely informed their illiterate imitators and followers that those were from Allah and from the Torah that Allah revealed to Moses in order to seek a little ephemeral gain. Their punishment would be severe for distorting the words of Allah, and they would be humiliated and disgraced for the gains they had unlawfully earned.

The noble verse vehemently threatened the Jewish scholars who dared to distort the Book of Allah, exchanged their religion for the short-lived gains of the world and claimed that what they wrote was from Allah.

The Almighty also stated that the writing was done by their hands- "what their hands have written-" (Q 2:79) to emphasize that it was done knowingly and deliberately, to negate any illusions that they ordered others to write what they did, and to depict their state as it was so that the hearer would almost witness and "see" them doing what they were doing.

Then, His saying: "'This is from Allah'" (Q 2:79) was meant to expose their lies and immorality; they distorted the words of Allah then claimed that that was from Allah so that their followers would accept them with conviction and assurance.

The Almighty then revealed the reason that prompted them to lie and distort Allah's words. He said: "seeking a fleeting gain." (Q 2:79) That is, they wrote the Book with their own hands and deceitfully and falsely attributed it to Allah in order to earn a meager worldly gain such as unlawful wealth, a pretense to erudition and knowledge, lust for authority and power, pleasing the public and common people- all that suited their desires and lusts.

The Almighty indicated that the gain they were seeking was a little "fleeting" gain since no matter how great the gain was, it would be worthless considering the punishment and torture that they would be facing, and the good rewards they were denied.

His saying: "So woe to them for what their hands have written, and woe to them for what they have earned" (Q 2:79) was a threat to them because of writing a corrupt distorted book and their unlawful exploitation of peoples' monies and wealth. It was a warning because of their means, i.e., the writing, as well as the end, i.e., unlawfully taking others' money and wealth.

Sheikh Al-Qasimi said: "Al-Raghib said: 'why was "earn" used in the future and "write' in the past (in the Arabic text)? The response would be in line with what the Prophet said: 'Whosoever committed an evil deed will have to bear its burdens as well as the burdens of those who committed it till Judgement Day. Thus, the misinterpretations that they had confirmed and which their illiterate followers embraced without verification would be a burden and a responsibility that would fall upon their shoulders. It was also expressed in writing, not orally, and what was written would remain even if what was said might be forgotten!" [82]

Thus, these noble verses have labelled the Jews with the vice of altering and distorting the words of Allah knowingly and deliberately. They also described them as hypocrites and deceitful and censured them for their unawareness and ignorance and lack of understanding and ill-conceived perception of Allah's knowledge and Omnipotence. They also warned them of the punishment that awaits them on account of their lies, transgressions against Allah and making permissible what Allah has prohibited.

B- Sura An-Nisa contains a verse that clearly shows that the Jews had distorted the words of Allah and offended the Prophet. The Almighty said: "Some Jews take words out of context and say, "We listen and we disobey," "Hear! May you never hear," and "Râ'ina!" [Herd us!]—playing with words and discrediting the faith. Had they said courteously, "We hear and obey," "Listen to us," and "Unẓurna," [Tend to us!] it would have been better for them and more proper. Allah has condemned them for their disbelief, so they do not believe except for a few." (Qur'an 4:46)

The meaning of the noble verse is: Among the Jews who were given a portion of the Scriptures are some who would take words out of context to make it applicable to meanings other than what they were originally intended to convey. They would do that by deletions, additions and misrepresenting the truth. And they would not stop at that, for when they had heard him who called for the truth, they would say: 'We listened and heard but disobeyed what you had called us to follow. Hear! May you never hear.' Then, they insulted and offended him further, saying: '"Râ'ina!" (Herd us) twisting their tongues to further insult and offend him and ridicule his faith. Had they said: 'We listened to the truth and obeyed instead of we listened and disobeyed,' or had they respectfully said: 'Listen to our response to your call, tend to us "Unẓurna," [Tend to us!] with compassion and kindness' instead of saying "Râ'ina!" [Herd us!] and twisting their tongues to insult and ridicule, it would have been much better for them, and it would have been more appropriate and advantageous for them in this world and in the Hereafter. However, they did not do what could have been beneficial for them. That is why, they became deserving of condemnation and disgrace for their persistent disbelief and obstinate rebelliousness. Only a few among them escaped this damnation because of their faith and unrighteousness.

Thus, the noble verse depicts a number of the dreadful and despicable deeds of the Jews and recounts some of their vices when they heard the Prophet's call to the straight righteous path.

The Almighty's "Some Jews" was a reference to the verses that have preceded this one: "Have you O Prophet not seen those who were given a portion of the Scriptures yet trade it for misguidance and wish to see you deviate from the Right Path? Allah knows best who your enemies are! And Allah is sufficient as a Guardian, and He is sufficient as a Helper." (Q 4:44-45)

Al-Alusi- may Allah rest his soul- said: "the Almighty emphasized His denunciation of those Jews and was quick to make the believers wary and distrustful of them and of mixing or socializing with them. He urged the believers to trust Him and feel self-sufficient and content by their allegiance to Him and His support of them." [83]

The Almighty's "Some Jews take words out of context" (Q 4:46) both points to their selling guidance for misguidance and details the many kinds of waywardness.

Interpreters looked at the meaning of distortion and recounted the following important views:

1- Imam Al-Razi said: "Distortion was done in many ways. One way was to change one word for another. Another way was to cast a false meaning and misinterpret a word to divert others from the true intended meaning to adopt a false meaning through various lexical tricks, very much like what heretics nowadays do with verses that are at variance with their beliefs. A third way was that they would go to the Prophet and ask him about a certain issue as though they were consulting him. When they left his presence, they would distort his words." [84]
2- The author of Al-Kashaaf said: "The Almighty's 'Some Jews take words out of context' meant that they would replace the words with other words. That is, they would substitute words that Allah has placed in certain contexts with other words, just as they did when they substituted the word الرجم/stoning with الحد" [85]
3- Imam ibn Kathir said: "The Almighty's 'Some Jews take words out of context' meant that they would interpret the words different from the intended original meaning, not in accordance with what Allah had intended. They did that knowingly and deliberately." [86]
4- The author of Al-Manar said: "Distortion can refer to two meanings: One meaning refers to interpreting what is said differently from the intended meaning. That was the most likely scenario because they were prompted to renounce the Prophet and deny his prophethood, while they knew his truthfulness. Thus, they interpreted-and they still interpret- things differently until the present day. They likewise interpret what was mentioned about Christ and attribute it to another person that they are still anticipating. The second meaning refers to taking a word or a group of words from one place in the Book and placing it/ them in a different place. That confusion did take place in the books of the Jews as what happened

> concerning Moses; they attributed to Moses things that were written about him a long time later. Some late interpreters among the People of the Scriptures confessed to that." [87]

From the aforementioned interpretations, we can conclude that taking words out of context could entail changing the words in their books by deletion or addition and interpreting texts incorrectly in a manner that was not supported by the appropriate and valid texts or maintained by sound rational minds. It also included perceiving the words of the Prophet in ways that differed from the intended meaning to intentionally ridicule and offend him. Ibn Abbas was quoted as saying: "The Jews went to the Prophet to seek his council on certain matters. He would tell them his views on those issues thinking that they would adopt them. However, when they left, they would distort his words."

Then, the Almighty reported that those Jews would not be content with distortion and taking words out of context. To the vice of distortion and alteration, He added other vices such as voicing their disobedience when they heard the call to the truth, their taking the Prophet lightly and ridiculing the religion of Islam. The Almighty said: "They said: 'We listen and we disobey,' 'Hear! May you never hear,' and 'Râ'ina!' [Herd us!]—playing with words and discrediting the faith." (Q 4:46) In other words, they would tell the Messenger when he called them to the righteous path, 'We heard what you said, Muhammad. We listened and we understood, but we couldn't obey you, even if what you said was the unadulterated, indubitable and certain truth.' That betrayed their deeply rooted, entrenched disbelief, their complete and total capitulation to malice and hatred, and their deliberate and utter denunciation and condemnation of the truth.

They were not content to merely display their rebelliousness and disobedience openly. Rather, they added two statements that betrayed their evil intention, their hypocrisy and their duplicity, even if they could have been taken as kind, thereby displaying their sarcasm for the Prophet and their ridicule of Islam through puns and other rhetorical devices.

The first statement "Hear! May you never hear," by which they meant to wish him deafness or death. This was apparently evil even though there could have been another meaning that implied goodness as in seemingly saying 'listen to us! May you never hear evil.' They- may Allah's damnation descend upon them- used to address the Messenger like that to ridicule him pretending that they wanted what was good for him while they were inwardly wishing him evil.

The second statement "Râ'ina!" (Herd us!) which the believers used to say to the Prophet to ask him to tend to their needs and provide them with good counsel. The Jews picked this word and twisted their tongues to change it from its intended meaning to another despicable and loathsome one, mainly, frivolity and triviality.

Al-Raghib said: "That was something they said to the Messenger to ridicule and mock him. They used it (Râ'ina) to describe him as frivolous and foolish pretending that they were saying a word which means keep or preserve us. They would pronounce the word

راعِنَا as though the ن/ noon is part of the word itself, not the pronoun نا by twisting their tongues, playing with words and discrediting the faith." [88]

And Al-Zamakhshari said: "It is possible that the word راعنا نكلمك meant watch us and wait. It might have been a Hebrew or Syriac word which they used to offend and curse one another, and they used it to discredit the faith and ridicule the Messenger. That is, they would talk to him in such a way that "seemingly" show respect and deference but, in reality, intended to ridicule and humiliate. They would play with words and twist their tongues to pronounce what was right and replace it with what was wrong. For example, they would use Râ'ina in place of "Unẓurna," and "may you never hear" in place of 'may you never hear something bad,' or they would twist their tongues to utter insults while pretending to be deferential. So, if you said: "How could they come up with something that could be interpreted in two different meanings after they had said: 'We listen and we disobey?' I will respond by saying that all the disbelievers were used to facing him acknowledging their disobedience and disbelief, but they would not curse or swear even though they may have indeed cursed him amongst themselves. They may have not uttered swearwords. However, since they had rejected the faith, they were made as though they did." [89]

What is indubitable, however, is that though these two statements could have been taken to mean something good, the Jews intended to use them to ridicule and disparage the messenger and discredit and denigrate the faith. That was what was well known about the Jews and their deeply ingrained malice to those whom Allah favored with His blessings and grace.

Ibn Attiyya said: "This tongue twisting to display things that are not really in one's heart is still apparent in the Children of Israel until now. There are many examples for this, but it is not appropriate to mention them in this document." Commenting on Ibn Attiyya's statement, Abou Hayyan said: "What Ibn Attiyya said is reported about the Jews of Al-Andalus. We have witnessed them, and we have also witnessed the Jews in Egypt behave in the same way. It is as though they bring up their young ones to follow in their footsteps. They teach them how to address the Muslims: how to appear respectful and deferential while being, in reality, demeaning and disparaging." [90]

The Noble Qur'an then stated the way they should have behaved and the sayings they should have uttered when they were called to the faith. The Almighty said (Q 4:46): ". Had they said courteously, "We hear and obey," "Listen to us," and "Unẓurna," [Tend to us!] it would have been better for them and more proper." In other words, it would have been far better and more beneficial for them in this world and in the Hereafter had they said we listened when they were invited to the faith instead of "We listen and we disobey." It would have been far better when they addressed the Prophet if they had asked him to listen to their response to his call, to look at them with patience, kindness and compassion and refrained from using dubious and twisted statements. However, because of their ill manners, they did not do that, and they were therefore deserving of Allah's condemnation in this world and the next because of their disbelief, ungratefulness, and rebelliousness. The Noble Qur'an stated this clearly: "Allah has condemned them for their disbelief, so they do not believe except for a few." (Q 4:46) Only the few who believed were not condemned.

Thus, we see that these noble verses have recounted that the Jews have distorted the words of Allah and the words of those people who commanded them to be fair and just. They also recorded their inappropriate behavior towards the Messenger and all who had called them to guidance and the upright path. Allah described them as circuitous and devious people who uttered ambiguous and equivocal statement and behaved impudently and insolently. He also depicted them as people who disparaged and ridiculed the faith using phrases that would ostensibly be taken as respectful and differential while in reality they were demeaning, derisive and condescending. People with such characteristics are truly deserving of condemnation and severe torture.

Seventh: Clinging eagerly to life and their cowardice to fight for the sake of Allah.

One of the ugly characteristics of the Jews at all times and in all places is their intense and eager clinging to life (to live a long-drawn-out life), their extreme love for life in this world regardless of its quality even if it were blemished with humiliation and disgrace. That voracious love for life and the world has led them to indescribable shameful cowardice, withdrawal and retreat from noble and honorable situations, and finding all kinds of pretexts to avoid fighting even for the sake of the truth. The Noble Qur'an has depicted these inherent vices of the Jews with precision and truthfully. Here are some of the verses that recount these attributes:

First: In Sura Al-Baqara the Almighty said: "You will surely find them clinging to life more eagerly than any other people, even more than polytheists. Each one of them wishes to live a thousand years. But even if they were to live that long, it would not save them from the punishment. And Allah is All-Seeing of what they do." (Q 2:96)
The meaning of the verse is: Muhammad! You will find that those Jews- who claim that they would be worthy of eternal life more than any other people- cling to life more eagerly than all others. More than any other people, they hate death the most, not just when they are enjoying good health but also when they are frail and unhealthy. They cling to life more eagerly than the polytheists who do not believe in the Afterlife, those whose greatest pleasure is enjoying the comforts and pleasures of this worldly life. They wish they could live for ages, as the Almighty said: "Each one of them wishes to live a thousand years." (Q 2:96) Thus, this honorable verse proves that they were untruthful when they claim that the eternal life is theirs alone, for if what they claim were true, they would have welcomed departing to eternity. However, they loathe death and don't even think about it. They feverishly cling to life even if they were leading an unhealthy, insalubrious debilitating life.

The reference to people is meant to include all people, and the superlative (af'al) in أَحْرَصَ (clinging…more) indicates that though life is instinctively precious all people, the Jews differ from others in the severity and reasons for their clinging to life and how they go about it. As the poet said:

"I see that we all seek life for ourselves,
are keen on it, and are passionately infatuated with it.
The coward's love of the self leads him to perishing,
and the brave's love of the self leads him to war."

Like the Jews, all people cling to life; however, the Jews cling to it more eagerly than all other people. Because of this unrestricted clinging, they are ready to sacrifice their faith, their dignity and everything else.

The Almighty denounced the life they ardently and keenly seek in order to chasten and castigate them. It is as though the Almighty was saying: "You avidly cling to life even if it abounded with misery and sorrow." He points to their unbridled desire to live regardless of how, even if their life is stripped of dignity and honor. One of the well-known sayings of the Jews is "Life is enough."

There is no doubt that such an intemperate clinging to life could lead to cowardice, timidity and submission in the face of grievance and injustice. A nation in which such a vice runs rampant would not be expected to distinguish between a respectful honorable life and a life of dishonor and humiliation.

The Almighty's "even more than polytheists" (Q 2:96) is a conjunction that functions as a conjoined clause that follows "more eagerly than any other people."(Q 2:96) Therefore, the meaning is they are more eager than all other people and even more eager than the polytheists.

The polytheists are those who associated partners with Allah. They were specifically mentioned even though they were amongst the "other people." That was to accentuate their chastisement and censure. Because they are People of the Book, their clinging to life more eagerly than the polytheists- who neither have Scriptures nor believe in the Resurrection-is proof of their humiliation and disgrace, their honor, and their lack of pride in their Scriptures that prohibit them from clinging to a disgraceful and dishonorable life.

Al-Zamakhshari said: "It is a severe chastisement because those polytheists do not believe in the Hereafter; they only know this present life. Therefore, to them, clinging eagerly to this life is understood and expected; after all, it is their paradise. But if those who are given the Scriptures cling to life more eagerly than them, that would be disgraceful and worthy of severe admonition and rebuke. If you said: 'Why did they cling to life more eagerly than the polytheists?' I would say: 'Because they will undoubtedly end in the fire, and the polytheists do not know that.'"[91]

Then, the Almighty revealed one of the signs of their voracious clinging to life. He said: "Each one of them wishes to live a thousand years." (Q 2:96) That is, they wish they could live for generations and reach that age that most people do not like reach as it is the most debilitating and humiliating age when life becomes most difficult.

The statement thus continues the verse that came before it to portray their exaggerated and rapacious desire to live long and to show their general penchant and propensity for this undesirable age. It is also meant to push back against what some might imagine that no matter how much they eagerly covet living, it would be highly unlikely that they would like to live for a thousand years, or more. This statement was therefore mentioned to prove that their clinging to life does, in fact, indicate their eagerness for that long drawn-out life where there is no happiness or comfort. It is the kind of life that the believers would shun.

Then, the Almighty showed that their long life would not save them from the punishment, for death will certainly find them no matter how long they live. The Almighty said: "But even if they were to live that long, it would not save them from the punishment." (Q 2:96) In other words, no one will escape the punishment that awaits, no matter how long they live.

The noble verse indicates their inevitable inescapable destiny. It puts an end to their covetousness and greed because death will find them, and they will be punished for their evil deeds.

The phrase "it would not save them" (Q 2:96) indicates that their long-drawn-out life will have no impact in lessening their punishment. And the statement "And Allah is All-Seeing of what they do" (Q 2:96) is a warning and a threat for them for the Almighty is the All-Knowledgeable; He is aware of all that they do, what they reveal and what they conceal, and He will reward them according to their deeds.

Second: In Sura Al-Ma'idah, the Almighty said: "And remember when Moses said to his people, "O my people! Remember Allah's favors upon you when He raised prophets from among you, made you sovereign, and gave you what He had never given anyone in the world. O my people! Enter the Holy Land which Allah has destined for you to enter. And do not turn back or else you will become losers." They replied, "O Moses! There is an enormously powerful people there, so we will never be able to enter it until they leave. If they do, then we will enter!" Two Allah-fearing men—who had been blessed by Allah—said, "Surprise them through the gate. If you do, you will certainly prevail. Put your trust in Allah if you are truly believers." Yet they said, "O Moses! Still we will never enter as long as they remain there. So go—both you and your Lord—and fight; we are staying right here!" Allah replied, "Then this land is forbidden to them for forty years, during which they will wander through the land. So do not grieve for the rebellious people." (Q 5:20-26)

These verses reveal the deeply rooted cowardice, the faint-heartedness and timidity, as well as the rebelliousness of the Children of Israel against their messenger. They preferred humiliation and disgrace as long as they were comfortable to dignity and honor if it meant fighting and warfare. The verses eloquently narrate a well know story. Here is a synopsis:

The Children of Israel marched in the direction of the Levant after Pharoah and his men drowned in front of their eyes. Allah inspired Moses to choose 12 leaders from among his people (representing the 12 tribes) and ordered him to send them to the Promised Land where the Canaanites used to live to gather information about the conditions of the inhabitants there. Moses did what Allah ordered him to do, and he said to the men he appointed to investigate the state of the Promised land and its mighty inhabitants: "Do not to tell anyone except me about what you see.' When those leaders entered the Promised Land and regarded the conditions of its inhabitants, they found them extremely mighty and powerful, well-built and huge and living in a fortified city. They returned to Moses and told him in front of the Children of Israel: "We went into the land to which you sent us, and it is a land that truly overflows with milk and honey. This is some of its fruits. However, the inhabitants are enormously powerful and strong, and their city is fortified." Each one of those leaders forbade his tribe to fight. Only two- Joshua ibn Noon and Kaleb ibn Yufnna [92] objected to what the other ten said. They asked the people to obey Moses, their Prophet, and to fight the Canaanites with him. However, the Children of Israel disobeyed the orders of these two leaders and insisted on their position to not fight. They wept and cried saying: "We wish we had died in Egypt or in the wilderness…" Then, they said: "Why did the Lord bring us to this land? To be killed with the swords of these mighty men and to have our children and women as booty for them?" Then, they said, "Let us appoint a leader and go back to Egypt." Moses urged them not to rebel and not to display that timidity and cowardice. He pressed them to fight against the mighty men, but they turned a deaf ear and a blind eye to his entreaties. Then, Allah told Moses that the Promised Land would be forbidden for forty years because of their rebelliousness and cowardice. During these years, they were destined to wander in the land.

This is a summary for that story as recounted in interpretation and history books. Some interpreters added details- that rational human beings find objectionable- concerning the characteristics of the mighty powerful Canaanites who were mentioned in the noble verses. We think it would be unbecoming to mention them- as Ibn Kathir said. [93]

To sum up, these verses mean: Remember, O honorable Messenger, when Moses (the one who spoke to Allah) said to his people, the Children of Israel, after their exodos from the land of Egypt, being saved from the Pharoah's ruthless tyranny and injustice and approaching the Promised Land: "People! Remember Allah's favors and thank Him for them. He raised many prophets from among you, and He made you free after you were enslaved to Pharoah and his men. He gave you favors that He had never given anyone else in the world. O my people! Enter the Holy Land that Allah had destined you to live in when you trust Him and follow His path. Do not turn back and disobey what His prophets brought you or else you will become losers in this world and in the Hereafter." However, the Children of Israel said to Moses: "The Holy land that you had commanded us to enter is inhabited by strong and powerful people that we could not fight against. We will not enter until they have departed from it. If they were to leave for some reason or another (without us being involved), we will enter it without fighting." Two Allah-fearing men said to them: "O people! Surprise them through the gate of the city and you will be victorious. Just trust in Allah's power and His help. Rely on Him, and be confident that you will be triumphant if you are truly believers." The Children of Israel were not convinced. They said to their Prophet: "We will never enter this land as long as these enormously powerful people dwell there. If you are determined to enter it, go with your Allah to fight and drive them out. As for us, we will be staying here." Moses presented his grievance to Allah for the cowardice and rebelliousness of his people: "Moses pleaded, "My Lord! I have no control over anyone except myself and my brother. So set us apart from the rebellious people." (Q 5:25) Allah responded saying: "Then this land is forbidden to them for forty years." (Q 5:26) During these years, they would wander through the land confused, perplexed and lost. He advised Moses not to grieve for those rebellious people.

In addition, the Almighty's "And remember when Moses said to his people, "O my people! Remember Allah's favors upon you" (Q 5:20) was a reminder to the Children of Israel- who lived during the time of the Prophet- of the vices of their predecessors that they might abandon them and avoid the punishments that fell upon their fathers because of their rebelliousness and cowardice. It was also meant to regale the Prophet for the harm and rebelliousness he had to suffer at their hands.

On commenting on the noble verse, Imam Ibn Jarir said: "'The Almighty was informing His Prophet of their departure from the truth, their bad choices, their differences with their prophets, and their slothfulness in returning to guidance despite Allah's abundant benevolence and favors, thus regaling His Prophet concerning the difficulties they had caused him.' The Almighty is saying to him: 'Do not worry about what you had to endure at their hands. They are accustomed to depart from Allah's ways and truth. Learn from what Moses, your brother, had to endure and suffer at their hands. Remember that Moses said to them: 'O my people! Remember Allah's favors upon you.'" (Q 5:20) [94]

Moses's words: "O my people! Remember Allah's favors upon you" was a pleasant and nice way to address them, an amiable way to prompt and urge them to be grateful for Allah's favors and blessings. He was trying to use this reminder so that Allah would even bless them more for their gratitude.

The Almighty's "He raised prophets from among you, made you sovereign, and gave you what He had never given anyone in the world" (Q 5:20) is a statement of three favors that He bestowed upon them.

The first one was: He raised many prophets from among them such as Moses, Aaron, Zachariah, John, and Jesus. The Almighty did not send as many prophets to any other nation in the world as He did with the Children of Israel. He consecutively sent a great number of prophets to them to bring them out of the darkness into the light and to rescue them from their immorality and depravity.

The second favor was: He made you sovereign. That is, He set them free after they were enslaved to the Pharoah and his people. He made you owners of dwelling places, and He gave you people to serve you after a time in which you owned nothing when you were in Egypt. This great blessing of freedom was one of the greatest favors that could only be appreciated for its great value by the dignified and magnanimous spirits that loath injustice and oppose unfairness.

The third favor was: The Almighty blessed them with favors that no other people in the world was given: He parted the sea for them in order to be able to march on dry land; they were rescued while their enemies drowned. He gave then manna and quails to get their nourishment and sustenance; and out of rocks He caused water to flow out of twelve springs so that each tribe would know their water source. There were many favors that the Almighty granted them. They should have hurried to follow His commandments and shun His prohibitions.

Moreover, to these three favors Moses added his plea to encourage and warn them at one and the same time. He said: "O my people! Enter the Holy Land which Allah has destined for you to enter. And do not turn back or else you will become losers." (Q 5:21) He urged them to enter the Holy Blessed Land- (most probably, Jerusalem) [95]- which was home to a great number of prophets such as Abraham. It then became the dwelling place for the Canaanites, the polytheists who defiled it with their disbelief and paganism.

Then, He added another incentive to lure them to enter the Holy Land and secure victory, i.e., "which Allah has destined for you to enter." It was He who destined and promised it for you provided that you believe, trust and obey Him. You should also fight for His sake and obey His commandments- just as He commanded you to pray and give alms- and the commandments of His messengers.

There could have not been a stronger confirmation or assurance of their victory as it proceeded from the Omnipotent, the All-Powerful.

Having lured them with the rewards of marching into the land, he warned them against cowardice, faintheartedness and retreating. He said: "And do not turn back or else you will become losers." (Q 5:21) That is, My people! Follow Allah's order and proceed to the Holy land that He ordered you to enter. Do not turn back the guidance that was brought to you and avert fighting for that would lead to losses in this world and in the Hereafter and deprive you of the blessings of the land that was destined to you.

Ibn Jarir said: "If someone said: 'Why would Moses order his people to enter the Holy Land and not to turn back or else they would become losers?' It was said that the Almighty's order was to fight against those disbelievers who inhabited the land. It was an order for them to enter it, and they were doomed to lose by forsaking it. Their position concerning Allah's commandment had two sides. First, they wasted the duty that Allah imposed on them to fight. Second, they disobeyed Allah's commandment when they refused to enter the land and when they said to their prophet: we will never be able to enter it until they leave. If they do, then we will enter!'" [96]

The noble verse "Do not turn back or else you will become losers" was a strong warning of a certain defeat and undeniable loss if they failed to comply with his orders after enumerating all the rewards he mentioned. Moses was empathetic and he, in fact, expected his people to refrain from fighting having experienced their cunning nature and bad manners on many occasions before. His former experiences with them prompted him to mention all the wonderful favors, the splendid memories, the strongest guarantees and the severest warnings as he commanded them to enter the Holy Land, hopefully they might comply with his order and proceed to fight with a true desire and a strong determination....

However, the cowardice, spinelessness and faintheartedness that characterize the Children of Israel never left them despite all the encouragements and intimidations that were mentioned. Using false excuses, they said their prophet: "O Moses! There is an enormously [97] powerful people there, so we will never be able to enter it until they leave. If they do, then we will enter!" (Q 5:22) This means: 'The land that you destined for us to enter, Moses, is inhabited by extremely enormous and strong people. We cannot fight them; they overcome all those who fought against them. It is not logical to throw ourselves at harm's way and try to enter their land.' In addition to this excuse for not entering, they said that they would definitely not enter that land as long as those powerful people live there. They said: "we will never be able to enter it until they leave. If they do, then we will enter!" (Q 5:22) Which means: 'We will never enter that land, Moses, as long as these powerful people are there. If they leave, we are ready to enter with comfort and peace, without toil, struggle or fighting."

It is unquestionable that what the noble verse recounted about them indicates their incredible cowardice and weakness for they did not want to achieve anything by using their physical and mental abilities. Rather, they wanted to get things through miracles and signs. A nation such as this is not worthy of a gracious life or a dignified existence since its people did not do the work that would qualify them to enjoy such a life.

Then, the Noble Qur'an reported that two Allah-fearing men denounced the reluctance of the Children of Israel to fight. They prompted them to obey their prophet, saying: "Two God-fearing men—who had been blessed by Allah—said, "Surprise them through the gate. If you do, you will certainly prevail. Put your trust in Allah if you are truly believers." (Q 5:23) That is: Two pious God-fearing men- who had been blessed by Allah with the blessing of faith and who trusted Allah and relied on Him- said to their people who refrained from entering the Holy Land: 'Our people! Those powerful giants have immense bodies without hearts, so do not fear them. Surprise them with your swords through the gate of their city and prevent them from regrouping in the desert to deny them the ability to fight. If you do that, you will overcome them.'

Describing these two men in such a fashion reflects that those who opposed them were not from among the God-fearing people who were blessed faith and assurance.

Al- Zamakhshari said: "If you ask 'How did they know that they would be victorious?' I would respond, saying: 'Moses informed them that they would. Also, the Almighty said:

'Allah has destined for you to enter.' Another reason is what they had been able to gather concerning Allah's constant support to ascertain the triumph of His messengers, what they had learned about Allah's support for Moses to vanquish his enemies and what they knew about the condition of those immensely powerful people." [98]

The Almighty's: "'Put your trust in Allah if you are truly believers'" (Q 5:23) was an invitation from the two God-fearing men to their people to trust their Creator and muster the resolve to enter through the gate to surprise their enemies if they were true believers and trust His promises. It is in the nature of the true believer to proceed and embark on doing something relying on, and trusting Allah. This is a basic principle in faith.

However, this advice was not well received by the Children of Israel. It fell on impervious unreceptive hearts and deaf ears. They were rebellious and disobedient. They reiterated their obdurate objection and adamant reluctance to enter the Holy Land. They said to their prophet: "O Moses! Still we will never enter as long as they remain there." (Q 5:22) That is, they did not heed the advice of the two men. They even declared their rebelliousness and objection: 'Moses! We will never enter- let alone invade- this land that you promised us at any time or under any condition as long as those people- whom we cannot fight- remain there.

To this declaration that betrayed their cowardice and fearfulness, they manifested a supercilious attitude, arrogant and brazen behavior and insolence and audacity towards their prophet. They said to him: "Go—both you and your Lord—and fight; we are staying right here!" (Q 5:24) That is: 'If you really care about this city, you and your Lord can go to fight and drive out its powerful inhabitants for we do not have a Lord if his Lordship will coat us this great price. We will be saying here for we do not really need any glory that would come by fighting the powerful people there. We do not need it.'

Saying this betrays their insolence and disrespect for their Lord and their carelessness and heedlessness in talking with their prophet. They said that mockingly taking Allah's commandments- that they received through His prophet- lightly and frivolously.

That is the case with the cowards and spineless. They become insolent and disrespectful. Cowardice and insolence are two sides of the same coin.

Now that Moses had become completely assured of the cowardice of the Children of Israel, utterly confident that they were adamant in their reluctance not to fight, and having heard various inappropriate responses from them, he turned to his Allah and pleadingly: "My Lord! I have no control over anyone except myself and my brother. So set us apart from the rebellious people." (Q 5:25) In other words, Moses complained and poured his grieving heart before Allah apologizing for the rebelliousness of his people. He said: 'Lord! You know that I can not force anyone to obey you, except for my brother and I.' He did not even mention the two Allah-fearing men that prompted their people before to "Surprise them through the gate" (Q 5:23) because he did not thoroughly trust that they would enter the land of those powerful people with him and fight alongside with him if others abandoned him. That was because some men may be willing to fight when there is a great number of fighters by their side, but they may withdraw and become unwilling to do so when they see fewer fighters. Therefore, he did not feel as comfortable to mention these two men like he felt concerning his brother and himself.

He did state that he had control over his brother, Aaron, just as he had control over himself. That was because his brother supported him with all his might throughout his resistance and struggle against the injustice of the pharaoh. Aaron stood by his side with all his might and will, and in every situation. He was also confident that Aaron was overshadowed with the spirit of the Almighty Allah.

Al- Zamakhshari said: "If you say 'Weren't the two men mentioned with him?' I would respond, saying: 'He wasn't completely confident of their position. He was not sure how steadfast they would have been because of what he had experienced firsthand at the hands of his people: their fickleness and their hardened cruel hearts. So, he only mentioned the infallible prophet, Aaron." [99]

The Almighty's saying: "So set us apart from the rebellious people" (Q 5:25) stated what Moses wished from his Allah after the Children of Israel disobeyed him. It meant: 'You are the Judge between us and those who disobeyed You. Give us and them according to what each deserves." That was a plea from Moses to Allah to punish them.

Allah responded to Moses's plea: He caused them to "visibly" go astray in the world just as they "inwardly" went astray from the paths of guidance. His decisive judgment was: "Then this land is forbidden to them for forty years, during which they will wander [100] through the land. So do not grieve for the rebellious people." (Q 5:26) That is, in response to Moses's plea, the Almighty said to Moses: 'Moses! This land is forbidden for them. They will not be able to enter it for forty years. During this time, they will wander helpless, lost and confused in the desert. They will not find their way. Do not grieve for them because of Our punishment. It was the result of their disobedience and refusal to obey Our commandments and their cowardice to fight.'

Thus, even though they were at the threshold of the Promised Land, their inappropriate actions led them to their wandering to toughen up by receiving whatever discipline they deserved and to learn that to be victorious, they had to pay a price.

Ibn Jarir said: "If someone said: 'How could he say 'which Allah has destined for you to enter' while you knew that they didn't enter it from His saying 'this land is forbidden to them?' How could it be that it was documented in the preserved tablet that it was a dwelling place for them, yet they were not allowed and were forbidden to enter it?' It could be argued that it was destined for them as a land and a dwelling place, and they did dwell there and it became theirs, as Allah said. It was Moses who said: 'Enter the Holy Land which Allah has destined for you to enter' (Q 5:21) by which he meant Allah destined to the Children of Israel, and those whom Moses ordered to enter it were from the Children of Israel." [101]

It is appropriate here to discuss the following issues:

First: The Jews' claims that the Holy Land- Palestine- is theirs based on the Almighty's saying: "Enter the Holy Land which Allah has destined for you to enter."

Second: The lessons that could be learned from these directives and advice.

To respond to the first point, we say: Interpreters have certain views concerning what was meant by "Allah has destined for you to enter." These are two well-known views:

The first: the meaning of 'Allah has destined' is He commanded you to enter it just as He commanded you to pray and give alms. So, the writing here is similar to His saying 'Establish prayer.' In other words, it is something of a duty imposed upon you. This is what Qatada and Al-Suddi believe.

The second: the meaning of 'Allah has destined' is that He decided to allocate this land as dwelling places for you, not the enormously powerful men, provided that you are faithful, obedient to the prophets, and ready to fight for what is right and just. If not- and, in fact, they were not- you will not be have this land. For this reason, after their prophet encouraged them by saying that the land was destined for them, he warned them against disobedience, cowardice and rebelliousness. He said: "Do not turn back or else you will become losers." (Q 5:21) Which means, "Do not disobey my commandments and resist from fighting or you will be losers, and you will be denied the land that Allah destined for you. Al-Alusi said: "Loss and disappointment as a result of turning back indicate the conditions stipulated in the Books concerning fighting as a necessary consequence of a firm steadfast faith." [102]

Ibn Abbas said: "It was a gift to them from Allah which He forbad because of their mutiny and rebelliousness." [103]

Fakhr al-Din al-Razi said: "The promise in His saying 'Allah has destined' was with the stipulation of obedience, so when the condition was not satisfied, the promise was denied." [104]

Regardless of the two views, the noble verse eloquently depicts the cowardice and timidity that the Children of Israel displayed. Their prophet displayed to them the most powerful incentives to encourage them to enter the Holy Land. As mentioned in the Qur'an, he said: "O my people! Enter the Holy Land which Allah has destined for you to enter." (Q 5:21) Then, he warned them against the adverse and unfavorable consequences if they opposed his order. He said: "And do not turn back or else you will become losers." (Q 5:21) Yet, despite all his encouragement to enter it and his intimidations and warnings against opposition and hesitancy, the Children of Israel turned back as losers; their mortified humiliated spirits would not let them move one step forward towards the land their prophet ordered them to enter. Moreover, to their cowardice and faintheartedness, they added their obdurate and adamant disobedience and rebelliousness. They said to their guide and prophet: "O Moses! There is an enormously powerful people there, so we will never be able to enter it until they leave. If they do, then we will enter!" (Q 5:22)

Then, the Qur'an reported that two righteous men stood by Moses and advised the Children of Israel to comply with his order. They also encouraged them to enter that land, saying: "Surprise them through the gate. If you do, you will certainly prevail. Put your trust in Allah if you are truly believers." (Q 5:23) Yet all of these advice and directives availed nothing. Instead, they received them with more stubbornness and rebelliousness. They obdurately confirmed that they would not enter the Holy Land as long as those powerful people were there, because entering this land entailed fighting and necessitated Jihad, and they were nor ready to do that. What they were ready to do was to usurp what their sick hearts desired, without labor or toil.

The Noble Qur'an portrayed the inconceivable fear that overwhelmed their hearts and their insolence and impudence towards their prophet: "O Moses! Still we will never enter as long as they remain there. So go—both you and your Lord—and fight; we are staying right here." (Q 5:24)

It was because of the persistence of the Children of Israel on their cowardice and rebelliousness that Allah punished them by forbidding them from entering it and to make them wander in the land. The Almighty said: "Then this land is forbidden to them for forty years, during which they will wander through the land. So do not grieve for the rebellious people." (Q 5:26)

Thus, we see that the Almighty's "Allah has destined for you" (Q 5:21) depicts the fainthearted, spineless and pathetic nature of the Children of Israel and how they had continued to disobey their prophet and refused to enter the Holy Land despite all the encouragements he promised and the punishments with which he threatened them.

In brief, the writing in the Almighty's "Allah has destined for you" can either be Obligatory ruling (writing), which meant they had to do it and they were obliged to enter it fighting and obeying their prophet,

Or, a Predestined ruling, which would mean that Allah ruled and destined that the land was theirs. In that case, there were conditions of belief, obedience and the obligation to fight and obey their prophet. However, that condition was not met. The Children of Israel didn't fulfil that condition. Rather, what they did was displaying disbelief to Allah and disobedience to their prophet. They were too cowardly and gutless to fight in the name of Allah. Even after Allah showed them His clemency and mercy and said to them: "Enter this city and eat freely from wherever you please; enter the gate with humility, saying, 'Absolve us.' We will forgive your sins and multiply the reward for the good-doers," they did not receive this wonderful favor with obedience and thanksgiving. Instead, they were ungrateful and ungrateful; consequently, Allah brought down upon them a humiliating punishment from heaven.

Therefore, we see that the Jews' claim that the Holy Land is theirs because of the Almighty's "Allah has destined for you" is baseless, groundless and unjustified.

The second issue which relates to their punishment to wander in the land for forty years is attributed to Allah's wisdom to make His penalty appropriate with the sins and transgressions they had committed. The Children of Israel had long been accustomed to humiliation and enslavement at the hands of pharaoh and his people. They therefore did not attach great value to freedom. They didn't appreciate it, their sense of pride waned and their inherent sense of human dignity ceased to exist. An easy comfortable life in humiliation, slavery and servitude was far better than dignity, self-esteem and pride in a life filled with fighting and jihad. Therefore, when their prophet called upon them to enter the Holy Land to lead a decent reputable life, they came up with all kinds of excuses, and they adamantly asserted that they would never approach that land as long as those powerful people were there.

It was therefore Allah's infinite wisdom to forbid them from entering this land because of their cowardice and rebelliousness. He condemned them to wander lost, confused and aimless until another generation- one that appreciated freedom and held it dearly- descended from them.

In his Introduction, Ibn Khaldun said: "From the context of this verse (Q 5:26) [105] it seems that the wisdom behind this punishment by wandering was deliberate and purposeful. It was meant to eliminate that generation that was brought up in humiliation, subjugation and disgrace and became so accustomed to these, in order to pave the way for a new generation to form during these 40 years in the wilderness, a generation that did not know suppression and enslavement, one that would not accept disgrace and humiliation like the previous generation. Thus, a new 'asabiyya (tribal solidarity)- which enabled them to pursue and overcome- replaced the old one. Thus, it appears that those 40 years were almost sufficient to eradicate one generation and replace it with another. Praise be to Allah the All-Knowledgeable." [106]

The author of Al-Manar tersely explained the wisdom behind this punishment, and we see it appropriate to mention here. In his conclusion to his interpretation of these honorable verses, he said: "The nations that are brought up in the cradle of oppression and get used to injustice, tyranny and oppression suffer moral humiliation, become week and corrupt, lose their strength and vigor and are stricken with disgrace and dishonor. They become comfortable with submissiveness and content with their timidity and subjugation. As time elapses with these nations in such conditions, these characteristics become as though genetically acquired and inherited. They become like natural instincts and intrinsic innate propensities. People in nations such as these become so caught up in these characteristics that they naturally feel drawn to them regardless of other forces that might play a role in freeing them from their tyranny. This is the nature of human beings in all they do or aspire to accomplish, good or bad, belief or disbelief."
The Prophet gave an example of the guidance he was bringing and the misguidance of those who were deeply overcome by their disbelief. He said: "My example is like that of a man who lit a fire. When it illuminated what was around him, moths and other insects that fall into the fire began to fall into it. He tried to hold them back, but they overcame him and rushed in. He said: 'That is my example and yours. I hold you back from the fire, 'Come out of the fire,' but you overcame me and rushed in."

The tyranny and injustices of the pharaohs corrupted the nature of the Children of Israel in Egypt. Consequently, their nature became stamped and tarnished with disgrace and humiliation. Allah showed them what no others had seen. He gave them signs of His Oneness and His abilities, His omnipotence. He demonstrated the truthfulness of His messenger, Moses, and He showed them how he took them out of the land of Egypt- to rescue them from slavery, torture and humiliation- to bring them to freedom, independence, affluence and happiness. Despite all of this, however, they would still revolt against Moses whenever they were hungry or when they were asked to do something that required labor and hard work. At such moments as these, they would feel nostalgic and long for Egypt. When Moses was away meeting his Allah, they made a golden calf out of their jewelry, and they worshipped it. Allah knew that they would not enter the land of the immensely powerful people because of their faint-heartedness and timidity. Hos pledge to their forefathers would only be fulfilled according to His Will and way of forming human nature. Thus, it was necessary that that generation that was brought up in slavery and idolatry was to perish, and another new generation would come after it, one equipped with the audacity of freedom and hope, the justice of the Law, and the discernment of the Divine signs. Allah would never annihilate any people until He had shown them His reasons for doing so. He was never unjust to others; they are the ones who wronged themselves.

It is according to this just and fair reasoning that Allah ordered the Children of Israel to enter the Holy Land after He had shown them miracles indicating His support to His messenger to them. Yet they were conceited and they rejected Allah's commandment. He therefore punished them and brought forth another generation capable of becoming the heirs through hard work that was consistent with Allah's Law that was revealed to them. That was a statement for the mutiny and rebelliousness they showed to Moses after he brought them clear and irrefutable evidence. It was also a revelation of Allah's wisdom behind forbidding that generation from entering the Holy Land. We should therefore take note of these examples that Allah manifested for us. We should learn that fixing a nation after it has been corrupted by injustice and oppression could only be possible by creating a new generation that is capable of combining the true free spirit of Bedouins with its pride and independence and the knowledge and application of the Law and virtues. In olden times, these were affected through the prophets. Now, after sealing the prophecy, heirs of those prophets- who combine Allah's law, discernment, and loyalty with a faithful inclination to straighten things, with a conviction that superseds all other desires and lusts- take upon themselves the duty of fixing nations." [107]

To respond to the third issue related to the lessons that can be drawn and learned from these directives, we can say that these noble verses comprised a unique style in calling others to Allah. They started with reminding the Children of Israel with their glories and the great blessings and amazing favors that Allah granted them to instill in them a feeling of pride and importance and to encourage them to respond favorably to what the Almighty had ordered them to do.

The verses also included warnings against cowardice, opposition and turning back as those would result in their loss during their life and after their death. Above all, the verses (Q 5:20-26) faithfully depicted and closely portrayed the true nature of the Children of Israel. They revealed- with clarity- their lack of will power, their faintheartedness, their cowardice, their inability to make good choices, their mutinous attitude towards their prophets, their reluctance to fight for the sake of Allah, and their arrogance in addressing their messengers. All of this made them deserving of severe and humiliating punishments.

That was bound to regale the Prophet for all the harms they had caused him. He warned them not to follow in the crooked footsteps of their forefathers or adopt their immoral and despicable ways in order to avoid the punishments that fell upon them.

Imam Ibn Kathir said: "This story included rebuking the Jews, uncovering their vices, opposing Allah and His messenger and refusing to obey him when he called upon them to fight. They were unwilling to face the enemies and fight them even though they had with them Allah's messenger, the one who spoke to Him, a favored among His creation at that time, who promised them with victory over their enemies. All of this, in addition to the torture, defeat and drowning that they witnessed engulfing the Pharoah and his men. Then, they refuse to fight some men who were almost 1/10th of the population of Egypt. Their vices and depravities were thus made known to all, both publicly and privately. Neither the pitch darkness of the night nor oblivion would be capable of covering their disgraceful scandals." Then, he said, "Where are they in comparison with what the companions said to their Messenger on the day of the Battle of Badr when he consulted them concerning fighting Quraysh? The said, 'O Messenger of Allah! If you were to cross this wide sea, we would all cross it with you, not a single man would desist. Do not worry about us meeting our enemies tomorrow. We will be patient and persist. May Allah show you what will be pleasing to your eyes. So, let us proceed and fight. Allah's blessings will be upon us'" [108]

From this story, we also learn that rebelliousness against Allah and His messengers would only lead to loss in this world and in the Afterlife, for when the Children of Israel were fearful of entering the Holy Land and disobeyed the commandment of Moses, their prophet, Allah punished them by wandering aimlessly in the desert for forty years.

Thus far, we have mentioned some of the noble verses that documented the Jews' voracious desire to cling to life, their cowardice to fight, their rejection of sound counsels, and their refusal to comply with their prophet's command. This led to undesirable consequences in this life and in the Hereafter.

Eighth: <u>Demanding that Moses, their prophet, make them a Allah like others.</u>

The Children of Israel lived in Egypt for a long time. During that time, they suffered greatly. They also became used to the paganism of the ancient Egyptians and their idol-worshipping, and they followed them just as the defeated follow those who conquer them and as followers submit and follow their leaders. The Almighty wanted to rescue and liberate them from their ignorance, disgrace and humiliation. He sent His Prophet, Moses, to invite pharaoh and his people to worship the Lord of the World. However, pharaoh was tyrannical, domineering and oppressive. He rejected both the signs and the warnings that Moses manifested. Finally, he drowned along with his men in the sea in front of the eyes of the Children of Israel who marched with their Prophet, Moses, leaving the land of Egypt and heading towards the Levant. No sooner had the Children of Israel crossed the sea in which pharaoh and his men drowned in front of their eyes- (while the wet sand was still clinging to the heels of their shoes)- than they caught sight of a group of people worshipping idols. Their deeply-ingrained paganistic nature overtook them, and they longed to do what those idol worshippers were doing. They asked their prophet and rescuer from the paganism and tyranny of pharaoh to make them a god similar to those gods that they saw the other people worship. Moses became furious and vehemently denounced their unawareness, their ignorance and their unthinkable and corrupt attitude. He showed them that what those people were doing was short-lived and doomed to destruction. He condemned and criticized them for desiring a god other than the All-Mighty One Who favored and honored them above all others at that time, the One Who granted them amazing favors and rescued them from the torture and suffering at the hands of pharaoh and his people. The Children of Israel pretended to be convinced with what their Prophet told them. However, their corrupt nature never left them; they worshipped the calf when Moses was away, as we will detail shortly.

The Noble Qur'an eloquently portrayed that situation in which they asked their Prophet to make them a Allah- an idol- similar to the ones that other people had. In Sura Al-A'raf, the Almighty said: "We brought the Children of Israel across the sea and they came upon a people devoted to idols. They demanded, "O Moses! Make for us a Allah like their Gods." He replied, "Indeed, you are a people acting ignorantly! What they follow is certainly doomed to destruction and their deeds are in vain." He added, "Shall I seek for you a Allah other than Allah, while He has honored you above the others?" And ⌜remember⌝ when We rescued you from the people of Pharaoh, who afflicted you with dreadful torment—killing your sons and keeping your women. That was a severe test from your Lord." (Qur'an 7:138-141) [109]

These-and the following- noble verses recount the story of Moses with his people, the Children of Israel, after the previous verses recounted his story with Pharaoh which ended in the destruction of Pharaoh and his people. The meaning of these verses is: "We brought the Children of Israel across the sea" with Our protection and ability. Then, they came upon a people who were worshipping idols. Their hearts yearned for paganism once again, and they said to their Prophet: "O Moses! Make for us a Allah like their Gods." Their Prophet rebuked them, saying, "Indeed, you are a people acting ignorantly!" That is, they did not have the awareness of the greatness and splendor of His Lordship, for the worshippers of those idols would be destroyed, and all that they did- by worshipping other than the One All-Powerful Omnipotent Allah- would be eradicated. He then chastised them even further, saying, "Shall I seek for you a Allah other than Allah, while He has honored you above the others?" That is to say, 'Allah had granted you favors that no other peoples in the world were granted. It was your duty to be thankful and appreciate these favors. It was your duty to remember with thanksgiving when He rescued you from the people of Pharoah who "afflicted you with dreadful torment—killing your sons and keeping your women." That torment and your rescue from it "was a severe test from your Lord."

The Almighty's saying: "We brought the Children of Israel across the sea" (Q 7:138) was a statement that depicted the great favor that Allah granted the Children of Israel, namely, crossing the sea after Moses stretched his hand with his staff over the sea, and the waters were divided and the sea became dry land for them to walk safely until they crossed it, in the company and protection of the Almighty Allah.

The Almighty's "they came upon a people devoted to idols" (Q 7:138) depicts the conditions of some polytheists they witnessed after they crossed the sea and were saved from their enemies. What was the result of witnessing that? They were expected to despise what they witnessed and show aversion to what they saw. After all, it was only a short time ago when they were afflicted with dreadful torment at the hands of the idol-worshippers, Pharaoh and his people. Also, they were rescued from their humiliation and disgrace at the hands of their Prophet, Moses, who called them to worship the One Almighty Allah Who would grant them even more favors.

However, the crooked serpentine nature of the Children of Israel was indeed deeply ingrained and would not depart from them. There they were: no sooner had their eyes caught sight of a people worshipping idols [110] than they found themselves irresistibly drawn to those idols. They asked their Prophet who saved them from their misery with the light of monotheism to make them an idol like the other people so they would worship it. The Qur'an recounted that when they saw that sight, they demanded, saying, "O Moses! Make for us a god like their gods." (Q 7:138) They said that because their faith was shaky and did not take root in their hearts. They were also under the sway of paganism because they grew so accustomed to idol worshipping during their subjugation in Pharoah's Egypt. Like physical diseases that affect the body, idol worshipping dominated both their souls and minds. That is the nature of the Children of Israel: as soon as they find the straight path, they depart from it and go astray; they soon decline, deteriorate and go speedily down the minute they ascend and rise; they may find the righteous path but they quickly relapse, regress and revert.

Using the imperative form in addressing their Prophet in "Make for us a god like their gods" (Q 7:138) was an undeniable proof for their arrogance and stupidity. Had they properly and decently asked him to make them an idol to worship, they would not have looked so strange. What happened was that they demanded from him- their Prophet, who had called them to monotheism and saved from their tyrannical and vicious enemy- to cast an idol for them himself.

Moses- by nature passionate and jealous in matters related to his Lord and faith- was upset because of their request. He responded in a disapproving and reproachful manner, surprised as he was, at what they said after having witnessed all the miracles they had seen. Rebuking them, he said: "Indeed, you are a people acting ignorantly." (Q 7:138) In other words, 'You, Children of Israel, by demanding this had proven that your ignorance had eclipsed your hearts and clouded your minds. You became unable to distinguish between the ostensible misguidance of these people and the honor, exaltation and grandeur of Divinity. If such ignorance and unawareness were to be recorded, it would only demonstrate the inconceivable and unimaginable ignorance that encompassed your lack of discernment and knowledge, your degraded perception and waning acuity, your corrupt and perverted reason, and your inability to calculate properly and evaluate things rationally.'

Having uncovered their ignorance and the travesty of what they were seeking and the dreadful consequences of those people whom they wanted to imitate, he explained to them in a style that comprised reasoning and justification, saying, "What they follow is certainly doomed to destruction and their deeds are in vain." (Q 7:139) In other words, Moses said, "Those people whom you want to imitate in their idol-worshipping are doomed to destruction. All that they do is destined to annihilation and obliteration because Monotheism will prevail in these lands and worshipping would be due to the One All-Powerful Omnipotent Allah."

Moses's response revealed their reprehensible desire and indicated that what they were seeking would only end in destruction and annihilation.

Imam Al-Razi said: "What is meant by 'their deeds are in vain' (Q 7:139) is that it would avail them nothing. Nothing good would come out of it. What is meant by true worshipping is that this act of worshipping would become continuous and entrenched in one's heart to the extent that the worshipper becomes happy and fulfilled by the remembrance of Allah and acquiring His knowledge. However, man may become preoccupied worshipping other than Allah and would thus become diverted from His remembrance. When that is the case, worshipping other than Allah becomes useless, worthless and unprofitable, as we have shown that what is truly meant by worshipping is that a firm confirmation of Allah's knowledge is firmly planted in the heart. Being preoccupied with worshipping other than Allah would remove His knowledge from the heart, and that would be the opposite of what is desired, and contrary to what should be sought. Allah knows!" [111]

Then Moses continued to denounce what they were seeking. He showed them that only Allah was worthy of worship and adoration. He said, "Shall I seek for you a god other than Allah, while He has honored you above the others?" (Q 7:140)

That is, Moses, peace be upon him, reminded his people with Allah's favors upon them, favors that should have driven them to worship and submit to Him Alone. He said, "Shall I seek another Allah other than Allah for you to worship? Another Allah other than Allah Who honored you above all the others? It was incumbent upon you to specifically worship Him Alone as He granted you, specifically, His various magnificent favors." The interrogative style in the noble verse betrays denunciation coupled with amazement at their seeking other than Allah Who blessed them with numerous favors and surrounded them with endless protection.

Then, he reminded them with Allah's favor when He rescued them from dreadful torment that was a test for them: would they be grateful and thankful, or would they rebel and disbelieve? The Almighty said: "We rescued you from the people of Pharaoh, who afflicted you with dreadful torment—killing your sons and keeping your women. That was a severe test from your Lord." (Q 7:141)

The Children of Israel should have profoundly appreciated that great favor as it involved a test for torment and suffering as well as one for rescue and salvation. Allah wanted to see how they would respond!

Thus, these noble verses most eloquently responded to what The Children of Israel sought and desired. They described them as ill-informed irrational, foolish and imprudent people. The verses started by depicting their ignorance of their God and their very nature as they demanded that their Prophet make them a Allah similar to the ones that other people were worshipping. Then, the verses continued to display that their request was unsound and corrupt, as it would only end in destruction and annihilation and, for this, such a request was both invalid and unsuitable to serve them with wealth Allah. Then, the verses displayed that true worship could only be to Allah Alone, the Omnipotent, the Creator and the One Who has the power to allow and prohibit. At the end, these verses reminded them with the favors that they were lavishly granted to alert them that what they had demanded from their Prophet amounted to meeting goodness and benevolence with denial and ungratefulness, to prompt them to reconsider their position, and to repent and offer true penitence to their Creator if they were truly people who could benefit from counsels and advice.

Ninth: Worshipping the calf instead of Allah:

Among the vices that reflect the ignorance of the Children of Israel, their crooked and twisted nature, their corrupt unsound mentality, their lack of vision and discernment and their reluctance to mend their ways was taking the calf-instead of Allah- as a Allah to worship and becoming wholeheartedly devoted to worshipping it.

The Noble Qur'an ridiculed the Children of Israel for this vice that their souls craved. It showed them its vanity and irrelevance in many of its verses.

Yet, before we start interpreting the verses that mentioned the worshipping of the Children of Israel of the calf and their indulgence in committing this dreadful vice, we believe it would be appropriate here to mention- in addition- a brief historical background related to the Children of Israel's worship of the calf.

After the Almighty drowned Pharaoh and his men in front of the eyes of the Children of Israel and saved them from his tyranny, their Prophet marched with them towards the Levant. The Almighty Allah wanted to honor them with His guidance, so He pledged to give Moses the Torah after forty days of fasting. Moses left his brother, Aaron, behind him during his absence. He asked Aaron, saying, "Take my place among my people, do what is right, and do not follow the way of the corruptors." (Q 7:142)

However, when Moses departed to get the Torah- which contained guidance and light for the Children of Israel- they took advantage of Aaron's leniency and flexibility and worshipped an idol of a calf that made a lowing sound which a Samiri molded out of their women's jewelry that they borrowed from the Copts of Egypt (i.e., the indigenous pre-Islamic Egyptians, obviously before Christianity, and the modern Coptic Christians). Aaron tried many ways to persuade them not to do that, but they opposed him, saying, "We will not cease to worship it until Moses returns to us." (Q 20:91) When he reiterated his advice to them, they attacked and almost killed him. Allah informed Moses that his people were lured by the Samiri to worship the calf. Moses returned to them, sorrowful and enraged. He most severely rebuked them and warned of the dreadful consequences of their action. They apologized and told Moses that they were seduced by the Samiri.

Moses thought that his brother, Aaron, was not strict and disobeyed his orders, so he admonished him harshly. Aaron, however, told Moses that he saved no effort in advising and guiding them, but they were people who did not appreciate good counsel.

Then Moses rebuked and admonished the Samiri, the chief plotter and culprit. After listening to what he had to say, Moses told him: "Go away then! And for the rest of your life you will surely be crying, 'Do not touch me!" Then you will certainly have a fate that you cannot escape. Now look at your Allah to which you have been devoted: we will burn it up, then scatter it in the sea completely." (Q 20:97) And all the Children of Israel witnessed when Moses fulfilled his pledge and burned the calf, scattered its dust in the sea and proved to everyone that it is Allah Alone Who is worthy of worship: "Your only god is Allah, there is no god worthy of worship except Him. He encompasses everything in His knowledge." (Q 20:98) Allah then revealed to Moses that the repentance of the calf-worshippers among his people would only be acceptable if they killed themselves. When they did, Allah forgave them. May be thankful.

This is a brief historical summary for the story of the Children of Israel taking the calf for a god to worship. Now, we will proceed to interpret the noble verses that mention this story. This is the first section:

A- In Sura Al-A'raf, the Almighty said: "In the absence of Moses, his people made from their golden jewelry an idol of a calf that made a lowing sound. Did they not see that it could neither speak to them nor guide them to the Right Path? Still, they took it as a god and were wrongdoers. Later, when they were filled with remorse and realized they had gone astray, they cried, "If our Lord does not have mercy on us and forgive us, we will certainly be losers." When Moses returned to his people, totally furious and sorrowful, he said, "What an evil thing you committed in my absence! Did you want to hasten your Lord's torment?" Then he threw down the Tablets and grabbed his brother by the hair, dragging him

> closer. Aaron pleaded, "O son of my mother! The people overpowered me and were about to kill me. So do not humiliate me and make my enemies rejoice, nor count me among the wrongdoing people." Moses prayed, "My Lord! Forgive me and my brother! And admit us into Your mercy. You are the Most Merciful of the merciful." Those who worshipped the calf will certainly be afflicted with wrath from their Lord as well as disgrace in the life of this world. This is how We reward those who invent falsehood. But those who commit evil, then repent and become true believers, your Lord will certainly be All-Forgiving, Most-Merciful." (Q 7:148-153)

The Almighty's "In the absence of Moses, his people made from their golden jewelry an idol of a calf that made a lowing sound" (Q 7:148) was a statement of what the Children of Israel did during Moses's absence when he went to receive the Torah from his Lord and left Aaron behind to lead them.

The jewelry الحُلِي [112]- a noun that refers to the gold and silver that are used for adorning purposes- was the jewelry that the women from among the Children of Israel borrowed from Egyptian women before their exodus from Egypt. When Allah drowned Pharaoh and his men, the women still had the jewelry in their possession. The Samiri gathered the jewelry from them claiming that it was not their legitimate possession. He cast them a calf with lowing sound and alleged that it was their god and the God of Moses. The Children of Israel worshipped it, instead of Allah.

Al-Hafiz Ibn Kathir said: "Interpreters differed among themselves on whether that calf transformed into one with flesh and blood and a lowing sound, or it remained as gold and air entered it so it made the sound of cow as it entered and exited! Allah knows!" [113]

The meaning is: During Moses's absence to receive the Torah, his people took a calf that with a lowing sound- like the cow's- as a god to worship.

Al-Zamakhshari said: "If you said: 'why was it said that Moses's people took their jewelry and made a calf out of it, while it was the Samiri who took it?' I would say: 'There are two sides to this. One to attribute the action to them as it is the case when the one who says something is the same as the doer of that thing. They also wanted- and all consented- to take the calf as a Allah. Second, it means they took it as a Allah and worshipped it. If you say: 'Why their jewelry while it was not theirs but was ostensibly obvious in their hands?' I would say 'They possessed the jewelry after those who perished just as they became owners of other properties. Consider His saying: 'So We lured the tyrants out of their gardens, springs, treasures, and splendid residences. So, it was. And We awarded it all to the Children of Israel." (Q 26:57-59)

The Almighty's "Did they not see that it could neither speak to them nor guide them to the Right Path?" (Q 7:148) was a strong rebuke for their ignorance and the corruption of their minds. The meaning is:

Those unable to discern and perceive were unaware that when they started to worship the calf, it was unable to do what humans could do. It could not talk or guide others to a straightforward righteous path. This is not the case with their Lord to Whom true worship is due. Among His characteristics are His directives to His prophets and messengers to what is good, beneficial and profitable for His creation and advising them against evil and wicked ways.

Then, the Almighty reinforced His admonition, saying, "Still, they took it as a god and were wrongdoers." (Q 7:148) In other words, they took the calf as a Allah to worship even though they could see that he was unable to speak to them or guide them to any path. By doing this, they were undoubtedly unjust to themselves for worshipping something other than the Almighty Allah and for their upsetting of values and proper measures.

Using كانوا to express their wrongdoing indicated the continuous nature of this injustice and wrongdoing and pointed to the fact that it was their habit even before they took the calf for a Allah. What they did was not novel or new for they had previously demanded from their Prophet as soon as they came upon a people devoted to worshipping idols, saying, """O Moses! Make for us a god like their Gods." He replied, "Indeed, you are a people acting ignorantly!" (Q 7:138)

The Almighty then revealed what they did when they perceived their misguidance. He said, "Later, when they were filled with remorse and realized they had gone astray, they cried, "If our Lord does not have mercy on us and forgive us, we will certainly be losers." (Q 7:149) That is, when they became remorseful for worshipping the calf and realized their errors and misguidance as if they had seen it with their eyes, they ruefully said: 'if Allah would not forgive and have mercy upon us, we would be losers.' In other words, they would be among those who would certainly be doomed to destruction.

Their remorse took place after Moses returned from his appointment with his Lord with the Torah. As evidence for this, when Aaron advised them to abandon worshipping the calf, they said: "We will not cease to worship it until Moses returns to us." (Q 20:91) Also, when Moses returned, he denounced and rebuked them for what they were doing. That was also evidence that they were persisting in worshipping the calf until Moses returned and enlightened them concerning their brazen wrongdoing and flagrant misguidance.

That is why, on interpreting the Almighty's "Later, when they were filled with remorse," (Q 7:149) Ibn Jarir said, "Those who worshipped the calf became remorseful when Moses came back and the surrendered to his judgement. Concerning those who feel remorseful for something they were unable to do, the Arabs use the expression 'he fell in his hands.' It is driven from الاستئسار (= capturing) in the sense of a man aiming a powerful blow to hit another man making him fall to the ground and can thereby capture him. So, the one on the ground is literally in the hands of his captor. That is why, he who is unable to do something or regrets what he was unable to do is said to have fallen into the other's hand." [114]

The Almighty expressed their intense sorrow by saying: "Later, when they were filled with remorse," (literally meaning when their mouths fell in their hands) because it is often the case of those who feel intense remorse to bite their hand in sorrow. Thus, the words were meant to indicate that their mouths fell in their hands, to specify the severity of their remorse.

The author of Taj Al-'Arus said: "In (Al-'Abab) which was not heard of before the Qur'an nor did the Arabs know of it, the meaning is: Something coming down from top to bottom and falling to the ground. Then the meaning widened to encompass سُقِطَ (=fall). Remorse takes place in the heart, but is reflected in what the hands do as in His saying: "And he remained clapping his hands with sorrow over what he had spent upon it." (Q 18:42) [115]

The Almighty then showed what Moses did upon his return from meeting his Lord when he knew his people's wrongdoing and transgression. He said: "When Moses returned to his people, totally furious and sorrowful, he said, "What an evil thing you committed in my absence! Did you want to hasten your Lord's torment?" Then he threw down the Tablets and grabbed his brother by the hair, dragging him closer. Aaron pleaded, "O son of my mother! The people overpowered me and were about to kill me. So do not humiliate me and make my enemies rejoice, nor count me among the wrongdoing people." Moses prayed, "My Lord! Forgive me and my brother! And admit us into Your mercy. You are the Most Merciful of the merciful." (Q 7:150-151)

The Almighty's "When Moses returned to his people, totally furious and sorrowful" (Q 7:150) was a statement of Moses's condition when he returned from the mountain and saw the calf that his people worshipped. He was enraged to see them worship other that the Almighty Allah, and he was saddened that his people were tempted and fell to worshipping a calf with a lowing sound.

Imam Al-Razi said: "The word sorrowful has two sides. First, sorrow indicates extreme anger, as Abi Al-Darda' and Atta' according to Ibn Abbas. As evidence, they recite the Almighty's "So when they enraged Us, We inflicted punishment upon them." (Q 43:55) In other words, they made Us furious. Second, the sorrowful could be a reference to a saddened and dejected person, as Al-Hassan and Al-Suddi maintained. As evidence, the quote Aiysha's Hadith: "Abou Bakr is a sorrowful man, meaning sad." Al-Wahedi maintained that the two meanings are close because anger may be engendered by sadness and sadness could give rise to anger. If what you hate comes from someone of a lower status, you would be angry; if it comes from one of a higher status, you will be saddened. One of these conditions is called sadness or sorrow and the other is called anger…" [116]

Moses rebuked his people, saying, "What an evil thing you committed in my absence!" (Q 7:150) This means that it was evil what you did after I left you for my appointment with my Allah. It was a dreadful thing to worship the calf and your hearts were filled with its love. You did not heed my pledge with you to worship Allah Alone and walk in accordance with my law.

His "in my absence" was an allusion to what they had seen concerning truly worshipping Allah Alone and not associating partners with Him after all of Moses's encouragements to the Children of Israel to shun what they desired when their eyes caught sight of the idol-worshippers and said: "O Moses! Make for us a god like their Gods." (Q 7:138) The successors have an obligation to follow those left to lead during their absence and not disobey them.

The Almighty's "Did you want to hasten your Lord's torment?" (Q 7:150) meant: Did you want to rush and worship the calf before coming to you with the Torah after forty nights? It was said that the Children of Israel felt that Moses took a long time before coming down from the mountain. During that interval, the Samiri deceived them and made that golden calf. They worshipped it, they sang and danced around it saying 'That was the true god who saved us from injustices.'

Al-Zamakhshari said: "it is said 'عجل عن الامر = to hasten/cannot wait' is to leave something unfinished...The meaning is 'You could not wait for your Allah's command, namely, waiting for Moses, keeping his covenant, and complying with his commandments, and you came to the conclusion that the time had come and I was not coming back and you said to yourselves that I died, so you changed your mind just like nations do after the death of their prophets!" It was also said that the Samiri told them when he had molded the calf: "This is your god and the God of Moses. Moses will not return because he died." It was also recounted that they counted twenty days and nights, made them forty, and then did what they did. [117]

The Almighty showed that Moses' wrath resulted in two things that revealed the severity of his anger. First, He said: "he threw down the Tablets." (Q 7:150) That is, Moses threw the tablets from his hands because of the extreme amazement and intense anger he experienced upon seeing his people devoted to worshipping the calf. His anger was caused for his Allah, his intense love for his faith and a denunciation of what his people did when they were worshipping the epitome of stupidity and idiocy.

The second thing Moses did was that he "grabbed his brother by the hair, dragging him closer." (Q 7:150) That is, Moses grabbed his brother by the hair of his head and dragged him towards him in anger thinking that he was not strict with them and did not prevent them from worshipping the calf. Aaron, however, entreated his brother in the name of brotherhood to calm down to explain to him the nature of the situation and absolve himself from the charge of being negligent and nonchalant. He pleaded: "O son of my mother! The people overpowered me and were about to kill me. So do not humiliate me and make my enemies rejoice, nor count me among the wrongdoing people." (Q 7:150) In other words, Aaron used that gentle reminder "O son of my mother," to appeal to the clemency of brotherhood, so that Moses would not rush to blame and ridicule him. He told Moses 'I saved no effort in trying to prevent them from worshipping the calf and I showered them with advice and admonition, but they did not listen to me. They overpowered and almost killed me when I insisted that they desist from worshipping the calf. So, do not do to me what they wished to do and offend and belittle me. It is important and natural that the bond of brotherhood that binds us together be strong in the presence of gloating enemies. Do not count me among the wrongdoers. I am innocent of what they did, and I advised them numerous times, but they do not like or listen to those who counsel them.'

At this point, Moses was convinced of Aaron's innocence of his allegation of negligence. He prayed: "My Lord! Forgive me and my brother! And admit us into Your mercy. You are the Most Merciful of the merciful." (Q 7:151)

That is, to please his brother, exonerate him from whatever allegations he had attributed to him, and to show those gloating people that he had forgiven his brother- now that he became confident of his innocence- Moses implored his Lord to forgive him his rush to judging his brother and all that he said that wronged his brother. He also implored his Lord to forgive Aaron any hint of negligence that he could be responsible for, since the Lord is All-Knowledgeable. He pleaded his Lord they be admitted into His mercy, for the Lord is the Most Merciful of the merciful.

Thus, the Noble Qur'an cleared Aaron of negligence and proved that he was exposed to harm as he tried to dissuade the calf worshippers from that practice. This corrects what is recounted in the Torah in Exodus, Chapter 32, where it is mentioned that it was Aaron who made an idol cast in the shape of a calf for the Children of Israel to worship while Moses was absent.

Then the Noble Qur'an issued its decisive ruling concerning the idol-worshippers. The Almighty said: "Those who worshipped the calf will certainly be afflicted with wrath from their Lord as well as disgrace in the life of this world. This is how We reward those who invent falsehood." (Q 7:152)

The meaning of the above-mentioned verse is: Those who took the calf for a Allah to worship and persisted in their misguidance will be deserving their Allah's wrath and punishment. We will not accept their repentance unless they kill themselves. They will also be afflicted with disgrace and ignominy in this life. This is the reward of those invent lies and falsehoods, anytime and anywhere, for disobeying Us, overstepping and trespassing. This is a recurrent punishment- as long as wrongdoing keeps recurring- for the Children of Israel and others.

Then Allah opened the door to all those who sought true penitence. He said: "But those who commit evil, then repent and become ˹true˺ believers, your Lord will certainly be All-Forgiving, Most-Merciful." (Q 7:153)

The meaning is: Those who have done evil deeds then regretted what they did, became remorseful, offered a true penitence and returned to Allah apologetically and in contrition, Allah will forgive them all these errors and cover all their mistakes. He will never divulge them or remember them anymore. He will have mercy on them and all those who-like them- offer true and faithful penitence.

Thus far, after chastising and admonishing the Children of Israel for their wrongdoing, these noble verses opened the door of repentance to them and to others to wake up and follow the path unto righteousness and abandon all the delusions, misguidance and ignorance they indulged in.

B- The second part of the verses that detailed the calf-worshipping that the Children of Israel indulged in is found in Sura Taha (Sura 20). It contained their deception at the hands of the Samiri, Moses' return to them sorrowful and angry, their insincere apologies and excuses, the Samiri's admission of guilt, his punishment and what Moses did to the calf that they took for a Allah other than Allah. The following are what the Almighty said (Q 20:83-98):

"Allah asked, "Why have you come with such haste ahead of your people, O Moses?" He replied, "They are close on my tracks. And I have hastened to You, my Lord, so You will be pleased." Allah responded, "We have indeed tested your people in your absence, and the Sâmiri has led them astray." So, Moses returned to his people, furious and sorrowful. He said, "O my people! Had your Lord not made you a good promise?[1] Has my absence been too long for you? Or have you wished for wrath from your Lord to befall you, so you broke your promise to me?" They argued, "We did not break our promise to you of our own free will, but we were made to carry the burden of the people's golden jewelry, then we threw it into the fire, and so did the Sâmiri." Then he molded for them an idol of a calf that made a lowing sound. They said, "This is your Allah and the Allah of Moses, but Moses forgot where it was!" Did they not see that it did not respond to them, nor could it protect or benefit them? Aaron had already warned them beforehand, "O my people! You are only being tested by this, for indeed your ⌜one true⌝ Lord is the Most Compassionate. So, follow me and obey my orders." They replied, "We will not cease to worship it until Moses returns to us." Moses scolded his brother, "O Aaron! What prevented you, when you saw them going astray, from following after me? How could you disobey my orders?" Aaron pleaded, "O son of my mother! Do not seize me by my beard or ⌜the hair of⌝ my head. I really feared that you would say, 'You have caused division among the Children of Israel, and did not observe my word.'" Moses then asked, "What did you think you were doing, O Sâmiri?" He said, "I saw what they did not see, so I took a handful of dust from the hoof-prints of the horse of the messenger-angel Gabriel then cast it on the molded calf. This is what my lower-self tempted me into." Moses said, "Go away then! And for the rest of your life you will surely be crying, 'Do not touch me!' Then you will certainly have a fate that you cannot escape. Now look at your Allah to which you have been devoted: we will burn it up, then scatter it in the sea completely." ⌜Then Moses addressed his people, "Your only Allah is Allah, there is no Allah ⌜worthy of worship⌝ except Him. He encompasses everything in His knowledge."

The interpretation of the noble verses:

The Almighty's "Why have you come with such haste ahead of your people, O Moses?" (Q 20:83) He replied, "They are close on my tracks. And I have hastened to You, my Lord, so You will be pleased." (Q 20:84) Which means: 'Why did you come with such haste ahead of your people and leave them behind, Moses? The leader should be behind his people when traveling to be able to watch them.' Moses responded apologetically, saying, 'They are close by and will be able to catch up with me. I only hastened and was ahead of them to please You.'

The story behind this is as follows: When Moses marched with the Children of Israel to the Levant after the destruction of Pharaoh, Allah made a pledge to grant Moses the Torah after he had fasted for forty nights. When that time period elapsed, Moses rushed to the mountain to receive the Torah, leaving Aaron behind to lead his people. Moses chose seventy men from his people to accompany him. When he drew closer to the meeting place, he was overpowered by the desire to go to Allah, so he hastened and was ahead of them. That was why Allah asked: "Why have you come with such haste ahead of your people, O Moses?" He replied, "They are close on my tracks. And I have hastened to You, my Lord, so You will be pleased."

Al-Zamakhshari said: "If you said 'Why you have come with such haste' is a question about the reason for that rush. The answer that would have been probable to the question would be to say: 'to make You more pleased with me and because I am eager to hear You talk to me.' However, as you see, his response 'They are close on my tracks" is not applicable to the question! I would say, however, that the Almighty confronted Moses with two things: First, denouncing rushing per se and, second, enquiring about the reason the necessitated it. Therefore, it was Moses's duty to present his excuse for doing so and to provide a reason for what he was admonished for. So, he explained that he just advanced a short distance ahead of them. He then followed this excuse by responding to the question: "And I have hastened to You, my Lord, so You will be pleased." (Q 20:84) [118]

Then, The Almighty informed Moses of what happened to his people after he left them. He said: "We have indeed tested your people in your absence, and the Sâmiri has led them astray." (Q 20:85) That is, the Almighty said to Moses: 'We plighted your people with calf worshipping after you departed, and the Samiri led them astray by calling them to worship it. Misguided himself, he led others astray.' There was no doubt that such news greatly saddened Moses, because his people- whom he had liberated from humiliation and slavery to become a nation devoted to Allah Alone and perform their mission in life in the best possible way- had relapsed into paganism as soon as he was absent. The long humiliation that they experienced throughout their lives must have corrupted the inclination to goodness; it must have left in their nature the overpowering propensity to be quickly led to evil without thinking or reasoning.

The Almighty recounted Moses's condition after learning about the temptation to which they succumbed. He said: "So, Moses returned to his people, furious and sorrowful." (Q 20:86) He harshly rebuked and scolded his people, saying (Q 20:86), "O my people! Had your Lord not made you a good promise that you could not deny? He had promised to bring you the Torah that contains light and guidance. He had promised you to enter the Holy Land. He had promised you to destroy your enemy, and you witnessed that yourselves. He had promised you goodness in this life and in the Hereafter if you truly faithful in worshipping Him. Why did you turn away from obeying and worshipping Him even though you live because of His favors and generosity?' He even chastised and rebuked them further, saying, "Has my absence been too long for you? Or have you wished for wrath from your Lord to befall you, so you broke your promise to me?" That is: 'Has it been such a long time ever since I left you, so you forgot Allah's favors upon you and your promise to me to remain firm and steadfast in your faith until I come back to you? It has not been that long! Did you deliberately do such a deed and broke your promise to me to bring Allah's wrath upon you?'

Ibn Jarir said: "They broke their promise to him, became devoted to the calf, abandoned following Moses's path, and said to Aaron when he forbade them from worshipping the calf and called upon them to follow in Moses's footsteps: '"We will not cease to worship it until Moses returns to us." (Q 20:91) [119]

Having been rebuked, they came up with strange excuses that reflected the impact of long servitude and subjugation upon them, their indiscriminate and undiscerning rush to pursue whosoever was calling, their vacillating and irresolute personalities and their foolishness and idiocy. How did they apologize?

"They argued, 'We did not break our promise to you of our own free will.'" (Q 20:87) [120] That is, the Children of Israel apologized to Moses saying, 'We did not break our promise and worshipped the calf out of choice and will. It was more than we could handle. Had we been left alone without the deception of the Samiri, we wouldn't have worshipped what he molded for us.'

Ibn Jarir said: "By His 'بِمَلْكِنَا' Allah indicated that they admitted their wrongdoing and they said: 'We could not push ourselves to do what was right. We had no control over ourselves until that test and we did what we did.'" [121]

Then, they explained that test that caused them to abandon their pledge with Moses to worship Allah Alone by the pretext that "we were made to carry the burden of the people's golden jewelry, then we threw it into the fire, and so did the Sâmiri." (Q 20:87) In other words, 'we borrowed the jewelry from them (Egyptian women) under the pretext that we had a feast that was approaching, but they remained in our possession after we left Egypt. So, the Samiri dug a hole, set fire in it, and ordered us to throw the jewelry in it to get rid of them since they were not legitimately ours. We threw the jewelry into the fire, and the Samiri also threw what he had in there.'

Imam Ibn Kathir said: "Obviously, these foolish people's excuse was that they would relinquish the jewelry of the Copts (being a burden), so they threw them and worshipped the calf. They thus avoided a minor offense to commit a graver and more brazen and audacious one." [122]

Then, the Almighty showed what the Samiri did with the jewelry. He said: "Then he molded for them an idol of a calf that made a lowing sound. They said, "This is your god and the God of Moses, but Moses forgot where it was!" (Q 20:88) That is, out of the jewelry that they threw into the fire, the Samiri molded for them an idol of a calf that made a lowing sound (like the cows'). It was said that Allah breathed life into the idol as a test for them.

It was also said that there was no life in the idol. It was only that the Samiri molded it with cleverness and made holes in it that would emit a lowing sound when the wind enters into it.

Ibn Abbas said: "No! By Allah. It was unable to make a sound at all. It was only that the wind would enter the idol from its behind and comes out of its mouth. That caused that lowing sound." [123]

What was the consequence of seeing the calf? No sooner had they witnessed its lowing sound than they forgot their Allah who rescued them from the land of slavery, humiliation and disgrace. They devoted themselves to the calf in worship, and they foolishly and without thinking or understanding the said: "This is your god and the God of Moses, but Moses forgot where it was!" (Q 20:88) That is, those who were tempted and succumbed to worshipping the calf said: 'This is your god and the God of Moses, so worship it because Moses forgot to seek it here and went to look for it at the mountain.'

That shows their arrogance and inappropriateness with their Prophet. It also indicates their stupidity and absurdity because they alleged that Moses- their Prophet who called them to worship Allah Alone- believed in the divinity of the calf and went to look for it.

It was said that it was the Samiri- not Moses- who forgot. In this case, the meaning is: the Samiri forgot and abandoned his seeming superficial faith and resented the religion that Allah sent to Moses, i.e., Islam.

We support the first view as it is the one that is closely related to the meaning of the verse.

The Almighty rebuked and chastised them for their absurdity and stupidity. He said: "Did they not see that it did not respond to them, nor could it protect or benefit them?" (Q 20:89)This means: 'Don't they realize that that calf that they worship does not respond to them if they ask for something? Don't they understand that it can't protect or benefit them either in this world or in the Hereafter? How can that be a Allah when it can't defend or benefit them.'

After the Almighty showed them that what they did was contrary to reason and sound thinking, He chastised them even further. He said: "Aaron had already warned them beforehand, "O my people! You are only being tested by this, for indeed your ⸢one true⸣ Lord is the Most Compassionate. So, follow me and obey my orders." (Q 20:90) They replied, "We will not cease to worship it until Moses returns to us." (Q 20:91)

This means that before Moses returned and reprimanded them, Aaron-peace be upon him-said to the calf worshippers: 'My people! Allah is testing your faith to see how steadfast in faith you are, to distinguish between the firm believer and the shaky one. Follow my orders and worship the One True Allah and abandon worshipping the calf. Comply with what I prohibit you from doing.' However, they did obey him and rejected his advice. They said: 'We will not desist from worshipping it until Moses returns to us and tells us what he thinks of it.'

Their response reflects their belittling the status of Aaron. It was as though they were telling his that he was not worthy of being followed or listened to and they would continue to worship the calf until Moses returned.

Imam Al-Razi said: "You have to realize that Aaron did a magnificent job in warning and advising his people. First, he warned them saying: "You are only being tested by this." Then, he called them to turn back to the knowledge of Allah: "indeed your one true Lord is the Most Compassionate." Third, he invited them to the follow him: "So, follow me." Then, he called them to follow and obey the law: "obey my orders." That was a great sequence of directives because to remove harm, it is necessary to eradicate doubts and come to the knowledge of Allah and obeying the law. Yet, though the sequence of these instructions was great, their ignorance and stubbornness cause them to receive it with indifference, apathy and indolence. They said: "We will not cease to worship it until Moses returns to us." [124]

The Almighty then demonstrated what transpired between Moses and Aaron after Moses harshly rebuked his people for their folly and imprudence. He said: "O Aaron! What prevented you, when you saw them going astray, from following after me? How could you disobey my orders?" Aaron pleaded, "O son of my mother! Do not seize me by my beard or the hair of my head. I really feared that you would say, 'You have caused division among the Children of Israel, and did not observe my word." (Q 20:92-94)

That is: Chastising his brother Aaron, Moses asked him: 'What prevented you from following me in anger when you saw them going astray and worship the calf? You could have fought against them alongside those who kept the faith! You could have scattered them! How could you disobey my orders when I asked you to 'take my place among my people and do right, and do not follow the way of the corrupters,' (Q 7:142) and to be strong and unyielding in matters of religion because your presence among them- now that they are worshipping other than Allah- is deemed reckless and lenient when neither are warranted.'

Aaron responded to his brother Moses pleadingly, "O son of my mother! Do not seize me by my beard or the hair of my head. I really feared that you would say, 'You have caused division among the Children of Israel, and did not observe my word." (Q 20:94) In other words; Aaron tried to appease his brother's anger by appealing to his mercy and compassion by saying: 'Son of my mother! Do not seize me by the beard or the hair of my head. I have not disobeyed your orders, neither have I been neglectful or inattentive to them. What caused me to remain with them despite their worshipping the calf was my fear that by fighting against them or taking the side of the faithful against the others, you might think that I divided them into two warring parties and did not follow your instructions to 'take my place among my people and do right, and do not follow the way of the corrupters.' (Q 7:142) That is why, I neither fought against them nor did I leave them. I remained with them advising and counselling until your return so could handle this matter yourself.

After Moses heard his brother's explanation and was persuaded by it, he agitatedly and angrily hurried to the Samiri, the chief culprit responsible for that sedition. He harshly chastised and vehemently rebuked him: "What did you think you were doing, O Sâmiri?" (Q 20:95) So, Moses said to the Samiri in a tone that reflected the enormity and seriousness of the situation: 'What have you been up to? What is your story? Why have you done what you did?' Moses talked to him in such a manner to show the Children of Israel- through his confession- the invalidity of what he did and to do make of him an example to others who are could comprehend.

He said: "I saw what they did not see, so I took a handful of dust from the hoof-prints of the horse of the messenger-angel Gabriel then cast it on the molded calf. This is what my lower-self tempted me into." (Q 20:96)

The Samiri said: 'I knew what they did not know, and I saw what they did not see. I saw Gabriel when he came to destroy Pharaoh mounting a horse that breathes life into anything that it gallops over. So, I took a handful of dust from the hoof prints of the horse and I threw it into hole where the melted jewelry was, and it became an idol of a calf with a lowing sound. Or, I threw it on the calf that was molded out of jewelry, and became alive. My lower-self tempted me to do that to tempt the Children of Israel to abandon worshipping Allah and worship the calf instead.'

According to this interpretation that is unanimously agreed upon by most exegetes, the ٱلرَّسُولِ (= messenger) that the Samiri saw was Gabriel. And the word أَثَرِ is a reference to the dust that he took from the hoof prints of his horse.

Abou Muslim Al-Asfahani has a different view. Al-Razi quoted him as saying: "Nothing in the Noble Qur'an indicates what exegetes mentioned. Here is another view: It could have been Moses who was intended by the word ٱلرَّسُولِ (= messenger), and the word أَثَرِ (dust' from the hoof-prints of 'the horse) refers to his doctrine and law that he was ordered to bring. This is the case when it is said that a man follows in the footsteps of another man to imitate and attempt to be like him. In this case, when Moses reproached the Samiri and enquired why he had misled and lured his people to worship the calf, he said: "I saw what they did not see." In other words, 'I knew that what you were following was not right, and I took a handful of dust (your doctrine and law), O Messenger, and I threw that away.' At this, Moses informed him of his torture in this world and in the Hereafter. And the fact that he called Moses "Messenger" even though he was an ungrateful disbeliever is reminiscent of those about whom Allah said: "O you to whom the Reminder is revealed! You must be insane!" even though they did not believe in the revelation. [125]

In sum, in interpreting the verses, what Abou Muslim is saying is that during the absence of their Prophet, the Samiri tempted the Children of Israel to throw the jewelry they had into the fire. When they did that, he molded an idol of a calf with intricate cavities which would cause the wind going in and out to make a lowing sound. They worshipped it instead of Allah. When Moses asked the Samiri: "What did you think you were doing, O Sâmiri? Why did you mislead them?" The Samiri replied saying: 'I became aware of things that others were unaware of. I knew that your law was not the right one. That is why, I resented whatever parts of it I used to believe in. I showed my people what I truly saw, namely, abandoning worshipping your Allah, Moses, to worship the calf that I molded for them instead.' Then Moses told him that his punishment for his misguidance in this life was to be denied pleasure of women in order prevent him from having descendants. That was what was meant by لَا مِسَاسَ 'Do not touch ⌜me⌝! In the Hereafter, you will suffer the punishment that is reserved for all those who relinquished worshipping Allah.

Imam Al-Razi adopted the interpretation of Abou Muslim. He said: "You ought to know that what Abou Muslim suggested only differed with the exegetes, but it is the closest to the truth for the following reasons:

First, Gabriel is not known by the name of "the Messenger," and he was not mentioned before to assume that the definite article "الـ" in ٱلرَّسُولِ refer to him.

Second, it necessitates "Implication" (the omission of something verbally but not in meaning) which is a handful ⌜of dust⌝ from the hoof-prints of ⌜the horse of⌝ the messenger. Implication is different from the original.

Third: It necessitates arbitrariness. How could the Samiri- to the exclusion of all others- be the one to see and know Gabriel? How could he have known that the dust of the hoof-prints of his horse had such an effect? They also mentioned that it was Gabriel who attended to the Samiri a long time ago. If that was the case, the Samiri would have had the sound understanding to know that Moses was a truthful Prophet and would not have resorted to deceitfulness and deception! If that was what he learned during his years growing up, what benefit was it then that Gabriel took care of him during his childhood years?

Fourth, if it were at all possible for unbelievers to know that that dust had such an effect, one may then say: 'Maybe Moses was also informed with something similar, and that was why he performed signs and miracles.' This is the attitude of those who deny miracles and say: 'Isn't it possible that they knew some of the medicines (tricks?) that could cause the occurrence of this miracle, and that was how they came up with that one?' That would cause the rejection and denial of miracles."[126]

The meaning according to Abou Muslim would be 'I was tempted to relinquish the guidance and light you are following without anyone asking me to do so.'

Imam Al-Alusi-may Allah rest his soul- responded to Al-Razi and Abou Muslim. Here it is briefly:

First, Calling Gabriel “messenger” was mentioned in the Noble Qur’an. The Almighty said: “Indeed, this Quran is the Word of Allah delivered by Gabriel, a noble messenger-angel.” (Q 81:19) Not being recurrent or mentioned previously does not mean that it was not common then. It might have been a common practice to call him “messenger” among the Children of Israel. Second, the use of the “المضاف /mudaf” (a noun that is added to another noun to create a relationship of possession) is countless and it occurs in Allah’s Book numerously. Third: Seeing Gabriel- to the exclusion of everybody else- was a test from Allah to the Samiri to accomplish something that was already known. His knowledge of its peculiar effect was due to the fear instilled in his heart to not throw it on anything. Fourth, the miracle indicated a claim of being sent by Allah. They asked ‘When did someone claim prophethood and performed signs and for some unknown reason was not known to those for whom he was sent? Allạh would certainly reveal the truth by showing someone who was not associated with the message. That was what was mentioned concerning the improbability of the delusion and fall of the Samiri after he had come to know the prophecy of Moses. The Almighty said: “And, although their hearts were convinced the signs were true, they still denied them wrongfully and arrogantly.” (Q 27:14) The Samiri’s disbelief was more or less comparable to that of Pharaoh’s, and he had witnessed his share of signs.” [127]

There are some reservations concerning Al-Alusi’s view despite its relevance. What exegetes say and demonstrate are acceptable so long as the effects are fixed and factual, not taken from the Isra’iliyyat (Israelite stories). The Book of Allah should not be interpreted except in terms of sound and discerning judgement or valid and true transmission. His claim concerning what exegetes had transmitted could not be acceptable except under another condition, namely, these interpretations were not taken from the “Isra’iliyyat,” and this condition is not satisfied here.

We are inclined to believe that Abou Muslim’s view is the closest one to the Noble Qur’an. Those who diligently read and research the Noble Qur’an would find these stories inconceivable from the Quranic text if they are to assume that such stories- narrated by interpreters- nonexistent. Also, they are not delivered by the Prophet through valid transmission in order to be accepted. Rather, they seem to belong to the Isra’iliyyat (Israelite stories) that we leave unto Allah, neither believing nor disbelieving them, fully aware that Allah’s words truthful, and what Abou Muslim wanted to say was right and truthful.

After Moses heard the Samiri’s excuses, he told him what Allah said: “Go away then! And for the rest of your life you will surely be crying, ‘Do not touch me! Then you will certainly have a fate that you cannot escape. Now look at your Allah to which you have been devoted: we will burn it up, then scatter it in the sea completely.” (Q 20:97)

The word "المساس"is a gerund that means “touching.” It meant: I will not touch or be touched. Whenever anyone touched him, both the person who touched and the touched become intensely feverish (as though on fire). So, whenever anyone wanted to touch him, he would panic and yell “do not touch me.”

It was also said that the meaning of "do not touch 'me" was forbidding him from mixing with others and preventing others from mixing with him, and that Moses drove him away from the Children of Israel, and he left into the wilderness as an outcast.

Al-Zamakhshari said: "He was punished with the worst kind of punishment. He was completely forbidden from mixing with other people. All were prohibited from associating with him; no one was allowed to meet, talk, help, confront or undergo any of the usual interactions. If a man or a woman touched him, they both become extremely heated and feverish because Allah had plighted him with such an incurable affliction. Therefore, people spurned and shunned him altogether. He was regarded as more despicable than a brutal murderer and more dreadful and loathsome than a vile beast in the wilderness." [128]

Al-Alusi said: "The mystery concerning punishing him in such a manner lies in the fact that it was the contrary of what he had hoped for, namely, to have the backing and support of the people. So, what he did was a reason for them to stay away, vilify and despise him. It was said that he was thus punished to make his punishment similar and congruent with the deed he perpetrated: he abandoned and forsook and he was abandoned and forsaken. That dreadful feverishness with which he was plighted was the epitome of untouchability." [129]

Abou Muslim has a different view about the Almighty's "do not touch 'me:" He said: "It might be possible that it meant 'I don't want to touch women.' Thus, Allah's punishment was to cut off his offspring to become without a child who would comfort him, keep him company and be a source of solace in life. Thus, Allah would deprive him from the adornments of this life which He mentioned in: "Wealth and children are the adornment of this worldly life." (Q 18:46) [130]

That was his punishment in this worldly life. As for his punishment in the Hereafter, Moses revealed in his: "Then you will certainly have a fate that you cannot escape." (Q 20:97) That is: You will not escape from the punishment that Allah prepared for you for your disbelief and corruption you caused in the land, just as He punished you in this world. You are one of those who lost in this life as well as in the Hereafter. What a horrible and humiliating loss!

Ibn Kathir, Abou Omer and Al-Hassan interpreted لَن تُخلِفَهُ/ you cannot escape as "You have an appointment on the Day of Resurrection that you will not be able to avoid."

Then, Moses said: "Now look at your god to which you have been devoted: we will burn it up, then scatter it in the sea completely." (Q 20:97) This means: Look at the calf that you worshipped and to which you devoted yourself for a long time. We will burn it up in front of your very eyes, then we will scatter its dust in the sea so that nothing would remain of it. You will see- along with those whom you deceived- its fate, to be an example and a lesson to those who are able to comprehend.

Once Moses completed his act of eradicating and destroying the idol, he showed them that Allah Only is worthy of worship. He said: "Your only god is Allah, there is no god worthy of worship except Him. He encompasses everything in His knowledge." (Q 20:98)

That is, Allah Alone is worthy of worship, adoration and exaltation. He is the All-Mighty, the All-Knowledgeable who is aware of everything on earth and in heaven.

Thus, the noble verses that we mentioned have labeled the Children of Israel with the vice of ignorance and narrow-mindedness. They have shown their inability to make sound judgements and their propensity to choose misguidance rather than guidance as they indulged in worshipping the calf, the epitome of stupidity and absurdity, and abandoned worshipping the One Who is Worthy of obedience, submission and worship, the One to Whom nothing on earth or in the heavens is concealed.

Tenth: Lack of sensitivity for religion and engaging in semantic bickering and argumentation.

Among the vices that were ascribed to the Children of Israel are their callousness and insensitivity to religion, their ungratefulness and belittling what Allah bestowed upon them, their non-compliance with the word of truth, their distrust of the truthfulness of their prophets and their semantic bickering either to get away with their non-compliance because of their lack of vision and perceptiveness to understand the law and its tenets.

The story in which their Prophet Moses asked them to sacrifice a cow is excellent evidence of the vices that we attributed to them. It reflects their rebelliousness against Allah's commandments as well as their lack of appreciation for the favors of their Creator. This story is mentioned is Sura Al-Baqara. The Almighty said:

"And remember when Moses said to his people, "Allah commands you to sacrifice a cow." They replied, "Are you mocking us?" Moses responded, "I seek refuge in Allah from acting foolishly!" They said, "Call upon your Lord to clarify for us what type of cow it should be!" He replied, "Allah says, 'The cow should neither be old nor young but in between. So do as you are commanded!'" They said, "Call upon your Lord to specify for us its color." He replied, "Allah says, 'It should be a bright yellow cow—pleasant to see.'" Again, they said, "Call upon your Lord so that He may make clear to us which cow, for all cows look the same to us. Then, Allah willing, we will be guided ˹to the right one˺." He replied, "Allah says, 'It should have been used neither to till the soil nor water the fields; wholesome and without blemish.'" They said, "Now you have come with the truth." Yet they still slaughtered it hesitantly! This is when a man was killed and you disputed who the killer was, but Allah revealed what you concealed. So, We instructed, "Strike the dead body with a piece of the cow." This is how easily Allah brings the dead to life, showing you His signs so that you may understand. Even then your hearts became hardened like a rock or even harder, for some rocks gush rivers; others split, spilling water; while others are humbled in awe of Allah. And Allah is never unaware of what you do." (Q 2:67-74)

Interpreters said: A rich man among the Children of Israel had a poor cousin as his sole heir. The poor man killed his rich cousin to inherit his wealth as he could not wait for him to die naturally. He carried the corpse to another village and threw it there. Then, he pretended to seek revenge, and he came to Prophet Moses accusing some people with the murder of his cousin. When Moses asked them, they denied having anything to do with the murder. They asked him to call upon his Lord to reveal to him the true killer. Moses entreated his Lord, and Allah inspired him to ask them to sacrifice a cow. So, Moses said: "Allah commands you to sacrifice a cow." (Q 2:67) [131]

The Noble Qur'an mentioned this story in an eloquent and appealing style, one that captures the hearts and inspires people to weigh and consider. The Almighty said: "Moses said to his people, "Allah commands you to sacrifice a cow." They replied, "Are you mocking us?" Moses responded, "I seek refuge in Allah from acting foolishly!" (Q 2:67)

The meaning of the noble verse is: Remember, O Children of Israel, for your own understanding and learning, when one of your ancestors was murdered and the killer was not known, and some of the folks of the murdered asked Moses to entreat Allah to reveal the true killer. When Moses said: "Allah commands you to sacrifice a cow," they were surprised and foolishly said: "Are you mocking us?" In other words, they asked if he was making them the target of his ridicule. He said: "I seek refuge in Allah from acting foolishly and say something that I was not commanded to say."

Interpreters say that the commandment to sacrifice a cow followed their contention over the murderer in order to know the identity of the true killer when they strike the dead body with a piece of the cow, as mentioned in the Almighty's "This is when a man was killed and you disputed who the killer was, but Allah revealed what you concealed." (Q 2:72)

The Almighty commanded them to sacrifice a cow- not other animals- because it was the same species that they worshipped, namely, the calf. In ordering them to do so, He was imparting the insignificance and lowly nature of the animal that they loved and worshipped. It was as though the Almighty was saying to them: 'the cows that are the essence of stupidity and dullness could not be worshipped instead of Allah. It is only good for tilling and watering the ground and for work and sacrifice.

Their response "Are you mocking us?" (Q 2:67) shows their folly, distrust of their Prophet, their lack of respect and reverence and their ignorance of the dominion and authority of the Almighty Who is Worthy of compliance, adoration and exaltation. Had they been with sound judgement, they would have obeyed their Prophet and waited to see the consequences. However, they were people who could not comprehend.

Since what they said betrayed their belief that Moses attributed to Allah something that he was not commanded to say, Moses responded, "I seek refuge in Allah from acting foolishly!" (Q 2:67) In other words, Moses said 'I seek refuge in Allah as I do not want to be counted among the foolish people who say lies and untruths about Him.' In this response, Moses absolves himself from jeering and mockery (a type of joking mixed with derision and ridicule with the mocked) since it is unbecoming for rational humans- let alone Allah's messengers- to indulge in this type of behavior. His response was also a way to turn their attention to the importance of appropriateness and deference for the Creator as he showed them that what they suspected was not appropriate except for those who are unaware of Allah's authority and power.

Interpreting the noble verse, the late Sheikh Muhammad Al-Khidr Hussein said:

"The noble verse has drawn the attention to the serious implications of taking religious matters lightly; mocking in religion is the kind of folly that brings the worst punishment to those who do it. It throws them to the torture of hellfire. It was for this reason that men of erudition and intellect have forbidden the use of verses in a mocking or joking context. They said: 'The Noble Qur'an was revealed to be recited with diligence and humility, and to comply with what is therein with acceptance and submission.'" [132]

What their Prophet advised them to do was enough to prompt them to sacrifice any cow to comply with Allah's commandment, but their twisted serpentine nature was deeply rooted. As the Qur'an mentioned, they asked: "Call upon your Lord to clarify for us what type of cow it should be!" (Q 2:68)

That is, the Children of Israel asked Moses to ask his Allah to show them what type of cow it should be and its description.[133] The reason behind asking about its type/description was their amazement at the idea of a cow slaughtered by their hands that would be used to strike a dead body with a piece of it to bring the dead back to life. It was as though they expected- due to their lack of understanding- that the cow that would be instrumental in revealing the identity of the killer should have a distinct quality distinguishing it from the rest.

The way they asked also revealed their arrogance and inappropriateness towards the Almighty and Moses, their Prophet. They said: "Call upon your Lord." It was as if the Almighty God is Moses' god, not theirs as well. It was as though that matter did not concern them; it was only an issue for Moses and his God. However, his response to those foolish people was judicious and prudent typical of a sagacious mentor. He said: "Allah says, 'The cow should neither be old [134] nor young but in between. So do as you are commanded!" (Q 2:68)

That is, after Allah informed Moses the description of the cow, Moses said: 'Allah says that the cow that He commanded you to sacrifice should neither be old الفارض nor young البكر. It should be middle aged العوان . So, stop asking questions and make haste to comply with what you have been commanded to do.'

The Almighty emphasized the sentence: "Allah says, 'The cow should قَالَ إِنَّهُ يَقُولُ إِنَّهَا بَقَرَةٌ" to denounce and condemn their stubbornness in pursuing these excessive questions and to revile them for their attempt to avoid compliance.

The Noble Qur'an did not mention that the cow should be middle aged العوان at first. Rather, it mentioned the other two qualities بَقَرَةٌ لَّا فَارِضٌ وَلَا بِكْرٌ (neither old nor young) to expose their stupidity and hint at their inability to understand a laconic and terse style. That is the reason for resorting to plenty of descriptions so as not to repeat these questions.

The Almighty's "do as you are commanded!" was meant to end excuses and urge compliance. It meant 'Obey what you were ordered to do in order to know the truth concerning the real killer in the easiest way possible. Do not limit and confine what Allah had provided lavishly. Do not persist in this line of questioning for it would not be in your interest.'

However, they persisted in asking questions. After knowing its age, they asked about the color. As the Qur'an mentioned, the said: "Call upon your Lord to specify for us its color." He replied, "Allah says, 'It should be a bright yellow cow—pleasant to see.'" (Q 2:69) The meaning is: Now that the Children of Israel knew the age of the cow, they asked their Prophet to ask his Lord to show them its color to facilitate the process of getting it. He replied, saying, 'The cow that I commanded you to sacrifice should be a bright yellow one that would make those who see it pleased.'

Ibn Jarir said: "Brightness when it comes to the yellow color is like the luminance of whiteness in its intensity and purity." [135]

Al-Zamakhshari said: "Brightness is mostly associated with the yellow spotless color. In emphasis, it is often said bright yellow as it is said pitch black...' Then he said: 'If you say what is the use of mentioning the color and saying bright yellow?" I would say: 'Emphasis! That is because the color indicates the appearance, the yellow color. It is as if we are saying intensely yellowish.'" [136]

Thus far, they should have known the characteristics of the cow as far as age and color are concerned. Yet, was that enough for them? Hardly! They started asking for the third time something that was completely unnecessary. As the Qur'an recounts, they said: "Call upon your Lord so that He may make clear to us which cow, for all cows look the same to us. Then, Allah willing, we will be guided to the right one." He replied, "Allah says, 'It should have been used neither to till the soil nor water the fields; wholesome and without blemish.'" They said, "Now you have come with the truth." Yet they still slaughtered it hesitantly!" (Q 2:70-71)

The meaning of the two noble verses is: After the Children of Israel knew the age and color of the cow, they asked Moses to make clearer to them which cow He had commanded us to sacrifice since the cows that were described previously with these two characteristics were too many, and they were unable to know exactly which cow to sacrifice. Allah willing, we will be able to find the right one once we are rightly guided, and we will obey what we were ordered to do. Then Moses answered saying: "Allah says, 'It should have been used neither to till the soil nor water the fields; wholesome and without blemish.'" That is, Moses said that Allah said that it is a cow that had not tilled the soil nor watered the fields, one that is without blemish, and with no other color that conflicts with its bright yellow color. When they found that its characteristics had been completed, they said: "Now you have come with the truth," the clear truth, and there are no doubts any longer. They looked for it and "Yet they still slaughtered it hesitantly!" because of their excessive questioning and their hesitancy.

The Almighty's "Call upon your Lord so that He may make clear to us which cow" (Q 2:70) marks their third question which they asked their Prophet in order to ascertain their knowledge concerning the cow and its description after getting to know its age and color.

It was as though they were saying that his responses to the previous questions were not sufficient, and it was therefore difficult to distinguish the cow. Therefore, he should ask his Lord to make clearer its description. Sensing that they might have overburdened him and went overboard, they justified their excessive questioning saying: "all cows look the same to us." (Q 2:70) That is, 'do not be upset for asking you many questions because there are many middle-aged yellow cows, and we are unable to choose the one that you want us to sacrifice.'

Sheikh Muhammad Al-Taher Ibn Assure said: "They did not apologize for the first and second questions, but they apologized for the third because the third time repeating the questions would bring about boredom." [137]

Their "Then, Allah willing, we will be guided to the right one" (Q 2:70) was to urge Moses, their Prophet, to entreat his Lord, a promise to comply and submit, an attempt to alleviate his boredom because of their excessive questioning and an excuse for their behavior and endless questions to avoid his anger. It was as though they were saying: 'Urgently entreat your Lord so that He may give us more guidance to the cow that you want us to sacrifice. And, Allah willing, with this clarification, we will be able to identify the cow and then we will be able to identify the true killer. We will then perceive the wisdom behind ordering us to sacrifice it.'

Ibn Jarir said: "The Almighty's 'Then, Allah willing, we will be guided' shows that they meant that Allah will clarify the confusion and mix up due to the similarity of cows. The meaning of we will be guided in that context was that they would be able to find the one particular cow that they were supposed to sacrifice to the exclusion of others." [138]

The Almighty's "'It should have been used neither to till the soil nor water the fields; wholesome and without blemish" indicated added features to the cow wanted. Such added characteristics were unnecessary had they obeyed their Prophet from the beginning. However, due to their repetitiveness, bad choices and lack of understanding the true purposes of the law, they themselves limited their own choices. Now, they were ordered to look for a certain specific cow with certain characteristics: middle aged, bright yellow cow, pleasing to the eye, one that did not till the soil or water the fields, without blemish and with no other color that would conflict with its bright yellow color.

And the Almighty's "used neither to till the soil" was a description for the cow, one [139]لَّا ذَلُولٌ تُثِيرُ ٱلْأَرْضَ indicating that it had not been trained. "To till the soil" means to move the soil to prepare it for farming and to throw the seeds therein. What was meant here was that the cow was not exposed to hard work, tilling the soil or watering the fields.

That is, it was a difficult cow that was not trained and subjugated to do field work: tilling the soil or watering the fields. It was a cow that was exempt from such toil. The لَّا in the Almighty's لَّاذَلُولٌ denotes negation. His emphasizes the first negation with وَلَا تَسْقِى ٱلْحَرْثَ (nor water the fields)

And the Almighty's مُسَلَّمَةٌ لَّا شِيَةَ فِيهَا (wholesome and without blemish) are two adjectives to describe the cow. The meaning is: this cow should be free of any blemishes and flaws. And it should not have any color- black or white- that would interfere with its yellow color. It should be yellow all over.

"The truth" in saying "Now you have come with the truth," was meant to indicate clarity of description without doubts and uncertainties. It was as though they were saying that 'only now have you offered the true description of the cow. You have distinguished it from others in terms of its color and other features. Now we have no more doubts concerning the cow.'

The expression "Yet they still slaughtered it hesitantly!" indicated that they got the cow and sacrificed it. Moses' people slaughtered the cow that Allah described for them after they had nearly abandoned complying with what they were commanded to do due to their doubts in the directives they received and their stalling and procrastination.

Al-Zamakhshari said: "Yet they still slaughtered it hesitantly!" demonstrated that because of stalling, procrastination and repeated inquiries, they almost abandoned the idea of sacrificing a cow. Their doubts and inquiries would have been endless, and they would have persisted on asking further questions. It was also said that they didn't want to slaughter the cow because of its high price. Others also said that they were afraid of revealing the identity of the killer." [140]

Then, Allah revealed the purpose behind the commandment to slaughter the cow. He said: "This is when a man was killed and you disputed who the killer was, but Allah revealed what you concealed. So, We instructed, 'Strike the dead body with a piece of the cow.' This is how easily Allah brings the dead to life, showing you His signs so that you may understand." (Q 2:72-73)

That is: 'Remember O Children of Israel when a man was killed and you contended among yourselves each one trying to absolve himself from the charge. The Almighty Allah undoubtedly exposed what you had concealed concerning the murderer and the murdered. He revealed the truth by asking Moses, His Prophet, to strike the dead body with any piece of the cow, and you did, so he came back to life and exposed the identity of his murderer. Similarly, just as the dead came back to life, Allah will bring the dead to life on Judgement Day to recompense them according to their deeds and to show you evidence of His Omnipotence and Supremacy. Hopefully, you may understand."

Most exegetes agree that the incident related to the murder and the discord and dispute that ensued between the people took place before the commandment to slaughter the cow. However, the Noble Qur'an mentioned it later to enumerate the many crimes that they perpetrated and to enhance interest in knowing the wisdom behind sacrificing it to make people readily accept it eagerness and enthusiasm.

Al-Zamakhshari said: "Why wasn't the story told in its logical sequence? It was appropriate to mention the murdered and striking him with a piece of the cow before commanding them to sacrifice it. It could have been said 'if a man is killed and you don't know who the killer was, then We say sacrifice a cow and strike the dead man with some of its pieces.' I would say: 'All the stories that relate to the Children of Israel are mentioned to enumerate their felonies and rebuke and chastise them. The two stories mentioned here- though related- independently rebuked them. The first rebuked them for their idleness, flippant attitude, and unwillingness to comply with orders speedily. The second chastised them for killing and doing something prohibited. However, the story of sacrificing the cow was presented before mentioning the murder because, had the order been reversed, it would have been one story and the duality of chastisement would have been lost." [141]

The Noble Qur'an ascribed the act of murder to all of them as shown in "when a man was killed" (Q 5:32) even though only some of them were guilty of the act of murder. This was done to demonstrate that the community- as a unified and cohesive whole- was to be regarded as one.

The murder was also ascribed to the Jews who lived during the time of the Prophet because they were descendants of those who had been around during the time of the murder. The Noble Qur'an oftentimes uses this style to recount and demonstrate that the descendants had followed in the footsteps of their forefathers in delusion and misguidance.

The Almighty's "you disputed who the killer was" (Q 2:72) was a statement that demonstrated what happened among them after the murder which we mentioned. The expression "فَادَّارَأْتُمْ فِيهَا" means you argued and differed with each other concerning the murder. Some of you denied the charge and accused others to absolve themselves from the crime.

The Almighty's "Allah revealed what you concealed" (Q 2:72) indicated that Allah will reveal what you have been trying to hide or conceal concerning the person you murdered then argued about his killer. The Almighty will reveal the true killer, and justice will prevail.

This statement "Allah revealed what you concealed" occurred in the middle between "you disputed who the killer was" and "Strike the dead body with a piece of the cow." It served the purpose of informing those addressed- even before getting to know what they would be ordered to do- that the identity of the true killer will undoubtedly be revealed.

The author of Liberation and Enlightenmentالتحرير والتنوير , said: "It was Allah's will to reveal the identity of the murderer even though this was not the first one to have his blood shed. He did this to honor Moses; He did not desire to have one of Moses' people die with Moses around and in their midst, especially because the murderers resorted to duplicity and conspired to show that they wanted to avenge his death. Had Allah not reveal the identity of the murderer, the people would have lost faith in Moses. They would have suspected his truthfulness, rejected the faith and became disbelievers. Revealing the identity of the true killer was, therefore, a way to honor Moses-peace be upon him- and to protect his people lest they go astray." [142]

The Almighty's "We instructed, 'Strike the dead body with a piece of the cow'" (Q 2:73) was to inform them of the method through which they would be guided to the real killer, and the pronoun "ه"in اَضْرِبُوهُ was meant to refer the person who was murdered.

And striking the dead body with a piece of the cow was evidence of Allah's power and authority as well as facilitating the task for them.

The meaning is: We said to Moses' people who argued and fought concerning the dead man: 'Strike the dead body with any of the pieces of the cow to bring him back to life.' They did, and Allah brought him back to life and he informed the people of his murderer. And just as he was brought back to life, Allah will resurrect the dead on Judgement Day to reward or punish them according to their deeds.

The verse thus revealed that the dead man who was struck with some of the pieces of the cow became alive again.

Imam Ibn Jarir said: "If someone said: 'What was behind the order to strike the murdered with a piece of the cow?' I would say: 'To come back to life and tell the Prophet of Allah and those who disputed the identity of the killer who the real killer was.' If he then said: 'Where was it that Allah ordered them to do that?' I would say: 'He left it to be inferred from the words that indicated that.' The meaning is: We instructed them to strike the dead body with a piece of the cow to come back to life. They struck him, and he came back to life. That was clear in the Almighty's 'This is how ⌜easily⌝ Allah brings the dead to life, showing you His signs so that you may understand.'" (Q 2:73) [143]

The Almighty's "showing you His signs so that you may understand" was clear evidence of Allah as the All-Powerful Omnipotent One. The people were able to witness with their own eyes how life was restored when the murdered was struck with a piece of the dead cow, how he was able to tell others the identity of the true killer, and how they were able to identify him according to what the murdered told them. All this was meant to urge them to use their mind and intellect in what was good and to convince them that He Who was able to bring one dead man to the world of the living was also capable of bringing all back to life. He is the all-Powerful, Omnipotent All-Mighty Allah.

The author of Al-Manar has a different view concerning the interpretation of the noble verse. He believes that "This is how ⌜easily⌝ Allah brings the dead to life" meant saving people from bloodshed. To him, it was not meant to truly bring the dead back to life after death. In his interpretation, he said: "The Almighty's 'We instructed, 'Strike the dead body with a piece of the cow. 'This is how easily Allah brings the dead to life' (Q 2:73) was a statement to bring to light what they were concealing. Many views were reported concerning this act of striking. It was said it was a gesture to strike the murdered with its tongue. It was also said it was meant to strike with its thigh or tail. They said that they struck him, and he came back to life and reported the person who killed him. From what has preceded, it is evident that this process was- to them- a way to decide whenever a dead body- whose killer was unknown- was found in some village and there was discord amongst them concerning the identity of the true killer. Whoever washed his hands and followed the law would be innocent of the dead man's blood, and whoever refused to do that would be considered guilty. According to this, bringing the dead back to life meant avoiding the shedding of blood that would have ensued because of the discord among them for the murder of that person. In other words, it was a process to save lives by complying with certain laws as the Almighty said: "whoever saves a life, it will be as if they saved all of humanity" (Q 5:32) and in His "There is security of life for you in the law of retaliation." (Q 2:179) Thus, bringing back to life in this context meant preserving life, as the meaning of the two verses indicate. [144]

It is our view that that what was meant by the Almighty's bringing back to life in His "This is how easily Allah brings the dead to life" (Q 2:73) was not the actual bringing back of the dead man to life after his death. Interpreting this as a means to avoid the shedding of blood and preserving lives seems implausible for the following reasons:

First: It differs from the interpretation of prior exegetes. Ibn Jarir narrated on the authority of Ibn Abbas. He said: "When the dead man was struck with pieces of it- meaning the cow- he became alive and sat. They asked who killed him, and he said that it was his nephews. Then he died again..." [145]

Second: the Noble Qur'an does not support what the author of Al-Manar said, neither in whole nor in part, neither implicitly or explicitly. That because the Almighty's "This is how easily Allah brings the dead to life" clearly -and without question- indicated that it meant bringing them back to life after their death. That is, the dead had actually died and bringing them back to life was meant to actually restore them back to life. Nothing exists in print that contradicts this meaning, and there is no evidence that conflicts with this meaning that could be reached with simple contemplation and scrutiny. Therefore, it would be inappropriate to distort the meaning and adopt other meanings or interpretations that are not warranted by the clarity of the text. It is quite arbitrary to say that what was wanted from the dead was to bring them back to life to execute retribution to avoid the shedding of blood among the living when- to express this meaning- the Almighty Himself said: "There is security of life for you in ˹the law of˺ retaliation, O people of reason, so that you may become mindful ˹of Allah." (Q 2:179)

This honorable verse (Q 2:179) indicates that retribution and making culprits pay for their crimes is bound to preserve people's lives without distortion or misleading of the intended message.

Third: interpreting the verse to mean bringing life back to the dead- as many exegetes said- instills faith in the soundness and authenticity of the resurrection in the hearts. This was amazing, i.e., bringing the dead back to life by striking his dead body with a piece of the cow to tell who killed him. Likewise, Allah brings the dead back to life by raising them up from their graves on Judgement Day to reward them for their deeds. This was a confirmation of the resurrection through witnessing; no one could deny it.

Fourth: The Almighty's "showing you His signs so that you may understand" (Q 2:73) is strong evidence that what was meant by bringing the dead back to life was actually bringing them back after their death because the word "signs" in this context- as exegetes said- is a reference to the Almighty's Sovereignty and power, His ability to create and make miracles that are beyond human ability and comprehension such as bringing back the dead and resurrecting them from their graves for their recompense.

Then, the Noble Qur'an revealed that these awe-inspiring, remarkable and astounding miracles that shake one's being, move hearts and inspire and instill faith did not impact the hardened hearts of the Children of Israel. Their hearts were not moved and their minds were not responsive even after witnessing these supernatural and amazing signs. The Almighty said: "Even then your hearts became hardened like a rock or even harder, for some rocks gush rivers; others split, spilling water; while others are humbled in awe of Allah. And Allah is never unaware of what you do." (Q 2:74)

This means: 'your hearts, O Children of Israel, toughened and hardened even after witnessing the signs that you witnessed, i.e., bringing the dead man back to life in front of your eyes. Your hearts are as solid and hard as a rock or even harder. For even rocks may have pours and holes that would gush rivers that benefit the creation. Other rocks would split and spill water to form wells and springs. Still, others would roll down from mountain tops to the foot of the valley, in humility and fear of Allah. Yet, you, O Children of Israel, have hearts that would not respond to instruction or guidance, ones that would not be steered to righteousness or submit and comply with that with which they were commanded, no matter the favors, the curses or the signs that you witness. Allah is never unaware of what you do.

The Almighty's "Even then your hearts became hardened like a rock or even harder" is a statement that indicated how the Children of Israel reacted: they didn't take anything into consideration, they were not affected or moved by directives or advice, they refused to submit to Allah's signs, and they breached the covenants they made.

The use of the word ثُمَّ (= then) which denotes sluggishness and slothfulness indicated the implausibility and unlikeliness that viciousness and cruelty would still gain the upper hand over them after all the signs that they had witnessed. It was as though the Almighty was saying to them-after recounting the story of the cow and the lessons and benefits they could have gained- 'even then your hearts, O Children of Israel, did not soften; rather, they hardened and you did not benefit from these signs. That was inconceivable and implausible.'

The Almighty's "مِنۢ بَعْدِ ذَٰلِكَ = Even then" expresses the heightened sense of shock and amazement that their hearts were that hardened even after the great number of favors and signs that the Noble Qur'an recounted in the previous verses.

The demonstrative ذَٰلِكَ refers to bringing the dead man back to life by striking him with a piece of the cow or it could have been a reference to all the favors and miracles referred to in the previous verses.

And the "أَوْ = or" in His "hearts ... like a rock or even harder" denotes differences and diversification in the qualities of their hearts. That is, there were various degrees of cruelty and hardness of hearts: some were as hard as rocks, others were even harder.

It was also said that "أَوْ = or" was meant to instill doubts in the hearts of the addressed, not the addressor. It was as if one person was saying to another: "The cruelty of those hearts is similar to the hardness of rocks, or even more."

It can also be taken as a means to exaggerate and emphasize, a hyperbole. Thus, the meaning could be your hearts became rigid and hardened like rocks, or even harder. There are no feelings in them. The rigidity of rocks and stones are well known; people know and understand that feeling of hardness in rocks, and that was why this simile was used.

Al-Zamakhshari said: "If you said: 'why was it said "even harder" indicating the superlative (a derivative in Arabic where the noun is driven from the trilateral verb in the form of (af'al)?' I would say: 'It is clearer and more indicative of intense cruelty. Also, it could be meant not to say the hardest, but to describe cruelty as most intense and severe. It is as if it were said: the stones are severe and intense in their hardness, but their hearts were even harder and crueler.'" [146]

The Almighty's: "for some rocks gush rivers; others split, spilling water; while others are humbled in awe of Allah" (Q 2:74) indicated preferring rocks over their cruel, harsh and hardened hearts. It was meant to reveal the reason that their hearts even exceeded the hardness of rocks. It was a matter that required explaining the reason for such a condition.

The Almighty seems to be saying to them: 'Despite the hardness and rigidity of these rocks, water causes some of them to have various cracks that make them gush water to useful springs and beneficial wells, and some of them humbly and submissively follow Allah's commandments. However, nothing useful or beneficial springs from your hearts that are neither affected by lessons and examples nor led to follow directives that guide the spirit.'

"And Allah is never unaware of what you do" (Q 2:74) cautioned and threatened them because the Almighty will reward them according to their deeds; He will inflict upon them the torture they deserve because of their denial of His favors and their non-compliance with His commandments. Thus, the noble verse ascribed to the Children of Israel this hardness of hearts, lack of discernment and judgement, and indifference and nonchalance to directives and warnings despite the great number of the signs they witnessed.

What could be learned from these lessons and warnings:

This story comprised many lessons and Divine interventions. Among these are:

1- Evidence of the deeply-ingrained harshness and cruelty of the Children of Israel, their arrogant and inappropriate attitude towards their prophets, their endless persistent and excessive inquiries, their unwillingness to submit and comply with what their prophets bring them, their procrastination and stalling when it was time to comply, and their deviation from the righteous path.
2- Evidence concerning the truthfulness of the Prophet (Muhammad) regarding what he was saying about His Allah, for he was informed of this story which he did not witness but which Allah had revealed to him. Such a revelation was a proof of his prophethood. It also showed the truthfulness of the prophecy of Moses and that he was a messenger sent by Allah.
3- Evidence that their procrastination in religion-related matters and their excessive questioning would only lead to more strict rulings. Had the Children of Israel slaughtered any cow, it would have been better for them. However, they kept on limiting their choices and, consequently, the Almighty limited theirs...

Ibn Jarir narrated on the authority of Ibn Abbas, he said: "Had the people chosen any cow, it would have been better for them. However, they were unnecessarily demanding and pernickety (fussy), and Allah was meticulous and demanding, in turn." [147]

Their procrastination, pedantic and nitpicking attitude led to limiting their chances for choosing and increasing the conditions of the requested cow. That was meant to discipline them for their stalling, their lack of sound judgement and their nonchalant attitude towards the law by either neglecting to obey it or for their inability to understand and appreciate it. Thus, it should be understood that what Allah asked them to do- at first- was to sacrifice a cow. The commandments that followed- being bright yellow, without a blemish and never labored in the fields- was a fortuitous statute, a mere incidental ruling- meant to discipline them for their stubbornness and chastise them for procrastination and excessive questioning.

Islamic teachings prohibit asking excessive questions. The Almighty said: "O believers! Do not ask about any matter which, if made clear to you, may disturb you. But if you inquire about what is being revealed in the Quran, it will be made clear to you. Allah has forgiven what was done in the past. And Allah is All-Forgiving, Most Forbearing." (Al-Ma'idah; Q 5:101) We also read in the Hadith: "Leave me as I have left you, or what destroyed those who came before you was their excessive questioning and their disagreement with their prophets. So, if I forbid you from something, avoid it, and if I command you to do something, do as much of it as you can." [148]

The author of Al-Manar said: "Our predecessors complied with this commandment, and they did not make things harder on themselves. Religion- to them- was innate, Hanafi and simple. However, those who succeeded them deliberately did what Allah has forbidden: they came up with rulings that were reached through their 'إجتهاد=Ijtihaad/personal reflection and deliberation .' Religion became burdensome to the nation; people became bored and they abandoned it." [149]

4- Imam Ibn al-Qayyim said that the story comprises many lessons:

A) It is inappropriate to receive Allah's commandment (when the wisdom it is not readily accessible to the commanded) with denial or rejection. When Moses, their Prophet, asked his people "Allah commands you to sacrifice a cow," they responded to that commandment, saying, "Are you mocking us?" That is, when they failed to understand the connection between that commandment and what they had asked him to do, they said: "Are you mocking us?" This demonstrated their utter ignorance of Allah and His Messenger (Moses). Moses informed them of Allah's commandment; he was not the one who commanded. Yet, even if he were the one who commanded them to do that, it would have been inappropriate for someone who believed in the Messenger (Moses) to receive his commandment in such a manner. When Moses said: "I seek refuge in Allah from acting foolishly!" and they were convinced that it was Allah who gave him that commandment, they started their stubbornness and excessive questions about its eyes and color. When these two questions were answered, they asked yet a third question. Now that these problems were solved, they 'hesitantly' did what they were commanded to do.
Among their worst vices and inappropriate behaviors was their saying to their Prophet: "Now you have come with the truth." If they meant to indicate that 'you did not come with the truth concerning the cow beforehand,' that would have been such a brazen, barefaced and shameless disbelief. If what they wanted to say was that 'now you have clearly pointed to the cow that we are commanded to sacrifice,' it was clearly due to their ignorance and witlessness since the statement was clear enough in saying: "Allah commands you to sacrifice a cow." The Messenger of Allah (Moses) came with the truth from the very beginning.

Imam Ibn Jarir said: "Some of the predecessors claimed that the people relinquished their faith and disbelieved Moses by saying: 'Now you have come with the truth.' It was claimed that that was a denial on their part that Moses came with the truth concerning the cow before that. That was not right because they complied with the order to slaughter the cow. Yet, what they said to Moses was witless and foolish, one of their lapses."

B) Evidence and proof of the accuracy and truth of what all prophets- from beginning to last- agree upon concerning the raising of the dead from their graves.
C) Providing signs, proofs and evidence for His servants in various ways, thereby enhancing the chances for guidance while cautioning those who go astray.
D) Informing us about the cruelty of that nation, its hardness and rigidity. It also informs us that faith did not take root in it.

On the authority of Wahab, Abdul-Samad Ibn Ma'qil said: "Ibn Abbas said: 'When Allah brought back the dead man to life, he told the people who killed him. The accused denied killing him and said: 'By Allah! We didn't kill him' even after they witnessed clear signs."

E) Giving the cruel unjust aggressor the opposite of what he intended to get, legally and practically. The killer craved to get the inheritance of the killed. He denied his involvement in the murder. Allah exposed and disgraced him, and He denied him the inheritance of the murdered.
F) The Children of Israel were deceived and lured twice by the cow to the exclusion of all other animals. They were lured to worship the calf, and they were also lured by the commandment to sacrifice the cow. Cows are amongst the most stupid animals. In fact, they are considered the epitome of stupidity and dullness.

At the conclusion of his analysis of this story, Imam Ibn al-Qayyim said: "It was apparent that that story came after the story of the calf. The commandment to slaughter the cow was to draw the attention that this kind of animal- which could be slaughtered, till the soil and water the fields- could not be a Allah to be worshipped in Allah's place. Rather, it was only suitable for slaughter, tilling the soil, watering the fields and other kinds of labor." [150]

5- Evidence of the Almighty Sovereignty, Dominion and Power. Bring the dead back to life by striking him with a piece of a slaughtered cow is evidence of the Almighty's authority and power over life and death. The act of striking was merely a means to reveal to people- through witnessing- the impact of Allah's ability, which was something they could not understand how it worked; they saw its supernatural and amazing consequences, yet they hardly knew its essence. Truthful are Allah's words: "Strike the dead body with a piece of the cow. This is how easily Allah brings the dead to life, showing you His signs so that you may understand." (Q 2:73)

Thus, this story had depicted the Children of Israel as people who procrastinated in religious matters bent on asking excessive questions, offending Moses, their Prophet, and not learning from the examples and lessons they were given. That was due to the cruelty of their hearts, their inappropriate conduct and their lack of discernment and acumen: "Whoever Allah allows to stray, none can guide." (Al-A'raf; Q 7:186)

In concluding our long discussion of the vices of the Children of Israel as portrayed by the Noble Qur'an, we say that their vices that we mentioned in this chapter were only examples of their wickedness and corruption which the successors inherited from their predecessors.

The Noble Qur'an mentioned these vices to record their deviation from the truth, their preference of misguidance and blindness over light and the straight path and to caution the believers against their wickedness and corruptions.

References

---

[1] Tafsir Al-Manar, Vol. 1, P. 370.
[2] Sura Al-Baqarah.
[3] Sura An-Nur: Verse 61.
[4] Tafsir Al-Manar, Vol. 1, P. 372.
[5] Liwaa Al-Islam Magazine, Vol. 11, Second Year.
[6] Al-Qurtubi said: "the نَقِيبٌ is a great man who would look for what his people in the tribe needed. He was thus called because he was well aware of who his people were and what they needed. Vol. 6. P. 112.
[7] Some say that this is a reference to Jerusalem- which is the most likely scenario. It is also said that it is a reference to Levant, or Jericho or Sinai and others.
[8] Go back to the interpretation of those noble verses under the section titled "Their keenness to live long and their cowardice to fight…" in this chapter.
[9] Tafsir Al-Kashshaaf, Al-Zamakhshari, Vol.1, P. 408.
[10] Tafsir Ibn Jarir, Vol. 6, P. 153. Al-Halabi Edition.
[11] Tafsir Ibn Jarir, Vol. 6, P. 155.
[12] Tafsir Al-Kashshaaf, Vol.1, P. 408.
[13] Al-Raghib, The Vocabulary of the Qur'an, P.491.
[14] خائنةdeceitful: You will always find deceit among a group or a sect of them.
[15] Tafsir Fakhr al-Din al-Razi, Vol. 3, P. 384, Al-Husyniyya Edition.
[16] Tafsir Ibn Kathir, Vol.1, P.436.
[17] Tafsir Ibn Jarir, Vol. 4.
[18] Tafsir Ibn Jarir, Vol. 1, P. 433.
[19] Sura Al-Anfal: Verse 58.
[20] We previously detailed the reasons for that battle and its consequences in Chapter "Punishing the Jews."

[21] We detailed the reasons for the battle Banu Nadir and its consequences in Chapter "Punishing the Jews."
[22] We talked in detail about the Battle of Banu Qurayza in the Chapter titled "Punishing the Jews."
[23] Sura Al-Baqarah: Verse 100.
[24] Tafsir Al-Kashshaaf, Vol.1, P. 227. Al-Halabi Edition.
[25] Tafsir Ibn Jarir, Vol. 1, P. 432.
[25a] Al-Razi's gloss on Qur'an 2:100 at the online website Tantawi helped create, www.altafsir.com, does convey that interpretation https://www.altafsir.com/Tafasir.asp?tMadhNo=0&tTafsirNo=4&tSoraNo=2&tAyahNo=100&tDisplay=yes&UserProfile=0&LanguageId=1
[26] Tafsir Ibn Kathir, Vol.1, P.423.
[27] Reasons for Revelation by Naysaburi, P. 76.
[28] Tafsir Al-Alusi, Vol. 1, P. 732.
[29] Tafsir Ibn Jarir, Vol. 1, P. 431.
[30] Sahih Al-Bukhari, The Book of Tafsir (Interpretation), Chapter, "Say, ⌜O Prophet, ⌝ 'Whoever is an enemy of Gabriel'," Vol. 6, P. 23.
[31] Musnad Ahmad ibn Hanbal, A Book by Ahmad ibn Hanbal, Vol. 1, P. 278.
[32] Tafsir Ibn Ashur "Liberation and Enlightenment),التحرير والتنوير Vol. 1. P. 8226.
[33] Tafsir Al-Kashshaaf, Vol.1, P. 226.
[34] Tafsir Ibn Jarir, Vol. 1, P. 439.
[35] Tafsir Al-Manar, Vol. 1, P. 394.
[36] Tafsir the noble verses by Sheikh Muhammad Abu Zahra. Liwaa Al-Islam Magazine, Vol. 11, Nineth Year.
[37] Tafsir Ibn Kathir, Vol.1, P.355.
[38] Tafsir Ibn Kathir, Vol.1, P.256.
[39] Tafsir Al-Qurtubi, Vol. 7, P. 403. Egypt Printing Press, 1938.
[40] Tafsir Al Fakhr Al-Razi, Vol. 4, P. 316, Al-Azhariyya Printing Press, 1308 H.
[41] Tafsir Al-Qurtubi, Vol. 7, P. 306.
[42] Tafsir Al-Qurtubi, Vol. 7, P. 307.
[43] Tafsir Al-Kashshaaf, Vol.1, P. 515.
[44] Tafsir Ibn Kathir, Vol.2, P.257.
[45] Tafsir Al-Alusi, Vol. 3, P. 147.
[46] Tafsir Al-Kashshaaf, Vol.1, P. 514.
[47] Tafsir Ibn Jarir, Vol. 1, P. 273.
[48] Tafsir Al-Kashshaaf, Vol.1, P. 514.
[49] "Relief to the Anxious from the Traps of Satan," Imam Ibn Al-Qayyim, P. 308.
[50] Sahih Al-Bukhari, Chapter "Do not Melt the Grease of Carrion," Vol. 3, P. 102. Also, in Muslim in the Book of Musaqat, Vol. 2, P. 1206, Al-Halabi Edition.
[51] Sahih Al-Bukhari, Chapter "Do not Melt the Grease of Carrion," Vol. 3, P. 102. Also, in Muslim in the Book of Musaqat, Vol. 2, P. 1207.
[52] Sura Al-Baqarah, verse 105.
[53] Tafsir Al-Kashshaaf, Vol.1, P. 228.
[54] Liwaa Al-Islam Magazine, Third Year, Vol. 5, P.6.
[55] Tafsir Al-Manar, Vol. 1, P. 421.
[56] Sura Al-Baqarah.

[57] Tafsir Ibn Jarir, Vol. 1, P. 443.
[58] Tafsir Al-Manar, Vol. 1, P. 397.
[59] Tafsir Al-Kashshaaf, Vol.1, P. 227.
[60] Tafsir Al-Manar, Vol. 1, P. 401.
[61] It is possible that ما/along is **related to** the magic promoted by the devils. In this case, the meaning would be: After the Jews cast Allah's Book, they followed the magic promoted by the devils during the time of Solomon, and they also followed the magic that was revealed to the two angels: Harut and Marut. Accordingly, the Almighty's saying: "the devils disbelieved. They taught magic to the people" would be a parenthetical sentence meant to acquit Solomon from the charge/allegation of using magic and attributing it to the devils to state that it was the devils who were taught magic and also taught it to the people to mislead them. There also other interpretations related to 'what had been revealed to the two angels," but we think that what we have mentioned is sufficient for our purposes.
[62] Babylon is a city in Iraq known for the widespread use of magic and wine.
[63] Tafsir Al-Kashshaaf, Vol.1, P. 228.
[64] مَثُوبَة to reward; it is a reward, something that is granted to others.
[65] Tafsir Al-Kashshaaf, Vol.1, P. 228.
[66] Tafsir Al-Aluci, Vol. 1, P. 384.
[67] Tafsir Ibn Kathir, Vol. 4, P.573.
[68] Fath Al-Bari by Ibn Hajar, Vol 12, P. 345, Al-Halabi Edition.
The meaning; Allah has answered my request by informing me about my condition (that I am bewitched).
[69] Interpretation of the Holy Qur'an by Ibn Al-Qayyim. Tafsir Sura Al-Falaq.
[70] Tafsir Al-Qurtubi, Vol. 2, P. 46.
[71] Sahih Muslim, The Book of Peace, Chapter on Magic, Vol.4, P. 1719. Report by Mr. Muhammad Fou'ad Abdul-Baqi.
[72] Liwaa Al-Islam Magazine, Third Year, # 3, P. 8.
[73] The Comprehensive Crown of the Fundamentals of the Hadiths of the Messenger by the honorable Sheikh Mansour Ali Nasif, Vol. 3, P. 30.
[74] الطمع/Reference here is made to desiring something badly.
[75] Corrupting the text: deviating from the right path. What was truthful and correct was likened to the right path; whatever was not correct or truthful was considered deviant and "corrupt."
[76] The pronoun in لَقُوا refers to the group of Jews who acted hypocritically. The pronoun in قَالُوا refers to those Jews who continued to believe in Judaism and who admonished the hypocrites for sharing with the believers what confirms the truthfulness of Muhammad.
[77] Tafsir Al-Razi, Vol. 1, P. 400.
[78] Tafsir Ibn Jarir Vol. 1, P. 370.
[79] Illiterate: those who do not read or write well.
[80] Tafsir Ibn Jarir Vol. 1, P. 375.
[81] الويل/ Woe: It is a term that denotes evil and perdition.
[82] Tafsir Al-Qasimi, Vol. 1, P. 174.
[83] Tafsir Al-Alusi, Vol. 2, P. 101.
[84] Tafsir Al-Razi, Vol. 10, P. 118. Abdul-Rahman Muhammad Edition.
[85] Tafsir Al-Kashshaaf, Vol.1, P. 267.

[86] Tafsir Ibn Kathir, Vol. 1, P.507.
[87] Tafsir Al-Manar, Vol. 5, P. 140.
[88] Al-Mufradat fi Gharib al-Quran, Al-Raghib P.198.
[89] Tafsir Al-Kashshaaf, Vol.1, P. 367.
[90] Interpretation of the Ocean by Abu Hayyan Al-Andalusi, vol. 3, P. 264.
[91] Tafsir Al-Kashshaaf, Vol.1, P. 235.
[92] The pronunciation of his name as mentioned in Tafsir Ibn Kathir, Vol. 2, P. 38.
[93] They claimed that one of them whose name was 'Awag Ibn 'Unuq was three thousand arm long and that 70 of Moses' men sat in the shade of one of them...etc.
[94] Tafsir Ibn Jarir, Vol. 1, P. 168.
[95] It was said that it was Jericho. It was also said it was the Levant. Ibn Jarir said: "It is best described as the Holy Land, as Allah's Prophet, Moses, said. It is certainly a land that falls between the Euphrates and Al-A'reesh in Egypt, as most interpreters, autobiographers and researchers agree." Vol. 6, P.172.
[96] Tafsir Ibn Jarir, Vol. 2, P. 172.
[97] The Arabic الجبارfrom the verb جَبَرَ (to force) is a term that is used to refer to a tall, enormously built haughty man who forces others and takes from them what he wants. The Arabic saying: "An enormous tree" which means extremely tall and its fruits could be reached by hand.
[98] Tafsir Al-Kashshaaf, Vol.1, P. 410.
[99] Tafsir Al-Kashshaaf, Vol.1, P. 411.
[100] Reference is made to a desert in which one is likely to wander aimlessly without direction or specific landmarks to guide them.
[101] Tafsir Ibn Jarir, Vol. 6, P. 127.
[102] Tafsir Al-Aluci, Vol. 6, P. 106.
[103] Tafsir Fakhr al-Din al-Razi, Vol. 3, P. 388.
[104] Tafsir Fakhr al-Din al-Razi, Vol. 3, P. 388.
[105] The reference is to the Almighty's: "Then this land is forbidden to them for forty years, during which they will wander through the land..."
[106] Ibn Khaldun Introduction, Chapter 19.
[107] Tafsir Al-Manar, P. 337.
[108] Tafsir Ibn Kathir, Vol. 2, P. 39.
[109] Verses: 138-141.
[110] Interpreters differ concerning those people who were "devoted to idols" when the Children of Israel passed by. Some say they were the Arabs of Lehem. Others say they were from Lehem and Guzam. It was also said that they were the Canaanites that Moses-peace be upon him- ordered his people to fight. It was also said that they were the Arabs that used to live close to Egypt's borders.
[111] Tafsir Al-Razi, Vol. 4, P. 291.
[112] Al-Qurtubi provides a note concerning the pronunciation of the word الخلي. Vol. 7, P. 284.
[113] Tafsir Ibn Kathir, Vol. 2.
[114] Tafsir Ibn Jarir, Vol. 9, P. 62.
[115] Tafsir Al-Qasimi, Vol. 7, P. 259.
[116] Tafsir Al-Razi, Vol. 4, P. 302.
[117] Tafsir Al-Kashshaaf, Vol. 1, P.510.

[118] Tafsir Al-Kashshaaf, Vol. 2, P.250.
[119]Tafsir Ibn Jarir, Vol. 16, P. 129.
[120] According to Naaf'I, Aasem and Issa بِمَلْكِنا which means "in our power." Ibn Kathir, Abou Omar and Ibn Aamer read it بملكنا in the sense of possession. And Hamza and Al-Kissa'I read it بمُلكنا in the sense of "ability." Al-Qurtubi, Vol. 11, P. 234.
[121] Tafsir Ibn Jarir, Vol. 16, P. 31.
[122] Tafsir Ibn Kathir, Vol. 3, P.162.
[123] Tafsir Ibn Kathir, Vol. 3, P.125.
[124] Tafsir Al-Razi, Vol. 22, P. 101.
[125] Tafsir Al-Razi, Vol. 22, P. 111.
[126] Tafsir Al-Razi, Vol. 22, P. 112.
[127] Tafsir Al-Aluci, "The Spirit of Meanings," Vol. 5, P. 598.
[128] Tafsir Al-Kashshaaf, Vol. 2, P.251.
[129] Tafsir Al-Aluci, Vol. 5, P. 298.
[130] Tafsir Al-Razi, Vol. 6, P. 81.
[131] Tafsir Ibn Kathir, Vol. 1, P.197. There are other views regarding this story by Ibn Jarir, Abou Hayyan and others, but we did not mention them because they do not differ from the interpretation we are providing except in some details.
[132] Liwaa Al-Islam Magazine, Vol. 7, Second Year, # 3, P. 8.
[133] The word ما(what) is used as an interrogative article to know the description
[134] الفارض A name to describe a cow that cannot bear because of age. It is thus called because it has reached a late stage, an old age. البكر Is a young one driven from البُكرة (the beginning of daylight), and it refers to a cow that has not born young yet. العوان Is a middle aged cow.
[135] Tafsir Ibn Jarir, Vol. 1, P. 235.
[136] Tafsir Al-Kashshaaf, Vol. 1, P.219.
[137]Tafsir Ibn Ashur "Liberation and Enlightenment), التحرير والتنوير Vol. 1. P. 532.
[138] Tafsir Ibn Jarir, Vol. 3, P. 358.
[139] ذَلُولٌ means flexible, easy and trained.
[140] Tafsir Al-Kashshaaf, Vol. 2, P.210.
[141] Tafsir Al-Kashshaaf, Vol. 1, P.220.
[142] Tafsir Ibn Ashur "Liberation and Enlightenment), التحرير والتنوير Vol. 1. P. 529.
[143] Tafsir Ibn Jarir, Vol. 1, P. 361.
[144] Tafsir Al-Manar, Vol. 1, P. 351.
[145] Tafsir Ibn Jarir, Vol. 1, P. 342.
[146] Tafsir Al-Kashshaaf, Vol. 1, P.221.
[147]Tafsir Ibn Jarir, Vol. 1, P. 347.
[148] Tafsir Ibn Jarir, Vol. 1, P. 347.
[149] Tafsir Al-Manar, Vol. 1, P. 346.
[150] Relief of the Distressed in the Traps of Satan إغاثة اللهفان, Vol. 2, P. 3.

Chapter Seven

The False Claims of the Jews
And
The Response Of The Noble Qur'an

When it comes to false claims, untruthful statements and insincere and dishonest assertions, the Jews seem to have a long and unparalleled history, one that is far-reaching and cannot be confirmed by anyone who is equipped with discernment and sound logical judgement.

The Noble Qur'an exposed these false claims and declarations that the Jews came up with. It demolished their excuses and shut their mouths, revealing their lies and falsehoods and exposing their vices, depravities and failings.

Before we begin to interpret the noble verses that mentioned their claims and allegations and responded to them, we would like to briefly mention a number of them. Here they are:

First: Their claim that the fire will not touch them except for a number of days.
Second: Their claim that they believe in what was sent down to them.
Third: Their claim that true guidance is in following their faith.
Fourth: Their claim that none except Jews will enter Paradise.
Fifth: Their claim that they are Allah's children and most loved.
Sixth: Their claim that Ezra was the son of Allah, parroting their rabbis.
Seventh: Their claim that their sins are forgiven.
Eighth: Their claim that they are not accountable for exploiting the Gentiles.
Ninth: Their outrageous accusation of Mary and their claim that they killed the Messiah.
Tenth: Their claim that Allah is tight-fisted.

These are some of their false claims and their despicable assertions. We present them as mentioned in the Noble Qur'an. Now, we will talk in detail About each claim and the decisive response to these allegations concerning those "attribute lies to Allah knowingly." (Q 3:78)

First: Their claim that the fire will not touch them except for a number of days:

Among the false contentions of the Jews is their claim that the Fire will not touch them except for a number of days. That is, they will not be punished for a long time because they believe that they are Allah's children and His most loved and that they are His chosen people, the one most favored among all nations. Thus, if Allah was to hold them accountable for their transgressions, it will be merely just as a merciful loving father punishes his spoiled children and loved ones: he will be harsh for just a little while, then he will resume normal loving behavior with them and will overlook their wrongdoing.

A) The Noble Qur'an recounted this claim and responded to it. In Sura Al-Baqara, the Almighty said: "˹Some of˺ the Jews claim, "The Fire will not touch us except for a number of days." Say, O Prophet,"Have you taken a pledge from Allah—for Allah never breaks His word—or are you ˹just˺ saying About Allah what you do not know?" But no! Those who commit evil and are engrossed in sin will be the residents of the Fire. They will be there forever. And those who believe and do good will be the residents of Paradise. They will be there forever."[1] (Al-Baqara; Q 2:80-82)

Commentators have recounted many reasons for the revelation of these verses, including what was narrated on the authority of Ibn Abbas who said: "The Jews used to say that this world is seven thousand years, and that we are only tormented for every thousand years for a day in the Fire, and they are only seven numbered days." So, Allah Almighty revealed: "And they said, 'The Fire will never touch us...'.[2]

Ibn Jarir narrated on the authority of Ibn Zayd who said: "My father told me that the Messenger of Allah said to the Jews: 'I ask you by Allah and by the Torah that Allah sent down to Moses on Mount Sinai, who are the people of Hell whom Allah mentioned in the Torah?' They said: 'Our Lord became angry with us, so we will remain in Hell for forty nights, then we will come out and you will replace us in it.' The Messenger of Allah said: 'By Allah, you have lied, we will never replace you in it.' So, the Qur'an was revealed in confirmation of the words of the Prophet and as a refutation and rejection of what they said. The Almighty said: "And they say: 'The Fire will not touch us except for a few days…' until His saying: 'They will abide therein eternally.'" (Q 2:81) [3]

Ibn Jarir also narrated on the authority of Ibn Abbas that he said regarding Allah the Almighty's saying: "And they say: 'The Fire will not touch us except for a few days…' That is, the enemies of Allah, the Jews, said, 'Allah will not admit us to the Fire except to fulfill the oath. The days in which we worshipped the calf were forty days. So, when those days have passed, the punishment and the oath will be cut off from us.' [4]

These are some of the reasons that were reported regarding the revelation of the noble verses, and the meaning is that the Jews said: 'O Muhammad! The Fire will not afflict us, and we will not taste its heat, except for a few days.' Say to them, O Muhammad! in response to their false claim, 'Have you taken a covenant from Allah regarding that so that its fulfillment will be certain? Or do you say falsehoods About Allah out of ignorance and audacity?' Then the Noble Qur'an invalidated their claim with a general principle that includes them and others, saying: It is not as you claim, but the truth is that whoever commits a sin and is overpowered by it and dies without repenting to Allah 'Then those are the companions of the Fire; they will abide therein eternally. And those who believe and do righteous deeds are the companions of Paradise; they will abide therein eternally.'

And the Almighty's statement that they said, 'The Fire will not touch us except for a few days' (Q 2:80) is a statement of a type of their arrogance and lies, as connected to their previous vices that the Holy Quran narrated. The pronoun in the Almighty's statement, 'And they said' refers to the Jews, About whom the discussion has already begun and has not yet ended.

Touching المس is the contact of one thing with another in a way that is felt. What is meant by the Fire النار is the Fire of the Hereafter. What is meant by "counted معدود is limited and few. It is said that something is counted to indicate little or few. And something uncounted to mean many. So, they claim that the Fire will not touch them except for a short period, which may be seven days, or it may be forty days, and after that they will go out to Paradise, because everything counted will come to an end.

Then, the Almighty Allah commanded His Messenger to respond to their claims. He said: "Say, O Prophet,'Have you taken a pledge from Allah—for Allah never breaks His word—or are you ˹just˺ saying About Allah what you do not know?'" (2:80) That is, tell them, O Muhammad, that such a confirmation that the Fire will not touch them except for a number of days could not be verified except from those who have secured a pledge from Allah. Ask them if they received such a confirmation from Allah that the Fire will not touch them except for a number of days and thus fulfilling such a pledge was a certainty, a fait accompli? For Allah would never breach His promises or are they just saying About Allah something that they do not know About?

The interrogation was meant to express denunciation and reproof. It was directed at their claim that the Fire will not touch them except for a number of days. It was as though the Almighty was telling them that what they were saying could only mean one of two things: either they secured a pledge from Allah or they were saying something About Allah without knowledge. Since pledge-taking did not actually happen, then you Jews were lying concerning your claim that the Fire will not touch you except for a number of days.

Imam Al-Razi said: "The Almighty's "Have you taken…" was not meant as an interrogation. Rather, it was a denunciation since it was unfit that Allah would make His Messenger's justification for annulling their claim come in the form of an interrogation. Rather, interrogation was intended to caution them through inference. That is, there was no way to get to the truth except through hearing (that such a pledge was uttered0, and since proof of hearing was nonexistent, it was imperative not ascertain such a confirmation (that it came from Allah). [5]

Yet, the Noble Qur'an responded to their claim in the form of an interrogation that they were saying About Allah what they did not know, since they could not prove that Allah promised them what they claimed He did, namely, that the Fire will not touch them except for a number of days, and there was no authentic text in their Book that confirms what they claimed.

Thus, the noble verse repealed their claim and utterly nullified it in a style that denoted denunciation and condemnation. Then, the Almighty said another verse that abolished their claim through proving what they negated. He said: "But no! Those who commit evil and are engrossed in sin will be the residents of the Fire. They will be there forever." (Q 2:81)

بَلَى =No" is a word that indicates a response, and it is used to prove that a verb was used in the negative form before it. The negated verb here was the Jews' saying "The Fire will not touch us except for a number of days." The use of "بَلَى =No" was used to prove that the Fire will touch them more than what they claimed for they will be there forever because of their disbelief and their lies.

The meaning of the verse is: It is not as you had claimed, O Jews, that the Fire will not touch you except for a number of days. In truth, you will reside in it forever, for everyone who is immersed in his sins and has been utterly enslaved and surrounded by them as a marquee surrounds those who are inside, and everyone who dies before believing and repenting for his sins will reside in the Fire forever.

Thus, the noble verse annulled their claim and proved what they negated in a way that would include them as well as those follow in their footsteps and claim what they claimed and show disbelief like them.

The word "سَيِّئَةً = evil" here refers to associating partners with Allah, as most commentators agree, since their predecessors' traces indicate that. And the Almighty's "engrossed in sin" to emphasize that once sin has overpowered an individual and he succumbs to it wholeheartedly, he would lose his faith, curbed his tongue, and he would be unable to say anything.

The Almighty's "They will be there (the Fire) forever" was a statement About the punishments that Allah has prepared for them on account of their disbelief and for lying to Allah. On Judgement Day, the Fire will be their eternal abode for preferring worldly life, disbelief and wrongdoing over those things which could have allowed them to enter Paradise, i.e., faith and good and righteous deeds.

After the Almighty recounted what He has prepared for them and other disbelievers like them who are given to slander and lies, he followed it with what He has prepared for those righteous and faithful ones. He said: "And those who believe and do good will be the residents of Paradise. They will be there forever." (Q 2:82) That is, those who believed in Allah and His messengers-, obeyed them, complied with Allah's commandments, did what Has asked them to do, and shunned what He has prohibited- those are the residents of Paradise, and they will be there forever. Thai is a favor that Allah bestows on those according to His will, for He is the Almighty and Most Benevolent Allah.

We can thus see that the noble verses aptly responded to the Jews' claims. They nullified their declarations that the Fire will not touch them except for a number of days and that they will go to Paradise after that. They also told them that they will reside in the Fire forever and informed all infidels that that is also their destiny. As for the righteous who have followed their messengers and believed, their abode will be Paradise where they will have their eternal abode.

B- In Sura Al-Imran we read that the Jews were invited to the Book of Allah to settle their disagreements, but they rejected that offer because of their belief that the Fire will not touch them except for a number of days. Here are the verses: "Have you not seen those who were given a portion of the Scriptures? Yet when they are invited to the Book of Allah to settle their disputes, some of them turn away heedlessly. This is because they say, "The Fire will not touch us except for a few days." They have been deceived in their faith by their wishful lying. But how 'horrible' will it be when We gather them together on the Day About which there is no doubt—when every soul will be paid in full for what it has done, and none will be wronged!" (Q 3:23-25)

Ibn Jarir narrated on the authority of Ibn Abbas, he said: "The Messenger of Allah, may Allah bless him and grant him peace, entered the school house upon a group of Jews, and called them to Allah. Then An-Nu'man ibn Amr and Al-Harith ibn Zayd said to him: 'What religion do you follow, O Muhammad?' He said: 'The religion and faith of Abraham.' They said: 'Abraham was a Jew.' Then the Messenger of Allah said to them: 'Come to the Torah, for it judges between us and you.' But they refused him. So Allah Almighty revealed About them: 'Have you not seen those who were given a portion of the Scripture? They are invited to the Book of Allah to judge between them' up to the Almighty's saying: 'And what they used to invent deceived them in their religion.'" [6]

Imam Al-Qurtubi said: "These arguments recounted that the verses under discussion were revealed because a group of Jews spurned the Muhammad's prophethood, so he said to them: 'Come to the Torah as it writes About my characteristics.' They rejected that." [7]

Imam Ibn Jarir said: "The first of the sayings in interpreting this, in my opinion, is the correct one to say: 'Allah, the Most High, informed About a group of Jews who were among the emigrants of the Messenger of Allah during his time, and who had been given knowledge of the Torah. They were called to the Book of Allah, which they acknowledged was from Allah and was in the Torah, to discuss matters over which they and the Messenger of Allah disputed. It may be possible that their dispute, over which they contended and then were called to the ruling of the Torah but refused to respond to it, was the issue related to Muhammad's prophethood. It may be possible that this was an issue related to Abraham, the friend of the Most Merciful, and his religion. It may be possible that this was a specific case, for they disputed with the Messenger of Allah over many issues. So, the Messenger called them to the ruling of the Torah, but he refused to respond to it. So, Allah exposed their lies and falsehoods and demonstrated their ingratitude and rudeness to what was in their Book and their reluctance and averseness to comply with their pledges." [8]

The meaning of the noble verses is: You have seen and witnessed, O Muhammad, those Jews who were given a portion of the Scriptures being invited to Allah's Book- (the Torah that Allah sent down to them to judge between them and settle all their disputes)- but they turned away and refused to accept it. They are people who are disposed to rejecting

Allah's orders and inclined to turn away from His rulings under the pretext that the Fire will only touch them for a number of days. They are prone to deception and wishful lying claiming that their forefathers will intercede on their behalf on Judgement Day. In fact, Muhammad, they will be severely and painfully punished on that Day. They will reside in the Fire forever when they are asked to present their account, and they will not be dealt with unjustly.

The Almighty's: "Have you not seen those who were given a portion of the Scriptures? Yet when they are invited to the Book of Allah to settle their disputes...?" (Q 3:23) was a statement to one kind of their stubbornness. They were invited to the Book in which they believe to settle their disputes; however, they refused to accept it and turned away because they were people who had gone astray and completely succumbed to wrongdoing.

The Almighty's expression "Have you not seen ...?" means that you have seen and verified the manners of those Jews. The interrogation was meant to be a denunciation, a scolding. The negation of the negative is an expression of a positive, a confirmation. The negation of "not seeing" was meant to confirm the act of seeing. The idea was expressed in such a light to show amazement at their conduct, to rebuke them for their words and deeds and to indicate the inappropriateness of perpetrating the deeds they performed and the words they uttered.

And the meaning of "those who were given a portion of the Scriptures" meant those who were familiar with the Torah, their Book, from which they had come to know the truth About your prophethood, O Muhammad, and the truth About what you have reported About your Allah. However, those rabbis who were given a portion of the Scripture neither benefited from this knowledge nor complied with its tenets or rulings. They merely used it in matters that suited their desires, and they ignored and refuted whatever was in opposition with these desires.

So, the noble verse chastised them further and rebuked them even more for persistently and knowingly abandoning the rulings of their Book because of their total capitulation to their delusions and submitting to their aberrations.

The "Book of Allah" to which they were invited to settle their disputes was the Torah. It was also said that it could have been a reference to the Qur'an. We are more inclined to believe the first view because the reasons for revelation support it, and most commentators agree with this view. Also, it enhances amazement at their conduct and annuls their justifications utterly since the Book that they turned away from and refused to follow its rulings WAS THEIR Book which came down to guide them and which they confirmed its truth.

The Almighty's "some of them turn away heedlessly" (Q 3:23) means that after being invited to the ruling of the Book of Allah, a large group of them turned away, rejected its rulings and teachings and abandoned them.

The use of ثُمَّ (=yet) which here expressed indolence indicated the implausibility of their turning away after learning that it was imperative to go back to the Book of Allah. It was their duty to willingly embrace the ruling of the Book of Allah because they were not ignorant or illiterate. However, they persisted on their blind stubbornness and wrongdoing. Thus, there was that great disparity between what they ought to have done on account of their knowledge and what they actually did when they turned away from the ruling of the Book of Allah.

The Almighty's "turn away heedlessly" indicated that this tendence to turn away from the truth was deeply-rooted, a second nature. It was not a temporary or incidental phenomenon; rather, it was something that was continuous and endless, inseparable from their manner of thinking.

Then, the Almighty showed the reasons that caused them to turn away from the rulings of Allah's Book. He said: "This is because they say, 'The Fire will not touch us except for a few days.'" In other words, the reason for their turning away from the truth, their refusal to abide by the rulings of the Book of Allah and not doing what was right was that they were making things easier for themselves by lessening the severity of the expected punishment, believing that they will not be punished for a long time, that the Fire will not touch them except for a number of days (either forty or seven days), and they will then be out of the Fire because they are Allah's children and His most favored ones and that their forefathers were prophets who will intercede on their behalf.

Their claim betrays their conceit and arrogance and regarding Allah's warnings frivolously and lightly. Those who take Allah's warnings lightly are devoid of the sanctity of faith and depleted of the holiness of religion. They would rush to commit transgressions heedlessly and nonchalantly. This is the case of peoples and nations and individuals when they disbelieve in Allah and become morally bankrupt.

The Almighty's "They have been deceived in their faith by their wishful lying" (Q 3:24) means that they were deceived by their deviant and thoughtless beliefs and their wishful thinking that the Fire will not touch them except for a few days.

Then the Almighty responded to their false claims and untrue allegations by proving that reward and punishment is only dependent on faith and good deeds. He said: "But how ⌜horrible⌝ will it be when We gather them together on the Day About which there is no doubt—when every soul will be paid in full for what it has done, and none will be wronged!" (Q 3:25) That is, what will they be like when We gather them together on that certain inescapable Day? They will certainly be shocked for the disappearance of their conceit and their unsound and corrupt illusions concerning the Day of Resurrection because they will be severely punished for their words and deeds, and they will reside in the Fire forever.

Thus, these noble verses eradicated their allegations and eliminated their claims. They responded to their conceit and arrogance in a way that closed their mouths shut so that those who will perish and those who will live will be aware why they will live or perish. Allah is the All- Hearing and Most Knowledgeable

Second: Their claim that they believe in what was sent down to them:

One of the false excuses the Jews made when invited to enter into Islam was their claim that "We are only called upon to believe in the Toral only. It is enough for us to believe in it and nothing else." The Noble Qur'an recounted this claim and responded to it. In Sura Al-Baqara, the Almighty said: "When it is said to them: "Believe in what Allah has revealed," they reply, "We only believe in what was sent down to us," and they deny what came afterwards, though it is the truth confirming their own Scriptures! Ask ˹them, O Prophet˺, "Why then did you kill Allah's prophets before, if you are ˹truly˺ believers?" Indeed, Moses came to you with clear proofs, then you worshipped the calf in his absence, acting wrongfully. And when We took your covenant and raised the mountain above you ˹saying˺, "Hold firmly to that ˹Scripture˺ which We have given you and obey," they answered, "We hear and disobey." The love of the calf was rooted in their hearts because of their disbelief. Say, O Prophet,"How evil is what your so-calledbelief prompts you to do, if you actually believe in the Torah!""" (Al-Baqara Q 2:91-93)

The meaning of these verses is: When the Jews- who lived during the time of Muhammad- were invited to believe in the Qur'an that Allah sent down to Muhammad, they would say: 'We only believe in what was sent down to us, namely, the Torah, which Allah sent down to Moses.' (Q 2:91) They would deny and denounce anything else, namely, the Noble Qur'an which confirmed their own Scriptures that commanded them to follow Muhammad. Then, the Almighty commanded His Messenger to impugn and dispute their claim that they believed in what was sent down to them. He said: "Ask ˹them, O Prophet˺, "Why then did you kill Allah's prophets before, if you are truly believers" (Q 2:91) in the Torah since it forbids you from killing them? Then, the Noble Qur'an once again impugned: "Indeed, Moses came to you with clear proofs." (Q 2:92) That is, Moses revealed clear signs of his truthfulness, but "you worshipped the calf in his absence," (Q 2:92) when he had an appointment to meet his Allah. You acted "wrongfully" for worshipping other than the Almighty Allah.

Then, the Noble Quran impugned them for claiming belief in what was sent down to them in yet another way other than the one mentioned before. The Almighty said: "And when We took your covenant and raised the mountain above you" (Q 2:93) and said: "Hold firmly to that ˹Scripture˺ which We have given you." (Q 2:93) In other words, be serious and diligent "and obey" (Q 2:93) willingly and cheerfully what you were commanded to do. However, your predecessors- whom you resemble and follow in their footsteps- said (Q 2:93) to their prophet "We hear" what you say but "disobey" your commandments. Their love of the calf was rooted in their hearts just as water seeps into all the parts of the human body. All of these deeds run counter to your claims that you believed in what was sent down to you. How dreadfully evil was what your so-called belief prompted you to do if you truly believed in the Torah, as you claimed! In fact, the Torah had nothing to do with your evil deeds, and you were worlds apart from believing in it.

The Almighty's "When it is said to them: 'Believe in what Allah has revealed,' they reply, 'We only believe in what was sent down to us'" depicted another type of the vices of the Jews. It demonstrated their turning away from the truth under the pretext that they asked to believe in nothing other than what Allah sent down to Moses, namely, the Torah. "[W]hat Allah has revealed" was a reference to the Noble Qur'an. It did not mention the receiver of the revelation, Muhammad, since that fact was well known or to emphasize the necessity and imperativeness that believing in the Book was sufficient to indicate that it was sent down from Allah. Once the belief that the Noble Qur'an came down from Allah was well established in one's soul, it would naturally follow that it was sent down to Muhammad.

Their saying: "We only believe in what was sent down to us" (Q 2:91) means "We believe only in the Torah that Allah revealed to our prophet Moses, nothing else. Their response betrayed their stupidity and stubbornness, because he who was calling them to believe was asking them to believe in all heavenly Books that Allah has revealed. However, they restricted themselves to believing in some of what Allah has sent down, namely, what was sent down to them (the Torah). As such, their belief was not congruent with what Allah commanded them: belief in ALL the revealed Books. There is no doubt that those who believe in some of the Revealed Books and disbelieve in others would be considered a disbeliever in all of them.

And the Almighty's "and they deny what came afterwards" (Q 2:91) was a statement of their clear disbelief of the Noble Qur'an after they hinted at that by their "We only believe in what was sent down to us." (Q 2:91) The pronoun ه in وَرَآءَهُ refers to "what was sent down to us," which is the Torah. That is, they said: 'We believe in what was sent down to us while, in fact, they disbelieve in what was revealed before the Torah and also what came down after it: the Noble Qur'an.

Ibn Jarir said: "The interpretation of وَرَآءَهُ in this context is before... Also, the meaning of the Almighty's 'they deny what came afterwards' is what was before the Torah and also the Revealed Books that Allah sent down to His messengers after it."[9]

The pronoun "it= هُوَ" in "it is the truth confirming their own Scriptures" refers to the Noble Qur'an which is metaphorically referred to in His "what came afterwards." (Q 2:91)And "the truth" means the ruling that corresponded and was in agreement with the reality. The Noble Qur'an was described as such for containing rulings that are in agreement with facts and reality.

The fact that the Qur'an confirmed what the Jews had, namely, the Torah indicated the prophethood of the Prophet. It confirmed the Torah that predicted the Prophet and mentioned characteristics that were only applicable to him alone. Thus, the Jews- who claimed to believe in what was sent down to them- were lying because they did not believe in Muhammad who was prophesied in their Torah which commanded them to believe in him and which the Noble Qur'an confirmed it in this regard.

Al-Zamakhshari said: "The Almighty's saying '"it is the truth confirming their own Scriptures' is a response to their 'We only believe in what was sent down to us' because if they disbelieved in what the Torah brought, they had disbelieved in the Torah itself." [10]

Then the Almighty commanded His Messenger to rebuke and impugn their claim that they are believers in what Allah has sent down to them by providing am inescapable proof. He said: "Ask them, O Prophet, "Why then did you kill Allah's prophets before, if you are truly believers?" (Q 2:91)

The meaning is: "Muhammad! Ask those Jews whom you called to believe in you who said: 'We only believe in what was sent down to us,' if you truly believe in what was sent down to you, the Torah, why do you kill Allah's prophets which the Torah prohibits and which commands you to follow and obey since Allah sent them to guide and lead you to what is good and profitable!

Killing them is the greatest evidence that you do not believe in what was sent down to you or in anything else. It only shows that you are disingenuous and untruthful because most of what Allah has revealed prohibits the killing of prophets and commands people to follow and believe them.

The meaning of the verse is indicated in the negation of the conditional statement, namely, their being believers, since there is no reason for killing the prophets except their disbelief in the Torah. This is the same case when you find no sense and reason in a man for doing what should not be done by a sensible and rational human being. In such a situation, you would ask: 'If you were truly reasonable, why did you do that?' In other words, you are indicating that he is not reasonable.

And the "ف" in فَلِمَ تَقْتُلُونَ 'Why then did you kill' in the response statement of the conditional sentence clarifies the point: If you are believers, why do you kill Allah's prophets?

The use of the present (the text in the Qur'an uses the present tense/تَقْتُلُونَ)- though perpetrated by their predecessors- is meant to bring this heinous crime to the forefront and to caution and remind them that these dreadful criminal acts happen again and again and that the successors blindly and thoughtlessly follow in the footsteps of their predecessors. The Jews who were contemporaneous with the Prophet tried to kill him, but the Almighty protected and saved him from their deceit and cunningness.

The Almighty called His prophets "Allah's prophets" (Q 2:91) to indicate their high esteem and great honor. This also indicated the appallingly horrific and shocking nature of the Jews' rebellion since they killed those whom they should have believed, obeyed and revered.

The Noble Qur'an also mentioned other crimes and atrocities that indicated that they did not believe in what was sent down to them. Among these was their worshipping the calf.

The Almighty said: “Indeed, Moses came to you with clear proofs, then you worshipped the calf in his absence, acting wrongfully.” (Q 2:92)

“Clear proofs/ٱلْبَيِّنَٰتِ” refers to the signs and miracles that indicated his honesty and the truthfulness of his prophecy such as the staff becoming a snake, the parting of the sea, springs of water gushing out of the rocks, etc.

These were called ٱلْبَيِّنَٰتِ because since no ordinary human being can make such miracles without Allah’s help, they were “proofs” of Moses’ truthful message and prophethood.

The meaning is: Children of Israel! Moses came to you with undeniable evidence that proved his truthfulness and the validity of his prophecy. It was incumbent upon you to believe him, but you didn’t. You took the calf as your Allah when he left for his appointment with his Allah even after you witnessed these signs that proved the truth of what he informed you About his Allah. You acted wrongfully because you abandoned Him who is worthy of worshipping and worshipped a good-for-nothing calf.

The noble verse disputed and annulled their claim that they believed in what was sent down to them because if they truly believed in their prophet who came to them with clear and undeniable proofs, they would not have abandoned what he commanded them to do, i.e., worshipping Allah, or done what he had prohibited them from doing, i.e., worshipping the calf.

The Noble Qur’an recounted another crime that impugned their claim that they “believe in what was sent down to” them: their unwillingness to accept the Torah out of stubbornness, defiance and conceit. The Almighty said: “And when We took your covenant and raised the mountain above you ˹saying˺, “Hold firmly to that ˹Scripture˺ which We have given you and obey,” they answered, “We hear and disobey.” The love of the calf was rooted in their hearts because of their disbelief. Say, O Prophet, “How evil is what your so-called belief prompts you to do, if you actually believe in the Torah!”” (Q 2:93)

The meaning of the noble verse is: Remember, O Children of Israel, when We took your covenant to comply with what is in the Torah and abide by its rulings obediently and willingly! Remember when We raised the mountain above you to show you one of Our greatest signs to fortify and strengthen your faith and prompt you to eagerly and willingly accept the teachings of the Torah! We said to you: “Hold firmly to what We have given you and obey Our commandments meticulously and with diligence. But you, O Children of Israel- who claim to believe in what was sent down to you- rejected the Torah that you were commanded to accept and said to your prophet: ‘we hear you, but we disobey your commandments.’ The love of the calf was rooted in your hearts and penetrated them just as water penetrates and seeps into the inner recesses of the body. You did not heed the light and guidance that the Torah brought you. Neither did you heed the clear glorious sign of raising the mountain above you. You rejected and disbelieved and yearned for the worship of the calf. You followed your predecessors’ path of stubbornness, ungratefulness and rejection of the truth that Allah sends down to you. If that is the case, how can you then claim that you believe in what was sent down to you?

The Almighty then commanded His Prophet to chastise and rebuke them. He said: "Say, O Prophet, "How evil is what your so-called belief prompts you to do, if you actually believe in the Torah!"" (Q 2:93)

The meaning of the Almighty's "We ... raised the mountain above you" (Q 2:93) is: We moved and suspended it in the air for you to witness with your own eyes a cosmic sign that should have prompted you to believe and obey if you had minds to understand and comprehend.

And His "Hold firmly to that ˹Scripture˺ which We have given you and obey" means: We said to you: 'take what we commanded you to do in the Torah with thoroughness and diligence, persevere in complying with what is in it, and listen and obey with understanding and commitment what you are commanded to do.' The Almighty's command to 'listen' is not a request to merely listen, but it is meant to be taken seriously and to prompt them to respond in accordance with the importance of the commandment. It emphasizes and confirms the Almighty's "Hold firmly to that Scripture..." (Q 2:93)

The Almighty then recounts their response which showed their stubbornness. He said: "they answered, 'We hear and disobey.'" (Q 2:93)

Al-Zamakhshari said: "If I asked: 'How similar is the Almighty's saying to their response? I would say, it is similar in as much as He said to them: 'Listen and your listening should be one indicating acceptance and obedience.' They said: 'We listened, but our listening is not to obey.'" [11]

Commentators differ in interpreting this verse: Did they actually utter these words or did they do something that replaced the utterance and thus it was just a metaphor for their action?

Al-Fakhr Al-Razi said: "The majority of exegetes believe that they actually uttered these words. Abu Muslim said: 'It is possible that they heard the commandment and rejected and disobeyed. That rejection was then expressed by these words even though they may have not uttered them, as in the Almighty's saying: "saying to it (the heaven) and to the earth, 'Submit, willingly or unwillingly.' They both responded, 'We submit willingly.' He said: 'The first view is more likely." [12]

The statement "The love of the calf was rooted in their hearts because of their disbelief" follows their "We hear and disobey" immediately. The word love (الاشراب)from drinking-metaphorically means mixing one color with another. It is as if one color is mixed with another color as in white tainted with red to indicate the mixing of the red with the white color.

Imam Al-Razi said: "'The love of the calf was rooted in their hearts' is a metaphor that can be interpreted in one of two ways. The first meaning: it might be that the love of the calf and the eagerness to worship it penetrated (mixed in) their hearts just as a dye colors a dress. And His saying: 'The love of the calf was rooted in their hearts' is meant to indicate the place where this mixing/penetration took place as in His saying: 'Indeed, those ... consume nothing but fire into their bellies.' The second meaning: just as drinking/water is indispensable element to the life of everything that comes out of the earth, that love was also an element to all the deeds that they perpetrated." [13]

The meaning of "The love of the calf was rooted in their hearts because of their disbelief" is: Those Jews who have been accustomed to mutiny and disobedience had the love of the calf intermingled with their hearts and souls. It was deeply rooted and they had imbibed it in their hearts to the extent that it ran through their being just as water amalgamates and melds in all organs of the body. The Arabic statement "وأشربوا في قلوبهم العجل" omits the word "love" from the noble verse which indicates their strong attachment to the calf as though they consumed (literally, drank) it.

Expressing the idea by using the word اشربوا indicates that their love of the calf was so consuming that they had no choice but to "drink" it, as though someone else forced them to "drink" it (this love).

The Almighty's "because of their disbelief" is evidence that their love of the calf was the result of prior acts of disbelief, a deeply-ingrained ungratefulness. Thus, the disbelief that led them to worship the calf was preceded by other acts of disbelief. In other words, it was disbelief upon disbelief.

Then, the Almighty commanded His Prophet to rebuke them. He said: "How evil is what your so-called belief prompts you to do, if you actually believe in the Torah!" (Q 2:93) In other words: Muhammad! Tell those Jews- who claim to believe in what was sent down to them- that what they believe in and prompts them to do the things they do is evil and dreadful: the killing of the prophets, worshipping the calf, rebelliousness and rejection, if they were true believers in the Torah as they claim. In fact, the Torah never commanded them to do any of those things. You are not believers in the Torah or any of the Books that Allah revealed because these Books do not encourage wrongdoing and transgression.

Thus, the noble statement annulled their claim "We only believe in what was sent down to us" (Q 2:91) after the Almighty has annulled it with the various previously mentioned proofs because when they claimed that- while still perpetrating dreadful and evil deeds incongruent with faith in any revealed Book, the Almighty commanded His Prophet to chastise them for all those deeds that contradict belief in what was sent down to them so that everyone would realize that their claims were groundless and unjustified.

Adding the word "faith," the Almighty said إِيمَـٰنُكُمْ (your so-called faith). He did not just say "faith" because it was fake and untrue. He therefore used the word to ridicule and deride them and belittle and mock their mentality.

The Almighty's "if you actually believe" (Q 2:93) was meant to impugn their belief in the Torah and dispute the validity of their claims. True belief commands worshipping Allah Alone, and it prohibits associating others with Him and forbids perpetrating evil and unrighteous deeds.

Thus, the statement has a negative meaning because of their claim that they believed in the Torah because it did not command anything that Allah abhors.

Imam Ibn Jarir said: "His saying 'if you actually believe' means: if you actually believed in what Allah sent down to you, as you claimed. However, Allah impugned them because the Torah prohibits all of this and commands the opposite of what they did. He therefore told them that if their belief in the Torah commands them to do what they did, then it was indeed evil and dreadful what the Torah commanded them to do. But Allah negated that the Torah would command them to perpetrate deeds that He abhors. Their so-called faith shows their going against Allah's commandments. It was their own wishes and desires that was behind their lawlessness, animosity and aggression." [14]

Thus, we can see that these noble verses had established numerous evidence and undeniable proofs of the Jews' lies and claims concerning their belief in what was sent down to them. They rebuked and censured them for their false claims and their untrue and corrupt statements.

The honorable Dr. Muhammad Abdu-Allah Draz had some powerful observations when he discussed these verses. He- may Allah have mercy upon his soul- said:

"Mentioning Jewish pilgrims, the Almighty said: "When it is said to them: "Believe in what Allah has revealed," they reply, "We only believe in what was sent down to us," and they deny what came afterwards, though it is the truth confirming their own Scriptures! Ask ⸢them, O Prophet⸣, "Why then did you kill Allah's prophets before, if you are ⸢truly⸣ believers?"

This is an excerpt from a chapter from the story of the Children of Israel. The principal elements that these few words highlight can be summed up in the following points:

1- A piece of advice from an advisor to the Jews: he invites them to believe in the Qur'an.
2- Their response to this advisor in a way that has two meanings.
3- The answer to the response (including the two meanings) from various angles.

I swear that if an eloquent lawyer were entrusted with the litigation in the language of the Qur'an in this case, and he were then guided to deduce these meanings that are stirring in the soul of the caller and the called, he would not be able to express them in these words. And perhaps after that he would not be able to fulfill the allusions, precautions, etiquette and morals surrounding them. The advisor said to the Jews: Believe in the Qur'an as you believed in the Torah. Did you not believe in the Torah that Moses brought because it was revealed by Allah? The Qur'an that Muhammad brought was revealed by Allah, so believe in it as you believed in the Torah.

Look at how the Qur'an has gathered this great meaning in this brief terse expression: "Believe in what Allah has revealed." (Q 2:91) The secret as that it had changed the speech from the explicit name of the Qur'an to its metaphor. So, it had made their call to believe in it a call to something with its proof, and in that way, it had brought out the proof and the invitation in one expression.
Then look at how he omitted the mention of the one to whom it was revealed. He did not say: Believe in what Allah revealed "to Muhammad," even though this is a complementary part of the description of the Qur'an intended for the call. Do you know why that was? ...

Because if it were mentioned, it would be, in the view of rhetorical wisdom, redundant, and in the view of guiding wisdom, corrupting!!

As for the first: because this specificity had no bearing on the obligation, the matter was managed according to the common measure and the middle limit, which was the pillar of evidence.

As for the second: because uttering this name to the enemies' ears was likely to bring out their grudges and stir up their hatred, which would have led to the opposite of what the caller intended in terms of reconciliation and reform.

The Jews' answer was that they said: 'What called us to believe in the Torah is not only that it was revealed by Allah, but that we believed in it because Allah revealed it to us, and the Qur'an was not revealed to us. So, you have your Qur'an, and we have our Torah, and every nation has its own law and method!'

This is the meaning that the Qur'an summarized in its statement: "We only believe in what was sent down to us." This is the first purpose. What added to the brevity of this statement is that the subject of the revelation, which is the Divine Name, was omitted from it, because it was mentioned previously.

It is clear that their limiting themselves to believing in what was revealed to them indicates their disbelief in what was revealed to others, and this is the second purpose, but they avoided stating it explicitly, because it would be heinous to record themselves as disbelievers, so the Qur'an wanted to highlight it. See how it highlighted it?

It did not make the consequence of their doctrine its doctrine, nor did it include the content of their statement in the sum of what it transmitted from their words, but rather it brought it out in the context of explaining and commenting on their statement: The Qur'an said: "and they deny what came afterwards." Isn't that the ultimate honesty in transmission? Then it was time for responding and discussing what they disclosed and what they concealed!

It did not start by disputing their claim in their faith of their Book. Rather, it temporarily left it as though it was a given. It did this to ascertain the necessity of believing in other Books, for how could their belief in their Book prompt them- or be a reason- to disbelieve in others that are just as worthy? No! "It is the truth." (Possibly Q 69:51, "And indeed this Qur'an is the absolute truth."?) And would "the truth" object to, or contradict, the truth"? Would belief in one necessitate disbelief in the other?

Then it goes on to say: 'The matter between this new Book and the Books that came before it is not like the matter between one truth and another. Something may be true and something else may also be true, so they do not contradict one another but, rather, they deal with two different matters. Thus, one does not necessarily bear witness to the other. As for this Book, it came as a witness and confirmation of the books that came before it. So how can someone who believes in it impugn others?'

Look at the perfection of the art of rhetoric: it is a word that was raised, and another that was placed in its place when needed; so, this word was a decisive factor in every excuse, and a blocking of every door of escape; rather, this word alone was like a movement to encircle the opponent, accomplished in one step, without any fuss or fanfare.

When it had satisfied the need to respond from this perspective, which it had presented in the course of objection and digression, it turned to responding to the original purpose that they boasted About, which was their claim to believe in what was revealed to them. It showed their blatant lies, denial and rejection, and it demonstrated that the disease of denial in them was an old disease, which they had imbibed in their hearts for centuries, until it became a chronic disease, and that what they had done today concerning disbelief in what was revealed to Muhammad was nothing but a connected link in the chain of their disbelief in what was revealed to them. It presented the horrific and undeniable historical evidence demonstrating their ignorance of Allah, their violation of the sanctity of His prophets, and their rebellion against His commands: "Then why did you kill the prophets of Allah before, if you were believers?" (Q 2:91)

Thus, the hearer who listens to their denunciation of what confirmed their Book can understand that they did not believe in their own Book. Would he who rejects those who believe in you believe in you?

Then, consider how the Noble Qur'an that has recorded the most despicable of vices against the Children of Israel- i.e., taking the calf, the epitome of stupidity, as a Allah to glorify, and described the cruelty of their hearts in disregarding Allah's commandments after prompting them to obey through magnificent and awesome signs- after all of this, it just describes them as acting "wrongfully" (Q 2:92) and that what they did was "evil" (Q 2:93). Is that all that can be said regarding all of these atrocities? Yes, these are two words that qualify to describe the crime, if understood appropriately!

<u>Third: Their claim that true guidance is in following their faith</u>:

One of the claims of the Jews is that the righteous path and true guidance can only be through following their faith. They claim that non-Jews are misguided and astray and that those who do not follow their faith and ways are far from the truth and are not rightly-guided.

The Noble Qur'an recounted their claims and answered their allegations and invalidated them in a clear way. It also guided them to the straightforward path that would lead them to true guidance, if they were to follow it. In Sura Al-Baqara, the Almighty said: "The Jews and Christians each say, "Follow our faith to be rightly guided." Say, O Prophet,"No! We follow the faith of Abraham, the upright—who was not a polytheist." Say, O believers, "We believe in Allah and what has been revealed to us; and what was revealed to Abraham, Ishmael, Isaac, Jacob, and his descendants; and what was given to Moses, Jesus, and other prophets from their Lord. We make no distinction between any of them. And to Allah we all submit." So, if they believe in what you believe, then they will indeed be rightly guided. But if they turn away, they are simply opposed ʿto the truthʾ. But Allah will spare you their evil. For He is the All-Hearing, All-Knowing. This is the natural Way of Allah. And who is better than Allah in ordaining a way? And we worship none butHim. Say, "Would you dispute with us About Allah, while He is our Lord and your Lord? We are accountable for our deeds and you for yours. And we are devoted to Him alone. Do you claim that Abraham, Ishmael, Isaac, Jacob, and his descendants were all Jews or Christians?" Say, "Who is more knowledgeable: you or Allah?" Who does more wrong than those who hide the testimony they received from Allah? And Allah is never unaware of what you do. That was a community that had already gone before. For them is what they earned and for you is what you have earned. And you will not be accountable for what they have done."[15] (Al-Baqara; Q 2:135-141)

Ibn Abbas said: "Abdullah ibn Suriya , the one-eyed- said to the Messenger of Allah: 'Our faith is true guidance, so follow us, Muhammad, if you want to be rightly guided.' Christians also said something similar to that. For this reason, Allah revealed (Q 2:135): 'The Jews and Christians each say, "Follow our faith to be rightly guided." Say, O Prophet, "No! We follow the faith of Abraham, the upright—who was not a polytheist."'"[16]

The meaning of the noble verse is: The Jews asked the Prophet and the Muslims to abandon their faith and follow theirs to be rightly guided and march on the righteous path. The Christians also made similar claims. Tell them, Muhammad, that that true guidance is not in following their faith but in following the faith of Abraham who was an upright man, not one of the polytheists. Therefore, you People of the Scripture, follow what we followed to be truly following in the faith of Abraham About whose guidance you do not dispute or differ.

The Almighty's "The Jews and Christians each say, "Follow our faith to be rightly guided" states the claims made by both the Jews and the Christians that guidance was in following their faith.

The use of أَوْ "or" indicated variation. That is, the Jews said to others that there is no religion except for Judaism and that Allah will not accept anything else. Therefore, follow Judaism, and you will be truly and rightly guided. On the other hand, the Christians asked them to become Christians to know true guidance. The Noble Qur'an expressed this variation saying: "The Jews and Christians each say, "Follow our faith to be rightly guided" to indicate- to the hearer-that each community impugned the faith of the other and considered it invalid or worthless. The Qur'an also recounted that. The Almighty said: "The Jews say, "The Christians have nothing to stand on" and the Christians say, "The Jews have nothing to stand on..." (Q 2:113)

The Almighty then instructed His Prophet to respond to them in a decisive manner. He said: "Say, O Prophet,"No! We follow the faith of Abraham, the upright—who was not a polytheist." (Q 2:135)

The word مِلَّةَ means faith, and حَنِيفًا (Hanif) originally refers to those who stay away from any deviant religion and follow the upright faith. Abraham was described as one who had an upright faith because he shunned the aberrant religions that existed during his time and adhered to the upright faith that Allah revealed to him.

Some exegetes believe that حَنِيفًا comes from straightforwardness.

Imam Al-Razi said: "Linguists have two opinions About the word حَنِيفًا "Hanif". First, the word means that Hanif is the straight one, and from this the lame person is called Ahnaf. They said: whoever submits to Allah and does not deviate from Him in anything is Hanif, and this is narrated from Muhammad bin Kaab Al-Qurazi. The second: That Hanif is the one who leans, because Ahnaf is the one who leans each of his feet towards the other with its toes, and Hanif means he leans, so the meaning is that Abraham was Hanif to the religion of Allah, that is, he leaned towards it, so the Almighty's statement "Rather, the faith of Abraham, the upright" means opposing the Jews and Christians and deviating from them..." [17]

There is no opposition between the two interpretations as they both negate any deviance or aberration on the part of the حَنِيفًا "Hanif." Both confirm upholding the path of the truth.

The meaning is: Tell those Jews, Muhammad, that true guidance is not in following your faith; rather, it is in following the of Abraham who did not lean towards any deviant religion but followed the upright faith and who was not in any shape, way or form amongst the polytheists.

The Almighty's saying: """No! We follow the faith of Abraham, the upright—who was not a polytheist" (Q 2:135) means: We follow the upright straightforward faith of Abraham. That statement disputed and abolished the claims that the Jews and the Christians made. The word بَلْ "No" negates what was purported in the previous statement, and the previous statement is what the People of the Scriptures said: "Follow our faith to be rightly guided." The word بَلْ "No" was used immediately after that statement to negate that claim and prove that true guidance was following the faith of Abraham and those who followed in his footsteps: Muhammad.

The two statements "No! We follow the faith of Abraham, the upright" and "who was not a polytheist" invited the Jews to follow Abraham's faith because of its uprightness and evasion of disbelief. This showed that their faith was not the upright one, but deviant and aberrant, and that their claim that they followed Abraham was unsubstantiated and groundless because they associated other Allahs with the Almighty and attributed to Him things that were unbecoming.

Imam Al-Razi said what could be summed up as: "The noble verse contains an answer that obliges them, which is the Almighty's saying: "Rather, the religion of Abraham, the upright." And the explanation of this answer is: If the path of religion is imitation, then it is better to follow the religion of Abraham because these disputing groups of people have agreed on the validity of the religion of Abraham, and taking what is agreed upon is better than taking what is disputed. Even if his method is deduction and contemplation, we have presented many proofs that what Muhammad brought is in agreement with what Abraham brought to the fundamental tenets of religion. [18]

The Almighty then guided the believers to a unified response and a united stance which signified pushing fanaticism aside and calling them to follow the Divine revelation- with which Allah sent His messengers with His good tidings and His warnings- without distinguishing or differentiating between any of them. It invited the People of the Scriptures to the true and righteous path. The Almighty said: "Say, O believers, "We believe in Allah and what has been revealed to us; and what was revealed to Abraham, Ishmael, Isaac, Jacob, and his descendants; and what was given to Moses, Jesus, and other prophets from their Lord. We make no distinction between any of them. And to Allah we all submit." (Q 2:136)

That is: O believers! Say to those Jews who claim that guidance is in following their faith that true guidance is not in following their faith which was distorted and tampered with. Tell them that true guidance is believing in Allah and in the Noble Qur'an that Allah sent down to us, in "what has been revealed to us; and what was revealed to Abraham, Ishmael, Isaac, Jacob, and his descendants," in the Torah that Allah revealed to Moses, and in the Injil (Bible; Gospels) that Allah revealed to Isa (Jesus). Our belief in these prophets is without distinction; we do not believe in some and disbelieve in others as you did, O Jews. We believe in all of them without distinction, and we submit to our Lord with humility, and we worship Him with faithfulness and loyalty.

Imam Al-Razi said: "If it is said: 'How is it permissible to believe in Abraham, Moses and Jesus while saying that their laws/doctrines were abrogated?' We say: 'We believe that each one of those laws was true in its time, so we are not required to contradict them. Rather, contradiction took place when the Jews acknowledged the prophethood of some at whose hands miracles happened, and they denied the prophethood of Muhammad even though he performed miracles. Contradictions appeared and distinctions emerged." [19]

The almighty's "Say … ' "We believe in Allah" was addressed to the believers.

The is the descendants is the grandchildren, a reference to the children of Jacob. They were thus called because they are the grandchildren of Abraham and Isaac. There were twelve grandchildren (tribes) as the Almighty said: "We divided them into twelve tribes—each as a community." (Q 7:160)

The intended meaning is the belief in what Allah has revealed to His prophets.

Imam Al-Qurtubi said: "The descendants: the children of Jacob. There were twelve children. Each one of them had a community, a group of followers. A tribe in the Children of Israel was like a tribe in the children of Ishmael. They were called descendants because the word سبط means followers; they were a group of followers. The word سبط also refers to trees to indicate that they were as numerous as the trees. This is shown in what was narrated About Ibn Abbas. He said: 'All the prophets of the Children of Israel except ten: Noah, Shu'ayb, Hud, Salih, Lot, Abraham, Isaac, Jacob, Ishmael, and Muhammad, may Allah's prayers be upon them.'"[20]

The Almighty's "and what was given to Moses, Jesus, and other prophets from their Lord" (Q 2:136) means: We also believe in the Torah that Allah revealed to Moses and the Injil (Bible) that He revealed to Jesus and all that Allah revealed to His prophets to confirm their prophethoods.

The Almighty mentions Jesus right after Moses without repeating the verb because Jesus came confirming the Torah- and there were only a few rulings that were abrogated- as the Noble Qur'an recounts About him: "And I will confirm the Torah revealed before me and legalize some of what had been forbidden to you" (Al-Imran; Q 3:50)

The Almighty also mentions belief in Allah before mentioning belief in the prophets because believing in the prophets is contingent upon believing in Allah.

He also mentions belief in what was revealed to us Muslims, namely, the Noble Qur'an, because belief in it should compromise the two aspects, the summery and the detail. As for what was revealed to the prophets before that (such as the Torah and the Bible), it is enough to believe in the summery.

The Almighty's "We make no distinction between any of them" (Q 2:136) means: We do not make any distinctions between the prophets; we do not believe in some and disbelieve others, as you did- O Jews- when you rejected Jesus and Muhammad. What you did was in fact a denunciation of all the prophets because whosoever disbelieves in one prophet has thereby disbelieved in all. That is why, we Muslims believe in all the prophets without distinction or discrimination.

Then, the Almighty showed that if the People of the Scriptures believed in what you, Muslims, have called upon them to believe in, they would become rightly guided.

However, if they denied and turned away, then they would be arrogant, rebellious and conceited. The Almighty said: "So, if they believe in what you believe, then they will indeed be rightly guided. But if they turn away, they are simply opposed ⌜to the truth⌝. But Allah will spare you their evil. For He is the All-Hearing, All-Knowing." (Q 2:137)

The فـ in فَإِنْ with which this noble verse begins connects what came afterwards to what had preceded since the believers' "We believe in Allah and what has been revealed to us; and what was revealed to Abraham…etc." should soften the hardened hearts and woo and win back the stray souls because it is devoid of stubbornness and fanaticism and because it is the truth that health and sound minds support and embrace. Yet, if they did not believe, it is only because of their unyielding obstinacy, crookedness and deviousness.

The Almighty's "فَقَدِ ٱهْتَدَوا/ they will indeed be rightly guided" (Q 2:137) was to encourage and entice them to pursue the truth that the believers embraced. In other words, if they believed like you, they would become rightly guided.

The word بِمِثْلِ in the verse "فَإِنْ ءَامَنُوا۟ بِمِثْلِ مَآ ءَامَنتُم بِهِۦ/ if they believe in what بِمِثْلِ you believe" means "the same thing." This means, if they believed in the same thing that you believe in, they would become rightly guided. This is just like what Arabs mean when they say مثلك لا يبخل to indicate that YOU would never be tight-fisted. Some interpreters view مثل is used here as an analogy to mean a "correspondence" or "parallel." Thus, the analogy was to two religions, two faiths, not necessarily the many things that Allah commanded us to believe in.

Imam Al-Qurtubi said: "The meaning is: If they had faith like you and believed in what you believed, they would have been rightly guided." [21]

Ibn Jarir said: "If they believed in what you believe, in all that you had witnessed from Allah and His prophets, they would have been rightly guided. The analogy was to point to two kinds of beliefs/faiths. His saying: 'if they believe in what you believe' was an analogy between the two faiths, not the believers.'" [22]

The Almighty's "But if they turn away, they are simply opposed ⌜to the truth⌝. But Allah will spare you their evil. For He is the All-Hearing, All-Knowing" was a declaration of their state when they turned away and rejected the truth. It was also a promise from Allah to His Prophet and the believers to have victory over them and to protect them from their evil. (Q 2:137)

The word شِقَاقٍ means strife, opposition and hostility. It is driven from the word شِق which means "side." It was to indicate that each of these groups was in a side that was different from the other group.

It was also said that the word شِقَاقٍ can be driven from a verb that means to make arduous and more strenuous. In this case, it would mean that each one of these groups was keen on making things harder and more difficult for the other group.

The meaning is: Muhammad! If those Jews- who claimed that true guidance is in following their faith- turned away from what you are inviting them to follow, it is because of their violation, opposition, stubbornness, and hostility. Nothing is clearer than the evidence you brought. Therefore, Allah will spare you their evil, and He will make you victorious and triumphant. He is the All-Hearing who hears everything they say About you, and He is the All-Knowing who knows all their envy and malice and all the plots they are devising against you and the believers. He will frustrate their attempts and foil and thwart their plots.

The Almighty expressed the intensity of their violations and opposition by saying: "they are simply opposed to the truth" (Q 2:137) to emphasize their opposition to the truth and to depict them as being entirely consumed by their opposing stance.

The Almighty also mentions that He will "spare you their evil" (Q 2:137) immediately after "they are simply opposed ʿto the truth" to emphasize His support and protection of the Prophet and the believers. This is because informing the believers that the People of the Book were hostile and antagonistic could cause them to become fearful due to their large numbers and great might. That is why, Allah promised His Prophet that no matter how mighty they might have been, they would not be able to harm him. The All-Mighty would spare him their evil.

Allah fulfilled His promise; He helped His Prophet gain victory over his enemies, and He spared him their evil and malice. The Prophet was able to sow the seeds of dissention and animosity between them, he expelled those who were deserving of being driven out, and he killed those who were deserving of death because of their treachery and betrayal. The noble verse comprised a promise of victory to the believers and a warning to the Jews and their likes of humiliation, disgrace and defeat.

Then, the Almighty showed that the religion of Allah, i.e., Islam, is the one that was worthy of embracing and following. He said: "This is the natural Way of Allah. And who is better than Allah in ordaining a way? And we worship none butHim." (Q 2:138)

The صِبْغَةً (dye) = natural Way means the condition of something- like cloth or other materials- when they are colored and dyed with a certain color. The word صِبْغَةً (dye) is used in the verse to mean faith and belief in what the verse expounded, i.e., His saying: "Say, O believers, "We believe in Allah and what has been revealed to us; and what was revealed to Abraham, Ishmael, Isaac, Jacob, and his descendants; and what was given to Moses, Jesus...etc." The word صِبْغَةً dye is used to refer to faith in what the verse mentioned in detail because faith mixes and intermingles with hearts like a dye blends and coalesces with the dyed material. Likewise, faith is reflected on the believer just as the effect of the dye is reflected on the material or the cloth. It is often said that 'someone became dyed with the religion if he perfected his faith and followed its teachings meticulously and diligently.

Al-Qadi said: "The Almighty's saying "the natural Way of Allah(Q2:138) صِبْغَةَ ٱللَّهِ is related to His "Say, ... "We believe in Allah" (Q 2:8) up to "And we worship none but

Him." (Q 2:138) He described their faith as صِبْغَةَ ٱللَّهِ the natural Way of Allah to reflect the striking and glaring clarity concerning the disparity between this religion that Allah chose and the religion that disbelievers chose for themselves; it was a discrepancy that was readily noticeable as colors and dyes can be easily perceived by the those of sound understanding and discernment." [23]

The interrogative style in the Almighty's "And who is better than Allah in ordaining a way?" (Q 2:138) indicates negation and denunciation. The meaning is: There is no one who has a better way than Allah, for He is the One Who dyes His servants with faith and purifies them from the horrible traces and effects of disbelief and misguidance. His is a fixed and everlasting dye; it will never disappear because once the beauty of faith enters the hearts, it will abide there forever. This is contrary to what the People of the Book receive at the hands of their rabbis, monks and scholars whose dyes are human ones that make many opposing and rival religions out of one.

Linguistically, this construction: "And who is better than Allah in ordaining a way?" essentially negates the possibility of the existence of a better religion than Allah's religion. In the meantime, it keeps the possibility for the existence of another religion that equals it in beauty: guidance to the truth and the straight path, virtue and uprightness, integrity and morality, sincere and upright worship, sound and rigorous counsel, and interactions that are based on the common good.

The Almighty's "And we worship none but Him" is a conjunction that follows "Say… 'We believe in Allah.'" The meaning is: Tell them, Muhammad, that we Muslims worship none but Allah and that His way is ours. We do not take our rabbis or scholars as Allahs who add to- or take away from- our religion; they permit and prohibit as they please and substitute polytheism with disbelief and monotheism.

Then, the Almighty commanded His Prophet to persevere in reminding them and impugn their claims. He said: "Say, "Would you dispute with us About Allah, while He is our Lord and your Lord? We are accountable for our deeds and you for yours. And we are devoted to Him alone. Do you claim that Abraham, Ishmael, Isaac, Jacob, and his descendants were all Jews or Christians?" Say, "Who is more knowledgeable: you or Allah?" Who does more wrong than those who hide the testimony they received from Allah? And Allah is never unaware of what you do. That was a community that had already gone before. For them is what they earned and for you is what you have earned. And you will not be accountable for what they have done." (Q 2:140-42)

The meaning of the noble verse is: Muhammad! Tell the People of the Scripture- who told you and your companions "Follow our faith to be rightly guided" (Q 2:135) and who claimed that their religion, not yours, is the only one that Allah accepts- tell them that if they dispute with you About Allah's religion, i.e., Islam, with which Allah sent you to the world as mercy and guidance, and if they claim that guidance is in following their Judaism or Christianity, and that Allah would not send His revelation to someone who doesn't belong to them because of their claim that they are closer to Allah than you and that they are Allah's children and His most loved ones- tell them that "He is our Lord and your

Lord," (Q 2:140) our Creator and yours, the One Who provides for us and for you, and the One Who will hold us accountable for our deeds and He will also hold you accountable for yours.

The Almighty's "We are accountable for our deeds and you for yours" (Q 2:139) means that we have our deeds and you have yours and reward and punishment depend on these deeds. Just as Allah is our Lord and your Lord, we will likewise be equal in the rewards and punishments in accordance with our deeds. Look at our deeds and yours, and you will find that ours are the righteous ones because we are loyal and faithful to Him in performing these deeds. So, do not be surprised if those who are loyal to Him receive the honor of prophethood.

The Almighty's "He is our Lord and your Lord? We are accountable for our deeds and you for yours" (Q 2:139) are two attestations that annul the allegations of the People of the Scriptures that they are more worthy to receive the prophethood. Allah's servants are all alike to Him. He is their Lord and they are His servants. There is no superiority except by piety, good deeds and loyalty in performing them. He is the All-Knowing; He gives His revelations to whomsoever He sees as most worthy. It was His will to send His revelation down to Muhammad, the illiterate Arab Prophet, and grant him an eternal immortal religion that provides light and guidance to people and lead them to success and happiness in this world and in the Hereafter.

The Almighty's "And we are devoted to Him alone" (Q 2:139) is a declaration of the Muslims' worthiness of the guidance and dignity they received. It means: We Muslims are loyal and devoted to Allah Alone; we are loyal in our worship and in our deeds; we do not associate other Allahs with Him. As for you, you have associated others with Allah, and you have gone astray: some claimed that Ezra was the son of Allah, while others declared that Jesus was the Son of Allah. We are the rightly guided ones.

The Muslims neither described their deeds as righteous nor alleged that the deeds of those addressed were not to prevent the addressed from feeling indignant and resentful. Rather, they presented their stance in accordance with the Almighty's "To you be your religion, and to me mine." Likewise, they did not say: We are loyal and you are not. Rather, they were content to attribute loyalty to themselves without mentioning others. That was a decent nonintrusive way to portray the addressed unloyalty to Allah. Informing a person that he has some common attributes with others then attributing one of those aspects to him alone indicates that that aspect that is attributed to him in particular is absent in the others. So, the meaning of the sentence is: We were loyal to Allah Alone in our deeds which were not tainted or had anything to do with polytheism as others' deeds.

Now that the Noble Qur'an impugned the unjust allegations that the People of the Scriptures levelled against Allah's religion, it followed it with disputing and abolishing their claims that their ancestors were Jews or Christians. The Almighty said: "Do you claim that Abraham, Ishmael, Isaac, Jacob, and his descendants were all Jews or Christians?" Say, "Who is more knowledgeable: you or Allah?" Who does more wrong than those who hide the testimony they received from Allah? And Allah is never unaware of what you do." (Q 2:140)

Ibn Jarir said: "This verse reflects Allah's demonstration to His Prophet of His opposition to the Jews and Christians whom Allah mentioned in many stories. Allah said to His Prophet: 'Muhammad! Tell those Jews and Christians: 'Do you argue with us concerning Allah and claim that your religion is better than ours and that you are guided while we are misguided and so you call us to follow your religion? Well! Present your evidence that this is true, and we will follow your religion. Do you claim that Abraham and others who came after him were Jews or Christians? Well! Bring your proofs and we will believe you. Allah made them Imams to follow their example!' Then, He said to His Prophet: 'Ask them, Muhammad- since they claimed that Abraham and those who came after him were Jews or Christians- if they were more knowledgeable About their religion than Allah!'" [24]

The Almighty's أم (=or) in the Arabic rendition of "Do you claim that Abraham, Ishmael, Isaac, Jacob, and his descendants were all Jews or Christians?" reverberates the Hamza أ in the previous verse "أَتُحَآجُّونَنَا فِى ٱللَّهِ" in two ways. It means: what is your intention? Are you disputing Allah's wisdom or are you claiming that the prophets who are mentioned in this verse were either Jews or Christians? The purpose behind the interrogative style was to impugn on both accounts. It was a denunciation of their dispute About Allah as well as rejection of their claims that Abraham, Ishmael, Isaac, Jacob and the descendants were Jews or Christians.

It was as if Allah was asking His Prophet to tell the Jews not to dispute Allah's religion without any solid reason, or claim that the prophets were following their faith, because their arguments were merely baseless and unsubstantiated claims that sound minds would find unacceptable.

The Almighty's ""Who is more knowledgeable: you or Allah?" means: Tell them, Muhammad, if they claim that Abraham, Ishmael, Isaac, Jacob and the descendants (those prophets mentioned in the verse) were Jews or Christians- that what they claimed was incongruent with what Allah knows because the Almighty has told us that they were submitting to Him and they had nothing to do with Judaism or Christianity. Tell them that, on his deathbed, Jacob asked his children to die submitting to Allah (Allah, i.e., embracing Islam), and that Torah and the Bible were revealed after all of those prophets. That was what Allah has informed us. [25] So, are you more knowledgeable of their faith than Allah? There is no doubt that they would not be able to claim that they are more knowledgeable. Rather, they would say Allah is more knowledgeable. In this case, we should tell them: 'then your claims are groundless.' Thus, the noble verse had abolished their claim eloquently, tersely and judiciously.

The Almighty's "Who does more wrong than those who hide the testimony they received from Allah?" means that the worst thing to do is concealing a testimony that they received from Allah, one that testifies that all those prophets were in submission to Allah (again, Allah, i.e., following Islam); they were neither Jews nor Christians.

Imam Ibn Jarir said: "If it were said: 'What testimony did the Jews or the Christians receive from Allah concerning Abraham, Ishmael, Isaac, Jacob and the descendants? The response is the testimony they received from Allah concerning them: what Allah revealed to them in the Torah and the Bible and in which He commanded them to their faith as upright and submissive. That is the testimony that they received from Allah. It is the testimony that they hid when Allah's Prophet invited them to Islam. They said to him: 'The Jews and Christians each claim that none will enter Paradise except those of their own faith." And they said to his companions: "Follow our faith to be rightly guided." That is why, Allah revealed these verses to show that they concealed the truth, came up with lies and falsehoods and made false claims concerning His prophets." [26]

It is also possible to offer another answer to this question that Ibn Jarir posed: Allah gave the people of the Book a testimony, mainly, that Abraham was an upright believer who had nothing to do with Judaism or Christianity. They received this testimony from the Qur'an, the miracle and the indubitable and irrefutable truth that is beyond suspicion or doubt. Therefore, it is possible that the verse is meant to denounce the People of the Book for not declaring that Abraham was neither a Jew nor a Christian as the Qur'an indicated.

It is also possible that that testimony- that they received from Allah and which they hid making them the most unjust and "wrong" amongst people- was his descriptions that were written in the Torah and the Bible. They knew these attributes that described him, but they denied and rejected them. Refusal to admit something that is supported with clear and indubitable evidence is considered hiding and concealing the testimony.

The late honorable Muhammad Al-Khader Hussein said what can be summed up as follows: "When the Almighty's words: 'They are' the ones who follow the Messenger, the unlettered Prophet, whose description they find in their Torah and the Gospel.[1] He commands them to do good and forbids them from evil, permits for them what is lawful and forbids to them what is impure, and relieves them from their burdens and the shackles that bound them..." up to the end of the noble verse- were revealed, some amongst the People of the Scriptures believed in what was mentioned concerning his (the Prophet's) descriptions and attributes. There were some who didn't deny that these attributes were mentioned in the two Books. However, they would still resist and claim that these referred to a prophet who has not come yet. A group of scholars and researchers in ancient and modern times examined all these prophesies in the two Books, the Torah and the Bible. They demonstrated the correspondence of these predictions and prophesies with the Prophet in such an undeniable way that the seeker after the truth would undoubtedly come to believe that Muhammad was the Prophet who was foretold and promised. Among these predictions is what is mentioned in the Book of Deuteronomy (18:18): "I will raise them up a Prophet from among their brethren, like unto thee, and will put my words in his mouth; and he shall speak unto them all that I shall command him."

The prophet who was to be considered as a counterpart to Moses- both in his message and the law that would be completed- was Muhammad. The brethren of the Children of Israel were the Arabs. They were both related through Abraham. And the Almighty's: "and will put my words in his mouth" was in agreement with the state of the Prophet who was illiterate and could not write." [27]

The verse concludes with a severe warning for their false and untruthful claims: "And Allah is never unaware of what you do." (Q 2:74)

The word غَافِل means oblivion and forgetfulness. The meaning is: Allah is aware of the deeds of those who concealed the truth. Nothing is beyond His knowledge. He will chastise them severely for hiding the truth, and He will discipline and punish them harshly for their false claims. The noble verse was a strong warning and a bleak threat to the People of the Scriptures.

In concluding these verses, the Almighty warned the People of the Scriptures against persevering in disbelief, opposition and rebelliousness relying on their connection to their predecessors who were among the prophets and the righteous. He said: "That was a community that had already gone before. For them is what they earned and for you is what you have earned. And you will not be accountable for what they have done." (Q 2:134)

The word "That" refers to the community of Abraham, Ishmael, Isaac, Jacob, and the descendants. And the word "community" refers to that group of people who were bonded together by one common goal, namely, faith.
The meaning of the noble verse is: Muhammad! Tell the people of the scriptures- those who claimed that true guidance is in embracing their faith and that Abraham and his people were Jews or Christians- tell them that those people represented a community that had already gone before and who had reaped the fruits of their deeds and what they sowed, good or bad. So, if that was the case for those About whom you boast and feel proud, it is incumbent upon you to follow the righteous path of faith and good deeds and abandon that reliance on the virtues of your fathers and forefathers for everyone is responsible for their own deeds on the Day of Resurrection. No one will be responsible for others' deeds, as the Almighty said: "Every person will reap only what they sowed." (At-Tur; Q 52:21)

The immediate purpose of the noble verse was warning those addressed against abandoning faith and obedience because of their reliance on their connection to their forefathers who were prophets and righteous people. This reliance was nothing but wishful thinking and unsound and corrupt judgement. As is written in the authentic Hadith: "Whosoever is slowed down by his actions, his lineage would not hasten (compensate) him."

The verse seems to be emphatic in saying: 'You have in front of you a religion to which you are called to follow, a religion that is supported with proofs and evidence. Look at these evidences that indicate its truth and grandeur. Do not reject it simply because of your claim that the prophets followed what you are following now. This claim will avail you nothing.

Thus, the noble verse (Q 52:21) impugned what the Jews claimed: that true guidance is in following their faith. It presented proofs and evidence to point to their falsehoods and lies and directed them to the true and upright religion. It invited them to embrace it and chastised them for disputing Allah's religion in ignorance and witlessness. It also warned them against deviating from the righteous and straightforward path, naively relying on the intercessions of their forefathers who were prophets and righteous people, for no one will avail anyone else on Judgement Day.

Fourth: Their claim that none except Jews will enter Paradise:

Among the claims that the Noble Qur'an reported concerning the People of the Book is that Paradise is restricted to them alone. The Jews claim that none except Jews will enter Paradise. Likewise, Christians claim that only Christians will enter Paradise. This betrays their conceit, arrogance and wishful thinking. The Noble Qur'an recounted- and impugned- this false claim. In Sura Al-Baqara, the Almighty said:

A) "The Jews and Christians each claim that none will enter Paradise except those of their own faith. These are their desires. Reply, O Prophet, "Show me your proof if what you say is true." But no! Whoever submits themselves to Allah and does good will have their reward with their Lord. And there will be no fear for them, nor will they grieve." (Al-Baqara Q 2:111-112)

The meaning of the two noble verses is: The Jews claimed that no one except the Jews will enter Paradise, and Christians also claimed that only Christians will enter Paradise. Both claims are groundless and unsupported; they lack judicious and sensible judgement. Their claims are mere "desires," wishful thinking, unproven and unverified. Ask them, Muhammad, to show their proof if what they claimed was true.

Then, the Noble Qur'an responded to their claims (Q 2:112): "بَلَى /But no!", for He will allow others- non-Jews and non-Christians- to enter the Paradise because Allah's mercy is not confined to a certain community of people; it is available to all those who are worthy of it: "Whoever submits themselves to Allah and does good will have their reward with their Lord. And there will be no fear for them, nor will they grieve."

The Almighty's "The Jews and Christians each claim that none will enter Paradise except those of their own faith" (Q 2:111) is yet another testimony of the corrupt and unsubstantiated claims and falsehoods of the People of the Book.

The word هُودًا refers to those who follow Judaism. The Noble Qur'an mentions them first because they came before them in time. The meaning is: the Jews claimed that no one except the Jews will enter Paradise, and Christians also claimed that only Christians will enter Paradise. However, the verse resorted to a stylistic device to briefly and tersely express the two claims in one statement: using the word أَوْ -in (وَقَالُوا كُونُوا هُودًا أَوْ نَصَارَىٰ تَهْتَدُوا)- before the second community of people, relying on the ability of the hearer to understand, and to prevent any confusion or ambiguity because of well-known enmity between the two teams, and the attempts of each team to mislead the other. A parallel verse to this is the Almighty's: "The Jews and Christians each say, "Follow our faith to be rightly guided." (Q 2:135) That is: the Jews said: 'Follow our faith to be rightly-guided,' and the Christians said: 'Follow ours to be rightly-guided.'

That is why, Imam Ibn Jarir said: "If it were said: 'How could the Jews and the Christians be grouped together in one statement despite the discrepancy of each other's claims: the Jews' claim that Christians will have no share in Allah's reward, and the Christians' claim that the Jews will have no reward with their Lord?' The answer to this is that since the meaning of the statement was clear and readily accessible to the addressed, the two teams were mentioned in the same statement: "The Jews and Christians each claim that none will enter Paradise except those of their own faith" (Q 2:111) [28]

The Almighty's: "These are their desires" (Q 2:111) is a parenthetical statement to indicate that their claims that Paradise is exclusively restricted to them were nothing but mere desires that they unrightfully- and without evidence- wish for, desires that they conceived and embraced because of their capitulation to Satan who deceived them with such illusions and falsehoods.

The demonstrative " تِلْكَ/ these" refers to what the Almighty's "The Jews and Christians each claim that none will enter Paradise except those of their own faith" indicated. It comprises many desires: the Jews' desire that Paradise is exclusively theirs and the Christians' desire that they alone are entitled to enter Paradise. Both groups believe that the Muslims are not worthy of Paradise. That is why, the plural form of the demonstrative is used: "These تِلْكَ are their desires."

Al-Zamakhshari maintains that many issues- that have been verbally enumerated and reported in the Qur'an- are referred to here. For example, the Almighty's: "The disbelievers from the People of the Book and the polytheists would not want you to receive any blessing from your Lord" (Q 2:105) and His: "Many among the People of the Book wish they could turn you believers back to disbelief because of their envy" (Q 2:109) and His: "The Jews and Christians each claim that none will enter Paradise except those of their own faith." (Q 2:111) "So, it was said; 'Why was it said "these تِلْكَ are their desires" when it is only ONE desire that is mentioned?' I would say: 'That was a reference to the desires that were mentioned, namely, wishing that the believers receive no blessings from their Lord, wishing that the believers turn back to disbelief, and their desire that none will enter Paradise except those of their own faith. These are their delusional and warped desires." [29]

The author of Al-Intisaf maintains: "The referred to entity is the same. That is, their claim: 'The Jews and Christians each claim that none will enter Paradise except those of their own faith.' The use of the plural was to signal that that desire had completely possessed them and their hearts were awash with it. It was indicative the fervor of their desire, their eagerness to attain it and how it had completely possessed and overtook them. The use of the plural emphasizes this notion that their hearts were overpowered and capitulated thoroughly to their desire. The plural indicated that even though the reference is to only one. It is like their saying 'I have the hungry with me,' wherein the adjective is in the plural even though it only refers to one. This is similar to what was recounted in the Almighty's 'These outcasts are just a handful of people,' (Q 26:54) [30] wherein He used the plural of قليل /a few. Also, this is similar to 'How many times has a small force vanquished a mighty army…' (Q 2:249) It is a style to emphasize the meaning of "few" by using the plural form to reveal magnanimity and abundance, an apt rhetorical device, eloquence at its best." [31]

Then, the Almighty commanded His Messenger to demand the evidence that verified the validity of what they claimed. He said: "Show me your proof if what you say is true." (Q 27:64)

That is, Muhammad! Ask those who claimed that Paradise is exclusively theirs to show proof that Paradise belongs to them alone if they were truthful concerning what they claimed. Since claiming that only they were worthy to enter Paradise can only be proven by Allah's revelation (not by wishful thinking), the Almighty commanded His Prophet to ask them for the proof from their Books to substantiate and verify their claims, a request that was bound to render them incompetent and helpless because their Books were devoid of any such proofs.

Imam Ibn Jarir said: "Though these words were apparently meant to ask those- who claimed that only 'the Jews and Christians … will enter Paradise-' to show proof for their claims, they were in essence a denunciation and a reproof to impugn their lies and falsehoods because they were incapable of showing any such proofs for their claims." [32]

It is also important to understand that this noble verse reminds and prompts us to avoid imitation in matters that are related to religion. It is incumbent upon us not to accept what others say without being supported by evidence and not to issue an opinion unless it is substantiated with proof.

The inappropriateness if imitation in matters pertaining to the basics or tenets of religion seems clear and self-evident: proof for a man's faith can be seen in such things that please and gratify his heart in Islam and such things that instill peace, comfort and tranquility. A man can derive his faith from his understanding of Allah's wisdom in perfecting His creation, in believing the truthfulness of the Messenger through listening to the Noble Qur'an, or contemplating the Messenger's life which no human could surpass or even come close to it. In sum, Islam for man should not be solely because he was brought up in Muslim environment or born to a Muslim father and mother.

As for imitation in matters that relate to the practical rulings (the branches), people's ability to distinguish right from wrong differs. Those who have the ability to understand proofs and the weightier rulings should not accept others' rulings unless they are coupled with proofs. If incapable, he should seek the counsel of established scholars who are well versed in religious 'Shari'a' matters, and who are well known for their upholding piety and righteousness." [33]

Then, the Noble Qur'an impugned their claim in a different way: displaying a general rule that based entering Paradise on faith and good works without favoring a certain nation, race or community. The Almighty said: “But no! Whoever submits themselves to Allah and does good will have their reward with their Lord. And there will be no fear for them, nor will they grieve.” (Q 2:112/2:62)

The word “بَلَىٰ =But no!” is used in the response to confirm what they denied, namely, that the Paradise is not only for them but others who are neither Jews or Christians will enter it as long as they are righteous and submit themselves to Allah.

The Almighty’s “ أَسْلَمَ وَجْهَهُ لِلَّهِ whoever submits themselves to Allah” means whoever abides by Allah’s commandments and worships Him with faithfulness and loyalty. The word أَسْلَمَindicates loyalty and submission.

The Almighty specifically mentions the face to the exclusion of other parts because it is the most dignified part and most venerable in the human body. If the face- which is the most revered in the human body- is submissive and loyal, then all the other parts are even more loyal and submissive.

The Almighty’s “هُوَ مُحْسِنٌ =does good” is a word that is driven from “perfection.” In other words, it means performing things in the best possible way and in correspondence with what is right and righteous. The meaning is: Your claims – both you Jews and Christians- that Paradise is exclusively yours are not right. What is truly right is that those who submit wholeheartedly to Allah and do good deeds honestly and with perfection will enter Paradise, as the Almighty said: Those “will have their reward with their Lord. And there will be no fear for them, nor will they grieve.” (Q 2:112/2:62)

The noble verse demonstrated the following:

A) It confirmed what they denied: others will enter Paradise.
B) It showed that they are not the people of Paradise unless they submit to Allah and do good deeds. This was to encourage them to embrace Islam and show them how different they were from those who will enter Paradise. It was also meant to encourage them to abandon their wicked deeds and desert their crooked ways.
C) It provided a statement to indicate that for Allah an acceptable deed should comprise two things:

First: It should be done exclusively for the sake of Allah.
Second: It should be in agreement with the doctrine that Allah accepts: the Islamic Shari’a (شريعة الاسلام).

Imam Ibn Kathir said: “If the deed is good but is not in accordance with the Islamic law, it would be rejected. That is why, the Messenger of Allah said: ‘Whoever does an action that is not in accordance with our wish, it will be rejected.’ For example, the works of the monks and their likes- even though they are supposed to be loyal to Allah- would be rejected until these deeds are in agreement with the Messenger who was sent to them and all other people. About them, the Almighty said: “And We will present to them whatever deeds they have done, and We will make them as scattered dust." (Q 25:23) And if the deed was "ostensibly" in accordance with the Shari'a, and was not for the sake of Allah, then it would also be rejected. This is the case of those hypocrites and frauds. That is why, the Almighty said: 'Whoever wants to meet his Lord, let him do righteous work and not associate anyone in the worship of his Lord.'" [34]

Thus, the two noble verses abolished their claim that Paradise is exclusively for them. They proved that such claims were the outcome of their delusions and wishful thinking, and they asserted that they had no proof to verify their claims. They also pointed to a general ruling, namely, that Paradise is not exclusively reserved for a certain community. Rather, it is attainable to everyone who submits to Allah and does righteous and good deeds.

B) There are also some noble verses in Sura Al-Baqara that respond and refute the claims of the Jews that no one except Jews will enter Paradise. The Almighty said: "Say, O Prophet,"If the eternal Home of the Hereafter with Allah is exclusively for you Israelites out of all humanity, then wish for death if what you say is true!" But they will never wish for that because of what their hands have done. And Allah has perfect knowledge of the wrongdoers. You will surely find them clinging to life more eagerly than any other people, even more than polytheists. Each one of them wishes to live a thousand years. But even if they were to live that long, it would not save them from the punishment. And Allah is All-Seeing of what they do." (Al-Baqara; Q 2:94-96)

The meaning of the honorable verses in brief is:

Mohammad! Tell those Jews who claimed that no one except Jews will enter Paradise that if Paradise is exclusively yours and no one else outside of your faith will enter it, "then wish for death if what you say is true" when you pray because those who are certain to go to Paradise would be eager to die to get there.

Then Allah revealed that this wish will never come to pass "But they will never wish for that," meaning death, "because of what their hands have done," that is, their disbelief and disobedience. "And Allah has perfect knowledge of the wrongdoers" who distorted and misled, coveted what wasn't theirs and denied it from others to whom it was right and lawful.

The Noble Qur'an informed us that their lust and hunger for life is consummate and unparalleled: "You will surely find them clinging to life more eagerly than any other people, even more than polytheists." (Q 2:96) That is, they cling to this life even more ferociously than the polytheists who know nothing except this worldly life. The statement "Each one of them wishes to live a thousand years" means that those Jews yearn to live an extremely long life, even beyond man's reasonable life span. However, a long life will not save anyone from the punishment. "And Allah is All-Seeing of what they do." Allah is aware of all their deeds, and He will give the punishment they deserve.

The Almighty's "Say, O Prophet, "If the eternal Home of the Hereafter with Allah is exclusively for you Israelites out of all humanity, then wish for death if what you say is true!" (Q 2:94) is a response to their false claim that only Jews will enter Paradise. The eternal Home is a reference to Paradise and all its pleasures. The meaning of خَالِصَةً (exclusively) is yours (the Jews) alone and no one else.

Imam Ibn Jarir said: "When it is said 'someone خَلِصَ for me, it means that this someone has become mine alone…" [35]

In the Almighty's "then wish for death," (Q 2:94) the word "wish" refers to a strong desire for something. As shown before, it is a word that is used to express a desire in one's heart. It can also be used as a word, a verbal utterance, as when one says I "wish" I can get this thing.

This second meaning is the one that is meant by the Almighty's "then wish for death." In other words, with your tongues mention a word that indicates that you love death and long for it. We believe that this is what is meant by this verse because the first meaning- that which reflects a heart's desire- is known only to Allah and a challenge would not target meanings that are associated with consciences or hearts.

The meaning of the verse: Tell those Jews, Muhammad, that if Paradise is exclusively for you-and no one else- as you claim, then say with your tongues that you wish for death in order to enjoy its eternal pleasures, if what you say is true. Otherwise, you are not truthful concerning your claim for it is inconceivable that a man would exchange the certain, assured everlasting pleasures of the Hereafter for pleasures mixed with pain and misery in this world.

Imam al-Razi said: "The inevitability of this view lies in the fact that the pleasures of life are few, petty and insignificant compared to the pleasures and blessings of the Hereafter. Moreover, few those pleasure as they were, they were not truly enjoyable because of the arrival of Muhammad and his differences, disputes and fights with them. Those who experience few petty pleasures with annoyance and nuisance (in this life) would certainly be eager for death when they learn About the certain undeniable and wonderful pleasures they would enjoy (in the Hereafter) when they die. And since death is the only way to attain these wished for pleasures, a man should be willing and eager to die. Therefore, if the Hereafter (Eternal Home) was exclusively theirs, they should have longed for death. However, Allah revealed that they were not eager to die and that they never wished to die. It was therefore imperative to impugn their claim that Paradise- (Eternal Home)- was exclusively theirs." [36]

The challenge to wish for death was to have them actually say with their tongues; "we wish to die," or something along the same meaning, as we mentioned before. This is the view of most interpreters.

On the authority of Ibn Abbas, it was said that could have been accomplished through getting together with the believers and each team would then invoke Allah's curse upon the liars.

We are inclined to support the first view because of its proximity to the meaning of the word that is mentioned in the verse. There is no mention of seeking to invoke Allah's curse in the verse; when the Qur'an mentioned this when talking to the Christian of Najran, the word was explicit and clear: "Now, whoever disputes with you O Prophet concerning Jesus (Isa) after full knowledge has come to you, say, "Come! Let us gather our children and your children, our women and your women, ourselves and yourselves—then let us sincerely invoke Allah's curse upon the liars." (Q 3:61) [37]

The Almighty then said that those Jews will never wish for death because of the evils they perpetrated: "But they will never wish for that because of what their hands have done. And Allah has perfect knowledge of the wrongdoers." (Q 2:95)

That is, the Jews do not wish for death because of the sins and transgressions they have committed. Allah is cognizant of all their evil deeds and their trespasses. He is aware of them, and He will reward and punish them accordingly. The noble verse is a statement from Allah that the Jews hate death and refuse to respond to the call to wish for it because they know that once they wish for it, death will certainly come to them. That is because the Messenger of Allah was always truthful regarding whatever he informed them. Therefore, they were cautious not to wish for death fearful of the descent of Allah's wrath upon them for the evils and sins they committed.

In his Interpretation, Ibn Jarir said: "We were informed that 'If the Jews wished for death, they would have died, and they would have seen their places in Hell. And if those who debate Allah's Messenger went out to invoke Allah's curse, they would have come back empty-handed to a place without folks, family or sustenance.' He said; 'Abu Karib, Zakharia ibn A'di, Abeed Allah ibn Omar, Abdul-Karim, ibn Abbas, and the Messenger said that.'" [38]

Imam Ibn Kathir said: "That was narrated by Imam Ahmad on the authority of Ishmael ibn Yazeed Al-Ruky and Furat on the authority of Abdul-Karim."[39]

Al-Zamakhshari said: "His saying 'But they will never wish for that' (Q 2:95) is a miracle because it foretells the unknown. If it is said: 'How do you know that they will not wish for it?' I would respond by saying: 'Had they wished for it, that would have been transmitted and recorded as were most of the other events. The transmitters from among the People of the Books would have, in droves, seized the chance to dispute and attack Islam. Yet no one had transmitted that.'" [40]

The Jews who were challenged by the Prophet to wish for death were unwilling to do so. They were the ones who constantly placed obstacles along the way to impede his message. They were the ones who insisted and persevered in denying and obstructing his prophecy.

No one from among those Jews who were contemporaneous with the Prophet dared to wish for death.

The Almighty's "because of what their hands have done" is a declaration of the reason for their unwillingness to wish for death. In other words, those Jews will never wish for death because of their disbelief in Allah's signs and their indulgence in sins and transgressions which rendered them deserving of severe punishment in the Hereafter.

And the Almighty's "And Allah has perfect knowledge of the wrongdoers" (Q 2:95) indicates a warning and a threat to them. The Jews were wrongdoers because of what their hands have done and because they lied to Allah claiming that Paradise is exclusively for them alone.

Then the almighty showed that those Jews who claimed that Paradise is exclusively theirs are most eager for a long-drawn-out life. He said: "You will surely find them clinging to life more eagerly than any other people, even more than polytheists. Each one of them wishes to live a thousand years. But even if they were to live that long, it would not save them from the punishment. And Allah is All-Seeing of what they do." (Q 2:96)

This noble verse describes them as more eager than all other people, even polytheists, to live a long life even one characterized with humiliation, dishonor and disgrace. Each one of them wishes to live a thousand years. Then, the Almighty reveals that this eagerness to live a lengthy life will not save them from their inevitable destiny in Hell. The Almighty said: "But even if they were to live that long, it would not save them from the punishment." That is, no matter how long one lives, one will not avoid the punishment that is prepared for them. Allah is All-Seeing, and He will inflict upon them the punishment they deserve.

From this exposition of these noble verses, we can see that they countered the Jews' claims that Paradise is exclusively theirs. They responded in a way that eliminated their arguments, exposed their claims, suppressed them and closed their mouths. They declared that Paradise is for those who submit to Allah and do good and righteous deeds. They were not this kind of people. That is why, they craved a long life and feared death for they knew that Hell and a miserable abode was waiting for them because of the evils they perpetrated, the sins they committed and the lies and falsehoods they spread.

Fifth: Their claim that they are Allah's children and most loved:

Among the falsehoods that the Noble Qur'an recounts concerning the People of the Scriptures is their claim that they are Allah's children and His most beloved. The Almighty said: "The Jews and the Christians each say, "We are the children of Allah and His most beloved!" Say, O Prophet, "Why then does He punish you for your sins? No! You are only humans like others of His Own making. He forgives whoever He wills and punishes whoever He wills. To Allah alone belongs the kingdom of the heavens and the earth and everything in between. And to Him is the final return." (Al-Ma'idah; Q 5:18)

Abn Jarir narrates on the authority of Ibn Abbas, he said: "N'umaan bin A'Da, Bahri bin Omero, and Shas bin A'ddi came to the Messenger of Allah and they talked to each other. The Messenger invited them to Allah and warned them against His wrath. They said: 'You can not frighten us, Muhammad. We are Allah's children and His most beloved ones.' Just as Christians claim. For this, Allah revealed: 'The Jews and the Christians each say, "We are the children of Allah and His most beloved- up to the end of the verse." [41]

The meaning of the noble verse is: The Jews said we are Allah's chosen people, His children and His most beloved. We therefore enjoy a higher status and receive more privileges and honor than the rest of humanity. Muhammad! Tell those liars that if you are Allah's children and His beloved ones as you claim, so why does Allah torment you because of the sins and transgressions you have committed? Then, you are not Allah's children; neither are you His beloved ones. You are only humans like others of His Own making, nothing more or less. And the Almighty forgives whoever He wants to forgive, and He punishes whoever He wants to punish. His is the heavens and the earth and all that is contained therein. And to Him all humans will return, and He will reward those who did good deeds and punish the wrongdoers. To Him, no person is better than another except by piety and faith. Therefore, believe in Muhammad, His Messenger, and abandon these false claims to become successful.

The Almighty's "The Jews and the Christians each say, "We are the children of Allah and His most beloved" (Q 5:18) is an account of the corrupt claims and untruthful falsehoods that the two groups declared.

1- Interpreters believe that the word 'children' in their claim "We are the children of Allah" refers to true 'biological' childhood. In fact, from their Book, the Jews refer to Allah's (God's) words to His servant Israel: "Israel is the first of my sons." (Exodus 4:22) So, they added extra shades of meaning and distorted what was said from its original sense. One of their sensible scholars, who embraced Islam, maintained that it was merely meant as a way to honor and dignify (Israel). Likewise, Christians quoted their Book when Jesus said "I will go to My Father and your Father"- meaning My Allah and your Allah- to mean other than what was intended. So, they also said: 'We are Allah's children and His most loved ones.'

2- Other interpreters believe that what is meant by "children" is following the doctrine, the faith: the Jews follow Ezra and his doctrine, and Christians follow Jesus and his doctrine. So, both groups are the children of Allah through this fellowship. Al-Zamakhshari favored this view. He said:

"The children of Allah are followers of the two children of Allah, Ezra and Jesus. It was said to the followers of Abi Khabib (Abdullah bin Al-Zubayer), the Khabibeans. And also, Raht (Musaylimah the Liar) used to say we are the children of Allah. Also, a king's kins, relatives and entourage would say 'we are kings.' For this reason, a believing man from the family of Pharaoh said: 'O my people, yours is the kingdom this day.'" [42]

Even though the two views differ in the interpretation of the meaning of "children," they agree on the Jews' perception and intension, i.e., their claim that they regard themselves as better and more privileged than the rest of humanity, that their relationship with Allah exceeds others' relationship with Him, and that they alone are entitled to be close to Him.

Then the Almighty impugned and refuted their claim in His response: "Say, O Prophet, "Why then does He punish you for your sins?" That is, tell those frauds and liars, Muhammad, that if you were truly Allah's children and His most beloved- as you claim- He wouldn't have punished you. A true lover would not torture his beloved. However, your situation is quite the opposite, for Allah has punished you for your sins by murdering, capturing and transforming you (into apes and pigs). In the Books that are between your hands, it is written that you will be punished in the Hereafter for your transgressions in this world. The Jews conceded that torture will befall them for only a few days, and the Noble Qur'an recounted that: "Some of the Jews claim, "The Fire will not touch us except for a number of days." (Q 2:80) And the Christians also admitted that the Almighty will reward each one according to their deeds.

Imam Al-Qurtubi said: "The Almighty responded to their claims and said: 'Why then does He punish you for your sins?'. To this, there was only two ways to respond: they could either admit that He punishes them, and they would then be told that they are not His children or most favored because a lover does not torment his beloved. But since you are admitting being tortured, this is proof for your lies. This is known as "reductio ad absurdum" (Contradictory proof which is a proof based on proving the validity of the required statement by invalidating its opposite or the invalidity of the required statement by proving its opposite). Or else, they would deny that He punishes them and thereby dispute what is mentioned in their Books and what their messengers brought them. That would also mean that they make transgressions permissible while admitting the torture that befalls the transgressors among them." [43]

Then, the Almighty responded to their claims and demonstrated to them the truth About their condition. He said: "No! You are only humans like others of His Own making. He forgives whoever He wills and punishes whoever He wills." (Q 5:18) This means: The truth is not as you claimed, you Jews; you are just like the rest of the people whom Allah created: if you believe and amend your works, you will be rewarded, but if you persisted in your disbelief, stubbornness and denial, you will be punished. No one is better than anyone else except by their faith and good deeds.

The noble verse (Q 5:18) then concludes the response to them. The Almighty said: "To Allah alone belongs the kingdom of the heavens and the earth and everything in between. And to Him is the final return." That is: Allah has the absolute power and authority to decide any matter according to His Knowledge, Prudence and Justice. All His creation is His subjects, His servants, and to Him all will return on Judgement Day when they present their accounts and receive their rewards for their good and evil deeds.

Thus, the noble verse has abolished the Jews' claim that they are Allah's children and His most beloved ones. It has also asserted that no one is better than another except by piety and good works.

Sixth: <u>Their claim that Ezra was the son of Allah, parroting their rabbis</u>:

The Noble Qur'an has recounted numerous false doctrines and untruthful claims that the People of the Scriptures reiterated. For example, the Jews said that "Ezra [44] is the Son of Allah," while the Christians claimed that "The Messiah is the Son of Allah." The Qur'an also mentions that the two groups took their rabbis and their monks as Lords besides Allah, and they sought to terminate and extinguish the light of Islam that spread throughout the land and guided those that went astray. The Noble Qur'an countered the claims, aberrations and distortions of the People of the Scriptures. It stopped their claims, confirmed their folly and misguidance and brought the believers blessed and good tidings. The Almighty said:

"The Jews say, "Ezra is the son of Allah," while the Christians say, "The Messiah is the son of Allah." Such are their baseless assertions, only parroting the words of earlier disbelievers. May Allah condemn them! How can they be deluded from the truth? They have taken their rabbis and monks as well as the Messiah, son of Mary, as lords besides Allah, even though they were commanded to worship none but One Allah. There is no god worthy of worship' except Him. Glorified is He above what they associate with Him! They wish to extinguish Allah's light with their mouths, but Allah will only allow His light to be perfected, even to the dismay of the disbelievers. He is the One Who has sent His Messenger with true guidance and the religion of truth, making it prevail over all others, even to the dismay of the polytheists." (At-Tawbah; Q 9:30-33)

Ibn Jarir narrated on the authority of Ibn Abbas, he said: "a group of Jews came to the Messenger of Allah: Salam bin Mishkam, An-Nu'man bin Awfa, Shas bin Qais, and Malik bin As-Saif. They said: 'How can we follow you when you have abandoned our Qiblah and you do not claim that Ezra is the son of Allah?' So Allah the Almighty revealed: 'And the Jews said, "Ezra is the son of Allah. And the Christians said that the Messiah is the Son of Allah…'" The Almighty's "And the Jews said, "Ezra is the son of Allah. And the Christians said that the Messiah is the Son of Allah…" is a statement that shows the false and incorrect claims of the two groups and their deviation from the upright and correct doctrine.

Imam Al-Baydawi said: "They said that 'Ezra is the Son of Allah' because after the events of Nebuchadnezzar, no one remained to preserve the Torah. When Allah brought him back to life a hundred years later, he dictated the Torah to them from memory. They marveled at this and said: 'No doubt
this is because he is the Son of Allah.'" [45]

On the other hand, the Christians' claim that 'The Messiah is the Son of Allah' can be attributed to the fact that created Him without a father, not in accordance with the natural biological laws governing conception and birth. They therefore called Him 'The Son of Allah.' In Sura Ali 'Imran, Allah showed them that Adam was without a father or a mother. He was thus worthier of this father-son relationship, but that was never attributed to him. Therefore, Jesus should be like Adam: "Indeed, the example of Jesus in the sight of Allah is like that of Adam. He created him from dust, then said to him, "Be!" And he was! This is the truth from your Lord, so do not be one of those who doubt." (Al-Imran; Q 3:59-60)

The Almighty then revealed that their claims cannot be supported with reason and sound judgement. He said: "Such are their baseless assertions." (Q 9:30) That is, those assertions concerning Ezra and Jesus were merely unsubstantiated claims that they blurt out without any judgement. Nothing confirms or validates these claims; they are only the fabrication of their imagination, their own delusional invention, valueless and without weight. Weighty and substantiated evidence indicate the impossibility for Allah to have a son, a father, or a partner: "There is none in the heavens or the earth who will not return to the Most Compassionate in full submission. Indeed, He fully knows them and has counted them precisely." (Q 19:93) [46]

The Almighty warned those who claim that He has offspring with severe punishment. He said: "and to warn those who claim, "Allah has offspring." They have no knowledge of this, nor did their forefathers. What a terrible claim that comes out of their mouths! They say nothing but lies." (Q 18:4) [47]

Al-Zamakhshari said: "If it is said that words come out of the mouth, so what is meant by 'Such are their baseless assertions قَوْلُهُم بِأَفْوَٰهِهِمْ (What their mouths utter)?' I would respond by saying that there are two views. The first view is that it was merely something that was said, some utterance that was unproven and unsupported, sheer noise, devoid of any meaning, much like empty words. A weighty and meaningful speech is uttered by the mouth and would have an impact on the heart. On the other hand, a meaningless speech would only be uttered by the mouth. The second view regards the speech as following a specific way or doctrine such as what is meant by 'Abu Hanifa's way,' meaning his style and teachings. It is as if it were said that that was their way and their doctrine: theirs was merely lip service not sincere and heartfelt. There is nothing in it- nothing profound or substantial- that would move the heart." [48]

Then the Almighty revealed that this baseless claim was due to their mimicking- parroting- those disbelievers who had preceded them: "only parroting the words of earlier disbelievers." (Q 9:30)

The meaning is: Those who claimed that Ezra is the Son of Allah had no evidence to support their claim. They were only parroting- in their appalling and horrendous disbelief- the words of those nations that came before them: the polytheists who said: "The angels are the daughters of Allah."

The Almighty's "May Allah condemn them" (Q 9:30) was a supplication to annihilate them thoroughly. Those with whom Allah fights are doomed to perish. And they were most deserving of this supplication because of the horrific nature of what they had uttered and what they had falsely attributed to the Almighty.

Ibn Abbas maintains that the meaning of "May Allah condemn them/ ' قَـٰتَلَهُمُ ٱللَّهُ " is may Allah curse them. Every time قَاتَلَ /death is mentioned in the Qur'an indicates a curse.

The Almighty's "أَنَّىٰ يُؤْفَكُون" means how can they be deluded 'from the truth and abandon worshipping the One Allah who is worthy of worship? How could they depart from monotheism and say preposterous and unacceptable things About Him, things that were neither proven nor reasonable? Jesus and Ezra were nothing but two of Allah's servants, the One who established this wonderful universe and managed all its affairs. How could they claim that About Him? What they said was conspicuously and glaringly untruthful. Rational and sound minds and righteous and pure hearts find it loathsome.

Then, the Almighty showed that these words that the Jews and Christians claimed were the result of parroting earlier disbelievers, not due to conviction or persuasion through proof or evidence. It was mere parroting their rabbis and monks who wanted to submerge monotheism and extinguish Allah's light. The Almighty said: "They have taken their rabbis [49] and monks as well as the Messiah, son of Mary, as lords besides Allah, even though they were commanded to worship none but One God (Allah). There is no god worthy of worship except Him. Glorified is He above what they associate with Him!" (Q 9:31)

The meaning is: Those Jews, who lied and attributed unacceptable things to Allah, took their rabbis and monks as lords besides Allah because if they made something permissible to them, they would embrace it even if Allah made it unlawful and forbidden. And if they forbade them something, they would shun it even if Allah made it lawful and permissible. Their obedience for their rabbis and monks was similar to the obedience of those who were obedient to Allah. Likewise, some took Jesus, Son of Mary, as a lord besides Allah, or as the Son of Allah.

The Almighty then showed that they were only commanded to worship none but One Allah, without associating any partner or son with Him. He said: "they were commanded to worship none but One Allah. There is no god worthy of worship except Him. Glorified is He above what they associate with Him!" (Q 9:31)

That is, they were commanded in their Books and by Moses and Jesus-peace be upon them- to worship Allah Alone with faithfulness and loyalty.

Imam Ibn Kathir said: "Imam Ahmad, al-Tirmidhi and Ibn Jarir said that when Udi bin Hatim received an invitation from the Messenger of Allah, he fled to the Levant. He had embraced Christianity during the days of ignorance. His sister encouraged him to embrace Islam. She prompted him to meet the Messenger of Allah. So, Udi came to Medina. He was a chief among his people Tai, and his father was Hatim al-Tai, who was well known for his generosity and open handedness. He came to the Prophet with a cross made of silver on his neck reading "They have taken their rabbis and monks … as lords besides Allah." He said: 'They did not worship them.' He said: 'No, they prohibited what was permissible and made permissible what was prohibited. And they followed them. That was how they worshipped them.' The Messenger of Allah said: 'What are you saying, Udi? Does it bother you when the phrase 'Allah is the greatest' is said? Do you know of any other Allah?' He then invited him to Islam. Udi became Muslim, and his face was glowing. He (Muhammad) said: 'The Jews are those who earned Your anger, and the Christians are those who went astray.'" (also a reference to Q 1:7) [50]

The Almighty then revealed the purpose behind the Jews' false claims and untruthful assertions. He said: "They wish to extinguish Allah's light with their mouths, but Allah will only allow His light to be perfected, even to the dismay of the disbelievers." (Q 9:32)

That is: those who rejected the truth from among the People of the Scriptures wanted to extinguish Allah's light with their mouths by repressing the guidance that Allah sent with His messenger and blocking the religion of truth with which he came. They sought to do this through their false claims and weak unsubstantiated assertions. They merely resembled those who might want to extinguish the rays of the sun or the light of the moon by blowing at them.

Al-Zamakhshari said: "In their quest to abolish Muhammad's Prophethood with their false statements, they resembled someone who wanted to blow at a splendid luminous light at the horizon. Allah wanted to make it all the more brilliant and luminous while that person was trying to blow it out and extinguish it with his mere breath." [51]

The Almighty thwarted the attempts of those disbelievers and rendered them helpless and disappointed while promising the believers the good tidings of victory. He said: "He is the One Who has sent His Messenger with true guidance and the religion of truth, making it prevail over all others, even to the dismay of the polytheists." (Q 9:33) That is, it was the Almighty who sent Muhammad, His Messenger, with the Qur'an that would guide people to what is good and beneficial to them. It was Allah who sent Muhammad with the religion of truth, Islam, to prevail and have supremacy over all other religions even to the disappointment of the polytheists who hated to see it spread and dominate. In Sahih Muslim on the authority of Thawban, he said: 'The Messenger of Allah said: 'Allah folded the earth for me, and I saw the east and the west. I was given the two treasures, the red and the white.'" [52]

Thus, the noble verses impugned the claims of the People of the Scriptures that neither Ezra nor Jesus were sons of Allah. They directed them to the straight path to follow, and they chastised and rebuked them for thoughtlessly and heedlessly following their rabbis and monks. They also promised the believers that the religion of truth will prevail even to. The dismay and disappointment of the disbelievers and the polytheists.

Seventh: <u>Their claim that their sins are forgiven</u>:

Among the Jews' false contentions and untruthful assertions is their claim that whatever sins they committed, despicable and horrific deeds they perpetrated, or unlawful gains they allowed themselves to acquire, they would be forgiven because they are Allah's chosen people, His children and most beloved ones.

The Noble Qur'an countered these false claims. It stopped their claims, impugned their assertions and revealed their falsehoods and lies. In Sura Al-A'raf, the Almighty said: "Then they were succeeded by other generations who inherited the Scripture. They indulged in unlawful gains, claiming, "We will be forgiven after all." And if similar gain came their way, they would seize it. Was a covenant not taken from them in the Scripture that they would not say anything About Allah except the truth? And they were already well-versed in its teachings. But the ˹eternal˺ Home of the Hereafter is far better for those mindful of Allah. Will you not then understand? As for those who firmly abide by the Scripture and establish prayer—surely, We never discount the reward of those acting righteously." [53] (Al-A'raf; Q 7:169-170)

Imam Al-Qurtubi said: "الخلْف/ (with the Sukkunسكون/ succeeded by) means children (whether it is singular or plural), whereas الخلَف(with the Fatha/ الفتح)means a substitute whether the reference is to a child or a stranger." Ibn al-A'rabi said: "الخلَف (with the Fatha) means the righteous whileالخلْف means the wrongdoer. That wordالخلْف is the one that is used when reference is made to inappropriate speech. It is the same word that is used in the well-known saying "He was silent for a thousand years, yet when he spoke, he uttered foul and inappropriate language." [54]

As Labid said: "Those who lived in their care are gone, and I am left behind خلْف like the skin of a mangy dog." The word عَرَض/ (with the Fatha) unlawful gains refers to worthless worldly possessions, while عَرْض (with the Sukkun) refers to money other than dirhams and dinars. The reference in this verse is to bribery and wicked earnings.

Al-Zamakhshari said: "The Almighty's 'يَأْخُذُونَ عَرَضَ هَٰذَا ٱلْأَدْنَىٰ/They indulged in unlawful gains' is meant to indicate the trifles and smidgeons of this world and its pleasing trivialities. It indicates contempt and disdain. The word الْأَدْنَى (from الدنو) may mean to come close because it is imminent and looming or it might mean دنو الحالة, which refers to a lowly status. The reference here is to the usury/bribes they received to issue distorted rulings to facilitate matters for the public." [55]

The pronoun in "مِنْ بَعْدِهِمْ/ were succeeded" refers to the Jews whom Allah described in the previous verse saying: "We dispersed them through the land in groups—some were righteous, others were less so. We tested them with prosperity and adversity, so perhaps they would return ˹to the Right Path˺"

That is: Worse people succeeded those whom We dispersed through the land. They inherited the Scripture, the Torah. They read and learned its teachings and the prohibitions and permissions it comprises. However, they were not impacted by the Scripture, and they rejected its rulings and knowingly made permissible what was prohibited. They craved the trifles of this world and its petty pleasures. They greedily indulged in and devoured unlawful gains. They claimed that Allah will forgive them their wrongdoing even as they wallowed in sins and reeled in transgressions. They declared that He will not punish them for unlawfully taking others' money and possessions because they are the offspring of His prophets and His chosen people favored above all else...etc.

The Almighty then reported that they were people who persisted on their wrongdoing and trespasses; they were not likely to offer penitence or express remorse for their actions. He said: "And if similar gain came their way, they would seize it." (Q 7:169) That is, they indulged in the trifles of this petty life heedless of Allah's commandments and doctrine as revealed in the Torah. They claimed that Allah will not punish them for their deeds. Moreover, they did not repent or express contrition; rather, if a new forbidden gain- like the others they had wrongfully and unlawfully acquired- presented itself to them, they would fervently rush to seize it anew, would make it permissible and devour it without penitence or remorse.

About the Almighty's "And if similar gain came their way, they would seize it," Mujahid said: "Whenever any of the pleasures of life is made manifest for them, they would take it whether it was lawful "halal" or unlawful "haram/forbidden." They would dream of forgiveness claiming, "We will be forgiven ⌜after all⌝" Yet, "And if similar gain came their way, they would seize it." [56]

Al-Suddi said: "Whenever the Children of Israel sought the service of a judge, they would bribe him. They got together and pledged not to accept bribes anymore. However, they still accepted bribes when their services were sought. Whenever asked why they did that (accepted bribes), they would respond saying that Allah would forgive them. The other members of the Children of Israel would then oppose this. When that judge died or was replaced by one of those who opposed the former judge, he would say: "And if similar gain came their way, they would seize it." [57]

The Almighty then impugned their claim that they "will be forgiven after all" while insisting on their disobedience and wrongdoing. He said: "Was a covenant not taken from them in the Scripture that they would not say anything About Allah except the truth? And they were already well-versed in its teachings." (Q 7:169) The meaning is: Allah had taken a covenant from those who took bribes and claimed that He will forgive them their deeds. He took a covenant that they would say nothing About Him except the truth and that they would not disobey His commandments, breach His covenant or trespass against Him. They studied, learned and understood what was in the Book. However, they did not abide by the pledges they made. Nor did they follow the commandments entailed in their Book; they did not do what they were asked to do, and they did not shun what was forbidden or prohibited. They studied the Book, but they were not affected by its teachings. They exchanged its teachings for the petty pleasures and trifles of life. What a miserable choice!

The statement "And they were already well-versed in its teachings" corresponds in meaning to the question that came before it: "Was a covenant not taken from them in the

Scripture…?" In other words, the Almighty had taken a covenant from them in the Torah, and they were well aware of its teachings and instructions.

Ibn Zayd said: "The one who was right would come to them with a bribe, so they would bring out the Book of Allah and rule in his favor according to its tenets. When the one who was wrong came, they would take the bribe from him and bring out for him the book that they had written with their own hands and rule in his favor." [58]

Then, the Almighty showed them the splendid eternal pleasures that He had prepared for the righteous ones, those who refrained from the consumption of the forbidden gain towards which the liars were racing to seize. He said: "But the eternal Home of the Hereafter is far better for those mindful of Allah. Will you not then understand?" (Q 7:169) The meaning is: The pleasures that the Almighty has prepared in the Hereafter for the righteous ones, those who faithfully worship Him openly and privately, are far exceed the petty and lowly gains that those Jews unlawfully and unjustly claim and preferred over Allah's eternal blessings and sumptuous rewards. "Will you not then understand?" (Q 7:169) Will you- who have consumed peoples' money unjustly and claimed that Allah will forgive your sins- not consider these clear instructions that sound minds- unspoiled by lusts and unpossessed by Satan- would undoubtedly perceive?

This points to the fact that it was the greed and lusts for worldly pleasure that drove the Children of Israel to say untruths and falsehoods About Allah, to consume unlawful gains without compunction, and to abandon and sell their religion for petty worldly pleasures.

Imam Al-Alusi said: "This verse aims to rebuke those successors for insistent claim that they will be forgiven while persisting on transgressions and sins. This persistence is seen in the use of the سـ in سَيُغْفَرُwhich is used to indicate emphasis, as researchers maintain. Ibn Abbas argues that that were admonished for claiming that Allah will forgive their sins which they still commit and never repent for.
Sunnis hold it important to chastise those who are untruthful. They maintain that Shadad ibn Aws that said that the Messenger said: 'An intelligent and strong person is the one who holds himself accountable and works for his eternity (what comes after death), whereas a weak and pathetic person is he who follows his desires and lusts and indulges in wishful thinking.' That is why, it is said that the Jews were chastised for consuming others' money, following their wishes and desires, claiming things that Allah never promised, lying and distorting Allah's judgements, indulged in unlawful gains, and saying untruths About Allah." [59]

Then the Almighty commended those who abide by the Scripture, those who seek what is permissible and avoid what is prohibited and those who refrain from saying untruths About Him. He said: "As for those who firmly abide by the Scripture and establish prayer—surely, We never discount the reward of those acting righteously." (Q 7:170) The word "Scripture" here refers to the Torah or the Qur'an or and of the Revealed Books. The meaning is, those who comply with and submit to the commandments of the Book that Allah revealed will be richly rewarded for Allah never overlooks the reward of the righteous who do good deeds.

Thus, the two noble verses reproved the Jews for lying and claiming untruths About Allah. They countered their claims that their sins are forgiven while still persisting on consuming unlawful gains. They directed them to the path of success that they should follow if they were among those who comprehend and learn from prior memories and examples.

Eighth: Their claim that they are not accountable for exploiting the Gentiles:

Among the Jews' false contentions and untruthful assertions is their claim that they are not accountable for exploiting the Gentiles. That is, those who do not embrace their faith have no right, their money is fair game to them, and they are not to be answerable if they were to unjustly pillage and unlawfully despoil or plunder their possessions.

The Noble Qur'an countered these false claims. It stopped their claims, impugned their assertions and revealed their falsehoods and lies. In Sura Al-Imran, the Almighty said:

"There are some among the People of the Book who, if entrusted with a stack of gold, will readily return it. Yet there are others who, if entrusted with a single coin, will not repay it unless you constantly demand it. This is because they say, "We are not accountable for exploiting the Gentiles." And so they attribute lies to Allah knowingly. Absolutely! Those who honor their trusts and shun evil—surely Allah loves those who are mindful of Him." [60] (Al-Imran; Q 3:75-76)

The meaning of the two noble verses is: Muhammad! There are some among the people of the Book who will readily and completely honor their trusts no matter how valuable and precious the stuff you entrust them with. And there are others who, if entrusted with few things, will keep them to themselves and not return them. The reason for unjustly legitimizing this is their claim that they are "not accountable for ⌜exploiting⌝ the Gentiles." That is to say, they are not answerable for taking away the money of the illiterate Arabs; no one can blame them for this. By saying this, Muhammad, they knowingly and consciously attribute lies to Allah. You, Muhammad, should refute and dispute what they claim and tell them that they are accountable for exploiting the Gentiles and that they will be held responsible for what they do because "Those who honor their trusts and shun evil—surely Allah loves those who are mindful ⌜of Him⌝."

The Almighty's "There are some among the People of the Book who, if entrusted with a stack of gold, will readily return it. Yet there are others who, if entrusted with a single coin, will not repay it unless you constantly demand it" is a statement to show two opposing groups among the People of the Scripture. The first group of people are those who would honor their trusts no matter how valuable and precious these trusts are. This was the group that rightly responded to the truth and believed in Muhammad, like Abdullah ibn Salaam and other believers like him from among the People of the Book.

Ibn Abbas said: "A man entrusted Abdullah Ibn Salaam twelve hundred ounces of gold, and returned completely when asked. Another man entrusted Finhas Ibn Azoura' one dinar, but he did not return it when asked. That is why the verse was revealed." [61]

The second group of people are those who do not return what they were trusted with, even if not valuable, unless they are constantly and repeatedly demanded to return them and various and numerous methods are used to affect this. This group was the one that rejected the truth, refused to follow Muhammad, and fought, in words and deeds, the Islamic call.

The words "stack" and "dinar" here refer to "big/great" and "small/few" amounts. That is, some are extremely honest and would return whatever they are entrusted with even if it was a great sum of money. One the other hand, some are extremely disloyal and deceitful to the extent that they would fulfill the pledge to return what they are entrusted with, even if little or insignificant. They will only return it after they are constantly and repeatedly asked to.

Imam Ibn Jarir said: "If it is said: 'Why would Allah inform His Messenger About such a thing when people know that there are honest and dishonest people when it comes to returning what they are entrusted with?' I would say: 'The Lord wanted to inform the believers of their nature in this verse to caution them against entrusting them with their money because many of them unlawfully and unscrupulously took the money of the believers without compunction or feeling guilty.'" [62]

The Almighty then reported the reason they justify their infidelity and disloyalty and take away and steal other people's money. He said: "This is because they say, "We are not accountable لَيْسَ عَلَيْنَا... سَبِيلٌ for exploiting the Gentiles." (Q 7:169)

The word سَبِيلٌ means a binding agreement. It originally means "a path." It was thus called because it refers to a method, a way or a path to obligate others and compel them to bear consequences. In other words, the reason for the disloyal group for not fulfilling promises and refusing to return what they were entrusted with is their claim that they are not to be held accountable or be blamed for taking the money of the illiterate Arabs by any means possible. They would not be censured or impugned if they trespassed against them for those Gentiles do not believe in their religion. The Jews claim that their Book permits them to kill and take the money away from those who oppose them, and by any possible means. Sanctity and honoring others' possessions are not to be extended to non- Jews

This contemptible and detestable attitude is deeply ingrained in the Jews. Their selfishness prompted them to distort their Book to agree with their wishes and desires. For example, the Torah forbad usury altogether, and it said "Do not take interest on the money which you let him (your brother) have." (Leviticus 25:37) The Jews distorted this text and added the "the Israelite" to it. The text now reads: "Do not take interest on the money which you let your Israelite brother) have." Thus, they now prohibit taking interest when they interact with each other, but they allow it when they are interacting with others because they do not feel or relate to the common good of brotherhood of humanity.

The Almighty's "And ⌜so⌝ they attribute lies to Allah knowingly" is a rejoinder to what they claimed that they are not accountable for exploiting the Gentiles. It impugns their claim because Allah never gave them that authority. No sound mind would support it either. Virtuous moral ethics should be applied to all people without discrimination or differentiation.

The meaning is: Those Jews who refuse to return what they are entrusted with on the pretext that they are not accountable for exploiting the Gentiles attribute lies to Allah, and they do that knowingly, because there is nothing in the Torah that gives them the right to exploit and deceive the Gentiles. Rather, what the Torah commands them to do is to gregariously and cheerfully return trusts to their owners.

The Prophet exhibited that trusts should be returned to the righteous and the unrighteous. Ibn Jarir narrated on the authority of Sa'eed Ibn Jubyer: "When the verse- 'There are some among the People of the Book who, if entrusted with a stack of gold, will readily return it. Yet there are others who, if entrusted with a single coin, will not repay it unless you constantly demand it. This is because they say, "We are not accountable for ⌜exploiting⌝ the Gentiles"'- was revealed, the Prophet said: 'The enemies of Allah have lied. Everything is under my feet except for trusts which should be returned the righteous and the wrongdoer.'" [63]

The Prophet's followers followed the principle of returning trusts to all men. They would not take anything from other peoples' money except lawfully.

Ibn Kathir said: "Abdul Razaaq said: Mu'amar said that Abi Ishaq al-Hamazani said that Abi Sa'sa'a Ibn Yazyd said that a man asked Ibn Abbas, saying: 'During battle, we get the chickens and lambs of the Dhimmi people.' Ibn Abbas said: 'What are you saying?' He said: 'That is okay with us.' Iban Abbas said: 'That is similar to 'We are not accountable for exploiting the Gentiles,' which is what the People of the Scripture said. Once they pay the Jizya, their money is not permissible unless they acquiesce.'" [64]

Also, Ibn Jarir said: "The Jews pledged allegiance to Muslim men during the pre-Islamic period, and when they converted to Islam, they demanded the rest of their money from them. The Jews said: 'You have no right over us, and we have no right to judge, because you abandoned your religion.' They claimed that they found that in their Book. So, Allah said: 'They attribute lies to Allah knowingly.'" (Q 7:169) [65]

Then Allah confirmed their lies by adding another compelling sentence that would bind and obligate them. He said: "Absolutely! Those who honor their trusts بَلَىٰ مَنْ أَوْفَىٰ بِعَهْدِهِۦ/ and shun evil—surely Allah loves those who are mindful of Him." (Q 7:170)

The word "بَلَى =But no!" is used in the response to confirm what the Jews denied by claiming "We are not accountable for exploiting the Gentiles." That is, it is not as you claimed, O Jews, that you are not accountable for exploiting them. In fact, you are. And you will be tortured for making their money permissible unlawfully and unjustly. And you will be rewarded if you believed in Allah and His Messenger, Muhammad, and fulfilled your trusts with the Arabs and others.

The Almighty justified this fair judgement by the general statement "Those who honor their trusts and shun evil—surely Allah loves those who are mindful of Him."

That is, those who fulfill their covenant with Allah and believe in His Prophet, Muhammad, follow his religion and shun the deceit and treachery that Allah has prohibited, will find favor in the sight of the Lord. Those who do not would incur Allah's wrath and displeasure, and they will be severely punished. Thus, the noble statement illustrates that Allah's love for His servants is fulfilled under two conditions:

First: Abiding by covenants, that is, it is incumbent upon man to comply with his pledges and promises. Foremost among these pledges is worshipping Allah Alone (monotheism) and believing in His messengers, especially Muhammad.

Second: Living in piety and the fear of Allah. That is, man should shun what Allah has prohibited and do only what Allah has made permissible.

The Jews were found lacking on both accounts. They did not fulfill the covenant that Allah took from them to believe in Muhammad. Consequently, they made permissible what Allah has forbidden, and they did not fulfill their trusts and they denied others their rights. They untruthfully claimed "We are not accountable for exploiting the Gentiles." Had they been pious and feared Allah, they would have abandoned what they were prohibited from doing and refrained from any kind of aggression and wrongdoing. Since they did not fear Allah and indulged in doing these things, they will be punished for their wrongdoing and loathsome despicable deeds.

Tafsir al-Manar said: "The response in the statement provides us with a general rule concerning religion, namely, fulfilling covenants and shunning all kinds of evil deeds bring a servant close to His Lord and make him worthy of His love. It is not because of any connection or relation to any specific people or nation. This rule betrays the error of the Jews in claiming that they are not accountable for exploiting the Gentiles. It also reveals that those who embrace this view are not people of virtue and piety which are the cornerstone of any upright religion." [66]

Thus, the Noble Qur'an vehemently and compellingly countered the Jews' claim "We are not accountable for exploiting the Gentiles" proving that they lie persistently and knowingly. It also recounted that fulfilling the trusts is a binding duty and incumbent on everyone, and that whoever fears Allah and abides by His covenants will be worthy of His love and pleasure.

Ninth: <u>Their outrageous accusation of Mary and their claim that they killed the Messiah</u>:

One of the Jews' most outrageous lies and contemptible slanders was attributing adultery to the pure Virgin and Immaculate Mary and their boastful claim that they had killed Jesus after they rejected His message, offended his character and pursed all possible means to harm Him.

The Noble Qur'an recounted what they said About the pure and Immaculate Mary and her Son, Jesus (Isa), and it fervently countered and impugned what they said About them to exalt and elevate the status of the Immaculate Mary and Jesus, the messenger. In Sura An-Nisa, we read: "They were condemned for breaking their covenant, rejecting Allah's signs, killing the prophets unjustly, and for saying, "Our hearts are unreceptive!"[1]—it is Allah Who has sealed their hearts for their disbelief, so they do not believe except for a few—and for their denial and outrageous accusation against Mary, and for boasting, "We killed the Messiah, Jesus, son of Mary, the messenger of Allah." But they neither killed nor crucified him—it was only made to appear so. Even those who argue for this crucifixion are in doubt. They have no knowledge whatsoever—only making assumptions. They certainly did not kill him. Rather, Allah raised him up to Himself. And Allah is Almighty, All-Wise. Every one of the People of the Book will definitely believe in him before his death. And on the Day of Judgment Jesus will be a witness against them." (An-Nisa Q 4:155-158)

The letter "baa/ب" in فَبِمَا نَقْضِهِم مِّيثَٰقَهُمْ (They were condemned for breaking their covenant) expresses the reason. The word "مَا" is for emphasis.

It is because of breaking their covenant, their rejection of Our signs, their killing of the prophets and attributing lies and falsehoods to Us that We did what We did to them: We condemned and transformed them (into apes and pigs), in addition to the other punishments that we inflicted upon them.

The word غُلْفٌ in قُلُوبُنَا غُلْفٌ is the plural of اغلف which means wrapped with a cover that prevents anything from penetrating inside.

The meaning is: Our hearts are covered with thick covers which make them immune and resistant to anything that Muhammad brought; nothing will penetrate to our hearts; they do not understand what Muhammad says. Thus, they are blameless for not following him since the Almighty created their hearts like this (covered with a thick mist), unmoved and unaffected by what Muhammad said.

The Almighty disputed this false claim and said: "it is Allah Who has sealed their hearts for their disbelief, so they do not believe except for a few." (Q 4:155) That is, it is not because their hearts are-by nature- covered, impenetrable and unreceptive that they disbelieve and fail to see the truth. Rather, it is the Almighty Allah Who has sealed their hearts because of their disbelief and wicked deeds. The Almighty created the human heart and inherently equipped it with the ability to choose good and evil. However, those Jews departed from what is good and righteous and pursued what is evil and wicked. They chose disbelief over belief because of their capitulation to their wishes and submission to their lusts. Allah has sealed their hearts because of their evil deeds and for knowingly, deliberately and persistently rejecting the truth. They do not believe except a little, and they do not pursue the truth or believe in all the messengers. They say: 'We believe in some, and we disbelieve others.' The faith of such people cannot be upheld or relied upon. Disbelieving some messengers amounts to disbelieving all messengers.

The noble statement "it is Allah Who has sealed their hearts for their disbelief, so they do not believe except for a few" is a parenthetical statement that is introduced to speedily impugn their false claims and fabricated untruthful assertions.

The Almighty mentioned two of their numerous crimes. He said: "their denial بِكُفْرِهِمْ and outrageous accusation against Mary." (Q 4:156)

The word بِكُفْرِهِمْ (their denial) here refers to their denial of Jesus (Isa), which is different from the "denial" that is mentioned in the Almighty's "it is Allah Who has sealed their hearts for their disbelief" because indicates all-encompassing and absolute denial.

Imam Al-Alusi said: "their denial (بِكُفْرِهِمْ) comes after- or coordinated to- their disbelief (بِكُفْرِهِمْ) (both are translated as بِكُفْرِهِمْ). The second بِكُفْرِهِمْ/disbelief refers to their denial of Isa (Jesus). The first بِكُفْرِهِمْ /disbelief is a reference to either absolute, downright denial/disbelief, or denial of/disbelieving in Muhammad because of the association with what the almighty mentioned About them "Our hearts are unreceptive." [67]

And the word بُهْتَانًا is a reference to the excessively extreme lies that sound minds find unacceptable and causes confusion and bewilderment to those targeted by it for its strangeness and novelty. And the meaning is: Among the reasons why Allah condemned the Jews and cast humiliation and disgrace upon them was their disbelief and rejection of Jesus, the messenger who was sent to guide them to the truth, to a straightforward path, and their outrageous accusations and lies About Mary, Jesus' Mother, and the terrible falsehoods they attributed to her, namely, begetting Jesus without a father. She was innocent of all of these charges and untruths.

She was brought up in the care of Allah's Prophet, Zachariah, and she was used to worshipping in her sanctuary that she barely left. At the birth of her Son, Jesus, Allah revealed clear evidence and verses that she was blameless, without blemish. She was innocent and far above any hint of suspicion, as the Qur'an most eloquently and articulately displays in Sura Maryam.

Then the Almighty recounted their lies About Jesus, and He revealed what was right and truthful. He said: "We killed the Messiah, Jesus, son of Mary, the messenger of Allah." (Q 4:157) That is, because of what they said, audacious and untruthful and criminally vicious and atrocious as it was, Allah condemned them and was wrathful and displeased with them as He was for their previous offenses and crimes.

What they said was in itself a crime because of the impudence and boastfulness they manifested in killing- according to their claim- one of Allah's prophets. Although this claim is in opposition to the truth and differs from facts, it indicates that they wanted to kill Him and that they sought all possible avenues to achieve their vile and despicable end. They connived with the Romans and slandered and disparaged Him attributing sorcery and witchcraft to Him. They attempted to deliver Him to His enemies to crucify Him. They even claimed that they did, in fact, deliver Him, but Allah thwarted their plan, foiled their plot and stopped their cunningness. He delivered His prophet, Jesus, from their evil and raised Him up to Himself unscathed.

There is no doubt that what the Jews attempted to do to Jesus- trying all possible means to kill Him and boastfully claiming that they actually did even though Allah raised Him up to Himself- is considered one of the gravest and most serious crimes. It is evidently clear in all doctrines and laws that whoever tries to commit a crime and pursues all possible ways to carry it out but fails to complete because of some factors beyond his control, should be considered a criminal deserving of punishment.

The Jews did pursue all means possible to kill Jesus as we showed. However, they were unable to carry out their scheme because of reasons beyond their control. This means that had there been some way left to carry out their dreadful crime, they would have undoubtedly seized it; they would have certainly rushed to see their plot unfold and come to fruition. They are, therefore, deserving of the punishment that is reserved for the criminal for thinking, intending and planning to commit what Allah has prohibited.

Imam Al-Razi said: "If it is said: 'The Jews rejected Jesus, deliberately attempted to kill Him and called Him a sorcerer and son of a sorceress.' How, then, could they say: 'We killed the Messiah, Jesus, son of Mary, the messenger of Allah'? 'There are two ways to respond to this question: the first, they said that sardonically and scornfully, just like Pharaoh mockingly said: 'Your messenger, who has been sent to you, must be insane.' (Ash-Shu'ara; Q 26:27) And as the disbelievers among Quraysh said to Muhammad: '"O you to whom the Reminder is revealed! You must be insane!" (Al-Hijr: Q 15 6) The second response is: it is plausible that Allah puts good words in place of their bad and vile words to elevate Jesus above what they mentioned About Him.'" [68]

The Almighty then disputed their claim. He said: "But they neither killed nor crucified him—it was only made to appear so." That is, what the Jews boastfully claimed, i.e., that they killed Jesus, was untrue and incorrect, a mere slander. They neither killed nor crucified Him. The truth is that they killed someone else who looked like Jesus. They thought it was Jesus and they killed and crucified him. They then said: "We killed Jesus, son of Mary." (Q 4:157)

Al-Zamakhshari said: "To what is the word شُبِّهَ =likened/it was only made to appear so' attributed? If you attribute it to Christ, then Christ is likened to him and not the one being likened. If you attribute it to the one killed, then the one killed was not mentioned. I say: It is attributed to the preposition and noun, which is 'to them', as in saying: 'It seemed to him,' as if it was said: But the likeningشُبِّهَ occurred to them, between Jesus and the one killed. It is possible to attribute it to the pronoun of the one killed, because their saying: 'We killed' indicates it, as if it was said: But it was likened to them who killed him." [69]

In his interpretation of "But they neither killed nor crucified him," the honorable Sheikh Hassanein Makhlouf said: "Most Jews claimed that they killed Jesus and crucified Him. However, Allah disputed and impugned their claim and said: "it was only made to appear so." In other words, the one who was killed looked like Jesus. So, when they went to kill him (that is, Jesus), they found that one who looked like Him, and they killed and crucified him thinking that it was Jesus. In fact, it was not Jesus because Allah raised Him up to the heavens and delivered Him from the evil of His enemies. They thought that the one they killed was Jesus as they were made to believe by their scholars and rabbis." [70]

Exegetes have many views concerning "التشبيه it was only made to appear so." The following are the two most important views:

The first view: Allah made one of those who betrayed and plotted to kill Christ- Judas Iscariot- look like Him. Judas was a traitor, and he spied on Jesus. He was the one who led the soldiers- who wanted to kill Him- to His place. He told the soldiers: 'He whom I kiss in front of you is Christ. Arrest and kill Him.' So, he entered Jesus' house to identify Him so they can kill Him. Allah raised Jesus up to Himself and made the hypocrite look like Him. The soldiers entered and killed him thinking that it was Jesus.

This view was mentioned in some Gospels, especially the Gospel of Barnabas, which recounts in detail the attempt to kill Jesus Christ. It said:

"When the soldiers and Judas came near the place where Jesus was, He heard the sound of the great multitude approaching. He retreated to the house in fear. The eleven disciples were asleep. When Allah saw that His servant was in danger, He ordered His Archangels Gabriel, Michael, Raphael and Uriel (Israfil and Azrael), His emissaries- to take Christ from the world. The holy and pure archangels came and took Christ from the window overlooking the south, and they placed Him in the third heaven that praises Allah forever. Judas violently rushed into the room from which Christ was raised up. All the disciples were asleep. The Almighty gave a strange commandment. Accordingly, Judas' voice and face changed and became similar to Christ's. Even we thought he was Christ. As for him (Judas), after he woke us up, he kept looking for the Master. We were amazed and we said to him: 'You are the master, teacher. Have you forgotten us now?' He said, smiling: 'Are you stupid that you do not recognize Judas Iscariot?' As he was saying this, the soldiers entered and arrested Judas because he was just like Jesus in every respect. When we heard what Judas said and saw the great number of the soldiers, we panicked and fled as though we were insane. John who was covered with a linen cover woke up and fled as well. When a soldier almost seized him, he left his linen cover and fled naked. Allah heard Christ's supplications and saved the eleven disciples from evil. The soldiers took Judas and tied him up as they were mocking him because he denied- even though he was truthful- that he was Christ. The soldiers sarcastically said to him: 'Do not fear, master! We came to make you king over Israel. We only tied you up because we know that you will reject the kingdom.' Judas said to them: 'Are you crazy? You have come with weapons and lamps to take Jesus of Nazareth. Have you tied me up to make me king? I am the one who led you to Him!' The soldiers became annoyed and impatient with him, and they started to humiliate Judas by hitting and kicking him, and they angrily led him to Jerusalem." [71]

The Gospel of Barnabas goes on to portray Judas- who was transformed into Jesus's likeness- when he met the governor and the King who thought that he was mad because of his claim (that he was not Jesus). Judas was killed in the end.

The second view: The Almighty Allah made one of Christ's loyal disciples look like Jesus when the Jews agreed to kill Him. Allah told Him that He will raise Him up to Himself. So, Jesus asked His disciples: "Who is ready to be transformed into My likeness, to die and be crucified, to enter Paradise?" One of the disciples volunteered. So, Allah made him look like Jesus, and he was killed and crucified.

Imam Ibn Kathir said: "Ibn Abi Hatim said: Ahmad bin Sinan told us, Abu Muawiyah told us, on the authority of Al-A'mash, on the authority of Al-Munhal bin Amr, on the authority of Saeed bin Jubayr, on the authority of Ibn Abbas, who said: ''When Allah wanted to raise Jesus to heaven, He came out to His companions. There were twelve men in the house, His disciples. He said to them: 'There is one among you who will disbelieve in me twelve times after having believed in me.' Then He said: 'Which of you will cast my likeness upon himself, so that he may be killed in my place and be with me in the same status?' Then a young man, one of the youngest among them, stood up and said: 'I will.' Jesus said to him, 'Sit down.' Then He repeated the same request to them, and the young man stood up and said, 'I will.' Jesus said, 'Sit down.' Then He repeated it to them, and the young man stood up and said, 'I will.' Jesus said, 'You are the one.' Then the likeness of Jesus was cast upon him, and Jesus was raised from a window in the house to heaven. Then the Jews came, and they took the one who looked like Him, killed him, and then crucified him. Some of them disbelieved in him twelve times after they had believed in him, and they split into three groups. A group said: 'Allah was with us as long as He wanted, then He ascended to heaven.' These were the Jacobites. The second group said: 'The Son of Allah was among us as long as He willed, then Allah raised Him up to Himself.' These were the Nestorians. The third group said: 'Allah's servant and messenger was among us as long as he wanted, then Allah raised Him to Himself.' These were the Muslims. The two infidel groups conspired against the Muslim group." Ibn Kathir said: "This is a correct chain of transmission to Ibn Abbas. Al-Nasa'i narrated it on the authority of Abu Kurayb on the authority of Abu Mu'awiyah, and it was mentioned by more than one of the predecessors that He said: 'Which one of you is willing to resemble Me and be killed in My place and become like Me in status in Paradise?'" [72]

The Almighty then said: "Even those who argue for this crucifixion are in doubt. They have no knowledge whatsoever—only making assumptions." (Q 4:157) That is, those from among the People of the Scriptures who differed concerning Jesus were in constant doubt regarding His reality. They were perplexed and confused as they lacked indubitable and irrefutable evidence About Him and His death. They were only pursuing their suspicions and assumptions stripped of any convincing evidence and unquestionable proofs.

The People of the Scriptures differed immensely concerning Jesus. There were those who denounced His prophethood downright and claimed that He was illegitimate. These were the Jews. Others said: He is the Son of Allah, claimed that there are Divine and human natures to Him and that Mary gave birth to the human element then the Divine element was bestowed upon Him. Others say that Mary gave birth to both natures, the human and the Divine... etc.

They also differed concerning the manner of His death. Some Jews said: "He was a liar, so we killed Him in truth." Others hesitantly said: "If the one that was killed is our friend, then where is Jesus?" Others said: "The face was that of Jesus, but the body resembled that of our friend." The People of the Scriptures still differ About the truth concerning Jesus and His crucifixion.

A while back, a German priest offered a proposal to the Ecumenical Council asking to exonerate the Jews from Christ's blood. He presented a document to the Council in support of his view. The Archbishop of the Anglican Church supported him. The Ecumenical Council held a meeting to express its view on this matter. It demonstrated that the document sharply and radically contradicts what is recounted in the Gospels concerning the absolute certainty that the Jews killed Jesus. The Council then attempted to devise a way that would not contradict what the document contained concerning exonerating the Jews or contradict the Gospels' condemnation of the Jews for killing Jesus. What did the members of the Council and its president say?

First: They said that the killing of Christ was in accordance with Allah's Will and that those who executed the plan to kill Him were complying to Allah's Will. However, they realized that such an explanation would not be acceptable by reasonable people since everything takes place according to Allah's Will.

Second: They said that Christ was not, in fact, killed by anyone. It was Christ Who killed Himself to redeem humanity. However, they also found that this would also be unacceptable because it is variance with what the Gospels recount.

Third: They said that those who were responsible for the killing of Christ were those who actually killed Him, the Romans. As for the Jews of that time, they were innocent of His blood.

Fourth: They said- as was also reported by international broadcasts- "The church- which rejects the persecution of mankind, perceives its common heritage with the Jews, always unaffected by political agendas and unbiased by policies, and is only driven and inspired by spiritual love for the Gospels- condemns hatred and antisemitism and denounces the persecution of the Jews at any time and by anyone." [73]

Thus, through cunningness and craftiness, the Jews were able to clutch an admission from some Christians that exonerated them from the blood of Christ.

The first goal behind the Jews' plan is to form a Jewish- Christian block that would stand in the face of the Muslims, support them in in usurping Palestine, and alleviate the intensity of the religious animosity between the Christians and the Jews considering that the mortal wound afflicting the Christian body is that Christ was killed and crucified by the Jews. Therefore, the Jews deliberately worked to confirm that document, and through their Christian allies at the time, when the Patriarch of Rome visited the Holy Land in Palestine.

As Muslims, we believe that exoneration the Jews from the blood of Christ is the right thing. The Qur'an testifies to that in the Almighty's saying: "But they neither killed nor crucified him." (Q 4:157) That does negate that they unjustly killed the prophets. Nor does this negate that they sought all possible criminal ways to kill and crucify Jesus. Had the Almighty not miraculously saved Him from their cunning connivance, they would have killed and crucified Him. They would not have proceeded to kill the one who was "likened" to Jesus had they not been fully convinced that their target was Jesus Himself.

As things stand, they were like a group of bandits that sought to kill a certain man. They prepared themselves for that deed and they took all the measures to pursue it. However, they were unable to achieve their goal because of factors beyond their control. It is therefore reasonable to suggest that they should be condemned- as bandits- by just doctrines and fair laws. And we would like to add here that what they wanted to kill was one of the most distinguished amongst the prophets, One Who was sent by Allah to guide them to the truth. Yet, they rejected Him, disbelieved in Him, conspired against Him and planned to kill Him. In fact, they did kill one whom they thought was the Christ. They have been boastful of their crime throughout the generations.

We can therefore perceive that absolving the Jews from Christ's blood is- under current circumstances- politically motivated, an action that some Christians undertook to curry favor with the Jews and benefit from their money and world. Even if what they call for is what actually happened, the real motive is unethical and immoral: benefitting financially and forming a vile block to conspire against Islam and Muslims and divert the attention of those who follow in their footsteps and cause them to turn a blind eye to thousands upon thousands of the displaced Muslim Palestinian refugees.

Thus, we see that the dispute among the People of the Scriptures concerning Jesus goes way back. It has not ended yet, and they are always in continuous suspicion and constant doubt regarding the matter of His death. The Noble Qur'an confirmed that Christ was neither killed nor crucified. The Almighty said: "They certainly did not kill him. Rather, Allah raised him up to Himself. And Allah is Almighty, All-Wise." (Q 4:157) In other words, the Jews did not really kill Jesus; they did not kill Him fully confident that it was certainly Jesus. The truth is: the Almighty Allah raised Jesus up to Himself and no harm befell Jesus at their hands. Allah is "Almighty;" anyone who resorts to Him will always find refuge, shelter and protection. He is "All-Wise" in all His rulings and judgement.

Commentators have two views concerning the Almighty's "certainly/
يَقِينًا:"

First: It describes something that is omitted. That is, they did not kill Him fully certain that their target was Jesus. Rather, they committed their crime doubting that it was Jesus. This is a more favored opinion on account of the doubt that overtook them and difference in opinion.

Second: It confirms what is negated. That is, they did not really kill Him. What is confirmed here is the negation, that is, negating that He was killed is a certainty, well confirmed. It is not a matter of mere speculation as you- People of the Scripture- claim.

The Almighty's: "Rather, Allah raised him up to Himself" (Q 4:158) is a response to their claim that they killed Him and a confirmation that He was unharmed by them. That is, He was not killed as you Jews claimed. Rather, Allah raised Him up to Himself.

Most exegetes believe that Allah raised up Jesus' body and soul, not just His soul. Some scholars believe that only His soul was raised up. We will examine this in detail shortly.

Then, the Almighty said: "Every one of the People of the Book will definitely believe in him before his death. And on the Day of Judgment Jesus will be a witness against them." (Q 4:159)

The word إن in "وَإِن مِّنْ أَهْلِ ٱلْكِتَـٰبِ إِلَّا لَيُؤْمِنَنَّ بِهِۦ قَبْلَ مَوْتِهِۦ /Every one of the People of the Book will definitely believe in him before his death" is used as a negative article. Exegetes have two views:

The first: The pronoun ـه in مَوْتِهِ refers to Jesus. In this case, the meaning is: Everyone among the People of the Book- Jews and Christians- will truly believe in Jesus at the end of time before His death, that is, the death of Jesus, and on the Day of Judgement, Jesus will be a witness that what He said to them was what Allah commanded Him to say, which is, to worship only Allah, My Lord and yours.

Commentators such as Ibn Jarir and Ibn Kathir favor this view. They confirmed its validity with many Hadiths such as what was narrated by the Sheikhan (the two Sheikhs) on the authority of Abu Hurairah, who said: "By Him in Whose Hand is my soul, the Son of Mary will soon descend among you as a just judge. He will break the cross, kill the pig, and abolish the jizya. Wealth will be so abundant that no one will accept it until a single prostration will be better than the world and everything therein." Then Abu Hurairah said: "Read if you wish: 'Every one of the People of the Book will definitely believe in him before his death. And on the Day of Judgment Jesus will be a witness against them." [74]

Ibn Kathir said: "There is no doubt that what Ibn Jarir mentioned was correct because the verses aim to abolish what the Jews claimed concerning killing and crucifying Jesus and the acceptance of such a claim by some ignorant Christians. So, the Almighty recounted that it was not so; it was merely made to appear so. They only killed the person who looked like Him, and they were not aware of that. He also recounted that Allah raised Him up to Himself, that He is alive and that He will descend before the Day of Judgement, as mentioned in the chain of transmission."[75]

The second: The pronoun ـه in مَوْتِهِ refers to "Every one of the People of the Book." The meaning is: No one from among the People of the Book will but believe in Jesus before his death (that is, the death of the person from among the People of the Book). That is because the truth will be revealed to him at his bed of death, with the groans of death, and the truth that he had denounced Him will be revealed and made manifest. He will then believe in Jesus, but this will avail him nothing since his belief came too late, at the time of the moans and groans of death.

This view is supported by Abi's (unknown reference by Tantawi) reading of the text: "'Every one of the People of the Book will definitely believe in him before THEIR death موتهم."

Informing them of the necessity of believing in Jesus before their death is a way to caution them. It is meant to alert them to the importance of believing at a time when such belief would be beneficial.

The statement: "And on the Day of Judgment Jesus will be a witness against them" means that He will be a witness against the Jews that they denounced and rejected Him.

We do not see any contradiction between the two views; they are both valid and correct. That is because at the time if his death, everyone from among the People of the Book will know that Jesus' Prophethood was truthful and that He was the servant of the Almighty and His messenger. Also, everyone of them witnessing the decent of Jesus in the fullness of time will believe in Him, follow Him and testify that He was truthful regarding what He said About His Lord.

Sura Al-Imran recounts some noble verses that point to the Jews' cunning and harmful intentions towards Jesus and how the Almighty delivered Him from their conniving and crafty intentions. The Almighty said: "When Jesus sensed disbelief from his people, he asked, "Who will stand up with me for Allah?" The disciples replied, "We will stand up for Allah. We believe in Allah, so bear witness that we have submitted." They prayed to Allah, "Our Lord! We believe in Your revelations and follow the messenger, so count us among those who bear witness." And the disbelievers made a plan against Jesus, but Allah also planned—and Allah is the best of planners. Remember when Allah said, "O Jesus! I will take you and raise you up to Myself. I will deliver you from those who disbelieve, and elevate your followers above the disbelievers until the Day of Judgment. Then to Me you will all return, and I will settle all your disputes." (Q 3:52-55) [76]

The Almighty's "When Jesus sensed disbelief from his people, he asked, "Who will stand up with me for Allah?" (Q 3:52) means: When Jesus felt that the Children of Israel were determined to pursue their path of disbelief and misguidance and insisted on their rejection and denunciation, He asked His people: 'Who will support Me in My call to follow Allah and proclaim His religion?' That was similar to what the Prophet used to say during the pilgrimage (Hajj) season before he migrated to Medina: "Is there anyone who would support me to deliver and convey the words of my Lord? Quraysh have prevented me from delivering the words of my Lord!" Allah therefore provided him with the Supporters to provide him with shelter and assist him in his call.

Then the Almighty said that the disciples told Jesus that they are His supporters and cohorts. He said: "The disciples replied, "We will stand up for Allah. We believe in Allah, so bear witness that we have submitted." (Q 3:52) They prayed to Allah, "Our Lord! We believe in Your revelations and follow the messenger, so count us among those who bear witness." (Q 3:53) That is, the disciples- who supported Him- said: 'We are believers, and we support and defend You. We believe in Allah, so count on us that we bear witness, as messengers do for and against their people.'

'We, O Lord, have believed in what was revealed to your messenger; we follow and trust Him. Count us among the believers, those who have pleased You and are considered worthy of your love and mercy."

Then, the Almighty recounted the Jews' crafty and conspiratorial plans to harm Jesus and His intervention to rescue Him from their devious plans. He said: "And the disbelievers made a plan against Jesus, but Allah also planned—and Allah is the best of planners." (Q 3:54) That is, those disbelievers among the Jews made plans, and Jesus sensed their conspiracy to inflict harm upon Him for they plotted to kill Him and pursued all means possible to carry out their plans. However, the Almighty thwarted their plans and saved Jesus by raising Him up- from their midst- to Himself. Thus. He saved Him from their schemes to kill and crucify Him and cast His image on someone else. They killed the one who looked like Him thinking it was Jesus. The Almighty is the "best of planners."

Then, the Almighty showed how He abolished and foiled their plans and saved Jesus from their harm. He said: "⸢Remember⸣ when Allah said, "O Jesus! I will take you and raise you up to Myself. I will deliver you from those who disbelieve, and elevate your followers above the disbelievers until the Day of Judgment. Then to Me you will all return, and I will settle all your disputes." (Q 3:55)

Al-Zamakhshari said: "إِنِّي مُتَوَفِّيكَ/ I will take you[1] and raise you up." This means: I will protect you and will not let the disbelievers kill You. I will keep you till the time I have set for You, but You will not get killed by them. إِنِّي مُتَوَفِّيكَ also means I will take You from the earth as in تَوَفَّيت مالي 'I took back my money.' It was also said that I will let you die in due time after descending from the heavens, but for now I will raise You up to Myself. Also, it may mean that I will let You die and raise You up in Your sleep so that no apprehension should overtake You, and You will wake up safe in the heavens." [77]

The meaning of the verse is: Remember, Muhammad, when Allah said to His Prophet Jesus: 'I will take You and raise You up to Myself, in body and soul, to live there until I give You permission to descend to the earth. I will deliver You from all the evil and harm that the Jews want to inflict upon You. I will protect you from their craftiness and their evil company. I will elevate those who follow and believe in You above the disbelievers until the Day of Judgement. That is, they will be elevated above the disbelievers on account of their faith and sound judgement as well as their physical and spiritual vigor. Then, you will all return to Me, and I will settle your disputes.

At this point, we would like to speak in. detail concerning the issue of raising Jesus up:

Exegetes maintain many views concerning raising Jesus. Two stand out as the most important among these views:

First: The meaning of "إِنِّى مُتَوَفِّيكَ/ I will take you and raise you up" is I will elevate Your status (rank) and Your spirit to My dignified exalted position to the angels' dwelling place, just as the spirits of the prophets are raised up to Me. This is the more prevalent meaning for this verse, and the Hadiths that occurred concerning Jesus' descent are Ahad Hadiths (اخبار آحاد as different from Mutawatur متواتر)- that cannot be reliable in matters of doctrine/ jurisprudence.

Second: The meaning of "إِنِّى مُتَوَفِّيكَ/ I will take you and raise you up" is I will take You from the earth, raise You up to the heavens, in body and spirit, to enjoy Your life there. Those who adopt this view- the majority of scholars and commentators- do not regard or interpret التوفي as death. Rather, they say that التوفي in the language means to take something totally. As such, the meaning of "إِنِّى مُتَوَفِّيكَ/ I will take you[1] and raise you up" is giving You all Your life in this world. Scholars also maintain that the famous Sunnah- (*the famous Hadith= what was narrated from the Messenger by a number of companions but did not reach the level of Twatur تواتر*)- indicated that Allah will descend to earth at the fullness of time to govern with Muhammad's law, then the Almighty will cause him to die after that.

The honorable Sheikh Hassanein Makhlouf said: " إِنِّى مُتَوَفِّيكَ وَرَافِعُكَ إِلَيَّ / I will take you and raise you up to Myself" means I will take You, body and spirit, and elevate You to My Dignified status. The coordination و/ and is meant to explain. When we say وفيت فلانا حقه, it means that I gave him in abundance and he got it all. Jesus was neither killed nor crucified. As the Almighty said: "But they neither killed nor crucified him—it was only made to appear so." The Almighty also said: "They certainly did not kill him." (Q4:157) Therefore, the Christians' belief in the killing of Jesus and His crucifixion amounts to blasphemy for sure. The Almighty said that He will raise up Jesus to Himself "raise you up to Myself." He also said: "Rather, Allah raised him up to Himself." (Q 4:158) It is predominantly believed that He was raised up to heaven, in body and spirit, untouched by death or slumber. The specific and exclusive distinction here is that He was raised physically in the flesh, and He will remain there as predestined. "Taking up," as expressed in this verse and as in the Almighty's saying in "But when You took Me up, You were the Observer over them" refer mostly to the correct sayings as narrated by Ibn Abas and Al-Qurtubi: Just as He was in the beginning miraculously born, an amazing and wondrous sign for people to witness, so was His end, a miracle and a marvel. Miracles are beyond human understanding and perception; they are simply Divine, proofs of the truthfulness of the prophets, peace be upon them." [78]

We are more inclined to adopt the second view for the following reasons:

First: The Almighty's "They certainly did not kill him. Rather, Allah raised him up to Himself" apparently indicates that raising Jesus involved both His body and His soul.

Second: Numerous Hadiths that had the validity of التواتر Twatur (Chain of Transmissions) occurred concerning the descent of Jesus to earth to spread justice- after it has been plagued with injustice- and to rule with Muhammad's law since there will be no other to follow his doctrine.

Imam Ibn Kathir dedicated a special chapter in his Tafsir in which he said: "Many Hadiths concerning the descent of Jesus, Son of Mary, to the earth in the fullness of time before the Day of Judgement mention that He will call to monotheism, to worship Allah Alone and assign no partners to Him."

Among these Hadiths was what was narrated by the Sheikhan (the two Sheikhs) on the authority of Abu Hurairah, who said: "The Messenger of Allah said: 'The Son of Mary will soon descend among you as a just judge. He will break the cross, kill the pig, and abolish the jizya. Wealth will be so abundant. One prostration will be made to the Lord of the World." [79]

Imam Ibn Kathir maintained that the Hadiths that occurred concerning the descent of Jesus to the earth have the validity of التواتر Twatur (Chain of Transmissions), as we indicated in the text that we investigated concerning his explanation of the Almighty's "Every one of the People of the Book will definitely believe in him before his death." The implication of these Hadiths is that Jesus will descend, body and soul, just as Allah raised Him up to Himself.

Thus, the noble verses impugned the Jews for the outrageous lies that they attributed to the Immaculate Virgin Mary. They also censured them for claiming that they killed Jesus, Son of Mary and Allah's messenger. The verses chastised them for their false allegations, brought the truth to light and abolished their lies and falsehoods, even to the dismay of the wicked.

Tenth: <u>Their claim that Allah is tight-fisted</u>:

The Noble Qur'an also recounted that among the Jews' most outrageous lies and contemptible slanders was their claim that Allah is tight-fisted. What the Qur'an says About them betrays their audacity and inappropriateness towards the Almighty, attributing things that are shocking and unbecoming to Him, and denying His great favors upon them and their ungratefulness to his innumerable and countless blessings.

Among the verses that described the Jews as liars are:

"'Some among the Jews said, "Allah is tight-fisted." May their fists be tied and they be condemned for what they said. Rather, He is open-handed, giving freely as He pleases. That which has been revealed to you O Prophet from your Lord will only cause many of them to increase in wickedness and disbelief. We have stirred among them hostility and hatred until the Day of Judgment. Whenever they kindle the fire of war, Allah puts it out. And they strive to spread corruption in the land. And Allah does not like corruptors."[80] (Al-Ma'idah; Q 5:64)

Ibn Abas said: "A Jew- called Shas bin Qais- said: 'Muhammad! Why is your Allah so tight-handed?' Allah revealed: ''Some among' the Jews said, 'Allah is tight-fisted.' " [81]

The Noble Qur'an attributed this claim to the Jews because they did not denounce what Shas bin Qais said; they accepted it.

The Almighty's recount of "'Some among the Jews said, Allah is tight-fisted'" (Q 5:64) indicates Allah's declaration of the Jews' inappropriate and daring audacity towards Him, a chastisement for their ungratefulness for all the countless favors and blessings He had bestowed lavishly upon them.

What they meant by claiming that Allah is tight-fisted was to indicate that Allah was penurious and ungenerous and that He withheld His favors and blessings from them, that He was miserly and parsimonious unable to stretch out His hand with gifts and offerings to them.

The notion of غل اليد وبسطها is a well-known euphemism for "tight-fistedness and open-handedness." This is what the Almighty said in this regard: "Do not be so tight-fisted, for you will be blameworthy; nor so open-handed, for you will end up in poverty." (Al-Isra; Q 17:29)

The reason: The hand is involved as a tool in performing most deeds, especially paying and spending money. So, they substituted the "cause" for the "reason" and attributed generosity and miserliness to the hand and the palm of the hand. The generous has therefore been called open handed and open-fisted (with a palm that is stretched). The miserly has been called tight-handed and tight-fisted. This is well known to Arabs.

Al-Zamakhshari said: the expression "'Tight-fistedness and open handedness' is a metaphor synonym to stinginess and generosity. The user of this expression does not mean to prove either stretching or clenching the hand. They are two statements that follow one reality. To him, there is no difference between the actual expression and what transpires in reality. A King may give or withhold with a signal, without using his hand, without clenching or stretching his fist... Clenching or stretching the hand are merely two expressions that occur successively to express stinginess and generosity." [82]

The Almighty's "May their fists be tied and they be condemned for what they said" is meant to impugn them for what they said, a prayer that they may become stingy and tight-handed and not spend for the sake of Allah.

The meaning is: It is not as the Jews claimed about Allah. Rather, it was the Jews who refrained and desisted from offering good things. They were condemned and cursed and became alienated from Allah's mercies and His favors because of their slanderous conduct and their attributing miserliness and stinginess to Him.

So, according to this interpretation, a prayer is raised that they may be stingy and tight-fisted. That is the meaning of "May their fists be tied."

Al-Zamakhshari said: "It is feasible that such a prayer to have their fists tied could be meant to invoke "actual" and "literal" tying: as captives in this world and as tortured and tied with the shackles of Hades in the Hereafter ." [83]

The Almighty, then, countered what they said and assured His definitive and ultimate generosity and open-handedness. He said: "Rather, He is open-handed, giving freely as He pleases." That is: He is not tight-handed as they claimed; rather, He is bountiful and generous, and he bestows lavishly and abundantly from His riches. The Almighty expressed His generosity by using His "two hands" to be more powerful in His response to their claim "Allah is tight-fisted," to fervently condemn and denounce them, to convey the notion that He gives without measure, lavishly and sumptuously, and to negate the notion of tight-fistedness concerning Him. One who uses both hands to give is indeed a cheerful and generous giver.

Al-Bukhari narrated on the authority of Abu Hurayrah, he said: "The Messenger of Allah said; 'The right hand of Allah is full. Spending does not diminish what He has in His hand. His generosity is by night and by day. Have you seen what He has spent since He created the heavens and the earth? What is in His right hand has not diminished. His throne is over the waters, and in His hand is the balance. He lowers and raises.' He also said: 'The Almighty said: 'Spend and give, and I will compensate you and give you in return.''" [84]

The Almighty's "giving freely as He pleases" is a statement that continues the statement before it to emphasize and ascertain His boundless generosity and to indicate that He spends in accordance with His Wisdom. withholding and restricting what He gives to some people does not conflict with His generosity and bountifulness because He gives and He withholds according to His Will upon which He established His creation.

Al-Zamakhshari said: "It was said that the Almighty was opulent and bountiful to the Jews, and they became the richest among the people. When they disobeyed Him and rejected Muhammad, He suspended His generosity. Then, Phinehas bin Azura said: 'Allah is tight-fisted.' The others accepted what he said." [85]

Then, the Almighty revealed their ungrateful rebellious attitude towards His Messenger. He said: "That which has been revealed to you O Prophet from your Lord will only cause many of them to increase in wickedness and disbelief."

The meaning is: That Noble Qur'an that We have revealed to you, all of the hidden and unknown things about those Jews, their Books and their history, and all those things that witness to the truth of your prophethood- all of this will only cause many of them to increase in their ungratefulness, hatred and rejection. They will show more disbelief in the verses of Allah because they are envious of the favors that Allah bestowed upon you. They resent you because you revealed their past and present ignominies and disgraces.

Thus, the favors and blessings that Allah gave you, Muhammad, will not only enrage and infuriate your enemies, but it will also increase their hostility and aggression, their disbelief and distrust, for the pious will find guidance in what was revealed to you, but the morose disbelievers will take no heed.

The noble statement portrays the stubbornness and denial with which many Jews confronted Muhammad and Allah's revelation to him. It also provides him with some comfort for the harm and slanders and lies he experienced at their hands.

The Almighty then showed that the enmity among the Jews would never cease; their conspiracies and schemes will return to haunt and afflict them. He said: "We have stirred among them hostility and hatred until the Day of Judgment. Whenever they kindle the fire of war, Allah puts it out." (Q 5:64)

That is: We have sowed perpetual animosity and everlasting hatred amongst the different Jewish sects. Their views were different and ununified and their attitudes and desires were at variance. Moreover, whenever they sought to wage a war on the Messenger and the believers, Allah frustrated their schemes, foiled their plots and cast terror in their hearts.

What this noble verse mentioned concerning the eternal animosity and hatred among the sects of the Jews is undoubtedly factual and true. Different Jewish sectors are still at variance warring with each other, the members of each sector betray evil and display animosity to members of other sectors. The hatred and enmity that is concealed and hidden is even far greater.

The cooperation and collaboration and the cunningness and deceit that the Jews employed at this generation to establish a state for them in Palestine is only temporary and transitory. Their presence in Palestine will not last long, regardless of the assistance and support they receive. Palestine will be restored once the Muslims truthfully fight them, follow the teachings of Islam and adequately prepare themselves to restore their usurped land.

History bears witness that the Muslims were exposed a great deal to the harm of the Jews and their aggression; however, the Almighty granted the believers victory over them because of their faithfulness and trust in Him as well as their adequate preparedness to confront their enemies.

The verse concluded with the Almighty's declaration that He hates their disobedience and corruption: "And they strive to spread corruption in the land. And Allah does not like corruptors." (Q 5:64)

That is: The Jews are known for their attempts to corrupt the land and entrap Islam and the Muslims. They have tried to erase the description of the characteristics of the Messenger from their Books. They also tried to sow the seeds of suspicion in the hearts of the Muslims concerning their faith. They stirred up dissentions and discords among them. However, Allah does not like the corruptors; He abhors them, disappoints them and thwarts their plans because they want to halt His Wisdom to make people righteous and the land opulent and prosperous.

Thus, the noble verse impugned the Jews for attributing stinginess to Allah. It revealed that the Almighty is bountiful, open-handed and magnanimous. It had also shown another aspect of the Jews' vices: their malice and stubbornness. Finally, the verse displayed that Allah does not like them for their corruption of the land.

Here, we would like to examine Allah's "And they strive to spread corruption in the land" to shed light on aspects of their perversion and corruption. We say:

The Jews' corruption in the land has been widespread, and it has taken many forms and methods. The following are some of these methods:

<u>First: Killing and assassination</u>:

The Noble Qur'an recounted in numerous verses that the Jews killed the prophets and those who wanted to establish justice among people. We have previously mentioned the verses that display this vice. [86]

Among Allah's prophets that the Jews killed were Zacharia and John. They also tried to kill Jesus and sought every possible way to do so, but the Almighty protected Him, and they failed for reasons beyond their control.

They also tried to kill the Prophet, but they were not successful for Allah rescued him from their wickedness and evil cunning intent.

Those who look at history in its various stages will soon realize that killing and assassination is second nature in the Jews throughout the generations. The following are some of the killings and assassinations they committed and which history recorded:

A- It was recorded in the Book # 78 which was written by Casasius, the historian, in chapter 32 in the second century BC (117) what can be summed up as follows:

During these years, the Jews deliberately and methodologically slaughtered the Greeks and the Romans, ate their flesh, stripped their skins and cut off their bodies into two haves from the head down. They also threw many of them to wild and ferocious animals. Two hundred twenty were killed.

B- Among the most acknowledged Jewish rituals is the shedding of blood of non-Jews and mixing this blood with the dough that is used for the Passover bread. This topic has been investigated, and it was found that the Jews have actually performed this criminal practice throughout the ages.

The fact that this crime was verified was one of the main reasons for their persecution by others. Some historians compiled the crimes that the Jews committed in this respect, and there were more that 200 crimes. [87]

One of the most well-known crimes was the one that took place in 1840. It was confirmed that they killed Father Toma and his servant. In sum, one of the Jewish rabbis wanted to get non-Jewish human blood to use for the Passover bread. They lured Father Toma and his servant, slaughtered them and drained their blood for that purpose. The murderers were convicted and sentenced to death. The Jews in Europe were concerned and they sent a number of their wealthiest to Muhammad Ali, the ruler of Egypt and Syria at the time. They offered him great amounts of money and precious gifts. He issued a decree to pardon the offenders who had perpetrated their crime in Damascus.

The investigations and trials related to this crime were published in many European books. They are also mentioned in detail in many modern books. [88]

There are many other crimes of similar nature that we do not have room to mention here.

C- Ever since their feet have trodden upon Palestinian soil, the Jews have perpetrated atrocious and appalling crimes, crimes that cause one to cringe and squirm. The following are some of the crimes they perpetrated against the Arabs of Palestine:

1- In May 8, 1948, the Jews attacked the village of Al-Majora, arrested 60 young men and executed them before the eyes of their folks.
2- In February 1951, the Jews placed explosives in the village of Sharfaat. Many men and women were killed.
3- 3- In October, 1953, the Jews attacked the village of Qubayya. They bombarded its houses with their artillery and killed women, children and old people.
4- The number of Arab villages that have been thoroughly destroyed from 1948 to 1955 have reached 187 village. The number of villages that were partly destroyed reached 15 village. All of these villages have been converted to Jewish settlements after a great number of its inhabitants were killed and those who remained alive were forced to leave. [89]

Three hundred thousand (300) Palestinian Arab inhabitants lived in 1947 in the area that the Jews occupied. In 1964, the number decreased to two hundred twenty thousand (220).

In other words, there were eighty thousand (80) less Palestinians because of the Zionist aggression.

D- To eradicate their opponents, the Jews used the most despicable and contemptible ways of cowardice and treachery. They do not face their enemy in broad daylight. Rather, the perpetrate their crimes through deception and trickery. As an example, in March of 1963, they sent a parcel containing explosives to six German experts in Cairo. They were all killed.

These are some of the evils that the Jews perpetrated in the land, crimes that comprise murder, assassination and conspiracies. If we were to trat this subject with some detail, we will need a huge voluminous book for that.

Second: Espionage:

Spying and espionage on various countries are amongst the most important ways that the Jews employ for their benefit to spread corruption in the land.

The Noble Qur'an recounted that they publicly demonstrated and displayed faith (with their tongues) while they concealed their disbelief. They would attend the meetings of the Messenger of Allah to listen to what he said and relay what they heard to their chiefs and others of the same faith.

The Almighty said: "O Messenger! Do not grieve for those who race to disbelieve—those who say, "We believe" with their tongues, but their hearts are in disbelief. Nor those among the Jews who eagerly listen to lies, attentive to those who are too arrogant to come to you." [90] (Al-Ma'idah; Q 5:41)

That is: They are spies for other people; they did not come to you and they did not listen to you except to spy on you. Ibn Isaac mentioned the names of some of those Jews who only pretended to be believers. They were hypocrites whose goal was to spy on the Muslims. He said: "Among those who showed allegiance to Islam and 'seemingly' embraced it- and they were a bunch of hypocrites allying with Jewish rabbis- were Sa'd bin Haneef, Zeid bin el-laseet, No'maan bin Oofy, Rafi' bin Hurymellah and Raf'eah bin zeid bin al-Taboot, etc.

Those hypocrites would attend the gatherings at mosques and listen to the conversations taking place among the Muslims. They mocked them and scorned their religion. One day, some of them got together in the mosque. The Messenger of Allah saw them and realized that they were murmuring among themselves in a low and inaudible voice, and they were sitting too close to one another. The Messenger of Allah ordered them out of the mosque, and they were violently driven out. Abu Ayyoub headed towards Amer bin Qeis, a Jew, grabbed his leg and pulled him out of the mosque. Then, he came to Abi Raffi and seized his dress and threw him out of the mosque while slapping him saying; 'Shame on you, hypocrite! Get out of the mosque of the Messenger of Allah.' That is, go back to where you came from. Emarah bin Hazim, a long-bearded man, went to Zeid bin Omer, and grabbed him by the beard and forcibly led him out of the mosque. Then, Emarah levelled a strong blow to his chest, and Zeid fell down, saying: 'you injured me, Emarah!' Emarah said: 'May Allah keep you far away!' [91]

Espionage has been and still is a Jewish propensity. They use it for any country to which they cultivate a liking or in which they dwell among their people. Some scholars view the expulsion of the Jews from Germany during the time if Hitler was meant to send them to various countries to be spies for Germany under the supervision of some Jewish experts. [92]

During the past two World Wars, the Jews were involved in espionage operations on the two warring camps. They were thus able to acquire the secrets of the two camps.

The Jews' spying on Arab countries, on the other hand, is a matter that necessitates caution and attentiveness. They employ men and women and they receive detailed and comprehensive training in using various tools and special receiving and transmitting equipments. They also get training in the art of photography, the use of explosives and how to send them in parcels. Many spying networks were exposed in the Arab countries.

To sum up, espionage is one of those activities that the Jews have perfected. It was- and still is- one of the most important methods that they have resorted to in order to gather secret information About countries and people to use to serve their ends, to entrap others and to spread corruption in the land.

<u>Third: Hiding and taking cover behind religions</u>:
A little while earlier, we mentioned that the Jews enter into other religions to spy on the people of these faiths. We would also add here that they pretend to embrace other religions for many other reasons. The most important of these reasons are to serve their own Jewish religious affiliation, their personal and self-interests and to spread evil among the nations that have different faiths other than their own.

The Jews "apparently" entered into all the other religions hypocritically to serve their own faith, Judaism. They entered Buddhism, Christianity, and Islam. Here are some examples for this:

A) Concerning entering into Buddhism, Dr. Ahmad Shalaby says: "My personal interactions and experiences made me aware that some of the men in the Far East who embraced it (Buddhism) worked for Israel with the same zeal and passion that any Jewish man displayed. At the beginning of my career in the Far East, I was appalled to find that some of the embassies in these countries in Indonesia vehemently and actively supported the cause of Israel to a great extent. It was no exaggeration to say that those countries had nothing to represent them in these buildings except the plaque fixed on the doors of the buildings. The majority of the activities and proceedings taking place inside the buildings, conversely, serve the Israeli cause. We were less surprised when we knew that among the employees in the embassy, even the most prominent government officials in these countries, were Buddhists from a Jewish origin, or Buddhists who had taken Jewish women for wives, or Buddhist wives that had Jewish blood in their veins. Some of those Buddhists were able to occupy the highest religious ranks and civil positions to the extent that priesthood was almost restricted to them." [93]

B) Let us now leaving Buddhism aside and turn to Christianity. We found that a great number of Jews declared embracing Christianity to protect themselves from persecution or to be able to spread their corruption and evil without causing suspicion.

One of the most prominent men who pretended to embrace Christianity to serve Judaism was Disraeli. That man was born at the beginning of the nineteenth century to a Jewish father and mother. He entered into Christianity at the age of twenty. He occupied many political and social positions until he became the Prime Minister of the United Kingdom.

This was the man who stole Egypt's share in the bonds of the Suez Canal for four Million pounds from Khedive Ishmael because of latter's debt. These bonds were worth double that sum of money. Disraeli then gave those bonds to the British government as a present. The British government made millions from that deal.

The primary goal of Disraeli behind this deal was to confirm and consolidate the existence of England in Egypt to protect the Jewish state that he worked so hard to establish for Zionism in Palestine.

Disraeli helped the Jews who entered Christianity to purchase some territories in Palestine. Thus, he laid the foundation for the establishment of a country to the Jews in Palestine.

Disraeli was not satisfied with his influence to merely establish a homeland for the Jews in the Holy Land; he wrote and sent poetry calling for it. In one of his writings, he says:

"You ask me about my dearest wish and I say 'It is the Promised Land.' And you ask me About those dreams that tickle my imagination, and I say: 'Jerusalem.' And you ask me About the thing that my heart craves, and I say: 'the synagogue.'"[94]

The Jews admitted that Disraeli offered them great services by pretending to embrace Christianity. This is a brief note of what a Jewish writer said about him:

"If one wants to fathom and understand Disraeli's passions, one must become acquainted with his history and life story. The events that surrounded his life revealed that the spirit of this man always hovered over the Jews. He was filled with compassion for them, and he would observe their rising up and their settling down, their every move, night and day."[95]

It was not Disraeli alone who hid behind Christianity to serve Judaism. There are scores of others like him who did what he did.

Those who read the books of the Jews will realize that their rabbis recommend that they enter into other religions to be able to better serve their own interest and spread corruption.

Let us read these recommendations that a high-ranking Jewish French rabbis issued in 1948. The Jews in France wrote to him saying:

"The French in Marseille threaten our synagogues. What shall we do?"

His response was:
"Dear brothers- We have received your message in which you informed us of your tribulations. This is what rabbis and rulers suggest. Since, as you said, the King of France is forcing you to embrace Christianity, go ahead and embrace it. However, keep the laws of Moses deeply entrenched in your hearts.
Since, as you said, they demolish your synagogues, make your children priests so they can demolish their churches. Do as we command you, and you will reach to the zenith of your power and glory."[96]

C) If we now leave Christianity and go to Islam, we will find that a great number of Jews have pretended to enter Islam to spy on Muslims as we showed a little while ago. They were as described in the Noble Qur'an: "When they meet the believers they say, "We believe." But in private they say to each other, "Will you disclose to the believers the knowledge Allah has revealed to you, so that they may use it against you before your Lord? Do you not understand?" (Al-Baqara; Q 2:76)

Among the Most famous Jews who pretended to have entered Islam and caused discord and disagreement among Muslims was Abdullah bin Saba' who died in the year 40 H. That man had nothing but resentment and malice to Muslims. He was the one who formed secret cells to shake and destabilize the Islamic faith in the hearts of the believers. He moved among Muslim communities to spread his venom and evil. He advocated for things that Allah has not called for or made permissible.

He then began to interpret Qur'anic verses in a despicable way to support his claims. Moreover, he came up with some Hadiths to support his views. Through cunning and craftiness, he was able to attract a large number of the feeble-hearted unsteady and shaky believers. He stirred up conspiracies and intrigues that led to the murder Othman Ibn Affan, the third Caliph.

D) Among the most dangerous groups that hid behind Islam to entrap it in modern times is the Donmeh Sect in Turkey. This sect is made up of Jews who had pretended to embrace Islam until they were able to eradicate the Ottoman Empire. Here is a brief note about them:

1- Donmeh is the name that was used to describe the Turkish Jews who live in Izmir and Salonika.
2- Those Jews pretended to be Muslims but concealed Judaism in their souls.
3- Those people who pretended to adopt Islam follow their Jewish leader, Sabbatai (Zevi) bin Mordechai, who claimed to be the Messiah in 1648. Then, he went to Palestine and from there he travelled to Egypt. He returned to Izmir in 1665 where he spread his disbelief and venomous views. In 1666, he departed to Constantinople where he was sentenced to death. He converted to Islam before that sentence was carried out, and Sultan Muhammad the Fourth pardoned him.
4- After he got out of prison, he spread his disbelief among the inhabitants of Izmir and Salonika, and he prompted all the Jews living in these two towns to pretend to be Muslims and conceal Judaism in their hearts until they realize their goals.
5- The members of this sect observe Jewish rituals secretively. The men have two names: one Jewish name that he keeps in complete confidentiality, and another name which he uses in his interactions with others who are not Jewish. These people do not associate with other Turks except in financial dealings. Their most important feast is August 9th, the day in which their leader, Sabbatai, was born.
6- This sect was most influential right before Sultan Abdul Hamid's era. When Sultan Abdul Hamid ascended the throne, he tried to curtail their influence and limit their activities. He prevented them from entering the Caliphate center, but they were able to overcome him through their deviousness and guile. Among the three who dethroned him was the Jewish Qurh So, the deputy in Salonika.

This Jewish deputy was the same who was delegated by the Jews with their leader, Herzl, in 1901 to meet Sultan Abdul Hamid to beg and bribe him. The begging was to give permission for the Jews to immigrate to Palestine. The bribe was 50 million gold pounds for the coffers of the country and five million pounds for the Sultan's private funds. Sultan Abdul Hamid rejected both: the supplication and the gift.

7- The Donmeh sect was one of the reasons why Turkey was defeated in the First World War. Britain was About to hold a peace treaty with Turkey during the war, but it was the Jews who stood in the way and prevented that from happening to eradicate Turkey, abolish its Caliphate and force Britain to borrow more from them. They actually accomplished what they wanted: Turkey lost the was and the disintegration of the Caliphate followed. The collapse of the Caliphate was one of the goals of the Jews to be able to flow (in large numbers) into Palestine.

8- The Donmeh sect in Turkey had the greatest impact on Turkey's denunciation of its Islamic faith, fighting the Arabic Language, liberating itself from any association with the Arabs and calling for Pan-Turanism to get rid of Islam. After Mustafa Kemal Ataturk came to power, Turkey became a secular country and would not acknowledge the Islamic religion or other religions. That Mustafa Kemal was nothing more than an agent devised by the Donmeh sect in Turkey.

9- Chaim Nahum, was serving as the Grand Rabbi of the ottoman empire at the time Ataturk's revolution. Nahum was able to open the door for the Jews to immigrate to Turkey to be close to Palestine. Then, he became the intermediary who oversaw the Allies' agreement with Turkey. He was then appointed as an ambassador to represent Turkey in America. However, Nahum declined this grave position and preferred to become the Grand Rabbi of the Jews in Egypt. He served in that capacity until his death in 1960.

The Jewish writer Eli Levi Abu Asal describes Nahum, saying:

"It was quite a coincidence that the election of Nahum Efendi came at the time of the intense upheavals that distraught the people of Turkey and violently shook the fundamental and prevailing values and lead to toppling Sultan Abdul Hamid and dethroning him. At the forefront of Nahum Efendi's accomplishments were his heroic struggle- with the help of America's ambassador- to abolition of the Red Passport which was issued particularly to limit the immigration of the Jews to Turkey. He was highly esteemed by Mustafa Kemal, and all his efforts were crowned with success. Among those was his ability to get a license to complete the buildings of the Israeli Engineering university in Haifa, and lifting up the restrictions that hampered Jewish interests." [97]

<u>Fourth: Stirring up seditions, wars and revolutions</u>:

Throughout the ages and in all places, Jews are known for stirring up seditions, fanning the embers of war and provoking revolutions against the status quo. History is a witness for what we say:

A) As for stirring up seditions and conflicts, we find that after the Prophet's migration, they fought his call using various methods. Most prominent among these methods were the religious argumentation and semantic bickering that they employed to stamp out trust between the Muslims.

They argued with the Prophet About Divinity-related issues, the angels, abrogation, changing the direction of the Qibla, Jesus and Abraham. They also disputed his prophethood. The purpose behind these arguments and debates was not to get to the truth. Rather, they merely wanted to arouse dissention and discord among the Muslims and sow the seeds of suspicion in their hearts concerning their Islamic faith. [98]

They attempted to stamp out trust between the Muslims, but Allah thwarted their attempts, prevented their evil and deviousness and cautioned the Muslims against their wickedness. He said: "O believers! If you were to yield to a group of those who were given the Scripture, they would turn you back from belief to disbelief." Up to "so that you may be rightly guided." [99] (Al-Imran; Q 3:100-103)

The Jews do not deny that they always seek to stir up discord and disagreements between people. Here is what one of their own leaders, Dr. Oscar Levi, says: "We, the Jews, are but the Masters of the world and its corruptors, the provokers of discord in it and its floggers."

In the Israeli University magazine issued in May 16th, 1907, we read this text: "In almost all major changes, we encounter the work of Jewish hands, whether apparent and conspicuous or secretive and concealed. Accordingly, the Jewish history extends and infiltrates world history in all its aspects, permeating it with thousands of conspiracies and intrigues." [100]

B) As for fanning up the flames of war, the Jews play an enormous role. History recounts that "It was they who pushed William, the Conqueror, to enter England so that they could follow in his footsteps. They were also responsible for inciting Alexander the Great to most of his conquests. They came with him to Egypt where they settled. They encouraged the Spanish King, Philip the Second, to annex Portugal to his kingdom to dwell in it under his banner. They also provoked the flames of the two World Wars in this century. They were the only ones who amassed great fortunes as a result of these wars." [101]

Even the Tripartite Aggression on Egypt in 1956 was the outcome of their conniving and guile. They held meetings and drew up plans with officials in the British and French governments to assail Egypt and destroy its military installations seeking vengeance for the nationalization of the Suez Canal.

C) As for stirring up revolutions, the Jews have the biggest share. Wherever they are, you will find unrest and turmoil followed by revolutions. That happened both in the east and in the west. They incite capitalism against communism or vice versa. Either case, they are the ones who benefit from such acts. Their aim is revolution and destruction.

As an example, let us consider the communist revolution that took place in October, 1917. Who prepared it and set it in motion? It was the Jews. The Communist Party that ascended to power after the success of the revolution consisted of seventeen members. Fourteen of them were Jews, and the other three were from a Jewish origin who were married to Jewish women.

The Communist movement itself was in general the work of the Jews. It was Karl Marx, a Jew, who was its leader and founder.

A short while ago, we also mentioned that the revolution that Ataturk headed against the Ottoman Empire was manipulated by the Jews.

The Jews have various methods at their disposal to enflame discord, wars and revolutions. Let us have a quick glance at their influence during this century. What do we see?

1- The Rothschild family possess most of the shares of the companies that exploit gold all over the world. This is a Jewish family that vehemently supports Zionism.
2- The Banks that are responsible for issuing currency in European countries and the United States are under the control of the Jews.
3- Diamond, nickel and copper mines are monopolized by the Jews.
4- The Jewish Sassoon Family controls the drug dealings and commerce all over the world. Ever since Israel established itself a country in Palestine, it has planted this poison and it has distributed it to other countries.

The wealth of the Jews in the United States in 1926 was estimated at 500 thousand million (500 billion) dollars. Of this, the Rothschild family alone had 300 thousand million (300 million) dollars. The other wealthy non-Jewish people who live in America possessed 25 million dollars.

We can thus see that with this enormous amount of money and influence, the Jews were capable of planting the seeds of discord, arousing wars and inciting revolutions to serve their self-interest.

Fifth: Their books and publications:

The Jews rely on what their books and publications command them to carry out their schemes, intrigues and evil deeds. These books inform them that the land and what is contained therein belongs to the Children of Israel alone, that other humans are mere slaves and servants for them, that any doctrine or faith other than their Jewish faith is corrupt and not upright, that all other nations will only seize power from them and they have to take it back, and that Allah forbids showing mercy and compassion to non-Jews. In Chapter One, we talked about the Jews' Holy Books and established evidence that they were distorted and altered.

Here, we would like to talk About some of the publications that their rulers have issued to corrupt the world in order to subjugate the world bring it under their sole control.

These publications were known as the Protocols of the Elders of Zion. Some writers translated them into Arabic. The following are some hints concerning these Protocols taken from the introduction of the translator.

1- Jewish leaders held twenty-three conferences between 1897 and 1951, the last of which was the one that was held in Jerusalem for the first time in August 14th of the same year to apparently look at the issue of the Jewish migration to Israel and its boundaries. The first conference was in the Swiss city, Bal, in 1897 headed by Herzl. It was attended by 300 of the most influential Jews representing fifty Jewish groups. In that conference, they made secret plans to subjugate the whole world under the rule of a king from David's lineage.

2- A French woman was able to steal these publications from one of the Jewish leaders in France. When she realized the evil and wickedness they contain, she delivered them to one of the Russian noblemen. This nobleman, in turn, gave them to Nilus, the Russian scientist, who made a few copies of it in 1902.

3- When these Protocols became widely spread, the criminal intensions of the Jews were divulged and many massacres took place against them in Russia. In one massacre alone, ten thousand Jews were killed. Herzl, their leader, was greatly upset and enraged. He issued a number of documents announcing that "Some secret documents were stolen from the Holy of Holies." The Jews rose everywhere announcing their innocence and claiming that they had nothing to do with these publications. Reasonable people found it hard to believe their claims.

4- These Protocols were printed again and again after that. The Jews were vigilant and cautious. As soon as copies resurfaced in the market, they would gather and burn them. Some British writers were able to publish these Protocols many times. The last time was in 1921. It was that last edition that some writers translated into the Arabic Language.[102] Here are some examples:

From the First Protocol:

Politics has nothing to do with morality. A ruler who has a strong code of ethics is not a clever politician, and he will, therefore, be unstable on his throne. Our right lies in power. The word "right" is an abstract idea that baseless and unjustified. It is a word that indicates nothing more than: 'Give me what I want to make me able to prove to you that I am more powerful than you.' The end justifies the means, and we have to- as we plan-pay no attention to what is good and ethical as much as what is necessary and useful. Our slogan should be "All the methods of violence and deception.'

From the Second Protocol:

Journalism is the greatest power with which we can direct people. Journalism shows the important demands of the people, displays the grievances of the complainers and engenders boredom for the mob. Thanks to journalism, we amassed gold without being seen.

From the Third Protocol:

We rule denominations by exploiting the feelings of envy and resentment in them. These feelings are our means to eliminate and sweep away everyone who stands in our way. When the time to crown our world leader comes, we will hold unto these means. That is, we will exploit the mob to destroy everything in front of us.

Remember the French Revolution which we call 'The Great One.' The secrets related to organizing it are well-known to us because we planned it with our hands. Ever since that time, we have been leading the nations ahead from one disappointment and discomfiture to another.

From the Eleventh Protocol:

It is Allah's mercy that His chosen people are dispersed. This dispersion- which appears to be our weakness before the world- has proven to be our strength that has brought us to the threshold of world authority.

From the Seventeenth Protocol:

We will diminish and tarnish the dignity of the clergy in order to succeed in harming their messages. It will not be too long before Christianity disintegrates altogether. Other religions will follow, and the king of Israel will become the Pontiff of the world.

These are some excerpts from the Protocols of the Elders of Zion. They betray the evils and malicious intent of the Jews for the world, their plans to destroy the world and subjugate its people, communities and nations. The extracts also reveal their wide knowledge of the methods through which they can exploit others' weaknesses to serve their goals and satisfy their greed and desires. They are seeking to topple governments in all countries and replace them with governments under Jewish control. They never desist from sowing the seeds of discord and dissention in all countries through secret political, religious, economic groups and clubs of diverse types.

Sixth: Secret Societies:

To achieve their goals, the Jews depend a great deal on secret societies and organizations (orders) and subversive movements. They institute these societies themselves and encourage others to launch them. They may infiltrate some societies that are already in existence. They do this to achieve their goals, spread their venom in these societies and direct their members to do whatever they want them to do. The Jews are almost always behind all of those secret societies that pose danger.

They were behind the Qarmatians and the subversive movements that caused a great deal of harm to the Muslims.

And they were behind tens of societies/organizations that came into existence in Europe centuries ago to abolish Christianity like the Knights Templar Order, the Black Mass Group, the Rosicrucian Order (Rosicrucianism), and Free Constructivism (Freemasonry). Many such secret societies (orders) were launched to serve Jewish interests and cause harm to others.

Mr. Muhammed Abdullah Annan talks About the effect (work) of the Jews in these secret societies. He says: "The role that the Jews played in inciting revolutions, creating secret societies and launching subversive movements has been tremendous. Even though it might be difficult to specifically and accurately identify it, we see the effect of the secret philosophical Jewish teachings clearly apparent in most of the secretive revolutionary movements.

The place in which all the secretive Jewish customs meet is in the philosophical spiritual belief of "Kabbalah." This is a Hebrew word that means traditions.

Kabbalah is a mixture of philosophical, spiritual teachings, sorcery and witchcraft known among the Jews from ancient times. In fact, the role that the Jews played- through secret societies and organizations- in modern revolutions is clear and can not be denied. With scrutiny and investigation, we see that it was a two-sided role. It relies on money and secretiveness at the same time. Ever since the Middle Ages, the Jews monopolized financial affairs in most European societies. At the same time, they spread a net of witchery and secrecy on them. Whenever the winds of political or social upheavals blew, they would come out of hiding and stand with- and support- the winning side to lay their hands on loots and spoils. Even if the Jews did not incite these revolutions or set these storms and upheavals in motion, they always knew how to direct them to serve their own self-interest. If we now know that these clandestine societies and subversive organizations aim to dismantle present-day religious, political and moral institutions, we should also mention- at the same time- that that has been the ultimate goal that world Zionism has been trying to achieve for generations." [103]

One of the most well-known secret societies that world Zionism launched to serve their ends was Freemasonry. Here is a brief note About it:

1- Freemasonry is a clandestine Jewish society that goes back in history to the first days of the Jews.

2- The “apparent/outward” goals of this society differ greatly from their real “concealed” ones. Outwardly, it is a charitable society launched to serve humanity and enhance brotherhood and love between its members regardless of religious ethnic considerations. Inwardly and in reality, however, it is “a Jewish organization-” as Rabbi Ishak Isaac Meyer Wise said, “and its history, degrees, teachings, interpretations and secret codes are nothing but Jewish thoughts from the beginning to the end.”

3- The influence of Freemasonry and its undertakings infiltrated most of the world from the eighteenth century up to the present time. They launched their Premier Banquet (Grand Lodge) in England in 1717. They called themselves the “Free Masons.” After launching this, they revealed some of their intensions. Among the goals of the Freemasons are:

A) Preserving Judaism
B) Fighting religions in general.
C) Spreading atheism and immorality among nations.

4- From Britain, the venom of Freemasonry spread to other countries. Other Grand Lodges were established in Paris, Germany, Holland, Switzerland, Russia, Sweden and India. In 1907, its Lodges in America increased to more than 50 comprising almost one million American.

5- Freemasonry does not welcome everyone. It only selects those who enjoy certain characteristics. Among these are: holding a high or middle position, having a background that does not follow religious teachings and descending from a family that is known for affluence or relatively comfortable financially.

6- When a person is accepted as a Freemason member, he has to make the following pledge:

“I swear by the Great Master of the universe not to betray the covenant of the organization, its secrets, signs, sayings, teachings and customs. I will keep them concealed in my chest forever. I swear by the Great Master of the Universe never to divulge the secrets of Freemasonry, neither by signals, nor speech, nor words. I will never write anything related to it, nor will I ever publish anything either in print, by carving or photographing. If I ever breach my pledge; I accept that my lips be scorched and to be killed.”[104]

This pledge indicates how careful the executives of Freemasonry are in keeping its undertakings secretive to ascertain they can serve Jewish interests in the easiest ways possible.

7- There are three ranks in Freemasonry:

A) Symbolic Freemasonry (Entered Apprentice): Followers of various religions- Muslims, Christians and others- are initiated in this rank. The members of this rank are powerless and have nothing to do with the internal affairs of Freemasonry. They merely recite slogans of freedom, fraternity and equality. They also perform some formalities in return for obtaining a job or a something they seek. This rank has thirty-three degrees. A member gets promoted until he gets to the highest degree in this rank. Usually, this degree is not attained until it has been proven that the member has abandoned his religion and country.

B) Kingly Freemasonry (Journeyman): Most of the members of this rank are Jews and they are called Fellow of the Craft. None except Jews will be passed to this degree unless they have achieved a great deal in serving Freemasonry.

C) Universal Freemasonry (Master Mason): This is the highest degree and its members are purely Jews who have spent most of their lives in Judaism. They are called the Master Masons. At their head is their chief- the Great Ruler- who is the source of authority for all Masonic Lodges. No one knows the members of this degree or its center of activities (headquarters).

Freemasonry has its signs, symbols, colors and secrets that correspond to the different degrees and ranks. These are known only to those who have become thoroughly involved in them.

8- Freemasonry vastly penetrated Arab and Islamic countries. Twenty years ago, joining its Lodges in Egypt was one the most important things one may be boastful About. Their members were amongst the wealthiest, the notables and those who held high positions.

In April 1964, the government of the Arab Republic of Egypt issued a decree to abolish all their Lodges all over the county. Their monies and possessions were seized and donated to the "Winter Assistance Charity."

This short exposition for Freemasonry, its goals and degrees reveal that these are Jewish societies that seek to eradicate governments and eliminate the values and institutions of non-Jewish peoples. They also seek to do away with religions and morality in their quest to serve Jewish interests.

There are other societies that were also launched by the Jews that are not less corrupt and destructive than Freemasonry, but we do not have enough room to discuss them here.

<u>Seventh: Spreading devices and immoralities</u>:

We mentioned that the Jews seek to eradicate religions, morality and spiritual values. This is because this will bring them riches, wealth and affluence, and it will aid them in attaining their goals and objectives. They use many different methods to spread devices and immoralities. Among these are:

A) Media: Such as journalism, broadcasts, publishing houses, the theater and all various sources of the media which the Jews have controlled for tens of years.

In a monthly magazine published by a Christian publishing press in 1846, we read the following:
"Daily journalism in Europe is to a large extent under the control of the Jews. If a man of letters or a writer takes a chance and tries to stand in their way, they get rid of him."

The Jews launched the "Times" Magazine in Britain in 1788. It has been under their control until now. This magazine is considered the most wide-spread magazine in the world. In addition to this magazine, the Jews have tens of other magazines and newspapers in Britain. The number of Jewish magazines and newspapers in France has reached 36. As for America, the Jews control all the media there. The number of magazines and newspapers under their control have reached 220.

Official statistics have proven that the Jews publish 819 newspaper and magazine in various languages and countries. This represents the majority of the world's newspapers and magazines. [105]

And the influence of the Jews in other media avenues such as broadcasts and the theater is no less that their influence in journalism. They use all these media methods to spread vice and depravity among individuals, communities and nations.

B) Cunning ideas and thoughts: The Jews are the cleverest among all people in propagating and spreading the principles, ideas, philosophies and theories that benefit them and harm others. They will soon adopt any idea or principle that benefits them, spread it and hold its advocate to the highest level among the greatest even if most unworthy as an individual.

They endorsed Nietzsche and elevated him to the top for mocking morals and virtues such as compassion and mercy and calling for violence and deriding and ridiculing values. This agrees with their evil Jewish spirit and its dark history. They also upheld Darwin and exploited his theory of evolution and natural selection to their benefit to ridicule and mock religions and morality since if everything starts as deficient and incomplete and then develops (as Darwin believes), then there is no sanctity to religions or morality, and there are no traditions to uphold or adhere to.

Al-Aqqad has poignantly expressed this meaning:
"You will not understand modern schools if you fail to understand this truth, i.e., the Jews are behind every call or idea that derides and mocks moral values and aims to destroy the principles on which human society is based throughout the ages. Karl Marx, a Jew, was behind Communism which essentially sought to eradicate religions and ethical values. Durkheim, a Jewish sociologist, attempted to eliminate the role of the family in

developing and nurturing virtues and moral integrity. Sartre, a key figure in the philosophy of existentialism that began as an aid to dignity of the individual, deviated into the animalism that harms the individual and the group. It is right and appropriate to study intellectual ideas and trends whenever a new one comes into existence in Europe; however, it is wrong and inappropriate to limit yourself to studying the titles and outward manifestations and trappings only without fathoming and understanding the inner and concealed elements of incidental coincidence and deliberate intended planning." [106]

You may say the same thing concerning Freud, another Jew who attributed all religious, moral and artistic inclinations to the sexual drive/instinct. Thus, the relationship between the individual and his society, family, universe and what is beyond, is reduced and degraded." [107]

Thus, we can see that spreading devious and sneaky thoughts is one of the most important methods that the Jews resort to disseminate vice and immorality among nations.

C) Women:

It is well-known that a Jewish woman would sell herself attain a goal or achieve some self-interest. The Jews rely tremendously on women to attain their goals and achieve their ends.

> The story of the beautiful Jewish Esther is a very well-known story. In brief, Esther's uncle, Mordecai, introduced her to one of the kings of Persia. She used her beauty and deceit to bring the king and her uncle close together. The Persians bowed down and paid homage to Haman, the king's minister. However, Mordecai refused to bow down or pay homage like others because he was friends with the king. Therefore, Haman sought to destroy him and all the Jews. He was able to obtain a decree from the king to eliminate all the Jews on the 13th of the month of Adar/arch. However, Esther and her uncle conspired against him. They were able to convince the king that Haman was trying to dethrone him and usurp him of his power and authority. Their plot succeeded and the king ordered Haman to be hanged. The Jews killed more than 15 thousand Persians on that day. Ever since that massacre, the following day- the 14th of Adar- has become a Jewish feast that is celebrated until now. The Jews have since been boastful of the Esther's accomplishments. Among their holy Books is the Book of Esther.
>
> Today, the Jews own the brothels in the world. They spread debauchery, decadence and depravity everywhere. There are tens of villages in the state of Israel in which sexual intercourse is not governed according to matrimonial relations. Rather, relationships between men and women are utterly licentious and dissolute and dissipated.
>
> These are some of the examples for the Jews' corruption of the land. We mention them to demonstrate and explain the Almighty's: "And they strive to spread corruption in the land. And Allah does not like corruptors." (Al-Ma'ida; Q 5:64)

Thus far, we have mentioned some of the false claims of the Jews as reported in the Noble Qur'an. The Noble Qur'an has impugned them, abolished their claims and thwarted all their plans "that those who were to perish and those who were to survive might do so after the truth had been made clear to both. Surely Allah is All-Hearing, All-Knowing." (Al-Anfal; Q 8:42)

References

[1] Verses 80-83.
[2] Tafsir Ibn Kathir, Vol. 1, P. 218.
[3] Tafsir Ibn Jarir, Vol. 1, P. 382.
[4] Lubab al-Nuqul fi Asbab al-Nuzul is a book written by Al-Suyuti, P.11.
[5] Tafsir Al-Razi, Vol. 3, P. 143.
[6] Asbab al-Nuzul , by Al-Suyuti, P.55.
[7] Tafsir Al-Qurtubi, P. 5.
[8] Tafsir Ibn Jarir, Vol. 4, P. 134.
[9] Tafsir Ibn Jarir, Vol. 1, P. 418.
[10] Tafsir Al-Kashaaf, Vol. 1, P. 224.
[11] Tafsir Al-Kashaaf, Vol. 1, P. 225.
[12] Tafsir Al-Fakhr Al-Razi, Vol. 1. P. 432.
[13] Tafsir Al-Fakhr Al-Razi, Vol. 1. P. 432.
[14] Tafsir Ibn Jarir, Vol. 1, P. 424.
[15] Al-Baqarah 135-141.
[16] Tafsir Ibn Kathir, Vol. 1, P. 8339.
[17] Tafsir Al-Razi, Vol. 1, P. 518.
[18] Tafsir Al-Razi, Vol. 3, P. 91.
[19] Tafsir Al-Razi, Vol. 3, P. 93.
[20] Tafsir Al-Qutubi, Vol. 2, P. 141.
[21] Tafsir Al-Qurtubi, Vol. 2, P. 143.
[22] Tafsir Ibn Jarir, Vol. 1, P. 569.
[23] Tafsir Al-Razi, Vol. 1, P. 522.
[24] Tafsir Ibn Jarir, Vol. 1, P. 573.
[25] The Almighty reflects this in these verses: "This was the advice of Abraham—as well as Jacob—to his children, ʿsayingʾ, "Indeed, Allah has chosen for you this faith; so, do not die except in ʿa state of fullʾ submission." Or did you witness when death came to Jacob? He asked his children, "Who will you worship after my passing?" They replied, "We will ʿcontinue toʾ worship your Allah, the Allah of your forefathers—Abraham, Ishmael, and Isaac—the One Allah. And to Him we ʿallʾ submit." **Also, His saying:** O People of the Book! Why do you argue Abut Abraham, while the Torah and the Gospel were not revealed until long after him? Do you not understand?
[26] Tafsir Ibn Jarir, Vol. 1, P. 575.
[27] Liwaa Al-Islam Magazine, Vol. 12, Third Year P. 827.

[28] Tafsir Ibn Jarir, Vol. 1, P. 491.
[29] Tafsir Al-Kashaf, Vol. 1, P. 230.
[30] Sura Ash-Shu'ara: Verse 54
[31] Tafsir Al-Kashaf, Vol. 1, P. 330.
[32] Tafsir Ibn Jarir, Vol. 1, P. 493.
[33] The interpretation of the noble verse by Sheikh Muhammad Al-Khidr Hussein: Liwaa Al-Islam Magazine, Third Year P. 7.
[34] Tafsir Ibn Kathir, Vol. 1, P. 154.
[35] Tafsir Ibn Jarir, Vol. 1, P. 426.
[36] Tafsir Al-Razi, Vol. 1, P. 433.
[37] Sura Al-Imran: Verse 61.
[38] Tafsir Ibn Jarir, Vol. 1, P. 427.
[39] Tafsir Ibn Kathir, Vol. 1, P. 127.
[40] Tafsir Al-Kashaf, Vol. 1, P. 225.
[41] Tafsir Ibn Jarir, Vol. 1, P. 110.
[42] Tafsir Al-Kashaf, Vol. 1, P. 409.
[43] Tafsir Al-Qurtubi, Vol. 1, P. 186.
[44] Izra: A Jewish monk who lived in Babylon in 457 BC. He collected the Books of the Torah and introduced the Kaldanian alphabet in place of Old Hebrew. He wrote Chronicles, Ezra and Nehemiah. The Jews venerated him because of his contributions to the Jurisprudence, statutes and law. They called him "the Son of Allah."
[45] Tafsir Al-BayDawi, P. 123.
[46] Sura Maryam: Verses 93-94.
[47] Sura Al-Kahf: Verses 4-5.
[48] Tafsir Al-Kashaf, Vol. 2, P. 30.
[49] Rabbis الاحبار is the plural of حبر and it refers to a scholar who perfecting speeches and words. الرهبان Monks is the plural of راهب and it refers to an ascetic worshipper. To Christians, the original meaning is abandoning worldly matters and isolating oneself from people.
[50] Tafsir Ibn Kathir, Vol. 3, P. 348.
[51] Tafsir Al-Kashaf, Vol. 2, P. 21.
[52] Sahih Muslim, The Book of Trials, كتاب الفتن Hadith # 19, Al-Halabi Edition, Muhammad Fouad abdul Baqi.
[53] Al-A'raf: Verses: 169-170.
[54] Tafsir Al-Qurtubi, Vol. 7, P. 10.
[55] Tafsir Al-Kashaf, Vol. 1, P. 516.
[56] Tafsir Al-Kashaf, Vol. 1, P. 516.
[57] Tafsir Ibn Kathir, Vol. 2, P. 260.
[58] Tafsir Al-Qurtubi, Vol. 7, P. 312.
[59] Tafsir Al-Aluci, Vol. 3, P. 150.
[60] Verses: 75-76.
[61] Tafsir Al-Razi, Vol. 7, P. 107.
[62]Tafsir Ibn Jarir, Vol. 3, P. 205.
[63] Tafsir Ibn Jarir, Vol. 3, P. 206.
[64] Tafsir Ibn Kathir, Vol. 2, P. 169.
[65] Tafsir Ibn Jarir, Vol. 3, P. 206.

[66] Tafsir Al-Manar, Vol. 3, P. 341.
[67] Tafsir Al-Aluci, Vol. 3, P. 4.
[68] Tafsir Al-Razi, Vol. 11, P. 77.
[69] Tafsir Al-Kashaf, Vol. 1, P. 396.
[70] Sfwat Albayaan/The cream of the explanation of the meanings of the Qur'an, by Hassanein M Makhlouf, P. 178.
[71] The Gospel of Barnabas, P. 313.
[72] Tafsir Ibn Kathir, Vol. 1, P. 574.
[73] Al- 'Arabi Magazine,مجلة العربي issue # 91, June, 1966, P. 30.
[74] Al-Bukhari, The Beginning of Creation, "The Decent of Jesus," Son of Mary, Vol. 4. P. 205. Also narrated by Muslim in the Book of Faith, "The Decent of Jesus Ruling by the Law of Muhammad," Vol. 1, P. 135. Imam Muslim mentioned almost ten Hadiths with the same meaning in the same chapter.
[75] Tafsir Ibn Kathir, Vol. 1, P. 577.
[76] Sura Al-Imran: verses 52-55.
[77] Tafsir Al-Kashaf, Vol. 1, P. 306.
[78] Sfwat Albayaan/The cream of the explanation of the meanings of the Qur'an, by Hassanein Makhlouf. If you desire to review more of these Hadiths, you may review **Al-Tasreeh bi ma tawatur fi nuzul al-Masih** (The Statement of What was Transmitted Abut the Descent of Christ) by Sheikh Muhammad Anwar Shah Kashmiri.
[79] Tafsir Ibn Kathir, Vol. 1, P. 578.
[80] Sura Al-Ma'idah: Verse 64.
[81] Tafsir Ibn Kathir, Vol. 2, P. 75.
[82]Tafsir Al-Kashaf, Vol. 1, P. 424.
[83] Tafsir Al-Kashaf, Vol. 1, P. 424.
[84] Al-Bukhari in his Book of Tafsir, when he interpreted Sura Hud "His Throne was on the Water."
[85] Tafsir Al-Kashaf, Vol. 1, P. 425.
[86] Review the Chapter: The Vices of the Jews, under "Their Inappropriateness to the Creator and their Killing of the Prophets."
[87] Review Abdu Allah Al-Tal's book "The danger of World Judaism on Islam and Christianity." Also, review "This is Why I hate Israel" by Colonel Amin Samy Al-Ghamrawi.
[88] Go back to the investigations that surrounded this case in "The Treasure Found in the Talmudic Rules," translated by Dr, Youssef Nasrallah. These investigations run from page 88 to 204.
[89] From "The State of Aggression" by Ali Muhammad Ali.
[90] We interpreted this verse in detail in the chapter titled "The Methods that the Jews use to Entrap Islam and Muslims."
[91] Biography of the Prophet, by Ibn Ishaq, Vol. 2, P. 174.
[92] "Zionism: The Highest Form of Colonialism," by Fathy Al-Ramly, P. 121.
[93] "Judaism" by Ahmad Shalaby, P. 294.
[94] "This is Zionism" by Israel Cohen, P.3.
[95] "Jewish World Awakening," by Eli Levy Abu Asal, P. 194.
[96] "Palestine and the New Tatar Invasion," P. 27, Iraqi Ministry of Culture and Guidance.
[97] "Jewish World Awakening," by Eli Levy Abu Asal, P. 170.

[98] We have explained this point in detail in the chapter titled "The Methods that the Jews use to Entrap Islam and Muslims" under "Their religious Argumentation."
[99] We interpreted these verses in the chapter titled "The Methods that the Jews use to Entrap Islam and Muslims." P. 265, Vol. 1.
[100] "Judaism" by Dr. Ahmad Shalaby, P. 288.
[101] "World Judaism and the Promised Land" by Ali Imam Atyyah, P. 10.
[102] Review the story of these Protocols in detail in the introduction of "The Jewish Threat" by Muhammad Khalifa Al-Tunsi.
[103] History of Secret Societies and Subversive Movements" by Muhammed Abdullah Annan, P. 115.
104 "Freemasonry - The Originator of The King Of Israel," by Dr. Mohammed Ali Al-Zoubi.

[105] "The Secret Government in Britain," P. 80.
[106] "World Zionism" by Abbas Mahmoud Al-Aqqad, P. 91.
[107] Introduction to "The Jewish Threat," by Muhammad Khalifa Al-Tunsi, P. 83.

Chapter Eight

Allah's Warnings To, And His Punishments Of, The Children Of Israel

In Chapter Five, we mentioned some of the favors that Allah granted the Children of Israel as recounted in the Noble Qur'an. We also saw how they did not receive these favors with gratitude and obedience to the Almighty. Rather, they were unappreciative and ungrateful.

In Chapters Six and Seven, we talked about the vices of the Children of Israel and their false, untruthful claims and how the Noble Qur'an impugned and responded to them.

In this Chapter, we will show- with Allah's help- some of the punishments that Allah visited upon them because of their ungrateful stance towards His favors, rejecting His verses and revelations, their trespassing against Him and their disobedience and non-compliance with His commandments.

The following are some of the punishments that the Almighty heaped upon them. We will mention them briefly before we discuss them in detail.

First: Dispersing and scattering them and sending them mighty ones who would make them suffer terribly until the Day of Judgement.

Second: Allah's warning and decree for corrupting the land twice.

Third: Forbidding them good things because of their aggression and violations.

Fourth: Allah's condemnation and punishment by reducing them to apes and pigs.

Fifth: They earned Allah's wrath and condemnation; He cursed them.

Sixth: They were stricken with disgrace and misery.

These are- in brief- some of the punishments that afflicted the Children of Israel because of their disobedience to Allah, their rejection of His revelations and their ungratefulness for His favors. We will now discuss each of these punishments in detail.

<u>First: Dispersing and scattering them and sending them mighty ones who would make them suffer terribly until the Day of Judgement</u>:

Amongst the severest punishments with which Allah afflicted the Jews on account of their disbelief, violations and corruption of the land was sending them those who would cause them to taste humiliating punishment until the Day of Resurrection. They will scatter and disperse them all over the land, rummage and plunder their homes. They will always be the object of other people's disdain and resentment.

The Noble Qur'an has recounted this punishment that Allah poured on them because of their corruption and because of corrupting the land. We read these noble verses in Sura Al-A'raf:

1) And remember, O Prophet, when your Lord declared that He would send against them others who would make them suffer terribly until the Day of Judgment. Indeed, your Lord is swift in punishment, but He is certainly All-Forgiving, Most Merciful. We dispersed them through the land in groups—some were righteous, others were less so. We tested them with prosperity and adversity, so perhaps they would return ˹to the Right Path˺." [1] (Al-A'raf; Q 7:167-168)

The meaning of the two verses: Remember, Muhammad, when your Lord informed the Children of Israel with His decision concerning them that He will- until the Day of Judgement- send others against them who would cause them to suffer terribly. They would humiliate, debase and disgrace them because of altering and distorting Allah's words, killing His prophets and persevering in committing vices and violations.

Then, the Almighty said: "Indeed, your Lord is swift in punishment, but He is certainly All-Forgiving, Most Merciful." (Q 7:167) That is, Allah is swift to punish those who insist on their disbelief and persevere in their stubbornness and ungratefulness like those Jews. However, He is forgiving and compassionate to those who abandon their wrongdoing and offer a true penitence. Thus, He combines encouragement with intimidation so that the transgressor would not lose heart on account of his prior transgressions if he approached Allah with true penitence and good deeds as the Almighty said: "And verily, I am indeed Forgiving to him who repents, believes (in My Oneness, and associates none in worship with Me) and does righteous good deeds, and then remains constant in doing them, (till his death)." (Taha; Q 20:82)

Then, the Almighty mentions their dispersion and scattering in the land because of their injustices, violation and ungratefulness. He said: "We dispersed them through the land in groups—some were righteous, others were less so." (Q 7:168)

That is, We have scattered, indeed torn apart, those Jews because of their disobedience and debauchery. We made them disconnected and divided nations. After their dispersion, they became groups with various beliefs. Some believed in Allah and the messengers and learned from the events and signs. Other groups were immoral and depraved. And others were ungrateful and unmindful of the punishments that befell their predecessors and deviated from the Right Path. This is the meaning of "some were righteous, others were less so." That the majority of them persisted on disbelief and depravity while only a group believed was a result of Allah's plan to test them with prosperity and adversity to return to the right path as the Almighty said: "We tested them with prosperity and adversity, so perhaps they would return ˹to the Right Path˺." That is to say, We tested them with many various blessings, and We plighted them with different hardships to bring them back to Allah's obedience and abandon the sins and transgressions they were prohibited from doing. Only some believed. Therefore, Allah's punishments will befall them until the Day of Resurrection.

What the two noble verses foretold- concerning Allah's informing the Children of Israel that He would send against them others that would make them suffer terribly until the Day of Judgement- history has verified and events have confirmed. The following are some examples of what had befallen the Jews because of their corruption and for corrupting the land. These are some of the punishments that other nations wreaked upon them throughout the ages.

First: After the death of Suliman in 975 BCE, his Kingdom was divided into two kingdoms: The Northern Kingdom (the Kingdom of Israel), in Samaria, [2] and it comprised ten tribes. And the Southern Kingdom (the Kingdom of Judah), in Jerusalem, which consisted of the tribes of Judah and Benjamin.

The conflicts and disagreements that lasted for a long time between the two Kingdoms ended when Sargon, the Assyrian King, attacked the Northern Kingdom of Israel in 721 BCE. He killed thousands of its men and took the rest captives and sent them beyond the Euphrates. He eliminated this Kingdom completely and forever.

The Southern Kingdom tried hard to fight for its existence. However, mighty nations raided it from the east and the south. The Assyrians attacked it in 677 BCE, murdered a great number of its men and led Manasseh, its king, as a captive to Babylon.

After some semblance of life finally came back to the Kingdom of Judah, Necho, Egypt's pharaoh, raided it in 610 BCE. He occupied it, killed Josiah, its King, and drove out the Assyrians.

And in 606 BCE, Nebuchadnezzar, the King of Babylon, attacked the Kingdom. He drove out Egypt's Pharaoh and occupied Jerusalem and its surrounding provinces. He ferociously humiliated its people. After being occupied for a while, the Jews revolted against him. Nebuchadnezzar realized that he must discipline and punish them severely. He attacked them once again in 599 BCE, killed thousands of them, drove the others and their families as captives to Babylon, and he plundered the Temple and took its treasures and possessions.

And for the third time Zedekiah bin Joakim, Judah's King, found it difficult to comply, so Nebuchadnezzar attacked the Jews once again in 586 BCE. He besieged Jerusalem. Once he entered the city, he murdered Zedekiah, its King, and slaughtered the rest of its inhabitants. He plundered the city, destroyed its walls, burned down the Temple and led whoever remained alive as captives to Babylon. Thus, the Kingdom of Judah was eradicated and its lands became the property of Babylon.

A western writer portrays the chain of adversities that led to the annihilation of the Kingdoms of Judah and Israel. He says: "It is a story of adversities and calamities, a story of temporary attainment of freedoms only to postpone the inevitable knockout. It is the story of unruly kings governing an unruly people. With 721 BCE, the Assyrians completely obliterated the Kingdom of Israel from existence. Its people were completely wiped out of history. The Kingdom of Judah kept on struggling until the Babylonians eradicated it in 586 BCE." [3]

Second; The Jews gained back some power under the rule of the Persians from 536 to 232 BCE. During that time, they returned to Palestine and they fell under the control of Alexander the Macedonian in 330 BCE.

In 320 BCE, Alexander's successor, Ptolemy, marched to them. He destroyed Jerusalem and demolished its walls. He sent one hundred thousand of them as captives to Egypt because of their revolt against him.

Third: Approximately in the year 200 BCE, the Jews fell under the control of the Syrian Seleucids after gaining victory over the Ptolemaic Kingdom. Some Seleucid rulers experienced mutiny and disobedience from the Jews. They punished them severely in many different places. One of the most prominent figures to torture the Jews between 170 and 168 BCE was Antiochus. He attacked Jerusalem, destroyed its walls, seized its riches and killed forty thousand of its men in three days. He also sold approximately the same number as slaves. None was able to escape from his brutality except those Jews who escaped to the mountains. Antiochus erected a castle on one of the mountains to be able to see any Jew approaching Jerusalem so he can kill him. He went as far as coercing a great number of them to abandon Judaism, and he made their Temple in Jerusalem a sanctuary to worship his gods.

Fourth: In the year 63 BCE, the Romans raided Jerusalem led by Pompeius. They occupied it until 614 AD. During the Roman occupation of Palestine, the Jews revolted many times against them. However, all these revolutions failed. Because of their rebellion and mutiny, the Jews tasted many kinds of torture, captivity, murder and displacement. The following are some of what the Jews experienced at the hands of the Romans:

A) When the Roman Pompeius entered Jerusalem in 63 BCE, he murdered a lot of its inhabitants, immensely humiliated its people and used catapults to destroy its walls and buildings…
B) In the year 75 BCE, the Jews revolted against the Romans. The Roman leader, Gabinius, attacked them, killed thousands, made unpopular changes in administrative and economic life abolishing the Jewish systems of operation and replacing them with other systems that stripped the Jews from any possible interference in the state's affairs.

C) In the year 37 BCE, the Romans entrusted Herod with punishing the Jews for stirring up discord and conflict. Herod besieged Jerusalem for many months. He then entered it and killed what he was able to kill from its people and seized whatever he could of its wealth and possessions. He led its Jewish prince, Antigonus, in shackles to the Roman governor, Antony, and was savagely killed. His death marked the end of the Maccabees, and Herod became the representative of the Roman Empire, the Wali (governor), over Palestine. Christ was born on the same year Herod died. [4]

D) In the year 70 AD, the Jews resumed their mutiny and revolt against the Roman Empire. The Roman Emperor, Vespasian, surrounded Jerusalem. He then went back to Rome leaving his son, Titus, behind to subjugate the Jews. Titus succeeded enormously in his mission. After a period of time, he was able to raid and enter Jerusalem. He destroyed the city, killed thousands of the Jews, burned the Temple and took the rest of the Jews captives to Rome.

E) In the year 106 AD, during the reign of the Roman Emperor, Trajan, some Jews returned to Jerusalem, and, once again, they began to get ready to revolt. When Hadrian became the Emperor of Rome in 117 AD, he transformed the city into a Roman colony, and he forbade the Jews from circumcision, reading the Torah and observing the Sabbath. The Jews, led by the Rabbi, Bar Kochba, revolted in 135 AD. Rome sent Julius Severus, an accomplished and strict Roman leader to quench the revolt. He occupied the city, vanquished the Jews, killed Bar Kochba and slaughtered 580 thousand Jew. The Jews were dispersed all over the land. To make the Jews forget Jerusalem, Hadrian eradicated the city and built the colony of Aelia Capitolina on the ruins of the destroyed city of Jerusalem. [5]

As a result of these severe punishments that the Romans inflicted upon the Jews, some fled to the south of the Arabian Peninsula, Egypt, North Africa, Spain, Europe and other places. Everywhere they settled they were exposed to the condemnation of the inhabitants of those lands because of their egotism, aloofness, prejudice, inciting discord and spreading vices.

It is probably appropriate here to quote what the author of "The History of the Israelites" wrote concerning the destruction of Jerusalem at the hands of Titus, the Roman. He said:

"The history of the Israelites as a nation ends here. After the destruction of Jerusalem, they were scattered all over Allah's land- as mentioned before- and their history through the remaining generations has become linked to the kingdoms that they inhabited. There, they suffered all kinds of torture, hardships and adversity. The Romans prohibited them from entering Jerusalem until Christians ascended the throne of the Roman Empire.

Constantine the Great restored to Jerusalem its name after it was replaced by another name. Empress Helena, Constantine's mother, took upon herself the responsibility of cleaning the city which remained in the hands of the Romans until 614 AD when it fell to the Persians at the hand of Khosrow II. In 637, it became subject to Muslim rule under the Caliph Umar bin Khattab..."[6]

F) Here, we would like to reveal a fact that that book has neglected to mention. That is, the Persians ruled Palestine approximately from 614 to 628 AD. That was made possible with the help of the Jews who killed a great number of the Christians who lived with them in Palestine after the victory of the Persians. When the Romans gained victory over the Persians under the leadership of Heraclius, the Jews were frightened and exceedingly alarmed. They presented precious gifts to Heraclius. They also pledged allegiance and loyalty to him. Thus, they were able to secure a pledge from him not to harm them. Heraclius was not aware of their trickery until he came to Palestine and the Christians informed him of the torture and killing that the Jews inflicted upon them during the Persian rule. They were able to convince him to dissolve the pledge he had taken with the Jews not to harm them. He then wrecked vengeance on them.

Let us go over how Al-Maqrizi, the historian, narrates this story. He says:

"Khosrow, the Persian Emperor, sent his armies to the Levantine and Egypt during the era of Fogha, the Roman Emperor. They ruined the churches in Jerusalem, Palestine, and most of the countries in the Levantine. They murdered the Christians there. They also advanced to Egypt and killed a great number of Christians. They also enslaved a countless number of them. The Jews helped them in fighting against the Christians and demolishing their churches. They came from Tiberias, Galilee Mountain, Nazareth, Tyre and Jerusalem and killed many, inflicted all kinds of torture on them and destroyed two churches in Jerusalem. Heraclius was able to defeat Khosrow. He then marched from Palestine to prepare the Levantine and Egypt and renew what the Persians had destroyed. The Jews came to him from Tiberias and other places, offered him precious gifts and asked him to pledge to provide them with safety and security. He did. However, when he entered Jerusalem and the Christians received him with Bibles, crosses, incense and candles, he saw the ruined city and its derelict ransacked churches. He was exceedingly saddened and pained. The Christians informed him of the collaboration of the Jews with the Persians and how they had tortured them and ruined their churches. They told him that they suffered more at their hands than at the hands of the Persians and that they had tried to kill them all. They urged Heraclius to avenge them and made this act of vengeance look good in his eyes. He objected because of his pledge to provide them with peace and safety. Christian monks and patriarchs convinced him that he would be without blemish and blameless in killing them and dissolving his pledge since they tricked him into making such a pledge when he was unaware of what they actually did. They also promised to offer an atonement for this by pledging to fast and demand all Christians to fast for one week every year henceforth. Heraclius agreed and he waged a war in which he eliminated most of them. In the Roman kingdoms in Egypt and the Levantine, the remaining Jews fled and disappeared. The Patriarchs and Bishops wrote to all the countries so that Christians would commit to observing a one-week-fast every year. They do that until today. This is known as the "Heraclius Week." Heraclius spent a great deal of money building and renovating and restoring the churches." [7]

We thus see that the Jews were the right hand of the Persians in their fight against the Romans and the Christians. These wars that took place between the Romans and the Persians ended at first with the victory of the Persians over the Romans in 614 AD. The polytheists in Mecca were delighted with the Persians' victory as they considered it a victory for their likes in matters of worship, i.e., the Persians. They were gleeful and boastful and they were happy to exhibit these feelings to the Muslims. However, the Almighty informed His Prophet that the Romans will vanquish the Persians after that. In fact, the Romans did prevail over the Persians in 629 AD, and the Muslims were delighted with that victory. The Noble Qur'an foretold the Muslims of that victory in the Almighty's: "The Romans have been defeated in a nearby land. Yet following their defeat, they will triumph within three to nine years. The whole matter rests with Allah before and after victory. And on that day the believers will rejoice at the victory willed by Allah. He gives victory to whoever He wills. For He is the Almighty, Most Merciful." (Q 30:2-5) [8]

We thus see that the Jews- a people of the Book- sided with the idol-worshippers in supporting the worshippers of Fire, the Persians, against the people of the Book, the Romans.

And here, we would like to briefly mention that the alliance between the Jews and the Persians was not a new thing. It was old. It was the Persian Cyrus the Great who fought against Nebuchadnezzar, the Babylonian, and vanquished him in 536 AD. He sympathized with the Jews and freed them from the Babylonian captivity. He brought them back to Jerusalem, and he built the temple for them. Thus, he had dominion over Palestine, and the Persians called the people of Judah "the Jews," and they called their doctrine "Judaism." Ever since, the word "Jew" is used to refer to those who adopt "Judaism" even if he is not one of the Children of Israel. This is the difference between a Jew and an Israelite." [9]

But why did Cyrus have compassion on the Children of Israel? The reason is that he is related to the Israelites. His mother- or stepmother- was the Israelite Esther who was born in Persia. When she was of age, her uncle, Mordecai, introduced her to Xerxes, the Persian King, who was infatuated by her beauty and married her to become Queen over Persia. She attended to his Crown Prince, Cyrus, and infused in him the love of Israel.

After Cyrus became King of Persia, he fought against Nebuchadnezzar, the Babylonian, and he set the Jews free as we mentioned a little while ago.

Fifth: Having mentioned some of the punishments that the Romans brought down on the Jews, we now continue to recount some of the punishments that the Muslims caused to befall them because of their deceitfulness, immorality and aggression. We say:

After the Prophet's migration to Medina, he treated the Jews living in Medina and adjacent neighborhoods well. He held a treaty with them which ensured the protection of all their rights. However, they breached their pledges and sought every possible trick to eliminate Islam and entrap the Muslims. The Prophet tried to convince them to abandon their aggression and immorality, but they did not respond to his invitations. So, he punished each group in proportion with their wrongdoing and treachery to secure safety for the Muslims. Among the penalties that the Prophet inflicted upon the Jews was dispelling Banu Qaynuqa and Banu Nadir from Medina, the killing of Banu Qurayza, the shedding of the blood of some of their prominent leaders like Ka'b bin al-Ashraf and Salam ibn Abi Al-Haqiq, fighting the Jews of Khaybar and then reconciling with them after many were killed and others entered into Islam and accepted the conditions that the Prophet stipulated.

The final words that the Prophet uttered before his death were those that he recommended for his companions: "Get the Jews out of the Arabian Peninsula; there should never be two religions there." [10]

During the Caliph Umar bin Khattab, most of the Jews were expelled out of the Arabian Peninsula following the recommendation of the Prophet.

Sixth: In concluding our presentation of some of the punishments that befell the Jews during different epochs for their wrongdoing and inciting dissention and discord, we now present some examples of what befell them at the hands some European countries:

A) In Britain: The Jews encountered many different kinds of torture, murder and displacement.

1- John, King of England, decreed that they be put in prison all over his kingdom.
2- King Henry the second ordered that the Jews be imprisoned and tortured because he found out that the Jews take parts of the official golden and silver coins when they receive them and then pay them to the merchants. That led to shortage in the official currency of the country.
This British King was not content with merely imprisoning and torturing the Jews. He issued a decree in 1230 AD demanding that the Jews pay one third of their transferred monies to the British Treasury.
3- When Edward III ascended the British throne in 1273 AD, he issued a decree forbidding the Jews from usury and mortgaging the land after realizing that the country's wealth was being directed solely to the pockets of the Jews. However, the Jews did not heed that decree. They

stole a great portion of the gold of the British currency. Two hundred Jews were condemned to death in 1281 after their crime was confirmed.

4- In 1298, the British people were extremely displeased with the Jews and many complaints circulated. King Edward the First issued a decree to send the Jews out of England within three months. However, the British people were unable to wait all this time. They began to kill tens, even hundreds- of them in Bork, the castle in which a great number of the Jews sought refuge. The British also burned more than 500 Jews. The King was forced to send the Jews out of the country even before the three months period had elapsed for fear that the people would eliminate them all over the whole country. Britain had no Jews for approximately three centuries. The Jews returned to Britain in 1656- during the despot Cromwell- who usurped the Kingdom from Charles the First because of the Jews who offered him great amounts of money to achieve his goals.

B) In France: The Jews were the target of the condemnation and resentment of the French people during many different epochs. That was because the Jews ruined their national economy and smothered it with their usury and immoral practices and interactions.

1- The economic conditions in France deteriorated during the time of Louis the Nineth. He issued a decree to abolish one third of the French debts to the Jews. Then, he ordered burning all their Holy Books especially the Talmud. One historian said: "They burned what was worth twenty-four loads of the Talmud." [11]
2- When Philip the Fair ascended the throne in France, the French viciously killed, pillaged and displaced many Jews until they were completely expelled out of France. However, they returned once again after they paid Philip two third of the debts they owed to France.
3- In 1321 AD, the French attacked and slaughtered many Jews. They ferociously tortured them. They were then driven out of France after their possessions were ransacked. They were unable to return until the mid-sixteenth century.
4- At the beginning of the Nineteenth Century, Napoleon tried to use to reach his goals, but they betrayed him. He became extremely resentful and he tortured a number of them ferociously. He said that they were the dregs and germs of the society. The Jews were not able to evade the brutality and viciousness of the French until the nineteenth and twentieth centuries.

C) In Italy: Patriarchs viciously fought against them. They called them "the Abhorred People." They incited the Italian people against them, and they killed and displaced many. The Popes had issued many decrees calling to regard them as blasphemous and unAllahly and to look at their religion that based on the Talmud as worthless and insignificant.

In 1242 AD, Pope Gregory the Ninth issued blazing accusations against the Talmud that discredited Christ and Christianity. He decreed that the Talmud be burned, and all available copies were burned.

In 1540 AD, the Italian people vehemently revolted against the Jews and killed thousands of them. They drove those who remained alive out of Italy.

D) In Spain: The Jews experienced many different kinds of torture, disgrace and brutality at the hands of the Spanish people and their kings. They were unable to enjoy any peace or quiet except during the time of the Islamic rule of Spain. We will only mention one of the numerous punishments that befell them in this country.

During the reign of King Ferdinand and his wife Isabella, resentment and antipathy against the Jews reached its peak due to their meddling in Spanish life, their exploitation of the country's economy and stirring up religious dissonance among the various religious sects and denominations. The King and his wife saw that ousting them out of Spain forever was the best course of action to protect the country from their evil.

On the 31st of March in 1492, King Ferdinand issued the following decree: "A good number of Jews live in our kingdom. We have established inspection courts twelve years ago. These courts exact penalties on civilians when necessary. According to the reports that these courts have provided, it has become evident that the collisions that take place between the Christians and the Jews cause a great deal of harm and will consequently lead to the eradication of the Catholic faith. We have therefore decided to banish the Jews, males and females, outside the borders of our kingdom and forever. All the Jews who are living in our country- without any discriminations concerning gender or age- should depart from it no later than the end of July of this year. They are not to attempt to return under any circumstances." [12]

It was because of this decree that the Jews were disgracefully driven out of Spain and were forced to leave their gold and possessions behind after infusing their venom in the country for almost seven centuries. There were almost half a million Jew when they were dispelled out of the country. Some Jews regard that decision and their consequent ousting and displacement worse than the destruction of Jerusalem.

D) In Russia: Almost half of the world's Jews lived there during the nineteenth century. During their stay there, they employed all their cunning and crafty methods to destroy and devastate. They opened bars, traded in liquor, lent money in return for extremely high interest, seized a lot of the country's wealth by illegal forbidden means, killed many of the Russian citizens, when possible, formed secret societies that aimed to eradicate the Russian Orthodox Rule and continued their activities until they succeeded through the Communist Revolution in 1917 AD. Most of the leaders of this revolution were Jews. The Russians, however, never forgot the aggression and exploitation of the Jews. They attacked them on numerous occasions and viciously and mercilessly killed them. The most famous massacres that took place against the Jews were in the years 1881 and 1882 AD when Russian peasants sought to thoroughly destroy the Jews.

When the Russian writer, Sergei Nilus, published a few copies of the Protocols of the Elders of Zion- which display Jewish criminal intent towards the world- in 1902 AD, they were extremely alarmed and frightened. Massacres against them were common in Russia. In one of them, approximately ten thousand Jew were killed.

E) In Germany: The Jews spread in many cities there ever since the Eighth century Ad, and they settled on the banks of the Rhine. They appallingly exploited the German people until they were almost able to seize its wealth through extremely dreadful usury and through the use of different methods to amass forbidden money. The Germans revolted against them at different times. And they used all methods of killing, robbery and expulsion.

The author of "The History of the Israelites" says: "The killing and slaughtering of the Jews were widespread until orders were issued to drive them out of Germany in subsequent times between the twelfth and fourteenth centuries to the extent that not even one Jew remained in it..." [13]

The final episodes of tortures, killings and displacements were at the hands of Hitler ever since he came to power in Germany in 1933 until his rule ended in 1945 AD.

The Jews were the target of the people's wrath and resentment in all the countries in which they settled and throughout history whether its old history, middle history or modern history. The world had dealt them dreadful blows and severe punishments that included torture, expulsion, imprisonment, killing and confiscation of money.

A western writer says: "All Christian nations participated in the persecution of the Jews and in inflicting various kinds of punishments on them. Cruelty and brutality to the Jews was considered one of the feats for which Christians praised and commended each other." [14]

Having presented some of the punishments that befell the Jews throughout the ages and with various nations, we would like to confirm that the Jews are the ones who have been responsible for all the persecutions they were exposed to, and that they deserve these punishments for the following reasons:

First: Their boundless selfishness and greed:

This made them believe that the world and all that is contained therein is their possession and that whenever they go to any country, they are entitled to rob it of its riches and treasures by any means possible. Money is the Jews' idol, their Allah, from olden times.

Karl Marx, a Jew and a Communist, says: "Money is the Allah to which Israel clings. No other Allah should exist besides money, for money reduces all the Allahs of humanity and transforms them to a commodity. Money is the general value, the essence, that forms in itself everything else. The Allah of the Jews has become a worldly Allah. This is the true Allah of the Jews."

Then, he says: "What is the worldly basis of Judaism? Practical interest and personal benefit. Thus, by liberating itself from trade and money and subsequently from practical Judaism, the new generation will also liberate itself."[15]

The Jews' selfishness, greed and unlawful consumption of peoples' money made them the object of world condemnation and wrath. Some prudent leaders understood the danger of their meddling in their countries and drove them out and cautioned his countrymen against their evil. Among those prudent leaders was Benjamin Franklin, one of the Presidents of the United States of America. He gave a speech in 1789 AD in which he said: "There is a great danger that threatens the United States of America. This danger is the Jews. Gentlemen! Wherever the Jews settle, we find them weakening the will of the people and shake honest commercial interactions. They do not mix or commingle with the people. They create a government within a government, and when they encounter opposition from some one, they strive to smother and repress the nation financially as happened in Portugal and Spain… If the Jews are not prevented from migrating by the power of the constitution, they will flow in huge numbers in less than one hundred years. They will govern and destroy us. They will change the shape of the government that we worked so hard and sacrificed our blood, lives, money and freedoms to form. If the Jews are not exempted from migration, two hundred years will not pass until we find our children workers in the fields that secure the food for the Jews… I warn you, gentlemen, if you fail to forever prevent the Jews from migrating, your children and grandchildren will curse you in your graves. Their mentality is different from ours, even if they lived among us for ten generations. A tiger cannot change its color... The Jews are a danger and a threat to this country. If they enter it, they will ruin and corrupt it…" [16]

To comment on this address, we would say that Franklin was very truthful and correct in his prediction. However, he miscalculated the period of time that was necessary to Transform America into a milking cow for the Jews. Franklin estimated that this period would be two hundred years (1989). The Jews, however, were able to harness America's politics, weapons, wealth, science, influence and treasures to serve their interests fifty years earlier than he expected.

Here is Dr. John Betty describing the Jewish penetrating influence in America. He says: "When the presidents of America work with them, they bow down before Judaism as if they are bowing down to an udder that has its sanctity… The Israeli minority has attained enough power and ambition that threatens America with a constant danger… It threatens to provoke a Third World War." [17]

<u>Second</u>: Their arrogance and conceit:

The Jews regard themselves as Allah's children and His most beloved, His chosen people. Ever since olden times, they have divided the world into two opposing sections: A) Israel, the elite amongst the people and the ones who are favored by Allah, and B) The Gentiles, the none- Jews (Goyim), a Hebrew word that refers to the pagans, the disbelievers, the impure and the unclean ones. This arrogance and conceit have led the Jews to disregard and neglect others' rights. Therefore, it is rightful for the Jews to rob non-Jews, to cheat, defraud, lie and even kill them if they discovered their crimes. The Noble Qur'an pointed to this vice that has overpowered the Jews: "There are some among the People of the Book who, if entrusted with a stack of gold, will readily return it. Yet there are others who, if entrusted with a single coin, will not repay it unless you constantly demand it. This is because they say, "We are not accountable for exploiting' the Gentiles." And so they attribute lies to Allah knowingly." [18] (Al-Imran; Q 3:75)

Jewish books, and the Talmud in particular, abound with commandments that allow the Jews to treat non-Jews in a manner that is different from the way they treat each other. In the Talmud, for example, we encounter: "If a Jew cheated a Gentile, and another Jew came and cheated the Gentile by increasing the price or decreasing the amount (weight), the two Jews should split the booty that Yahweh sent to them." [19] Yahweh is the Allah of the Jews.

As a consequence of this conceit and arrogance that characterizes the Jews and causes them to waste and neglect others' rights and humiliate and dishonor them, people from among the Gentiles rose and defended their rights and inflicted the worst and severest forms of punishment on them for their false arrogance and conceit.

<u>Third</u>: Their isolation, tribal solidarity and fanaticism and betrayal of the countries they live in:

They are prejudiced and biased fanatics. They are not brought together because of their love for one another. Rather, what brings them together is their hatred for others who do not share their faith. They are also brought together by feelings of resentment and wrath towards the whole world. Isolation, fanaticism and racism have become inextricable Jewish traits.

Dr. Weizmann, the first Israeli President, describes this trait of isolation in the Jews: "The Jews in Motol (his birthplace) in Russia used to live like the other Jews in hundreds of big and small cities: isolated, withdrawing and secluded, in a world unlike the world in which other people around them live."

Perhaps, the most accurate description that urged them to become isolated and withdrawn was what Salomon Schechter mentioned in his speech at the Higher Jewish Theological School, where he said: "The meaning of integration into nations is the loss of identity, and this type of integration with the consequences that result from it is what I fear more than I fear massacres and persecutions." [20]

This isolation and tribalism led to grave consequences. They looked at all the other people from other nations with suspicion, distrust, caution and hostility. They were therefore stamped- everywhere and throughout the ages- with distrusting any religious or worldly organization, and they were branded by their unloyalty to the countries in which they live and partake of their products and blessings. Their loyalty was merely confined to their own groups and their personal gains and self-interest, no one else. That is because a Jew is first and foremost a Jew before anything else, no matter what his nationality might be and regardless of any outward beliefs or doctrines he seemingly adopts. If his nationality conflicts with his Judaism, he would stick to Judaism and try to spread destruction and devastation in the country in which he is one of its people, especially if he could escape punishment. World Zionism commands the Jews everywhere to pledge their allegiance- first and foremost- to Israel, not to the countries in which they live.

Golda Meir, a former Israeli Prime Minister, says: "The Jews who live outside of Israel are dispersed scattered groups that live in banishment. They are Israeli citizens, first and foremost, and they should pay allegiance and have absolute loyalty to this new state regardless of the official nationality that they have. A British Jew who chants "Long Live the Queen" -because of his British citizenship- cannot be a Zionist at the same time." [21]

Numerous are the situations in which the Jews were informants and spies on the countries in which they lived for the benefit of their enemies. One of the most glaring examples for this is the disloyalty of the Jews who were living in Germany towards Germany during the First World War. One of the fruits of their deception was the defeat of Germany and granting the Jews the Belfour Declaration in 1917 that the British Government issued as a reward for the Jews' complicity and betrayal of Germany.

Hitler enumerated the deceptions of the Jews to Germany. He mentioned forcibly taking the people's money by usury and extortion, corrupting education, controlling the banks and trade companies, dominating publishing presses, and meddling in the politics of the country for the benefit of other countries and against the wellbeing of Germany. At the top of their treacheries came their spying against Germany, something that many of them perfected.

Hitler concludes his long speech about the Jews, saying: "If it were destined for a Jew to overcome the countries of this world, his crown would be 'Humanity's Funeral.' And when our planet continues its march in the universe as it has done for millions of years, there will be no humans left on its surface… That is why, I believe that I dealt with them as our Creator wished: by defending myself against the Jew, I strive to defend the work of the Creator." [22]

Thus, the destruction and displacement- that the Jews suffered throughout the generations because of their isolation, their fanaticism and their betrayal of the countries that gave them shelter- were fair and just.

<u>Fourth</u>: Their persecution of others when they had the ability- hidden or manifest- to do so:

The history of the Jews is stained with crimes of killing, slaughter, looting, treachery and brutality. It is a history that is filled with massacres against the peoples that they defeated. In this, they were promoted by the commandments of their books to kill, humiliate and dishonor others whenever they are able to do so. In Deuteronomy, we read: "When you march up to attack a city, make its people an offer of peace. If they accept and open their gates, all the people in it shall be subject to forced labor and shall work for you. If they refuse to make peace and they engage you in battle, lay siege to that city. When the Lord your Allah delivers it into your hand, put to the sword all the men in it. As for the women, the children, the livestock and everything else in the city, you may take these as plunder for yourselves. And you may use the plunder the Lord your Allah gives you from your enemies. This is how you are to treat all the cities that are at a distance from you and do not belong to the nations nearby. However, in the cities of the nations the Lord your Allah is giving you as an inheritance, do not leave alive anything that breathes. [17] Completely destroy them…" (Deuteronomy 20:10-17) [23]

The Jews have applied these instructions in the worst possible way throughout their history. In Rome alone, they killed one hundred thousand Christians in 204 AD at the behest of Emperor Marcus Aurelius.

And why should we go so far back to bring evidence for their brutality when we have the wars in Palestine vividly itched and alive in our memory. One contemporary writer says: "The Deir Yassin Massacre was one of the most atrocious that the Jews had perpetrated. They killed two hundred and fifty, mutilated their bodies, slaughtered the children in the arms of their mothers, …" Many similar massacres have taken place in Palestinian cities such as Haifa, Jaffa and Kfar Qasim.

In his book "The Study of History," the British historian, Arnold Toynbee, wrote: "If the atrocity of a sin and the degree of the crime that the culprit perpetrates are juxtaposed against his discerning ability, the Jews would have the least excuse for what they perpetrated in 1948. Yet, the Jews are well aware of what they have perpetrated. Thus, their great tragedy can be summed up as such: The lesson that they learned as a result of their confrontation with the Nazi Germans did not make them avert the wicked deeds of those Nazis. Rather, it pushed them to continue those deeds. Those wicked deeds that the Jews perpetrated against the Palestinian Arabs included the killing of women, children and men and led them to flee from their country." [24]

The truth is: The improper and untruthful conceptions of the Jews, their overwhelming egotism and boundless selfishness, their conniving and crafty attitude, their corrupt morality and demeanor, their despicable and dreadful fanaticism, their cruelty of heart and their brutality and their nonchalance to killing and humiliating others- all of these made them the object the world's wrath and resentment. Because of these despicable and appalling behaviors, Allah has sent those who would make them suffer terribly until the Day of Judgement, and they would be hopelessly scattered and vastly dispersed.

At this juncture, I would like to share something that the Jewish historian Josephus wrote and which I like: "There is no nation on earth- throughout all of history, ever since the beginning of the creation and until now- that has endured as much calamities and tribulations as the Children of Israel. However, these calamities and tribulations are their own making." [25]

Allah's warning to them for causing corruption in the land twice:

Sura Al-Isra' contains noble verses that mention Allah's warning to the Children of Israel to punish them for corrupting the land and steering off the right path. The Almighty says:

"And We warned the Children of Israel in the Scripture, "You will certainly cause corruption in the land twice, and you will become extremely arrogant. When the first of the two warnings would come to pass, We would send against you some of Our servants of great might, who would ravage your homes. This would be a warning fulfilled. Then ⌜after your repentance⌝ We would give you the upper hand over them and aid you with wealth and offspring, causing you to outnumber them. If you act rightly, it is for your own good, but if you do wrong, it is to your own loss. "And when the second warning would come to pass, your enemies would ⌜be left to⌝ totally disgrace you and enter that place of worship as they entered it the first time, and utterly destroy whatever would fall into their hands. Perhaps your Lord will have mercy on you if you repent, but if you return to sin, We will return to punishment. And We have made Hell a ⌜permanent⌝ confinement for the disbelievers." (Q 17:4-8) [26]

We will consider these noble verses in the light of four major perspectives:

First: A historical synopsis of the history of the Children of Israel from the time of David in 1055 BCE approximately until the second destruction of Jerusalem at the hands of the Roman Emperor Titus in the year 70 AD.

Second: An interpretation of the noble verses.

Third: The most famous interpretation of exegetes concerning whom Allah sent twice against them. We will investigate their views, and we will consider which should be adopted.

Fourth: Our commentary on the views of a contemporary researcher who sees that the two times they corrupted the land was in Islam.

Let us now look at the first perspective.

First:

1- The Noble Qur'an mentions in Sura Al-Baqara what the chiefs of the Children of Israel said after Moses: "They said to one of their prophets, 'Appoint for us a king, ⌜and⌝ we will fight in the cause of Allah.'" (Al-Baqara; Q 2 246) They demanded with persistence. He expected them to cower if ordered to fight, but they said to him: "'How could we refuse to fight in the cause of Allah, while we were driven out of our homes and separated from our children?'" Then, the Noble Qur'an showed that their prophet told them that Allah appointed Talut (Saul) to be their King. They protested and said: "'How can he be our king when some of us are more deserving of kingship than he, and he has not been blessed with vast riches?'" Their prophet responded to their objection, saying: "Allah has chosen him over you and blessed him with knowledge and stature." Then, the Noble Qur'an concludes the story by stating that the smaller force fighting alongside Saul won victory over their enemies, and that David killed Goliath, the leader of the enemies of the Children of Israel. The verses continue to confirm that Allah blessed David with kingship and wisdom and taught him what He willed. Historians believe that the victory of the Children of Israel over Goliath and his army marked the establishment of their first kingdom with Saul as its king. He remained their King for two years. Then, he died in 1055 BCE. His era was marked by numerous wars and continuous conflicts.

2- After Saul's (Talut) death, David became King over the Children of Israel. He ruled over them for approximately forty years. Hebron was the capital of his Kingdom during the first seven years. As for the remaining thirty-seven years- period of his rule, Jerusalem became the capital. The Israeli Kingdom immensely flourished during his reign; its territories stretched, magnificent and luxurious buildings were erected, and indomitable fortifications were built. The Kingdom witnessed an era in which opulence, peace, safety and power abounded and prevailed.

3- After David's death, his son, Suliman (Solomon) [27], became King over the Children of Israel. They prospered and became even more secure and powerful.

A writer describes the conditions of the Children of Israel during Suliman's reign. He says:

"During the time of Suliman, the Israelites became more dominant and formidable. Their Kingdom stretched from the Red Sea to the Great Euphrates. Neighboring nations feared them… He sent his ships to the far ends of the world. They brought back gold, silver and precious stones. His rule lasted for forty years during which the Israelites enjoyed great prosperity, opulence and happiness. They became inebriated with goblets of pleasures and victory." [28]

In conclusion, the time during which David and Suliman- peace be upon them- ruled the Children of Egypt was considered their golden era and the most prosperous and opulent of all times as their Kingdom's borders widened and stretched, and their influence and impact became weightier. They were privileged with abundance and sumptuousness.

There are many verses in the Noble Qur'an that indicate that Allah lavishly bestowed enormous material comfort and magnificent blessings on David and Suliman. In Sura An-Naml (Q 27:15-16), we read: "Indeed, We granted knowledge to David and Solomon. And they said in acknowledgment, "All praise is for Allah Who has privileged us over many of His faithful servants." And David was succeeded by Solomon, who said, "O people! We have been taught the language of birds, and been given everything we need. This is indeed a great privilege."

4- After the death of Suliman in 975 BCE, Rehoboam, his son, succeeded him. Seditions, dissonance and disagreements became widespread during his era- as historian report. The Kingdom was in a state of disturbance. That led to its division into two Kingdoms: The Kingdom of Judah and the Kingdom of Israel.

   A) Jerusalem was the capital of the Kingdom of Judah, and Rehoboam was its King. It consisted of the tribes of Judah and Benjamin. Twenty-one King succeeded each other in ruling it.

Its end was at the hands of Nebuchadnezzar who invaded and destroyed it in 588 BCE. He led the survivors as captives to Babylon where they stayed for almost fifty years. What Nebuchadnezzar did to the Children of Israel is called the first destruction of Jerusalem.

   B) Samaria (now Nablus) was the capital of the Kingdom of Israel. It was established like its sister, the Kingdom of Judah, in 970 BCE. Its King was Jeroboam, Rehoboam's brother, and it comprised the other ten tribes. Nineteen kings ruled over it, until its end at the hands of Sargon, The King of Assyria, who invaded it, gained victory over it and banished its Jewish inhabitants to beyond the Euphrates in 721 BCE.

5- In 538 BCE, a war broke out between Cyrus the Great, King of Persia, and Nebuchadnezzar, King of Babylon. It ended with the victory of the King of Persia who issued an order in 526 BCE giving the Jews the permission to return to Jerusalem. However, most of the Jews had grown accustomed to their life in Babylon and were hesitant to return. Only a few returned, and they were mostly from the tribes of Judah and Benjamin. Those who returned rebuilt the Temple with the approval of Cyrus in 416 BCE approximately.

Ever since that time, the word "Jew" became associated with those who embrace Judaism, even if not from among the Children of Israel. This is the difference in meaning between "Jewish" and "Israeli."

Under the surveillance of the Persians, the Jews went about their business supervised by their rabbis. Ceaseless skirmishes between the Jews and the Persians marked this period until the end of the Persian rule in 322 BCE.

6- In that year, Alexander the Macedonian (Alexander the Great) defeated the Persians and drove them out of Syria and Palestine. When he entered Jerusalem, the Jewish rabbis received him, and they pledged allegiance to him. Jerusalem and adjacent territories were under his rule until his death.

7- When Alexander the Great died in the year 323 BCE, his Kingdom was divided among his commanders. Jerusalem fell to Ptolemy, the King of Egypt. He ruled Jerusalem with ferocity and violence despite the resistance of the Jews. Because of their repeated rebellions and uprisings, he was compelled to destroy a great portion of it. He also killed a lot of its inhabitants and sent one thousand Jew to Egypt in 320 BCE.

The Ptolemaic Kingdom rulers succeeded each other in ruling Jerusalem for a long time. Some treated the Jews harshly and with cruelty, and others treated them with kindness and leniency until the Seleucids vanquished the Ptolemaic Kingdom in 198 BCE.

8- The Seleucids were extremely cruel and harsh with the Jews. When Antiochus, the Seleucid, occupied Jerusalem, he destroyed its walls, seized its wealth and possession, killed eighty thousand Jews and severely humiliated and degraded their rabbis.

9- In 168 BCE, the Jews, headed by Matthias, their rabbi, revolted against the Seleucids without success. Matthias died a year later. Rabbi Maccabias, His son, took over and led the revolting Jews anew. To this Rabbi the Maccabi family (movement) is attributed. They were a group of Jewish rabbis who were known for their shrewdness and astuteness. They were more military-like than religious. They were able to take over the rule of Jerusalem for a period of time.

10- In 63 BCE, disagreements among the Maccabees became so pronounced and their influence waned. The Romans seized that chance and, led by Pompeius, they attacked Jerusalem.

Ever since then, Jerusalem became under Roman rule until the Persians occupied it in 614 AD. Then, it fell to the Romans in 628 AD. Then, the Muslims conquered it in 636-638 AD (15-16 H) during the time of Umar bin Khattab. It remained an Arabic

Islamic country until the Jews seized a big part of it in 1948 AD (1368 H) to establish their state there.

Thus far, we hope to have shed some light on the overall history of the Jews and Palestine ever since King David until the present time.

The second Perspective: An interpretation of the noble verses.

The Almighty's "And We warned the Children of Israel in the Scripture, "You will certainly cause corruption in the land twice, and you will become extremely arrogant." (17:4)

This means that We have disclosed to the Children of Israel and informed them in their Book, the Torah, of a sure revelation. We made it known to them through Moses, their prophet, that they will cause corruption in the land of the Levantine twice as the Almighty said: "You will certainly cause corruption in the land twice, and you will become extremely arrogant." That is, you will disobey Allah, become arrogant and refuse to comply with His commandments twice. You will become extremely and undeservedly haughty, and that would lead you to loss and destruction.

Among the signs of their corrupting the land was twisting and distorting the Torah, their non-compliance with its teachings, their killing of the prophets, their aggression towards those who seek fairness and justice among people, and indulging in immoralities and iniquities.

If it is said: "What is the benefit of Allah informing the Children of Israel in the Torah that they are twice corrupting the land and that He is punishing them for that by sending enemies against them to destroy them?"

The response is: Informing them of His plans indicates that Allah is not unjust to people. He only punishes them for the wrong they do and the corruption they cause. He pardons and forgives many, and His mercy can also extend to those corruptors who return and repent. Yet, there are also other benefits to informing them: He is cautioning the rational and sensible people in all nations not to commit depravities and aggressions since this can lead a nation to perdition. They- in turn- should caution their nations, enlighten their people and give them the discernment to understand the grave consequences of disobedience and corruption in order to avert Allah's punishment.

The third benefit of informing them is to demonstrate that vanquished nations can restore their might and former glory if they become vigilant and commit to obey Allah and comply with what the prophets have brought them.

Also, among the benefits of declaring this in the Noble Qur'an is to alert those Jews who were contemporaneous with the Prophet- as well as other disbelievers and polytheists like them- to one of Allah's ways of dealing with His creation, i.e., corrupting the earth, disobeying His commandments, transgressing, and disobeying His prophets- all of these will lead to loss in this world and in the Hereafter. So, it is imperative for the Jews and other people to believe in Muhammad- whose prophethood has been verified and confirmed- to secure happiness in this world and in the Hereafter.

Then, Allah revealed that he would send those who would conquer them and violate and desecrate what they hold sacred and revered. They would destroy them utterly as a punishment for what they did. The Almighty said: "When the first of the two warnings would come to pass, We would send against you some of Our servants of great might, who would ravage your homes. This would be a warning fulfilled." (Q 17:5)

That is: When the time comes to fulfill the first punishment for corrupting the land for the first time, Children of Israel, We would send against you powerful men, "some of Our servants of great might," who would cause you a great deal of harm as they would "ravage your homes;" they would kill you, take your wealth, violate your honor, destroy your homes, take your wives and everything. And "This would be a warning fulfilled." That is: This punishment- for corrupting the land- would be inevitable and unavoidable; you would not escape from it.

The Almighty's "We would send against you some of Our servants of great might, who would ravage your homes" is, most likely, a reference to Goliath and his fighters as we will explain when we handle the third perspective.

The Almighty then showed them that He would grant them victory over their enemies and provide them with wealth and offspring if they act rightly, repent and strive to amend the corruption that they caused the first time. He said: "Then after your repentance We would give you the upper hand over them and aid you with wealth and offspring, causing you to outnumber them." (Q 17:6)

The meaning is: Then, We gave you back, Children of Israel, the ability and the power to overcome those who humiliated and shamed you after you repented, returned to Allah and followed what He commanded you to do. You restored your wealth and your families from those who killed you and ransacked your homes. With Our Grace and Compassion, We "aid you with wealth and offspring" after your wealth was usurped and your children enslaved "causing you to outnumber them." We made you outnumber your enemies and caused your numbers to increase more than before. It was therefore your duty to appreciate this favor and make the best of it. It is Allah's way to aid the weak and raise the lowly and make them kings and inheritors when they fear Him, walk along the straight path, renounce depravities and shun evil desires.

The Almighty said: "We certainly help Our messengers and the believers, both in this worldly life and on the Day the witnesses will stand forth for testimony—" (Q 40:51) [29]

Therefore, you should remember Allah's favors, O Children of Israel. You should be exceedingly thankful and believe in Muhammad, His Prophet, whose truth you know just as you know your own children.

The Almighty's "If you act rightly, it is for your own good, but if you do wrong, it is to your own loss" (Q 17:7) explains what has preceded. It is as if the Almighty is saying: We helped you, O Children of Israel, overcome your enemies, and We profusely bequeathed Our blessings upon you after you amended your ways and came back to your faith. We did this to learn one of Our fixed, unalterable and permanent ways, i.e., the consequence of corrupting the land is ruin and destruction while the consequence of charity and obedience is ruling the land and copious and abundant blessings. We also want you to remember that if you act rightly and comply with Allah's commandments, you will attain happiness in this worldly life and in the Hereafter.

In this worldly life, We will give you the upper hand over your enemies, and We will abundantly increase your wealth, offspring and numbers.

In the Hereafter, you will abide in "Gardens under which rivers flow." (see Q 5:85, 5:199, 9:100, 20:76, etc.) However, if you do wrong and disobey your Lord, you will only harm yourselves, for Allah will send mighty men against you, and they will severely torture you in this world, and you will have an evil end in the Hereafter.

Then, the Almighty revealed that they would significantly corrupt the land once again and that they would be subjected to those who would humiliate and debase them because of their rebellion and non-compliance. He said: "And when the second warning [30] would come to pass, your enemies would be left to totally disgrace you and enter that place of worship as they entered it the first time and utterly destroy whatever would fall into their hands." (Q 17:7)

The meaning is: When it is time for the second punishment for corrupting the land, Children of Israel, we will send your enemies against you to totally humiliate and disgrace you. They will يَسُئُوا وُجُوهَكُم; that is, they will make your faces reflect those signs of doom and gloom that you feel inwardly. They will enter the Aqsa Mosque as conquerors ravishing and disgracing you, just as your enemies did before, and they will utterly and fiercely destroy whatever falls into their hands. Imam Al-Razi said: "The Almighty linked the offence and humiliation to their faces because the inward feelings and psychological states felt in the heart are often reflected outwardly on the face. If one is joyful at heart, the face becomes glowing, lustrous and radiant. If fear and sadness overwhelm the heart, traces and signs of gloom, despondency and despair are reflected on the face. For this reason, the humiliation and offence are associated with the face. Similar meanings to this abound in the Qur'an as in the Almighty's: "Then when they see the torment drawing near, the faces of the disbelievers will become gloomy." [31] (Al-Mulk; Q 67:27)

Among the examples of them corrupting the land this second time are killing Zachariah and John, attempting to kill Jesus, persevering in transgressions and evil deeds, allowing what Allah had forbidden and all the other vices that permeated and prevailed among them throughout the ages and everywhere.

Most exegetes believe that this time it was Nebuchadnezzar, the Babylonian, who was sent against them the second time. We will elucidate in detail who was sent to them when we explain the third point.

Then, the Almighty showed that the destruction that befell them for corrupting the land twice could be for their own good, a way to lead them to penitence and righteousness if they became responsive to the truth, learned from previous examples and past events and understood that Allah's way with His creation is fixed, constant and unchangeable: good deeds lead unto happiness and corruption leads unto perdition and annihilation. The Almighty said: "Perhaps your Lord will have mercy on you if you repent, but if you return to sin, We will return to punishment. And We have made Hell a permanent confinement for the disbelievers." (Q 17:8)

Abu Hayyan said: "This plea is not meant to restore a country to them. Rather, it is to demonstrate that Allah's mercy will overshadow those who obey Him." [32]

The meaning is: Perhaps Allah will pardon and have mercy on you after His vengeance against you, Children of Israel, if you act rightly, do good deeds, worship Him truthfully, and shun depravities and transgressions. You have learned that Allah does not allow calamities to befall unless there are inequities and transgressions, and He does not lift them without penitence. For this reason, He said: "but if you return to sin, We will return ..." That is: If you return to disobeying Me, disregarding My commandments and violating My sanctities for a third time after you have been clothed with My compassion, We will return to murder and torture, humiliate and disgrace you, and send enemies against you who would severely punish you in this worldly life.

In fact, they did return to wrongdoing, and Allah did return to punishing them. They did not believe in Muhammad, and they concealed what was reported concerning him in the Torah and the Bible. They sought to kill him. So, Allah instructed Muhammad to punish them because of their treachery and injustice. He killed Ban Qurayza, drove Banu Qaynuqa and Banu Nadir out of Medina and levied the Jizya tax on the rest. They would pay the tax, willingly submitting, fully humbled.

Ibn Abu Abbas said: "They returned (to their wrongdoing), so Allah sent the believers against them."

Then, they returned to their corruption during the ages that followed the advent of Islam, and Allah sent others from His servants who humiliated and displaced them. The Jews are still the object of people's contempt, resentment and hatred because of their selfishness, racism, ill manners and corruption in the land. And Allah has truthfully said: "And remember, O Prophet, when your Lord declared that He would send against them others who would make them suffer terribly until the Day of Judgment." (Al-A'raf; Q 7:167) He also reveals their end: "And We have made Hell a permanent confinement for the disbelievers." (Q 17:8) That is, Hell will be their abode; it is there that We have prepared an eternal prison for them, one from which they cannot escape. So, in this worldly life, they have faced annihilation and destruction. In the Hereafter, they will suffer in the eternal fire that surrounds them from every side. That is because of their corruption and for corrupting the land.

The third perspective:

The most well-known views concerning whom Allah sent against the Children of Israel these two times. We will examine these views and figure out what the most reasonable view is.

Exegetes have certain views concerning the servants that Allah sent against the Children of Israel in those two times. The most famous are the following:

First: Ibn Jarir relates on the authority of ibn Abbas and ibn Mass'oud. He said: "Allah pledged [33] the Children of Israel in the Torah: 'You will certainly cause corruption in the land twice.' (Q 17:4) The first corruption (of the two) was the killing of Zachariah. Allah sent Sahabeen, King of the Nabataeans, and his warriors. His family was of a Persian origin and they were known for their valor and might. The Children of Israel made the necessary preparations. Nebuchadnezzar came with kindness and modesty and entered the city and joined their assemblies. He heard them say that if their enemies knew the terror they felt, they would not have wanted to fight against them. Nebuchadnezzar invigorated his army and attacked. This is the Almighty's "When the first of the two warnings would come to pass, We would send against you some of Our servants of great might, who would ravage your homes. This would be a warning fulfilled." (Q 17:5) Then, the Children of Israel got ready to fight the Nabataeans, and they had the upper hand over them and restored some of what they lost. That is what the Almighty said: "We would give you the upper hand over them and aid you." (Q 17:6) [34]

However, we believe that this view is improbable:

A) The invasion of the Nabataeans and Nebuchadnezzar took place approximately six centuries before the killing of Zacharia. It is historically confirmed that Nebuchadnezzar gained victory over the Children of Israel three times. The first was in 606 BCE, the second in 699 BCE and the third in 588 BCE. In the third time, he killed many of them, took those alive as captives and completely destroyed Jerusalem as we indicated previously.

As for Zacharia, it is well-known that he lived during the time of Jesus or around His time. The Noble Qur'an tells us that it was Zacharia who attended to Mary, the mother of Jesus.

Therefore, suggesting that their first corruption was for the killing of Zacharia and that the Nabataeans and Nebuchadnezzar were sent against them implies a contradiction with the established and fixed historical facts.

B) History does not tell us that after the invasion of the Nabataeans and Nebuchadnezzar the Children of Israel restored their might and attacked the Nabataeans, killed them, and seized what they had. What history tells us is that Cyrus, the King of Persia, was the one who gave them permission to return to Jerusalem after his victory over Nebuchadnezzar in 526 BCE.

This should not be considered as gaining the "upper hand" over the Nabataeans of Nebuchadnezzar since they did not gain victory over them because of their own power or might. That did not take place, not even once in order to be able to claim that they had the "upper hand." Their return to Jerusalem- as a result of the permission that Cyrus, King of Persia, gave them- should not be considered a victory since they lived under their control until 322 BCE. That is, they moved from on submission to the Babylonians to another, i.e., the Persians.

Therefore, suggesting that they were able to gain the "upper hand" over the Nabataeans or Nebuchadnezzar is apparently untrue.

C) This view is also clearly untrue because Sahabeen, the King of the Nabataneans, whom historians call Sennacherib, was King of Assyria. He was the one who invaded the Kingdom of Judah in 713 BCE. That was one hundred years before Nebuchadnezzar invaded it. Nebuchadnezzar's first invasion was in 606. Nebuchadnezzar was not contemporary with Sennacherib.

Second: Ibn Jarir relates on the authority of Ibn Zeid, he said: "Their corruption in the land was twice: killing Zacharia and killing John. Allah sent Shapur II (Shapur the Shouldered) who was one of the kings of Persia for the killing of Zacharia. And He sent Nebuchadnezzar for the killing of John." [35]

Ibn Asakir in his History of Damascus relates on the authority of Ali ibn Abi Talib concerning the Almighty's 'You will certainly cause corruption in the land twice.' (Q 17:4) He said: the first is for the killing of Zacharia and the other one was for the killing of John." [36]

We believe that these claims by Mujahid and Ali ibn Abi Talib are weak; they are neither supported by the verses of the Qur'an nor are they validated by historical facts. That is because the time that elapsed between the killing of Zacharia and the killing of John was just a short period of time and would, therefore, not have been sufficient for them to corrupt the land twice or give them the chance to have the "upper hand" over their enemies after the first one as the Almighty said in: "We would give you the upper hand over them and aid you." (Q 17:6) In addition, Shapur II and Nebuchadnezzar existed six centuries before the killing of Zacharia and John.

Third: Ibn Jarir, Ibn Abi Sheiba, Ibn Al-Munzir and Ibn Abi Hatim relate on the authority of Mujahid concerning 'We would send against you some of Our servants of great might.' (Q 17:5) He said: "Some Warriors came from Persia to spy on the Children of Israel and listen to their talk. The Persians went back without fighting. The Children of Israel were victorious. That was the first one. When it was time for the second one, the King of Persia sent an army headed by Nebuchadnezzar, and they destroyed them. That was the second one." [37]

We also believe that this view contradicts what the Qur'an displays. The noble verses clearly indicate that the Almighty sent those mighty ones against the Children of Israel. They humiliated them, and they ransacked their homes after the first corruption took place. This punishment lasted for a long time during which they were severely punished. However, the current view that we examined states that there was no fighting between Persia and the Children of Israel.

This view is also at odds with historical facts that indicate that the Children of Israel did not win any battle fought against Persia.

Fourth: Ibn Jarir and Ibn Abi Hatim relate on the authority of Ibn Abbas concerning "When the first of the two warnings would come to pass, We would send against you some of Our servants of great might, who would ravage your homes. This would be a warning fulfilled." (Q 17:5) He said: In the first one, Allah sent Goliath against them. He ransacked and pillaged their homes and severely humiliated and mortified them. They asked the Almighty to send them a king to fight for Allah's cause. He sent Saul to them, and they fought Goliath and Allah granted them victory. Goliath was killed at the hands of David who became King over the Children of Israel. When they corrupted the land the second time, Allah sent Nebuchadnezzar who ravaged their homes and places of worship. After the first and second corruptions, Allah said: "Perhaps your Lord will have mercy on you if you repent, but if you return to sin, We will return to punishment." (Q 17:8) They returned and Allah sent the believers against them." [38]

Ibn Jarir and Ibn Abi Hatim relate on the authority of Qataada. He said: "The first time, Allah sent Goliath against them. He sent Saul and David and aided the Children of Israel gain the upper hand and "caus(ed) you to outnumber them." (Q 17:6) That was at the time of David. "And when the second warning would come to pass," the second punishment, "your enemies would be left to totally disgrace you يَسُـُٔوا۟ وُجُوهَكُمْ and enter that place of worship" (Q 17:7) as they did before. They would utterly destroy whatever would fall into their hands. So, in the second one, Allah sent Nebuchadnezzar, the most despicable of all Allah's creatures. He killed many, enslaved the rest, utterly destroyed Jerusalem and severely humiliated and disgraced them." [39]

This view- related by Ibn Abbas and Qataada- is the one that we favor the most. We will discuss it in detail in a little while.

So far, we have mentioned the most well-known views of the exegetes concerning the identity of those who were sent against the Children of Israel because of their corruption of the land at two occasions. We examined them, discarded weak and unsupported justifications and accepted proven and corroborated evidence. We have not mentioned other interpretations due to their lack of evidence.

Before we begin to indicate the view that we choose to adopt, we would like to provide you with the following propositions:

1- First proposition: This can be summed up as follows: the Messenger of Allah did not mention in his Hadiths what was meant by those whom Allah sent against the Children of Israel for twice corrupting the land. Otherwise, exegetes would have mentioned it.

2- Second proposition: This can be summed up as follows: Corrupting the land at the hands of the Children of Israel took place many times. What the Almighty's "And We warned the Children of Israel in the Scripture, 'You will certainly cause corruption in the land twice'" (Q 17:4) mean is to mention two incidents of this corruption. However, corruption took place many times, and they were punished for it every time. This is evidenced in the Almighty's "but if you return to sin, We will return to punishment." (Q 17:8) Also, the Almighty's "And remember, O Prophet, when your Lord declared that He would send against them others who would make them suffer terribly until the Day of Judgment" (Q 7:167) indicates that sending those who would make them suffer will continue until the Day of Judgement.

3- Third proposition: Going back to history will help in determining what was meant by twice corrupting the land for which the Children of Israel were warned in the Book. This will also help us determine who those servants- that were sent against them for their first and second corruption- were.

4- Fourth proposition: The views of historians and exegetes- concerning the meaning of twice corrupting the land and those whom Allah has sent against them- were different in accordance to what various people would consider regarding the corruption that the Children of Israel caused and the subsequent punishments enacted by Allah.

5- Fifth proposition: The intention behind these verses is to reveal one of Allah's methods in dealing with nations at times of righteousness and unrighteousness (corruption). The Noble Qur'an has poignantly and most tersely and succinctly expressed this idea in His: "If you act rightly, it is for your own good, but if you do wrong, it is to your own loss." (Q 17:7)

It is unquestionably true that this is the way that is followed with all nations without change or alteration everywhere and throughout the generations.

Since this is what is meant by these verses, we can conclude that understanding these verses should not be limited to the two specific times of their corruption nor the specific identity of those sent against them each time that corruption took place.

I like what Imam Ibn Kathir said in this regard: "What Allah informed us in His Book was more sufficient than in other books before it. Neither Allah nor His Messenger made us in need of more information. Allah informed that when they transgressed and did injustices, Allah sent their enemies against them to ravage and ransack their homes and severely humiliate and debase them. Allah is not unjust to His servants; it was them who were defiant and disobedient, and it was them who killed the prophets and scholars." [40]

And Imam Al-Razi said: "You ought to understand that knowing the identity of the specific people sent against them is not very relevant. The idea that is being conveyed here is that when they committed many transgressions, Allah sent others against them to kill and annihilate them." [41]

In his Interpretation of the Ocean, Abu Hayyan said: "Allah informed the Children of Israel in the Torah that they would become disobedient and ungrateful for His favors, and that He would send against them a nation that would defeat, kill and humiliate them. Then, He would have compassion upon them, strengthen them and enable them to restore their former position. They would return to their sins and transgressions once again; they would become ungrateful and unjust and they would kill and some would disbelieve. Then, Allah would once again send another nation that would pillage and ravage their homes, and kill and drive them away. History has proven this." [42]

After mentioning the five propositions above, we now go back to prove the validity of the view that we are inclined to adopt concerning the servants that Allah sent against the Children of Israel after the first and second corruptions. We say:

A) The view that we choose is: The servants that Allah sent against the Children of Israel after corrupting the land were Goliath and his warriors. This view is the one that exegetes have adopted, and we are inclined to choose it for the following reasons:

First: The way that the Noble Qur'an mentions the story of the fighting that took place between Saul (Talut), the leader of the Children of Israel, and Goliath, the leader of their enemies, indicates that the Children of Israel were in overwhelmed and defeated by their enemies. This meaning is clear in the Almighty's "Have you not seen those chiefs of the Children of Israel after Moses? They said to one of their prophets, "Appoint for us a king, and we will fight in the cause of Allah." He said, "Are you not going to cower if ordered to fight?" They replied, "How could we refuse to fight in the cause of Allah, while we were driven out of our homes and ˹separated from˺ our children?" (Q 2:246)

In other words, what they said- as mentioned in the Qur'an- "'How could we refuse to fight in the cause of Allah, while we were driven out of our homes and 'separated from' our children?'" strongly indicates that they were miserably and mortally defeated at the hands of their enemies even before fighting with Goliath to the extent that they were driven out of their homes and were separated from their children.

Second: Some interpreters stated that the enemies that compelled the Children of Israel out of their homes and separated them from their children were Goliath's people. They stated that they vanquished the Children of Israel and killed a great number of them before the Children of Israel gained the upper hand over them under the leadership of Saul.

Imam Al-Alusi said: "The reason why the Children of Israel asked their prophet to send them a king to fight for Allah's sake was that Goliath's people, a mighty, powerful and strongly built opponent, defeated them, took a lot of their lands and levied the Jizya (taxes paid by non-Muslims) on them." [43]

Third: The Almighty's "We would give you the upper hand over them and aid you" (17:6) indicates that He granted victory to the Children of Israel after they repented. They gained the upper hand over their enemies who humiliated and ravaged their homes.

This meaning is in agreement with the Noble Qur'an's story that under the leadership of Saul (Talut), the Children of Israel achieved victory over Goliath and his warriors and that David killed Goliath. The Almighty said: "When they advanced to face Goliath and his warriors, they prayed, "Our Lord! Shower us with perseverance, make our steps firm, and give us victory over the disbelieving people." So, they defeated them by Allah's Will, and David killed Goliath. And Allah blessed David with kingship and wisdom and taught him what He willed." (Al-Baqara; Q 2:250-251)

That victory was a great blessing to the Children of Israel. It happened after they were driven out of their homes and were separated from their children, after objecting to leaving Saul as King over them and after only a few fought alongside with him. There was no doubt that such a victory should have prompted them to obey Allah and thank Him for His favors.

Fourth: The Almighty's "We would give you the upper hand over them and aid you with wealth and offspring, causing you to outnumber them" (Q 17:6) seem to apply more to the era during which King David and his son, King Soliman, ruled over the Children of Israel. During their reign- which lasted almost eighty years- their Kingdom flourished and prospered, and their authority and influence were unchallenged. Allah gave them great abundance and many children, and He made them stronger than their enemies in strength and in number.

After their reign, their Kingdom was split into two parts: the Kingdom of Judah and the Kingdom of Israel. Conflicts, discords and deterioration plagued them until the Assyrians defeated the Kingdom of Israel in 721 BCE. Nebuchadnezzar also vanquished the Kingdom of Judah in 588 BCE. Their history henceforth was nothing but an endless chain of calamities, tragedies and punishments that were inflicted upon them from various nations throughout different epochs because of their corruption and corrupting the land. We discussed that in detail when we examined the first perspective.

Thus far, we hope to have been able to reach the correct choice- which we have chosen and which investigators have supported- that those whom Allah sent against the Children of Israel after their first corruption of the land were Goliath and his warriors.

B) As for the servants that Allah sent against the Children of Israel after their second corruption of the land, interpreters tend to think that they were the Babylonians headed by Nebuchadnezzar. We have shown before that Nebuchadnezzar attacked the Children of Israel three times: the first was in 606 BCE, the second was in 599 BCE and the third was in 588 BCE. The third time, he killed thousands of them, demolished their Temple and took those who were alive captives to Babylon, as we detailed when we treated the first perspective.

This view has been adopted by a large number of exegetes. It is not far-fetched since it describes the severe punishments that they were subjected to. However, we tend to believe that it was the Romans headed by Titus who were sent against them the second time they corrupted the land. Here are the most important reasons why we believe so:

First: Those who study history will soon realize that the vices of the Children of Israel- before the Romans inflicted punishments on them- were graver and more unmistakable than those that they perpetrated before Nebuchadnezzar humiliated them. That was why, the Roman's punishments were even more severe and cruel. For example, before the Roman's cruel punishments under the leadership of Titus, they had already murdered Allah's prophets Zachariah and John. They had also attempted to kill Jesus, and they saved no effort to accomplish this. They failed for reasons beyond their control. Vices and depravities had run rampant among the Children of Israel to the extent that Jesus cursed them. [44] Hence the Romans' devastating and shattering blows that eradicated their very existence were appropriate punishment for them for their disobedience and violations of Allah's commandments and for not forbidding one another from doing evil.

Second: Exegetes mention that the reason Allah sent Nebuchadnezzar against them for corrupting the land the second time was because of killing John. Previously, we have repeatedly shown that Nebuchadnezzar was living more than five centuries before John, and Jerusalem was under the control of the Romans during John's time. The Children of Israel killed John during the Romans' reign. They also killed his father, Zacharia, during their reign.

Therefore, what the interpreters related concerning sending Nebuchadnezzar after their second corruption is applicable to the times of the Romans, not to the time of Nebuchadnezzar because he lived five centuries before John as we mentioned.

Third: The Romans' blows that were directed to the Children of Israel were in themselves harsher and crueler than the blows that Nebuchadnezzar levelled at them. For example, the number of Jews killed at the hands of the Romans under Titus reached a million Jew. [45] The number of captives reached one hundred thousand, as historians relate. On the other hand, the number of deaths and captives at the hands of Nebuchadnezzar was much less. Historians describe the calamities and tribulations that the Jews suffered at the hands of Titus in harsher colors than those they suffered at the hands of Nebuchadnezzar.

A writer describes what befell the Jews at the hands if Titus. He said: "Titus was in his thirties when he stood at the head of his army in front of the walls of Jerusalem in the year 70 AD. The city started to suffer the brunt of the siege. At the same time, it started to grunt and groan because of a worse calamity, i.e., the civil war. Some Jewish eccentrics, fanatics and gangsters occupied some neighborhoods in the city and started to savagely launch attacks against other neighborhoods. Blood flowed in the streets, and a Jewish famine started. They would crawl on their hands and feet like pallid withering ghosts preceded by rumors that they had swallowed up their gold. The soldiers would cut open their stomachs after killing them to look for the gold... When Titus and his warriors entered the city, he issued a decree declaring that they can kill, steal and burn. He also decreed that the money, wealth, possessions and women of the Jews are permissible. The Romans burned and destroyed the Temple of the Jews. Christ's prophecy was fulfilled: "This land will see misery, and wrath will descend upon its people. They will fall dead by the sword, and they will march captives to Egypt. Jerusalem will be trodden underfoot." [46]

Fourth: The consequences of the Nakba (disaster) that the Romans caused the Jews at the hands of Titus were far more horrific than those caused by Nebuchadnezzar because after the brutality, abuse and captivity for fifty years that they experienced at the hands of Nebuchadnezzar, they returned to Jerusalem once again with the help of Cyrus, the King of Persia. They started to increase and multiply again. However, after the brutality and abuse of the Romans, they were exterminated, dispersed and scattered all over the land, and they were rendered unable to stand as a nation again. In 135 AD, the Romans destroyed Jerusalem completely. They plowed the land and mixed it with salt in order to turn it into a barren soil unable to produce food. In place of the Jewish Temple, Hadrian, the Roman Emperor, built a pagan temple. Christianity was not recognized then. That temple remained until Christianity came to Jerusalem, and the Christians thoroughly destroyed the Roman temple during the time of Emperor Constantine. The author of the "History of the Israelites" stated this when he concluded his description of what Titus did to them: "At this juncture, the history of the Israelites as a nation ends. After the destruction of Jerusalem as mentioned before, they were dispersed throughout the land of Allah. Their history afterwards is linked to the history of the kingdoms in which they settled or lived..." [47]

Therefore, the adversities and hardships that Titus and other Romans inflicted upon the Jews were- in our opinion- harsher and crueler than those that Nebuchadnezzar caused them. Perhaps we are not exaggerating to suggest that the blow that the Roman Emperor, Titus, levelled at them was the worst punishment they suffered ever since the death of Soliman in 975 BCE up to the end of the first century AD.

For these reasons, we tend to believe that the servants that Allah sent against the Children of Israel- following their second corruption of the land- were the Romans with Titus as their commander.

However, regardless of our propensity to believe that Goliath and his warriors were sent against them the first time and that the Romans with Titus as their leader who were sent against them the second time, we still reiterate what we mentioned before, i.e., these noble verses aim to show one of Allah's cosmic ways of dealing with nations in times of righteousness and also during times of depravity and corruption.

A nation that obeys its Creator and follows the righteous, straightforward and correct paths to attain its legitimate rights will be aided by Allah in this worldly life, and it will also enjoy eternal bliss and happiness in the Hereafter. The Almighty said: "We certainly help Our messengers and the believers, both in this worldly life and on the Day the witnesses will stand forth for testimony." (Q 40:51) [48]

As for a conceited and arrogant nation that favors blindness over discernment and guidance, blocks its ears from the word of truth and justice, transgresses and violates those that attempt to direct and straighten its paths and fails to use its potential to forge ahead- such a nation is surely doomed to degradation and destined to disgrace and annihilation.

"Indeed, Allah would never change a people's state of favor until they change their own state of faith. And if it is Allah's Will to torment a people, it can never be averted, nor can they find a protector other than Him." (Q 13:11) [49]

<u>The Fourth perspective</u>:

A new view for the interpretation of the noble verses:

During our examination of the Children of Israel's corruption of the land and the servants that Allah sent against them after their first and second corruptions, we mentioned some of the views that interpreters have stated concerning them. We also stated our position concerning these views. Those who examine what those interpreters reported concerning these noble verses will find them in agreement on two issues:

First: The two times in which the Children of Israel corrupted the land took place prior to Islam.

Second: The servants that Allah sent to punish them for these two corruptions were also prior to Islam. Any disagreements among the interpreters are not related to these two issues.

However, one scientist wrote an essay in which he disagreed with other interpreters on the interpretation of these noble verses. He said: "These two incidents were not before

Islam; they were during Islam. The first time was during the time of the Messenger of Allah and his Companions, and the other one is during our own time…"[50]

In order for the reader to understand this view, we thought it would be wise to share his text.

His eminence said: "The Almighty said: 'And We warned the Children of Israel in the Scripture, "You will certainly cause corruption in the land twice, and you will become extremely arrogant. When the first of the two warnings would come to pass, We would send against you some of Our servants of great might, who would ravage your homes. This would be a warning fulfilled. Then ˹after your repentance˺ We would give you the upper hand over them and aid you with wealth and offspring, causing you to outnumber them. If you act rightly, it is for your own good, but if you do wrong, it is to your own loss. "And when the second warning would come to pass, your enemies would be left to totally disgrace you and enter that place of worship as they entered it the first time and utterly destroy whatever would fall into their hands. Perhaps your Lord will have mercy on you if you repent, but if you return to sin, We will return to punishment. And We have made Hell a permanent confinement for the disbelievers. Surely this Qur'an guides to what is most upright, and gives good news to the believers—who do good—that they will have a mighty reward.'" (Al-Isra; Q 17:4-8)

Interpreters have agreed that they caused this corruption twice: in the past before Islam when they became arrogant and haughty, killed the prophets, and disbelieved the messengers. Yet, they differed concerning the exact occurrence of their first and second corruptions as well as the identity of those sent against them.

There are two issues that I am interested in illuminating here:

<u>First:</u> These two times were not before Islam; they were during Islam.
<u>Second:</u> The first time was during the time of the Messenger of Allah and his Companions. The second time is at the present time when we will totally disgrace them نَسُئُوء وُجُوهَم and enter the Mosque as conquerors ravishing and debasing them, just as we did before, and we will utterly and fiercely destroy whatever falls into our hands, Allah willing.

I would like to assure those who are astonished by this view and see it at odds with what is commonly believed and what exegetes find acceptable. What is commonly accepted is not readily supported with evidence and proofs. However, this issue is of mere historical implications and going against commonly accepted views or interpretations would hardly be viewed as distortion or taking words out of context. Now, I will try to prove the first point. I say:

Talking about Al-Isra' الاسراء is good tidings and foretelling the future:

It is well-known that Al-Isra الاسراء happened to the Prophet in Mecca before his migration. It is a Meccan Sura except for known verses. At that time, the Muslims were in Mecca. They were few and weak. The Children of Israel had nothing to do with the

Muslims at that time. They had no influence nor posed any threat in Mecca that would warrant talking about them in such detail in a Meccan Sura.

So, what is the secret behind Allah's telling of الاسراء- (taking His servant Muhammad by night from the Sacred Mosque to the Farthest Mosque)- in the first verse at the beginning of the Sura then completely stopping anything related to it and beginning to talk about the Children of Israel, His favors and promises and an important role they will play.

What is the relationship between these verses and the events taking place? The mystery is that in Al-Isra, the Almighty informs His Prophet and the persecuted and oppressed Muslims in the land of Mecca of good tidings: they will soon become more powerful and influential when the capital of polytheism and the capital of the People of the Book surrender and become indebted to them. The Almighty said: "Glory be to the One Who took His servant Muhammad by night from the Sacred Mosque to the Farthest Mosque." (Q 17:1) He did not say from Mecca to Jerusalem because the Ka'ba at that time was not a mosque; it was a building around which idol-worshippers and polytheists performed their rituals. Also, the Temple of David and Soliman in Judah and Israel was not a mosque; it was just a house around which the Children of Israel consumed forbidden gain and spread corruption.

The Almighty, however, foretold in Al-Isra that there would be a transfer from one mosque to another to bring the Muslims the good tidings that their position would improve and their state would be elevated; the country wherein they were humiliated and regarded as weak and where their sanctities were violated would become a place for a sacred mosque and a house of peace and Islam. Its glamor, luminance and influence would even reach the capital of the People of the Book, and the Temple of David and Soliman would become the Farthest Mosque, for the Muslims are worthier of it. "None has the right to guardianship except those mindful of Allah." (Al-Anfal; Q 8:34)

Here, the answer and the relevance of the Almighty's "And We gave Moses the Scripture" (Q 17:2) and "And We warned the Children of Israel in the Scripture" (Q 17:4) and the first verse in Al-Isra becomes clear.

The theme is connected even though the topic shifted from foretelling the fate of the Temple to the fate of its people:

<u>Sura the Children of Israel</u>: It is more fitting that Sura Al-Isra الاسراء is called the Sura of the Children of Israel as it did not talk about Al-Isra -except to foretell that the Ka'ba and the Temple would become a sanctified place and a mosque for Muslims- as much as it talked about the Children of Israel and the hardships they caused the Muslims. The Almighty said: "And We warned the Children of Israel in the Scripture, "You will certainly cause corruption in the land twice." (Q 17:4) We may have noticed that the Almighty does not mention the Children of Israel in Meccan Suras except to mention their stance towards Moses and his commandments and their stance with Pharaoh and his soldiers. However, in Medina Suras, the Almighty mentions them a lot. He mentions many forms and types of corruption and corrupting; He mentions breaching their pledges, their

disbelief in Allah's miracles and signs, their unjust killing of the prophets, their saying that their hearts are unresponsive, their injustices and wrongdoing, their hindering others from Allah's way, their acceptance of usury and extreme high interest and their unlawful exploitation of others' wealth.

He also talks about their violation of the Sabbath, their fear of death and consuming lust for a long life, their choosing a fleeting gain over Allah's revelations, their killing each other and driving one another from their homes; their aggression and animosity and their claiming that they could not be held accountable for exploiting the Gentiles.

Corruption Twice: We notice here that Allah warned that they would cause corruption in the land twice: if the first warning comes to pass, this (X) would happen, and if the second warning comes to pass, this (X) would happen. This means that these two times are not what was previously recorded about them. They will take place in the future for those to whom the Book was revealed. What is said is to foretell, an insinuation at what is yet to come in the future; it is to inform the unknown and tell what has not taken place yet; otherwise, they had caused corruption seventy times before, and the two times that are mentioned in the verse had taken place already as confirmed by the miracle of the Noble Qur'an and the truth that Muhammad brought.

The first: The Almighty said: "When the first of the two warnings would come to pass, We would send against you some of Our servants...etc." (Q 17:5) This time is not completely applicable except in that role they played during the era of the Prophet and his Companions and how Allah had punished them and those whom He sent against them.

They had corrupted the land, and they had broken their promises to Allah and His Messenger. Upon his arrival to Medina, the Prophet made a covenant with them: "They are a nation with the Muslims. The Muslims have their religion, and the Jews have their religion. There will be support and righteousness among them, no injustice and no condescending. Whoever fights the people of this treaty or attacks Yathrib... etc." (Al-Madinah Newspaper)

Yet, despite this attention, reconciliation and equity, the Jews were filled with degenerate wanton envy, deceit and cunning, and they set out to plant suspicion concerning the Prophet, his integrity and his message claiming that the polytheists are more guided than the believers.

They befriended the enemies of the Prophet and they exposed the sanctities of the believers. They even attempted to kill the Messenger and incited Quraysh and Ghatafan. They encircled Medina to eradicate the Messenger of Allah, eliminate his message and his followers. They joined them, breached their pledge with Allah and His Messenger at a very crucial moment during the Battle of Al-Ahzaab (the Parties/ the Confederates). Therefore, Allah sent His servants, the believers, against them. They drove Banu Al-Nadir away, killed Banu Qurayza and took them captives, and then they entered Khaybar. The Messenger of Allah made a treaty with them and kept them until they were driven out by Omar during his Caliphate. Allah had promised the believers to enable them against their enemies, and He did. This was the first time which is only fit to describe the followers and Companions of the Messenger of Allah.

A) They are the ones that are worthy of being honored with "Our servants" (Q 17:5) because they were the followers of His servant whom He took by night from the Sacred Mosque to the Farthest Mosque (Al-Isra الاسراء). On the other hand, the followers of Nebuchadnezzar, Shapur II, Sahabeen, Sennacherib, etc., were pagans and were unworthy of the honor of being linked to Allah in His "Our."

B) They were the ones whom Allah described in His Book as "And those with him (Muhammad) are firm with the disbelievers and compassionate with one another" (Al-Fath; Q 48:29)

C) They were the ones for whom disciplining the Jews only caused them to "ravage (their) homes." (Q 17:5) As for the followers of Nebuchadnezzar, it was mentioned that they killed seventy thousand Jews for killing Zacharia, and that they went into the sanctuary and plundered its gold, etc. This was more of an invasion than a mere ravaging of homes.

Giving them the upper hand: The Almighty said: "We would give you the upper hand over them and aid you..." (Q 17:6) One thousand and three hundred years later- after Allah sent His servants, the believers, to discipline them and ravage their homes- the Jews were given the upper hand.

After this period of time which the Almighty indicated its length by His saying ثُمَّ (then) which in subordination indicates procrastination and delaying, the Jews were given the upper hand. They were given three things that they never experienced before in history:

1- Money that is liberally granted to them from many countries in the world.
2- Immigrant and warriors that have been selected for their zeal, proficiency and ability to build their country.
3- وَجَعَلْنَاكُمْ أَكْثَرَ نَفِيرًا/ Causing you to outnumber them: The Jews have never throughout their history enjoyed the backing and support they enjoy today. No nation on earth receives the assistance they get, and many nations rush to their rescue; if they become angry, America, England, France and all western nations become angry with them. The east and the west agreed- and they have never before agreed on anything- to establish Israel and divide Palestine, and they kept quiet and silent-and they have never done that before- as they witness the tragedies of the refugees, the afflicted and the displaced.

All this confirms that what we are suffering today is the "upper hand" mentioned in the verse. All that exegetes have mentioned is far-fetched and does not fit these descriptions.

A chance to choose: "If you act rightly, it is for your own good, but if you do wrong, it is to your own loss." (Q 17:7) The Almighty decided to give the Jews the upper hand. He decided to give them the chance to choose and determine their end: those who act rightly will have a good end and those who do wrong will have an unpleasant one. He then decided that they will never abandon their corruption and wrongdoing. Accordingly, He immediately decided their inevitable well-known fate. The Almighty said: "And when the second warning would come to pass, your enemies would be left to totally disgrace you and enter that place of worship as they entered it the first time." (Q 17:7)

The Almighty knows that they will not receive His favors with thanksgiving and gratitude nor show gratefulness for being given the upper hand and abandon their corruption. He knows that they will return to their deeply ingrained corruption which will earn then Allah's wrath and the resentment of His servants. That would alienate them from His mercy and compassion. So, the Almighty said: "And when the second warning would come to pass," We will send against you Our first servants who entered the mosque and on whose successors you gained the "upper hand," and they will totally disgrace you/ يَسُـُٔوا۟ وُجُوهَكُم and "enter that place of worship" impressively and majestically "as they entered it the first time" and triumphantly and jubilantly "utterly destroy whatever would fall into their hands." (Q 17:7)

This is our expected role, the work that we hope Allah would honor us to accomplish in the near future; we hope that Allah would torture them at our hands, disgrace them, grant us victory over them and give His believers the chance to vent for the pain they feel inside their chests.

The Almighty warned that He will gather them together to eradicate them. He said: "but when the promise of the Hereafter comes to pass, We will bring you all together." (Al-Isra; Q 17:104)

Good tidings for the believers: Their fate, their end is confirmed, and it will come to pass soon as predicted by the Almighty's "فَإِذَا جَآءَ/ when the promise…comes to pass:"

1- The use of " فـ" (but) indicates a chronological order and sequence of events.
2- Using "إِذَا" (when) indicates that it will undoubtedly come to pass.
3- And the good tidings of victory that are confirmed all over in this Sura.

Following these verses, the Almighty said: "Surely this Quran guides to what is most upright, and gives good news to the believers—who do good—that they will have a mighty reward." (Al-Isra; Q 17:9) And at the end of the Sura, the Almighty said: "And We said to the Children of Israel after Pharaoh, "Reside in the land, but when the promise of the Hereafter comes to pass, We will bring you all together." (Al-Isra; Q 17:104)

Our Thoughts on the Article

Those who read this article will realize that the writer believes that it is the Noble Qur'an, not the Torah, that is meant by "the Scripture/ٱلْكِتَـٰبِ." Under the heading "Corruption Twice," he said:

"We notice here that Allah warned that they would cause corruption in the land twice: if the first warning comes to pass, this (X) would happen, and if the second warning comes to pass, this (X) would happen. This means that these two times are not what was previously recorded about them. They will take place in the future for those to whom the Book was revealed. What is said is to foretell, an insinuation at what is yet to come in the future; it is to inform the unknown and tell what has not taken place yet…etc."

This view, which the honorable Sheikh adopts, that "Scripture" refers to the Qur'an, cannot occur to anyone who prudently and cautiously reads the honorable verses because the Almighty says: "And We gave Moses the Scripture and made it a guide for the Children of Israel." (Al-Isra; Q17:2) Then, the Almighty says: "And We warned the Children of Israel in the Scripture, "You will certainly cause corruption in the land twice…etc." (Al-Isra; Q 17:4)

The word "Scripture" mentioned in the second verse refers to the same "Scripture" mentioned in the first one, i.e., the Torah which Allah gave Moses and made it a guide for the Children of Israel.

This meaning- inferred from the verses- and which anyone who prudently contemplates Allah's Book will soon adopt- has been accepted by most exegetes. A few of those interpreters added that it could also refer to the tablets, and we have explained in our second perspective the reason for informing the Children of Israel in the Torah that they corrupt the land twice.

By proving that it is the Torah that is meant by "Scripture" in the Almighty's "And We warned the Children of Israel in the Scripture," (Q 17:4) we have thus abolished the notion that it refers to the Qur'an. Also, we have consequently abolished the notion that the two incidents of corruption occurred during Islam, and that they foreshadow the future of what is to be revealed to Muhammad.

We also have some observations concerning some of what the article mentions:

First: The honorable Sheikh says: "What is the secret behind Allah's telling of الاسراء- (taking His servant Muhammad by night from the Sacred Mosque to the Farthest Mosque)- in one verse at the beginning of the Sura then completely stopping to talk about الاسراء until the end of the Sura and then begin to talk about the Children of Israel, mentioning His favors and promises and an important role they will play? What is the relationship between these verses and the events…?"

We say that the Almighty mentioned Al-Isra (الاسراء) as a sign, among many, to prove the truthfulness of His Messenger's prophethood and message. Polytheists used the sign of الاسراء (Al-Isra) to implant doubts- in those who had sickness in their hearts- concerning the message of the Prophet and the truthfulness of his prophethood. They also used it as a pretext to mock the Messenger and those who believed in him. That is why, the Almighty was saying- to those who had disease in their hearts and hindered others from Allah's path, as well as those who mocked His honorable Prophet- that should they not desist from their corruption in the land and refrain from placing obstacles to hinder the Muhammadian Call, they would face the same terrible consequences that the Children of Israel encountered before them when they corrupted the land twice and became extremely arrogant. After each one of these two times, Allah sent against them those who severely punished them, killed them, and ravaged and destroyed their homes utterly.

Then, the Almighty talks about the Noble Qur'an, the Muhammadian Call and the light and guidance therein that would lead to success in this worldly life and happiness and bliss in the Hereafter. He says: "Surely this Quran guides to what is most upright and gives good news to the believers—who do good—that they will have a mighty reward. And it warns those who do not believe in the Hereafter ˹that˺ We have prepared for them a painful punishment." (Al-Isra; Q 17:9-10)

The reader of the honorable Sura would realize that it elaborates the morals, principles and ethics of the Noble Qur'an. The Almighty says: "For your Lord has decreed that you worship none but Him. And honor your parents" (Q 17:23) up to "This is part of the wisdom which your Lord has revealed to you O Prophet. And do not set up any other Allah with Allah ˹O humanity˺, or you will be cast into Hell, blameworthy, rejected." (Q 17:29) (all from sura Al-Isra)

Then, the Almighty chastises those polytheists, saying: "When you O Prophet recite the Quran, We put a hidden barrier between you and those who do not believe in the Hereafter. We have cast veils over their hearts—leaving them unable to comprehend it—and deafness in their ears. And when you mention your Lord alone in the Quran, they turn their backs in aversion." (Al-Isra; Q 17:45-46)

The Almighty then commands His Messenger to hold fast and not to heed those who were trying to shake him away from the truth: "Had We not made you steadfast, you probably would have inclined to them a little, and then We truly would have made you taste double punishmen˺ both in this life and after death, and you would have found no helper against Us." (Al-Isra; Q 17:73-74)

Then, the Almighty elaborates and states that the Noble Qur'an is the greatest sign for the truthfulness of His Messenger: "Say, ˹O Prophet, ˺ "If all humans and jinn were to come together to produce the equivalent of this Quran, they could not produce its equal, no matter how they supported each other." (Al-Isra: 88)

Then, the Almighty mentions their suggestions to His Prophet demanding to show them special signs that would confirm his truthfulness concerning his prophethood as they were not content with the Noble Qur'an. He says: "They challenge 'the Prophet', "We will never believe in you until you cause a spring to gush forth from the earth for us" up to "Say, Glory be to my Lord! Am I not only a human messenger?" (Al-Isra; Q 17:90-93)

At the end of this Sura, the Almighty shows His Prophet one of His constant and perpetual ways, one that has been applied ever since the beginning, namely, that He grants victory to those who act with righteousness and destroys the unrighteous and the ungodly. For example, He brought Moses nine clear proofs, yet Pharoah did not believe and persevered in his injustices and tyranny. Allah drowned him and gave the land to the Children of Israel after him to show the arrogant and haughty disbelievers who refuse to accept the truth that their fate would be like that of pharaoh if they do not abandon their twisted and crooked behavior.

The Almighty then concludes the Sura with a statement about the status of the Noble Qur'an. He said: "We have sent down the Quran in truth, and with the truth it has come down. We have sent you O Prophet only as a deliverer of good news and a warner. It is a Quran We have revealed in stages so that you may recite it to people at a deliberate pace. And We have sent it down in successive revelations. Say, O Prophet, "Believe in this Quran, or do not. Indeed, when it is recited to those who were gifted with knowledge before it was revealed, they fall upon their faces in prostration…" (Al-Isra: Q 17:105-107)

This short exposition of the Sura reveals that it is given to assure the prophethood of the Messenger and the truth of the Noble Qur'an that was revealed to him. It also displays that those who seek other signs have not been able to contemplate, understand and know its true worth, and if they persisted in their ungracious denunciation and rejection, they would be exposed to what other nations have experienced and what was inflicted upon the Children of Israel after they had twice corrupted the land.

Second: What the honorable Sheikh mentioned that the verses in Al-Isra الاسراء are Meccan and that at that time, the Muslims were few and weak. He also said that the Children of Israel had nothing to do with the Muslims at that time. They had no influence nor posed any threat in Mecca that would warrant talking about them in such detail in a Meccan Sura.

While we agree with him that the verses are Meccan and that the Muslims in Mecca at that time were weak and outnumbered, we disagree with his view that the Children of Israel had nothing to do with the Muslims that would warrant talking about them in such detail.

These are among our reasons for our disagreement with him:
The lack of commercial interactions or residential connection between the Muslims of Mecca and the Jews and the absence of danger or threat should not necessitate that the Noble Qur'an abandon talking about the Children of Israel in detail. There were more important things than these: the identical position of the people of Mecca and the Jews in relation to religion and the truth. They both adopted an ungrateful, rebellious and obstinate position concerning the heavenly revelations. The Noble Qur'an demonstrated to the

people of Mecca that the Almighty Allah revealed the Torah to Moses to guide the Children of Israel. However, they did not follow it, and they corrupted the land. They were like donkeys carrying books containing knowledge but unaware of what they had. As a result, Allah sent against them those who humiliated and subjugated them for their non-compliance with Allah's commandments. So, if the people of Mecca would still follow the same deviant and crooked path that the Children of Israel chose to follow after Muhammad came to them with guidance and the upright religion, they would be subjected to the same painful punishment that afflicted them.

This detailed delineation that the Noble Qur'an used in talking about the Children of Israel here was also used, in even much more detail, in other Meccan Suras such as Ash-Shu'ara (sura 26), Al-A'raf (sura 7), Taha (sura 20), Al-Qasas (sura 28), and many other Meccan Suras that mentioned them in detail.

Therefore, we believe that that detailed delineation of the Children of Israel in this Meccan Sura (Al-Isra) was important: it demonstrated the identical positions of the people of Mecca and the Children of Israel concerning the upright religion, the religion of truth, and the opposition of the two groups to an immortal divine doctrine, i.e., the religion of Islam, not to a transient law or a worldly custom. The Sura also brought the Muslims good tidings and demonstrated the favorable consequences of their positive response to Allah and His Messenger.

Third: The honorable Sheikh said: "The Almighty said: "When the first of the two warnings would come to pass, We would send against you some of Our servants...etc." (Q 17:5) This event perfectly fits the role they played at the time of the Prophet and his companions and Allah's punishment for them."

We do not agree with his view for the following reasons:

A) What exegetes mean by the word 'land' in the Almighty's "And We warned the Children of Israel in the Scripture, "You will certainly cause corruption in the land twice" (Q 17:4) is the land of the Levant where the Jews dwelt when the torah was revealed. It does not refer to the Arabian Peninsula, as the honorable Sheikh suggests, as it was not their home or the place where they settled when the Torah was revealed.

B) We do not deny that they caused corruption during the time of the Prophet. However, their corruption then was less than the corruption they caused before. As evidence for this is the many vices that they committed and which the Noble Qur'an attributed to them. Among these were their killing of some of Allah's prophets such as Zacharia and John and attempting to kill Jesus and saving no effort to do so. They only failed to kill Him for reasons outside their control.

Their corruption in the land before the emissary of the Prophet was, therefore, much more appalling and atrocious than their corruption after him.

C) Their corruption in the land during the time of the Prophet and his companions would usually be covert and take the form of hypocrisy and treachery. They would not openly display it because of their fear of the Muslims. However, their corruption before that was overt, open and visible; it was characterized by unconcealed injustice and unfairness, discernable noncompliance and defiance, intentional aggression and deliberate belligerence as indicated in His "and you will become extremely arrogant." (Q 17:4)

This indicates that their corrupting in the land twice was a reference to the time before the Prophet.

D) The noble verse says: "and you will become extremely arrogant." This arrogance and haughtiness that the verse attributes to them does not apply to their condition during the time of the Prophet or his companions. That is because during that period of time, those represented just a part of the Jews that were spread across the land. They were so weak that some of them joined the Khazraj while others joined the Aws. Whenever a war erupted between the two groups, those who allied themselves with the Khazraj would fight against and kill their fellow Jews who sided with the Aws, and those who allied themselves with the Aws would fight against and kill their cousins who sided with the Khazraj. The Noble Qur'an mentioned that in "But here you are, killing each other and expelling some of your people from their homes, aiding one another in sin and aggression; and when those ⌜expelled⌝ come to you as captives, you still ransom them—though expelling them was unlawful for you." (Al-Baqara; Q 2:85)

Then, the Almighty's "When the first of the two warnings would come to pass" (Q 17:5) after saying "you will become extremely arrogant" apply to the greater and more serious corruptions that they caused prior to Islam when they acted aggressively, atrociously and arrogantly in the land.

E) The punishments that were inflicted upon them during Muhammad and his companions were minimal and negligible compared to the punishments that they received at the hands of the Babylonians, the Romans and others. The punishments they encountered during the Prophet's time were only restricted to those Jews who inhabited the Arabian Peninsula. On the other hand, the punishments that the Babylonians and the Romans inflicted upon them encompassed all the Jews who were gathered in one place, i.e., the Levant.

Also, the punishments they received at the hands of the Muslims at the beginning of Islam were during different scattered periods of time. They were also in proportion to the offense. For example, the Prophet was content to merely drive Banu Qaynuqa out of Medina for breaking their promises. He still allowed them to take a lot of their wealth with them. Also, the Prophet drove Banu Al-Nadir out of Medina because of their treachery and betrayal. With the exception of weapons, he allowed them to take all the wealth that their camels can carry.

As for Banu Qurayza, who joined Al-AHzaab and betrayed the Muslims at a most difficult time, the Muslims had to kill them. The Prophet fought against the Jews of Khaybar for inciting Al-Ahzaab against the Muslims. After the Muslims' victory over them, the Prophet made an agreement with certain conditions. So, what are these scattered, limited and fair punishments that the Prophet inflicted upon the Jews for their aggression against the Muslims in comparison with the sweeping, all-encompassing and devastating calamities that befell Jewish men, women, children and their possessions at the hands of various nations like the Babylonians, the Assyrians, the Seleucids, the Romans and others. We talked in detail about this before. [51]

Thus, we can see that the corruption that the Jews caused the first time was related to what they did before Islam. We can also see that the servants that Allah sent against them to humiliate and punish them for their corruption were also before Islam.

Fourth: The honorable Sheikh confirmed that the description of those who punished the Jews the first time can be applied only to the companions of the Messenger of Allah because they are the ones who are worthy of this honor…and they are the ones who merely went into their house to punish them. The followers of Nebuchadnezzar, on the other hand, were said to have killed seventy Jew for the murder of Zacharia… This was an invasion, not a mere جوسا ransacking/ pillaging of their homes."

We disagree with the honorable Sheikh for many reasons. The most important are:

A) All people, believers or disbelievers, and those whom Allah sent to punish the Children of Israel after corrupting the land the first time are His servants regardless of their faith or lack thereof.

As evidence for this is the Almighty's "They will have layers of fire above and below them. That is what Allah warns His servants with. So fear Me, O My servants!" (Az-Zumar; Q 39:16)

In this verse, Allah linked His servants, believers and disbelievers, in general, to Himself. There are other verses in which Allah makes this link between Himself and His servants whether they are believers or not.

B) The honorable Sheikh says: "To punish the Jews, they merely went into their house جاسوا to punish them." He does not indicate the connotations or meanings of the word الجوس. However, what we can understand from what he says is that الجوس -in his opinion- means going among the houses without noticeable fighting.

This interpretation- in our opinion- is not supported in the context of the verses. It is also at odds with the most well-known views of linguists and exegetes.

The *context* does not support his interpretation because the verse mentions great corruption and excessive tyranny on the part of the Children of Israel when they corrupted the land the first time. It also mentions that after that they were disciplined and punished for that corruption: Allah sent against them some of His most powerful servants. Allah also revealed the mission of those servants: they "would ravage your homes." (Q 17:5)That is, these mighty servants would raid your homes, O Children of Israel, to ransack, pillage, plunder, kill, vandalize and demolish them. This is applicable to what happened to the Jews and the sweeping, all-encompassing and devastating punishments that were inflicted upon them by the Babylonians, the Romans and others. They are not applicable to the punishments that the Muslims inflicted upon them during the Prophet's era because those were measured punishments characterized by fairness and restraint and only affected those who were deserving of such punishments.

As for being at odds with the most well-known views of linguists and exegetes concerning the meaning of الجوس, we offer the following proofs:

1- Imam Ibn Jarir said: "Some people with knowledge of the meanings of the Arabs' words from Al-Basra would say: the meaning of جاسوا is: 'they killed.' They use the following line from a poem by Hassan ibn Sabet:

And among us is he who met with the sword of Muhammad
and swept through the enemy جاس *with it, killing them with his sword.*

He also said: "It might also be possible to mean that they went back and forth in their houses to kill them." [52]

2- Al-Zamakhshari said: "He attributed الجوس (which is going throughout their homes causing corruption) to them. So, destroying the Mosque and burning the Torah are some of the overall meaning of الجوس that is attributed to them." [53]

3- Al-Razi said: "Concerning the Almighty's they would 'ravage your homes,' Al-Lyth said الجوس means going back and forth in their homes causing corruption, and the homes is a reference to the homes in Jerusalem." Then, Al-Razi said: "Exegetes differ in their interpretation of the word جاسوا : Ibn Abbas views it as 'searched for.' To Ibn Qutayba, it means they plundered and destroyed. And to Az-Ujaj, it means they went through the homes to check to see if there was anyone left without being killed… "[54]

4- Ibn Manzour said: "الجوس : جاس /جوسا/ جوسانا which means to go back and forth. In the Quran, they would ravage your homes, means they went back and forth raiding them الجوسان . Al-Fara' said: 'They killed you between your homes.' Az-Ujaj said that they would ravage your homes means they went through the homes to check to see if there was anyone left without being killed…" [55]

5- Al-Zamakhshari said: "they would ravage your homes means they went through your homes causing damage and destruction as in a person who nonchalantly passes among people heedless of them and doing what he pleases.."[56]

These texts indicate that الجوس means going back and forth between the homes to kill and destroy.

Even if we were to accept the honorable Sheikh's view concerning the meaning of الجوس, we have to ask him: Was the cost for the Muslims to punish the Jews merely going into and through their homes?

What is evident for us is that punishing the Jews cost the Muslims more than that: They encircled Banu Qaynuqa more than ten days and drove them out of Medina after arguments and negotiations. As for Banu Al-Nadir, the Muslims surrounded them, burned their vegetations and forced them to depart from Medina. The Jews of Banu Qurayza were surrounded by the Muslims and they were killed in accordance with the ruling of Sa'd ibn Mu'dah. There was a ferocious fight between the Jews of Khaybar and the Muslims which ended in the capitulation of the Jews. Thus, punishing the Jews did cost more than going into their homes as the honorable Sheikh believes.

C) The Almighty said: "And when the second warning would come to pass, your enemies would ˹be left to˺ totally disgrace you and enter that place of worship as they entered it the first time, and utterly destroy whatever would fall into their hands." (Q 17:7) This verse indicates that the Mosque would be taken from the Jews by force and those who would take it would destroy and devastate it. These are acts and descriptions that that applied to the Babylonians and the Romans and others who, when they entered Jerusalem before Islam, they demolished it and destroyed its Temple.

However, when the Muslims entered Jerusalem during the Umar Ibn Khattab in 16 H (638 AD), there were no traces of the Jews. They did not take the Mosque from the Jews; they took it from the Christians, the Romans at the time, who occupied the Levant for hundreds of years. When they entered, they abolished paganistic symbols and purified the land for the worshippers. The Muslims never demolished or destroyed the Mosque or anything else in Allah's land as shown in His "utterly destroy whatever would fall into their hands." (Q 17:7)

Accordingly, the actions, characteristics and devastating punishments- that the Children of Israel experienced after their corrupting the land the first time- apply to those servants who humiliated them before Islam, like the Babylonians and the Romans; they do not apply to the companions of the Messenger of Allah, as the honorable Sheikh suggests.

Fifth: Under the subtitle *Giving them the upper hand,* the honorable Sheikh said: "The Almighty said: 'Then … We would give you the upper hand over them … causing you to outnumber them." (Q 17:6) The Jews were given the upper hand over us after one thousand three hundred years of Allah's punishment to them when He sent His servants the believers and companions of the Prophet who went through their homes... etc.

We disagree with his eminence for the following reasons:

A) The meaning of the Almighty's 'Then … We would give you the upper hand over them' indicates that they abandoned their immorality and corruption and that Allah gave them the upper hand over their enemies. This is one of Allah's fixed and eternal characteristics: He grants victory to those who offer true penitence and multiplies them. However, this meaning that the verse reflects cannot be applied to the Jews in our times. They are still corrupt and corrupting, disbelievers and tyrannical. However, this description can be attributed to the few believers among the Children of Israel who obeyed Talut (Saul) and fought alongside with him as well as those who supported and sustained David and when they advanced to face Goliath and his warriors, they prayed: "they prayed, "Our Lord! Shower us with perseverance, make our steps firm, and give us victory over the disbelieving people. So, they defeated them by Allah's Will…" (Al-Baqara; Q 2:250)

So, the Almighty's 'Then … We would give you the upper hand over them' (Q 17:6) is more fit to apply to those among the Children of Israel who fought with patience, steadfastness and unshakable faith with Saul. That is why, Allah granted them victory.

B) The honorable Sheikh maintains that the Jews were given the upper hand and granted three things that they never experienced before in history: Money that is liberally lavished upon them, immigrant and warriors that are selected for their zeal…etc.

This is applicable to their condition during the era of Soliman and David when Allah was bountiful and munificent: He gave them immense wealth, increased their offspring and made them outnumber their enemies. It is no exaggeration, perhaps, to suggest that during the reign of Soliman and David, the Children of Israel enjoyed the only golden age they have enjoyed throughout their history. What followed after this golden era and up to the present time is nothing but an endless chain of blows, calamities and disasters as we detailed when handled the first perspective. The world's resentment and scorn for them will continue and its hatred and vengeance will go on until the Judgement Day. This is due to their selfishness and their corruption of the land. The Noble Qur'an stated this clearly: "And ʿremember, O Prophet, ʾ when your Lord declared that He would send against them others who would make them suffer terribly until the Day of Judgment." (Al-A'raf; Q 7:167)

However, no matter how much money and support the Jews receive from the great countries of الكفر(Kufr), they will not outnumber us; they are not أَكْثَرَ نَفِيرًا compared to us, the Muslims. Neither are they wealthier or richer if we compare the treasures that we have- on the surface of the earth and under it- and our abilities to work which brings more wealth and money because of our great numbers. This is contingent upon our ability to efficiently manage what we possess. And when the Muslims fully comply with their Islamic teachings and conduct their lives appropriately and as Allah has commanded them, and when they fully and responsibly shoulder the responsibilities with which they are entrusted, and when they are mindful of Allah, then He will bountifully pour upon them blessings from the heavens and the earth.

Sixth: The Honorable Sheikh says: "The Almighty has decided that He will bring them together to annihilate them. He said: 'but when the promise of the Hereafter comes to pass, We will bring you all together.'" (Al-Isra; Q 17:104)

It seems clear that the honorable Sheikh interprets ٱلْـَٔاخِرَةِ in the honorable verse فَإِذَا جَآءَ وَعْدُ ٱلْـَٔاخِرَةِ جِئْنَا as the second time they caused corruption in the land.

We believe that the word ٱلْـَٔاخِرَةِ refers to the Hereafter, as displayed by the context of the verse and as interpreters tend to believe:

1- Al-Zamakhshari said: "'but when the promise of the Hereafter comes to pass' (Q 17:104) refers to the Hour/Judgement Day. Then, 'We will bring you all together,' (Q 17:104) mixed together, you and them, to be judged and to distinguish and separate between those who will enjoy bliss and happiness and those who will be wretched and miserable." [57]
2- Imam Al-Razi said: "The Almighty's 'but when the promise of the Hereafter comes to pass' refers to Resurrection Day when 'We will bring you all together,' from here and there." [58]
3- Al-Qurtubi said: "'but when the promise of the Hereafter comes to pass,' that is, the Day of Judgement, 'We will bring you all together,' that is, We will bring you from your graves from all places.

<u>Seventh</u>: The honorable Sheikh says: "I would like to assure those who might be astonished by this view and see it at odds with what is commonly believed and what

exegetes find acceptable. What is commonly accepted is not readily supported with evidence and proofs. However, this issue is of mere historical implications and going against commonly accepted views or interpretations would hardly be viewed as distortion or taking words out of context."

In response, I would like to first indicate that it is an obvious departure from what a prudent and judicious reader of the Qur'an would understand, both implicitly and explicitly, that the intended meaning of the Almighty's reference to 'Scripture' in His "And We warned the Children of Israel in the Scripture" (Q 17:4) is the Torah, NOT the Noble Quran.

Second: Historical facts do not support his view. At the time of the Muslims' conquest headed by Umar Ibn Khattab, the Farthest Mosque was under the control of the Christians, not the Jews. The Mosque was taken by force from the hands of the Christians, not the Jews, for the Jews had no noticeable presence in Palestine. The Muslims did not destroy or demolish it. On the contrary, they conserved and kept its sanctities safe and well-kept.

If to this we add that the verses indicate that giving the Jews "the upper hand" (Q 17:6) would be a consequence of straightening their paths, becoming righteous and charitable, working hard and offering penitence for their sins as reflected in His "If you act rightly, it is for your own good, but if you do wrong, it is to your own loss," (Q 17:7) then I would add to this that the Jews' occupation of Palestine today was due to their righteous deeds, being moral and virtuous and a case of rightful owners taking and restoring what belongs to them.

However, all of this is in sharp contrast of the reality that we can touch with our hands and see with our eyes. The Jews at the present time are the same Jews throughout the ages: corrupt and corrupting, belligerent and aggressive, and tyrannical and oppressive. They flagrantly and brazenly attacked the Muslims of Palestine. Infidel countries provided them with various types of assistance. Our anticipated role, Allah willing, is to eliminate all manner of disagreements and discord amongst ourselves to enable the religion of Allah to be firm and steadfast in the land through unity, strength, hard work and true worship and conduct our business unwaveringly with legitimate means and with resoluteness and stanchness. Then the believers will be gladdened with Allah's victory.

Now that we have disagreed with the writer in some of what his article contained, we should also admit that the article was written in a kind Islamic spirit and with a powerful religious passion that indicate his loyalty, faithfulness and sound upright intentions... We ask Allah to guide us all to what is upright and truthful.

Third: Forbidding them good things because of their aggression and violations.

A) Among the punishments that the Almighty imposed upon the Children of Israel was forbidding them from eating certain foods though they were permissible before. That was because of their violations, injustices, manipulating Allah's doctrines and their selfishness that prompted them to "indulge in unlawful gains, claiming, "We will be forgiven after all." (Al-A'raf; Q 7:169) The Almighty displayed what he has forbidden in His Book. In Sura Al-An'am (sura 6), the Almighty said:

"For those who are Jewish, We forbade every animal with undivided hoofs and the fat of oxen and sheep except what is joined to their backs or intestines or mixed with bone. In this way We rewarded them for their violations. And We are certainly truthful. But if they deny you O Prophet, say, "Your Lord is infinite in mercy, yet His punishment will not be averted from the wicked people." (Q 6:146-147) [59]

The Almighty's "For those who are Jewish, We forbade every animal with undivided hoofs" is a statement that reflects what the Almighty forbade the Children of Israel for their violations. This same statement refutes the Jews' assertions and impugns them for claiming that Allah did not prohibit anything and that they were the ones who forbade themselves from eating certain foods that Israel forbade itself. That is why, this verse was revealed to show some of the things that were previously permissible but have now been forbidden by Allah because of their aggression, violations and immorality.

The Almighty's "every animal with undivided hoofs" is a reference to animals and birds (with undivided hoofs) such as camels ostriches, geese and ducks, as Ibn Abbas, Saied Ibn Jubair and Qatada stated.

Imam Al-Razi said: "The almighty's 'For those who are Jewish, We forbade every animal with undivided hoofs' indicates that this act of prohibition was specifically directed to them. Two perspectives indicate that: First: The Almighty's 'For those who are Jewish' should do so and so is a style of restriction in the language wherein the thing that is to be done precedes the doer of the action. Second: Had this act of prohibition targeted all, then the statement 'For those who are Jewish, We forbade ..." would have been pointless." [60]

Then, the Almighty states what other animals and birds were forbidden them besides those with undivided hoofs. He said: "and the fat الشحم of oxen and sheep except what is joined to their backs or intestines الحوايا or mixed with bone."

The word الشحم refers to the fat that animals have in their body. And the word الحوايا refers to what is inside the stomach (the intestines)."[61]

The meaning is: Just as We forbad the Children of Israel every animal with undivided hoofs, We also forbad them the excessive fats of sheep and lambs which are easily extracted, but We allowed those that are joined to their backs or intestines or those fats that are mixed with bone. Those are allowed.

Then, the Almighty states that that prohibition was due to their violations. He said: "We rewarded them for their violations. And We are certainly truthful." That is: forbidding those Jews from ostriches, birds, cows and sheet and these restrictions that We imposed on them was the result of their injustices, violations and trespassing against Allah.

Qatada said: "Allah forbad them these as a punishment, to reprimand and chastise them."

This piece of news concerning this Jewish canon was not known to the Prophet and his people because of their illiteracy, and the Jews used to lie to him claiming that Allah did nor forbid them these things to punish them. For this reason, the Almighty confirmed this information. He said: "We are certainly truthful." That is: We are truthful, Muhammad, in everything with which We informed you: We forbad the Jews certain foods, and they are liars in claiming that they forbad themselves because Israel did so.

However, despite the fact that all fats- except for those that Allah allowed - are forbidden them, they employed fraudulent and dishonest ways to avert Allah's laws; they would liquify those fats and use them in various ways, or they would sell them and use their money to eat and satisfy their other needs. In many Hadiths, the Prophet cursed them for their duplicitous ways to make lawful and permit what Allah had forbidden. Ibn Abbas said: "The Messenger of Allah was sitting behind the Maqam, and he raised his eyes to the sky and said: 'May Allah curse the Jews three times. He forbade them from eating fat, but they sold it and ate its price. Allah has not forbidden a people from eating something without forbidding them its price." [62]

Jabir ibn Abdullah said: "I heard the Messenger of Allah say in the year of the conquest: 'Allah has forbidden the sale of wine, carrion (dead animals), pigs and idols.' It was said: 'O Messenger of Allah: What do you think of the fat of dead animals? Have you seen that they are used to grease hides, coat ships, and people use them for lighting?' He said: 'No. This is forbidden.' Then, the Messenger of Allah said: 'May Allah curse the Jews! When Allah forbade them their fat, they melted it down and ate its price.'" [63]

Then Allah cautioned them against disbelief and aggression. He said: "But if they deny you O Prophet, say, "Your Lord is infinite in mercy, yet His punishment will not be averted from the wicked people." (Al-An'am; Q 6:147) That is, If those Jews and polytheists did not believe what We informed you that We forbade them certain foods as punishment for them, Muhammad, tell them that Allah has infinite and boundless mercy and that He does not rush to judge and punish the disbeliever or chastise the noncompliant. However, those who insist on wrongdoing and persevere in perpetrating wicked deeds will not avoid His punishment.

The noble verse was revealed to upbraid and censure them for their violations and aggression in order to return to the upright and straightforward path if they were people who could comprehend and learn from past lessons.

B) There are noble verses in Sura An-Nisa which also show that Allah forbade the Children of Israel certain foods because of their violations and wrongdoing. The Almighty says: "We forbade the Jews certain foods that had been lawful to them for their wrongdoing, and for hindering many from the Way of Allah, taking interest despite its prohibition, and consuming people's wealth unjustly. We have prepared for the

> disbelievers among them a painful punishment. But those with solid knowledge among them and those with true faith believe in what has been revealed to you O Prophet and what was revealed before you—˹especially˺ those who establish prayer—and those who pay alms-tax and believe in Allah and the Last Day, to these people We will grant a great reward." [64] (An-Nisa; Q 4:160-162)

The Almighty's "We forbade the Jews certain foods that had been lawful to them" (Q 4:160) offers a reason for the punishments that were imposed on them. The noble verse shows that the Almighty has punished the Jews by forbidding certain foods that were lawful to them before on account of grave injustices they committed and atrocious crimes they perpetrated. The previous and following verses detail these injustices for which the Almighty has punished them in this worldly life and in the Hereafter.

Among the violations that the Almighty has mentioned in previous verses are breaking their covenants, disbelieving and denying Allah's signs, killing the prophets unlawfully, hurling outrageous accusations against Mary, and boasting about killing Jesus, as they thought. The punishments that Allah inflicted upon them for these violations and crimes were of two types. Some were in this life and the Noble Qur'an pointed to it this in "We forbade the Jews certain foods that had been lawful to them." The verse in Sura Al-An'am- (Q 6:146) which we have explained previously- talks in detail about the foods that Allah has forbidden them.

The other type of punishment is mentioned in the Noble Qur'an in the Almighty's: "We have prepared for the disbelievers among them a painful punishment." (Q 4:161)

The Almighty's "We forbade the Jews certain foods … for their wrongdoing…etc." (Q 4:160) reflects that it was because of their wrongdoing, not anything else, that Allah prohibited certain things that were lawful and permissible before so that they might return and abandon their evil deeds and relinquish their egotism.

The use of the indefinite طَيِّبَٰتٍ (foods) is an indication that Allah did not deny them ALL foods, but only some as He disclosed in Sura Al-An'am. The verse also impugns them for claiming that Allah did not forbid them anything and that these were prohibited for Noah, Abraham and other prophets.

Then, the Almighty reveals yet another type of their violations after revealing many others before. He said: "and for hindering وَبِصَدِّهِمْ many from the Way of Allah." (Q 4:160)

The word صَدّ means to prevent or hinder. In other words, We have cursed and denounced them and forbade them foods that were lawful before because they did not follow the righteous path and because they hindered and prevented others from the way of Allah. This is also one of the violations that they committed and for which Allah punished them.

Then, the Almighty mentions some of the other reasons which necessitated forbidding them certain foods. He mentions their "taking interest despite its prohibition, and consuming people's wealth unjustly." (Q 4:161) That is, among the reasons why We cursed them and forbade certain foods was taking interest. Even though their prophets prohibited them from doing this, they did not comply with their commandments. They still took interest and used duplicitous and dishonest ways to do this. Another reason for denying them certain foods was their unjust consumption of people's wealth through bribery, treachery, cunning and fraudulence. As the Almighty depicted them in His Book, they are the "devourers of unlawful gains." (Al-Ma'ida: Q 5:42) This is a reference to illicit money. And since they are people who are utterly possessed by their egotism and controlled by their lusts, they indulged in usury and attempted to amass wealth by all possible mean, legally and illegally. Usury was their favorite way of transaction as it is the best method to amass money without toil or the risk of loss. It is a kind of slothfulness that oftentimes leads to betting and gambling. For this reason, these societal vices are often found where usury is used. And wherever Jewish transactions are conducted, there abounds the unjust consumption of people's money; it is not a- give- and- take kind of transaction, no reciprocity or mutual interest. Rather, their transactions are based on monopoly, domination and bribery... whatever they called or however they are described. Dealings without honor, without integrity.

Then Allah shows their reward in the Hereafter. He says: "We have prepared for the disbelievers among them a painful punishment." (Q 4:161) That is, because of their wrongdoing and violations, We have prepared a painful punishment for those disbelievers among the Jews. This is because of their corrupted beliefs and mischievous spirits and their lust to enjoy life's pleasure without heeding Allah's tenets and complying with His commandments and prohibitions.

The Almighty then promises fairness to those who are worthy among them and He brings them good tidings. He says: "But those with solid ٱلرَّٰسِخُونَ knowledge among them and those with true faith believe in what has been revealed to you O Prophet and what was revealed before you—especially those who establish prayer—and those who pay alms-tax and believe in Allah and the Last Day, to these people We will grant a great reward." (Q 4:162)

The word رسوخ means being steadfast, resolute and unwavering. The expression "with solid ٱلرَّٰسِخُونَ knowledge" refers to those who are not affected or influences by suspicions or doubts. Rather, they are steadfast and resolute and discerning. They know the truths and facts behind their knowledge, and they cling and commit wholeheartedly to them. Nothing could shake their firm and solid knowledge, neither doubt nor suspicion or inkling whatsoever.

The meaning of the verse is: Even though those Jews, Muhammad, have committed endless violations and injustices, there are yet those with solid knowledge of religion and comply with its tenets and follow the truth. There are those among them- and others as well- who believe in you. They believe in the Qur'an which was revealed to you. They believe in the Heavenly Books (the correct ones) which were revealed to others before you and which prompt people to establish prayer in awe and reverence, give alms to the needy and destitute, believe in Allah and the Last Day. Such people as these will be granted a great reward that in only known to the All-Knowledgeable.

Thus, these noble verses that Allah has mentioned in His Book have clearly and thoroughly displayed some of the punishments that the Almighty has inflicted upon the Children of Israel because of their violations, injustices and transgression. They also demonstrated fairness and justice to those who are worthy and brought them good tidings of great rewards.

Fourth: Allah's Punishment of the Jews by Transforming Them:

Among the punishments that Allah Almighty has inflicted upon the Jews is transforming them into apes and pigs, cursing them and becoming wrathful with them on account of their transgression, disobeying His commandments, and being consumed by their greed and desires.

The Almighty recounts these punishments in several verses. Among them is His saying in Al-Ma'idah (sura 5): "Say, 'Shall I inform you of [what is] worse than that as penalty from Allah ? [It is that of] those whom Allah has cursed and with whom He became angry and made of them apes and pigs and slaves of Taghut. Those are worse in position and further astray from the sound way. And when they come to you, they say, "We believe." But they have entered with disbelief [in their hearts], and they have certainly left with it. And Allah is most knowing of what they were concealing. And you see many of them hastening into sin and aggression and the devouring of [what is] unlawful. How wretched is what they have been doing. Why do the rabbis and religious scholars not forbid them from saying what is sinful and devouring what is unlawful? How wretched is what they have been practicing." (Q 5:60-63)

The Almighty's "Shall I inform you of [what is] worse than that as penalty from Allah ? [It is that of] those whom Allah," (Q 5:60)is a response to those Jews who came to Mohammad and asked him about the prophets he believes in. He told them, "We believe in Allah Almighty and what was revealed to Abraham, Ishmael, Isaac, Jacob, and the Descendants and what was given to Moses and Jesus and what was given to the prophets from their Lord. We make no distinction between any of them, and we are Muslims (in submission) to Him." (Q 2:136; Q 3:84) When he mentioned Jesus, they denounced His prophecy and said, "we do not believe in Jesus and we do not believe in those who believe in Him. We do not know of a religion that is more evil than your religion. Allah Almighty then revealed "Say, 'O People of the Scripture, do you resent us except [for the fact] that we have believed in Allah and what was revealed to us and what was revealed before and because most of you are defiantly disobedient?' (Q 5:59) Say, 'Shall I inform you of [what is] worse than that as penalty from Allah? [It is that of] those whom Allah has cursed and with whom He became angry and made of them apes and pigs and slaves of Taghut. Those are worse in position and further astray from the sound way.'" (Q5:60) [65]

It is the Jews [66] who have begrudged the believers' entering into the religion of Allah and believed in His prophets without differentiation- who are apparently being addressed here.

The demonstrative ذَٰلِكَ "that" refers to what the Jews begrudge the believers for, which is following the religion of Islam which commands them to believe in Allah and His prophets.

"Mathoba" -from "Thaba," which means 'to return," means a reward. It is generally used for rewarding someone for something good and beneficent. It is used here as "rewarding" or, rather, punishing something that is bad by way of sarcasm and making fun of them. This is similar to the Almighty's "Give them tidings of a painful torture." (See Q 3:21, 3:177, 4:18, 4:138, 9:3, 9:34, etc.)

The meaning is: Mohammad, tell those Jews who have taken Islam lightly and begrudge you for believing in Allah and what has been revealed to you, and what has been revealed before- tell them shall I inform you of far worse for what you begrudge us as a punishment from Allah? Then Allah revealed: "[It is that of] those whom Allah has cursed and with whom He became angry and made of them apes and pigs and slaves of Taghut." This means what is even far more evil than the religion that you begrudge us for is the religion of those whom Allah has cursed and who arose His anger and made of them apes, pigs and slaves of Taghut.

Imam Al-Razi says, "If it is said: those to whom this religion- the religion of Islam- is attributed are destined to an evil (ending), and it is a well- known fact that it is not so, we would say: the judgement of the Jews is in accordance with their sayings and beliefs. They came to the judgement that this religion is evil. In response, it is said (to them): even if this is true, Allah's curse and His wrath and His transforming your appearances is even more evil."

In this honorable verse (Q 5:60), the Almighty attributes despicable characteristics to them:

First, The Almighty cursed them, that is, He alienated them from His mercy and compassion.
Second: He became angry with them, that is, He became indignant and displeased with them on account of their disbelief and their indulgence in sin even after clear signs were made manifest to them.
Third: The Almighty made of them apes and pigs and slaves of Taghut. In other words, He changed some into apes and others into pigs for trespassing and disobeying His commandments.

Some commentators maintain that the Almighty links the people of the Sabbath to apes and those who disbelieved in Jesus' Table- (reference is to the Last Supper)- to pigs. Others say that the transformations occurred to the people of the Sabbath: their (the Jews') youth were reduced into apes, and their elders were reduced into pigs. [67]

The Qur'an supports- along with the majority of exegetes- that they were- in fact- made apes and pigs and then they became extinct since the transformed would not have an offspring.

Abdullah Ibn Mas'ood- may Allah be pleased with him- said, "We asked the Prophet SAW if apes and pigs are descendants of the Jews. He (the Prophet) said, 'Allah has not caused a nation to perish- or, he said, He transforms some and gives them no offspring, and the apes and pigs were there from before.'" [68]
It was said: it was their hearts that were transformed, not that they were transformed into apes. It was a parable that Allah gave them similar to others He has given before such as "Like a donkey carrying books."

Mujaded maintains: "their forms (appearance) were not transformed. Rather, it was their hearts that were transformed; they cannot accept exhortations and instructions nor can they comprehend reproach and rebuke.

The Almighty's "slaves of Taghut" [69] refers to أُوْلَٰئِكَ "them." The meaning is as follows: He made of them slaves of Taghut. "Taghut" is a name for anything that is worshipped, honored or glorified, other than Allah Almighty. It can be an idol, a man, a demon or any other false Allah.

Having mentioned these traits about them, He moves from condemning them for their hatred for Muslims for entering (accepting) Islam into mentioning what is even more despicable and censure provoking, i.e. the attitude of their fathers towards their Prophets and Allah's punishment for them for their immorality and rebellion: He incurred upon them a punishment that was worse that His punishment for the unjust profligates and debauched: He cursed them and became wrathful and made them apes and pigs and slaves of Taghut.

Having described them, the Almighty condemned and allocated them a harsh awful destiny for their departure from the righteous path, the "Right Way." He said: "These are far worse in rank and farther astray from the Right Way." (Q 5:60) That is, those accursed who have been reduced into pigs and apes are assigned a far worse place in this life and in the life to come (the Hereafter) because their abode will be in Hell, while the believers will enjoy Paradise. Those accursed ones who have gone astray have been the most misguided ones and they have departed far away from the upright religion. The use of Al-taf Deel- (=the superlative: the verbal noun in the form ' af'al,' to indicate -usually- that two things share a characteristic, and one of them has more of that characteristic than the other, such as: uglier, more expensive, better, shorter)- in شَرٌّ وَأَضَلُّ far worse in rank and farther astray- is meant to indicate absolute and unquestionable deviation.

Imam Ibn Jarir said: "As for His saying 'These are far worse in rank and farther astray from the Right Way,' the word 'These' refers to those whom He has described, that is, those whom Allah has cursed and with whom Allah has become wrathful and reduced into apes and pigs and slaves of Taghut. All of these are descriptions that apply to the Jews of the Children of Israel. The Almighty says: You Jews who have these descriptions will have the worst place in this world and the Hereafter compared to those you begrudged their faith in Allah. You, Jews, have persisted in pursuing the crooked and unrighteous path, and you have deviated far away from discernment and understanding. Thus, Allah is informing those Jews- whose description was stated in the previous verses- of their wicked deeds and their loathsome moralities and that they have earned His wrath and displeasure because of the abundance of their sins and transgressions to the extent that He transformed some into apes and others into monkeys. Now, He is asking His Prophet, saying: 'Ask them, Muhammad, are those who believe in Allah and His Books, those whom you ridicule and mock evil? Or is it those whom Allah has cursed?' The message is subtly intended for them! [70]

Then, the Noble Qur'an demonstrated some of the vices that made the Jews deserving of this transformation and cursing. The Almighty said: "When they come to you believers they say, "We believe." But they are committed to disbelief when they enter and when they leave. And Allah knows what they hide." (Q 5:61)

Qatada said: "This verse was revealed concerning those Jews who would come to the Prophet and inform him that they had become believers and acknowledge the message he brought while, in reality, they were still committed to disbelief, insisting on their misguidance. The Almighty informed him about their reality and that they leave his assembly as they enter it without learning or keeping anything in their hearts or benefiting from his exhortations, urgings or advice."[71]

The meaning of the noble verse (Q 5:61) is: Those hypocrites come to you, believers, and falsely and deceitfully tell you and your Prophet that they believe that Islam is the upright religion and that Muhammad is a messenger from Allah. In reality, they come to you cloaked in disbelief and they leave your assemblies with hearts that are still filled with disbelief. They leave as they enter not availing themselves of anything they hear, untouched by sermons or exhortations.

"And Allah knows what they hide." (Q 5:61) That is, Allah is aware of their inward thoughts and the cunning and disbelief that they really conceal in their hearts, even if they pretend and appear to be otherwise. When they come to you, they merely want to gather information and spy on you. And when they leave, they say to their evil associates: " 'We are definitely with you; we were only mocking" the believers and their Prophet. (Al-Baqara; Q 2:14)

The significance of the wordقَد in قَد دَّخَلُواْ بِٱلْكُفْرِ وَهُمْ قَدْ خَرَجُواْ بِهِۦ ("When they come to you believers"; Q 5:61) -when mentioning entering those assemblies- is that it denotes that their past or prior duplicity was not that far after all and that the signs of their hypocrisy and deceit were ostensible and clear.

Also, the word هُمْ-when talking about leaving these assemblies- implies confirmation of their disbelief and negates any likelihood that the Prophet had anything to do with them leaving his assemblies in such a loathsome state of disbelief. It is used to emphasize that it was "them" who left with disbelief; it was their very choice.

It was necessary to confirm that this state of disbelief (with which they entered and left) was their own choice in contrast to what was expected and known. It was well, known that those who came to the Prophets assemblies would enjoy peace and serenity and their hearts would be filled with joy for accepting the truth and complying with it. Whenever a man went to the Prophet intending to offend and insult, these intensions soon evaporated when he sat in his presence and listened to his sayings and saw his deeds. His original intensions were replaced by true faith and sincere love because of the virtues, honor and integrity that he had heard and seen.

Those Jews and their likes were different, however. They were not moved or affected by what they heard from the Prophet and his companions. That was essentially because their bad intensions, cunning and denial of the truth prevented them from discernment, learning and understanding. Rather, their bad intensions drove them to treachery and deceitfulness. They did not have the mentality to perceive and discern nor the contrite heart to consider and submit.

Then, the Almighty mentioned some of their other vices and inequities that led them to be reduced and alienated from His mercy. He said: "You see many of them racing towards sin, transgression, and consumption of forbidden gain. Evil indeed are their actions!" (Q 5:62) This means: You see, Muhammad, a lot of those Jews take their religion lightly and frivolously. They rush into perpetrating violations and wrongdoings. They do not hesitate to do what Allah has prohibited them from doing. They rush into transgressing against Allah; they do not make lawful what Allah has made lawful, and they do not prohibit what Allah has prohibited. They rapaciously consume 'forbidden gain,' that is, illicit profit, ant they yearn for it.

The Almighty's "Evil indeed are their actions!" is a denunciation and reproof of their previous deeds. That is, the deeds that those Jews have performed, i.e., rushing into violations and aggressions and consuming forbidden gain are malicious and evil as they defile and desecrate the spirits, vandalize and sabotage society's systems and order, and shakes and threatens the very foundation of a nation.

Then, the Noble Quran mentioned one of the vices of their scholars and rabbis. The Almighty said: "Why do their rabbis and scholars ٱلرَّبَّٰنِيُّونَ وَٱلْأَحْبَارُ not forbid them from saying what is sinful and consuming what is unlawful? Evil indeed is their inaction!" (Q 5:63)

The ٱلرَّبَّٰنِيُّونَ "rabbis" are the scholars who have authority and influence over the Jews, and it was also said that they are the ascetics. The ٱلْأَحْبَار are their jurists.

The meaning is: Did those rabbis and scholars prevent those Jews rushing to violations from committing transgressions and consuming what is unlawful? What an evil thing they did by leaving most of them free to commit violations and consume illicit profits! It was indeed evil to be inactive and fail to encourage what is good and forbid what is evil.

Censuring their scholars was even more poignant and effectively agonizing than what was said concerning the majority before. The Almighty rebuked the majority of the Jews saying: "لَبِئْسَ مَا كَانُوا يَعْمَلُونَ/Evil indeed are their actions!" And He rebuked their rabbis and scholars saying: "لَبِئْسَ مَا كَانُوا يَصْنَعُونَ/Evil indeed is their inaction!" The word الصنع/make is stronger and more poignant than العمل/ work because العمل/work is not to considered الصنعmake unless it becomes fixed and stable and controlling. So, the Almighty made the offense of the workers unsticking, not deeply-rooted, while He regarded the offense of those who were inactive- permitting violations to continue to spread unchecked- as a fixed sin, a deeply rooted violation.

Among the Qur'anic verses that stated transforming the Jews into apes and monkeys are: "You are already aware of those of you who broke the Sabbath. We said to them, 'Be disgraced apes!'" (Al-Baqara; Q 2:65) and His saying: "But when they stubbornly persisted in violation, We said to them, "Be disgraced apes!" (Al-A'raf; Q 7:166)

So far, these noble verses that we have examined mentioned some of the punishments that Allah inflicted upon the Jews: He cursed them, He was indignant and wrathful with them, and He reduced them to monkeys and pigs. All of this was because of going beyond their limits and encroaching against Him, rushing into violations and wrongdoing, the inactivity of their rabbis and scholars and their neglecting to warn them against their encroachments.

Fifth: They earned Allah's wrath and condemnation; He cursed them:

In many of the verses of His Noble Book, the Almighty stated that the Children of Israel have earned His wrath and censure because of their disbelief and violations, their failure to encourage what is good and forbid what is evil and committing other offenses and wrongdoings that would destine their perpetrators to disgrace and loss in this world and in the Hereafter. Among the verses that stated Allah's cursing and condemnation of the Children of Israel are:

"The disbelievers among the Children of Israel were condemned in the revelations of David and Jesus, son of Mary. That was for their disobedience and violations. They did not forbid one another from doing evil. Evil indeed was what they did! You see many of them taking the disbelievers as allies. Truly wicked are their misdeeds, which have earned them Allah's wrath. And they will be in everlasting torment. Had they believed in Allah, the Prophet, and what has been revealed to him, they would have never taken those ⸢pagans⸣ as allies. But most of them are rebellious." [72] (Al-Ma'idah; Q 5:78-80)

The Almighty's "The disbelievers among the Children of Israel were condemned in the revelations of David and Jesus, son of Mary" (Q 5:78) is a statement of the curse/condemnation that was pronounced against the Children of Israel by two of Allah's honorable prophets.

Condemnation/cursing اللعن entails alienating and driving away as an indication of resentment and aggravation. This is Allah's punishment in the Hereafter. In this worldly life, His punishment is denying His mercy and granting success. To people, اللعن (cursing) is wishing harm to someone else." [73]

Ibn Abbas said: "They were cursed by every tongue. They were cursed during Moses' time in the Torah. They were cursed during David's time in the Book of Psalms. They were also cursed in the Gospel during Jesus' time, and they were cursed during Muhammad's time in the Qur'an." [74]

Imam Al-Razi said: "Considering the word 'curse,' most exegetes refer to the Sabbath Breakers or the People of the Table (that spread with food from heaven sent down to Jesus). As for the Sabbath Breakers, those were David's people – the people of Ayla- who violated the sabbath by hunting whales/large fish and not complying with Allah's commandments as mentioned in Sura Al-A'raf (Q 7:162-167). David said: 'Allah curse them and make them an example,' and they were reduced into apes. As for the People of the Table, when they ate from the Table and did not believe, Jesus said: 'Allah curse them as you cursed the Sabbath Breakers,' and they were transformed into pigs." [75]

That curse continued to plague them afterwards because of their perseverance in the paths of transgressions and violations.

Then, the Almighty showed the reason for cursing them. He said: "That was for their disobedience and violations." (Q 5:78) That is, this severe admonition and stern condemnation that were inflicted upon them was on account of their disobedience, their continuous noncompliance with His commandments, their violations and for doing what they were prohibited from doing.

Then, the Almighty showed another one of their vices for which they were condemned and cursed. He said: "They did not forbid one another from doing evil. Evil indeed was what they did." (Q 5:79) In other words, those Jews whom Allah cursed did not forbid one another from wrongdoing and indulging in the sins and violations they committed. What an evil thing it was to commit such sins and perpetrate these violations abandoning encouraging what is good and forbidding what is evil.

Al-Zamakhshari said: "If you say: 'How could not forbidding one another from doing evil be interpreted as violation and disobedience?' I will respond by saying: 'Since Allah commanded us to forbid one another from doing evil, non-compliance with such a command is considered a violation. Forbidding one another from doing evil is a definite way to end corruption. Not doing so would lead to the opposite consequence.' Now, if you say: 'What is the meaning of describing the evil with فعلوه (something they did), and not do the forbidding after the act?' I would say: 'It means that they do not forbid one another from repeating an evil act they have done or wanted to do, just as when you see the signs to pursue an evil act underway, and all the components of the evil act in place, so there is no denying or stopping it. It may also be feasible to suggest that they do not end, stop or prevent themselves from an evil act they did; rather, they indulge in and insist on doing it.'" [76]

The history of the Children of Israel abounds with violations and disobedience in various shapes and forms. These violations and wrongdoings were not individual actions; rather, they characterized the whole society, and their occurrence have become common and familiar. No one can deny these violations, and no one tries to eradicate them. When a nation descends to such a low stage, when evil is perpetrated by the old and the young, and when no one tries to change this with his hand (by force), tongue (speech) or heart, such a nation is destined to collapse and become annihilated, one deserving of punishment in this world and in the Hereafter.

A virtuous upright society, on the other hand, is one that encourages what is good and righteous and forbids what is bad and ungodly. In such a society, there are who are clothed with such virtues. Their unwavering faith, strong morals and convictions, sound judgement and discernment drive them to openly proclaim these virtues fearing nobody except Allah. In such a virtuous society, there are also those who are desirous and eager to listen with conviction and approval. Such willing listeners are the bulwark, the defenders of those counsellors and advisors ready to guard and push away any harm from them in order to be able to relay Allah's messages.

These characteristics have been missing in the Israeli society. For this reason, Allah descended His wrath and displeasure on its individuals. The Prophet stated this in many Hadiths. Abou Daoud narrated on the authority of Abdullah bin Mas'ud, he said: "The first defect (in religion) that affected the Children of Israel in the way that a man would meet another man and say to him: 'Fear Allah and abstain from what you are doing! This is not lawful.' Then, he would meet him the following day and find him the same way with no changes. However, that would not prevent him from eating with him, drinking with him, and sitting in his assemblies. When it came to this, Allah led their hearts into evil ways on account of their association with others.' Then, he recited 'The disbelievers among the Children of Israel were condemned in the revelations of David and Jesus, son of Mary. That was for their disobedience and violations. They did not forbid one another from doing evil. Evil indeed was what they did!'" (Q 5:78-79)

Then, the Prophet said: "Nay, by Allah, you either enjoin good and forbid evil and catch hold of the hand of the oppressor and persuade him to act justly and stick to the truth, or Allah will involve the hearts of some of you with the hearts of others and will curse you as He had cursed them." [77]

Then, the Almighty showed how they had allied themselves with the disbelievers against the Muslims. The Almighty said: "You see many of them taking the disbelievers[1] as allies. Truly wicked are their misdeeds, which have earned them Allah's wrath. And they will be in everlasting torment. Had they believed in Allah, the Prophet, and what has been revealed to him, they would have never taken those ⸢pagans⸣ as allies. But most of them are rebellious." (Q 5:80-81)

The meaning is: You see, Muhammad! A lot of those Jews whom Allah has cursed and condemned take the disbelievers, the idol worshippers, as their allies. They instigate them to fight against you. They have earned My wrath and My displeasure for the wickedness of their deeds. On Judgement Day, they will be tormented forever. Had those Jews who sided with the disbelievers believed in Allah and Moses, His prophet, whom they claim they follow and believe in the Torah that was revealed to him, they would not have taken them as allies. Believing in Allah, His prophet and His Books should have prevented them from allying themselves with the polytheists. However, most of them are rebellious violators, unwilling to obey Allah, His messengers and His Books. They oppose His revelations.

And there are numerous noble verses that state the condemnation of the Children of Israel and earning Allah's wrath because of their immoralities and decadences.

1- In Sura Al-Baqara, the Almighty said:
"Miserable is the price they have sold their souls for—denying Allah's revelation and resenting Allah for granting His grace to whoever He wills of His servants! They have earned wrath upon wrath. And such disbelievers will suffer a humiliating punishment." (Al-Baqara: Q 2:90)

2- In Sura An-Nisa, the Almighty said:
"Have you O Prophet not seen those who were given a portion of the Scriptures yet believe in idols and false Allahs and reassure the disbelievers that they are better guided than the believers?" (An-Nisa: Q 4:51)

3- Also, in Sura An-Nisa, the Almighty said:
"Some Jews take words out of context and say, "We listen and we disobey," "Hear! May you never hear," and "Râ'ina!" [Herd us!]—playing with words and discrediting the faith. Had they said ˹courteously˺, "We hear and obey," "Listen to us," and "Unẓurna," [Tend to us!] it would have been better for them and more proper. Allah has condemned them for their disbelief, so they do not believe except for a few." (An-Nisa: Q 4:46)

4- And in Sura Al-Ma'idah, the Almighty said:
"But for breaking their covenant We condemned them and hardened their hearts. They distorted the words of the Scripture and neglected a portion of what they had been commanded to uphold." (Al-Ma'idah; Q 5:13)

There are many other noble verses that have clearly stated Allah's wrath and condemnation has descended upon them for breaching their covenants, abstaining from forbidding one another from wrongdoing, distorting the words of the Scripture, indulging in depravities and decadence and ever trespassing beyond bounds. "Allah never wronged them, but they wronged themselves." (Al-Imran: Q 3:117)

Sixth: They were stricken with disgrace and misery.

Allah extolled the Islamic nation as the best community that was ever raised for humanity. He attributed many honorable traits that made it worthy of such praise and high status.

They are an upright community, one that enjoins what is good and virtuous and forbids what is bad and ungodly. They believe in Allah. He censured and condemned the Jews and ascribed the worst descriptions to them. He warned them of a severe and terrible punishment. He struck them with disgrace and humiliation for disbelieving His signs, killing the prophets and trespassing beyond bounds. In Sura Al-Imran, the Almighty said:

"You are the best community ever raised for humanity—you encourage good, forbid evil, and believe in Allah. Had the People of the Book believed, it would have been better for them. Some of them are faithful, but most are rebellious. They can never inflict harm on you, except a little annoyance. But if they meet you in battle, they will flee and they will have no helpers. They will be stricken with disgrace wherever they go, unless they are protected by a covenant with Allah or a treaty with the people. They have invited the displeasure of Allah and have been branded with misery for rejecting Allah's revelations and murdering His prophets unjustly. This is a fair reward for their disobedience and violations." [78] (Al-Imran; Q 3:110-112)

The word "كان kana" in the noble verse may be understood as denoting a complete verb (which requires only the nominative) denoting "it happened." In other words, it means it was "found" that you are the best community ever raised for humanity. It might also be "كان/Kaan," the incomplete (that should take both the nominative and the accusative). In this case, it means: you were regarded in Allah's eyes as the best community ever raised for humanity. [79]

The words of this noble verse are addressed to the believers who were contemporaneous to the Prophet as well as those who have come after them and followed the teachings of Islam until the Day of Judgement. For this reason, Ibn Kathir said: "It is correct to suggest that this verse is a general one directed to all the nation, according to each century. Their best century was when the Messenger of Allah was sent, then those who followed him and then those who followed them. As the almighty said in another verse: "And so We have made you ˹believers˺ an upright community so that you may be witnesses over humanity and that the Messenger may be a witness over you." [80] (Al-Baqara; Q 2:143)

Numerous Hadiths that mention the virtues of the Islamic community have been recounted. Among these are what is narrated by Imam Ahmad, At-Tirmidhi, Ibn Magha on the authority of Mo'awyya ibn Hedah, who said that the Messenger of Allah said: "You are best among seventy nations and most generous to your Allah." [81]

The Almighty then reveals why the Islamic community is the best one ever raised for humanity. He said: "you encourage good, forbid evil, and believe in Allah." (Q 3:110)

The meaning is: You were found to be the best community that Allah has ever raised for humanity because "you encourage good" through your decent words and pleasant and favorable deeds, and you "forbid evil," that is, you shun every evil word or action that religions find unacceptable and believers find loathsome. You also "believe in Allah," that is, you trust Allah and faithfully worship Him Alone. So, the description of the Islamic community as being the best nation is contingent upon fulfilling two elements:

First: Encouraging good and forbidding evil for these are the bulwarks, the fortifications of religion. No nation can be solidly established on virtue and righteousness except by embracing them. The Children of Israel were deserving of condemnation because they abandoned them.

Second: Believing in Allah. This belief cannot be realized unless accompanied with belief in Allah's messengers, His Books and the Last Day. Otherwise, it would not be true belief in Allah. Goodness cannot be applied to those who are deficient in one of these two elements. A nation that neglects to encourage what is good, abstains from forbidding what is bad and does not believe in Allah cannot be a good virtuous nation. It can hardly be described as such; there is no goodness except in virtues, justice and the truth. And these are only possible with the existence of faith in Allah as well as the existence of a large number of people supplicating that goodness prevail and evil desist. These supplications and pleas would have a powerful impact to ascertain that virtues prevail and vices disappear. It is as though the Almighty mentions "belief in Allah" after "encouraging good and forbidding evil" to prompt people to strive for these virtues since their burdens and costs are only bearable by those who believe and seek Allah's face and faithfully and laboriously strive to reach Him. This belief in Allah is the incentive- for those who encourage what is good and prohibit what is bad- to proclaim Allah's messages with courage and without fear or trepidation.

Then, the Almighty encouraged the People of the Scripture to believe in His Messenger. He said: "Had the People of the Book believed, it would have been better for them." (Q 3:110)

That is: Had the People of the Scripture believed in Muhammad and what he brought from Allah, and had the abandoned their arrogance and obstinacy, it would have been better for them in this world and in the Hereafter. They would have been accredited that trait of "goodness" that the Islamic community has attained. But they did not believe, and they were denied this status for their lack of true and upright faith and for exchanging what is better and sublime for what is worse and worthless.

Then the Almighty mentioned that some of the People of the Scripture chose belief over disbelief. He said: "Some of them are faithful, but most are rebellious." (Q 3:110)

That is: Among the People of the Scripture, there is a group who believed in Allah and Muhammad, His Messenger, and embraced the truth he brought. However, the majority of the People of the Book are refused to believe in Allah and His honorable Messenger. They are resistant to the truth, defiant and insisting on disbelief.

So, the noble verse gives justice to the few of the People pf the Book who believed like Abdullah Ibn Salaam and others who entered into Islam and embraced it. It also censures the majority of the People of the Scripture who denounced the truth and deviated from the straight path.

The Almighty then informed the believers the good news that this corrupt majority of the People of the Book that disobeyed Allah's commandments and displayed hostility towards the believers will not inflict any major harms on them, only a little annoyance. The Almighty said: "They can never inflict harm on you, except a little annoyance." (Q 3:111) That is, they will only annoy you a little like say bad things and try to sow doubt between you to divert the shaky from the truth. This further assures the believers because there are two categories for harm:

First: It can destroy the very fabric of the society, weaken its strength, violate its dignity when matters fall into the enemy's hands and they are free to do whatever they please.

Second: Harm that does not affect the society or lead to its collapse or annihilation. Hurtful offensive speech or trying to shake the faith of the weak unsteady believers fall into this such a category. The Almighty assured the believers that the Jews would not inflict this kind of harm on them. He said: "They can never inflict harm on you لَن يَضُرُّوكُمْ إِلَّآ أَذًى, except a little annoyance." (Q 3:111) He uses the present tense with لَن (an article that is used to negate the future) to indicate that that will not happen in the future.

However, the unlikelihood of this kind of harm to occur is contingent upon the Islamic community's adhering to the two important basic principles (mentioned earlier): belief in Allah and offering pleas and supplications for goodness and virtue to prevail. So, if the Muslim community does not want to be afflicted by any harms from the Jews, it must faithfully and loyally worship its Lord, embrace the Sunna (teachings) of its Prophet, abide by the tenets of its Book, and be well prepared to fight Allah's enemy and their own. If the Muslim community does not do this, their enemy will inflict harm upon it, its very foundation would be shaken and its enemy would be become enabled to do what they please.

Then, the Almighty gave the believers the good tidings of victory if their enemies and those like them fight against them. He said: "But if they meet you in battle, they will flee and they will have no helpers." (Q 3:111)

"يُوَلُّوكُمُ ٱلْأَدْبَارَ" is a euphemism for defeat: "They will flee" because the defeated is known to turn their back towards the victorious in order to flee into a safe resort to avoid death or captivity.

The meaning is: Those Jews and those who allied themselves with them will not be able to harm you, believers. They may just annoy you a little but in a way that would not affect you as long as you cling to your religion. So, if they fight against you and you hold fast to your religion, Allah will grant you victory over them. He would cast terror in their hearts, and they will flee in defeat. They will have no supporters as long as you remain loyal and obedient to the commandments of your Allah, and as long as they persist on their rebellion and wrongdoing. Allah is committed to defend those who obey Him.

The use of ثُمَّ in ثُمَّ لَا يُنصَرُونَ "they will have no helpers" (Q 3:111) indicates laxity in rank of importance since being informed that their enemies are doomed to defeat is greater than being informed that they will flee.

Al-Zamakhshari has aptly and most fittingly explained this meaning. He said: "If it is said: 'Why not the jussive (the Majzoum case المجزوم) in ثُمَّ لَا يُنصَرُونَ 'they will have no helpers?' I would say: 'It was meant to postpone the ruling of the reward to inform them of the good news first. It is used to emphasize that He informed you that they will be defeated.' Now, if it is said: 'What is the difference in meaning between the nominative case (Marfoo'/المرفوع) and the Jussive case (Majzoum/المجزوم)?' I would say: 'If it were in the Majzoum caseالمجزوم , negating (denying) the victory of the enemy would have been conditioned by fighting in order for them to flee. However, using the nominative case (Marfoo'/المرفوع) assured an absolute promise of denying the enemy's victory. It was to ascertain that He said that their story and state with which He informed you after fleeing was that they would be helpless, powerless and defeated. They would never be able to rise or stand again. It was just as He informed them about the conditions of Banu Qurayza, Banu Nadir, Banu Qaynuqa and the Jews of Khaybar.' If you said: 'What was subordinated to declaring the news?' I would say: 'The conditional statement and the reward. It was as if it was said: I inform you that if they fought against you, they would be defeated, and I inform you that they will have no helpers.'" [82]

This noble verse (Q 3:111) brought the faithful believers three good predictions:

First: They were safe and protected against severe harm from the Jews, one that would affect their being, their pride or their dignity.

Second: If the People of the Scripture were to fight against them, the believers would be victorious.

Third: After their victory over them, the People of the Book, especially the Jews, would have no ability or power to avenge themselves.

All these predictions came to pass. Just as the Almighty informed them, the early Muslims who clung fervently and wholeheartedly to their faith fought against the Jews of Banu Qaynuqa, Banu Qurayza, the Jews of Khaybar and others. They gained victory over them, and the Jews turned their backs towards the Muslims and fled. Allah destined one group to evacuate and depart, another group was annihilated and destroyed and a third stayed but in submission and humiliation.

If someone said: "But what we witness now is that the Jews- whom no one suspects are cowards and eager for prolonged lives- have triumphed over the Muslims and established a state in one of the most precious of all the Islamic countries, Palestine. Has Allah forsaken His promise?"

The answer is: Allah's promise has not- nor will it ever be- changed or forsaken. The Almighty fulfilled this promise for our righteous predecessors who truly and devotedly believed in Him, those who enjoined what is good and forbade what is evil. However, it is the Muslims of this generation that have changed. They have neglected their religion, they do not establish prayers, they have indulged in lusts desires, they have followed Satan's footsteps, they have become divided to parties and sects, they have stopped encouraging what is righteous and good, they have abstained from forbidding what is bad and ungodly, they have not been harsh enough on the infidels nor merciful enough among each other, they have not adequately prepared themselves to fight against Allah's enemy and their own as were their predecessors, and they have not adequately shouldered the responsibility as mandated by the teachings and instructions of Islam. Because of this, their state has changed from good to evil, and Allah sent against them (the Muslims) those who neither fear them nor show them mercy because "Indeed, Allah would never change a people's state of favor until they change their own state of faith." (Ar-Ra'd; Q 13:11) When the Muslims return to their religion and thoroughly apply its commandments and prohibitions on themselves, Allah will restore their dignity and self-esteem. "Allah will certainly help those who stand up for Him. Allah is truly All-Powerful, Almighty." (Al-Hajj; Q 22:40)

From this we realize that stopping the harm that could affect the Islamic community is contingent upon its firm and steadfast belief in its Allah and its commitment to follow the teachings and guidance of His Messenger.

Then, the Almighty showed some of the punishments that He inflicted upon the Jews. He said: "They will be stricken with disgrace wherever they go, unless they are protected by a covenant with Allah or a treaty with the people." (Q 3:112)

The word الذلة means disgrace, ignominy and humiliation. They are surrounded and utterly wrapped in it.

And the word حبل is a reference to the 'rope' that links two things. It is used in the sense of a covenant because people are connected and associated together by covenants just as tangible connections can take place by means of a rope.

Imam Ibn Jarir said: "The 'rope/ covenant' that Allah mentions in this place is the reason why they, their children and possessions are protected from the believers. That was the covenant offered them before they went into the Islamic countries." [83]

The meaning is: Those Jews have been besieged by disgrace in all aspects and wherever they exist or go except when they are protected by a covenant with Allah or a treaty with the people.

Interpreters explain that "a covenant with Allah" is a reference to the Jizya (الجزية= a type of taxation historically levied on non-Muslim subjects of a state governed by Islamic law), which links them to the Muslims. They say that levying the Jizya was a covenant with them from Allah, that Allah established it, and it was therefore necessary to keep and fulfill such a pledge. It was also a covenant from the Muslims since they represent one of the two parties (in the equation). They were the ones who implemented it with the Jews.

According to this covenant, the Muslims protect their rights, lives and possessions. Also, they have the same rights and duties just like the Muslims. The Muslims protect them and their possessions in return for a sum of money, called the Jizya, which is paid every year.

"A treaty with the people" is the pledges or agreements that they have with any nation they live in, Muslim or infidels. If these treaties are issued by Muslims, they can also be called "covenants with Allah," since it is Allah who has allowed them. If they are issued by non-Muslims, they are only treaties with people, whether or not they are in agreement with Allah's law.

The overall meaning of the verse is: Allah has stricken the Jews with disgrace and misery everywhere they go, everywhere and at all times because of their disbelief and rebellion. Their ability to self-determination and governance have been stripped from them; they live all over the land in the protection of other nations and according to treaties that they have with these nations.

Someone may say: They now have status, prestige and authority after they have been able to acquire international recognition by establishing the State of Israel.

The response to this is: Even though this State has been established, they still live under the protection of the other infidel world powers. These are the countries that protect them and provide the means for them to survive and become strong. This is also a case to which the phrase "A treaty with the people" is applicable. The Jews have no power or authority; neither do they have self-esteem. They are commanded and controlled, harnessed to live in that part of the land to be the center, or springboard for these nations- that provide them with protection- to attack and fight the Muslims if the chance offered itself to them. If the Muslims changed their own state of faith, held tight to their faith, united and with common goals, these countries and those that protect them would be in fear and terror of the Muslims. We have great hope in Allah that the Muslims would become vigilant and aware of the dangers that surround them and push them away. We have great hope that they will hold firmly together to the rope of Allah to regain their strength and prestige.

Then, the Almighty displayed two more punishments that He inflicted upon them for their disbelief and trespassing beyond bounds against Him. He said: "They have invited the displeasure of Allah and have been branded with misery وباءوا بِغَضَبٍ مِّنَ ٱللَّهِ وَضُرِبَتْ عَلَيْهِمُ المسكنة "

"باءوا" is taken from البواء which means become deserving of or equal to. This means that they became deserving, or they earned- His displeasure.

"المسكنة" has the pattern of 'maf'ala' indicating silence because a poor, miserable and despondent person is usually inactive because of his psychological condition. "المسكنة," then, reflects a person's psychological state which demoralizes and dispirits him causing a state of inactivity, helplessness and dejection regardless of wealth or physical strength.

The meaning is: In addition to being struck with disgrace wherever they went, they have also earned Allah's wrath and became deserving of His anger. They have also been stricken with misery which causes them to feel small and demoralized regardless of their physical strength and wealth.

Then, the Almighty mentioned the reasons that made worthy of these punishments. They were, He said: "for rejecting Allah's revelations and murdering His prophets unjustly. This is a fair reward for their disobedience and violations..." (Q 3:112) That is, their continuous defeats, being struck with Allah's wrath and misery, becoming the object of His anger and denunciation- all these and other punishments are because of their rejection of Our revelations, killing Our prophets deliberately, insisting on their wrongdoing. They would not have had the audacity to perpetrate these violations had they not relished and enjoyed committing these transgressions and gotten used to aggression and wrongdoing. It is easy for those with such proclivities to commit all kinds of offenses and crimes and, consequently, become deserving of Allah's most severe punishments. This is what has become of the Children of Israel.

Imam Ibn Jarir said: "Allah informed His servants what He has done to the People of the Book, i.e., striking them with disgrace and misery in this world in addition to the severe and painful punishment He has kept in store for them in the Hereafter because they have transgressed against Him beyond bounds and made permissible what He has prohibited. He is cautioning them to return and repent. He is also cautioning our nation not to adopt their ways or follow in their footsteps and conduct ourselves as they did. Otherwise, Allah's wrath and displeasure is our lot." [84]

So far, we have mentioned some of the punishments that Allah inflicted upon the Children of Israel on account of their disbelief, injustices, violations and rejection of Allah's commandments. "The evildoers certainly did not wrong Us, but wronged themselves." (Q 2:57)

References

---

[1] Verses 167- 168.
[2] Samaria is modern day Nablus.
[3] "Judaism" by Dr. Ahmad Al-Shalabi, P. 93.
[4] "The History of the Israelites" by Shaheen Macarius, P. 70 (margin), 1904.
[5] "World Judaism" by Abdullah Al-Tal, P. 36.
[6] "The History of the Israelites" by Shaheen Macarius, 1904.
[7] Sermons and Considerations in Mentioning Plans and Monuments, by Al-Maqrizi, Vol. 4, P. 392.
[8] Sura Al-Rum (sura 30): Verses 2-5.
[9] The story of beliefs between heaven and earth" by Suleiman Madhar, P.318. Taken from "The History of the Arabs before Islam" by Gawad Ali, Vol. 6, P. 95.
[10] Sahih Al-Bukhari: "Expelling the Jews," Vol. 4, P. 120.

[11] "The History of the Israelites" by Shaheen Macarius, P.83.
[12] "The Danger of World Judaism on Islam and Christianity" by Abdullah Al-Tal, P. 118.
[13] "The History of the Israelites," P. 88.
[14] "Judaism" by Dr. Ahmad Al-Shalabi, P 73.
[15] "Jewish Question" by Carl Marx, translation by Muhammad Etani, P. 55.
[16] "World Judaism and its Constant War against Christianity" by Elia Abou Al-Rous, P. 130.
[17] الستار الحديدي حول امريكا/ "The Iron Curtain Around America" from "That is why I hate Israel , P. 183.
[18] We interpreted this noble verse in Chapter" The Jews' False Claims and the Qur'an's Response."
[19] "World Judaism" by Abas Mahmoud Al-Aqqad, P. 44.
[20] "Judaism" by Dr. Ahmad Al-Shalabi, P. 33.
[21] From a printed lecture on "The Jews and the State of Israel."
[22] "Mein Kampf" by Adolf Hitler.
[23] Deuteronomy, Chapter 20: 10-17.
[24] "The State of Terrorism" by Ali Muhammad Ali, P. 39.
[25] "Palestine: Our Country" by Mustafa Murad Al-Dabaagh, Vol. 1, P. 657. Al-Talee'a Printing Press: Beirut 1965.
[26] Sura Al-Isra: Verses: 4-8.
[27] Suliman was born in Jerusalem in 1033 BCE. He died in 975 BCE, approximately.
[28] "The History of the Israelites" by Shaheen Macarius, P. 23.
[29] Sura Ghafir: Verse 51.
[30] وعد الآخرة the reference is to the punishment for the second violation. It means: When the second punishment befall you, We will send the mighty men to humiliate and dishonor you. This is a continuation of verse 5 (Al-Isra) فَإِذَا جَآءَ وَعْدُ أُولَىٰهُمَا which refers to the first of the two warnings.
[31] Al-Razi's Interpretation, Vol. 2, P. 159.
[32] Interpretation of the Ocean by Abu Hayyan Al-Andalusi, Vol. 6, P. 9.
[33] The meaning is God informed them that they will cause corruption twice. The structure is similar to the Almighty's "And We warned the Children of Israel in the Scripture, "You will certainly cause corruption in the land twice."
[34] Ibn Jarir's Interpretation, Vol. 15, P. 17.
[35] Ibn Jarir's Interpretation, Vol. 15, P. 22.
[36] Ad-Durr Al-Manthur by Al-Suyuti, Vol. 4, P. 163.
[37] Ad-Durr Al-Manthur by Al-Suyuti, Vol. 4, P. 165.
[38] Ad-Durr Al-Manthur by Al-Suyuti, Vol. 4, P. 163.
[39] Ad-Durr Al-Manthur by Al-Suyuti, Vol. 4, P. 163.
[40] Ibn Kathir's Interpretation, Vol. 1, P. 35.
[41] Imam Al-Razi's Interpretation, Vol. 20, P. 156.
[42] Interpretation of the Ocean by Abu Hayyan Al-Andalusi, Vol. 6, P. 9.
[43] Al-Alusi Interpretation Book, "The Spirit of Meanings," Vol. 2, P. 141.
[44] Jesus' condemnation is reported in Sura Al-Ma'idah: "The disbelievers among the Children of Israel were condemned in the revelations of David and Jesus, son of Mary. That was for their disobedience and violations. They did not forbid one another from doing evil. Evil indeed was what they did!" (Al-Ma'idah: 78-79)

[45] "The History of the Israelites," P. 76.
[46] From an article by Mr. Omar Tala't Zahran titled "The destruction of Jerusalem" published in Al-Azhar Magazine, Vol. 21, P. 47.
[47] "The History of the Israelites" by Shaheen Macarius, P.77.
[48] Sura Gafer: Verse 51.
[49] Sura Ar-Ra'd: verse 11.
[50] The writer of the article is the honorable Sheikh Abdul-Mu'iz Abdul Sattar. The title of the article is: "The Sura of Al-Isra talks about the End of Israel." It was published in Al-Azhar Magazine, Vol. 28, P. 689.
[51] Review what we wrote when we interpreted the Almighty's "And ˹remember, O Prophet, ˺ when your Lord declared that He would send against them others who would make them suffer terribly until the Day of Judgment" (Al-A'raf: 167)
[52] Ibn Jarir Interpretation, Vol. 15, P. 27.
[53] Al-Kashaf Interpretation, Vol. 2, P. 181.
[54] Al-Razi Interpretation, Vol.5, P. 382.
[55] Lisan Al-Arab, Vol.25, P. 43, Beirut Edition.
[56] Asas al-Balagha by Al-Zamakhshari, Vol. 1, P. 141. Dar al-Kutub Printing Press, 1922.
[57] Al-Kashaf Interpretation, Vol. 2, P. 966. Dar Al-Kitaab Al-Arabi, Beirut.
[58] Al-Razi Interpretation, Vol.5, P. 453.
[59] Verses: 146-147.
[60] Al-Razi Interpretation, Vol.3, P. 16.
[61] Ibn Jarir Interpretation, Vol. 8, P. 75.
[62] Ibn Kathir Interpretation, Vol. 2, P. 185.
[63] Ibn Kathir Interpretation, Vol. 2, P. 185.
[64] Verses: 160-162.
[65] Al-Alusi Interpretation. Vol. 6, P. 156.
[66] It was said: the infidels. It was said to the believers.
[67] Al-Razi Interpretation, Vol.12, P. 36.
[68] Ibn Kathir Interpretation, Vol. 2, P. 73.
[69] The Almighty's "slaves of Taghut" has various interpretations. Hamza reads it as 'a sea of Taghut' meaning they were made to be a whole nation, not a sole individual, as slaves. Abi reads it as 'they worshipped Taghut.' There are other interpretations by Al-Zamachshari, Al-Razi and others.
[70]Ibn Jarir Interpretation, Vol. 6, P. 295.
[71] Al-Razi Interpretation, Vol.12, P. 38.
[72] Sura Al-Ma'idah, Verses: 79-82
[73] Mufradaat Al-Raghib Al-Asfahani, P. 451.
[74] Ibn Jarir Interpretation, Vol. 6, P. 317.
[75] Al-Razi Interpretation, Vol.12, P. 63.
[76] Al-Kashaf Interpretation, Vol. 1, P. 430.
[77] Riyad Al-Saleheen, by Al-Nouri, Chapter: "Enjoining Good and Forbidding Evil," P. 92.
[78] Verses from 110-112.
[79] It might also be used to mean "become," that is, you believers who came from pre-Islamic times and were contemporaneous with the Prophet have 'become' the best community ever raised. It might also be redundant; in this case, it means: you ARE the

best community ever raised. Other interpretations were also stated. However, what we mentioned in examining the verse is what is most commonly believed by the exegetes.

[80] Ibn Kathir Interpretation, Vol. 1, P. 391.

[81] Ibn Kathir Interpretation, Vol. 1, P. 391.

[82] Al-Kashaf Interpretation, Vol. 1, P. 320.

[83] Ibn Jarir Interpretation, Vol. 2, P. 48.

[84] Ibn Jarir Interpretation, Vol. 4, P. 51.

Conclusion

Palestine And The Various Stages Of The Zionist Invasion

This Chapter with which we conclude our dissertation on The Children of Israel in the Qur'an and the Sunna deals with a topic on which hundreds of books, articles and research have been written especially after the establishment of the State of Israel in 1948. Because of the numerous books and research articles the I perused on this topic, I wonder where to start. How can I extract from these countless books and research what might give the reader a clear, condensed and concise idea about the various stages of the Jewish invasion of Palestine.

Most of my investigation concerning the Children of Israel in the previous chapters focused on expounding the noble verses that mention them in the Qur'an and examining their actions during the Prophet's era in relation to their betrayals, conspiracies and violations that led each group of them to the punishments which they deserved.

My study in this brief chapter will essentially be a historic investigation to complete what I mentioned concerning their history and conditions in the first Chapter. My goal is to help reveal the crooked methods and the various conspiracies that World Judaism has played throughout the ages until it was able to establish a state in Palestine, in the heart (center) of the Islamic World, in 1948, after killing thousands of its children and displacing hundreds of thousands of its Muslim inhabitants.

My study in this chapter will include the following:

A) A brief summary about the history of Palestine since the Islamic Conquest in 15 H (636 AD) and up to 1367 H (1948 AD).
B) Judaism and Zionism and the steps they took to establish a state for them in Palestine.
C) The stage of dreams and wishful thinking to establish the State of Israel. This stage extends from the first destruction of Jerusalem in 586 AD until the end of the Nineteenth Century.
D) The stage of practical planning and actual preparation to declare the establishment of the State of Israel. This stage extends from 1897 AD to 1948 AD.
E) The stage of declaring the establishment of the State of Israel and the consequent hopes of the Jews.
F) What are the main reasons for the tragedy of Palestine, and how can we restore it?

We will now elaborate in detail each one of these points:

A) History of Palestine:

In the year 15 H (Hijra), Jerusalem was conquered. After the Muslims conquered Damascus, they directed some of their warriors commanded by Abu Obayda A'mer bin Al-Jaraah to Palestine. They were able to occupy a number of its cities. They continued marching until they reached Elia' (Jerusalem). There, a fierce war ensued between the Muslims and the Romans who ferociously tried to defend Jerusalem. However, the Romans' enormous efforts were in vain as they were forced in the end to surrender on the condition that the Commander of the Faithful himself would negotiate its surrender.

Abu Obayda wrote to Umar bin al-Khattab asking him to come himself to negotiate the surrender of Jerusalem. Umar consented and got the key to Jerusalem from Patriarch Sophronious.

Imam Ibn Kathir talked about Umar's coming from Medina to take Jerusalem. He said what can be summarized as: "Umar mounted a horse to rush from Medina leaving Ali bin Abu Talib as his deputy in Medina. He rode until he reached Jabiyah where he gave a long eloquent speech. Some of what he said was 'People! Improve your inward lives and your outward lives would be improved. Be mindful of your end, and you will be able to take care of your worldly lives. Be aware that he who seeks Paradise should stick with the group, for Satan will come to the one who forsakes the group, and he departs from the company of two. No one should be alone with a woman; otherwise, Satan would be the third companion. He who delights in doing righteous things and is saddened by doing an ungodly thing is a believer.'

Umar made peace with the people of Aelia and departed on his way to Jerusalem. When he reached Damascus, he was received by Abu Obayda and other commanders. He marched and made peace with the Christians of Jerusalem and stipulated that they expel the Romans in three days. Then, he entered the mosque from the door through which the Messenger of Allah entered on the night of the Isra'. He prayed the greeting of the mosque in the niche of David. He also prayed with the Muslims the morning prayer the next day. He first recited Sura Sad (sura 38) and prostrated and the Muslims also did so. (He recited) a second Sura (the Children of Israel/ Al-Isra'; sura 17), when he came to the Rock and asked Ka'b Al-Ahbar about its location. Then, he removed some dirt from the Rock using the edge of his cloak, and the Muslims also did like him. The Romans made the Rock a landfill because it was the Qibla for the Jews that even menstruating women would throw the cloth they used there…" [1]

Umar issued a covenant to safeguard the inhabitants of Al-Quds (Jerusalem). It is known as the Covenant of Umar (Al-Ohdah Al- Umariya):

"In the name of Allah, the most Merciful, the Compassionate. This is the security accorded by the servant of Allah, Umar, to the inhabitants of Aelia. He guarantees all the people of Jerusalem without distinction, be they ill-disposed or well the security of their persons, possessions, churches and whatever relates to their faith. Their churches will not be transformed into dwelling houses, they will not be destroyed, nor will anything be taken from them or the ground on which they stand. Their crosses and possessions will be safe. They will not be coerced in their religion and none of them will be troubled or hurt. No Jews will live in Aelia with the Christians. The inhabitants of Aelia will pay Jizya (poll tax) like those in other towns. They have to drive out the Byzantines and bandits. Those of them who leave the city will be given safe conduct for themselves and their possessions until they reach a safe place, but those of them who prefer to remain are also secure, but they have to pay the same poll tax as the inhabitants of Aelia. Those inhabitants of Aelia who desire to accompany the Byzantines leaving their chapels and crosses behind will enjoy the same safe conduct until they reach a safe place. Those who want to stay may remain there on condition that they pay the same poll tax as the inhabitants of Aelia. If they desire, they may leave with the Byzantines or return to their families, and they will not be required to pay anything before the harvesting of the next crop. He asks Allah to witness that he will guarantee to them everything contained in this covenant. He promises them the protection of the apostle of Allah, his caliphs, and the faithful, if they pay the required poll tax. Signed (as witness) by: Khalid ibn-al-Walid, Amr ibn-al-Ass, Abdurrahman ibn-Auf and Muawiya ibn-Abi Sofyan in year 15H (638 AD)." [2]

Palestine remained Islamic and Arabic since the Islamic conquest in 15 H (636 AD) until the Crusades in 1099 AD, when the Crusaders were able to capture Palestine and gain control over it until 1187 AD. Then, God helped the hero Saladin Al-Ayyubi to restore it from the Crusaders after many Battles. The Battle of Hattin-which ended in the defeat of the Crusaders in March 25th in the year 583 H (1187 AD)- was the most prominent of these battles. Many other battles followed which ended in Saladin capturing Jerusalem on Friday, July 27th in the year 583 H (1187 AD).

A historian comments on the impact of the Jews on the Crusades. He says:

"Examining these battles reveals that the Jews were behind the Crusaders' invasion of the Holy Lands. Now that the Jews had failed in returning to the Holy Land, they attempted to do this in the shadow of the Christians. They used wealth and money as a means to achieve their goal. They concealed their religious and patriotic sentiments behind money. They represented the most booming and thriving trade centers on the northern coast of the Mediterranean. So, they helped the Crusaders launch this adventure under the name of the cross to open the trade roads to the east through Palestine. However, the Jewish mantra was, in fact, mightier than money and stronger than the cross. Nonetheless, Saladin Al-Ayyubi soon recaptured Jerusalem after the Battle of Hattin, and one city after the other started into his hand and the hands of those who came after him. Palestine remained an Islamic Arabic country until the State of Israel was established." [3]

In the year 1257 AD, the Mongol ruler Hulagu invaded Bagdad and continued marching towards Damascus. He then tried to invade Egypt, but the Muslims were able to vanquish him under the command of the al-Malik al-Muzaffar (Qutuz). Palestine became under the rule of the Mamluks. In 1517 AD, the Turkish Ottomans conquered

the Mamluks, and Palestine became an Ottoman province. This lasted until 1917 AD. In December 9th, 1917, the British the command of General Allenby occupied Jerusalem. He entered the city through Hebron (Al-Khalil) and said his well-known statement: "Now the Crusades have ended." Ever since, Palestine was under British rule until they delivered it to the Jews in May 15th, 1948.
This is a summary of the history of Palestine since the Islamic Conquest until the Jews usurped the biggest portion of it and establish their state there.

B) <u>We now move to examine Judaism and Zionism</u>:

Judaism and Zionism are, in fact, two sides of the same coin. However, it has become customary for some researchers to regard Zionism as the political side, the national aspect of Judaism, or the executive apparatus for World Zionism that strives to destroy the world and control is destiny.

The word Zionism is related to Mount Zion which is located south of Jerusalem. This mountain was home of the Jebusites. When David became King over the Children of Israel, he dispelled the Jebusites from it for a period of time. Zion became a holy place for the Jews as they believed that the Lord dwelled in it. In the Book of Psalms, it is written: "*Sing the praises of the Lord, enthroned in Zion.*" (Psalms 9:11)
In the British Encyclopedia, this text is written under the word "Zionism:"

"The Jews seek to save Israel, gather their people in Palestine, restore the Jewish state, rebuild the Temple, and once again reinstate the throne of David with one of David's descendants as King." [4]

In the Jewish Encyclopedia, this text is written under the word "Zionism:"

"The Jews yearn to get together and come to Jerusalem. They seek to vanquish the enemy and reestablish worship there (in place of the Farthest Mosque). They want to want to establish their rule there." [5]

Consequently, the goal of Zionism is to fulfill the Jewish ambition which aims to seize Palestine to make it the center of their Jewish State and rebuild their Temple which is called "The Temple of Soliman" in place of the venerated Farthest Mosque where they can worship and practice their religious rituals.

A Zionist is the Jew who prefers to live in Palestine more than any other country. He is an individual who helps the Jews financially and spiritually to reside and settle in Palestine.

Zionism- as an idea and a movement that calls for and encourages the return of the Jews to Palestine- in not a new idea; it is an old one. The seeds for this idea were planted- as some Jews maintain- when the Assyrians conquered the Kingdom of Israel in 721 BCE, followed by the first destruction of Jerusalem at the hands of Nebuchadnezzar in 586 BCE and taking the Jews as captives to Babylon.

Some writers maintain that "It was those Jews taken to Babylon who planted the seeds of Jewish fanatic racism and that they deserve the most credit for the idea to return to Zion and for advocating the myth they are God's chosen people and His most beloved."

The Jewish writer, Alfred Lilienthal, says in his book "The Price of Israel" that the idea of the State of Israel remained alive in the hearts of the Jews through their chants and hymns. In Psalms 37, the singer says:

'By the rivers of Babylon we sat and wept when we remembered Zion. There on the poplars we hung our harps, for there our captors asked us for songs, our tormentors demanded songs of joy; they said, "Sing us one of the songs of Zion!" How can we sing the songs of the Lord while in a foreign land? If I forget you, Jerusalem, may my right hand forget its skill. May my tongue cling to the roof of my mouth if I do not remember you, if I do not consider Jerusalem my highest joy... Daughter Babylon, doomed to destruction, happy is the one who repays you according to what you have done to us. Happy is the one who seizes your infants and dashes them against the rocks.'" [6]

C) The following stages are presented to the reader in order to be able to realize the efforts that Zionism exerted ever since the first destruction of Jerusalem in 538 and up to the end of the Nineteenth Century to seize Palestine:

1- In the year 163 BCE, the Maccabean Revolt, led by the Jewish Rabbi, Mathathias, and his children, essentially aimed to create an independent state for the Jews. They were able to rule for a period of time, but it was destined to cease to continue as the Romans completely eradicated them in 37 BCE. We talked in detail about this movement in the First Chapter.

The Jews have- up to the present time- taken pride in the Maccabean Revolt. Ben Gurion said that "Thanks to the revolts of the Maccabeans before the birth of Christ, the Jews enjoy political freedom in the Twentieth Century."

2- 117 AD, Bar Kokhba headed a movement that called the Jews to get together and unite to create a state for them in Palestine, to rebuild the Temple and crown a king from David's offspring. However, notwithstanding all the zeal and enthusiasm that that movement stirred, it was doomed to fail and destined to utter annihilation.

3-In 361 AD, the Jews employed all the possible means with the Roman Emperor Julian to rebuild their Temple and grant them independence. Julian promised to attend to their demands, but he died unexpectedly before he was able to fulfill his promises with them.

During the Fourth Century one of the Persian Kings made a covenant with them to grant them independence if they paid allegiance to him. However, he persecuted, humiliated and oppressed them when he sensed their duplicity and betrayal.

4- The efforts of the Jews to achieve their dream to returning came to a halt during the Middle Ages because of the persecutions that were inflicted upon them. Their plans stopped, and their efforts were focused on instilling the idea of returning in their souls through prayers and supplications in the temples. They also tried to consolidate their old traditions and special rituals and instill them in the hearts and minds of their people. They were helped in doing this by their isolated style of living in their specific neighborhoods in which they resided for hundreds of years.

In these isolated and detached milieus, a number of their scholars and rabbis who established studies for Jewish thought became prominent. Among those were Eleazar Qallir in the seventh century, Saadia Gaon (282-942 AD), Musa bin Maymun (1135-1204 AD), Isaac Luria (1534-1572) and many others.

The Jewish inactivity and lackadaisical attitude, their abandonment of disciplined and orderly planning and their discontinuing serious efforts can be attributed to the inopportune political and social circumstances at the time, as one of their intellectuals said. They used these centuries to prove their presence through creating tens of societies and organizations throughout this stage in their history, a stage that was characterized by adopting a general defensive policy. The most famous among these societies are the Kabbalah, the Freemasons, the Knights Templar, the Pink Cross and other clandestine societies that the Jews founded to serve and cater for their best interest." [7]

5- During the Sixteenth Century, the Jews resumed some of their activities. In 1532 AD, David Robin and Solomon Molcho, his disciple, started a movement to gather the Jews and bring them to Palestine to create a state for them there.

6- In 1566 AD, Joseph Nasi, a Spanish Jew, asked the Ottoman Sultan to sell him a wide stretch of land close to Tiberius for a high price. His goal was to establish the first colony for the Jews- who were persecuted in other countries- to occupy and settle in. However, the Ottoman Sultan denied his request vehemently. [8]

7- In 1604 AD, the movement 'Menashe Bnei Israel' arose in Britain. Its goal was to bring the Jews of the world to Britain. Then, arrangements would be made to prepare a home for them in Palestine to which they can immigrate to and settle in It is most likely that this movement was the first nucleus for modern Zionism which found a fertile soil for it in Britain. It grew and flourished there and, in three centuries, it became able to harness all the powers of the British to achieve the goals of the Jews.[9]

8- In 1626 AD, the members of a violent movement led by Shabnai Levy ardently sought to establish a homeland to the Jews in Palestine. Despite its zeal and vehemence, it failed to attain its goals. Some Jews were even opposed to- and fought- it. They called upon their fellow brothers to accept living in the countries in which they settled advising them to be content with the religious aspects of their Jewishness and to ignore its political side.

9- In the year 1663 AD, the persecution of the Jews in Germany, Italy, Holland and Egypt increased. Many Jews escaped to Palestine and settled there as immigrants subject to the Ottoman administration of which Palestine was one of its governates.
10- After the French Revolution which erupted in July 14th 1789, the activities of the Jews demanding creating a homeland for them in Palestine increased because they were behind the French Revolution, as they admitted in their Protocols, and the waves of persecution that the French inflicted upon them before the Revolution decreased or even became non-existent after the revolution. Furthermore, the Jews started to control France after that, a fact that prompted Napoleon Bonaparte to called the Jews of the world to join him to restore their former glory and reclaim their lost rights for thousands of years. This invitation which was directed to the Jews was published in the official French newspaper in April 20th 1799. However, due to consecutive events, Napoleon was unable to do anything for them. Moreover, his call was, in reality, intended to distance them from France after realizing that they were in control of all its major affairs and after seeing that they went beyond bounds to incite the feelings of the Jews to rebuild their former country in Palestine.
In 1797 AD, one of their leaders in France gave a rabble-rousing speech in which he talked about their hopes and aspiration and demanded that they work hard and seriously to return to Palestine. The following is an excerpt from the speech:

"Brothers: Do not ever lose sight of the fact that your sighs and moans have reached the very heavens for all the unspeakable injustices and persecutions you have endured. You are about to rid yourselves, once and for all, of this state of humiliation and degradation which uncouth people have caused you. We have seen resentment and hatred accompanying us everywhere. The time has come to break the shackles of disgrace and degradation which our enemy has placed around our necks. The time has come to get rid of that unbearable yoke. Yes! It is time now to stand and occupy that status that befits us among the nations of the world. Let us proceed, brothers, to renew the Temple of Jerusalem. Our numbers, in the millions, are scattered all over the countries of the world. We have in our possession enormous and vast wealth, so we should seize every opportunity and means to restore our land. The chance is here, and it is our duty to seize it. We should adopt the following means to achieve this sacred goal: establishing an assembly elected by the Jews residing in the following fourteen countries: Italy, Switzerland, Hungary, Poland, Russia, the Netherlands, Great Britain, Spain, Wales, Sweden, Germany, Turkey, Asia and Africa. That committee that represents the Jews living in these countries will make the necessary decisions and recommendations, and it is incumbent upon all the Jews to accept these decisions and give them the power of laws that should be strictly followed and obeyed. The countries that intend to accept these with an agreement with France are Lower Egypt (While preserving a vast area extending from the city of Acre to the Dead Sea, and from the south of the Dead Sea to the Red Sea. This is a more convenient center that would enable us- through the navigation coming from the Red Sea- to control Indian, Arabian, north and south Africa trade routes. There is no doubt that Ethiopia will not hesitate to willingly and cheerfully establish commercial relations with us. These were the countries that offered gold, ivory and precious stones to King Soliman. Also, being in close proximity to Aleppo and Damascus is bound to facilitate our trade, and by virtue of the location of our country on the Mediterranean, we can easily with France, Italy, Spain and other European countries. Since our country would be in the center of the world, it would become the storehouse to all the produce that these rich lands produce. As for the other arrangements and agreements related to our proposals to the Sublime Porte (Ottoman Porte/ Al-Bab Al-Alie), these should not be openly announced. We will be obliged to keep this issue to the best judgement of the French government. Brothers: You should not save any effort or desist from offering any sacrifice in our pursuit to attain this goal, i.e., returning to our country where we can live in the light of our own special doctrines and renew our holy country for which our ancestors are known for their sacrifices and the valor and gallantry they displayed. I look at you now and I see the fire of faith raging in your chests. My Israeli fellows: the time has come to end our miserable condition. The opportunity has now presented itself. Beware it slips through your fingers."[10]

This is the speech that one of the Jewish rabbis gave a century and half before the establishment of the State of Israel. In it, the dreams, imagination and ambitions of the Jews to annex Lower Egypt are obviously reflected.

11- During the Nineteenth Century, the Jews continued to exert great efforts and use various means to settle in Palestine. In 1840, the Jews of Western Europe sought to obtain an official declaration from Britain to establish a homeland for the Jews in Palestine. Lord Shaftesbury sent a memorandum to the Prime Minister of Britain during the London Conference in 1840 asking Britain to commit to establish a state for the Jews in Palestine. As a result of these crafty and scheming endeavors, England declared its protection of the Jews residing in Palestine, and the British Prime Minister at the time sent a memo indicating that to the British consul in Jerusalem. One year after that conference, another conference was held in Dublin which declared, among its various resolutions: "Asking for British intervention for the purpose of helping the Jews to settle in Palestine."
12- In 1854 AD, the English Chief Rabbi and Mr. Moses Montefiore, the Jewish Minister, conducted a large campaign to collect donations to buy land in Palestine for the Jews to settle there. The first amount of money they were able to collect for this purpose was more than 30 thousand dollars. With this amount of money and others, the purchase of some lands in Palestine was made possible. This was the first seed in the Holy Lands.
13- In the year 1856 AD, Moses Montefiore [11] visited Palestine and purchased a huge citrus plantation near the city of Jaffa. He employed only Jews to work in that plantation. Then, he started to purchase tens of houses in Jerusalem specifically for Jews. These dwelling places were known by the name Mishorim. That was in 1858 AD. Rothschild's family- well-known for its unparalleled wealth and affluence- followed the same course. They bought huge stretches of land in Palestine, and they offered them as presents to the Jews of East Europe to settle in Palestine. There were many wealthy Jews who spent millions of their money to help Jews settle in Palestine.
14- In 1869 AD, an organization by the name the Israeli Alliance Organization was founded in France. Its goal was to spread the Hebrew language among the Jews of the world so that their children would grow with thorough knowledge of the language and thereby become eager to promote working to return to Palestine. This organization

succeeded tremendously in spreading the Hebrew language. It was also able to build many schools and settlements for the Jews in Palestine.
15- In 1882 AD, they founded an organization called Lovers of Zion (Hovevei Zion) after the massacres that that were inflicted upon the Jews in Russia. One of the most important goals of the organization was to send Jews to Palestine. About this organization, Weizmann[12] says in his memoirs: “In reality and in essence, the Zionist movement started in Russia. It was the Jews of Russia who were the backbone for the Jewish existence in Palestine since this movement started.” [13] It was through this organization that the first group of Russian Jews immigrants infiltrated to Palestine where they started the first agricultural settlement near Jaffa. They called it Rishon LeZion, that is, the First in Zion. Ben Gurion calls it the first immigration.

These are the most important efforts exerted by the Jews throughout the centuries and until the end of the Nineteenth Century. Some writers commented on these efforts, saying: “During this stage, Jewish activities increased and became condensed, the money was collected and the first wave of immigrants started to come to Palestine. However, this stage was not well thought out or well planned. It was mainly conducted on an individual basis or by societies and organizations that did not plan seriously for this stage. Historians believe that the idea that has taken root has ended with the publication of Herzl’s “The Jewish State” and the success of the World Conference in Bale (French) or Basel (German) in Switzerland in 1897 AD.” [14]

D) The stage of practical planning and actual preparation to declare the establishment of the State of Israel:

A lot of researchers maintain that the stage of actual preparation for establishing the state of Israel and acknowledging it started with the World Jewish Conference in Bale (Basel) in Switzerland in 1897 AD and ended with the founding of the State of Israel in May 15th, 1948 AD.
The following are the most important efforts that World Zionism exerted during this stage as well as the most important aids that were offered by countries of infidelity to establish a state for it in Palestine.

In August 20th 1897 AD, the first Zionist Conference was held in Bale in Switzerland with Theodore Herzl as its president. 196 Jewish deputies from all over the world attended the conference. They sat around one table, and they examined the means to restore the state of Israel. Herzl defined the goals of the conference, saying: “We have gathered here to lay the cornerstone for the principles that gather the Jewish people together and the state of Zion that was eradicated twenty centuries ago.”[15] The conference lasted for three days. The attendees left the conference with some resolutions the most important was the following:
“Zionism hopes to establish a country for the Jewish people, one that is acknowledged from two perspectives: Officially and legally. By establishing such a country, the Jewish people would safe from persecution. This country should be Palestine.”

Among the most important resolutions reached was encouraging the Jews all over the world to participate in the following conferences, strengthen the agricultural movement in Palestine, increase the purchase of lands owned by the Jews in the Holy Lands, revive the Hebrew culture, arouse racist sentiments among the Jews in the world and prompt other governments to materially and morally support the Jews' struggle to achieve these objectives.
After announcing these resolutions, Herzl wrote an article in his newspaper which he used to publish in Austria. In that article he said: "If I were asked to summarize the resolutions of the Bale Conference, I would say, or even loudly declare, that I founded the Jewish State. This may arouse a wave of laughter here and there, but the world will undoubtedly see that, in five or fifty years, the establishment of the Jewish State in accordance with the will of the Jews." The man's prophecy came true. Twenty years after the first conference for Zionism was held, the Jews were able to obtain the Belfour Declaration. Also, fifty years later came the resolution to divide Palestine between the Arabs and the Jews in 1947 AD.

The Jews have taken great pride in Herzl's efforts and achievements. They consider him the prophet of Zionism and its greatest founder. About him, Weizmann, the first president for the State of Israel, said: "Herzl's greatness is manifest in his fervent and positive effort which is exemplified in his utter commitment and dedication in the service of the Zionist idea."

Conferences to serve Zionism and enable the Jews to occupy Palestine followed annually. In 1898 AD, the second conference- attended by 349 Jewish representatives from all over the world- was held. A large number of rabbis attended that conference. Among its most prominent resolutions was establishing a big company that was responsible for purchasing lands in Palestine, distributing these lands among the immigrants and advocating for the organizations that encourage spreading the Hebrew Language in the world. In 1899 AD, the third conference in Bale was held. Hundreds of Jews attended it. The most important resolutions for this conference were organizing Zionistic propaganda in European countries in particular, increasing the purchase of lands in Palestine and increasing the establishment of settlements for the workers there. In 1900 AD, the fourth conference was held in London. The intended aim behind holding the conference in London was to secure direct communication with the British government to urge it to pressure Sultan Abdul- Hamid to facilitate the purchase of lands in Palestine for the Jews. That was because when Sultan Abdul-Hamid realized that the Jews were expanding their attempts to purchase lands in Palestine, he began to hinder them and instituted obstacles on their way. "In that conference, the "Jewish National Fund" was founded. Its aim was to pursue the purchase of lands in Palestine or, according to the strange expression that they used, re-purchase lands in Palestine. The Jewish National Fund was one of the most active in the World Zionist Organization."[16]

Ben Gurion described the gains that World Zionism was able to achieve up to the end of the Nineteenth Century. He said: "By the end of the Nineteenth Century, we had 13 new settlements in Palestine. The first seeds for the Jewish State were planted. However, the principal element, i.e., Jewish workers, was not adequate enough. That deficiency was addressed and satisfied with the second wave of immigrants which arrived in the first years of the present century and whereby a firm and stable foundation for the state was laid. An independent Jewish force that had its economic, military and cultural stamp was formed in Palestine."[17] Herman Shapiro describes the ambitions that the Jews were able to achieve in Palestine until the end of the Nineteenth Century. He said: "The end of the past century marked the beginning of establishing the state. We have laid the foundation for the house of Israel. After us, our children will build the walls. Our grandchildren will then install the doors."

At the dawn of the Twentieth Century, World Zionism adopted a practical, well- studied and carefully deliberated course to institute the State of Israel in Palestine. In 1901 AD, the Jews held their fifth annual conference in Bale in Switzerland. The conference was attended by hundreds of Jews. Among its most important resolutions was: "Approving the establishment of a Hebrew university in Palestine to spread the Jewish culture among the Jewish inhabitants. Dr. Chaim Weizmann, who was considered the pioneer for the Zionist movement, adopted that proposal and executed it.

Also, during that year, the Jews bargained once again with Sultan Abdul-Hamid, and they tried to convince him- through enticements and temptations- to help them establish the Jewish State in Palestine. Herzl, their leader, accompanied with many of the elders of Zion went to him. They offered him huge financial aids to help save the empire from fiscal collapse and fund it with the money it needed afterwards in return for allowing them to establish a Jewish state in Palestine. However, despite the Sultan's dire need for money, he responded to Herzl and his entourage in a way that disappointed them. He said:

"I advise Dr. Herzl not to take any further steps concerning that matter or to push me to abandon even one inch of the land to the Jews. This land is not my personal property to do what I please. It is the peoples' land. My people had struggled and fought for this land and soaked it with their blood. Let the Jews keep their millions. If my empire is torn apart, they would get Palestine for free. They cannot take away any part of this empire unless it becomes a lifeless corpse. I cannot dissect my country's body while it is alive."[18]

Yet, despite that decisive response by Sultan Abdul-Hamid, Herzl continued to maneuver and implore the German and Russian Caesars. However, all his pleas and schemes failed because of Sultan Abdul-Hamid's determination, shrewdness, insight and profound understanding of Jewish ambitions.

In 1902 AD, after lengthy negotiations with the Jews, Sultan Abdul Hamid agreed to the following: "The Ottoman Empire grants the Jews a promise to allow them to immigrate to the various Asian countries of the Empire provided that the Jewish immigrants become subjects of the Ottoman Empire, undertake their military service and to live dispersed- not together- in the countries of the Ottoman Empire, with five families at the most in one region. Palestine is an exception; it is forbidden for them." The Jews were flabbergasted because of what the Sultan had offered them. They rejected his proposal altogether, and they started scheming to get rid of him by all possible means. Finally, they were able to get their atheist cronies in the Turkish army to revolt against Sultan

Abdul-Hamid. That ended with dethroning him. Among the three who men who delivered the Sultan the decree to dethrone him was a Jew by the name of Emmanuel Carasso.That was how World Zionism avenged itself on Sultan Abdul-Hamid

In 1903 AD, the sixth conference for the Jews was held. Most of the discussions during that conference revolved around the possibility of establishing a Jewish state in any other place other than Palestine such as Sinai, Cyprus or Uganda. However, the Jews of Eastern Europe, in general, and the Jews of Russia, in particular, were able to refute any suggestion calling for settling the Jews in any other region in the world other than Palestine. They came out of the conference with a resolution stating that "Palestine is the only eternal national homeland for the Jewish people." In that year, the Jews started to seriously look for a country that would assist them to reach that goal. It did not take them long. They found the object of their desire in Britain. They soon turned their faces towards Britain to help them establish a homeland for them in Palestine.

Chaim Weizmann was the orchestrator of the idea of getting close to and befriending Britain because its people were the firmest believers that the Jewish State should be founded in Palestine in accordance with the Torah that the British understand. Also, at that time, England was dominating many countries in the world and World Zionism had the strongest influence in Britain at that time. Britain welcomed that clinging tendency and found it beneficial to her. Thus, colonial interests reconciled with the ambitions of World Zionism.

In August 1905 AD, the seventh conference was held with David Wolfensohn as president after the death of Herzl in 1904. Among the most important resolutions of this conference was increasing the furtive immigration to Palestine and establishing a big Hebrew library there. In the year 1907, the ninth conference headed by Max Nordau, a Hungarian Jew. It was held in Hamburg, Germany. At that conference, a bank for agricultural loans and settlements run by cooperative systems were to be established, and working to establish the settlement of Tel Aviv was also announced. That settlement kept on growing until it became the capital of Israel. In 1911, the tenth Zionist conference headed also by Nordau was held. Among its most important resolutions was creating a company to improve the land. Its goal was to purchase Arab land and offer them to Jewish immigrants. In 1913, the eleventh conference was held in Austria. In it, the attendants agreed to establish the Hebrew University in Jerusalem.

Many conferences followed thereafter. They constituted a great change in the history of the Jews because they enabled them to congregate to revive their ambitions after being scattered and dispersed for more than twenty centuries. Now they had an official representative to speak on their behalf, and by virtue of these conferences, they had come up with well-deliberated plans to seize Palestine and harness the help of many countries to serve their goals and aspirations.

When the blaze of World War 1 raged, the number of the settlements owned by the Jews were forty agricultural colonies extending over a stretch of land that reached two hundred thousand acres with almost twelve thousand Jews working on them. The number of the Jews who resided in Palestine at that time were more than ninety thousand, with approximately half of them living in Jerusalem. The Jews realized that the Great War was a precious opportunity for them to fulfill their ambitions. They started to wait in anticipation of the winning side to come close and ingratiate to it. They finally settled on England, and they started to support it because they saw that England would be victorious. A great number of the Jews joined the military service in the British army. They would wear the British army uniform and carry the hexagonal star as their slogan. Dr. Weizmann succeeded in producing Acetone- which he prepared in British labs- to manufacture explosives. The British used the Jews to spy for them. One of their most famous organizations in reconnaissance was 'Nelly' (Nili) whose members were mostly from the Jews of Palestine.

Moreover, the Jews were able to drag America to enter the First World War to support Britain and its allies. [19] The Jews were rewarded for their services to Britain with the Balfour Declaration that required the British to work to create a homeland for the Jews in Palestine. Here is the text of the Declaration:

"Dear Mr. Rothschild: [20] The government of his Majesty the King looks favorably upon the establishment of a homeland for the Jewish people in Palestine. It will do its best to facilitate the attainment of this goal. It should be understood that nothing will be done to change the civil and religious rights of non-Jews in Palestine, nor the rights and political position that Jews enjoy in any other countries."

The Jews were extremely thrilled by this Declaration, and they regarded it as a turning point in their history. Their fervent and impassioned zeal for this promise was beyond bounds as they came to realize that acknowledging such a Declaration had put an end to their suffering and fulfilled the prophecies of their Holy Book. As a result of this Declaration, the Jews doubled their efforts to realize their ambitions in Palestine. They asked Britain to acknowledge a special citizenship for the Jews and to be granted autonomy. Then the Jews took one more step to convince the League of Nations to acknowledge that Declaration. And they got what they wanted. In April 1920, a peace treaty with Turkey was signed in San Remo. The Balfour Declaration was part of that treaty and, consequently, it was given an international recognition having been recorded with the League of Nations.

But who wrote the Balfour Declaration? Weizmann admitted in his memoirs that he wrote it with the help of some other Jews. He also said that, after writing it, he delivered it to Balfour in 7, 18, 1917 AD.

In conclusion: The Balfour Declaration was "An unlawful promise from someone who did not own what he gave to someone who unlawfully received what he had no right to get what he was given. The two parties- the unlawful giver and the unlawful receiver- were able, by force and deceit, to strip the rightful owner of his legitimate and lawful right." Britain then adopted the process of enabling the Jews to seize Palestine until she delivered it to them in 1948.

In December 9, 1917, the British were able to occupy Jerusalem. At the beginning of 1918, they were able to occupy the remaining parts of Palestine which became subject to the British Mandate. The Mandate lasted for three years during which a number of officers known for their Jewish tendencies were in charge of the military rule. During this period of time, the Jews were able to carry out a large number of their projects. In 1920, the British government ended its military rule and placed a civil one instead. It lasted until May 14th, 1948. Most of the rulers who were in charge of the administration of Palestine during this period were either people with a Jewish origin or known for their advocacy for the Jews. Some of them were even hand-picked by the Jews to facilitate their tasks. The number of Jewish immigrants legally allowed to reside in Palestine during this period was more than 600 thousand immigrants. In short, the British Mandate over Palestine aimed to place it under such administrative, economic and political circumstances that would guarantee the establishment of a homeland for the Jews there. The British in Palestine at that time were nothing more than guardians of Jewish interests to execute and carry out their demands. With conceit and arrogance, Weizmann said in his memoirs: "We, the Jews, sought to establish a country for us in Palestine. We chose the British to govern it with the help of the League of Nations. We were the ones who temporarily delivered Palestine to the British. It was not the British who gave Palestine to us. Britain had embraced the Jewish movement since its inception. It shouldered the responsibility to carry out its goals and made an agreement to deliver Palestine to the Jews free of its Arab inhabitants in 1934. But for the consecutive revolutions of the Arabs of Palestine, that agreement would have been realized." [21]

The first English High Commissioner to govern Palestine in 1920 was Herbert Samuel who was chosen by the Jews because of his Jewish origin. When Samuel arrived in Jerusalem, he headed directly to the Jewish Temple to pray with them (the Jews). He was the High Commissioner for Palestine for five years. During this period of time, the nonconcrete and abstract Balfour Declaration was transformed into a tangible palpable reality. He established the Jewish Agency which was a Jewish government replete with complete apparatuses that comprised more than 200 members from all over the world. He regarded the Hebrew Language as the official language. He facilitated the flow of Jewish immigrants to Palestine, and their numbers reached 156 thousand Jews during his time as Commissioner. He handed the Jews all facilities for industries and farming. He appointed a Jew to supervise the Endowments/ Zakat (Awqaf) of Muslims. He granted vast stretches of the country's lands to the Jews. He gave the Jews privileges (liens) to use the waters of the Jordan River to produce electricity, and the Russian Jew, Pinhas Rutenberg, was appointed to be in charge. That lien was given for seventy years. He also gave them the lien to one of the most important projects: exploiting the waters of the Dead Sea because of its immense minerals that could be used in various industries. In short, Samuel harnessed his financial and political prestige to carry out Zionistic ambitions and greed.

In 1924, he was succeeded by Lord Plumer who followed in his predecessor's footsteps providing the Jews with the assistance they needed while making it more cumbersome for the Arabs. He granted the Jews privileges to extract the minerals from the Red Sea.

He also facilitated the purchase of lands for them. Other rulers from England came after them. They all followed the same pre-planned strategy, prepared by World Zionism, and executed by the British government. All of those commissioners were faithful servants and obedient soldiers to the Jews.
The Arabs of Palestine realized that their country was on its way to become a Jewish colony ever since the English had trodden on its soil in 1917. They also witnessed with their own eyes that the British treat the Jews in the same way a compassionate loving father treats his only spoiled son: they opened the doors of immigration to them, they gave the land without measure, they gave them free access to utilize the waters, they appointed them in the best and most important ranks, etc. The Arabs of Palestine revolted because of the injustices that befell them at the hands of colonialism and Zionism. The following are some of their revolutions from 1920 to 1939:

1-In April 1920, in a conflict between the Arabs and the Jews that took place in Jerusalem, a big number of Jews were killed. There were trials for the two parties in the conflict, and a large number of Arabs were sentenced to imprisonment.
2-In May 1921, the Jews attacked the Arabs in Jaffa which resulted in the killing a big number of them. These skirmishes lasted for fifteen days.
3-In August 1929, the Jews carried out widespread demonstrations especially in Jerusalem. They provoked the Arabs sentiments by flying the Zionist flag near the Farthest Mosque. The initial altercations turned into violent confrontations that comprised most of the cities of Palestine. They lasted for fifteen days during which the Muslims directed violent attacks to Jewish settlements. During these clashes, a great number of Arabs and Jews were killed. However, most of the Arabs who were killed then were killed at the hands of the British. It is known as the "Buraq Uprising."
4-In November 1933, the Arabs organized huge demonstrations in Palestinian cities to express their opposition to Britain's policies in widely opening the doors of immigration to the Jews. Many Arabs and Jews were killed.
5- In November 2nd, 1935, in an immense uprising led by Sheikh Izz Al-Din Al-Qassam, the Arabs declared their rebellion against the British Commissioner. They took refuge in a forest near the city of Jenin. The British forces surrounded Sheikh Al-Qassam and his companions. In the fight that ensued, Sheikh Al-Qassam was killed and those of his companions who were still alive were sentenced to imprisonment for various terms.
6- Then came the Great Revolt (the Palestinian Revolution) in which the Arabs sacrificed their blood and money. It extended from 1936 to 1939.

During this period, Palestinian fighters carried their weapons and sought refuge in the mountains. Volunteers from outside Palestine arrived to help them. The revolution started with guerrilla wars against the British and the Jews. The number of British soldiers in Palestine at that time were seventy thousand. However, the Muslim rebels were able to gain victory over the armies of colonialism and Zionism in many battles. When Britain with its army and weapons failed to quench the revolution, it resorted to intrigues and deceits. The British were able to get the Arab Kings and Presidents to intervene to end the revolution.

In October 1936, Arab Kings and Princes issued the following communique: "To our sons, the Arabs of Palestine: We were profoundly saddened by the current prevailing situation in Palestine. In agreement with our brethren, the Arab Kings, and Prince Abdullah, we urge you to reestablish peace and serenity in order to prevent further bloodshed, fully confident of the good intentions of our friend, the British government, and its persistent desire to achieve justice. Be assured that we will continue and persevere in helping you." [22]

The revolution calmed down after this communique. It lasted for six months during which three thousand Arabs were killed and seven thousand were wounded. In addition, eight-thousand-woman, old men and children were killed. Following this, in November 4, 1936, the English formed a committee headed by British Lord Peel (sic; The Commission was established in April, 1936, and arrived in Palestine on November 11, 1936) to examine the Palestinian question. The committee listened to what the Arabs and the Jews had to say. It returned to London and published its report in July 1938. The report included a proposal to divide Palestine between the Arabs and the Jews. It also included a proposal to annex the Arabic section to the east Jordan Principality.

After the publication of the report, the Arabs resumed their revolution in 1937. They killed a great number of the English. Among those killed was Andrews, the English Commissioner of the Galilee region.
The English violently tried to quench the revolution. They absolved the Arab Higher Committee, arrested a great number of Palestinian leaders, and destroyed villages and houses. Still, the revolution kept on raging until 1939. Britain then held a conference in London in February 7, 1939. Representatives from Arab countries, Palestinian Arabs, and Jewish leaders attended that conference. However, the conference failed one month after it was held. Then, the English published a book in March 17th, 1939. Among its proposals was: "Placing restrictions on the immigration of the Jews to Palestine so that the number of Jewish immigrants would not exceed 75 thousand in a period of five years."The Jews rejected that proposal and called upon Churchill, their friend, to denounce it. He attacked it in the British House of Commons, and because of Churchill's deprecation, the British government ignored the good proposals that would have been in the Arabs' best interest.

In September 9th, 1939, the Second World War erupted. The Jews used this to realize their ambitions, organize their ranks and prepare the necessary plans to attain their goals and achieve their objectives in Palestine. Among the most important steps they took to do so was bringing various weapons to their settlements in Palestine to use them when needed.

The English welcomed the idea of the Jews' joining their ranks to fight along with them. The number of Jews who joined the British army reached 86 thousand man and 5 thousand women. All of those worked to serve the British army.At the end of the Second World War all these thousands of the Jews were discharged. Every one of them kept their weapon as a gift from the British army. The following are some of the efforts that were exerted by both Britain and America during the war to satisfy the greed and ambitions of World Zionism:

1-In 1940, the British Labor Party decided to ask the government to open the doors of Palestine to the Jews.
2-In 1942, sixty-two members of the U.S. Senate and one hundred and eighty members from the House of Representatives presented a memorandum asking the United States to help the Jews in establishing a state for them in Palestine.
3-In 1943, the British Labor Party decided to ask the government to facilitate the immigration of the Jews to Palestine to the necessary numbers to establish a Jewish state.
4- In 1944, President Roosevelt issued an official statement asking to open the doors of immigration of Palestine to unlimited numbers of Jews. In that statement, he displayed his empathy and the empathy of the American people towards the afflicted Jews.
5- In May 7th, 1945, The Second World War ended with Germanys defeat. In September 2nd of the same year, the Allies gained victory over Japan. America was at the forefront of the victorious countries, and she became more enthusiastic than Britain to establish a state in Palestine for the Jews. As soon as World War I1 ended, Truman, the U.S. President at the time, issued a memorandum asking the British government to allow one hundred Jew to immigrate to Palestine right away. Then, five thousand American priests a petition to the United States' government asking her to interfere and open the doors of immigration, without restrictions- to Palestine.
6- In December 1946, the Arab League sent a memorandum to the U.S. government asking her to lessen her enthusiasm towards the Jews and to show the true nature of the Palestinian cause. In January 1st, 1947, the U.S. government sent its response to the Arab League: "The United States government and the American people have supported the idea of creating a homeland for the Jews in Palestine ever since the end of World War I. Our stance today, that is, calling to take the necessary steps to bring this idea to fruition, is in correspondence with our traditional policy. As for encouraging Jewish immigration to Palestine from regions occupied by America in Europe, a lot of those persecuted Jews look to Palestine as refuge for them." That memorandum was the clearest statement and the most poignant evidence showing America's support for Zionism and her collaboration with Britain in conspiring to make Palestine a Jewish state.

During these years, the Arab countries demonstrated their opposition to the policies of Britain and the United States concerning Palestine. Also, Palestinian fighters revolted frequently against the English and the Jews. Through these uprisings, they were able to disturb Britain peace and cause her great losses in lives and money.

In February 1947, Britain pretended to be completely unable to find a solution to the Palestinian problem. It decided to bring the case to the United Nations. World Zionism seized the chance of sending the Palestinian Cause to the United Nations and used all possible means to influence the members of the United Nations to vote in accordance with what they pleased. While examining the case in the United Nations, strange intrigues and conspiracies took place. Truman, the President of the United States at that time, played a big role in these conspiracies.

After consultations and negotiations, the decision to divide Palestine between the Arabs and the Jews was presented to the United Nations in November 29th 1947. Thirty-three members accepted it, while fifteen members rejected it mostly from Arab and Islamic countries. On top of the countries that agreed to the decision were America and Russia.

Thanks to that international decision, Britain succeeded in fulfilling what she always wanted for the Jews. The falsehoods of World Zionism triumphed over the rights of the Arabs and Muslims, and the Jews obtained an official promise (Declaration) from several countries to have a state established for them in the heart of the Islamic world. The British then announced that they would stop their mandate over Palestine in May 15th 1948 with the exception of the city of Haifa from which they would depart at the beginning of August 1948.

The Arab countries rejected the decision to divide. Demonstrations broke out in all Arabic and Islamic countries. The Arab League started to prepare an army of volunteers to rescue Palestine. The Organization for the Holy Struggle was formed under the leadership of Abdul Qadir al-Husani. The forces of this organization blew up the Jewish Agency building, and they were able to control roads and communications in Palestine and isolate Jerusalem where a hundred and twenty thousand Jews resided. When the British realized that the Arabs were winning and the Jews were hiding in their hidey-holes, they committed criminal acts that boosted the Jews' morale. Among these acts:

A) Delivering the city of Haifa to the Jews in April 21st 1948 even though they had earlier announced that they would depart from that city at the beginning of August of the same year. As a result of this, one hundred thousand Arabs were obliged to depart from it.

B) Delivering the city of Jaffa to the Jews in April 21st 1948 even though it was determined that the time to evacuate it was May 15th 1947. That took the Arabs by surprise, and they were unable to sufficiently prepare themselves to confront the Jews who attacked the city by surprise with the help of the British. Hundreds of the children of Jaffa fell dead as a result of the treachery of the British and the Jews. The battle lasted for a few days, and the Arabs of Jaffa left to other places.

C)The British were content to merely give Haifa and Jaffa to the Jews, but they also gave them the two cities of Safed and Tiberias also before the appointed time. They also lavishly provided the Jews with all the weapons that they left when they departed from these cities. They fought with them in every battle.
Ferocious fights between the army of Holy Struggle and the Jews lasted for a long time. When the Jews were unable to confront the fighters in the open fields, they started attacking the children and the women. Among the villages in which a large number of its inhabitants died as a result of the Zionist treachery were Deir Yasin, Qobiyya, Kafr Qasim and other villages.

In May 15th 1948, Ben Gurion announced the birth of the State of Israel. A little while later, America was the first country to acknowledge it. On the same day, the Arab states officially declared war on Israel. These wars took four stages:

A) The First Stage: It started on the day the Arab armies entered Palestine in May 15th 1948 and ended on the first day of the first truce in June 11th 1948. During this period, the Arab forces were victorious; they were able to march and infiltrate the Israeli settlements. Some of these forces was even a few miles away from Tel Aviv, the capital of Israel. Had the war continued, Israel would have surrendered in a week.

B) The Second Stage: It started on the day the first truce ended in July 9th 1948, and it ended with the acceptance of the second truce in July 18th 1948. During this stage, the Jews gained the upper hand because of the tragedy of delivering Lod and Ramla and the lack of military unity against the Jews who were provided and equipped with a lot of weapons by the British during the first period of the truce.

C) The Third Stage: It started on the day the Jews breached the truce on October 14th 1948 and attacked the Egyptian forces in southern Palestine. This war lasted intermittently until January 7th 1949 when Egypt agreed to negotiations for a new truce with the Jews in Rhodes. Other countries followed suit, negotiated with the Jews and held truce with them.

D) The Fourth Stage: It was concluded in March 1949 when General Glubb, the Commander of the Jordanian Army, gave the Jews the southern part of Negev which is located on the Gulf of Aqaba near Um Rash-Rash Seaport which the Jews received from Glubb thereby separating the Arab World in Asia from the Arab World in Africa for the first time in history.

Now, after this brief review of the history and various stages of the Zionist invasion of Palestine, and after being defeated an abysmal unmatched defeat and the Arab and Islamic nations have experienced unparalleled humiliation and disgrace due to the June 1967 war, we have to ask: What are the principal reasons for the tragedy of Palestine? How can we restore it as an Islamic Arabic country once again?

To answer the first part of this question, we say, the most important reasons that led to the tragedy of Palestine and the loss of the war are:

1-The weakening and dwindling of religious motives in the hearts of a lot of Muslims. That has led to laxity in morality, the collapse and disintegration of will power, lack of gallantry, enthusiasm and fervor, negligence and disregarding obligations and duties to Allah, trespassing and sinning against Him, thinking of nothing except the pleasures and lusts of life, and nonchalance concerning the afflictions that befall the Islamic World. We have even seen those who call themselves Muslims pay no attention whatsoever to the tragedy of Palestine.

2- Negligence to identify the threat that surrounds the Islamic World due to the spread of World Zionism, the invasion of the Holy Land, not confronting this danger from the very beginning seriously with steadfastness and resolve, and being uninformed of the deeply-ingrained malice and evil what World Zionism has in store for the Islamic World. Some Arabs took this Jewish threat lightly and displayed weakness and lack of resolve during their official meetings with British and American representatives

concerning the Palestinian Cause. They even appeared as frail and hesitant mediators while the Jewish leaders displayed seriousness, resolve and strength. Some Arab officials were deceived by the duplicity of the British who deluded them into believing that the Jews will only take a small portion of Palestine. Through various methods, they were able to control them and make them treat the Palestinian cause with empty words and push other loyal believers from participating in defending Palestine under the pretext that they were fanatics, given to exaggeration and far from being shrewd and insightful.
3-The financial and moral efforts that the Arab and Islamic worlds exerted to keep Palestine an Arabic Islamic state were far less than the efforts that World Zionism made to seize Palestine from their legal owners and change it into a Jewish state. For example, if we look at the money that the Jews collected in order to capture and control Palestine, we will find that it was immensely more than the money that the Arab and Islamic countries collected to defend the Holy Land. This lack of willingness to give had attracted the attention of some foreigners. Mr. Crossman, a member in the British House of Commons, asked one of his Muslim Arab friends, saying: "Is there anything in the religion of Islam that prevents cooperation between the Muslims?" His friend replied in the negative, and he asked him why he was asking such a question. Crossman said: "Then, why don't you help each other? You don't even give anything to the displaced refugees?" [23]

4- One of the most important factors that led to the Arabs' loss in the Palestinian war was the lack of unity amongst their leaders. They have been unwilling to come to a consensus in a firm, loyal and efficient way. The Arab forces engaged in these wars under various and unified leaders with weak, hesitant and oscillating policies. They did not fight in solid ranks as a one unified "concrete structure" (As-Saf; Q 61:4—"Surely Allah loves those who fight in His cause in ʿsolidʾ ranks as if they were one concrete structure.") Thus, the opportunity to defeat their enemy slipped through their fingers. There is no doubt that when the Arab forces entered the Palestinian war in 1948- and thereafter- they were more equipped and numerous than the Jews. However, this supremacy in might and numbers did not find the adequate leadership that could lead to faithfully, fervently and passionately save Palestine. On the contrary, it was the target of conspiracies that tore it apart and enabled its enemy. If anyone claims that the Arab forces were united, it was only "apparently" or "ostensibly" united, and the harms outweighed the benefits. The Israeli Prime Minister, Ben Gurion, admitted that their victory in the Palestinian war was due to their shrewd politics not to their military might. In an address to the Knesset, he said: "For our success in establishing the State of Israel, we owe 97% to policy and only 3% to the war and the army."[24]

5- Also, one of the most important reasons for losing the war in Palestine was signing the two truces between the Arabs and the Jews because of the pressure that England and America placed on some Arab countries. At first, the Arabs were victorious as the Egyptian army progressed towards Tel Aviv, the Iraqi army was only a few miles away from it and the Jordanian army still had control over Lod and Ramla. The Jews were in a very difficult position because the Arab fighters had surrounded them. The Jews raised white flags as a symbol for their surrender. The Jews of Haifa asked some Arabs to negotiate with the Iraqi army concerning their surrender. In Tel Aviv, the Jews were in a state of fright and panic; they even asked their leaders to surrender immediately. Ben Gurion, the Prime Minister of Israel at that time, was forced to address them. He said: "I have a definitive promise from England and America that the truce will held in three days. If this did not take place, you can come and strangle me." [25] Before three days had passed for Ben Gurion's address, the first truce was signed in June 11th 1948. During the second truce which was signed in July 18th 1948, the Jews were able to get the weapons and instruments that were not available before. They were able to lift the siege imposed on the Jews of Jerusalem, and- through their proxies- forced the Iraqi forces to retreat far from their positions. They also convinced the Jews of Haifa not to surrender, and they were able to remove the Jordanian forces from Lod and Ramla. In short, during the two truces, the Jews were able to turn the situation head over heels. Had the Arab leaders rejected these two truces altogether and continued to fight regardless of the circumstances, the Jews would not have been able to do what they were able to do.

6- The Arab armies and volunteer organizations that participated in defending Palestine were in essence doing this because of patriotic and political motives not religious ones. Religious zeal and fervor for Palestine did not fill the hearts of the fighters, empowered their feelings and emotions or dominated their beliefs, conduct and ethics. On the other hand, the Jews consider their wars in Palestine as purely religious wars and that death on its soil is a great honor for them. They exploited these religious aspects in the conflict to impact the British and the Americans to help them attain their goal and create a state for them in Palestine which God granted to them alone. Through this Jewish religious propaganda, World Zionism was able to collect hundreds of millions of dollars that they spent in Palestine. Also, through such propaganda, it was able to harness clergymen in England, America and other countries of infidelity (Kufr) to serve its interests.

7- These reasons that we have examined are- in general- internal causes for the crisis of Palestine. There are also external reasons. The most important are: The goals and interests of British colonialism have met those of the Jews in the Palestinian cause. Then, America joined them at the beginning of this century. That is because colonialism aims to:

A) Making the Jewish State a basis for it (colonialism), a poisonous dagger that can be brandished in the face of Arab countries whenever they sense mutiny or resistance.
B) Making the Jewish State a wedge that separates the Arab countries in Asia from the Arab countries in Africa to cut off land connection between the two continents.
C) Making the Jews an obstacle to hinder the Arab countries from forging ahead in their vast territories which are located in the most important geographic, commercial and military centers in the world and whose numbers are ever-increasing and which colonialism wants to control and exploit.

The attempts of colonialism to create a foreign state in the heart of the Arab World is not new. Rather, these attempts were going on for decades. In 1907, Campbell Bannerman who was Prime Minister of the United Kingdom formed a committee composed of some historians, jurists and politicians from several countries. He addressed that committee and identified its mission. This is an excerpt from that address:

"Empires are formed, become bigger and stronger then start to disintegrate gradually and finally disappear. History abounds with examples for this, examples that do not change for all nations. There were the Roman, Greek, Indian and Chinese Empires. Before them, there were the Babylonians, the Assyrians and the Pharaohs… and others. Do you have any means that can prevent our empire from falling? Or delay the fate of European colonialism after it has reached that far (the zenith)?"
After spending seven months researching and investigating, the committee presented a report to the Ministry of British Colonies.

Here is an excerpt:
"The threat against colonialism in Asia and Africa is insignificant. The greatest threat lies in the Mediterranean." Accordingly: Those countries with common mutual interests should work to keep this region and its people the way they are, i.e., in a state of disunity, backwardness and ignorance… They should also work to separate the African section in this region from the Asian one. The committee therefore recommends the creation of a strong foreign human barrier that would represent the land bridge that connects Asia with Africa, where a friendly power for colonialism, antagonistic to the inhabitants of the region, would be instituted in this area close to the Suez Canal."

England kept looking for that foreign human barrier that would become the land bridge that connects Asia with Africa… Deliberations led England to choose the Jews and create a state for them in Palestine, a state that would be friendly to England and hostile to the inhabitants of the region. Ever since, and after Palestine became under the British Mandate, the British kept trying to make Palestine a national homeland for the Jews. And, throughout the Mandate, Britain contrived to place Palestine in certain political, economic and administrative conditions that would facilitate the creation of this homeland to the Jews. We discussed this in detail before. Other countries of infidelity, especially America- which exerted gigantic efforts to create a state for the Jews in Palestine and spent hundreds of millions of dollars for that purpose- joined England. Thus, we see that usurping Palestine and grabbing it from its people and giving it- by duplicity and deceit, to the Jews, was one of the goals of England to consolidate its influence in Arab and Islamic countries.
We now proceed to respond to the second part of the question: How can we restore Palestine as an Arab Islamic country once again? We say:

1-We should be aware a decisive war will take place between the Muslims and the Jews in which the Muslims will be victorious as long as they cling steadfastly to their religion, obey the teachings of their Quran, and follow the ways of their Prophet. Al-Bukhari and Muslim relate on the authority of Abdullah bin Umar that the Messenger of God said: "You will fight the Jews and they will hide behind the stone which will yell: Servant of Allah! There is a Jew behind me…Kill him." [26] In another Hadith by the two Sheikhs, Abu Hurayra related that the Messenger of God said: "The hour will not come until the Muslims fight the Jews, and the Muslims will kill them. The Jews will hide behind trees and stones, and the trees and stones will shout: 'O Muslim, servant of Allah! There is a Jew hiding behind me. Come and kill him. Except for the Ghardaq [27] since they are from the trees of the Jews."[28] These two authentic Hadiths inform the Muslims that a ferocious fight will take place between the Muslims and the Jews before the Hour has come, and that the Muslims will be victorious when they follow God's commandments. God will honor them; He will inform the stones and trees behind which the Jews hide to tell the Muslims about their hiding places, and that they have to kill them.

2- We should rest assured that the plight that has afflicted us in Palestine can be changed and reformed once we have true faith, strong determination and the resolve to restore our Holy Land and adopt all the efficient means and do everything to fulfill that objective. Our Holy country has fallen into the hands of the aggressors more than once. With Allah's help and assistance, we were able to restore it. After all, tens of countries were under the yoke of colonialism after the end of the last World War, but they were able to gain their freedom, independence and dignity. The catastrophe (nakba) of Palestine has alerted the Muslims to the dangers encompassing them and taught them lessons of which they were unaware. It made them aware of the evil and malice that World Zionism and the countries of infidelity have in store for them. It drove them to strive and work hard to preserve their honor and dignity after long years of humility and disgrace.

3- The two nations, i.e., the Arab and the Islamic nations, should unite under one leadership, entrust and place this leadership in faithful and loyal hands. They should encourage and support this leadership when it does well and act rightly, but they should also redirect, reform and correct the course if they deviate or err. They should stay away from discords and avoid the disagreements that may take place among leaders, kings and presidents. I want to say that saving Palestine from the Zionist cancer requires an army under a unified leadership, with a well- defined goal, adequately, strongly and thoroughly prepared from all aspects, with a staunch and unfaltering belief in the holiness and sanctity of the war that it will wage and unaffected and untouched by the disagreements amongst the politicians that rule these Arab countries.
We have lessons to learn from in the Battle of the Yarmuk and other Islamic battles. In the Battle of the Yarmuk, seeing his leaders fighting separately, Khalid bin El-Waleed gathered them and said: "This day is one of the days of Allah; there should be no conceit and no arrogance. Fight faithfully for Allah, and perform your duty and work in His name. You are spread out. Do not fight dispersed and scattered. That is not right. It is more profitable for the polytheists. I know there are disagreements between you, but let us get united under one banner. Let me lead you. They did, and they were victorious on that day thanks to Khalid."

4- The two nations, i.e., the Arab and the Islamic nations, should make great efforts to keep the Palestinian Cause at the forefront. All media outlets in every country should propagate and publicize the Palestinian Cause. Its history should be taught in schools, institutes and universities, and the maps of Palestine and pictures of its holy places should be circulated everywhere so that the tragedy of Palestine remains alive in. the hearts and minds. This generation that is contemporary with the tragedy of Palestine will come to an end. Other generations will follow. If we fail to keep this tragedy alive in their minds and link it to their hearts from a religious, political, cultural and economic perspectives, this tragedy of Palestine would be completely forgotten and will soon disappear from the hearts just as the tragedy of Al-Andalus did with the passage of days and years. Palestine is one of the Holy Muslim countries. It is the home of the Farthest Mosque (the Aqsa Mosque) to which the Prophet was taken in Al-Isra, the first of the two Qiblas and one of the three mosques to visit. In the Hadith: "Do not prepare a mount (travel) to visit any mosque except three: the Sacred Mosque, Aqsa Mosque, and this mosque of mine." [29] There are also a lot of temples and holy places in Palestine. There are the tombs of some prophets such as Abraham, Moses and David. There also the tombs of a large number of the Companions such as Abu Obeida ibn Al-Jarah, Ebada ibn al -Samit, Al-Fadel ibn Al-Abaas, Sadad ibn Aws, and others. There is no doubt that a piece of Muslim land that contains all such sanctities should be worthy of repeatedly brought to the forefront everywhere and at all times.

5- The two nations, i.e., the Arab and the Islamic nations, should take a firm and resolute stance concerning those countries that have supported Zionism; they should use all the various weapons and methods available to stop these countries from supporting the Jews. One of the most important weapons is petroleum which is abundantly available in our countries. If we use it well, the countries of infidelity would cease their support to oppressive Zionism. This weapon, and others, will not bring forth the desired results until the Arabs are united and stand as a solid rank, a concrete structure, to confront colonial conferences and World Zionism.

6-The Arab and the Islamic nations should strengthen and reinforce the Palestinian fighters from all aspects. These fighters should be chosen from among the loyal and faithful ones who are strong believers in Allah, their religion and their country. They should be equipped with all the facilities that they could use to violently shake the Zionists (through guerrilla wars) because these wars threaten the security, stability and economy of Israel and all its structures. This jihad will be the prelude to that decisive jihad that the Islamic nation should wage against Israel to purge the Holy Land from the Jews. Many countries have adopted the guerrilla war technique against the occupiers and were able to gain victory in the end. They were able to grab their freedom and independence despite their oppressor' reluctance. A good example for this is Algeria, the country of the million martyrs. Algeria waged such a jihad against France and forced it to depart and leave the country.

7-We should wage our next Palestinian war on a religious struggle (jihad) basis, not on a patriotic one only. That is because Palestine is a holy Islamic country, as we mentioned before. It is the land of all Muslims, and it is the obligation and duty of each Muslim on the face of world to defend and protect it. The Jews have widely exploited the religious aspect to confirm their fabricated existence in Palestine. They convinced western countries, especially England, that Palestine is their Promised Land and that this land was theirs alone, according to what is mentioned in the Torah. The Arabs, on the other hand, neglected that important religious aspect, and they waged the Palestinian war on national and patriotic motives. Some of their writers even scorned those religious aspects. That is why, they were destined to failure. We do not deny the impact of patriotic motives to achieve success, but what we vehemently reject is the reliance on patriotic motives alone to the exclusion of the moral, spiritual and religious aspects. Those who do not care much about the religious and moral aspects will not succeed, even if they were to possess the mightiest power on earth. The Constitution admitted the importance of spiritual and religious aspects/energy: "We always have to remember that it is the spiritual energy- that nations derive from their high moral values that spring from their revealed religions or their cultural heritage- that are capable to perform wonders. These spiritual energies imbue the nations' highest aspirations with the greatest momentum and drive. They also equip these nations with the shields of patience and courage with which they can confront all odds, conquer all hardships and overcome all hindrances. If financial and material aspects are necessary and essential to ascertain progress, the spiritual and moral motives are the only ones that can grant this progress and clothe it with the highest principles and the noblest goals and objectives."

8- Before and after this, if the Arab and the Islamic nations want to restore Palestine, they themselves should return to the teachings of Islam and apply them on themselves thoroughly. They should fight vices and inequities and establish their lives, systems, dealings and interactions on the basis of the upright religion. They should adequately and thoroughly prepare themselves to fight Allah's enemy and their enemy. If they do this, victory will be theirs. The noble verses that testify to this are countless: "O believers! If you stand up for Allah, He will help you and make your steps firm." (Muhammad; Q 47:7)
Also, the Almighty said: "Allah will certainly help those who stand up for Him. Allah is truly All-Powerful, Almighty." (Al-Hajj; Q 22:40) And His: "We certainly help Our messengers and the believers, both in this worldly life and on the Day the witnesses will stand forth for testimony." (Ghafir; Q 40:51) And one of the Messengers recommendations to his nation which he directed to Ibn Abbas is: "Keep Allah (in your heart) and He will keep (preserve) you. Keep Him and you will find Him in front of you." And Umar bin Khattab advised Sa'd ibn Abu Waqaas, saying: "I command you and all those soldiers with you to conduct yourselves with righteousness and fear of Allah for the fear of Allah is the best weapon against the enemy and the most potent in jihad. I command you and those fighting alongside with you to be vigilant and stay away from sins and transgressions. The Muslims are victorious because of the transgressions of their enemy and their disobedience to Allah. Otherwise, we would not have been able to gain victory because they outnumber us and their weapons are more efficient. Therefore, if we transgress, they will have the upper hand over us. Be aware that Allah is the One who protects your march. He knows what you do. Stary away from sins and transgressions. You are fighting in the Name of Allah. Do not say that our enemy is evil or worse than us, and that we will not be harmed if we do evil. Remember when the Children of Israel did evil and transgressed against Allah, He sent servants of great might against them and they "ravaged (their) homes." Ask Allah to provide you with His help and assistance. Ask Him to grant you victory over your enemy. I ask Him on our behalf and yours..." [30]

Allah's prayers and peace be upon our Master Muhammad and his family and companions.

The Jewish Threat

The American President (sic; Franklin was never U.S. President but is recognized as "The First American Diplomat"[31]) Benjamin Franklin, cautions the United States of America against the Jewish threat. He says: "There is a great danger that threatens the United States of America. This danger is the Jews. Gentlemen! Wherever the Jews settle, we find them weakening the will of the people and shake honest commercial interactions. They do not mix or commingle with the people. They create a government within a government, and when they encounter opposition from some one, they strive to smother and repress the nation financially as happened in Portugal and Spain… If the Jews are not prevented from migrating by the power of the constitution, they will flow in huge numbers in less than one hundred years. They will govern and destroy us. They will change the shape of the government that we worked so hard and sacrificed our blood, lives, money and freedoms to form. If the Jews are not exempted from migration, two hundred years will not pass until we find our children workers in the fields that secure the food for the Jews… I warn you, gentlemen, if you fail to forever prevent the Jews from migrating, your children and grandchildren will curse you in your graves. Their mentality is different from ours, even if they lived among us for ten generations. A tiger cannot change its color... The Jews are a danger and a threat to this country. If they enter it, they will ruin and corrupt it…"[31a]

References

---

[1] Al-Bidayah wa Al-Nihaya, by Ibn Kathir, Vol. 7, P. 55. Al-Sa'da Printing Press.
[2] Al-Farook Omar by Muhammad Husein Heikal. (Farook because he distinguished truths and falsehoods)
[3] Judaism by Dr. Ahmad Shalaby, P. 68.
[4] "Facts about Palestine" issued by the Arab Higher Committee for Palestine in 1954 (P. 114).
[5] The previous reference.
[6] "This is Zionism" By Israel Cohen, P. 23.
[7] "Israel: An Idea, a Movement, a State," by Hani al-Hindi and Mohsen Ibrahim, P. 33.
[8] World Zionism and the Promised Land, P. 134.
[9] "The Danger of Judaism," by Abdullah Al-Tell, P. 158.
[10] "The Danger of Judaism," by Abdullah Al-Tell.
[11] Moses Montefiore was an extremely wealthy Jew who donated millions of dollars to promote the settling of the Jews in Palestine. He used his financial and political influence for this goal. He visited Palestine a number of times to learn the conditions of the Jews there and to help them by any means possible. He embraced the Orthodox creed in order to be able to serve the Jews behind the veil of religion. He was born in 1784 AD, and he died in 1885 AD.
[12] Weizmann was the first President of Israel. He deserves the most credit for establishing the State of Israel. He was instrumental in obtaining the Balfour Declaration. He

represented the Jews in international conferences. He was born in Russia in 1874, and he died in 1951 AD.

[13] Weizmann's Biography, P. 14.

[14] "Israel: An Idea, a Movement, a State," by Hani al-Hindi and Mohsen Ibrahim, P. 49.

[15] The Jews consider Herzl the founder of the Zionist movement. He fervently sought to establish the state of Israel. He also published a book which was titled "The Jewish State" and which caused an uproar in the world. He also represented the Jews in their world conferences. He worked as a writer and an attorney. He was born in 1860 and died in 1904 AD.

[16] System of Government in Israel, P. 13.

[17] The Annual Book of the Israeli Government, year 53-54, the Introduction, P. 8.

[18] The Jewish State and its Relation to the Holy Land by Mr. Mousa Habib, P. 89.

[19] "Our Cases in the United Nations" by Mr. Khairy Ahmad explains in detail how America entered the First World War and the Jews' role in this.

[20] Rothschild was the richest man in the world at that time. He was a fanatic Jew who spent millions of his money to help settle the Jews in Palestine. He was the one who lent the British government 4 million dollars to buy the shares of the Suez Canal from Khedive Ismael.

[21] Weizmann's Biography, P. 28.

[22] The Great Conspiracy by Emil Al-Ghori.

[23] Facts about the Palestinian Cause, P. 173. Published by the Higher Arab Organization to Save Palestine, 1954 AD.

[24] The previous reference, P. 190.

[25] The previous reference, P. 190.

[26] Related by Al-Bukhari in Fighting the Jews," Vol. 4, P. 56. Also, related by Muslim in "Tribulations and the Signs of the Hour," Vol. 4, P. 2229.

[27] Gharqas: a kind of tree known to grow in the Levant.

[28] Related by Al-Bukhari in "The virtues of Struggling" Vol. 4, P.1. Also, related by Muslim in "Tribulations and the Signs of the Hour," Vol. 4, P. 2229. Muhammad Abdul-Baqi edition.

[29] Related by Al-Bukhari, Muslim, Abu Dawoud and al-Tirmidhi.

[30] The Unique Contract by Bin Abd Rabu, 10:49.

[31] "Franklin served from 1776 to 1778 on a commission to France charged with the critical task of gaining French support for American independence. French aristocrats and intellectuals embraced Franklin as the personification of the New World Enlightenment. His likeness appeared on medallions, rings, watches, and snuffboxes, and fashionable ladies adopted the 'coiffure a la Franklin' in imitation of the fur cap he wore instead of a wig. His popularity and diplomatic skill—along with the first American battlefield success at Saratoga—convinced France to recognize American independence and conclude an alliance with the thirteen states in 1778. Franklin presented his credentials to the French court in 1779, becoming the first American Minister (the eighteenth century American equivalent of Ambassador) to be received by a foreign government." https://history.state.gov/milestones/1776-1783/b-franklin

[31a] "From a speech he gave in 1789 in celebration of the Feast of the Constitution," is Tantawi's "reference". There was never a "Feast of the Constitution," nor did Franklin ever make such a "speech" or write anything comparable to this Antisemitic screed. See

discussion in The Introduction, including these citations: "Benjamin Franklin vindicated: an exposure of the Franklin 'prophecy." *International Benjamin Franklin Society*, 1939, Pamphlet, American Jewish Congress, New York. https://ia601202.us.archive.org/23/items/306346/306346.pdf;
Antisemitism in Europe: hearing before the Subcommittee on European Affairs of the Committee on Foreign Relations, United States Senate, One Hundred Eighth Congress, first session, October 22, 2003. https://www.govinfo.gov/content/pkg/CHRG-108shrg95528/html/CHRG-108shrg95528.htm;
Saul J. Singer. "Benjamin Franklin And The Jews," *The Jewish Press*, June 28, 2023. https://www.jewishpress.com/sections/features/features-on-jewish-world/benjamin-franklin-and-the-jews/2023/06/28/

Index

A

B

C

D

E

F

G

H

I

J

K

L

M

N

O

P

Q

R

S

T

U

V

W

Y

Z

www.ingramcontent.com/pod-product-compliance
Lightning Source LLC
Chambersburg PA
CBHW080225140626
46555CB00019B/2887
* 9 7 9 8 9 9 9 0 9 9 6 0 0 *